The Insider's Guide to Old

BOOKS

MAGAZINES

NEWSPAPERS

TRADE CATALOGS

RON BARLOW & RAY REYNOLDS

Windmill Publishing Company
El Cajon, California 92020

Printed in the United States of America.

ISBN 0-933846-05-3

NOTICE

This Price Guide is a compilation of asking prices. It is
not a guarantee of what you can buy or sell your books,
magazines, newspapers or catalogs for.
Used book dealers base their prices on one or more of
seven factors: sale of past copies; auction prices; other
dealer's catalogs; price guides; dealers' prices at book
fairs; dealers' shop prices; and pricing by intuition.
Demand for a book, magazine, newspaper or trade
catalog will vary according to geography.
Where, when, how, and to whom an item is sold is the
final determinate of value.

To order additional copies of this book
Send $19.95 plus $3 postage & handling to
Windmill Publishing Company
2147 Windmill View Road
El Cajon, California 92020.

CONTENTS

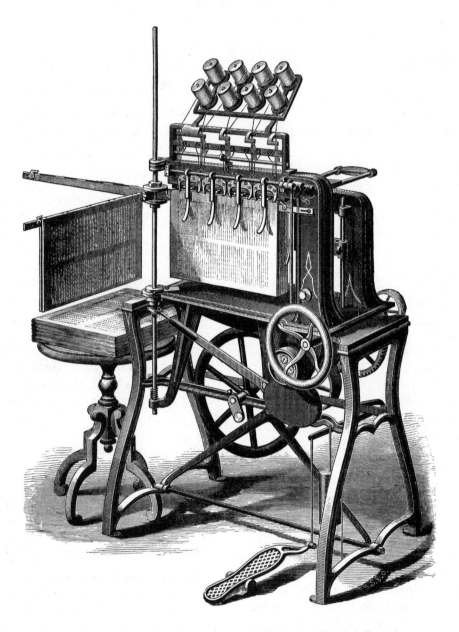

Smyth's Book-Sewing Machine, the invention of Mr. D. M. Smyth of Hartford, Conn., is represented in Fig. 3868. ———— This apparatus is remarkable not only for the great ingenuity of its construction, but for the rapidity with which it operates and the strength of its finished work. It is
capable of sewing 60 signatures per minute, and inserts 8 separate threads if need be, any one of
which may be cut or broken without impairing the holding of the others. The machine, which is
represented in perspective in Fig. 3868, uses 8 spools, and is capable of sewing any book in length
within the compass of its supporting-bar and up to 8 inches in thickness.

Smyth's Book-Sewing Machine, circa 1880.

INTRODUCTION

Last month I interviewed a veteran book and paper dealer in his booth at a local antique show. During the course of a long and serious conversation about the antiquarian book business, I asked him which price guide he consulted most often.

"I've been using *B. B. Sky's* guide for a number of years now," he answered.

"Really," I replied, "I've got a half dozen others on my desk, but I haven't heard of that one. Where can I get a current edition?"

The old bookman's eyes twinkled through his tiny bifocals as he winked and stroked his beard.

"I just look up at the big blue sky for a moment," he said, "and the right price just pops into my head."

So there you are...another confirmation that no hard and fast prices exist in the antiquarian book business...or for that matter in the old magazine, newspaper or trade catalog field either. Each transaction can be a game of wits between buyer and seller. One man's retail is often another man's wholesale.

This is what makes the field so exciting. A book or paper rarity can easily change hands four or five times between its discovery at a flea market and the final sale to a library, bookshop, museum or collector.

Why are we printing yet another price guide? Because **more than 5 million** different book titles have been published in the United States during the last century. The average used-book store stocks only 25,000 volumes and a typical guide lists about the same number. It's obvious that collectors, dealers, librarians and historians need all the help they can get. Another hundred price guides would not cover the entire field.

Moreover, *The Insider's Guide to Old Books, Magazines, Newspapers and Trade Catalogs* is the first and only price guide to combine all of the above, in one comprehensive, yet affordable volume that emphasizes older publications. You will find dozens of collecting tips as well as numerous articles on how to buy, sell, and trade for a profit. We've even thrown in a chapter on starting a used bookstore.

One thing we've learned in many years of dealing is that in any given specialty, at a given time, only a small number of titles are actually in demand; the rest are simply clutter. This guide tells you what is collectible.

When you do turn up a possibly worthwhile find, there are several things you need to know.

• Does the title appear often in dealer catalogs?

• Has a copy sold recently at auction?

• Is it a staple item in shops or shows?

• Is it a desirable early edition, or a later reprint?

• How should I describe its condition?

• What is a rough estimate of its value?

• Where can I sell it for a fair price?

The Insider's Guide is designed to answer these important questions. The prices recorded are from shops, shows, auctions and dealer catalogs, with a dash of "Blue Sky" intuition thrown in. We emphasize that these prices are not written in stone. They are recorded to help you buy and sell in an informed manner.

Condition is a critical factor in book collecting. The difference in price between a "Good" first edition with no dust jacket and a "Fine" example in its original spotless dust wrapper might be hundreds, even thousands of dollars. Don't overrate your finds.

Unless otherwise noted, most of the books listed in this guide are in "Very Good" to "Fine" condition. Do not assume that dust jackets are present unless it is so stated.

"First edition" status also involves a caveat. Some dealers have used the term in error, not knowing that a previous edition exists. Further research may be necessary (See Bibliography).

Ray Reynolds, a retired college journalism instructor and former used-book store owner, still operates a part-time business dealing in old books and ephemera. He is the author of *California the Curious*, a trivia collection, and *Cat's Paw Utopia*, a historical narrative. Ray lives in rural San Diego County with his wife Mary, a librarian.

Ronald Barlow is an author-publisher specializing in antiques and Americana. (His four previous titles appear on the back page.) Ron has owned several retail stores and brings a business slant to his writing. He lives in the foothills of El Cajon, California, with his wife and partner, Lynda.

ABBREVIATIONS

1st - first edition
1st ed - first edition
1st prntg - 1st printing

abr - abridged
aeg - all edges gilt
Am, Amer - American
anon - anonymous
app - appendix
arc - advanced reading copy
auth - author
av - average
auct - auction
autog - autograph

b/w - black and white
bce - book club edition
bd - bound
bg, bdg - binding
bds - boards (hard covers)
bib - bibliography
bkplt - bookplate
bkstrp - back strip
buck - buckram
bxd - boxed

c - copyright
ca - circa (about)
capt - caption
cat - catalog
chip, chpd - chipped
cl - cloth
col - colored or color
comp - compiler
cond - condition
cont - contemporary
cont'd - continued
conts - contents
cor - corrected
cov - cover, covers
cpy - copy or copies
CWO - check with order

dba - doing business as
dec - decoration
ded - dedication
disb - disbound
DJ - dust jacket
dlr - dealer
doc - document
dup - duplicate
dw - dust wrapper (same as DJ)

ed - edition, edited, editor
eng - engraving, engraved
Eng - English
ep - endpapers
est - established
ex lib - library copy

F - fine
F - folio
fac - facsimile
fe - fore edge
ff - following
first - first ed
fldg - folding
fly - flyleaf
fp - full page
fr - fair
front, frontis - frontispiece
fox - foxed or foxing

G - good
gte - gilt top edge
G-VG - good to very good

hc - hardcover

illus - illustrations, illustrated
imp - imprint
impr - impression
ins - inscribed, inscription
intro - introduction
le, ltd - limitd edition
LEC - Limited Editions Club
lea - leather
lg - large
lev - levant
litho - lithograph, lithography
lr - large
loc - located
lt - light
ltd - limited edition

M - mint
mag - magazine
marg - margin, marginal
ms, mss - manuscript
mtd - mounted

nd - no date given
NF - near fine
NM - near mint
np - no place or publisher given
ny - no year given

ob - oblong
op - out of print
orig - original
o/w - otherwise

p, pg, pp - page, pages
pb - paperback
photo - photographs
pict - pictoral
ppd - post paid
port - portrait
pref - preface

pres - presentation copy
priv pr - privately printed
prtn, prntg - printing, printed
pub - publisher, published

rb - rebound
ref - reference
remmk - remainder mark
repr - repaired
repro - reproduction
rev - revised, revised edition
rpt - reprint, reprinted

ser - series
sev - several
sg sgd sgnd - signed
sl - slight slightly
sm - small
stn - stain, stains

t, tp - title page
teg - top edge gilt
tr, trans - translation, translated
tpd - tipped in

unbd - unbound
unfin - unfinished
unk - unknown
univ - university
up - uncorrected proof

VF - very fine
VG - very good
vol - volume, volumes

waf - with all its faults
w - with
wl - want list
wn - worn
wrps - wrappers (soft cover)

x-lib - library copy

BOOK SIZES
4to (quarto) aprox. 12 inches high.
8vo (octavo) approx. 9 in. high.
12mo (duodecimo) approx. 7 to 8
 inches high.
16mo approx. 6 to 7 inches high.
24mo approx. 5 to 6 inches high.
32mo approx. 4 to 5 inches high.
48mo approx. 4 inches high.
64mo approx. 3 inches high.
Miniature, below one inch high.
Folio, approx 13 in. or higher.
Elephant folio, 23 in. or larger.
Atlas folio, 25 inches.
Double elephant folio, larger than
 25 inches.

GLOSSARY

ALBUMEN PRINT. Most photographs produced between 1850 and 1890 were made on albumen paper coated with egg white. This paper was sold commercially in ready-to-use form after 1872. Some books of the period had actual photographs tipped in.

ADVANCE COPY. Also known as a review copy. Sent in paper binding or cloth binding with a review slip tucked in. Reviewers get them before official publication day, bound and published in a plain paper cover for advance publicity.

ANNOTATION. In a bibliography or catalog, a descriptive or evaluative note following an entry.

AQUATINT. An intaglio process of etching in which acid-resistant granules are applied to a copper or steel plate before etching. Makes soft, watercolor effects possible. Black or sepia aquatints can be handcolored after printing.

AUTHORIZED EDITION. An edition which was not pirated or otherwise published illegitimately.

AUTHOR'S PROOF. One that is returned to the publisher after the author has made corrections. Occasionally available on the market.

BACK LIST. A publisher's list of older titles still in print because of continuing demand. Books thought to be out of print can sometimes be found on back lists.

BACKED, RE-BACKED. The re-covering of a book's spine.

BACKSTRIP. The cloth (sometimes leather) covering of a book's spine. Often where the first signs of wear appear.

BEVELLED BOARDS. Covers of a book which have been cut at an angle.

BIND. To fasten leaves together with staples, glue, thread or wire and adhere to covers to form a pamphlet, book, or magazine.

BINDER'S BOARDS. The stiff pasteboard used for a book's covers. Usually covered with cloth, paper or leather.

BINDING COPY. A used book that needs rebinding.

BLANK. A page, either at the front or back of a book that has no printing or illustration. The flyleaf is a blank which follows the free front endpaper. Absent front blanks lower a book's value more than the absence of rear blanks, because it is assumed that significant inscribed information may have been lost. Rear blanks are often the result of a manuscript ending before a full signature of 8 or 16 pages is reached. It is cheaper for the printer to leave these excess pages blank than to remove them from the printing and trimming cycle.

BLEEDING. Printing an image past the edge of a page is sometimes done deliberately, especially in the case of photographs. Accidental bleeds can destroy text.

BLIND STAMPING OR BLIND TOOLING. An ungilded or uncolored raised design made by a bookbinder on the covers of a book. Also called blind embossing.

BLURB. A term coined by Gelett Burgess in 1907 that refers to puffery on a book's dust jacket or in the publisher's advertising. A brief publicity notice.

BOARDS. Early books were bound between two pieces of wood. Today the "wood" is thick cardboard. Wooden boards went out in the 16th Century.

BOOK JACKET. Usually called a dust jacket, sometimes a dust wrapper. However, dust wrapper really means the actual covers of a book, made of either stiff or limp paper. A book jacket is, of course, removable from the covers.

BOOK PLATE. An ownership label usually pasted in the inside cover of a book. When present, bookplates can increase a book's value. Removal, but with signs of once being present, reduce value.

BOOK SCOUT. A "dealer" without a store. A self-employed picker who searches auctions, fairs, flea markets, estate sales, etc., for books, often previously ordered by a dealer or a collector. Scouts are sometimes more knowledgeable than dealers.

BOOKWORM. Beetle larvae that ordinarily like the paste and glue of a book. The alum in modern paste is distasteful to such larvae.

BOUND GALLEY. Uncorrected page or galley proofs of a book.

BOWDLERIZING. Altering a book's text to remove passages and/or illustrations offensive to the publisher, editor, or morals of the times. From Thomas Bowdler, 1725-1825, who cleaned up Shakespeare for children.

BOX, SLIPCASE, SOLANDER. Containers of individual books or of sets, made of wood or cardboard. Used principally by private presses and for limited editions. A slipcase protects a book while showing its spine. A solander is shaped like a book and opens like a book. A book can be examined without removing it from the solander.

BREAKER. A book suitable to be taken apart for the sake of removing color plates, engravings or maps. Some people view breaking books as downright sinful. If purists had their way, most picture framers would be out of work. Nine-five per cent of all antique prints are from broken books.

BROADSHEET, BROADSIDE. An unfolded sheet of paper which has printing on only one side. (Broadsheet sometimes refers to single sheets with printing on both sides.)

BROWNING. The discoloration of paper because of age. Too much browning is a matter of individual taste.

BUCKRAM. A coarse and heavy fabric, of cotton, hemp or linen, that is stiffened with glue and used to bind books. It was popular in the mid-19th Century.

BULK. The thickness of a book without its covers. Book paper varies from 200 to 2,000 pages to the inch. One way to make a book look bigger than it should be is to use thick but light paper. Printers express bulk as the thickness of any chosen paper in thousanths of an inch, or pages per inch, (ppi).

CABINET CARDS. A new photo size introduced in 1867: 3 3/4 x 5 1/2 image mounted on 4 1/4 x 6 1/2 inch card stock. Popular into the early 1880s, cabinet cards are mounted as illustrative matter on pages of some books of the period.

CALENDERING. A process which gives paper a smooth and glossy surface by passing it between rollers during manufacturing.

CALF, CALFSKIN. The most common type of leather used for binding books. Most American books, before 1830, were bound in sheepskin. Calfskin has no grain and looks well undyed, but it can be dyed any color. It can also be polished, scored, grained, diced or given a woven texture.

CANCEL. A part of a book, usually a leaf, that has been inserted as a replacement for a part at fault. The replacement is called a cancellans; the original part a cancelland.

CARTE DE VISITE. A visiting-card-sized paper photograph patented in 1854 and widely used during the Civil War. More than 100,000 carte de visite photographs of Abraham Lincoln were distributed during the 1860 presidential campaign. Book dealers frequently encounter carte de visites in estate lots.

CARTOUCHE. A usually oval frame design used with maps to enclose a caption.

CASE BIND. To bind by gluing signatures to a case (cover) made of binder's board covered with fabric, cloth or leather, thus yielding a hard cover book.

CHAPBOOK. Originally, crude pamphlets hawked by "chap-men" or "chaps" from the 17th to the 19th Century. Now applied by private presses to books or pamphlets six or seven inches tall, issued today in limited editions.

CHROMOLITHOGRAPHY. The making of a lithographic print in colors. Usually implies a color print made from a series of hand drawn images on limestone printing plates, but can also mean any color print other than a woodcut or etching.

COLLATE, COLLATION. To collate is to ensure that every original leaf of a book is present. Collation refers also to checking that the pages are in their proper order.

COLLOTYPE. A photograph produced in large volume by a photomechanical process utilizing gelatin plates. Many mass-produced cabinet card photos produced between 1870 and 1900 used the collotype process.

COLOPHON. From the Greek, meaning "finishing stroke." It is an inscription, usually at the end of a book, identifying its source and other facts about its publication.

COMB BIND. To bind with a flexible plastic comb-shaped strip inserted through holes in a stack of paper.

COMMISSION. The costs of a book published on commission are paid by the author, who sometimes hires a "vanity press."

CONCORDANCE. The alphabetical index to all the words in a text, showing where each word can be found. The Bible and Shakespeare are the most obvious examples.

CONJUGATE LEAVES. Leaves, originally a single sheet of paper, which have been folded once. The leaves belong to each other, although separated by many pages in the book. (Also see leaf.)

CONSIGNMENT. Shipping books to a dealer or other person with the understanding that money will change hands only when the books are sold and money paid to the seller. The seller charges a percentage of the money paid. Twenty-five per cent is fairly usual.

COPPERPLATE ENGRAVING (See also INTAGLIO.) An image with fine details with sharply defined lines which may taper to a fine point at the ends. The ink is clearly raised above the surface and can be felt with the finger. A delicate plate tone, which contrasts with the hard lines, is a feature of soft copperplate technique. Even finer detail can be achieved with steel engraving. Both are often confused with etching, pen and ink, and photo-gravures. Both may be simulated by a print run which makes a deep rectangular impression upon the previously printed image, thus duplicating those made by early hand presses.

COPYRIGHT. A right granted by the Federal Government, for exclusive publication, distribution or sale of literary or artistic material. Copyrights secured before January 1, 1978, may last a total of 75 years, including an extension. For works created after that date, the copyright lasts the lifetime of the holder and for 50 years afterward. Works not protected by copyright are those which have been published without a copyright notice, or on which the copyright has run out and are thus in the public domain. These may be reprinted freely by anyone. A copyright notice is printed on the back of a book's title page in the United States.

CUT. An illustration printed with the text of a book. The term also refers to the engraving from which the illustration is printed.

DAMPSTAIN. Water stain.

DECKLE EDGE. The rough, or feathered edge of hand-made or machine-made paper.

DECORATED BOARDS. Unclothed covers (boards) may be covered with paper printed in fanciful, geometric or colorful designs.

DEFINITIVE EDITION. The most authoritative version of the complete works of an author.

DENTELLE. Patterns tooled into the leather covers of a book, or around the inner edge of covers. The designs are usually lacy and in gilt.

DISBOUND. Now lacking binding, which has been removed. Not the same as "unbound," which means there was no binding.

DISCARD STAMP. Usually a stamp of a library on a withdrawn book, either on an endpaper, title page or page edges.

DUST JACKET. The paper cover placed around a book's covers both to protect the book and to provide promotional space. Often used as equivalent to "dust wrapper," although "wrapper" refers to book covers made from paper rather than from boards. Dust jackets can play a major part in book appraisal.

DUODECIMO. A page size referring to books approximately 7 3/4 inches high.

EDITION. All the copies of a book which are printed from the same plates and type. If multiple printings are made, each printing is called an impression, the plates and type not having been altered. Significant changes in plates or type result in a second, third, etc., edition. See also ISSUE and POINTS.

ELEPHANT FOLIO. The largest book size; often up to two feet in height.

EMBOSSING. A raised rather than indented design on a book cover.

END PAPERS. Leaves at the beginning and end of a book. The first leaf is pasted to the inside front cover. The rear end paper is not pasted but is normally an unnumbered page.

ENGRAVING. Any illustration or decoration made from an incised metal plate or wood block. See also HALFTONE.

EPHEMERA. Any non-book, non-magazine or non-trade catalog. Usually means short-lived printed material, such as flyers, pamphlets, posters, playbills, dance programs, clippings, etc. Now often referred to as "paper collectibles."

ERRATUM. A misprint or other error in a printed book. Plural is errata. Errata slips with corrections are sometimes inserted or pasted into a book.

EX-LIBRARY. Discarded by a library. Not often of interest to collectors. Dealer catalogs should always mention such a condition, which is usually indicated by card pockets, discard stamps or extreme shelf wear.

EXPURGATED EDITION. (See also Bowdlerizing) Amended by removal of obscene, objectionable or erroneous passages.

EXTRA-ILLUSTRATED. Also called Grangerized. A book into which, after publication, additional illustrations have been either laid-in or tipped (pasted) in.

FACSIMILE. An exact reproduction of a book, usually done by a photocopying process. It is a reprint only if the printing is done from the book's original plates.

FIRST EDITION. The total run of a press from the first setting of the type of a book. Related terms are IMPRESSION, ISSUE, STATE, POINT.

FIRST SEPARATE EDITION, or SEPARATE. Applied to gatherings of material that previously appeared in magazines, etc., with other matter, and now appear for the first time in book form.

FIRST THUS EDITION. Not to be confused with a true first edition. Catalog writers use this term to describe editions which are NOT stated first, second or third editions, but which have added illustrations, gone into paperback, have a new introduction, etc. Also stated "1st ed. thus." A misleading term at best.

FIRST TRADE EDITION. The first printing of a book, for trade distribution, that has been already printed in a limited or private edition.

FLY LEAF. Unprinted page or pages at the beginning and end of a book. Not to be confused with endpapers.

FOLIATION. The numbering of the pages of a book. Also called pagination.

FOLIO. A page size referring to a book approximately 15 inches high. Exceeded only by the elephant folio, which can be two feet or more tall.

FORE EDGE. The edge of a book opposite its spine. Fore-edge painting is an embellishment in which a scene is painted on the fore edge. When the pages are fanned, the painting becomes visible.

FORMAT. The shape, size, type design, and general makeup of a book.

FOXED, FOXING. Reddish brown stains that appear in aging paper. Older books are "permitted" some foxing. What is too much foxing depends on various other qualities of the book.

FRONTISPIECE. Older books frequently have their first illustration facing the title page. They are sometimes removed and framed, reducing the book's value.

GALLEY PROOFS. Copies of long, narrow columns of type which will be made up into final pages after proofing by editors and author. They are the next step after an edited manuscript and may be quite valuable.

GHOST. A faint image appearing on a printed sheet where it was not intended to appear. A ghost may indicate a missing plate.

GUTTER. The inner margin of a page: the space between the type and the binding.

HALFTONE. An illustration composed of a series of almost invisible mechanical dots. The dots are created by a photographic screen process.

HARDBACK, HARDBOUND, HARDCOVER. A synonym for stiff, clothbound books. Almost all hardbacks are covered with cloth or paper textured to resemble cloth.

HEADBAND. A decorative band, usually of cotton or silk, that is fastened inside the spine of a book to strengthen it at the head or foot.

HINGE. An inside or outside joint of a book's binding. Purists use only "joint" when referring to the outside hinge.

HOLOGRAPH. A document of any kind written completely by hand by the original author.

HORNBOOK. A paddle or tablet-shaped primer of colonial days in which the primer was protected by a sheet of transparent horn. Produced into the early 19th Century.

HURT BOOKS. Publishers occasionally sell somewhat damaged or shopworn new books to booksellers at a lower price than normal wholesale.

ILLUMINATION. Decoration of old manuscripts and early printed books with ornamental letters and colored illustrations. Most often found on vellum in gold, silver or watercolor.

IMPRESSION. The number of copies of an edition printed at one time without alterations or corrections.

IMPRIMATUR. A 16th and 17th Century license to print, usually by the Catholic Church. The imprimatur was carried on the first page of a book.

IMPRINT. Information identifying the book's source publisher, printer, date, place, etc.) placed on the title page, the copyright page or at the end of a book. Early American books with full imprint information are often quite valuable.

IN PARTS. Books were sometimes issued serially, by the week or month, in the 19th Century. A Dickens novel ran serially in 19 parts in 1836 and 1837. The term was sometimes applied also to regular numbers of magazines, but is only applicable to the building of a single book.

INSCRIBED COPY. A copy signed by the author and carrying a message, short or long. Some authors are eager inscribers, lessening in some cases the value of the inscription. When the inscription is to someone of note, the book is called a presentation copy.

INTAGLIO. A diecut, engraved or carved design sunk below the surface of a plate. The ink is captured in these furrows and produces a very sharp-edged image. Usually printed on soft paper. Copper is the most widely used metal for intaglio plates.

JAPON VELLUM. An imitation of expensive hand-made Japanese paper. Used for special editions, it cannot be cleaned as real vellum can.

JOINT. See HINGE.

JUSTIFYING. The arrangement or spacing of type for an even margin.

KEEPSAKE. An American 19th Century gift book, often elaborately illustrated and with much verse content.

LABELS. Before book titles were stamped into bindings, leather or paper labels were glued on. Still used at times for decorative effect. Library labels are of course to be shunned.

LAID IN. An errata slip or other piece of paper not affixed to a book but inserted. Not to be junked without inspection.

LAID FINISH. Paper with a surface consisting of parallel lines to simulate handmade stock.

LEAF. A single sheet of paper. Two pages of a book numbered consecutively, e.g., pages 7 and 8 equal one leaf.

LETTERPRESS. A method of printing from raised surfaces that involves individual pieces of type or a plate made from the type. Unlike modern offset printing, the inked type or plate is impressed directly upon the paper.

LEVANT. Also known as MOROCCO LEATHER. A kind of leather made from goatskin.

LIBRARY BINDING. A type of reinforced binding ordered by libraries for books which endure hard wear.

LIMITED EDITION. An edition purportedly limited to a stated number of copies, from two to 1,000 or more. Often they are numbered and signed by the author and/or illustrator. Sometimes an abused term, since only the publisher knows how many copies are actually printed.

LIMP BINDING. A vellum, cloth or suede binding that does not use boards.

LINE ENGRAVING—LINE CUT. Unscreened engraving, either photo or mechanical, used when the illustration has no gray tones between black and white. Pen and ink drawings are handled this way. Prior to the refinement of photography, line cuts were engraved directly on metal or wood by skilled craftsmen.

LIST PRICE. The publisher-set retail price of a book.

LITHOGRAPHY. A no-cut printing method involving the principle that grease and water do not mix. A chemically coated plate attracts ink in the image areas and repels ink in the non-image areas. Before 1890 most lithographic work was done by an artist drawing directly with an oil pencil on a limestone plate. The oil attracted the printer's ink and the damp limestone repelled it. Multiple color work was achieved by drawing on a separate stone for each color desired. Careful registration placed each color in the required position on the printed piece. Modern lithography is called "offset" printing because the image is transferred (or offset) to a rubber roller—from the printing master—before it imprints the paper.

LITTLE MAGAZINES. Magazines of small circulation and usually literary and ephemeral. Collectible because prominent writers often appear in them early in their careers.

LOSS LEADER. A book sold near or below actual cost. Frequently used in book promotion to attract customers into retail stores, or by book clubs to sign up new subscribers.

MARBLED PAPER. Paper that, by swirling floating ink on top of water, develops a marble-like veining. Used in the past for end papers and board covers. Today this tedious process can be imitated by offset printing.

MADE-UP COPY. A copy of a book which has had missing leaves or plates (or Xerox copies) glued or pasted in to make it complete. Oddly, such copies are sometimes called "sophisticated."

MARGINALIA. Hand-written notes in a book's text. If the writer is identifiable as important, the writing is other than a defect.

MEZZOTINT. Engraving, usually on copper, that involves scraping or polishing surfaces to produce dark velvet-like prints with richly modulated highlights. The artist starts with a roughened plate which would print black, and then softens the tones to grey and white by burnishing out the raised, grained surface. Often confused with photogravures, lithos and aquatints. Mezzotints can also be made on steel.

MISBOUND. A bound part of which pages have been misplaced by the printer.

MONOGRAPH. A specialized subject study, of partial or full book length.

MOROCCO. Goatskin tanned reddish with sumac. Used for bookbinding.

MOUNTED. Denoting the strengthening of damaged leaves or the light pasting-down of illustrations on a blank page.

OCTAVO, (abbreviated 8vo). A page size made from a printer's sheet folded into eight leaves. Commonly 5 x 8 inches to 6 x 9½ inches.

OFFPRINT. An extract from a book or magazine, stapled or glued and sometimes bound.

OFFSET. A printing process that differs from letterpress in that the plate, or letters, do not make a direct impression upon the paper. In offset printing, a rubber roller transfer ink from a sheet metal or paper plate to a blanket roller which prints the final image. (See also LITHOGRAPHY.)

PARTS. See IN PARTS.

PERFECT BINDING. A process by which pages folded into signatures are trimmed, notched and glued (rather than sewn) to a paper cover with no air space between the spine and the binding. Pages that come loose in this process prove daily that the word "perfect" is a misnomer.

PERMANENT WANTS. A phrase not used lightly by used book dealers with special interests. When you find a dealer's "permanent" want ad, it can still be valid months, or even years, later.

PHOTOGRAVURE. A widely used, but expensive, photo mechanical printing process begun after 1880. A copper plate is photo-engraved. The individual dots in the photogravure differ in lightness and darkness by the depth at which they are engraved. Transparent brown inks are often employed which produce soft, glowing images. Photogravure sections from early newspapers are much sought after.

PICTORIAL CLOTH. As early as the 1830s, pictures were printed directly on cloth covers of books. Pictorial paper covers started in 1852. Overdone, such covers are called yellowbacks.

PIRATED EDITION. A book printed without the author's permission and with no payment to the author. These books are often printed in a country other than where the book was originally produced.

POINTS. Facts about a particular issue of a book which help determine the book's value. Points may be errors in the text or a binding change. First editions which have certain errors (points) may be much more valuable than otherwise. Some collectors are known as "point maniacs."
Examples:
> The first issue of F. Scott Fitzgerald's *The Great Gatsby* has the word "chatter" instead of "echolalia" on page 60.

> The first issue of Jack London's *Call of the Wild* has vertically ribbed cloth.

> The first issue of Margaret Mitchell's *Gone With The Wind* has "Published May, 1936" on the copyright page, rather than June.

> The first issue of Ernest Hemingway's *Men Without Women* weighs more than the second issue.

POINTS. Also, in printing, the term refers to a unit of type measurement. For example, 3 point type is about 1/32 of an inch tall; 12 point type is 5/32nds of an inch tall.

PRESENTATION COPY. A signed & inscribed copy by an author or publisher, presented to someone as a gift.

PRESS RUN. The total number of pieces printed.

PRIVATE PRESS. A non-commercial press, usually small, run for esthetic rather than economic reasons.

PROVENANCE. The history of a book's ownership.

PRIVATELY PRINTED. A publication paid for by the author or other interested party. "Vanity presses" cater to situations in which commercial publishers

have turned down a manuscript. However, vanity publishers do little, if any, promotion. Most such books are disasters, except in terms of ego support.

PROOF. A test sheet made by the printer to reveal errors and predict results.

QUARTO, (4to). A page size obtained by folding a full sheet into four leaves. Up to 12 inches tall.

QUOTE. In the used book business, a formal statement of the asking price by a book's owner, usually quoted to a book dealer for resale. "Quotes" also include all pertinent information relating to date, edition and condition.

READING COPY. A book whose text is still intact, although the binding and covers are in poor shape. Sold only for the facts it contains.

REBACKED. Replacement of a book's original backstrip or spine.

RECASED. Removal of a book from its covers for regluing and change of endpapers.

REMAINDERS. Publishers may sell part or all of an out-of-print book to booksellers at reduced prices, usually through "remainder houses." Rarely, the remainders are not books, but unbound sheets of a book, which the new owner binds and sells. Looking through the reduced priced remainders at a local book store can alert a budding author or self-publisher to what is not selling well on the general market.

REPRINT. A double meaning word often used loosely. It can be a new impression from the same setting of type, or a later edition using new type, but with few, if any, changes in text.

RESERVE. The minimum price set by a book owner when consigning valuable goods to an auction. Placing too high a reserve can result in no bidders. Placing too low (or no) reserve can mean a windfall to insiders given preference by the auctioneer.

RETURNS. Books not sold which are returned to the publisher for cash or credit.

REVIEW COPY. A book sent by a publisher to potential reviewers before publication.

RIGHTS. Copyright rights and rights spelled out in a publisher's contract with an author.

ROYALTY. Money paid periodically to an author by his or her publisher. It is usually a percentage of the list price of all copies of the book sold.

SADDLE STITCH. To bind by stapling sheets together where they fold at the spine, as in a comic book.

SEARCH SERVICE. An agency usually without a large inventory of its own, offering to find books sought by individuals or institutions. Most searches are free, the agency adding a fee to the price of the located book. Nowadays about $25 is the minimum price one can expect to pay for a book obtained this way.

SECOND EDITION. An edition using a set of plates wholly new, the first edition plates having been disposed of. Or an updated version of the first edition, utilizing some original text and illustrations and stated as the second edition. (See First Thus Edition.)

SEXTODECIMO, (16mo). A page size ranging between 6 and 7 inches tall. Made by folding a printer's sheet into 16 leaves or 32 pages.

SIGNATURE. A sheet of printed paper that is folded into 8 or 16 pages (4 or 8 leaves) and then is sewn or glued to other printed signatures and bound and trimmed. The word derives from an outdated custom of printing a number or letter at the bottom of a page.

SELF-COVER. A book or pamphlet whose cover is made from the same paper, so that the cover is printed at the same time as the contents.

SLICKS. Magazine on coated paper, as opposed to pulps, which are printed on newsprint.

SLIPCASE. A tailor-made box of cardboard or pasteboard. It protects a book while showing the spine. (See "Box" listing.)

SPINE. The back of the book, connecting covers. Also called backbone or backstrip.

STATE. The part of an edition in which a point or points occur related to a change in type or makeup. SEE POINTS.

STEEL ENGRAVING. An image with sharply defined lines which may be delicate or bold, but very severe compared to pencil or litho work. Finer details than can be achieved in copperplate engraving. A feature common to all early handpresses is the deep impression the four edges of the printing plate made in the paper. Often confused with pen and ink etchings and photo-gravures.

SUBSIDIARY RIGHTS. Rights to sell a book to reprint publishers, film studios, book clubs, magazines, etc.

THREE DECKER. A work, usually a novel, published in three volumes in cloth binding. Common in England in the second half of the 19th Century.

TIPPED IN. A plate, leaf, illustration, errata slip, etc., lightly attached to a book page, usually by hand and pasted only along the top edge of the insert. A technique often used to lower the initial expense of printing fine art books by enabling all color work to be printed on one giant sheet and then tipped in on individual pages of black and white copy.

TOOLING. Cover impressions made for decoration, usually on leather. When the indentation lacks color, this is called blind tooling.

TRADE EDITION. An edition meant for general distribution, as against textbook, library, book club or limited edition markets. Differs from mass market paperbacks in size and are printed on a finer quality paper.

TRADE LIST. A publisher's list of titles, with prices.

TRADE PAPERBACKS. Usually non-fiction paperbacks meant for sale in bookstores or by mail, as against mass market outlets such as supermarkets. Defined by larger size and better paper.

UNCUT AND UNOPENED. Commonly misunderstood terms. In an uncut book the edges of the leaves have not been cut or trimmed. In an unopened book the pages have not been separated, making reading the book impossible without cutting the still-folded leaves. Cutting or trimming such a book can actually lower value.

VANITY PUBLISHER. Also known as a subsidy publisher. The author subsidizes (pays for in advance) most or all of the costs of publication, as well as most of the promotional costs. This leaves the vanity publisher with a sizeable profit, whether or not any books are actually sold.

NEW YORK BOOK BINDERY.

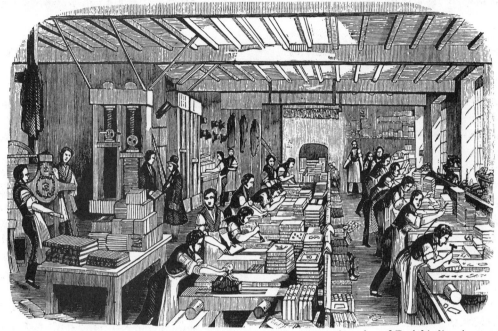

☞ This old establishment is chiefly devoted to the finer and more costly styles of Book-binding in **TURKEY MOROCCO, RUSSIA, ENGLISH, FRENCH** and **AMERICAN CALF,** and especially those unique and economical half Calf and Morocco styles. In all cases the very best of *Stock* and *Workmanship*, with *strength* and *beauty* combined, may be relied upon.

VARIANT. Any copy of a book which is in some way different from most copies of the book in the same edition. If the variants are numerous, that part of the edition is sometimes called a state. Points and variants are closely related. (See POINTS for examples.)

VELLUM. Parchment prepared from the skin of a calf, sheep, lamb or goat. Untanned skin is treated so that it can be written or printed on. Modern vellum, as used in printing and artwork, is 100 per cent rag paper of a translucent quality.

WATERMARK. The distinctive design or trademark created within certain paper during manufacture. Readily seen when held up to a strong light.

WOODCUT. The oldest known printing method. Reached its greatest popular use in the 15th and 16th centuries. Gradually replaced by copperplate engraving. The first woodcuts were carved from planks. Wood engravings are made from end-grain maple and were developed in the 1800s for commercial printing. Woodcuts are bold and poster-like in appearance. Wood engravings are delicate, line-shaded, renderings.

WOVE FINISH. A relatively smooth finish on paper achieved by moderate calendering. A term used to differentiate regular paper from "laid" stock, which has subtle parallel lines within.

WRAPPERS. A paperbound book is said to be "in wrappers." The wrappers may, or may not, be stiff. (See DUST JACKET.)

AGE BEFORE BEAUTY?

Millions of books were printed prior to the 19th Century but ninety-nine percent of them are of British or European origin and have little or no value to collectors. If a book lacks demand, if it adds nothing to history, if it is not illustrated, beautifully bound, or unique in some way, cool off...unless, or course, you just want to own an ancient tome.

Early American Imprints are valuable. The "Imprint" includes the name of the book's **publisher** and the **place** and **date** of publication. Early imprints of books and other printed matter in American states, cities and regions are always in demand. Such items are obviously scarce, but they still turn up in attics, garages and estate sales.

Here is a list of early imprints extracted from John Clyde Oswald's *Printing in the Americas*. It lists the probable or certain year in which the **first printing took place in each state**. If you find a book complete with the necessary points (publisher's name, place, date), published within a decade of these examples, it may be worth consigning to a major auction house!

Buyers of imprints often focus on the output of certain commercial publishers who were active at various times from the Civil War to the 1930s. Here are a few worth keeping an eye out for. With the date of their earliest publications, they are:

Lee and Shepard, Boston, 1862.

James Osgood, Boston, 1866.

Estes and Lauriat, Boston, 1872.

Thomas Bird Mosher, Portland, Maine, 1891.

Copeland and Day, Boston, 1893.

Stone and Kimball, Chicago, 1893.

Mitchell Kennerley, New York, 1897.

Caxton Printers, Caldwell, Idaho, 1903.

Boni and Liveright, New York, 1917.

Alabama, 1811
Alaska, 1852
Arizona, 1859
Arkansas 1819
California, 1834
Colorado, 1859
Connecticut, 1709
Delaware, 1761
District of Columbia, 1789
Florida, 1783
Georgia, 1763
Hawaii, 1872
Idaho, 1839
Illinois, 1814
Indiana, 1804
Iowa, 1836
Kansas, 1834
Louisiana, 1764
Maine, 1785
Maryland, 1700
Massachusetts, 1638
Michigan, 1797
Minnesota, 1846
Mississippi, 1798
Missouri, 1803

Montana, 1862
Nebraska, 1854
New Hampshire, 1757
New Jersey, 1723
New York, 1693
New Mexico, 1834
North Carolina, 1794
North Dakota, 1853
Ohio, 1793
Oklahoma, 1835
Oregon, 1846
Pennsylvania, 1685
Rhode Island, 1715
South Carolina, 1731
South Dakota, 1858
Tennessee, 1786
Texas, 1813
Utah, 1849
Vermont, 1778
Virginia, 1689
Washington, 1852
West Virginia, 1790
Wisconsin, 1827
Wyoming, 1867

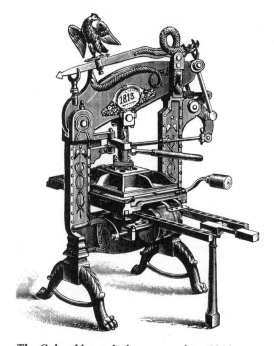

The Columbian printing press, circa 1813.

CONDITION, CONDITION, CONDITION!

In real estate it's location, location, location. Likewise the physical condition of a used book or magazine is a crucial factor in most buy-sell situations. "Good" is simply not good enough for collectors. However, to assert that Fine or Very Good condition is a "must" in all transactions ignores the reality of the marketplace..

Highlighting and underlining generally lowers value, but marginal scribbling sometimes raises the price. For example, genealogies increase in value when additional information has been scrawled in margins or at the end of a book. If the scribbler was the author, or an important personality, the sky might be the limit.

A missing page in a scarce volume can be replaced with a photo copy. Institutions often buy such items and arrange to get Xeroxed pages from other institutions. Most collectors know where to find such facsimile pages and will do so. Condition is more of a concern to buyers of literary first editions, art books, private press books and illustrated books than to seekers of Americana, historical or technical works.

Children's books are very hard to locate in fine condition. Collectors will accept defective copies, sometimes paying surprisingly high prices for scarce titles.

The absence of many pages in the case of a truly great book may be overlooked. A copy of the first illustrated edition of *The Canterbury Tales* sold for $84,000 although 36 leaves were missing.

Rebound copies can scare away collectors, although decorators and others will buy, provided the binding is especially nice. It is like remodeling a house before you sell it—quite a gamble at best. Rebinding a book means that the retail price must be at least twice the cost of rebinding, which runs from $25 to $150 per volume.

Owner's names on 19th Century and earlier books do not generally detract from value. An owner's name on a 20th Century book might, or might not, be considered a defect. (There is always the chance that the inscriber may in time turn out to be an important figure.)

Dust jackets, or dust wrappers, date back to the 16th century, when a plain paper wrapper was folded around some books to protect their costly vellum covers. Vellum is an animal parchment prepared from calfskin, kidskin or lambskin. It "rubs" easily, warps in warm weather and is subject to soiling.

Nothing was printed on early protective dust jackets. It was the responsibility of booksellers to hand-letter a title on each wrapper.

The first use of a printed dust jacket dates from the 1850s. These early commercial dust jackets carried only the book's title and they were printed and affixed before they reached the bookseller. Toward the end of the 19th Century falling profits accelerated wider use of dust jackets. Publishers saw them as a way around expensive embossed and decorated bindings which were currently in vogue. From then on, the cheaper "trade" bindings were often covered with colorful paper dust jackets.

Today finicky book collectors insist on original dust jackets—preferably not chipped, creased, torn, taped, faded, price-clipped or otherwise blemished.

There was a time not many years ago, when a few rare book dealers fought the tide and actually threw away all dust jackets. But the fad did not catch on. Today a hotly pursued rarity, minus its dust jacket, might sell for $100 in very good condition, but go for as high as $5,000 in a fine original jacket.

Modern dust jackets are promotional devices that often contain artwork and biographical information which is not repeated inside the book. So it follows that collectors may not be satisfied with just *any* dust jacket. For example, only the first edition of Thomas Wolfe's **Look Homeward, Angel** carried a dust jacket with a photograph of the author. That's the **only** dust jacket a Wolfe fan will accept.

GRADING YOUR FINDS

There is no national standard of what the terms *Mint, Excellent, Fine, Very Good, Good, Fair, Poor* or *Reading Copy* mean to book dealers. The closest thing to an accepted trade terminology can be found in the **Antiquarian Bookman Weekly**, but its definition of "Fine" stipulates *no defects* in a book, yet allows minor tears and wear?

Grading magazines and newspapers is even more difficult than grading old books, because potential defects are far more numerous.

The books, magazines, newspapers and trade catalogs listed in our book have been drawn, in part, from dealer catalogs. Different catalogers use different grading systems. We have combined the clearest features of various systems in our listings.

Book Grading Terms

MINT: As new, fresh from the publisher and probably unread. No defects. If there is a dust jacket, it must be perfect.

FINE: Showing slight signs of age or spine wear. Dust jacket may have a tiny tear or minor rubbing. Generally a bright and tight copy.

VERY FINE: Used when above defects are at an absolute minimum.

VERY GOOD: Still no major defects, such as a sizeable tear. Normal handling and wear are now obvious. Spine may show slight stress.

GOOD: All contents still intact; no major defect. This is the average used book, well worn, perhaps with minor tape repairs, small spine tears and a little page browning.

FAIR: Worn, or torn, jacket or cover. May lack endpapers or half-title page. A small part of cover may be gone. Marks and stains are expected.

POOR or READING COPY: Text is still complete, but it has all the major defects above, and probably several more. It is only good for information content, not collectible and too ugly to appear on a book shelf.

Condition Grades of Magazines

MINT: Straight from the publisher, probably unopened. No mailing label.

FINE: Very slight traces of wear, the lightest fading of cover or spine. No writing or mailing label. No browning.

VERY FINE: A minimum of wear traces and fading.

VERY GOOD: If lamination is present, peeling may be obvious. All cover luster is gone, there is slight browning and spine may be a bit loose. No tape repairs.

GOOD: Color cover badly faded, spine rolling, cover folded too often. Some pages may be brittle. Creases and flaking present. but nothing is missing.

FAIR: Major defects. Badly worn, torn and soiled. Part of the cover may be missing. Stains common. However, the item is still complete. Equals the reading copy of a hardcover book.

Newspaper Grading

The grading system of the Newspaper Collectors Society of America is as follows:

VERY FINE: Newspaper can have a minor tear but it cannot extend into the body affecting any articles. Small amounts of staining or mottling may be present. The texture of the paper can show some usage and have some fold lines.

FINE: Newspaper can have some staining, mottling or browning and can have some spine separation. The texture of the paper will show signs of handling (limp, wrinkles, etc.). Margins can show some wear or even a portion may have a small area torn away, but it must not affect any part of the text.

GOOD: The spine is separated completely. The texture of the paper will show obvious wear and tear. Considerable staining, mottling and browning are present. Small areas of the page missing, including portions of text. Only a truly rare paper is collectible in this condition.

POOR: Anything less than the definition of "good." Paper entirely separated at the half-fold, brittle, flaking, etc. Has no collector value unless it is the only known example of the paper.

Many newspaper collectors use a simpler grading system. If a 20th Century newspaper is solid, intact, relatively clean with no stains and only mild browning, it is in "collectible condition."

A newspaper printed before 1870, on rag stock, that has become limp from use, with pieces missing and lots of wrinkles, might only be worth 25 percent of one that is in "collectible condition."

Trade Catalogs

Buyers of trade catalogs are not as particular about condition as are the collectors of old books and magazines. Catalog buyers are generally "users" rather than collectors. They are interested in the practical value of catalogs as direct sources of information or as items suitable for reproduction.

Catalog dealers often place disclaimers at the front of their lists stating that normal signs of wear, such as chips, creases, pencil notations, company stamps and owner inscriptions are to be expected and are not noted in descriptions. The most damning defect which can be found in any trade catalog is a missing page or a clipped illustration. Likewise tears or bold marks which might hinder the reproduction of illustrations should be noted.

THE DEFECTORY

A checklist of imperfections commonly found in books, magazines, newspapers and trade catalogs follows on the next page.

Newcomers to selling such merchandise tend to rate their offerings as being in better condition than they actually are (and veteran dealers have been known to overlook less than obvious defects.)

THE DEFECTORY, applied faithfully to all offerings will help, rather than hinder a sale.

An honest description builds confidence and eliminates costly returns. When a customer feels that your terminology has overlooked obvious defects you have lost him forever.

COMMON DEFECTS

A checklist of imperfections commonly found in books, magazines, newspapers and trade catalogs.

Common defects
browning
book plate removal
clippings, pasted in
crayon
dirt
erasures
foxing
gluing
holes
insect damage
liquids
mending
marks
pen
pencil
price stickers
re-backing
re-covering
remaindering
repair tape
rusty staples
soiling
water/damp stains

Binding defects
bindery tears
centerfold loose or
detached
disbound partly
or in toto
loose binding
re-binding poor
re-jointing poor
staples loose or
missing

Spine wear
bent, bowed or
broken spines cut
clipped, crinkled
discolored
fraying, flaking
loose, missing all or part
library, other stickers
rips, tears
rolling, rounding
splitting

Page defects
art work by readers
bookplates of inconsequential
persons
brittle
browning
copyright, other pages
  missing
cropping, clipping, creasing,
or crumbling
discoloring
edges frayed, nicked
endpapers missing, damaged
ends folded over
illustration registration poor
illustration plates missing
illustration color running
library stamps
loose, detached
repair tape
rips, tears, cuts
signatures, inscriptions of
inconsequential persons
scribbling, underlining

thumbwear
yellowing

Cover defects
chipping
clipping
corners dogeared, bumped,
creased or folded
cracked leather
detached, missing
discolored
dry leather
fading color
flaking
gouging
labels (library, subscriptions)
laminated plastic peeling,
detached
luster lost
ripped, torn, scratched, rubbed
soiling
warping
wear (shelf, handling)
wrinkles

Dust jacket defects
chipping
clipping
color fading
flap worn, torn, missing
fraying
gloss gone
holes
rips, tears
rubbing
tape repair

Note:
Any of the above defects can affect value. Most of the prices quoted on the following pages are for books in very good, or better, condition. Be sure to adjust your estimates accordingly.

FIRST EDITIONS

For the past hundred years most publishing houses have seemingly conspired to make their first editions impossible to distinguish from later print runs. The first edition of a book technically includes all copies printed from the first setting-up of type. Theoretically copies printed 50 years apart could both be first editions, provided the type had remained intact.

Realistically, however, the term "first editions" has meant to dealers and collectors only those copies printed between the starting of the first run and its first stop (for additions, corrections, price changes, or any other reason). This first impression, or printing, is what collecting modern fiction, in particular, is all about.

If the first impression contains some typographical or textual peculiarity, then the impression is known as an issue or state. (The difference in meaning is minor. "Issue" is used when publication is complete, "state" before any copies are circulated.) The term for the peculiarity is "point". A true first edition must have all the right "points." A few examples of points are:

Opinions of Olliver Allston, by Van Wyck Brooks, has different color dust jackets on first edition copies. However, only one color would be considered a "first state" printing. Once the press stopped, and changes were made, the book became a "2nd state" of the first edition.

Ethan Frome, by Edith Wharton, has a line of broken type in all but the first issue.

The Good Earth, by Pearl Buck, has the word "fleas" instead of the proper "flees" on page 100 of the first issue.

The Song of Hiawatha, by Henry Wadsworth Longfellow, contains advertisements in its first issue that are dated November 1855. Later copies printed in 1855 are not "true" firsts.

Some collectors do not get excited about points; others are fanatical about them. Dealers and collectors frequently amass a considerable number of bibliographies and other reference books that spell out hundreds of points. Entire books have been written on identifying the first editions of individual authors.

Without consulting reference books, one may hope that a book is a first edition if the date on the title page agrees with the date on the copyright page. But many times the title page has no date, and copyright page entries can be tricky. Publishers often change copyright dates when any new material is added. A first edition checklist follows:

1. If more than one date is listed, the odds are that the copy is not a first. The earliest date listed may mean that the work was first published in a magazine, which is therefore, the "truest" first.

2. If the publisher obtains a copyright date late in the year, say in December, and does not get around to publishing the book in the following year, the printed copyright date would not indicate the actual first edition date, which could be two years later.

3. Phrases like "Illustrated Edition", "First Illustrated Edition", "First Edition With Preface", "New Edition", etc., may appear on the copyright page, but none of them are used on the first impression—the collector's first. They are merely selling devices used to give the illusion of an early edition.

4. Reprints and book club editions—printed months or even years after the true "first"—may retain the phrase "first edition", for the same marketing reasons, but they are not firsts.

Publishers' quirks and code changes in their handling of firsts are legion. For this reason many reference books citing "points" and other pertinent data have been published for bibliophiles, particularly about books published in the early part of the 20th Century. Check out a copy of H. Boutell's *First Editions of Today and How to Tell Them*, Spoon River Press' *First Editions: A Guide to Identification*, or Bill McBride's *Identification of First Editions-A Pocket Guide*.

One valuable reference book which collectors usually overlook, because it does not list points, is the massive set of the *National Union Catalogue of Printed Books*, which lists, in chronological order of publication, every book contained in the Library of Congress. However, only the largest public libraries and college libraries carry this huge set, published from 1953 to 1983.

In 1991, *"Firsts"*, a sophisticated monthly magazine for collectors of modern first editions, began publication. Each month an article discusses (and prices) the firsts of a modern author and reports recent dealer catalog prices on many other collectible writers. Write to: Firsts Magazine Inc., 575 N. Lucerne Boulevard, Los Angeles CA 90004.

The imprint of any of the following publishers on a book means that with few exceptions it is a reprint. Just a few short years ago reprints by these houses were disdained by antiquarian bookmen. But today a nicely jacketed early copy—especially of a juvenile title—could pay for a fine dinner out.

Altemus	Collier	Hurst
Blakiston	Cupples & Leon	Saalfield
Blue Ribbon	Fiction Library	Sun Dial
A. L. Burt	Goldsmith	Tower
Cassel	Grosset & Dunlap	Triangle

LIMITED EDITIONS

The Franklin Library, a "limited edition" publisher, reportedly paid Erskine Caldwell $50,000 to sign his name on 25,000 sheets of paper, each of which became a page in a "limited edition" of a Caldwell novel. Ray Bradbury signed 13,000 sheets, and John Cheever 12,600 sheets for other "limited editions."

By a sort of "gentleman's agreement" within the trade today, a book printing that exceeds 2,500 copies is not considered a limited edition. A firm like the Franklin Library, which does not individually number the copies of its "limiteds", apparently takes advantage of this ambiguous situation.

The limited edition fad became popular at the turn of the century. Elbert Hubbard's Roycroft Press (1899-1928), frequently printed more than 1,500 copies of his "limited editions" (which he had advertised as being limited to only 200 copies).

A few kind words about limited edition books are, however, in order. The author's signature is probably genuine, whereas autographed and inscribed copies of mass-produced trade books are more suspect. Assuming the trade copy signature and inscription genuine, the number of such copies is not known; while if the limited edition has been numbered, one can be reasonably assured his investment is safe.

In addition to being signed and numbered (lower than 2,501 copies) a legitimate limited edition comes with a slipcase or box, is illustrated and often fancily bound. However, getting heavily invested in new issues is chancy because only a small percentage of authors ever reach the stardom required to recover retail prices.

Robin Smiley, in "Firsts" magazine, tells the story of Ernest Hemingway's only limited edition. His publisher, Scribner's, issued 31,050 trade copies of *A Farewell to Arms*. Hemingway had achieved a high level of popularity by 1933, so it was decided that these copies would be supplemented by a limited edition of 510 (of which 10 were for Hemingway's personal use). These limited edition copies were larger than the trade edition copies and, as usual, boasted a slipcase, but no dust jacket. Today, Smiley recounts, "A trade copy in very good to fine dust jacket is worth from $400 to $1,500. A limited edition copy which has lost its box is worth about $2,500. If it has a box in nearly pristine condition, the price rises to nearly $6,000. In essence, the only difference between a $2,500 copy and a $6,000 copy is the condition of the box."

Ordinary book club editions (usually printed on cheap stock and plainly bound) are loathed by dealers and collectors alike. **The Limited Editions Club** is an exception. Compared to some other present day so-called "limited edition" publishers (who have no limits) the Limited Editions Club always states the exact number of copies printed (usually between 1,500 and 2,000). Their books are quality productions, usually signed by the illustrator or designer.

Dealing strictly in limited editions and maintaining a good reputation since its inception in 1929, the Limited Editions Club has turned out more than 500 titles. Significantly, most of the titles do not draw unusually high prices (an average being $75 to $200), so dealers' prices may vary. Ironically, a book published in a trade run of 50,000 copies may be harder to find in a used bookstore than a limited edition copy of the same book. Those 50,000 copies suffered the fate of heavy wear and loss that all trade copies are subject to, while the limited edition sat safely in its box on a collector's shelf, and probably was never read.

Another limited-edition-producer of both books and prints was Eugene Connett's **Derrydale Press**. Prior to its inception in 1927 the quality of American books on sporting subjects was appallingly mediocre. Connett "found a need and filled it" with quality books for sportsmen that have yet to be surpassed.

Derrydale books of field and stream were issued in limited editions of less than 1,251 copies. Mr. Connett's formula was to produce "easy-to-read, dignified volumes which would appeal to conservative people." He also designed them to last. "Make a book for your customer's great-grandchildren" was his important credo.

At a recent auction the following prices were paid for Derrydale books in very good to fine condition. *Early American Sporting Books*, inscribed by author, $500; *Western Angler* by Roderick Haig-Brown, $400; *Atlantic Salmon Fishing* by Charles Phair, $700. Other Derrydale books at the auction sold between $60 and $600. The rarest and most deluxe editions of some Derrydales sell for between $5,000 and $10,000. A complete list of Derrydale values may be found in the latest edition of Ralf Coykendall's *Sporting Collectors Price Guide*.

Small presses and private presses sometimes acquire rights to the unpublished work of an esteemed author. Their subsequent limiteds sell briskly. A certain number of copies are signed and numbered, another group is hardbound, but unsigned, and finally a few hundred are paperbacked. The consummate collector simply has to own all three. Happy hunting!

COLLECTIBLE ILLUSTRATORS

Illustrators are society's visual historians. A well rendered illustration tells its audience a story without using any words.

The technical difference between a "fine artist" and a commercial illustrator is the fact that a painter's work need not convey any particular message; it can stand on its own as an object of subjective beauty.

Conversely, the illustrator is paid to produce a picture which will enhance or enliven an author's text. Fine art is not necessarily meant for reproduction, while the illustrator's art is expressly produced for mass publication.

The father of 20th century illustration in America was **Howard Pyle (1853-1911)**. His stories and artwork appeared in Scribner's and Harper's even before he had graduated from art school.

Pyle was a stickler for historically accurate illustration—a trait which he passed on to many of his students. Among them were N. C. Wyeth and Jessie Wilcox Smith. Norman Rockwell also acknowledged Howard Pyle's influence on his work. Pyle wrote and illustrated 25 children's books between 1886 and 1908.

Charles Dana Gibson (1867-1944) sold his first illustration to *Life* magazine in 1886, just two years after beginning his studies at the Art Students League in New York.

By the time of the 1895 World's Fair, Gibson's crisp pen and ink drawings had replaced millions of color lithographs as standard Victorian parlor decor. His story-telling black and white sketches expressed a wide and deep understanding of American society.

The *New York World* claimed that "Gibson's pen has sent mustaches out of fashion and synthesized the ideal American girl."

The "Gibson Girl" remained the national standard of perfection until **Howard Chandler Christy** created the "Christy Girl" in 1906.

Harrison Fisher's "American Beauties" captured the stage in 1909 and his work is currently the most collectible of all three illustrators.

Maxfield Parrish (1870-1966) was a second generation artist whose rich colorful fantasies emerged in the 1890s to fill the pages of *Scribner's, Collier's* and *Harper's* magazines., His talents extended to many book illustrations, from fairy tales to Kenneth Grahame's *Dream Days* and *Golden Age*. All of Parrish's work is collectible today, including posters, covers, magazine illustrations and Mazda light bulb ads.

Also in tune with the naturalness and truthful detail found in most art of the period was the work of **Jessie Wilcox Smith (1863-1935).** Her wonderful drawings of children graced the pages of *Little Women, Water Babies* and *Heidi*. Her cover art and illustrations appeared in *Good Housekeeping, McClures* and many other magazines.

Frederic Sackrider Remington (1861-1909) finished his studies at the Yale School of Fine Arts in 1880 and promptly headed west to capture the last real cowboys and Indians on canvas. Once there, he lived the life of his subjects and participated in everything from cattle drives to mule ranching and gold prospecting.

In 1885 Remington moved to New York where his illustrations appeared regularly in *Harper's Weekly* and *Century Magazine*. Over his lifetime he produced 23 notable bronzes, completed more than 2,700 paintings and drawings, and wrote several books.

He was also a war correspondent for the Hearst newspapers during the Spanish American War. While in Cuba he met Rough Rider, Theodore Roosevelt, whose books and articles he later illustrated. After his death the *New York Herald* called him "an exalted realist, a Courbet of the Southwest."

Palmer Cox did not receive any formal art school training. Born in Quebec in 1840, he traveled to San Francisco at the age of 23 and worked at various railroad and ship carpenter jobs while submitting short stories and cartoons to California newspapers. After some success he moved to New York in 1875 where he wrote and illustrated 13 Brownie books between 1887 and 1913. His little elves appeared on dozens of products and in most all of the children's magazines of the period.

Joseph Christian Leyendecker was born in Germany in 1874 and moved to Chicago as a child. After graduation from the Art Institute he went to work for Cyrus Curtis at the *Saturday Evening Post* where he created 300 covers over a 40 year period. Leyendecker also is well known for his advertising art, including illustrations for Arrow Shirt and Hart, Shaffner & Marx.

Space limits us to these brief thumbnail sketches of a few famous illustrators, but we have listed dozens more alphabetically, throughout this guide, with current prices for their most popular books. You will also find additional entries in the Magazine Section. Other price guides and reading material appear in the Bibliography.

For nearly 50 years, art critics and collectors had looked down at book and magazine illustration as a utilitarian device. But in 1979 several auction houses started offering the work of commercial illustrators along with traditional fine-art fare. Today, collecting original illustration art and reproductions is much in vogue. The illustrated book, in particular, has become a major collectible.

Lithography, the most common technique used in reproducing original illustrations, is almost 200 years old. Invented by Alois Senefelder in 1798, the process did not immediately catch on. Woodcuts remained the preferred vehicle for illustration in America until after the Civil War. *Leslie's Illustrated* and *Harper's Weekly* successfully employed the medium during the Civil War to convert on-site artist's sketches into realistic battle scenes for news-hungry readers. Several engravers could work at once on a large rendering, each producing a separate, smaller, woodblock which was locked in place along with others to form a two-page spread.

Stone lithography was used for colorful labels, greeting cards, bonds, bank notes, letterheads and other advertising pieces. Lithography was also used to produce Winslow Homer's *Campaign Sketches*. In Homer's book one can see the subtle texture of the porous limestone that reproduced original drawings made on it with lithographic pencils and crayons.

Between 1885 and 1890 photo-engraving spelled the end of woodcuts and wood engraving in most books. In 1880 the first photographic halftone (a mechanical dot pattern) was printed in the *New York Journal Graphic* newspaper. By this time, pen and ink sketches could be photographically reproduced in as much detail as hand-engraved pieces of the 19th century.

Lithography and letterpress technology advanced rapidly after steam-powered cylinder presses were introduced in 1866. Newspapers were flying off new rotary presses at the rate of 30,000 an hour!

The Golden Age of illustration, 1890 to 1915, was led by *Harper's, Leslie's, Scribner's* and *Century* magazines. Commercial illustrators of the day flourished by the hundreds, but only a few dozen did well at book illustration.

The austerity of World War I eliminated many established magazine publishers and forced full-color illustration out of books. With the exception of some children's books, black and white again became standard fare. Scratchboard, graphite pencils, pen and ink, and charcoal were popular mediums during in this period.

After World War II mass market magazines such as *The Saturday Evening Post, Colliers, Cosmopolitan, Redbook* and *Ladies' Home Companion* gave way to specialty magazines. Color in children's books expanded its thrust into general book illustration. Airbrush, watercolor, felt-tip-pens, paper collage and prisma color pencil illustration rapidly gained prominence over former mediums.

Three important reference books on the commercial illustrator's art are James J. Best's *American Popular Illustration: A Reference Guide* (Greenwood Press, 1984); Anne Gilbert's *American Illustrator Art* (House of Collectibles, 1991) and *The Illustrator in America, 1880-1980*, by Walt Reed, Roger Reed and Fred Taraba.

The market for original illustration art is centered in New York City, where several specialty galleries and auction houses hold annual sales. At a recent event conducted by Illustration House, a gallery at 96 Spring Street, some record prices were made.

Norman Rockwell's study for *Freedom of Speech* brought $407,000. (The previous record for a Rockwell painting was $264,000.) N. C. Wyeth's *Moose Call*, a painting of an American Indian in a canoe, brought $99,000. J. C. Leyendecker's rendering of a western couple, *Watcher's of the Plains*, sold for $52,800.

A leading dealer, who pioneered the market for American illustrator paintings and drawings, is Judy Goffman at 18 East 77th Street, New York, NY 10021.

The Society of Illustrators' Museum of American Illustration is located at 128 East 63rd Street, New York.

To keep abreast of this market you might subscribe to: *Antiques & the Arts Weekly*, 5 Church Hill Road, Newton CT 06470; *The Illustrator Collector News*, Box 1958, Sequim WA 98282 and current auction catalogs from *Illustration House*, 96 Spring St., 7th Floor, New York NY 10012-3923.

Most fine art price guides also list auction prices realized for leading illustrators. Davenport's *Art Reference and Price Guide* is a good one to check for unfamiliar artists. The latest edition contains data on more than 100,000 artists. Write to Davenport at 1036 Britten Lane, #202, Ventura, CA 93003.

Richard Hislop's *Art Sales Index* should be available at large libraries. It contains sales information from 271 worldwide auction houses.

The vast majority of illustrators were free-lance individuals and some were never listed in major biblio- graphic sources. Here are 120 illustrators who are actively collected in both original and reproduced form:

John Wolcott Adams
Constantin Alajalov
Joan Walsh Anglund
Peter Arno
Stanley Arthurs
Boris Artzybasheff
Ingre Aulaire
James Avati
W. J. Aylward
McClelland Barclay
Ludwig Bemelmans
Anna Whelan Betts
Esther Franklin Betts
Walter Biggs
Reginald Birch
Mahlon Blaine
Franklin Booth
Will Bradley
Frank W. Brangwyn
Paul Bransom
George Brehm
Arthur W. Brown
Charles Bull
Harrison Cady
Randolph Caldicott
C. F. Chambers
Howard Chandler Christy
Fanny Young Cory
Walter Crane
Palmer Cox

James Daugherty
Marguerite de Angeli
W. W. Denslow
Steve Dohanos
Edmund Dulac
Harvey Dunn
Nick Eggenhofer
Harrison Fisher
James Montgomery Flagg
Thomas Fogarty
H. J. Ford
Frank Frazetta
A. B. Frost
Charles Dana Gibson
Robert Giusti
William J. Glackens
Elizabeth Shippen Green
Kate Greenaway
Johnny Gruelle
Jules Guerin
Bessie Pease Gutmann
Oliver Herford
Greg Hildebrant
Tim Hildebrant
Winslow Homer
Maud Humphrey
Lynn Bogue Hunt
Peter Hurd
Will James
Burris Jenkins, Jr.

Roger Kastel
A. L. Keller
Richard Kemble
Rockwell Kent
W. H.D. Koerner
Marie Lawson
Robert Lawson
Lois Lenski
Joseph C. Leyendecker
Reginald Marsh
James McMullan
Stanley Meltzoff
Grace and Carl Moon
Rowena Morrill
Willard Mullin
Thomas Nast
John R. Neill
Peter Newell
Kay Nielsen
Violet Oakley
Rose O'Neill
Maxfield Parrish
Russell Patterson
Clara Peck
Edward Penfield
Joseph Pennell
Maude Petersham
Coles Phillips
Willy Pogany
Leo Politi

Beatrix Potter
Howard Pyle
Arthur Rackham
John Rae
Henry P. Raleigh
Frederic Remington
Boardman Robinson
Norman Rockwell
Charles M. Russell
Mead Schaeffer
Frank Schoonover
Maurice Sendak
Ernest Thompson Seton
Ben Shahn
Joan Sloan
Jesse Wilcox Smith
Alice B. Stephens
Sarah J. Stilwell
Arthur Szyk
W. L. Taylor
Hugh Thomson
Diana Thorne
Murray Tinkelman
Lynd Ward
Kurt Weise
John Whitcomb
Milo Winter
Andrew Wyeth
N. C. Wyeth
F. C. Yohn

CHILDREN'S BOOKS

Children's books are probably the most popular form of collectible illustrator art. Their history dates back to the 17th century juvenile title, **Orbis Pictus**, which was filled with woodcuts of people at play and other interesting objects to encourage reading.

By the middle 1700s a few London printing houses had begun to specialize in juvenile literature, but the emphasis was on highly moralistic tales. Gradually, however, the works of Puritan authors were superseded by more exciting classics such as **Gulliver's Travels** and **Robinson Crusoe**.

The tide continued to turn in 1807 when a banker named William Roscoe wrote a best-seller entitled **The Bufferly's Ball and the Grasshopper's Feast**. In the same year Mrs. Catherine Dorset penned **The Peacock at Home**, which sold more than 4 million copies in 12 months. By the 1820s **Old Mother Hubbard** and **The Tale of Cock Robin** had both been mass-produced in hand colored editions—by child labor.

In the mid 1800s color lithography gradually began to replace earlier watercolor-tinted woodcuts and steel engravings in some children's books. The Germans excelled in chromolithography and most fine color printing was done in Germany and then bound up with the text after being shipped back to England or America for distribution.

Also of Germanic origin were the brothers Grimm and their "shocking" 1812 to 1815 series of fairy tales which were later illustrated in English language versions by such notables as George Cruikshank (1792-1878), Arthur Rackham (1867-1939), John R. Neill (1878-1943), Johnny Gruelle (1880-1938) and Jesse Wilcox Smith (1863-1935).

In the middle 1860s there was a relapse back into black and white dullness in children's books. Then, in the 1870s, British illustrators led a color revival in the industry. Three of the most prominent artists of the period were Randolph Caldicott (1846-1886), Kate Greenaway (1846-1901) and Walter Crane (1845-1915).

America was not without its share of children's book publishers during the 19th century. In the early 1800s it was a common practice for bookshop owners to print original (or pirated) editions for their own inventory and then sell the surplus to the trade at large. Many small sized "toy books", with hand colored plates, were issued by Yankee merchants and printers in the 1850s.

The Night Before Christmas— a poem penned in 1822 by a New York doctor named Clement. C. Moore—was later made famous by the McLoughlin Brothers and their chief illustrator, Thomas Nast.

An already ancient collection of nursery rhymes, **Mother Goose's Melodies**, was issued in a color-litho edition by Porter & Coates, of Philadelphia, in the 1870s. Subsequent editions illustrated by Kate Greenaway (of A, B, C, fame), Maud Humphrey (1868-19??) and Maxfield Parrish (1870-1966) have appeared onward to this day.

To make a long story short; it is estimated that more than a hundred children's book publishers were thriving in the United States by the year 1870.

Chief among these firms was a giant book, board game, paperdoll and postcard publishing house named after its founder, John McLoughlin, a Scottish immigrant.

Starting in 1828 with a used handpress, John McLoughlin wrote and printed his own small instructional pamphlets of conduct and morals for children. Later editions were bound into larger books and by 1848 McLoughlin was able to retire, leaving the business to his two sons—Edmund and John, Jr.

The McLoughlin Brothers continued to expand their father's successful operation and by the late 1880s were the world's largest publisher of children's books. They employed the cream of America's illustrators, including Thomas Nast (1840-1902), Palmer Cox (1840-1924) and Howard Pyle (1853-1911).

At their peak of production in the 1890s the McLoughlins employed a staff of 75 artists. However, they did not list illustrators' names in any of their books or pamphlets. (Perhaps this was because most books were group efforts and the policy eliminated rivalry.)

In 1920 a third generation of McLoughlins sold out to Milton Bradley, a leading manufacturer of toys, games, crayons and other grammar school supplies. Bradley used the McLoughlin label for three more decades and then the once-famous name passed into history.

Space limits us to a very brief history of the Golden Age of children's books. However, there are dozens of authoritative volumes available for collectors seeking further enlightenment, (see Bibliography).

The important thing to remember is that if you come across illustrated children's books of the 1870s-1930s it may be worth your time to do further research.

STORMY LITERATURE

Once "Banned in Boston" assured a new book of hefty sales and of becoming a "storm center" of public opinion. There have been dozens of storm centers over the decades, resulting in high demand for some and oblivion for others. Let's have a look at these controversial collectibles.

THE STORY OF LITTLE BLACK SAMBO

First published in England in 1899, this children's book's setting was laid in an imaginary land, a mixture of India and Africa. Author-illustrator Helen Bannerman's hero, Sambo, was hardly controversial. He had pleasing features, dressed well, was intelligent and had loving parents. Because a friend's mistake weakened the book's copyright, more than 50 editions have been published with which Mrs. Bannerman had no connection.

In the United States the term "Sambo" as used in *Uncle Tom's Cabin,* had become a derogatory term, a fact unknown to Mrs. Bannerman. American illustrators drew Sambo and his family as plantation-slave stereotypes. The book was extremely popular, and charges that it was racist did not appear until the 1940s. Today, though generally relegated to a special section in libraries, the classic story of *Little Black Sambo* is still being published and remains a brisk seller.

Perhaps critic Selma Lanes hit the mark when she pointed out that the book introduced blacks to American children as human beings. They were human beings, not racist stereo-types, in Helen Bannerman's original version. The villains may well have been those American illustrators, who exaggerated Sambo's features.

The first edition of *Little Black Sambo* appeared in an issue of 500 copies, with 27 colored wood engravings. A good copy is worth in the neighborhood of $2,000 today, and early editions are growing in value.

FOREVER

The 17-year-old heroine of Judy Blume's 1975 novel, cautiously and carefully yields her virginity, but splits with her boy friend when sex is not enough to hold them together. Moralistic? Beneath the surface, definitely. But several critics felt *Forever* to be "a manufactured sex manual disguised as a novel." Another reader said the book had "all the right messages, but all the same...it is pornography." Even Miss Blume's friendly biographer, Maryann Weidt, admits that the plot of *Forever* is "methodical" and that the characters are strictly one-dimensional. *Forever's* publisher classed it as adult fiction, although Mrs. Blume intended it as a cautionary tale for 13 and 14-year-olds. In the 1980s, Mrs. Blume, a mother now waxing conservative, suggested that girls shouldn't read her book until they finished high school.

Today the price of a very good first edition is $15-$25.

THE IMPENDING CRISIS

In 1857, six years after *Uncle Tom's Cabin* antagonized Southern slaveholders, a louder fury greeted Hinton Rown Helper's *The Impending Crisis*. The son of a failing South Carolina farmer, Helper charged caustically (and with plentiful statistics) that the slave-holding aristocracy had impoverished the small southern farmer and would soon doom the South.

Published, prudently, in New York City, the book was ceremoniously burned in front of many southern courthouses. In the South, merely owning a copy was a criminal act. Three men were reportedly hanged in Arkansas for possessing a copy. A railway company denied "Helperites" tickets, and one state denied them any chance of becoming policemen. A Congressman told the House that a certain book distributor should be hanged. In Helper's former home-state of North Carolina it became a felony-punishable by death on second offense--to bring any literature into the state which tended to incite slaves.

Helper himself despised blacks. He would have taxed slaveowners and used the money to ship slaves back to Africa. (In a later book, Helper even suggested that blacks be exterminated.)

A fine first edition of *The Impending Crisis* is worth $80.

THE WELL OF LONELINESS

"A Book That Must Be Suppressed" screamed the banner headline of London's *Daily Express* in 1928. Sales of Radclyffe Hall's new novel, *The Well of Loneliness* skyrocketed. "I should rather give a healthy boy or a healthy girl a vial of prussic acid than this novel." said the editor of the Express. Using an 1847 law, a British judge banned Hall's book as obscene, and it suffered the same fate in New York for ten years.

The Well of Loneliness explored lesbianism for the first time in an English novel. The author was a mannish middle-aged, wealthy, devout Catholic whom friends called "John" or "Johnny." In her then-sensational novel, she poured forth 500 pages of polemic and stereotype asserting that lesbianism is inborn.

Her publisher, seeing a ban ahead, shipped the book's plates to Paris, where British tourists routinely bought a copy on their way home. In the United States, *The Well* sold briskly, but fearful conservative reaction was not confined to Britain. One American mother said that such a ballyhoo had been roused by the book that "Young boys and girls can no longer remain ignorant of certain facts which ordinarily would never have come to their notice."

The price today of a British first edition (in large format, bound in black and with a plain cover) ranges from $250 to $300. A 1928 American limited first edition in slipcase is worth $350.

THREE WEEKS

A new kind of novel appeared in the U. S. in 1907, with the publication of English author Elinor Glyn's *Three Weeks*. It told how the youth "Paul, whom books did not worry much," has a torrid affair with the middle-aged wife of a Russian diplomat. Called only "The Lady," she dresses in black and has an extremely red mouth. In prose innocuously purple by today's standards, she undulates on a tiger rug "round and all over" the adolescent, Paul. An instant best-seller, though tut-tutted throughout Britain, *Three Weeks* gave rise to a popular lyric:

> Would you like to sin
> With Elinor Glyn
> On a tiger skin?
> Or would you prefer
> To err with her
> On some other fur?

Although *Three Weeks* was ruled obscene and swept from bookstore shelves in Massachusetts, it sold briskly in other American cities. By the mid-1930s, according to Miss Glyn, 5,000,000 sales had markedly improved her financial condition. As late as 1932, however, a Mickey Mouse cartoon was suppressed in the U. S. because in it a cow, resting in a pasture, is reading *Three Weeks*.

The price of a British first edition today is $15-$30.

THE ADVENTURES OF HUCKLEBERRY FINN

More than a century after Mark Twain's classic tale was published, it still ranks high on many school lists of controversial books. Objections are made to "racist," "anti-religious," and "frank" language. To such protests, Twain replied that he wrote the book exclusively for adults. The satirist recalled that he was allowed as a child to read the Bible unexpurgated, which probably soiled his mind for good.

Noted critic Lionel Trilling defends the book by stating simply that a national history is not made up only of "pleasant and creditable things." However, when a parent in Pennsylvania objected to the novel in 1983, a school committee decided that many 9th grade students do not understand satire as a literary device. Therefore, the book was only used afterwards in the 11th and 12th grades.

Today the price of a very good first edition is $1,000-$3,000.

WHERE THE WILD THINGS ARE

Are monsters frightening or funny? If they do frighten kids for a moment, is that bad?

Maurice Sendak's *Where the Wild Things Are* raised these questions in the early 1960s. His book argued that childhood is not all innocence; that children have nasty fantasies, personal troubles and angry moments. Little Max, Sendak's hero, goes to bed without supper when, in a wolf suit, he threatens to eat his mother. She calls him a "wild thing." So of course Max dreams of a land full of wild things, monsters who make him king. He leads them in howling revels, then sends them to bed without supper.

Famed psychologist Bruno Bettelheim first said the book was too scary for children; then, like others, he changed his mind. Sendak's editor called *Where the Wild Things Are* the first American picture book for children to recognize that children have powerful emotions. One admiring critic wrote, "Boys and girls may have to shield their parents from his book. Parents are easily scared."

The price of a very good first edition is $1,500-$2,400.

CATCHER IN THE RYE

Hundreds of times, J. D. Salinger's 1951 novel. *Catcher in the Rye*. has been tossed disgustedly on some school official's desk by many an angry parent. Many times, the parent has succeeded in getting the book removed from the required reading list, or put on a closed shelf or pulled from the library entirely.

Protagonist Holden Caulfield's flight from insensitive grownups and his two days underground in Manhattan may have enraptured thousands of young readers, but charges of bad language, sacrilege and sexual perversion keep flying. A Kentucky high school teacher, told he could not use the book in class, protested that the principal (a member of Citizens for Decent Literature) hadn't read the book. The teacher was fired for his observation.

In Oklahoma eight parents complained, but 2,000 supported a teacher who added the novel to the required reading list. The practical principal kept the teacher...but fired the book.

In 1978 a Washington State school board banned the book when a protester cited "785 profanities" in it.

Curiously, a reviewer in the prominent Catholic weekly, "America," defended *Catcher*, saying that Holden's language was remarkably restrained, compared to what modern young people were using. Sexual matters, he said, were treated tastefully, and *Catcher* was not "an immoral, corrupting book."

Today's price of a first edition is $1,000-$1,500.

LADY CHATTERLEY'S LOVER

The only reason *Lady Chatterley's Lover* is such a well-known book today is because it was banned here and in England upon publication in 1928.

A couple of stimulating scenes between the main characters, a British society matron and her husband's handyman, were just too hot for public consumption.,

Author D. H. Lawrence signed and numbered the 1,000-copy first edition, which was printed in the liberal-minded city of Florence. Today a very good to fine copy of this scarce edition might fetch in excess of $3,000. Worn and shaken examples have shown up at auction over the years, and brought from $300 to $800.

Several unauthorized printings appeared late in 1928. One pirated version published in New York is worth $100-$150.

By 1932 most censors had relented and the first authorized English edition was printed in London. It is worth about $50. Meanwhile, because of all the fuss, *Lady Chatterley's Lover* remains one of the most notorious books of the 20th century.

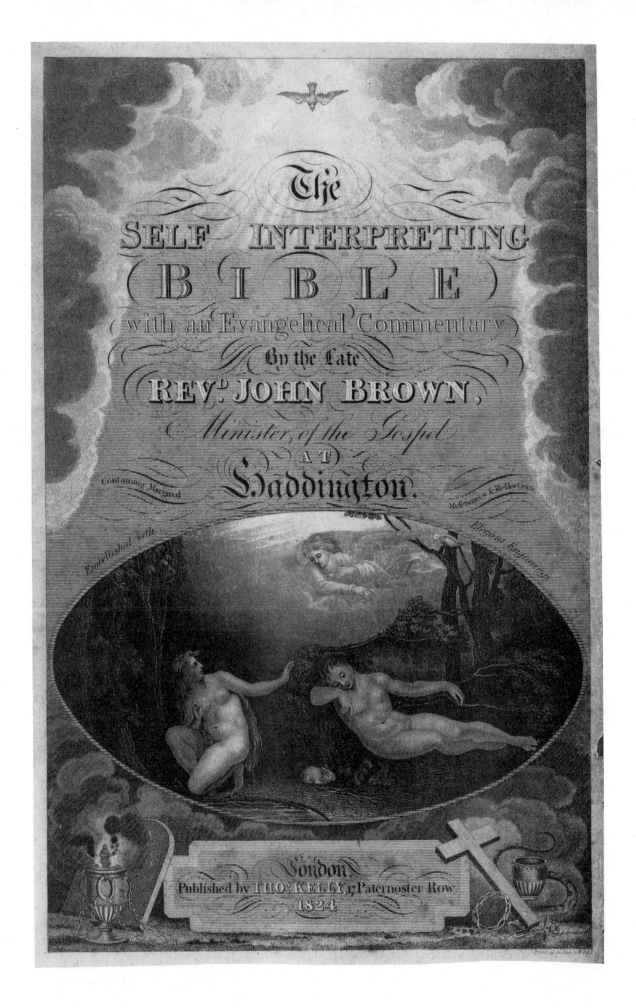

The
SELF INTERPRETING
BIBLE
with an Evangelical Commentary
By the Late
REVᴰ JOHN BROWN,
Minister of the Gospel
AT
Haddington.

Containing Marginal
References & Reflections

London,
Published by THOˢ KELLY, 17, Paternoster Row
1824

COLLECTIBLE BIBLES

Of course everyone knows that the Bible has been the world's number one best-seller ever since Martin Luther's version was printed in 1534. By the year 1574 more than 100,000 copies had been sold and within a comparatively short span of years the "Good Book" was translated into several hundred different languages.

So, it's easy to see why so few versions are worth a second glance today. In fact, in 30 years of antique dealing and book collecting, I have never bought or sold a 19th or 20th century Bible for more than $50. Even today one can purchase Bibles printed as early as 1590 for a relatively low sum.

There are, however, sleepers in this specialty which are worth knowing more about. The quickest way to become familiar with individual volumes which have achieved auction prices of over $100 is to browse through several volumes of *American Book Prices Current* at your public library. You will find such entries as: "Bible Translated into Ojibwa Indian. NY, 1875. $125," or "Mohawk Indian edition. $300." Any American Indian Bible is worth a professional appraisal. Some have brought big money. The Rev. John Eliot's *Natic Indian Language Edition*, Cambridge, Mass., 1663, sold at Christie's New York auction house a few years back for $300,000.

The *Jane Aiken Bible*, four volumes, published in Philadelphia in 1808. Unopened, some damp stains, and a defective spine is worth $2,000. A copy of the 1611 *King James*, lacking four pages, and with many closely cropped, sold for $34,650 recently. Modern Bibles designed by Bruce Rogers are very collectible. In 1949 Rogers designed one, of which only 975 copies were printed, that was auctioned for $600. Others by Rogers have gone for as much as $3,000.

American Book Prices Current describes and prices dozens of English-language Bibles dating from 1540 to 1945. Special limited editions, examples with elaborate bindings, those containing lists of subscribers, and folio sized volumes are all valuable if printed before 1800. Common, limp-leather-bound *King James* Bibles from 1850 to present have no resale value.

Foreign language editions, however, are worth careful scrutiny. A few recent sales: *The Bible in Chinese*, New Testament 1823, Malacca approx. $1,650. *The Bible in Dutch*, 1748, 1 vol. $475. Another Dutch Bible, 17th century with handwritten notes, Elephant folio size, brought $900.

Bibles with misprints are also collectible. *The Geneva Bible* of 1560 contains the following passage in Genesis 3:7; "The eyes of them bothe were opened..and they sewed figge-tree leaves together, and made themselves breeches." It appears that way, (breeches), in all editions of The Geneva Bible but not in any other version.

A devilish misprint is found in the so-called *"Wicked Bible"* printed in London in 1632. The seventh commandment dropped the word "not" making it read "Thou shalt commit adultery." A careless printer's error or a monstrous practical joke?

Any Bible illustrated by Gustav Dore, the French graphic artist and designer who lived from 1833 to 1883, is collectible; especially the 2-volume folio edition published by Tours in 1866 ($350 and up).

The location where an American Bible was published can make it valuable even if it boasts no other virtues. Each of 24 towns in Massachusetts produced its own edition. Even small towns like Zenia, Ohio, had their home-grown versions.

Breaking up Bibles for the value of individual pages, or frameable color plates, is a long-established practice. In 1921 bookseller Gabriel Wells broke up an incomplete copy of the 15th Century Gutenberg Bible and got rich selling one leaf at a time. The last copy to turn up at an auction sold for 4.9 million dollars. Single pages from this edition bring $10,000 to $15,000 today.

When you mat or frame an old biblical print, it's best not to tell your customer it was removed from the "Good Book." They will be happier thinking that some 19th Century publisher printed the pictures individually.

A few years ago you could not give away those large family Bibles which formerly graced nearly every Victorian parlor table. Today nicely bound and highly illustrated examples are selling in antique stores for $50 to $100. The "marriage", "birth" and "death" pages from these volumes are valuable as genealogical records and qualify some family Bibles for sale to distant relatives or genealogists. Check with your local Genealogical Society.

The American Bible Society at 1865 Broadway, New York, NY 10023, has a collection of 40,000 Bibles in 19,900 languages, dating from as early as the 1400s. Edwin A. R. Rumball-Petre lists all the important Bibles in the world in his book, *Rare Bibles*, published in 1938 and revised in 1954.

The standard reference on American Bibles is *The English Bible in America*, by Margaret T. Hills, New York, 1972. This bibliography lists 2,600 editions printed in the United States between 1777 and 1957.

VINTAGE PAPERBACKS

The end of the Civil War set in motion the first wave of paperback book publishing in the United States. Many titles were self-published accounts of spies, battles, prison life and day-to-day hardships borne by soldiers on both sides of the conflict.

Popular fiction was also available. In 1885 a newsstand publisher named Norman Munro put out a 16-page catalog of "Popular novels issued in a convenient form for the pocket."

By the late 1930s modern paperback novels and their seductively colorful covers had evolved. Titles such as *Odd John: He Had to Be Stopped, for all Women Were his Playthings* could hardly be passed up for a mere 25¢.

Pearl Buck's *The Good Earth* was issued in a trial edition of 2,300 copies by Pocket Books in 1938. Today a fine copy of this pioneer paperback is worth a month's wages. In 1992 an exceptionally well-preserved example sold at auction for $6,100.

Collectors generaly concentrate on paperbacks published between 1939 and 1959. Most vintage paperbacks were numbered and the first 100 titles of individual publishers are hotly sought after.

Pocketbooks, the 1939 pioneer, was joined over the next three decades by Ace, Avon, Ballantine, Bantam, Dell, Popular Library, Gold Medal, Lion, Signet and several other publishing houses.

As competition for market share increased, casualties occurred. Some collectors seek "dead" imprints such as Eton Books, Bonded Mysteries, Bart, and Black Knight. Fine copies of these start at $8 and run to $35 or more.

Most vintage paperback titles were reprints of already popular works. However, original titles—termed PBO, or Paperback Originals—were issued in considerable numbers. Many of these were the first published works of writers who later became quite well known.

Dell published over 100 "First Editions", including *The Sirens of Titan* by Kurt Vonnegut ($40); *The Nothing Man* by Jim Thompson ($90) and *April Evil* by John D. MacDonald ($45). Many less-important paperback originals, in fine condition, sell in the $10-$20 range at shops (and 25 cents at garage sales).

"Fine" is a key word in this field. Condition is perhaps the most challenging factor in paperback collecting. Pocket-sized books were subject to a lot more wear and tear than conventional hardbacks. Titles with missing pages, cover creases, rolled spines or water damage drop sharply in value. Collectors will pay top dollar for 50-year-old books that look like new.

The field is so broad that a beginning collector often finds it difficult to select a "niche". Specializations range from mystery to sex to science fiction. One can collect paperbacks with a movie-tie-in, "peephole" covers, or cowboy plots.

Should you choose "firsts" there is the first western *Oh, You Tex*, by William McLeon Raine (Pocket Books, $15), or the first Gothic Romance, *Rebecca*, by Daphne DuMaurier (Pocket Books, $8). The first science fiction collection, *The Pocket Book of Science Fiction*, goes for $35. The first Agatha Christie mystery, *The Murder of Roger Ackroyd*, is worth $140. And the first movie-tie-in, *Wuthering Heights*, by Emily Bronte (Pocket Books) is quoted at $100.

If you choose illustrators as a specialty you will run into lots of competition while scouring thrift shops, yard sales and flea markets for covers by Frank Frazetta, James Avati, Stanley Meltzoff, Frank McCarthy, James Bama, Robert McGinnis, Walter Brooks, Harry Bennett and a host of other paperback artists.

Be forewarned that not every cover artist signed his work—and those that did often had their names cropped off in the final design.

Some authors and illustrators felt safer using pseudonyms. In the early 1960s I owned an artist's supply store in San Diego and a couple of my best customers worked for a sleezy sex novel publisher. The whole crew, including the company's top executive, spent a month in the slammer before the A.C.L.U. came to their aid. It really put a dent in my sales of flesh-colored paints.

One popular author, Mike Avallone, used 15 different names and Gore Vidal sometimes wrote as "Edgar Box".

If you are serious about the book business you will need to pick up a few good references on pseudonyms.

Another niche is Ace Books' double novels. In the 1950s and 1960s Ace combined a paperback original with a reprint. Two novels in one were printed back to back, each with its own cover art. Where the first novel ended, the second one began, upside-down.

Prices for fine copies can run into three figures. A couple of examples: Ace double book No. 1. *The Grinning Gismo* and *Too Hot for Hell* ($140); *Junkie* and *Narcotic Agent* ($250).

Not all Ace doubles are high flyers; many can still be found in the $12 range.

Another niche in paperback collecting consists of 1,322 titles that were issued by the Council on Books in Wartime. These *Armed Service Forces Editions* were sent to local and overseas servicemen by 70 participating publishers.

Most *Armed Service Forces* titles can be purchased for under $10 in fine condition, but there are dozens of higher priced examples, e.g.:

The Return of Tarzan, Edgar Rice Burroughs, ($200).
Selected Stories of Edgar Allan Poe, an original ($75).
Selected Short Stories of Ernest Hemingway, an original and printed in only one edition, ($75).
Selected Poems of Carl Sandburg, an original ($20).

Dust jackets on paperbacks is another exciting area to explore. Poor sellers were sometimes revived with dust jackets. A successfully filmed book could find its paperback editions dressed up with a jacket. Bantam added dust covers to over 20 titles. Some examples:

The Great Gatsby by F. Scott Fitzgerald. (Alan Ladd was a top movie draw at this time, and his stone-faced portrayal of Gatsby graces the added jacket.) A fine copy is worth $75.

A dust-jacketed *Babbit*, by Sinclair Lewis, is $28.

Ring Lardner's *The Love Nest and Other Stories* goes for $100 in fine condition.

Books by famous authors are always in demand. Look for Ray Bradbury, Dashiell Hammett, and Ross MacDonald. Movie and TV tie-ins—released in conjunction with a movie or a popular television show—are also valuable. They usually feature a photographic cover or a photo section inside. The first clue to older paperbacks is that they either bear no cover price or will have a printed price of 25¢ or 35¢.

We have scattered a number of paperback first editions among the authors listed in this book, but specialized price guides and periodicals are a must for further study. These are currently available:

Books are Everything is a quarterly magazine published by paperback expert R. C. Holland. Write BAE, P.O. Box 5068, Richmond, KY 40475.

Paperback Parade is a similar bimonthly publication. Gryphon Publications, P.O. Box 209, Brooklyn, NY 11228-0209.

Paperbacks at Auction, published by Gorgon Books, lists prices for thousands of books auctioned over the last year. Gorgon Books, 102 Joanne Dr., Holbrook, NY 11741.

Huxford's Paperback Value Guide contains the values of nearly 25,000 paperback books. Collector Books, P.O. Box 3009, Paducah, KY 42002-3009.

Hancer's Price Guide to Paperback Books is another valuable source. Wallace-Homestead, Radnor, PA 19087.

Over My Dead Body by Lee Server is a good guide to paperbacks. Chronicle Books, 275 Fifth St., San Francisco, CA 94103.

The Official Price Guide to Paperbacks by Jon Warren prices 41,000 books published from 1939 to 1981. House of Collectibles, 201 East 50th St., NY, NY 10022.

BOOK AUCTIONS

Auctions have long been a primary source of stock for antique dealers and bookstore owners. Being a quick source of cash, they have also been called a dealer's dumping ground for dead or damaged goods.

But once in awhile a legitimate estate will pass across across the auction block, along with the usual array of goodies consigned by dealers, pickers and institutions.

Basically, there are two types of auction sales: *uncataloged* auctions—where items are put on the block at random or by request—and *catalog sales*, where each lot is individually numbered and described on a printed sheet and sold in its proper sequence.

Sophisticated, big-city auction houses usually catalog their inventory several weeks before a sale and mail these catalogs to subscribers—who later receive a "prices realized" list. Bookmen covet these catalogs for their accurate descriptions—including "points" and corresponding prices.

Many beginning dealers and collectors are unaware that *uncataloged* household, farm, estate and business auctions are conducted several days a week in most cities and counties throughout the land. Look in the yellow pages of local and metropolitan area phone books for the names and addresses of auctioneers. Write to them and request that your name be placed on their mailing lists for future sale announcements.

Also call or write to county officials for information regarding sheriff's or public administrator's auction sales. Watch the weekend classified ad section of local and out-of-town newspapers for advertisements of upcoming auction events.

At uncataloged sales a front row seat can help you spot the goodies in box-lots that might have been hiding under a table during the preview—which is held an hour or two before the actual selling begins.

Sometimes, if boxes of old books are taking up too much of his valuable time, an auctioneer will start offering volumes by the shelf-full, room-full, or wagon load—all for a single winning bid.

Needless to say, dealers who bring a truck or trailer to every auction they attend are often well-rewarded for the effort. If you overbuy, a vehicle can be rented, or the auctioneer may be able recommend a local hauler.

At the auction preview watch for:

1. Missing pages, plates, and dust jackets.
2. Marks, labels, stains, underlining, owners' names, wear, tear, cracks, rebinding, clipped ads, etc.
3. Box lots hidden under tables by other bidders.

A few rules to remember:

1. Do not exceed your predetermined maximum bid (about one-third of retail) on all but the most desirable items. You need a triple markup to make a living as a book scout or bookstore owner.
2. Do not bid on items you have not personally examined (otherwise, you are buying blindfolded.)
3. Don't believe anything anyone says at an auction (they have their own interests at heart.)
4. Don't believe the auctioneer (half the stuff is his).
5. Don't pay any attention to what known dealers are willing to bid (they may be drunk, in love, or buying for a rich collector).
6. When the hammer falls you've bought it..."as is, where is." So double check just before the bidding starts. During display hours, books are stolen, laid-in items are removed, dust jackets are torn, and items are switched from one box to another to confuse the competition..

An annual catalog of catalogs called *American Book Prices Current* is available at most large public libraries. In it are prices realized for books from 30 international auction houses. A.B.P.C. separates the wheat from the chaff by listing only books published before the year 1900 and by confining entries to those volumes which brought $100 or more.

If you think you have a rare book, it will pay to consult several back issues of *American Book Prices Current* and then consider consigning your find to one of the specialist firms listed below. (American Book Prices Current, Bancroft-Parkman Inc., 121 East 78th St., New York, NY 10021). Most large libraries have a set of A.B.P.C. behind the counter.

Here are a few auction houses from whom you can order catalogs. A fee is usually charged.

Baltimore Book Auctions
2112 North Charles Street
Baltimore MD 21218

Berkshire Book Auctions
PO Box 746
Sheffield MA 01257

New Hampshire Book
Auctions
PO Box 460
92 Woodbury Road
Weare NH 03281

Pacific Book Auction
Galleries
139 Townsend St, Ste 305
San Francisco CA 94107

Superior Galleries
9478 W Olympia Blvd
Beverly Hills CA 90212

Swan Galleries
10 East 25th Street
New York City NY 10010
(212) 254-4710

THE USED BOOK BUSINESS

You're approaching middle age, the kids are through college and your mortgage is about paid off. Maybe it's time to throw caution to the wind and go into the used book business?

About 10,000 souls are presently engaged in this vocation. My guess is that a third of these happy bibliophiles make a living at the trade while the rest are in business for fun, or a tax writeoff. Some are motivated to dispose of personal collections, much like their counterparts in the general antiques trade. Others start from scratch or buy an existing shop.

The appeal of both kinds of business is the interesting people you have an opportunity to meet, the vast amount of knowledge one can soak up in a very short time, and the unceasing thrill of a treasure hunt.

Monetary profit, though, is often elusive. So here we offer a chapter on tips of the trade.

Very little capital is required to start a used or antiquarian book business. You can work from home with a roomful of carefully selected volumes or rent a low cost space in an antique mall. After a year or two of dilettante dealing, you might be ready to make the leap into full time entrepreneurship.

If you have purchased this price guide you already know where to find old books. You probably spend much of your weekend at flea markets, auctions, and library and estate sales. What you may not know is that many books purchased by dealers for resale are bought from book scouts and other dealers. Much of this intercourse is conducted discreetly, by mail.

For those hardy souls who have actually rented a storefront location, the buying becomes much easier. People walk through their doors every day with armloads of books they want to turn into cash. Many customers will trade books--two of theirs for one of yours. The inventory can grow rapidly, especially if you run a "Cash For Used Books" advertisement in the local newspaper.

If you really plan to make a living at the business, it will pay you to develop a wholesale clientele of other bookstore owners in addition to your walk-in retail trade. To do this you must be willing to sell clean, tight books at less than one half of "price guide" values.

Why do dealers buy from each other? Because there have been over 20 million books published in the last 200 years, and the average bookman only has shelf space for 25,000 volumes. When a customer requests a title that is not in stock, the dealer advertises in the "wanted" section of several trade tabloids. Thousands of book scouts make money filling these want-ad requests.

Several computer search services have been launched (and sunk) over the years, but publications such as *Bookseller*, *A.B. Bookman*, *Antique Week,* and *Paper Collector's Marketplace* remain the best source for both buying and selling contacts.

However, a computer is an extremely useful tool in the trade. Programs such as *Bookmaster Professional* (TAS Software, 3285 Route 88, Newark, NY 14513) provide a system of inventory control, bookkeeping, book quote print-outs and instant catalog production, along with on-line book search capability.

When printing a catalog of old books, trade catalogs, magazines or newspapers that you plan to offer by mail, remember to include a "blurb" with each item. A flattering highlight of contents is often more important than the actual title. Sell the "sizzle," not the steak.

It is also important to group catalogued items in related categories, under a headline. Today's buyers will not wade through hundreds of mixed entries to find their favorite author or subject. **Bold headlines** can add interest to boring listings.

Mail your fliers and catalogs to every public library within a hundred miles of your shop. Then zero in on individual collectors, other book dealers, and nationwide libraries which have special collections (ask your librarian for help here.)

Used and rare book dealers base their prices on one or more of seven factors: sale of past copies; auction prices realized; other dealers' catalogs; price guides; dealers' prices at book fairs; dealers' shop prices; and pricing by intuition.

Demand for a book, magazine, newspaper or trade catalog will vary according to geography. Technical books and old tool catalogs are good sellers in New England, where industrial history is revered. You stand a better chance of selling a Civil War item in Alabama than in Montana (where a book about cattle ranching or fly fishing will be much more welcome.)

Unless you are a well-established mail order dealer, selling to a library or other institution will almost always involve showing the items. Do this if you can, or have someone you trust do the job. Incidentally, institutions are notoriously slow payers; allow up to 90 days (and repeated billings) before getting apprehensive.

If you are serious about opening a shop, we recommend Dale Gilbert's *Complete Guide to Starting a Used Book Store*, (Upstart Publishing Company, a divison of Dearborn Publishing Group, 12 Portland Street, Dover, NH 03820.)

In Dale's book, you will learn how to choose a location, build display shelves, deal with customers, hire and fire employees, and all the other nitty gritty of a retail shopkeeper's daily existence. If you would like to own a similar book related to the antiques trade, get a copy of Ronald Barlow's *How To Be Successful in the Antique Business*. It has been the beginner's Bible of the trade since 1980. (Send $11.95 to Windmill Publishing Co., 2147 Windmill View Road, El Cajon CA 92020).

HOW AND WHAT TO BUY

The best advice we can offer a beginning dealer is to start with the subject(s) you know best, and then accumulate at least 5,000 additional nonfiction titles on popular subjects such as cooking, crafts, cowboys and Indians, county histories, the Civil War, etc.

Of course you can begin mailing out printed lists or small catalogs with a few hundred selected titles; however, your chances of success will be greatly enhanced in direct proportion to the size and quality of your stock and trade. You can't sell very much from an empty wagon.

Many customers will not buy anything from your initial printed list, but will respond with a note or phone call, asking for some other title. That's where a large inventory can save the day. The real payoff is further down the road. Eventually you will accumulate a list of active customers, cross-filed by subjects wanted. When you begin to seek out, and offer these "wanted" titles, your book business will prosper.

"Americana" is always in demand. Specialized books, pamphlets, catalogs, maps and broadsides about American history, folklore, towns, states, territories, mining and the westward movement all fall under the broad brush of "Americana."

No matter who the writer is, there is little demand for reprints of novels or poetry. First editions are the key to sales here. Pass up most book club editions and reprints by stock publishers.

The tighter the focus of a book, the more likely it is to sell. A "how to" book will move more quickly than general information. Regional history is good, but local material is better. Any book bearing a date earlier than 1800 has value for someone, in that it has simply survived the ravages of time.

Very generally speaking, retail prices are about double wholesale prices in the used book business. There are many exceptions; most are based on whether the dealer is buying for shelf stock or to fill a customer's order. Common titles are bought for less than 25 cents on the dollar (and they sit forever.) Very desirable volumes that might enhance a dealer's shop (or catalog) are bought for 50 to 75 per cent of retail value.

Collectors and institutions often pay dealers a 10 per cent commission to buy for them at auctions. You won't make much money doing this, but it builds good will and forces you to attend auctions where you might pick up a bargain or two. (See chapter on auctions.)

Professional book scouts visit thrift stores regularly and make away with most of the good stuff. Or they leave a business card which states that they are cash buyers of certain types of material. Print a short "wanted" list on your business card. (A folding style will allow plenty of room.) Carry a pocketful everywhere.

When buying from fellow dealers, always present your resale number and business card *before* a sale is written up, but don't suggest to a dealer that the price of an item be lowered for you. Most dealers do not work on tremendous volume, and each sale is an important contribution toward rent/food/bed. But some dealers, if your purchases run to a tidy sum, will give you a 10 or 20 per cent discount automatically. One dealer's retail price may be another dealer's wholesale. You can make money here if you know what *your* customers will pay.

Some shopkeepers who have very large bookstores (like a barn) do not know the value, or location, of every item on their shelves. When entering such stores, ask the proprietor where the subject section is that you are seeking, rather than asking for a specific title. Browsing may turn up more books which are suitable for resale. The more casually you approach a transaction, the lower the price may be. If you are going to haggle, put the book you most covet on the bottom of the stack.

Library sales are great places to pick up bargains, often by the box full. Libraries "withdraw" unwanted books from their shelves, and usually these books are clearly stamped WITHDRAWN, but not always. Some sensitive librarians prefer not to deface the endpaper or title page of a beautiful or valuable book. Somewhere, however, in the book or on the page edges, there is probably evidence of "ex-library" status--a marking which of course lowers the book's value on the market, unless it has exceptionally nice illustrations or is purchased for research.

Before buying or selling, ask yourself who would want this item, and why? The more general or "dated" the title is, the least likely it is to sell. Small niches are rich veins to mine. Look for books on "beekeeping," not "bookkeeping." Seek "fire fighting," not "flower gardening." The world is full of common books on everyday subjects.

Technical titles often outsell old novels by a wide

margin. In addition to local history, be on the lookout for books on early tools, trades, techniques, the decorative arts and forgotten crafts.

Do not spend your nest egg on Victorian novels, general history, science, math, biographies, medicine, law, accounting, travel or etiquette books. Almost nobody wants them. Also in low demand are books on religion.

Bibles, prayer books, sermons and theological debates were the largest body of books published in early America. Only one out of a hundred such books is worth a second look (See Bible chapter).

In any given subject area, only a small number of volumes ever published are actually in demand. The common titles (those you most often encounter) are books that will sit on your shelves forever. So conserve capital and buy quality rather than quantity.

The first check you write on your new business account should be for a subscription to *A.B. Bookman's Weekly*, the trade publication of specialist book dealers (P. O. Box AB, Clifton, NJ 07015.) Each issue contains several thousand title listings of "Books Wanted" and a smaller number of "Books for Sale." More than 7,000 advertisers use this weekly stock market of the old-book trade to conduct a substantial part of their business. You would be wise to read a dozen issues before you do any serious buying for resale. Check your local library or order a sample copy from AB.

In a recent newspaper interview, a successful dealer said his "secret weapon" was a subscription to another, somewhat cheaper, publication. *The Bookseller.* (P. O. Box 8183, Ann Arbor MI 48107). It's worth a look.

MAIL ORDER MANNERS

Perhaps 50 per cent of all antiquarian book transactions are conducted by mail. Some dealers specialize as "book finders." They solicit offers of books for sale (from scouts and other dealers) that match the titles on their want lists. These offers are called "quotes."

In "quoting" books, it's best to quote items individually on 3 x 5 index cards or within a 3 by 5 inch area on the back of a postcard. This "quote" should contain the following facts in order:

1. Source of listing of the wanted item (where you saw the dealer's want ad.)
2. The item's title and author.
3. Publishing details: publisher, place, date, edition number and copyright date.
4. Description: including condition, hardback or soft-back, with or without dust jacket, condition of dust jacket, illustration data, introduction or preface writer's name, number of pages, ads in back, etc.

5. The number of copies you have available.
6. Price, plus shipping and insurance costs.

Print your logo, or name and address, at the top of each quote card. You can photocopy them in groups for future mailing. It often takes as many as 10 or 15 quotes to sell a book. These Xerox copies can be time savers.

Hold all the books you have quoted (for at least three weeks) before reshelving, or requoting to another search company. The buyer may be waiting for other quotes which might be cheaper, or offering the same item in better condition.

A California bookseller entering the mail order business was shocked at the wide variation in quotes she received from a recent want ad. On a relatively common detective novel from the 1970s she got four quotes, ranging from $6 to $24. She bought the low quote and was well satisfied with the copy she received. Expect wide variations in quoted prices when you do business by mail.

When shipping by United Parcel Service, don't use a post office box address. Use a street address, or there will be a mix-up. Ask your customer which method of shipment he or she prefers. On books priced under $10 or $20, 4th class bookpost will usually suffice. More expensive items should be shipped priority mail, or by UPS (which automatically insures items to $100).

Shoving a customer's book into a padded Jiffy bag for mailing is not a good idea. Support it with a stiff cardboard insert which is larger than the book or magazine. Better yet, use a box instead of a bag. Don't ever wrap an item in newspapers. The ink rubs off in transit and your customer will probably return the soiled book. An inner wrap of poly-ethylene or Saran wrap is added protection against moisture and keeps packing material from creeping in between pages or soiling the book.

SELLING DIRECTLY TO DEALERS

Almost to a man (or woman), dealers, scouts and writers on book collecting say that selling to a dealer is the most effortless way to dispose of any book and, in many cases, the most profitable. This is true most of the time, but reference books listing *collector clubs, museums, libraries, historical societies* and *trade associations* can yield good results too. (Ask your local librarian for help. She probably has most of these volumes behind the counter.)

Before offering books, magazines, newspapers or trade catalogs to the proprietor of a store, check out his or her inventory. If the shop is overstocked in the subject you plan to offer (or if it does not deal in the subject at all) take your wares farther down the street.

If you are selling a special collection, invite a number of dealers to bid on it, but be prepared to have some dealers decline your offer. They may figure you are just after a free appraisal. If you tell them you will set an "asking price" on the collection, they will be more likely to respond. Some will want to buy only one or two items, and will make an offer. Don't lower the collection's value by allowing piecemeal purchases. Always try to move related books, etc., in groups when possible (unless you own a retail store).

The professional buyer "picks and chooses." The smart seller makes you "take them all."

If a certain title is in heavy demand, don't wait too long to sell it. The first offer is often the best (or the only one) you will receive. As demand grows and sales results are published, more copies come out of the woodwork. Market values tend to drop very fast on fad items. Fashions in book, magazine and newspaper collecting change nearly as often as women's shoe styles. What is eagerly sought after today may become tomorrow's largest occupier of dead shelf space.

OPENING A SHOP

We've covered all the ins-and-outs of mail-order dealing, but haven't begun to advise you of the sundry responsibilities of running a bookstore.

Opening a shop is easy...too easy in fact. Take a long hard look before you leap! Ask yourself if you are really a "people person"? You are going to be trapped (sometimes for hours at a time) behind the counter, listening to a lot of stuff you've heard many times before.

If you are approaching retirement age maybe a ten-hour shopkeeper's day is not your cup of tea.

Employees are much like one's children, not always a joy to be around. And partners can be the worst of all possible problems; getting rid of one is comparable to a bad divorce.

Landlords run the gamut from could-care-less absentees to the smelly, loud-mouthed variety that spends an hour a day bending your ear and drinking your coffee.

Shopping center leases are extremely restrictive. They contain provisions for uniform signs, no sidewalk displays, fireproof wall coverings, parking lot maintenance, cooperative advertising, fixed hours and a host of other undreamed rules (that mail-order entrepreneurs don 't have to put up with).

A compromise between "mail-order" and an "open shop" might be to rent a small space in a well-situated antique mall. The heavy traffic can expose your stock to thousands of people a year. The trick is to figure out what the clientele wants before you go out and buy all the wrong stuff. You can't afford to waste any precious shelf space on slow-moving items.

Some dealers confine their selling effort to shows. These events range from weekend flea markets to prestigious antiquarian booksellers' conventions. One couple we know has done very well following the paper antiques and postcard circuit. Show advertising appears several months in advance in trade publications.

Store layout requires more common sense than creative talent. The cash register and wrapping counter must be adjacent to the front door because customers should be greeted as they enter (and leave).

Good lighting is very important; you can't buy what you can't see. Take a close look at a department store or super-market ceiling on your next shopping trip.

Aisles must be at least 40 inches wide; a full four feet would be even better. This distance allows browsers to pass one another without bumping posterior body parts and lets far-sighted folks back up enough to read shelf labels. It also allows light to fall upon those hard-to-read spines. A well-lighted shop is as important as your stock in trade

Shelving can be anything smooth that does not sag over a four foot span. Check out what types of fixtures other bookstores are using. Be sure to connect any tall free standing shelf units to 2 x 6 inch posts which are firmly attached to the ceiling. (People have been killed by toppling book cases.)

The size of your store can determine potential profits. You might gross $25,000 to $50,000 from 500 square feet of floor space or three times as much from the recommended minimum of 1,500 square feet of selling area (a 30 ft. by 50 ft. room). A two or three time turnover of inventory is your goal, but a shop can survive on a once a year turnover if the rent does not exceed 7% of gross sales.

You could do a lot worse than locating your new enterprise next door to an existing bookstore. In many cities antique shops or used bookstores are concentrated on one avenue or within a two or three square block area.

Tourist traffic is the number one choice for almost any business, but rents are formidable in these busy locations. The next best spot might be near a post office, restaurant, movie theatre, supermarket or drug store.

The more people who see your store, every day, the better are your chances of success.

Treat your customers as you would expect to be treated and word-of-mouth will be all the advertising you need. A clean, well-lighted establishment, with ten or twenty thousand carefully selected titles arranged alpha-betically upon clearly labeled shelves, is the minimum prerequisite. Coffee, cookies, chairs and reading tables are icing on the cake.

ABBAZIA, D. *Mr. Roosevelt's Navy.* Naval Institute Press, 1975 1st ed. Fine in fine dust jacket. $25-$30.

ABBEY, EDWARD. *Jonathan Troy.* New York, 1954. Author's 1st book inscribed & dated by author. Very Fine in near perfect dust jacket and box. $1,800. Another copy in lesser condition. Damaged dust jacket. Endpaper spots, otherwise Near Fine. $650.
Fire on the Mountain. London, 1963 1st English ed. Near Fine in dust jacket. $375.
Desert Solitaire. McGraw-Hill, 1968 1st ed. F in DJ. $350.
Appalachian Wilderness. New York, 1970 1st edition. Elliott Porter photos. Very Good in clipped dust jacket. $125. Fine in dust jacket. $195.

ABBOTT, CARLISLE. *Recollections of a California Pioneer.* New York, Neale, 1917 1st edition. Gilt-decorative cloth. $80-$100.

ABBOTT, JOHN S. *Life of Gen. Ulysses C. Grant.* Boston, 1868 1st ed. Minor foxing, cover stains. $25-$35.

ABELL, MRS. L. G. *The Skillful Housewife's Book Cookery, etc.* New York, 1846. Disbound. $40. Another edition, New York, 1852. Good. $50. A tight, very good, 1852 copy. $100.

ABERNETHY, BYRON R. *Private Ellis Stockwell, Jr., Sees the Civil War.* Univ of Oklahoma Press, 1958 1st ed. Very Good in dust jacket. $28.

ABET, LT JAMES W. *Through the Country of the Comanche Indians in the Fall of the Year 1845.* San Francisco. 1970. Illustrated. Fine in dust jacket. $15.

AB-SA-RA-KA. Anon. (Mrs. H. B. Carrington). Philadelphia, 1868. $100-$250.

ACCOUNT BOOKS and BUSINESS LEDGERS with hand-written entries of the day. Various trades, from dentist to wheelwright. 1850s to 1900s examples are worth from $50 to $175.

ACKERLEY, J. R. *The Prisoners of War.* London, 1925 1st edition. Very Good in dust jacket. $60.

ACTON, MISS ELIZA. *Modern Cookery in All Its Branches.* Revised by Mrs. S. J. Hale in 1864. Philadelphia. Gold-stamped cloth. Only American edition of the 1845 London work. The first to give real measurements and approx. cooking time for recipes. VG. $100-$200. Fair. $50.

ADAMIC, LOUIS. *Two-Way Passage.* NY 1941. G-VG. $7.

ADAMS, ANDY. *A Texas Matchmaker.* Boston, 1904 1st ed. Very Good. $20-$40.
The Outlet. Boston, 1905. Good-VG. $20.
Cattle Brands: A Collection of Campfire Stories. Boston 1916. VG. $20. Houghton, 1906 ed. Good. $10.
Why the Chisholm Trail Forks. Austin, TX, 1956. VG in dust jacket. $28.

ADAMS, ANSEL. *My Camera in Yosemite Valley.* 24 photos and essay. Boston, 1949 1st ed. $100 auction.
This is the American Earth. San Francisco, 1960. VG in DJ. $75. 4th edition, 1960. Fine in dust jacket. $45.
These We Inherit-Parklands of America. Sierra Club, 1962. Fine in dust jacket. $60.
The Land of Little Rain. Boston, Houghton Mifflin, 1950. Yellow cloth. Near Fine. $93 auction.
Fiat Lux: The University of California. New York, McGraw-Hill, 1968 1st edition. Very Good in rubbed dust jacket. $50 auction.
The Negative. New York, 1964 New edition, Signed. Very Good in dust jacket. $40.
The Print. NY, 1967 New ed. VG in dust jacket. $15.
The Portfolios of Ansel Adams. Garden City 1973 3rd printing. Fine. $35. NY Graphic Soc. 1981. Signed. $100.
Photographs of the Southwest. No place, 1976 1st ed. Signed by Adams & Powell. VG in dust jacket. $40.
Yosemite and the Range of Light. NY, 1979 1st printing. Very Good in dust jacket. $80-$125.

ADAMS, CHARLES. *The Complete Guide to Blacksmithing, Horseshoeing, Carriage & Wagon Building & Painting, etc.* Chicago, 1902. $45.

ADAMS, EMMA. *To and Fro in Southern California.* Cincinnati, W.M.B.C. Press, 1887 1st ed. Orig. gilt-dec. cloth. Good-Very Good. $45-$80.

ADAMS, HARRIET. (See Appleton, Victor; Hope, Laura Lee and Keene, Carolyn).

ADAMS, HENRY. *The Education of Henry Adams*. Boston & NY, 1918 1st ed. VG, cover stains. $20. Near Fine. $80. *Mont-Saint Michel and Chartres*. NY, 1957. Limited Editions Club. One of 1,500 copies. Samuel Chamberlain photos, signed by him. Fine in slipcase. $125.

ADAMS, LEONIE. *High Falcon and Other Poems*. NY, 1929 1st ed. Very Good in dust jacket. $100.

ADAMS, RAMON F. *Western Words*. Norman, OK, 1946 3rd printing. Fine in dust jacket. $25.
Come and Get It: The Story of the Old Cowboy Cook. Norman, OK, 1952 1st ed. Fred Egenhoffer illus. VG. $30.
The Best of the American Cowboy. Norman, OK, 1957 1st ed. Fine in dust jacket. $23.
Rampaging Herd, A Bibliography of Books on the Cattle Industry. Univ. of Oklahoma, 1959 1st ed. VG. $150.
Old-Time Cowhand. NY, 1961 1st ed. VG. $30-$40.
From the Pecos to the Powder. Norman, OK 1965 1st ed. Very Good in dust jacket. $20.
The Cowman and His Code of Ethics. Austin, TX, 1969. Encino Press Limited ed. VG in dust jacket. $35.

ADAMS, RICHARD. *Watership Down*. New York, 1972 1st American ed. 1st book, signed. VG in vg DJ. $125. Unsigned, Fine in dust jacket. $35-$45.
Shardik. NY, 1974 1st American ed. Signed. Fine in DJ. $35. Same, unsigned. $15.
The Tiger Voyage. NY, 1976 1st American ed. Illus. VG in DJ. $15. Fine in fine dust jacket. $60.
The Plague Dogs. Penguin, 1977 1st ed. Fine, no DJ. $13.
The Ship's Cat. NY, 1977 1st ed. Alan Aldridge illus. VG in dust jacket. $55.

ADAMSON. *Sportsman's Game & Fish Cook Book*. New York, 1957 1st ed. Very Good in dust jacket. $11.
Grandmother in the Kitchen. New York, 1965 1st ed. VG in dust jacket. $18.

ADAMSON, JOY. *Born Free, a Lioness in Two Worlds*. NY, 1960, Pantheon in chipped dust jacket. $8.
Living Free. Collins, 1961. Very Good. $9.

ADDAMS, CHARLES. *Addams and Evil*. NY, 1947. Near Fine in dust jacket. $45.
Homebodies. NY, 1954 1st ed. VG in DJ. $25. Another, 2nd printing. $20.
Dear Dead Days: A Family Album. NY, 1959 1st ed. Fine in good dust jacket. $35.
Black Maria. NY, 1960 1st ed. Very Good in DJ. $33.
Mother Goose. NY, 1967 1st ed. Very Good in DJ. $35.

ADDAMS, JANE. *Twenty Years at Hull House*. NY, 1910 1st ed. Macmillan. Fine. $10. 1923 ed. VG. $7.
Spirit of Youth and the City Streets. NY, 1916. Good. $5.
The Long Road of Woman's Memory. New York, 1916 1st edition. Very Good. $12-$24.

ADDINGTON, SARAH. *Tommy Tingle-Tangle*. Volland, 1927. Gertrude A. Kay illus. VG in vg DJ. $50.
The Boy Who Lived in Pudding Lane. Atlantic Monthly, 1923 2nd printing. Fine. $30.

ADE, GEORGE. *Artie*. Chicago, 1896 1st edition. Author's 1st book. J. J. McCutcheon illustrator. Uncut. Fine. $50. 1898 edition. Good. $18.
Forty Modern Fables. NY, Chicago, 1900 1st ed. Illus. VG. $10. 1902 ed. Fine, no dust jacket. $18.
More Fables. NY, Chicago, 1900 1st ed. G-VG. $10.
Fables in Slang. Herbert Stone, 1901. Fine. $25.
Breaking Into Society. Harper, 1904 1st ed. VG. $12.
In Pastures New. McClure, 1906 1st ed. Fine. $18.
People You Know. NY, Harper, 1903 1st ed. VG. $12.
The Girl Proposition. NY, Harper, 1904 ed. VG. $18.
Knocking the Neighbors. NY, 1912. G-VG. $9-13.
The Old-Time Saloon. NY, 1931 1st ed. VG. $25-$35.

ADLEMAN, ROBERT and GEORGE WALTON. *Rome Fell Today*. Boston, 1968 1st ed. VG in dust jacket. $22.

ADLER, MORTIMER. *What Man Has Made of Man*. NY, 1937 1st ed. VG in dust jacket. $35.
The Idea of Freedom. Doubleday, 1958 1st ed. VG in clipped dust jacket. $35.

THE ADVENTURES OF A YANKEE. Anon. (John Ledyard). Boston, 1831. $325-$425.

THE ADVENTURES OF ROBIN DAY. Anon. (R. M. Bird). Philadelphia, 1839. 2 vols. $200-$350.

AESCHYLUS. *The Oresteia*. LEC. 1961. Good. $24.

AESOP'S FABLES. Wm. Heinemann, London, 1912. Arthur Rackham illus. $175-$250. Lon., 1895. Charles Robinson illus. $45. NY, 1908. Perkins illus. $35-$50. NY, 1931. Bennett illus. $30-$40. NY, 1933. Artzybasheff illus. $60-$80. Heritage Press, 1941. Lawson illus. VG in case. $30. McLoughlin Bros. circa 1880s. $45-$60.

AGAWA, H. *The Reluctant Admiral*. Tokyo, 1979. Fine in dust jacket. $18-$25.

AGRICULTURE, U. S. DEPARTMENT OF, YEARBOOK. 1870-1950 editions average $8-$10 each.

AIKEN, JOAN. *Selected Poems*. NY, 1929 1st ed. Fine in chipped dust jacket. $150.
Mr. Arcularis: A Play. Cambridge, 1957 1st ed. VG. $35.
The Fortune Hunters. NY, 1965 1st ed. Fine in DJ. $20.
Tom, Sue and the Clock. NY, 1966 1st ed. Julie Mass illus. Fine in dust jacket. $25.
Midnight is a Place. NY, 1974 1st ed. Fine in DJ. $20.
Arabel's Raven. NY 1974 1st American ed. Quentin Blake illus. Very Good. $15.

AINSLEE, KATHLEEN. *Oh! Poor Amelia Jane!* London, circa 1900. Illus. by author. Some soiling, o/w VG. $125.

AINSWORTH, ED. *The Cowboy in Art.* NY, 1968 1st ed. Very Good in dust jacket. $100.
Painters of the Desert. Palm Desert, CA, 1960 1st ed. VG in chipped dust jacket. $275.

AINSWORTH, WILLIAM. *The Tower of London.* London, 1840 1st ed. George Cruikshank illus. VG. $400.
The Star Chamber. London, no date. VG. $175.

AIRCRAFT YEARBOOK. 1921-1940 editions VG-Fine. $40-$65 each. 1941-1944 editions. G-VG. $30-$45 each.

AIRNEWS YEARBOOK. Vol. 1. NY, 1942. Good. $24.

AIRD, CATHERINE. *The Religious Body.* NY, 1966 1st ed. Fine in torn dust jacket. $30.
A Most Contagious Game. 1967 1st ed. Fine in DJ. $30.

AKELEY, MARY L. *Carl Akeley's Africa.* Blue Ribbon, 1931. Illus. Few water stains. $24.

ALBEE, EDWARD. *The Zoo Story and Other Plays.* London, 1962 1st ed. Near Fine in dust jacket. $100.
Who's Afraid of Virginia Woolf? London, 1964 1st British ed. Fine in fine dust jacket. $70.
Tiny Alice. London, 1966 1st British ed. VG in DJ. $50.
A Delicate Balance. NY, 1966 1st ed. Signed by author. Fine in fine DJ. $75. Another, signed. $28.

ALBION, ROBERT G. *The Rise of New York Port, 1815-1860.* NY, 1939 1st ed. VG in torn dust jacket. $65.

ALBRIGHT, NANCY. *The Rodale Cookbook.* Rodale, 1977 12th ed. Very Good in dust jacket. $8.

ALCOHOLICS ANONYMOUS. Works Publication Co., 1939 1st edition. Fine in good, taped dust jacket. $7,500.
1st edition, 14th printing. Works Publication Co., 1951. Fine in good dust jacket. $75.
NY, 1955 Revised 2nd ed., 1st prtg. F in fine DJ. $80. AA. Pub. Co. NY, 1972 2nd ed. 13th printing. VG in DJ. $45.
The Little Red Book. Minn, 1949. $50-$75.

ALCOTT, LOUISA MAY. *Flower Fables.* Boston, 1855 1st ed. Author's 1st book. Gift binding. Good plus. $350.
Hospital Sketches. Boston, 1863 1st ed. Sunned, rubbed. $100-$150. Little Brown, 1909 ed. Fine. $12-$15.
An Old Fashioned Girl. Boston, 1870 1st Amer. ed. $100.
Eight Cousins: or, The Aunt-Hill. Boston, 1875 1st ed. 2nd issue. Good. $150. 1890 ed. $35. 1930s ed. $12.
Jo's Boys, and How They Turned Out. Boston, 1886 1st edition. Good. $45. Worn copy. $25-$35.
Silver Pitchers and Independence: A Centennial Love Story. Boston, 1876 1st ed. Fine, as new. $175.

May Flowers. Little Brown, 1887 edition. $25-$45.
A Garland for Girls. Boston, Roberts Bros., 1888 1st ed. Green Satin. Rubbed, some leaves spotted. Good. $75.
Jack and Jill. Roberts Bros., 1891. Good $10.
Proverb Stories. Roberts Bros., 1887. Dusty, foxing. $25.
Little Women. Boston, 1922. Jesse Wilcox Smith illus. VG. $50. Little Brown, 1923 edition. Alice B. Stephens illus. VG. $25. Little Brown, 1938 3rd edition. Orchard House, Jesse Wilcox Smith illus. Very Good. $25.
Rose in Bloom. 1930s editions. $15-$30.
Under the Lilacs. Boston, 1928. M. Davis illus. VG. $25.
Little Men. 1871 1st edition, 1st issue. All points. Torn preliminary pages else Very Good. $135. Winston, 1928. Clara M. Burd illustrator. Good. $25.
Aunt Jo's Scrap Bag. Boston, 1878 1st ed. VG. $100. Grosset & Dunlap, 1929. Good. $10.

ALCOTT, WM. A. *The Young Housekeeper, or Thoughts on Food and Cookery.* NY, 1855. G-VG. $75-$125. Another, Boston, 1849 9th edition. Fair cond. $40.

ALDERMAN, CLIFFORD. *Annie Oakley and the World of Her Time.* Macmillan, 1979 1st ed. Fine in DJ. $10.

ALDIN, CECIL. *Dogs of Character.* London, 1927 1st ed. Illus. by author. Very Good. $150.
The Cecil Aldin Book. London, 1932 1st ed. Fine. $100.
Hunting Sketches. NY, 1936 1st American ed. Fair in torn dust jacket. $85.

ALDINGTON, RICHARD. *Images Old and New.* Boston, 1916 1st American ed. Paperback. VG. $40.
Fifty Romance Lyric Poems. Aldington as editor. Crosby Gaige, 1928. One of 900 copies signed by Bruce Rogers. Some rubbing, o/w Fine. $60.
At All Costs. London, 1930 signed 1st ed. VG, $40.
All Men Are Enemies. Lon., 1933 1st. F in torn DJ. $50.
The Rejected Guest. NY, 1939. 1st American ed. Very Good in worn dust jacket. $15.

ALDISS, BRIAN. *Greybeard.* NY, 1964 1st. VG in DJ. $125.
The Hand-Reared Boy. London, 1970 1st edition, Very Good in dust jacket. $25-$40.
Soldier Erect. NY, 1971 1st Amer. ed. Fine in vg DJ. $20.

ALDRIDGE, ALAN (Editor). *The Beatles Illustrated Lyrics.* 1969, Delacorte Press, VG. $40. No. 2. 1971. VG in DJ. $40

ALDRICH, THOMAS BAILEY. *Daisy's Necklace.* New York Derby & Jackson, 1857 1st edition. Inscibed by author. Good-Very Good. $200.
The Story of a Bad Boy. Boston, 1870 1st issue. VG, in Cambridge box. $250.
The Writings of Thomas B. Aldrich. Boston, 1897 1st ed. 8 volumes. Illustrated. $75.
A Sea Turns and Other Matters. Boston & New York, 1902 1st edition. Soiled, no dust jacket. $25.

ALDRIDGE, JAMES. *Goodbye UnAmerica.* No place, 1979 1st American ed. VG in DJ. $28.

ALEXANDER, A. S. *The Veterinary Adviser.* NY, Orange Judd, 1950 reprint of 1929 ed. VG. $15.

ALEXANDER, HELEN. *The Helen Alexander Cook Book.* NY, 1926 1st ed. Good. $15.
Helen Alexander's Hawaiian Cook Book. Honolulu, 1938 1st ed. Decorative green cloth cover. VG. $30.

ALGER, HORATIO. *Ragged Dick, or Street Life in New York With the Bootblacks.* Boston, 1868 1st ed., 1st issue. Very Good. $700-$850.
Mark The Match Boy. Boston, 1869 1st ed. VG. $35.
Strive and Succeed. Boston, 1872. $75-$100.
From Canal Boy to President. Boston, 1881. Wear, poor hinges. $50.
Ben's Nugget; or A Boy's Search for Fortune. Pacific Coast Series. Philadelphia, H. T. Coates, 1882 1st ed. Near Fine. $99 auction.
Tony The Tramp. NY, 1911. VG. $5.
The Errand Boy. Burt, 1888. Ads in back. Three full page illus. G-VG. $12-$20.
Do and Dare. Winston, no date. (Original publication, 1884). Browned o/w VG in DJ. $14.
The Erie Train Boy. No place. No date. Reprint of 1890 edition. VG in DJ. $18.
Adrift in New York. World, no date. DJ. $15.
The Young Adventurer. Reprint of 1878 ed. Burt, no date. Chimney Corner series. VG in original DJ. $18.
A Collection of mixed titles. 1904-1915. VG. $9-$15 each. Nine different titles. Various publishers: Donohoe, World, Hurst, Burt. $5-$8. Street & Smith paperbacks. No dates. $8 each.

AUCTION LOTS OF HORATIO ALGER.
Risen from the Ranks. 1st ed. (1874). • *The Telegraph Boy.* (1879). • *Paul Prescott's Charge.* (1865). • *Strive and Succeed; or, The Progress of Walter Conrad.* (1872). • *Strong and Steady; or, Paddle Your Own Canoe.* (1871). • *Randy of the River, or The Adventures of A Young Deckhand.* 1st ed. (1906). Together 6 vols. Original dec. or pictorial cloth. Various places; various dates. First published by Loring, next 4 by Porter & Coates,

last by Chatterton-Peck. Much wear to earlier vols., else all good to very good. 6 vols. $50-$100. *Jed the Poorhouse Boy.* • The Young Salesman. with jacket. • *Shifting for Himself.* • *Try and Trust.* • *Young Outlaw.* • *Brave and Bold.* • *Adrift in New York.* • Plus 12 others. Together, 19 vols. Original pictorial cloth. New York: Hurst & Co. (n.d., c. 1900) Rubbing & wear to some covers, many with contents darkening, jacket lacking most of spine strip, else all about very good. 19 vols. $70-$120. *Dan the Newsboy.* (1893). • *The Train Boy.* (1883). • *Mark Manning's Mission: The Story of a Shoe Factory Boy.* (1905). • *Tony, the Hero.* (1890). • *Strong and Steady: The Story of a Successful Boy.* n.d. • *Tom Thatcher's Fortune.* • Plus 5 others. Together, 11 vols. Some illus. Original pictorial cloth. New York: A. L. Burt, various dates. Wear to some cov., generally VG. 11 vols. $45-$90.

ALGREN, NELSON. *Somebody in Boots.* NY, 1935 1st ed. Author's 1st book. VG in DJ. $600-$900.
The Man With the Golden Arm. NY, 1949 1st ed. VG to Fine in dust jacket. $45-$75. Good-VG in DJ. $15-$25.
Chicago: City on the Make. Garden City, 1951 1st ed. VG-Fine in dust jacket. $20-$50.
A Walk on the Wild Side. 1956 1st ed. DJ, Fine. $40.
Who Lost an American? NY, 1963 1st ed. VG in DJ. $20.
The Neon Wilderness. London, 1965 1st English ed. VG in dust jacket. $30.

ALLBEURY, TED. *Moscow Quadrille.* London, 1976 1st ed. Very Good in dust jacket. $20.
The Alpha List. London, 1979 1st ed. NF in DJ. $35.

ALLEN, BETSY. *The Secret of Black Cat Gulch.* (Connie Blair no. 4) Grosset & Dunlap, 1948 1st ed. VG in dingy dust jacket. $35. Later copy. $20.
The Brown Satchel Mystery. (Connie Blair no. 9) Grosset & Dunlap, 1954. VG in dust jacket. $40.

ALLEN, BILLIE. *The Desert and Two Stones, California & Arizona Desert Trails.* Harlow Press, 1969 1st edition. Red cloth. Fine. $15.

ALLEN, C. L. *Bulbs and Tuberous-Rooted Plants.* NY, Orange Judd, 1925 edition. VG, slight faded. $25.

ALLEN, GAY W. *Melville and His World.* NY, 1971 1st ed. Near Fine in dust jacket. $45.

ALLEN, HERVEY. *Anthony Adverse.* NY, 1933 1st ed. Fine. $30. Another, soiled, signed by author. $20.
Bedford Village. NY, 1944 1st ed. Good in fair DJ. $40.
Toward the Morning. NY, 1948 1st ed. $40.

ALLEN, HUGH. *The Story of the Airship.* Goodyear Tire & Rubber, 1932. Near Fine. $60-$90. Poor-fair. $8. Lakeside Press, 1942 ed. Very Good. $16.
House of Goodyear. Akron, 1936 2nd ed. VG in DJ. $20.

ALLEN, IDA BAILEY. *Ida Bailey's Modern Cook Book*. 1924. $30-$40. Garden City. 1933 reprint. G-VG. $10. *The Common Sense Cook Book*. 1939. $20-30. *Cook Book for Two*. Doubleday, 1957 rev. ed. VG. $10. *Luscious Luncheons and Tasty Teas*. Minneapolis, Buzz Co. circa 1930 1st ed. In string-tied wrappers. Fine. $45.

ALLEN, JAMES LANE. *The Blue-Grass Region of Kentucky and Other Kentucky Articles*. NY, 1892 1st ed. VG. $85. Same, ex-library. Good. $15. *A Kentucky Cardinal*. NY, 1895 1st edition. VG. $30. *The Choir Invisible*. NY, 1897, 1st ed. VG. $45. *Summer in Arcady*. Macmillan, 1896. Cover soil. $10. *Flute and Violin*. Harper, 1891. Pyle illus. VG. $30. *The Reign of Law*. Macmillan, 1900 1st ed. G in DJ. $45. Same, no dust jacket. $6-$12. *Bride of Mistletoe*. No place, 1909. No DJ. $10. *The Doctor's Christmas Eve*. NY, 1910 1st ed. Good. $13. Same, Fine in dust jacket. $45-$80. *A Cathedral Singer*. NY, 1916 1st ed. Fine. $25. *The Kentucky Warbler*. NY, 1918 1st ed. VG in DJ. $60. Another, Good, no dust jacket. $15.

ALLEN, IVAN. *Atlanta From the Ashes*. Atlanta, 1928 Limited edition with letter signed by author. VG. $40.

JOSIAH ALLEN'S WIFE. (Also see Holley, Marietta.) *Samantha at Saratoga*. 1887 1st edition. G-VG. $8-$15. *Samantha Among Colored Folks*. NY, 1904. Good. $35. *Samantha In Europe*. 1895. Very Good. $24. *Samantha at the Saint Louis Exposition*. Dillingham, 1904 1st ed. Very Good. $14.

ALLEN, LEWIS. *History of Short Horn Cattle*. Buffalo, 1878, 1886 eds. Illus. $50-$100.

ALLEN, P. S. *King Arthur & His Knights*. Rand McNally, 1924. J. R. Neill illus. VG. $45. Same, 1936 ed. VG. $25.

ALLEN, RICHARD S. *Covered Bridges of the North East*. Brattleboro, 1957. Good in DJ. $16. *Covered Bridges of the Middle Atlantic States*. Bonanza, 1965 reprint. Fine in DJ. $14.

ALLEN, ROBERT. *Lucky Ford: The History of Patton's 3rd U. S. Army*. NY, 1947. Good plus. $50.

ALLINGHAM, MARGERY. *Flowers for the Judge*. Doubleday Doran, 1936 1st ed. Good in DJ. $22. *Pearls Before Swine*. NY, 1943 1st ed. VG. $15. Another, Fine in dust jacket. $30. *More Work for the Undertaker*. NY 1949 1st ed. VG in dust jacket. $20. *No Love Lost*. NY, Crime Club, 1954 1st American. edition. Fine in dust jacket. $45. *The Estate of the Beckoning Lady*. NY, 1955 1st ed. Near Fine in dust jacket. $38.

ALLSOPP, FRED W. *Folklore of Romantic Arkansas*. Grolier Society, 1931. 2 vols. Very Good. $75.

ALMANACS. (See Magazine Section, by author or title).

ALPERS, A. *Dolphins: The Myth and the Mammal*. Boston, 1961. Very Good. $13.

ALSOP, STEWART and THOMAS BRADEN. *Sub Rosa*. New York 1946. Good-VG. $4-$15.

ALTGELD, JOHN P. *Our Penal Machinery and Its Victims*. Chicago, 1886 New, revised ed. Very Good. $40. *Live Questions: Including Our Penal Machinery & Its Victims*. Chicago, 1890 1st ed. Good. $35.

ALTOWAN: OR INCIDENTS OF LIFE AND ADVENTURE IN THE ROCKY MOUNTAINS. Anon. (Sir William D. Stewart). New York, 1846. $500-$850.

ALTSHELER, JOSEPH. *Sun of Saratoga*. NY, 1897 1st ed. Author's 1st book. Very Good. $150. *In Hostile Red*. New York, 1904. Special subscription. Very Good. $25. *The Recovery*. Frank Lovell Co, 1908. VG. $25. *The Sun of Quebec*. Appleton, 1919. Good. $15. *The Tree of Appomattox*. NY, 1928. VG. $35. *The Hosts of the Air*. Appleton, 1942. Good. $10. Various other Appleton reprints. $14 ea.

ALTROCCHI, JULIA COOLEY. *The Old California Trail: Folklore & Furrow*. Caxton Printers, 1945. G-VG. $30.

AMBLER, ERIC. *Judgement at Deltchey*. London, 1951 1st edition. Fine in worn dust jacket. $40. *State of Siege*. NY, 1956 1st American ed. Fine in DJ. $35. *The Light of Day*. New York, 1962 1st edition. Near Fine in dust jacket. $15.

AMEND, OTTILIE. *Jolly Jungle Pictures*. P. F. Volland, 1929. Eleanore Barte illus. Good. $35.

AMBRUS, VICTOR. *Little Cockerel*. Harcourt, 1968 1st American edition. Very Good-Fine in dust jacket. $20-$30.

AMERICAN ANNUAL OF PHOTOGRAPHY. 1930-1948. Covers scuffed. Good plus. $15 each. 6 vols. for 1938, 1942, 1943, 1944, 1945, 1946. Good to VG. The lot, $75.

AMERICAN ARMIES AND BATTLEFIELDS IN EUROPE: A History, Guide and Reference Book. Washington, 1938. Maps in pocket. Very Good. $60

AMERICAN BOOK PRICES CURRENT. Vols. for 1971, 1972, 1974. $30. Vols. for 1977 and 1978. $40 each. Vols. for 1984, 1985, 1986. $15 each. 12 vols. 1960-70. Red cloth. $110 auction.

THE AMERICAN BOY'S BOOK OF SPORTS & GAMES. A Repository of In and Outdoor Amusements. NY, 1864. Good-Very Good. $35-$50.

AMERICAN BUREAU OF ETHNOLOGY. Reports for years 1884-1884, 1888-1889, 1891-1892, 1894-1895, 1899-1900, 1900-1901, 1905-1906, 1906-1907, 1911-1912, 1926-1927. $125 each. Issue of 1899-1900. $300.

THE AMERICAN CRUISER. Anon. (Capt. George Little). Boston, 1846. Very Good. $120-$140.

AMERICAN FIREMARKS. Insurance Co. of North America, 1933. Very Good. $40.

AN AMERICAN FAMILY COOK BOOK. By a Boston housekeeper. NY, James Miller, 1864. Gold dec. green. cloth. 330 pgs. Good-VG. $80-$120.

AMERICAN GUIDE SERIES (WPA). *Colorado*. Hastings House, 1945 3rd printing. VG. $18. 1941 ed. Fair. $8. *Michigan*. Oxford Univ., 1943 2nd printing. VG. $24. *Minnesota*. Viking, 1938 1st ed. VG, no DJ. $29. *Wisconsin*. Duell, Sloan. 1941 1st ed. Good. $18. *Los Angeles*. Hastings House, 1941. VG. $18. *WPA Guide to Washington*. GPO 1st ed., 1937. Fine. $30. First editions of State Guides in good to very good condition, with maps and dust jacket intact, bring an average of $20-$35 each. Those of the least populated states bring much more, e.g., Alabama $60. Delaware $80. Iowa $75. Nebraska $80. North Dakota $150.

THE AMERICAN HERITAGE BOOK OF INDIANS. 1961. Introduction by J. F. Kennedy. VG in slipcase. $17-$25.

AMERICAN HERITAGE COOK BOOK. 2 volumes, A.H., 1964. Very Good. $35.

AMERICAN HERITAGE PICTURE HISTORY OF THE CIVIL WAR. 2 vols., 1960. Very Good. $22.

AMERICAN HOME BOOK OF SMART INTERIORS. No place, 1939 4th ed. Good-VG. $26.

THE AMERICAN HOME COOK BOOK. "By an American Lady" NY, 1854. Good-VG. $40-$85.

THE AMERICAN HOYLE. 1864. By Trumps. 518 pages. $75 auction.

THE AMERICAN PRACTICAL COOKERY BOOK. Phil., 1859. John E. Potter. 50 engravings. G-VG. $100-$150.

THE AMERICAN SHOOTER'S MANUAL. Anon. (Jesse Kester). Philadelphia, 1827. $2,000-$3,000.

THE AMERICAN SODA BOOK. American Soda Fountain Co. Circa 1910. 1,000 formulas plus ads. Good. $35.

THE AMERICAN SOLDIER IN THE CIVIL WAR. NY, 1895. Binding worn and shaken. $70.

AMIS, KINGSLEY. *Lucky Jim*. NY, 1954. 1st American ed. Author's 1st book. Near Fine in DJ. $250-$275. *I Like It Here*. NY, 1958 1st American ed. VG in DJ, $20. *James Bond Dossier*. Lon., 1965 1st ed. VG in DJ. $50. *The Anti-Death League*. London, 1966 1st ed. Signed. Near Fine in dust jacket. $100. *The Green Man*. NY, 1970 1st Amer. ed. VG in DJ. $20.

AMMONS, A. R. *Carson's Inlet*. Ithaca NY, 1965. Advance copy. Fine in dust jacket. $65. *Selected Poems*. Ithaca NY, 1968 1st ed. VG in DJ. $40.

AMSDEN, CHARLES. *Navaho Weaving: Its Technique and History*. 1949 1st edition. $150-$250. 1949 reprint. $35-$50. 1974. $20.

AMUNDSEN, ROALD and L. ELLSWORTH. *First Crossing of the Polar Sea*. Doubleday, 1928. VG. $45. Another, Foldout map torn loose. Reading copy. $20. *My Life as an Explorer*. Garden City, 1927. $20-$35.

AMUNDSEN, ROALD and others. *Our Polar Flight*. NY, 1925 1st ed. Fine. $175. London, no date. Good. $25.

ANDERS, W. *Hitler's Defeat in Russia*. Chicago, 1953 1st ed. Good-VG in dust jacket. $20-$30.

ANDERSEN, HANS CHRISTIAN. *Stories for the Household*. London, Geo. Routledge and Sons, 1866. First collected edition in English 8vo., 220 wood engravings. Near Fine. $300. Note: from 1846 onwards there were many translations of Andersen's fairy tales, but the above edition was the first definitive one, being the "largest and most complete collection that has yet been made." *Hans Andersen's Fairy Tales*. London, 1916. 40 plates by Harry Clarke. VG. $165. Albert Whitman, circa 1920. McCracken illus. Near Fine. $28-$35. NY, Doran, 1924. Kay Nielsen illus. Near Fine. $200-$375. Grosset & Dunlap, 1945. Junior Library. Arthur Szyk illus. Worn slipcase. $35. London, 1932. Rackham illus. Red cloth, 288 pgs. Fine. $195. NY, Routledge, circa 1880. 10 color plates. VG. $45. Philadelphia, no date, Mc Kay. Rackham illus. 288 pgs. Red cloth, gold stamped. VG in DJ. $150-$250. Philadelphia, no date, Altemus pub. Carse illus. 371 pages. $45. Garden City, 1932. Kay Nielsen. $50-$95. *It's Perfectly True and other Stories*. Harcourt, 1938 translation by Paul Lysec. VG, no DJ. $20. *The Snow Queen*. London, ca 1910. Dulac illus. VG. $125. Dial, 1982. 2nd printing. Susan Jeffers illus. F in DJ. $25. *The Little Mermaid*. Natick, MA 1984. Chichiro Iwasaki illus. Very Good in dust jacket. $15.

ANDERSON, ANNE. *The Patsy Book*. Nelson, no date. Illus. by author. Good. $40.

The Wonder Story Book. London, no date. Illus. VG. $45.
Rosie Posie Book. Nelson, no date. VG. $65.
Sleeping Beauty. Nelson, no date 1st. Illus. by auth. G $18.

ANDERSON, BERNICE G. *Topsy Turvy's Pigtails*. Chicago 1938. Esther Friend illus. Some wear. $45.

ANDERSON, CHARLES C. *Fighting by Southern Federals*. NY, 1912 1st ed. Good-VG. $50-$95.

ANDERSON and COLLIER. *Riding & Driving*. Macmillan. 1936. Very Good. $40.

ANDERSON, EVA G. *Chief Seattle*. Caldwell ID, 1943 1st edition. Color plates, map. $75-$120. Same, Caxton, 1950. Very Good. $25.

ANDERSON, FREDERICK IRVING. *The Book of Murder.* NY, 1929, 1st ed. Short stories. VG. $175.

ANDERSON, J. R. L. *Death on the Rocks.* NY, 1973 1st ed. Fine in dust jacket. $20.
Death in the Caribbean. Lon., 1977 1st ed. Fine. DJ. $25.

ANDERSON, JOHN L. *A Fifteenth Century Cookry Boke*. Scribners, 1962. VG in dust jacket. $20.

ANDERSON, MARGARET. *The Unknowable Gurdjieff*. NY, 1962 1st ed. VG in dust jacket. $30.

ANDERSON, MAXWELL. *Key Largo*. Washington, DC, 1939 1st ed. Near Fine in DJ. $100.
The Star-Wagon. Wash. DC, 1937 1st ed. in DJ. $85.

ANDERSON, MARIAN. *My Lord, What a Morning*. NY, 1941 1st ed. in DJ. $40. 1956 and 1958 editions. $15-$25.

ANDERSON, N. *Pilots' Airplane Manual*. Civil Aeronautics Bulletin No. 27. Washington, 1940. 150 pages. $20.

ANDERSON, POUL. *Vault of the Ages*. Philadelphia, 1952 1st ed. Author's 1st book. VG in DJ. $40. Another, signed by author. VG in dust jacket. $75.
Murder Bound. NY, 1962 1st ed. Page borders browning, Very Good in dust jacket. $75.
The Star Fox. Garden City, 1965 1st ed. VG in DJ. $70.
Brain Wave. Walker, 1969 1st American edition. hardcovered. Very Good in dust jacket. $75.
Tau Zero. Doubleday, 1970 1st ed. VG in worn DJ. $100.

ANDERSON, SHERWOOD. *Windy McPherson's Son*. No place, 1916 1st ed., 1st book. Fine in slipcase. $450.
Winesburg, Ohio. NY, 1919 1st ed. Near Fine. $350.
Same. 1st edition, 1st issue, rebound in morocco. $400.
Same, Modern Library, 1919. Good. $8.
Return to Winesburg. Univ. of North Carolina, 1967 1st ed. Very Good in dust jacket. $25.

The Triumph of the Egg. Huebsch, 1921 1st ed. VG. $35.
Horses and Men. NY, 1923 1st ed. Fine in DJ. $200.
Dark Laughter. NY, 1925 1st ed. VG in DJ. $125.
Tar, A Midwest Childhood. 1926 1st ed. VG in DJ. $75.
Same, no dust jacket. $16-$30.
Hello Towns! Liveright, 1929 1st ed. NF in DJ. $140.
Kit Brandon. Scribner, 1936 1st ed. VG in DJ. $40.
Home Town (Photos). NY, 1940 1st ed. G-VG. $40.
The Portable. NY, 1949. Fine. $15.

ANDREWS, BENJAMIN. *History of the United States*. Scribner, 1895. Howard Pyle illus. VG. $25.

ANDREWS, JANE. *Seven Little Sisters Who Live on T*. Ginn & Co., 1887. Good plus. $12.
Each and All: Seven Little Sisters Prove Sisterhood. Boston, 1900. Very Good. $18.

ANDREWS, RALPH. *This Was Logging*. Seattle WA, 1954. One of 2,000 copies. Photographs. G-VG. $35.
Picture Gallery Pioneers - First Photographers of the West 1850-1875. Superior, 1964 1st ed. Fine in DJ. $30.
Photographers of the Frontier West. Seattle, 1965 1st ed. Fine in dust jacket. $35.

ANDREWS, ROY CHAPMAN. *Camps and Trails in China*. NY, 1919. VG. $75. Signed copy. $95.
Across Mongolian Plains. Blue Ribbon, 1921. $15.
On The Trail of Ancient Man. NY, 1926 1st ed. Hinges cracked, o/w Very Good. $40.
An Explorer Comes Home. NY, 1947 1st ed. $13.

ANGEL, MARIE. *Beasts in Heraldry*. Stephen Greene Press, 1974 1st ed. Illus. by author. Very Good. $85.

ANGEL, MYRON, (Editor). *History of Nevada with Illustrations and Biographical Sketches*. Oakland, Thompson & West, 1881 1st edition. Rebound. in Morocco. 680 pages. Near Fine $500 auction.

ANGELL, ROGER. *Stone Arbor*. Boston, 1960 1st ed. Author's 1st book. VG in dust jacket. $50.
The Summer Game. New York, 1972 1st edition. Near Fine in dust jacket. $50.
Five Seasons. NY, 1977 1st ed. VG in DJ. $18.

ANGELO, VALENTI. *Nino*. NY, 1938 1st ed. VG. $20-$25.
Golden Gate. NY, 1939 1st ed. signed. $28.
Look Out Yonder. NY, 1943 1st ed. VG in DJ. $25.
Angelino and the Barefoot Saint. NY, 1961 1st ed. Illus. by author. Fine in dust jacket. $45.

ANGELUCCI, ENZO. *Airplanes, From the Dawn of Flight to the Present Day*. NY, 1973 1st edition. VG in DJ. $35.

ANGER, KENNETH. *Hollywood Babylon*. Bell Publications, 1981 1st ed. As new in DJ. $12.

ANGLE, PAUL. *Here I Have Lived*. Springfield IL, 1935 1st ed. Signed. VG in DJ. $30. Same. New Brunswick NJ, 1950. Very Good in sunned dust jacket. $15.

ANGLE, PAUL and EARL MIERS. *Fire the Salute! Abe Lincoln Nominated!* Kingston P., 1960. VG in box. $25.

ANGLUND, JOAN W. *The Brave Cowboy*. NY, 1959 1st ed. Illus. by author. Very Good in dust jacket. $20.
In A Pumpkin Shell. NY, 1960. Illus. by author. Good. $9.

ANISOARA, STAN. *The Romanian Cook Book*. Citadel Press, 1951 1st ed. Very Good in dust jacket. $30.

ANNO, MITSUMASA. *Anno's Counting Book*. NY, 1977. Illus. by author. Very Good in dust jacket. $45.
Anno's Counting House. NY, 1982 1st American edition. Illustrated by author. $20.
Anno's Math Games. NY, 1987 4th printing. Illustrated by author. Fine. $30.
Anno's U.S.A. NY, 1983 1st ed. Illus. by author. F in fine DJ. $45. Same. One of 1,000 copies. Signed in slipcase. Fine. $150. Ex-library copy of 1st trade ed. F in DJ. $15.

ANNUAL OF ADVERTISING ART. For 1926, 1930, 1932, 1933. $60-$75 each.

ANNUAL REPORT OF THE AMERICAN HISTORICAL ASSOC, 1931. USGPO, 1932. Vol. 1. 452 pgs. $15.

ANTHONY, IRVIN. *Paddle Wheels and Pistols*. Macrae-Smith, 1929 1st ed. Good-VG. $10-$20.

ANTONINUS, BROTHER (William Everson). *The Residual Years*. New Directions, 1948 1st ed. VG in DJ. $125.
Man-Fate: The Swan Song of Brother Antoninus. New Directions, 1974 1st ed. Fine in DJ. $20.

ANYONE CAN BAKE. Royal Baking Powder. 1927-1929 eds., cloth cover. Good-VG. $15-$20 ea.

APPLETON, L. H. *Indian Art of the Americas*. NY, 1950 1st edition. Illus. In dust jacket. $80-$150.

APPLETON, VICTOR. *Moving Picture Boys and the Flood*. Grosset & Dunlap series 6. Fine in DJ. $25.
Don Sturdy in the Tombs of Gold. Grosset & Dunlap series 3. Fine in dust jacket. $25.
Tom Swift and His Giant Robot. Grosset and Dunlap series 4. Fine in dust jacket. $20.
Tom Swift and His Ultrasonic Cycloplane. Grosset & Dunlap series 10, 1st ed. Fine in dust jacket. $20.
Tom Swift and His Motor Boat. VG. $13.
Tom Swift and His Submarine Boat. VG. $13.
Tom Swift & His Ocean Airport Whitman. VG in DJ. $36.
Tom Swift and His Deep Sea Hydrodome. Orange spine, pictorial cover. $8.

VICTOR APPLETON was a pseudonym. Edward Stratemeyer and Howard Garis (an employee) were the real authors of the *Tom Swift* juvenile series. Edward Stratemeyer also wrote (or outlined) the *Rover Boys* adventures. His daughter, Harriet Adams (better known as Carolyn Keene and Laura Lee Hope) wrote most of the *Bobsey Twins* and all the *Nancy Drew* books.

Harriet took over her father's fiction syndicate in 1930 and continued to issue many of the 1,200 books he had written or commissioned under many pen names including Franklin W. Dixon of *Hardy Boys* fame.

Tom Swift juvenile titles published in the 1920s and 1930s sell for $25 to $60 each in very good condition with original dust covers. Without dust jackets they are worth $10 to $24 a copy.

The original *Tom Swift* series began in 1910 and ended in 1941. A second series ran from 1954 to 1971. Simon and Schuster published a third series from 1981 to 1984. Books of the later 1930s and 1940s bring from $7 to $15 each without dust jackets. 1950s titles are worth less. Both command a 50 to 100 per cent premium if found in undamaged dust jackets, which were discontinued in 1961.

There are some $100-$200 sleepers among early issues. Serious juvenile series collectors often consult *Heffelfinger's Bayport Companion* for price variations. Write to Charles Heffelfinger, Midnight Press, 7011 18th St, Tampa, FL 33610. Nancy Drew fans use *Farah's Guide to Nancy Drew*. From Dave Farah, 3110 Park Newport, Apt 412, Newport Beach, CA 92660. A magazine devoted entirely to juvenile series books, called *Yellowback Library*, is available from Yellowback Press, P. O. Box 36172, Des Moines, IA 50315.

Tom Swift Jr. and His Space Solartron. Orange spine, pictoral cover. $8.
Tom Swift Jr. and His Megascope Spare Prober. Orange spine, 1st ed. Near fine. $15.
Tom Swift Jr. and the Asteroid Pirates. Orange spine, 1st edition. Near fine. $15.
Tom Swift and His Airline Express. No. 29 Grosset & Dunlap, 1926. VG in DJ. $40.
Tom Swift & His Magnetic Silencer. NF, BLB. scarce. $135.
Tom Swift. Series 34. Tan Book. $60.
Tom Swift. Series 35 Tan Book 1st ed. Reinforced DJ. $200.
Tom Swift Series 36. Orange Book. 1st in orig. DJ. $150.
Various Tom Swift titles. 1954-1961. $2-$8.
Hardy Boys 3 in 1 Edition. VG. $15.
Hardy Boys, Footprints Under the Window. Wrap spine jacket. Very Good. $11.
Hardy Boys, The Wailing Siren Mystery. Wrap spine jacket. Very Good. $13.

APPLETON'S CYCLOPEDIA OF APPLIED MECHANICS. NY, 1896. 2 vols. Revised ed. Good-VG. $50.

APPLETON'S DICTIONARY OF MACHINES. Appleton, 1867. 2 vols. 4,000 engravings on wood. G-VG. $50.

APPLETON'S GENERAL GUIDE TO U. S. & CANADA. Appleton, 1886 revised ed. VG. $18-$20.

APPLETON'S JUVENILE ANNUAL 1869. Foxing. $75.

THE ARABIAN NIGHTS ENTERTAINMENT. 1924 ed. Frances Brundage illus. $35. 4 vols. Limited Ed. Club, 1954. One of 1,500 copies. Arthur Szyk illus. F. $200. Worn, stn. $55. (Also see Burton, Richard .)

ARBUS, DIANE. *Aperture, 1972*. 80 plates. VG in DJ. $85.

ARCHIBALD, JOSEPH. *The Smoke Eaters*. NY, 1965. Good-VG. $15.
Commander of the Flying Tigers: Claire Chennault. No place, 1966. Very Good. $14.

ARCHITECTURAL LEAGUE OF NEW YORK. *Year Book and Catalogue*. 1907, $40. 1926, $50. 1928, $45.

ARDIZZONE, EDWARD. *Little Time and the Brave Sea Captain*. Illus. by author. London, 1939. Reprint. Paperback edition. Good. $20.
Peter the Wanderer. NY, 1964 1st U. S. ed. Illus. by author. Ex-library copy in dust jacket. $10.
Old Ballad of the Babes in the Wood. NY, 1972 reissue. VG-Fine in dust jacket. $25-$35.
Tim and Ginger. Walck, 1965 ed. Illustrated by author. VG in edge worn dust jacket. $30.
Young Ardizzone. Macmillan, 1970 1st American ed. Fine in fine dust jacket. $40.

ARESTY, E. *The Delectable Past (Cookery)*. New York, 1964. Good-VG in dust jacket. $10-$25.

ARMER, LAURA ADAMS. *Dark Circle of Branches*. Longmans, 1933. Illus. by author. Ex-lib. VG in DJ. $25.
Waterless Mountain. NY, 1975. Newbery Medal in 1931. Fine in dust jacket. $16.

ARMES, ETHEL Stratford Hall, the Great House of the Lees.. VA, 1936. 1 of 1,200 copies, signed. Fair in fine DJ. $75.

ARMITAGE, MERLE. *Fit For a King: the Merle Armitage Book of Food*. R. McGhee ed. NY, 1939 1st edition. Good. $30. Very Good. $60.
Accent on America. NY, 1944. One of 325 copies, signed by author. Very Good. $25.
Rendevous With the Book. NY, 1949 1st ed. VG. $45.
Stella Dysart of Ambrosia Lake. Duell, 1959 1st limited ed. Very Good in dust jacket. $25.

ARMITAGE, MERLE (Editor). *The Art of Edward Weston*. NY, 1932 1st ed. 30 full page Weston photos. Staining, marking, rebacked, recased. Signed by Weston. $600.

ARMOUR, J. OGDEN. *The Packers, the Private Car Lines and the People*. Philadelphia, 1906 1st ed. VG. $60-$120.

ARMSTRONG, HARRY. *Principles and Practice of Aviation Medicine*. 1937, 1939 and 1941 editions. Illustrated. Very Good in dust jacket. $50-$100 each.

ARMSTRONG, LOUIS. *Satchmo. My Life in New Orleans*. NY, 1954 1st ed. VG in worn dust jacket. $25.
Swing That Music. Longmans, 1936 1st ed. in DJ. $100.

ARMSTRONG, MARGARET. *The Man With No Face*. NY, 1940 1st ed. Owner inscription, o/w VG in DJ. $100.
The Blue Santo Murder Mystery. NY, 1941 1st ed. Near Fine in dust jacket. $85.

ARMSTRONG, NEIL with MICHAEL COLLINS and EDWIN E. ALDRIN. *First on the Moon*. Boston, 1970 2nd printing. Good in dust jacket. $17.

ARMSTRONG, TOM and others. *200 Years of American Sculpture*. David R. Godine, 1976. Very Good. $60.

ARMY FOOD AND MESSING. Harrisburg, 1943 3rd ed. Worn, stained. $20.

ARNO, PETER. *Whoops, Dearie*, NY, 1921 1st ed. Author's 1st book. Very Good. $40.
Arno's Parade, NY, 1929. One of 150 copies. Signed by author. Cover loose. $60.

ARNOLD and EAKER. *Army Flyer*. NY, 1942, 1st edition. Good -VG. $15-$20.

ARNOLD, WILLIAM. *Ventures in Book Collecting*. Scribners, 1923 1st ed. Good-VG in DJ. $25-$40.

ARROWSMITH, JAMES. *The Paper Hanger's Companion*. Directions, etc. Philadelphia, 1866. 108 pgs. Worn. $50.

ART AT AUCTION-THE YEAR AT SOTHEBY'S. *Annuals from 1967 to 1988*. $25 each.

ARTHUR, ROBERT. *The Third Marine Division*. Wash. DC, 1948 1st ed. 385 pages. Good-VG. $55-$85.

ARTHUR, RUTH. *A Candle in Her Room*. NY, 1966. 7th printing. Margery Gill illus. Ex-library. Good in DJ. $9.
Miss Ghost. NY, 1979 1st Amer. ed. Ex-lib. VG in DJ. $7.

ARTHUR, T. S. *Ten Nights in a Barroom*. Bos., 1854 1st edition, Hinge cracked o/w Good. $100. 1897 edition, Altemus. Loose binding. $5.

ARTISTIC GUIDE TO CHICAGO AND THE WORLD'S COLUMBIAN EXPOSITION, 1892. 420 pgs. $15-$30.

ARTZYBASHEFF, BORIS. *Behind Moroccan Walls*. Macmillan, 1931. Illus. by auth. Ins. Cov. foxed, else. VG. $70.
Seven Simeons. NY, 1937. 1st ed. Illustrated by author. Ex-library. Fine in dust jacket. $40.

ARTZYBASHEFF, BORIS. (Illustrator). *Funnybone Alley*. By Alfred Kreymborg. NY, 1927, 1st trade ed. Good. $45. Same 1st ed. One of 500 copies. VG. $100.
The Circus of Dr. Lao. By Charles G. Finney. Viking, 1945 1st ed. Edge wear, o/w Very Good. $50.

ASBJORNSEN, PETER. *East of the Sun & West of the Moon*. Doran. $200-$250. NF in dust jacket. $300-$400.
Folk & Fairy Tales. NY, Armstrong, 1883. VG. $45-$60.

ASH, EDWARD C. *Dogs: Their History and Development*. London, 1927 1st ed. 2 vols. Illus. VG. $250.
Dogs and How to Know Them. London., 1926 2nd ed. Very Good. $35-$40.

ASHBROOK and SATER. *Cooking Wild Game*. NY, 1945. Scarce, in dust jacket. $35.

ASBURY, HERBERT. *The Gangs of New York*. Garden City, NY, 1927. Fine. $75.
Ye Olde Fire Laddies. NY, 1930. G-VG, $45.
Gem of the Prairie. No place, 1940. G-VG. $35.

ASHBERY, JOHN. *Some Trees*. New Haven, 1956 1st ed. Fine in dust jacket. $200.
Rivers and Mountains. NY, 1966 1st ed. Fine in DJ. $100.
Self-Portrait in a Mirror. NY, 1975. VG in DJ. $20.
As We Know: Poems. NY, 1979 1st ed. Inscribed, Fine in dust jacket. $100. Unsigned. $30.

ASHBY, THOMAS. *The Valley Campaigns*. NY, 1914 1st edition. Good-VG. $75-$150.

ASHFORD, DAISY. *The New York Visiter, or Mr. Salteena's Plan*. No place, 1919. Novel by 9-year-old. Preface by J. M. Barrie. VG in DJ. $30. 1951 ed. $15.

ASHLEY, CLIFFORD. *The Yankee Whaler*. Boston & NY, 1926 1st ed. G-VG. $250-$400. 1938 2nd ed. Good. $50-$75. 1942 reprint, Halcyon. VG in DJ. $25-$50.
Whaleships of New Bedford. Boston, 1929 1st ed. VG-Fine in dust jacket. $150-$200.

ASHLEY, ROBERTA. *Cool Cooking*. New York, 1972 1st ed. Recipes contributed by rock stars. $35-$50.

ASIMOV, ISAAC. *Pebble in the Sky*. NY, 1950 1st edition, 1st book. Inscribed by author. VG in very good DJ. $225. Another, not inscribed. $38.

The Stars Like Dust. NY, 1951 1st ed. VG in DJ. $150.
Foundation. Gnome Press, 1951 1st edition. 1st issue. Rebound. $150.
Foundation and Empire. Gnome Press, 1952 1st edition, 1st issue. Rebound. $125.
The Currents of Space. New York, 1952 1st edition. Very Good in Good dust jacket. $165.
The Death Dealers. NY, 1958 1st ed. VG. $23.
Nine Tomorrows. NY, Bantam, 1960 1st. Paper. VG. $8.
The Sensuous Dirty Old Man. NY, 1971 1st ed. VG in poor dust jacket. $50.
The Universe From Flat Earth to Quasar. Walker & Co, 1966 1st ed. Fine in dust jacket. $10-$12.
The Beginning and the End. Doubleday, 1977 1st ed. Fine in dust jacket. $15.

ASINOF, ELIOT. *Eight Men Out, 1st Black Sox and the 1919 World Series*. Rinehart, 1963 1st ed. VG in DJ. $38.

ATALANTIS. Anon. (William Gilmore Sims). New York, 1832. Good-VG. $350-$750.

ATECO SIMPLIFIED CAKE DECORATING. August Thomson & Co, 1940 5th ed. Good-VG. $25.

ATGET, EUGENE (Photographer). *A Vision of Paris*. NY, 1963. Words by M. Proust. VG to Fine in DJ. $125-$175.

ATHERTON, GERTRUDE. *Rezanov, A True Romance of Old California*. NY, Stokes, 1906. Torn jacket, o/w near fine. $50-$80.
My San Francisco. Indianapolis, 1946 1st ed. VG. $15.

ATHERTON, LEWIS. *Main Street on the Middle Border*. Iowa University Press, 1954 1st ed. VG in DJ. $18-$20.
The Cattle Kings. Iowa University Press, 1961 1st ed. Fine in dust jacket. $19-$25.

ATLAS, CHARLES. *Secret of Muscular Power and Beauty*. No place, 1926. Very Good. $25.

ATLAS OF EARLY AMERICAN HISTORY: THE REVOLUTIONARY ERA, 1760-1790. Edited by Lester Cappon. Princeton Univ. Press, 1976. Fine in DJ. $200.

ATLAS OF ENGLISH HISTORY. London, 1892. School atlas with partly colored battle maps. Nice. $35.

ATLAS OF LAND FORMS. By H. Curran. NY, 1974 2nd ed. Light foxing, o/w Very Good. $30.

ATLAS OF THE AMERICAN REVOLUTION. Text by Don Higginbotham. Commentary by Kenneth Nebenzahl. Chicago, 1974. Very Good in dust jacket. $135.

ATLAS OF THE LEWIS & CLARK EXPEDITION. Univ. of Nebraska, 1983 1st ed. 14 x 20 folio, 184 pgs. Fine. $75.

ATLAS OF THE PHILIPPINE ISLANDS. U. S. Coast Guard and Geodetic Survey. No place, 1900. Cover worn, joints weak, Interior Fine. $125.

ATLAS OF SUSQUEHENNA COUNTY, PA. Pomeroy & Co., 1872. 34 colored maps. Duct tape on cover, maps loose, small tears. $125.

BELMOUNT COUNTY, OHIO. 1888 ATLAS. 14 x 17 in. with 70 hand-colored plates to 17 x 28 in. $295.

THE CAMBRIDGE PHOTOGRAPHIC ATLAS OF THE PLANETS. Cambridge Univ. Press, 1982. VG in DJ. $22.

CIVIL WAR ATLAS, TO ACCOMPANY STEELE'S AMERICAN CAMPAIGNS. 1941, West Point. 136 maps. Good-Very Good. $35.

COLLEGIATE ATLAS. NY, circa 1890. 57 maps, some double-page, colored. Very Good. $50.

CRAM'S UNIVERSAL ATLAS, GEOGRAPHICAL, ASTRO-NOMICAL & HISTORICAL. Chicago, 1889. VG. $125.

CRAM'S UNRIVALLED FAMILY ATLAS. Chicago, 1883. Light wear. $130.

CRAM'S UNIVERSAL ATLAS. Chicago, 1897. Good. $85.

CRAM'S MODERN ATLAS. NY, Chicago, 1902. Good. $45.

CRAM'S UNIVERSAL FAMILY ATLAS, 1884. VG. $65.

CRAM'S UNRIVALED ATLAS OF THE WORLD. Census edition, 1911. $28. 1892 edition. $110. 1897 ed. VG. $120.

DUTTON, CLARENCE. ATLAS TO ACCOMPANY MONOGRAPH ON HISTORY OF GRAND CAÑON. 22 double-page plates in color, 17 x 20 in. Wash., 1882. Worn binding, foxed to margins, o/w VG. $1,200-$1,800.

C. A. GASKELL FAMILY & BUSINESS ATLAS OF THE WORLD. Chicago, 1895. Good. $150-$175.

GOODE'S SCHOOL ATLAS. Revised and enlarged. Rand McNally, 1932 4th ed. Cover worn. Good. $10.

HAGSTROM'S ATLAS OF THE CITY OF NEW YORK. No place, 1945 4th ed. Very Good. $6.

HISTORICAL ATLAS OF KNOX COUNTY INDIANA. Vincennes, 1903, Hardacre. 14 x 16 in. VG. $250.

INDIANA, COMBINATION ATLAS OF MIAMI COUNTY, 1877. Kingman Bros. Fair. $90.

NEW HISTORIC ATLAS OF CASS COUNTY INDIANA, 1878. Kingman Bros. Poor. $85.

OFFICIAL ATLAS OF THE CIVIL WAR. Yosoloff, 1958 1st ed. 14 x 17 in. Fine in fair dust jacket. $55.

JOHNSON'S ATLAS. 1863. Full leather, folio, 99 hand-colored maps 14 x 18 in., 18 x 28 in. VG. $900-$1,200.

JOHNSON'S NEW ILLUSTRATED FAMILY ATLAS. NY, 1862. Near Fine. $700.

THE LIBRARY ATLAS. NY, 1876. 108 maps. $75.

MAPPING THE TRANSMISSISSIPPI WEST, 1540-1861. Carl Wheat. 5 vols. of 6. 14 x 10 in., many folding maps. One of 1000 sets. San Francisco, 1957-1967. Ex-library. $2,475 auction.

MITCHELL'S SCHOOL ATLAS. Philadelphia, 1847. Spine chipped. $250.

MITCHELL'S NEW GENERAL ATLAS. Philadelphia, 1881. Cover shaken. Good. $150.

NEW HISTORICAL ATLAS OF SENECA COUNTY, OHIO. D. J. Stewart. Philadelphia, 1874. 14 ½ x 17½ in. 55 pgs. Worn covers, spine gone. $200.

THE NEW REFERENCE ATLAS OF THE NEW WORLD. Hammond, 1927. Colored maps. Very Good. $10.

PORTER COUNTY INDIANA. 1895 ATLAS. 16 x 19 in. with approx 70 hand-colored maps. Farm & business photos, etc. $150.

RAND-MCNALLY & CO'S NEW IDEAL STATE AND COUNTY SURVEY AND ATLAS. Illinois ed. 1911. One large map missing. Cover fair, contents Very Good. $50.

RAND-MCNALLY STANDARD ATLAS OF THE WORLD. 1890. Good. $35.

RAND-MCNALLY & CO. NEW HANDY ATLAS. 1896. Very Good. $15.

RAND-MCNALLY FAMILY ATLAS. Chicago, 1891 German ed. Rebound. $65.

RAND-MCNALLY UNIVERSAL ATLAS. 1900 revised ed. Very Good. $35.

TUNISON'S PEERLESS UNIVERSAL ATLAS OF THE WORLD. Chicago, 1910. Hinges, covers poor, contents Very Good. $75.

ATWOOD, EVANGELINE. *We Shall be Remembered.* Anchorage, Alaska Methodist Univ. Press, 1966. VG. $35.

AUCHINCLOSS, LEWIS. *Law for the Lion.* Boston, 1953 1st ed. Very Good in dust jacket. $25.

Portrait in Brownstone. Boston, 1962 1st ed. VG. $15.
The Rector of Justin. Boston, 1964 1st ed. VG in DJ. $20.
Tales of Manhattan. Boston, 1967 1st prtn. VG. DJ. $12.
The Winthrop Covenant. Boston, 1976 1st ed. Signed. Near Fine in dust jacket. $40.

AUDEL'S CARPENTERS AND BUILDERS GUIDE. Audel & Co, 1946 4 vols. Good-VG. $20.

AUDEL'S HOUSEHOLD HELPS, HINTS & RECEIPTS: 3,000 REFS. NY, Audel & Co, 1913 ed. G-VG. $12-$20.

AUDEN, W. H. *Poems*. London, 1930 1st ed. VG. $300.
Dance of Death. London, 1933 1st ed. Fine in DJ. $225.
The Shield of Achilles. NY, 1955 1st ed. VG in DJ. $25.
Homage to Cleo. NY, 1960 1st Amer. ed. VG in DJ. $25.

AUDEN, W. H. and CHRISTOPHER ISHERWOOD. *The Dog Beneath the Skin*. London, 1935 1st ed. Near Fine in chipped dust jacket. $100.

AUDSLEY, GEORGE ASHDOWN. *The Organ of the Twentieth Century*. NY, Dodd, Mead, 1919 1st ed. Cover damage, insects. Good. $60 auction.

AUDUBON, JOHN JAMES. *The Birds of America*. NY, 1840-44. 7 vols. 500 plates. $25,000 and up. Macmillan, 1937 edition. 500 color plates. Spine faded, G-VG. $90-$150. Macmillan, 1962 edition. 435 illus. G-VG. $45. Easton Press ed., 1981. Baby elephant folio, green leather bound. As new. $390. Abbeville Press, 1981. One of 2,500 copies in baby elephant folio. Signed by Roger Tory and Virginia Peterson. Fine. $350. Original pages from the rare 1827-38 elephant-folio-sized edition sell for thousands of dollars. They are hand-colored on rag paper.

AUDUBON, JOHN WOODHOUSE. *Audubon's Western Journal: 1849-1850*. Cleveland, Arthur Clark, 1906 reprint. Fine $200. Ex-library. $60-$90.
The Drawings of John Woodhouse Audubon. Adventures Through Mexico and California, 1849-1850. 1 of 400. Grabhorn Press, San Francisco, 1957. Near Fine. $275.

AUDUBON, MARIA. *Audubon & His Journals*. Scribner, 1897 1st ed. 2 vols. $125. Presentation copy. $250.

AUER, J. JEFFERY. *Antislavery and Disunion, 1858-1861*. NY, 1963. Very Good in dust jacket. $20.

AURTHUR, ROBERT. *Third Marine Division*. 1948 1st ed. Very Good. $58. Later editions. $35.

AUSTEN, JANE. *Pride and Prejudice*. London, G. Allen, 1894. Thomson illus. $50-$85. NY, Heritage Press, 1920, LEC in slipcase. $25. 1950. Sewell, illus. VG. $13.
The Complete Novels of Jane Austen. NY, no date. Modern Library. Very Good in dust jacket. $14.

AUSTIN, ALMA H. *The Romance of Candy*. NY, 1938. 1st ed. Very Good in dust jacket. $60.

AUSTIN, MARGOT. *Tumble Bear*. New York, 1940 1st ed. Illus. by author. Very Good. $25.
Trumpet. Dutton, 1943 4th printing. Very Good in dust jacket. $16.
Lutie. Dutton, 1944 1st ed. VG in DJ. $18.
Peter Churchmouse. Dutton, 1944 36th printing. Good in chipped dust jacket. $14.

AUSTIN, MARY. *Land of Little Rain*. Boston, 1903 1st ed. Author's 1st book. E. B. Smith illustrator. Good-VG. $150-$175. Fine. $300.
The Basket Woman: A Book of Fanciful Tales for Children. Boston, 1904 1st ed. Ex-library. $15.
The Flock. Boston, 1906 1st ed. E. Boyd Smith illus. Ex-library. $65. Same, VG-Fine. $95-$165.
A Small Town Man. New York, 1925 1st edition. Very Good in dust jacket. $20.

AUSTIN, OLIVER. *Birds of the World*. Golden Press, NY, 1961. Good to Near Fine. $30-$40.

THE AUTOCRAT OF THE BREAKFAST TABLE. Anon. (Oliver Wendell Holmes). Boston, 1858. $500-$600.

AUTOMOBILE MANUALS AND SALES LITERATURE. (See Catalog Section).

AUTOMOBILE CLUB OF AMERICA, YEAR BOOK, 1908. Annual report, etc. NY. 117 pages. $25.

AVARY, MYRTA LOCKETT. *Dixie After the War*. NY, Doubleday, 1906 1st ed. 434 pages. Green cloth gilt-dec. cover. Very Good. $40.

AVEDON, RICHARD (Photographer). *Observations*. NY, Lucerne, 1959. Truman Capote comments. Good in slipcase. $165. London, 1959. VG in case. $250.
Avedon: Photographs, 1947-1977. NY, 1978 1st ed. 162 Photos. Fine in dust jacket. $150.

AVERILL, NAOMI. *Choochee*. NY, 1937 1st ed. Illus. by author. Fine in DJ. $125. Same in repaired cond. $25-$40.

AVERILL, NAOMI (Illustrator). *A Child's Story of the World*. By D. C. Peattie. New York, 1937 1st edition. Very Good in dust jacket. $60.

AXELROD, GEORGE. *Will Success Spoil Rock Hunter?* NY, 1956 1st ed. Illus. from play. Fine in good DJ. $50.

AYER'S AMERICAN ALMANAC. 1881 EDITION. $13. (See Magazine Section for more Almanacs.)

AYERS, C. *Huxley (T. H.)*. NY, 1932. Ex-library. VG. $13.

B

BABINGTON, S. H. *Navajo Gods and Tom-toms*. NY, 1950 1st ed. Illus. maps, etc. VG in dust jacket. $35-$45.

BAAS, JOH. HERMANN. *Outlines of the History of Medicine and the Medical Profession*. Translation by H. E. Handerson. NY, 1889, Vail. "One of the most important single volume texts on medical history." G-VG. $100.

BABBITT, NATALIE. *The Search for Delicious*. NY, 1969 1st ed. Illus. by author. Ex-library. VG in DJ. $15.
Goody Hall. NY, 1971. Illus. Ex-library. VG in DJ. $15.
The Eyes of the Amaryllis. NY, 1977. Fine in DJ. $12.

BABCOCK, HAVILAH. *Tales of Quails 'n Such*. NY, 1951. 1st ed. Signed. Review copy. Fine in DJ. $150. Another, unsigned. Very Good in dust jacket. $55.
I Don't Want to Shoot an Elephant. NY, 1958. 2nd printing. Inscribed by author. Near Fine in DJ. $75.
My Health is Better in November. NY, 1966 7th printing. Very Good. $35.

BACHE, RICHARD MEADE. *Life of General George Gordon Meade*. Philadelphia, 1897 1st ed. 20 maps. Ex-library, o/w Very Good. $42.
American Wonderland. Phil., 1871 1st ed. Claxton, Remsen & Haffelfinger. Green cloth. Good. $45.

BACHELLER, IRVING. *Eben Holden*. Boston, 1900 1st ed., 1st state (round-topped pine cones on spine). $125. Reprints, same year. Good. $5-$8.
D'ri and I. Boston, 1901 1st ed. Wear, foxing. $35.
Eben Holden's Last Day a-Fishing. NY, 1907 1st ed. Fine in dust jacket. $75.
Turning of Grigsby. Harper, 1913 1st ed. VG. $15-$20.
A Man for the Ages. Bobbs Merrill, 1919 1st. VG. $12.
Coming Up the Road. No place, 1928. Good-VG. $17.

BACON, JOSEPHINE. *Ten to Seventeen*. NY, Harper, 1908. J. W. Smith illus. $25-$45.
Biography of a Boy. Harper, 1910. Rose O'Neill illus. Very Good. $25-$40.
On Our Hill. NY, 1918. T. M. Bevans illus. $18-$24.

BACON, FRANCIS. *Bacon's Novum Organum*. Oxford, 1879 2nd revised edition. Edited by Thomas Fowler. Good. $35. American Home Library ed., 1902. Very Good. $5.

BACON, PEGGY. *The Ballad of Tangle Street*. New York, 1929. 1st edition. Illustrated by author. Very Good in fair dust jacket. $85.
The Terrible Nuisance. NY, 1931. 1st ed. Illus. by author. Good in dust jacket. $50.
The Good American Witch. NY, 1957 1st ed. Illus. by author. Review copy. Fine in dust jacket. $35.
The Oddity. NY, 1962. 1st ed. Illus. by Author. Ex-library. Very Good in dust jacket. $10.
The Ghost of Opalina. Boston, 1967 1st ed. Illus. by author. Fine in dust jacket. $65.

BACON, PEGGY (Illustrator). *The Cat That Jumped Out of the Story*. By Ben Hecht. Philadelphia, 1947 1st ed. Very Good. $25-$35.
Wholly Cats. By F. McNulty. NY, 1962 1st ed. VG. $22.

BADEN-POWELL, SIR ROBERT. *Reconnaissance and Scouting*. London, 1844. Author's 1st book. VG. $800.
Aids to Scouting. Aldershot, 1909. Revised ed. VG. $120.
Scouting for Boys. No place. 1913. 6th ed. Original wrappers. VG. $120. 1937, 18th ed. Cloth cover. Fair. $12.
Indian Memories: Recollections of Soldiering, Sport, etc. London, 1915 1st ed. Near VG. $65-$85.

THE BADMINTON LIBRARY OF SPORTS AND PASTIMES. 11 vols. of the series. London, Longmans, Green. 1896-1904 later printings. G-VG. $150 all. Cycling Number. 1887 1st Amer. ed. $50-$75.

BAEDEKER'S TRAVEL GUIDES.
U. S. with Mexico. 1899 2nd ed. Ex-library. $45.
Northern Italy. 1903 12th ed. $25. 1906. $17.
Southern Italy & Sicily. 1903. Ex-lib. $14. 1912. $35.
Berlin & Environs. 1910. Fine. $60.
Belgium & Holland. 1905 14th ed. $15.
Austria & Hungary. 1905 10th ed. $30.
Italy. 1909 2nd ed. Buckram binding. $32.
N. France. 1909. $35.
Norway, Sweden, Denmark. 1912 10th ed. $45.
Switzerland. 1913. $45.
United States 1909 4th ed. $45-$75.
Great Britain. 1901, 1910. $12-$25.
Paris & London. 1910. $24.
London. 1908, 1911. $15-$25.
Southern Germany. 1907 to 1929. $15-$25.

BAER, BUGS and HENRY MAJOR. *Hollywood*. No place, 1938. Henry Major caricatures, Baer captions. One of 800 copies, signed by Baer. Good-VG. $85.

BAGNASCO, ERMINO. *Submarines of World War II*. Naval Institute Press, 1977. Good-VG. $40.

BAGNOLD, ENID. *National Velvet*. NY, 1935 1st ed. Minor wear to DJ. $40-$50. Repr. DJ. $15. No DJ, VG. $3-$5.
The Loved and Envied. NY, 1951 1st American ed. Cecil Beaton Very Good in dust jacket. $35. 1972 ed. $15.
Alice and Thomas and Jane. London, 1966. Reprint. Laurian Jones illus. Fine in dust jacket. $24.

BAGROW, LEO. *History of Cartography*. Harvard, 1966 Revised, enlarged. VG in dust jacket with box. $150.

BAILEY, ARTHUR. Juvenile books, all published by G& D. 1st eds. 1916-1929. *The Tale of Old Mr. Crow, The Tale of Cuffy Bear, The Tale of Paddy Muskrat*, etc. No dust jacket. $10-$15. In bright covers, up to $25 each.

BAILEY, CAROLYN *Peter Newell's Mother Goose*. NY, Holt, 1905. Very Good. $50-$75.
L'il Hannibal. Platt & Munk, 1938. Very Good. $35.
Miss Hickory. NY, 1946 1st ed. Ruth Gannett illus. Newbery medal. VG in DJ. $30-$65. Good. $20.
Finnegan II, His Nine Lives. NY, 1953. Kate Seredy illus. Good in dust jacket. $25.

BAILEY, E. STILLMAN. *The Sand Dunes of Indiana*. 1917. 165 pgs., 95 illus. VG. $35. 1924 ed. Fine, no DJ. $15.

BAILEY, G. C. *The Complete Airman*. NY, circa 1920. Worn binding. $25.

BAILEY, H. C. *The Red Castle Mystery*. NY, Crime Club, 1932 1st ed. Near Fine in good dust jacket. $150.
Case for Mr. Fortune. NY, 1932 1st ed. VG. $29.
Mr. Fortune Wonders. NY, Crime Club, 1933 1st American ed. VG in dust jacket. $45.
The Great Game. NY, 1939 1st. Ex-lib. in DJ. $13.
The Bishop's Crime. NY, Crime Club, 1941 1st ed. VG in good dust jacket. $40-$95.
The Best of Mr. Fortune Stories. NY, Pocket Books, 1942 1st ed. Very Good. $15.
Mr. Fortune Finds a Pig. NY, 1943 1st ed. NF in DJ. $50.

BAILEY, WILLIAM L. *Our Own Birds*. Lippincott, 1869. Revised, edited by E. D. Cope. Good. $100.

BAIN, ALEXANDER. *The Senses and the Intellect*. NY, 1879. Good. $35.

BAIN, JOHN JR. *Tobacco in Song and Story*. Caldwell, 1896. Suede cover. Good. $15. Very Good. $35.
Tobacco Leaves. Caldwell, 1903. Worn calf. $35-$65.

BAKER, CHARLES H. *The Gentleman's Companion*. Derrydale Press, 1939. 2 vols. in faded box. Good-VG. $75-$150. Same, 1946 edition. $10-$25.

BAKER, D. W. C. (Editor). *A Texas Scrapbook*. NY, 1875 1st ed. Very Good. $275.

BAKER, DOROTHY. *Young Man With A Horn*. Cambridge, 1938. $15. Tower reprint, 1946. VG in dust jacket. $9.

BAKER, GEORGE (Cartoonist). *The Sad Sack*. NY, 1944. Very Good in dust jacket. $14.

BAKER, L. C. *A History of the United States Secret Service*. Philadelphia, 1867 1st ed. Very Good. $75. Worn. $35.

BAKER, RAY STANNARD. *Boys Second Book of Inventions*. Doubleday, 1917 ed. Very Good. $10.

BAKER, THOMAS H. *The Memphis Commercial Appeal*. Baton Rouge, 1971, LSU Press. Fine in DJ. $20.

BAKER, WILL. *The Boy Ranchers on the Trail*. Cupples, 1921. Good. $5. *Western Stories for Boys*. 1934. G. $7.

BALDRIDGE, CYRUS LEROY. *Time and Chance*. John Day, 1947 1st ed. Fine in dust jacket. $14.

BALDWIN, HANSON W. *Sea Fights and Shipwrecks*. NY, 1955. Very Good. $18.

BALDWIN, JAMES. *Story of Seigfried*. Scribner, 1882. H. Pyle illus. VG. $100-$150. 1929 reprint. VG. $50-$75.
Story of Rowland. Scribner, 1883. Birch illus. $65-$90. Same, 1911. Peter Hurd illus. $35.
Story of the Golden Age. Scribner, 1887. H. Pyle illus. Very Good. $75-$100.

BALLANTINE, STUART. *Radio Telephony for Amateurs*. Mc Kay, 1922 1st ed. Good. $14.

BALLOU, M. M. *The New Eldorado: A Summer Journey to Alaska*. Boston, 1889 1st ed. Cover stain, o/w VG. $50.

BALSHOFER, FRED J. and ARTHUR C. MILLER. *One Reel a Week*. University of California Press, 1967. Fine. $45.

BANCROFT, GEORGE. *Literary & Historical Miscellanies*. NY, 1855 1st ed. VG. $50. *History of the United States*. NY, 1882. 2 vols. Fine. $175.

BANCROFT, HUBERT HOWE. *The Works of Hubert Howe Bancroft*. San Francisco, 1886-1890. 39 volumes, 1st ed. Howe drew upon a personal library of 41,000 volumes and first hand interviews with all the players in the drama of the West, settlers, prospectors, etc. and his own team of field workers who covered the state doing research. Sets have

sold at auction for $1,500-$3,000. Individual volumes for up to $100 each.
The Native Races of the Pacific States of North America. NY, 1875 Vol. IV: Antiquities. VG. $65. 5 vols. VG. Auction. $75-$100.
The History of California in Seven Volumes. San Francisco, 1886-1890. Hinges cracked, o/w VG. $295.
History of Arizona & New Mexico. San Francisco, 1889. Very Good. $75-$120.
History of Alaska, 1730-1886. San Francisco, 1886. Very Good. $150-$225.
History of Utah. San Francisco, 1890. Good-VG. $50.

BANDELIER, ADOLF. *The Delight Makers.* Pueblo Indians. NY, Dodd Mead, 1916 2nd ed. Near Fine. $100-$150. Another, Very Good. $70.

BANDINI, RALPH. *Horizons: Stories of Big Game Fish of the Sea.* NY, Derrydale Press, 1939 1st ed. Illus. No. 281 of 950 copies. Very Good. $80-$125.

BANG, ASTA and EDITH RODE. *Open Sandwiches and Cold Lunches.* NY, 1949 1st American ed. VG. $15.

BANG, MOLLY. *The Buried Room and Other Stories.* NY, 1977 1st ed. Signed by author. Fine in dust jacket. $18.
The Grey Lady and the Strawberry Snatches. NY, 1980 3rd printing. Fine in dust jacket. $20.
Dawn. NY, 1983 2nd printing. Signed by author. Very Fine in dust jacket. $30.

BANGS, ARTHUR. *A World Atlas of Military History to 1500.* NY, 1973. Fine in dust jacket. $45.
A World Atlas of Military History, 1860-1945. NY, 1973. Fine in dust jacket. $45.

BANGS, JOHN KENDRICK. *The Enchanted Typewriter.* NY, 1899 1st ed. Peter Newell illus. Near Fine. $55.
The Dreamers: A Club. NY, 1899 1st ed. Edward Penfield illus. Very Good. $35.
Mr. Munchausen. Platt, 1901 1st ed., 1st state. Peter Newell illus. VG-F. $50. Same, 4th state. $25.
A House-Boat on the Styx. Harper, 1896 1st ed. signed. Good. $100. Unsigned. VG. $50. 1899 ed. VG. $10.
Molly and the Unwiseman Abroad. Philadelphia, 1910. Grace Wiederseim illus. 10 full color pgs. VG. $135.
Songs of Cheer. Boston, 1910 1st ed. VG in DJ. $45

BANKS, CHARLES. *A Child of the Sun.* Herbert, 1900. Good plus. $18.

BANKS, CHARLES and OPIE READ. *Complete History of the San Francisco Disaster and Mount Vesuvius Horror.* C. E. Thomas, 1906. Soiled, worn. Good-VG. $10-$15.

BANKSON, RUSSELL. *The Klondike Nugget.* Caldwell, Caxton Printers, 1935 1st ed. Very Good. $65.

BANNERMAN, HELEN. *Little Degchie-Head.* London, 1903 1st ed. Illus. by author. Spine soiled, cloth fading. $400.
The Story of the Teasing Monkey. NY, 1907 1st American ed. Good. $200.
Little Black Sambo. NY, 1901 1st Amer. Ed. VG. $300-$400. Platt & Munk, 1930. Fine. $100-$125. Platt & Munk, 1932 ed. Eulalie illus. Little Library series. Soft cover. Fine. $60. Simon & Schuster, 1948 6th ed. VG. $20. Circa 1920 ed. Florence White Williams illus. Chicago, Saalfield. Soiled. $60. Early edition with 1918 inscription, but no date. Pages printed on one side, color illus. Stokes pub., NY. VG. $100 auction. Platt & Munk, 1928. $50.
All About Little Black Sambo. Cupples, circa 1917. Johnny Gruelle illus. $95-$150. Later reprint, no date. $65.
Little Black Sambo and Other Stories. Rand McNally, 1939. VG. $40. Saalfield, 1942. Linen pictorial. Oversize quarto. Small dark spot on cover. $150.
A New Story of Little Black Sambo. Whitman, 1932. Juanita C. Bennett illus. Paperback. VG. $100.
The Story of Little Black Quasha. London, 1940. Illus. by author. Hinge cracked. Overall VG. $120.
Little Black Sambo (Movable Pages). NY, 1943. J. Wehr illus. Plastic-bound. VG. $185 auction; $285 dealer.
The Story of Little Black Quibba. London, 1940s. $140.
Little Black Sambo, A Surprise Book. Dell, NY, 1950. Tony Rivera, ed. Paperback. Some browning. $30. No place. 1966 reprint of London 1899 ed. Illus. by author. VG in vg DJ. $50. NY, Platt & Munk, 1972 edition. VG in DJ. $50. Whitman, no date. Enlarged picture edition. Cobb X. Shinn illus. Tape repair, light soiling. $110.
Little Black Bobtail. No place, no date. Reprint of London 1909 ed. Illus. by author. Good plus. $40.
Little Black Mingo. No place, no date. Reprint of London 1902 ed. Illus by author. Good plus. $40.

BANNING, WILLIAM. *Six Horses.* NY, Century Co., 1930. Good, some foxing. $30.

BANTA, NATHANIEL MOORE. *Nature Neighbors: Embracing Birds, Plants, Animals, Minerals.* Chicago, 1914 Limited ed. 1 of 2,500. 5 vol. set. Good plus. $125.

BANTA, R. E. *The Ohio.* 1949. Rivers of America series. Edward Shenton illus. Fine in dust jacket. $27.
Hoosier Caravan. Indiana Univ. Press. 1951 1st ed. VG. $18. Same, in VG DJ. $29. Rev. ed., 1975. VF in DJ. $18.

BANTA, WILLLIAM and J. W. CALDWELL. *Twenty-seven Years on the Texas Frontier.* Council Hill, OK, 1933 revised ed. Soft cover. Fine. $75.

BARAGWANATH, ALBERT. *100 Currier & Ives Favorites.* NY, Crown, 1978 1st ed. Very Fine. $15.

BARAKA, AMIRI (Leroi Jones). *Tales.* Grove Press, 1967. 1st ed. Fine in dust jacket. $75.

BARBER, EDWIN A. *American Glassware Old & New.* Philadelphia, 1900, David Mc Kay Co. Good-VG. $55.
Pottery & Porcelain of the U.S. NY, 1893. Good. $45.

BARBER, ELMER D. *Osteopathy Complete. Fully Illustrated.* Kansas City Mo, 1898. 3rd ed. $50.

BARBEAU, MARIUS. *Indian Days in the Canadian Rockies.* Toronto, 1923 1st edition. Kihn illustrator. Very Good in dust jacket. $100.
Alaska Beckons. Caxton, 1947. Very Good. $40.

BARBER, EDITH. *Edith Barber's Cook Book.* No place, 1955. Good-VG. $15-$20.

BARBER, EDWIN ATLEE. *The Pottery and Porcelain of the United States.* NY, 1901 2nd ed. Revised, enlarged. Fine. $150. Another, worn, good. $45.

BARBER, H. L. *The Story of the Automobile: Its History and Development From 1760 to 1917.* Chicago, 1917 1st ed. Good-VG. $20-$35.

ASSOCIATED MASTER BARBERS. *Standardized Textbook of Barbering.* Chicago, 1939. Good-VG. $25-$35.

BARBER, JOEL. *Wild Fowl Decoys.* New York, Windward House, 1934 1st ed. Near Fine. $80-$120. G-VG. $50-$75.
Long Shore. Derrydale Press, 1930s. Fair. $50. Fine. $400.

BARBEY, VICE ADM. DANIEL. *McArthur's Amphibious Navy.* Naval Inst. Press, 1969 1st ed. As new in DJ. $45.

BARBOUR, JOHN. *Footprints on the Moon.* Associated Press, 1969 1st ed. Includes map & moon poster. Fine in dust jacket. $15-$20.

BARBOUR & PETERSON. *Kentucky Birds - A Finding Guide.* University of Kentucky, 1973 1st edition. Fine in Good dust jacket. $15.

BARBOUR, RALPH H. *Kitty of the Roses.* Lippincott, 1904 1st ed. Very Good. $45.
Hitting the Line. Appleton, 1917 1st edition. Rockwell Color plates. Fine. $45.
Left End Edwards. Dodd Mead, 1924 reprint. VG. $10.
Right End Emerson. Dodd Mead, 1922 1st ed. Brown cloth. Bumped corners, shelf wear. $12.

BARHAM, RICHARD HARRIS. *The Ingoldsby Legends, or Mirth and Marvels.* London, Richard Bentley, 1840-1847. 3 vols., 12mo. 19 engraved plates by Cruikshank and Leech. Full red morocco, raised bands on spines. Fine. $400. Also see Ingoldsby, Thomas for other examples.

BARKER, CATHERINE. *Yesterday Today: Life in the Ozarks.* Caldwell, ID, 1941. Caxton. VG in DJ. $20.

BARKER, LILLIAN. *The Quints Have a Family.* NY, 1941. Very Good in dust jacket. $20.

BARNARD, GEORGE N. *Sherman's Campaign.* Early photographic views. 1977 reprint of 1866 ed. VG. $35.

BARNEBY, W. HENRY. *Life and Labour in the Far West.* London, 1884 1st ed. with map. $150-$200.

BARNES, DJUNA. *Ryder.* NY, 1928. 1st ed. VG in DJ. $35.
Night Wood. NY, 1937 1st ed. VG in dust jacket. $100.
The Antiphon. London, 1958 1st ed. Fine in chip DJ. $85.

BARNES, LINDA. *Dead Heat.* NY, 1984 1st ed. Near Fine in DJ. $100. Fair in poor DJ. $15.

BARNUM, PHINEAS T. *The Humbugs of the World, etc.* New York, 1866. Very Good. $50.
Struggles and Triumphs. Hartford, J. B. Burr, 1869 ed. $50-$80. Johnson, 1872 ed. VG. $65. Buffalo, 1879 ed. Worn. $25-$35.
Forty Years Recollections. 1872. Good. $27.
Lion Jack: Perilous Adventure. NY, 1887. VG. $50.
Dollars and Sense: How to Get On. Bos., 1890. VG. $45.
Barnum's Own Story for the Boys and Girls of America. 514 pgs. of animals, etc. Illus. Chicago, R. S. Pale, 1891 1st ed. Near Fine. $60 auction (est. $80-$120).

BARON, STANLEY. *Brewed in America: History of Beer and Ale in U. S.* Boston, 1962 1st ed. VG in DJ. $35-$50.

BARR, LOUISE FARROW. *Presses of Northern California and Their Books, 1900-1933.* Book Arts Club, 1934 1st ed. Faded, o/w VG. $100-$150.

BARRETT, JOHN. *The Panama Canal. What It Is What It Means.* Pan American Union, 1913. Joseph Pennel sketch. Pre-canal opening. Near Fine. $35.

BARRIE, JAMES M. *When a Man's Single.* London, Hodder Stoughton, 1888 1st ed. Blue buckram case. Fine. $85.
A Window in Thrums. London, 1889 1st ed. 217 pgs. Blue cloth covers. Fine. $40.
An Edinburgh Eleven. London, 1889 1st ed. Office of British Weekly. Very Good. $125.
The Little White Bird. Scribners, 1902 1st Amer. ed. $50-$75. 1903 trade ed. $15. Scribners, 1912, Rackham color plates. $175-$200. Same, 1913, B&W illus. $25-$40.
Peter Pan in Kensington Gardens. London, 1906 1st trade ed. Arthur Rackham illus. VG. $350-$400. Scribners, 1906 (1925) cloth with pictorial paper label. 16 plates. VG in DJ. $100. Many editions after 1906 (to 1940) are priced at $40-$95 each. Grosset & Dunlap, 1911. $22.
Peter and Wendy. New York, Scribner's, 1911 1st American ed. 12 illus. by Bedford. Orig. gilt-dec. green cloth covers. Good-VG. $88 auction. (est. $100-$150).

The Little Minister. London, Cassell & Co., 1891 1st ed. 3 vols. Pinkish brown cloth, rubbed. $225. NY, 1899 Caldwell. Good. $24. Grosset & Dunlap movie edition. No date. Good. $10.
Quality Street. London, 1912 1st trade ed. 23 color plates. Stained covers. Good. $100. VG. $120-$160.
The Admirable Crichton. London, 1914 1st ed. Hugh Thomson illus. Near Fine. $75-$150.

BARROWS, JOHN R. *Ubet*. Cowboy Narrative. Caxton, 1934. R. H. Hall illus. Near Fine in DJ. $80-$120.

BARROWS, MARJORIE. *The Child Life Story Book*. Rand McNally, 1932. Illus. by author. Very Good. $30.

BARRUS, CLARA. *Nursing the Insane*. Macmillan, 1908 1st ed. Very Good. $50.

BART, BELLE. *The Heavens Proclaim: Being an Analysis and Explanation of the New Astrology*. Roycroft Press 1928. Near Fine. $75.

BARTLETT, A. *Baseball and Mr. Spalding*. NY, 1951 1st ed. Very Good in dust jacket. $28.

BARTLETT, JOHN. *A Collection of Familiar Quotations*. Cambridge, John Bartlett, 1855 1st ed. Royal blue cloth. Near Fine. $250.

BARTLETT, CAPT. ROBERT A. *The Log of Bob Bartlett*. G. P. Putnam, 1928 3rd edition. Signed by author. Very Good. $15.

BARTON, CLARA. *The Red Cross: A History*. Wash, DC, 1898. Very Good. $35.

BARTON, LUCY. *Historic Costume for the Stage*. Boston, 1935. Illus. Very Good. $25.

BARUCH, DOROTHY. *Dumbo of the Circus*. D. C. Heath, 1948 1st ed. Good. $18.
Pinocchio. D. C. Heath, 1940 1st. G-VG, ex-library. $12.

BARWELL, MRS. (LOUISE MARY BACON). *Advice to Mothers on the Treatment of Infants*. Philadelphia, 1853 Revised, enlarged ed. Good-VG. $100.

BAR-ZOHAR, MICHAEL. *The Hunt for German Scientists, 1944-1960*. London, 1967. Fine in dust jacket. $25.

BARZUN, JACQUES. *A Catalogue of Crime*. No place, 1989 Revised enlarged edition. Bibliography 5,045 entries. Fine in dust jacket. $50.

BASEBALL REGISTER, OFFICIAL. *Sporting News*. 1940 edition. Blue cloth covers. Very Good. $39. 1976 edition. Paper covers. Fine. $12.

BASHKIRTSEFF, MARIE. *Last Confessions*. Stokes, 1901 1st ed. Very Good. $15.

BASKIN, ESTHER. *The Poppy & Other Deadly Plants*. New York, 1967 1st ed. L. Baskins illus. Fine in DJ. $22.

BATES, H. E. *Down the River*. Holt, 1937 Advance Review Copy. 81 wood engravings by Agnes M. Parker. VG in dust jacket with browned spine. $150.

BATES, M. *The Natural History of Mosquitoes*. NY, 1949. Ex-Library. Very Good. $15.

BATTLES AND LEADERS OF THE CIVIL WAR. No place, 1887 1st ed. Good. $150-$200. 1888, 8 vol. set. VG. $185. Pictorial edition, Century, 1894. Very Good. $50-$75.

BATTY, JOSEPH. *Practical Taxidermy & Home Decoration*. NY, 1880, Orange Judd. Good. $40. 1906 edition, 203 pgs. Fine. $50.

BAUER, FRED. *Cake-Art-Craft. Cake Decorating*. Chicago, 1924 1st ed. A classic text. Good-VG. $50-$100.

BAUM, DWIGHT JAMES, (Editor). *Great Georgian Houses of America*. NY, 1933 1st ed. Endpapers foxed, o/w Very Good. $100.

OZ BOOKS

When L. Frank Baum died in 1919, he had just finished his 14th book about the mythical kingdom. His widow allowed Baum's publisher, Reilly & Lee, to hire another writer to keep Oz alive. Ruth Plumly Thompson, then only 20 years old, turned out 18 additional titles. John R. Neill, who had illustrated all but three of the Oz books, traded his drawing board for a typewriter and added three more titles. After Neill's death, Jack Snow wrote three books, Rachel R. Cosgrove one, and the team of Eloise McGraw and Lauren Wagner penned one more.

A true first issue of the first edition of *The Wonderful Wizard of Oz* must possess a title page date of 1900 and an 11-line colophon (not 13) on the back end paper. There are several different bindings of the first edition. The true first edition, first issue, must read George M. Hill Co., Chicago and New York, have 261 pages, and be illustrated by W. W. Denslow.

The original plates of *The Wonderful Wizard of Oz* were taken over by Bobbs-Merrill publishers in 1902. *The New Wizard of Oz*, printed from these plates, is so close to being a first edition that one expert calls it a "sub-edition" rather than a second edition. But the fact that *The New Wizard of Oz* had a new cover, new title page, new end-drawings and only 15 of the original 24 color plates, persuaded Bobbs-Merrill to label it "second edition."

BAUM, FRANK L. *The Master Key*. Indianapolis, 1901. Fanny Y. Cory illus. VG overall, $200.

Dot and Tot in Merryland. Chicago, 1901. Denslow illus. $500-$800. Bobbs-Merrill, 1903. $200-$300.

Life & Adventures of Santa Claus. Indianapolis, 1902 1st ed. Mary C. Clark illus. Signed. Fine. $550.

The Sea Fairies. Reilly & Britton, 1911. 1st ed., 1st issue. J. R. Neill illus. Good. $200.

Dorothy & the Wizard of Oz. Reilly & Britton, 1908 1st ed., 1st issue. John R. Neill illus. DJ damaged. $6,160 (auction). Chicago: Reilly & Britton, 1908 1st ed., 2nd issue. John R. Neill illus. Minor wear. $300-$600. Reprints. Reilly & Lee, 1908-1945. $50-$75 in DJ.

The Emerald City of Oz. Chicago: Reilly & Britton, 1910 1st ed., 1st printing. Minor wear. $990 (auction). Same, Chicago, 1910 Later printing. John R. Neill illus. Light cover stain. Good. $75. VG. $150-$200. 1940s. $35-$40.

Glinda of Oz. Chicago: Reilly & Lee, 1920 1st ed. John R. Neill illus. Fine. $440 (auction). 1920 reprint in color. $100. No color. $30-$50.

The Laughing Dragon of Oz. Racine, WI: Whitman, 1934 Unauthorized 1st ed. Milt Youngren illus. Minor wear. $357 (auction). Same, Racine, WI, 1934 1st ed. as Big Little Book. VG. $155.

Little Wizard Series. Chicago, 1913. Complete set of six 1st eds. John R. Neill illus. Various conditions $1,870.

The Lost Princess of Oz. Chicago: Reilly & Britton, 1917 1st edition, 1st printing. Slightly worn. $605 (auction). Another, better copy, with DJ. $3,740, (auction). Junior edition, 1939. $25. 1941 ed. Fine in DJ. $100.

The Magic of Oz. Chicago: Reilly & Lee, 1918 1st ed., 1st printing. John R. Neill illus. Minor flaws. $412 (auction). Reilly & Lee, circa 1930 reprint. J. R. Neill illus. Worn, shaken. Good. $60. VG in DJ. $120. 1919. No color. $40.

The Marvelous Land of Oz. Chicago: Reilly & Britton, 1904 1st ed., 1st printing. John R. Neill illus. Minor wear. $522 (auction). Dealer. $800. Same, 2nd state. $250-$275.

The New Wizard of Oz. Indianapolis: Bobbs-Merrill, 1903 2nd ed., 3rd printing. W. W. Denslow illus. $1,320 (auction). 1903 5th ed. Indianapolis. Denslow illus. Good. $100. Bobbs-Merrill, 1939 movie version. VG in DJ. $150.

Ozma of Oz. 1907 1st ed., 2nd printing. $4,840 (auction). Avg. dealer price. $500-$800. Same, no DJ. $100. 1907 reprint, R&B. $100-$200. Same, 1907, Reilly & Lee. $75.

The Patchwork Girl of Oz. Chicago: Reilly & Britton, 1913 1st ed., 1st state. John R. Neill illus. Minor wear. $605 (auction). Reilly & Lee, 1913. Reprint. Good plus. $40. Chicago 1935, Post. John Neill illus. VG. $45.

Queen Zixi of Ixi. NY, 1905 1st state. F. Richardson illus. 16 color plates. Near VG. $300.

Rinkitink in Oz. Chicago: Reilly & Britton, 1916 1st ed., 1st issue. John R. Neill illus. Minor wear. $605 (auction). 1920s edition in DJ. $125. Junior Edition, 1939. G. $50.

The Road to Oz. Chicago: Reilly & Britton, 1909 1st edition, 1st issue. John R. Neill illustrator. Fine. $1,045 (auction). R&B 1909 reprint in DJ. $100-$175. Reilly-Lee, 1939. Junior edition. Very Good. $75.

The Royal Book of Oz. Chicago: Reilly & Lee, 1921 1st ed., 1st printing. John R. Neill illus. on DJ. $5,720 at auction. Dealer price usually $250-$350. Reprint by Reilly & Lee, 1921. Color. $100. No color. $35-$50.

The Scarecrow of Oz. Chicago: Reilly & Britton, 1915 1st ed., 1st printing. $770 (auction). Rpt. of same year. $150.

Tik-Tok of Oz. Reilly & Lee (after 1935). J. R. Neill Illus. Endpaper removed, slight soiling. $50. Very Good. $75.

The Tin Woodman of Oz. Chicago: Reilly & Britton, 1918 1st edition, 1st printing. John R. Neill jacket and illus. $1,980 (auction). Reilly & Britton, Chicago, 1918 1st edition, 1st issue. Pencil scribbling on one page. Hinges cracking. Covers slightly rubbed, soiled. $125. 1937. Near Fine in dust jacket. $125. 1918 reprint. $100-$150.

Visitors From Oz. Chicago: Reilly & Lee, 1960 1st ed. Dick Martin illus. Jean Kellog, adaptation for children. $302 (auction).

The Wizard of Oz. Chicago, 1900 1st ed., 2nd state of first Oz book. W. W. Denslow illus. Repaired hinges, Some cloth discoloration. $4,000. Donohoe, 1913 edition. Denslow illus. Some marks on blank pgs. Loose hinge. $125. G&D, 1939 in DJ. $35. 1956. Dale Urley illus. Good. $15. 1982 ed. Michael Hague illus. VG in DJ. $22.

The Land of Oz, a Sequel to the Wizard of Oz. Chicago, 1904 (printed in 1914). VG. $95. Same, 1935. $40.

Jack Pumpkinhead and the Sawhorse of Oz. Rand-McNally, 1939 1st ed. VG. $20.

The Wonderful Wizard of Oz. George M. Hill, 1900 1st ed. Front fly endpaper inserted in facsimile. Cov. wn., spine ends repaired. $800. Same. Chicago & NY George M. Hill, 1900 1st, 2nd state. Minor wear. $1,320 (auction). Same, 1st ed., 1st state. $5,000 up.

BAUR, JOHN E. *Christmas on the American Frontier, 1800-1900*. Caxton Printers, 1961. VG. $50-$80.

BAXTER, DOW VAWTER. *On and Off Alaskan Trails*. No place, 1937. 184 pgs., photo illus. Very Good. $65.

BAY, KENNETH. *Saltwater Flies, Popular Patterns*. Lippincott, 1970 1st ed. VG in dust jacket. $14.

BAYLOR, BIRD. *Yes is Better Than No*. NY, 1977 1st ed. Very Good in dust jacket. $50-$75.

BAZIN, GERMAIN. *The History of World Sculpture*. NY, 1968. Over 1,000 color photos. $40.

BEACH, REX. *The Spoilers*. A. L. Burt, 1906. Good. $7.

The Ne'er-do-well. NY, 1911 1st ed. $15-$35.

The Iron Trail. Harpers, 1913 1st ed. VG. $13.

The Auction Block. NY, 1914 1st ed. VG. $13.

The Winds of Chance. NY, 1918 1st ed. VG. $15.

Confessions of an Agitated Sportsman. NY, 1921. Photo on cover. VG-Fine. $12-$25.

The Miracle of Coral Gables. Hartford CT 1926. Edward Wilson, illus. Limited ed. VG. $30.

BEACH, S. A. *The Apples of New York*. Albany, 1905 1st ed. 2 volumes, nicely illustrated. $60-$120.

BEADLE, J. H. *Mysteries and Crimes of Mormonism*. No place 1871. Cover worn, G. $20. 1882 ed. VG $20-$35. *Life in Utah: or Mysteries of Mormonism & Polygamy*. Philadelphia, 1870 1st ed. Very Good. $50-$80.

BEAGLE, PETER S. *A Fine and Private Place*. NY, 1960 1st ed. Author's 1st book. Review copy. Fine in DJ. $100-$150. Same with no dust jacket. Fine. $75.
I See By My Outfit. NY, 1965 1st ed. NF in DJ. $35.
The Last Unicorn. NY, 1968 1st ed. Fine in DJ. $80.

BEALS, CARLETON. *Brimstone & Chili: Experiences in the Southwest and Mexico*. No place, 1927. Reading copy. $15. Better copies. $25 up.

BEAM, PHILLIP. *Winslow Homer's Magazine Engravings*. NY, Harper-Row, 1979 1st ed. Fine in DJ. $16-$20.

BEAMISH, RICHARD. *The Boy's Story of Lindbergh: the Lone Eagle*. Philadelphia, 1928 1st ed. F in DJ. $15-$20.

BEAN, EDWARD. *Bean's History and Directory of Nevada County, Calif*. CA, Daily Gazette, 1867. Fair. $300-$500.

BEARD, DANIEL C. *The American Boy's Handy Book*. NY, 1882 1st ed. VG. $225. 1902. VG. $45. 1920. $15.

BEARD, JAMES. *The Fireside Cook Book*. 1949. 5th printing. Good-VG. $20-$30.
Cook It Outdoors. 1953. Good-VG. $15-$25.
James Beard's Treasury of Outdoor Cooking. Ridge Press, 1960 1st printing. Good in dust jacket. $25.
Beard on Food. NY, 1974. Very Good. $15-$25.

BEARDSLEY, AUBREY. *His Best Fifty Drawings*. London, 1955 1st ed. Very Good in dust jacket. $25.
Selected Drawings. Grove Press, 1967 1st ed. VG. $48.
Brian Reade. NY, 1967. VG in dust jacket. $25.
The Uncollected Work of Aubrey Beardsley. London, John Lane, 1925 1st ed. Darkening, warped. $45. (auction).

THE BEATLES QUIZ BOOK. London , 1964 Paper. VG.$35.

BEATON, CECIL. *Air of Glory*. Lon., 1941 1st. Good. $35.
Chinese Album. London, 1945-46. Good. $40.
Ballet. NY, 1951 1st Amer. ed. 100 Photos. F in DJ. $60.
Cecil Beaton's Fair Lady. NP 1964 1st ed. NF. $100.

BEATON, CECIL and KENNETH TANNIN. *Persona Grata*. London, 1954 2nd impression. DJ lightly worn. $50.

BEATON, JANE. *Woman's Own Book of Casserole Cooking*. London, 1967. $15.

BEATSON, SIR GEORGE THOMAS. *Ambulance Handbook -Principles of First Aid*. St. Andrew, 1915. 414 pgs., illustrated. Very Good. $12-$15.

BEATTY, CLYDE and EDWARD ANTHONY. *The Big Cage*. NY, London, 1933 2nd ed. Signed by Beatty. VG. $50. Same, unsigned. Ex-library copy. $15.

BEATTY, JEROME. *Shirley Temple*. Saalfield, 1935. VG in Good dust jacket. Lots of photos. $65.

BEAUVOIR, SIMONE DE. *Force of Circumstance*. NY, 1965 1st ed. in English. VG in dust jacket. $28.
The Coming of Age. NY, 1972 1st American ed. VG. $28.

BEAUMONT, NEWHALL. *The History of Photography, 1839 to Present*. NY, 1964 Revised ed. Torn DJ. $25.

BECK, HENRY C. *Fare to Midlands*. NY, 1939 1st ed. Folding map. Very Good in dust jacket. $50-$75.

BEE, CLAIR. *Clutch Hitter*. (Chip Hilton No. 4). Grosset & Dunlap, 1949 1st ed. Red cloth. Bumped corners, shelf-wear, o/w Very Good in chipped dust jacket. $20.
Hoop Crazy. (Chip Hilton No. 5). Grosset & Dunlap, 1950 1st ed. Very Good in dust jacket. $20.

BEEBE, LUCIUS. *Mixed Train Daily: A Book of Short-line Railroads*. Howell-North, 1961. VG in DJ. $28.

BEEBE, LUCIUS and CHARLES CLEGG. *Hear the Train Blow*. NY, 1952 1st ed. 870 Illus. Very Good. $35.
Narrow Gauge in the Rockies. Berkeley, 1958 2nd ed. VG in worn dust jacket. $25.
The American West. NY, 1955 1st ed. NF in vg DJ. $65.
Mansions on Rails: The Folklore of the Private Railway Car. No place, 1959 1st ed. Fine in vg DJ. $50.
U.S. West, the Saga of Wells Fargo. NY, no date. Reprint ed. Very Good. $30.

BEEBE, WILLIAM. *Two Bird-Lovers in Mexico*. Boston, 1905 1st ed. Author's 1st book. Very Good. $250.
Jungle Peace. NY, 1918 1st ed. Very Good. $35.
Edge of the Jungle. NY, 1921. 1st ed. Very Good. $35.
Galapagos: World's End. NY, 1924 1st ed. VG. $30.
Arcturus Adventure. NY, Lon., 1926 1st ed. VG. $35-$65.
Pheasants—Their Lives and Homes. Doubleday, 1932. 2 vols. bound in one. Very Good. $80-$100.
Half a Mile Down. NY, 1934. Illus. VG in DJ. $40.
High Jungle. NY, 1949. 1st ed. Fine. $25.

BEECHER, CATHERINE. *Treatise on Domestic Economy*. Boston, 1843 revised ed. 42 woodcuts. Frayed, shaken. $65. Very Good. $115. 1867 5th ed. $65.
Miss Beecher's Domestic Receipt Book. NY, 1849 3rd ed. Very Good. $95. 1855 edition. Very Good. $195.

BEECHER, CATHERINE and HARRIET B. STOWE. *American Woman's Home, or Principles of Domestic Science*. NY, 1869. Good-VG. $55-$85. A fine tight copy. $150. A fair copy with bad hinges. $40.

BEECHER, HENRY WARD. *Norwood, or Village Life in New England*. NY, 1868. $25-$35.
Star Papers. J. C. Derby. New York, 1855. Green cloth. 1st ed. Good-VG. $10-$20.

BEECHER, MRS. H. W. *Motherly Talks with Young Housekeepers*. NY, 1875. J. B. Ford. Good-VG. $50-$85.

BEEDING, FRANCIS. *The Seven Sleepers*. Boston, 1925 1st American ed. Signed by John Palmer & Hilary Saunders. Very Good. $60.
Murdered One By One. NY, 1937 1st ed. Ex-library in stained dust jacket. $10.
The 12 Disguises. NY, 1942 1st ed. in DJ. $15-$35.

BEER, THOMAS. *The Fair Rewards*. NY, 1922 1st ed. Author's 1st book. VG in dust jacket. $100.
Hanna. NY, 1929 1st ed. Spine faded, o/w VG in DJ. $25.

BEERBOHM, MAX. *The Poet's Corner*. London, 1904. 20 Caricatures. Rebacked. Very Good. $125.
Zuleika Dobson. London, 1911 1st ed. Paper. VG. $38.
Christmas Garland. London, 1912. Inscribed, NF. $50.
And Even Now. London, 1920 1st. Uncut, DJ poor. $75.
Things New and Old. London, 1923 1st ed. F in DJ. $250.
A Peep Into the Past. 1923 private printing. 16 pgs. $50.
Works. London, 1922-1924. 10 vols. One of 750 sets. Signed by Beerbohm. Two volumes have DJs. $450.
Observation. London, 1925 1st ed. Illus. by author. Over 50 plates. VG to Fine in DJ. $200-$300. Good, no DJ. $65.

BEERS, CLIFFORD W. *A Mind That Found Itself*. NY, 1914 3rd ed. Inscribed. Very Good. $75.

BEERS, F. W. CO. *Various Atlases* of Eastern United States published in 1860s & 1870s. $150-$225 each.

BEETON, ISABELLA. *Mrs. Beeton's Book of Household Management: A Guide to Cookery in All Branches*. London, 1906 New revised, enlarged ed. Illus. 2,056 pp. Leather backing in pieces. $75-$150. NY, 1969. Facsimile of 1861 ed. Very Good in dust jacket. $45.
Mrs. Beeton's Cookery Book. London, 1930s ed. Color plates. Good in good DJ. $50. 1910 ed. in poor cond. $20.
Mrs. Beeton's All About Cookery. Ward-Lock, 1950s reprint. 640 pgs. Very Good. $15.
Mrs. Beeton's Everyday Cookery and Housekeeper Book. NY, 1984 reprint of 1865 ed. Fine. $25. Ward, Lock & Co. Circa 1880 new enlarged ed. 570 pgs. Incl. ads. VG. $100.

BEGG, ALEXANDER. *Dot It Down. A Story of Life in the North-West*. Toronto, Hunter, 1871 1st. VG. $70-$100.

BEHAN, BRENDAN. *The Quare Fellow*. London, 1956. 1st book. Near Fine in dust jacket. $150.
Brendan Behan's New York. NY, 1964 1st ed. Paul Hogarth illus. Fine in dust jacket. $45.

BEHRMAN, S. N. *No Time for Comedy*. NY, 1939 1st ed. Very Good in dust jacket. $100.

BEL GEDDES, NORMAN. *Magic Motorways*. NY, 1940 1st ed., 1st printing. Many illus., photos. Very Good. $65.

BELDAM, G. W. *Great Golfers: Their Methods at a Glance*. London, 1904 2nd printing. Photos. Fine. $125.

BELDEN, ALBERT. *The Fur Trade of America*. NY, Peltries Pub Co., 1917 1st edition. 591 pgs. Some wear. Hinges weak. Good-VG. $125.

BELDEN, GEORGE P. *Belden, The White Chief, or 12 Years Among the Wild Indians*. 1870 1st ed. Good. $40. 1872 printing. Fair. $18.

BELL, CURRER (See Bronte, Charlotte).

BELL, ERNEST A. *Fighting the Traffic in Young Girls*. Bell, 1910 1st ed. VG. $16. Good. $10. Another, gilt-lettered green cloth, pictorial cover label, no place (L. H. Walter 1911 First ed. Very Good. $28 (auction).

BELL, LOUIS. *The Telescope*. NY, McGraw Hill, 1922 7th printing of 1st ed. Good-VG. $30-$50.

BELL, MAJOR HORACE. *On the Old West Coast, Further Reminiscences of a Ranger*. Morrow, 1930 1st ed. Library binding. Good-VG. $45.

BELL JOSEPHINE. *Death in Retirement*. NY, 1956 1st ed. Near Fine in dust jacket. $18.
Death on the Reserve. NY, 1966 1st ed. Fine in DJ. $13.
Wolf! Wolf! London, 1979 1st British ed. Fine in DJ. $23.

BELLAMY, EDWARD. *Looking Backward: 2000-1887*. Boston, 1888. 1st ed., earliest printing. VG. $250.
Equality. NY, 1897 1st ed. Near Fine. $85.

BELLE, BART. *The Heavens Proclaim*. Roycroft, 1928. A Good copy. $20.

BELLE, FRANCIS P. *Life and Adventures of Celebrated Bandit Joaquin Murieta*. Chicago, 1925 Limited. edition. $75. 1937 2nd edition. $40.

BELLEW, FRANK. *The Art of Amusing. Merry Games, Odd Tricks, etc.* NY, Carleton, 1866 1st ed. Some foxing and soil, else Very Good. $100-$150.

BELLIN, MILDRED G. *The Jewish Cook Book*. NY, 1947 7th printing. Revised and enlarged. VG in DJ. $15.

BELLOC, HILAIRE. *The Bad Child's Book of Beasts*. London, 1903. B.G.T. Blackwood illus. Fine. $60.
Mr. Petre. New York, 1925 1st edition. Very Good. $13.
The Highway and Its Vehicles. London, 1926. One of 1,250 copies. 131 plates, Light foxing, o/w Fine. $250.
The Missing Masterpiece. NY, 1929 1st ed. Drawings by G. K. Chesterton. Very Good. $50.

BELLOW, SAUL. *The Victim*. NY, Vanguard, 1947 1st ed. Author's 2nd book. Black cloth in DJ. VG plus. $300.

BELLOWS, GEORGE. *George W. Bellows: His Lithographs*. NY, 1927 Catalog Raisonne. In slipcase. $150.

BEMELMANS, LUDWIG. *The Golden Basket*. NY, 1936 1st ed. Illus. by author. VG in dust jacket. $100.
Madeline. NY, 1939 1st ed. Illus. by author. VG. $100.
Small Beer. NY, 1939 1st ed. Illus. by author. Arthur Fiedler copy, signed. Fine. $70.
Fifi. NY, 1940 1st ed. Illus. by author. VG in DJ. $60.
Rosebud. NY, 1942. Illus. Mended front, poor DJ. $12.
Now I Lay Me Down to Sleep. NY, 1945. One of 400 copies. Illus. by author. Spine dark, o/w VG. $100.
Hotel Bemelmans. NY, 1946 2nd printing. Illus. by author. VG in dust jacket. $14.
A Tale of Two Gumps. NY, 1947 1st ed. Illus. by author. Backstrip gone. Good. $75.
The Happy Place. NY, 1952 1st ed. Illus. VG in DJ. $75.
The High World. NY, 1954 1st ed. Illus. VG in DJ. $16.
Parsley. NY, 1955 1st ed. Illus. Fine in DJ. $150.
Welcome Home. NY, 1955 1st ed. Illus. Fine in DJ. $150.
Bemelmans' La Bonne Table. NY, 1964 1st ed. Illus. by author. VG in DJ. $40. Good, no DJ. $16.

BENCHLEY, ROBERT. *The Treasurer's Report And Other Aspects of Community Singing*. NY, 1930. 1st ed., 1st printing. Fine. $70.
After 1903 What? NY, 1938. 1st ed. Good in DJ. $40.

BENET, STEPHEN VINCENT. *The Devil and Daniel Webster*. NY, 1937 1st. H. Denison illus. VG in DJ. $45.

BENET, WILLIAM ROSE. *Adolphus, The Adopted Dolphin*. Houghton Mifflin, 1941. In DJ. $18-$36.

BENEZIT, E. *Dictionnaire Critique et Documentaire des Peintres, Sculpteurs*. 8 vols. Dictionary of Painters, etc. France, 1960. Very Good. $350.

BENJAMIN, A. CORNELIUS. *An Introduction to the Philosophy of Science*. NY, 1937 1st ed. VG. $30.

BENJAMIN, ASHER. *The Practice of Architecture*. Boston, 1835. Published by author. 2nd edition. Fair. $300.

BENNETT, A. G. *Whaling in the Antartic*. NY, Holt, 1932 1st ed. Very Good. $35-$45.

BENNETT, CHARLES H. *The Book of Blockheads*. London, 1863 1st ed. Very Good. $600-$650.
Lightsome and the Little Golden Lady. London, 1867 1st ed. Illus. by author. Ex-lib Very Good. $100-$120.
Shadow and Substance. London, 1860 1st ed. Illus. by author. Very Good. $175-$200.

BENNETT, COLIN. *Handbook of Kinematography. The History & Practice of Motion Picture Projection*. London, 1911 1st ed. Very Good. $75.

BENNETT, JUANITA. *A New Story of Little Black Sambo*. Whitman, 1939. Loose covers. $65.

BENSON, HENRY C. *Life Among the Choctaw Indians*. Cincinnati, 1860 1st ed. Very Good. $250-$350.

BENTLEY, E. C. *Elephant's Work*. NY, 1950 1st ed. Near Fine in dust jacket. $25.
Trent's Own Case. NY, 1946. VG in dust jacket. $15.

BENTON, FRANK. *Cowboy Life on the Sidetrack*. Denver, 1903 1st ed. Pictorial cover. Very Good. $90-$125.

BENTON, JOEL. *A Unique Story of a Marvelous Career. Life of Phineas T. Barnum*. Phil., 1891. Good-VG. $25.

BENTON, THOMAS HART. *The Artist in America*. No place, 1939. Very Good. $14.

BENTWRIGHT, JEREMIAH. *The American Horse Tamer*. NY, 1858. Very Good. $85.

BERCOVICI, KONRAD. *Story of the Gypsies*. NY, 1928. $30. Same, 1931. Very Good. $20.

BERENS, S. *Nansen in the Frozen World*. Peary's exped. Hoilman & Co. 1897. Illus. cover. Minor wear. $45.

BERGAUST, ERIK. *Reaching for the Stars*. (Biography of Werner Von Braun). Garden City, 1960 1st ed. Good. $20.

BERGMAN, RAY. *Trout*. Philadelphia, 1938 1st ed. VG. $100. NY, 1952 2nd ed. 21 color plates. VG. $15. Knopf, 1962 ed. Fine in dust jacket. $18.
Fresh Water Bass. NY, 1942 1st ed. Wm. Penn. Fine. $50.
With Fly, Plug and Bait. NY, 1947 1st ed. VG. $35.

BERKELEY, STANLEY. *A Bow-Wow Book*. Illus. by author. Soft cloth pgs. No date, 1st ed. VG. $50-$75.

BERLANT, ANTHONY and MARY H. KELENBERG. *Walk In Beauty: The Navajo and Their Blankets*. Boston, 1977. Illus. Very Good in dust jacket. $85.

BERNARD, BRUCE (Editor). *Photodiscovery: Masterworks of Photography, 1840-1950*. Abrams, 1980. VG in DJ. $75.

BEROLZHEIMER, RUTH (Editor). *International Cook Book*. Chicago, 1938. Good-VG. $25.
The American Woman's Cook Book. 1938 & 1942 eds. Good-VG. $12-$15. Combined with U. S. Regional cookbook , white damask cover. 2 vol. set. VG. $36 pair.

BERRIGAN, DANIEL. *Time Without Number*. NY, 1957. Author's 1st book. VG in DJ. $30-$40. Signed. $75.
Encounters. NY, Cleveland, 1960. Insc. Fine in DJ. $50.
World for a Wedding Ring. NY, 1962. VG in DJ. $20.

BERRIGAN, PHILIP. *Prison Journals of a Priest Revolutionary*. NY, 1970 1st ed. Fine in dust jacket. $12.

BERRIGAN, TED. *In The Early Morning Rain*. London, 1970 1st ed. One of 100 copies, signed. VG. $40.

BERRY, BOLLAY, and BEERS (Editors). *Handbook of Meteorology*. NY, 1945 1st ed. $30-$60.

BERRY, WENDELL. *The Unforeseen Wilderness*. Kentucky, 1971 1st ed. Gene Meatyard photos. Signed by Berry & Meatyard. VG in clipped DJ. $250. Same, unsigned. $75.
Nathan Coulter. H. Mifflin, 1960 1st ed. in DJ. $150-$175.

BERRYMAN, JOHN. *The Dispossessed*. NY, 1948 1st ed. in dust jacket. $150-$250.
Stephen Crane. NY, 1950 1st ed. in dust jacket. $75-$125.

BERTILLON, ALPHONSE. *The Bertillon System of Identification*. No publisher, 1896. Translation. 80 plates. Good plus. $75.

BERTON, PIERRE.*The Great Railway, 1871-1881*. Toronto, 1971 5th printing. Near Fine in dust jacket. $25.
The Impossible Railway: The Canadian Pacific. NY, Knopf, 1972 1st Amer. ed. VG in DJ. $18-$30.

BERYMENSKI, LEO. *The Death of Adolph Hitler*. NY, 1968 1st ed. Good in dust jacket. $16.

BESANT, ANNIE. *Some Problems of Life*. London, 1900 1st ed. VG. $20. NY, 1906. 1st American ed. VG. $20.
Super-Human Men in History. Lon., 1913 1st. VG. $20.
Esoteric Christianity. Madras, 1913. VG. $15.

BESTER, ALFRED. *Who He?* No place, 1953 1st ed. Fine in dust jacket. $40.

BESTON, HENRY. *The Book of Gallant Vagabonds*. NY, 1925. Illus. Very Good in dust jacket. $15.
The Outermost House: A Year of Life on the Great Beach of Cape Cod. Garden City, 1928. 1st ed. Photo illus. Near Very Good. $35.
Herbs of the Earth. Doubleday, 1935 1st. VG in DJ. $35.
The St. Lawrence. NY, 1942. 1st ed. Rivers of America series. Illus. Very Fine. $35. Another, No DJ. $25.

BETHURUM, TRUMAN. *Aboard a Flying Saucer*. Los Angeles, 1954. Very Good. $20.

BETJEMAN, JOHN. *Summoned by Bells*. London, 1960 1st ed. Michael Tree illus. Fine in dust jacket. $25.
High & Low. Bos., 1967 1st Amer. Poems. VG in DJ. $45.
Archie and the Strict Baptists. Philadelphia, 1977 1st American ed. Gill illus. Ex-library. Fine in DJ. $20.

BETTEN, E. L. *Upland Game Shooting*. Philadelphia, 1940 1st ed. Lynn Bogue Hunt illus. Very Good. $60.

BETTER HOMES & GARDENS COOKBOOKS.
All-Time Favorite Bread Recipes. 1965-1980. $5-$10.
Bread Cook Book. 1965-1980. $5-$10.
Dessert Cook Book . 1965-1980. $5-$10.
Homemade Cookies Cook Book. 1965-1980. $5-$10.
Pies and Cakes. 1965-1980. $5-$10.
100's of Baking Ideas. 1965-1980. $5-$10.
Junior Cook Book. 1955 1st ed. $14-$18.
New Jr. Cook Book. 1979 4th ed. $12-$16.
Complete Step by Step. 1980 10th ed. $8-$12.
B.H.& G. Cook Book. 3-ring binder, 1935-1968. $12-$25.

BETTY CROCKER COOK BOOK. (See Crocker, Betty).

BEVERIDGE, ALBERT J. *The Life of John Marshall*. Bos., NY, 1916 4 vols. in 2 books. VG. $50. 1919 ed. Fine. $35.
Abraham Lincoln. Boston, 1928. 4 vols. One of 1,000 copies. VG. $350. 1928 trade editions. $40-$60 per set.

BEYER, WALTER and OSCAR KEYDEL. *Deeds of Valor*. Perrien Keydel, 1901. Good. $60.

BIANCO, PAMELA. *The Starlit Journey*. NY, 1933. 1st ed. Illus. by author. Good. $24. Another, VG in DJ. $50.

BIANCO, MARGERY WILLIAMS. *Poor Cecco*. NY, 1925 1st ed. Arthur Rackham illus. 1st issue (pictorial end papers). DJ and Box. $300-$500. No DJ.$120-$175.
The Adventures of Andy. NY, 1927 1st edition. Leon Underwood illus. VG. $35.
The Little Wooden Doll. NY, 1931 31st printing. Pamela Bianco illus. Very Good in dust jacket. $12.
A Street of Little Shops. NY, 1932. G. Paul illus. G. $10.
Winterbound. Viking, 1936 1st ed. Decorations by Seredy. Very Good in dust jacket. $45.

BICKEL, KARL A. *The Mangrove Coast*. NY, 1942. 32 photos by Walker Evans. Ex-lib. Cover with DJ pieces pasted on. Contents Good. $125.

BICKHAM, GEORGE. *The Universal Penman*. NY, 1941 Fac. of 1743 ed. Many illus. 1 of 1,000. VG in DJ. $125.

BIDDLE, GEORGE. *Artist at War*. NY, 1944. Good plus in dust jacket. $28.

BIDWELL, GEN. JOHN. *Echoes of the Past About California and In Camp and Cabin.* by Steele. Lakeside Press, 1928. Good-VG. $35. LA, 1948 Ltd. ed. $30-$65.

BIEBER, MARGARETTE. *The History of the Greek and Roman Theater.* 1939 1st ed. Illus. Fine in DJ. $100.

BIERCE, AMBROSE. *In The Midst of Life.* NY, 1898 1st ed. Near Fine. $125.
Fantastic Fables. NY, 1899 1st ed. Covers soiled. $150.
Great Battles of the World. Philadelphia, 1901 1st ed. John Sloan illus. Ex-lib, o/w Fine. $275.
The Dance of Death. San Francisco, 1877 2nd ed. Very Good. $40-$60.
The Shadow on the Dial and Other Essays. San Francisco, 1909 1st ed. Good plus. $50. Very Good. $71. Another, unopened. $150.
Battle Sketches. London, 1930 1st ed. One of 350 copies. Dark endpapers, o/w Fine. $200.
Tales of Soldiers & Civilians. Limited Editions Club, 1943. Paul Landacre illus. Joseph H. Jackson, ed. One of 1,500 copies, signed by Landacre. NF in slipcase. $150.

BIERSTADT, EDWARD. *Curious Trials and Criminal Cases From Socrates to Scopes.* No place, 1928. VG. $25.

BIG LITTLE BOOKS. Whitman Publishing Company of Racine, Wisconsin originated the concept of these thick little hard-bound books of comic and adventure stories for preteen children. The first *Big Little Book* was introduced in 1933 and sold for ten cents. Today prices range from $5 to $50 with the average book in very good condition falling between $15 and $35.

Whitman assigned each of its books a serial number. Other publishers, such as Saalfield, Goldsmith and World Syndicate, copied Whitman's successful format. All are collectible. Below is a small sampling of titles. Many others may be found in general antiques price guides.

Tarzan of the Screen (778). VG. $30.
The Tarzan Twins (no #). VG-Fine. $47.
Tarzan Escapes (1182). N. Mint. $90.
Buck Rogers-Planetoid Plot (1197). Fine-VF. $50.
Buck Rogers-Planetoid Plot (1197). Fine. $40.
Buck Rogers-Moons of Saturn (1143). V. Good. $30.
Buck Rogers-25th Century A.D. (742). V. Good. $25.
Flash Gordon-Witch Queen of Mongo(1190). VG-F. $35.
Flash Gordon-Tournaments of Mongo(1171). F-VF. $47.
Flash Gordon-Planet Mongo (1110). Good-VG. $15.
Flash Gordon-Monsters of Mongo (1166). VG. $35.
Dick Tracy-Boris Arson Gang (1163). Fine-VF. $45.
Mickey Mouse in Blaggard Castle (725). VG. $30.
Jane Withers in Keep Smiling (1463). VG-Fine. $22.
Billy the Kid (773). Near Mint. $42.

The Silver Streak (1155). Near Mint. $40.
Little Orphan Annie-Punjab the Wizard (1162). VF. $60.
Dirigible-ZR90 (1464). VG. $12.
Lone Ranger-Menace of Murder Valley (1465). VG. $20.
Lone Ranger & His Horse Silver (1181). VG. $18.
Gene Autry in Law of the Range (1453). Fine. $28.
Tom Mix-Stranger From the South (1183). N. Mint. $49.
Tom Mix-Fighting Cowboy (1144). V. Fine. $65.
Buck Jones-Roaring West (1174). VG-Fine. $24.
Prairie Bill-Covered Wagon (758). N. Mint. $45.
Buffalo Bill Plays a Lone Hand (1199). Fine. $18.
Tailspin Tommy-Great Air Mystery (1184). V Fine. $45.
Tailspin Tommy-Hunting Pirate Gold (1172). Fine. $23.
Two Gun Montana (1104). Fine-VF. $25.
Mickey Rooney & Judy Garland (1493). VG. $15.
Skeezix in Africa (1112). Fine. $21.
Skeezix at Military Academy (1408). VF. $24.
Skippy (761). VG-Fine. $18.
Bringing Up Father (1133). V. Fine. $40.
Mutt and Jeff (1113). V. Fine. $50.
Mandrake the Magician (1167). Fine-VF. $34.
Jungle Jim (1138). V. Fine. $45.
Erik Noble-Forty Niners (722). V. Fine. $15.
OG-Son of Fire (1115). $12.
Smilin' Jack-Stratosphere Ascent (1152). VG-Fine. $22.
Smokey Stover-Foo Fighter (1421). Fine-VF. $21.
Junior G Men (1442). Very Fine. $26.
Alley Oop & Dinny (763). VG. $10.
Mac of the Marines in Africa (1189). VF. $20.
Ace Drummond (1177). Fine. $12.
Danger Trails in Africa (1151). Fine-VF. $18.
Hall of Fame of the Air (1159). V. Fine. $20.
Detective Higgins (1484). Fine-VF. $20.
Don Winslow (1107). Fine. $23.
Dan Dunn-Crime Never Pays (1116). Fine. $20.
Terry & the Pirates (1156). Fine-VF. $32.
Little Annie Rooney-Orphan House (1117). F-VF. $24.
Radio Patrol Trailing the Safeblowers (1173). F-VF. $18.
S.O.S Coast Guard (1191). V. Fine. $22.
Moon Mullins-Plushbottom Twins (1134). VG-Fine. $12.
Li'l Abner in New York (1198). VG-Fine. $18.
Treasure Island-Jackie Cooper (1141). Good-VG. $9.
The Arizona Kid (1192). N. Mint. $27.
G Men on the Job (1168). Fine. $15.
Chester Gump-City of Gold (1146). VG-Fine. $15.
Chuck Malloy Railroad Detective (1453). Fine. $12.
Hairbreath Harry in Dept Q. T. (1101). Fine-VF. $21.
Captain Easy-Soldier of Fortune (1128). Fine. $19.
Tiny Tim (767). Good-VG. $8.
Blaze Brandon-Foreign Legion (1447). Fine-VF. $16.
Bronc Peeler-Lone Cowboy (1417). N. Mint. $32.
Black Silver Pirate Crew (1414). Fine. $15.
Sombrero Pete (1136). Fine-VF. $15.
Foreign Spies-Doctor Doom (1460). Fine-VF. $15.
Mickey Mouse (717) . Fair-Good (no spine). $35.
Jim Starr Border Patrol (1428). V. Fine. $20.
Fightin' Heroes (1401). VG-Fine. $11.

Men of the Mounted (755). V. Good. $8.
Story of Jackie Cooper (W714). Good-VG. $9.
Boss of the Chisholm Trail (1153). N. M.-Mint. $34.
Walt Disney's Mickey Mouse & Boy Thursday (845).
Very Fine. $25.
Pioneers of the Wild West (No #). V. Good. $5.
Buffalo Bill-All Pictures (No #). V. Good. $5.
Little Jimmy's Gold Hunt (1087). VG-Fine. $10.
Adventures of Pete the Tramp (1082). VG. $8.
Adventures of Tim Tyler (1053). VG-Fine. $18.
The Laughing Dragon of Oz. 1934 1st ed. VG. $150.

BIGGERS, EARL DERR. *Seven Keys to Baldpate*. Bobbs-Merrill, 1913 1st ed. Author's 1st book. Fine. $100.
Keeper of the Keys. Bobbs-Merrill, 1932 1st ed. $55-$75.
Love Insurance. Bobbs-Merrill, 1914 1st ed. $40-$80.
Earl Derr Biggers Tells Ten Stories. Bobbs-Merrill, 1933 1st ed. VG-Fine. $95-$125.

BIGGS, JOHN. *The Guilty Mind*. NY, 1955 1st. VG. $20.

BIGHAW, MADGE A. *Sonny Elephant*. Little Brown, 1930 1st ed. Very Good. $14.

BILL, ALFRED HOYT. *The Beleaguered City: Richmond, 1861-1865*. NY, 1946 1st. Cov. fading, o/w VG. $20-$30.

BILLINGS, JOHN D. *Hardtack & Coffee*. Boston, 1887 1st edition. Illustrated. Very Good. $225. Lakeside Classic, 1960 reprint. Fine. $25-$38.

BINDER, PEARL. *Muffs and Morals*. NY, no date. Costume history. Illus. Very Good. $24.

BINKLEY, WILLIAM C. *Expansionist Movement in Texas, 1836-1950*. Berkeley, Univ. of CA, 1925. Near Fine. $250.

BINNS, ARCHIE. *The Roaring Land*. Mc Bride, 1942 1st ed. Very Good. $12-$14.

BINYON, LAURENCE. *Collected Poems*. No place, 1931. 2 vols with two signed letters. VG in poor DJ. $70.
English Water-Colours. London, 1933. 24 Photogravures. Near Fine. $45.
Japanese Colour Prints. (with J. Sexon). No place, 1978. Reprint. Very Good. $20.

BIRCHMORE, FRED. *Around the World on a Bicycle*. Athens, GA, 1939 1st ed. One of 2,500 copies. Fine. $45.

BIRD, ISABELLA. *Unbeaten Tracks in Japan*. NY, 1881 1st American ed. 2 vols. Illus. VG-Fine. $165.
The Golden Shersonese. NY, 1886. Near Fine. $80.
A Lady's Life in the Rocky Mountains. NY, 1879-1880 1st American ed. Near VG. $90. London ed. $30-$60.
The Hawaiian Archipelago. London, 1876, John Murray. 2nd edition. VG. $50.

BIRD, JOSEPH. *Protection Against Fire & the Best Means of Putting Out Fires in Cities, Towns & Villages*. NY, 1873 1st ed. Good-VG. $90-$100.

THE BIRDS OF NORTH CAROLINA. State Geological and Economic Survey, Vol. IV, 1919. 24 color plates. $90.

BIRMINGHAM, STEPHEN. *Young Mr. Keefe*. Boston, 1958 1st ed. Author's 1st book. VG in DJ. $50.

BIRNEY, HOFFMAN. *Grim Journey: The Story of the Donner Party*. NY, 1934 1st ed. VG in DJ. $25.
Vigilantes. PA, 1929 1st ed. Good-VG. $20-$24.

BIRREN, FABER. *Color Dimensions. Creating New Principles of Color Harmony*. Chicago, 1934 1st ed. VG. $50.
New Horizons in Color. NY, Reinhold, 1955. VG. $25.

BISHOP, CLAIRE. *The Man Who Lost His* Head. NY, 1942 5th ed. Robert McCloskey illus. Signed. VG. $16.

BISHOP, FREDERICK. *The Illustrated London Cookery Book*. London, 1852. Engravings, foldout. Shaky hinges o/w Good. $125.

BISHOP, LEANER. *History of American Manufactures*. NY, 1864. Vol 1 only. Good. $25-$35.

BISHOP, NATHANIEL H. *Voyage of The Paper Canoe*. Boston, 1878 1st ed. Maps, illus. Very Good. $125.
Four Months in a Sneak Box. Bos., 1879 1st ed. VG. $60.

BISHOP, RICHARD E. *Bishop's Wildfowl*. MN, Brown & Bigelow, 1948 1st ed. Leather bound. $150-$200.

BISHOP, ROBERT. *American Folk Sculpture*. Bonanza, 1985 reprint of 1974 1st ed. Fine in DJ. $25-$35.
Centuries and Styles of the American Chair. New York, 1972. Very Good. $35.

BISSELL, RICHARD. *A Stretch on the River*. Boston, 1950 1st ed. Author's 1st book. NF in dust jacket. $75.
The Monongahela. Rivers of America Series. NY, 1952 1st ed. Rinehart. VG, no dust jacket. $25.
You Can Always Tell a Harvard Man. NY, 1962 1st ed. Fine in dust jacket. $10.
My Life on the Mississippi, Or Why I Am Not Mark Twain. Boston, 1973 1st ed. Fine in DJ. $25.

BITTING, A. W. & KATHERINE G. *Canning & How to Use Canned Foods*. Wash. DC, 1916. Rubbed. $20.

BITTING, KATHERINE G. *Gastronomic Bibliography*. San Francisco, 1939 1st ed. VG to Fine. $200-$350.

BLACK, ROBERT C. *The Railroads of the Confederacy*. Chapel Hill, 1952. Fine. $40.

BLACKBRIDGE, JOHN. *The Complete Poker Player*. 1880. 142 pgs. Hardcover. Very Fine. $275 auction.

BLACKMAR, FRANK W. *Spanish Institutions of the Southwest*. Baltimore, Johns Hopkins Press, 1891. Rubbed, dull, frayed. $150.

BLACKMORE, R. D. *Erema*. London, 1878 1st ed. Illus. Inscribed. Very Good. $50.
Lorna Doone. NY, 1902. Clifton Johnson illus. VG. $23. Many editions printed in 1880s, 1920s.
Slain by the Doones. Dodd Mead, 1895 1st U. S. ed., later issue. Good-VG. $20.

BLACKSTONE, ELLA M. *The American Woman's Cook-Book*. Laird & Lee, 1910 1st edition. Very Good in dust jacket. $19.

BLACKWOOD, ALGERNON. *A Prisoner in Fairyland*. NY, 1913 1st ed. Very Good. $25-$35.
John Silence. No place, 1914 2nd Amer. ed. 1 of 500 $45.
The Empty House. London, 1916. VG. $30.
Shocks. NY, 1936 1st ed. VG in DJ. $45.
The Promise of Air. NY, 1938. Fine in DJ. $50.
The Doll and One Other. Arkham House, 1946 1st ed. VG-Fine in dust jacket. $35-$70.

BLAINE, JOHN. *Rick Brant Juvenile Titles*. Grosset & Dunlap, no dates. 10 different. No DJs. $3-$5 each. Number 15 in Rick Brant series. VG in vg DJ. $25.

BLAISDELL, ALBERT. *Stories of the Civil War*. Boston, 1890. Illus. Good-VG. $15-$30.

BLAKE, FORRESTAL. *Johnny Christmas*. NY, 1948. VG in dust jacket. $25-$50.

BLAKE, WILLIAM. *The Poetical Works of*. London, 1913 1st ed. Illus. Very Good. $30.
Songs of Innocence. London, 1926 Facsimile ed. Illus. VG. $65. Another Very Good in dust jacket. $100. London, 1954 Limited edition. Boxed. $125.
Land of Dreams. NY, 1928. Bianco illus. VG. $30.

BLAKELY, H. W. *The 32nd Infantry Division in WWII*. Madison WI, 1955. Fine in dust jacket. $130.

BLAKINGAME, W. *The U.S. Frogmen of World War II*. NY, 1964. Good plus. $25.

BLANC, CHARLES. *Art in Ornament and Dress*. NY, 1877. Illus. Very Good. $85.

BLANCHAN, NELTJIE. *Bird Neighbors*. New York, 1900. 52 color plates. Good. $40.
Birds. Wise, 1930. 35 color plates. VG. $25.
The Bird Book. Garden City, 1932 1st ed. VG. $25.

BLANCK, JACOB. *Peter Parley to Penrod*. American juvenile books bibliography. 1974. Classic ref. Fine. $165.
Johnson's American 1st Editions. 1942 4th ed. VG. $195.
Bibliography of American Literature. New Haven CT. No date. 7 volumes. Very Good. $375.

BLAND, DAVID. *A History of Book Illustration*. Cleveland, World Pub, 1958 1st ed. Ex-library. Good-VG. $60-$90.

BLANDING, DON. *Vagabond's House*. NY, 1934. Signed by author. Faded spine, else Very Good. $20.
Drifter's Gold. NY, 1939. Dodd-Mead 1st ed. Signed by author. Very Good, no dust jacket. $15.
Floridays. Dodd-Mead, 1942 2nd ed. Fine, no DJ. $10.
14 mixed titles. Mostly 1st eds. in DJ. Auction lot. $100.

BLANK, CLAIR. *Beverly Gray, Reporter (No. 10)*. Grosset & Dunlap, 1940 1st ed. VG in worn DJ. $25.
Beverly Gray's Scoop (No. 24). McLoughlin, 1954. Worn, bumped, yellowed. Good-VG. $15.
Beverly Gray, Sophomore (No. 2). A.L. Burt, 1934. VG in DJ which lists 4 titles. $75.
Beverly Gray's Journey. Very Good. $10.

BLASSINGAME, JOHN W. *The Slave Community*. Oxford Univ., 1972 1st ed. Fine in dust jacket. $14.

BLAVATSKY, H. P. *The Secret Doctrine*. London, 1893 3rd revised ed. 4 vols. Vol. 1 shaken, o/w Good. $75. 1913 6th edition. $35. No place, 1952, 2 vols. Bumped corners. $28.
Nightmare Tales. London, no date. Theosophical Publ. House. Foreword by Annie Besant. Very Good. $55.
Key to Theosophy. 1920 1st ed. Very Good. $35.
The People of the Blue Mountains. Garden City, 1965. David Erdman ed. Harold Bloom commentary. VG. $35.

BLEGVAD, LENORE. *Moon-Watch Summer*. NY, 1972 3rd printing. Erik Blegvard illus. Fine in DJ. $28.

BLISH, JAMES. *Earthman Come Home*. NY, 1955 1st ed. Very Good in dust jacket. $35.
Black Easter. NY, 1968 1st ed. G-F in DJ. $95-$300.
Midsummer Century. London, 1972. Fine in DJ. $22.

BLISS, DOUGLAS PERCY. *A History of Wood Engraving*. London, J. M. Dent, 1928 1st ed. Ex-lib. VG. $50-$80.

BLOCK, HERBERT. *The Herblock Book*. No place, 1952 1st book. Inscribed by author/cartoonist. Typed letter signed laid in. Fine in dust jacket. $35.

BLOCK, LAWRENCE. *The Girl With the Long Green Heart*. NY, Gold Medal, 1965 1st ed. Fine. $20.
In the Midst of Death. Dell paperback, 1976. Fine. $20.
Burglars Can't Be Satisfied. NY, 1977. Fine in DJ. $20.
Burglars Can't Be Choosers. NY, 1977 Limited ed. Signed, Fine in dust jacket. $25.

The Burglar Who Studied Spinoza. NY, 1980. Fine in DJ.
$20. Book Club ed. Fine in dust jacket. $6.
A Stab in the Dark. NY, 1981 1st ed. Fine in DJ. $100.
Eight Million Ways to Die. NY, 1982 1st. F in vg DJ. $65.
The Burglar Who Painted Like Mondrian. Arbor House,
1983 1st ed. Signed. Fine in dust jacket. $30.

BLOCK, ROBERT. *Pleasant Dreams*. Arkham House, 1960
1st ed. Fine in dust jacket. $165.
Deadbeat. Simon & Schuster. 1960 1st ed. Near Fine. $80.
American Gothic. NY, 1971 1st ed. Fine in DJ. $45.
Blood Runs Cold. NY, 1974 1st ed. VG-F. DJ. $45-$100.
Cold Chills. NY, 1977 1st ed. Fine in DJ. $45.
Unholy Trinity. Santa Cruz CA, 1986 1st ed. F in DJ. $32.

BLUE JACKET'S MANUAL, USN. Naval Institute, 1943
11th ed. Fine. $6-$8. Appleton, 1918 6th ed. Fr, stain. $10.

BLUM, DANIEL. *Pictorial History of the American Theater*.
NY, 1951. Very Good. $15-$22.

BLUMENTHAL, JOSEPH. *The Printed Book in America*.
Boston, 1977. 70 plates. Fine in dust jacket. $15.

BLUNDEN, EDMUND. *Undertones of War*. London, 1928
1st ed. Very Good in dust jacket. $150.
Retreat. London, 1928 1st ed. Signed, VG in DJ. $100.
After the Bombing. London, 1928 1st ed. Signed, VG in
dust jacket. $100.

BLUNT, WILFRED S. *My Diaries 1888-1914*. NY, 1921
2 vols 1st ed. Fine. $100.
The Art of William Blake. Columbia University Press,
1959. Very Good. $12.
Cockerell. NY, 1965 1st American ed. VG in DJ. $60.

BLYTON, ENID. *The Children of Cherry Tree Farm*.
London, 1940 9th ed. Harry Rountree illus. VG in DJ. $20.
More Adventures of Pip. London, probably 1940s.
Raymond Shepard illus. VG in edge worn DJ. $38.
Secret of Moon Castle. Blackwell, 1953. $8.
Mystery of the Vanished Prince. Methuen, 1952. F. $12.

BOATNER, MARK. *Civil War Dictionary*. McKay, 1961
2nd ed. Very Good in dust jacket. $22.

BOCCACCIO, GIOVANNI. *The Decameron*. NY, 1925.
John Payne translator. Clara Tice illus. 48 plates. 2 vols.
VG-Fine. $150-$300. Limited Edition Club, 1940, 2 vols.
Signed by illus. F. Kredel. Fine in slipcase. $250-$350.
Garden City reprint, 1949. Kent illus. VG in DJ. $10.

BOCUSE, PAUL. *Paul Bocuse in Your Kitchen*. NY, 1982
1st American ed. Very Good in dust jacket. $13.

BODE, CARL. *Midcentury America: Life in the 1850s*.
Southern Illinois University, 1972. Illus. VG in DJ. $25.

BODENHEIM, MAXWELL. *Naked on Roller Skates*.
Liveright, 1930. 1st ed. VG in chip dust jacket. $45.

BODINE, A. AUBREY. *My Maryland*. Camera Magazine,
1952. Fine in good dust jacket. $30.
The Face of Maryland. Baltimore, 1961 1st ed. 144
Photos. Inscribed. Near Fine in dust jacket. $50.

BODSWORTH, FRED. *Last of the Curlews*. New York,
1955. T. M. Short illus. Good in good dust jacket. $25.

BOESCH, MARK. *The Lawless Land, Storyof Vigilantes*.
Philadelphia, 1953. VG in dust jacket. $18.

BOGAN, LOUISE. *Body of This Death*. McBride, 1923 1st
ed. Author's 1st book. In dust jacket. $250-$500.

BOGGS, MAE HELENE. *My Playhouse Was a Concord
Coach*. 1822-1888 newspaper stories. Oakland, CA, 1942
1st ed. Ex-library. Very Good. $150-$250.

BOHR, NIELS. *Atomic Physics and Human Knowledge*.
NY, 1958. Good in chipped dust jacket. $13. Fine. $30.

BOK, EDWARD. *The Americanization of Edward Bok*. NY,
1922. One of 1,250. Signed. Hinges loose, sunned. $25.
Twice Thirty. NY, 1925. Very Good. $12.

BOLAND, MARY A. *A Handbook of Invalid Cooking*. NY,
1893. Good. $35.

BOLLAND, SIMPSON. *The Iron Founder, The Art of
Moulding*. John Wiley, 1896 revised edition. 382 pages,
illustrated. Good-VG. $14.

BOLLES, ALBERT S. *Industrial History of the United
States*. Norwich, 1878 3rd edition. Good. $35. Fine. $125.

BOLTON, ETHEL S. *American Samplers*. Boston, 1921 1st
ed. MA Society of Colonial Dames. VG. $200.
American Wax Portraits. No place, 1929. Ex-library.
Shelfwear, foxing. Limited ed. Contents VG. $15.

BOLTON, HERBERT E. *Coronado, Knight of Pueblos and
Plains*. NY, Whittlesey, 1949 1st ed. VG in DJ. $75.
Font's Complete Diary. Founding of San Francisco.
Berkeley, University of Calif. Press, 1931 1st edition. Fine
in sunned jacket. $80-$10.
*Rim of Christendom. Biography of Eusebio Francisco
Kino*. NY, Macmillan, 1936 1st ed. Near Fine in clipped
dust jacket. $100-$120.

BOLTON, ISABEL. *Many Mansions*. NY, 1952. 1st ed. Fine
in dust jacket. $25.

BOND, JOHN. *Mussolini, the Wild Man of Europe*.
Washington DC, 1929. Very Good. $37.

BOND, NELSON. *Mr. Mergenthwirker's Lobblies*. NY, 1946 1st ed. Author's 1st book. Good in DJ. $45.
Thirty-First of February: 13 Flights of Fantasy. NY, 1949. Very Good in dust jacket. Signed by author. $115.
Nightmares and Daydreams. Arkham House, 1968 1st ed. Fine in dust jacket. $30-$45.

BONE, STEPHEN. *The Little Boy and His House*. NY, 1936 1st ed. Mary Adshead illus. Good. $45.

BONNE, JOSEPHINE. *The Continental Cook Book*. NY, 1928 1st American ed. Worn. $15.

BONNER, WILLIAM H. *Pirate Laureate*. Captain Kidd. Rutgers Univ. Press, 1947 1st ed. VG in DJ. $22.

BONTEMPS, ARNA and JACK CONRAY. *Slappy Hooper, the Wonderful Sign Painter*. Boston, 1946 1st ed. Ursula Koering illus. Very Good in clipped dust jacket. $28.

BONZON, PAUL JACQUES. *The Runaway Flying Horse*. NY, 1976. William Pene DuBois illus. VG in DJ. $20.

THE BOOK OF BIRDS. National Geographic Society, 1937, 2 volumes. Good-VG. $25-$40.

A BOOK OF COMMANDMENTS FOR THE GOVERNMENT OF THE CHURCH OF CHRIST. Anon. (Joseph Smith, Jr.) Independence MO, 1833. $25,000-$30,000.

BOOKMAN'S PRICE INDEX. Vols. 1, 8, 9, 10, 11 and 12. $20-$30 each. 18 volumes. 1973-1983. $250-$350 all.

BOOKS IN PRINT. 1970s-1990s volumes. $8-$15 each.

BOOTH, GEORGE C. *The Food and Drink of Mexico*. Ward Ritche, 1964 2nd printing. VG in dust jacket. $20.

BOOTH, MARY. *History of the City of New York*. NY, 1867 2nd printing. Very Good. $50-$75.
Uprising of a Great People. NY, 1861. Good-VG. $35-$60.

BOOTHBY, GUY. *Pharos the Egyptian*. NY, 1899 1st American ed. Very Good. $25.
Farewell Nikola. Lippincott, 1901 1st Amer. ed. VG. $18.

BOOTHE, CLARE. *Kiss the Boys Goodbye*. NY, 1939 1st ed. Very Good in dust jacket. $75.

BORDER BEAGLES. Anon. (William Gilmore Sims). Philadelphia, 1840. $300-$400.

BOREIN, EDWARD. *Etchings of the West*. Santa Barbara CA, 1950 1st ed. One of 1,001. NF in slipcase. $250.

BORN, MAX. *Atomic Physics*. NY, 1936 1st ed. Translated. Good plus. $45. 1946 4th edition. $25-$35.

BORRETT, WILLIAM C. *Historic Halifax - Tales Told Under the Old Town Clock*. Ryerson Press, 1948 1st ed. Very Good in dust jacket. $10.

BORTHWICK, J. D. *Three Years in California*. 1851 gold miners' experiences. Edinburgh, 1857 1st ed. Worn, cracked hinges. $300-$500.

BORUP, GEORGE. *A Tenderfoot with Peary*. NY, 1911 1st ed., Stokes. 46 illus. Very Good. $35.

BOSSERT, H. *Ornament in Applied Art*. NY, 1924. 122 color plates. Ex-library. Rubbed. $185.

BOSTON BUSINESS DIRECTORY. No. 25. Littlefield Pub., 1895. 696 pgs. Good. $25.

BOSTON, LUCY. *The Children of Greene Knowe*. London, 1954 1st ed. Peter Boston illus. Fine in DJ. $250.
The River at Greene Knowe. NY, 1959 1st American ed. Peter Boston illus. Fine in dust jacket. $45.
A Stranger at Greene Knowe. New York, 1962 3rd American printing. Pewter Boston illustrator. Very Good in dust jacket. $20.
The Stones of Green Knowe. NY, 1976 1st American ed. Peter Boston illus. Fine in dust jacket. $45.

BOSWELL, JAMES. *The Life of Samuel Johnson*. The first edition was published in London in 1791. $3,000-$4,500. Boston, 1807, 1st Amer. ed. $175. 1887, J. B. Alden, 4 vol set. $50. Various limited ed. sets, 1930s-1940s. $75-$175.

BOSWORTH, CLARENCE. *Breeding Your Own, Raising Colts*. 1939 Derrydale, Ltd. ed. Good plus. $60.

BOTKIN, B. A. (Editor). *A Treasury of Mississippi River Folklore*. NY, 1955. VG in DJ. $25. Bonanza, 1978. $13.
Sidewalks of America. Indianapolis, 1954 1st ed. VG-Fine in dust jacket. $30.
A Civil War Treasury of Tales, Legends, and Folklore. NY, 1981. Very Good in dust jacket. $20.

BOTSFORD, HARRY. *Fish and Game Cook Book*. NY, 1947 1st ed. Very Good in dust jacket. $20.

BOUCHER, ANTHONY. *The Case of the Baker Street Irregulars*. NY, 1940. Fine in dust jacket. $175.

BOULLE, PIERRE. *A Noble Profession*. NY, 1960 1st American ed. Near Fine in dust jacket. $20.
The Virtues of Hell. NY, 1974 1st American edition. Fine in dust jacket. $15.

BOURKE, JOHN G. *On the Border With Crook*. NY, 1892 2nd ed. Good plus. $65. 1891 1st ed. $200.
The Snake Dance of the Moquis of Arizona. Chicago, 1962. Facsimile of 1884 ed. Fine. $35.

BOURKE-WHITE, MARGARET. *Machines and Men in Russia*. NY, 1932. Photos by author. Rubbed. $35.
Shooting the Russian War. NY, 1942. Photos by author. Poor. $15. Very Good in dust jacket. $45.
They Called It "Purple Heart Valley". Simon & Schuster, 1944 1st ed. Fine, no dust jacket. $35.

BOVEY, MARTIN. *The Saga of the Waterfowl*. Wash. DC. 1949 1st ed. Fine in dust jacket. $30.

BOWDITCH, NATHANIEL. *The New American Practical Navigator*. NY, Blunt. 1847-1861 eds. $150-$230.

BOWEN, FRANK C. *The Sea: Its History and Romance*. McBride, 1927, 4 vol. set. Very Good. $100.
America Sails the Seas. NY, 1938, 1st illus. ed. $50.
Men of the Wooden Walls. 1952 edition. Good. $25.

BOWER, B. M. *The Gringos*. 1913 1st edition Good. $30.
Boy's Book of Cowboys. Harper, 1910. VG. $12.
Flying U's Last Stand. Grosset & Dunlap, 1915. Good. $4.
Rim O' The World. Little Brown, 1919 1st ed. VG. $35.
The Eagle's Wing. Little Brown, 1924 1st edition. VG. $35.

BOWERS, CLAUDE. *Jefferson in Power*. Boston, 1936 1st ed. Illus. Good. $15.

BOWLES, ELLA. *Homespun Handicrafts*. Philadelphia and London, 1931, 1st ed. VG in worn dust jacket. $20.

BOWLES, SAMUEL. *Across the Continent: A Summer's Journey to the Rocky Mountains*. Springfield, MA, 1865. Map torn, bumped, shaken. $65. Another, VG. $85.

BOWMAN, ELIZABETH S. *Land of the High Horizons*. Southern Pubs, 1938 1st ed. Good. $15.

BOWMAN, HEATH. *Hoosier, A Composite Portrait*. Bobbs-Merrill, 1941 1st ed. VG in dust jacket. $24.

BOY MECHANIC. 1,000 THINGS FOR BOYS TO DO. Popular Mechanics, Chicago, 1913-15. 3 vols. Good-VG. $20-$30 each.

BOY SCOUT BOOKS: *Boy Scouts of America Handbook for Boys*. Doubleday, Page, 1911 1st ed. Fair. $25.
The Boy Scouts Year Book. NY, 1920. F. K. Mathiews, editor. VG in worn dust jacket. $95.
Pioneering Merit Badge Series. BSA, June, 1932. $20.
National & World Jamborees in Pic. NY, 1937. VG. $30.
Handbook for Scout Masters. No place, 1938. 2 vols. $45. 1957 edition. Very Good. $8.
Boy Scout Handbook. 1928 ed. with N. Rockwell cover. $25. NY, 1943 and 1944, 36th & 37th printing. Rockwell covers $5-$15. 1950s-1970s eds. in average cond. $5-$8.
Handbook for Boys. 1913. $40. 1949-1955. Fine. $12 ea.
Fieldbook for Boys and Men. 1970 edition. 560 pgs. $8.

BOYD, JAMES P. *Life of General Sherman*. Publisher's 1891 1st ed. Very Good. $20.
Marching On. New York, 1927 1st ed. VG-Fine. $20-$40.
Drums. NY, 1928 1st ed. Wyeth illus. Fine in DJ. $200. Same, 1929. No dust jacket. Very Good. $40.
Long Hunt. NY, 1930. One of 260, signed. Good. $135.

BOYD, THOMAS. *Poor John Fitch, Inventor of the Steamboat*. Putnam, 1937 1st edition. Very Good no dust jacket. $14.

BOYER, MARY G. *Arizona in Literature*. Glendale, CA. A. H. Clark, 1935. VG-Fine. $75.

BOYINGTON, G. "PAPPY". *Baa Baa Black Sheep*. NY, 1958. Good plus. $18-$20.

BOYKIN, EDWARD. *Congress and the Civil War*. McBride, 1955. Good. $15.

BOYLE, KAY. *Monday Night*. NY, 1938 1st. F in DJ. $65.

BOY'S KING ARTHUR AND HIS KNIGHTS OF THE ROUND TABLE. NY, 1880. Gilt dec. cover. Faded. $35.

THE BOY'S STORY BOOK. NY, 1859. Anon. Hand-colored engravings. Worn. $200.

BRACKETT, OLIVER. *English Furniture Illustrated*. NY, 1950 Revised ed. 240 plates. Very Good. $50.

BRADDON, MARY ELIZABETH. *Lady Audley's Secret*. Tauschnitz, 1862 1st ed. Very Good. $60.

BRADEN, JAMES A. *The Auto-Boys on the Road*. 1920, Saalfield. Very Good. $7.
Far Past the Frontier. Saalfield, 1902. Good. $4. Same, 1936 ed. Very Good in dust jacket. $12.

BRADFORD, ERNIE. *Four Centuries of European Jewelry*. London, 1967. Illus. Good-VG in dust jacket. $40.

BRADFORD, GAMALIEL. *Confederate Portraits*. Boston, 1914 1st ed. Very Good. $35.
Bare Souls. No place, 1924 1st ed. Good. $7.
Lee, The American. Boston, 1927. Good. $20.

BRADFORD, NED (Editor). *Battles and Leaders of the Civil War*. Fairfax, 1979 1st ed. Illus. Fine in DJ. $16. Another, Hawthorn, 1956. $20.

BRADFORD, NED & PAM. *Boston's Locke-Ober Cafe*. History and recipes. New York, 1978 1st edition. Very Good in dust jacket. $35.

BRADFORD, WILLIAM. *The Bradford History of Plymouth Plantation*. Boston. VG. $75. 1898 & 1899 eds. Good. $45. 1953 ed. $15.

BRADLEY, ALICE. *The Candy Cook Book*. Boston, 1917, Little Brown 1st ed. Good-VG. $20. 1924 ed. Worn. $12.

BRADLEY, MARY ALICE. *Electric Refrigerator Recipes & Menus*. 1927 1st ed. General Elec. Co. Good. $25. 1927-1929 3rd to 5th editions. Good-VG. $10-$20.

BRADLEY, M. GENERAL OMAR. *A Soldier's Story*. New York, 1951. Signed by author. Good plus. $130. Another, unsigned in Good cond. $15.

BRADLEY, HELEN. *And Miss Carter Wore* Pink. NY, 1972 1st ed. Illus. by author. Fine in dust jacket. $30.

BRADLEY, J. *Accounts of Religious Revivals in Many Parts of the United States*. Albany, NY, 1819. VG. $285.

BRADLEY, VAN ALLEN. *Gold in Your Attic*. NY, Fleet Pubs., 1958 2nd printing. Fine in DJ. $25. G. ex-lib. $10.
Music for Millions. Regnery, 1957 1st ed. Fine in DJ. $14.

BRADLEY, WILL (Book Designer). *The Leather Bottle*. Concord MA, circa 1902. Fine. $100.
A Dissertation Upon Roast Pig. By Charles Lamb. Concord MA, circa 1902. Fine. $100.
A Love Song. Concord MA, 1903. Fine. $100.

BRADLEY, WILL (Illustrator). *Rip Van Winkle*. By Washington Irving. NY, 1897. Very Good. $125.
The Open Boat. By Stephen Crane. NY, 1898 1st edition. Near Fine. $750.

BRAIDER, DONALD. *The Niagara*. Rivers of America Series. NY, 1972 1st ed. Very Good. $20.

BRAINE, JOHN. *Room at the Top*. London, 1957 1st ed. Author's 1st book. Near Fine in dust jacket. $50.

BRAINE, SHEILA. *Moving Animals: A Novel Book for Children*. London, circa 1900. 6 chromolithos. Pages detached but working pull-tabs. $88 auction.

BRAIVE, MICHEL. *The Photograph: A Social History*. NY, 1966 1st American ed. Ex-library. $35.

BRAKE, HEZEKIAH. *On Two Continents, a Long Life's Experience*. Topeka, Crane & Co., 1896. VG. $75.

BRAMWELL, CLARENCE. *The Construction of a Gasoline Motor Vehicle*. NY, Grossman, 1901 only ed. Rare. $175.

BRANCH, E. DOUGLAS. *The Cowboy and His Interpreters*. NY, 1926 1st ed. Illus. by Will James, C. M. Russell and Joe de Young. Very Good. $250.
Hunting of the Buffalo. Appleton, 1929 1st ed. VG. $50.
Sentimental Years, 1836-1860. Appleton, 1934. G. $15.

BRAND, MAX. *Destry Rides Again*. Dodd Mead, 1930. Bumped corners. Ink inside cover, o/w VG. $100.
The Jackson Trail. NY, 1932. Minor cover wear. $30.
Happy Jack. Dodd Mead, 1936 1st ed. Library stamp, o/w Good. $60. Another, Good in DJ. $40
The Streak. NY, 1937 1st ed. Near Fine in DJ. $125.
Singing Guns. NY, 1938 1st ed. Good in DJ. $60.
The Dude. Grosset & Dunlap, 1940. Good in DJ. $18.
Max Brand's Best Stories. NY, 1967 1st ed. Robert Easton, editor. VG plus in dust jacket. $18.
Dead Man's Treasure. NY, 1973. 1st ed. Fine in DJ. $30.
Collected Works. Published by Walter Black. 29 vols., No date. Mint in packing boxes. $245.

BRAND, MILLEN. *The Outward Room*. NY, 1937 1st ed. Fine in dust jacket. $45.
Local Lives: Poems About The Pennsylvania Dutch. NY, 1975 1st ed. Good. $10.

BRANDEIS, MADELINE. *The Little Indian Weaver*. Grosset & Dunlap, 1928 motion picture edition. Good. $10.
Little Rose of the Mesa. Grosset & Dunlap, 1935 ed. Decorative cover. Good-VG. $12.

BRANDT, BILL (Photographer). *Camera In London*. London, NY, 1948 1st ed. Fine in DJ. $250.
Literary Britain. London, 1951 1st ed. VG in DJ. $125.
Perspective of Nudes. NY, 1961 1st ed. 90 Photos. VG in torn dust jacket. $175.
Shadow of Light. NY, 1977 1st American ed. expanded from British ed. 1966. 144 b/w plates. VG in DJ. $75.
Nudes, 1945-1980. Boston, 1980 1st ed. Fine in DJ. $85.
Portraits. Austin TX, 1982 1st ed. Fine in DJ. $40.

BRANT, JOHN. *True Story of the Lindberg Kidnapping*. NY, 1932 1st ed. VG in DJ. $35.

BRASHER, REX. *Birds and Trees of North America*. NY, 1962 2 vols. 740 color plates. Bumped, o/w VG. $125.

BRASSAI (Photographer). *Camera in Paris*. London, NY, 1949 1st ed. Light foxing, o/w Fine in DJ. $285.
The Secret Paris of the Thirties. NY, 1976 1st American ed. Fine in dust jacket. $75.

BRASSEY, LADY. *Around the World in the Yacht Sunbeam*. NY, 1878. Original blue cloth boards. $18. Rebacked, new endpapers. Very Good. $25.

BRATON, O. S. *Three Years With Quantrill: A True Story*. McCorkle, circa 1914. Brite covers. Very Fine. $35.

BRAYLEY, ARTHUR. *A Complete History of the Boston Fire Department, 1630-1888*. Boston, 1889 1st ed. Good, hinges cracked, rubbing. $125.
History of the Granite Industry of New England. 2 vols. Boston, 1913 1st ed. Very Good. $125.

BRAYTON, MATTHEW. *The Indian Captive. A narrative of the adventures and sufferings of Matthew Brayton, in his thirty-four years of captivity among the Indians.* Cleveland, 1860 1st ed. $750-$1,200. 2nd edition, Fostoria, OH, 1896. $100-$150.

BRAZER, ESTHER STEVENS. *Early American Decoration.* Springfield MA, 1947 2nd ed. VG in fine DJ. $100. 1961 3rd ed. As new in dust jacket. $35.

BREARLEY, H. C. *Time Telling Through the Ages.* NY, 1919. Illus. Very Good. $45.

BREASTED, JAMES HENRY. *Development of Religion & Thought in Ancient Egypt.* NY, 1912 1st Am. ed. VG. $27.

BREHME, H. *Picturesque Mexico.* NY, 1925. 256 Photos. Fading. Backstrip weak. $25.

BREIHAN, CARL W. *The Complete and Authentic Life of Jesse James.* NY, 1953 1st ed. Fine in DJ. $30.
Quantrill and His Civil War Guerrillas. NY, 1959. G. $8.
The Bandit Belle. Seattle, 1970. Illus. VG. $15.
Billy the Kid: Date With Destiny. Seattle, 1970 1st. F. $40.

BREMER, FREDRIKA. *The Homes of the New World: Impressions of America.* NY, 1853 2 vols, 1st American ed. Some water staining. Near VG. $125. VG. $300.

BRENNEN, JOSEPH. *Parker Ranch of Hawaii, Saga of a Ranch and a Dynasty.* Day, 1974 1st ed. Fine in DJ. $15.

BREWER, REV. E. COBHAM. *Character Sketches of Romance Fiction and Drama.* Selmar Hess, 1892 1st ed. 4 vols, ½ leather. Very Good. $85.

BREWER'S DICTIONARY OF PHRASE AND FABLE. NY, late 1940s. Very Good. $25.

BREWINGTON, M. V. *Shipcarvers of North America.* Barre VT, 1962. Dust jacket stained. $50-$85.

BRIAZAK, NORMAN J. *The UFO Guidebook.* Citadel, 1978 1st ed. Fine in dust jacket. $12.

BRICE, WALLACE. *History of Fort Wayne.* IN, 1868 1st ed. Biographies of F. W. Pioneers. 357 pgs. G-VG. $95-$125.

BRIDGE, ANN. *The Dangerous Islands.* NY, 1963 1st ed. Fine in dust jacket. $20.
The Episode at Toledo. NY, 1966 1st American ed. Fine in dust jacket. $18.

BRIDGMAN, L. J. *Guess?* A book of riddles. NY, Caldwell, 1901. Very Good. $95 up.
Santa Claus Club. NY, Caldwell, 1907. VG. $25 up.
Mother Goose & Her Wild Beast Show. Boston, 1900. Very Good. $20.

A BRIEF DESCRIPTION OF WESTERN TEXAS. Anon. (W. G. Kingsbury). San Antonio, TX. $900-$1,500.

BRIGGS, RAYMOND. *Mother Goose Treasury.* Coward McCann, 1966 1st American ed. VG. $50-$75.
Father Christmas Goes on Holiday. NY, 1975 1st American ed. Fine in dust jacket. $35.
The Snowman. New York, 1978 1st American edition. Fine in dust jacket. $60.
Unlucky Wally Twenty Years On. London, 1989 1st ed. Illus. by author. Very Good. $20.

BRIGHAM, CLARENCE. *Paul Revere's Engravings.* NY, 1969. Full page plates. VG-Fine. $65-$120.

BRIGHT, ROBERT. *The Friendly Bear.* Doubleday, 1957 1st ed. Very Good in torn dust jacket. $20.

BRILLAT-SAVARIN. *The Handbook of Dining.* NY, 1865. VG. $50. Another, Fine. $150.
The Handbook of Gastronomy. NY, 1884 and Boston 1915. Good-VG. $120-$175 ea.

BRININSTOOL, E. A. *Trail Dust of a Maverick.* Los Angeles, 1921 2nd ed. Inscribed. $75.
Fighting Red Cloud's Warriors. Columbus OH, 1926 1st ed. Near Fine. $55.
A Trooper With Custer. Hunter-Trader-Trapper Co., 1925. Orig. gold cloth. VG. $60. 1926 2nd ed. VG. $25-$35. 1952 Bonanza reprint, dust jacket. $16.

BRINK, CAROL RYRIE. *Mademoiselle Misfortune.* NY, 1936. Reprint. Kate Seredy illus. VG in worn DJ. $12.
Baby Island. NY, 1937 1st ed. H. Sewell illus. Fine. $65.
Lad With a Whistle. Macmillan, 1941 1st ed. Robert Ball illus. Very Good in dust jacket. $25.

HANS BRINKER OR THE SILVER SKATES. NY, McLoughlin, no date. May Post illus. Foxing, spots. $50.

BRINNIN, JOHN M. *The Sorrows of Cold Stone.* Poems 1940-50. Dodd Mead, 1951 1st printing. Rubbed, in worn dust jacket, o/w Very Good. $45.

BRITTEN, MRS. EMMA HARDINGE. *Nineteenth Century Miracles.* (A study of spiritualism). NY, 1884. VG. $75.

BROBECK, FLORENCE. *The Best-Of-All Cook Book.* Chicago, 1960. $15-$20.

BROCK, ALICE MAY. *Alice's Restaurant Cookbook.* Random House, 1969 1st edition. with record. $25-$35. 4th edition, same year. Very Good in dust jacket. No record. $12-$15.

BRODER, PATRICIA J. *Taos: A Painter's Dream.* Boston, 1980. Very Good in dust jacket. $200.

BRODIE, FAWN M. *No Man Knows My History, Joseph Smith*. Knopf, 1963 7th ed. Fine, no dust jacket. $15.

BROEHL, W. G. II. *John Deere's Company - The History of*. NY, 1984, Doubleday. 890 pgs. VG in DJ. $39.

BRODERICK, JAMES. *Galileo, the Man, His Work, His Misfortunes*. London, 1964. VG in dust jacket. $20.

BROLASKI, HARRY. *Easy Money*. Gambling. 1911. 328 pgs. Very Fine. $100 auction. 1936 ed. of 96 pages. $50.

BROMFIELD, LOUIS. *The Green Bay Tree*. NY, 1924 1st ed. Author's 1st book, Good plus. $50.
The Rains Came. NY, 1937. Very Good. $5.
Mrs. Parkington. NY, 1943. Good in DJ. $5.
The Farm. 1945 edition. Tower Books. Good in DJ. $8.
What Became of Anna Bolton? London, 1945 1st English ed. Very Good in torn dust jacket. $20.
Out of the Earth. NY, 1950 1st ed. Illus. VG in DJ. $20.

BRONTE, CHARLOTTE (Currer Bell). *The Professor*. NY, 1857 1st American ed. Good-VG. $75-$100.
Twelve Adventurers and Other Stories. London, 1925. A Fine copy, $20.
Jane Eyre. Paris, 1923 3rd ed. E. Gabin illus. $195. NY, 1943, Random House. Very Good. $12.
The Professor, A Tale. NY, Harper, 1857 1st American ed. Orig. purple cloth. Sunning spine o/w VG. $93 auction.

BRONTE, EMILY (Ellis Bell). *Wuthering Heights*. London, 1907 paperbound. VG. $75. London, 1905, J. M. Dent. Edmund Dulac illus. Fine. $20. 1931, Random House. Fine. $21. 1943, Random House. VG. $12.

BROOKE, IRIS. *English Costume from the 14th Through the 19th Century*. NY, 1937. Fine in worn DJ. $50.

BROOKES, L. ELLIOTT. *The Automobile Hand Book*. Chicago, Drake, 1905 1st ed. Very Good. $35-$60.

THE BROOKLYN DODGERS ANNUAL VICTORY BOOK. 1942 edition. $600. 1941 edition. $250.

BROOKS, GWENDOLYN. *A Street in Bronzeville*. NY, 1945 1st ed. Author's 1st book. VG in DJ. $375.
In the Mecca. Harper, 1968. Inscribed. N F in DJ. $65.
The Tiger Who Wore White Gloves. Chicago, 1974 1st ed. Paperbound. Cover crease, o/w Fine. $100.

BROOKS, JOE. *Bass Bug Fishing*. No place 1947 1st edition. Very Good in dust jacket. $20.
The Complete Book of Fly Fishing. No place, 1958 1st ed. Fine in dust jacket. $13.
Fly Fishing. No place, 1966 1st ed. Fine in DJ. $15.
Salt Water Game Fishing. 1968 1st edition. Very Good in dust jacket. $15.

BROOKS, JOHN. *The Fate of the Edsel and Other Business Adventures*. NY, 1963 1st ed. VG in dust jacket. $15.
The Telephone. The First Hundred Years. Harper & Row, 1976 1st ed. Fine in dust jacket. $10-$15.

BROOKS, NOAH. *First Across the Country: The Story of the Exploring Expedition*. Lewis & Clark, 1804-1806. NY, 1901 1st ed. One of 1,050 copies. Very Good. $75.
The Boy Emigrants. Scribner's, 1929. Harvey Dunn illus. Fine in dust jacket. $25.

BROOKS, RICHARD. *The Brick Foxhole*. NY, 1945. Author's 1st book. Very Good in dust jacket. $125.

BROOKS, WALTER. *Freddy the Pied Piper*. NY, 1946. 1st ed. Kurt Wiese illus. Good. $40.
Freddy the Magician. NY, 1947 1st ed. Kurt Wiese illus. Good. $40.

BROSNAN, CORNELIUS. *Jason Lee: Prophet of New Oregon*. Macmillan, 1932 1st ed. VG, no DJ. $15.

BROSSARD, CHANDLER. *Who Walk in Darkness*. NY, 1952 1st ed. Author's 1st book. Near Fine in DJ. $75.
The Spanish Scene. NY, 1968 1st ed. VG in DJ. $28.

BROUGH, JAMES. *"We Were Five" The Dionne Quintuplets Story*. Simon & Schuster, 1964 Book Club edition. Very Good in dust jacket. $15. No dust jacket. $8.

BROUGHTON, JAMES. *The Playground*. Center Press, 1949 1st ed. Zev illus. VG in worn DJ. $50.

BROWN, ABBIE FARWELL. *A Pocketful of Posies*. Houghton-Mifflin, 1902 1st ed. Fanny Cory illus. VG. $15.

BROWN, ALICE. *Meadow-Grass*. Boston, 1895 1st edition. VG. $65. Same, 1896. Good. $15.

BROWN, BELMORE. *Conquest of Mount McKinley*. Houghton Mifflin, revised ed., 1951. Fine in DJ. $15.

BROWN, BOB. *You Gotta Live*. London, 1932 1st ed. Presentation copy by author. VG in repaired DJ. $150.
The Complete Book of Cheese. 1955. $15-$20.

BROWN, CORA, ROSE and BOB. *America Cooks*. NY, 1949. Good-VG. $12-$15.

BROWN, DEE. *Bury My Heart at Wounded Knee*. NY, 1970 1st ed. VG in dust jacket. $25.
Creek Mary's Blood. NY, 1980 1st edition. Very Good in dust jacket. $20.

BROWN, DEE and MARTIN SCHMITT. *Trail Driving Days*. Scribners, NY, 1952 1st ed. VG in DJ. $75. 1952 reprint, Bonanza. Very Good in dust jacket. $15.

BROWN, G. S. *First Steps to Golf*. Boston, ca 1924. F. $77.

BROWN, HARRIETT. *Grandmother Brown's Hundred Years, 1827-1927*. Little Brown, 1929 1st ed. VG. $14.

BROWN, HELEN. *Helen Brown's West Coast Cook Book*. Boston, 1952 1st ed. Ward Ritchie design. VG in DJ. $15. *Helen Brown's Holiday Cook Book*. Boston, 1952 1st ed. M. F. K. Fisher Introduction. VG in DJ. $15.

BROWN, JOHN. *Twenty-Five Years a Parson in the Wild West*. Fall River MA, 1896. Self-published. Good-Very Good. $100-$150.

BROWN, JOHN M. D. *Rab and His Friends and Marjorie Fleming*. Boston, 1876. Illus. Near Fine. $65.

BROWN, MARCIA. *The Sun: A Tale from Russia*. NY, 1972 1st ed. Illus. by author. Near Fine in DJ. $20. *All Butterflies*. NY, 1974 1st ed. Illus. Fine in DJ. $75. *The Blue Jackal*. New York, 1977. Illustrated. Near Fine in dust jacket. $25.

BROWN, MARCIA (Illustrator). *Cinderella*. By Charles Perrault. NY, 1954. Signed by Brown. VG plus. $90. *Shadow*. By Cendras. NY, 1982 1st ed. Fine in DJ. $30.

BROWN, MARGARET WISE. *The Indoor Noisy Book*. Scott, 1942. L. Weisgard illus. No backstrip, o/w VG. $14. *The Golden Egg Book*. Simon & Schuster, 1947. L. Weisgard illus. VG. $25. Good. $12. *Goodnight Moon*. NY, 1947. Clement Hurd illus. VG. $12. *The Sleepy Little Lion*. NY, 1947. Ylla photos. Good. $22. *The Quiet Noisy Book*. New York, 1950. Very Good in fair dust jacket. $15. *The Dark Wood of the Golden Birds*. NY, 1950. Leonard Weisgard illus. Very Good in dust jacket. $50. *The Duck*. NY, 1952 1st ed. Photo illus. VG. $50. *The Color Kittens*. Little Golden Book. 1958. Good. $15. *The Steamroller*. NY, 1974 1st ed. Evaline Ness illus. Fine in dust jacket. $30. *The Fish With the Deep Sea Smile*. NY, 1988. Reprint. Roberta B. Rausch illus. As new in dust jacket. $30.

BROWN, MARION. *The Southern Cook Book*. Chapel Hill NC, 1951 1st ed. Very Good in dust jacket. $25.

BROWN, MARSHALL. *Wit & Humor, a Choice Collection*. Chicago, 1879. Worn, shaken. $16. *Wit & Humor of Bench & Bar*. Chicago, 1899. G. $30.

BROWN, NELLIE. *Recipes From Old Hundred*. 200 years of New England cooking. New York, circa 1930. $15-$20.

BROWN, ROBERT C. *The Remarkable Adventures of Christopher Poe*. Chicago, 1913 1st ed. M. Wilson Craig illustrator. Good. $125.

BROWN, THOMAS. *The Taxidermist's Manual*. NY, Orange Judd, no date. American revised version of 1870s English edition. Rubbed. $45.

BROWN, WILLIAM H. *The History of the First Locomotives in America*. NY, 1871 1st ed. Inscribed 10 plates, six folding. Very Good. $300. Another, with broken binding. Fair-Good. $100.

BROWNE, BELMORE. *The Conquest of Mount McKinley*. NY, 1913, Putnam's. 1st ed. Very Good. $100.

BROWNE, CHARLES. *The Gun Club Cook Book*. NY, 1930 1st ed. VG. $40. Same, 1931 revised ed. L. Holton illus. Near VG. $35. 1939 edition, Very Good. $10.

BROWNE, D. J. *The American Poultry Yard. Origin History of Breeds*. NY, C. M. Saxon, 1850 1st ed. Numerous woodcut illus. Good-VG. $88 auction.

BROWNE, GEORGIANA. *Water Babies' Circus and other Stories*. Boston, 1940. Walt Disney Studio illus. VG. $25.

BROWNE, J. *Four Years in Secessaria: Adventures Within and Beyond Union Lines*. Hartford CT, 1865 1st ed. Foxing, o/w Very Good. $40.

BROWNE, J. ROSS. *Adventures in the Apache Country*. NY, 1869 1st ed. Worn spine, signatures loose, o/w Good. $225. Another, rebound with original backstrip. $150. 3 vols. Travel journals, writings. pub. 1965-1969. $25 each.

BROWNE, JUNIUS HENRI. *Great Metropolis: A Mirror of New York*. Hartford, 1869. Very Good. $20-$35.

BROWNING, ELIZABETH BARRETT. *Aurora Leigh*. NY, 1857 1st American ed. Good to VG. $225. *Napoleon III in Italy and Other Poems*. New York, 1860 1st edition. Near Fine. $90. *Sonnets From the Portuguese*. NY, 1936. Willy Pogany illus. 8 tipped-in color plates. Fine in vg DJ. $125. Another, NY, 1948 LEC. VG in orig. box. $80.

BROWNING, JOHN and CURT CENTRY. *John M. Browning, American Gunmaker*. 1964 1st edition, Doubleday. Very Good. $55.

BROWNING, ROBERT. *The Ring and the Book*. London, 1868 1st ed. 4 vols. Repaired hinges. Good plus. $275. *Fifine at the Fair*. London, 1872 1st ed. VG. $25. *The Pied Piper of Hamelin*. London, 1919. Greenaway illus. Near Fine. $275. G & D , 1936. Good-VG $20-$40. Lippincott, 1934, Rackham ilus. $150. 1939. $35.

BROWNLOW, WILLIAM G. *Sketches of the Rise, Progress and Decline of Secession*. Philadelphia, 1862 1st ed. Covers rubbed, fading. $40.

BROWNS, G. *The Trial of Captain Kidd*. London, 1920 1st ed. Notable British Trials Series. VG in DJ. $45.

BRUCE, C. G. *The Assault on Mount Everest*. NY, 1923 1st American ed. Illus. Near VG. $125.

BRUCE, LENNY. *How to Talk Dirty and Influence People*. Chicago, 1965 1st ed. Fine. $70.

BRUFF, J. GOLDSBOROUGH. *Gold Rush Journals*. Columbia, 1949. VG in DJ. $85. Same, 1st ed., 1944. 2 vols. Very Good. $200.

BRUGUIERE, FRANCIS. *San Francisco*. Crocker, 1918 1st ed. Fine in dust jacket. $132 auction.

BRUNDAGE, FRANCIS. *What Happened to Tommy*. 1921, Stecher. Good. $22.

BRUNO, HARRY. *Story of American Aviation*. NY, Halcyon, 1944 ed. Very Good. $14.

BRUNNER, JOHN. *Devil's Work*. NY, 1970 1st ed. VG in clipped dust jacket. $35.

BRUNSWICK-BALKE-COLLENDER CO. *Handbook of Rules for Billiards*. New York, 1911. Good-VG. $60-$75.

BRUNTON, PAUL. *Quest of the Overself*. London, about 1930. Very Good. $45.

BRYAN, DANIEL. *The Mountain Muse: Comprising The Adventures of Daniel Boone*. Harrisonburg, VA, 1813. Tiny 16mo. Darkened, scuffed, fair. $75.

BRYANT, BILLY. *Children of Ol' Man River*. Lee Furman, 1936 1st ed. Good, rebound. $15.

BRYANT, CHARLES. *History of the Great Massacre by Sioux Indians in Minnesota*. Cincinnati, Rickey & Carroll, 1864 2nd ed. Cover wear, foxing, loose pgs. $60.

BRYANT, EDWIN. *What I Saw in California: Journal of a Tour by Emigrant Route, 1846*. Santa Ana, Fine Arts Press, 1936. Very Good. $90-$120.

BRYANT, WILLIAM CULLEN (Editor). *Picturesque America*. NY, 1872. 2 vols. Lavishly illustrated with steel and wood engravings. Good-VG. $195-$350. Slightly scuffed and light foxing. 2 vols. at auction. $220.

BRYANT, WILLIAM CULLEN (In Magazines). *North American Review*. Sept 1817 "Thanatopsis". $75-$85. Same, March 1818. "To a Waterfowl". $35-$45.

BRYCE, GEORGE. *The Remarkable History of the Hudson's Bay Company*. NY, 1901 3rd ed. Near Fine. $45. 1968 Reprint. Very Good. $20.

BRYCE, JAMES. *The American Commonwealth*. London, 1888 3 vols. 1st ed with suppressed chapter on Tweed. Spotted edges, some rubbing, o/w VG. $150.

BUCHAN, SIR JOHN. *Sir Walter Raleigh*. London, 1897. Endpaper foxed, o/w Very Good. $65.
Prester John. Doran, 1910. Henry Pitz illus. VG. $30.
The Thirty-Nine Steps. London, 1915 1st ed. Good. $150.
The Watcher By the Threshhold. NY, 1918. Later ed., with three added stories. Very Good. $35.
A History of the Great War. Boston, 1922. Limited ed. Signed. Very Good. $135.
History of the Great War. Boston, 1922 4 vols. VG. $125.
A Book of Escapes and Hurried Journeys. Boston, 1923. Illus. Fine. $35.
The Three Hostages. Bos. 1925. 1st Amer. ed. VG. $30.
Courts of the Morning. London, 1929 1st ed. VG. $55.
The Island of Sheep. London, 1936 1st ed. F in DJ. $200.
Mountain Meadow. Boston, 1941. Very Good in DJ. $25.

BUCHAN, WILLIAM. *Domestic Medicine*. Williams, 1828. 495 pgs., Leather worn, o/w Very Good. $100.

BUCHANAN, LAMONT, Ed. *A Pictorial History of the Confederacy*. New York, 1951 1st edition. Worn covers, o/w Good. $25. Bonanza, 1963 reprint. Very Good in chipped dust jacket. $20.

BUCK, FRANK. *Bring'Em Back Alive*. NY, 1930 1st ed. Photos. Fine. $45.

BUCK, FRANKLIN. *A Yankee Trader in the Gold Rush*. Boston, 1930. Very Good in dust jacket. $50-$65.

BUCK, PEARL S. *The Good Earth*. 1936 1st ed., John Day Pub. 1st printing ("fleas" spelled "flees" on pg. 100) $350-$600. Photoplay edition, Grosset & Dunlap, 1936. $75.
Fighting Angel. 1936 1st ed. in dust jacket. $28.
The Patriot. 1939 1st ed. in dust jacket. $16.
Dragon Seed. John Day, 1942. Good. $10.
Death in the Castle. New York, 1965 1st edition. Fine in dust jacket. $20.
Oriental Cookbook. NY, 1972 1st ed. $25-$35.
Christmas Miniature. John Day, 1957 1st ed. juvenile. VG in worn dust jacket. $25.

BUCK, SOLON J. *Travel and Description, 1765-1865*. Together With a List of County Histories, Atlases and Biographical Collections and a List of Territorial and State Laws. Springfield, IL, 1914 1st ed. Very Good. $50.

BUCKBEE, EDNA BRYANT. *The Saga of Old Tuolumne*. NY, Press of the Pioneers, 1935 1st ed. VG. $75-$95.
Pioneer Days of Angels Camp. CA, 1932 Ltd ed. VG. $65.

BUCKE, RICHARD MAURICE. *Cosmic Consciousness*. NY, 1923 4th corrected ed. Good. $25.

BUCKINGHAM, NASH. *De Shootinest Gentlemen*. Derry-dale Press, 1934 1st ed. One of 950 copies. Fine. $600. NY, 1941 1st separate ed. Fine in DJ. $175. Putnam, 1943 edition. VG. $50. Nelson, 1961 ed. VG in dust jacket. $45.
Mark Right! Derrydale Press, 1936. One of 1,250 copies. NF. $300. Another, Putnam's, no date. VG in DJ. $65.
Ole Miss. Derrydale Press, 1937. One of 2,500 copies. Near Mint. $400. Putnam's, 1946 edition. VG. $75.
Blood Lines. Derrydale Press, 1938 1st ed. One of 1,250 copies. VG. $165-$250. Another, broken hinge. $30. NY, 1947 1st trade ed. Fine in DJ. $45.
Tattered Coat. Putnam's, 1944. 1 of 995 cpy. Signed with insc. F in acetate wrapper. $165. Same, 2nd ed. VG. $30.
Game Bag. NY, 1945 1st ed. One of 1,250 copies. Signed, VG. $160. Putnam's, 1945 1st trade ed. in DJ. $25-$45.
Hallowed Years. Harrisburg PA, 1953 1st ed. Very Good in dust jacket. $110-$145.

BUCKMASTER, HENRIETTA. *Let My People Go: Story of the Underground Railroad*. 1941 1st ed. VG. $45.

BUCKLEY, JAMES. *Buckley's New Banjo Book, Complete with Instructions*. Boston, 1860. Good-VG. $50.

BUDGE, E. A. WALLIS. *The Mummy*. Cambridge, England, 1893 1st ed. Illus. NF. $75. 1974 reprint. Fine in DJ. $15.
The Book of the Dead. London, 1898 3 vols. VG. $150.
Osiris and Egyptian Resurrection. London, 1911 2 vols. 1st ed. Illus. Fine. $275.
The Nile: Notes for Travelers in Egypt and Sudan. London, 1912 12th ed. $35-$75.
From Fetish to Gods in Ancient Egypt. Oxford Univ. Press, 1934 1st ed. VG plus. $175.

BUECHNER, FREDERICK. *A Long Day's Dying*. NY, 1949 1st ed. Very Good in dust jacket. $50.
Return of Ansel Gibbs. NY, 1958 1st ed. VG in DJ. $40.
Sacred Journey: Spiritual Memoir. San Francisco, 1982 1st ed. Very Good. $20.

BUECHNER, THOMAS. *Norman Rockwell, Artist and Illustrator*. Abrams, 1970 1st ed. Fine in DJ. $150-$200. Same, no DJ. $75. 1983 edition. Fine in DJ. $60.

BUEL, J. W. *Life and Marvelous Adventures of Wild Bill. The Scout*. Chicago, 1880. $900-$1500.
Heroes of the Plains: or Lives & Adventures of Wild Bill, Buffalo Bill, etc. St Louis MO, 1881 1st ed. VG. $75-$85.
The Border Outlaws. St Louis, 1881 1st ed. has a separate title page in same book: "The Border Bandits". $75.

BUENGER, WALTER L. *Secession and the Union in Texas*. Univ. of Texas Press, 1984 1st ed. VG in DJ. $30.

BUFFALO COOKERY. Ladies Auxiliary, St. Lukes Sunday School, Wyoming. 1916 2nd ed., Brown & Whitaker, OH. Good-VG. $25-$35.

BUGIALLI GIULIAN. *Giuliano Bugialli's Classic Techniques of Italian Cooking*. NY, 1982. VG in DJ. $25.

BUGS BUNNY IN RISKY BUSINESS. Whitman, 1948 1st edition. Very Good. $15.

BUGS BUNNY & THE BIG RED APPLE. Whitman, 1950 1st edition. Fine. $9.

BUICK MOTOR CO. *Buick Owner's Manual*. 1933. 52 pgs. $15-$30. (Also see Catalog Section).

BUILDING STONE, BRICKWORK, LIGHTING. Intl Textbook Co. Scranton, PA, 1903. Good-VG. $10-$20.

BULAU, ALWIN. *Footprints of Assurance*. Macmillan, 1953. Firemarks, illustrated. Very Good. $15-$20.

BULEY, R. CARLYLE. *The Old Northwest, The Pioneer Period 1815-1840*. Indiana Univ. Press, 1983 4th printing. 2 vols. 1,320 pgs. $25.

BULLA, CLYDE ROBERT. *Moon Singer*. New York, 1969 1st edition. Inscribed by Trina Schart Hyman, illustrator. Very Fine in dust jacket. $40.

BULLARD, ROBERT LEE. *Personalities and Reminiscences of the War*. NY, 1925 1st ed. VG. $40-$65.

BULLOCK, JOHN. *The American Cottage Builder*. NY, 1854. Designs, plans. Good. $145.

BULWER-LYTTON, LORD EDWARD. *A Strange Story*. Boston, 1862 1st American ed. Very Good. $60.
The Ring of Anasis. New York, 1863 1st American edition. Very Good. $65.

BUNIN, IVAN. *The Well of Days*. NY, 1934 1st American ed. Near Very Good in dust jacket. $35.
The Elaghin Affair and Other Stories. NY, 1935 1st American ed. Very Good in dust jacket. $45.

BUNNER, HENRY C. *Love in Old Clothes*. NY, 1897. Illus. Very Good. $12.
Zadoc Pine & Other Stories. NY, no date, Good. $10.

BUNYAN, JOHN. *Pilgrim's Progress*. London, 1849, Chiswick Press. $300. Pickering 1849. Fair. $15. 1890s edition thermolitho plates. $30. NY, 1942 Heritage Press ed. $20. 1939 edition, Robert Lawson illus. $65. Various limited editions in fine bindings by famous illustrators, 1899-1949. $100-$500 and up.
Complete Works of John Bunyan. John Ball, 1850 revised edition. Good. $15.

BURBRIDGE, GEOFFREY and MARGARET. *Quasi-Stellar Objects*. San Francisco, 1967. VG in chipped DJ. $20.

BURD, CLARA M. (Illustrator). *Wonder Stories*. by C. S. Bailey. Milton Bradley, 1920. Very Good. $35.
Dickens' Stories About Children. Chicago, 1929 1st ed. Very Good in dust jacket. $50.
A Child's Garden of Verses. by R. L. Stevenson. Saalfield, 1930. Very Good in fair dust jacket. $65.

BURDETT, CHARLES. *Life of Kit Carson*. Philadelphia, 1869. Illus. Good-VG. $40. 1902 ed. $30.

BURDICK, ARTHUR. *The Mystic Mid-Region: Deserts of the Southwest*. NY, 1904 1st ed. Good-VG. $25-$50.

BURDICK, USHER. *The Last Battle of the Sioux Nation*. Fargo ND, 1929 1st ed. VG in dust jacket. $40.

BUREAU OF AMERICAN ETHNOLOGY-1886, 1889. GPO 1891 *Pueblo & Navajo Indians of New Mexico and Arizona*. Good. $95. Another, 1902-1903. GPO 1907. *Games of North American Indians*. 847 pgs. Good. $125. Another, 1882-1883 . GPO. 1886. *Pictographs, Pottery and Ceramic Art of the Zuni, Moki and Pueblo Indians*. VG. $150. 1884-85, 1888. *Chiriqui Textiles. Maya Codices, Osage, Eskimo*. Good. $95. Fair only brings half the value. Fine bindings, more. Many bear ex-library stamps. Other 1879-1908 editions in Good to Very Good condition fall in the $50-$85 range.

BURGESS, GELETT. *The Burgess Nonsense Book*. NY, 1901 1st ed. Illus. by author. Very Good. $150.
Goop Tales. NY, 1904 1st ed. illus. by author. Good. $45.
The Maxims of Methuselah. Stokes, 1907. L. D. Fletcher decorations. Good-VG. $35.
New Goops & How to Know Them. NY, 1951 2nd printing. Very Good. $20.

BURGESS, R. F. *The Sharks*. NY, 1970. VG in DJ. $10.

BURGESS, THORNTON W. *Old Mother West Wind*. NY, 1914 1st ed. Near Fine. $50. 1919. $20-$30.
How Unc' Billy Possum Met Buster Bear. Cole & Winthrop, 1914. Good-VG. $25.
Billy Mink. 1924 1st ed. in dust jacket. $50-$75.
The Adventures of Johnny Chuck. Boston, 1916. Harrison Cady illus. Near VG. $30.
The Adventurs of Buster Bear. Boston, 1916 1st ed. Harrison Cady illus. Good-VG. $20.
The Adventures of Prickly Porky. Boston, 1916. $15.
The Adventures of Paddy the Beaver. Boston, 1917. Harrison Cady illus. VG. $60. Same, G & D, 1917. $9.
The Adventures of Bobby Coon. 1918 1st ed. Little Brown. Good-VG. $17-$35.
Mother West Wind "When" Stories. Boston, 1917 1st edition. Very Good. $35.
Happy Jack. Little-Brown, 1918 1st ed. Harrison Cady illus. VG-Fine. $40.
The Burgess Bird Book. Boston, 1919 1st ed. Louis Agassiz color illus. Slight wear. Very Good. $60.

The Adventures of Poor Mrs. Quack. Boston, 1922. Harrison Cady illus. Near VG. $20.
Buster Bear's Twins. G & D, circa 1923. VG in DJ. $25.
The Burgess Animal Book for Children. Little Brown, 1920 1st ed. Good, light soil. $15.
White Foot, the Wood Mouse. Boston, 1922 1st. VG. $25.
Old Mother West Wind. Little-Brown, 1923. Cady illus. Very Good in dust jacket. $15.
The Adventures of Old Mr. Toad. Boston, 1925. Harrison Cady illus. Good in DJ. $20.
Mother West Wind's Animal Friends. Little Brown, 1924 ed. Good. $10.
Happy Jack Squirrel's Bright Idea. Egger, 1928. VG. $22.
The Adventures of Chatterer The Red Squirrel. Boston, 1928. Harrison Cady illus. Near Fine. $20.
Mother West Wind's Neighbors. Boston, 1930. VG in tattered dust jacket. $22.
The Adventures of Peter Cottontail. Little Brown, 1941 1st ed. Harrison Cady illus. Bedtime Story Book Series. Very Good in dust jacket. $46.
The Adventures of Grandfather Frog. Little Brown, 1946. Cady illus. Hinges weak, o/w VG in DJ. $30.
Old Mother West Wind. Boston, 1960. Golden Anniv. ed. Harrison Cady illus. Very Good. $15.
Now I Remember. Boston, 1960 3rd printing. Signed. VG in DJ. $30. An unsigned copy without DJ. Very Good. $10.

BURKE, BILLIE and CAMERON SHIPP. *With a Feather on My Nose*. Appleton, 1949. Inscribed by Burke. VG. $75.

BURKE, EDGAR. *American Dry Flies*. Derrydale Press. (1930s?) Ltd ed. VG-Fine. Auction. $375.

BURKE, JOHN. *Beatles in "A Hard Day's Night"*. Dell paperback, 1964 1st ed. Very Good. $15.

BURKETT, CHARLES. *Farm Crops*. NY, Orange Judd, 1910. Good-VG. $25-$35.
Farm Stock. NY, Orange Judd, 1910. Good-VG. $25-$35.

BURKETT, DOROTHY LOUISE. *Canary Birds, A Compleat Guide*. NY, Orange Judd, 1931 ed. Good-VG. $20.

BURMAN, BEN. *Children of Noah*. NY, 1951. One of 500, signed by author. $35.
Children of the North - Glimpses of Unknown America. Messner, 1951 1st ed. Fine in dust jacket. $14.

BURNAM, DANIEL and E. H. BENNETT. *Plan of Chicago*. Prepared by direction of Commercial Club. Chicago, 1909, Lakeside Press. One of 1,650 copies. Some wear. Rear cover dampstained. $650.

BURNETT, FRANCES HODGSON. *That Lass O'Lowrie's*. Scribner, 1877 1st ed. 1st state, author's 1st book. A. Fredericks illus. Good. $75-$100.
Sarah Crewe. Scribner's, 1888 1st ed. Brown cloth, gilt dec. Shelfworn, hinge crack. Good-VG. $40.

Little Lord Fauntleroy. The first edition, 1886, is identified by two points: 1, the insignia of the DeVinne press is on page 210, and 2, there are 14 pages (not 16) pages of ads in the back. Scribner's printed 10,000 copies of the 1st edition. 1st ed., 1st state (as above) $400-$750. 1st English ed. Nov, 1886. $150-$250. 2nd printing of 1886 ed. VG-Fine. $100-$150. NY, 1886. $30-$50. 1889 reprint by Scribner. VG. $15-$35. 1942 reprint. VG. $35. (The book is still in print today).

Editha's Burglar. Boston 1888 1st ed. Henry Sandham illus. Hinge cracked, foxing. $25. VG in DJ. $45.

The Pretty Sister of Jose. NY, 1889 1st ed. Good. $40.

One I Knew Best of All. Scribner, 1893 1st ed. VG. $60.

Piccino and Other Child Stories. NY, 1894 1st ed. Reginald Birch illus. VG. $25.

Two Little Pilgrims' Progress. NY, 1895 1st ed. VG. $40.

In the Closed Room. Grosset & Dunlap, 1904. Jessie Wilcox Smith illus. Good. $60-$95.

The Good Wolf. NY, 1908. Harold Sichel illus. Good. $25.

Little Hunchback Zia. Stokes, 1916 1st edition. Very Good in dust jacket. $40.

Queen Silver Bell. Century, 1906 1st ed. VG. $60.

The Land of the Blue Flower. NY, 1909 1st ed. S. De Ivanowski illus. Fine. $40.

My Robin. Stokes, 1912 1st ed. Good in poor DJ. $40.

The Children's Book. NY, 1915. Rubbed, o/w VG. $35.

A Little Princess. 1940 reprint. Birch illus. Good. $12. Philadelphia, 1963 reprint. Tasha Tudor illus. Fine in DJ. $30. Good. $18.

BURNETT, ALICE HALE. *A Day at the County Fair*. 1916, New York Book Co. Juvenile. Very Good. $7.

BURNETT, PETER H. *Recollections and Opinions of an Old Pioneer*. NY, Appleton, 1880 1st ed. Orig. brown cloth, gilt-dec. Good-VG. $120-$160.

BURNETT, W. R. *Little Caesar*. NY, London, 1929 1st ed. Author's 1st book. Very Good. $25.
Little Men, Big World. NY, 1951 1st ed. VG in DJ. $20.

BURNHAM, MAJOR FREDERICK. *Scouting on Two Continents*. NY, 1926 1st ed. (Some are signed.) $25-$45.

BURNINGHAM, JOHN. *Borka*. London, 1966 reprint. Kate Greenaway medal. Ex-library. Fine. $45.
Seasons. London, 1969 1st ed. Illus. by author. VG. $65.
Trubloff the Mouse Who Wanted to Play the Balalaika. NY, 1985. 1st ed. Fine in DJ. $25.

BURNS, GEORGE with HOBART, CYNTHIA. *I Love Her, That's Why!* 1955. 2nd printing. Illus. Good. $7.
Gracie: A Love Story. NY, 1988 3rd ed. Fine in DJ. $20.

BURNS, JOHN HORNE. *Lucifer With a Book*. London, 1949 1st ed. Very Good in dust jacket. $20.
The Cry of Children. NY, 1952 1st ed. VG in DJ. $15.

BURNS, WALTER NOBLE. *A Year With a Whaler*. NY, 1919 edition. Near VG. $30. 1913 1st ed. in DJ. $50-$100.
The Saga of Billy the Kid. Garden City, 1926 1st ed. VG-Fine. $35-$55. 1940s reprints by Grosset & Dunlap, and Garden City Pub. $25.
Tombstone. Doran, NY, 1929. Will James Illus. VG. $40.
The Robinhood of El Dorado. NY, 1932 1st ed. $15.

BURR, FRANK and R. J. HINTON. *Life of Gen. Phillip H. Sheridan*. Providence, Reid, 1888. Scuffed cover. $30.

BURROUGHS, EDGAR RICE. *Tarzan of the Apes*. New York, 1915 edition in dust jacket $75-$150. Same, no dust jacket. Good. $10-$15.
The Beasts of Tarzan. McClurg, 1916 1st ed. Must have 1916 on title page and March 1916 on copyright page with W. F. Hall Printing Company. $150-$300 without DJ. $3,000-$5,000 with a very good dust jacket. The A. L. Burt 1916 reprint. Good, no DJ. $9-$18.
The Return of Tarzan. A. C. McClurg, 1915 1st ed. VG, no DJ. $550. A. L. Burt reprint, 1915. VG in DJ. $15. NY, 1916 reprint. VG. $10. A. L. Burt, 1918 reprint. Good. $8-$10. 1920s reprint. St John illus. Red cloth covers. VG. $18. 1967 ed., Anderson & Moore illustrators. VG. $16.
A Princess of Mars. McClurg, 1917 1st ed. Exterior VG, several pages have torn corners. $250. Grosset & Dunlap reprint, 1917. Good-VG, no DJ. $12-$16.
Son of Tarzan. McClurg, 1917 1st ed., 1st issue. Worn cover. Good. $95. A. L. Burt, 1918 reprint. Fair-G. $8-$10.
Tarzan and the Jewels of Opar. McClurg, 1918 1st ed. Good. $125. 1919 2nd ed. VG. $85-$125.
Jungle Tales of Tarzan. Chicago, 1919 1st ed. A. G. McClurg. Hinge weak, o/w Good plus. $100. Same, Very Good to Fine. $475. Another, Good, no DJ. $25. Grosset & Dunlap reprints of the 1940s (not dated). $10-$15.
The Warlord of Mars. Chicago, 1919 1st ed. VG plus $450. Burroughs, 1947 reprint. No DJ. $14. G&D. $6.
Tarzan the Untamed. McClurg, 1920 1st ed., 1st printing. Good. $95. VG. $125.
Tarzan the Terrible. McClurg, 1921 1st ed. Good-Very Good. No dust jacket. $15-$25.
Thuvia, Maid of Mars. McClurg, 1920 1st ed. VG. $90. 1921 reprint. $30.
At the Earth's Core. McClurg, 1922. Worn, o/w VG. $75.
Tarzan and the Golden Lion. McClurg, 1923 1st ed., 1st state. Good $150-$200. Another, soiled cover. Good. $50. Grosset & Dunlap reprint. 1920s. VG. $15.
The Land That Time Forgot. Grosset & Dunlap, 1924 reprint. Good, No DJ. $15.
The Chessmen of Mars. Grosset & Dunlap 1924 reprint. VG in DJ. $85.
Tarzan and the Ant Men. Grosset & Dunlap, 1924. Allen St. John illus. Fine in good DJ. $40. Another, VG, no DJ. $10. 1940s reprint. VG, no DJ. $10.
Tarzan at the Earth's Core. Metropolitan, 1930 1st ed. Good. $125.
Tarzan the Invincible. Tarzana CA, 1931 1st ed. G. $38.

Tarzan and the City of Gold. ERB Inc. 1933 1st ed. VG in fair DJ. $250. Whitman, 1954 ed. VG. $6-$10.
Tarzan & the Leopard Men. ERB, 1935 1st ed. VG. $60.
Tarzan the Terrible. McClelland & Stewart (Canada). No date, 1st Canadian ed. Allen St. John illus. Good. $25.
Tarzan and the Lost Safari. Whitman, 1957 1st ed. VG-Fine. $9-$15.

BURROUGHS, EDGAR RICE (In Magazines). *Blue Book*. Feb, 1936. From "Tarzan & Immortal men", $35.
Argosy. Jan, 1939. Article with story. $10.

BURROUGHS, JOHN. *Locusts and Wild Honey*. Boston, 1879. Corners chipped. $40.
Camping & Tramping with Roosevelt. Boston & NY, 1907. Foxed. $12-$14. Same, VG-Fine. $25-$35.
My Boyhood. Doubleday, 1922 1st ed. $18.
Time and Change. Boston & NY, 1912 1st ed. Fine in nice dust jacket. $30.

BURSON, WILLIAM. *A Race for Liberty: or My Capture, Imprisonment & Escape*. Wellsville, OH, 1867. Orig. cloth. Good. $175.

BURT, STRUTHERS. *Powder River*. Rivers of America Series. NY, 1938 reprint. Fine in dust jacket. $19.

BURTON, KATHERINE. *Paradise Planters: The Story of Brook Farm*. NY, 1939. 1st ed. VG in DJ. $30.

BURTON, RICHARD F. *Ultima Thule, or A Summer in Iceland*. London, 1875 1st ed. Ex-library. Foxing. $400.
The Kasidah of Haji Abdu El-Yezdi. Mosher Press, 1915. As editor-translator. One of 250 copies VG. $125. 1931 edition. David McKay. Very Good. $50.
The Book of 1,000 Nights and a Night. Heritage Press, circa 1934. 6 vols in 3. Angelo illus. VG in fair DJs. $50.
The Arabian Knights. 12 volume set published in 1897. Good. $135. 4 vols. 1954. Fine in slipcases. $200.
The City of Saints. New York, 1862. 1st American edition. Wom, shaken. $100.

BURTON, VIRGINIA LEE. *Mike Mulligan and His Steam Shovel*. Boston, 1939 1st ed. Illus. by author. Very Good in dust jacket. $90-$150.

BURTON, WILLIAM. *Josiah Wedgwood and His Pottery*. NY, 1922 1st ed. Illus. One of 1,500 copies. VG. $95-$125.
A General History of Porcelain. London, 1921 2 vols. Illus. Very Good in dust jacket. $150.

BURY, VISCOUNT and LACY HILLIER. *Cycling*. Boston, Little Brown, 1887 1st American ed. Highly illus. by Pennell and Bury. Fine. $75.

BUSHELL, STEPHEN W. *Oriental Ceramic Art*. NY, 1980. Facsimile of 1896 ed. Illus. Good-VG in DJ. $60.

BUTLER, CLEORA. *Cleora's Kitchens; Eight Decades of Great American Food*. Oklahoma, 1986. Black author's autobiographical cookbook. Good-VG. $25. Fine. $40-$50.

BUTLER, ELLIS PARKER. *The Incubator Baby*. NY, 1906 1st ed. May Wilson Preston illus. Good. $20.
The Great American Pie Company. NY, 1907. Fair. $15.

BUTLER, T. B. *The Philosophy of the Weather*. Appleton, 1856. Very Good. $75.

BUTTERFIELD, CONSUL W. *History of Seneca County*. Sandusky, OH, 1848 1st ed. 248 pgs. Rebacked, spotted cover. Good. $250-$350.
History of the Girtys. Cincinnati, OH, 1890 1st ed. 426 pgs. Orig. cloth covers. $300-$400.

THE BUTTERICK BOOK OF RECIPES & HOUSEHOLD HELPS. Butterick Pub. Co., 1927. Worn cover. $20.

THE BUTTERICK COOK BOOK. Butterick Pub. Co, 1911. Very Good. $10.

BUTTERWORTH. *The Patriot Schoolmaster*. Appleton, 1894. Very Good. $27.

BUTTERWORTH, BENJAMIN. *The Growth of Industrial Art*. Washington, 1892. Folio 200 plates. $400.

BUTTERWORTH, HEZEKIAH. *Zig-Zag Journeys in the White City*. 1894 1st ed. Gilt-dec. cover. $65.

BUZZATI, DIN. *The Bears' Famous Invasion of Sicily*. Pantheon, 1947. Illus. by author. Very Good. $95.

BYAM, WALLY. *Trailer Travel. Adventurous Living*. NY, McKay, 1960 1st ed., Illus. Very Good. $25.

BYATT, A. S. *The Game*. NY, 1967 1st American ed. Fine in dust jacket. $75-$150.

BYINGTON, LEWIS F. *The History of San Francisco*. S. J. Clarke, 1931 1st ed. Vol II only. Fine, no DJ. $15.

BYNE, MILDRED and ARTHUR. *Spanish Gardens and Patios*. Illus. Philadelphia, Lippincott, 1924 1st ed. Ex-library, else Very Good. $60-$90.

BYRD, DOUGLAS. *The Science of Baseball. A Text Book*. Chicago, 1922. Illus. Minor wear. $35.

BYRD, RICHARD. *Little America*. Putnams, 1930. One of 1,000 signed. VG. $150. Fine. $300-$400. Same year, 3rd printing. $25.

BYRN, EDWARD. *The Progress of the Invention in the 19th Century*. NY, Munn & Co., 1900. Illus. VG. $35

C

CABELL, JAMES BRANCH. *The Eagle's Shadow*. NY, 1904 1st ed. Author's 1st book. VG plus. $100.
Line of Love. NY, Harper, 1905 1st edition. Howard Pyle illus. Pictorial green cover. $50-$100.
Jurgen. NY, 1926. 2nd ed. Light foxing, sunning. G. $15.
The Works of James Branch Cabell. NY, 1927. Storisende edition, 18 vols. Light shelfwear. $300-$400.
Cream of the Jest: A Comedy of Evasions. New York, 1927. Good-Very Good. $25-$40.
Between Dawn and Sunrise. NY, McBride, 1930 1st ed. Fine in dust jacket. $50.

CABLE, GEORGE WASHINGTON. *Old Creole Days*. NY, 1879 1st ed, 1st issue. Very Good. $195. 1890 ed. $35.
John March, Southerner. NY, 1894. VG. $28.
The Grandissimes. NY, 1898. VG. $18.
Cavalier. NY, 1901 1st ed. VG. $15.
Gideon's Band. NY, 1914 1st ed. VG. $30.

CADILLAC MOTOR CAR COMPANY. *Operator's Manual*. 1928. 62 pgs. $30. (See catalog section for sales literature.)

CAFFIN, CHARLES H. *Photography As a Fine Art*. NY, 1901 1st ed. Very Good. $110.
American Masters of Sculpture. Doubleday, 1903 1st ed. Good-Very Good. $15-$25.

CAGE, JOHN. *Silence. Lectures and Writings*. Middletown, CT, 1961 1st ed. Signed by Author. Fine in DJ. $100.
For the Birds. Boston & London, 1981. Signed by Author. Fine in dust jacket. $35.

CAINE, HALL. *The Christian*. No place, 1897. Fine. $10.
The Prodigal Son. NY, 1904. Fine. $15.
The Life of Christ. NY, 1938 edition. Fine. $7.

CAIN, JAMES M. *The Postman Always Rings Twice*. NY, 1934. 1st ed. VG in DJ. $400.
The Moth. NY, Knopf, 1948 1st ed. VG in DJ. $45-$65.
Rainbow's End. London, 1975 1st British edition. Fine in dust jacket. $20.
The Baby in the Icebox. NY, 1981. Fine in DJ. $20.

CALDECOTT, RANDOLPH. *Old Christmas*. London, 1882 1st ed. Illus. by author. VG. $25.
A Sketchbook of Randolph Caldecott. London, NY, 1883. Illus. by author. VG. $70.

Randolph Caldecott's Sketches. London, 1890 1st ed. Illus. by author. VG. $30.
Caldecott's Collection of Pictures and Songs. London, no date. Color illus. Very Good. $45.

CALDER, ALEXANDER. *Animal Sketching*. Pelham New York, 1926. Author's 1st book. Illustrated by author. Very Good in dust jacket. $100.
Calder: An Autobiography. London, 1967. VG in DJ. $50.

CALDWELL, ERSKINE. *Tobacco Road*. NY, 1932 1st ed. Very Good in DJ. $300-$700. 1940 ed., boxed. $75.
God's Little Acre. NY, 1933 1st ed. VG in DJ. $150-$300. Same, no dust jacket. $50-$65.
We Are The Living. NY, 1933 1st ed. Good-VG. $50.
Journeyman. NY, 1935 1st ed. Near VG. $35. G&D. $8.
Kneel to the Rising Sun. NY, 1935 1st. Minor wear. $20.
Say, Is This the USA. Bourke-White photos. NY, 1941 1st edition. Very Good. $75.
All Night Long. Duell, 1942 1st ed. VG in DJ. $40.
A Place Called Estherville. 1949 1st edition. Very Good in dust jacket. $35.
Close to Home. NY, 1962 1st ed. Grey cloth, Yellow boards. Very Good in dust jacket. $25.

CALIFORNIA ARTISTS COOKBOOK. 200 recipes by 107 artists. 216 pgs. Abbeville Press, 1982. VG in DJ. $45.

THE CALIFORNIA HERITAGE COOK BOOK. Junior League of California. Garden City NY, 1976 1st ed. Very Good in dust jacket. $13.

CALIFORNIA ILLUSTRATED. By a returned Californian. Anon. (J. M. Letts). NY, 1852. $550-$850.

CALIFORNIA SKETCHES, WITH RECOLLECTIONS OF THE GOLD MINES. Anon. (Leonard Kip). Albany NY, 1850. Good-Very Good. $850-$1,000.

CALLAGHAN, MORLEY. *Strange Fugitive*. NY, 1928 1st ed. Author's 1st book. Good-VG. $80-$100.

CALLAHAN, GENEVIEVE. *The California Cook Book*. NY, 1946 2nd printing. VG in DJ. $20.

CALVERTON, V. F. *Where Angels Feared to Tread*. Indianapolis IN, 1941 1st ed. VG. $30.

CALVIN, J. ROSS. *River of the Sun*. Albuquerque, NM, 1946 1st ed. Near Fine in DJ. $35. Fine in Fine DJ. $55. *Sky Determines*. Albuquerque, NM, 1948 revised edition. Near Fine. $45.

CALVINO, ITALO. *The Baron in the Trees*. NY, 1959 1st American ed. VG in dust jacket. $35.
The Watcher. NY, 1971 Review copy. Inscribed. Fine in fine DJ. $350. Another, unsigned. VG. $30.
Italian Folktales. NY, 1980 1st Amer ed. Fine DJ. $25.

CAMERA ANNUAL. 1942 edition. Good-Very Good. $18.

CAMERON, WILLIAM E. *The World's Fair, Being a Pictorial History of the Columbian Exposition*. Ferguson, 1893 1st ed. Very Good. $25.

CAMP FIRE GIRLS, THE BOOK OF. New York, 1938. Thin color printed cloth covers. Very Good. $25.

CAMP, RAYMOND. *Fishing the Surf*. Boston, 1941 1st ed. Fine in dust jacket. $35.
Hunter's Encyclopedia. Harrisburg, 1948 1st ed. VG. $20.
Duck Boats: Blind Decoys. NY, 1952 1st ed. VG. $45.
Game Cookery. NY, 1958 1st ed. Fine. $35.
Fireside Book of Fishing. No place, 1959 1st ed. VG. $20.

CAMP, WALTER. *Authors and Inventors*. Juvenile series. P.F. Collier, 1903 1st ed. Very Good. $7.
Great Men and Famous Deeds. Collier, 1903 1st. VG. $7.
Official Football Rules. NY, 1914. Illus. Paperback. $25.

CAMPBELL, A. J. *American Practical Cyclopaedia*. Campbell, 1872 revised ed. Leather cover. Good. $12-$14.

CAMPBELL, HANNAH. *Why Did They Name it...? A History of Brand Names*. Fleet Press, 1964 1st. F in DJ. $12.

CAMPBELL, J. L. *The Miracle of Peille*. NY, 1929 1st ed. Presentation copy. Signed by author. VG in fair DJ. $45.

CAMPBELL, JOHN. *Cloak of Aesir*. Shasta Press, 1952 1st edition. Fine in dust jacket. $38.
The Black Star Passes. Fantasy Press, 1953 1st edition. Near Fine in dust jacket. $60-$90.

CAMPBELL, JOSEPH. *The Masks of God: Primitive Mythology*. No place, 1959. VG. $18.
The Masks of God: Oriental Mythology. 1962. VG. $18.

CAMPBELL, MARIE. *Folks Do Get Born*. NY, 1946 1st ed. Clare Leighton illus. VG in good DJ. $45.

CAMPBELL, ROY. *The Wayzgoose: a South African Satire*. London, 1928 1st ed. VG in DJ. $30.
The Georgiad. London, 1931 1st ed. Signed. $125.
Pomegranates. London, 1932 1st ed. illus. Fine. $100.

CAMPBELL, RUTH. *The Cat Whose Whiskers Slipped*. Volland, 1925. 5th ed. Illus. Worn. o/w VG. $20. 1938 edition, Very Good. $25.
Small Fry and Winged Horse. Volland, 1927. VG. $30.

CAMUS, ALBERT. *The Stranger*. NY, 1946 1st American ed. Near Fine in dust jacket. $125
Resistance, Rebellion & Death. NY, 1961 1st American ed. Translated, VG in DJ. $30.
Notebooks, 1935-1942. London, 1963. NF in DJ. $40.
A Happy Death. NY, 1972 1st American ed. Good. $8.

CANBY, HENRY S. *The Brandywine*. Rivers of America Series. NY, 1941 1st edition. Wyeth illus. Very Good. $32.

CANFIELD, DOROTHY. *Hillsboro People*. NY, 1915 1st edition. Very Good. $15.
Understood Betsy. NY, 1917 1st ed. A. C. Williamson illus. Very Good. $38.
Home Fires in France. NY, 1918 1st ed. VG. $30.
Seasoned Timber. NY, 1939 1st edition in case. $16.

CANFIELD, KID. *Card Sharpers: Tricks Exposed*. 1910. 102 pgs. Very Fine. $55 auction

CANIFF, MILTON. *Terry and War in the Jungle*. Whitman, 1944 1st edition. Fine. $22.
Terry and the Pirates. NY, 1946. Illus. by author. Very Good in dust jacket. $35.

CANIFF, STEVE. *Operation Eel Island*. (Steve Canyon). Grosset & Dunlap, 1959. VG in worn DJ. $26.

CANNING, VICTOR. *The Kingsford Mark*. NY, 1975 1st ed. Fine in repaired dust jacket. $10.
Vanishing Point. London, 1932 1st British ed. Fine in repaired dust jacket. $18.
The Burning Eye. New York, 1960 1st edition. Near Fine in dust jacket. $20.

CANNON, R. *The Sea of Cortez*. Menlo Park, 1973. Near Fine in dust jacket. $20.

CANTOR, EDDIE. *Between the Acts*. Simon & Schuster, 1930 1st edition. Very Good in dust jacket. $35.

CAPA, ROBERT. *Slightly Out of Focus*. NY, 1947 1st ed. Fair, no DJ. $28. VG. $40. Fine in dust jacket. $125.
Images of War. NY, 1964. Fine in dust jacket. $95.

CAPEK, JOSEPH. *Harum Scarum*. New York, 1963 1st edition. Very Good. $25.

CAPEK, KARL. *The Markropoulos Secret*. Boston, 1925 1st American edition. Good. $25.
Letters From Spain. New York, 1932 1st American edition. Near Very Good. $50.

War With the Newts. Putnam, 1937 1st American. Light foxing, o/w VG in DJ. $145. London, 1937 2nd ed. $50.
Tales From Two Pockets. NY, 1943 1st American ed. Very Good in dust jacket. $60.
Krakatit: An Atomic Phantasy. NY, 1951 1st American edition. Very Good. $65. London, 1948. VG in DJ. $60.

CAPON, R. F. *The Supper of the Lamb*. Recipes. NY, 1969. Very Good in dust jacket. $20.

CAPP, AL. *Hardhat's Bedtime Story Book*. New York, 1971. Fine. $15.

CAPT. SMITH AND PRINCESS POCAHONTAS: AN INDIAN TALE. Anon. (John Davis). Philadelphia, 1805. $2,000-$2,500.

CARAS, ROGER. *Wings of Gold: U. S. Naval Aviation*. Philadelphia, 1965 1st ed. Very Good in DJ. $20-$25.

CARELL, PAUL. *Hitler Moves East, 1941*. Boston, 1964 1st American ed. VG in DJ. $100. Good. $50.
Foxes of the Desert. No place, 1960 1st ed. F in DJ. $85.
Scorched Earth: Hitler's War on Russia. London, 1970 1st ed. Fine in dust jacket. $45.

CAREY, A. MERWYN. *American Firearms Makers*. NY, 1953. Very Good in dust jacket. $15-$25.

CAREY, THOMAS A. *Orange Culture in California*. San Francisco, 1882. With ads. Fair. $50.

CARLETON, HENRY GUY. *The South Fifth Avenue Poker Club*. Ivers & Co., NY, 1888. 107 pgs. VG. $450 auction.

CARLETON, WILL. *Poems*. Chicago, 1871. #341 of 1,000 copies. Author's first book. Good. $125.
Farm Ballads. Harper, 1873 1st ed. VG. $14. Fine. $28.
Farm Legends. Harper, 1875 1st ed. Good-VG. $14-$24. Signed by Author. $50.
Farm Festivals. 1881 1st ed. VG. $35.
City Ballads. 1885 ed. G-VG. $15-$29.
City Legends. 1890 1st ed. Fine. $28.

CARLISLE, D. T. *The Belvedere Hounds*. NY, Derrydale Press, 1935. 1 of 1,250 copies. Spine wear, o/w VG. $50.

CARLSON, NATALIE SAVAGE. *The Family Under the Bridge*. NY, 1958. Garth Williams illus. Ex-lib. VG. $10.
Carnival in Paris. New York, 1962. Rocker illustrator. Fine in dust jacket. $12.

CARLYLE, THOMAS. *Oliver Cromwell's Letters and Speeches*. NY, 1846. Good. $58.
The Works of Thomas Carlyle. Croxly edition, 10 vols. no date. Good. $40.
Reminiscences. London, 1881. 2 volumes. Good. $45.

CARMAN, BLISS. *Ballads of Los Haven*. Boston, 1897 1st ed. Unopened. Signed. VG. $125.
Echoes From Vagabondia. Boston, 1912 1st ed. NF. $50.
April Airs. Boston, 1916 1st ed. Signed. G-VG. $125.

CARMAN, HARRY (Editor). *American Husbandry*. Columbia University, 1939. $25.

CARMICHAEL, HOAGY. *The Stardust Road*. Rinehart, 1946 1st ed. Very Good in dust jacket. $24.

CARMER, CARL. *Listen for a Lonesome Drum*. Farrar & Rinehart, 1936 1st ed., Very Good. $10.
The Hudson. NY, 1939. Rivers of America series. Illus. Signed inscription. Fine. $100. Unsigned. G-VG. $20.
The Tavern Lamps Are Burning. David McKay, 1964. Very Good in dust jacket. $15.

CARNEY, CLEVE. *The Master Cake Baker*. Illinois, Calumet Baking Powder Co., 1927 1st. 108 pages. G. $15.

CARPENTER, CHARLES. *History of American Schoolbooks*. Univ. of Pennsylvania Press, 1963. As new. $15.

CARR, JOHN. *Pioneer Days in California*. Eureka, CA, Times Pub. Co., 1891. 452 pgs. Worn frayed. $250.

CARR, JOHN DICKSON. *The Murder of Sir Edmund Godfrey*. New York, 1936. 1st edition. Internal spotting, fair dust jacket. $350.
The Man Who Could Not Shudder. NY, 1940 1st ed. Very Good in slightly frayed DJ. $250.
Death Turns the Tables. New York, 1941 1st edition. Very Good in frayed dust jacket. $175.
The Case of the Constant Suicides. NY, Harpers, 1941 1st edition. Good in DJ. $35.
A Graveyard to Let. New York, 1949 1st edition. Fine in slightly torn dust jacket. $85.
Below Suspicion. NY, 1949 1st ed. VG in chip DJ. $18.
The Long Divorce. New York, 1951 1st edition. Ex-library. Very Good. $15.
Maiden Murders. NY, 1952. VG in DJ. $20.
The Third Bullet. NY, 1954. VG in fair DJ. $35.
Captain Cut-Throat. NY, 1955. Fine in DJ. $25.
Various Collier reprints. No dates. Dark blue cloth. Gilt skull decoration. $5.

CARRANCE, LYNWOOD. *Logging the Redwoods*. Caxton Printers, 1975 1st ed. Photos. Fine in DJ. $19.

CARRICK, ALICE VAN LEER. *Shades of Our Ancestors: American Profiles and Profilists*. Boston, 1928. VG. $65.
A History of American Silhouettes 1790-1840. Tuttle, 1968 reprint. VG in dust jacket. $20-$30.

CARRICK, ROBERT W. *Pictorial History of the Americas Cup Races*. NY, 1964. Very Good in dust jacket. $10.

CARRIGHAR, SALLY. *One Day at Teton Marsh*. NY, 1947 1st edition. Near Fine in dust jacket. $30.
Moonlight at Midday. NY, 1959. VG in DJ. $40.

CARRINGTON, FRANCES. *Army Life on the Plains*. Philadelphia, 1911 2nd edition. Very Good. $55.
My Army Life and the Fort Kearney Massacre. Philadelphia, 1910 1st edition. Rubbed, Good-VG. $75-$125.

CARRINGTON, H. *Higher Psychical Development*. NY, 1920. Very Good. $35.
The Physical Phenomena of Spiritualism. Boston, 1920 3rd edition. Good. $38.

CARROLL, JAMES. *Madonna Red*. Boston, 1976 1st ed. Author's 1st book. Near Fine in DJ. $50.

CARROLL, LEWIS. *Alice's Adventures in Wonderland*. NY, 1866 1st American edition. Tenniel illus. VG-Fine, $3,500-$6,500. London, 1875 edition. Good. $35. Winston pub, 1923 ed. VG. $38. Garden City, 1930s. Jackson illus. VG. $35. Dial New Edition, 1935. Hudson illus. Good. $55. Harper, 1901, Peter Newell illus. $130. 1941 Facsimile ed. league of Amer. Good. $22. 1946. Special edition. Random House Very Good. $18. NY, 1977. Color illus. Fine. $25. Limited Editions Club. 1932. Signed by Alice Hargreaves. Full red leather. Headcap chipped. $275. Doubleday, circa 1907. Rackham illustrator. $80-$175.
Through the Looking Glass. NY, 1872 1st American edition. VG in DJ. $1,500. 1901 ed., NY & London. Peter Newell illus. VG. $125. McLoughlin ed. no date. $30. Macmillan, 1889 reprint. Good. $15. VG. $25. Harper, 1902. Peter Newell illus. VG. $65-$150.
The Hunting of the Snark. NY, London, 1903 1st ed. Peter Newell illus. VG. $135. Harper, 1903. Good. $75. NY, 1914 edition, H. Holiday illus. G-VG. $20-$30. NY, 1970 edition. Helen Oxenbury illustrator. Very Good-Fine in dust jacket. $35-$45.
Sylvie and Bruno. Macmillan, 1890 1st ed. Gilt-dec. red cloth. Bumped, fly leaf gone, o/w VG. $50.
Collected Verse. Macmillan, 1933. Shelfwear. VG. $25.

CARROLL, PAUL VINCENT. *Shadow and Substance*. NY, 1937 1st ed. Near Fine in dust jacket. $35.

CARRYL, GUY WETMORE. *Fables for the Frivolous*. Harper, 1898 1st ed. Peter Newell illus. Fine, $85.

CARSON, RACHEL. *Under the Sea Wind*. NY, 1941 1st ed. Author's 1st book. VG in DJ. $150.
The Sea Around Us. Oxford Univ., 1951 1st ed. $20.
Silent Spring. NY, Houghton Mifflin, 1962 1st edition. Near Fine in dust jacket. $95.

CARSTENSEN, GEORGE and CHARLES GILDEMEISTER. *New York Crystal Palace*. NY, 1854. Plates, drawings. One plate torn, chip spine. $175.

CARTER, FORREST. *Gone to Texas*. NYU, 1975 1st edition. Very Good in dust jacket. $35-$75.

CARTER, JIMMY. *The Blood of Abraham*. Boston, 1985 1st ed. Inscribed. Very Good in dust jacket. $75.
An Outdoor Journal. 1988. Signed. Fine in DJ. $125.

CARTER and MUIR. *Printing and the Mind of Man*. NY, 1967 1st ed. VG in dust jacket. $150-$300.

CARTER, SUSANNAH. *The Frugal Housewife: or the Complete Woman Cook*. Philadelphia, 1796. Calf-backed boards, $1,000.

CARTER, W. C. and A. J. GLOSSBRENNER. *History of York County (PA) From Erection to Present*. Harrisburg, 1930 New edition. $45.

CARTIER-BRESSON, HENRI (Photographer). *The Decisive Moment*. New York, 1952. Fine in dust jacket with caption booklet. $435.
Europeans. NY, 1955. Includes caption. booklet. $350.

CARTLAND, BARBARA. *The Audacious Adventuress*. London, 1971 1st ed. Fine in dust jacket. $15.

CARTWRIGHT. *The Boy's Book of Ships*. E. P. Dutton, 1925. Very Good. $14.

CARVALHO, SOLOMON H. *Incidents of Travel and Adventure in the Far West*. No place, 1954 Reprint of 1857 edition. Illus. by author. VG. $60.

CARUSO, DOROTHY. *Enrico Caruso, His Life and Death*. Simon & Schuster, 1945 1st ed. VG in dust jacket. $10.

CASEY, BRIG. GEN. SILAS. *Infantry Tactics*. Vol. 3. NY, Van Nostrand, 1862. 189 pgs. with fold-outs. Good. $100.

CASH, W. F. *The Mind of the South*. NY, 1941 1st ed. Near Fine in clipped dust jacket. $150.

CASKODEN, EDWIN. *When Knighthood Was in Flower*. NY, 1898 subsequent ed. Very Good. $12.-$14.

CASPERY, VERA. *Laura*. Boston, 1943 1st ed. VG $25.
The Man Who Loved His Wife. NY, 1966 1st ed. Fine in dust jacket. $18.

CASS, BEVIN. *History of the 6th Marine Divison*. Washington, 1948 1st ed. Very Good. $95.

CASS, ELEANOR B. *The Book of Fencing*. Boston, 1930, Lothrop, Lee & Shepard. 1st ed. Very Good. $50-$80.

CASSELL'S DICTIONARY OF PRACTICAL GARDENING. London, 1900. 4 vols. Black/white, color illus. $60.

CASSON, H. N. *The History of the Telephone*. Chicago, 1910 1st ed. Very Good. $18-$24.

CASTENADA, CARLOS. *Teachings of Don Juan*. NY, 1973 1st ed. Very Good in dust jacket. $13.
Tales of Power. NY, 1974 1st ed. VG in DJ. $20.

CASTLE DISMAL: OR, THE BACHELOR'S CHRISTMAS. Anon. (William G. Sims). New York, 1844. $250-$350.

CASTLEMAN, ALFRED. *The Army of the Potomac*. Milwaukee, Strickland, 1863. Very Good. $250.

CASTLEMON, HARRY. *The Mail Carrier*. Philadelphia, 1879. Boy Trapper Series. Good-Very Good. $15.
Frank in The Mountains. Hentry T., 1868. VG. $23.

CATE, MARGARET DAVIS. *Early Days of Coastal Georgia*. Fort Frederica, 1956 2nd ed. Fine in DJ. $16. 1970 6th edition. $12.

CATHER, WILLA. *April Twilights*. Boston, 1903 1st ed. Author's 1st book. Spine label & most of front label gone. Minor joint wear. $650.
Alexander's Bridge. Boston, NY, 1912 1st ed. Fine, $75.
O Pioneers. NY, 1913 1st ed. VG. $175.
A Lost Lady. NY, 1923 1st ed, 1st printing. Near Fine in dust jacket. $175.
My Antonia. Houghton-Mifflin, 1924 1st. Sg. VG. $225.
Death Comes for the Archbishop. NY, 1927 1st edition. $100-$400. 1929 edition. $55-$100.
Lucy Gayheart. NY, 1935 1st ed. Near Fine in DJ. $25. Another, signed. $275.
Sapphira and the Slave Girl. NY, Knopf, 1940 1st trade edition. VG-NF in dust jacket. $60-$125.
The Old Beauty & Others. NY, 1948. 1st. VG in DJ. $35.

CATLIN, GEORGE. *North American Indians. Letters and Notes, 1832-1839*. London, 1841 1st ed. $500-$1,500 at auction. 1926 ed., Edinburgh, John Grant. $600 auction.
Episodes From Life Among the Indians. University of Oklahoma, 1959 1st ed. Fine in dust jacket. $65.
Life Among the Indians. London & Edinburgh, no date. Circa 1890s. Very Good to Near Fine. $65-$85.

CATON, JOHN DEAN. *The Antelope and Deer of America*. New York, 1877 1st edition. Inscribed. Very Good. $250. Another, worn, no inscription. Ex-library. $80.

CATREVAS, CHRISTINE. *Fairy Tales for Little People*. Sears, 1927. Charlotte Becker illus. Good plus. $25.

CATTON, BRUCE. *The War Lords of Washington*. NY, 1948 1st ed, 1st book. VG in DJ. $25.
Army of the Potomac. NY, 1952. VG. $7. In DJ. $12.
Hallowed Ground. Garden City, 1956 1st ed. Good in dust jacket. $10. Very Good in dust jacket. $25.
Grant Takes Richmond. Book Club Edition, 1969. Very Good in dust jacket. $10.
American Pictorial History of the Civil War. NY, 1960 2 vols, boxed. Good. $45.
Grant Moves South. Boston, 1960 1st ed. Good in DJ. $8. Same. Signed presentation copy in dust jacket. $35.
The Coming Fury. Doubleday, 1961 1st ed. F in DJ. $38.
The Centennial History of the Civil War. Garden City, 1961. 3 vols. 1st ed. Near Fine in DJ. $35.
Terrible Swift Sword. NY, 1963. Good-VG. $6.
Grant Takes Command. Boston, 1968 1st ed. Worn cover, o/w Fine in dust jacket. $25.
Waiting for the Morning Train. Doubleday, 1972. Very Good in dust jacket. $30.
The Civil War. Fairfax ed, 1980. $6.

CAUSLEY, CHARLES. *Figgie Hobbin*. New York, 1973 1st edition. Trina Schart Hyman illustrator. Repaired dust jacket, else Very Good. $25.

CAUTHORN, HENRY S. *History of the City of Vincennes, Indiana, 1702-1901*. VG-Fine. $35-$45.

CAVENDISH, MARSHALL. *The Marshall Cavendish Illustrated Encyclopedia of World War II*. 25 vol. set. 1972. Good-Very Good. $75-$135. Fine. $150.

CAWEIN, MADISON. *The Giant and the Star*. Boston, 1909 1st ed. One of 1,000 copies. VG. $40.

CELLINI, BENVENUTO. *Life of Benvenuto Cellini*. NY, 1906, Brentanos. 2 vols. VG. $20. Heritage, 1960. $12.
The Autobiography of Benvenuto Cellini. NY, 1946, limited edition signed by S. Dali. $250. NY, 1948, Doubleday. Dali illus. VG. $60-$100.
The Life of ...Written by Himself. Verona, Limited Editions Club, 1937. Signed by illus., Fritz Kredel. Fine in dust jacket. $100.

CENDRAS, BLAISE. *Sutter's Gold*. NY, 1926 1st ed. G-VG in dust jacket. $25-$50.

CERAM, C. W. *Gods, Graves and Scholars*. Knopf, 1952. Good, no dust jacket. $7. Very Good. $12.
Archeology of the Cinema. NY, 1965 1st ed. F in DJ. $45.

CERVANTES, MIGUEL DE. *The Adventures of Don Quixote*. Hundreds of editions followed the 17th century 1st edition. Illustrations and fine bindings are value makers. NY, 1890, Collier. Dore illus. Good. $75. 1906, John Grant pub. VG. $60. NY, 1928 Houghton Mifflin. VG in DJ. $15. London, 1930, Nonesuch Press. $200-$450. Heritage Press, 1939. 682 pgs, Very Fine in case. $20. Most modern editions fall in $25-$50 price range.
The History of Don Quixote. Dore illus. Gilt pictorial cloth. San Francisco, J. Dewing, circa 1885. Cracked hinges, else VG. $50-$80.

CHADWICK, HENRY. *The Sports and Pastimes of American Boys*. NY, 1884 1st ed. Fine $85-$125.
The Game of Baseball. New York, 1868. The first clothbound book on baseball. Very scarce. $500-$3,000.

CHADWICK, LESTER (Edward Stratemeyer). 14 novels in *Baseball Joe* series. 1912-1928. Average $10-$20 each.

CHADWICK, MRS. J. *Mrs. Chadwick's Cook Book*. New York, 1853 1st ed, 2nd printing. Very Good. $175.

CHAGALL, MARC. *The Ballet*. Tudor, 1969 1st ed. Original litho tipped in. Fine in slipcase. $300.
Other Chagall books with original lithos, sell for $500-$2,500 based on number of plates & if signed by Chagall.

CHALLAMEL, AUGUSTIN. *History of Fashion in France*. NY, 1882. 21 hand-colored plates. Some fox o/w G. $135.

CHALMERS, MARY. *Here Comes the Trolley Car*. NY, 1955 1st ed. Illus & signed by author. Cover foxing, o/w Very Good. $45.

CHALMERS, PATRICK. *The History of Hunting*. Philadelphia, no date. 1st ed. Illus. VG in DJ. $25.
Gun Dogs. London, 1931 1st ed. Fine. $75.

CHAMBERLAIN, GEORGE AGNEW. *African Hunting Among the Thongas*. NY, 1923 1st ed. Good. $50.
Overcoat Meeting. NY, 1949 1st ed. Signed. $40.

CHAMBERLAIN, H. D. *Riding & Schooling Horses*. NY, 1934. Derrydale Press. No. 32 of 950 copies. Spine dull, slightly soiled. $60.
Training Hunters, Jumpers & Hacks. NY, 1952 1st edition. Very Good. $35.

CHAMBERLAIN, SAMUEL. *Tudor Homes of England*. New York, 1929. Illustrated. Four pages missing, o/w Very Good. $120.
Cape Code in the Sun. H. House, 1937 1st ed. VG. $22.
Ever New England. H. House 1946, 4th imp. VG. $7-$10.
Bouquet of France: An Epicurean Tour of French Provinces. Gourmet, 1960. Illus. by author. VG. $30.

CHAMBERS, ROBERT W. *The Maid-at-Arms*. NY, 1902. H. C. Christy illus. Presentation copy. Light spine fading, corners rubbed. $60. 1902, Trade ed. $20-$35.
Common Law. Knopf, 1911 1st edition. Very Good-Fine, no dust jacket. $10-$20.
Quick Action. Appleton, 1914 1st ed. Good-VG. $20-$30.
Little Red Foot. Burt, New York, 1921. Reprint. Very Good in fair dust jacket. $15.
Street of Ascalon. 1912, Gibson illus. $30-$35.

CHAMPLIN, H. S. *The American Fireman*. Boston, 1875 1st edition. Good -Very Good. $100-$125.

CHANDLER, ALFRED and JOHN C. SHARP. *A Bicycle Tour in England and Wales With Appendix Information on the Use of the Cycle in Europe and the United States*. Boston, 1881 1st ed. Very Good. $100.

CHANDLER, ANNA CURTIS. *Pan the Piper & Other Marvelous Tales*. Harper, NY & London, 1923 1st ed. Good-Very Good. $25.

CHANDLER, RAYMOND. *The Big Sleep*. NY, 1939 1st ed. Light shelfware, o/w Fine in restored DJ. In slipcase, $5,000. Same, no slipcase. $2,500. Another, DJ trimmed, minor wear and browning, $1,800. Same, without dust jacket. $150.
Farewell, My Lovely. NY, 1940 1st ed. Slightly soiled edges, o/w fine in chip DJ. $2,500. Same, no DJ. $250. Later reprints in dust jacket. $20-$40.
The Lady in the Lake. NY, 1943 1st ed. VG in Good dust jacket. $500. Grosset & Dunlap, 1946 ed. VG in DJ. $35.
The High Window. NY, Knopf, 1943 1st ed. VG-Fine. No DJ. $100-$200.
Spanish Blood. World, 1946. VG in chip DJ. $25-$45.
The Little Sister. Boston, 1949 1st Amer. ed. Near Fine in DJ, $200. Same in pb, 1950, Pocket Book. VG. $20.
The Simple Art of Murder. London, 1950 1st English ed. VG in vg DJ. $100-$300.
Pick-Up on Moon Street. NY, 1952 1st ed. Paperbound. Near Fine. $15.
The Long Goodbye. Houghton-Mifflin, 1954 1st American edition. Fine in fair DJ. $200. Same, London, 1959. Penguin paperback. $22.
Playback. London, 1958 1st ed. Near fine in vg DJ. $100.
Omnibus. NY, 1959 Book Club ed. Fine in fine DJ. $15.
Killers in the Rain. NY, 1965 1st. Paperbound. NF. $10.
Farewell, My Lovely and The Lady in the Lake. NY, 1967. 1st Modern Library edition. Fine in DJ. $25.

CHAMPNEY, LIZZIE W. *Three Vassar Girls Abroad*. Boston, 1883 1st ed, Estes & Lauriat. Good-VG. $35-$45.

CHANDOHA, WALTER (Photographer). *Walter Chandoha's Book of Kittens and Cats*. NY, no date. Very Good. $20.

CHANTRAINE, CHARLES. *La Cuisine Chantraine*. Brussels restaurant recipes. New York, 1966. Very Good in dust jacket. $12-$15.

CHAPEL, CHARLES E. *Guns of the Old West*. NY, 1961 1st ed. Coward-McCann. Very Good in DJ. $55.
The Art of Shooting. A. S. Barnes, 1960. VG in DJ. $20.

CHAPEL, CHARLES EDWARD. *Finger Printing*. Coward-McCann, 1941 2nd printing. Musty, otherwise Very Good in ragged dust jacket. $25.

CHAPIN, HOWARD M. *American Privateers*. Providence, 1928 1st ed. Blue cloth cover. Very Good. $35.

CHAPLIN, RALPH. *Bars and Shadows; Prison Poems of Ralph Chaplin*. Leonard Press. 1922. VG in DJ. $10. *Somewhat Barbaric*. Dogwood Press, 1944 1st edition. Signed, presentation copy. Fine in fine dust jacket. $75. *Wobbly: The Rough and Tumble Story of an American Radical*. University of Chicago, 1948 1st edition. Near Fine to Fine in dust jacket. $25-$50.

CHAPMAN, A. W. *Flora of the Southern United States*. Ivison, 1872 revised edition. Very Good. $15.

CHAPMAN, FRANK. *Bird-Life: A Guide to the Study of Our Common Birds*. NY, 1899. F. $45. 1900, wraps. $25. NY & London, 1915 ed. Color plate illus. $50-$60. *Warblers of North America*. NY, 1907 1st ed. Ex-lib. $55. Appleton, 1914 2nd edition. Good. $55. *Camps and Cruises of an Ornithologist*. Appleton, 1908 1st ed. Good-Very Good. $20-$40. *Color Key to North American Birds*. NY, 1912 Revised edition. Pencil marks. Good plus. $25-$35. *Autobiography of a Bird Lover*. Appleton, 1933 1st ed. Good-VG. $10-$25. Fine. $50.

CHARLOT, JEAN. *The Mexican Mural Renaissance, 1820-1915*. Yale Univ Press, 1963 1st ed. Very Good. $25. Same in dust jacket. $50-$75.

CHARPENTIER, HENRY and SPARKES. *Life A La Henri*. (Famous restauranteur). NY, 1934. Very Good. $35.

CHARTERIS, LESLIE. *The Saint Intervenes*. NY, 1934 1st edition. Near Fine. $35. *Prelude for War*. NY, 1938. VG. $20. *The Saint Steps In*. New York, 1943 1st edition. Very Good in dust jacket. $40. *Vendetta for the Saint*. NY, Crime Club, 1964 1st ed. Near Fine in dust jacket. $38. *Count on the Saint*. New York, 1980 1st edition. Near Fine in dust jacket. $15. *Salvage for the Saint*. NY, 1983. Fine in fine DJ. $20.

CHARYN, JEROME. *Once Upon a Droshky*. NY, 1964 1st ed. VG-Fine in dust jacket. $40-$60. *The Man Who Grew Younger*. NY, 1966 1st ed. Inscribed. Fine in dust jacket. $100. *Tar Baby*. 1973 1st ed. VG in dust jacket. $14.

CHASE, A. W. *Dr. Chase's Recipes*. Ann Arbor, 1866. This title went through 41 editions within a few short years and is overvalued by many dealers. $20-$75. McKay, 1931 revised edition. Very Good. $20. *Dr. Chase's Family Physician, Bee Keeper, etc.* 1863-1879 eds. $40-$70.

CHASE, EDWARD. *Memorial Life of General William Tecumseh Sherman*. R. S. Peale, 1891 1st ed. VG in red cloth covers. $60-$80.

CHASE, ERNEST D. *The Romance of Greeting Cards*. Rust Craft, 1956 1st ed. Fine in dust jacket. $20.

CHASE, STUART. *A Study of Two Americas*. NY, 1931. Diego Rivera illus. Very Good. $75.

CHATLEY, HERBERT. *The Force of the Wind*. London, 1919 2nd edition. Good. $26.

CHATTERBOX ANNUALS. 1881-1915. Very Good. $25 each. 1926, worn, scuffed. $19.

CHATTERTON, E. KEBLE. *King's Cutters and Smugglers*. Lippincott, 1912. Good-Very Good. $35-$75. *Fore and Aft*. London, 1912, VG. $65. *The Romance of a Ship*. London, 1913. Good. $15. *Sailing Ships & Their Story*. London, 1914. Illustrated Good-Very Good. $20-$40. *Whalers and Whaling*. Philadelphia, 1926. G-VG. $40. *Sailing Models Ancient & Modern*. Lon., 1934 1st. $100.

CHAUCER, GEOFFREY. *Troilus and Cressida*. Literary Guild, 1932. Eric Gill illustrator. Fine in dust jacket. $50. Good, blue cloth. $30. *The Works of Geoffrey Chaucer*. Cleveland, 1958. Facsimile edition. of William Morris Chaucer. Very Good in dust jacket. $100. *Canterbury Tales*. G. C. Pub. 1930 deluxe ed. Rockwell Kent illus. Very Good. $25-$40. NY, 1930, folio, 2 volumes. Rockwell Kent signed. $350. 1934 reprint. Kent illustrator. Fine in dust jacket. $12-$15.

CHENEY, EDNAH, D. (Editor). *Life, Letters and Journals of Louisa M. Alcott*. Boston, 1890. Good. $48.

CHENEY, EMMA C. *Young Folks History of the Civil War*. Estes-Lauriat, 1887 edition. Good. $10.

CHENEY, SHELDON. *The New World Architecture*. No place, 1930 1st ed. Rubbed, corners bumped. $50. *Expressionism in Art*. NY, 1934. Good. $40.

CHENNAULT, A. *A Thousand Springs*. General Chennault and the Flying Tigers. NY, 1962. Good. $20.

CHERRY, P. P. *The Western Reserve and Early Ohio*. Akron, Fouse, 1920. Shelfworn ex-library, o/w VG. $50.

CHERR, P. *The Lion in Fact and Fiction*. No place, 1966. Fine in dust jacket. $13.

CHESTER, W. T. *Chester's Complete Trotting and Pacing Record...through 1883*. NY, 1884. Cracked hinges. $100.

CHESTERTON, GILBERT. *The Man Who Was Thursday*. NY, 1910 Later edition. Very Good. $45. *Manalive*. NY, London, 1912 1st edition. Very Good. $40.

The Incredulity of Father Brown. NY, 1926 1st American ed. VG plus. $35. London, 1926 1st ed. VG. $40.
The Well & the Shallows. Sheed Ward, 1935 1st ed. VG plus in dust jacket. $65.

CHESTERTON, G. K. (Illustrator). *The Missing Masterpiece.* By Hilaire Belloc. 41 drawings. Very Good. $50.

CHESTNUTT, CHARLES. *The Wife of His Youth.* Houghton-Mifflin, 1899 1st ed. Very Good. $100.
The Conjure Woman. Boston, 1920 2nd ed. VG. $100.

CHEVIGNY, HECTOR. *Lord of Alaska: Baranov and the Russian Adventure.* No place, 1942 1st ed. G-VG. $12. Later editions sell at same price.

CHEVROLET. *Owner's Manual, 1942.* $15.
(See Catalog Section for additional items).

CHICAGO 1933 WORLD'S FAIR. OFFICIAL GUIDE BOOK. Blue cloth, stamped silver. Very Good-Fine. $75.
SOUVENIR BOOK. 1934. 110 views. Very Good. $25.

CHIDSEY, DONALD. *The American Privateers-A History.* Dodd-Mead, 1962. Ex-library. Dust jacket. $10.

CHILD, JULIA. *Julia Child and Company.* NY, 1978. Signed. Very Fine in DJ with minimal edge wear. $40.

CHILD, JULIA, SIMONE BECK, L. BERTHOLLE. *Mastering the Art of French Cooking.* NY, 1961 2nd printing. $20-$25. 1970 edition. 2 vol set. $40.

CHILD, LYDIA MARIA. *The First Settlers of New England.* Boston, 1829 1st ed, 1st issue. Uncut, binding repaired. Water stain. $65.
Mother's Book (Cook Book). 1831. $300-$350.
An Appeal in Favor of That Class of Americans Called Africans. Boston, 1833 1st. Disbound, some foxing. $95.
The American Frugal Housewife, Dedicated to Those Who Are Not Ashamed of Economy. NY, 1847. $100.
The Right Way, the Safe Way, Proved by Emancipation. NY, 1860. $30. 1969 reprint. $12.

CHILDERS, J. S. *War Eagles.* NY, Lon., 1943. VG. $25-$45.

CHILTON, PUBLISHER. *Automobile Directory.* 1922. $35.
Automobile Multi-guide. 1930. 536 pages. $30.

CHIPMAN, GEN. N. P. *The Tragedy of Andersonville: The Trial of Captain Henry Wirz, The Prison Keeper.* San Francisco, 1911. Very Good. $75.

CHITTENDEN, HIRAM M. *The Yellowstone National Park.* 1899 3rd ed, Robert Clark Co. VG. $25.
The American Fur Trade of the Far West. NY, Harper, 1902, 3 volumes. $550-$650. NY, 1935. 2 volumes. 2nd

edition. Very Good. $150. Fine in case. $200. 1954 reprint, Stanford. 2 vols. Very Good. $80-$120.
The History of Early Steamboat Navigation on the Missouri River. NY, 1903 Ltd ed. 2 vols. $200-$350. Minneapolis, 1962 reprint in one vol. Fine in DJ. $40.

CHOATE, ANN H. and HELEN FERRIS. *Juliette Low and the Girl Scouts.* NY, 1928. Good-VG. $18.

CHOMSKY, NOAM. *Language and Mind.* NY, 1972. Revised ed. Very Good in dust jacket. $25.

CHORLTON, WILLIAM. *The American Grape Grower's Guide.* NY, Orange Judd, no date, circa 1852, 2nd edition. 204 pgs. Worn and spotted. $45. Another, 1856. $35.

CHRISTENSEN, ERWIN O. *Early American Woodcarving.* Cleveland, 1952 1st ed. Faded spine, o/w Good. $35.
The Index of American Design. Macmillan, 1950. Fine in dust jacket. $20-$35.
Primitive Art. NY, 1955 1st ed. Profusely illus. VG in DJ. $85. Another, Bonanza Books. Good. $30.

CHRISTIE, AGATHA. *The Murder of Roger Ackroyd.* Lon., 1926 1st ed. $450-$550.
The Big Four. NY, 1927 1st ed. $75-$150.
Hound of Death and Other Stories. London, 1933. Published only in England. 1st ed. VG in DJ. $175.
Appointment With Death. NY, 1938 1st American ed. Rubbed, o/w Fine. $50.
And Then There Were None. NY, 1940 1st ed. VG in very good dust jacket. $250.
The Moving Finger. NY, 1942 1st. VG in fair DJ. $125.
Remembered Death. NY, 1945 1st American ed. VG in fair dust jacket. $35-$60.
Hickory Dickory Dock. London, 1955 1st. VG in DJ. $28.
Dead Man's Folly. London, 1956 1st ed. VG in DJ. $35.
4:50 From Paddington. London, 1957 1st ed. (Miss Marple). Very Good in dust jacket. $35.
Cat Among the Pigeons. London, 1959 1st ed. Fine in DJ. $40. Same, 1960 1st American ed. VG in DJ. $18.
The Pale Horse. New York, 1962 1st American edition. Very Good in dust jacket. $25.
The Clocks. Dodd Mead, 1963 1st American ed. Bumped corners. VG in dingy DJ. $25.
A Caribbean Mystery. London, 1964. Fine in DJ. $30.
At Bertram's Hotel. London, 1965 1st ed. (Miss Marple). Very Good in dust jacket. $35.
Endless Night. London, 1967 1st. Edge staining, o/w F in clipped DJ. $25. Same, NY, 1968 1st Amer. F in DJ. $20.
By the Pricking of My Thumbs. London, 1968 1st English ed. Fine in dust jacket. $40.
Nemesis. NY, 1971 1st American ed. Fine in DJ. $20.
Curtain. Dodd Mead, 1975 1st American edition. VG in clipped dust jacket. $15.
Elephants Can Remember. NY, 1972 1st American ed. Fine in dust jacket. $15.

Sleeping Murder. London, 1976 1st British edition. Near Fine in dust jacket. $25.

CHRISTIE, AGATHA (In Magazines). *Cosmopolitan*. Oct, 1948. Short story, $15-$25.

CHRISTY, HOWARD CHANDLER. *The American Girl*. NY, 1906. 16 color plates. Illus. by author. $65-$125.
The Christy Girl. Bobbs-Merrill, 1906. Color illustrations. Very Good. $45-$90.
Our Girls. Moffat, 1907. Illus. by author. Cover soiled, loose. 18 color illus. $75.
Drawings. NY, 1905. $100-$150. Same, 1913. $50-$95.

CHRISTY, HOWARD CHANDLER (Illustrator). *Wanted-A Matchmaker*. By Paul Leicester Ford. New York, 1900. Margaret Armstrong decorations. Very Good. $45.
An Old Sweetheart of Mine. By James Whitcomb Riley. Indianapolis, 1902. Near Fine. $40.
Wanted: A Chaperon. By Paul Leicester Ford. NY, 1902 1st edition. Very Good. $70.
The Man in Lower Ten. By Mary Roberts Rinehart. Indianapolis, 1909 1st ed. Auth. 1st crime fiction. VG. $45.
The Girl I Loved. By J. W. Riley. New York, 1910. Good in poor dust jacket. $60.
The Lady of the Lake. By Sir Walter Scott. Bobbs-Merrill, 1910. Endpaper missing, o/w Good. $50.

A CHRISTMAS GIFT FROM FAIRY LAND. Anon. (James Kirk Paulding). New York, 1838. $200-$250.

CHURCH, JAMES R. *University Foot-Ball. The Play of Each Position. With Portraits*. NY, 1893, Scribners. 1st edition. Fine. $100.

CHRYSLER, WALTER P. *Life of an American Workman*. Dodd Mead, 1950 reprint. Very Good in DJ. $10.

CHURCH, THOMAS. *History of Philip's War. The Great Indian War of 1675-76*. Exeter, NH, 1836 2nd edition. Full leather, scuffed, foxed. $45.

CHURCHILL, WINSTON (1871-1947). American historical novelist. The book *Richard Carvel (1899)* was his biggest success. Other titles are: *The Celebrity (1898), The Crisis (1901) and Coniston (1906)*. These books sell for $2 without dust jackets, and $5 with DJs intact. His books are often confused with those by the British statesman, Sir Winston Churchill.

CHURCHILL, SIR WINSTON. *London to Ladysmith via Pretoria*. NY, 1900 1st Amer. ed. 1 of 3,000 copies. $100.
Savrola. Churchill's only novel. NY, 1900 1st ed. G-F. $300-$1,200. Same, London, 1900. Good-F. $200-$1,000.
The Unknown War. NY, 1931 1st ed. Good. $65.
The Dawn of Liberation. No place, 1945. Good, Ex-library. $22.

Blood, Sweat and Tears. Putnam's 1941 1st American edition. Original dark blue cloth. Fine. $100.
The Second War. Putnam's 1948-1953 1st ed. 6 vols. Small tears in dust jacket. $375. Another, Good-Very Good in dust jacket. $150.
Painting as a Pastime. New York, 1950 1st American edition. Very Good in good DJ. $20. London, 1948, 1st? 18 color plates of Churchill's paintings. Very Good. $50.
A History of the English-Speaking Peoples. London, 1956-1958. 4 volumes, 1st English edition. Near Fine in dust jackets, $500. Same, Good-VG in DJ. $200.

CIARDI, JOHN. *The King Who Saved Himself From Being Saved*. NY, 1965. Edward Gorey illus. Signed by Gorey. Fine in dust jacket. $35-$45.
Someone Could Win a Polar Bear. Philadelphia, 1970 1st edition. Edward Gorey illustrator. Very Good in dust jacket. $25-$35.

CINDERELLA. Garden City, 1938. Leonard Weisgard illustrated. Corners bumped, o/w Very Good in slightly torn dust jacket. $35.

CINEMATOGRAPHIC ANNUAL. Cinematographic Annual. Vol. 11, 1931. Hollywood. Good in DJ. $15.

CITY DIRECTORIES.
San Francisco, 1854. Le Count & Strong. 264 pgs. 16 inserted ads. $550 auction.
San Francisco, 1867. Langley. 698 pgs. $110.
Janesville, WI, 1866. Good. $75.
Boston, MA, 1895. $25.
Logansport, IN, 1915. $24.
Auburn, IN, 1940. $15.
Buffalo, NY, 1953. $15.

CLAIBORNE, CRAIG. *The New York Times Cook Book*. New York, 1961 1st edition. $15-$20. Book Club edition, 1971. $10.

CLAIRE. *My Company Cook Book*. New York, 1932 1st edition 416 pgs. Good. $12.
Gimbels Cook Book. New York, Greenberg Pub. Co., 1932. 416 pages. Very Good. $15.

CLARK, JERRY E. *The Shawnee*. University of Kentucky Press, 1976 1st edition. Fine. $14.

CLARK, JOE. *Back Home-Photo Essay of Tennessee*. Tenn Squire Assoc, 1965 1st ed. Fine in DJ. $18.

CLARK, KENNETH. *The Gothic Revival*. London, 1928. Very good. $60. Near Fine. $75.
The Nude-A Study in Ideal Form. NY, 1971 4th printing. Book Club ed. Poor DJ. $16.
The Best of Aubrey Beardsley. London, 1979 1st English edition. Fine. $18.

CLARK, ROLAND. *Gunner's Dawn*. Derrydale Press, 1937. One of 950 copies. Fine. $700. Countryman Press, 1945 reprint. In worn slipcase. $50.

CLARK, THOMAS. (Editor). *The Southern Country*. Indianapolis, 1948 1st edition. VG in torn DJ. $20.

CLARK, WILLIAM. *Boy's Own Book Extended. A Complete Cyclopedia, Gymnastics, Parlor Magic etc.* NY & Boston, Francis pub, 1859. $100.

CLARKE, ARTHUR C. *Interplanetary Flight: An Introduction to Aeronautics*. New York, circa 1950 1st American edition. Good. $25.
Expedition to Earth. NY, Ballantine, 1953 1st ed. Fine in DJ. $300. London, 1955 1st British ed. $100.
Earthlight. NY, 1955 Paperback. 1st ed. Fine. $35.
City and the Stars. NY, 1956 1st. NF in DJ. $50-$100.
A Fall of Moondust. NY, 1961 1st edition. Fine in good dust jacket. $175.
Tales of Ten Worlds. NY, 1962 1st edition. Very Good in worn dust jacket. $50.
A Space Odyssey. NY, NAL, 1968 1st edition. VG in DJ. $100-$150. Same, no date. Easton Press ed. Leather. $30.

CLARKE, HARRY (Illustrator). *Tales of Mystery and Imagination*. Edgar Allan Poe. NY, 1925. Sunned, rubbed. $120.
Selected Poems of Algernon Swinburne. London, NY, 1928. Fine. $125.
Fairy Tales of Hans Christian Andersen and Charles Perrault. NY, no date. Good. $60.

CLARKE, HELEN. *Longfellow's Country*. NY, Doubleday, 1913 subsequent ed. Gilt-dec. grn. cloth. Fine. $28.

CLARKE, KIT. *Where the Trout Hide*. New York, 1889. Worn. $90.

CLARKE, S. A. *Pioneer Days of Oregon History*. Portland, 1905 1st ed. 2 vols. Ex-library. Good-Very Good. $65.

CLAYTON, DONALD D. *The Dark Night Sky: A Personal Adventure in Cosmology*. NY, 1975. Good in DJ. $22.

CLAYTON, H. J. *Clayton's Quaker Cook Book*. No place, 1883. $350-$450.

CLEAVELAND, AGNES. *No Life for a Lady*. Boston, 1941 1st ed. G-VG, no DJ. $30-$50. 1952 edition, F in DJ. $25.

CLEAVER, ELDRIDGE. *A Soul on Ice*. NY, 1968 1st ed. Author's 1st Book. Near Fine in DJ. $75. G-VG. $20-$25.
Eldridge Cleaver. Random House, 1969 1st ed. Near Fine in dust jacket. $25-$35. G-VG in dust jacket. $20.

CLEAVES, FREEMAN. *Old Tippecanoe - William Henry Harrison*. Scribner's 1939 1st ed. VG in poor DJ. $30.

CLEMENS, SAMUEL. (See Twain, Mark).

CLEVELAND, BESS. *Alaskan Cookbook*. Howell-North, 1960 1st ed. Very Good in dust jacket. $20.

CLEWS, HENRY. *Fifty Years in Wall Street*. NY, 1908. Very Good. $45.

CLINE, W. *The Muzzle-Loading Rifle, Then and Now*. Huntington, WV, 1944. Overall VG. $40.

CLINGER, FRED. *The History of the 71st Infantry Division*. Augsburg, Germany, 1946. Good plus. $110.

CLOUSTON, J. STORER. *The Man From the Clouds*. Doran, 1919, Good-Very Good. $20-$25.
The Chemical Baby. London, 1934 1st ed. VG. $30.

CLOVER, SAMUEL T. *Paul Traver's Adventures*. Way & Williams, 1897 edition. Good. $15.
On Special Assignment. Boston, 1903. Laskey illustrator. Very Good. $30-$50.
A Pioneer Heritage. Los Angeles, 1932. VG. $45.

CLYMER, FLOYD. *Henry's Fabulous Model A Ford*. No place, 1959. Good -Very Good. $10.
Clymer's Historical Motor Scrapbook. No place, no dates Nos. 1, 2 and 3. The set. $24.
Album of Historical Steam Traction Engines. Calif, 1949 1st edition. Good-VG. $14.

COATES, ROBERT M. *The Outlaw Years*. Literary Guild, 1930. Illus. Good. $15.
The View From Here. Harcourt, 1960 1st edition. Very Good in dust jacket. $25.
Beyond the Alps. NY, 1961 1st ed. VG in DJ. $20.
The Man Just Ahead of You. NY, 1964. Good in DJ. $8.

COATSWORTH, ELIZABETH. *The Cat and the Captain*. NY, 1927, 1st edition. Author's 1st book. Gertrude Kaye illus. Very Good. $35.
The Sun's Diary. NY, 1929 1st ed. VG in DJ. $45.
The Cat Who Went to Heaven. Macmillan, 1930 1st. VG in DJ. $95. Same, 1931 3rd ed. Ward illus. VG in DJ. $20.
Houseboat Summer. NY, 1942 1st Davis illus. VG. $20.
The Kitten Stand. NY, 1945. Keeler illus. Good DJ. $30.
The Blue Cat of Castletown. New York, 1949 1st edition. Janice Holland illus. Very Good. $50.
Night and the Cat. NY, 1950 1st ed. Foujita illus. Corners bumped, o/w VG in worn DJ. $30. Another in VG DJ. $55.
They Walk in the Night. NY, 1969 1st edition. Wood engravings by Stefan Martin. VG in dust jacket. $20.
Under the Green Willow. NY, 1971, 1st ed. E. and J. Domanska illus. Fine in dust jacket. $30.

COBB, HUMPHREY. *Paths of Glory*. NY, 1935 1st ed. Author's 1st book. signed, VG in dust jacket. $50.

COBB, IRVIN S. *The Works of Irvin S. Cobb*. Doran, 1923. 8 vols. One vol signed. Minor wear. $35. Same, Review of Reviews, 1928. 8 vols. Fine. $34.
Intellectually She Rolls Her Own. No place, 1924. McCutcheon, illus. VG in dust jacket. $20.

COBB, JOHN S. *A Quarter Century of Cremation in North America*. Boston, 1901 1st ed. Ex-lib. Overall VG. $125.

COBB, TY. *My Life in Baseball*. NY, 1961 1st ed. VG in vg dust jacket. $30.

COBLEIGH, ROLFE. *Hand Farm Devices and How to Make Them*. New York, Orange Judd, 1938 edition. Fine in dust jacket. $18.

COCKRAN, JACQUELINE. *The Stars at Noon*. Little Brown, 1954 4th printing. VG in dust jacket. $12.

COCKRAN, SAMUEL. *Simon Kenton*. VA, Shenandoah, 1932 1st ed. Very Fine in dust jacket. $28.

CODMAN, COL. CHAS. R. *Drive*. By Patton's Aide-de-camp. Little Brown, 1957 1st ed. $25.

CODMAN, JOHN. *The Mormon Country. A Summer With the Latter Day Saints*. NY, 1874 1st ed. Very Good. $35.

CODY, WILLIAM F. *Story of the Wild West*. Philadelphia, 1889 ed. VG. $60. 1902 edition, Thomas. VG. $15.
Life and Adventures of "Buffalo Bill". NY, 1904. Good. $20. Chicago, 1917. Good-Very Good. $30-$38.
Buffalo Bill's Own Story. 1917 1st ed. Pictorial cover. Good-Very Good. $25.
True Tales of the Plains. NY, 1908, VG. $75.

COFFIN, MARGARET. *The History and Folklore of American Country Tinware 1700-1900*. NY, 1968. Illus. Good-VG in dust jacket. $25-$35.

COFFIN, ROBERT P. TRISTAN. *Kennebec: Cradle of Americans*. NY, 1937 reprint. VG no DJ. $20.
Mainstays of Maine. NY, 1933. VG. $15-$20.

COFFMAN, MRS. EVA M. *Mrs. Coffman's Cook Book*. 1889. Good. $50-$60.

COGLEY, Thomas. *History of the 7th Indiana Cavalry Volunteers*. Laporte, IN 1876. Original green cloth. $250.

COLBERT, E. *Chicago and the Great Conflagration*. Cincinnati, 1872 1st ed. Illus. Foldout map. Spine weak, foxing, o/w Very Good. $45.

COLBURN, ZERAH. *The Locomotive Engine: Rules for Estimating Capabilities, etc*. Philadelphia, 1853. Worn, good. $45. 1875 edition, as new. $40.

COLBURN, FRONA EUNICE. *In Old Vintage Days*. San Francisco, 1937. Dorothy Payne illus. Signed by author. Dark spine, else Very Good. $75.

COLE, G. D. H. and MARGARET. *The Murder at Crome House*. NY, 1927 1st ed. Good plus, $13.
Mrs. Warrender's Profession. NY, 1939. 1st American ed. Good in dust jacket. $45.
Toper's End. NY, 1942 1st ed. VG in slightly wn DJ. $30.

COLE, MARGARET. *Robert Owen of New Lanark*. NY, 1953. 1st American ed. Very Good in dust jacket. $25.

COLE, WILLIAM. *Beastly Boys and Ghastly Girls*. Cleveland, 1964 12th printing. Tomi Ungerer illus. Near Fine in dust jacket. $15.

COLEMAN, J. WINSTON. *Kentucky, A Pictorial History*. Univ. of KY, 1972 2nd ed. Fine in DJ. $22.

COLEMAN, WILL H. *La Cuisine Creole*. NY, 1885. Very scarce cookbook. $250-$400. Later editions. $35-$40.

COLERIDGE, SAMUEL TAYLOR. *Rime of the Ancient Mariner*. NY, 1877. Doré illus. $150. 1885-1893 eds illus by Patton. $65-$95. Roycroft limited edition of 1899. $50-$75. Various limited editions 1900-1964. Signed by famous illustrators $250-$1,000. 1971 ed. Walter Hodges illus. Fine in DJ. $40. NY, 1964 Chilmark Press. Boxed, as new. $150. Doubleday, 1928. Pogany illus. $75.

COLES, MANNING. *Diamonds to Amsterdam*. Doubleday Crime Club. 1940 1st ed. Review copy. Browned acidic paper, o/w VG in edgeworn dust jacket. $50.
Drink to Yesterday. Ohio, World Pub., 1946 1st ed. VG in torn dust jacket. $10.
Let the Tiger Die. NY, Crime Club, 1947 1st ed. Fine in fine dust jacket. $14.

COLLIER, BASIL. *The Airship*. NY, 1974. Illus. G in DJ. $18.

COLLIER, JOHN. *His Monkey Wife*. London, 1930 1st ed. Author's 1st book. Near VG. $75. Same, 1933 reprint, Macmillan. Very Good in dust jacket. $6. New York, Appleton, 1931. Good. $15.

COLLIER, RICHARD. *Duce! A Biography of Benito Mussolini*. No place, 1971. VG. $20.

COLLIER'S JUNIOR CLASSICS. Vols. 1-10. 1962. Very Good. $30 set.

COLLIER'S PHOTOGRAPHIC HISTORY OF WORLD WAR II. No place, 1946. Good. $35.

COLLIER'S PHOTOGRAPHIC HISTORY OF THE EUROPEAN WAR. No place, 1915. Good. $18.

COLLINGWOOD, STUART D. *The Life and Letters of Lewis Carroll*. Century, 1899 ed. Ex-library. G-VG. $35.

COLLINS. *Our Volunteer Firemen 1736-1881*. Ephrata Science Press, Ltd. ed. 1982. 1 of 1200 copies. Mint. $95.

COLLINS, HERBERT R. *Threads of History: Americana Recorded on Cloth*. Washington DC, 1979. Bibliography of fabric imagery. Fine in dust jacket. $75.

COLLINS, JACKIE. *The World Is Full of Married Men*. World, 1969 1st book. VG in DJ. $15.

COLLINS, JOHN S. *Across the Plains in '64*. Omaha, 1904 1st edition. Very Good. $35.
My Experiences in the West. Lakeside Press, 1970. Map in rear. Very Good. $25.

COLLODI, CARLO. *Pinocchio*. Lippincott, 1917. Maria L. Kirk illus. Worn, soiled covers. $8. Another, Boston, 1904. Charles Copeland illus. VG. $15. 1924 edition. Frances Brundage, illus. Saalfield Pub. 247 pgs. Mint. $25. Garden City, 1932. Petersham illus. Good. $15. Very Good. $30.

COLMAN, LOUIS (Editor). *Alexandre Dumas Dictionary of Cuisine*. Simon-Schuster, 1958. G-VG in DJ. $15-$20.

COLUM, PADRAIC. *The Big Tree of Bunlahy*. NY, 1933 1st ed. Jack Yeats illus. Very Good. $34.
The Peep-Show Man. Macmillan, 1924 1st ed. Lois Lenski illus. Very Good in dust jacket. $40-$50.
The Boy Who Knew What the Birds Said. New York, 1930. Good-Very Good. $15.

COLVIN, IAN. *Master Spy: the Story of Admiral Wilhelm Canaris*. NY, 1957. Good in dust jacket. $15.

COMBE, GEORGE. *Essays on Phrenology*. London, 1819 1st ed. Weak hinges, lightly foxed. $175.
Lectures on Phrenology. NY, 1851. Good. $35.
A System of Phrenology. NY, 1897 2nd ed. VG. $30.

COMBS, BARY B. *Westward to Promontory*. Palo Alto CA, 1969 1st edition, 1st printing. Very Good in dust jacket. $32. 2nd printing. $13.

COMER, GEORGE N. *Penmanship Made Easy*. Boston, 1871 6th ed. Good-Very Good. $25.

COMMAGER, HENRY STEELE. *Illustrated History of the American Civil War*. London, 1976. VG in DJ. $25.
Official Atlas of the Civil War. Yosoloff, 1958 1st ed. Fine in fair dust jacket. $55.

COMPILATION OF NARRATIVES OF EXPLORATION IN ALASKA. Washington DC, 1900. 856 pages, folding maps. Binding worn, spotted. Some insect holes. $195.

A COMPLETE COURSE IN CANNING. Baltimore, 1914, 1914 3rd ed. Good-Very Good. $20.

COMPLETE DOG BOOK, CARE, HANDLING AND FEEDING. 1947 revised edition, AKC pub. Very Good in dust jacket. $10-$14.

COMPLETE STORY OF THE SAN FRANCISCO HORROR. 1906. H. D. Russell. Good. $15.

COMPTON, MARGARET. *Grand Union Cook Book*. Grand Union Tea Co., 1902. Brown, brittle, torn. Poor. $20.

COMSTOCK, HARRIET. *Joyce of the North Woods*. Doubleday, 1911 1st ed. Illus. Good. $10.

COMSTOCK, HELEN. *The Looking Glass in America, 1700-1825*. NY, 1968. Illus. G-VG in DJ. $40.

COMSTOCK, HENRY B. *The Iron Horse*. Galahad, 1971 1st ed. Illus. Fine in dust jacket. $15.

COMSTOCK, JOHN H. *How to Know the Butterflys of Eastern United States*. NY, 1904. Color illus. VG. $35.

COMSTOCK, WILLIAM. *Bungalows, Camps & Mountain Houses*. NY, 1908. Building plans. VG. $75-$125.

CONDON, EDDIE. *We Called It Music*. NY, 1947. Fine in dust jacket. $30.

CONDON, RICHARD. *The Manchurian Candidate*. NY, 1959 1st ed. Very Good in dust jacket. $35.
Some Angry Angel. NY, 1960 1st ed. VG in DJ. $35.
A Talent for Loving. NY, 1961 1st ed. VG in DJ. $35-$60.
An Infinity of Mirrors. NY, 1964 1st ed. VG in DJ. $35.
Prizzi's Honor. NY, 1982 1st ed. Fine in NF DJ. $35.

CONFECTIONER'S HANDBOOK. Anonymous. Dick & Fitzgerald, NY, 1870s. $45.

THE CONGRESSIONAL CLUB COOK BOOK. Wash, D.C., 1927. 800 pgs. Near VG. $45. 1961 6th edition. $20.

CONKLIN, ENOCH. *Picturesque Arizona*. Mining, Indians, flora & fauna. NY, Mining Record, 1878. 380 pgs. $300.

CONKLING, ROSCOE and MARGARET. *The Butterfield Overland Mail*. Glendale CA, 1947, 3 volumes. Fine in dust jacket. $600.

CONNELL, EVAN S. *Son of the Morning Star. Custer and the Little Big Horn*. North Point Press, 1984 1st ed. Fine in DJ. $50-$100. 7th edition, same year. $15.

CONNELLY, MARC. *The Green Pastures*. Farrar, 1929 1st edition. Fine in dust jacket. $75.

CONNER, HOWARD M. *Spearhead, WW II History of the 5th Marine Division*. Infantry Press, 1950 1st edition. Very Good. $85.

CONNETT, EUGENE. *Early American Hunters*. Derrydale, NY, 1928. One of 375 copies. Very Good. $150.
Any Luck. NY, 1933 1st ed. Fine in dust jacket.$90.
American Big Game Fishing. Derrydale Press, 1935. One of 1,850 copies. $350.
Duck Shooting Along the Atlantic Tidewater. Morrow, 1947 1st edition. G-VG. $50-$95. Same, 2nd edition. $35.
Yachting in North America. NY, 1948. VG. $30-$55.
Wildfowling in the Mississippi Flyway. New York, 1949. Fine in fine dust jacket. $250. Same, no DJ. $125-$175.
My Friend the Trout. NY, 1961 1st edition. Near Fine in soiled dust jacket. $40.

CONNOLLY, JAMES B. *Out of Gloucester*. NY, 1903 1st edition. Near Fine. $40.
The Book of the Gloucester Fishermen. NY, 1927 1st ed. Illus. Near Fine. $30. 1928 edition. $25.

CONNOR, RALPH. *The Sky Pilot*. G&D, 1899. G-VG. $6.
Black Rock. New York, 1900. Very Good. $15.
The Men From Glengarry. Revell, 1901 1st ed. VG. $18.
Glengarry School Days. G&D, 1902. Good. $10.

CONRAD, BARNABY. *Gates of Fear: Exploits of the World's Bullrings*. New York, 1957 1st edition. Very Good in dust jacket. $20-$30. Same, Signed, inscribed with drawing. Good in dust jacket. $65.
Encyclopedia of Bullfighting. Bos., 1961. VG in DJ. $30.
The Death of Manolete. Boston, 1958 1st. DJ chips. $25.
Matador. Houghton Mifflin, 1952 BCE. Fine in DJ. $8.

CONRAD, JOSEPH. *Lord Jim, A Romance*. New York, 1900 1st American edition. Very Good. $110.
Tales of Hearsay. New York, Doubleday, 1925 1st American edition. Very Good in dust jacket. $50.
The Rover. Doubleday, 1923 1st Amer. trade ed. VG. $35.

CONSTANCE, ARTHUR. *The Inexplicable Sky*. Werner Laurie, 1956 1st ed. Very Good. $15.

CONWAY, DANIEL MONCURE. *The Life of Thomas Paine*. New York, 1892. 2 volumes. 1st edition. Near Very Good. $85.

COOK, DAVID. *Hands Up, Thirty-five Years of Detective Life*. Denver, 1897 enlarged 2nd edition. Dull, frayed spine, else Very Good. $125-$175.

COOK, FREDERICK. *Through the First Antarctic Night*. NY, 1909. Inscribed. VG. $125.
My Attainment of the Pole. New York, London, 1912. Illustrated. Very Good. $45. Another, signed. Very Good. $125. Same, 1913 edition. Inscribed. Worn. $50.

COOKBOOKS

A few pioneer American cook books of the 18th and 19th century are worth hundreds of dollars (you will find them listed by author, or title, among other books in this volume) but most cook books published during the past 75 years fall in a general price range of $9 to $20 each (See author or title.)

Specialist dealers often cite one of the following bibliographies when cataloging an important cook book:

Gastronomic Bibliography, Katherine Bitting, San Francisco, 1939.

Culinary America - 100 Years of Cookbooks Published in the United States 1860-1960, by Bob and Eleanor Brown, New York, 1961.

Bibliography of American Cookery Books, 1742-1860, by Eleanor Lowenstein, Mass., 1972.

Other price guides worth owning are:

A Guide to Collecting Cookbooks, by Robert Allen. Collector Books, Paducah, KY. 1993.

Cookbooks Worth Collecting, by Mary Barile. Wallace-Homestead, Radnor, PA. 1994.

Price Guide to Cookbooks and Recipe Leaflets, by Linda Dickinson. Collector Books.

COOK, JAMES H. *Fifty Years on the Frontier as Cowboy, Hunter, Guide, Scout & Ranchman*. Univ. of Oklahoma, 1957 reprint. Fine. $42. 1925 3rd printing, Yale Univ. Press. Photo illus. Good-VG. $25-$35.

COOK, JOEL. *America Picturesque and Descriptive*. PA, Henry Coates, 1900 1st. 3 vols. F in red cloth DJ. $60 set.

COOK, JOHN ESTEN. *A Life of Gen. Robert E. Lee*. NY, 1871 2nd ed. Near VG. $250.
The Life of Stonewall Jackson. NY, 1876 2nd. VG. $300.

COOKE, EDMUND VANCE. *I Rule the House*. Poems. NY, Dodge Pub., 1910 1st ed. Near Fine. $20.
Chronicle of the Little Tot. NY, Dodge Pub., 1905 1st ed. Very Good. $30.

COOKE, PHILIP ST. GEORGE. *Calvalry Tactics*. New York, 1862. $90-$120.
The Conquest of New Mexico and California. NY, 1878 1st edition. $175-$250.

THE COOK'S OWN BOOK. AN AMERICAN FAMILY COOK BOOK. 2,500 Receipts. NY, 1865. Worn. $150.

COOLBRITH, INA. *Songs From the Golden Gate*. Boston, 1895. 1st ed. Sunned, slight foxing. $50.

COON, HORACE. *Columbia-Colossus on the Hudson*. E. P. Dutton, 1947 1st edition. Very Good. $14.

COOPER, A. *In and Out of Rebel Prisons*. 1888. $35-$55.

COOPER, ELLWOOD. *Forest Culture and Eucalyptus Trees*. San Francisco, Cubery, 1876 1st ed. Good. $100.

COOPER, JAMES FENIMORE. *The History of the Navy of the United States*. Philadelphia 1839 2 vols. Spines split, sunned. $100 Rebound set $200. NY, Stringer Townsend, 1856 edition. Good. $50. Putnam, 1854. 3 volumes. $60.
The Battle of Lake Erie. Soft cover. Cooperstown NY, 1843 1st ed. $300-$400.
Lives of Distinguished American Naval Officers. 2 vols. Philadelphia, 1846 1st ed. $400-$500.
The Pathfinder: or, The Inland Sea. London, 1840 1st ed, 3 vols. VG. $1,000. Same, 2 vol. Philadelphia 1840. $275. Philadelphia, 1840 1st ed, first issue, no copyright notice in Vol 1. 2 vols. $650. NY, 1965 LEC. Boxed. $50-$70.
The Last of the Mohicans. Scribners, 1919, Wyeth illus. $125-$150. Same, 1925. $40-$65. NY, 1932 LEC. $65. NY, 1937 Scribners. Wyeth illus. VG. $20. Another, 1939 Ex-lib. Good. $10. Ginn & Co., 1904. $12.
The Deerslayer. Philadelphia 1841 1st edition, 2 vols. $2,400. Scribner's, 1925 edition. N. C. Wyeth illustrator. Good, no dust jacket. Ex-library. $10-$14. Same, Very Good-Fine. $75-$150. 1927 ed. $35-$65.
The Leatherstocking Saga. Allan Nevins, editor. Kingsport Press, 1954. Very Good in slipcase. $25.
The Works of James Fenimore Cooper. In 10 volumes. New York, P. F. Collier, 1892. 8,000 pgs. Green gilt-dec. cloth. Illustrated. Very Good. $75 set.

COOPER, FREDERICK TABER. *Argosy of Fables*. New York 1921 1st ed. Paul Bransom illus. Very Good. $75.
Riders' California. A Guide-book. New York, London, 1925. 28 maps intact. Good. $50.

COOPER, LENNA F. *The New Cooking*. Battle Creek MI, 1922, 8th ed, revised. Good. $13.

COOPER, MADISON. *Sironia, Texas*. Boston, 1952 1st ed. Very Good. $50.

COOPER, SUSAN. *Mandrake*. London, 1964 1st ed. Author's 1st book. Very Good in dust jacket. $70.
Dawn of Fear. NY, 1970 Reprint. Ex-library. $12.
The Dark Is Rising. New York, 1975. 2nd edition. Signed. Fine in dust jacket. $30.

COOPER-OAKLEY, I. *The Comte De St. Germain*. London, 1927. 2nd printing. Illus. Very Good. $38.

COPELAND, ROBERT M. *Country Life: A Handbook of Agriculture, Horticulture, etc.* NY, Orange Judd, 1867. 912 pgs. Orig green cloth, gilt spine. Shelfworn, $50-$65.

COPLEY, FRANK. *Frederick Taylor, Father of Scientific Management*. New York, Harper, 1933 1st edition, 2 vols. Very Good. $75.

COPPARD, A. E. *Adam and Eve & Pinch Me*. Golden Cockerell, 1921 1st edition. Author's 1st book. VG. $35.
Pink Furniture. London, 1930 1st edition. Nancy B. Gurney illustrated. Fine in dust jacket. $100. Another, no dust jacket. $50.
Fearful Pleasures. Arkham House, 1946 1st edition. Very Good in dust jacket. $75.

CORBETT, BERTHA L. *The Sunbonnet Babies*. Minn., 1900 1st edition. Good. $38.

CORBETT, JAMES J. *The Roar of the Crowd*. NY, 1925 1st edition. Illus. Very Good. $150.

HELEN CORBITT'S COOK BOOK. Boston, 1957 Book Club ed. Very Good in dust jacket. $8.

COREY, FANNY Y. (Illustrator). *The Master Key*. by L. F. Baum. Indianapolis, 1901. 12 color plates. VG. $200.
The Fanny Corey Mother Goose. NY, 1913, 1st edition. Anonymous. Spotted, several pages torn. Good. $160.

CORLISS, WILLIAM. *Mysteries of the Universe*. NY, 1967. Illus. Very Good. $16.

CORN, WANDA M. *The Art of Andrew Wyeth*. Fine Arts Museum, 1973 1st ed. Fine in DJ. $28-$35.

CORNEBISE, A. E. *The Stars and Stripes: Doughboy Journalism in World War II*. No place, 1984. As new in new dust jacket. $20.

CORNELIUS, MRS. MARY HOOKER *Young House-keeper's Friend Cook Book*. 1845, 1846, 1859, 1863, 1864, 1868 and 1871 editions. $55-$75 each.

CORRIGAN, DOUGLAS. *That's My Story*. NY, 1938 1st edition. Signed presentation copy. VG in dust jacket. $50. Another, no dust jacket. $20.

CORSON, JULIET. *The Cooking Manual of Practical Directions for Economical Every Day Cooking*. NY, 1877 1st edition. Good-Very Good. $45.
Miss Corson's Practical American Cookery and Household Management. NY, circa 1885. Illus. $100-$175.

CORSON, RICHARD. *Fashions in Hair: the first 6,000 Years*. New York, 1969. 3,500 illustrations. Very Good in dust jacket. $45-$65.

COSNAN, MADELEINE. *Fabulous Feasts: Medieval Cookery & Ceremony*. NY, 1976 1st printing. Very Good in dust jacket. $35.

COSTELLO, AUGUSTINE E. *Our Firemen*. (New York City F.D.) NY, 1887. VG. $200. Fair, pages gone. $45.

COSTELLO, D. F. *The World of the Porcupine*. Lippincott, 1966. Fine in dust jacket. $18.

COTTON, HENRY. *A History of Golf*. Lippincott, 1975. 1st edition. Illus. Very Good in dust jacket. $15.

COUES, ELLIOTT. *Birds of the Northwest*. Boston, 1877. Very Good. $45-$65.
Fur Bearing Animals. Wash. DC, 1877 1st edition. $75.

COUES, ELLIOTT (Editor). *Forty Years a Fur Trader on the Upper Missouri; Charles Larpenteur, 1833-1872*. New York, 1898. No. 548 of 950 copies. NF. $300-$500.

COULTER, ELLIS M. *The Civil War and Readjustment in Kentucky*. Chapel Hill, 1926 1st edition. Very Good in dust jacket. $85. Another, no dust jacket. $60.

COULTON, G. G. *Chaucer and His England*. New York, 1957. Very Good in dust jacket. $22.

COULTER, JOHN (Editor). *The Complete Story of the Galveston Horror*. Tornado, Flood, Cyclone. 1900, United Publishing. Good-VG. $11.

COUNT JULIAN: OR, THE LAST DAYS OF THE GOTH. Anon. (Walter S. Landor). Baltimore, 1845. $350-$450.

COUNTY HISTORIES. (See "History" or Author.)

COURTINE, R. *The Hundred Glories of French Cooking*. NY, 1973 1st edition. Very Good in dust jacket. $25-$30.

COURTNEY, W. S. *The Farmers' and Mechanics' Manual*. Revised by George E. Waring. New York, 1878. 25th thousand. Illus. Near Very Good. $65.

COUSSENS, PENRHYN. *A Child's Book of Stories*. NY, Duffield, 1911 1st ed. 10 color plates by Jessie Wilcox Smith. Good-Very Good. $65-$100.

COVARRUBIAS, MIGUEL. *Prince of Wales & Other Famous Americans*. NY, 1925. 1st edition. Illus. by author. Carl Van Vechten introduction. Bumped corners, foxing, o/w Very Good. $150.
Island of Bali. NY, 1937 1st ed. Profusely illus. by author. Very Good to Fine in dust jacket. $70-$150.
Indian Art of Mexico and Central America. New York, 1954 1st edition. $80. 1971 edition. $90. 1957 edition. Fine in dust jacket. $150.

COVARRUBIAS, MIGUEL (Illustrator). *Mules and Men*. By Zora Neale Hurston. Philadelphia, 1935 1st edition. Extremities worn, o/w Very Good. $300.

All Men Are Brothers. By Pearl Buck. Heritage Press, 1948. Fine in vg slipcase. $35.
John and Juan in the Jungle. By Ivan Sanderson. NY, 1963. 25 color paintings. Near Fine. $35.

COWARD, NOEL. *This Happy Breed*. NY, 1947 1st edition. Fine in dust jacket. $40.
Qiuadrille. NY, 1955 1st American ed. Fine in DJ. $50.
Present Indicative. Doubleday, 1937 1st American edition. Near mint, in slipcase. $300-$375.

COWBURN, PHILIP. *The Warship in History*. NY, 1965. Good in dust jacket. $15.

COWLES, FLORENCE A. *Seven Hundred Sandwiches*. Boston, 1928. Good. $10.
Early Algona. Des Moines, 1929. Good. $20.

COX, CHARLES E. *John Tobias, Sportsman*. NY, Derrydale Press, 1937. Alden Ripley illus. VG. $95.

COX, PALMER. *Brownies, Their Book*. NY, 1887. Illus. by author. 1st ed., 1st state. $200-$300. 1887 reprint. VG. $75-$150. 1892 2nd issue of 1st ed. $65. 1915 reprint. Good. $35.
Comic Yarns in Verse. Prose and Picture. Hubbard Bros., 1889. Very Good. $75-$100.
Another Brownie Book. NY, 1890. Illus. by author. Much spine wear. $100. 1941 reprint. VG in DJ. $45.
Brownies Around the World. NY, 1894. Illus. by author. Very Good. $100. Repaired spine, Good. $30.
Brownies Abroad. New York, 1899. Illustrated by author. Much spine wear. $100. Same, VG. $150-$200.
Brownies in the Philippines. NY, 1904 1st edition. Illus. by author. Very Good. $100.
Brownies at Home. Century, 1893. VG. $150-$200. 1942 27th printing. Very Good in dust jacket. $45.
The Brownies and Prince Florinel. NY, 1918 1st ed. As new in dust jacket. $275. Same, no DJ. $100-$130.

COXE, GEORGE HARMON. *Silent Are the Dead*. NY, 1941 1st ed. VG in worn. dust jacket. $40.
The Charred Witness. New York, 1942 1st edition. Very Good plus in dust jacket. $45.
The Jade Venus. NY, 1945 1st ed. Near Fine in DJ. $30.
Eye Witness. NY, 1950. Fine in dust jacket. $25.

CRABB, ALFRED LELAND. *Supper at the Maxwell House*. Bobbs-Merrill, 1943 3rd ed. Ex-library. Rebound. VG. $7.
A Mockingbird Sang at Chickamuaga. Bobbs-Merrill, 1949 1st edition. Very Good in dust jacket. $25.

CRADDOCK, HARRY. *The Savoy Cocktail Book*. New York, 1930 1st ed. VG. $35. 1983 reprint. $25.

CRAIG, WILLIAM N. *Lilies and Their Culture in North America*. Chicago, 1928 1st ed. Illus. Very Good. $20.

CRAM, JACK and DANIEL BRIMM. *Civil Pilot Training Manual*. Civil Aeronautics Bulletin No. 23. Washington, 1940. 257 pages Illus. $20.

CRAM, GEO. F. (See Atlas).

CRAMP, HELEN. *The Institute Cook Book*. Smithsonian Co., Oakland, CA, 1913. 505 pgs. G-VG. $20-$30.

CRANE, HART. *White Buildings*. NY, 1926 1st ed 2nd issue. Author's 1st book. VG-Fine. $300-$400.
The Bridge. NY, 1930 1st trade ed. VG in DJ. $200-$500.
The Collected Poems. Liveright, 1933 1st. Very Good in dust jacket. $100-$200.

CRANE, LEO. *Desert Drums. The Pueblo Indians of New Mexico, 1540-1928*. Little Brown, 1928 1st ed. VG. $28.

CRANE, ROY. *Buzz Sawyer and Bomber 13*. Whitman, 1946 1st edition. Fine. $18.

CRANE, STEPHEN. *Maggie: A Girl of the Streets*. (As Johnston Smith). NY, 1893 1st, paperbound. Author's 1st book. VG-F. $4,000-$14,000. 1896 Hardcover. VG. $150.
The Red Badge of Courage. New York, 1895 1st edition, 1st state. Near Fine. $1,000-$2,000. 1896 2nd ed. $100.
The Third Violet. Appleton, 1897. Orig. cloth. $20-$60.
The Open Boat and Other Stories. NY, 1898 1st edition. Will Bradley illus. Near Fine. $350-$700.
War Is Kind. NY, 1899 1st. Will Bradley illus. NF. $750.
Whilomville Stories. NY, 1900 1st edition. Peter Newell illustrator. Very Good. $125-$175.
O'Ruddy, a Romance. NY, 1903 1st ed. Near Fine. $135.
The Works of Stephen Crane. NY, 1925-1926 1st ed. One of 750 sets. 12 vols Wilson Follett, editor. Fine in vg slipcase. $475.

CRANE, STEPHEN (In Magazines). *Scribner's*. June, 1897. "The Open Boat". $20-$30.
McClure's. Feb, 1898. Short story. $17.

CRANE, WALTER. *Little Red Riding Hood • Jack and the Bean Stock. • The Forty Thieves. • Puss in Boots. • Mother Hubbard. • Valentine and Orson. • The Three Bears*. Together, 7 vols. Illus. throughout with color woodblocks from drawings by Crane. 11½x9¼, original pictorial wrappers. London: John Lane, (c.1900). The Re-Issue Series of Walter Crane's Picture Books. First 3 with yellow wrappers, the last 4 with white. Last 3 with much wear to spine, a corner chipped, else good, others very good to near fine with just a bit of wear to spines. $200-$300 auction.
This Little Pig Went to Market • The Fairy Ship • King Luckie Boy's Party. Illus. throughout with color woodblocks from drawings by Crane. 11½x9¼, original pictorial wrappers. Chicago: Stone & Kimball, (c. 1895). American issue of the first series of Walter Crane's Picture Books. Normal darkening to wrappers, a few short tears, 3rd with wraps neatly detached from contents as a unit, otherwise very good. $150-$250 auction.
Flora's Feast of Flowers. London, 1889 1st edition. $140.
Baby's Bouquet. Warne, NY, London, circa 1900. VG in dust jacket. $75. No jacket. $30.
Cinderella's Picture Book. NY, Dodd. $25-$45.
Columbia's Courtship. Prang. (1892). 12 pls. $150-$200.
Floral Fantasy. Harper, 1899. Illus. by Crane. $125.
Walter Crane's Picture Book. Dodd, 1890s. $75.

CRAVEN, AVERY. *The Coming of the Civil War*. Univ of Chicago Press. 1963. Very Good. $13.

CRAWFORD, F. MARION. *Works of F. Marion Crawford*. NY, 1920 24 vols. Cloth faded. $100 set.

CRAWFORD, MARY C. *Old Boston Days and Ways*. Boston, 1909 1st ed. Illus. Fine. $15.

CRAWFORD, LEWIS F. *Rekindling Camp Fires: The Exploits of Ben Arnold*. ND. Capital Book Co., 1926 1st edition. Fine. $100-$150.

CRAY, ED. *Levi's, The Shrink-to-Fit Business*. Houghton-Mifflin, 1978 1st ed. 286 pages. As new. $10.

CREASY, JOHN. *The Gelignite Gang*. New York, 1955. Fine in dust jacket. $30.
The Toff and the Deep Blue Sea. London, 1955 1st English ed. Not pub. in U. S., until 1967. Near Fine. $25.
Strike for Death. London, 1958 1st edition. NF in DJ. $35.
The Killing Strike. NY, 1958 1st ed. Near Fine in DJ. $13.
Death of a Racehorse. NY, 1959 1st ed. NF in DJ. $13.
The Inferno. NY, 1965 1st American edition. Review copy. Fine in soiled dust jacket. $28.
The Toff and the Great Illusion. New York, 1967. Fine in dust jacket. $20.

CREEKMORE, HUBERT. *The Fingers of Night*. NY, London, 1946 1st ed. VG in DJ. $35.

CREELEY, ROBERT. *The Gold Diggers*. Divers Press, 1954 1st ed. Auth. 1st book. Good, paperbound. $75. Fine. $150.
The Island. NY, 1963 1st ed, 2nd issue. Fine in DJ. $35.
Poems, 1950-1965. London, 1966 1st ed. Fine in DJ. $50.
Mary's Fancy. New York, 1970 Limited edition, signed. Fine in dust jacket. $50-$70.

CRESY, EDWARD. *An Encyclopaedia of Civil Engineering*. London, 1865. 1,752 pages. $75.

CRICHTON, MICHAEL. *The Andromeda Strain*. NY, 1969 1st edition, 1st book. VG in near fine DJ. $40. G in G. $20.
The Great Train Robbery. New York, 1975 1st edition. Fine in dust jacket. $20-$50.
Eaters of the Dead. NY, 1976 1st ed. NF in DJ. $45.

CRISCO, THE STORY OF. Proctor & Gamble, 1914 3rd ed. Includes recipes. Good. $20. 17th edition. $10-$12.

CRISPIN, EDMUND. *The Moving Toyshop*. Philadelphia, 1946 1st ed. Near Fine in frayed DJ. $45. Same, London, 1946 1st British edition. Very Good in dust jacket. $125. *Obsequies at Oxford*. Philadelphia, 1945 1st edition. Very Good in dust jacket with tear. $75.

CROCKER, BETTY. *Betty Crocker's $25,000 Recipe Set*. 1933 spiral bound hard-cover. VG. $22.
Betty Crocker's Picture Cook Book. McGraw-Hill, 1950 1st edition, 1st printing. 449 pages. $40-$50. Same year, 6th & 7th printing. $15-$25.
Betty Crocker's Cook Book for Boys and Girls. NY, 1957. G-VG. $12-$16.
Betty Crocker's New Picture Cook Book. New York, 1961, $15-$30.
Betty Crocker's Cooking Calendar. NY, 1962. Ring bound. Very Good. $10.
Betty Crocker's Cook Book. 1950, General Mills, 1st ed. 448 pgs. $20. 1970, 2nd printing 480 pgs. $10-$15.
Betty Crocker's Kitchen Gardens. Mary M. Campbello. Scribner's, 1971. Very Good in dust jacket. $35. Paperback edition. $18.
Betty Crocker's 40th Anniversary Cook Book. 7th ed., Prentice Hall, 1991. $13.
Various other Betty Crocker titles. 1957-1988. $6-$12.

CROCKETT, DAVY. *Adventures of Davy Crockett*. NY, 1934. John Thomason illus. Very Good. $20.

CROFTON, A. *Poker: Its Laws and Principles*. 1915. 92 pages. Very Good. $150 auction.

CROFTS, FREEMAN WILLS. *Mystery in the Channel*. London, 1931 1st ed. VG. $50.
Antidote to Venom. London, 1938 1st ed. VG. $35.
Silence for the Murderer. London, 1949 1st ed. Fine in very good dust jacket. $75.

CROLL, PAULINE. *Just for You: Ryhmes by,* Chicago, 1918 1st ed, Volland. Mary Basset, illus. G-VG. $35.

CRONIN, FRANCIS. *Under the Southern Cross: Saga of the American Division*. Washington, 1951 1st ed. VG-Fine. $75-$125. Later editions. G-VG. $10-$15.

CRONISE, TITUS FREY. *The Natural Wealth of California*. San Francisco, 1868. Good-VG. $60-$120.

CROSS, AMANDA. *The James Joyce Murder*. New York, 1967 1st edition. Fine in dust jacket. $50-$75.
Poetic Justice. NY, 1970 1st ed. Fine in DJ. $40.
The Thebes Mysteries. NY, 1971 1st ed. Fine in DJ. $40.
Death in a Tenured Position. New York, 1981 1st edition. Fine in dust jacket. $15.

CROSS, REUBEN. *The Complete Fly Tyer*. Rockville Center 1971. Contains "Fur, Feather and Steel" and "Tying American Trout Lures". Fine. $25.

CROTHERS, SAMUEL. *Miss Muffet's Christmas Party*. Houghton, 1902. Olive Long illus. Very Good. $35.
The Children of Dickens. Scribners, 1925. J. W. Smith illus. VG. $75-$125. 1940 reprint. $25.

CROUSE, RUSSEL. *Mr. Currier & Mr. Ives, Their Lives and Times*. Doubleday Doran, 1930 1st edition. One of 301 signed copies. Very Good. $60. Garden City Pub., 1937 reprint. Very Good. $20.

CROWEN, MRS. T. J. *Every Lady's Cook Book*. NY, 1857. Illus. Good-Very Good. $95-$145.

CROWINSHIELD, B. B. *Fore and Afters*. Boston, 1940. (Yachting), 64 photo plates. VG. $75.

CROWLEY, ALEISTER. *Works of Aleister Crowley*. London, 1905 3 vols. Reprinted by Yogi Pub. Fine. $65.
Clouds Without Water. London, 1909 1st ed. Privately printed. Fine. $200.
777. London, 1909 1st ed. Fine. $700.
Ambergris. London, 1910 1st ed. Fine in dust jacket. $300.
Moonchild. London, 1929 1st. Mandrake Press. Fine. $200.
The Confessions of Aleister Crowley. New York, 1970 1st American edition, 2nd printing. John Symonds and Kenneth Grant, editors. VG in DJ. $50.

CROWLY, MRS. J. C. *Jennie June's American Cookery Book*. NY, 1878. Illus. $100-$150.

CROZIER, R. H. *The Confederate Spy*. Louisville KY, 1885 5th edition. Worn edges, o/w Good. $35.

CULLEN, COUNTEE. *Color*. Harper, 1925 1st ed. Author's 1st book. Very Good. $250. Later ed., no date. $18-$30.
Copper Sun. NY, 1927 1st ed. Marbled bds. No DJ. Corners bumped. VG. $60-$75. Others quote $25-$300.
One Way to Heaven. Harper, 1932 1st. Near Fine. $100.
The Medea. NY, 1935 1st edition. Dust jacket chip, spine faded, o/w Very Good. $125.

CULPEPER, NICHOLAS. *The Complete Herbal*. Birmingham, England, 1953. Facsimile of 1653 ed. VG. $90.

CULVER & GRANT. *Book of Old Ships. Saga of the Sailing Ship*. Garden City, 1935 rpt. Color illus. VG in DJ. $16.

CUMMINGS, E. E. *The Enormous Room*. NY, 1922 1st ed. Author's 1st book. Near VG. $150.
Puella Mea. Golden Eagle Press, 1923. VG. $45-$75.
Eimi. Covici Friede, 1931 1st edition. One of 1,381 copies, signed. Good. $175.
Fairy Tales. NP, 1965. John Eaton illus. VG in DJ. $20.

CUNNINGHAM, EUGENE. *Triggernometry: A Gallery of Gunfighters*. NY, 1934 1st edition. Overall VG. $95. Caxton, 1947 reprint. Good. $45. 1975 reprint. $35.

CUPPY, WILL. *The Decline and Fall of Practically Everybody*. No place, 1950 1st edition, William Steig cartoons. Near Fine in dust jacket. $15.

CURRIER & IVES. *Railroad, Indian and Pioneer Prints by*. NY, Antique Bulletin, 1930. No. 99 of 500. $50-$80.
Currier & Ives Album. Doubleday, 1942. Poor binding. Interior good. $10-$25.
One Hundred Currier & Ives Favorites. New York, Crown, 1978 1st edition. Good. $15.

CURTIS, CAPT. PAUL A. *Guns and Gunning*. Philadelphia, 1934 1st edition. Good-Very Good. $16-$25. 2nd edition, Knopf, 1943. Very Good. $15.

CURTIS, DAVID A. *Queer Luck: Poker Stories*. 1900. 235 pages. Excellent. $100 auction.
The Science of Draw Poker. 1901. 216 pgs. Ex. $200.
Stand Pat, Mississippi Poker Stories. 1906. 269 pages. Very Fine. $170 auction.

CURTIS, EDWARD S. (Author/Photographer). *The North American Indian*. Preface by Theodore Roosevelt. 20 volume set published 1907-1930. One of 250 sets actually published; $30,000 to $60,000 at auction. (Many have been broken and individual pages sold.)
Portraits From North American Indian Life. Promontory Press, 1972. Very Good, no dust jacket. $58.
The North American Indian: The Southwest. Amaranth Press, 1980. One of 250 copies. Fine. $95.

CURTIS, GEORGE TICKNOR. *Life of Daniel Webster*. Appleton, 1870 1st edition, 2 volumes, green cloth cover. Very Good. $35.

CURTIS, GEORGE W. *Prue and I*. New York, Dix, Edwards, 1856. Orig. brown cloth, worn. $25.
The Potiphar Papers. New York, 1853 1st edition. Hinges worn. $20.

CURTIS, MATTOON. *The Story of Snuff & Snuff Boxes*. New York, 1935. Illustrated. Fine in dust jacket. $50. Another, Very Good. $35.

CURTIS, NEWTON M. *From Bull Run to Chancellorsville Story of the 16th NY Infantry*. New York, 1906, signed by author. $80. Unsigned, VG. $40. Unsigned, Fine. An unopened copy. $90.

CURTISS, DANIEL. *Western Portraiture and Emigrant's Guide*. New York, J. H. Colton, 1852 1st edition Original cloth, rebacked. $100-$150. Another dealer offers same book in orig. cloth. Very Good . $350.

CURTISS, GLENN H. *The Curtiss Aviation Book*. NY, 1912 1st ed. Fine. $125.

CURWOOD, JAMES OLIVER. *Steele of the Royal Mounted*. Triangle Books, 1911. Good in dust jacket. $10.
The Valley of Silent Men. Grosset & Dunlap, 1920. Dean Cornwell illus. VG-Fine in DJ. $12. Cosmopolitan, 1920 1st edition. Very Good. $25.
Back to God's Country. Grosset & Dunlap, 1920. Photoplay scenes. Good. $7.
The Country Beyond. Cosmopolitan, 1922 1st. VG. $15. Grosset & Dunlap reprint, 1922. $6-$8.
A Gentleman of Courage. Cosmopolitan, 1924 1st ed. R. W. Stewart illus. Very Good. $15.

CUSHING, FRANK. *My Adventures in Zuni*. Santa Fe NM, 1941 1st ed. of 400. VG in DJ. $260. Same, Palo Alto, Amer. West, 1970 Limited Edition. $45.

CUSHING, HARVEY. *Surgery, Its Principles and Practise*. Philadelphia, 1910. 6 vols. Ex-library. VG. $40.
Consecratio Medici and Other Papers. Boston, 1928 1st edition. Fraying, o/w Very Good. $45-$100.
From a Surgeon's Journal, 1915-1918. Boston, 1936 1st edition. Near Fine. $100. Another, Good. $35.
The Life of Sir William Osler. London, 1940. 2 vols in one. Spine fade, o/w VG. $30-$40. 1925 1st ed. 2 vols. Very Good. $100-$200.

CUSHMAN, DAN. *Stay Away Joe*. NY, 1953 1st ed. Very Good in dust jacket. $20-$35.
The Great North Trail. McGraw Hill, 1966 1st ed. Very Good in dust jacket. $15-$25.

CUSTER, ELIZABETH B. *Boots & Saddles, or Life in Dakota With Gen'l Custer*. NY, 1885 1st ed., 1st state. $75-$95. Same year, 2nd printing. VG. $35-$70.
Tenting on the Plains, or General Custer in Kansas and Texas. New York, 1895. Woodcuts. Cracked hinge, spine dark. $38. University of Oklahoma, 1971 reprint. $20.
The Boy General. The Life of Major Gen. George Armstrong Custer. Scribner's, 1901 1st ed. Good. $14.

CUSTER, GENERAL GEORGE. *My Life on the Plains*. NY, 1874 1st edition. Spine fade. $75-$175. London, 1963 reprint. Fine in case. $50.

CUTLER, CARL C. *The Story of the American Clipper Ship*. NY, 1930 1st ed. Illus. Near VG. $25.
Queens of the Western Ocean. USN Inst. Press, 1967. $35.

CYCLING FOR HEALTH AND PLEASURE. Anon. NY, 1896. Rev. edition. Illus. Soiled covers. $50.

CYR, ELLE. *The Children's Third Reader*. Ginn & Co., 1901. Very Good. $12.

D

DABNEY, OWEN P. *True Story of the Lost Shackle or Seven Years with the Indians*. Salem, Capital Printing Co., circa 1897. Paperback, darkened, else VG. $150.

DACUS, J. A. *Life and Adventures of Frank and Jesse James, the Noted Western Outlaws*. St. Louis, 1880 1st ed. 383 pages. G-VG. $100-$200. Worn, dark. $50. Later editions appeared from 1881-1883, (published in various other cities) and are worth considerably less.
Illustrated Lives and Adventures of Frank and Jesse James and the Younger Brothers. N. D. Thompson, 1881 1st ed. Fair. $15. Good-VG. $30-$45.
Annals of the Great Strikes in the United States. Chicago, 1877 1st ed. Good-VG. $100-$150.

DADANT, C. P. *First Lessons in Beekeeping*. Amer. Bee Journal, 1947 revised edition. VG. $8-$10.

DAHL, ROALD. *The Gremlins*. NY, 1943 1st ed. Author's 1st book. Fine in near fine dust jacket. $425.
James and the Giant Peach. NY, 1961. Reprint. Nancy E. Burkert illus. Very Good in worn dust jacket. $30.
Charlie and the Chocolate Factory. New York, 1964. J. Schindelman illus. Very Good in worn dust jacket. $45.
The Magic Finger. NY, 1966 1st ed. William Pene du Bois illus. Fine in dust jacket. $40.
Fantastic Mr. Fox. NY, 1970 1st ed. VG in DJ. $20.

DAHLBERG, EDWARD. *From Flushing to Calvary*. NY, 1932. Fine in dust jacket. $30.
The Sorrows of Priapus. New Directions, 1957 1st ed. Ben Shahn illus. Fine in dust jacket. $25.
Because I Was Flesh. London, 1965 1st ed. Inscribed. Fine in dust jacket. $100.
Do These Bones Live? Harcourt, 1941 1st. DJ. $25-$75.

DAHNKE, MARY. *The Cheese Cook Book*. No place, 1942. Very Good. $18.

DALBEY, ED & WALTER. *Pictorial History of the City of Richmond, Indiana*. Nicholson Printing Co, 1896. 198 pages. 188 illustrations. Worn, else Very Good. $200.

DALE, EDWARD E. *The Range Cattle Industry*. Norman OK, 1930 1st edition. Some foxing, otherwise Very Good. $100-$175. 1960 1st printing of new edition. Fine in dust jacket. $50.

DALGLIESH, ALICE. *The Davenports and Cherry Pie*. Scribner's, 1949 1st ed. Flavia Gag illus. VG in DJ. $40.

DALI, SALVADOR. *The Secret Life of Salvadore Dali*. NY, 1942 1st edition. Near VG. $150. Same, Good. $60.
Hidden Faces. Dial, 1944 1st ed. VG in DJ. $85. Morrow, 1974 1st American edition. Very Good in dust jacket. $75.
Diary of a Genius. Doubleday, 1965 1st. Good in DJ. $65.
Dali by Dali. Abrams, 1970 1st ed. Fine in fine DJ. $75.

DALI, SALVADOR (Illustrator). *Fantastic Memories*. By Mari Sandoz. Garden City, 1944. Slightly stained cover, very worn dust jacket. $60.
The Maze. By Mari Sandoz. Doubleday, 1945 1st edition. Fine in dust jacket. $85.
The Autobiography of Benvenuto Cellini. Doubleday, 1946. 1 of 1,000 copies, signed. NF in worn slipcase $200.
Wine, Women and Words. By Billy Rose. New York, 1948 1st edition. Good. $50.
On the Verge. By Mari Sandoz. 1959 1st edition. VG. $75.
Jerusalem Bible. No place, 1970. VG in DJ. Boxed. $155.

DALI, SALVADOR (In Magazines). *Esquire*. Dec, 1942. Article by Dali. $28.

DALRYMPLE, DYRON. *Doves and Dove Shooting*. NY, 1949 1st edition. Fine in dust jacket. $14-$20.
Modern Book of Black Bass. Winchester, 1972. G. $10.
North American Game Animals Crown, 1978. Good. $10.

DALY, ELIZABETH. *Deadly Nightshade*. NY, 1940 1st edition. Very Good plus in dust jacket. $135.
Murders in Volume 2. NY, 1941 1st. NF in fair DJ. $165.
The Book of the Dead. NY, 1944 1st ed. F in DJ. $50-$75.
Somewhere in the House. New York, Rinehart, 1946 1st edition. Fine in dust jacket. $80-$100.

DALY, R. W. *How the Merrimac Won*. New York, 1957 2nd edition. Good. $19.

DALY, THOMAS A. *Canzoni*. Phil., 1906 1st ed. VG. $75. McKay, 1967 4th printing. John Sloan illustrator. VG. $15.
Madrigali. Philadelphia 1912. Signed with drawing by John Sloan. Very Good. $2,000.
A Little Book of Humorous Verse. 1926. Good-VG. $10.
Selected Poems. New York, 1936 1st edition. Very Good in dust jacket. $20.

DANA, CHARLES. *Recollections of the Civil War*. NY, 1898 1st ed. Slight edge wear, o/w VG. $25.

DANA, CHARLES L. *The Peaks of Medical History*. NY, 1926 1st ed. Signed, inscribed. $175. Unsigned. $50-$75. *Text-book of Nervous Diseases & Psychiatry*. NY, 1904 6th edition. Fine. $20.

DANA, FREEMAN, *Murder at the New World's Fair*. Random House, 1938 1st edition. VG in dust jacket. $300.

DANA, JULIAN. *Sutter of California*. NY, 1938, Halcyon House reprint. Fine in DJ. $20.
The Sacramento River of Gold. No place, 1939. Ex-library. Worn cover. $15.

DANA, RICHARD H. *Two Years Before the Mast*. NY, Harper, 1840 1st ed., 1st issue. Unbroken head on page 9. Good. $700-$1,000. Boston-NY, 1911. Smith color plates. $18. John Winston 1902 edition. Fair. $18. Limited Editions Club, 1947, signed by artist. VG. $50. Photoplay edition, 1945. World Pub. VG. $8. Chicago, Lakeside Press, 1930. 1 of 1,000. Signed by Wilson. $150-$200. Grabhorn, 1936. 1 of 1,000. NF. $200. VG. $65-$100. Houghton Mifflin, 1911. Near Fine. $50. LA, Ritchie Press, 1964. 2 vols., Weinstein illustrator. In slipcase. $40.

DANGERFIELD, STANLEY. *Your Poodle and Mine*. Rocklif, 1954 1st ed. VG. $10-$12.

DANIEL, M. DANIEL. *Babe Ruth: The Idol of the American Boy*. Racine, 1930, Whitman 1st edition. Good-Very Good. $45-$85.

DANIEL, PETE. *The Shadow of Slavery: Peonage in the South 1901-1969*. University of Illinois Press, 1972. Inscribed. Very Good in dust jacket. $18.

DANIELSON, RICHARD. *Martha Doyle and Other Sporting Memories*. New York, 1938 Limited edition, Derrydale. Good. $40.

DANTE, ALIGHERI. *The Divine Comedy*. Illustrated Modern Library, 1944. George Grosz illus. VG. $26. NY, 1957. Gustav Dore illus. VG. $20.

D.A.R. COOK BOOK. 1949, Valley Forge Commission, 1st edition. Spiral bound. $12-$15.

DARRAH, WILLIAM C. *Stereo View, A History of Stereographs in America*. Gettysburg, 1964. VG in DJ. $45.

DARROW, CLARENCE. *Farmington*. Chicago, 1904 2nd edition. Signed by author. $300.
Infidels & Heretics. Boston, 1929 1st ed. VG in DJ. $50.
Plea in Defense of Loeb and Leopold. Girard, KS. Haldeman, Big Blue Book. Paper darkened, o/w VG. $35.

Clarence Darrow's Two Great. Trials. (Scopes and Dr. Sweet). Girard, KS. Big Blue Book. Paperbound. Paper darkened, otherwise Very Good. $35.

DARWIN, CHARLES. *Descent of Man and Selection in Relation to Sex*. London, 1871 1st edition, 2nd issue. 2 volumes. VG. $160. Same, NY, 1871. G-VG. $100-$150.
Expression of Emotion in Man and Animals. London, 1872 1st ed., 2nd issue. VG. $280. Same, NY, 1873 1st American ed. G-VG. $95-$150. Same, NY, 1920. $35.
Different Forms of Flowers. NY, 1877 1st American edition. Very Good. $20.
The Power of Movement in Plants. NY, 1881 1st American ed. Ex-library, shelfwear. Good. $35.
Fertilization of Orchids. NY, 1895 2nd ed. $20.
Complete Works. 1879 Appleton. 15 vols. 3/4 leather. VG. $20 each. $300 set. 1896 revised ed. Good. $10 each vol.
The Structure and Distribution of Coral Reefs. NY, 1897 3rd edition. Piece of map missing. $45.
Geological Observations. Appleton, 1897 3rd. VG. $30.
Animals Under Domestication. NY, 1898 2 vols. $25.
Life & Letters of Charles Darwin. NY, 1898 2 vols. Authorized edition. $95.
The Different Forms of Flowers On Plants of the Same Species. NY, 1903. Near Fine. $38.
The Variation of Animals & Plants Under Domestication. NY, 1905. 2 vols. Good plus. $35.
On the Origin of Species. Limited Editions Club, 1963. Paul Landacre illustrator. One of 1,500 copies. Fine in slipcase. $250. 1963 Heritage edition in case. $35. Facsimile of 1st edition. Harvard, 1964. Very Good. $25-$50. Franklin Center, PA, 1978. Tooled, full leather, gilt edges. Wrinkled pages o/w Very Good. $18. New York, Appleton, 1871 5th edition. $25-$35.

DARY, DAVID. *Entrepreneurs of the Old West*. Knopf, 1986 1st American edition. Fine in DJ. $16-$20.

DASENT, GEORGE W. *Popular Tales From the Norse*. Routledge reprint, 1900s. Engraved frontis. VG. $12.
East O' The Sun, West O' The Moon. McKay, 1921. Good-Very Good. $20-$30.

D'AULAIRE, INGRI and EDGAR. *Children of the Northern Lights*. New York, 1935 2nd edition. Illustrated by author. Very Good in dust jacket. $45.
Ola. Doubleday, 1936 1st edition. Folio. Fine. $75.
Animals Everywhere. NY, 1940 1st edition. Illus. by author. Ex-library. Good. $60-$100.
Leif the Lucky. NY, 1941. Illustrated by author. $35.
Benjamin Franklin. NY, 1950 1st edition. Illustrated by author. Good in dust jacket. $50.
D'Aulaire's Trolls. Doubleday, 1972 2nd printing. Illus. by author. VG in good DJ. $32.

DAUGHERTY, JAMES. *Andy and the Lion*. NY, 1938 1st ed. Illus. by author. Very Good in dust jacket and box. $75.

DAVID, JOHN P. *The Union Pacific Railway: A Study in Railway Politics*. Chicago, 1894. Ex-lib. Shelfwear. $50.

DAVIDIS, FRAU HENRIETTE. *Praktisches Kochbuch fur die Deutchen in Amerika*. Milwaukee, 1879. Cookbook. 400 pages in German, Gothic script. VG. $75.

DAVIDOFF, Z. *The Cigar*. McGraw-Hill, 1967 1st. VG. $21.

DAVIDSON, J. B. *Farm Machinery & Farm Motors*. NY, Orange Judd, 1914 ed. 513 pages. 376 illus. Good. $45.

DAVIDSON, JOHN. *The Last Ballad and Other Poems*. London, NY 1899. Very Good. $35.

DAVIDSON, ORLANDO. *The Dead-Eyes: The Story of the 96th Infantry Division (WWII)*. Washington, 1947 1st ed. Very Good. $78. Same, 1981 ed. New. $32.

DAVIDSON & STUVE. *Complete History of Illinois, 1673-1873*. Springfield, 1874. 944 pages. Covers worn, few tattered pages. $125.

DAVIDSON, WINIFRED. *Where California Began*. San Diego, 1929. Author inscription. Near Fine. $45.

DAVIES, HUNTER. *The Beatles Authorized Biography*. London, 1968 1st ed. Good in good DJ. $15-$18.

DAVIES, L. P. *The Paper Dolls*. NY, 1954 1st ed. Fine in nicked dust jacket. $20.
A Grave Matter. NY, 1967 1st ed. Fine in DJ. $15.

DAVIES, VALENTINE. *Miracle on 34th Street*. NY, 1947 1st edition. Published at same time as release of film. Fine in clipped DJ. $100. Another, VG in dust jacket. $35.

DAVIS, ADELLE. *Let's Cook It Right*. NY, 1947. Good in DJ. $7. 1956-1962 revised editions. Fine in DJ. $10.
Let's Eat Right to Keep Fit. NY, 1954. $15-$20.

DAVIS, BURKE. *The Gray Fox: Robert E. Lee and the Civil War*. NY, 1956. Very Good. $28.
Our Incredible Civil War. NY, 1960 1st. VG in DJ. $28.
Jeb Stuart, The Last Cavalier. Bonanza, 1960s reprint. Fine in dust jacket. $14.
The Billy Mitchell Story. Philadelphia, 1969 1st ed. VG in poor dust jacket. $25.
Sherman's March. NY, 1980. VG in dust jacket. $20.
The Long Surrender. NY, 1985 1st ed. Good. $20.

DAVIS, DANA. *The Firemen*. Boston, James French, 1858. Good-Very Good. $120.

DAVIS, DANIEL. *A Manual of Magnetism, Including Galvanism, Electro-Magnetism, etc*. Boston, 1848 2nd edition. Worn. $75. 1865 13th edition. Spine missing. $50.

DAVIS, HENRY E. *The American Wild Turkey*. Georgetown, 1949. Fine in dust jacket. $250.

DAVIS, JEFFERSON. *Rise & Fall of the Confederate Government*. NY, 1881 1st ed. 2 vols. $50-$100.

DAVIS, JULIA. *The Shenandoah*. Rivers of America Series. NY, 1945 1st ed. Farrar & Rinehart. $20.

DAVIS, MARY LEE. *Uncle Sam's Attic*. Wilde, 1930 1st edition. Good. $10.
We Are Alaskans. Wilde, 1931 1st ed. VG. $14.
Sourdough Gold. Wilde, 1933. Folding map. $30-$45.

DAVIS, RICHARD HARDING. *Gallegher and Other Stories*. NY, 1891 1st edition. Author's 1st book. VG. $75.
The West From a Car Window. NY, 1892 1st ed. F. Remington illus. Near Fine. $100-$150. VG. $50-$70. Good. $18. Another, 1892. Soiled, but near VG. $25. London, no date, circa 1892. VG. $75.
Van Bibber and Others. NY, 1892 1st edition. $40.
In the Fog. NY, Russell, 1901 1st ed., 1st state. Pierce illus. Decorative. boards. VG. $30.
About Paris. NY, 1895 1st. C. D. Gibson illus. VG. $20.
Ransom's Folly. Scribner's 1902. H. C. Christy illus. Spine fading, o/w VG. $15-$30.
Bar Sinister. NY, Scribner's, 1903 1st ed. G-VG. $20-$40.
The Scarlet Car. NY, 1907 1st ed. Steele illus. VG. $25.
Vera, the Medium. NY, 1908 1st ed. Steele illus. VG. $15.
The White Mice. NY, 1909 1st ed. Gibbs illus. VG. $25.
Once Upon a Time. NY, 1911. Ex-lib. Hinge mended. $25.
The Deserter. Scribner, 1917. Valentine illus. $30.

DAVIS, VERNON. *The Garden Book*. Farm life series. New York, Orange Judd, 1915 1st edition. Original cloth. Very Good. $20.

DAVIS, WALTER and DANIEL DURRIE. *An Illustrated History of Missouri*. St. Louis, Hall & Co., 1876. 639 pages. Spine faded, rubbed. $150.

DAVIS, WILLIAM HEATH. *Seventy-Five Years in California*. San Francisco, John Howell, 1929 edition. Worn, marked, frayed. $60. Argonaut Edition, extra illus. 2nd ed. with new illustrations, etc. No. 198. John Howell, 1929. Near Fine. $250-$350.

DAVIS, WILLIAM MORRIS. *The Coral Reef Problem*. NY, 1928 1st edition. Spoiled cover, hinge poor. $40.

DAWSON, ELMER A. *Buck's Winning Hit*. (Buck & Larry Baseball Stories, no. 2). Grosset & Dunlap, 1930. Very Good in dust jacket. $100.
Gray Grayson titles. G&D, 1920s. $8-$12 each.

DAWSON, W. F. *Saga of the "All American" 82nd Airborne Division*. Atlanta, 1946. Good plus. $165. 1978 ed. $40.

DAWSON, WILLIAM LEON. *The Birds of California, 580 Species*. Booklovers' Edition. Los Angeles, 1923. 4 vols. Shelfwear, VG. $200-$250.
The Birds of Ohio. Columbus, 1903. 2 vols. $125.

DAY, AVANELLE & LILLIE STUCKEY. *The Spice Cookbook*. New York, 1964. $30-$40.

DAY, CYRUS L. *The Art of Knotting and Splicing*. U. S. Naval Institute, 1964 2nd ed. Illus. Soiled DJ. $20.

DAY, DONALD. *Will Rogers, A Biography*. 1949 1st edition. $20. 1962 edition. Very Good. $15.
Big Country Texas. NY, 1947 1st ed. VG-Fine in dust jacket. $25-$35. No dust jacket. $12-$15.

DAY, J. WENTWORTH. *Speed, The Authentic Life of Sir Malcolm Campbell, Illustrated*. London, 1932. VG. $45.

DAYAN, MOSHE. *Diary of the Sinai Campaign*. NY, 1966. Good in dust jacket. $14.

DEADERICK, BARRON. *Strategy in the Civil War*. Harrisburg PA, 1951 1st ed. VG. $20. Fine. $50.

DEAMICIS. *The Heart of Boyhood*. Whitman, 1918. F. $20.

DE ANGELI, MARGUERITE. *Ted and Nina Go To The Grocery Store*. NY, 1935 1st ed. Author's 1st book. Illus. by author. VG in dust jacket. $75.
Ted and Nina Have a Happy Rainy Day. Doubleday Doran, 1936. Illus. by author. VG in DJ. $35.
Coppertoed Books. NY, 1938 1st ed. Illus. by author. Signed. Very Good in dust jacket. $60.
Skipjack School. NY, 1939 1st edition. Illus. by author. VG in dust jacket. $40.
Yonie Wondermosey. NY, 1944 1st ed. Very Good. $25.
Bright April. Garden City, 1946. Illus. by author. Signed. VG in torn dust jacket. $32.
Just Like David. NY, 1951. Reprint. Illustrated by author. Ex-library. Very Good in dust jacket. $8.
A Little Book of Prayers and Graces. Doubleday, 1952. Inscribed. Illus. by author. Overall VG. $16.
Turkey for Christmas. Westminster, 1954 ed. Illus. by author. Ex-lib. VG. $20. 1949 1st edition. VG in DJ. $50.
A Book of Nursery and Mother Goose Rhymes. NY, 1954. Inscribed. Illus. by author. VG in dust jacket. $45.

DE ANGELI, MARGUERITE (Illustrator). *The Little Duke*. By Charlotte M. Yonge. NY, 1927. VG. $30.
The Covered Bridge. By Cornelia Meigs. NY, 1936 1st edition. Near Very Good. $35.
The Old Testament. Doubleday, 1960 1st. VG in DJ. $32.

DEATHERAGE, CHARLES. *Early History of Greater Kansas City*. Diamond Jubilee edition, 1928. Vol. I. Kansas City, MO, 1927. 701 pages. VG, map intact. $150.

DE BAYE, BARON J. *The Industrial Arts of the Anglo-Saxons*. London, 1893. Translation. Illus. G-VG. $175.

DE BRUNHOFF, JEAN. *Babar & His Children*. New York 1938 1st U. S. edition. Illustrated by author. Very Good in worn dust jacket. $225. Same, Good, no dust jacket. $95 auction.
Babar and Father Christmas. NY, 1940 1st ed. Illus. by Author. VG-Fine. $150-$250.
Babar and Zephir. NY, no date. Illustrated by author. Inscribed. Very Good in chipped dust jacket. $40.

DE BRUNHOFF, LAURENT. *Babar's Cousin*. NY, 1948 1st American edition. Illustrated by author. Very Good in very good dust jacket. $35.
Babar the Gardener. NY, 1969. Author Illus. VG. $19.
Pique-Nique Chez Babar. Paris, 1949 1st ed. Soiled. $38,

DE CAMP, L. SPRAGUE. *The Wheels of If*. Shasta Pub. Co, 1948 1st ed. Signed. VG in dust jacket. $225.
Let Darkness Fall. Phil., 1949 1st ed. Fine in DJ. $25-$65.
Solomon's Stone. NY, 1957 1st ed. VG in nicked DJ. $50.
The Glory That Was. New York, 1960 1st edition. Very Good in dust jacket. $50.
The Tritonian Ring. Philadelphia, 1977. Fine in DJ. $15.

DE DIENES, ANDRE (Photographer). *The Nude*. London, 1967. Good in dust jacket. $30.
Sun-Warmed Nudes. Lyle Stuart, 1968 4th printing. Fair in dust jacket. $37.
Marilyn, Mon Amour. St. Martin's 1985 1st ed. Photos. As new in dust jacket. $45.

DEDRA, DON. *A Mile in His Moccasins*. McGrew, 1960 1st ed. Signed by author. VG in rubbed dust jacket. $16.

DEEPING, WARWICK. *The Ten Commandments*. NY, 1931 1st ed. Very Good in dust jacket. $10.
Folly Island. No place, 1939 1st ed. Fine in DJ. $25.

DEERE, JOHN. *Operation, Care and Repair of Farm Machinery*. John Deere. 11th-13th editions, 1930s. $24 each. 24th-25th editions, 1940s. $15 each. (Also see Catalog Section).

DEFOE, DANIEL. *Robinson Crusoe*. London, 1856. Illus. Very Good. $85. London 1882, 2 volumes. VG. $120. McLoughlin, 1893. Chromos. Very Good. $100-$150. NY, Cosmopolitan, 1920. Wyeth illus. VG. $95-$110. Philadelphia, 1923. Abbot illus. VG. $15. NY, Limited Editions Club, 1930. Boxed. $165-$185. 1928 edition. Illustrated by Winter. Good-Very Good. $12-$15.
The Works of Daniel Defoe. London, 1895. 16 volumes. Yeats illus. Near Fine. $245.

DEFOREST, JOHN W. *History of the Indians of Connecticut*. 1851. Brown cloth. Very Good. $100.

DE GOUY, LOUIS. *The Derrydale Cook Book of Fish and Game*. Derrydale Press, NY, 1937 2 volumes. One of 1,250 copies. VG. $200. 2nd printing, 308 pages. VG. $50. *The Gold Cook Book*. NY, 1947 1st ed. VG. $20.

DE GRAF, F. W. *Head Hunters of the Amazon*. Duffield, 1923 1st ed. Soiled covers. Good. $20.

DE GRAZIA, TED. *The Rose and the Robe*. Tucson, 1968. Illustrated, inscribed by author. Fine in DJ. $125.

DE KRUIF, PAUL. *Hunger Fighters*. NY, 1928 1st edition. Fine in dust jacket. $25.

DELAFIELD, CLELIA. *Mrs. Mallard's Ducklings*. Lothrop Lee & Shepard, 1946 1st ed. Good in DJ. $25.

DELAFIELD, E. M. *The Provincial Lady in America*. NY, London, 1934 1st ed. Signed. $75.

DE LA MARE, WALTER. *Down-Adown-Derry*. London, 1922. Dorothy Lathrop illus. Very Good plus. $70.
Peacock Pie. London, 1924. C. Levat Fraser, illustrator. One of 250 copies, signed by author and Fraser. VG in DJ. $100. Holt, 1925. W. Heath Robinson illustrator. VG in fair dust jacket. $50-$75. Another, No dust jacket. $15.
Three Mulla-Mulgars. NY, 1925 2nd printing. Dorothy Lathrop illus. Near Fine in good dust jacket. $12.
Broomsticks and Other Tales. NY, 1925 1st American edition. Very Good in dust jacket. $65.
A Child's Day: A Book of Rhymes, 1923 2nd edition and *Ding Dong Bell*. 1924 1st American edition. Signed. Sold together at auction. $77.

DELAND, MARGARET. *The Old Garden and Other Verses*. Walter Crane illus. Near Fine. $85. Same, Boston, 1894 1st American edition. Crane illus. $50.
Awakening of Helena. Harper, 1906 1st edition. $20.
Dr. Lavendar's People. Harpers, 1903 1st ed. VG. $20.
Partners. Harper, 1913 1st ed. Charles Dana Gibson illus. Fine in torn dust jacket. $45.
The Vehement Flame. Harper, 1922 1st edition. Signed by author. Fine, minor wear. $65.

DELANEY, JOHN. *The Blue Devils in Italy: A History of the 88th Infantry Division in World War II*. Washington, 1947 1st ed. Fine. $95.

DELANO, ALONZO. *Across the Plains and Among the Diggings*. New York, Wilson, 1936 reprint. $80-$120.

DE LA ROCHE, MAZO. *White Oak Harvest*. Boston, 1936. Tipped in card signed by author. Very Good. $30.
The Building of Jalna. Boston, 1936. Tipped in card signed by author. Very Good. $30.
Return to Jalna. Boston, 1946 1st edition. Very Good in dust jacket. $14.

DELBANCO, NICHOLAS. *The Martlet's Tale*. Philadelphia, 1966 1st edition. Author's 1st book. VG in dust jacket. $75.

DELINEATOR HOME INSTITUTE. *New Delineator Recipes*. 1930. Good. $10.

DELISSER, GEO. P. *Delisser's Horseman's Guide*. New York, Dick & Fitzgerald, 1875. Good-VG. $35.

DELLENBAUGH, FREDERICK. *The Romance of the Colorado River*. NY, Putnam's, 1903 2nd ed. 399 pages. Lite cover soil, o/w Very Good. $75.
Freemont and '49. New York, Putnam's 1914. Good-Very Good. $65.

DE LOUP, MAXIMILIAN. *The American Salad Book*. NY, 1906 3rd edition revised. Good-VG. $20.

DEL REY, LESTER. *Mission to the Moon*. Winston, 1956 1st edition. Very Good in dust jacket. $55.
The Mysterious Sky. NY, 1964 1st edition. Very Good in worn, chipped dust jacket. $14.
Rocket From Infinity. New York, 1966 1st edition. Fine in dust jacket. $30.

DEMAREST, PHYILLIS G. *The Wilderness Brigade*. NY, 1947 1st edition. Cover spots, o/w Good. $15.

DE MAUPASSANT, GUY. *Mademoiselle Fifi*. Modern Library 1st ed., 1917. VG-Fine in dust jacket. $100.
A Woman's Life. NY, Heritage, 1939 reprint. Nonesuch Press. Very Good in slipcase. $18.

DEMING, HENRY. *The Life of Ulysses S. Grant*. Hartford CT, 1868. Water stained. $15.

DE MONVEL, MAURICE B. *Joan of Arc*. McKay, 1918. Illustrated by author. Very Good. $30. Another, Paris, 1924. Cobden G. $100. Century 1931. VG. $60. NY, 1980. Translation. Illus. by author. Near Mint. $25-$50.

DEMPSEY, JACK. *Round by Round*. NY, 1940. Photos. Signed twice. Very Good plus. $25-$35.
Dempsey by Himself. As told to Bob Considine & Bill Slocum. NY, 1960 1st edition, 1st printing. Presentation copy, signed by Dempsey. Fine. $35-$65.

DENLINGER, MILO. *The Complete Dalmatian*, and others. Mr. Denlinger was the author-publisher of several titles on various breeds. 1947-1954 1st editions in DJs. $25-$50. 2nd and 3rd editions without jackets. $10-$12.

DENISON, GRACE. *American Home Cook Book*. Grosset and Dunlap, 1932. Good-VG. $18.

DENNIS, MORGAN. *The Morgan Dennis Dog Book*. NY, 1946. Illus. by author. Good plus. $20.

DENSLOW, W. W. (Illustrator). *The Wonderful Wizard of Oz*. By Frank L. Baum. Chicago, 1900 1st ed., 2nd state. Very Good-Fine. $2,000-$3,000. 1st state. $5,000 up.
Around the World in a Berry Wagon. Berry Bros. (varnish maker), 1909. Paperback. Anon. VG. $225.
Ballads of a Book-Worm. By Irving Browne. Roycrofters, 1899. Hand-illuminated title page. Initials designed by Denslow are hand-drawn and illuminated. One of 31 copies, signed by E. Hubbard. Fine $350-$650. Same, unsigned. $150.

DENSLOW, W. W. *Denslow's Mother Goose*. NY, 1901 1st edition, 1st state. Illus. by author. VG-Fine. $200-$400.
The Night Before Christmas. Donohoe, 1902. $95-$175.
Dennslow's Scarecrow & the The Tin Man. Donohoe, 1913. $35-$75.
House That Jack Built. Dillingham, 1903. $85-$160.

DENSLOW, W. W. and DUDLEY BRADGON. *Bill Bounce*. NY, 1906. Denslow illus. 16 color plates. $95-$250.

DENSLOW, W. W. and PAUL WEST. *Pearl and the Pumpkin*. NY, 1904. Denslow illus. 16 color prints tipped in. Near VG. $75. Very Good-Fine. $150-$200.

DENVER WESTERNER'S BRAND BOOK. No. IV. 1954 1st trade edition. One of 500 copies. Fine in DJ. $50.

DE PACKMAN, ANNA. *Early California Hospitality: The Cookery Customs of Spanish California*. Fresno, 1952. Near Fine in vg DJ. $75.

DE PAOLA, TOMIE. *Fight in the Night*. Philadelphia, 1868 1st ed. Illus. by author. Fine in DJ. $30.

DEPARTMENT OF AGRICULTURE YEARBOOKS: 1870-1950. Average asking price. $8-$15 each.

DEPUY, FRANK A. *New Century Home Book*. New York, 1900. Good. $28.

DE QUINCEY, THOMAS. *Confessions of an English Opium Eater*. London, 1822 1st ed. $2,000 up. Phila., 1843. G-VG. $45. Same. NY, 1950, Heritage Press. $30.
Note Book of An English Opium Eater. 1866. VG. $35.
California and the Gold Mania. No date, 1940s. $40.

DERBY, GEORGE (As John Phoenix). *Phoenixiana of Sketches and Burlesques*. No place, 1856. Signed by author. VG. $25. Grabhorn, 1937 Limited. ed. $95-$150.

DERLETH, AUGUST. *In Re: Sherlock Holmes*. Mycroft and Moran, 1945 1st ed. 1st collection of Solar Pons stories. Fine in clipped dust jacket. $125.
Bright Journey. Scribner's, 1940 2nd ed. VG. $12.
Wind Over Wisconsin. NY, Scribner's, 1938 1st ed. Inscribed by author. Very Good. $65.

Someone in the Dark. Arkham, 1941 1st. VG in DJ. $140.
Mischief in the Lane. NY, 1944 1st. Fine in fair DJ. $75.
Something Near. Arkham House, 1945 1st ed. Good. $60.
The Memoirs of Solar Pons. Sauk City, Mycroft, 1951 1st ed. Signed and inscribed. Near Fine in DJ. $175.
The House on the Mound. Duell, 1958 1st ed. Fine. $60.
Mask of Cthulhu. Arkham House, 1958 1st edition. Fine in fine dust jacket. $120.
Lonesome Places. Arkham House, 1962 1st edition. Very Good in mended dust jacket. $50.
Dwellers in Darkness. Arkham House, 1976 1st edition. Very Fine in very good DJ. $50. Same, no dust jacket. $25.

DERLETH, AUGUST (Editor). *Dark of the Moon Poems of Fantasy & the Macabre*. Arkham House, 1947. One of 2,500 copies. VG in DJ. $75.

DEROSSO, H. A. *The Rebel*. Whitman, 1961 1st edition. Fine illustrated boards. $14.

THE DERRYDALE COOK BOOK OF FISH & GAME. Derrydale 1947. by L. P. Degouy. 2 vols. 1st edition. Limited to 1,250 sets. $200.

DE SAINT-EXUPERY, ANTOINE. *The Little Prince*. Harcourt, 1943 1st American ed. Very Good in very good dust jacket. $50-$100.

DETMOLD, EDWARD J. *Pictures From Birdland*. NY, London 1899 1st ed. Illus. by author and brother Maurice. Author's 1st book. VG-Fine. $300-$600.
The Book of Baby Pets. London, 1910 1st ed. Illus. by author. Foxing. Good-VG. $150-$375.
Our Little Neighbors. London, no date. Covers worn, o/w Very Good. $350-$400.

DETMOLD, EDWARD (Illustrator). *The Fables of Aesop*. NY, 1909 1st American ed. VG-Fine. $150-$225.
News of Spring. By Maurice Maeterlinck. NY, 1913 1st American ed. Hinge cracked, soiled. $125.
Fabre's Book of Insects. By Fabre. NY, 1937. VG. $50.

DE TOCQUEVILLE, ALEXIS. *The Old Regime and the Revolution*. NY, 1856 1st American ed. VG. $50-$150.
Democracy in America. NY, 1841 4th ed. 2 vols. $125. Same, NY, 1945 edition. 2 volumes boxed. VG. $30.

DEUTSCH, ALBERT. *Our Rejected Children*. Boston, 1950 1st edition. Inscribed. Very Good. $25.

DEVOL, GEORGE H. *Forty Years a Gambler. On The Mississippi*. Cincinnati, 1887 1st ed. G-VG. $180-$230. 1926 reprint. VG. $100.

DEVOTO, BERNARD. *The Crooked Mile*. Minton, 1924 1st edition, 1st book. Good. $40.
Across the Wide Missouri. Bos., 1947 1st VG in DJ. $55.

Mark Twain's America. M. J. Gallagher illus. Boston, 1932 reprint. Good-VG. $20.

DEVRIES, PETER. *No But I Saw the Movie*. Boston, 1952 1st ed. Inscribed. Near Fine in dust jacket. $35.
Through the Fields of Clover. Boston, 1961 1st ed. Signed presentation copy. Fine in chip dust jacket. $30.
Into Your Tent I'll Creep. Boston, 1971 1st ed. Signed presentation copy. Fine in dust jacket. $35.

DEWEY, JOHN. *Moral Principles in Education*. Boston, 1909 1st ed. Near Fine. $50.
Quest for Certainty. NY, 1929 1st. VG in worn DJ. $35.

DEWINDT, HARRY. *Through the Gold Fields of Alaska to the Bering Strait*. NY, 1898 1st ed. Ex-library. VG. $45.

DE ZEMLER, CHARLES. *The Story of Man and His Hair*. No place, 1939. Good-VG. $25-$35.

DICK, EVERETT. *The Sod-House Frontier*. New York, 1937 1st edition. Very Good. $40.

DICK, PHILIP K. *The Cosmic Puppets*. NY, Ace, 1957 1st edition. Near Fine. $15-$25.
The Man in the High Castle. NY, 1962 1st ed. VG in vg DJ. $150-$200. Book Club ed., 1962. Fine in DJ. $10-$15.
The Crack in Space. NY, Ace, 1966 1st ed. Very Good. $10. Fine. $25-$35.
A Scanner Darkly. NY, 1977 1st ed. Fine in DJ. $65-$75.
Radio Free Albemuth. NY, 1985 1st ed. NF in DJ. $15.
The Cosmic Puppets. Ace Double, 1957 1st ed. $20.
Seven House, 1986 1st hard cover ed. As new in DJ. $45.

DICK, PHILIP K. (In Magazines). *Fantastic Story*. July, 1953 1st appearance. $20.
Rolling Stone. Nov. 6, 1975. Article by, interview with. Signed. $50.
Playboy. Dec 1980. Story,"Frozen Journey". Signed. $65.

DICK, WILLIAM. *Encyclopedia of Practical Receipts and Processes*. 6,400 domestic and industrial. Dick and Fitzgerald, 1879. Worn, sunned. Good. $35.

DICKENS, CHARLES. *Sketches by Boz*. 1st ed. of Dicken's first book. 2 vols. in orig. dark olive cloth covers with stamped gilt shield. London, John Macrone, 1836. Fine and bright, but loose in bindings. $12,500. Another, Boz, Second Series, complete in one volume. London, 1837. Rebacked, slight soil. VG. $1,500. Same, ex-library copy, rubbed. $750. New edition, London, Chapman & Hall, 1839. NF. $450. 1850 ed. New preface. Good. $125.
Oliver Twist. First edition, first issue. London, Richard Bentley, 1838. 3 volumes. Title page authorship credits to "Boz". Orig. cloth, reddish brown, horizontal ribs. Light foxing, fading, soil. A good set. $5,000. Another set, rebound by Birdsall in brown morocco. Minor defects.

$3,500. Same, rebound in red morocco with ads removed. Clean and bright. $3,000. Same, rebacked, repaired. $2,000. 1846 edition, Bradbury & Evans. One vol. ed. Spine faded. $200. Early American edition of Oliver Twist. Philadelphia, Lee and Blanchard, 1839. 2 vols. Red cloth, hinges repaired. $550. Cincinnati, 1839 in 2 vols. Orig. floral cloth. Hinges cracked, rubbed, foxed. $350. Minton Blach, no date, Teague illus. Issued w/o DJ. VG. $35.
The Life and Adventures of Nicholas Nickleby. London, 1839 1st ed., Chapman and Hall. 39 plates by Phiz. Leather and marbled boards. Lightly foxed and rubbed. $600. Another, bound from the parts. Red calf. $200-$250. 1839, Chapman and Hall, but Hablot Brown plates inserted. G-VG. $200-$375. Auction $165. Philadelphia, Lea & Blanchard, 1839. Rebound in calf. $195.
Master Humphrey's Clock. London, Chapman and Hall, 1840 1st ed., 1st issue. Bound from 88 weekly parts. 3 vols. in red morocco-backed boxes. $2,500. Another set in publishers orig. bold-ribbed brown cloth. Light soil, corners bumped. $1,250. Same in much faded cond. $500.
The Old Curiosity Shop. London, no date, Hodder and Stoughton. Color illus. by Frank Reynolds. 1 of 350 signed by Reynolds. Near Fine. $350. Lea & Blanchard, 1841 1st American ed. G-VG. $200-$250. Ticknor and Fields, 1867 ed. Good. $75. Heritage reprint, 1941. VG, no case. $14.
Barnaby Rudge. Philadelphia, E. Littel and Co., 1842. Early edition with no illus. Limp boards, worn. $375. Ticknor and Fields, 1867. Good. $75.
American Notes for General Circulation. London, Chapman and Hall, 1842 1st ed. In orig. reddish-brown ribbed cloth. Smooth repair of spines. Good plus. $650. Another, rebound in morocco and marbled boards. Faded spine but near fine. $500. New York, J. Winchester, 1842 1st Amer. ed. New World ed. Sewn periodical in a red morocco slipcase. $750. Philadelphia, Lee and Blanchard, 1842. Boz' works-No. 21. Handbound and lettered title, uncut copy. $350. Appleton & Co., 1868 ed. NF. $90.
The Life and Adventures of Martin Chuzzlewit. London, Chapman and Hall, 1844 1st ed. 40 plates. Rebacked and repaired. 20 numbers bound in 19 printed wraps. Housed in fold box. $1,250. Another in orig. blue pebble cloth. Hinge repair. $650. Various other bindings of 1844 ed. $200-$450. Ticknor & Fields, 1867 edition. Good. $75.
A Christmas Carol. London, Chapman and Hall, 1843 1st ed., 1st issue. Orig. cinnamon cloth, blind-stamped and gilt. Slight wear. VG. $8,500. Another, light soil. $7,500. Another 1843 ed. with four inserted hand-colored plates. Rare green and red title pg. $12,500. Another in crimson morocco. Signed by Dickens. $4,900. Roycroft Press, 1902. Suede leather ed. Fine. $38. McKay, 1914 ed. Gilt-dec. blue cloth. VG. $40. Philadelphia, Lippincott, no date. Arthur Rackham illus. Square octavo. Inscribed, 1917. G-VG. $175. Saalfield, 1929 ed. Peat illus. G-VG in DJ. $20-$35. Various U. S. publisher's editions. 1915-1950, many in red cloth binding. G-VG. $35 each.
The Christmas Books. Full set "A Christmas Carol", "The Chimes", "The Cricket on the Hearth", "The Battle of Life" and "The Hunted Man". 1843-1848 ed. Bound in ¾

morocco. F in case. $5,000. Same set, 12th ed., Chapman & Hall, 1845. 5 books, 3 are 1st ed. Very nice. $1,250.

The Chimes. Philadelphia, Lea and Blanchard, 1845 1st illus. Amer. ed. 12mo, 96 pages. Orig. ecru cloth. Good and tight. $500. London, Hodder & Stoughton, circa 1913. Seven color illus. Bright red cloth, gilt-dec. In orig. box. VG. $450. Same, faded spine, over-opened. VG. $100.

The Battle of Life. London, Bradbury and Evans, 1846 1st ed; 1st state. Foolscap, octavo. Engraved title and frontpiece by Maclise. Only 4 copies of this first state are known to exist. Full green morocco in slipcase. $45,000. Same 1846 book in 4th state. Orig. red cloth. $250. Another, soiled but VG. $200.

The Haunted Man & The Ghost's Bargain. London, Bradbury & Evans, 1848 1st ed. Foolscap, octavo. Litho front. Orig. red cloth. VG. $350. Another, light soiling. VG. $250. Another in deluxe binding by Riviere. Fine. $550. Another with rough endpapers, dampstained. $125.

The Posthumous Papers of the Pickwick Club. New York, James Turner, 1838. First American one-volume ed., bound from parts. 52 plates. Contemporary calf binding. Scuffed, rubbed, but VG. $450. Another in orig. cloth. Worn, repaired, foxed. $200. 2 volume set by E. P. Dutton, NY, no date. Color and black and white illus. Printed in Edinburgh and London. $275. Oxford Press ed., 1933. 2 vols. Minor wear. $250. New York, Hodder & Stoughton, no date. Near Fine. $125. NY, 1930. Brock illus. VG in faded dust jacket. $85.

Dombey and Son. London, Bradbury and Evans, 1848 1st ed. Orig. green cloth. Rebacked. Light stain. $600. Same, but rebound. G-VG. $250-$300. Another, pages loose but present. $80. London, Chapman and Hall, no date. Early edition. Clean, bright copy. $200. New York, Limited Editions Club, 1957. 1 of 1,500 copies signed by illustrator, Henry C. Pitz. 2 vols. Near Fine. $75.

David Copperfield. "The Personal History of David Copperfield" London, Bradbury and Evans, 1850 1st ed. in the orig. monthly parts. 20 bound in 19 with 40 inserted plates by Browne. In green-black morocco slipcase. $8,500. Same, in orig. cloth binding. Some spotting. $1,250. Another, rebound in green morocco. Fine. $850. London, 1866 "Peoples Edition" in 2 vols. VG. $100. Phil., Lea & Blanchard, 1851. Rubbed spine, o/w Fine. $40.

Bleak House. London, Bradbury and Evans, 1853 1st ed. 20 original parts, bound in 19 with 40 inserted plates by Phiz. Orig. printed blue wraps, showing some soil and wear. $2,000. Same, with 4 missing ads and one leaf gone. $1,200. Another, rebound in calf. H. K. Browne illus. $250-$300. Philadelphia, 1853. Getz. Paperbound. G. $35.

Hard Times. London, Bradbury and Evans, 1854 1st ed. Original olive moire, ribbed cloth. Clean and tight. $1,000. Appleton, New York, 1871. Paperbound with additional Christmas stories. VG. $60. Limited Editions Club, 1966. One of 1,500 signed by illus., Charles Raymond. Fine in original slipcase. $60-$75.

Little Dorrit. London, Bradbury and Evans, 1857 1st ed in orig. parts. H. K. Browne illus. Morocco fold-down box.

$2,500. Another with chipping and repair to spines. $1,800. Another rebound in half brown morocco. Some ads missing. Near fine. $300. Copyright edition 1856-57 in four vols., Leipzig. Some foxing. $200.

A Tale of Two Cities. London, Chapman and Hall, 1859 1st ed. in orig. 7/8 monthly party. H. K. Browne illus. Shows little wear. Brown morocco pull-off case. $8,500. Same with 16 inserted plates by Phiz. Orig. red cloth, slightly soiled. $5,000. Another 1859 edition with Phiz illus. Rebound in calf over marbled boards. Book plate removed, cellophane tape repair. $500. T. B. Peterson and Brothers, "1859 First U. S." ink notation on wraps. 1st Philadelphia edition, untrimmed in wraps. $1,250.

Great Expectations. London, Chapman and Hall, 1861 1st ed., 1st issue. 3 vols. In orig. purple cloth. Near fine. $35,000. Another set, rebound in crushed red morocco. $12,500. Same with vol. 3 being 2nd ed. $6,000. Boston, Gardner A. Fuller, 1862 early American reprint, "Thirtieth Thousand" on title page. Orig. brown cloth. Good. $250. Limited Editions Club, 1937. One of 1,500 copies signed by illus., Gordon Ross. Near Fine. $150.

A Child's History of England. London, 1852-54. 1st ed., 1st issue. Some stain and wear. 3 volumes. $500.

The Cricket on the Hearth. London, 1846 1st ed., 2nd state. VG. $250. NY, circa 1882, Lovell. Paperbound w/ads. $35. NY, circa 1900, Putnam's. Limp leather. Near Fine. $50. Harper, 1927. Gilt-dec. red cloth G-VG. $35.

The Life of our Lord. Simon & Schuster, 1934 1st American edition. Very Good in worn dust jacket. $20. Another, Fine in dust jacket. $40-$50.

The Mystery of Edwin Drood. London, Chapman and Hall, 1870 1st ed. Publisher's green cloth binding. VG. $450. Another, rebound. Slight wear. $225. NY, Heritage Reprint, 1941. Very Fine in slipcase. $18.

Works of Charles Dickens. Estes & Lauriat, 1890 40 vols., One of 1,000 sets. Tenniel, Stone, Cruikshank illus. Rubbing, fraying, o/w VG. $300. London, NY, circa 1895. 38 vols. Gadshill ed., with 4 additional vols. Notes by Andrew Lang. VG. $700. London, Chapman and Hall, 1903-1906. Biographical edition. 19 vols. Many engravings by orig. illustrators. Green morocco. Clean, bright. $2,750. Boston, Ticknor and Fields, 1867-1874. Library edition. 27 volumes. VG. $750.

DICKEY, JAMES. *Deliverance*. Boston, 1970 1st ed. Signed. Near Fine in dust jacket. $100. Same. Franklin Library edition. Fine. $60.

Zodiac. Doubleday, 1976 1st. Signed. F in slipcase. $50.

The Owl King. NY, 1977 1st ed. One of 100 copies, signed. Near Fine. $150.

Ducky the Hunter. NY, 1978 1st ed. Marie Angel illus. Fine in dust jacket. $35.

DICKINSON, EMILY. *Poems, Second Series*. Boston, 1891. Very Good. $150 and up.

Letters of Emily Dickinson. Boston, 1894 1st ed., 1st printing. M. L. Todd edition. 2 vols. Near Fine. $500.

The Single Hound. No place, 1914 2nd ed. VG. $35.
The Poems of Emily Dickinson. Centenary Ed. Boston, 1930 1st ed. Fine in dust jacket. $125.

DICKINSON, PETER. *The Glass-Sided Ant's Nest*. NY, 1968 1st ed. Fine in dust jacket. $35.
The Sinful Stones. NY, 1970 1st ed. Near Fine in DJ. $25.
The Lizard in the Cup. London, 1972. Fine in fine DJ. $30. Book Club edition, Harper. $5.
The Green Gene. New York, 1973 1st American edition. Fine in dust jacket. $25.
The Lively Dead. NY, 1975 1st edition. Fine in DJ. $15.
The Last House Party. London, 1982 1st British ed. Fine in DJ. $35. American edition in dust jacket. $20.

DICKSON, CARTER (John Dickson Carr). *The White Priory Murders*. NY, 1934 1st ed. Very Good. $25.
The Judas Window. New York, 1938 1st edition. Very Good in worn DJ. $550.
Reader Is Warned. New York, 1939 1st edition. Very Good in worn dust jacket. $125.
Nine and Death Makes Ten. NY, 1940 1st ed. Near Fine in dust jacket. $275.
The Department of Queer Complaints. NY, 1940 1st ed. Fine in taped dust jacket. $750.
The White Priory. New York, Pocket, 1942 1st edition. paperback. Near Fine. $13.
A Graveyard to Let. New York, 1949 1st edition. Very Good in dust jacket. $50.

DICKSON, W.K.L. & ANTONIA. *The Life and Inventions of Thomas A. Edison*. New York, 1894 1st edition. Very Good. $75.

DICTIONARY (See Webster, Noah).

DICTIONARY OF AERONAUTICAL TERMS. ENGLISH, FRENCH, JAPANESE, GERMAN. Washington, USAAF, 1942. $25.

DICTIONARY OF AMERICAN BIOGRAPHY. NY, 1946. 22 volumes in 11. Shelf wear. $350.

DICTIONARY OF AMERICAN SLANG. H. Wentworth and S. Flexner, NY, 1960. VG. $25.

DICTIONARY OF AMERICANISMS. John Bartlett, Boston, 1859. Marginal notes. Good. $30.

DICTIONARY OF AMERICANISMS. M. M. Matthews, editor. Chicago, 1921. 2 vols. VG. $80.

DICTIONARY OF THE BIBLE. Willliam Smith, editor. National Pubs., 1869 revised edition. Fair, leather. $16.

DICTIONARY OF THE BIBLE. By Isaiah Thomas. Worcester MA, 1798. Fair-Good. $75.

OXFORD ENGLISH DICTIONARY. London, Oxford, 1933. 13 vols. Faded. $400. Short version, 1978. 2 vols. $25.

DICTIONARY OF PHILOSOPHY AND PSYCHOLOGY. Peter Smith, 1960. 3 volumes. Reprint. Ex-library. Very Good. $150.

DIDIER, CHARLES. *Twixt Cupid & Croesus*. Baltimore, Jno. Williams, 1896. Didier illus. G-VG. $70-$100.

DIETZ, F. and A. *Gay Nineties Cook Book*. Richmond VA. 1945. VG in DJ. $25.

DIETZ, FRED. *A Leaf From the Past, Dietz Then and Now*. NY, 1914. $35.

DIGGES, JEREMIAH. *Cape Cod Pilot*. Mass. Guide Series. (WPA) 1937. Soiled cover. $20.

DILLE, JOHN. *Americans in Space*. American Heritage, 1965 1st ed. Good. $12.

DILLEY, ARTHUR U. *Oriental Rugs and Carpets: A Comprehensive Study*. New York, 1931. 79 plates. Ex-library. Good. $55.

DILLON, JOHN B. *History of Indiana from Earliest Exploration to 1856*. Bingham-Dohert, 1859 1st edition. 637 pages, rebound. Very Good. $35.

DIMAGGIO, JOE. *Lucky to be a Yankee*. Rudolph Field, 1946 1st edition. G-VG in DJ. $75. Grosset & Dunlap, 1951 edition. Very Good. $20.

DIMOCK, A. W. *The Book of the Tarpon*. NY, 1926. F. $75.

DINGEE-MC GREGOR. *Science of Successful Threshing*. J. I. Case Threshing Machine Co, 1904. Fine, no DJ. $45.

DIRECTORY OF ARCHITECTS & CLASSIFIED HANDS IN THE BUILDING TRADES. Clark W. Bryan & Co., pub. Springfield, MA, 1889. 8vo, yellow boards. $300.

DISEASES OF THE HORSE. U. S. Dept. of Agriculture, 1890. Fair-Good. $20-$25.

DISNEY, DOROTHY CAMERON. *The Golden Swan Murder*. New York, 1939 1st ed. VG in dust jacket. $33.
Crimson Friday. New York, 1942 1st edition. Very Good in dust jacket. $38.
A Compound for Death. New York, 1943 1st edition. Very Good in dust jacket. $45.

DISNEY, DOROTHY MILES. *Murder on a Tangent*. NY, 1945 1st ed. VG in sunned dust jacket. $25.
Who Rides a Tiger. NY, 1946 1st ed. VG in DJ. $18.
Fire at Will. NY, 1950. Good in dust jacket. $13.

DISNEY, WALT

The Disneyana field is enormous and interactive. Only a fraction is represented here. When Disney books and magazines rise in price on the used book market, prices of collectible Disney toys and games also rise, and vice versa. Several price guides have been published on Disney items.

The "classic" period for collectors is from the late 1920s through the early 1940s. That period saw the arrival of Mickey Mouse, Donald Duck, Goofy and Pluto, and the screening of "Snow White and the Seven Dwarfs" (1937), "Pinocchio" (1940), "Fantasia" (1940), "Dumbo" (1940, and "Bambi" (1942).

The Adventures of Mickey Mouse. McKay, 1931, Book 1. Many small defects, but VG for "this fragile item." $125. Another, fewer defects. $200.

Mickey Mouse Story Book. Philadelphia, 1931 1st ed. Soiled. Good. $65. Overall. VG. $100.

Mickey Mouse Stories No. 2. McKay Co. 1934. G. $75.

Mickey Mouse Stories, Book No. 2. Philadelphia, David McKay, 1934 1st ed. 6 x 8½ cloth backed stiff wraps. Creased covers, small piece gone. $95 auction.

Mickey Mouse. A "Big Little Book" Racine, Whitman, 1933 1st ed. Rubbed, but near fine and bright. $300 auction. (est $150-$250).

Three Little Pigs. NY, Blue Ribbon Books, 1933 1st ed. Illus. by Walt Disney Studios. 10 x 7½ pictorial boards. Light wear in slightly torn DJ. Auction. $300. Another, Crayon on 6 pp. Backstrip part gone. o/w VG. $75.

Who's Afraid of the Big Bad Wolf. McKay, 1933. Stiff wraps. Illus. VG. $65.

Mickey Mouse the Mail Pilot. Whitman, 1933, Big Little Book. Very Good. $100.

The Three Orphan Kittens. Whitman, 1935. Bumped corners, darkened pgs., o/w VG. $85.

The Tortoise and the Hare. Whitman, 1935, 1st ed. Orig. color boards. Some chipping. In orig. cartoon. $125.

Mickey Mouse in King Arthur's Court. Pop-up. Blue Ribbon Books, 1933 1st edition. Near Fine. Seldom found in this condition. $1,000.

The Pop-Up Minnie Mouse. Blue Ribbon Books, 1933 1st edition. Chipped and stained. $135 auction.

The Pop-Up Mickey Mouse. Blue Ribbon Books, 1933 1st edition. Near Fine. $650.

Walt Disney Annual. Racine. Whitman, 1937 1st ed. 10¼x13½ in Jacket. Minor defects, rubbing. VG. $770.

Mickey Mouse Presents Walt Disney's Silly Symphonies Stories. Whitman, 1936, Big Little Book. Good. $25. Another, fine. $100-$150.

Nursery Stories from Walt Disney's Silly Symphony. Whitman, 1937 1st ed. Near Fine. $175.

The Story of Bashful. Whitman, 1938 1st ed. Fine. $125.

Little Red Riding Hood and the Big Bad Wolf. Philadelphia, 1934, McKay, $40.

Donald Duck. Racine, Whitman, 1935 1st ed. The first Donald Duck book! Pictorial linen wrappers, 9½x13. Chipped, missing corners. $110 auction.

Donald Duck Hunting for Trouble. Racine, WI, Whitman, 1938 1st ed. Disney illus. 4¼x3½ pictorial cover. G-VG. $50-$75.

Mickey Mouse and Mother Goose. Racine, WI, Whitman, 1937 1st ed. 8¾x6½ cloth-backed cover. $40-$80.

Snow White and The Seven Dwarfs. Movie Book. 1938, Disney. Good. $28-$35.

Story of Donald Duck. Whitman, 1938 1st ed. VG. $15.

Pinocchio. Whitman, 1939. Chipped edge. $15. Disney Studio, 1940 4th ed. Good. $25.

Walt Disney's Version of Pinocchio. Random House, 1939 1st ed. Torn, DJ, else VG. $250.

Dance of the Hours. From Fantasia. Disney Studio illus. NY, 1940 1st ed. Corner, edge wear. Contents VG. $45.

Walt Disney's Bambi. NY, Simon & Schuster, 1941 1st ed. 11 x 8¼. Includes 4 detachable plates. Color illus. Rubbed spine, chipped jacket, o/w VG. $143 auction.

Bambi. D. C. Heath, 1944 1st ed. VG. $15.

Donald Duck Lays Down the Law. Whitman, 1948 1st ed. Very Good. $18.

Uncle Remus. Little Golden Book, 1947. Fine. $10.

Minnie Mouse and the Antique Chair. Whitman, 1948. Illus. VG. $35.

Pinocchio. NY, 1948, Mickey Mouse Club Book. G. $15.

Mickey and the Beanstalk. Whitman, 1948. Fine. $50.

Alice in Wonderland. Whitman, 1951 1st edition. Very Good in dust jacket. $20.

Walt Disney's Guide to Disneyland. 1959. G-VG. $23.

Lady and the Tramp. by Ward Greene. NY, Simon & Schuster, 1953 1st ed. Inscribed by Walt Disney. $2,500.

101 Dalmatians. Whitman, 1960 1st. VG plus in DJ. $15.

Treasures of Disney Animation. Abbeyville Press, no date, 1st ed, 4th printing. VG. $75.

Walt Disney's Vanishing Prairie. NY, no date. Good. $15.

Mickey Mouse Movie Stories. Abrams, 1988. F in DJ. $30.

Mickey Mouse in Color. Pantheon, 1988 1st edition. In new condition. $20-$30.

Beauty and the Beast. Disney, 1991 1st ed, 3rd printing. Story by A. L. Singer for film. Ron Diaz illus. Signed by Singer, Diaz, Paige O'Hara (Beauty) and Bradley Pierce (Beast). As new in DJ. $28.

Disney Animation: The Illusion of Life. Abbeyville Press, no date. 1st ed, 3rd printing. VG. $70.

Disney's America on Parade. NY, Harry Abrams, no date. Very Good. $15.

Walt Disney's Mickey Mouse Memorabilia: The Vintage Years. NY, Abrams, 1986. VG. $40.

Disney Art Exhibition Catalog. 1940. 24 pgs. 9x11. L.A. County Museum. VG. $138 auction.

Disneyland Stamp Book. 1956. 32 pgs. 8x11. 50 stamps pasted in. VG. $99 auction.

Fantasia Program Book. 1940. 32 pgs. 9x12. $154.

Mickey Mouse and Silly Symphony Folio of Songs. 1933. 32 pgs. 9x12. Fine. $120 auction.

Fantasia. Deems Taylor, 1940. 158 pages. 13x10. 1st ed. in dust jacket. VG-Fine. $517 auction.

Goofy: The Good Sport. Signed and illustrated by Jack Kinney. 1985, 96 pages. 8x11. 1st edition. Very Fine in dust jacket. $330 auction.

He Drew As He Pleased. by Albert Hunter. 1940. 190 pgs. 9x12 sketchbook. No DJ. Light cover wear. $990 auction.

Pop-Up Minnie Mouse. 1933. 9x7. 3 color pop-ups. No dust jacket. Minor wear. $440 auction.

Walt Disney's Wonderful. World of Reading Book No. 100. Special Limited ed. 1986. 44 pgs. 9x12. #9 of 30 copies. Very Fine. $495 auction.

DISNEY BOOKS SOLD AT AUCTION

A Walt Disney Flip Book. 3 x 3½ color cover, b&w illus. on each page. Excellent. $15.

Disney's America on Parade (1975). 9 x 11½, hardcover, 144 pgs., Abrams. Excellent. $22.

Donald Duck And His Friends (1939). School reader, 6¼ x 8½, 104 pgs., Heath. Full-color illus. throughout, school labeled. Fine. $40.

Donald Duck And His Nephews (1940). School reader, 6¼ x 8½, 72 pgs., Heath, full-color illus. VG. $48.

Donald Duck Gets Fed Up (1940). Better Little Book. Whitman (1462). VG. $18.

Donald Duck Sees Stars (1941). Better Little Book. Whitman (1422). VG. $18.

Little Red Riding Hood And The Big Bad Wolf (1934). 8 x 10, 32 stiff pgs., illus. color and b&w, printed in England. Good. $55.

Mickey Mouse And The Dude Ranch Bandit (1943). BLB Whitman (1471), 430 pgs. Fine. $46.

Mickey Mouse Annual (1930). Restored copy of the first English annual, 6½ x 9, Dean & Son, London. Good. $120.

Mickey Mouse Annual (1946). 6 x 8½, hardcover, 188 pages, Dean & Son. VG. $45.

Mickey Mouse Bellboy Detective (1945). Better Little Book. Whitman (1483). Fine. $30.

Mickey Mouse Birthday Book (1953), Simon & Schuster, 8½ x 11, hardcover, 64 pgs. Stories include Mickey And the Beanstalk and other classics. VG. $67.

Mickey Mouse Book No. 4 (1934). 10 x 10, softcover, 48 pgs., David McKay, repaired. Good. $140.

Mickey Mouse On Sky Island (1941). Better Little Book. Whitman (1417). Good. $15.

Mickey Mouse Sticker Fun (1983). Golden Book, 11½ x 12, 16 pgs. of story and four pgs. of gummed punch-outs. Near mint. $22.

Mickey Never Fails (1939). School reader, 6 ¼ x 8½, hard cover, 104 pgs., Heath, Boston. VF. $51.

Peter Pan And Wendy (1952). Little Golden Book. 2nd edition. Fine. $12.

Pinocchio's Christmas Party (1939), 8 x 10 ¾, 16 pgs. Department store giveaway, imprinted "Spear" (Pittsburgh). Excellent. $38.

Pluto The Pup Picture Story (1937), Whitman (894), 9¼ x 13, 12 pgs., linen-like paper. VF. $48.

School Days In Disneyville. School reader, 6¼ x 8½, hardcover, 104 pgs., Heath, Boston. VF. $78.

Snow White And The Seven Dwarfs Jingle Book (1938). 4 x 5½, 20 pgs. Premium book imprinted "Olson's Bakery" (Los Angeles). Hake states "First we've seen this book with b&w cover rather than a color cover. $50.

Story of Walt Disney World, The (1978). 11 x 11, 48 pgs. Very Fine. $30.

The Story of Casey Jr. (1941). 7 x 9½, 28 pgs., hardcover, b&w and color illus. Garden City Publishing. Fine. $23.

The Tortoise And The Hare (1935). 9 x 10, hardcover, b&w and color illus., Whitman. Very Fine. $48.

Walt Disney Annual (1937). 10½ x 14, hardcover, 124 pgs., Whitman, color illus. includes The Big Bad Wolf and The Country Cousin. Good. $100.

Walt Disney Presents A Mickey Mouse Alphabet (1938). 9½ x 13, linen-like paper, full-color, Whitman (889). VeryGood. $47.

Walt Disney's Donald Duck (1935). 9½ x 13, 16 pgs., Whitman (978). Considered to be the first Donald Duck book. Fine. $280.

Walt Disney's Elmer Elephant (1936). 6¼ x 8¾, hardcover, 48 pgs., David McKay. Poor. $24.

Walt Disney's Famous Seven Dwarfs (1938). 12½ x 13, 12 pgs., Whitman. VG. $82.

Walt Disney's Mickey Mouse Decorate-A-Tree (1979). Golden Book, 8½ x 12, full-color, Western Publishing. Seven sheets of punch-outs. Near Mint. $26.

Walt Disney's Pedro From the Walt Disney Feature Production "Saludos Amigos'." (1943). 7 x 8¼, 32 pgs., hardcover, Grosset & Dunlap. Fine. $66.

Walt Disney's Pinocchio (1940). School reader, 6¼ x 8½, 90 pgs., Heath. Excellent. $78.

Walt Disney's Sleeping Beauty (1957). Little Golden Book. 1st ed. Excellent. $22.

Walt Disney's Version of Pinocchio (1939). 8 x 11, hardcover, 4th printing., Random House. Near Mint minor moisture markings. $50.

Water Babies' Circus And Other Stories (1940). School reader, 6¼ x 8½, 78 pgs., Heath. VF. $35.

Zorro And The Secret Plan (1958). LGB. 2nd printing. Excellent. $20.

THE DISPENSER'S FORMULARY. NY, 1925. More than 2,500 soda fountain recipes. $75.

DISRAELI, BENJAMIN. *Coningsby: or The New Generation*. London, 1844 1st ed. Rebound. $250. 1859 edition, Routledge. Fair. $24.

DITCHFIELD, P. H. *Picturesque English Cottages and Their Doorway Gardens*. Philadelphia, 1905. Poor exterior, inside clean. $60.

DITMARS, RAYMOND L. *The Reptile Book*. NY, 1907. Good-Very Good. $40-$50.
Reptiles of the World. NY, 1922. G-VG. $20-$30.

The Reptiles of North America. 1936 revised edition. Worn, shaken, foxed. $30.

The Book of Living Reptiles. Lippincott, 1936. VG. $10. Fine in dust jacket. $18.

The Fight to Live. NY, 1938. Advance review copy. Fine in dust jacket. $25.

Book of Insect Oddities. Lippincott, 1938. Helen Carter illus. Fine in DJ. $30. VG in DJ. $18.

The Making of a Scientist. NY, 1938. VG plus. $15.

A Field Book of North American Snakes. NY, 1939. VG in dust jacket. $10.

Snakes of the World. NY, 1951. VG. $15.

DIVINE, A. D. *Behind the Fleets*. London, 1940. G. $16.
Dunkirk. 1948. Good-VG. $15-$18.

DIXON, AUBREY. *Communist Guerrilla Warfare*. New York, 1954 1st ed. VG in dust jacket. $28.

DIXON, EDWARD. *Scenes in the Practice of a New York Surgeon*. Dewitt, 1855. Very Good. $65.

DIXON, FRANKLIN W.

The real authors of *Ted Scott* and the *Hardy Boys* series were Edward Stratemeyer and his daughter Harriet Adams (a.k.a. Carolyn Keene of *Nancy Drew* fame). Thru the years the pair and their prolific staff penned more than 1,500 titles under a variety of names including Franklin Dixon and Victor Appleton.

A few random samples of dealer prices follow but a general rule of thumb for pricing *Hardy Boys* titles is: 1920s-1930s. $25-$50 each (in very good condition with original dust covers intact). Fine examples bring more. Books of the later 30s and 40s command $10 to $15 without jackets and twice the money with good dust covers. The 1950s bring $6 to $12. (Dust jackets were discontinued in 1961).

There are some $100-$200 sleepers among early issues. Serious juvenile series collectors often consult *Heffelfinger's Bayport Companion* for price variations. Write to Charles Heffelfinger, Midnight Press, 7011 18th St, Tampa, FL 33610. Nancy Drew fans use *Farah's Guide to Nancy Drew*. From Dave Farah, 3110 Park Newport, Apt 412, Newport Beach, CA 92660. A magazine devoted entirely to juvenile series books, called *Yellowback Library*, is available from Yellowback Press, P. O. Box 36172, Des Moines, IA 50315.

Through the Air to Alaska. NY, Grosset & Dunlap, 1930. No dust jacket. Good-VG. $10.

Brushing the Mountain Top. Grosset & Dunlap, 1934 1st edition. VG in worn dust jacket. $60.

Castaways of the Stratosphere. Grosset & Dunlap, 1935 1st ed. VG in vg dust jacket. $75.

The Missing Chums. Series 4, no. 10. G & D. VG in DJ. $200. Same, series 4, no. 21. G & D. VG in DJ. $35. Same, 1957 reprint. VG in dust jacket. $10.

While the Clock Ticked. Series 11, no. 20. Fine in DJ. $30.

Yellow Feather mystery. Series 33, no. 33. G & D 1st ed. Near fine in VG. dust jacket. $25.

A Figure in Hiding. (Hardy Boys no. 16). Grosset & Dunlap, 1937 1st ed. Worn at spine, brown spotting page edges, o/w VG in chipped dust jacket. $100.

The Hidden Harbor Mystery (Hardy Boys no. 14). G&D (1935) 9th prntg 1941. Orange spine, Gretta cover art. $90.

Ted Scott, Flying Against Time. 1st prntg. VG in DJ. $40.

Hardy Boys. no. 37. VG in dust jacket. $10.

The House on the Cliff. G&D, 1935 printing of 1927 orig. G in good DJ. $150. Same, 1943 printing. Browned paper, worn DJ. $55. 1957 edition. VG in DJ. $12.

The Secret of Skull Mountain. (Hardy Boys no. 27). G&D, 1948. Wartime paper is browned. 1st ed. DJ. $45.

The Mystery of Cabin Island. (Hardy Boys no. 8). G&D, 1933 ed. of 1929 orig. white DJ $100. Same, no date. $8.

The Secret of Pirates Hill. (Hardy Boys no. 36). G&D, 1956 1st ed. VG in DJ. $45. Good, no jacket. $6.

The Secret Warning. (Hardy Boys no. 6). G&D, 1943 printing of 1928 orig. Browned, o/w VG in DJ. $65.

The Sign of the Crooked Arrow. (Hardy Boys no. 28). G&D, 1949 1st ed. Brown cloth in DJ. VG. $45.

The Twisted Claw. (Hardy Boys no. 18). G&D, 1939 1st edition. Yellow spine. VG in dust jacket. $200.

What Happened at Midnight. (Hardy Boys no. 10). G&D, 1934 7th prntg. Thick ed., white spine DJ, stained. G-VG. $175. Same, 1941 printing. Yellow spine. DJ. VG. $125.

DIXON, ROYAL. *The Human Side of Birds*. Stokes, 1917 1st ed. Bumped, rubbed. Good-Very Good. $25.

DIXON, THOMAS. *The Clansman*. NY, 1905 1st. Author presentation copy. VG. $100. "Birth of a Nation" photoplay version. VG in good DJ. $40. 1922 reprint, Grosset & Dunlap. Good. $8.

The Leopard's Spots. Garden City 1902 1st ed. Author inscribed copy. Worn, soiled covers, o/w good. $100.

DIXON, WINIFRED H. *Western Hoboes: Ups and Downs of Frontier Motoring*. NY, 1923. Near VG. $20.

DMITRI, IVAN. *Flight to Everywhere*. Whittlese, 1944 1st edition. Very Good. $25.

DOBELL, C. *Antony van Leeuwenhoek and His Little Animals*. Harcourt, 1932 1st edition. Very Good. $75. NY, 1958 reprint. Fine. $25.

DOBIE, J. FRANK. *Vaquero of the Brush Country*. Dallas, 1929 4th edition. Illus. $40.

Coronado's Children. Dallas, 1930 1st ed. Illus. VG. $35.

On the Open Range. Dallas, 1931 1st ed. One of 750 copies. Spine faded, small hole in margin. $400.

Mustangs and Cowhorses. Austin, TX, 1940 1st. F. $85.

The Longhorns. Boston, 1941 1st trade edition. Inscribed. Fine in dust jacket. $250.

The Voice of the Coyote. Boston, 1949 1st edition. Illus. Near Fine in dust jacket. $75.

The Mustangs. Boston, 1952. DJ spine faded. $35.

Tales of Old-Time Texas. Little-Brown, 1955 1st ed. Barbara Latham illus. Very Good. $35.

I'll Tell You a Tale. Boston, 1960 1st ed. Inscribed Fine in dust jacket. $200. Another, Near Fine. $95.

Guide to Life & Literature of the Southwest. Dallas, 1965 5th printing. Revised and enlarged. Illus. Ex-library. $18.

Some Part of Myself. Boston, 1967, Little Brown, second printing. Very Good in worn dust jacket. $20.

DOBLHOFER, ERNST. *Voices in Stone - Decipherment of Ancient Writings.* Viking, 1961 1st ed. Fine in DJ. $14.

DOBSON, AUSTIN. *The Story of Rosina.* NY, 1895 1st American ed. Hugh Thomson illus. VG. $85.

Rosalba's Journal and Other Papers. London, 1919 1st edition. Near Fine. $20.

DOCKHAM'S AMERICAN REPORT. Directory of Textile & Dry Goods Trade. Boston, 1900. 35th edition. VG. $60.

DOCTOROW, E. L. *Welcome to Hard Times.* NY, 1960 1st ed. Author's 1st book. VG in dust jacket. $250.

Drinks Before Dinner. NY, 1979 1st ed. Fine in DJ. $20.

World's Fair. NY, 1985 1st ed. Fine in DJ. $10.

DOD, KARL. *The Corps of Engineers: The War Against Japan.* G.P.O., 1968. Very Good. $40.

DODD, GEORGE. *Days in the Factories; or the Manufacturing Industry of Great Britain Described and Illustrated.* London, Chas. Knight, 1843. 548 pages. Orig. cloth, cover detached. $200.

DODGE, GRENVILLE. *How We Built the Union Pacific Railway & Other Railway Papers.* Denver, 1965. Reprint of 1911-1914 private ed. Fine in DJ. $55.

Personal Recollections of President Abraham Lincoln, General Grant & General Sherman. CA, 1914. VG. $60.

DODGE, JACK. *Jack Dodge, His Life and Times.* Sherman Danby, 1937 1st ed. VG, no DJ. Signed by author. $14.

DODGE, MARY MAPES. *The Land of Pluck.* NY, 1894. 1st ed. Illus. Soiled cover, o/w VG. $24.

When Life is Young. Century, 1894 1st ed. Illus. VG. $25.

Rhymes and Jingles. Scribner's, 1927. Illus. VG. $18.

Hans Brinker or the Silver Skates. Garden City, 1932. N. C. Wyeth and Peter Hurd illustrator. Near Very Good. $45. Harper, 1924 1st edition. L. Rhead illustrator. Good-Very Good. $25-$35. Saalfield, undated reprint. Very Good. $5. Scribner's, 1926. Color illustrations. $25.

DODGE, RICHARD IRVING. *Our Wild Indians.* Hartford CT, 1883. Illus. Fine $70-$150.

Black Hills. NY, 1876 1st ed. Green cloth. $150.

The Plains of the Great West. NY, 1877. $75.

DODGE, THEODORE A. *A Bird's Eye View of Our Civil War.* Boston, 1883 1st ed. Spine ends chip. $25.

DODS, MATILDA L. *The Art of Cooking.* 1880. $50-$65.

DOLAN, J. R. *The Yankee Peddlers of Early America.* Potter, 1964. Good-Very Good. $25.

DOLBIER, MAURICE. *The Magic Shop.* No place, 1946 1st ed. Fritz Eichenberg illus. VG in DJ. $13.

DONAHEY, WILLIAM. *Alice and the Teenie Weenies.* Chicago, 1927. Good. $25.

Teenie Weenie Neighbors. 1945 2nd ed. Clean, tight. $20.

DONALD, J. *Outlaws of the Borders.* No place, 1882 1st ed. Covers worn. Interior Good. $85. Chicago. VG. $100

DONALDSON, PASCHAL. *Odd Fellows Text Book and Manual.* Moss, revised ed., 1873. Illus. VG. $20.

DONAT, ALEXANDER. *The Holocaust Kingdom: A Memoir.* New York, 1965. Very Good in dust jacket. $20.

DONNE, BURT. *Play Ball! An Up To The Minute Book on How to Play All Positions.* NY, 1947 1st ed. Good. $50.

DONNELLY IGNATIUS. *The Antediluvian World.* NY, 1882 1st ed. 1st book. Near VG. $55.

Atlantis. NY, 1882 18th ed. Cover wear, o/w VG. $45.

The Golden Bottle. D. Merrill, 1882 1st ed. VG. $125.

Ragnarok: The Age of Fire and Gravel. Peale, 1887. Very Good in dust jacket. $30.

The Great Cryptogram. Chicago, 1887 1st ed. Good. $40.

DORSEY & DEVINE. *Fare Thee Well. A Look at Two Centuries of American Hostelries.* Crown, 1964 1st ed. Illus. Fine in dust jacket. $20.

DORSON, R. M. *Peasant Customs & Savage Myths.* Chicago, 1968 2 vols. Fine. $60.

DORIN, PATRICK C. *The Canadian Pacific Railway.* Seattle, 1974 1st ed. Fine in fine DJ. $25.

DORST, J. *Migration of Birds.* Boston,1962. F in DJ. $33.

DOS PASSOS, JOHN. *1919.* NY, 1932 1st ed. F in DJ. $30.

The Big Money. NY, 1936 1st edition. VG in fair DJ. $75.

The Garbage Man. NY, Harper, 1926 1st ed. 1st issue in hard cover. VG-Fine. $200-$400. 2nd state in DJ. $95.

One Man's Initiation. London, 1920 1st edition. $85.

DOS PASSOS, JOHN (In Magazines). *Esquire*. Jan, 1936. Short story. $28. Sept, 1953. Short story. $14.

DOSTOEVSKI, FEODOR. *Poor People*. Modern Library 1st edition, 1917. Good-Fine in dust jacket. $120.
A Gentle Spirit. 1931 Translation by Constance Garnett. One of 495 copies. Fine in slipcase. $120.
Stavrogin's Confession. NY, 1947. VG in DJ. $20.
The Idiot. Heritage edition, 1956. Eichenberg illustrator. Fine, but no case. $10.
Crime and Punishment. Heritage reprint, 1950. Fine in slipcase. $13. Literary Guild, 1953. Very Good. $8.

DOUGLAS. *Hickory Ridge Boy Scouts Great Hike*. NY, 1913. Good. $12.

DOUGLAS, AMANDA. *Santa Claus Land*. Boston, 1873. Good-VG. $40.

DOUGLAS, LLOYD C. *Magnificent Obsession*. Chicago, 1929 1st edition. 1st novel. Near Fine in dust jacket. $100.

DOUGLAS, NORMAN. *In the Beginning*. NY, 1928 1st American edition. Very Good in dust jacket. $35.
South Wind. New York, Heritage reprint, 1939. Fine in slipcase. $18.

DOUGLAS, WILLIAM O. *Of Men and Mountains*. NY, 1950 1st ed. VG. $25. Another, signed. $40.
Beyond the High Himalayas. Doubleday, 1952. Book Club edition. VG in good dust jacket. $5.

DOUGLASS, FREDERICK. *My Bondage and My Freedom*. NY & Auburn, 1855 1st ed. Rubbed, but VG. $195. Chicago, 1970 reprint. Scuffed covers. $20.
Life and Times. Hartford, 1881. Illus. Very Good. $35.

DOWNES, WILLIAM HOWE. *The Life and Works of Winslow Homer*. Boston, 1911 1st ed. 266 illus. VG. $60.

DOWNEY, FAIRFAX. *Portrait of an Era as Drawn by C. D. Gibson: a Biography*. New York, 1936 1st edition. Illustrated. Very Good. $45.

DOWNING, A. J. *Cottage Residences of North America*. NY, 1860 4th edition. Good. $80.
Fruit and Fruit Trees of America. NY, 1870. Illustrated. Very Good. $60-$70. Wiley, 1892. Very Good. $45.
The Fruits and Fruit Trees of North America. NY, 1857 Revised edition. Fair. $125.

DOYLE, ARTHUR CONAN. *The Adventures of Sherlock Holmes*. London, 1892 1st ed. Sidney Paget illus. Morocco bound. Spine fading, o/w Fine in slipcase. $1,250. NY, 1892 1st American edition, later issue. Inscribed and dated by Doyle on title page. 16 tipped-in plates. VG in slipcase. $2,750. Same, no inscription. VG. $145-$250.

The Memoirs of Sherlock Holmes. London, 1894. The second collection of Holmes stories. Few repairs, o/w VG. $500. NY, 1894 1st American ed. VG. $145.
The Exploits of Brigadier Gerard. NY, 1896 1st American ed. Near Fine. $45.
The Hound of the Baskervilles. London, 1902 1st ed. Sidney Paget illus. Very Good in slipcase, $1,500. NY, 1902 1st American ed. Near VG. $60.
The Adventures of Gerard. NY, 1903 1st American ed. Near Very Good. $18.
The Return of Sherlock Homes. McClure, 1905 1st American edition. Published one month before English edition. Good. $500.
A History of the Great War. NY, 1916-1920 1st American ed. 6 vols. Little bumping, shaking, o/w VG. $275.
The British Campaign in France and Flanders, 1915-1916. London, 1918 2 vols. Fold-out maps VG. $20.
The Case for Spirit Photography. NY, 1923 1st American edition. Near Very Good. $50.
The White Company. NY, 1891 1st American ed. $100. Same, 1922, Cosmopolitan. Wyeth illus. VG in DJ. $55.

DOYLE, ROBERT A. *Straight Razor Collecting, An Illustrated History and Price Guide*. Paducah, KY, 1980. $50.

DRABBLE, MARGARET. *A Summer Bird Cage*. NY, 1964 1st American ed. Author's 1st book. VG in good DJ. $85.
The Needle's Eye. NY, 1972 1st Amer. ed. NF in DJ. $30.

DRAGO, HARRY. *Outlaws on Horseback*. NY, 1964. One of 150 signed copies. Mint in VG slipcase. $250. Another, 1964 trade edition. Unsigned, Good-VG in DJ. $20
Great American Cattle Trails. NY, 1965 1st edition. Good-VG in dust jacket. $30.
Steamboaters. NY, 1967. Fine in dust jacket. $18.
Canal Days in America. Bramwell, 1972 1st ed. Very Good-Fine in dust jacket. $15-$30.
Wild, Wooly, and Wicked. NY, circa 1960. DJ. $35.

DRAKE, MAURICE and WILFRED. *Saints and Their Emblems*. London, 1906. 12 plates. Covers worn. $125.

DRAKE, SAMUEL ADAMS. *The Making of the Great West*. NY, 1887 1st ed. VG. $45. 1894 reprint. Good. $10.
Our Colonial Homes. Boston, Lee & Shepard, 1894 1st edition. Fair, stains. $15.
Old Boston Taverns. Boston, 1917. Illus. Very Good. $20.

DRAKE, ST. CLAIR and H. CLAYTON. *Black Metropolis, A Study of Negro Life*. NY, Harcourt Brace, 1945 1st ed. Very Good in dust jacket. $50.

DRANNAN, CAPT. WILLIAM F. *31 Years on the Plains and in the Mountains*. Chicago, 1899 1st ed. G-VG. $75-$150. Many editions were published within ten years of the first. 1901-1904 copies sell in the $20-$40 range. Most authorities say Drannan was, at best, a senile braggart.

DREISER, THEODORE. *The Color of a Great City*. NY, 1923 1st ed. Near Fine. $200. Good-VG. $75.
Sister Carrie. NY, 1907 2nd ed. G-VG. $100-$200. NY, 1939 LEC. Sgnd by illus. F in case. $100. Unsigned. $15.
An American Tragedy. NY, 1925 Limited edition. 2 vols. Signed. Very Good in poor box. $125.
Chains. NY, Boni-Liveright, 1927 1st ed. VG. $23.
The Bulwark. Doubleday, 1946 1st. VG in DJ. $13-$30.

DREISER, THEODORE (In Magazines). *Cosmopolitan*. April 1898. Short story. $20-$30.
Esquire. Sept 1935. Short story. $20-$30.

DRESS GOODS, WHITE GOODS, CLOTHING. International Textbook Company, 1905. Merchandise display lessons, etc. Good-VG. $15-$25.

DRESSLER, ALBERT. *California's Pioneer Circus, Joseph Andrew Rowe, Founder*. San Francisco, Dressler, 1926 1st ed. No. 792 of 1250 copies. VG. $50-$80.

DREVENSTEDT, J. V. *The American Standard of Perfection*. Amer. Poultry Assoc. 1898 ed. G-VG. $12-$15.

DREW, JAMES M. *Blacksmithing*. Webb Books, 1943 3rd edition. Fine in wraps. $10.

DREXEL, ARTHUR. *The Drawings of Frank Lloyd Wright*. Bramhall House, 1962 1st ed. VG in DJ. $75.

DREYFUS, ALFRED. *Five Years of My Life*. NY, 1901 3rd edition. Good. $45.

DRIGGS, HOWARD. *Westward America*. NY, 1942. 40 plates by Jackson. VG. $40. Another, signed. $60.
The Old West Speaks. 1956, Englewood. Jackson illus. Good. $10. Another, VG-Fine. $25-$40.

DRIGGS and KING. *Rise of the Lone Star*. 1936, Stokes. Very Good in dust jacket. $25.

DRINKWATER, JOHN. *Abraham Lincoln: A Play*. Boston, 1919. Very Good. $85.
Costwold Characters. New Haven, London, 1921. Good-Very Good. $60-$90.
Charles James Fox. NY, 1928 1st ed. Very Good. $15.

DRISCOLL, CHARLES B. *Country Jake*. Macmillan, 1946 1st ed. Signed by author. Fine in dust jacket. $12.

DRUMMOND, JAKE. *Death Comes to Tea*. Boston, 1940 1st edition. Very Good in dust jacket. $30.
High Tension. NY, 1950 1st ed. VG in fair DJ. $18.
Murder on a Bad Trip. NY, 1968 1st ed. Fine in DJ. $13.

DRURY, ALLEN. *Advise and Consent*. Franklin Mint, 1976. Fine leather. $15.

DRURY, JOHN. *Old Chicago Houses*. Univ. of Chicago Press, 1941 1st ed. Very Good. $18. Fine. $35.
Old Illinois Houses. 1948. Fine. $20.
Midwest Heritage. 1948. Very Good. $35.

DRYFHOUT and FOX. *Augustus Saint-Gaudens - The Portrait Reliefs*. Grossman, 1969 1st ed. F in DJ. $16-$20.

DUBIN, ARTHUR. *More Classic Trains*. Milwaukee, 1974 1st edition. Very Good in dust jacket. $50-$65.

DUBOIS, W. E. B. *Suppression of the African Slave to the USA*. NY, 1896 1st ed. Harvard dissertation. Ex-library. Full leather. Hinge break, title label missing. Slight endpaper foxing. $2,200.
Souls of Black Folk. Chicago, 1903 1st. VG. $250-$325.
The World and Africa. NY, 1947 1st ed. Good in DJ. $35.
Ordeal of Mansart, Mansart Builds a School, Worlds of Color. NY, 1957-1961 3 vols. Fine in NF DJs. $250-$275.

DUBOIS, WILLIAM P. *The Great Geppy*. NY, 1940 1st edition. Illus. by author. VG in facsimile dust jacket. $60.
The Flying Locomotive. NY, 1941 1st ed. VG in DJ. $75.
Twenty One Balloons. NY, 1947 1st ed. Illus. by author. Very Good in dust jacket. $40.
Bear Party. NY, 1951 1st ed. Illus. by author. Good. $36.
Squirrel Hotel. NY, 1952 1st ed. Illus. by author. Fine in dust jacket. $50.
Lion. New York, 1956 1st edition. Illustrated by author. Very Good in dust jacket. $150.
Petunia's Treasure. NY, 1975 1st ed. Illus. by author. VG in dust jacket. $18.
Periwinkle. NY, 1976. Illus. by author. Fine in DJ. $18.
The Forbidden Forest. NY, 1978 1st ed. VG. $38.

DUCHAILLU, PAUL. *Stories of the Gorilla Country*. Harpers, 1868 1st ed. Illus. ads. Very Good. $95.
The Land of the Midnight Sun. NY, 1881 2 volumes 1st edition. Fine. $75.

DUDLEY, CHARLES M. *60 Centuries of Skiing*. Stephen Daye Press, 1935. Illus. Spine wear. o/w VG. $25.

DUFF, CHARLES. *A Handbook on Hanging*. Boston, 1929. Very Good. $25. London, 1955 revised ed. $25.

DUFFEY, E. B. *The Ladies' and Gentlemen's Etiquette: a Complete Manual etc*. Phil., 1877. Good-VG. $20-$40.

DUFFIELD, J. W. *Radio Boys, Flying Service*. No date. Very Good in dust jacket. $20.
Radio Boys Under the Sea. Circa 1920. Very Good. $8.

DUFFUS, R. L. *The Santa Fe Trail*. NY, 1930 1st edition. Good-VG. $25-$35. Later editions, 1936-1943. $20-$25.
The Valley and its People. New York, 1944. Very Good in dust jacket. $50-$75.

DUFFY, CLINTON (Warden). *88 Men and 2 Women*. NY, 1962. Anchor ed. 1st ed. VG. in chip DJ. $23.
Pocket Dictionary of Prison Slanguage. No Place, 1941. Good-Very Good. $30-$40.
The San Quentin Story. 1950 1st ed. VG. $10.

DUFFY, HERBERTS. *William Howard Taft*. NY, Balch, 1930 2nd edition. Very Good. $10.

DUGGAR, B. M. *Mushroom Growing*. NY, Orange Judd, 1915. Very Good. $20.

DUGMORE, A. R. *The Romance of the Newfoundland Caribou*. Lippincott, 1913 1st ed. Illus by author. VG. $75.
The Wonderland of Big Game. London, 1925 1st ed. G-VG. $40-$50. (Other wildlife titles by author.) $40-$75.

DUKE OF WINDSOR. *A King's Story*. No place, 1951. VG in very good dust jacket. $30.

DULAC, EDMUND (Illustrator). *The Rubaiyat of Omar Khayyam*. Edward Fitzgerald, translator. NY, London, circa 1910. One of 200 copies. Tipped-in color plates. VG. $300. Doran, 1928 ed. 12 plates. Very Good. $50.
The Poetical Works of Edgar Allen Poe. NY, circa 1912. Near Fine. $175.
Stories for the Arabian Nights. London, circa 1920. 34 color plates, tipped in. Cover mottling, o/w VG. $90.
The Kingdom of the Pearl. Brentano, 1920. Signed limited ed. Rebound in slipcase. VG. $500.
4 Plays for Dancers. By William Butler Yeats. NY, 1921 1st American ed. VG in DJ. $150.
Treasure Island. Doran, circa 1927. 12 color tipped-in plates. Very Good. $90.
The Masque of Comus. By John Milton. Limited Editions Club. No date. One of 1,500 copies. Fine in slipcase. $225,
Edmund DuLac's Fairy Book. Doran, no date. 9 tipped-in color plates. Light rubbing, edge wear, $150.
The Sleeping Beauty and Other Tales. By Arthur Quiller-Couch. London, no date. One of 1,000. Signed by Dulac. Tipped-in color plates. Rebacked in morocco. VG. $950. 1920s ed. NY, Doran. 16 tipped in plates. $90-$120.

DULIN, R. *Battleships: U. S. Battleships in World War II*. Annapolis MD, 1976. Very Good. $39

DULL, PAUL. *A Battle History of the Imperial Japanese Navy, 1941-1945*. Annapolis MD, 1978. VG. $25. Book Club ed. Very Good in dust jacket. $10.

DULL, MRS. S. R. *Southern Cooking*. Ruralist Press. Atlanta, 1928 1st ed. Green cloth. 350 pgs. VG. $30.

DUMAS, ALEXANDRE. *The Nutcracker of Nurenberg*. McBride, 1930. Hasselriis illus. Very Good. $35.
The Three Musketeers. NY, Limited Editions Club, 1953. One of 1,500 copies. Edy Legrand illus. F in slipcase. $45.

The Complete Works of Alexander Dumas. 30 volume set. Collier's, 1902. Cloth gilt tops. Very Fine set. $120.
Camille. London, LEC, 1937. Signed by Marie Laurencin, illus. $300 auct. Same, a fine copy in slipcase. $475 dealer.

DU MAURIER, DAPHNE. *Rebecca*. NY, 1940. Movie scenes. Very Good. $7.
King's General. 1946 1st ed. Shaken. $14.
Mary Jane. 1954 edition in DJ. Good-VG. $12.
My Cousin Rachel. Doubleday, 1952 1st American ed. VG in ragged edge, taped dust jacket. $20.
The Parasites. Doubleday, 1950 1st American ed. VG in edgeworn dust jacket. $25.

DUMKE, GLENN S. *Boom of the Eighties in Southern California*. San Marino, 1944 1st ed. Fine. $40.

DUMONT, A. S. *My Airships*. NY, 1904 1st ed. Good. $90.

DUMONT, DWIGHT L. *Antislavery Origins of the Civil War*. Univ. of Michigan Press, 1959. Very Good. $18.

DUNBAR, EDWARD E. *The Romance of the Age or The Discovery of Gold in California*. NY, 1867, Appleton 1st edition. Very Good. $65.

DUNBAR, PAUL LAWRENCE. *Lyrics of the Hearth Side*. Dodd Mead, 1899 1st ed. VG plus. $150.
Poems of Cabin and Field. NY, 1900. Photos. VG. $125.
Howdy, Honey, Howdy. NY, 1905 1st edition. Photos. Near Very Good. $150.
"Joggin' Erlong". Toronto, 1906 1st Canadian ed. illus. John Rae decorations. VG. $100.
Lyrics of Lowly Life. Dodd-Mead. 1898 2nd ed. Very Good. $35-$45. 1908 ed. cover stained. $50.
The Complete Poems of--. NY, 1924. Good. $30. Dodd-Mead, revised ed. 1944. Very Good. $15.
Little Brown Baby: Poems for Young People. NY, 1957. Illus. Ex-library. Almost VG. $35.

DUNBAR, SEYMOUR. *A History of Travel in America*. Indianapolis, 1915 1st ed. 4 vols. Fine. $250. Good. Ex-lib $75. Fair. $28. 2nd ed NY, 1937 in 1 vol. $30-$50.

DUNCAN, DAVID DOUGLAS (Photographer). *The Private World of Pablo Picasso*. Ridge Press, 1958 1st ed. Good in DJ. $25. Grosset & Dunlap, 1974 ed. VG in DJ. $75.
The Kremlin. NY, 1960 1st. Color photo. VG. $30-$50.
Yankee Nomad. NY, 1966 1st ed. Mended DJ. VG. $30.
War Without Heroes. NY, 1970 1st ed. Over 250 photos. Fine in dust jacket. $135.

DUNCAN, GREGORY. *Dick Donnely of the Paratroopers*. Whitman, 1944. Very Good in dust jacket. $10

DUNCAN, ISIDORA. *My Life*. NY, 1927. Good plus. $20. Same, signed and numbered. $40. Liveright, 1942 ed. $6.

DUNCAN, CAPTAIN RICHARD. *Stunt Flying*. Chicago, 1930 1st ed. Very Good in dust jacket. $45.

DUNHAM, JACOB. *Journal of Voyages*. New York, 1851. Little worn and shaken, some foxing. $250.

DUNHILL, ARTHUR. *The Pipe Book*. NY, Macmillan, 1924 1st Amer. ed. 262 pages. Gilt dec. cover. G-VG. $50-$75. London, 1977 5th printing. Revised ed. VG in DJ. $30.

DUNN, PAUL H. *The Osmonds*. Salt Lake City, 1975. Signed by all nine Osmonds. Fine in fine DJ. $50.

DUNNE, IDA LEE. *The American Hostess Cook Book*. New York, 1949. Recipes and biographical data, from Bess Truman to Tom Dewey.$25-$40.

DUNSHEE, KENNETH H. *Enjine! Enjine!* NY, 1939 1st edition. Paperbound. Good-VG. $45.
As You Pass By. Firefighting. NY, 1952. G-VG. $8-$12.

DUPUY, ERNEST. *WWII: A Compact History*. New York, 1969. Very Good in dust cover. $20.

DUPUY, R. E. *St. Vith-Lion in the Way: The 106th Infantry Division in WWII*. Washington, 1949 1st ed. VG-Fine in dust jacket. $75-$95. Later editions. $25.

DUPUY, T. N. *Military History of World War II*. NY, 1962. 14 vol. set. Very Good-Fine. $48.
Air War in the Pacific: Victory in the Air. New York, 1964. Fine in dust jacket. $10.

DURANT, JOHN. *The Yankees*. NY, Hastings House. 1949 1st ed. Very Good in dust jacket. $69.

DURANT, JOHN and ALICE. *Pictorial History of the American Circus*. A. S. Barnes, 1957. Very Good in dust jacket. $35.

DURANT, WILL. *Transition*. New York, 1927. Review copy. Author's 2nd book. One of 1,000 copies. Fine in fine dust jacket. $100.

DURANT, WILL and ARIEL. *The Lessons of History*. NY, 1968 1st ed. Inscribed Good in dust jacket. $25.

DURHAM, MARILYN. *The Man Who Loved Cat Dancing*. NY, 1972 1st ed. Author's 1st book. Near Fine in DJ. $50.

DURHAM, VICTOR G. *The Submarine Boys on Duty*. 1909, Saalfield. Juvenile. Very Good. $7.

DURRELL, GERALD. *Island Zoo*. Philadelphia, 1963 1st American ed. Good-VG. $17.
The Overloaded Ark. New York, 1963. Good in DJ. $6.
The Donkey Rustlers. Lon., 1968 1st ed. Fine in DJ. $15.

DURRELL, LAWRENCE. *Prospero's Cell*. London, 1945 1st edition. Very Good in dust jacket. $25.
Zero and Asylum in the Snow. Paperback, 1946 1st edition, Rhodes. $145. 1st American edition, Berkeley, 1947 Very Good in dust jacket. $75.
Mount-Olive. London, 1958 1st ed. VG in dust jacket. $50.
Dark Labyrinth. London, 1961 1st edition. VGin DJ. $50.
The Alexandria Quartet. London, 1962. 1st collected ed. No. 348 of 500 signed. Near Fine in slipcase. $850.
Nunquam. London, 1970 1st edition. Fine in DJ. $20.

DUSTIN, FRED. *The Custer Tragedy*. Ann Arbor MI, 1939 1st ed. One of 200. Includes 3 maps in pocket. $395. Ann Arbor, 1965 edition with maps. $40.

DUTCH, ALEXANDER and LAURA HARRIS. *Freddy and the Fire Engine*. Moveable pictures with side pull-tabs. NY, Crown Pub, 1945 1st ed. $80-$120.

DUTTON'S HOLIDAY ANNUAL, 1893. Children's stories with 6 full-page chromos. $38.

DUVAL, JOHN. *Early Times in Texas*. Austin, TX, 1892 1st edition. Very Good. $175.

DUVAL, MATHIAS. *Artistic Anatomy*. London, 1892 6th edition. Wood engravings. Very Good. $65.

DUVOISIN, ROGER. *Donkey-Donkey*. Chicago, 1933 1st edition. Illus. by author. Good. $36. Same. NY, 1940 1st edition. Revised. Illus. by author. Good in DJ. $35.
Chanticleer. NY, 1947 1st. Illus. by auth. VG in DJ. $20.
See What I Am. NY, 1974 1st edition. Fine in DJ. $30.

DWIGGINS, W. A. (Illustrator). *Tales by E. A. Poe*. Chicago, 1930. One of 1,000 copies. Near Fine in slipcase. $150.
The Strange Case of Dr. Jekyll and Mr. Hyde. By Robert Louis Stevenson. NY, 1929. One of 1,200 copies, signed by Dwiggins. VG in slipcase. $125.

DWYER, CHARLES P. *The Economic Cottage Builder*. Buffalo, 1856. Slight foxing, o/w VG. $295.
The Immigrant Builder. How to Construct Dwellings in the Bush and on the Prairie... Philadelphia, 1878 10th ed. 145 pages. Light rubbing. $200.

DYKSTRA, ROBERT. *The Cattle Towns*. Knopf, 1968 1st edition. Fine in dust jacket. $20.

DYLAN, BOB. *Tarantula*. New York, no date, 1st edition. Author's 1st book. NF in DJ. $50-$60. 1971 ed. $20-$30.

DYER, FREDERICK. *A Compendium of the War of the Rebellion*. Des Moines IA, 1908 1st ed. Very Good. $95.

DYKE'S AUTOMOBILE & GASOLINE ENGINE ENCYCLOPEDIA. Chicago, 1924. Very Good. $45-$75.

E

EARHART, AMELIA. *Our Flight in the Friendship*. NY, London, 1928. Signed by author. Near VG. $275.
The Fun of It: Random Records of My Own Flying and of Women in Aviation. NY, 1932 1st ed. With broadcast record in pocket. Signed. Cover silver-fished, soiled dust jacket. $850-$1,000. Unsigned. Good. $150. Same, 2nd printing. Very Good. $550.
Last Flight. Arranged by George Putnam. NY, 1937. 1st ed. in DJ. $35-$65. 3rd printing. Good-Very Good. $20.
Soaring Wings. Putnam, 1939 1st ed. G-VG. $10-$20.

EARLE, ALICE MORSE. *Home Life in Colonial Days*. NY, 1898. Good. $30. 1902 ed. $20.
Stage Coach & Tavern Days. Macmillan, 1900 1st ed. Good-Very Good. $25-$45. 1901 edition. $10.
Sun Dials & Roses of Yesterday. Macmillan, 1902 1st ed. Fair, ex-lib. $10. Another, inscribed 1 of 100. $50.
Two Centuries of Costume in America. NY and London, 1903, 2 vols. Spine strip gnawed, inside clean. $55. Another set, in very good condition. $85-$95.

EARP, JOSEPHINE. *I Married Wyatt Earp*. Glen Boyer, editor. Tucson, 1976 1st ed. VG in Fair DJ. $30.

EAST O' THE SUN & WEST O' THE MOON. Frances Brundage, illus. No date, Saalfield. 248 pgs. $18.

EASTER, JOHN. *The Chargres: River of Westward Passage*. Rivers of America Series. NY, Rinehart, 1948 1st ed. Very Good in dust jacket. $20.

EASTLAKE, CHARLES. *Hints on Household Taste in Furniture, Upholstery and Other Details*. London, 1868. Faded cloth, soil. $90. 1869 revised ed. $50. Boston, 1874 2nd American ed. Near Fine. $55.

EASTMAN, CHARLES. *Indian Boyhood*. NY, 1902 2nd impression. Very Good. $35. Later reprints. $15-$25. Signed. $30-$45.
Red Hunters and the Animal People. 1904 1st ed. $50.
Smoky Day's Wigwam Evenings. Little Brown, 1912 reprint. Good-Very Good. $20-$30.

EASTMAN, MAX. *Leon Trotsky: Portrait of a Youth*. NY, 1925 1st ed. Fine. $35.
Kinds of Love. NY, 1931 1st ed. Fine in DJ. $65.
Sense of Humor. Scribner, 1921 1st ed. $50-$100.

The End of Socialism in Russia. Boston, 1937 1st edition. Very Good in dust jacket. $45. Another, signed. $50.
Reflections on the Failure of Socialism. NY, 1955. Inscribed. Very Good in dust jacket. $35.
Love and Revolution. NY, 1964 1st. Signed. F in DJ. $65.

EATON, ALLEN H. *Handicrafts of the Southern Highlands*. NY, 1937. Illus. Very nice. $125. 2nd printing in DJ. $60.

EATON, CLEMENT. *A History of the Southern Confederacy*. New York, 1954. Very Good in dust jacket. $28.

EATON, E. HOWARD. *Birds of New York*. Various full color editions, published from 1909 to 1925. $50-$125.

EATON, SEYMOUR. *The Roosevelt Bears, More About Teddy B., Bears Abroad,* and *Bear Detectives*. 4 books, various dates, 1906-1909. First editions. Philadelphia, Edward Stern. usual minor defects, o/w VG. $385 auction.
More About the Roosevelt Bears. Stern, 1907. $60-$95.
The Traveling Bears in Outdoor Sports. Barse, 1915. $40-$60.

EBERHART, MIGNON. *Hasty Wedding*. Doubleday, 1938 1st ed. Very Good in dust jacket. $25.
Escape the Night. NY, 1944 1st ed. Near Fine in DJ. $28.
Wings of Fear. NY, 1945 1st ed. VG in DJ. $20.
Another Man's Murder. NY, 1957 1st ed. F in DJ. $20.
Enemy in the House. NY, 1962 1st ed. Fine in DJ. $25.
RSVP Murder. NY, 1965 1st ed. Fine in DJ. $20.
El Rancho Rio. NY, 1970 1st ed. Fine in DJ. $15.

EBERLEIN, HAROLD and A. E. RICHARDSON. *The English Inn, Past and Present*. Philadelphia, 1926 1st. ed. Very Good. $35.

EBERLEIN, HAROLD D. *American Antiques*. Garden City, 1927. Illus. Very Good in dust jacket. $25.
Manor Houses & Historic Homes of Long Island. Philadelphia, 1928. Very Good. $60.

EBERLEIN, H. D. and A. MC CLURE. *The Practical Book of Period Furniture*. Philadelphia, no date. Near Fine in good dust jacket. $75.

ECKERT, ALLAN W. *The Frontiersman*. Boston, 1967 1st ed. Very Good in dust jacket. $20.

The Crossbreed. Little Brown, 1968 1st. VG in DJ. $35.
Wilderness Empire. Boston, 1969. Illus. VG in DJ. $27.
The Court Martial of Daniel Boone. Little Brown, 1973 1st ed. Corners bumped, else VG in dust jacket. $40.

ECKHARDT, G. H. *Pennsylvania Clocks and Clockmakers.* NY, 1955. VG in DJ. $30-$40. Bonanza reprint. Fine in dust jacket. $15.

ECKSTEIN, GUSTAV. *Noguchi.* NY, 1931 1st ed. Near VG. $45. Fair-Good. $15-$25.
The Pet Shop. Harpers, 1944 ed. Autographed by author. Very Good in dust jacket. $25.

EDDINGTON, ARTHUR S. *Space, Time, and Gravitation.* Cambridge, 1921 1st ed. Very Good. $50.
The Expanding Universe. NY, 1933. Good. $26.
Stars and Atoms. London, 1927 1st edition. $20-$50. 1942 3rd edition. Warped boards. $14.
Relativity Theory of Protons and Electrons. NY, 1936 1st American edition. $95.

EDDISON, E. R. *The Worm Ourobouros.* Boni, 1926 1st American ed. Near Fine in Near Fine DJ. $225. Same without DJ. $95. Same in VG cond. $50.

EDDY, MARY BAKER. *Poems.* Boston, 1910 1st ed. F. $35.
Miscellaneous Writings 1883-1896. Boston, 1914. Good-Very Good. $28.
Science and Health. Boston, 1875 1st ed. $1,000-$1,800. Lynn MA, 1878 2nd edition. $500. Boston, 1941. One of 1,000 copies. Designed by William Dana Orcutt. Fine in slipcase. $2,000. Auction, 1994. $1,200.

EDGERTON, HAROLD E. and JAMES R. KILIAN, JR. *Flash! Seeing the Unseen by Ultra High-Speed Photography.* Boston, 1954 2nd edition. Revised, enlarged. Signed by Edgerton. Fine in dust jacket. $85.
Moments of Vision: The Stroboscopic Revolution in Photography. MIT, Press, 1979 1st ed. Very Good in DJ. $30.

EDMINSTER, FRANK. *The Ruffled Grouse.* Macmillan, 1947 1st ed. Very Good. $38.
American Game Birds of Field and Forest. NY, 1954. Signed. Worn dust jacket. $50.

EDMONDS, S. EMMA. *Nurse and Spy in the Union Army.* Hartford CT, 1865 1st ed. 12 wood-engraved plates. NF. $125. Another, faded but VG. $50. Same, rebound. $25.

EDMONDS, WALTER D. *Rome Haul.* Boston, 1929 1st ed. Author's 1st book. VG in DJ. $50-$60, 1943 rpt. VG. $8.
Mostly Canallers. Little Brown, 1934 1st. VG in DJ. $40.
Chad Hanna. Boston, 1940 1st edition. Fine in DJ. $30.
Young Ames. Little Brown, 1942 1st ed. Fine in DJ. $20.
The Boyds of Black River. Book Club Edition. Dodd-Mead, 1953. Fine in dust jacket. $8.

Drums Along the Mohawk. Boston, 1936 1st edition. $30-$75. Little Brown, 1937 reprint. Good. $8.

EDWARDS, AMELIA. *A Thousand Miles Up the Nile.* NY, 1877 1st American edition. Illustrated. Fading, rubbing, o/w Very Good. $175. Same, 2nd edition. $30-$40.

EDWARDS, CLARENCE E. *Bohemian San Francisco. Its Restaurants and Their Most Famous Recipes.* Paul Elder, 1914 1st ed. VG. $35. Another dealer quotes. $85.

EDWARDS, EMORY. *Modern American Locomotive Engines.* Philadelphia, 1890. VG-Fine. $25.

EDWARDS, EUGENE. *Jack-Pots.* Gambling. 1900 Hard cover, 342 pgs. VG. $160. Same, Very Fine. $325.

EDWARDS, FRANK. *Flying Saucers-Serious Business.* NY, 1966 1st ed. Very Good. $13.
Strange People. 1961 1st ed. Near Fine in DJ. $12.

EDWARDS, LEO. *Jerry Todd and The Talking Frog.* NY, G&D, 1925 1st. Chipped, rubbed; creased DJ. $55 auction.
Poppy Ott and the Stuttering Parrot. Grosset & Dunlap, 1926. Good, no dust jacket. $10.

EDWARDS, WILLIAM B. *Civil War Guns.* Castle Books, 1978 Illustrated. Very Good. $35. Earlier editions $20-$35.
Story of Colts Revolver. 1953 1st ed. in dust jacket. $45.

EDWIN, JONATHON HOYT. *Buckskin Joe.* Hunter, scout. Univ. of Neb. Press, 1966. VG in DJ. $45.

THE EFFECTS OF NUCLEAR WEAPONS. U. S. Atomic Energy Commission. USGPO June 1947. Paperback $22.

EGGLESTON, EDWARD. *The End of the World, A Love Story.* NY, Orange Judd, no date, circa 1872. Good. $30.
The Mystery of Metropolisville. NY, no date, circa 1873. 320 pgs. Worn, frayed. $30.
The Hoosier Schoolboy. NY, 1883 1st ed., 1st issue. G. D. Bush illus. Very Good. $75.

EGGLESTON, GEORGE CARY. *The Big Brother, A Story of Indian War.* Putnam's Sons, 1875 1st. G-VG. $15-$30.
A Captain in The Ranks. Barnes, 1904. Very Good. $15.
The History of the Confederate War. New York, 1910, 2 volumes. Very Good. $125.

EICKEMEYER, CARL & LILIAN W. *Among the Pueblo Indians.* NY, 1895 1st edition. Merrian. VG. $45-$60.

EINSTEIN, ALBERT. *Relativity, the Special and General Theory.* NY, 1920 1st American ed. Translation. VG-Fine. $75-$250. Good. $55. 4th edition. London, 1921. $15.
Out of My Later Years. Philosophical Library, 1950 1st edition. Worn but Very Good in dust jacket. $20.

EINSTEIN, CHARLES. *The Fireside Book of Baseball*. NY, 1956 Book Club Edition. Very Good. $22.
The 2nd Fireside Book of Baseball. NY, 1958 1st ed. VG in vg DJ. $25. Fine in dust jacket. $40.
Willie Mays, Coast to Coast Giant. NY, 1963 1st edition. Very Good in dust jacket. $20.

EIPPER, PAUL. *Circus: Men, Beasts, and Joys of the Road*. Literary Guild, 1931 reprint. Very Good. $15.

EISELEY, LOREN. *The Immense Journey*. NY, 1957 1st edition. Author's 1st book. VG in DJ. $60.
The Unexpected Universe. NY, 1969. Good-VG. $6.
The Night Country: Reflections of a Bone-Hunting Man. NY, 1971. E. Fisher illus. Near Fine in DJ. $15.
The Star Thrower. NP, 1979 5th printing. VG in DJ. $15.

EISENBERG, JAMES. *Commercial Art of Show Card Lettering*. Van Nostrand, 1952 reprint. Ex-library. Good-Very Good. $10-$15.

EISENHOWER, DWIGHT. *The White House Years*. 1963 1st ed. VG-Fine in dust jacket. $10-$20.

EISENHOWER, JOHN. *The Bitter Woods*. NY, 1969. VG in DJ. $30. Same, Good in dust jacket. $12.

EISSLER, MANUEL. *The Modern High Explosives; Nitroglycerine and Dynamite*. NY, 1884. 3/4 morocco. Slight wear, o/w Very Good. $75.

ELDER, PAUL. *The Old Spanish Missions of California*. San Francisco, 1913. Special ed. Wn. Contents VG. $100.

ELIOT, GEORGE (Mary Ann Evans). *The Mill on the Floss*. NY, 1860 1st American edition. Near Very Good. $150. Edinburgh and London, Blackwood, 1860 1st ed. 3 vols. with 16 ads. Earliest issue. G-VG in cloth slipcase. $350.
Impressions of Theophrastus Such. Harper, 1879 1st American edition. Good-Very Good. $35-$50.
Silas Marner. The Weaver of Raveloe. Harper, 1861 1st Amer G-VG. $50-$95 London, LEC. 1 of 1,500. 1953. $70.
Daniel Deronda. London, 1876 1st ed. 1st issue. 4 vols. leather & cloth. VG. $395. One volume reprints. $6-$12.
Romola. McClurg, special edition, 1906. Very Good. $16.

ELIOT, ELIZABETH. *Portrait of a Sport: The Story of Steeplechasing in Great Britain and the U. S*. Woodstock VT, 1957 1st ed. VG in DJ. $25.

ELIOT, T. S. *Murder in the Cathedral*. NY, 1935 1st ed. Near Fine in clipped dust jacket. $100.
Old Possum's Book of Practical Cats. London, 1939 1st ed. Rubbing, light soiling, o/w VG, no DJ. $250. Harcourt Brace, 1939 1st American edition. Fine in dust jacket. $150.
Notes Toward a Definition of Culture. New York, 1949 First American edition. Fine in dust jacket. $65.

The Elder Statesman. London, 1959 1st ed. Fine in fine dust jacket. $75. NY, 1959 1st American ed. in DJ. $60.
Collected Poems 1909-1935. NY, 1946, Harcourt. VG. $7.

ELLET, MRS. E. F. *The New Cyclopaedia of Domestic Economy...5,000 Receipts*. CT, 1872. Many engravings. Good-Very Good. $95-$125.

ELLIOT, BEN G. *The Gasoline Automobile*. McGraw Hill, 1932 4th edition. Very Good. $12.

ELLIOTT, HENRY W. *Our Alaska Province*. NY, 1886 1st edition. Illustrated. Very Good. $75.
Our Arctic Province: Alaska and the Seal Islands. NY, 1897. Illustrated. Very Good. $28.

ELLIOTT, MAUDE HOWE. *Art and Handicraft in the Woman's Building of the World's Columbian Exposition*. Chicago, 1894. Illus. $90.

ELLIS, AUDREY & M. CAVAIANI. *Farmhouse Kitchen*. Chicago, 1973. Good-Very Good. $15-$20.

ELLIS, E. S. *The Indian Wars of the United States*. Chicago, 1902. Rear cover stain, o/w Good-VG. $20.

ELLIS, L. F. *Victory in the West*. London, 1962. Vol. 1: Normandy. VG-Fine in DJ. $75-$125.
The War in France and Flanders. London, 1953 1st ed. Very Good in dust jacket. $95-$130.

ELLIS & RUMELY. *Power and the Plow*. NY, Doubleday-Page, 1911. No dust jacket. $28.

ELLIS, WILLIAM D. *The Bounty Lands*. World, 1952 1st edition. Signed by author. VG in worn dust jacket. $40.

ELLISON, CHARLES. *Fundamentals of Window Display*. Scranton, PA, 1937. Very Good. $15.

ELLSBERG, EDWARD. *On the Bottom*. NY, 1929. Literary Guild edition. Very Good. $19.
Hell on Ice: Saga of the Jeanette. NY, 1938 1st. VG. $9.

ELLSWORTH, and DICKERSON. *The Successful Housekeeper*. Harrisburg PA, 1883 2nd printing. Good. $45.

ELLUL, JACQUES. *The Meaning of the City*. Eerdmans, 1970. Very Good in dust jacket. $20.

ELLWANGER, GEORGE. *The Pleasures of the Table: An Account of Gastronomy etc*. NY, 1902 1st. Illus. VG. $85.

ELMAN, ROBERT. *Advanced Hunting Tips*. Winchester, 1979 revised ed. Very Good in dust jacket. $8.
All About Deer Hunting. Winchester, 1976 1st ed Fine in dust jacket. $10.

ELMER, ROBERT. *Target Archery*. NY, 1945 1st ed. VG in dust jacket. $35.

ELSIE'S COOK BOOK. (Elsie the Cow). Bond Wheelright, 1952 1st ed. VG, no DJ. $18.

ELVIS YEARBOOK. Malibu CA, 1960. Very Good. $40.

EMDE and DEMAND. *Conquerors of the Air*. New York, 1968. Very Good-Fine in dust jacket. $30-$40.

EMERSON, ALICE B. *Ruth Fielding Homeward Bound*. Cupples & Leon, 1919. Good-VG. $9.

EMERSON, EDWARD R. *The Story of the Vine*. NY, London, 1902 1st ed. Rubbing, o/w Fine. $35.

EMERSON, RALPH WALDO. *Nature: Addresses and Lectures*. Boston, 1849 1st ed. Near Fine. $200.
Letters and Social Aims. Boston, 1876 1st ed., 1st printing. Very Good. $75.
The Conduct of Life. Boston, 1860. Good. $24. Another, 1st issue, with catalog at end. Very Good. $200.

EMERSON, RALPH WALDO (In Magazines). *Literary World*. May 1879. Ralph Waldo Emerson Issue. $30-$40.

EMERY, STEWART. *Commando of the Clouds*. Cupple, 1943. Very Good in dust jacket. $8.

EMINENT WOMEN OF THE AGE. Hartford, 1869. VG. $45.

EMMET, BORIS and TOM JENCK. *Catalogues and Counters, A History of Sears Roebuck Co*. Univ. of Chicago, 1950. VG-Fine. $12-$25.

EMMETT, CHRISTOPHER. *Texas Camel Tales*. No place, 1969 reprint. Fine in dust jacket. $55.

EMMONS, MARTHA. *Deep Like the Rivers: Story of My Negro Friends*. No place, 1969 1st edition. Inscribed by author. Very Good in dust jacket. $60.

EMMOTT, ELIZABETH. *The Story of Quakerism*. Headley Bros., 1916 1st ed. Very Good. $12.

EMORY, J. *The Life of Rev. John Wesley*. Ohio Weslyan Univ., 1869. Good with bright covers. $35.

EMORY, LIEUT. COL. WILLIAM. *Notes of a Military Reconnaissance, from Fort Leavenworth, Missouri, to San Diego, California*. Washington, 1848 1st ed. Senate Issue. 416 pgs. Rebound. $400-$700. Fair. $150.

EMSLEY, MICHAEL and KJELL SANDVEL. *Rain Forests and Cloud Forest*. Abrams, NY, 1979. Kjell Photos. Very Good in good dust jacket. $75.

ENCYCLOPEDIAS. Ninety-nine out of one hundred old encyclopedia sets are absolutely worthless. Like the ubiquitous *Reader's Digest* condensed books, millions are printed and few ever destroyed; the market is glutted.

The first edition of the *Encyclopedia Britannica*, published in Edinburgh in 1771, is worth $800 and up. A current year's edition might fetch the same money if you find someone about to buy a set from a door-to-door salesman. Good sets of *World Book, Britannica,* and *Americana* which are less than five years old still have value as reference books and are frequently priced at $300 to $500. Sets more than five years old rarely bring more than $5 or $10 per volume and are not worth their display space in a used book store.

Exceptions to this rule are some Victorian encyclopedias. A few European editions of the 1880s contain full-page color plates and line engravings which can be matted and sold to picture framers and interior decorators.

ENCYCLOPEDIA BRITANNICA. NEW WERNER ED. Akron, 1904 9th ed. 30 vols. $150.

ENCYCLOPEDIA BRITANNICA. NY, 1911 11th ed. 32 "Handy Vols." Chip, wear, few tears at spine tops. $125.

CENTURY DICTIONARY AND ENCYCLOPEDIA. NY, 1900. 10 vols. Nicely rebound. Fine. $250.

PEOPLE'S CYCLOPEDIA OF UNIV. KNOWLEDGE. 1891, 4 vol set, wood engravings & 75 double pg. Color plate maps. Good-Very Good. $50.

THE SCIENTIFIC AMERICAN CYCLOPEDIA OF RECEIPTS, NOTES & QUERIES. No place, 1899. Spine damage, o/w Very Good. $20.

ENCYCLOPEDIA OF ABERRATIONS. By Edward Podolsky. NY, 1953. VG in chipped dust jacket. $23.

STANDARD ENCYCLOPEDIA OF THE ALCOHOL PROBLEM. Westerville, Ohio, 1925. E. H. Cherrington, editor. 1st edition. 6 volumes. Illustrated. Very Good. $250.

THE CONCISE ENCYCLOPEDIA OF AMERICAN ANTIQUES. NY, 1960. By Helen Comstock. Very Good. $25.

THE LAROUSSE ENCYCLOPEDIA OF ANIMAL LIFE. NY, 1967. Very Good. $12.

ASIMOV'S BIOGRAPHICAL ENCYCLOPEDIA. Isaac Asimov. Doubleday, 1964 1st ed. VG plus. $28.

THE ILLUSTRATED ENCYCLOPEDIA OF AMERICAN BIRDS. By L. A. Hausman, New York, 1944 1st edition. Very Good in dust jacket. $14.

THE ENCYCLOPEDIA BOTANICA. By Dennis Brown. NY, 1978 1st printing. Dust jacket. $33.

THE BROWNING ENCYCLOPEDIA. Lon, 1949. VG. $10.

AN ENCYCLOPEDIA OF CANDY AND ICE CREAM MAKING. By S. I. Leon. New York, 1959 1st edition. Ex-library. $25.

AN ENCYCLOPAEDIA OF CIVIL ENGINEERING. London, 1865. Very thick, 1,752 pages. $75.

ENCYCLOPEDIA OF COMEDY. Philadelphia, 1896. Hinge broken, some wear. Good. $8.

ENCYCLOPEDIA OF THE GREAT COMPOSERS AND THEIR MUSIC. NY, 1962 2 vols. BCE. VG in DJ. $15.

ENCYCLOPEDIA OF DOLLS. 1973. Near Fine in DJ. $40.

ENCYCLOPEDIA OF WORLD DRAMA. McGraw-Hill, 1972. 4 vols. Very Good. $58.

INTERNATIONAL ENCYCLOPEDIA OF FILM. Roger Manvell, editor. New York, 1972 1st American edition. Very Good on dust jacket. $20.

WISE FISHERMAN'S ENCYCLOPEDIA. A. J. McClane. NY, 1951 1st ed. Fine. $35.

THE ENCYCLOPEDIA OF FOOD. NY, 1923, Ex-lib. $50.

AN ENCYCLOPEDIA OF FREEMASONRY. Allbert G. Mackey. NY, 1918. 2 vols. New, revised ed. VG. $85.

LAROUSSE GASTRONOMIQUE ENCYCLOPEDIA. of Food, Wine and Cookery. NY, 1961. $20-$25.

THE NEW GARDEN ENCYCLOPEDIA. E. D. Seymour, editor. NY, 1946. 1,380 pages. Very Good. $15.

NEW ILLUSTRATED ENCYCLOPEDIA OF GARDENING. NY, no date. Color plates. $15.

THE GROCER'S ENCYCLOPEDIA. NY, 1911. Good. $75.

THE STANDARD CYCLOPEDIA OF HORTICULTURE. NY, 1917. by L. H. Bailey. 6 volumes in dust jacket. Slight wear. $150. 1943 edition in 3 volumes. $55.

THE GOOD HOUSEKEEPING ENCYCLOPEDIA. Alice Carroll, editor. 1950. Very Good. $6.

THE ENCYCLOPEDIA OF THE HORSE. by C. E. G. Hope. London, 1973. Fine in dust jacket. $40.

THE HUNTER'S ENCYCLOPEDIA. By Raymond Camp. Harrisburg, 1948 1st ed. Fine in dust jacket. $40.

THE UNIVERSAL JEWISH ENCYCLOPEDIA. New York, 1939-1943. 10 volumes. Illustrated. Very Good. $225 set.

ENCYCLOPEDIA OF KNOTS & FANCY ROPEWORK. 1958. Very Good. $45.

APPLETON'S CYCLOPEDIA OF APPLIED MECHANICS. NY, 1896 2 vols. Revised ed. Good-VG. $50.

MOTOR ENCYCLOPEDIA. Cincinnati, 1928. Good. $15.

MUSIC LOVER'S ENCYCLOPEDIA. Ruper Hughes, compiler. NY, 1939. Cover wear. $18.

ENCYCLOPEDIA OF FOLK, COUNTRY AND WESTERN MUSIC. NY, 1969. Illus. VG in dust jacket. $12.

STANDARD ENCYCLOPEDIA OF THE WORLD'S OCEANS AND ISLANDS. NY, 1962 1st ed. $18.

ENCYCLOPEDIA OF PHYSICAL CULTURE. By Bernarr McFadden, 1925 2nd ed. 5 vols. VG plus. $85.

THE READER'S ENCYCLOPEDIA. NY, 1948. William Rose Benet, editor. 4 vols, Very Good. $40.

THE ILLUSTRATED ENCYCLOPEDIA OF THE WORLD'S ROCKETS & MISSILES. London, 1979. Bill Gunston, editor. Very Good in dust jacket. $30.

THE ENCYCLOPEDIA OF SOUTHERN HISTORY. Baton Rouge, 1979. Roller and Twyman. 1st ed. VG. $85.

ENCYCLOPEDIA OF THE VIOLIN. NY, 1926. VG. $60.

ENCYCLOPEDIA OF WATER LIFE. Amsterdam, 1949. English text. Very Good. $27.

ENCYCLOPEDIA OF ARTISTS OF THE AMERICAN WEST. By Peggy and Harold Samuels. No place, 1985. Fine in dust jacket. $40.

ENCYCLOPEDIA OF THE FAR WEST. 1991. F in DJ. $40.

ENCYCLOPEDIA OF WESTERN OUTLAWS. Norman, OK, 1979. Fine in fair dust jacket. $35.

THE MARSHALL CAVENDISH ILLUSTRATED ENCYCLOPEDIA OF WORLD WAR II. No place, 1972. 25 vols. Very Good. $125. Another set, Good. $80.

THE SIMON AND SCHUSTER ENCYCLOPEDIA OF WORLD WAR II. By T. Parrish. NY, 1978. F in DJ. $25.

ENDICOTT, WENDELL. *Adventures With Rod & Harpoon Along the Florida Keys*. NY, 1925. Photos. VG. $75. *Adventures in Alaska and Along the Trail*. NY, 1928 1st edition. Very Good in dust jacket. $50.

ENGELHARDT, ZEPHYRIN. *Franciscans in Arizona*. Holy Childhood Indian School. MI, 1899. VG plus. $200.
Franciscans in California. Harbor Springs MI, 1897. Inscribed by Author. Worn, cracked hinge. $125.
Missions & Missionaries of California. Santa Barbara, 5 vols. 1913, 1915, 1916, 1929, 1930. Folded maps intact. Very Good plus. $450.

ENGEN, RODNEY. *Kate Greenaway, A Biography*. NY, Schocken Bks, 1981 1st ed. VG in DJ. $20.

ENGLISH, GEORGE. *History of the 89th Division U.S.A. 1917, 1918, 1919*. War Soc. of 89th, 1920 1st ed. F. $69.

ENRIGHT, ELIZABETH. *Kintu*. NY, 1935 1st ed. Author's 1st book. Good. $50.
Thimble Summer. NY, 1938 1st ed. Newberry Medal winner. Good. $38.
Gone-Away Lake. NY, 1957 1st ed. Beth and Joe Krush illustrators. Fine in dust jacket. $80.
Tatsinda. NY, 1963 1st ed. Irene Hass, illus. F in DJ. $25.

ENSER, A.G.S. *A Subject Bibliography of the Second World War*. No place, 1977. As new. $45.

THE ENTERPRISING HOUSEKEEPER. Enterprise Mfg. Co., Philadelphia, 1900. A recipe book distributed at the 1901 Pan-American Exposition. 80 pgs. 12mo. $20-$40.

ENYEART, JAMES. *Edward Weston's California Land-scapes*. Weston photo illustrations throughout. Boston, Little Brown, 1984 1st edition. Fine in original shipping box. $100-$150.

ERAS, VINCENT. *Locks and Keys Throughout the Ages*. Amsterdam, 1957. A modern classic on this subject. Only edition. $100.

ERICHSEN, HUGO, M.D. *Cremation*. Detroit, 1887 1st ed. Illustrated. Very Good. $90.

ERSKINE, A. R. *History of the Studebaker Corporation*. South Bend IN,1924. Fine Copy, $50. Soiled copy. $25.

ERSKINE, JOHN. *The Private Life of Helen of Troy*. Indianapolis,1925 1st ed. Signed. Good in DJ. $18.
Adam and Eve. 1927, Bobbs-Merrill. Good. $15.

ERSKINE, MARGARET. *Dead By Now*. NY, 1954 1st ed. VG plus in dust jacket. $23.
A Graveyard Plot. NY, 1959 1st ed. Fine in DJ, $20.
Give Up the Ghost. NY, 1969 1st ed. Fine in DJ. $23.

ERTE (Artist). *Erte at Ninety: The Complete Graphics*. With selected writings. Dutton, 1972 1st. VG in good DJ. $150.
Things I Remember. London, 1975. VG in DJ. $75.
Sculpture. Dutton, 1986 1st ed. Near Fine in DJ. $150.

ESARY, LOGAN. *History of Indiana From its Exploration to 1922*. 3 vols. Dayton, 1923. VG. $90. Worn copy. $70.
The Indiana Home. Banta, 1943 1st ed. VG. $18. Ind. Univ. Press, 1953 limited edition. One of 1,550 copies. Very Fine in slipcase. $58. 1976 reprint. Very Good. $8.

ESCOFFIER COOK BOOK. 1956 18th edition. VG. $10.

ESCOFFIER, A. *Guide to Modern Cookery*. London, 1907 1st English ed. VG. $125. New York, 1941. Cloth. Very Good. $28. Vinyl cover. $14.

ESQUIRE'S HANDBOOK FOR HOSTS. New York, 1949. Scuffed. Good. $20.

ESENWEIN, J. B. (Editor). *Adventures to Come*. 1st ed. McLoughlin, 1937. Good in dust jacket. $45. No DJ. $12.

ESSAME, H. *The Battle for Germany*. NY, 1969 1st ed. VG in dust jacket. $20-$25.
Patton: A Study in Command. NY, 1969 1st ed. VG in DJ. $24. Book Club edition. VG in DJ. $15.

ESTES, ELEANOR. *The Moffats*. NY, 1941. Reprint. Louis Slobodkin illus. Fine in DJ. $22.
Rufus M. NY, 1943. Reprint. Louis Slobodkin illus. Fine in dust jacket. $16.
Pinky Pye. NY, 1958 1st ed. illus by Edward Ardizzone. Very Good. $16.
The Witch Family. NY, 1960. Edward Ardizzone illus. Ex-library. Good in dust jacket. $10.
The Lollipop Princess. NY, 1967 1st ed. Illus. by author. VG in dust jacket. $32.
Miranda the Great. NY, 1967 1st ed. Edward Ardizzone illustrator. Ex-library. Good in dust jacket. $10.

ETS, MARIE HALL. *Mister Penny*. NY, 1935 1st ed. Illus. by author. Exterior poor, interior Good. $16.
The Story of a Baby. Viking, 1939 1st ed. Illus. by author. VG-Fine in dust jacket. $35-$65.
Mr. T. W. Anthony Woo. NY, 1951 1st ed. Illus. by author. Fine in dust jacket. $100.
Play With Me. NY, 1955 1st ed. Illus. by author. VG. $25.
Mister Penny's Race Horse. NY, 1961 3rd ed. Illus. by author. VG in torn dust jacket. $16.

EUSTIS, CELESTINE. *Cooking in Old Creole Days*. NY, 1903 1st ed. No backstrip, o/w VG. $40.

EVANS, ALBERT. *A La California: Sketches of Life in the Golden State*. San Francisco, Bancroft, 1873 1st edition. Original brown cloth, gilt-lettered. Very Good. $75-$100.

EVANS, BILLY. *How to Umpire*. American Sports Pub., 1940 ed. $25-$35. 1917 first edition is worth a bit more.
Umpiring From the Inside. Self-published, 1947 1st ed. Good-Very Good. $100-$150.

EVANS, CHARLES. *American Bibliography*. A chronological dictionary of all books, pamphlets & periodical publications printed in the United States from the genesis of printing in 1639 to and including the year 1820. With bibliographical and biographical notes. Privately printed by the Blakely Press, Chicago, 1903-1934. 15 consisting of the original 12 covering 1639-1799, vol. 13, comp. by Cliffore Shipton, pub. by the American Antiquarian Society in 1955, and 2 short-title index volumes. pub. by AAS in 1969. 3 vols. are numbered and signed by Evans. VG in faded spines. $800.

EVANS, C. S. (Editor). *Cinderella*. London, 1919. Rackham color plate. $150-$225 in DJ. Same, Lippincott, 1919. $150-$200 in DJ.
Sleeping Beauty. London, 1920. Rackham illus. $125-$175 in DJ. Same, Lippincott, 1920. $125-$175 in DJ.

EVANS, EASTWICK. *Pedestrious Tour of Four Thousand Miles Through the Western States and Territories*. Concord, NY, Joseph Spear, 1819 1st. NF. $522 auction.

EVANS, GEORGE. *Upland Shooting Life*. NY, 1971 1st ed. Near Fine in dust jacket. $30.
The Best of Nash Buckingham. (Evans, editor). 1973, Winchester Press. DJ tears, smudges, contents good. $45.

EVANS, JOHN HENRY. *100 Years of Mormonism*. Utah, Deseret, 1909. Good. $15.

EVANS, MARY ELIZABETH. *My Candy Secrets, etc.* NY, 1919 1st ed. G-VG. $45.

EVANS, WALKER (Photographer). *The Mangrove Coast*. By K. A. Bickel. NY, 1942. 32 photos of Florida West Coast. Ex-lib. Cover with dj pieces pasted on. Good. $125.
First and Last. NY, 1978 1st ed. VG in DJ. $85.

EVENTS OF THE CENTURY & GREAT CENTENNIAL EXPOSITION AT PHILADELPHIA, 1876. U. S. Cent. Pub, 1877. Good. $18.

EVERETT, MARSHALL (Editor). *The Wreck and Sinking of the Titanic*. L. H. Walter, 1912 1st ed. Good. $10.
The Great Chicago Theater Disaster. Chicago, 1904 1st ed. Black cloth. Very Good. $18.

EVERITT, CHARLES. *Adventures of a Treasure Hunter*. Boston, 1951 1st ed. Very Good in dust jacket. $12-$20.

EVERITT, GRAHAM. *English Caricaturists and Graphic Humorists of the 19th Century*. London, 1893 2nd ed. Very Good. $70.

EVERS, HENRY. *Steam and the Locomotive Engine*. NY, Putnams, 1873 1st ed. Ex-library. VG. $25.

EVERS, J. *Touching Second*. Reilly Britton, 1910. Ink on endpapers. $85-$100.

EVERSON, GEORGE. *The Story of Television*. W.W. Norton, 1949 1st ed. Fine in dust jacket. $18.

EVERSON, WILLIAM. *The Residual Years*. NY, New Directions, 1st ed. 1948. 1 of 1,000. VG in DJ. $95-$125.

EVERSON, W. K. *The Art of W. C. Fields*. 1967 edition, Very Good in dust jacket. $15.
Pictorial History of Western Film. 1969 1st ed. VG. $15.

EVERTON and RASMUSON. *Handy Book for Genealogists, 4th Edition*. Everton, 1962. VG in dust jacket. $10.

EVERY MAN HIS OWN DOCTOR, A MEDICAL HANDBOOK. Anon. NY, 1871, Hunter & Co. G-VG. $50.

EVERYMAN HIS OWN MECHANIC. 1900. Good. $22.

EWALD, CARL. *Two Legs*. Scribners, 1906 1st American edition. Very Good. $20.
The Old Willow Tree and Other Stories. Stokes, 1921 1st American ed. Very Good in dust jacket. $15.

EWEN, DAVID. *Book of Modern Composers*. 1943. A Fine copy, signed by printer. $25.
Journey to Greatness, The Life of Gershwin. Holt, 1956 1st edition. Very Good. $30.

EWERS, HANNS. *The Sorcerer's Apprentice*. Day, 1927 Limited edition. M. Blaine, illus. Good-VG. $50-$100.

EWERS, JOHN C. *Indian Life on the Upper Missouri*. Univ. of Oklahoma Press, 1968 1st ed. VG in DJ. $35.

EWING, H. H. *Jacknapps, Daddy Darwin's Dovecott and Other Stories*. Boston, 1893 1st edition. Very Good. $25.

EWING, P. V. *Pork Production*. Orange Judd, 1918. Good-Very Good. $10-$15.

EXCLESHYMER, ALBERT & D. SCHOMAKER. *A Cross-Section Anatomy*. NY, 1911 1st ed. VG. $100-$200.

EXLEY, FREDERICK. *A Fan's Notes*. NY, 1968 1st ed. Author's 1st book. Near Fine in DJ. $85-$100.
Pages From a Cold Island. New York, 1975 1st edition. Fine in dust jacket. $35.

EXPERIENCED ENGLISH HOUSEKEEPER. London, 1776. By Elizabeth Raffald. Illus. Cookbook, etc. $1,500.

EYRE, ALICE. *The Famous Freemonts & Their America*. No place. Fine Arts Press, 1948 1st ed. Signed. Very Good in dust jacket. $75.

F

FABRE, J. H. *The Glow-Worm and Other Beetles*. NY, 1919
1st edition. Very Good. $18.
The Heavens. Philadelphia, no date (1920s). Good. $25.
The Life of the Spider. NY, 1928. Worn. $25.
Fabre's Book of Insects. NY, 1927. VG. $16-$20.
Fabre's Book of Insects, Retold. NY, Tudor Pub., 1937.
Illus. Very Good. $40 auction.

FAGAN, JAMES O. *Confessions of a Railroad Signalman*.
Boston, 1908 1st ed. Illus. Very Good. $40.

FAIRBANKS, DOUGLAS. *Laugh and Live*. Britton Pub.
1917 2nd printing. $9-$12.

FAIRBANKS, JONATHAN L. and ELIZABETH BATES.
American Furniture, 1620 to the Present. NY, 1981.
Illus. Good-VG in dust jacket. $65.

FAIRBROTHER, NAN. *The Cheerful Day*. NY, 1960 1st ed.
Very Good in dust jacket. $15.
A House in the Country. NY, 1965 1st American ed. VG
in dust jacket. $18.

FAIRCHILD, DAVID. *World Was My Garden: Travels of
a Plant Explorer*. Scribners, 1938 1st edition. Very Good
in dust jacket. $14.
Garden Islands of the Great East - Collecting Seeds.
Scribner's, 1943 1st ed. VG in dust jacket. $12.

FALCONER, WILLIAM. *Mushrooms: How to Grow Them*.
Philadelphia, John Gardiner, 1891. $45. NY, Orange Judd,
1891. $45. 1907 reprint. Very Good. $35.

FALES, WINIFRED. *The Household Dictionary*. Boston,
1920 1st ed. Good-VG. $20.

FANNIN, COLE. *Lucy and the Mad Cap Mystery*. Whitman,
1963 1st ed. Fine. $12.
Roy Rogers, King of the Cowboys. Whitman, 1956 1st ed.
Very Good. $15.

FARINA, RICHARD. *Been Down So Long It Looks Like Up
To Me*. NY, 1966 1st ed. Fine in dust jacket. $100.
Long Time Coming. NY, 1969 1st ed. Fine in DJ. $30.

FARIS, JOHN T. *Old Roads Out of Philadelphia*. Lippincott,
1917 4th impression. Very Good. $20.

Old Trails & Roads in Penn's Land. Philadelphia, 1927
edition. Illus. Very Good. $30.
Romance of Forgotten Towns. NY, 1924 1st ed. VG. $25.
Old Gardens in and About Philadelphia. 1932 1st ed
Very Good $35.

FARJEON, ELEANOR. *Come Christmas*. Rachael Field illus.
F. A. Stokes, 1928. 62 pgs. Chip. $30.
Dark World of Animals. London, 1945 1st ed. T. Stoney
illus. VG in dust jacket. $75.
Mrs. Malone. NY, 1962. Edward Ardizzone illus. Fine in
dust jacket. $25.

FARJEON, JEFFERSON. *The Judge Sums Up*. Crime Club,
1942 1st edition. Slightly spotted pages. VG in fair DJ. $60.
Death in the Inkwell. NY, 1942 1st. Fair in inked DJ. $37.
Death in Fancy Dress. New York, No date 1st edition.
Very Good in dust jacket. $40.

FARLEY, WALTER. *The Black Stallion and Satan*. NY,
1949 1st ed. Very Good in dust jacket. $32.
The Black Stalion's Filly. NY, 1952 1st. VG in DJ. $25.
The Black Stallion Revolts. NY, 1953 1st. VG in DJ. $35.
The Black Stallion's Sulky Colt. NY, 1960 1st ed. VG in
dust jacket. $35.
Son of the Black Stallion. NY, 1974 1st. In DJ. $14-$20.

FARM JOURNAL COOK BOOKS, 1959-1980. *Various
titles*, up to 431 pgs. Fair-Good. $8. Good-VG. $10-$20.

FARMER, FANNIE MERRITT. *The Horsford Cook Book*.
Rumford Chemical Works, 1895. Good-VG. $50.
The Boston Cooking-School Cook Book. Boston, 1896
1st ed. One of 3,000 copies. $700-$1,200. Same, 1897.
Two printings of 5,000 copies each $250-$350. Boston,
1906, Little Brown. 648 pgs. VG. $25. 1930 edition, 831
pgs. VG. $25-$30. Bumped corners, shaken. $12-$14.
Chafing Dish Possibilities. Boston, 1898 1st ed. VG-Near
Fine. $120-$200. Same edition, signed. $250. Another, 2nd
printing. Fine. $135.
A Book of Good Dinners etc. Dodge, 1905, 1914. $30-$40.
Food and Cookery for The Sick and Convalescent. 1907
Good-Very Good. $35-$45.
Catering for Special Occasions With Menus and Recipes.
Philadelphia, 1911. Kewpie drawings by A. Blashfield.
Near Fine. $150.
A New Book of Cookery. Boston, 1912 1st ed. $40-$60.

The Boston Cooking School Book. Little-Brown, 1935-1942. Good-Very Good. $20-$25.

The Fanny Farmer Junior Cook Book. Wilma Perkins, editor. Boston, 1942 1st ed. Poor. $12. Boston, 1957 New, revised edition. Good in torn dust jacket. $10.

The Fanny Farmer Cook Book. Boston, 1965 11th printing. Revised by Wilma Perkins. Very Good. $8.

FARMER, PHILIP JOSE. *The Maker of Universe*. NY, 1965 Ace paperback original. Very Good. $25.

The Gates of Creation NY, 1966 Ace paperback. VG. $25.

Lord Tyger. NY, 1970 1st ed. Signed. NF in DJ. $95.

Tarzan Alive: A Definitive Biography of Lord Greystoke. NY, 1972. Waterstains on DJ. $50.

The Adventure of the Peerless Peer. Aspen Press, 1974 1st ed. Tarzan rescues Sherlock Holmes, Fine in DJ. $45.

A Feast Unknown. Fokker, 1975 1st ed. paperbound. Richard Corben illus. Signed by Farmer. VG. $95.

The Dark Design. Putnam, 1977 1st. Signed F in DJ. $35.

To Your Scattered Bodies Go. Gregg, 1980 1st ed. Signed. As new. $40.

The Magic Labryinth. Berkley, 1980 1st edition. Signed, in dust jacket. $25.

FARMERS ALMANAC. (See Magazine Section).

FARNHAM, ELIZA W. *California, In-Doors and Out. How We Farm, Mine and Live in the Golden State*. NY, Edward Dix, 1856 1st. Frayed spine ends, o/w VG. $100.

FARR, FINIS. *Black Champion: The Life and Times of Jack Johnson*. NY, 1964 1st ed. Illus. Fine in VG DJ. $45.

Margaret Mitchell of Atlanta, Author of "Gone With the Wind". Morrow, 1965 1st ed. Fine, no DJ. $20.

FARRAR, EMMIE F. *Old Virginia Houses: The Mobjack Bay Country*. NY, 1955. Illus. VG in DJ. $25.

Old Virginia Houses Along the James. Hastings House, 1957 1st ed. Fine, no DJ. $20.

FARRAR, S. *The Housekeeper (cookbook)*. 1872. $70-$85.

FARRELL, JAMES T. *Young Lonigan*. NY, 1943 1st ed. Author's 1st book. VG plus. $100.

My Days of Anger. Vanguard, 1943 1st ed. VG in DJ. $15.

The Young Manhood of Studs Lonigan. NY, 1944. G. $4.

Bernard Clare. NY, 1946 1st ed. VG in DJ. $10.

FARNOL, JEFFREY. *The Broad Highway*. London, 1910. Brock illus. Good. $25.

The Amateur Gentlemen. NY, A. L. Burt, 1913. VG. $4.

Peregrine's Progress. Boston, 1922 1st ed. VG in DJ. $15.

FARRINGTON, S. KIP. *Atlantic Game Fishing*. NY, 1937. Inscribed. 7 color plates by Lynn Bogue Hunt. Ernest Hemingway introduction. Photo illus. Good with slight foxing. $185. Same book in Fine condition. $250.

Railroads of the Hour. Coward-McCann, 1958 1st ed. Autographed. Very Good in worn dust jacket. $35.

FARSON, ROBERT. *The Cape Cod Canal*. CT, Wesleyan Press, 1977 1st ed. Fine in dust jacket. $35.

FAULK, ODIE *Destiny Road*. The Gila Trail. Oxford Univ. Press, 1973 1st ed. Very Good. $25.

FAULKNER, EDWARD H. *Plowman's Folly*. Grosset & Dunlap, 1944 reprint. VG in dust jacket. $7.

FAULKNER, JOSEPH. *The Life of Philip Henry Sheridan*. NY, 1888 1st edition. Good. $25.

FAULKNER, WILLIAM. *Sartoris*. NY, 1929 1st ed. Small dust jacket defect, o/w Fine $3,600. VG in DJ. $1,500.

As I Lay Dying. Jonathan Cape, 1930 1st ed. G plus. $125.

Light in August. Harrison Smith, 1932 1st ed. Near Fine in dust jacket. $400. Same, no dust jacket. $135.

Pylon. Smith Hass, 1935 1st ed. in DJ. $300-$450.

The Wild Palms. NY, 1939 1st ed. Edges browned, sunned. $200. Another. Spine slightly worn. DJ rubbed, o/w Fine. $550.

Viking Portable Faulkner. NY, 1946. VG in DJ. $210.

The Sound and the Fury and As I Lay Dying. NY, Modern Library, 1946. Near Fine in DJ. $50.

Intruder in the Dust. NY, 1948 1st ed 1st printing. VG in chipped, worn dust jacket. $95-$150.

The Collected Stories of William Faulkner. NY, 1950 1st edition. Very Good. $125.

Requim for a Nun. NY, 1951 1st ed., 1st printing. VG in worn dust jacket. $75. Fine in very good DJ. $85.

The Town. NY, 1957 1st ed., 1st printing. VG in chip, torn dust jacket. $60. Fine in near fine dust jacket. $100.

The Mansion. NY, 1959 1st ed., 1st printing. VG in chip dust jacket. $60. Fine in near fine dust jacket. $150.

The Reivers. NY, 1962 1st ed., 1st printing. VG in DJ. $45.

The Wishing Tree. NY, 1964 1st ed. Don Bolognese illus. Faulkner's only children's book. VG. $50.

Selected Letters of William Faulkner. NY, 1977 1st trade ed. Very Good in dust jacket. $23.

May Day. 1978 1st trade ed. Notre Dame. Fine in DJ. $60.

FAULKNER, WILLIAM (In Magazines). *Harper's Aug, Sept 1931, Apr 1932, Sept 1933. Feb 1934, Dec 1935*. Short stories. $20-$23 each.

Story. May-June 1942, March-April 1943, July-Aug 1943. Short stories. $30-$35.

Collier's. Dec 1935. Short story. $20.

The Saturday Evening Post. Nov 23, 1940. $20-$30.

FAWCETT. CLARA. *Paper Dolls: A Guide to Costume*. NY, Lindquist, 1951 1st ed. Signed. Fine. $65.

FAY, BERNARD. *Franklin, the Apostle of Modern Times*. Boston, 1929 1st ed. Good. $20.

FEDERAL WRITERS PROJECT. *New York City Guide*. NY, 1939 1st ed., 1st printing. Lacks map, o/w Good. $25.
Death Valley. Boston, 1939. Plates, folding map. Very Good in dust jacket. $30.
Arizona. 1st ed. No date. Good plus, in chip DJ. $50.
New Hampshire. 1st ed. No date. VG in good DJ. $40.
North Carolina - Guide to Old North State. Univ. of North Carolina, 1939 1st ed. Fine. $28.
WPA Guide to North Carolina. Univ of N. Carolina, 1939 1st ed. VG, no dust jacket. $18.
(Also see WPA Guides, listed under "W".)

FEIKEMAN, FEIKE. *The Golden Bowl*. Webb, 1st ed. No date. Author's 1st book. $65.
The Giant. NY, 1951 1st ed. Fine in DJ. $35.

FEININGER, ANDREAS (Photographer). *The Anatomy of Nature*. NY, 1956. Dampstains, DJ worn. $35.
The World Through My Eyes. NY, 1963 1st. 165 b/w. color plates. Fine in chip DJ. $35.
The Complete Photographer. NY, 1965 2nd printing. $12.

FELLOWS,.CHARLES. *The Culinary Handbook*. Chicago, 1940. Very Good. $25.

FELTON, HAROLD. *Legends of Paul Bunyan*. NY, 1947 1st edition. R. Bennett illus. VG in dust jacket. $25.

FENTON, ROBERT W. *The Big Swinger, E. R. Burroughs and Tarzan*. Prentice Hall, 1967 1st ed. VG in DJ. $35.

FENNER, T. *Cabin and Plantation Songs*. 1870, complete scores. Clean, tight. $35.

FERBER, EDNA. *Show Boat*. NY, 1926 1st ed. One of 1,000 copies. Very Good. $23.
Cimarron. Doubleday, 1930 1st. VG in tattered DJ. $18.
Saratoga Trunk. NY, 1941 1st ed. In DJ. $20-$40.
Giant. NY, 1952 1st ed. VG to Fine in DJ. $30-$45.

FERENCZI, SANDOR. *Sex in Psychoanalysis*. Boston, 1922 2nd edition. Light foxing. $35.

FERGUSSON, ERNA. *Our Southwest*. NY, 1946 3rd printing. Very Good. $9.
Murder & Mystery in New Mexico. Albuquerque NM, 1948 1st ed. Signed. Fine. $75.

FERGUSSON, HARVEY. *Blood of the Conquerors*. NY, 1921 1st ed. VG in DJ. $25.
Rio Grande. NY, 1933 1st ed. Fine. $35.
Home in the West: An Inquiry Into My Origins. Duell, 1944 1st ed. Fine in frayed DJ. $25.

FERMI, L. and G. BERNARDINI. *Galileo and the Scientific Revolution*. NY, 1961 1st ed. Fine in DJ $30. 1962 3rd printing. $15.

FERRIS, JAMES C. *The X-bar-X Boys Seeking Lost Troopers*. (no. 20). Grosset & Dunlap, 1941 ed. Red cloth in edgeworn DJ with flap listing 19 titles. VG. $50.

FERRIS, RICHARD. *How it Flies, or the Conquest of the Air*. NY, 1910 1st ed. 475 pgs. Illus. Good-VG. $50.

FERRIS, WARREN. *Life in the Rocky Mountains: A Diary of Wanderings, 1830-1835*. Denver, Old West Publishing, 1940 1st ed. VG in soiled dust jacket. $250. auction.

FESSENDEN, THOMAS G. *The New American Gardener*. Boston, 1828 1st ed. With ads browning, o/w VG. $200.

FIELD, BEN. *The Exciting Adventures of Mister Jim Crow*. 1928. E. B. illus. $18.

FIELD, EUGENE. *The Love Affair of a Bibliomaniac*. NY, 1896 1st ed. Very Good. $25-$40.
A Little Book of Tribune Verse. Denver, 1901. One of 750 copies. Very Good. $50.
The Works of Eugene Field. Revised ed., Scribner's, 1901. 10 vol. set. Very Good. $30.
Poems of Childhood. NY, 1904. Maxfield Parrish illus. VG in DJ. $175. 1956 reprint. Scuffed. $24.
The Tribune Prime. Boston, privately printed, 1901. Author's 1st book. Good-VG. $35.
Christmas Tales and Christmas Verse. NY, 1912 1st ed. Florence Storer illus. VG. $100. 1919 edition. $35.
Sugar Plum Tree & Other Verses. Saalfield, 1930. Fern Bisel Peat illus. Edge, spine wear, o/w VG. $45.
The Gingham Dog & Calico Cat. Lowe, 1944. VG. $16.
Hoosier Lyrics. Chicago, 1905. Fine. $15.

FIELD, HENRY. *Old Spain and New Spain*. NY, Scribner's, 1891 3rd ed. Fine. $28.
The Story of the Atlantic Telegraph. NY, Scribner's, 1893. Very Good. $35. 1866 1st ed. $55-$95.

FIELD, RACHEL. *Taxis and Toadstools*. Doubleday, 1926. Illus by author. Near VG in repaired DJ. $33.
The Magic Pawnshop. NY, 1927. Illus by author. Flyleaf missing, edges worn. $12.
Polly Patchwork. NY, 1928 1st ed. VG in DJ. $100.
Hitty, Her First Hundred Years. No place. 1929. Dorothy Lathrop illus. Inscribed by Field. VG. $125.
The Yellow Shop. NY, 1939. Illus by author. VG. $15.

FIELDER, MILDRED. *Treasure of Homestake Gold*. North Plains, 1975 2nd ed. Fine in DJ. $17.
Railroads of the Black Hills. Bonanza. Fine in DJ. $20.

FIELDING, HENRY. *The History of Tom Jones*. Dodd Mead, 1930. VG in DJ. $35. London, 1934 1st ed. VG. $25. Modern Library edition, 1943. $6. Limited Editions Club, 1952. One of 500 signed by illus. $100. NY, Heritage reprint, 1952. Fine in slipcase. $13.

FIELDING, MANTLE. *Dictionary of American Sculptors and Engravers*. Greensfarm VT, 1974. Good-VG. $25.

FIFE, GEORGE B. *Lindbergh, The Lone Eagle*. World Pub, 1933 ed. Fine in Very Good dust jacket. $15.

FILIPPINI, ALESSANDRO. *The Table-How to Buy Food, How to Cook, etc.* NY, 1890 2nd ed. by Delmonico's Restaurant chef. Very Good. $32.
100 Ways of Cooking Eggs. NY, 1892 1st ed. VG. $25.
The International Cookbook. New York, Doubleday, 1906 1st ed. $45. auction.

FILM DAILY YEAR BOOK OF MOTION PICTURES, 1930. 12th annual ed. 1,100 pgs. Ads, actor lists. VG. $65.

FINCH, CHRISTOPHER. *The Art of Walt Disney From Mickey Mouse to the Magic Kingdoms*. NY, Abrams, 1973 1st ed. Profusely illus. VG. $135-$175. Another, poor cond. $20. 1975 edition. Very Good. $75.

FINCH, JOHN B. *The People Versus the Liquor Traffic*. Nat. Temperance Society, 1887 1st ed., green cloth, Good. $8.

FINCK, HENRY. *Food and Flavor*. Cookbook. Harper, 1924. 604 pgs., green cloth. Very Good. $25.

FINGER, CHARLES J. *Frontier Ballads*. NY, 1927 1st ed. Paul Honore illus. Signed by Honore & Finger. VG. $175.
High Water in Arkansas. NY, 1943. Henry Pitz illus. Very Good. $12.

FINLEY, MARTHA. *Elsie and the Raymonds*. Dodd, Mead, 1889. Very Good. $15.
Elsie's Widowhood. Burt, 1908. Sequel to *Elsie's Children*. Very Good. $20.
Elsie at Home. Donohue, 1897. Very Good. $8.
Elsie Dinsmore. Dodd, Mead, ca 1900. No. 1. $12-$14.

FINLEY, REV. JAMES B. *Life Among the Indians or, Personal Reminicensces*. Ohio, no date. 1st ed. Good. $38.

FINLEY, W. and I. *Wild Animals as Pets*. NY, London, 1936. Fine in dust jacket. $15.

FINN, FRANK. *That Office Boy*. Benziger, 1915. NF. $12.

FINNEY, CHARLES. *The Circus of Dr. Lao*. Viking, 1935 1st ed. Fine in vg DJ. $130. 1945 edition. Viking. Boris Artzybasheff illus. G. $50. Limited Edition Club, 1982, one of 2,000. Very Good in box. $75.
Revivals of Religion. No place, 1978. VG in good DJ. $14.

FIRST STEAMSHIP PIONEERS. Ed. by a Committee. San Francisco, 1874 1st ed. 393 pgs. Biographies of better known passengers of the steamer "California" on her first trip to CA. Morocco cov. Auction. $600. (est. $250-$350).

FISCHER, HANS. *The Birthday*. Harcourt, 1954. Illus. by author. Soiled dust jacket, o/w Very Good. $28.

FISCHER, OTTOKAR. *Illustrated Magic*. Macmillan, 1944 reprint. Very Good. $14.

FISHER, ALBERT K. *The Hawks and Owls of The United States in Their Relation to Agriculture*. Washington DC, GPO, 1893 1st ed. Inscribed. 26 color plates. VG. $275.

FISHER, GEORGE T. *Snuff and Snuff-Takers*. London, 1846. Ads and illus. Near VG. $125.

FISHER, HARRIET WHITE. *A Woman's World Tour In a Motor Car*. Philadelphia 1911 1st ed. 70 illus. VG. $45.

FISHER, HARRISON. *The Harrison Fisher Book*. New York, 1908. 80 full pages. illus. by author. Like new. $75.
American Belles. NY, Dodd, 1911. Folio. $175-$250.
Dream of Fair Women. NY, 1907. Illus. $125.
Same, Bobbs-Merrill, 1909. $175-$225.
A Book of Sweethearts: Pictures By Famous American Artists. G & D, 1908. Worn, shaken, stained. $40.
Bachelor Belles. NY, 1908 1st ed. Good. $95. VG. $175.
Harrison Fisher's American Beauties. Bobbs-Merrill, 1909 1st ed. Illus. by author. Fine in worn, chip DJ. $600. Same, no DJ. $150-$250. G&D, 1909. $100-$150.
Harrison Fisher's American Girls in Miniature. New York, 1912. $55-$75.
Maidens Fair. NY, Dodd, 1912. $200-$350.
Harrison Fisher Girls. NY, 1914 1st ed. 12 color plates by author. Very Good. $40.
Pictures in Color. Scribners, 1910. Folio. $350-$450.
Fair Americans. Scribners, 1911. 22 plates. $175.

FISHER, HARRISON (Illustrator). *A Checked Love Affair*. By Paul Leicester Ford. NY, 1903. Fine. $45.
Love Finds a Way. By Paul Leicester Ford. NY, 1904. Corners bumped, o/w Near Fine. $45.
Nedra. By George Barr McCutcheon. Dodd Mead, 1906. Signed by author. VG-Fine. $15. Same 1905. $20-$40.
Hiawatha. H. Longfellow. Indianapolis, 1906. Good. $95.

FISHER, M. F. K. *Serve It Forth*. NY, 1937 1st ed. Author's 1st book. VG. $100. Same, inscribed by author. $300.
The Art of Eating. NY, 1937, 1954 1st printing. Near Fine in dust jacket. $40-$65.
Consider the Oyster. New York, 1941 1st edition. Very Good in good dust jacket. $40.
How to Cook a Wolf. NY, 1942, 1943 1st ed. 5th printing. Good in vg DJ. $35. Same, 1942, but 2nd edition. VG in DJ. $32. 1951 revised ed. VG in dust jacket. $60.
The Gastronomical Me. NY, 1943. VG in DJ. $20.
Here Let Us Feast. NY, 1946 1st ed. VG in DJ. $35-$65.
An Alphabet for Gourmets. NY, 1949 1st. G in DJ. $85.
The Art of Eating: The Collected Gastronomical Works of M.F.K. Fisher. NY, 1954. Ex-lib. VG in good DJ. $30.

The Story of Wine in California. Berkeley, 1962. Illus. Very Good in dust jacket. $60.

FISHER, SYDNEY G. *The True Benjamin Franklin*. Lippincott, 1899. Good plus. $10.

FISHER, VARDIS. *Toilers of the Hills*. Houghton Mifflin, 1928 1st ed. Very Good $75.
  In Tragic Life. Caxton, 1932 1st ed. VG. $50-$75.
  Passions Spin the Plot. Caxton, 1934 1st ed. One of 2,000 copies. Very Good in dust jacket. $110.
  We Are Betrayed. Caxton, 1935 1st ed. One of 1,225 copies. VG in repaired dust jacket. $105.
  No Villain Need Be. Caxton, 1936 1st ed. One of 2,200 copies. Very Good in dust jacket. $95.
  The Idaho Encyclopedia. Caxton, 1938 1st. F in DJ. $300.
  Tale of Valor. Garden City, 1938 1st ed. VG in DJ. $35.
  City of Illusion. Caxton, 1941 1st ed. One of 1,000 copies. Very Good in dust jacket. $115.
  The Mothers: An American Saga of Courage. NY, 1943 1st ed. Very Good in dust jacket. $75.
  Intimations of Eve. Vanguard, 1946 1st edition. Near Fine in dust jacket. $17.
  Idaho, A Guide in Word and Picture. Federal Writers Project, 1950 2nd ed. revised. VG. $50.
  Love and Death: The Complete Stories. NY, 1959 1st ed. Fine in dust jacket. $40.

FISKE, DWIGHT. *Without Music*. NY, 1933. Worn cov. $25.

FISKE, JOHN. *Excursions of an Evolutionist*. Boston, 1884. Near Fine. $24.
  The Discovery of America. No place, 1895 1st ed. 2 vols. Fine. $14. Cambridge ed. of 1902. 3 vols. $30.
  The Mississippi Valley in the Civil War. Boston, 1900 1st edition. $25-$50.

FITCH, MICHAEL H. *The Chattanooga Campaign*. Wisconsin Historical Comm. 1911. Worn cover. $38.

FITCHETT, LAURA. *Beverages & Sauces of Colonial Virginia*. Neal Pub, NY, 1906. G-VG. $75.

FITTS, JACK. *Captain Kidd's Gold: The True Story*. A.L. Burt, 1888. Good plus. $11.

FITZGERALD, EDWARD (Translator). See *Rubaiyat ...*

FITZGERALD, F. SCOTT. *This Side of Paradise*. New York, 1920 1st edition. Author's 1st book. Hinge repaired, o/w Very Good. $160. Another, Near Fine. $700. Same, 1923. Inscribed to his nurse. $1,950. New York, 8th printing. Inscribed. $1,200.
  The Beautiful and the Damned. 1922 1st ed. $75.
  The Great Gatsby. Scribner's, 1925 1st edition, 1st issue. Fine in fine dust jacket. $4,500-$5,000. Same, no dust jacket. $175-$450.

All the Sad Young Men. NY, 1926 1st ed., 1st state. Near VG in fine DJ, slipcase. $3,000. Same, not 1st state. $150.
  Tender is the Night. NY, 1934 1st ed. Fair DJ. $50-$350.
  Taps at Reveille. NY, 1935 1st ed., 1st state. Near Fine in chipped dust jacket and clamshell case. $1,500.

FITZGERALD, F. SCOTT (In Magazines). *Smart Set*. Sep, 1919. "Babes in the Woods," 1st story. $35-$50.
  American. Sept, 1922. "What I Think and Feel at 25." With photos. $75.
  Metropolitan. Dec, 1922. "Winter Dreams." $20-$30.
  Famous Story Magazine. July, 1926. Part of "The Great Gatsby." $13.
  Saturday Evening Post. Feb 21, 1931. "Babylon Revisited." $20-$30.
  American Magazine. Apr, 1936. Short story. $19.

FITZGERALD, KEN. *Weathervanes and Whirligigs*. NY, Clarkson Potter, 1967 1st ed. VG in DJ. $20.

FITZGERALD, ZELDA. *Save Me The Waltz*. NY, 1932 1st ed. Author's 1st book. VG in vg DJ. $750-$1,500. London, 1953 1st English ed. Very Good in dust jacket. $95.

FITZHUGH, PERCY K. *Hervey Willetts*. Grosset & Dunlap, 1927. Shelfworn, but VG in poor DJ. $25.
  Lefty Leighton. (Buddy Books). G&D, 1930. G-VG in chipped dust jacket. $50.
  Skinny McCord. G&D, 1928. Scouting title. Very Good in dust jacket. $50.

FITZPATRICK, SIR PERCY. *Jock of the Bushveld*. NY, 1908. Very Good. $20.

FLACK, MARJORIE. *Angus and The Ducks*. NY, 1930. Illus. by author. Very Good. $45.
  Ask Mr. Bear. Macmillan, 1939. Illus. by author. VG in worn dust jacket. $18.
  The New Pet. Doubleday, 1943. Illus. by author. VG. $22.

FLAGG, JAMES MONTGOMERY. *The Well-Knowns*. Doran, 1914 1st edition. Illustrated by author. No. 21 of 248 copies. Very Good. $200.
  Boulevards All the Way. NY, 1925 1st ed. Illus. G. $30.
  Roses and Buckshot. Putnam's, 1946 2nd. VG in DJ. $15.

FLAHERTY, ROBERT. *Igloo Life*. NY, privately printed, 1923 1st ed. Illus. Good. $30.

FLAMINI, ROLAND. *Scarlett, Rhett and a Cast of Thousands*. Macmillan, 1976 4th ed. Fine in dust jacket. $12.

FLAMMARION, CAMILLE. *Urania*. Estes & Lauriat, 1890 1st ed. Very Good. $125.
  Popular Astronomy. NY, 1925. Reprint of 2nd ed. of 1907. Translation. Very Good. $75.
  Dreams of an Astronomer. NY, 1923. Very Good. $35.

FLANAGAN, EDWARD M. *The Angels: A History of the 11th Airborne Division, 1943-1946*. Wash., 1946. Good plus. $150. Same, San Francisco, 1988. As new in DJ. $30.

FLANAGAN, ROY C. *The Story of Lucky Strike*. Lucky Strike, 1938 1st ed. Fine. $10-$12.

FLAUBERT, GUSTAV. *Madame Bovary*. NY, Heritage reprint, 1950. Very Fine in slipcase. $13. Franklin Library for Oxford Univ. Press. 1979. Leather bound. $25.

FLECKER, JAMES ELROY. *Hassan*. London, 1924 1st ed. Illus. Very Good in dust jacket. $90.

FLEISCHER, NAT. *Jack Dempsey, the Idol of Fistiana*. NY, 1929. Photos. Fine. $80.
How to Box. No place, 1929, paperbound 1st ed. Foreward by James J. Corbett. near VG. $45. 1942 5th ed. VG. $20.
Training for Boxers. No place, 1932 8th ed. Paperbound. Foreward by Jack Dempsey. G. $35. 1937 9th ed. VG. $20.
The Heavyweight Championship: An Informal History of Heavyweight Boxing from 1719 to the Present. NY, 1949 1st ed. Light foxing, o/w VG in DJ. $55.
The Ring. Record Book and Boxing Encyclopedia. Fleischer, 1959 1st ed. Autographed. Fine. $55.
Modern Wrestling. 1945 2nd rev. ed. Paperback. VG. $20.
Louis Legend: Biography. 1956. Very Good. $25.

FLEISCHMAN, SID. *Longbeard the Wizard*. Boston, 1970 1st ed. Charles Bragg illus. Signed by author with sketch. Very Good in dust jacket. $20.
The Hey Hey Man. Boston, 1979 1st ed. Nadine Westcott illus. Signed by author. Near Fine in dust jacket. $22.

FLEMING-BURCKEL. *Who's Who in Colored America*. Burckel, 1950 7th ed. $16.

FLEMING, HOWARD. *Narrow Gauge Railways in America*. No place, 1876 2nd ed. Very Good. $100.

FLEMING, IAN. *Casino Royale*. NY, 1954. 1st American ed. Author's 1st book. VG in rubbed dust jacket. $80.
Moonraker. J. Cape, 1955 1st ed. Very Good. $75.
Diamonds are Forever. NY, 1956. In DJ. $75-$175.
Thunderball. London, 1961 1st English ed. F in DJ. $175.
The Spy Who Loved Me. NY, 1962 1st American edition. Fine in dust jacket. $85.
You Only Live Twice. London, 1964 1st ed., 1st issue. NF in worn dust jacket. $45. NY. G-VG in DJ. $15-$30.
The Man With the Golden Gun. NY, New American Library, 1965 1st American ed. Fine in DJ. $25-$45.
Octopussy and the Living Daylights. London, 1966 1st English ed. Fine in dust jacket. $25-$50.
Gilt Edged Bonds. Macmillan, 1961 VG in DJ. $35.

FLEMING, JOAN. *He Ought To Be Shot*. NY, Crime Club, 1955 1st ed. Near Fine in fair dust jacket. $18.

Malice Matrimonial. NY, 1959 1st ed. F in inked DJ. $18.

FLETCHER, INGLIS. *The Queen's Gift*. Bobbs Merrill, 1952 1st ed. Very Good in dust jacket. $50.
The Scotsman. Bobbs Merrill, 1957 1st ed. VG in DJ. $25.

FLETCHER, JOHN GOULD. *The Burning Mountain*. NY, 1946 1st ed. VG. $10. Same in VG dust jacket. $25.

FLINT, TIMOTHY. *The History and Geography of the Mississippi Valley*. Cincinnati, 1832 2nd ed. $85.
Indian Wars of the West. Cincinnati, 1833 1st. VG. $185.
Life and Adventures of Daniel Boone. 1868. $20-$30.

FLOHERTY, JOHN. *Flowing Gold--the Romance of Oil*. NY, 1945 1st ed. Ex-library. Cover soiled, o/w VG. $17.

FLORENCE. *Gentlemen's Handbook on Poker*. 1892. 195 pgs. Very Fine. $170 auction.

FLORIN, LAMBERT. *Ghost Towns of the West*. Promontary Press, 1971. VG in DJ. $20-$24.
Ghost Town Album. Bonanza Books, NY, 1962. Very Good in dust jacket. $15-$20.
Boot Hill. Seattle, 1966 1st ed. G-VG in DJ. $20-$30.
Ghost Town Trails. Bonanza reprint, 1960s. F in DJ. $15.

FLOURNOY, THEODORE. *From India to the Planet Mars*. Translation. NY, 1900 1st ed. in English. Good. $50.

FLUGEL, J. C. *The Psychology of Clothes*. London, 1950 3rd impression. Very Good, $35.

FLYNN, ERROL. *My Wicked, Wicked Ways*. NY, 1959. 1st ed. No dust jacket. $10.

FLYNT, JOSIAH. *The World of Graft*. NY, 1901. Inscribed, Very Good. $35.

FOLEY, DORIS. *The Divine Eccentric, Lola Montez and the Newspapers*. Westernlore, 1969 1st ed. Fine in DJ. $12.

FONSECA, LEW. *How to Pitch Baseball*. Chicago, 1942 1st ed. Illus. Very Good. $50.

FOOTE, AGNES COPE. *The Sea Bird Island*. Boston, 1935. Andrew Wyeth Illus. Signed by Wyeth. Fine. $300.

FOOTE, JOHN TAINTOR. *Blister Jones*. Indianapolis, 1913 1st ed. Jay Hambidge illus. Good. $13.

FOOTE, SHELBY. *Tournament*. NY, 1949 1st ed. 1st novel by Foote. VG to Fine in dust jacket. $75-$175.
Follow Me Down. Dial, 1950 1st edition. Very Good in dust jacket. $30.
Jordan County. Dial, 1954 1st ed. VG in DJ. $35.
The Civil War. No place, 1958 Vol. 1, 1st ed. VG. $13.

FOOTNER, HULBERT. *Rivers of the Eastern Shore, Maryland*. NY, 1944 reprint. Very Good. $19.
New Rivers of the North. NY, 1912 1st. G-VG. $30-$40.
The Doctor Who Held Hands. NY, Doubleday Crime Club, 1929 1st ed. Fine in dust jacket. $75.
The Murder of a Bad Man. NY, 1936 1st ed. G plus $8.
Queen of Clubs. In six parts in Argosy Magazine. November 5, 1927-December 10, 1927. VG plus $50.

FORBES, ESTHER. *Mirror For Witches*. London, 1928 1st ed. Robert Gibbins engravings. VG in DJ. $38.
Johnny Tremain. Boston, 1943 1st ed. VG in DJ. $40.
Paul Revere and the World He Lived In. Boston, 1942. Illus. Good-VG. $12-$18.

FORBUSH. EDWARD HOWE. *Useful Birds & Their Protection*. Bost., 1905 1st. & 1907 2nd. G-VG . $20-$35 ea.
Birds of Mass. & Other States. 1925-1929. 3 vols. $95.

FORD, BERT. *The Fighting Yankees Overseas*. Boston, 1919. Fine. $25.

FORD, COREY. *Salt Water Taffy*. Putnam, 1929 2nd ed. VG in fair dust jacket. $20.
You Can Always Tell a Fisherman. NY, 1958 1st ed. Fine in dust jacket. $75.
Uncle Perk's Jug. NY, 1964 1st ed. Ex-lib. $75.
Donovan of OSS. Little Brown, 1970 1st ed. F in DJ. $15.
The Best of Corey Ford. NY, 1975. J. Samson, editor; signed by him. Fine in DJ. $20.

FORD, GERALD R. *Humor and the Presidency*. NY, 1987. Signed.Fine in fine dust jacket. $75.
A Vision for America. No. 67 of 100 copies, total run of 500. Castle Press, Northridge, 1980 1st ed. Signed by Ford. Near Fine. $120-$180.

FORD MOTOR COMPANY. *Instruction Book for Ford Model T Cars*. Detroit, 1912. 46 pgs. 5th ed. $25. (Also see Catalog Section).

FORD, PAUL LEICESTER. *Janice Meredith: A Story of the American Revolution*. NY, 1899 1st ed. 2 vols. VG. $150.
Wanted--A Matchmaker. NY, 1900. Howard Chandler Christy illus. Very Good. $45. Fine. $95.
Wanted: A Chaperon. NY, 1902 1st ed. Howard Chandler Christy illustrator. VG. $70. Same, 2nd printing. $25-$40.
A Story of Untold Love. NY, 1902 1st. Signed. VG. $85.
A Checked Love Affair. NY, 1903. H. Fisher illus. F. $45.
His Version Of It. NY, 1905. Henry Hutt illus. Fine. $45.
A Warning to Lovers: Sauce for the Goose. NY, Dodd Mead, 1906. Good-Very Good. $35.

FORESTER, C. S. *Lord Hornblower*. Boston, 1946 1st American ed. Andrew Wyeth cover. VG in DJ. $30-$50.
Randall & The River of Time. London, 1951 1st English ed. Good in dust jacket. $35.

The Captain From Connecticut. Boston, L-B, 1941 1st ed. Good in DJ. $23. 1942 reprint. Good. $9.
The Good Shepherd. Boston, 1955 1st ed. in dust jacket. $20-$30. Book of the Month Club ed. Fair in DJ. $9.
The Age of Fighting Sail. The Story of the Naval War of 1812. NY, 1956 1st ed. Very Good, no dust jacket. $22.

FORESTER, FRANK (H. W. HERBERT) *The Horse of America*. NY, 1847 2 vols. VG. $175.
Frank Forester's Fish & Fishing in the U. S. NY, 1850 1st American ed. Light foxing, spine chip. $30.
The Complete Manual For Young Sportsmen. NY, 1856 1st edition. Good. $35.
Fishing With Hook & Line: A Manual for Amateur Anglers. NY, no date Paperback. Good. $50.

FORNEY, JOHN W. *Life and Military Career of Winfield Scott Hancock*. Philadelphia, circa 1880. Poor-Fair. $25.

FORREST, G. *Every Boy's Book of Sports and Games*. NY, 1864 1st ed. 600 illus. Good-VG. $75-$150.

FORRESTER, GLENN. *The Falls of Niagara*. Van Nostrand, 1928 1st ed. Very Good. $14.

FORSEE, AYLESA. *William Henry Jackson--Pioneer Photographer of the West*. NY, 1964 1st ed. Photo illus. Fine in dust jacket. $50.

FORSTER, AUGUST. *American Culinary Art*. Private press, 1951. 418 pgs. Cookbook. $30-$45.

FORSTER, E. M. *A Passage to India*. London, 1924 1st ed. one of 200 copies, signed. Fine in slipcase. $1,700.
The Hill of Devi. NY, 1953 1st American ed. F in DJ. $20.
Battersea Rise. NY, 1955 1st American ed. VG in DJ. $35.
The Life to Come and Other Stories. Norton, 1972 1st American ed. Fine in DJ. $20.

42ND DIVISION - SUMMARY OF OPERATIONS IN THE WORLD WAR (WWI). GPO 1st ed. 1944. Fine. $35.

FOSTER, HAROLD. *Prince Valiant in the New World*. New York, 1976. Illus. by author. Near Fine in DJ. $25.

FOSTER, J. W. *Prehistoric Races of the United States*. 1873 2nd ed. Worn but good. $60. 1874 3rd ed. VG. $60.

FOSTER, R. F. *Practical Poker*. 1904. Very Fine. $75.

FOWKE, GERARD. *Evolution of the Ohio River*. Fowke, 1933 1st ed. Fine. $15.
Archaeological History of Ohio. 1902. 760 pgs. Fine. $95.

FOWLER, GENE. *Timberline*. NY, 1933 1st edition. VG. $25.
Salute to Yesterday. NY, 1937. Light endpaper foxing, bookplate. Signed. $45.

Good Night, Sweet Prince (John Barrymore). Viking, 1944 8th printing. Book Club ed. Very Good. $25.
Schnozzola, The Story of JimmyDurante. 1961 1st ed. Very Good in dust jacket. $15.

FOWLER, NATHANIEL C., JR. *About Advertising And Printing. A Concise, Practical And Original Manual On The Art of Local Advertising.* Boston, 1889. Good. $75.

FOWLER, ORSON S. *Phrenology Proved, Illustrated and Applied.* NY, 1837 2nd ed. Poor. $30.
Phrenology and Physiology Explained and Applied to Matrimony. NY, 1842 4 vols in one. Good. $75.
Phrenology and Marriage. NY, 1842. VG. $35.
Fowler's Works on Education and Self Improvement, etc. NY, 1844. Good. $50.
Fowler's Practical Phrenology. NY, 1849. VG. $30.
The House: A Pocket Manual. NY, 1859. Illus. G. $45.
The Practical Phrenologist and Recorder & Delineator. No place, 1869. VG. $85.
The Human Science of Phrenology, Self Culture, Mental Philosophy, etc. NY, 1873. Near VG. $30.

FOX, BROOKS and TYRWITT. *The Mill* (Windmill). NY Graphic Soc., 1976 1st ed. Illus. VF in dust jacket. $28.

FOX, CHARLES PHILIP. *Ticket to the Circus. Story of Ringlings.* Bramwell House, rev. ed., 1959. VG in DJ. $15.

FOX, FRANCES MARGARET. *How Christmas Came to Mulvaneys.* 1905, 4th printing. Very Good. $20.
The Wilding Princess. 1929 1st ed., Volland. J. E. Perkins, illus. Near Fine in dust jacket. $75.
Nannette. 1929 1st. Johnny Gruelle, illus. G-VG. $30-$40.
Little Bear's Ups and Downs. Rand McNally, 1936. Francis Beem, illus. $27.
Doings of Little Bear. 1937 reprint. W. Carr, illus. $32.

FOX, HELEN M. *Gardening For Good Eating.* New York, 1943. Very Good. $25.

FOX, JOHN, JR. *The Little Shepherdof Kingdom Come.* NY, 1903 1st edition, 1st printing. Near Fine. $50. 1931 edition. N. C. Wyeth illus. Very Good. $100.
A Knight of the Cumberland. NY, 1906 1st ed. NF. $35.
The Trail of the Lonesome Pine. NY, 1908 1st ed., 1st state. Fine. $60-$80. Grosset & Dunlap ed. $10.
Mountain Europa. Scribner, 1910. G-VG. $10-$15.

FOX, RICHARD K. *Poker: How to Win.* 1905. 90 pgs. (facsimile cover). $210.
Police Gazette Card Player. 1888. 73 pgs. VG. $290.

FOX, UFFA. *Sailing, Seamanship and Yacht Construction.* NY, 1936 3rd ed. Spine separated, o/w VG. $25.
Sail & Power. Scribner's, 1937 1st American ed. Some damping, o/w Very Good in dust jacket. $65.

Racing, Cruising and Design. Scribner's, 1938 1st American ed. Fine in dust jacket. $75.
Thoughts on Yachts & Yachting. Scribner's, 1939 1st American ed. Fine in dust jacket. $75.

FOX, WILLIAM. *New York at Gettysburg.* 3 vols. NY, 1900. Good-Very Good. $75-$150.

FOXFIRE BOOKS. *Various titles.* by Anchor Publishing. Nos. 1 thru 5, 1972-1979. Paperback. $4-$10 each.

FRANCATELLI, CHARLES ELME. *Francatelli's Modern Cook Book.* Pre-1873 9th ed. reprint. (Chief cook to British queen). $300-$350.
French Cookery: The Modern Cook. Philadelphia, 1846 1st American ed. Very Good. $220. 1878 ed. $35.

FRANCE, ANATOLE. *The Crime of Sylvester Bonnard.* NY, 1890. Lafcadio Hearn translation. G-VG. $40-$60.
The Red Lily, 1917. Modern Library. 1st ed. 1917. Very Good-Fine in dust jacket. $100.
At the Sign of the Reine Pedaugue. NY, 1928. Frank Pape, illus. Fine. $25.
The Revolt of the Angels. London, no date 1st ed. Frank C. Pape, illus. Very Good. $45.
Thais. NY, no date. Frank C. Pape, illus. VG. $30.

FRANCIS, DEVON. *Mr. Piper & His Cubs.* 1973 Iowa Univ. Press, 1st ed. Good-VG. $20-$25.

FRANCIS, DICK. *Banker.* London, 1952 1st ed. Fine in DJ. $50. Same, NY, 1982 1st American ed. VG in DJ. $15-$20. Another, signed by author. Very Fine. $30-$50.
For Kicks. NY, 1965 1st ed. VG plus in nicked DJ. $325. Same, London. $275.
Flying Finish. NY, 1966 1st ed . Fine in DJ. $150-$250.
Blood Sport. NY, 1968 1st American ed. Fine in DJ. $100.
Rat Race. London, 1970 1st British ed. F in DJ. $100-$125.
Knock Down. London, 1974 1st. F in DJ. $75. NY, 1974 1st Amer. ed. Signed. Edge foxing, poor DJ, o/w VG. $50.
Risk. London, 1977 1st ed. Signed. VG in fine DJ. $30. NY, 1978. Fine in dust jacket. $50.
Whip Hand. London, 1979 1st ed. VG in DJ. $45.

FRANDSEN, J. H. and E. A. MARKHAM. *The Manufacture of Ice Cream and Ices.* NY, London, 1915. G-VG. $40.

FRANK LESLIE'S ILLUS. HISTORICAL REGISTER OF THE CENTENNIAL EXPOSITION. 1876. $125.

FRANK, HELENA (Translator). *Yiddish Tales.* No place, 1912. Hinge cracks. Good. $17.

FRANK, ROBERT (Photographer). *The Americans.* NY, 1969. Jack Kerouac introduction. Photographs. NF. $125.
The Lines of My Hand. Lustrum Press, 1972. Ex-library. Paperbound. Fair. $85.

FRANKFURTER, FELIX. *The Case of Sacco and Vanzetti.* Boston, 1927. Good. $30.

FRANKLIN, BENJAMIN. *The Works of the Late Benjamin Franklin.* NY, 1807. Rough covers. $20.
Life of Benjamin Franklin, Written by Himself. C. M. Saxton, 1860 1st ed. Light foxing. Good. $12-$15.
Papers of Benjamin Franklin. Yale Univ. 1959 1st ed. Vol 1. Very Good in dust jacket. $28.
The Autobiography of Benjamin Franklin. NY, Grosset and Dunlap, Cameo Classic. 1940s. Blue cloth. Fine in good slipcase. $10. Chicago, Lakeside, 1903. $150.

FRANKLIN MINT BOOKS, 1973-1980. Set, *100 "Greatest" Books of All Time.* Prospectus included. Near M. $5,000.
54 different titles. Fine in leather bindings. $40-$65 each.
36 signed 1st editions. $40 each, or $1,130 for the lot. Various single titles in slightly used condition have been offered in the $17-$25 range. See individual author headings for more examples.

FRAPRIE, FRANK and F. C. O'CONNOR. *Photographic Amusements.* Boston, 1937. Illus. VG in DJ. $25.
American Annual of Photography 1934. Fine. $15.

FRASER, LOVAT (Illustrator). *Peacock Pie.* By Walter de la Mare. NY, 1924. Very Good. $100.
The Book of Lovat. 1st trade ed. VG in dust jacket. $100.

FRASER, SAMUEL. *The Strawberry.* NY, Orange-Judd, 1926 1st ed. Very Good. $12.

FRASER, WALTER J. *Patriots, Pistols and Petticoats.* Charleston County Bicentennial Commission, 1976. Inscribed. Very Good in dust jacket. $15.

FRAZER, J. G. *The Golden Bough.* London, 1926 3rd ed. 12 vols with DJ. Fine. $700. In one volume, NY,1947. VG in DJ. $15. Another, 1951. Fine in DJ. $18. Set of 13 vols., 1976, VG in DJ. $260.

FREECE, HANS F. *The Letters of an Apostate Mormon to His Son.* NY, privately printed, 1908. VG. $85.

FREEDMAN, A. M. and HAROLD KAPLAN, eds. *Comprehensive Textbook of Psychiatry.* Williams & Wilkins. 1967 1st ed. Very Good. $60.

FREELING, NICHOLAS. *Because of the Cats.* NY, 1984. Near Fine in fair dust jacket. $25.
Double Barrel. NY, 1964 1st ed. Fine in good DJ. $18.
Criminal Conversation. Lond., 1965 1st. NF in G DJ. $45.
The Dresden Green. London, 1986 1st ed. Fine in DJ. $15.
The Kitchen. NY,1970 1st Amer. ed. NF in good DJ. $20.

FREEMAN, DON. *Come Again Pelican.* Viking, 1961 1st ed. Autographed by author. VG in dust jacket. $60.

Hattie the Backstage Bat. NY, 1970 1st ed. Illus. by author. Very Good in dust jacket. $20.

FREEMAN, DOUGLAS S. *R. E. Lee: A Biography.* NY, 1936. 4 vols. Near Fine in slipcase. $125.
Lee's Lieutenants. NY, 1942-44, 3 vols. G-VG. $50-$90. Scribner's 1970 reprint, 3 vols. Fine in dust jacket. $30.
Lee's Dispatches: Unpublished Letters of General Lee. Putnam, circa 1956, new ed. Fine. $20.

FREEMAN, HARRY. *A Brief History of Butte, Montana.* H. Shepard, 1900 1st ed. Very Good. $65-$95.

FREEMAN, LARRY. *New Light on Old Lamps.* NY, 1945, Century House. Very Good. $10-$20.
Cavalcade of Toys. (Ruth and Larry) NY, 1942. $12.
Louis Prang: Color Lithographer. NY, 1971. $25.

FREEMAN, R. AUSTIN. *A Certain Dr. Thorndyke.* NY, 1928 1st ed. Fine. $60.
Dr. Thorndyke's Cases. NY, 1931 1st ed. Good. $25.
Dr. Thorndyke Intervenes. NY, 1933 1st. F in DJ. $185.
The Stoneware Monkey. London, 1938 1st. F in DJ. $175.

FREEMAN, ROGER. *The Mighty Eighth* NY, 1970. VG. $65.
B-17 Flying Fortress at War. New York, 1977. $15-$30.

FREIDEL, FRANK. *Harvard Guide to American History.* Harvard Univ. Press. 1974. 2 vols. VG in DJ. $50.

FREMLIN, COLIN. *Possession.*NY, 1969 1st. NF in DJ. $15.
Appointment With Yesterday. Philadelphia, 1972 1st edition. Near Fine in dust jacket. $15.

FREMONT, JOHN C. *Memoirs of My Life.* Chicago, 1887 1st ed. Vol. 1. Only vol. published. VG. $100. Another, lacking maps & some plates. $60.

FRENCH & HORNBY. *Old Concord.* Little Brown, 1918 edition. Illus. History. Fine. $18.

FRENCH, WILLIAM. *Some Recollections of a Western Ranchman, 1893-1899.* NY, Argosy, 1965 ed. 1 of 750. 2 vols., boxed. Near Fine. $200.

FREUD, ANNA. *The Ego and Mechanisms of Defense.* NY, 1966 Revised ed. VG. $20.

FREUD, SIGMUND. *Totem and Taboo.* NY, 1918 1st ed.in English. A. A. Brill translator. Near Fine. $175. Another, Dodd & Mead, no date. Good. $25.
A General Introduction to Psychoanalysis. NY, 1920 1st American ed. VG. $125.
Group Psychology and the Analysis of the Ego. NY, 1920s. 1st American ed. VG. $45.
Beyond the Pleasure Principle. NY, 1924 1st American ed. Very Good-Fine. $40.

The Interpretation of Dreams. Basic Books, 1955. 1st U. S. printing of Strachey translation. VG in DJ. $100.
Jokes and Their Relation to the Unconscious. NY, 1960 1st Amer. ed. James Strachey, translator. VG in DJ. $35.

FRIED, FREDERICK. *Pictorial History of the Carousel*. 1964, Bonanza. Good in dust jacket. $25. Barne's, 1970 reprint. Fine in dust jacket. $30.
Artists in Wood. Potter, 1970 1st ed. VG in DJ. $50. Fine in dust jacket, ex-library. $32. Fair. $12.

FRIEDMAN, BRUCE JAY. *Stern*. NY, 1962 1st ed., 1st book. Fine in dust jacket. $60.
Mother's Kisses. NY, 1964 1st ed. Fine in dust jacket. $10.
Black Angels. NY, 1966 1st ed. VG in dust jacket. $30.

FRIEDMAN, JACOB. *Common Sense Candy Teacher*. (Recipes). Jonas Bell, 1915 6th ed. Good. $18.

FRIEDMAN, MORRIS. *The Pinkerton Labor Spy*. NY, 1907 1st ed. Near Fine. $20.

FRIGIDAIRE RECIPES. 1928 1st ed. 77 pgs. Fine in DJ. $20. 1929 2nd ed. VG in dust jacket. $12-$15.

A FROG HE WOULD A-WOOING GO. McLoughlin Bros, 1902. Repaired, Good. $48.

FROISETH, JENNIE (Editor). *The Women of Mormonism: Or, The Story of Polygamy as Told By The Victims Themselves*. Detroit, 1886. Illus. Good. $25.

FROM DANISH KITCHENS. By the Ladies of St. Johns Luthern Church. Seattle, circa 1940. $14.

FROME, DAVID. *The Strange Death of Martin Green*. NY, 1931 1st ed. Near VG. $14. Same in worn DJ. $50.
Mr. Pinkerton at the Old Angel. 1939 1st ed. VG in faded dust jacket. $28.
Mr. Pinkerton Finds a Body. NY, 1941 1st. PB. F. $15.

FROST, A. B. *A Book of Drawings*. NY, 1904. Verse by Wallace Irwin. Joel C. Harris introduction. 39 plates by author. Near Fine. $150. Good-VG. $60.

FROST, A. B. (Illustrator). *The Story of a Bad Boy*. By Thomas Bailey Aldrich. Boston, 1895. G-VG. $35.
Uncle Remus. Appleton, 1911. Very Good. $45.
Pomona's Travels. By Frank A. Stockton. No place, no date. Light cover soiling, o/w VG. $45.

FROST, HONOR. *Under the Mediterranean*. Prentice-Hall, 1963. Fine. $24.

FROST, JOHN. *Pictorial History of California: History of the State from period of the Conquest by Spain*. Auburn CA, 1850 1st ed. Very Good. $150-$250.

FROST, L. *The Court-Martial of General George Armstrong Custer*. Norman, OK, 1968. Fine in vg DJ. $45.

FROST, ROBERT. *Mountain Interval*. NY, Henry Holt, 1916 1st ed. 1st state. VG, no dust jacket. $250.
A Boy's Will. London, 1913 1st ed. 1st issue. Author's 1st book. Sydney Cox inscription. VG. $3,000. Same, but 2nd issue. $200. Same, NY, 1915 1st American ed. 1st issue. $295. 2nd issue. $125.
West Running Brook. NY, 1928 1st ed. 1st state. Signed by Frost. Fine in later DJ. $500. Same, but 2nd state. Fine in dust jacket. $75.
Collected Poems. NY, 1930 1st ed., 1st printing. VG in vg dust jacket. $250.
A Witness Tree. NY, 1942 1st ed. Fair DJ, o/w NF. $55.
A Masque of Reason. Holt, 1945 1st ed. Good in DJ. $40.
Complete Poems of Robert Frost. NY, 1949. One of 500 copies, signed. Fine in repaired slipcase. $350-$475.
You Come Too. NY, 1959. 1st edition. T. W. Nason engravings. Clipped DJ, o/w Fine. $45.
In the Clearing. NY, 1962 1st. Near Fine in clip DJ. $40.

FROTHINGHAM, OCTAVIUS. *Transcendentalism in New England*. NY, 1876 1st ed. VG. $60.

FRYER, JANE E. *The Mary Frances Cookbook*. Winston, 1912. Blue cloth, pictorial label. G-VG in poor DJ. $200.

FUCHIDA, MITAUO and M. OKUMIYA. *Midway: The Battle that Doomed Japan*. Annapolis MD, 1955. Very Good in dust jacket. $22. 1981 edition. $20.

FUCITO, SALVATORE and BARNET J. BEYER. *Caruso and the Art of Singing*. NY, 1922 1st edition. 13 plates. Very Good. $150.

FULLER, BUCKMINSTER. *Nine Chains to the Moon*. Lippincott, 1938. Signed. $195-$235. Unsigned. $25-$50.
Ideas and Integrities. NY, 1963 1st ed. Illus. F in DJ. $35.
How Little I Know. 1966, October, 1st ed. Paperbound. VG-Fine. $50-$95.
Synergetics. New York, 1975 1st edition. Inscribed. Very Good in dust jacket. $100.

FULLER, J. F. C. *The Generalship of Ulysses S. Grant*. NY, 1929. Very Good. $45.
Grant and Lee. Indiana Univ, 1957. VG in DJ. $25.

FULLER, MARGARET. *Love Letters of Margaret Fuller*. NY, 1903 1st ed. Fine. $25.

FUNDERBURK, T. R. *The Fighters, The Men & Machines of the First Air War*. NY, 1965, Grosset. VG in DJ. $30.

FUTRELLE, JACQUES. *The Thinking Machine*. NY, 1907 1st ed. Weak hinge, o/w Good plus. $150. Another copy in Very Good cond. $350.

G

GABOR, MARK. *The Pin-Up, a Modest History*. Dell, 1972 1st ed. Very Good in dust jacket. $18.

GADDIS, WILLIAM. *The Recognitions*. NY, 1955 1st ed., 1st book. Inscribed by Gaddis. Near Fine in DJ. $400.
J. R. NY, 1975 1st ed. Fine in DJ. $100.

GADDIS, THOS E. *Birdman of Alcatraz*. NY, 1955 1st ed. Very Good in dust jacket. $29.

GAG, WANDA. *Millions of Cats*. NY, 1928 1st ed. Illus by author. Very Good in dust jacket. $200.
Three Tales from Grimm. Coward McCann, 1936. VG. $65. 2nd edition, NY, 1943. VG in DJ. $50.
Nothing At All. NY, 1941 1st ed. Illus by author. Gag's 1st color book. Fine in xeroxed DJ. $80.
The Sorcerer's Apprentice. NY, 1979. Margot Tomes illus. Fine in dust jacket. $30.
The ABC Bunny. NY, 1933 7th printing. Illus. by author. Ex-library. Reading copy. $15. 1970s 16th printing. $8.
Snow White and the Seven Dwarfs. London, 1938 1st ed. Translation. Illus. by author. Fine in fine DJ. $135.

GAINES, ERNEST J. *The Autobiography of Miss Jane Pittman*. Dial, 1971 1st ed. Fine in DJ. $75.
A Gathering of Old Men. NY, 1983 1st edition. Fine in dust jacket. $50-$100.

GALE, ZONA. *Friendship Village: Love Stories*. NY, 1909 1st ed. Very Good. $35.
Mothers to Men. NY, 1911 1st ed. G-VG. $10-$20.
Neighborhood Stories. NY, 1914 2nd printing. Fine. $35.
A Daughter of the Morning. Bobbs Merrill, 1917 1st ed. Good-VG. $12-$24.

GALELLA, RON. *Jacqueline*. NY, 1974 1st ed. Photographs. Very Good in dust jacket. $30.

GALLAGHER, THOMAS. *Fire at Sea: The Story of the Morro Castle*. NY, 1959. Good plus in DJ. $18.

GALLICO, PAUL. *The Snow Goose*. NY, 1941 1st American ed. VG in DJ. $40. 1946 edition. Near Fine. $35.
Thomasina. NY, 1957 1st ed. VG in DJ. $30.
Mrs. 'Arris Goes to Paris. NY, 1960 1st American ed. Fine in fine dust jacket. $18.

The Poseidon Adventure. NY, 1969 1st American ed. Fine in clipped dust jacket. $15-$25.
The Boy Who Invented Bubble Gum. London, 1974 1st English ed. Fine in dust jacket. $18.

GALSWORTHY, JOHN. *The Eldest Son*. NY, 1912 1st American edition. Very Good. $25.
A Bit o' Love. NY, 1915 1st American ed. Near Fine. $20.
Swan Song. Scribner, 1928 Trade ed. VG in DJ. $18.

GALT, JOHN. *Annals of the Parish*. T. N. Foulis, 1919. H. Kerr illus. Very Good. $25.

GAMOW, GEORGE. *A Star Called the Sun*. New York, 1964. Very Good in dust jacket. $18.

GANDY, LEWIS CASS. *The Tabors*. NY, 1934. Inscribed, presentation copy. Very Good. $25.

GANSSER, EMIL. *History of the 126th Infantry WWI*. Grand Rapids, MI, 1920 1st ed. Illus. photos, maps, F. $65.

GARCES, FRANCISCO. *A Record of Travels in Arizona and California, 1775-1776*. San Francisco, 1965 reprint by John Howell Books. Fine. $70-$85.

GARD, WAYNE. *Sam Bass*. Boston, 1936 1st edition. Good-Very Good. $45-$55.
Frontier Justice. University of Oklahoma, 1949. Very Good in dust jacket. $15.
The Chisholm Trail. Norman, OK, 1954 1st ed. Very Good-Fine in dust jacket. $35-$45.
The Great Buffalo Hunt. No place, 1959. Illus. Very Good in dust jacket. $15.

GARDNER, ALBERT. *Winslow Homer*. 1961 1st ed. illus. Ex-library. moderate wear. $18.

GARDNER, JOHN. *The King's Indian*. Knopf, 1974 1st ed. Shelfworn, but Very Good in dust jacket. $30.

GARDINER, PAUL. *A Drummer's Parlor Stories*. NY, A. P. Gardiner, 1898. Illus. Very Good. $25.

GARDNER, E. C. *Illustrated Homes, Real Houses and Real People*. Boston, 1875. Minor wear. $75.

GARDNER, ERLE STANLEY. Fine or Near Fine copies of books in "The Case of" series are worth from $100-$250 when inscribed by Gardner. Not inscribed titles in the series run from $25-$100 depending on condition. (7) different titles beginning with "The Case of", All 1st eds., all inscribed by Gardner. Fine or Near Fine. $175-$250 each. (26) different titles beginning "The Case of", All 1st editions in Fine or Near Fine condition. $20-$50 each. (4) 1950s reprints of above. $8 each.

The Case of the Counterfeit Eye. Morrow, 1935 1st ed. A Good copy. $75.

The Case of the Dangerous Dowager. NY, 1937 1st ed. Near VG in fair DJ. $150.

Murder Up My Sleeve. NY, 1937 1st ed. NF in DJ. $125.

The Case of the Velvet Claws. NY, 1940 1st ed. Paperback. VG. $25.

The Case of the Turning Tide. Morrow, 1941 1st ed. Good in DJ. $60-$70.

The Case of the Black-Eyed Blonde. Morrow, 1944 1st ed. Good in dust jacket. $75-$100.

The Case of the Crooked Candle. NY, 1944. Ink stamp on edge, o/w VG in good DJ. $6.

The Case of the Borrowed Brunette. Morrow, 1946 1st edition. Good in DJ. $60.

The Case of the Restless Redhead. Morrow, 1954 1st ed. VG in DJ. $45-$65.

The Case of the Runaway Corpse. Morrow, 1954 1st ed. Good in DJ. $40-$55.

The Case of the Singing Skirt. Morrow, 1959. Advance Review Copy. DJ. Fine. $65.

The Case of the Waylaid Wolf. NY, 1959. 1st ed. Endpaper stamps, o/w VG in fine DJ. $32. Another, VG in ragged edge DJ. $18.

Hunting the Desert Whale. Morrow, 1960 2nd ed. Fine in dust jacket. Ex-library. $18.

Hovering Over Baja. NY, 1961 1st. VG in fine DJ. $30.

This Desert Is Yours. NY, 1963 1st ed. Illus. Very Good in very good dust jacket. $20

The Case of the Careless Cupid. NY, 1968 1st ed. Fine in dust jacket. $25.

GARDNER, ERLE STANLEY (In Magazines). *Black Mask.* 1923-1943. Gardner stories appeared in many issues of this magazine. G-VG. $10-$15 each.

Detective Fiction Weekly. 32 issues, 1929-1935. Gardner story in each issue. $20-$35 each.

Argosy All-Story Weekly. 10 issues, 1930-1933. Gardner story in each issue. VG-Fine. $20-$35 each.

Detective Story Weekly. 1932-1935. Stories in 16 issues. $20-$25 each.

Argosy Magazine. 1933. Stories in 4 issues. $20-$25 each.

Black Mask Nov. 1934. Story. (Also, story by Carroll John Daly). Near Fine. $85.

Cosmopolitan. Sept 1937 1st printing, precedes book publication of "Murder Up My Sleeve", VG. $35.

Writer's 1937 Yearbook. "Doping It The Hard Way". Essay on writing. Very Good. $20.

GARDNER, HELEN. *Art Through the Ages.* Harcourt, 1959. Ex-library copy. $12.

GARDNER, ISABELLA. *Birthdays From Ocean.* Cambridge MA, 1955 1st ed. Author's 1st book. VG in DJ. $50.

GARDNER, JOHN. *Understrike.* New York, 1965 1st ed. Fine in dust jacket. $23.
A Complete State of Death. NY, 1969 1st American ed. Near Fine in dust jacket. $20.
The Return of Moriarty. NY, 1974 1st ed. NF in DJ. $23.

GARDNER, LEONARD. *Fat City.* NY, 1969 1st ed. Author's 1st book. VG in dust jacket. $40.

GARDNER, MARTIN. *The Annotated Alice.* No place, 1960. Reprint. Fine in dust jacket. $20.

GARDNER, RALPH. *Horatio Alger, or the American Hero Era.* Mendota CA, 1964. VG in DJ. $40.

GARDNER, ROBERT E. *Arms Fabricators, Ancient and Modern.* No place, 1935 1st ed. G-VG. $95.

GARIS, HOWARD R. *The Curlytops & Their Pets.* Cupples Leon, 1921. VG in DJ. $5-$7. Other Curlytops titles, 1918-1924. G to VG, no dust jacket. $5-$7 each.
Adventures of Uncle Wiggily, the Bunny Rabbit Gentleman. Newark, Graham, 1924 1st ed. L. Campbell, color illus. Red boards, pictorial label. VG. $80.
Uncle Wiggily's Bungalow. A. L. Burt, 1930. Very Good in Good. DJ. $15.
Uncle Wiggily and Flying Rug and 3 other volumes pub by Whitman in 1940s, VG in DJs. $110.
Uncle Wiggily's Story Book. No place, 1939. Lansing Campbell illus. VG. $20.
Uncle Wiggily's Picture Book. NY, 1940. Lang Campbell illus. Very Good. $25.
Uncle Wiggily's Fortune. Platt & Munk, 1942. Rache illus. Good plus. $15.
Uncle Wiggily's Happy Days. Platt & Munk, 1947. VG in dust jacket. $17.
Uncle Wiggily Goes Camping. Whitman, 1940 1st ed. Lansing Campbell illus. VG. $10.
Uncle Wiggily and His Friends. Platt & Munk, 1955. Illus. Very Good. $5.
The Face in the Dismal Cavern. McLoughlin, no date. Pictorial, oversize. VG. $15.
Uncle Wiggily in the Country. Platt & Munk, no date. Good plus. $15.
Uncle Wiggily and Grandaddy Longlegs. Ohio, (1942) American Crayon Co. Good. $10.

GARLAND, HAMLIN. *Crumbling Idols.* 1894 1st edition. Fine. $45-$70.
Boy Life on the Prairie. 1899 Border ed. Good. $12.
Hesper. Harper, 1903 1st ed. VG. $16.

Trail Makers of the Middle Border. NY, 1926 1st ed. Constance Garland illus. Very Good. $15.
Mystery of the Buried Crosses. NY, 1939 1st ed. Very Good plus. $39.

GARLAND, JAMES A. *The Private Stable*. Boston, 1903. Illus. Good plus. $125.

GARNETT, DAVID. *No Love*. NY, 1929 1st ed. VG. $16.
Pocahontas. NY, 1933 1st ed. Very Good. $15.
Beany-Eye. London, 1935 1st ed. One of 110 copies. signed. Very Good. $60.
Aspects of Love. NY, 1956 1st Amer. ed. Fine in DJ. $45.

GARNETT, RICHARD. *Twilight of the Gods*. NY, 1924 1st ed. Henry Keen illus. Near Fine in DJ. $200. Same, Bodley Head edition. Very Good in gilt decorated cloth. $100.

GARNETT, T. S. *Major-General J. E. B. Stuart*. NY, 1907 1st ed. Neale Pub. Very Good. $175.

GARRATT, ALFRED C. *Myths in Medicine and Old-Time Doctors*. NY, 1884 1st ed. Rubbed. $45.
Medical Battery Guide. Philadelphia, 1867. Woodcut illus. Good. $150-$200.

GARRETT, GARET. *Other People's Money: the Greatest American Racket*. Reprint of Saturday Evening Post series. NY, 1931. Very Good. $15.

GARRETSON, MARTIN S. *The American Bison*. NY, 1938 1st ed. Illus. Near Fine. $35.

GARRETT, PAT. *The Authentic Life of Billy, The Kid*. Santa Fe, NM, 1882 1st ed., 1st state. 137 pgs., blue pictorial wraps, ad inside back cover, misnumbered back pages. $4,000. NY, 1927 edition. $65-$85. 1946 ed. Good. $25. Norman, OK, 1954 reprint. $12-$15. More than 500 books have been published which contain material about the life of William Bonney, (Billy, the Kid), 1859-1881.

GARTH, DAVID. *Road to Glenfairlie*. NY, 1940 1st ed. VG in dust jacket. $25.

GARWOOD, DARRELL. *Crossroads of America, Kansas City*. W. W. Norton, 1948 1st ed. VG in DJ. $15.

GASKELL, ELIZABETH C. *The Life of Charlotte Bronte*. Tauchnitz, 1857 2 vols. Good-VG. $30-$40.

GASKELL, C. A. *Gaskell's Guide to Writing, etc.* New York, 1883. Very Good. $50.
Gaskell Family & Business Atlas of the World. Chicago, 1895. Good. $150-$175.

GASQUE, JIM. *Bass Fishing, Technique, Tactics and Tales*. NY, 1945 1st ed. Inscribed. Near Fine. $50.

GASS, PATRICK. *Gass's Journal of the Lewis and Clark Expedition*. Chicago, McClurg, 1904 reprint of 1811 edition. Near Fine. $120-$180.

GATES, DORIS. *Blue Willow*. NY, 1940 1st ed. Paul Lantz illus. Very Good. $32.

GAUGIN, PAUL. *Noa Noa*. NY, no date. Translated. Greenburg, South Seas ed. Merle Armitage bookplate. Near VG in slipcase. $200.

GAULT, W. P. *Ohio at Vicksburg*. Columbus, 1906 report of Battlefield Commission. 374 pgs. Rough covers. $45.

GAUTIER, THEOPHIL. *One of Cleopatra's Nights*. NY, 1882 1st American ed. Good-VG. $150.

GAUVREAU, EMIL. *Billy Mitchell*. NY, 1942. Very Good in dust jacket. $15.

GAVIN, JAMES M. *On to Berlin. Battles of an Airborne Commander 1943-1946*. Viking, 1978 1st American ed. Fine in DJ. $14. Book Club ed., same year. Fine in DJ. $8.

GAY, JOHN. *The Beggar's Opera*. Paris, Limited Editions Club, 1937. One of 1,500, signed by illustrator. VG in good slipcase. $50. Heritage Press, 1937 reprint. Fine in good slipcase. $14.

GEBLER, ERNEST. *The Plymouth Adventure, Chronicle of the Mayflower*. Doubleday, 1950 1st ed. VG in DJ. $12.

GEE, ERNEST. *Early American Sporting Books*. Derrydale Press Ltd ed., 1940. Inscribed to author's wife. Auction. $500. Not inscribed. $30-$60.

GEHMAN, R. *The Sausage Book*. P-H, 1969 1st ed. VG in DJ. $15. Another inscribed by author. $25.

GELATT, RONALD. *The Fabulous Phonograph*. Philadelphia, 1955 1st ed. Near Fine in DJ. $40.

GELLHORN, MARTHA. *Liana*. NY, 1944. VG in DJ. $8.
The Honeyed Peach. NY, 1953 1st. Near Fine in DJ. $35.

GENDERS, ROY. *Perfume Through the Ages*. NY, 1972 1st American ed. Cover stained, o/w Very Good. $8.

GENERAL FOODS KITCHENS COOKBOOK. NY, 1959. Good. $10. Very Good. $18.

GENTHE, ARNOLD. (Photographer). *Pictures of Old Chinatown*. NY, 1908. Text by Will Irwin, 1st. VG. $200.
Old Chinatown: A Book of Pictures. NY, 1913 Enlarged 2nd ed. Inscribed. 91 Gravures. VG. $425.
The Book of the Dance. NY, 1916. Images of great female dancers. Good. $125. 1920 2nd printing. $75.
Impressions of New Orleans: A Book of Pictures. NY, 1926 1st ed. Photographs. VG in fair DJ. $145-$175.
Isidora Duncan, Studies. New York, 1929 1st edition. Very Good in slipcase. $75.

GEORGE, HENRY JR. *The Menace of Privilege*. NY, Macmillan, 1905 1st ed. Fine. $75.
The Complete Works of Henry George. NY, Doubleday, Page Co., 1904. 10 vols. Spines are faded. $100-$150.

GERHARD, WILLIAM. *Theatre Fires and Panics*. NY, Wiley, 1896 1st ed. Good-VG. $50-$75.

GERNSHEIM, HELMUT. *Lewis Carroll - Photographer*. New York, 1949. Very Good. $50.
The History of Photography. London, Oxford, 1955 1st ed. Very Good in poor dust jacket. $275.
The Origins of Photography. NY, 1982 1st ed. 191 plates. Fine in dust jacket and slipcase. $95.

GERSTELL, G. *How to Survive an Atomic Bomb*. Combat Forces Press, 1950 1st ed. VG in dust jacket. $25.

GERTSCH, W. J. *American Spiders*. NY, 1949. Very Good in dust jacket. $38.

GESELL, ARNOLD. *The Mental Growth of the Preschool Child*. Macmillan, 1925 1st ed. Lightly shelfworn. $50.
Infant & Child in the Culture Today. Harper, New York, 1943. Very Good. $10.
Vision: Its Development in Infant and Child. NY, 1949 1st ed. Very Good in dust jacket. $30.

GIBBINGS, ROBERT. *Iorana! A Tahitian Journal*. Boston, 1932 1st American ed. Woodblock illus. by author. One of 385 copies, signed. VG in slipcase. $125.
Lovely is the Lee. NY, 1945. Illus. by author. VG. $20.
Blue Angels and Whales. Dutton, 1946 1st ed. Very Good in dust jacket. $24.

GIBBONS, EUELL. *Stalking the Blue-eyed Scallop*. NY, 1964. Catherine Hammond illus. VG in vg DJ. $25.

GIBBS, WILLIAM. *Spices & How to Know Them*. Dunkirk NY, 1909 1st edition. Photo illus. Very Good. $55.

GIBRAN, KAHLIL. *The Earth Gods*. New York, 1931 1st ed. Very Good. $30.
Spirits Rebellious. NY, 1947. VG. $50.
Tears and Laughter. NY, 1949. Fine. $13.

GIBSON, CHARLES DANA. *Drawings*. New York, 1896. Illus. by author. Good. $90. Russell, 1897. $95-$135.
Pictures of People. NY, 1897. Illus. by author. VG. $175. Soiled cover and contents. $65-$95.
Sketches and Cartoons. NY, 1898. Illus. by author. Few loose plates, o/w Very Good. $90.
The Education of Mr. Pipp. NY, 1899. Illus. by author. Covers worn. Good. $90. Very Good. $120-$145.
Americans. NY, 1900. Illus. by author. Covers worn, otherwise Good. $90.
A Widow toHer Friends. NY, London, 1901 1st ed. Illus. by author. Folio. Very Good. $135.
Our Neighbors. NY, London, 1905 1st ed. Illus. by author. Folio. Very Good. $125.
The Gibson Book. NY, 1907 2 vols. Over 900 plates. Very Good-Fine. Folio. $125-$200.
80 Drawings of the Weaker Sex. NY, 1903. $95-$150.

GIBSON, CHARLES DANA. (Illustrator). *About Paris*. by Richard Harding Davis. NY, 1895. Very Good. $20.
The Streets of Ascalon. By Robert W. Chambers. Appleton, 1912 1st ed. Very Good plus. $40.

GIBSON, C. R. *Electricity Today: Its Work and Mysteries*. Phil., 1907 1st ed. Illus. Spotted cover, o/w VG. $75.

GIBSON, LOUIS. *Convenient Houses With 50 Plans for the Housekeeper, Architect and Housewife*. NY, Crowell, 1889. Ex-library. Light rubbing. $50.

GIBSON, RALPH. (Photographer). *The Somnambulist*. Los Angeles, 1970 1st ed. Author's 1st book. Inscribed. Near Fine. $120. NY, 1973 2nd ed. Paperbound. Good. $35.
Deja-Vu. NY, 1973. Very Good. $40.

GIBSON, WILLIAM H. *My Studio Neighbors*. Harper, 1898. Drawings by author. Very Good. $50.

GIDDINGS, J. LOUIS. *Ancient Men of the Arctic*. NY, Knopf, 1967 1st ed. Ex-library. Fine cond. $20.

GILBERT, A. C. *The Man Who Lives in Paradise*. NY, 1954 1st ed. (Toy trains). Good in dust jacket. $40.

GILBERT, ANTHONY. *Death Against the Clock*. NY, 1958 1st ed. Fine in dust jacket. $25.
The Fingerprint. NY, 1965 1st ed. Fine in DJ. $18.
Mr. Crook Lifts the Mask. NY, 1970 1st ed. F in DJ. $15.

GILBERT, J. WARREN. *The Blue and Gray A History of the Conflicts During Lee's Invasion and Battle of Gettysburg*. No place, circa 1922. Good-VG. $22.

GILBERT, MICHAEL. *He Didn't Mind Danger*. NY, 1948 1st American ed. VG in dust jacket. $35.
Death Has Deep Roots. London, 1951 1st. VG in DJ. $30.
The Crack in the Teacup. NY, 1966 1st ed. F in DJ. $25.
Game Without Rules. NY, 1967 1st. Fine in fine DJ. $45.
The Etruscan Net. London, 1969 1st ed. VG in DJ. $35.
Star of Execution. London, 1971 1st British ed. Fine in dust jacket. $75.
The Body of a Girl. London, 1972 1st ed. VG in DJ. $30.

GILBERT, PAUL T. *Bertram and His Fabulous Animals*. NY, 1937. Inscribed. Good. $22.
Bertram and His Funny Animals. Rand McNally, 1934 (1937). VG in dust jacket. $25.

GILBERT, WILLIAM S. *Bab Ballads*. London, 1904. Illus. by author. Very Good. $25. Later editions. $12-$17.
The Story of the Mikado. London, 1921 1st ed. Good in chipped dust jacket. $125.
Gilbert and Sullivan Operas and the Bab Ballads. NY, 1932. W. S. Gilbert illus. Fly leaf gone, stained. $20.
Yeoman of the Guard. London, 1979. Illus. Fine. $15.

GILBRETH, FRANK B., JR., *Cheaper by the Dozen*. Crowell, 1948. Illus. Very Good. $8.
Of Whales and Women. NY, 1956. VG in DJ. $18.

GILL, BRENDAN. *The Trouble of One House*. New York, 1950 1st ed. Good plus in torn DJ. $30.
Here at the New Yorker. Random House, 1975 1st ed. Fine in dust jacket. $12.

GILL, ERIC. *Art-Nonsense and Other Essays*. London, 1929. Very Good. $125.
Autobiography. London, 1940. Good-VG. $50.
It All Goes Together: Selected Essays. Devin-Adair, 1944. Very Good in dust jacket. $15.
Letters of Eric Gill. London, 1947 1st ed. Fine in DJ. $15.
All the Love Poems From Shakespeare. NY, 1947. One of 499 copies. Full leather. Fine. $40.

GILL, ERIC (Illustrator). *Troilus and Cressida*. By Geoffrey Chaucer. Literary Guild, 1932. Fine in DJ. $50.
The Tragedy of Hamlet. By William Shakespeare. Limited Editions Club. 1933. Rebound. Fine. $235.

GILLETTE, MRS. F. L. *The American Cook Book*. 1886, 1887, 1889. Good-VG. $40-$60.

GILLETTE, MRS. F. L. and HUGO ZIEMANN. (See *White House Cook Book*). 1887-1894. G-VG. $50-$65. 1897 edition, $30-$35. 1905 ed. $25-$30. 1909 enlarged ed. $35. 1911-1924. $20-$24.

GILPATRIC, GUY. *The Glencannon Omnibus*. NY, 1944. "Scotch and Water","Half Seas Over", and "Three Sheets in the Wind". Fine. $20.

GILPIN, LAURA (Photographer). *The Pueblos: A Camera Chronicle*. NY, 1941. G in DJ. $95. Another, NF. $200.
Temples in Yucatan: a Camera Chronicle of Chichen Itza. Hastings House, 1948. DJ torn, o/w Good. $75.

GINGRICH, ARNOLD. *The Well-Tempered Angler*. NY, 1965 1st edition. Fine. $40.
The Fishing in Print. NY, 1974. Mint in fine DJ. $25.

GINSBURG, CHRISTIAN D. *The Essenes*. London, 1968 2 vols. in one. Very Good. $25.

GIOVANNI, NIKI. *Gemini*. Indianapolis, 1971. 1st ed. Fine in clip DJ. $40. Another, inscribed. $75.
The Women and the Men. NY, 1975 1st ed. Very Good in dust jacket. $50.
Cotton Candy on a Rainy Day. NY, 1978 1st ed. Fine in dust jacket. $35.

GIRL SCOUTS. *Handbook for Girl Scouts*. A. B. Powell. 1917 1st edition. $40-$50. 1920 edition. $20-$30. 1921-1925 printings. $8-$12.
How Girls Can Help Their Country. Adapted from British version, 1913. $55-$85. 1916 revised edition, by Juliette Low. $40-$65.
Scouting For Girls. 1921 1st edition. $20-$35. 2nd-5th editions. $8-$12.
Girl Scout Handbook. 1940s. $8-$12. 1950s. $6-$10.

GISSING, GEORGE. *New Grub Street*. London, 1891 1st ed. 3 vols. Faded spines, o/w Fine. $2,800.
The Private Papers of Henry Ryecroft. Westminster, 1903 1st ed. Good-VG. $75-$175.
Veranilda: A Romance. London, 1904 1st ed. NF. $60.
Will Warburton. London, 1905 1st ed. VG. $85.

META GIVEN'S MODERN ENCYCLOPEDIA OF COOKING. 1951-1956 5th & 6th editions. G-VG. $10-$14 each.

GIPSON, FRED. *Hound Dog Man*. NY, 1949. Signed copy in Very Good condition. $50.

GLAAB, C. N. and L. H. LARSEN. *Factories in the Valley*, Neenah-Menasha, 1870-1915. Madison WI, 1969 12th ed. Very Good in dust jacket. $20.

GLASGOW, ELLEN. *The Descendants*. NY, 1897 1st ed. Published anonymously. Near Fine. $150-$200.
The Shadowy Third. NY, 1923 1st ed. VG. $30.
They Stooped to Folly. NY, 1929 1st trade ed. Near VG in good dust jacket. $45.
Vein of Iron. Harcourt, 1935 1st ed. Near Fine. $13.
In This Our Life. NY, 1941 1st ed. Fine in DJ. $40.

GLASPELL, SUSAN. *Plays*. Bos., 1920 1st ed. F in DJ. $25.
Norma Ashe. Lippincott, 1942 1st ed. VG in DJ. $45.
Lifted Masks. NY, Stokes, 1912 1st ed. Fine. $50.

GLASSCOCK, C. B. *The Big Bonanza*. Indianapolis, 1931 1st ed. Very Good. $40-$50.
Gold in Them Hills. Indianapolis, 1932. Good. $25.
A Golden Highway. Bobbs Merrill, 1934 1st ed. Very Good in dust jacket. $15.
Here's Death Valley. Bobbs-Merrill, 1940 1st ed. Very Good in poor dust jacket. $20.
Then Came Oil. 1938 1st ed. Bobbs Merrill. G-VG. $50.
Lucky Baldwin 1933. 308 pgs. VG. $35.
Motor History of America. 1945, CA, Clymer rpt. $15.

GLASSE, HANNAH. *The Art of Cookery Made Plain and Easy*. No place, 1758 6th ed. Hinges repaired. Good. $300.

GLAZIER, CAPT. WILLARD. *Three Years in the Federal Cavalry*. NY, 1870 1st ed. G-VG. $55. 2nd edition, 1874. Good-Very Good. $25.
Battles for the Union. 1883 reprint of the 1873 ed. $35. Another with damage and loose pgs. $20.
Headwaters of the Mississippi. Chicago, 1893. Good-Very Good. $20-$35.
Ocean to Ocean on Horseback. Philadelphia, 1896. $25.

GLEASON, DUNCAN. *The Islands and Ports of California*. NY, 1958. Illus. by author. Near Fine in chip DJ. $30-$40.

GLOVER, ELLYE HOWELL. *Dame Curtsey's Book of Candy Making*. McClurg, 1913. VG. $30.

GLUECK, SHELDON and ELEANOR T. GLUECK. *Unraveling Juvenile Delinquency*. NY, 1950 1st edition. Very Good. $25.

GODDEN, GEOFFREY. *The Illustrated Guide to Lowestoft Porcelain*. NY, 1969. VG in dust jacket. $60.

GODDEN, RUMER. *Chinese Puzzle*. London, 1936 1st ed. Fine in dust jacket. $50-$60.
The River. Boston, 1946 1st ed. VG in DJ. $12. London, 1946 1st ed. VG in DJ. $20.
Mooltiki: Stories and Poems From India. London, 1947 1st ed. Fine in DJ. $36.
Dolls' House. NY, 1948 1st ed. Dana Saintsbury illus. Very Good. $25.
St. Jerome and the Lion. NY, 1961 1st ed. Jean Primrose illus. Near Fine in dust jacket. $25.
Little Plum. NY, 1963 2nd printing. Jean Primrose illus. Very Good in dust jacket. $12.
The Kitchen Madonna. NY, 1967. Carol Barker illus. Very Good in dust jacket. $25.
In This House of Brede. NY, 1969 1st American ed. Fine in dust jacket. $20.

GODEY'S LADYS BOOK (See Magazine Section).

GODFROY, CLARENCE. *Miami Indian Stories*. Godfroy, 1963. Good-Very Good. $24.

GODSELL, PHILIP H. *Arctic Trader. 20 Years with Hudson Bay*. A. L. Burt, 1934 reprint. Very Good. $12.

GOETHE, JOHANN WOLFGANG VON. *The Works of*. 5 vols. illus. with wood and steel engravings. Philadelphia, Barrie, 1885. Very Good. $100-$150 set.

GOETSCHIUS, PERCY. *Counterpoint Applied*. Schirmer, 1930 reprint. Fine, no dust jacket. $13.

GOETZMANN, WILLIAM. *Exploration and Empire*. NY, 1967 2nd printing. VG plus in dust jacket. $50.

GOFFSTEIN, M. B. *Brookie and Her Lamb*. NY, 1967. Very Good in dust jacket. $13.
Two Piano Tuners. NY, 1970 1st ed. Ex-lib. Good. $7.
Laughing Latkes. NY, 1980 1st ed. Ex-lib. VG in DJ. $8.

GOGARTY, OLIVER ST. JOHN. *Mourning Became Mrs. Spendlove*. NY, 1948 1st American ed. Fine in DJ. $35.
An Offering of Swans. London, no date. Signed presentation copy. $23.

GOLD MEDAL FLOUR COOK BOOK. Washburn, Crosby Co., 1910. Covers worn. Good. $10. Various other editions, 1900-1910 in Very Good condition. $20.

GOLDBERG, ISAAC. *Tin Pan Alley*. NY, John Day Co, 1930 1st ed. VG-Fine. $40.

GOLDBERG, RUBE. *The Rube Goldberg Plan for the Postwar World*. NY, 1944 1st ed. Near Fine. $65.
Rube Goldberg to Europe. NY, 1954 1st ed. VG. $10.

GOLDEN RULE BAZAAR. *Encyclopedia of Cookery & Reliabale Recipes*. San Francisco & Portland, OR, 1892. 400 pgs., browned. Good. $25.

GOLDING, LOUIS. *Honey for the Ghost*. Dial, 1949 1st ed. Fine in dust jacket. $10.
The Glory of Elsie Silver. London, no date, 1st ed. Inscribed. Very Good in dust jacket. $25.

GOLDING, WILLIAM. *Lord of the Flies*. NY, 1955 1st American ed. Near Fine in pictorial DJ. $250-$350. London, 1954 1st ed. VG in DJ. $1,000-$1,500.
Free Fall. London, 1959 1st edition. Very Good in dust jacket. $85. Fine. $100-$150.
Spire. NY, 1964 1st American ed. VG in vg DJ. $20.
The Hot Gates. NY, 1966 1st ed. Fine in DJ. $20.
The Marathon Man. NY, 1974 1st ed. Fine in DJ. $40.

GOLDMAN, EMMA. *Anarchism & Other Essays*. NY, 1910. 30 pgs. damp spot, o/w Very Good. $50.

GOLDSMITH, ALFRED N. *Radio Telephony*. NY, 1918. Illus. Good plus. $18.

GOLDSMITH, OLIVER. *Goody Two-Shoes*. London, 1881
Facsimile of 1766 ed. Covers heavily rubbed, soiled. $40.
The Deserted Village. Harper, 1902 edition. Illus. $45.
Miscellaneous Works. Putnam reprint, 1850, 4 vols.
Good-Very Good. $30-$40.

GOLDWATER, BARRY. *People & Places*. 1967 1st ed. Near
Fine in Very Good dust jacket. $14.

GOLF FOR OCCASIONAL PLAYERS. Anon. New York,
1922. Fine. $75.

THE GOLFER'S YEARBOOK, 1930. By W. D. Richardson
& others. NY, 1930. Photos of Jones, Hogan, etc. VG. $40.

GONDOR, EMERY. *Ten Little Colored Boys*. NY, Howell,
Soskin, 1942 1st ed. VG. $187 auction.

GONE WITH THE WIND COOKBOOK. (Gift with Pebeco
toothpaste). No place, 1939. G-VG. $35. Same. No date
(1940) 47 pgs. $30.

GOOD HOUSEKEEPING HOUSEKEEPING BOOK. 1947
1st ed. McKay. G-VG in dust jacket. $10-$12.

GOOD HOUSEKEEPING BOOK OF MENUS, RECIPES,
ETC. 1962 edition. Cloth. Fair-Good. $12.

GOOD HOUSEKEEPING'S COMPLETE BOOK OF
NEEDLECRAFT. Vera P. Guild. 1959. VG. $18.

GOOD HOUSEKEEPING COOK BOOK. By Dorothy B.
Marsh. 1933-1958 editions. Good-VG. $5-$20.

GOOD HOUSEKEEPING NEEDLEWORK MANUAL.
Springfield, MA, 1905. $20.

GOODLOE, A. C. *College Girls*. NY, Scribners, 1895.
Gibson illus. Very Good. $15-$30.

GOOD WIFE'S COOK BOOK. NP, 1911. Paperbound. $40.

GOODMAN, BENNY. *Benny, King of Swing*. No place,
1979. Signed copy. Good in good DJ. $150.

GOODMAN, PAUL. *Growing Up Absurd*. NY, 1960 1st ed.
Fine in dust jacket. $25.
Utopian Essays and Practical Proposals. NY, 1962 1st
ed. Very Good in dust jacket. $28.
Making Do. NY, 1963 1st ed. Fine in DJ. $15.

GOODRICH, LLOYD. *Winslow Homer*. Whitney Museum
of Art, NY, 1944. Very Good. $48.
The Graphic Art of Winslow Homer. New York, 1968,
Paperbound. Very Good. $30.
Raphael Soyer. NY, Harry Abrams, 1972 1st ed. Ex-
library, else extremely good. $60.

GOODRICH, SAMUEL. *Winter Evening*. Boston, 1830 1st
ed. 8 hand-colored plates, tipped-in provenance, Original
boards, new leather spine. $100.
A Pictorial Geography of the World. Boston, 1847 2 vols.
14th thousand. 1,008 pgs. Illus Spine chip. $50.
History of the Indians of North & South America. NY,
1844 1st ed. Illus. Corner wear, foxing, some paint spots.
Good plus. $50.
Peter Parley's Georgraphy for Children. Hartford, 1832.
Paperback, worn, stain. $125.
The First Book of History: For Children and Youth.
Boston, 1843. Worn. Good. $75.
*The BalloonTravels of Robert Merry & His Young
Friends Over Various Countries in Europe*. NY, 1855 1st
ed. Extra-illustrated. Fiction. $50.
Peter Parley's Annual. London, 1882. Color plates. Good-
Very Good. $30.

GOODRICH and TUTTLE. *Illustrated History of the State of
Indiana*. IN, R. S. Peale, 1875 ed. 748 pgs. Good. $30.

GOODSPEED, C. E. *Anglng in America*. Boston, 1939.
Major bibliography. Spine discolored, o/w VG. $200.

GOODSPEED, E. J. *History of the Great Fires of Chicago
and the West*. NY, 1871. Scuffed. $50-$100.

GOODWIN, C. C. *The Comstock Club*. Leonard, 1891 1st ed.
Good-Very Good. $40.
The Wedge of Gold. Salt Lake, 1893. Good. $70.

GOODWIN, THOMAS S. *The Natural History of Secession*.
NY, 1864. Slightly shelfworn. $20.

GOODWIN, MAUD. *The Head of a Hundred*. Boston, 1897-
1900. J. W. Smith illus. $65-$95.

GOODWIN, WILLIAM B. *The Truth About Leif Ericsson
and The Greenland Voyages*. Bos., 1941. Worn DJ. $25.

GOODYEAR, W. A. *The Coal Mines of the Western Coast
of the United States*. San Francisco, Bancroft, 1877 1st ed.
Green cloth, gilt title. Very Good. $125

GORDIMER, NADINE. *The Soft Voice of the Serpent And
Other Stories*. NY, 1952 1st ed. Fine in vg DJ. $100.
The Lying Days. NY, 1953 1st ed. Poor DJ. $80.
A Sport of Nature. NY, 1958 1st American ed. Near Fine
in clip dust jacket. $60.
A Guest of Honour. NY, 1970 1st ed. Fine in DJ. $35.
Livingstone's Companions. NY, 1971 1st edition. Very
Good in dust jacket. $45.
The Conservationist. Viking, 1975 1st American ed. Fine
in dust jacket. $25.

GORDON, CAROLINE. *The Garden of Adonis*. NY, 1937
1st ed. Very Good, no dust jacket. $30.

The Forests of the South. NY, 1945 1st ed. Near Fine in DJ. $195. 1949 printing. Very Good in dust jacket. $70.
How to Read a Novel. NY, 1947 1st ed. VG in DJ. $40.
The Malefactors. NY, 1956 1st ed. F in near fine. DJ. $65.
The Collected Stories of Carolina Gordon. NY, 1981 1st edition. Very Good in dust jacket. $20.

GORDON, ELIZABETH. *Flower Children: The Little Cousins of Field and Garden*. Chicago, Voland, 1910. Very Good. $35-$55.
Bird Children. Volland 1912, M.T. Ross illus. $45-$75. 1939 revised ed. Very Good. $20.
Some Smiles. A Little Book of Limericks. 1911 1st ed. M. T. Ross illus. $45-$75.
Mother Earth's Children. NY, 1914. Illus. Good. $20.
Wild Flower Children. Volland, 1918 17th ed. Pictorial boards. Very Good. $60.
The Turned-Into's. Volland, 1920. Later edition. Janet L. Scott illus. VG plus. $30.
Really So Stories. Volland, 1924 1st ed. John Rae illus. Near Very Good. $20-$30.
Buddy Jim. Wise Parslow, 1935. John Rae illus. $20-$30.

GORDON, GEN. J. B. *Reminiscences of the Civil War*. New York, 1904. Scuffed, poor. $35.

GOULD, JOHN. *Birds of Europe*. London, 1966. 160 color plates. Fine. $45.
Birds of Asia. London, 1969. Fine in dust jacket. $85.

GORES, JOE. *A Time of Predators*. NY, 1969 1st ed. Author's 1st book. Near Fine in vg DJ. $75-$100.
Dead Skip. NY, 1972 1st ed. Near Fine in DJ. $50.
Final Notice. London, 1974 1st English ed. VG in DJ. $25.
Gone, No Forwarding. NY, 1978 1st ed. VG in DJ. $25.

GOREY, EDWARD. *The Unstrung Harp*. NY, 1953 1st ed. Author's 1st book. NF in VG DJ. $200. Illus. by author. Very Good in dust jacket. $125.
The Listing Attic. NY, 1954 1st ed. VG in DJ. $50.
The Doubtful Guest. Garden City, 1957 1st edition. Illus. by author. Very Good in dust jacket. $60.
The West Wing. NY, 1963 1st ed. Illus. by author. Poor backstrip. Good. $24.
The Utter Zoo Alphabet. NY, 1967 1st edition. Illus. by author. VG in dust jacket. $25.
The Jumblies. NY, 1968. Illus. by author. VG in DJ. $40.
The Awdrey-Gore Legacy. NY, 1972. Inscribed by author. Very Fine in near fine dust jacket. $55.

GOULD, E. W. *Fifty Years on the Mississippi*. St. Louis, Nixon-Jones, 1889 1st ed. VG. $350.

GOULD, MARY E. *Early American Woodenware and Other Kitchen Utensils*. No place (MA), 1942 1st ed. Fine. $45.
The Early American House: Household Life in America, 1620-1850. Tuttle, 1965 Revised edition. VG in DJ. $40.

GOULD, ROBERT FREKE. *History of Free Masonry*. London, 1884-1887 3 vols. Vol. 2 lacks spine cover. Each vol. has 500 plus pgs. Leather bound, gold embossing. $150. 1903 History in one vol. $40.

GOURMET'S OLD VIENNA COOK BOOK. Langseth-Christensen. 2nd printing, 1964. Good-VG. $20.

GOVER, ROBERT. *The 100 Dollar Misunderstanding*. NY, 1962 1st ed. VG to Near Fine in DJ. $25-$45.
Here Goes Kitten. Grove, 1964 1st ed. Fine in DJ. $15.
The Maniac Responsible. Grove, 1963 1st ed. Fine in dust jacket. $15.
Poorboy at the Party. NY, 1966 1st ed. Fine in DJ. $15.

GOWER, RONALD. *Last Days of Marie Antoinette*. London, 1885. Extra-illus. with over 75 engravings, etchings, color plates. Fine. $250.

GOWLAND, PETER. *How to Photograph Women*. Crown, 1953 1st ed. 142 pgs. Very Good. $7.

GOYEN, WILLIAM. *House of Breath*. NY, 1950 1st ed. Author's 1st book. Near Fine in vg DJ. $100.
Come the Restorer. NY, 1974 1st ed. VG in DJ. $15.
In a Further Country. NY, 1955 1st ed. Inscribed. VG in dust jacket. $150.
The Collected Stories of William Goyen. NY, 1975. Advance review copy. Inscribed. Near Fine in DJ. $150.

GRAHAM, FRANK. *A Quiet Hero (Lou Gehrig)*. NY, 1942 1st ed. Very Good. $28.
The New York Yankees. An Informal History. NY, 1943 1st ed. Illus. G in DJ. $28. Revised and expanded edition, Putnam, 1958. Fine in dust jacket. $50.

GRAHAM, G. *Outlaws: Thrilling Accounts of Heroic Animals*. Privately printed, Oklahoma, 1939 2nd ed. enlarged. Signed. $48.

GRAHAM, HARVEY. *The Story of Surgery*. NY, 1939. Good. $10. Very Good. $16. Fine. $45.

GRAHAM, COLONEL W. A. *The Custer Myth*. Stackpole, 1953. Good in DJ. $30. VG to NF in DJ. $75-$95.

GRAHAM, TOM (Sinclair Lewis). *Hike and the Airplane*. Stokes, NY, 1912 1st ed. Author's 1st book. Art Hitchins illus. Repaired pages o/w Good Plus. $2,200-$3,000.

GRAHAME, KENNETH. *The Wind in The Willows*. London, 1908 1st ed. $2,000 and up. NY, 1st Amer. ed. $75-$100. Scribner's, 1924 ed. Nancy Barnhart illus, blue cloth. Ex-library. VG. $40-$70. 1933 Scribner's reprint. VG in DJ. $30. 1940 Limited Edition by Heritage Press. $50 up. 1966 ed. World Pub. F. $35-$65. NY, Ltd. Eds. Club, 1940. 1 of 2,020 signed by Bruce Rogers. Fine in slipcase. $1,000.

Dream Days. NY, London 1899. Maxfield Parrish illus. G-VG. $45-$75. Another, London, 1930. Ernest H. Shepard illus. One of 275 copies. Signed by author and illustrator. Very Good. $300.

GRAMATKY, HARDIE. *Hercules.* NY, 1940 1st ed. G. $20.
Homer and the Circus Train. NY, 1957 3rd printing. Signed. Very Good. $25.

GRAND DIPLOME COOKING COURSE. Danbury Press, 1972, 20 volumes. Very Good. $50.

GRANT, GORDON. *Greasey Luck: A Whaling Sketchbook.* NY, 1932. Illus. signed by author. Good. $35.
Old Man & Other Colonel Weatherford Stories. Derrydale Press, 1934. One of 1,150. Good plus. $45.
Life and Adventures of John Nicol, Mariner. NY, 1936. Farrar. Good-VG. $40-$50.

GRANT, JESSE R. *The Days of My Father. General Grant.* NY, London, 1925 1st ed. Good. $30.

GRANT, MAXWELL. *The Shadow Laughs.* Street-Smith, 1931 1st ed. Stain & scuff, o/w Very Good. $115.

GRANT, ULYSSES S. *Personal Memoirs of U. S. Grant.* NY, 1885-1886 1st d. 2 vols. Rubbing, scuffing, endpaper missing. VG. $85. Fine. $150. Fair set, taped spines. $40. Very good set in green cloth. $65. Scuffed covers, else VG. $60-$100 at auction.

GRAPHIC GRAFLEX PHOTOGRAPHY. Morgan & Lester, 1947 8th ed. 443 pgs. Fine, No dust jacket. $35.

GRASS, GUNTER. *The Tin Drum.* NY, 1962 1st American ed. Near VG in fair dust jacket. $35.

GRAU, SHIRLEY ANN. *The Black Prince and Other Stories.* NY, 1955 1st ed. Auth's 1st book. VG in DJ. $75.
The Hard Blue. NY, 1958 1st. VG in good plus DJ. $40.
Keepers of the House. NY, Knopf, 1964 1st ed. F. $35.

GRAUMONT & HANSEL. *Encyclopedia of Knots and Fancy Rope Work.* Cornell, 1958 4th ed. VG in DJ. $18.

GRAVES, JOHN WOODCOCK. *John Peel: The Famous Cumberland Hunting Song.* NY, Derrydale Press, 1932. Robert Ball illus. One of 950 copies. VG. $80.

GRAVES, RALPH H. *Triumph of an Idea, The Story of Henry Ford.* Doubleday Doran, 1935 revised ed. Good-Very Good. $12.

GRAVES, ROBERT. *Proceed, Sergeant Lamb.* London, 1941 1st ed. Near Fine in vg dust jacket. $150.
Hercules, My Shipmate. New York, 1945 1st American edition. Very Good in dust jacket. $35.

King Jesus. NY, 1946 1st American ed. VG in DJ. $40.
The White Goddess. NY, 1948 1st ed. Fine in chip DJ. $75.
The Islands of Unwisdom. NY, 1949 1st ed. VG in chip dust jacket. $20.
Watch the Northwind Rise. NY, 1949 1st ed. VG in chip dust jacket. Signed. $40.
Homer's Daughters. London, 1955 1st ed. VG in DJ. $60.
They Hanged My Saintly Billy. NY, 1957 1st American ed. Very Good in good dust jacket. $25.
Man Does, Woman Is. NY, 1964 1st American edition. Very Good in dust jacket. $30.
Collected Short Stories. NY, 1964 1st. NF in DJ. $35.

GRAVES, RICHARD. *Oklahoma Outlaws: A Graphic History.* Frontier, 1968 2nd printing. Fine, paperbound. $30.

GRAY, ASA. *A Manual of Botany of the Northern United States.* Boston, 1848 1st ed. Very Good. $220.
How Plants Grow. NY, 1858 1st ed. Cover soiled, edges worn. Good plus. $85.
Elements of Botany for Beginners. 1887 Revised ed. Good-VG. $30.

GRAY, HENRY. *Anatomy of the Human Body.* Lea-Febige, 1936 23rd edition. Fine in simulated green leather. $17.
Anatomy, Descriptive and Surgical. 1862, 2nd American edition. $75-$125.

GRAY, JAMES. *The Illinois.* Rivers of America Series. NY, 1940 1st ed. No dust jacket. $20.
Pine, Stream & Prairie. NY, 1945 1st ed. NF in DJ. $15.

GRAY, MONROE, ARTLEY & ARBUTHNOT. *The New Fun with Dick & Jane.* S. Foresman, 1956. Fine. $20. Scott, 1940-47 editions. $30-$50.

GRAY, THOMAS. *Elegy in a Country Churchyard.* First published in London in 1751. 1884 ed. Estes & Lauriat. VG. $24. Several limited editions were published 1900-1931. They average $50 in very good condition. More if signed by illustrator. Dutton, NY, 1931. John Vassos, illus. In chipped DJ. $50. Signed. $150. Limited Editions Club, 1938. Agnes Parker illus. Fine in slipcase. $82 auction.

GRAY, WOOD. *The Hidden Civil War, the Story of the Copperheads.* Viking, 1942 1st ed. VG. $35.

THE GREAT AMERICAN WRITERS' COOKBOOK. Oxford, MS, 1981. Recipes from Norman Mailer, William Faulkner, James Dickey, etc. Comb binding. As new. $35.

GREELEY, HORACE. *Hints Toward Reform.* NY, 1850. Presentation copy. Fading, spots. $350. Trade copy. $35.
The American Conflict: A History of the Great Rebellion. Hartford, 1864-1866 2 vols. Good-VG. $40-$50.
Recollections of a Busy Life. No place, 1869 2nd. G-VG. $20-$30. 1868 1st ed., NY. Original cloth cover. NF. $85.

GREELEY, HORACE and OTHERS. *The Great Industries of the United States*. Hartford CT, 1872. 1,304 pgs. Nearly 500 illus. Good. $50-$75. Very Good. $100-$125.

GREELY, ADOLPHUS. *Three Years of Arctic Service*. NY, 1886 1st ed. 2 vols. Light foxing, shelf wear. $150-$250.
Handbook of Arctic Discoveries. No place, 1897. $10.
Handbook of Alaska. NY, 1909. Fine. $30. G. $17-$25.
Handbook of Polar Discoveries. 1910 5th ed. VG. $20.
The Polar Regions in the Twentieth Century. Boston, 1928 1st ed. Poor DJ. $85. Same, taped map, no DJ. $40.

GREEN, ANNA KATHARINE. *The Circular Study*. NY, 1900 1st ed. Scuffed, o/w VG. $45.
The Filigree Ball. Bobbs-Merrill 1903 1st ed., 1st issue. C. M. Relyea illus. Near Fine. $40. Inscribed by author. $160.
The Woman in the Alcove. Bobbs-Merrill, 1906 1st ed. Arthur I. Keller illus. Near VG. $25. Inscribed. $170.
The Mayor's Wife. Indianapolis, 1907 1st ed. Alice B. Stephens illus. Good-VG. $35.

GREEN, BEN. *Biography of the Tennessee Walking Horse*. Nashville TN, 1960. Very Good. $60.
Some More Horse Tradin'. No place, 1972 1st ed. One of 350 copies. VG in slipcase, $150. Another, Fine. $300. Trade edition. Signed. Fine in dust jacket. $60.

GREEN, FITZHUGH. *Our Naval Heritage*. Century, 1925 1st ed. Very Good. $25.
Dick Byrd: Air Explorer. NY, 1928. G-VG. $10-$15.
The Film Finds Its Tongue. Putnam's, 1929. VG. $75.

GREEN, HENRY. *Living*. NY, 1929. Near VG. $100.
Back. London, 1946 1st ed. VG in clipped DJ. $100.
Nothing. NY, 1950 1st Amer. ed. VG to F in DJ. $25-$45.

GREEN, JONATHAN. *An Exposure of the Arts and Miseries of Gambling*. Cincinnati, 1843 1st ed. (1st Book on gambling publilshed in U. S.) Very Good. $1,000.
Gambler's Tricks With Cards: Exposed and Explained. 1850. 114 pgs. Very Fine. $900.

THE GREEN MOUNTAIN BOYS. (Daniel Pierce Thompson). 2 vols. 1839 1st ed., first state. $600-$800. Boston, 1856 rev. ed. 2 vols in one. Poor-Good. $40-$60.

GREEN, WILLIAM. *Augsburg Eagle: Story of the Messerschmidt*. Garden City, 1971. VG in DJ. $36.

GREENAWAY, KATE. *Under the Window*. London, 1878 1st edition, 1st issue. $135-$225. Later printing. Warne & Co. No date. $75. Another, Routledge. Circa 1878. $150.
Marigold Garden. London, 1885 1st ed. $125-$250. NY, 1888 edition. $75.
Language of Flowers. London, George Routledge & Sons, 1884 1st ed. Orig. olive green pictorial boards. VG. $60 auction. Dealers asking $120-$175.

Kate Greenaway's Alphabet. George Routledge & Sons, no date (1885). Very Good. $125-$195.
Almanacks for 1883 to 1927. George Routledge & Sons, London. 12 to 24 pgs. ea. $95-$150 each.
Kate Greenaway Pictures. London, 1921. 20 plates with tissue covers. Very Good. $150-$200. Fine. $250-$300.
Mother Goose. London, no date, circa 1900. $65-$95. Same, NY, McLoughlin, circa 1882. $125-$150.

GREENAWAY, KATE (Illustrator). *Little Ann and Other Poems*. By Jane and Anna Taylor. London, 1880s 1st ed. VG. $150. 2nd ed., circa 1909. London, Frederic Warne. Rubbed, soiled. Good. $60-$80.
The Queen of Pirate Isle. By Bret Harte. Boston, 1887 1st U.S. ed. Shelf wear, o/w NF. $125-$150. Same, London, circa 1886. Very Good to Near Fine. $175. 1931 edition. VG. $50. 1955 edition. Very Good. $35.
The Pied Piper of Hamelin. By Robert Browning. London, No date. Near Fine. $275. Warne. $95-$150.

GREENBAUM, FLORENCE K. *The International Jewish Cook Book*. New York, 1919 2nd ed. Good-VG. $30.

GREENE, LT. COL. CHARLES S. *Thrilling Stories of the Great Rebellion*. Philadelphia, 1864. Ex-lib. G. $15-$25.

GREENE, DAVID L. and DICK MARTIN. *The Oz Scrapbook*. NY, 1977 1st ed. 2nd printing. Fine in fine dust jacket. $40-$75.

GREENE, GRAHAME. *The Man Within*. London, 1929 1st ed. Author's 1st book. VG in DJ. $1,350. Same, Doubleday, VG in dust jacket. $600. 1947 ed. in dust jacket. $30.
Stamboul Train. London, 1932 1st ed. Near VG. $30. Another, lightly foxed. $100.
Journey Without Maps. Garden City, 1936 1st ed. VG in chipped dust jacket. $45.
The End of the Affair. London, 1951 1st British ed. Good in DJ. $50. Another, Fine in clipped DJ. $125.
Loser Takes All. London, 1955 1st ed. NF in DJ. $25. 1957 1st U.S. edition. Near Fine. $35.
The Little Train. London, Lee & Shepard, 1958 1st ed. Dorothy Craigie illus. Fine and very scarce. $247 auction.
The Potting Shed. NY, 1957 1st ed. Fine in DJ. $69-$125.
The Comedians. New York, 1966 1st American edition. Very Good in dust jacket. $35.
The Honorary Consul. London, 1973 1st ed. Fine in very good dust jacket. $40.
The Little Steamroller. NY, 1974 1st American ed. Edward Ardizzone illus. Fine in dust jacket. $75.

GREENE, MAX. *The Kansas Region Forest, Prairie, Desert, Mountain, Vale, and River*. New York, Fowler & Wells, 1856 1st ed. Good-VG. $200-$400.

GREENEWALT, CRAWFORD. *Hummingbirds*. Garden City, 1960. 69 plates. Light foxing, o/w Very Good. $80.

GREENHOW, ROBERT. *The History of Oregon and California and Other Territories on the Northwest Coast*. Boston, Little & Brown, 1844 enlarged edition. Folding map. Rebound in 3/4 calf. $200 auction.

GREENSLET, FERRIS. *The Lowells and Their Seven Worlds*. Boston, 1946 1st ed. VG in good DJ. $23.

GREENWALT, EMMET. *California Utopia: Point Loma, 1897-1942*. San Diego, 1974. VG in DJ. $15.

GREENWOOD, GRACE. *Victoria, Queen of England*. NY, Alden, 1884. Good-VG. $20.

GREER, CARLOTTA. *Foods and Home Making*. Bos. 1928. A typical home economics textbook of the period. $8-$15.

GREER, WILLIAM R. *Gems of American Architecture*. A spoof on outhouse designs. St. Paul, MN, 1935. G-VG. $15.

GREEY, EDWARD. *Young Americans in Japan, or the Adventures of Jewett Family*. Boston, 1883. Illus. G. $75.

GREGORIETTI, GUIDO. *Jewelry Through the Ages*. NY, no date. Illus. Very Good in dust jacket. $75.

GREGORY, ANNIE R. *Woman's Favorite Cook Book*. "Three Volumes in One". Circa 1902. Covers worn and detached. Poor. $20.

GRENFELL, WILFRED T. *Northern Neighbors: Stories of The Labrador People*. Boston, 1906 4th ed., Author ink sketch on endpaper. Signed. $65.
Adrift on an Ice Pan. NY, 1909 1st ed. VG. $10.
Labrador Days. NY, 1932 1st ed. Very Good. $9.

GREGORY, LADY. *Irish Folk History Plays*. NY, 1912 1st American ed. Near Very Good. $40.

GRESHAM, WILLIAM LINDSAY. *Nightmare Alley*. NY, 1946 1st ed. Author's 1st book. VG-NF in DJ. $40-$70.
Monster Midway. NY, 1953 1st Amer. ed. VG in DJ. $25.

GREY, ZANE. *The Spirit of the West*. A. L. Burt, 1906. Illus. Good. $50.
The Young Forester. NY, 1910 1st ed. Light foxing. $160.
Desert Gold. Photoplay edition, 1913. G&D. $6-$12.
The Last of the Plainsmen. 1911 2nd ed., G&D. $6-$12.
The Spirit of the Border. 1906. A. L. Burt. $6-$12. Grosset & Dunlap 1941 reprint. Fine in DJ. $10.
The Young Lion Hunter. 1911, G&D. $6-$12.
The Shortstop. NY, 1914 4th ed. VG in DJ. $30.
Tales of Fishes. NY, 1919 1st ed. Photo cover, color frontis. Very Good. $50-$150.
Tappan's Burro. NY, Harper, 1923 1st ed. F in DJ. $100.
Tales of Lonely Trails. NY, Harper, 1922 1st ed. VG. $100-$150. Same, later printing. Good. $45.

Wanderer of the Wasteland. New York, Harper, 1923 1st edition. Fine in fine dust jacket. $200-$300. Very Good, no dust jacket. $30.
Tales of Southern Rivers. NY, 1924 1st ed. Good-Very Good. $120-$150.
To the Last Man. Harper, 1922. Spaulding illus. Good, no dust jacket. $12.
The Thundering Herd. NY, 1925 1st. Good in DJ. $200.
The Vanishing American. NY, 1925 1st ed. Very Good in dust jacket. $35-$75.
Tales of Fishing Virgin Seas. No place, 1925 1st ed. Spine bumped, o/w VG. $125.
Tales of Anglers' El Dorado. NY, 1926 1st ed. VG. $135.
Under the Tonto Rim. NY, Harper, 1926 1st std.. G. $35.
Forlorn River. Grosset & Dunlap, 1927. Fine. $13.
Wild Horse Mesa. NY, 1928 1st ed. Fine. $30.
Fighting Caravans. NY, 1929 1st ed. Near Fine in mended dust jacket. $175.
The Shepherd of Guadaloupe. NY, 1930 1st ed. VG. $33.
Tales of Tahitian Waters. NY, 1931 1st ed. Rebound, repaired tape. $225. Another, bumped corners. $400.
Western Union. NY, 1939, G & D. VG. $25-$35.
30,000 On the Hoof. NY, 1940 1st ed. Fine, no DJ. $35. Near Fine in DJ. $175. Good. Signed. $300.
The Drift Fence . Grosset & Dunlap, around 1940. Very Good in dust jacket. $28.
Desert Gold. Grosset & Dunlap, 1941 reprint. Fine in DJ. $10. 1913 1st ed. Very Good. $45.
The Zane Grey Omnibus. NY, Lndon, 1943 1st. F. $125.
The Deer Stalker. NY, 1949. Good in DJ. $55.
Lost Pueblo. NY, 1954 1st ed. Good in DJ. $60.
Stranger From Tonto. NY, 1956 1st ed. Good in DJ. $60.
The Arizona Clan. NY, 1958 1st ed. Good in DJ. $60.
Horse Heaven Hill. NY, 1959 1st ed. Good in DJ. $55.
The Ranger & Other Stories. NY, 1960 1st ed. Very Good in dust jacket. $55.
The Zane Grey Cookbook. 1976, Prentice Hall 1st ed. Near Fine. $25-$75.
The Reef Girl. No place, 1977 1st ed. Grey's last novel. As new in as new DJ. $65.
Collected Works. published by Walter Black. 54 vols. No date. Mint in packing boxes. $485.
G & D, reprints of many Grey novels, VG. $13 each.

GREY, ZANE (In Magazines). *The Country Gentlemen*. May 4, 1920. Nonfiction/fishing/photos. $23.
The Country Gentlemen. Nov 13, 1920. Beginning of novel. $13.
American Magazine. July, 1924. Memoir/photos. $23.
American Magazine. Nov, 1924. Nonfiction. $23.
American Magazine. Apr, 1926. Nonfiction/fishing. $23.
American Magazine. Nov, 1926, Feb-May, 1927. Novel. $14 each of five parts.
American. April-Oct, 1929. "The Drift Fence, serial novel. Seven issues. $120.
American. Aug, 1931-Feb, 1932. "West of thePecos", serial novel. Seven issues. $120.

GRIFFIN. *Japanese Food and Cooking*. Tuttle, 1963 14th ed. Very Good in dust jacket. $10-$12.

GRIMM, JACOB and WILHELM. *Grimm's Fairy Tales* has gone through many editions since its 1812-15 German printing. The 1909 English translation by Mrs. E. Lucas with color illustrations by Rackham is worth $300-$500 in the 1st trade ed. Limited editions signed by Rackham sell for over $1000. Other artists of note are Johnny Gruelle, 1914. $100-$175. E. Abbott, $50 and up. Andree, $50 and up. Grosset & Dunlap, 1943 reprint. Very Good. $18.
Hansel and Gretel. Reilly, 1908, Neill illus. $40-$75. Doran, no date. $100. Doubleday, 1923, Rackham illus. $150. Knopf, 1944, Chappell illus. $45. NY, 1925, Nielsen illus. Red cloth covers. 250-$350. 1925 reprint. $95-$150.
Household Stories. No date, Am. Pub. (1894) W. Crane illus. $50-$100. Same Macmillan, 1882. $125-$200. 1914 edition. $50-$75.
Fairy Tales of Bros. Grimm. Lippincott, no date. Rackham illus. $55-$95. Same, Doubleday, 1909. $250-$400.
The Golden Bird. Macmillan, 1962. Sandro Nardini illus. Includes five additional stories. Very Good. $38.
The Juniper Tree & Other Tales. NY, 1973, Farrar, Straus & Giroux. 2 vols. in slipcase. $50-$100.

GRIMSHAW. *Locomotive Catechism*. 1916 ed. VG. $50.

GRIMSLEY, WILL. *Golf, Its History, People and Events*. NJ, 1966. 2nd printing. VG in glassined DJ. $50.

GRINNELL, GEORGE. *The Story of the Indian*. Appleton, 1895 1st ed. Illus. Good. $75.
(with Theodore Roosevelt) *Trail and Campfire*. Boone & Crockett, 1897 1st ed. Near Fine. $2,003.
American Big Game. NY, 1904 1st ed. Very Good. $135.
American Game Bird Shooting. New York, 1910 1st ed. Fine. $50-$95.
Fighting Cheyennes. NY, Scribner's, 1915 1st ed., 11 maps, 431 pgs. Orig. cloth, shelfworn. $110.
Trials of the Pathfinders. Scribner's, 1911 1st ed. G. $50.
Indians of Today. NY, 1911 Revised ed. Fine. $75.
American Duck Shooting. NY, 1918. Good. $50.
When Buffalo Ran. Yale University, 1920. Good. $40.
Two Great Scouts and Their Pawnee Battalion. Cleveland, 1928. Fine. $175.

GRINNELL, JOSEPH. *Gold Hunting in Alaska*. David Cook, 1901 1st ed. VG in marbled boards. $25-$50. NF. $75.

GRINNELL, JOSEPH with DIXON and LINSDALE. *Fur-Bearing Mammals of California Their Natural History*. University of Calif. Press, 1937 1st ed. 2 vols. in dust jackets. $120 auction.

GRISWOLD, LESTER. *HandiCraft - Simplified Procedure and Projects*. (American Indian). Griswold, 1942 1st ed. Very Good. $20. 8th edition, same year. Very Good. $12.

GROSLIER, BERNARD. *The Art of Indochina*. NY, 1962. 60 tipped-in color plates. VG in dust jacket. $35.

GROEBER, KARL. *Children's Toys of Bygone Day*. NY, 1928. Near Fine in dust jacket. $150.

GROSS, MILT. *Dunt Esk*. NY, 1927. Very Good. $15.
Dear Dollink. NY, 1945 3rd printing. VG in DJ.$15.
Yankee Doodles. House of Kent, 1948 1st ed. Very Good in dust jacket. $40.

GROSSINGER, J. *The Art of JewishCooking*. NY, 1958 5th prntng. Author was Catskill resort hostess. VG in DJ. $15.

GROSVENOR, GILBERT and A. WETMORE. *The Book of Birds*. National Geographic Society, 1937 2 vols, Exterior fair, contents good. $75.

GROSZ, GEORGE. *A Little Yes and a Big No*. Dial, NY, 1946 1st ed. Autobiography, illus. by author. VG in good dust jacket. $60-$75 .
Ecce Homo. NY, 1966 2nd printing. Henry Miller introduction. Many plates. VG to Fine in DJ. $25-$45.

GROSZ, GEORGE (Illustrator). *The Voice of the City*. By O. Henry. Limited Editions Club, NY, 1935. One of 1,540 signed. Fine in slipcase. $210.
1,001 Afternoons in New York. By Ben Hecht. Viking, 1941. Very Good plus in dust jacket. $75.
The Divine Comedy. By Dante. Illustrated Modern Library, 1944. Good. $25.

GROUT, A. J. *Mosses With Hand-Lens & Microscope*. NY, 1903, published by author. 1st ed. of a classic text. $25.

GROVE, EULALIE. *The Sunbonnet Babies Primer*. Chicago, 1902. Covers worn, Good. $57.
Mother Goose. Volland, 1915 1st ed. Full-page color illus by F. Richardson. Very Good. $50-$65.

GROVE'S DICTIONARY OF MUSIC. Five volumes amd American supplement. 3rd edition. 1935. Very Good. $70. 1911 2nd edition. $75.

GRUBER, FRANK. *Silver Jackass*. Reynal, 1941 1st ed. Fine in Fine dust jacket. $85.
The Honest Dealer. New York, 1947 1st edition. Fine in good dust jacket. $35.
Tales of Wells Fargo. NY, 1958. Paper. Near Fine. $20.

GRUBER, FRANK (In Magazines). *Black Mask*. Oct 1938, Feb 1939 & March 1939. Story in each issue. $50-$75 ea.

GRUELLE, JOHNNY. *Raggedy Ann Stories*. Volland, 1920 1st ed. in DJ. $100-$175. Reprint same date. $75.
Friendly Fairies. Chicago, Donohue, 1919. Reprint in dust jacket. $80. Voland, 1919 original. $150.

Raggedy Ann and Andy and the Camel With the Wrinkled Knees. Volland, 1924. Orig. ed. in DJ. $100-$125. Reprint, same date. $30-$50 (More in DJ).

Raggedy Andy's Number Book. Chicago, 1924. $30-$50.

Raggedy Ann's Wishing Pebble. Donohue, 1925. Illus. by author. $25-$50 Same, later edition, Volland. $50-$75.

Paper Dragon. Volland, 1926. Illus. by author. VG. $90.

Orphant Annie Story Book. Bobbs-Merrill, 1921 1st ed. Illus. by author. Very Good. $50. In dust jacket. $100.

Wooden Willie. Voland, 1927. Illus. by author. Contains a rag doll as black faced mammy. $50. In DJ. $75-$100.

Raggedy Ann's Magical Wishes. Volland, 1928 1st ed. in DJ. $75-$150. Donohue, reprint, same date. $45.

The Cherry Scarecrow. Volland, 1929 1st ed. in DJ. $75-$100. Donohue reprint, same date. $30-$50 in DJ.

Johnny Gruelle's Golden Book. Chicago, No date. Extremities worn. $35. VG. $80.

Raggedy Ann in the Deep Deep Woods. Voland, around 1930. Covers worn, mended. $25. 1st ed. $100 up.

Raggedy Ann's Lucky Pennies. Donohue, 1932. Corners bumped. $35. Volland, 1932 1st ed. in DJ. $100 up.

Raggedy Ann and the Golden Butterfly. NY, 1940. Illus. by author. Good plus in heavily chip DJ. $85.

Raggedy Ann and Andy and the Nice Fat Policeman. NY, 1942, Johnny Gruelle Co. Very Good in DJ. $45. Another in poor dust jacket. $25.

Raggedy Ann Stories. 1947 ed., Johnny Gruelle, NY. Torn DJ. $25-$40. Bobbs-Merrill, 1960-1961 ed. VG. $10-$14.

Raggedy Ann's Merriest Christmas. Wonder Books, 1952 ed. Very Good. $10.

Raggedy Ann and Andy: The Wrinkled Knees. Bobbs Merrill, 1960. Very Good. $7.

Raggedy Ann and the Happy Meadow. Bobbs-Merrill, 1961. Very Good. $10.

Raggedy Ann and the Golden Ring. Bobbs-Merrill, 1961 reprint. Very Good. $10.

GRUSON, EDWARD. *Word for Birds: Lexicon of North American Birds*. Quadrangle, 1972 1st ed. Illus. Fine in dust jacket. $14.

GUERNDALE, R. *Draw Poker Without a Master*. 1889. Fine. $250 auction.

GUEST, EDGAR. *All That Matters*. Reilly, 1922. Fine. $10.
Over Here, War Time Rhymes. 1918 1st ed. Fine. $10.
Friends. Chicago, 1926. Fine. $8.
The Passing Throng. Reilly & Lee, 1923 1st ed. VG, signed by author. $18.
A Heap O' Livin. Reilly, 1916 1st ed. VG. $10.
Harbor Lights of Home. Reilly, 1928 1st ed. VF. $10.
Collected Verse of Edgar Guest. Reilly & Lee, 1938 4th ed. Signed by Guest. Very Good. $24.

GUEST, JUDITH. *Ordinary People*. NY, 1976 1st ed. Author's 1st book. NF in DJ. $25. Another, VG in DJ. $13.

GUEVARA, CHE. *Che Guevara on Guerilla Warfare*. 1961, Praeger, 1st ed. Very Good. $8-$10.

GULD, VERA P. *Goodhousekeeping's Complete Book of Needlecraft*. 1959. Very Good. $18.

GUILES, FRED L. *Norma Jean*. No place, 1969. Very Good in dust jacket. $11.

GULICK, BILL. *Snake River Country*. Caxton, 1971 2nd ed. Very Good in dust jacket. $25.

GULLY, JAMES M. *The Water Cure in Chronic Disease*. NY, 1849 1st American ed. Foxed, worn. $35.

GUNSTON, BILL. *Classic Aircraft Bombers*. Grosset & Dunlap, 1978. Fine in fine dust jacket. $25.

GUNN, DOUGLAS. *Picturesque San Diego, Historical and Descriptive Notes*. Chicago, Knight, 1887. 98 pgs. & 72 plates. Rebacked. $175.

GUNN, JOHN C. *Dunn's Domestic Medicine and Poor Man's Friend*. 1837 9th edition. $60 and up, according to condition of leather binding.
Gunn's New Domestic Physician or Home Book of Health. 1861 and later editions. $40 and up.

GUNN, THOM. *Fighting Terms*. Fantasy Press, 1954 1st ed. Inscribed. Very Good. $20.
The Sense of Movement. University of Chicago, 1959 1st ed. Fine in vg dust jacket. $125.
Jack Straw's Castle and Other Poems. NY, 1976 1st ed. Fine in dust jacket. $25.

GUNNISON, J. W. *The Mormons, or Latter Day Saints*. 1852 1st ed. VG. $150-$200. Philadelphia, 1856. Text foxed, worn covers. Good plus. $70.

GUNTHER, JOHN. *The Red Pavilion*. NY, 1926 1st ed. Author's 1st book. Near Fine. $50.

GUPTILL, ARTHUR. *Norman Rockwell, Illustrator*. New York, 1971 Reissue of 1946 1st edition. Fine in fine dust jacket. $30 8th printing, 1975. Very Good in torn dust jacket. $12.

GUSTE, ROY F. *Antoine's Restaurant*. Cookbook and history. Carbery-Guste, 1978 1st edition. Very Good in dust jacket. $25.

GUTHEIM, FREDERICK. *The Potomac*. Rivers of America Series. New York, 1949 1st edition, Rinehart. Very Good, no dust jacket. $20.

GUYER, JAMES. *Pioneer Life in West Texas*. Brownwood, 1938. Red cloth, 185 pgs. Fine. $75.

H

HABBERTON, JOHN. *Some Folks.* NY, 1877 1st ed. Illus. Near Very Good. $25.
A Romance of California Life. No place, 1880. VG. $40.
The Jericho Road. Chicago, 1887. Good. $15.
Helen's Babies. A.L. Hurst, 1876. VG. $23. 1920 reprint of 1876 1st edition. Very Good. $18-$20.

HABENSTEIN, ROBERT and W. M. LAMERS. *Funeral Customs the World Over.* Milwaukee, 1960. Fine in chip dust jacket. $95.

HABERLY, LOYD. *Pursuit of the Horizon: A Life of George Catlin.* NY, 1948 1st ed. 17 plates. Near Fine in slightly worn DJ. $50. Another in VG condition with portions of dust jacket pasted down. $25.

HABSBURG-LOTHERINGEN. G. VON and A. VON SOLODKOFF. *Faberge, Court Jeweler to the Tsars.* NY, 1979. Illus. Good-VG in dust jacket. $50.

HACKWOOD, FREDERICK. *Good Cheer* (food and drink). London, 1911. Good. $25.

HADEN, CHARLES T. *A Medical Guide for the Use of Families.* London, 1832 2 volumes in one, 2nd edition. Good-VG. $150.

HADER, BERTHA and ELMER. *The Old Woman and the Crooked Sixpence.* NY, 1928 1st ed. Illus. by authors. Near Very Good. $35.
Midget and Bridget. NY, 1934 1st ed. Illus. by authors. Small end paper spots. $30.
Billy Butter. New York, 1936 1st edition. Illustrated by authors. Very Good. $30.

HAEBERLE, ARMINIUS T. *Old Pewter.* Boston, 1931. VG in chipped dust jacket. $40-$90.

HAFEN, LEROY. *The Overland Mail 1849-1869.* Clark, 1926 1st ed. Illus. Very Good. $115.
Broken Hand: The Life of Thomas Fitzpatrick: Mountain Man, Guide and Indian Agent. Denver, 1931 1st ed. Fine. $350.
Ruxton of the Rockies. University of Oklahoma, 1950 1st edition. Fine in fine dust jacket. $45.
Handcarts to Zion. No place, 1960. Good in DJ. $15.

Mountain Men & The Fur Trade of the Far West. Glendale CA, Arthur Clark Co, 1965-1972. 10 volume set. Fine. $1,750.

HAFEN, LEROY and ANN W. HAFEN. *Pike's Peak Gold Rush Guidebooks of 1859.* Glendale CA, 1941 1st edition. As new. $125.

HAGEN, WILLIAM T. *The Sac and Fox Indians.* Norman, Univ. of Okla. Press, 1958 1st ed. Near Fine in DJ. $75.

HAGGARD, HOWARD. *Devils, Drugs and Doctors.* NY, 1926 6th printing. VG. $30. Good, no DJ. $15.
The Doctor in History. Yale University Press, 1934 1st ed. Very Good. $25.

HAGGARD, H. RIDER. *She.* London, 1887 1st. VG. $600.
The World's Desire. London, 1890. Good. $25.
Cleopatra. London, 1893. G-VG. $75-$95.
People of the Mist. Longmans, 1894 1st ed. Cover soil, o/w Very Good. $75.
Ayesha: The Return of She. NY, 1905 1st American ed. Some soiling. $75.
The Lady of the Heavens. Lovell, 1908 1st American ed. Very Good. $225.
Marie. Longmans, 1912 1st ed. VG. $26.
The Ivory Child. Cassell, 1916 1st ed. VG. $125.

HAHNEMANN, SAMUEL. *Organon of Homeopathic Medicine.* Wm. Radde, 1843 1st ed. VG. $35.

HAIG-BROWN, RODERICK. *Pool and Rapid: The Story of a River.* London, 1936. Signed. Very Good. $35.
The Western Angler. Derrydale, 1939 2 vols. One of 950 sets. Lacks map, o/w Fine. $475. Another, soiled. $375.
Panther. London, 1946. Near Fine in good DJ. $18.
Salt Water Summer. No place, 1948 1st ed. VG. $10.
Measure of the Year. Morrow, 1950, 1st. Fine in DJ. $60.
Fisherman's Winter. No place, 1954. Fine in DJ. $25. NY, 1954 1st ed. Very Good. $45.
Fisherman's Summer. No place, 1959. VG in DJ. $10.
The Whale People. NY, 1963. Illustrated. Cloth soiled, o/w Very Good. $15.
Fisherman's Fall. Morrow, 1964 1st ed. VG in DJ. $50.
A Primer of Fly Fishing. NY, 1964 1st ed. F in DJ. $60.
Fisherman's Spring. NY, 1975 New ed. Mint in DJ. $25.

HAIG, ARTHUR. *Wheels*. Doubleday, Garden City NJ, 1971 1st ed. Very Good in dust jacket. $20.

HAINES, DONALD H. *The Southpaw*. Farrar & Rinehart, 1931 4th printing. Some wear and ink notations, o/w Very Good in dust jacket. $15.

HAINES, EDITH. *Tried Temptations-Old New*. A Cookbook. NY, Farrar & Rinehart, 1931. 230 pages. VG. $10.

HAINES, FRANCIS. *The Nez Perces*. University of Oklahoma, 1955 1st ed. VG in good DJ. $60.
Appaloosa, the Spotted Horse, in Art and History. Austin TX, 1963. Very Good in dust jacket. $38. Another, signed. Fine in dust jacket. $60.
The Buffalo. NY, 1970. Very Good. $15.

HAKLUYT, RICHARD. *The Principal Navigations, Voyages and Discoveries of the English Nation*. Cambridge Univ., 1965. 2 vol. facsimile of 1589 ed. VG in DJ. $95.

HALDEMANN, JULIUS. Publisher of depression era paperback series of *Little Blue Books*. Value $1-$3 each.

HALE, REV. E. and MISS SUSAN. *A Family Flight Around Home*. Boston, Lothrop, 1884. Very Good. $25.

HALE, SARAH. *The Good Housekeeper*. No place, 1839 1st edition. Good-VG. $175-$500.
Mrs. Hale's New Cook Book. 1851. $225-$275. Same, 1873 edition. $95-$125.
Mrs. Hale's Receipts for the Millions. 1851. $110-$250.

HALE, WILLIAM H. *Horizon Cookbook*. American Heritage, 1968. 2 vols. in box. Fine. $50.

HALEY, J. EVETTS. *The Heraldry of the Range*. Canyon TX, 1949 1st ed. VG in dust jacket. $450.
Some Southwestern Trails. El Paso, 1948. H. D. Bugbee illus. Pictorial cloth. In worn slipcase. $375.
Life on the Texas Range. University of Texas, 1952 1st edition. Fine in fine slipcase. $150.
Jeff Milton: A Good Man with a Gun. University of Okla. Press, 1948 1st edition, 1st issue. G-VG. $30-$60. Very Good in vg dust jacket. $100-$150.

HALL, A. N. *The Handy Boy*. NY, 1937, Lathrop, Lee & Shepard. Revised ed. $25.

HALL, BEN. *The Golden Age of the Movie Palace*. Potter, 1961. Very Good. $14.
Best Remaining Seats. Potter, 1961 1st edition. Very Good in dust jacket. $30.

HALL, CARRIE & ROSE KRETSINGER. *The Romance of the Patchwork Quilt in America*. Idaho, 1947. VG. $25. Another, worn. $16.

HALL, DONALD. *Dark Houses*. NY, 1958 1st ed. Inscribed. Very Good in dust jacket. $50.
String Too Short To Be Saved. NY, 1961 1st ed. VG. $20.

HALL-DUNCAN, NANCY. *The History of Fashion Photography*. NY, 1979 1st edition. Preface by Yves Saint-Laurent. Fine in clipped dust jacket. $85.

HALL, HAMMOND. *The Young Electrician*. Macmillan, 1910 1st ed. 289 pages. $35.

HALL, H. M. *Woodcock Ways*. NY, 1946. Ralph Ray illus. Very Good. $25. Another, in dust jacket. $35.

HALL, JAMES NORMAN. *Kitchener's Mob*. Boston, 1916 1st ed. Author's 1st book. Signed. Very Good. $75.
High Adventure. No place, 1918 1st ed. Very Good. $38.
Dr. Dogbody's Leg. NY, 1939. 1 of 1,500. VG. $45.

HALL, MANLY P. *Lectures on Ancient Philosophy*. Los Angeles, 1929 1st ed. Illus. Fine in vg DJ. $75.
Reincarnation. Los Angeles, 1939 1st ed. VG. $15.

HALL, RADCLYFFE. *The Well of Loneliness*. NY, 1928 1st American ed. Limited ed. boxed. VG. $350. 1929 edition in 2 vols. One of 225 copies. Signed. Good. $350. 1928 British 1st edition. in large format, bound in black with plain cover. $250-$350.

HALLEY, WILLIAM. *The Centennial Year Book of Alameda County, California*. Oakland, William Halley, 1876 1st ed. 586 pages including ads. G-VG. $100-$150.

HALLIBURTON, RICHARD. *The Glorious Adventure*. Garden City, 1927 reprint. Very Good. $12.
New Worlds to Conquer. Indianapolis, 1929 1st ed. Inscribed. VG. $25. Another, ex-library. Good. $8.
Seven League Boots. Indianapolis, 1935. Signed. G. $30.
Second Book of Marvels - The Orient. Indianapolis, 1938 1st ed. Signed. Fair. $30.

HALPER, ALBERT. *The Foundry*. NY, 1934 3rd printing. Very Good in dust jacket. $20.
This is Chicago. NY, 1952 1st ed. Fine in vg DJ. $13.
The Golden Watch. NY, 1953 1st ed. Fine in DJ. $30.
Goodbye, Union Square. Chicago, 1970 1st. F in DJ. $8.

HALSMAN, PHILIPPE. *The Frenchman*. New York, 1949. Softcover. Good. $12.
Piccoli: A Fairy Tale. NY, 1953 1st ed. Paul Julian illus. Inscribed by Halsmann. VG in dust jacket. $50.
The Jump Book. NY, 1959 1st ed. Near Fine in DJ. $35.

HALSTEAD, MURAT. *The Story of Cuba*. Chicago, 1898. Illus. Very Good. $60.
Illustrious Life of William McKinley. Photo illus. cover. A common book at $5-$8.

HALSTEAD, BRUCE W. *Poisonous and Venomous Marine Animals of the World*. Washington, Government Printing Office, 1965. 3 vols. Illus. Fine. $150.

HAMBIDGE, JAY. *Dynamic Symmetry: The Greek Vase*. Yale, 1920 1st ed. Good. $25.

HAMBLETON, JACK. *Charter Pilot*. (Bill Hanson no. 4) Longmans Green, 1952 1st ed. Juvenile. Very Good in ragged dust jacket. $15.

HAMERTON, PHILIP GILBERT. *Etching and Etchers*. Boston, 1876. Illus. Near VG. $100.

HAMILTON, A. V. *The Household Cyclopaedia of Practical Receipts, etc.* Springfield, 1875. Illus. $50-$95.

HAMILTON, CARL. *In No Time at All*. Iowa State University. Press, 1975 1st edition, 6th impression. Fine in dust jacket. $15.

HAMILTON, EDWARD P. *The French and Indian Wars*. Garden City, 1962 1st. Tipped in letter from author. $35.

HAMILTON, W. T. *My Sixty Years on the Plains*. NY, 1905. Charles Russell illus. Very Good. $125.

HAMMETT, DASHIELL. *Red Harvest*. NY, 1929 1st ed. Author's 1st book. Near VG. $250. In Dust Jacket. $2,500.
The Maltese Falcon. NY, 1930 1st ed. VG plus. $250-$500. In Dust Jacket. $2,500. Grosset & Dunlap reprint, 1930. Good in DJ. $65. Modern Library edition, 1934. Very Good in dust jacket. $45-$55.
The Glass Key. NY, 1931 1st edition, 4th printing. Slight wear, Bookplate. VG. $150.
The Thin Man. NY, 1934 1st ed., 5th printing. Covers slightly discolored, o/w VG. $150. Same, good, $75.
Omnibus. NY, 1935 1st collected edition of Red Harvest, Dain Curse, Maltese Falcon. VG in fair DJ. $30.
The Big Knockover. NY, 1966 1st ed. Edited, with introduction, by Lilian Hellman. Fine in vg DJ. $75.

HAMMETT, DASHIELL (In Magazines). *Black Mask*. Dec 1922, Oct 1923 and various issues 1925-1930. $20-$30 each. "The Maltese Falcon" ran in five parts in *Black Mask*, Sep 1929 through Jan 1930. All five issues, in VG condition, name your price.
American Magazine. July 1932. "Sam Spade". $75.

HAMMOND, GEORGE (Editor). *Adventures of Alexander Barclay: Memorandum Diary, 1845-1850*. Denver, 1976 1st ed. VG in very fine DJ. $40.
The Treaty of Guadalupe. Berkeley CA, Grabhorn Press 1st edition. Illus. $200.
Digging For Gold Without a Shovel: The Letters of Daniel Wadsworth. Denver, 1976 1st ed. One of 1,250 copies. Fine. $35.

HAMMOND, JOHN. *Quaint and Historic Forts of North America*. Philadelphia, 1915 1st ed. G-VG. $50-$80.

HAMNER, LAURA L. *Short Grass and Longhorns*. Univ. of Oklahoma, 1943 2nd ed. Photos. VG. $45.

HAMPTON, TAYLOR. *Nickel Plate Road. History of a Great Railroad*. OH, World Pub., 1947. Fine in DJ. $28.

HANDBOOK OF ARCHITECTURAL PRACTICE. Amer. Inst. of Architects. Wash., 1927. G-VG. $20.

HANDY, W. C. *Father of the Blues*. No place, 1941 1st ed., 1st printing. Spine a bit dark. o/w VG. $150.

HANEY, JESSE. *Haney's Manual of Sign, Carriage and Decorative Painting, etc.* NY, 1870. 12mo, 95 pages. Worn, rear cover gone. $100.

HANNAH, BARRY. *Geronimo Rex*. NY, 1972 1st ed. Author's 1st book. Near Fine in DJ. $100.
Airships. NY, 1978 1st ed. Fine in DJ. $50.

HANSEN, HARRY. *The Chicago*. Rivers of America Series. NY, Farrar & Rinehart. 1942 reprint. VG in DJ. $20.

HARBESON, GEORGIANA B. *American Needlework*. NY, Bonanza, 1938. 400 illus. VG in DJ. $35.

HARBORD, JAMES. *The American Army in France, 1917-1919*. Boston, 1936. Illus. Maps. Fine. $40.

HARD, WALTER. *The Connecticut*. Rivers of America Series. NY, Rinehart, 1947 1st ed. 310 pgs. VG in DJ. $20.

HARDING, A. D. *Wolf and Coyote Trapping*. St. Louis MO, 1909 1st ed. Illus. $25.

HARDINGE, EMMA. *Modern American Spiritualism*. New York, 1870 2nd ed. VG. $75. Same, 3rd edition. $25.

HARDISON, THEODORE. *Poker, a Work Exposing*. 1914. 120 pages. VF. $210 auction.

HARDY BOYS SERIES. (See Dixon, Franklin W.)

HARDY, MARY EARLE. *Little Ta-Wish Indian Legends from Geyserland*. Rand McNally, 1914. Illus. Fine. $45.

HARDY, THOMAS. *Life's Little Ironies*. NY, 1894 1st American ed. VG. $50-$100.
Wessex Poems and Other Verses. London, 1898 1st ed. Near Fine. $150.
Human Shows Far Phantasies. Macmillan, 1925 1st ed. Green cloth. Some shelfwear. VG in chipped DJ. $50.
The Mayor of Casterbridge. NY, LEC. 1964. 1 of 1,500, signed by illustrator. Fine in slipcase. $125.

HARGRAVE, CATERINE P. *A History of Playing Cards and a Bibliography of Cards and Gaming.* 1930. 468 pages. Very Fine in dust jacket. $220.

HARKNESS, PETER. *Andy the Acrobat.* (Alert juvenile series). Grosset & Dunlap, 1907 ed. Worn, but VG in dingy dust jacket. $18.

HARLAND, MARION. *Common Sense in the Household.* 1871 1st edition. $200-$300.
Breakfast, Luncheon and Tea. NY, 1875 1st ed. $50-$95.
Dinner Year-Book. 1878. $115-$135.
A Complete Housewife's Guide. 1886. $45-$55.
Eve's Daughters. 1884, $25-$55.

HARLAND, MARION, MARIA PARLOA. Mrs. D. A. LINCOLN, others. *The New England Cook Book.* Charles Brown, 1905. Soiling, wear, interior VG. $38.

HARMSWORTH, ALFRED C. *Motors and Motor-Driving.* London, probably 1931 3rd edition. Revised, enlarged. Illus. Very Good. $75.

HARPENDING, ASBURY. *The Great Diamond Hoax.* San Francisco, 1913 1st ed. Illus. $50.

HARPER'S HOUSEHOLD HANDBOOK. Harper, NY, 1913. VG in DJ. $25. Without dust jacket. $15.

HARPER'S MONTHLY/WEEKLY. (See Magazine and Newspaper sections).

HARPER'S PICTORIAL HISTORY OF THE CIVIL WAR. Puritan Press, Chicago, no date. 2 vols. Fine. $700. 2 vols. 1866, 1868. Poor. $125. Vol. 1 only. Loose, shaken and worn. $125. Fairfax, 1975 reprint of 1866 edition. 836 pages in one volume. Fine in DJ. $35.

HARPER'S PICTORIAL HISTORY OF THE WAR WITH SPAIN. 32 parts, with full color plates. Each tabloid, 16 pages. Minor spotting, complete. VG. $288.

HARRIMAN, MARGARET C. *The Vicious Circle, The Algonquin Round Table.* NY, 1951. Al Hirschfeld illus. Fine in vg dust jacket. $20.

HARRIS, A. C. *Alaska and the Klondike Gold Rush.* Washington DC, 1897 1st edition. Illustrated. Very Good in fine dust jacket. $245.

HARRIS, BENJAMIN. *The Gila Trail: The Texas Argonauts and the California Gold Rush.* Norman OK, Univ. of Okla. 1960 1st ed. VG-Fine in DJ. $25-$45.

HARRIS, FRANK. *My Reminiscences as a Cowboy.* NY, Boni, 1930. Paperback. VG-Fine. $20-$35.
My Life and Loves. Castle reprint, 1966. Fine in DJ. $20.

HARRIS, JOEL CHANDLER. *Uncle Remus, His Songs and His Sayings: the Folk-Lore of the Old Plantation.* NY, 1881, 1st ed. Author's 1st book. F. S. Church and J. H. Moser illus. 1st Uncle Remus book. Good. $650-$875. 1884 edition, Near Fine. $75. 1921 edition, Appleton-Century. Worn, no dust jacket. $20. NY, 1941 edition. Chipped dust jacket. $10. Same, NY, London, 1920. Thomas Nelson Page introduction. A. B. Frost, E.W. Kemble illus. Large gift edition. Near Very Good. $100. Limited Editions Club, 1957. One of 1,500 signed by illustrator. Near Fine in case. $125.
Nights With Uncle Remus: Myths and Legends of the Old Plantation. Boston, 1883 1st edition. Rebound $150. 1917 edition, Milo Winter illus. VG. $75.
Free Joe and Other Georgian Sketches. NY, 1887 1st edition. Near Fine. $300.
Uncle Remus and Friends. Boston, 1892 1st edition. A. B. Frost illustrator. Very Good in original pictorial cloth cover. $400. Houghlin Mifflin 1914 edition. VG. $70.
On the Plantation: A Story of a Georgia Boy's Adventure During the War. New York, 1832 1st American edition. E. W. Kemble illus. Fine. $200.
The Chronicles of Aunt Minervy. NY, 1899 1st edition. Near Very Good. $75.
On The Wing of Occasions. NY, Doubleday, 1900 1st ed. Very Good. $60.
A Little Union Scout. NY, 1904 1st ed. George Gibbs illus. Near Fine. $75-$125.
Told by Uncle Remus: New Stories of the Old Plantation. NY, 1905 1st ed. Illus. by A. B. Frost, J. N. Conde, Frank Verbeck. VG. $300.
Uncle Remus and the Little Boy. Boston, 1910 1st ed. J. M. Conde illus. Near Fine, uncut. $600.
Nights With Uncle Remus. Boston, 1917. Milo Winter illus. Very Good. $75.

HARRIS, JOEL C. and F. A. ALDERMAN (Editors). *Library of Southern Literature.* Atlanta, 1913. 16 vols. Spine poor on some vols, o/w Fine. $250.

HARRIS, JULIA COLLIER. *The Life and Letters of Joel Chandler Harris.* Boston, 1918 1st ed. Illus. VG. $45.

HARRIS, MARK. *Trumpet to the World.* NY, 1946 1st ed., Author's 1st book. VG in dust jacket. $50.
The Southpaw. NY, 1953 1st ed. VG in good DJ. $65.
Bang the Drum Slowly. NY, 1956 1st ed. VG in vg DJ. $45. Fine in dust jacket. $100.

HARRIS, SHELDON. *Blues Who's Who.* NY, 1979. Fine in dust jacket. $40-$70.

HARRISON, CONSTANCE C. *Woman's Handiwork in Modern Homes.* NY, 1881. Very Good. $65.

HARRISON, T. R. *Principles of Internal Medicine.* Philadelphia, 1950 1st edition. Very Good plus. $95.

HARRY, GERARD. *The Peltzer Case*. Famous Trial Series. New York, 1928. Illustrated. Spine frayed, corners bumped, foxing. $10.

HARSHBARGER, G. *McCall's Garden Book*. NY, 1968, Simon & Schuster. Deluxe edition in slipcase. $25.

HART, H. M. *Old Forts of the Southwest*. Superior, 1964 1st ed. Very Good in dust jacket. $20-$30.
Old Forts of the Far West. Superior, 1964 1st ed. Near Fine in dust jacket. $23.
Pioneer Forts of the West. Superior, 1967 1st edition. VG in dust jacket. $32.

HART, MOSS and GEORGE S. KAUFMAN. *George Washington Slept Here*. NY, 1940 1st ed. F in DJ. $150.

HART, WILLIAM S. *My Life East and West*. NY, 1929 1st edition. Good plus. $22. Another, inscribed. $70.

HART, WILLIAM S. and MARY HART. *Pinto Ben and Other Stories*. NY, 1919. Illus. $50.

HARTE, BRET. *The Luck of Roaring Camp*. 1870 1st ed., 1st issue, without the story "Brown of Calaveras." $500-$700. 2nd issue, same year with story "Brown." $150 up. 1871 edition. VG. $45. 1892-1903 editions. $20-$24. San Francisco, 1916 limited ed. $200. Haddon Craftsman, 1941 ed. VG. $50-$90. Boston, Large 11x14, 1872. $150.
Heathen Chinee. Boston, 1871. Near Fine. $125 up.
Poems by Bret Harte. Fields & Osgood, 1871 1st edition. Very Good. $14.
Echoes of the Foothills. Boston, 1875 1st ed. Fine. $50.
The Queen of the Pirate Isle. London, probably 1886. Kate Greenaway illus. Fine. $250-$300. Near Fine. $175. Same, 1887 1st American ed. VG in vg DJ. $150.
Snowbound at Eagles. Boston, 1886 1st ed. Good. $30.
Trent's Trust and Other Stories. Boston, 1903 1st edition. Fine in dust jacket. $110.
The Writings of Bret Harte. Boston, no date. 1897-1914. 20 volumes. Good. $275.
Cressy and Other Tales. 1896, Standard Library Edition. Very Good. $15.
Bret Harte Complete Poems. London, 1887. VG. $45.
The Story of a Mine, etc. No place, 1896. Spine faded, o/w Very Good. $17.
Salomy Jane. NY, 1910. Fisher illus. VG. $50.
Bret Harte's Tales of the Gold Rush. Heritage Press, 1944. Good. $7-$10.

HARTE & TWAIN. *Sketches of the Sixties*. San Francisco, 1927. Worn dust jacket. $100.

HARTFORD CT. BUSINESS DIRECTORY, 1897. Hardbound. With ads, Colt, etc. 781 pages. $49.

HARTMANN, F. *Premature Burial*. London, 1896. Fine. $60.

HARVARD CLASSICS, 1909-1910. 50 vols. and booklet. Sunned spines, o/w VG. $175. Another, 19 vol. set. Published from 1903-1916. by P. F. Collier. Good. $35.

HARVARD CLASSICS SHELF OF FICTION. New York, 1917 20 vols. One of 2,131 sets. Very Good. $75.

HASKELL, FRANK A. *The Battle of Gettysburg*. Boston, 1958. Bruce Catton, editor. Very Good in DJ. $17.

HASKINS, SAM (Photographer). *Five Girls*. NY, 1962 1st ed. Photographs. VG in DJ. $35-$45.
Cowboy Kate & Other Stories. NY, 1965 1st ed. Photographs. Fine in dust jacket. $50.

HASLUCK, PAUL N. *Violins and Other Stringed Instruments. How to Make Them*. Cassell, 1908. $45.
How to Write Signs, Tickets & Posters. Philadelphia, 1918. Good-VG. $35.
Metal Working Illustrated. London, 1904. Fair. $75.

HATCHER, HARLAN. *Lake Erie*. Bobbs-Merrill, 1945 1st edition. American Lakes series. VG. $19-$25. Signed. $30.
The Western Reserve. Indianapolis, 1949 1st edition. Signed by author. VG in Good DJ. $35.

HATCHER, JULIAN. *The Book of the Garand*. Washington, 1948 1st ed. Fine in dust jacket. $75.

HAUPTMANN, GERHART. *The Heretic of Soana*. NY, 1923 1st American ed. Very Good. $28.

HAVEN, CHARLES and FRANK BELDEN. *History of the Colt Revolver and Other Arms*. NY, 1940. Illus. G. $150. Bonanza reprint, 1960s. Fine, no dust jacket. $45.

HAVIGHURST, WALTER. *The Upper Mississippi: A Wilderness Saga*. NY, 1937, Farrar. Rivers of America Series. VG, no dust jacket. $18-$24.
Land of Promise. Macmillan, 1946. VG in DJ. $18.
Annie Oakley of the Wild West. London, 1955 1st English edition. $16-$20.
Wilderness For Sale: The Story of the First Western Land Rush. NY, 1956 1st ed. 372 pages. VG in DJ. $25.

HAWES, C. B. *The Dark Frigate*. Bos., 1923 1st ed. G. $32.
Whaling. NY, 1924 1st ed. Very Good. $35-$45.

HAWKE, DAVID. *Benjamin Rush, Revolutionary Gadfly*. Indianapolis, 1971 1st ed. Very Good in DJ. $20.

HAWKES, JOHN. *The Blood Oranges*. New Directions, 1971 1st ed. Fine in dust jacket. $65.
Death, Sleep and the Traveler. New Directions, 1974 1st edition. Fine in dust jacket. $30.
Adventures in the Alaskan Skin Trade. NY, 1985 1st ed. Signed. Fine in fine dust jacket. $50.

HAWKINS, N. *New Catechism of the Steam Engine*. NY, Audel, 1904 revised ed. $28.

HAWKS, FRANICS L. *Narrative of the Expedition of an American Squadron to Japan, 1852-1854 by Commodore Perry*. D. Appleton, NY, 1856 1st ed. 11 folding maps. Original red cloth. Rubbed, staining. $1,500.

HAWLEY, HARRIET SMITH. *The Goose Girl of Nurnberg*. Los Angeles, 1936. Willy Pogany illustrator. Near Very Good. $35.

HAWLEY, WALTER A. *Oriental Rugs, Antique and Modern*. NY, Dodd-Mead, 1922. VG. $70-$100.

HAWLEY, WALTER AUGUSTUS. *Early Days of Santa Barbara, California, to Dec. 1846*. Santa Barbara, 1910 1st ed. Light wear. $150.

HAWTHORNE, JULIAN. *Rumpty-Dudget's Tower*. Stokes, 1924 (1925). Cloth with pictorial label. G-VG. $45.

HAWTHORNE, NATHANIEL. *Fanshaw and Other Pieces*. Boston, no date, 2nd. Author's 1st book. Near Fine. $225.
Grandfather's Chair: A History for Youth. Boston, 1842 2nd ed. revised, enlarged. Chipping, foxing. $100.
Famous Old People: Being the Second Epoch of Grandfather's Chair. Boston, 1842 2nd edition. Chipping, foxing. $70.
Tanglewood Tales. Boston, 1887. VG. $75. Same, 1921, Hampton. Sterritt illus. VG. $48. 1938, Dulac illus. $150.
The Scarlet Letter. 1883, H. M. Co. Good. $10.
The House of the Seven Gables. Boston, 1851 1st ed. March ads. $700-$800. 2nd printing, May ads. $250. Another, 1851, bound by Zaehnsdorf, elaborate. $150. Heritage Press reprint, 1935. $15.
Tales & Sketches. Houghton, 1900. Red cloth. $50-$95.
Mosses From An Old Manse. Houghton, 1900. Orig. red cloth. $50-$95. Same, 1903 ed. $40-$55.
The Works of Nathaniel Hawthorne. Boston, 1883. 15 vols. Standard Library ed. $100. New York, Houghton Mifflin, 1900. No. 187 of 500. 22 volumes. Signed by Rosa Hawthorne and artists. $1,250 set.
Wonder Book for Boys and Girls. Houghton Mifflin, 1902. Pictorial green cloth cover. Very Good. $75. 1893 edition, Walter Crane illus. $100-$150.

HAY, JOHN. *Castilian Days*. Boston, NY, 1903 1st printing. Bumped corners. $30.
The Pike County Ballads. Houghton, 1912. N. C. Wyeth illus. Penned dedication. $100.

HAY, NICOLAY. *Abraham Lincoln*. NY, Appleton, 1914. 10 volume set. Very Good. $150.

HAY, T. R. *Hood's Tennessee Campaign*. NY, 1929 1st ed., Neale Pub. Co. Very Good. $175.

HAYCOX, ERNEST. *Outlaw*. Boston, 1939 1st ed. NF. $30.
Earth Breakers. Boston, 1952 1st ed. VG in DJ. $35.
Brand Fires on the Range. Derby CT, 1959. Paperback original. 1st printing. Fine. $25.
The Best Western Stories of Ernest Haycox. NY, 1960. Paperback original. Fine. $25.
The Border Trumpet. NY, no date. Armed Services edition. Very Good. $25.

HAYCRAFT, HOWARD. *The Life and Times of the Detective Story*. No place, 1941 1st edition. Near Fine in Fair dust jacket. $55.
The Art of the Mystery Story. NY, 1946 1st edition. Near Fine in dust jacket. $55.
Murder for Pleasure. New York, 1974 reprint. Very Good in dust jacket. $25.

HAYNES & YAGGY. *The Royal Path of Life. The Aims and Aids to Success and Happiness*. Western Pubs, 1879 edition. Leather. Very Good. $18.

HAYHOW, ERNIE. *The Thunderbolt Across Europe: A History of the 83rd Infantry Division, 1942-1945*. Munich, 1946. Fine in fine dust jacket. $120.

HAZZARD, SHIRLEY. *Cliffs of Fall and Other Stories*. NY, 1963 1st American ed. VG in fair dust jacket. $25.

HEADLEY, J. T. *Farragut and Our Naval Commanders*. NY, 1867. Fair. $30-$50.
Great Riots of New York. 1873 ed. VG. $25.
Achievements of Stanley and Other African Explorers. Hubbard, 1878 1st ed. VG. $18-$22.

HEADLEY, P. C. *Life of Napoleon Bonaparte*. Lee & Shepard, 1886. Ex-library. Good. $12.

HEAGERTY, JOHN J. *Four Centuries of Medical History in Canada*. Toronto, 1928 2 vols. Fine. $80.

HEARN, LAFCADIO. *La Cuisine Creole*. No place, 1885 1st edition. $400-$425.
Two Years in the French West Indies. Harper, 1890 1st edition. Good. $150.
Kokoro. Cambridge, 1896 1st ed. Fine. $200.
Gleanings in Buddha Fields. NY, 1897. VG. $23-$50.
Kwaidan. Houghton-Mifflin, 1904 1st ed. VG. $200.
Exotics and Retrospectives. Boston, 1907. Page foxing. Very Good. $50.

HEATH'S GREATLY IMPROVED INFALLIBLE COUNTERFEIT DETECTOR AT SIGHT. Laban Heath & Co., 1870 3rd ed. 40 pages. Very Good. $110.

HEARN, WILLIAM E. *The Aryan Household, Its Structure and Its Development*. London & New York, 1891. Original cloth. $30.

HEAT MOON, WILLIAM L. *Blue Highways-A Journey into America*. Little-Brown, 1982 1st ed. VG in DJ. $15. Same, Fine in dust jacket. $35-$75.

HECHT, ANTHONY. *A Summoning of Stones*. NY, 1954 1st ed. Author's 1st book. VG in DJ. $75.

HECHT, BEN. *Erik Dorn*. Putnam, 1921 1st ed. Good. $75.
Fantazius Mallare. Chicago, 1922. One of 2,025 copies. Wallace Smith illus. Good. $50.
Gargoyles. NY, 1922. Illus. Shaken spine, o/w VG. $60.
A Book of Miracles. NY, 1939. Uncorrected proof copy in wraps. About Very Good. $50.
1,001 Afternoons in New York. Viking, 1941. George Grosz illus. VG plus in dust jacket. $75.
The Cat That Jumped Out of the Story. Philadelphia, 1947 1st ed. Peggy Bacon illus. Near VG. $25.

HECHT, BEN and GENE FOWLER. *The Great Magoo*. NY, 1933. Very Good in fair dust jacket. $75.

HECHTLINGER, ADELAIDE. *The Great Patent Medicine Era*. NY, 1970. Fine in dust jacket. $45.

HECKETHORN, C. W. *"Rouge et Nori." The Gambling World*. NY, 1898 1st American edition. $50.

HEDIN, SVEN. *My Life as an Explorer*. Garden City, 1925. Ex-library. Very Good. $12.
Riddles of the Gobi Desert. Lon. 1933. About Fine. $15.
Jehol, City of Conquerors. NY, 1933. Very Good. $15.

HEFNER, HUGH. *Playboy Annual #1*. HMH Publications, 1956 1st ed. 130 pgs. Good, No DJ. $20. Good in DJ. $30.

HEGAN, ALICE C. *Mrs. Wiggs of the Cabbage Patch*. Century, 1902. Very Good. $15.

HEGEL, GEORG W. F. *The Phenomenology of Mind*. London, 1931, 2nd revised ed. J. B. Baillie translation. Very Good. $50.

HEILNER, VAN CAMPEN. *A Book on Duck Shooting*. Philadelphia, 1939 1st ed. Lynn Bogue Hunt illus. Good in DJ. $95. 1940, 4th printing. $50.
Our American Game Birds. Garden City, 1941. Illus. by Lynn Bogue Hunt. VG in DJ. $75. Another, shaken. $50.

HEIMANN, ROBERT K. *Tobacco & Americans*. New York, 1960. Good-VG in DJ. $20-$30.

HEINEMANN, RICHARD W. *Siegfried and the Twilight of the Gods*. 1911 1st ed. 30 color plates by Arthur Rackham. Light cover soil, o/w Very Good. $150.

HEINL, R. D. *Soldiers of the Sea*. Annapolis, 1962 1st ed. Fine in rubbed dust jacket. $100.

HEINLEIN, ROBERT. *Sixth Column*. Gnome, 1949 1st ed. Very Good in dust jacket. $50.
The Puppet Masters. NY, 1951 1st ed. VG in DJ. $225.
The Star Beast. NY, 1954 1st ed. NF in vg DJ. $150.
Tunnel in the Sky. NY, 1955 1st edition. VG-Fine in dust jacket. $65-$175.
Time for the Stars. Scribner's, 1956 1st ed. VG. $80.
Double Star. NY, 1956 1st ed. NF in nicked DJ. $1,250.
Orphans of the Sky. Putnam, 1964 1st American edition. Loose page, o/w Very Good. $75.
The Moon Is a Harsh Mistress. NY, 1966 1st ed. Near Fine in soiled dust jacket. $750.

HELDE, FLORENCE P. *The Shrinking of Treehorn*. NY, 1971 1st ed. Edward Gorey illus. Fine. $75.

HELK, PETER. *Great Auto Races*. As told and painted by. NY, 1975, Abrams. VG in dust jacket. $150.

HELLER, JOSEPH. *Catch 22*. NY, 1961 1st ed. Author's 1st book. Near Fine in dust jacket. $150-$450.

HELLMAN, LILLIAN. *The Little Foxes*. London, 1939 1st British ed. Good in fair dust jacket. $100.
Toys in the Attic. NY, 1960. Fireside Theatre Book Club edition. Fine in dust jacket. $45.

HELM, THOMAS. *Hurricanes: Weather at Its Worst*. NY, 1967. VG in worn dust jacket. $18.

HELMERICKS, C. *Hunting in North America*. 1956 1st ed. Worn dust jacket. $15.

HELPER, HINTON R. *The Land of Gold: Reality versus Fiction*. Baltimore, MD, 1855. Near VG. $75.
The Impending Crisis in the South. NY, 1857 1st ed. Abolitionist letter laid in. Fine. $80.

HEMINGWAY, ERNEST. *A Farewell to Arms*. NY, 1929 1st ed. 1st state. Good. $100. Same, Fine in DJ. $700-$900. Same, 1st ed. 1st issue. Spotted cloth, worn labels. Good. $60. Same, London, 1929 1st British ed. VG-Fine in DJ. $125-$200. Photoplay edition, 1930s. Very Good. $5.
Death in the Afternoon. NY, 1932 1st ed. VG-Fine in DJ. $250-$600. 1950 4th Impression. VG, No DJ. $20.
Winner Take Nothing. NY, 1933 1st ed. VG in DJ. $400.
Green Hills of Africa. NY, 1935 1st ed. Good. $100.
To Have and Have Not. Grosset & Dunlap, 1943 reprint. Good-VG. $5.
For Whom the Bell Tolls. NY, 1940 1st ed. 1st issue. VG-Fine in DJ. $150-$250. Same, 1st ed. 1st issue. Good. $65. Another, not 1st state. $30. Same, 1st ed. 1st state. DJ spine piece missing, o/w Fine in DJ. $100.
The Old Man and the Sea. NY, 1952 1st ed., 1st issue. VG-Fine in DJ. $125-$450. Same, 1st British ed. 1952. $90. Same, LEC, 1990. Eisenstadt photogravures. One of 600 copies signed by Eisenstadt. Fine in slipcase. $680.

The Wild Years. Dell paperback, 1962 1st ed. F. $15-$20.
Islands In the Stream. Scribner's, 1970 2nd edition. Very Good in dust jacket. $9.
Ernest Hemingway. Selected articles and dispatches of four decades. NY, 1967. VG in DJ. $20.

HEMINGWAY, ERNEST (In Magazines). *Scribner's*. March, 1927. "The Killers," his first story in an American magazine. $30-$40.
Scribner's. Aug, 1930. "Wine of Wyoming." $20-$30.
Hearst's International Cosmopolitan. May, 1932. "After the Storm". $30-$45.
Esquire. Apr, 1934. "Article by. $15-$25.
Hearst's Intl Cosmopolitan. Apr, 1934. "One Trip Across". $20-$35. Oct, 1939. "Under the Ridge". $20-$35.
Esquire. Jan, 1936. Nonfiction about Africa. $28.

HENCK, JOHN. *Field Book for Railroad Engineers*. Appleton, NY, 1874. Thin leather, worn. $25.

HENDERSON, MRS. L. R. S. *The Flight Brothers*. Chicago, Reilly & Britton, 1912 1st edition. with 6 color plates by Emilie Nelson. Rubbed, but VG. $60 auction.

HENDERSON, MRS. MARY F. *Practical Cooking & Dinner Giving*. NY, 1878. Good. $75. 1976 reprint. VG. $50.

HENDERSON, PETER. *Gardening for Pleasure*. NY, Orange Judd, 1875. Clean bright, ex-library. $30.
Gardening for Profit. NY, Orange Judd, 1884 & 1893 eds. VG. $35 each. Fair. $15-$25.

HENDERSON, W. A. *Modern Domestic Cookery and Useful Receipt Book*. Boston, 1844. Good. $145.

HENDRICK, BURTON J. *Statesmen of the Lost Cause*. Little Brown, 1939 1st ed. Very Good. $20.
Lincoln's War Cabinet. Little Brown, 1946 1st ed. F. $18.

HENDRYX, JAMES B. *Gun Brand*. NP, 1917. Illus. G. $7.
Connie Morgan in Cattle Country. NY, 1924 2nd printing. F. E. Schoonover illus. Good. $13.
Blood on the Yukon Trail. NY, 1930 1st ed. VG. $25.

HENLE, FRITZ. (Photographer). *Mexico*. Chicago, NY, 1945 2nd ed. Good. $50-$65.

HENLEY'S TWENTIETH CENTURY FORMULAS. Revised and enlarged. Hiscox Gardner, editor. Henley Pub., 1935. Worn cover, dark spots. $10.

HENLEY, WILLIAM ERNEST. *Poems of*. NY, 1920, Scribner's. VG. $7.
A Song of Speed. London, 1903 1st ed. $125.

HENRETTA, J. E. *Kane and The Upper Allegheny*. Philadelphia, 1929. Limited edition, 600 copies. $70-$85.

HENRICKSON, ROBERT. *The Great American Chewing Gum Book, History of the World of*. Radnor PA, Chilton, 1976 1st ed. $25.

HENRY, MARGUERITE. *King of the Wind*. Chicago, 1938 1st ed. Wesley Dennis illus. Inscribed by author. VG. $25.
Geraldine Belinda. Platt & Munk, 1942. Gladys Blackwood illus. Very Good. $27.
Justin Morgan Had a Horse. Chicago, 1945. Wesley Dennis illus. Very Good. $30.
Misty of Chincoteague. NY, 1947 1st ed. Wesley Dennis illus. Good plus. $16-20.
Star Sea-Orphan of Chincoteague. Rand McNally, 1949 1st ed. Wesley Dennis illus. Very Good. $40.
Born to Trot. Rand McNally, 1950 1st ed. Signed. Wesley Dennis illus. Very Good. $17.
Brighty of the Grand Canyon. Rand McNally, 1953 1st ed. Wesley Dennis illus. Fine in good DJ. $20.
Black Gold. Chicago, 1957 1st ed. Wesley Dennis illus. Good in dust jacket. $35.

HENRY, O. (William S. Porter). *Cabbages and Kings*. NY, 1904 1st ed., 1st issue. O'Henry's 1st book. Good. $200. Very Good in dust jacket. $500.
Roads of Destiny. NY, 1909 1st ed. Weak hinges, bumped spine, o/w Very Good. $40.
Waifs and Strays: Twelve Stories by. Doubleday, 1917 1st ed. One of 200 copies. Silk endleaves. In slipcase. $125.
Heart of the West. McClure, 1907 1st ed. VG. $60.
The Complete Writings of O. Henry. New York, no date, 12 volumes. $65.

HENRY, O. (In Magazines). *McClure's*. Dec, 1899. Story Written in prison, 1st in a national magazine. $60-$75.
Everybody's. Oct, 1902. Two "Little Stories of Real Life", Very Good. $15-$25.
Cosmopolitan. May, 1904. Short story. $20-$30. Sep, 1910. $20-$30. Oct, 1912. $20-$30.

HENRY, ROBERT S. *Story of the Confederacy*. Indianapolis, 1931. Maps intact. Very Good. $40.
The Story of Reconstruction. Indianapolis, 1938. Very Good. $23.

HENRY, WILL. *No Survivor*. NY, 1950 1st ed. VG in very good dust jacket. $10-$20.
Who Rides With Wyatt? NY, circa 1955 1st ed. G-VG in worn dust jacket. $22.
San Juan Hill. NY, 1962 1st ed. Fine in DJ. $18.
Custer's Last Stand. Philadelphia, 1966 1st ed. G-VG in dust jacket. $15.
Alias Butch Cassidy. NY, 1967 1st. Fine in fine DJ. $35.
The Gates of the Mountains. NY, 1963 1st ed. Fine in fine dust jacket. $25.

HENSHALL, JAMES A. *Ye Gods & Little Fishes*. Cincinnati, Ohio, 1900. Fine. $150.

Bass, Pike, Perch and Others. New York, 1903 1st ed. Very Good. $30-$40.

Book of the Black Bass. Bass Angler's pub, 1978 reprint. Very Good. $14.

HENTY, GEORGE A. *Through Russian Snows*. NY, 1895 1st American ed. Near Fine. $45.

On the Irawaddy. NY, 1896 1st American ed. VG. $45.

By Pike & Dyke. NY, 1897 1st ed. Some foxing, cover spots, o/w Very Good. $25-$30.

Both Sides of the Border. NY, 1898 1st American ed. Ralph Peacock illus. VG plus. $50.

With the Allies to Pekin. NY, 1903 1st ed. VG. $35.

The Cornet of Horse. Sampson Low (British), 1906 1st ed. Illus. Good plus. $35.

Various boy juvenile titles. American, British publishers. 38 different titles. $4-$10 each.

HEPPENHEIMER, T. A. *Colonies in Space*. Stackpole, 1977. Very Good in dust jacket. $16.

Toward Distant Suns. Stackpole, 1979. VG in DJ. $16.

HERALDSON, DONALD. *Creators of Life-A History of Animation*. NY, 1975. VG in dust jacket. $60.

HERBERT, FRANK. *Dragon in the Sea*. NY, 1956 1st ed. VG in DJ. $80. Book Club edition, Same year. $10.

The God Makers. NY, 1972 1st ed., VG in DJ. $30.

Heretics of Dune. NY, 1984 1st ed. Signed, 1 of 1,500. VG in slipcase. $75. 2nd impression, 1984. F in DJ. $10.

Chapterhouse of Dune. NY, 1985 1st ed. Signed, 1 of 750 copies. Fine in slipcase. $75.

HERBERT, HENRY WILLIAM. *Horse and Horsemanship of the United States*. NY, 1857. 2 vols 1st ed. Rebound. One hinge weak, o/w Very Good. $175.

Hints to Horse Keepers. NY, 1859 1st ed. Woodcuts. Shaken. Good. $65.

HERBST, JOSEPHINE. *Nothing is Sacred*. NY, 1928 1st ed. Author's 1st book. VG. $120-$125.

Rope of Gold. NY, 1939 1st ed. Fine in DJ. $125.

New Green World. London, 1954 1st ed. Very Good in worn dust jacket. $24.

HERFORD, OLIVER. *The Bashful Earthquake and Other Fables*. NY, 1898. Illus. by author. VG. $45.

The Simple Jography: How to Know the Earth and Why It Spins. Boston, 1909 1st ed. John Luce. VG. $35.

Neither Here Nor There. Doran, 1922 1st ed. VG. $12.

Cupid's Almanac and Guide to Hearticulture for This Year & Next. Boston, 1908, 3rd impression. $45.

Confessions of a Caricaturist. NY, 1917 1st ed. Illus. by author. Very Good. $30.

Sea Legs. Alphabet Book. Illustrated by author. Philadelphia, Lippincott, 1931 1st edition. Very Good in rubbed DJ. $56 auction.

HERGESHEIMER, JOSEPH. *The Lay Anthony*. NY, 1914 1st edition. Author's 1st book. Very Good. $50. Another, inscribed. Fine. $125.

The Three Black Pennies. NY, 1917 1st ed. VG in DJ. $30. Another, signed by author & illus. No. 3 of 175. Fine in worn slipcase. $150.

Tampico. NY, 1926 1st ed. Fine in fine DJ. $25.

Quiet Cities. New York, 1928 1st edition. Fine in fine dust jacket. $32.

Sheridan. Boston, NY, 1931. Near VG. $38.

Berlin. NY, 1932 1st edition. One of 125 copies, signed. Very Good. $45.

HERLIHY, JAMES. *The Sleep of Baby Filbertson*. NY, 1959 1st ed. Author's 1st book. Near Fine in DJ. $100.

Midnight Cowboy. New York, 1965 1st ed. Very Good to Near Fine in dust jacket. $20-$25.

HERNDON, SARAH R. *Days on the Road Crossing the Plains in 1865*. NY, Burr Printing, 1902. VG. $200.

HERNDON, WILLIAM. *Exploration of the Valley of the Amazon*. Washington, 1854. 2 vols. One spine nearly detached. $45. Another set, good, some foxing. $125.

HERODOTUS. *The Histories of Herodotus*. Nonesuch Press, 1935 limited ed. One of 675 copies. G-VG. $200. Another, Fine in dust jacket. $500. Limited Editions Club, 1958. One of 1,500 signed by illus. Fine in slipcase. $200. Various Trade editions from 1800s. $15-$45 depending upon quality of binding.

HERR, MICHAEL. *Dispatches*. NY, 1977 1st ed. VG to Fine in dust jacket. $60-$100.

HERRLINGER, R. *History of Medical Illustration From Antiquity to 1600*. NY, 1970. Fine. $80. Another, in slipcase. $125.

HERSCHEL, JOHN F. W. *Familiar Lectures on Scientific Subjects*. NY, 1872. 3rd American printing. Ex-library. o/w Very Good. $85.

HERSHEY, JOHN. *A Bell for Adano*. NY, 1944 1st ed. Inscribed, signed. Fine in fine dust jacket. $43.

Hiroshima. NY, 1946 1st ed. Ex-library. Edges worn, o/w Very Good. $25. Another, Fine in DJ. $45.

A Single Pebble. Knopf, 1956 1st edition. Very Good in worn dust jacket. $22.

HERSHEY'S 1934 COOKBOOK. Original. edition. Good-Very Good. $25-$40. 1971 reprint by Hershey. Fine. $8.

HERTER, GEORGE & BERTHE. *George the Housewife*. Herter's, MN, 1965 2nd. Bright gold dec. cover. VG. $35.

Bull Cook & Historical Recipes. Herter, 1973 6th ed. Vol II. 584 pages. Fine, paperback. $12.

HERTER & HOFFMEISTER. *History and Secrets of Professional Candy Making*. 1964 1st ed. White cloth. Very Good. $24.

HERTZ, EMANUEL. *The Hidden Lincoln*. Viking, 1938 1st ed. VG in dust jacket. $20.

HERTZLER, VICTOR. *Hotel St. Francis Book of Recipes*. San Francisco, 1910. Limited edition. VG. $90.

HERVEY, A. B. *Sea Mosses. A Collector's Guide and An Introduction To The Study of Marine Algae*. Boston, 1881. 20 color plates. $75.

HESS, FJERIL. *Toplofty*. (Girl Scout approved). Macmillan, 1939 1st ed. Very Good in dust jacket. $18.

HESS, JOHN D. *Combat Story of the 743rd Tank Battalion*. 1945 1st ed. Very Good. $80.

HESSE, HERMAN. *Demian*. NY, 1923 1st ed. Translation. Author's 1st book. Very Good. $100.
Narcissus and Goldmund. NY, 1968 1st American ed. Translated. Near Fine in dust jacket. $45.
If the War Goes On. NY, 1971 1st American ed. Very Good in dust jacket. $25.

HESS & KAPLAN. *The Ungentlemanly Art. History of American Political Cartoons*. Macmillan, 1968 1st ed. Fine in DJ. Signed by Kaplan. $18.

HEUVELMANS, B. *On the Track of Unknown Animals*. NY, 1959. Fine in dust jacket. $35.
In the Wake of the Sea Serpents. NY, 1969. F in DJ, $33.

HEWETT, EDGAR. *Ancient Life in the American Southwest*. Bobbs-Merrill, 1930 1st edition. Fine. $40. Another, Good. $14.
Ancient Andean Life. Bobbs-Merrill, 1939 1st ed. Near Very Good. $60.

HEWETT, EDGAR and B. DUTTON. *The Pueblo Indian World*. Albuquerque, 1945 1st ed. Illus. $35.

HEYERDAHL, THOR. *Kon-Tiki*. Rand McNally, special edition for young people, 1960. Very Good in dust jacket. $16. Another, signed by author. $30. 1950 Book Club edition. Very Good in dust jacket. $5. Allen-Unwin, 1964 24th edition. Fine in dust jacket. $14.
The Art of Easter Island. NY, 1975 1st ed. VG-Fine in dust jacket. $50-$125.

HEYWARD, DUBOSE. *Porgy*. NY, 1925 1st ed. Very Good, no dust jacket. $25.
Mamba's Daughters. NY, 1929 1st ed. VG in fair DJ. $20-$30. Book Club edition. $7.
Angel. Doran, 1926 1st ed. Good. $20.

HIBBEN, F. C. *Treasure in the Dust: Exploring Ancient North America*. NY, 1951. Illus. Very Good. $10. Another, inscribed. $25.

HICKENLOOPER, FRANK. *Illustrated History of Monroe County, Iowa*. Albra IA, 1896. Soiled, else VG. $125.

HICKS, GRANVILLE. *I Like America*. NY, Modern Age, 1938. Fine in dust jacket. $45.

HICKS, JOHN E. *Adventures of a Tramp Printer*. Mid-America Press, 1950. Fine, no dust jacket. $15.

HIGGINS, GEORGE V. *The Friends of Eddie Coyle*. NY, 1972 1st ed. Author's 1st book. NF in DJ. $25-$75. *The Digger's Game*. NY, 1973 1st. Near Fine in DJ. $15. *Cogan's Trade*. NY, 1974 1st ed. Near Fine in DJ. $15.

HIGGINS, VIOLET MOORE. *The Little Juggler and Other French Tales Retold*. Racine WI, 1917 1st ed., Whitman. Near Fine. $35.

HIGGINSON, THOMAS WENTWORTH. *Army Life in a Black Regiment*. Boston, 1870 1st ed. VG. $150-$275. Same, 1960 reprint. VG in DJ. $25-$30. Same, 1982 reprint. Fine in dust jacket. $45.

HIGHSMITH, PATRICIA. *A Game For the Living*. NY, 1958 1st ed. Near Fine in dust jacket. $50.
The Tremor of Forgery. London, 1969 1st English ed. Fine in dust jacket. $20.
The Snail Watcher & Other Stories. Garden City, 1970 1st ed. Graham Greene introduction. Fine in DJ. $30.

HILL, ALICE POLK. *Tales of the Colorado Pioneers*. Denver, 1884 1st ed. Hinge crack, bumped corners. $175.

HILL, CHARLES T. *Fighting a Fire*. NY, 1887. Fire station organization. Good-VG. $60. Same, 1904. $50.

HILL, FREDERICK TREVOR. *Lincoln, Emancipator of the Nation*. NY, 1928 1st ed. Very Good. $20.
Washington: The Man of Action. NY, Appleton, 1914 1st ed. 27 color litho plates. Very Good. $88 auction.

HILL, GRACE LIVINGSSTONE. *House Across the Hedge*. Lippincott, 1932. Fine in dust jacket. $10.
Head of the House. G & D, no date. VG in DJ. $15.
Where Two Ways Met. Lippincott, 1947. VG in DJ. $6.

HILL, JANET M. *Salads, Sandwiches and Chafing Dish Dainties*. 1899 1st ed. $55-$70.
Practical Cooking and Serving. NY, 1902 1st $25-$30.
The American Cook Book. Boston Cooking School, 1929 edition. Fine, no dust jacket. $10-$12.
Cooking for Two. 1930 revised ed. $20-$30. 1948 edition. Very Good in dust jacket. $9.

HILL, JIM DAN. *The Minute Man in Peace and War: A History of the National Guard*. Stackpole. 1946. Fine in fine dust jacket. $25.

HILL, LORNA. *The Little Dancer*. Thos. Nelson, 1957 1st American ed. Slight soil in edgeworn dust jacket. $14.

HILL, RUTH BEEBE. *Hanta Yo*. Doubleday, 1979 1st ed. Fine in dust jacket. $25.

HILL, THOMAS E. *Hill's Manual of Social and Business Forms*. Hill Standard Book Co., 1882 1st ed. VG. $25-$35. 1891 edition. Good. $20. Reading copy. $10.

HILL, W. R. *The Great Flood of 1903*. Kansas City MO, Enterprise Pub. Co., 1903. Good. $35.

HILLARY, SIR EDWARD. *High in the Thin Cold Air*. Doubleday, 1962 1st ed. Fine in dust jacket. $14.

HILLER, CARL. *From Teepees to Towers: A Photographic History of American Architecture*. 1967 1st. G in DJ. $20.

HILLER, E. O. *New Dinners for all Occasions*. Volland, no date. Lavender deluxe covers, tied with matching yarn. Very Good in box. $45.

HILLER, LEJAREN A. (Photographer). *Bypaths in Arcady*. By Kendall Banning. Chicago, 1915. One of 540 copies. Very Good. $125.
Surgery Through the Ages: A Pictorial Chronicle. NY, 1944 1st ed. P. Benton and J. Hewlett. VG. $100.

HILLER, MRS. ELIZABETH O. *Fifty-Two Sunday Dinners*. Fairbank Co., 1913. Decorative cloth, Good. $22. NY, 1915 edition. Very Good. $12.

HILLERMAN, TONY. *Dance Hall of the Dead*. NY, 1973 1st ed. Fine in dust jacket. $850.
The Great Taos Bank Robbery. Univ. of New Mexico Press, 1973 1st ed. Fine in slipcase. $160.
The Spell of New Mexico. Univ. of New Mexico Press, 1978 2nd printing. Signed. Fine in clip DJ. $40.
Rio Grande. Portland OR, 1975 1st ed. Robert Reynolds photos. Fine in clip dust jacket. $125.
People of Darkness. NY, 1980 1st ed. Fine in DJ. $150.
The Dark Wind. NY, 1982 1st ed. Fine in DJ. $65. Another, signed by author. $200.

HILLES, HELEN T. *To the Queen's Taste*. NY, 1950. Very Good in dust jacket. $11.

HILLICK, M. C. *Practical Carriage and Wagon Painting*. Chicago, 1903 3rd ed. Worn, cracking. $75.

HILLGROVE, THOMAS. *A Complete Guide to the Art of Dancing*. NY, 1863. Corner wear, o/w VG. $60.

HILTON, JAMES. *Lost Horizon*. London, 1933 1st ed. Near Fine in DJ. $1,500. Same, NY, 1933 1st American ed. Fine in dust jacket. $200-$600.
Goodby, Mr. Chips. Little Brown, 1934 reprint. $10. Same, but 1st edition, 1st state. Signed by author. Fine in dust jacket. $200.
So Well Remembered. Little Brown, 1945 1st ed. G-VG in dust jacket. $6-$12.
Nothing So Strange. Boston, 1947 1st ed. VG in DJ. $23.

HIMES, CHESTER. *Cotton Comes to Harlem*. NY, 1965 1st edition. Fine in fair DJ. $50. Another, in Fine jacket. $75.
Pinktoes. Putnam, 1965 1st edition. VG in DJ. $45.

HIND, ARTHUR M. *A History of Engraving & Etching From the 15th Century to 1914*. Boston, 1927 3rd revised ed. Ex-library. Hinge broken. $65.
An Introduction to a History of Woodcut. Boston, 1935. 2 vols. Near Fine in broken box. $100.

HIND, H. LLOYD. *Brewing, Science and Practice*. NY, 1938. 2 vols. Illus. Near Fine. $125.

HINDS, WILLIAM A. *American Communities: Brief Sketches of Economy, Zoar, Bethel, etc*. Oneida, 1878. Good. $75.

HINES, SHERMAN and RAY GUY. *Outhouses of the East*. Nova Scotia, Canada, 1978. Fine. $15.

HINMAN, WILBUR F. *Corporal Si Klegg and His Pards*. N. G. Hamilton, 1891 revised ed. Good. $21.

HINTON, RICHARD. *John Brown and His Men, Roads They Traveled to Harper's Ferry*. NY, Funk & Wagnalls, 1894 1st ed. Orig. red cloth. $60-$90.

HINTON, S. E. *The Outsiders*. NY, 1967 1st ed. Author's 1st book. VG in vg DJ. $125. Another, Fine in DJ. $250.

HIRST, HENRY B. *The Book of Cage Birds*. Philadelphia, 1843 2nd edition. $75.

HIRTZLER. *Hotel St. Francis Cook Book*. Chicago, 1919 1st ed. Gilt-decorated cloth cover. Good. $90.

HISCOX, GARDNER D. *Horseless Vehicles, Automobiles, Motor Cycles, etc*. New York, 1900 1st ed. VG. $125.

HISLOP, CODMAN. *The Mohawk*. Rivers of America Series. NY, 1948 1st ed. VG no dust jacket. $23.

HISTORY OF THE AMERICAN FIELD SERVICE IN FRANCE 1914-1917. 3 vols. Boston, 1920 1st. Fine. $85.

HISTORY OF BEAVER COUNTY, PA. Knickerbocker Press, 1904. 2 vols. Very Good. $150.

HISTORICAL & BIOGRAPHICAL RECORD OF WOOD COUNTY, OHIO. 1976 reprint of 1897 2 volume set. Very Good. $45.

HISTORY OF BOONE COUNTY, MISSOURI. St. Louis, Western Hist. Co., 1882. 1,144 pages. Illus. 3/4 leather. Rebacked. Very Good. $160.

PORTRAIT AND BIOGRAPHICAL RECORD OF BOONE & CLINTON COUNTIES, INDIANA. A. W. Bowen, 1895. 908 pages. Leather bound. Portraits, Biographies. Very Good. $125.

HISTORY OF THE 11th AERO SQUADRON, U.S.A., 1917-1919. Written & illus. by members. No place, 1922. Rubbed, contents Fine. $95.

BIOGRAPHICAL & HISTORICAL RECORD OF KANE COUNTY ILLINOIS. Chicago, 1888. 1,115 pages. Spine missing, poor covers. $145.

HISTORY OF THE CITY OF CLEVELAND, 1796-1806. J. H. Kennedy. Cleveland, 1896 1st. 605 pgs. Good. $75.

HISTORY OF THE CITY OF DENVER, ARAPAHOE COUNTY & COLORADO. Chicago, Baskin & Co., 1880. 652 pgs. Orig. 3/4 leather, gilt-stamped cover. VG. $400.

HISTORY OF THE CITY OF NEW YORK, 1609-1909. John W. Leonard. NY, 1910. 954 pages. Worn cover. $90.

HISTORY OF CONCORD, N. H. James O. Lyford, editor. Illus. Rumford Press, NH, 1903. 1,477 pgs. Good. $120.

HISTORY OF CONTRA COSTA COUNTY, CALIFORNIA. Munro-Fraser. San Francisco, 1882. 710 pages. Illus. 1st ed. in orig. sheepskin. Covers detached. $300.

HISTORY OF CUMBERLAND & ADAMS COUNTIES, PA. 1974 reprint of 1886 edition. Very Good. $75.

HISTORY OF THE TOWN OF DOUGLAS MASSACHUSETTS. Wm. A. Emerson. Boston, 1879. 3/4 leather covers, 359 pages. 100 pages of genealogy. Signed. $65.

HISTORY OF DELAWARE COUNTY. Ohio, 1975 reprint of 1880 history. Illus., maps. Fine. $45.

HISTORY OF ERIE COUNTY, PA. Chicago, 1884 1st ed. 1,006 pages. $75.

HISTORY OF THE GREAT LAKES. ILLUSTRATED. John B. Mansfield editor. Chicago, J. H. Beers, 1899. 2 volumes. 928 & 1213 pages. 5 double maps. Full leather with gilt stamping. Near Fine. $450.

HISTORY OF HANCOCK COUNTY, OHIO. Jacob Spaythe, 1903. 311 pages. Very Good. $85.

HISTORY OF HARFORD COUNTY, MARYLAND. Preston, Baltimore, 1972 reprint of 1901 ed. Fine. $35.

HISTORY OF HENNEPIN COUNTY & THE CITY OF MINNEAPOLIS. George E. Warner, et. al., North Star Pub. Co., 1881, 731 pgs. map intact. G-VG. $135.

COMPLETE HISTORY OF ILLINOIS, 1673-1873. Davidson & Stuve. Springfield, 1874. 944 pages. Covers worn, few tattered pages. Good. $125.

NEW CENTENNIAL HISTORY OF THE STATE OF KANSAS. Charles R. Tuttle. Inter-State Book Co., 1876. 708 pages. Some illus. Rubbed, soiled cover, else G. $135.

HISTORY OF MASSACHUSETTS. Geo. Lowell Austin. Boston, 1885. 597 pages. Green decorative cloth cover. Stained, hinge crack. $25.

ILLUSTRATED HISTORY OF MONROE COUNTY, IOWA. By Frank Hickenlooper. Albia IA, 1896. Soiled, else. Very Good. $125

HISTORY OF MONTGOMERY COUNTY, PA. 1975 reprint of 1884 1st ed. 2 vols. 1,197 pages. VG. $80.

AN ILLUSTRATED HISTORY OF MISSOURI. by Walter Davis and Daniel Durrie. St. Louis, 1876. 639 pages. Good. $150.

HISTORY OF NEVADA WITH ILLUSTRATIONS AND BIOGRAPHICAL SKETCHES. Oakland, Thompson & West, 1881 1st ed. Rebound in morocco. 680 pages. Near Fine. $500 auction.

SOUVENIR HISTORY OF NIAGARA COUNTY, NY. 25th Anniversary edition. 1902. Good. $18.

HISTORY OF OHIO. Rowland H. Rerick. Madison WI, 1905 1st ed. 3/4 leather. Bumped corners. Good. $50.

HISTORY OF THE STATE OF OHIO. Carl Wittke, editor. OH, 1941-42. 6 vol. set. Fine. $150.

HISTORY OF THE RED CROSS. THE TREATY OF GENEVA. Washington. 1883. Ex-library. Good. $25.

HISTORY OF RHODE ISLAND AND NEWPORT. Edward Peterson. 1853 1st edition. Good. $95.

PICTORIAL HISTORY OF THE CITY OF RICHMOND, INDIANA. By Ed and Walter Dalbey. Richmond IN, Nicholson Printing Co., 1896. 198 pages, of which 188 are illustrated views of bldgs., etc. Worn, else very good. $200.

HISTORY OF ROSS AND HIGHLAND COUNTIES (OHIO). 1978 reprint of 1796 illustrated history. 642 pages, maps, etc. Very Good. $55.

HISTORY OF SACRAMENTO COUNTY CALIFORNIA WITH BIOGRAPHICAL SKETCHES OF MEN AND WOMEN. Los Angles, 1923 1st ed. Near Fine. $75-$100.

AN ILLUSTRATED HISTORY OF SACRAMENTO. Win. J. Davis. 808 pages, many engravings. Chicago, Lewis Pub., 1890 1st ed. Fine. $200-$300.

HISTORY OF SENECA COUNTY. Consul W. Butterfield. Sandusky, 1848 1st ed. 248 pages. Rebacked, spotted cover. Good. $250-$350.

HISTORY OF SENECA COUNTY. By W. Lang. Springfield, 1880. 6 x 9 inches, 691 pages. Worn, stained. $75.

HISTORY OF SOLANO COUNTY. San Francisco, 1879. Munro-Fraser. Includes 20 lithographed portrait plates. Very Good. $357 auction.

HISTORY OF THE 77th DIVISION. NY, 1919. Written in the field, France. Near Fine. $50.

A HISTORY OF TECHNOLOGY. Editor, Charles Singer and others. London, 1954-58. 5 vols. 1st ed. Profusely illus. Very Good in dust jackets. $200.

HISTORY OF THE 3rd DIVISION, U. S. ARMY. 1919 1st ed. Army. Good. $14.

HISTORY OF VAN WERT AND MERCER COUNTIES, OHIO, 1882 1st ed. Fair, water stained covers. $129.

HISTORY OF A VILLAGE, RIDGEWOOD NEW JERSEY. 1964 1st ed. 165 pages. Fine in DJ. $15-$20.

A HISTORY OF THE CITY OF VINCENNES, 1702-1901. Terre Haute, 1902. VG. $35. Fine. $45.

HISTORY OF WAYNE COUNTY INDIANA. Cincinnati, 1872. Andrew Young. 459 pages. $110.

HISTORY OF YORK COUNTY, PA. 1973 reprint of 1886 1st ed. 772 pages plus new material. VG. $45-$80.

HITCHCOCK, HENRY RUSSELL. *In The Nature of Materials. The Buildings of Frank Lloyd Wright 1887-1941*. NY, 1942. Inscription from author to an artist. $125. *Latin American Architecture Since 1945*. NY, Museum of Modern Art, 1955. Illus. VG in DJ. $20.

HITLER, ADOLF. *My Struggle (Mein Kampf)*. London, 1933 5th printing in English. VG. $90. 1939 ed. $16-$24. *Mein Kampf*. Reynal & Hitchcock, 1941 21st ed. Cover stains, o/w Good plus. $12. *My New Order*. Reynal & Hitchcock, 1941 1st ed. VG, no dust jacket. $14. *Blitzkrieg to Defeat: Hitler's War Directives*. Holt, 1964 1st ed. Very Good in dust jacket. $20.

HITTELL, JOHN S. *A History of the City of San Francisco*. A. L. Bancroft, 1878 1st ed. Faded spine, worn. Good-Very Good. $100-$150.

HITTEL, T. *Adventures of James Capen Adams*. NY, 1911 ed. New introduction and postscript. VG. $130.

HITTELL, THEODORE H. *History of California*. San Francisco, 1898. 4 vols. G-VG. $10-$150. Earlier 2 vol. set. 1885 1st ed. Good-VG. $150-$200.

HOBBS, JAMES. *Wild Life in the Far West. Adventures of a Border Mountain Man*. Hartford, 1873. Soiled, rubbed. Good-VG. $100-$150.

HOCHWALT, A. F. *The Modern Setter*. Private printing, 1923 2nd ed. Good. $40.

HODGE, FREDERICK (Editor). *Handbook of American Indians North of Mexico*. 2 vols. Washington, Govt. Printing Office, 1907-1910 1st ed. Original sheep. Worn spine. Very Good. $150-$250. Part 1 only, 4th printing, 1912. Very Good. $60.

HODGSON, FRED T. *Practical Carpentry*. New York, 1883. Good-Very Good. $20. *The Carpenters' Steel Square*. NY, 1893. $25. *Builders' Architectural Drawing Self-Taught*. Chicago, Good-VG. 1904. $25. *Easy Steps in Architecture & Architectural Drawing*. Chicago, 1913. Good-VG. $30. *The Builders' Guide & Estimators' Price Book*. NY, 1882 1st ed. Good-VG. $25. *Practical Bungalows and Cottages*. F. Drake, 1916 revised ed. Very Good. $15.

HODGSON, WILLIAM HOPE. *The House on the Borderlands and Other Novels*. Arkham House, 1946. Near Fine in as new DJ. $350. *Carnacki, the Ghostfinder*. Arkham House, 1947 1st ed. Fine in dust jacket. $150. *Deep Waters*. Arkham House, 1967 1st. Fine in DJ. $75. *Poems of the Sea*. London, 1977. Limited ed. Illus. F. $68.

HOEHLING, A. A. *Great Ship Disasters*. Chicago, 1971. Very Good in dust jacket. $19.

HOFF, A. C. *Bread & Pastry Recipes of the World Famous Chefs*. Los Angeles, CA, 1913. Good-VG. $25.

HOFFER, ERIC. *The True Believer*. No place, 1951 1st ed. Good to Very Good. $12. *Working & Thinking on the Waterfront*. Harper, 1969. Very Good in dust jacket. $20.

HOFFMAN, W. *Draw Poker, The Standard Game*. NY, 1913. 113 pages. Very Good. $45 auction.

HOGARTH, WILLIAM. *The Complete Works of William Hogarth*. London, 2 vols., no date, circa 1880. 150 steel engravings. VG. $250. Another, with James Hannay intro. Lon. Printing & Pub. Co. (circa 1850). Single vol. in full brown morocco. $60-$80. (Many 1880s folio volumes are broken for individual plates, which sell for $15-$25 each.)

HOLBROOK, STEWART. *Holy Old Mackinaw*. NY, 1938 1st ed. Signed. Good plus. $35.
Lost Men of American History. NY, 1946. VG. $9.
The Story of American Railroads. NY, 1947 3rd printing, Crown. VG in DJ. $18. 1959 5th printing. $12.
The Columbia. New York, 1956 1st edition. Rivers of America series. $18-$35. Signed, in DJ. $30-$50.
The Old Post Road. NY, 1962 1st ed. VG to Near Fine in dust jacket. $20-$35.

HOLDER, CHARLES F. *Life in Open: Sport With Road, Gun, Horse & Hound etc.* NY, 1906 1st ed. F. $50-$95.
Big Game at Sea. Outing, 1908. VG. $38.
Recreations of a Sportsman On the Pacific Coast. NY, 1910 1st ed. Good-VG. $25-$75.
Salt Water Game Fishing. NY, 1923. Good. $10.

HOLE, CHRISTINA. *Witchcraft in England*. London, 1947. VG. $25. NY, 1947 1st U. S. edition. VG. $20-$30.
English Home-Life, 1500 to 1800. London, 1949. Illus. Good-Very Good in torn dust jacket. $25.
Haunted England. London, 1950. Good. $15.

HOLLAND, DAN. *Trout Fishing*. Crowell, 1949 1st edition. C. Ford, photos. Good. $16.

HOLLAND, MRS. MARY. *Economical Cook and Frugal Housewife*. London, 1853 16th ed. Fine. $175.
Our Army Nurses (Civil War). Boston, 1895 1st ed. Overall Very Good. $175.

HOLLAND, RAY. *My Gun Dogs*. Houghton-Mifflin, 1929. Very Good. $25. 1st ed. Fine. $60.
Shotgunning in the Uplands. NY, 1944 2nd printing. Lynn Bogue Hunt illus. VG. $70. Same. One of 250 copies. Signed. Very Good. $250.
Good Shot. No place, 1946 1st ed. Fine in DJ. $23.
Bird Dogs. NY, 1948 1st ed. Illus. Fred McCaleb illus. Foxing on early pages. Good. $15. Same, Very Good. $30.
Scattergunning. NY, 1951 1st ed. VG in DJ. $45.
7 Grand Gun Dogs. NY, 1961 1st ed. One of 260 copies. Fine, boxed, $250.

HOLLAND, RUPERT SARGENT. *Yankee Ships in Pirate Waters*. Macrae-Smith, 1931. Frank Schoonover illus. Very Good in dust jacket. $20.
Historic Railroads. 1927, Grosset & Dunlap. Good. $25.

HOLLAND, W. J. *To the River Plate and Back*. NY, 1913 1st ed. Illus. VG plus. $110. Another, worn. $50.

HOLLEY, GEORGE W. *Niagara: Its History and Geology*. NY, 1872 2nd ed. Folding maps, lithographs. Covers badly stained. $25. Same year, 1st ed. Very Good. $75.

HOLLEY, MARIETTA (Also see Allen, Josiah's wife). *My Wayward Pardner*. Hartford CT 1880. Good. $25.
Samantha at The World's Fair. NY, 1893, Funk & Wagnall. Very Good. $12.
Samantha on the Race Problem. Boston, 1892. Ornate colored cover. G-VG. $40. Fine. $70.
Samantha Among the Brethren. NY, 1890, Funk & Wagnall. Edge wear, o/w good. $9.

HOLLING, HOLLING C. *The Book of Indians*. Platt & Munk, 1935. Illus. by author. Very Good in chip dust jacket. $35. Good in DJ. $14.
The Book of Cowboys. Platt & Munk, 1936 1st ed. Illus. by author. VG in DJ. $25. Good. $12.
Paddle-to-the-Sea. Boston, 1941 1st ed. Illus. by author. VG in worn in dust jacket. $70.
Minn. of the Mississippi. Boston, 1951 1st ed. Illus. by author. Fine. $40.

HOLLING, L. and H. C. (Illustrators). *Little Folks of Other Lands*. By Watty Piper. NY, 1956. VG. $35.
Road to Storyland. Platt & Munk, 1952. VG in DJ. $40.

HOLLOWAY, E. S. *The Practical Book of Furnishing The Small House or Apartment*. Phila., 1922. Near VG. $85.

HOLLOWAY, LAURA C. *The Hearthstone: or Life at Home*. A household manual. Chicago, 1887. G-VG. $45.

HOLLY, H. W. *The Carpenter's & Joiner's Hand-Book*. NY, 1883 revised edition. Good-VG. $20-$35.
The Art of Saw Filing. NY, 1882 4th edition. $25.

HOLMAN, HAMILTON. *Zachary Taylor, Soldier in the White House*. Bobbs-Merrill, 1951 1st ed. Very Good in dust jacket. Illus. $15.

HOLMES, EFNER TUDOR. *The Christmas Cat*. NY, 1976. Tasha Tudor illus. Fine. $35.

HOLMES, OLIVER WENDELL JR. *The Common Law*. Boston, 1881 1st edition. Rebound in morocco, Very Good. $400. A rough copy. Fair. $200.

HOLMES, OLIVER WENDELL, SENIOR. *The Professor at the Breakfast Table*. Boston, Ticknor & Fields, 1860 1st ed., 1st state, orig. embossed cover. VG. $195. Same year, reprint. Good-VG. $45-$75.
Songs of Many Seasons, 1862-1874. Boston, R. Osgood & Co., 1874. Very Good. $50-$75. Another, signed by author. $150.
Autocrat of the Breakfast Table. Boston, 1858 1st ed., 1st issue. $75-$150. Houghton, 1894. Pyle illus. $125.

Elsie Venner, A Romance of Destiny. Ticknor, 1861 1st edition. 2 vols. Good. $125.

The Writings of Oliver Wendell Holmes. Boston, 1891 14 vols. One of 275 sets. Near Fine. $550.

The One-Hoss Shay. Houghton-Mifflin, 1892 & 1905. Howard Pyle illus. Very Good. $50-$100.

Illustrated Poems of Oliver Wendell Holmes. Boston, 1885. Howard Pyle illus. Very Good. $30-$45.

HOLZWORTH, J. *Wild Grizzlies of Alaska*. Putnam's, 1930 1st ed. Illus. Good plus in DJ. $75.

HOMANS, JAMES E. *Self-Propelled Vehicles*. NY, Audel, 1904. Early classic. Fine in DJ. $75. 1902 edition. G-VG. $50. 1910 edition. $22.

HOME COMFORT COOKBOOK. Wrought Iron Range Co., St. Louis, No date. Very Good. $20.

HOME QUEEN WORLD'S FAIR SOUVENIR COOK BOOK. Geo. F. Cram Pub. Co., 1883 1st ed. VG. $250. Same, 1898 4th ed. $40-$50.

HOME, DANIEL DUNGLAS. *Incidents in My Life*. NY, 1864. Probably 5th ed. Bad spine, o/w Very Good. $40.

Lights and Shadows of Spiritualism. NY, 1879 1st American ed. Lacks flyleaf, half-title. Good. $45.

HOMES, GEOFFREY. *Forty Whacks*. NY, 1941 1st ed. Near Fine in chipped dust jacket. $75.

HONEY, W. B. *The Art of the Potter*. New York, 1955 1st edition. Illustrated. Fine. $30.

Ceramic Art of China & Other Countries. NY, 1954 1st ed. Very Good in dust jacket. $35.

THE NEW HOOD COOK BOOK. H. P. Hood & Sons, Dairy Products, 1941. 394 pages. A tall red book. VG. $15.

HOOD, JOSEPH F. *When Monsters Roamed the Sky*. Grosset & Dunlap, 1968 1st ed. Fine in DJ. $15.

HOOK, F. A. *A Romance of the Clipper Ships*. NY, 1972 3 vols. Mint in dust jacket and slipcase. $225.

HOOTON, ERNEST. *Poor Man's Relations*. NY, 1942. Fine in Very Good dust jacket. $15.

Why Men Behave Like Apes & Vice Versa. Princeton, 1940. Very Good. $15.

HOOVER, HERBERT CLARK. *A Remedy for Disappearing Game Fishes*. NY, 1930 1st ed. Harry Cimino illus. One of 990 copies. VG. $75.

Challenge to Liberty. NY, 1934 1st ed. VG. $20.

Memoirs of Herbert Hoover, 1929-1941. Macmillan, 1952 1st ed. $20-$35. Another. Inscribed by author. VG in dust jacket. $200.

HOOVER, J. EDGAR. *Masters of Deceit*. NY, 1960 6th printing. Signed. VG in torn DJ. $35.

A Study of Communism. NY, 1962 4th printing. Inscribed, Very Good. $45.

HOPE, ANTHONY. *The Dolly Dialogues*. Russell, 1901. Howard C. Christy, illus. Good. $8. VG. $25-$35. NY, Holt, 1894. Arthur Rackham illus. $50.

Tristram of Blent. McClure, 1901. Good. $10.

The Prisoner of Zenda. London, no date 1st ed. VG. $30. Same, 1898. Gibson illus. G & D. $10-$15.

HOPE, ARTHUR. *A Manual of Sorrento and Inlaid Work for Amateurs*. Chicago, 1876. 47 pages + ads. VG. $35.

HOPE, BOB. *I Owe Russia $1,200*. No place, 1936. Inscribed. Fine in dust jacket. $35.

5 Women I Love. Doubleday, 1966 1st ed. VG in DJ. $25.

HOPE, THOMAS. *Costume of the Ancients*. London, 1812, New ed. enlarged. 2 vols. Foxing, hinges repaired. $150.

HOPE, LAURA LEE (HARRIET ADAMS). *The Outdoor Girls in a Motor Car*. Grosset & Dunlap, 1913. Illus. Good. $5.

The Moving Picture Girls at Oak Farm. Grosset & Dunlap, 1914. Good. $15.

The Outdoor Girls at Hostesss House. NY, 1919 1st ed. R. Owen illus. VG. $20.

The Bobbsey Twins and Baby May.(no. 17) Grosset & Dunlap, 1924 1st ed. Last title on DJ list. VG. $30. Another, not a 1st edition, No DJ. $5.

The Bobbsey Twins and Their Schoolmates. Grosset & Dunlap, 1928. DJ. Good plus. $12.

The Blythe Girls: Margy's Mysterious Visitor. Grosset & Dunlap, 1930. Good in DJ. $15.

Bobbsey Twins (All below have green covers):
The Bobbsey Twins' Wonderful Secret. G&D, 1932. $8.
In a Radio Play. 1937. VG in DJ. $9.
In Echo Valley. 1943. VG in DJ. $9.
In a Rainbow Valley. 1950. VG in DJ. $9.
On a Bicycle Trip. 1954. VG in DJ. $9.

Edward Stratemeyer (See Appleton, Victor) wrote the first *Bobbsey Twins* book in 1904. His daughter Harriet Adams took over the series soon after and one or two titles appeared every year until 1979. The series has sold 50 million copies.

HOPKINS, ALBERT. *Home Made Beverages*. NY, 1919 2nd printing. (Includes alcoholic drinks) Hinge cracked. $20.

HOPKINS, ALBERT A. *The Lure of the Lock*. NY, Museum of Mechanics & Tradesmen, 1954, (still in print). $15-$20.

HOPKINS, G. MANLEY. *Poems: Second Edition, With Additional Poems*. Oxford University Press, 1930. Fine in rubbed dust jacket. $150.

Some Poems. London, 1945 1st ed. booklet. $50.

HOPPE, WILLIE. *Thirty Years of Billiards*. NY, 1925. Some foxing, rubbing, o/w Very Good. $60.

HOPWOOD, JOHN A. *Monkey Family*. Chicago, 1930. Illus. by author. Very Good. $35.

HORAN, JAMES D. *Confederate Agent*. NY, 1954 1st ed. Crown Pub. VG-Fine in DJ. $20-$40.
Timothy O'Sullivan: America's Forgotten Photographer. Doubleday, 1966. Fine. $60.
The Pinkertons: The Detective Dynasty. NY, 1967 1st ed. Crown. Fine in DJ. $40-$60. Bonanza, 1957 printing. Good-VG. $10-$15.
North American Indian Portraits. NY, 1975. 120 color plates. Very Good. $15.
Mathew Brady, Historian With a Camera. Crown Pub., 1955. Very Good in dust jacket. $25.
The Great American West. Pictorial History. Crown Pub, 1959 1st ed. VG in DJ. $20.
Across The Cimarron. NY, Crown, 1956 1st ed. VG in fair dust jacket. $30.

HORGAN, PAUL. *Great River. (Rio Grande)*. Rinehart, 1954 1st ed. Rivers of America series. 2 vols, slipcased. Near Fine in good DJ. $35. Book Club edition. Fine, no DJ. $12.
The Centuries of Santa Fe. NY, 1956 1st ed. Very Good in dust jacket. $15-$30.
Lamy of Santa Fe. Farrar & Strauss, 1975 1st ed. VG, no dust jacket. $10.

HORN, CALVIN. *New Mexico's Trouble Years*. Albuquerque NM, 1963 1st edition. Inscribed. VG in DJ. $35.

HORN, HENRY. *Drumming as a Fine Art. Commercial Travelers, Their Lives on the Road*. New York, 1882. Chipped, worn. $50.

HORN, TOM. *Life of Tom Horn, Government Scout & Interpreter*. Denver, 1904 1st ed. Cloth. $45-$80. Chicago, 1987 reprint. Fine. $35. Another, 1957 ed. Good. $30.

HORNADAY, W. T. *The American Natural History*. Scribner's, 1904 1st ed. Good-VG. $40-$50.
The Minds and Manners of Wild Animals. NY, 1922. Inscribed. Good. $25. Same, unsigned. $15.
Campfires in the Canadian Rockies. New York, 1923. Very Good. $100.

HORNBECK, JAMES (Editor). *Design For Modern Merchandising. Stores, Shopping Centers, Showrooms*. NY, 1954 1st ed. Very Good. $35.

HORNE, CHARLES F. *Great Men & Famous Women*. 1894 set of engravings in 8 volumes. VG. $85-$100.

HORNE, LENA and RICHARD SCHICKEL. *"Lena."* Doubleday, 1965. Inscribed, VG. in DJ. $75.

HORNER, HARLAN H. *Lincoln and Greeley*. Univ. of Illinois Press, 1953 1st ed. Good. $10.

HORNUNG, CLARENCE. *Handbook of Early American Advertising Art*. Dover Pub., 1947 1st ed. Orig. cloth. $50. (Still in print today).
Wheels Across America. NY, Barnes, 1966 4th printing. Very Good in dust jacket. $25.

HORNUNG, E. W. *Dead Men Tell No Tales*. London, 1899. Paperback. Very Good. $115.
Mr. Justice Raffles. NY, 1909 1st ed. VG. $40.
The Crime Doctor. Indianapolis, 1914. Frederic D. Steele illus. Very Good. $12.

HOSMER, JAMES K. *A Short History of the Mississippi Valley*. Boston, 1901 1st ed. Good. $25. Another, with minor cover stains. $12.

HOTEL PLANNING AND OUTFITTING. Anon. Chicago, 1927-1928. Plans & views of famous resorts & hotels. $75.

HOUDIN, ROBERT. *Card Sharpers: Their Tricks Exposed*. 1902. Green cover, 189 pages. Very Fine. $85 auction.

HOUDINI, HARRY. *Miracle Mongers and Their Methods*. No place, 1920 1st American ed. VG in original DJ. $86.
The Right Way To Do Wrong. Boston, 1906 1st edition. in wraps. $175.
A Magician Among Spirits. NY, 1924. Inscribed to Dick Fuller. Good. $1,175. Another, unsigned. $200.
Houdini's Big Little Book of Magic. Whitman, 1927. American Oil Co. Very Good. $25.

HOUGEN, J. H. *The History of the Famous 324th Infantry Division in World War*. No place. 1979. Fine. $40.

HOUGH, EMERSON. *The Story of the Cowboy*. NY, 1897 1st ed. C. M. Russell illus. Fine. $38. Appleton, 1923. Story of West series. Good. $18.
A Man's Story. Ticknor, 1889 1st ed. VG. $40.
The Mississippi Bubble. Bowen Merrill, 1902 1st ed. Henry Hutt illus. Very Good. $20.
The Way to the West. No place, 1903 1st ed. Frederic Remington illus. Near Fine. $100. Very Good. $85.
54, 40 or Fight. Bobbs-Merrill. 1909 1st ed. VG. $15.
The Magnificent Adventure. Appleton, 1916 1st ed. Pictorial cover. Near Fine in dust jacket. $125.
Plain People. Dodd Mead, 1929 1st ed. Signed. Fine in dust jacket. $28.

HOUGH, HENRY BEETLE. *An Alcoholic to His Sons*. Simon-Schuster, 1954 1st ed. Fine in dust jacket. $16.

HOUSEHOLD DISCOVERIES AND MRS. CURTIS' COOK BOOK. Success Pub., 1902. G. $35. (Later editions omitted outhouse plans). 1909-1914. G-VG. $15-$25.

HOUSEHOLD, GEOFFREY. *A Time to Kill*. Boston, 1951
1st American ed. Near Fine in DJ. $28.
The Courtesy of Death. Boston, 1967 1st American ed.
Fine in dust jacket. $25.
Doom's Caravan. Boston, 1971 1st American ed. Fine in
good dust jacket. $18.

HOUSEHOLD SEARCHLIGHT RECIPE BOOK. Topeka,
1939 12th ed. G-VG. $12-$14 1958 ed., 320 pgs. $10-$15.

HOUSE, HORNER D. *Wild Flowers of New York*. 2 vols.
Albany NY, 1923 2nd printing. VG. $95-$125.

THE HOUSEKEEPER'S COOK BOOK AND KITCHEN
GUIDE. Anon. NY, circa 1875. Paperbound. $25.

HOUSTON, EDWIN J. *Elements of Physical Geography*.
Eldridge & Bro., 1899 revised ed. Very Good. $14.

HOW TO KEEP A HUSBAND, OR CULINARY TACTICS.
San Francisco, 1872. 2nd cookbook ever published in
California. Paperbound. $600.

HOWARD, MRS. B. C. *Fifty Years in a Maryland Kitchen*.
NY, 1944. Revised by Florence Brobeck. G-VG. $15.

HOWARD, CLIVE and J. WHITLEY. *One Damned Island
After Another: A History of the 7th Air Force in WWII*.
No place, 1946 1st ed. Good plus. $45. Without DJ. $28.

HOWARD, MAJOR GEN. OLIVER OTIS. *Autobiography
of Oliver Otis Howard*. 2 vols. Baker & Taylor, 1907 1st
ed. Very Good, no dust jacket . $75.

HOWARD, MARIA W. *Lowney's Cook Book*. Boston,
W. M. Lowney Co, 1912 revised ed. 425 pages with ads.
Good-VG. $25.

HOWARD, ROBERT E. *Skull-Face and Others*. Arkham
House, 1946 1st Limited ed. VG in chip DJ. $27.
Conan the Conqueror. NY, 1950 1st ed. Near Very Good
in faded dust jacket. $80.
The Sword of Conan. NY, 1952 1st edition. Half of dust
jacket missing. $30.
The Coming of Conan. Gnome Press, 1953 1st ed. Good
in dust jacket. $100.
King Conan. Gnome Press, 1953 1st edition. Good in
dust jacket. $100.
Conan the Barbarian. NY, 1954 1st ed. Edgewear. Good
plus in dust jacket. $60. VG-Fine in DJ. $80-$100.

HOWE, HENRY F. *Salt Rivers of the Massachusetts Shore*.
Rivers of America series. NY, 1951 1st ed. Rinehart. No
dust jacket. $20.

HOWE, JULIA WARD. *Passion Flowers*. Boston, 1854 1st
ed. Author's 1st book. Gift binding. Near Fine. $200.

A Trip to Cuba. Boston, 1860 1st edition. Good. $25.
Later Lyrics. Boston, 1866 1st ed. Very Good. $30.
From the Oak to the Olive. Boston, 1868. Near VG. $45.

HOWELS, JOHN MEAD. *Lost Examples of Colonial
Architecture*. NY, 1931 Limited. ed. 1 of 1,100. $50.

HOWELLS, WILLIAM DEAN. *Suburban Sketches*. Boston,
1871 1st ed. Author's 1st book. VG. $100. 1872 new
enlarged ed. Good. $22.
Venetian Life. Boston, 1892 2 vols. 1st trade ed. VG. $50.
Riverside Press ed. of 1907. 2 vols. One of 550 copies.
Very Good. $100.
The Rise of Silas Lapham. Boston, 1885 1st ed., 1st
printing. Near Fine. $275. 1951 Modern Library edition.
Very Good in dust jacket. $10.
Roman Holidays and Others. Harpers, NY, 1908 1st ed.
Green. gilt decorative cloth. Fine. $35.

HOWLAND, CHESTER. *Whale Hunters Aboard the Grey
Gold*. Caxton, Idaho, 1957. Very Fine in DJ. $45.

HOWLAND, JOHN. *James Whitcomb Riley in Prose and
Pictures*. Chicago, 1903 1st ed. Fine. $45.

HOYLE (author unknown); Edmond? *Hoyles Games
Improved*. Boston, 1814. $120.
American Hoyle. by "Trumps". 1864. 518 pages. VF. $75.
Hoyle's Games. Circa 1940. 278 pgs. Worn. $100 auction.
Hoyle's Improved Edition of Rules For Fashionable
Games. NY, 1830. $75.

HOYNINGEN-HUENE, G. (Photographer). *African Mirage:
The Record of a Journey*. NY, London, 1938. Good in
worn dust jacket. $70.

HRDLICKA, ALES. *Old Americans*. Baltimore, 1925 1st ed.
Very Good. $40.
Alaska Diary, 1926-1931. Lancaster PA, 1943 1st edition.
Ex-library. $40.

HUBBARD, ELBERT. *Time and Chance*. Roycroft, 1899.
2 vols. Very Good. $88.
As It Seems to Me. Roycroft, 1897 1st ed. Suede. Fox. $65.
Ballads of a Book Worm. By Irving Brown. Roycroft,
1899. Hand-illuminated. One of 850 copies signed by
Hubbard. Rebound. Fine. $175.
A Message to Garcia. East Aurora, 1899. 1st. 1 of 1,000.
Suede binding. Fine. $65. Later editions have little value.
The City of Tagaste. Roycroft, 1900. One of 940 copies.
Signed by Hubbard and artist. VG. $225-$275.
Hamlet. by Shakespeare. Roycroft, 1902. Inscribed by
Elbert Hubbard. $50.
Gray's Elegy. Roycroft, 1903. Illustrated. Half-calf in
case. Fine. $50.
Consecrated Lives. Roycroft, 1904. 1st edition. Very
Good. green suede. $28.

Joaquin Miller. Roycroft, 1903 1st ed. Suede cover. Very Good-Fine. $25-$35.

White Hyacinths. Roycroft, 1907 1st ed. Good suede. $28.

Little Journeys to the Homes of Great Orators. Roycroft, 1903. Very Good. $14.

Health and Wealth. Roycroft, 1908 1st edition. Suede covers. Very Good. $15.

Pig Pen Pete, or Some Chums of Mine. Roycrofters, 1914. Leather covers worn. $25.

Little Journeys to the Homes of the Great Lovers. No place, 1916. VG in chip DJ. $13.

The Complete Writings of Elbert Hubbard. Roycroft Press, 1908-1915. 19 of 20 vols. (vol. 15, missing). Top, bottom, rib wear. One spine needs repair. One of 1,000 signed. $350.

Abe Lincoln & Nancy Hanks. Roycrofter, 1920. Very Good to Fine. $15-$25.

Elbert Hubbard's Scrap Book. NY, 1923 1st edition in original leather box. $35-$65. Rev. ed. No box. VG. $15.

Poor Richard's Almanac. By Benjamin Franklin. East Aurora, 1924. Nice. $30.

Little Journeys to the Homes of The Great. Memorial ed. Wise & Co. No date. 14 volumes and guide. Roycrofters. Very Good. $100.

1916-1928 Editions. 14 vols. Good. $30-$40.

Little Journeys to the Homes of Great Scientists: Tyndall. 1905, Roycroft. VG. $14.

Little Journeys to the Homes of Famous Women. 1908. Good-Very Good. $20-$35. 1911 ed. $12-$15.

Elbert Hubbard's Scrapbook. Roycroft, 1923. Leather or cardboard cover. Good-VG. $8-$12.

HUBBARD, ELBERT (In Magazines). *The Philistine*. Mar, 1899. "A Message to Garcia". $15-$25.
The Goodrich. Feb, 1913. Article. $45.

HUBBARD, JEREMIAH. *Forty Years Among the Indians*. Miami, OK, 1913. Very Good $350.

HUBBARD, KIN. *Abe Martin's Home Cured Philosphy*. Abe Martin, circa 1907. Good, stain. $12.
Abe Martin on the War and Other Things. Abe Martin, 1919 1st ed. Good. $15.
These Days by Abe Martin. Kin Hubbard, circa 1920. Good. $14.
Kin Hubbard's Legislature Sketches. 1905 1st ed. $18
Abe Martin - Hoss Sense and Nonsense. IN, 1926 1st ed. Hubbard, illus. VG in Good DJ. $22.
Abe Martin of Brown County, Indiana. IN, 1906 1st ed. Gingham cloth, paper label. Light soil, o/w good. $37.

HUBBARD, L. RON. *Buckskin Brigade*. Macauley, 1937 1st ed. Author's 1st book. VG in DJ. $2,000.
Slaves of Sleep. Shasta Publishing Co. 1948 1st ed. Very Good in dust jacket. $300-$350.
Final Blackout. Hadley, 1948 1st ed. VG to Fine in DJ. $200-$350. No dust jacket. $125.

Dianetics. Hermitage, 1950 1st ed. Near Fine in dust jacket. $200-$500. 1951 ed. VG in DJ. $45-$80.
Self-Analysis. No place, 1951 1st ed. Paperbound with "wheels". Fine, $150.
Return to Tomorrow. NY, 1954 Ace original paperback 1st ed. Fine. $125.

HUBBARD, WILLIAM. *A Narrative of the Indian Wars in New England*. Mass, 1801 reprint of 1677 edition. Rebound in simple leather. $125.

HUBBLE, EDWIN. *The Realm of the Nebulae*. Yale Univ. Press, 1937 2nd printing. Ex-lib. Near VG. $40. 1958 edition. Very Good. $5-$10.
The Observational Approach to Cosmology. Oxford, 1937 1st ed. Very Good. $20.

HUDSON OWNER'S MANUAL. *1949-1954 editions*. $15-$20 each. (Also see Catalog Section).

HUDSON, THOMAS JAY. *The Law of Psychic Pnenomena*. Chicago, 1893. Cover spotting, flyleaf out, o/w Good. $25.
The Law of Mental Medicine. Chicago, 1903 1st edition. Very Good. $35.

HUDSON, W. H. *Idle Days in Patagonia*. London, 1893 1st edition. Very Good. $85.
Green Mansions. London, 1904 1st ed., 1st issue. Endpapers foxed, hinges worn, lightly soiled. $350. 1944 Modern Library edition. $8-$10.
The Land's End. No place, 1908 1st ed. Illus. VG. $40.
Adventures Among Birds. NY, 1915 1st American ed. Very Good. $30.
Far Away and Long Ago. NY, 1918 1st ed. Good. $18.
The Purple Land. LEC 1943. Raul Rosarivo illus. Signed by Rosarivo and Alberto Kraft. Slightly soiled. $125.
The Book of a Naturalist. NY, 1919 1st American ed. Zane Grey's copy. Very Good overall. $200.
Birds of La Plata. London, 1920 2 vols. 1st ed. One of 200 copies, signed by author. Ex-lib. $250.
Green Mansions. Modern Library. 1944. VG in DJ. $10.

HUFFARD & CARLISLE. *My Poetry Book, for Boys & Girls*. Winston, 1934 1st ed. Pogany illus. G-VG. $25-$35.

HUGHES, DOROTHY B. *The Fallen Sparrow*. NY, 1942 1st ed. Very Good in dust jacket. $65.
The Blackbirder. NY, 1943 1st ed. VG in DJ. $50-$75.
Ride the Pink Horse. NY, 1946. Chip DJ. $35.
The Expendable Man. NY, 1963 1st ed. Fine in DJ. $35.

HUGHES, LANGSTON. *The Sweet Flypaper of Life*. NY, 1955. One of 2,920 copies. Fine in chip DJ. $175.
The First Book of Jazz. NY, 1955 1st ed. Fine in DJ. $125. Same, Very Good. $35.
Simple Stakes a Claim. London, 1958 1st British edition. Very Good in dust jacket. $85.

HUGHES, LANGSTON & ARNA BONTEMPS. *The Poetry of the Negro, 1746-1949*. NY, 1949 Definitive anthology. Very Good in dust jacket. $95.

HUGHES, NORMAN. *Practical Handbook of the Hand Telephone*. New York, 1894. Very Good. $75.

HUGHES, TED. *The Hawk in the Rain*. NY, 1957 1st American ed. Near Fine in dust jacket. $60-$100.
The Earth-Owl and Other Moon-People. London, 1963 1st ed. R. A. Brandt illus. Fine in dust jacket. $60.
Moon-Whales and Other Moon Poems. Viking, 1976 1st ed. Leonard Baskin illus. Near Fine in DJ. $30.

HUGHES, THOMAS. *Tom Brown at Oxford*. Boston, 1861 1st American ed. 2 vols. Upper spine wear, o/w VG. $125.
Thomas Brown's School Days. NY, 1911. $15-$20.

HUGHES, WILLIAM CARTER. *The American Miller & Millwright's Assistant*. Philadelphia, 1851 2nd. $60-$75.
New Revised Edition. 1894. Good-VG. $40-$50.

HUGO, VICTOR. *Les Miserables*. London, 1887 5 vols. VG. $175. NY, Limited Editions Club, 1938. NF. $100.
The Complete Works of Victor Hugo. Paris, circa 1896. 10 vols. Fine. $125.
The Hunchback of Notre Dame. A. L. Burt, no date. Photoplay ed. Very Good. $30.

HUIE, WILLIAM B. *The Klansman*. NY, 1967 1st ed. VG in DJ. $20. Fine in dust jacket. $30.

HULBERT, ARCHER BUTLER. *The Old National Road: A Chapter of American Expansion*. Columbus, OH, 1901. Illustrated. Very Good. $85.
Historic Highways of America. Cleveland, Arthur Clark Co., 1902-1905. 16 vols., folding maps, original navy cloth. A fine set, inscribed by author. $950.
The Ohio River. NY, 1906 1st ed., fold map. Good. $75.

HULME, F. E. *The History, Principles & Practice of Heraldry*. NY, 1969. Fine. $30.

HUME, H. HAROLD. *Citrus Fruits and Their Culture*. NY, Orange Judd, 1915 6th ed. 587 pages. VG. $35.

HUMFREVILLE, J. *Twenty Years Among Our Hostile Indians*. NY, 1903. Endpapers cracked, spine wear. $150.

HUMPHREY, MAUD. *Baby's Record*. NY, Stokes, 1898 1st ed. Baby information record. 12 chromolithos. Silver-dec. cloth. Near Fine. $275-$350.
Treasury of Stories, Jingles and Rhymes. NY, Stokes, 1894. Color illus. $140-$160.
Favorite Rhymes from Mother Goose. NY, Stokes, 1891 1st edition. Color illus. cloth-backed pictorial covers. Rubbing, stains. Very Good. $150.

Children of the Revolution. NY, 1900. Illus. by author. Very Good. $200-$250.
Little Continentals. Rebound, 6 color plates. VG. $95.
Other books illustrated by this popular artist often command prices from $100-$300.

HUMPHREY, HUBERT. *The Education of a Public Man*. No place, 1976 1st ed. Inscribed. Fine in fine DJ. $45.

HUNEKER, JAMES. *Mezzotints in Modern Music*. NY, 1899 1st ed. Author's 1st book. Very Good. $100.
The Letters of James Gibbons Huneker. Scribner's, 1922 1st ed. Very Good. $8.
Painted Veils. Boni, 1920 1st ed. One of 1,200 copies. Slight soiling. $45.

HUNGERFOLRD, EDWARD. *Wells Fargo: Advancing the American Frontier*. NY, 1941 1st ed. VG in DJ. $35. 1959 edition. Near Fine. $30.

HUNT, W. BEN. *Indian Silver-Smithing*. NY, 1960-76, Collier. Very Good. $28.

HUNT, BLANCHE SEALE. *Little Brown Koko Has Fun*. American Colortype, 1952 1st ed. VG. $25. Another, Chicago, 1953. Good-VG. $38.

HUNT, FRAZIER. *The Tragic Days of Billy the Kid*. NY, 1956 1st ed. Fine in dust jacket. $40.
Cap Mossman, Last of the Great Cowmen. Hastings House, 1951 1st ed. Fine in darkened dust jacket. $50.

HUNT, FRAZIER and ROBERT HUNT. *Horses and Heroes*. The horse in America for 450 years. Illus. Fine. $75.

HUNT, JOHN W. *Wisconsin Gazetteer*. Cities, towns, villages, lakes, post offices, etc. Madison WI, 1853. 14 x 18 map intact. $350.

HUNT, LEIGH. *The Town: Its Remarkable Characters and Events*. London, 1848 1st ed. 2 vols. Illus. VG. $195.

HUNT, LYNN BOGUE. *An Artist's Game Bag*. Derrydale Press, 1936. One of 1,225 copies. Illustrated by author. Worn spine. $350.

HUNT, LYNN BOGUE (Illustrator). *Grouse Feathers*. NY, Derrydale Press, 1935 1st ed. One of 950 copies. F. $260.
Our American Game Birds. By V. C. Heilner, Garden City, 1941. Very Good in dust jacket. $75.
Pacific Game Fishing. By Skip Farrington, Jr. NY, 1942 1st ed. Very Good in dust jacket. $65.
Shotgunning in the Uplands. By Ray P. Holland. NY, 1944 2nd printing. Very Good. $60.

HUNTER, DARD. *Paper Making Through Eighteen Centuries*. NY, 1930 1st ed. Very Good. $65.

Papermaking, The History and Technique of an Ancient Craft. NY, 1943. Ex-library. $65.
Papermaking in Pioneer America. Philadelphia, 1952 1st ed. Very Good. $95.

HUNTER, J. MARVIN. *The Trail Drivers of Texas*. No place, 1920, 1923 1st eds. 2 vols. Very Good in DJ. $400.

HURLIMANN, BETTINA. *Three Centuries of Children's Books in Europe*. Cleveland, 1938 1st American edition. Very Good in dust jacket. $35.

HURST, FANNIE. *Imitation of Life*. NY, 1933 1st ed. G. $5.
White Christmas. NY, 1942 1st ed. VG. $15.
A President is Born: A Novel. NY, 1928 1st ed., Harper. Near Fine in dust jacket. $25.

HURSTON, ZORA NEALE. *Jonah's Gourd Vine*. Phil., 1934. Author's 1st book. Very Good. $1,000.
Tell My Horse. Philadelphia, 1935 1st ed. Near Fine. $250.
Mules and Men. Philadelphia, 1935 1st ed. Miguel Covarrubias illus. Extremities wear, o/w VG. $300.

HUSBAND, JOSEPH. *The Story of the Pullman Car*. Chicago, 1917 1st ed. VG. $30. 1974 reprint, Grand Rapids. Very Good in dust jacket. $20.

HUSMANN, GEORGE. *American Grape Growing and Wine Making*. NY, Orange Judd, 1915 4th revised ed. VG. $50.

HUTCHENSON, W. H. *Gene Autry and the Golden Ladder Gang*. Whitman, 1950 1st ed. Good in DJ. $14.

HUTCHINGS, J. M. *Scenes of Wonder and Curiosity in California: A Tourist's Guide to the Yosemite Valley*. NY, San Francisco, 1870. Over 100 engravings. VG. $90-$120.

HUTCHINGS, MARGARET. *The Book of the Teddy Bear*. Boston, 1965. VG in dust jacket. $25.

HUTCHINGS, J. M. *In the Heart of the Sierras, the Yosemite Valley*. Oakland CA, 1888. Folding map is torn, little foxing, tight copy, $150.

HUTCHINS, R. E. *Strange Plants and Their Ways*. NY, 1958. Very Good in dust jacket. $13.

HUTCHINSON, C. C. *Resources of Kansas. Fifteen Years Experience*. Cattle, sheep, new towns, etc. Topeka, 1871. Very Good, map split. $150.

HUTCHINSON, HORACE G. *The Book of Golf and Golfers*. London, 1899 1st ed. 71 Photos. VG plus. $250.

HUTCHINSON, RUTH. *New Pennsylvania Dutch Cook Book*. Harper & Row, 1958 Book Club ed. Good-Very Good in dust jacket. $12-$15.

HUTCHINSON, W. H. *A Bar Cross Man*. University of Oklahoma, 1956 1st ed. Signed. VG. $50.
Oil, Land and Politics. University of Oklahoma, 1965. 2 vols. Fine in box. $50.

HUTCHISON, G. A. *The Boy's Own Book of Indoor Games and Recreations*. Lippincott, 1890. G-VG. $50.

HUTCHISON, LT COL G. S. *Machine Guns, Their History and Tactical Employment*. London, 1938. VG. $35.

HUTH, H. *Nature and the American: Three Centuries of Changing Attitudes*. Berkeley, 1957. Fine in DJ. $33.

HUTT, HENRY. *She Loves Me*. Indianapolis, 1911 1st ed. Fashion color plates by author. Very Good. $125.

HUTTON, ALFRED. *The Sword and the Centuries*. NY, 1901. Fading spine, few spots, Very Good. $195.

HUXLEY, ALDOUS. *The Cicadas and Other Poems*. 1931 1st U.S. edition. Very Good in dust jacket. $20.
Brave New World. London, 1932 1st ed. One of 324 copies signed. Near Fine. $1,975. Unsigned. Good in dust jacket. $400. NY, 1932 1st American edition. VG in DJ. $300-$500. Ex-library copy. VG. $20.
Ends and Means - Inquiry into the Nature of Ideals. Chatto & Windus, 1937 1st ed. Good-VG in DJ. $50-$75. Book Club ed. 1937. No DJ. $10.
Ape and Essence. NY, 1948 1st American edition. Fine in vg dust jacket. $5.
After Many a Summer. London, 1939 1st ed. Near Fine in dust jacket. $65.
Doors of Perception. London, 1954. Minor wear, mildew, o/w Very Good. $55.
The Letters of D. H. Lawrence. NY, Viking, 1932 1st ed. Very Good. $37.
Heaven & Hell. London, 1956 1st ed. VG in DJ. $55.
Brave New World Revisited. NY, 1958 1st ed. Fine in dust jacket. $10. NY, 1932 1st ed. in DJ. $65-$85.

HUXLEY, THOMAS HUXLEY. *Lay Sermons, Addresses and Reviews*. London, 1870 1st ed. Near Fine. $100. NY, 1871 edition. Very Good. $25.
Critiques and Addresses. London, 1883 1st edition. Spine slightly faded. $45.
Man's Place in Nature and Other Anthropological Essays. NY, no date. Engravings. Good plus. $10.

HUXTABLE, ADA. *Kicked a Building Lately?* Quadrangle, 1976 1st ed. Very Good in dust jacket. $30.

HUYSMANS, J. K. *Down There*. NY, 1924 1st American ed. One hinge loose, o/w Very Good. $55.

HUZEL, DIETER K. *Peenemunde to Canaveral*. Prentice-Hall, 1962. Introduced by W. Von Braun. VG. $45.

I

IBSEN, HENRIK. *Peer Gynt*. Philadelphia, Lippincott, no date. Arthur Rackham illus. Torn DJ o/w VG. $60-$90.

ICKS, ROBERT J. *Famous Tank Battles*. New York, 1972. Very Good. $25.

ILES, FRANCIS. *Before the Fact*. London, 1932 1st ed. VG. $85. Same, paperbound. Very Good. $15.

ILES, GEORGE. *Flame, Electricity and the Camera*. NY, 1900 1st ed. Illus. Very Good. $60.

ILLENBERGER and KELLER. *Cartoonists Cook Book*. Hobbs Dorman, 1966. Fine in dust jacket. $12-$15.

ILLINOIS TERMINAL RAILROAD CO. *Directory Industries, Historical & Statistical Data*. Springfield, 1947. Profiles of towns and businesses. 136 pages, paperbound. Very Good. $75.

ILLINOIS - TOWN, COUNTY, STATE, NATIONAL AND GENERAL ATLAS. Warner and Beers, 1872. 95 large pages, some loose. $200.

ILLUSTRATED HISTORY OF THE HASTY PUDDING CLUB THEATRICALS. Cambridge, 1933. VG. $75.

ILLUSTRATED HISTORY OF INDIANA. Indianapolis, Morrow, 1879. Good. $95.

INDIANA HISTORICAL SOCIETY. *Publications*. Vols. 1-7 and 10-16. Indianapolis, 1895-1952. 13 illustrated volumes. Usually found separately in wraps. VG. $300.

INDIANA SOCIETY OF CHICAGO. *Group of 12 Publications*. Indianapolis, Bobbs-Merrill, 1911. 12 volumes by various authors, illus., maps, etc. orig. red cloth with gilt stamping. Contents: After the flood, Gene Stratton-Porter; Verses & jingles, George Ade; Short furrows, Kin Hubbard; Mrs. Miller, James Whitcomb Riley; Redemption of Anthony, Majorie Benton Cooke, Her weight in gold, George Barr McCutcheon; Who's Hoosier (2 vol.), Wilbur D. Nesbitt; Dog & the child & the ancient sailor man, Robert A. Wason, Style & the man, Merideth Nicholson; Sweet alyssum, Charles Major; & History of Indiana; John T. McCutcheon. This famous set is complete. 1 vol. dampstained, else Very Good. $650.

INFANTRY DRILL REGULATIONS. 1941 1st edition. Government Printing Office. 208 pages. $8-$10.

INGE, WILLIAM. *Bus Stop*. NY, 1955 1st ed. Very Good in dust jacket. $40.
The Dark at the Top of the Stairs. NY, 1958 1st ed. Very Good in dust jacket. $40.
Good Luck, Miss Wyckoff. Boston, 1970 1st ed. Very Good in dust jacket. $15.

INGELOW, JEAN. *Mopsa*. Maria L. Kirk, illus. 1910. $18.

INGERSOLL, ERNEST. *Crest of the Continent*. Chicago, 1888. Good-VG. $18-$30.
Gold Fields of the Klondike and Wonders of Alaska. NY, 1897 1st ed. 487 pages. VG-Fine. $50.
Knocking Round the Rockies. Harper, 1882 1st ed. Good, ex-library. $15.

INGERSOLL, ROBERT. *Crimes Against Criminals*. Roycroft Press, 1906 1st ed. $10.
Ingersoll's Greatest Lectures. Freethought Press, 1944 edition. $5.
The Gods and Other Lectures. Peoria, 1874 1st edition. Good-VG. $60-$80.
Works of Robert Ingersoll. 1909 Dresden edition. 12 volumes. $100.

INGERSOLL, RALPH. *The Battle is the Payoff*. NY, Harcourt, 1943. Good-VG in dust jacket. $10-$12.
Top Secret. NY, 1946. Good-VG in dust jacket. $8-$12.

INGHAM, G. THOMAS. *Digging Gold Among the Rockies*. Philadelphia, 1880 1st ed. $150. Same, 1888 ed. $35-$50.

INGHAM, TRAVIS. *Rendezvous by Submarine*. NY, Doubleday, 1945 1st ed. Very Good $28.

INGOLDSBY, THOMAS. *The Ingoldsby Legends*. Philadelphia, 1856. 2 vols. Worn. $100. New York, circa 1880s, Cruickshank illus. 2 vols. $50. London, 1898 and 1905 editions with Rackham illus. $100-$200. New York, 1907 limited ed. Rackham illus. $1,500. Trade edition. $300. London, 1930, Rackham illus. $100. London, Richard Bently pub., 1840-1847. 3 vols., 12mo. 19 engraved plates by Cruikshank and Leech. Full red morocco, raised bands on spines. Fine. $400.

INGRAM, J. S. *The Centennial Exposition*. Philadelphia, 1876. Very Good. $38.

INMAN, COLONEL HENRY. *The Old Santa Fe Trail*. NY, 1897 1st ed. Remington illus. Good-VG. $125. 1898 edition. $75.
Great Salt Lake Trail. Minneapolis, 1966 reprint with William Cody. $35.

INNES, HAMMOND. *The Wreck of the Mary Deare*. NY, 1956 1st American ed. Near Fine in DJ. $25.
The Doomed Oasis. NY, 1960 1st. Fine in DJ. $20-$30.
Atlantic Fury. NY, 1962 1st ed. Near Fine in DJ. $28.
The Strode Adventurer. NY, 1965 1st ed. VG in DJ. $35.

INNES, MICHAEL. *Appleby's End*. London, 1945 1st ed. Very Good in dust jacket. $30.
Appleby Talks Again. NY, 1956 1st ed. NF in DJ. $50.
Death on a Quiet Day. NY, 1957 1st ed. NF in DJ. $30.

INTERNATIONAL COOK BOOK. Boston, 1929. Decorative cloth. Good. $20.

INTERNATIONAL HARVESTER CO. *Harvest Scenes of the World*. Chicago, 1913. Photos of people and animals at work. Paperbound. Good. $20.

INTERNATIONAL INSTITUTE COOK BOOK. International Institute, MA, 1938. Spiral bound. G-VG. $9-$12.

INSIGNIA AND DECORATION OF THE U. S. ARMED FORCES. National Geographic Society, 1943. $45.

IRISH, WILLIAM (Cornell Woolrich). *The Dancing Detective*. Lippincott, 1946 1st ed. Fine in DJ. $450.
Waltz Into Darkness. Lippincott, 1947 1st ed. Very Good-Near Fine in dust jacket. $95-$125.
Dead Man Blues. Lippincott, 1948 1st. Fine in DJ. $250.
Phantom Lady. P. F. Collier, 1943 reprint. VG. $14.
Strangler's Serenade. Book Club ed. W. J. Black, 1951. Very Good in dust jacket. $15.
Eyes That Watch You. New York, 1952 1st edition. Fine in dust jacket. $285.

IRVINE, W. *Apes, Angels & Victorians*. NY, 1955. Very Good in dust jacket. $13.

IRVING, DAVID. *The Rise and Fall of the Luftwaffe*. Boston, 1974 1st ed. VG in dust jacket. $25.
Trail of the Fox-Field Marshall Erwin Rommel. 1977 1st ed. Very Good in dust jacket. $20-$25. Same year, 2nd ed., Congdon. No dust jacket. $12.

IRVING, JOHN. *Setting Free the Bears*. NY, 1968 1st ed. Author's 1st book. VG in dust jacket. $350.
The World According to Garp. NY, 1978 1st edition. Fine in dust jacket. $60.

IRVING, PIERRE. *Life and Letters of Washington Irving*. 1st ed., 1862. 4 vols. Ex-library. $38.

IRVING, WASHINGTON. *A History of the Life and Voyages of Christpher Columbus*. NY, 1831 Revised ed. 2 vol. set. Ex-library. Good. $23.
Knickerbocker's History of New York. New York, 1894 2 volumes. E. W. Kemble illustrator. Van Twiller edition. Very Good. $150-$450. NY, Russell, 1900. Parrish illus. $95-$150. Heritage, 1940. In slipcase. $13.
A Tour of the Prairies. Philadelphia, 1835 1st ed., 1st state. Good-VG. $80-$120.
The Alhambra. NY, 1895. Joseph Pennell illust-rator. VG in DJ. $140. 1909, Lippincott pub. George Hood illus. Good-VG. $50. 1926, Warwick Goble illus. Fine. $40.
Astoria, or Anecdotes of an Enterprise. NY, 1849 edition. Putnam's. Good plus. $55. London, 1861 revised edition. Good. $40. First edition, 1st state. 2 vols. Folding maps. Philadelphia, 1836. Very Good. $300-$500.
The Life and Works of Washington Irving. NY, Lovell, 1883 1st ed. 3 vols. illus. Gilt-dec. grn. cloth. VG. $95.
Tales of a Traveler. NY, 1895 2 vols., Arthur Rackham illus. Good-VG. $60-$120.
Old Christmas. New York, 1908. Cecil Aldin illustrator. Good-VG. $45-$85.
The Legend of Sleeping Hollow. NY, 1931. Bernhardt Wall etchings. One of 1,200 copies. $40. Another, Philadelphia, 1928. A. Rackham illus. $75-$160.
Rip Van Winkle. London, 1893, Macmillan. VG. $95. Altemus, 1900. G. Browne illus. VG. $35. McKay, 1921. Wyeth illus. VG in DJ. $75-$150. Limited Ed. Club, 1930. Sgnd by F. Goudy. $60. Doubleday, 1905. Rackham illus. VG in DJ. $150-$225. Same, 1916 24 color plates. $95-$140 in DJ.

IRWIN, WILL. *The City That Was*. NY, 1908 3rd printing. Cracked hinges, interior Very Good. $25.

ISHERWOOD, CHRISTOPHER. *The Condor and the Cows. A South American Travel Diary*. NY, 1949 1st ed. Photo illus. Very Good in dust jacket. $45.
People One Ought to Know. London, 1982 1st ed. Fine in DJ. $12. Doubleday, 1982 1st Amer. ed. Fine in DJ. $20.

ISHAM, FREDERIC S. *Under the Rose*. Bobbs Merrill, 1903 1st ed. Christy illustrator. $15-$25.
Black Friday. Bobbs Merrill, 1904. Harrison Fisher, illus. Very Good. $16.

IVERSON, MARION DAY. *The American Chair, 1630 to 1890*. NY, 1957. Very Good in dust jacket. $45.

IVIMY, JOHN. *The Sphinx and the Megaliths*. NY, 1975 1st ed. Very Good in dust jacket. $15.

IVINS, VIRGINIA WILCOX. *Pen Pictures of Early Western Days*. Privately printed, 1908. William Ivins illus. G. $100.

J

JABLONSKI, EDWARD. *Flying Fortress*. NY, 1965 Book Club ed. Fine in dust jacket. $15.
Ladybirds, Women in Aviation. NY, 1968 1st ed. Good-Very Good in dust jacket. $20.
Warriors with Wings. Indianapolis, 1966 1st ed. Fine in dust jacket. $20.

JACKSON, CHARLES. *Lost Week*end. Farrar Rinehart, 1944 1st ed. Fine in dust jacket. $20-$30.

JACKSON, HELEN HUNT. *Mercy Philbrick's Choice*. Boston, 1876 1st ed. Very Good. $50.
A Century of Dishonor. NY, 1881 1st ed. VG. $100.
Glimpses of Three Coasts. Boston, 1886 1st edition. Near Very Good. $45.
Ramona. Boston, 1884 1st edition. $400-$500. Monterey edition, 1900, Boston 2 volumes. Very Good-Near Fine in dust jacket. $75-$150. Boston, 1890 signed presentation copy. Very Good. $100. 1939 edition, 4 color plates. $25. 1932 edition, Good. $10. 1945 ed. Wyeth illus. $25-$40.
Glimpses of California Missions. No place, 1919. $16.
California and the Missions. Boston, 1927. H. Sandham illus. Near Fine. $45.

JACKSON, HOLBROOK. *The Eighteen Nineties*. NY, 1923 1st American ed. Near VG. $25. Knopf, no date. Fine. $60.
The Anatomy of Bibliomania. London, 1930, 2 vols. Ltd edition. 1000 copies. Fine. $75. NY, 1950 reprint. Very Good in dust jacket. $30.
Bookman's Holiday. London, 1945 1st ed. VG in DJ. $10.

JACKSON, JOSEPH HENRY. *Tintypes in Gold: Four Studies in Robbery*. NY, 1939. VG. $15.
Bad Company. NY, 1940 1st ed. Illus. VG in DJ. $30.
Anybody's Gold. No place, 1941 1st ed. E. H. Suydam illus. Inscribed by author. VG. $25.
Christmas Flower. NY, 1951 1st edition. Illustrated. Fine in dust jacket. $16.

JACKSON, KATHRYN. *Animals' Merry Christmas*. Simon Schuster, 1950 1st edition. Giant Golden Book. Good-Very Good. $20-$40.

JACKSON, ROBERT. *Before the Storm*. London, 1972. Fine in dust jacket. $18.
Fighter: The Story of Air Combat. NY, 1979. Very Good in dust jacket. $18

JACKSON, SHIRLEY. *The Road Through the Wall*. New York, 1948 1st edition. Author's 1st book. Near Very Good in dust jacket. $150.
Hangsaman. NY, 1951 1st ed. Paperbound NF. $103. Another in cloth with worn DJ. $60.
Love Among the Savages. New York, 1953 1st edition. Fine in dust jacket. $35.
Raising Demons. New York, 1957 1st edition. Near Fine in dust jacket. $35.
The Sundial. NY, 1958 1st ed. Near Fine in DJ. $75-$95.

JACOB, H. *Six Thousand Years of Bread*. NY, 1944 1st ed. Illus. Very Good in dust jacket. $25.

JACOBI, CARL. *Revelations in Black*. Arkham House, 1947. Author's 1st book. Fine in dust jacket. $55-$110.

JACOBS, W. W. *The Castaways*. NY, 1917 1st ed. G. $20.
Snug Harbor. NY, 1931 1st ed. Illus. $13.

JACOBSTEIN, M. *The Tobacco Industry in the United States*. Columbia Univ. Press, 1907 1st ed. Inscribed. Back flyleaf missing. $88.

JACOBUS, M. W. *The Connecticut River Steamboat Story*. Hartford Historical Society, 1956. Slight soil. $35.

JAFFE, BERNARD. *Crucibles Lives & Achievements of Great Chemists*. NY, 1934 3rd printing. G-VG. $8.
Men of Science in America. 1958 ed. G-VG. $20.
Michelson and the Speed of Light. New York, 1960 1st edition. Good. $12.

JAMES, ALICE. *Catering for Two*. 1898, 1906. $30-$40.

JAMES, DIAN. *Dining in New York*. John Day, 1931 3rd ed. 125 restaurants. Good-VG. $15.

JAMES, ED. *The Game Cock*. NY, 1873. Good. $40.

JAMES, GEORGE W. *What the White Race May Learn From the Indian*. Chicago, Forbes & Co., 1908. Illus., red cloth, Very Good. $125.
Through Ramona's Country. Boston, 1909 1st edition. Very Good. $60.
California, Romantic and Beautiful. Boston, 1914 1st edition. Very Good. $50.

JAMES, HENRY. *A Passionate Pilgrim, and Other Tales.* Boston, 1875 1st ed., first book. $1,000 and up.

Confidence. Osgood, Boston, 1880 1st American. ed. Good-Very Good. $200-$300.

The Ambassadors. NY, 1903 1st American ed. Harper. Good-Very Good. $100-$150.

The Outcry. NY, Sept, 1911 1st ed. VG in DJ. $75-$125.

English Hours. H. M., Boston, 1905. ½ leather. Illus. Good. $65. Very Good-Fine. $75-$100.

Views and Reviews. Boston, 1908 1st ed. Ball Pub. Good-Very Good. $25-$50.

Travelling Companions. Boni & Liveright, 1919 1st ed. Very Good. $30.

The Short Stories of Henry James. NY, 1948. Modern Library. Very Good in dust jacket. $15.

JAMES, MARQUIS. *The Cherokee Strip: A Tale of an Oklahoma Boyhood.* NY, 1945 1st ed. VG. $25. Viking, 1945 3rd edition. $9.

Andrew Jackson, The Border Captain. Bobbs-Merrill, 1933 1st ed. Very Good. $16.

Life of Andrew Jackson. Bobbs-Merrill, 1938 new edition. Faded spine. $10.

Mr. Garner of Texas. Bobbs-Merrill, 1939 1st. VG. $10.

JAMES, P. D. *Cover Her Face.* NY, 1962 1st ed. Fine in rubbed dust jacket. $150.

Death of an Expert Witness. London, 1977 1st edition. Fine in dust jacket. $65-$90.

A Taste for Death. NY, 1986 1st American ed. Near Fine in dust jacket. $85. Same, London, 1986 1st edition. $65.

The Skull Beneath the Skin. Scribner's, 1982 1st American ed. Signed. Fine in DJ. $55.

JAMES, WILL. *Cowboys North and South.* NY, 1924 1st ed. Author's 1st book. Illustrated by author. VG plus. $100. Grosset & Dunlap reprint, 1924. $8-$15.

Smoky the Cow Horse. No place, 1926, 1st printing, 1st state. Cover stains o/w Very Good. $250. Scribner's 1926 edition, no dust cover. $16. 1929 illus. ed. $35.

Lone Cowboy: My Life Story. NY, 1930 1st ed. Spine fading, wear, o/w VG. $35-$50. 1946 ed. Rebound. $15.

Big Enough. NY, 1931 1st ed.ition Illus. by author. Signed. Cover stained, back soiled. $100. Same, Unsigned. Near Fine. $60.

Sun Up. NY, 1931. Ex-library. Good. $10.

Uncle Bill. Scribner's 1932 1st ed. VG, no DJ. $14.

All in the Day's Riding. NY, 1933 1st ed. Illus. by author. Near Fine. $375. Same, NY, 1933 1st ed. Cloth soiled, o/w Good. $60.

In the Saddle With Uncle Bill. NY, 1935 1st ed. Spine faded, o/w Very Good. $60.

Cow Country. NY, 1927 1st ed. VG in DJ. $65. 1940s reprint, Grosset & Dunlap. Fine in dust jacket. $8.

JAMES, WILLIAM. *The Principles of Psychology.* NY, 1896. 2 vols. VG. $85. Same, 1913 ed. 2 vols. VG. $50.

JAMESON, MALCOLM. *Atomic Bomb.* Bond Charteris Pub., 1945. Very Good. $75.

JANE'S ALL THE WORLD'S AIRSHIPS. London, 1910 2nd year of issue. Photos. Very Good. $450.

JANE'S ALL THE WORLD'S AIRCRAFT. Pre-1960 eds., over $100 in VG condition. 1942 ed. Fore edge stain. DJ. $95. 1958-1959 ed. $50-$80 in good condition. 1978-1979 edition. Very Good. $35.

JANE'S FIGHTING SHIPS. NY, 1942 VG in DJ. $125. Same, shaken, rubbed, no dust jacket. $40. Same, 1954-55. Good plus. $40. Annual vols. 1965-1990 $25 each.

JANESVILLE, WISCONSIN. *City Directory, 1866.* Spine missing. $75.

JANSSON, TOVE. *Finn Family Moomintroll.* London, 1950 1st ed. Illustrated by author. VG in DJ. $75.

Moominsummer Madness. London, 1955 1st ed. Illus. by author. VG in facsimile dust jacket. $35.

Who Will Comfort Toffle? London, 1960 1st ed. Illus. by author. VG in DJ. $75. NY, 1969 2nd ed. VG. $50.

The Summer Book, NY, 1974 1st American ed. Illus . by author. Fine in dust jacket. $15.

JANVIER, THOMAS. *Mexican Guide.* NY, 1890. All maps present. Very Good. $30.

Legends of the City of Mexico. NY, 1910 1st ed. Good plus. $25. Very Good. $35.

Aztec Treasure House. Harper, 1890 1st ed. VG. $95. Same, 1918. B. Kutcher illus. Very Good. $37.

JARRELL, RANDALL. *Pictures From an Institution.* NY, 1954 1st ed. Near VG in dust jacket. $85.

A Sad Heart at the Supermarket. NY, 1962 1st ed. Very Good in dust jacket. $75.

The Bat-Poet. Macmillan, 1964 1st ed. Fine. $40. 5th printing, same year. New in dust jacket. $15.

The Animal Family. No place, 1965 1st ed. Maurice Sendak illus. Near Fine in good dust jacket. $35.

The Ginger Bread Rabbit. NY, 1967 1st edition. Garth Williams illus. VG-Fine. $25.

Fly by Night. Farrar & Strauss, 1976 1st ed. Illus. by Maurcie Sendak. Fine in dust jacket. $12.

JEFFERS, LEROY. *The Call of the Mountains: Rambles Among the Mountains and Canyons of the United States and Canada.* NY, 1922 1st ed. Photos. Near VG. $40.

JEFFERS, ROBINSON. *Roan Stallion, Tamar and Other Poems.* NY, 1924 1st ed. $500-$750. 7th printing. $25.

The Women at Point Sur. Boni, 1927 1st ed. VG. $35. Signed and numbered. $200-$400.

Cawdor and Other Poems. NY, 1928 1st edition. Very Good. $100-$200. Same book, another dealer. $35.

Give Your Heart to the Hawks. NY, 1933 1st ed. VG in fair dust jacket. $50.

Solstice and Other Poems. NY, 1935 1st edition. Near Fine in dust jacket. $65. Grabhorn Ltd ed. Signed. $250.

The Selected Poetry of Robinson Jeffers. NY, 1938 1st edition. $100-$150. Another dealer offers Fine at $50.

Medea. NY, 1946 1st ed. Near Fine in DJ. $25.

JEHL, FRANCIS. *Menlo Park Reminiscences.* (Thomas A. Edison laboratory). Dearborn, MI, 1937-1941 1st edition. 3 volumes. NF. $85. Another, 1936. 430 pages. 1 vol. $35.

JEKYLL, GERTRUDE & LAWRENCE WEAVER. *Gardens for Small Country Houses.* London, 1920. 400 Photos. Hinge cracks, inside clean. $60.

JELL-O DESSERT BOOKLETS. 1904. Playing card cover, 14 pages. $75-$100.
1905 to 1918. Various 20 page cookbooks. illustrated by Rose O'Neill. $50-$60.
1920s. Dessert recipes. 6 to 20 pages. $12-$15.
1930s. New Jell-O recipes. 23 to 47 pages. $14.
1933-1934. Wizard of Oz series. $40-$50 each.
1935-1941. Ice Cream recipes, etc. $10-$15 each.

JENKINS, S. *The Greatest Street in the World: Broadway.* NY, 1911 1st ed. Highly illustrated. Near Fine. $85.

JENKS, TUDOR. *Century World's Fair Book for Boys & Girls.* Century, 1893. Castaigne illus. $35-$75.
Magician One Day. Altemus, 1905. $50-$80.
Timothy's Magical Afternoon. Altemus, 1905. John R. Neill illus. Very Good. $30.
Galopoff The Talking Pony. Philadelphia, 1901 1st ed. Very Good. $16.
Rescue Syndicate. Altemus, 1905. $35-$60.

JENNINGS, PRESTON. *A Book of Trout Flies.* Crown, 1935. G-VG. $75. Derrydale Press, 1935. Handcolored plates. Very Good-Fine. $350. 1970 4th ed. $25.

JEPSON, WILLIS L. *A Manual of the Flowering Plants of California.* Berkely, 1925 1st ed. VG in DJ. $35.

JESSE JAMES IN NEW ORLEANS. Street & Smith, 1898. Paperbound. $25.

JESSUP, ELON. *The Motor Camping Book.* New York, 1921 1st edition. With 100 illustrations. $50. Same, 1922. Good-VG. $30.

JEWETT, SARAH ORNE. *Marsh Island.* Houghton, 1885 1st ed. No wear or foxing. Very Good. $125.
The White Heron. Boston, 1886 1st ed. VG. $100.
The Country of the Pointed Firs. Boston, NY, 1896 1st ed. Near Very Good. $185.
The Normans. NY, 1898. Illus. Very Good. $25.

The Queen's Twin and Other Stories. Boston, 1899 1st edition. Very Good. $75.

The Tory Lover. Boston, 1901 1st ed. VG. $145.

Play Days: A Book of Stories for Children. Houghton-Mifflin, 1906. Very Good. $38.

JOB, THOMAS. (Translator). *Giants in the Earth.* NY, Harper, 1929 1st edition in dust jacket. $25-$50.

JOHN DEERE. *Operation, Care and Repair of Farm Machinery.* 4th ed. 1930s. $18. 26th ed. 1940s $8-$14. (Also see Trade Catalog section.)

JOHN, UNCLE. *The Boy's Book of Sports and Games.* Philadelphia, 1851. 7 plates. Good. $50.

JOHNSON, CLIFTON. *Highways & Byways of the South.* NY, 1904. Illus. Good. $13.
Old-Time Schools and School-Books. NY, 1904 1st ed. Very Good. $25.
Highways & Byways of the Pacific Coast. New York, 1908. Good. $10.
Highways & Byways of California. Macmillan, 1915 edition. Illus. Very Good. $22.

JOHNSON, CROCKET. *Harold and the Purple Crayon.* NY, 1955. Illus. by author. Rubbed. Good. $75.
Harold's Trip to the Sky. NY, 1957. Illus. by author. Rubbed. Good. $50.
Harold's Fairy Tale. NY, no date. Reprint. Illus. by author. Very Good. $12.

JOHNSON, DOROTHY. *The Bloody Bozeman.* NY, 1971, McGraw-Hill 1st ed. American Trails Series. Very Good in dust jacket. $15-$20.

JOHNSON, ELIZABETH. *Stuck With Luck.* Boston, 1967 1st ed. Trina Schart Hyman illus. VG in DJ. $25.

JOHNSON, GENE. *Ship Model Building.* Cornell Maritime Press, 1953. Includes loosely inserted folding plate. $20.

JOHNSON, HARRY. *New and Improved Bartender's Manual.* NY, 1900. Good-VG. $50.

JOHNSON, JAMES WELDON. *The Book of American Negro Spirituals.* NY, 1925 1st ed. VG-NF. $65-$85.
God's Trombones. Viking, 1927 1st ed. VG. $85-$100. 1932 reprint. Very Good. $15.

JOHNSON, JAMES WELDON (In Magazines). *Harper's.* Sept, 1897. Article on race prejudice. $13.
The Freeman. Dec 1, 1920. "The Creation". $12-$18.
Century. Nov, 1927. Article on lynching, $15.

JOHNSON, JOSEPH. *Narrative of Military Operations.* NY, 1875. Maps, illus. Near VG. $325. 1874 ed. Fair. $75.

JOHNSON. *20 Years of Hus'ling*. Thompson, no place, 1900. W. W. Denslow illus. VG. $75-$120.

JOHNSON, LOUISA. *Every Lady Her Own Flower Garden*. New Haven, CT, 1844. Good-VG. $25-$50.

JOHNSON, MARTIN. *Camera Trails in Africa*. NY, 1924. Fine. $35. Fair. $10.
Safari. NY, 1928. Spine faded, o/w Fine. $20.

JOHNSON, MERLE. *High Spots of American Literature*. NY, 1929 1st ed. Fine. $125.
American First Editions. NY, 1929 1st ed. One of 1,000 copies. Near Fine. $50. Same, 1932. $35. 1936. $25.

JOHNSON, OSA. *Bride in the Solomons*. Boston, 1944. Photo illus. Very Fine. $35.
Tarnish, The True Story of a Lion Cub. Wilcox, 1944. A. Jansson illus. Good-VG in DJ. $20.

JOHNSON, OWEN. *The Lawrenceville Stories*. NY, 1967 1st ed. Very Good in dust jacket. $25.
Skippy Bedelle. Boston, 1922 1st ed. VG in DJ. $20.

JOHNSON, ROBERT U. (Editor). *Battles and Leaders of the Civil War*. NY, 1888, 8 vols. VG plus. $185. 1887 1st edition. Good. $150-$200.

JOHNSON, ROSSITER. *Campfire and Battlefield*. NY, 1896. Repaired spine. Illus. $70. Another, Rebound, Very Good. $125. Another, binding loose, cover stains, prelim. pages gone. $50.

JOHNSON, SAMUEL. *The Idler*. London, 1761 2 volumes. Very Good. $100.
The Poetical Works of Samuel Johnson. London, 1785 new ed. Very Good. $85. 1824 edition, 12 vols. $75.
Letters of Samuel Johnson. 2 volumes. Harper, 1892 1st edition. $40.
Dictionary of the English Language. 1967. $85.

JOHNSON, W. FLETCHER. *The Life of Sitting Bull, etc.* Edgewood Publications, 1891 1st edition. Near Fine. $80. Very Good. $50. Good. $18-$35. Fair. $14.
The Life of William Tecumseh Sherman. Edgewood Publications, 1891. Good. $40.
A History of the Johnstown Flood. No place, 1899. Illus. with photos. VG. $19. Edgewood, 1889 1st. G, no DJ. $14.

JOHNSON, WENDELL. *People in Quandaries*. NY, 1946 1st ed. Very Good in dust jacket. $23.

JOHNSTON, ALVA. *The Legendary Mizners*. New York, 1953. Reginald Marsh illus. VG in good dust jacket. $25.

JOHNSTON, ANNIE FELLOWS. *The Little Colonel's Holidays*. L. C. Page 1901 1st ed. VG. $30.

Miss Santa Claus of the Pullman. Century, 1913 1st ed. Reginald Birch illus. Near Fine. $25.
The Little Colonel's Christmas Vacation. No place, 1919. Very Good. $15.
The Road of the Loving Heart. Boston, 1922 1st ed., Winifred Bromhall illus. VG. $30.
The Land of the Little Colonel. Boston, 1929 1st ed. Ex-library. Very Good. $25. Fine in slipcase. $50.
The Little Colonel. A. L. Burt, 1935. Photos from film starring Shirley Temple, Lionel Barrymore. Inscribed by author. DJ tattered. $25. 1940 38th edition in DJ. $8.
The Little Colonel at Boarding School. L. C. Page, 1939. Very Good in dust jacket. $30.

JOHNSTON, J. P. *Twenty Years of Hus'ling*. Chicago, Thompson, 1900 ed. Denslow illus. Fair cond. $18.

JOHNSTON, MARY. *To Have and To Hold*. Houghton-Mifflin, 1900 1st ed. VG-Fine. $25-$40.
The Long Roll. Houghton-Mifflin, 1911 1st edition. Fine. $15-$30. Same, 1917 edition. N. C. Wyeth, illus. VG. $20.
The Witch. Boston, NY, 1914 1st ed. Near VG. $35.

JOHNSTON, RICHARD. *Follow Me! The Story of 2nd Marine Division in World War II*. NY, 1948 1st ed. VG in DJ. $120. No jacket. $75-$90. Later editions. $30-$35.

JOHNSTON, S. PAUL. *Horizons Unlimited*. (History of Aviation). NY, 1941 1st ed. VG in DJ. $25.
Flying Squadrons. New York, 1942 1st edition. Very Good in dust jacket. $35.

JOHNSTON, STANLEY. *Queen of the Flat-Tops - USS Lexington*. Blakiston, 1942. Very Good. $7-$15.

JOHNSTOWN HORROR, THE. Anon. 1889 Newspaper pub. Very Good. Gilt illus. boards. $16.

JOLAS, EUGENE. *Vertical: Yearbook for Romantic-Mystic Ascensions*. Gotham, 1941. One of 400 copies. $30.
Transition Workshop. NY, 1949. G-VG. $15-$30.

JOLLY JUMP-UPS, THE. McLoughlin Bros, 1942 1st ed. VG-Fine. $20-$25.

JONES, ADNAH. *History of South America*. London, 1899 1st ed. Green cloth, large fold-out map. Good. $20.

JONES, DANIEL W. *Forty Years Among the Indians: A True Yet Thrilling Narrative*. Salt Lake City, 1890 1st edition. Stained, rubbed. Good-VG. $55-$75.

JONES, DAVID. *Journal of a Visit to Indian Nations West of the Ohio River*. NY, 1865. 1 of 250 copies. VG. $250.

JONES, E. A. *Old Silver of Europe and America*. Philadelphia, 1928 1st ed. 96 gravure plates, VG. $75-$95.

JONES, EDGAR D. *Lincoln and the Preachers*. NY, Harper & Bros., 1948 1st ed., Very Good in dust jacket. $12.

JONES, EVAN. *A Food Lover's Companion*. NY, 1979 1st ed. Fine in dust jacket. $12.

JONES, GWYN. *A History of the Vikings*. NY, 1968 1st American ed. Illus. Worn dust jacket o/w VG. $153.

JONES, HOLWAY R. *John Muir and the Sierra Club - Battle for Yosemite*. Sierra Club, 1965 1st edition. Fine in dust jacket. $75.

JONES, JAMES. *From Here to Eternity*. NY, 1951 1st ed. Author's 1st book. Near Fine in DJ. $100-$150.
The Pistol. NY, 1958 1st ed. VG in DJ. $25-$40.
The Thin Red Line. NY, 1962 1st ed. Fine. $45.
Go to the Widow-Maker. NY, 1967 1st ed. VG in DJ. $20.

JONES, LEROI. *Tales*. NY, 1967 1st ed. Fine in DJ. $35.
Black Magic: Poetry 1961-67. Indiana, 1969. Very Good in dust jacket. $40.

JONES, MRS. C. S. and WILLIAMS, H. T. *Ladies Fancy Work Hints and Helps to Home Taste and Recreations*. NY, 1876. Soiled, bumped, dark. $45.

JONES, ROBERT T. *Golf is My Game*. NY, 1960 1st ed. illus. VG in DJ. $100. Same, no dust jacket. $28.
The Basic Golf Swing. NY, 1969 1st ed. Fine in DJ. $30.

JONES, ROBERT T. and O. B. KELLER. *Down the Fairway*. NY, 1927. Very Good. $86.

JONES, STEPHEN. *Drifting - Voyages in Dooryards, Alleys, Bayous, Canals, etc.* NY, Macmillan, 1971 1st edition. Fine in dust jacket. $16-$24.

JONES, VIRGIL. *Gray Ghosts and Rebel Raiders*. NY, 1956 1st ed. Illus. VG in dust jacket. $30-$40. Fine. $50.
The Civil War at Sea. NY, 1960 1st ed. Vol. 1 only, of 3 volume set. Good. $25.
Ranger Mosby. N.C. University, 1944 1st ed. $45-$85. 4th printing. Very Good. $15-$30.

JORDAN, DAVID S. & BARTON EVERMAN. *American Food & Game Fishes*. New York, 1908, Doubleday reprint. Very Good. $65.

JORDAN, WILFRED (Editor). *Colonial & Revolutionary Families of Pennsylvania*. NY, 1936, Lewis Hist Pub. Very Good. $80.

JORDANOFF, A. *Illustrated Aviation Dictionary*. NY, Colliers, 1942. VG. $12. Same, 1st edition in DJ. $20-$25.
Flying and How To Do It. G & D, 1940. G-VG. $12-$15.
Power and Flight. NY, 1944 1st edition. Very Good. $18.

JORDON, ROBERT P. *The Civil War*. National Geographic Society. 1969 1st ed. $20. 1983 6th ed. Fine in DJ. $10.

JOSEPH, FRANZ. *Star Fleet Technical Manual*. NY, 1975 1st edition, Ballantine. Very Good. $28-$35.

JOSEPHSON, MATTHEW. *The Robber Barons: The Great American Capitalists*. 1861-1901. NY, 1934 1st edition. Very Good in dust jacket. $40.
Union House, Union Bar. New York, 1956 1st edition. Very Good. $13.
Edison, a Biography. NY, 1959. Fine. $14.

JOSEPHUS, FLAVIUS. *Works of Flavius Josephus*. Baltimore, 1839. Whiston Trans. Worn, loose covers. $25. Various other editions thru 1900. $15-$35.

JOSEPHY, ALVIN. *The Long and the Short and the Tall: Marine Corps Combat inWW II*. Knopf, 1946 1st ed. Good-VG. $25-$40. 1979 reprint. $20.

JOYCE, JAMES. *Ulysses*. Paris, 1922 1st ed. on heavy rag paper. Signed and numbered. $5,000 - $20,000. First English language edition. Egoist Press, Limited to 2,000 copies. $1,500-$2,500. NY, 1935 Limited Editions Club. One of approximately 250 copies. Illus. by Matisse. Signed by Joyce and Matisse. Very Good plus in custom made box. $2,500-$4,500. NY, 1934 1st American edition. VG-Fine in dust jacket. $150-$250.
Finnegan's Wake. NY, 1939 1st American edition. Very Good-Near Fine in dust jacket. $250-$450. London, 1939 1st trade edition. Very Good. No dust jacket present. $200-$600. Another, in DJ and box. $1,000. Near Fine. $1,250. Signed, in box. $3,900.
Haveth Children Everywhere. Paris and New York, 1930 Ltd edition in slipcase. $800-$900.
Stephen Hero. New Directions, 1944 1st American ed. Very Good. $70-$85. Good. $25.
Pomes Penyeach. Paris, 1927 1st ed. Near Fine. $300.

JOYLAND. Children's cloth book, no date. Very Good. $35.

JUDSON, KATHERINE B. *Myths and Legends of the Pacific Northwest*. No place, 1910 1st ed. Illus. VG in DJ. $60. Stained, no dust jacket. $30.
Myths and Legends of California and the Old Southwest. Chicago, 1912 1st ed. Near VG. $30.
Early Days in Old Oregon. No place, 1916. No dust jacket. Good. $30.

JUNGLE ABC. Children's linen book. 1915. VG. $22.

THE JUNGLE BAND. Child's cloth book, circa 1900. 12 double pages. Very Good. $40-$60.

JUSTER, NORTON. *The Phantom Toll Booth*. NY, 1966 8th printing. Jules Pfeiffer illus. Very Good in DJ. $15.

K

KAEL, PAULINE. *The Citizen Kane Book*. Boston, 1971 1st ed. Fine in vg dust jacket. $30-$35.

KAEMPFFERT, WALDEMAR. *A History of American Invention*. New York, 1924 1st edition. 2 volumes. Over 500 illustrations. Very Good. $68.

KAFKA, FRANZ. *Metamorphosis*. London, 1937 1st English edition. Blue cloth on brown boards. Very Good-Fine. $500-$1,500.
America. London, 1938 1st English edition in DJ. $275.
The Great Wall of China. Schocken, 1946 1st American edition. Inscribed VG in dust jacket. $20-$40.
In The Penal Colony. Schocken, 1948 1st American ed. Fine. $13. Limited Editions Club. One of 800 signed by the illus. Very Good in box. $250.
Diaries. Schocken, 1949 2 volumes. Vol. 1, 2nd printing. Vol. 2, 1st ed. Very Good in dust jacket. $35.
The Castle. New York, 1969 Modern Library. Very Good in very good dust jacket. $15. Same. Limited Editions Club, 1987. One of 800, signed by Michael Hafftka, illustrator. Mint in box. $350.

KAHN, EDGAR. *Cable Car Days in San Francisco*. Stanford University, 1940. Fine in torn dust jacket. $30. Same, 1944. $25. Another, 1946. $20.

KAHN, HERMAN. *On Thermonuclear War*. Princeton University Press, 1960 1st ed. Fine in DJ. $35.
The Year 2000: A Framework for Speculation. New York, London, 1967 1st edition. 8-line inscription by author. Very Good. $68.

KAHN, ROGER. *The Boys of Summer*. NY, 1971 1st ed. VG in DJ. $25-$35. 1972 edition in dust jacket. $18.

KALEP, E. *Air Babies*. Saalfield, 1938 Juvenile. Introduced by Amelia Earhart. Good. $30.

KALLIR, OTTO (Editor). *Grandma Moses, My Life's Story*. NY, 1952 1st ed. Good-VG. $30-$50.

KALLNER, ESTHER. *Moonshine - Its History and Folklore*. Bobbs Merrill, 1971 1st ed. Fine in dust jacket. $10.

KALT, WILLIAM D. *Awake the Copper Ghost*. Banner, 1968 1st ed. Very Good. $14.

KANBE, HARNETT. *Plantation Parade - The Grand Manner of Louisiana*. Bonanza, 1960s reprint. Very Good in dust jacket. $10-$12.

KANDER, MRS. SIMON. *The Way to a Man's Heart: The Settlement Cook Book*. No place, 1931 19th ed. Good-Very Good. $15. 1949 29th ed. $10-$15.

KANE, ELISHA KENT. *Arctic Explorations in Years 1853, 54, 55*. Philadelphia, 1856 2 volumes. Very Good. $150. 1881 edition, Very Good. $55.

KANE, HARNETT T. *Bayous of Louisiana*. Morrow, 1944 7th ed. Good, no dust jacket. $9.
Queen New Orleans. Morrow, 1949 1st edition. Signed by author. Very Good in dust jacket. $25. Rebound. $8.
Gentlemen, Swords and Pistols. NY, 1951 1st ed. Very Good in dust jacket. $15-$20.
Spies for the Blue and Gray. Garden City, 1954 1st edition. Very Good in dust jacket. $35.
The Golden Coast. NY, 1959 1st ed. Illus. Good. $6.
Gone are the Days. Bonanza, 1989 reprint. As new in dust jacket. $13. Bramwell, 1960 reprint. $15.

KANITZ, WALTER. *The White Kepi: A Casual History of the French Foreign Legion*. Chicago, 1956 1st. Fine. $35.

KANT, IMMANUEL. *Critique of Pure Reason*. NY, 1896 1st American ed. Translated by F. Max Muller. NF. $50.

KANTOR, MACKINLAY. *The Voice of Bugle Ann*. NY, 1935. Good in DJ. $5. VG in DJ. $18.
Glory For Me. Coward-McCann, 1945 Book Club ed. $6.
Andersonville. NY, 1955 1st edition. VG in DJ. $75.
Spirit Lake. World, 1961 1st ed. VG in DJ. $18.

KARASZ, ILANKA. *The Twelve Days of Christmas*. NY, 1949. Very Good in dust jacket. $20

KAROLEVITZ, R. F. *Doctors of the Old West*. Seattle, 1967 1st edition. Fine in dust jacket. $15.

KAROLEVITZ, ROBERT. *The 25th Division and World War II*. Baton Rouge, 1946. Good. $95.

KARPINSKI, LOUIS. *The History of Arithmetic*. Chicago, 1925 1st ed. Near Fine. $35.

KARSH, YOUSUF (Photographer). *Faces of Destiny: Portraits by Karsh*. NY, 1946 1st ed. Fine in vg DJ. $50.
This is Newfoundland. Toronto, 1949. Karsh portraits. Scenes by Cyril Marshall. Good in poor DJ. $45.
Faces of Our Time. University of Toronto, 1971 1st ed. Very Good in dust jacket. $40.

KATCHER, PHILIP. *Armies of the American Wars, 1753-1815*. NY, 1975. Very Good. $70.

KAUFFER, MC KNIGHT. *The Art of the Poster*. London, 1924. Very Good plus. $325.

KAUFMAN & COOPER. *The Art of Creole Cooking*. Doubleday, 1962 reprint. Good. $10.

KAUFFMAN, HENRY J. *The Pennsylvania-Kentucky Rifle*. Harrisburg, 1960, Stackpole. Very Good. $32.
American Copper and Brass. Camden, 1968 1st ed. Thomas Nelson. $35. Bonanza, 1979. $12.
The Colonial Silversmith. NY, 1969, Galahad Books. Very Good. $15.
The American Pewterer. Camden, NJ, 1970. Illus. Very Good in dust jacket. $27.
The American Fireplace. Galahad, 1972 2nd edition. $25.

KAUFMAN, GEORGE S. and MOSS HART. *The Man Who Came to Dinner*. NY, 1939 1st ed. Photos of production. VG, no DJ. $40. Same in VG dust jacket. $100.

KAUFMAN, MURRAY. *Murray the K Tells It Like It Is Baby!* Holt-Rinehart, 1966 1st ed. Superman, Beatles, etc. Illus. bds. Very Good. $20.

KAUTSKY, TED. *Ways With Watercolor*. Reinhold, 1949 1st edition. Spiral bound. Very Good. $15.

KAVANAGH, PATRICK. *Terry Flynn*. NY, 1949 1st ed. Near Fine in dust jacket. $60.

KAYE-SMITH, SHEILA. *Superstition Corner*. NY, 1934 1st edition. Very Good. $10.
Ember Lane. London, 1940 1st ed. Good. $15.

KAZANTZAKIS, NIKOS. *The Last Temptation of Christ*. NY, 1960 1st American ed. VG in DJ. $45. 2nd ed. $12.

KEARTON, CHERRY. *The Island of Penguins*. McBride, 1931 1st U. S. edition. Good-VG. $25.

KEATING, H. R. F. *Inspector Ghose Draws a Line*. London, 1979 1st ed. Signed. Fine in clipped dust jacket. $30.

KEATS, EZRA JACK. *Whistle for Willie*. NY, 1964. Illus. by author. Very Good in dust jacket. $9.
A Letter to Amy. New York, 1968. Illustrated by author. Ex-library. Good. $7.

Hi Cat. Macmillan, 1970 1st edition. Illustrated by author. Fine in dust jacket. $40.
Clementine's Cactus. NY, 1982 1st ed. Illus. by author. Very Good in dust jacket. $10.
Goggles. Mcmillan, 1969 1st ed. No page numbers. Very Good-Fine in dust jacket. $30.

KEELER, HARRY STEPHEN. *Find the Clock: A Detective Story of Newspaper Life*. NY, 1927 1st ed. Signed. Rubbed hinges, o/w Very Good. $50.
Matilda Hunt Murder. Dutton, 1931 1st. VG in DJ. $85.
The Man With the Crimson Box. NY, 1940 1st ed. VG in good dust jacket. $45.
The Case of the Canny Killer. NY, 1946 1st ed. Near VG in chip dust jacket. $37.

KEELEY, LESLIE E. *The Morphine Eater*. Dwight, IL, 1881. Signed presentation copy. $125.

KEENE, CAROLYN (aka, Harriet Adams & Laura Lee Hope). The real author of the enduring Nancy Drew series of popular juvenile titles was Harriet Adams. She wrote her first book, *The Bobbsey Twins*, in 1904, for her father's Stratemeyer syndicate. She took over the syndicate's 1,200-title "fiction mill" in 1930 and continued to write Nancy Drew books until her death in 1982 at the age of 89.

Like the Hardy Boys series, Nancy Drew books were published in numerous formats and reprint editions. Expertise is needed to distinguish 1st editions. Dust jackets on true firsts are mandatory for high value.

Serious Nancy Drew collectors often refer to *Farah's Guide to Nancy Drew Books* for pricing rarer editions. Write to Dave Farah, 3110 Park Newport, Apt 412, Newport Beach, CA 92660. A magazine devoted entirely to juvenile series books, called *Yellowback Library*, is available from Yellowback Press, P.O. Box 36172, Des Moines, IA 50315.

The Mystery of the Brassbound Trunk. Nancy Drew mystery. Grosset & Dunlap, 1929 1st edition. VG in DJ. R. H. Tandy illus. $200. Same, no dust jacket. $60. Same, 1929. Not 1st ed. No DJ. $20. Same, 1940. $12.
The Clue of the Tapping Heels. Nancy Drew mystery. Grosset and Dunlap, 1929 1st ed. VG in DJ. R. H. Tandy illus. $160. Same, 1929. Not 1st ed. No DJ. $20.
Mystery at Lilac Inn. Grosset and Dunlap No. 4. 1936 1st edition. Fine in dust jacket. $25.
Clue in the Cobweb. Grosset and Dunlap, 1939 1st ed., purple binding. VG in dust jacket. $85.
Clue of the Leaning Chimney. Grosset and Dunlap, 1949 2nd printing. VG in dust jacket. $35-$45.
Riddle of the Frozen Fountain. Grosset and Dunlap, 1964. VG in pictorial binding. $25-$35.
By the Light of the Study Lamp. Series 1, no. 9. G&D. Fine in dust jacket. $35.
Secret of the Lone Tree Cottage. Series 2, no. 10. G&D. Fine in DJ. $35. 1934 edition in purple cloth, 5 titles on dust jacket. $135.

Clue of the Tapping Heels. Series 16, no. 21. Grosset & Dunlap. Fine in dust jacket. $20.

Scarlet Slipper Mystery. Cameo. Series 32. VG in DJ. $23.

In The Shadow of the Tower. (Dana Girls, no. 3). G&D, 1934 1st ed. Very Good. Purple cloth in dust jacket which lists only 3 titles. $75.

The Clue in the Diary. (Nancy Drew no. 7). Grosset & Dunlap, 1932, early copy, 3rd printing. Blue cloth, spotted cover, stained. $150.

Clue of the Broken Locket. (Nancy Drew no. 11). Grosset & Dunlap, 1934. Dust jacket lists 18 titles. VG. $35.

The Message in the Hollow Oak. (Nancy Drew no. 12) G&D, 1935, 1936-A. Loose hinges in DJ with missing spine area, o/w Very Good. $145.

Nancy's Mysterious Letter. (Nancy Drew, no. 8). G&D, 1932, 1933-A. Blue cloth, thick edition, stained dust jacket which lists 9 titles. $200.

Clue in the Jewel Box. (Nancy Drew no. 20). Grosset & Dunlap, 1943 2nd printing. VG in dust jacket. $50.

The Secret of the Wooden Lady. (Nancy Drew no. 27). G&D, 1950 1st ed. G-VG in dust jacket. $30.

The Secret of the Swiss Chalet. (Dana Girls, no. 20). G&D, 1958. Green cloth in dust jacket. VG. $22.

The Hidden Window Mystery. (Nancy Drew, no. 34). Grosset and Dunlap, 1957B-2. Blue tweed cloth in Very Good dust jacket. $40.

Nancy Drew nos. 1-34 in glossy jackets. Circa 1950s. $350 for mixed-spine set of 34 books.

Various *Nancy Drew* titles, Grosset & Dunlap reprints of various dates. 20 different titles. Good to Very Good. $10-$15 each, e.g.:

Haunted Lagoon. 1959. $10-$15.

Nancy Drew with yellow spine picture covers and blue endpapers. Grosset & Dunlap. $6-$9 each.

The Nancy Drew Cook Book. Clues to Good Cooking. Grosset & Dunlap, 1977. Ex-library. VG. $15.

KEENE, JOHN H. *The Boy's Own Guide to Fishing*. Boston, 1894. Very Good. $45.

KEEPING, CHARLES. *Alfie Finds The Other Side of the World*. New York, 1968 1st edition. Illustrated by author. Fine in dust jacket. $60.

Joseph's Yard. NY, 1969 1st American ed. Illus. by author. Fine in dust jacket. $75.

The Christmas Story. NY, 1969 1st American ed. Illus. by author. Very Good in dust jacket. $35.

Through the Window. NY, 1970 1st ed. Illus. by author. Very Good in dust jacket. $40.

Richard. London, 1973 1st edition. Illustrated by author. Fine in dust jacket. $75.

KEESEY, REV. W. A. *War as Viewed from the Ranks*. Exp. & News Co., 1898 1st ed. Signed by author. Good. $28.

KEESLING, B. F. *Keesling's Cook Book*. Keesling-Closs, 1914 3rd ed. Many ads. Good-VG. $25.

KEIGHTLEY, THOMAS. *World Guide to Gnomes, Fairies, Elves & Other Little People*. No place, 1978. Reprint of 1878 edition. Very Good. $25.

KEITH, ELMER. *Six Gun Cartridges and Loads*. No place, 1936. Very Good in dust jacket. $90.

Keith's Rifles for Large Game. Standard Pubs., 1946 1st ed. Very scarce. Good-VG. $250-$550.

Big Game Rifles & Cartridges. Plantersville, SC, 1946. Very Good in good dust jacket. $90-$125.

Elmer Keith's Big Game Hunting. Boston, 1948 1st edition. Good plus. $25-$30.

Six Guns by Keith. Bonanza, 1961 5th edition. Very Good plus in dust jacket. $40.

Hell, I Was There. Peterson, 1979 1st ed. Fine in DJ. $35.

KELEHER, WILLIAM A. *The Maxwell Land Grant*. Santa Fe NM, 1942 1st ed. Inscribed, Very Good. $160.

Turmoil in New Mexico, 1846-1868. Santa Fe NM, 1952 1st ed. Fine in dust jacket. $85-$100.

Memoirs: 1892-1969. Albuquerque NM, 1962 Revised ed. Fine in dust jacket. $40-$50.

KELLER, HELEN. *Optimism*. NY, Crowell & Co., 1903 1st ed. Fine in original dust jacket. $75.

KELLOGG, J. H., M. D. *Plain Facts for Old and Young*. Burlington IA, 1882 ed. Sexual transgressions, etc. by the Battle Creek reformist. Very Good. $25. 1881 1st edition. Fair, leather. $10.

Plain Facts - Natural History & Hygiene. I. F. Segner, 1891 revised ed. Fine. $18.

KELLAND, CLARENCE BUDINGTON. *Mark Tidd, Editor*. NY, 1917 1st ed. Good. $9.

Rhoda Fair. NY, 1926 1st ed. Good. $6.

Death Keeps a Secret. NY, 1953 1st edition. Near Fine in dust jacket. $20.

KELLEY, DOUGLAS. *22 Cells in Nuremberg*. No place, 1947 1st ed. Very Good in dust jacket. $20.

KELLOGG, JOHN HARVEY. Various *Health and Temperance* titles, 1877-1920s. $40-$50 each.

KELLOGG, ROBERT. *Life and Death in Rebel Prisons*. 1866. Chipped spine, cover worn. $40.

KELLOGG, STEVEN. *The Mystery of the Missing Red Mitten*. NY, 1974. Signed, with sketch. Fine in DW. $20.

KELLOG'S FUNNY JUNGLELAND MOVING PICTURES. 1932. Children's booklet. $20.

KELLY, CHARLES. *Salt Desert Trails: A History of the Hastings Cutoff*. Salt Lake City, 1930 1st ed. Illus. Very Good. $95-$150.

The Outlaw Trail: the Story of Butch Cassidy's Wild Bunch. NY, 1954. Illus. Good in DJ. $10.
Holy Murder. New York, 1934 1st edition. Very Good in worn dust jacket. $180.

KELLY, EMMETT. *Clown*. Prentice Hall, 1954 ed. Good. $15. Same. 1st ed., advance reader copy in DJ. Fine. $40.

KELLY, FANNY. *Narrative of My Captivity Among the Sioux Indians*. Hartford, 1871 1st edition. $150-$250. Chicago, 1880 2nd ed. Covers worn, o/w Good to VG. $25. Hartford, Mutual Pub. Co., 1871. Red cloth, 285 pages. Worn but good. $45.

KELLY, FRED C. *The Wright Brothers*. Harcourt, 1943 1st edition. Very Good in dust jacket. $25.
George Ade, Warmhearted Satirist. Bobbs Merrill, Indiana edition, 1947 1st ed. Fine in DJ. $20.
Life and Times of Kin Hubbard. Farrar Straus, 1952 1st edition. Fine in DJ. $16.

KELLY, WALT. *Pogo*. Simon-Schuster. 1950 1st. VG. $16.
The Pogo Sunday Book. Simon-Schuster, 1956 1st ed. Very Good. Paperback. $16-$24.
I Go Pogo. Simon Schuster, 1952 1st ed. VG. $18-$24.
The Pogo Stepmother Goose. New York, 1954 1st printing. Very Good. $25.
The Pogo Peek-a-Book. NY, 1955 1st ed. VG. $20-$30.
Positively POGO. NY, 1957 1st printing. $20-$35.
Deck Us All With Boston Charlie. NY, 1963 1st ed. Paperbound. Edges dark. VG. $25.
Jack Acid Society Black Book. Simon & Schuster, 1962 4th printing. Very Good. $10.
The Pogo Poop Book. NY, 1966 1st ed. VG. $15.
Pogo Romances Recaptured. 2 in 1 vol. Fireside, 1975 1st edition. Very Good. $12.
Most Pogo original paperbacks, 1st editions in Very Good-Fine condition, range in value from $20 to $45. A hardback, *Ten Ever-Lovin, Blue-Eyed Years with Pogo* is worth $75 as a first in dust jacket The 7th edition, 1965 paperback. $12-$14.

KELSEY, D. M. *History of Our Wild West & Stories of Pioneer Life*. Thompson-Thomas, 1901 1st ed. Illustrated boards. 542 pages. Very good. $35.

KELTON, ELMER. *The Good Old Boys*. Doubleday, 1978 1st ed. Fine in poor dust jacket. $40.

KEMBLE, EDWARD W. (Illustrator). *Samantha on the Race Problem*. By Samantha Holley. Bos, 1892. Fine. $75.
On the Plantation. By Joel C. Harris. NY, 1892 1st ed. Very Good-Fine. $300-$450.
Knickerbocker's History of New York. By Washington Irving. NY, 1894 2 vols. Van Twiller edition. $150-$450.
Danny's Own Story. By Don Marquis. Garden City NY, 1912 1st ed. Very Good plus. $100.

KEMBLE, FRANCES ANNE. *Journal of a Residence on a Georgian Plantation in 1838-1839*. NY, 1863 1st American edition. Rebacked. VG. $125. Another with three pages. missing. Good. $35.

KENDRICK, BAYARD. *The Whistling Hangman*. NY, Crime Club, 1937 1st ed. Ex-library in DJ. $15.
Death Knell. NY, 1945 1st ed. Near Fine in worn DJ. $40.
Flames of Time. Scribner, 1948 1st ed. VG in DJ. $35.

KENLON, JOHN. *Fires and Firefighters*. Doran, 1913. Good-Very Good. $50.

KENNAN, GEORGE. *Tent Life in Siberia*. NY, 1873. VG plus. $50. 1888 edition. $20.

KENNEDY, DIANA. *The Cuisines of Mexico*. Harper & Row, 1972 1st ed. 378 pages. VG in DJ. $22.

KENNEDY, JAMES HARRISON. *History of the City of Cleveland, 1796-1896*. Cleveland, 1896 1st edition, Numbered 256. Needs rebinding. $75.

KENNEDY, JOHN F. *Why England Slept*. NY, 1940 1st ed. Author's 1st book. VG in vg DJ. $250-$450. Same, London 1st English ed. VG. $90.
Profiles in Courage. New York, 1956 1st edition. Near Fine in near fine dust jacket. $225. Very Good in DJ. $75.

KENNEDY, LUDOVIC. *Pursuit: The Chase & Sinking of the Battleship Bismarck*. NY, 1974. VG in worn DJ. $16.

KENNEDY, NANCY. *Ford Times Cookbook*. Ford, 1968 1st ed. Very Good. $10-$12.
Ford Treasury of Favorite Recipes. Simon & Schuster, 1950 1st ed. Very Good. $15.

KENNEDY, RICHARD S. *The Window of Memory*. Univ. of N. C. 1962 1st ed. VG in dust jacket. $16.

KENNEDY, ROBERT F. *Just Friends & Brave Enemies*. Harper, 1962 1st ed. Very Good $15.
The Pursuit of Justice. NY, 1964 1st ed. Signed. Very Good in dust jacket. $60.
13 Days: Memoir of Cuban Missile Crisis. NY, 1969 1st ed. Fine in dust jacket. $20.

KENNERLY, B. *The Eagles Roar*. New York, Harper, 1942. Good-Very Good. $16.

KENT, CORITA. *Damn Everything But the Circus*. NY, Holt, Rinehart, 1970 1st ed. Illus. by author. Signed by Corita. VG in clipped DJ. $45 auction.

KENT, LOUISE. *Village Greens of New England*. NY, 1948 1st ed. Very Good. $13.
Mrs. Appleyard and I. Boston, 1968. Good. $10.

KENT, ROCKWELL. *This is My Own*. 1910 1st ed. Stained. $16. 1940 Duell, Sloane. Fine. $28.
N by E. Brewer, NY, 1930 1st ed. Very Good in DJ. $70. Another, in Poor dust jacket. $30.
Rockwellkentiana. NY, 1933 1st ed. Illustrated by author. Fine in dust jacket. $75. Very Good in DJ. $35-$50.
Rockwell Kent's Greenland Book. NY, 1935 1st. F. $65.
Salamina. NY, 1935 1st ed. Signed. G-VG in DJ. $60-$175. Soiled DJ, unsigned. VG. $25.
A Northern Christmas. NY, Amer. Artist Group, 1941 1st ed. 24 pages. Paper bds. VG. $35.

KENT, ROCKWELL (Illustrator). *Candide*. By Voltaire. NY, 1928. One of 1,470 copies. $75-$150.
The Ballad of Yukon Jake. NY, 1928. Near Fine. $35.
Moby Dick. By Herman Melville. NY, 1930. Very Good in dust jacket. $75.

KENT, WILLIAM W. *The Hooked Rug*. NY, 1941. Illus. Very Good in dust jacket. $65.

THE KENTUCKY HOME COOK BOOK. Maysville, KY, 1899 1st ed. Good-VG. $30-$45.

A KENTUCKY HOUSEWIFE'S COOK BOOK. Anon. 1839. $300-$500.

KEPES, GYORGY. *Language of Vision*. Chicago, 1944 1st ed. Slight wear, o/w Very Good. $30.
The Nature and Art of Motion. No place, 1965 2nd ed. Very Good in dust jacket. $45.
Structure in Art and Science. NY, 1965 2nd printing. Very Good in dust jacket. $25.

KEPHART, HORACE. *Our Southern Highlanders*. Photo illus. NY, Outing Pub., 1913 1st edition. VG. $55 auction.

KEPLINGER, JOHN. *The Jewelry Repairer's Handbook*. NY, 1902. Small 12mo, cloth, 96 illustrated pages. $50.

KEPPEL, FREDERICK. *The Golden Age of Engraving*. NY, 1910 3rd printing. Hinges reinforced. Fair. $18.

KERFOOT, J. B. *American Pewter*. 1911 1st edition. Good plus. $30. Bonanza reprint. Good. $20.

KEROUAC, JACK. *On the Road*. NY, 1957 1st ed. Viking. VG-Fine in DJ. $400-$900. Same, 3rd ed. VG in DJ. $55.
The Dharma Bums. NY, 1958 1st edition. VG in rubbed dust jacket. $125-$175.
Dr. Sax. Grove, 1959 1st ed. Signed. Paperback. Good. $500. Same, unsigned, no DJ. $250.
The Subterraneans. NY, Grove, 1958 Hardbound Trade edition. Very Good, no DJ. $195.
Maggie Cassidy. Avon paperback, 1959 1st ed. VG. $40.
Lonesome Traveler. NY, 1960 1st ed. Larry Rivers illus. Very Good plus. $25. Same in dust jacket. $30-$60.

Visions of Gerard. NY, 1963 1st ed. Near Fine in vg dust jacket. $100-$150. Same, review copy. $200.
Pic. Grove 1971 1st ed. Fine in slipcase. $75.
Visions of Cody. NY, 1972 1st ed. Fine in DJ. $90.

KERR, GRAHAM. *The Complete Galloping Gourmet Cookbook*. Grosset and Dunlap, 1972. Good in fair DJ. $13. 1969 3rd ed. Fine in dust jacket. $8.

KERRIGAN, EVAN E. *American War Medals and Decorations*. Macmillan, 1971 revised ed. Very Good in dust jacket, ex-library. $10.

KERTESZ, ANDRE (Photographer). *Sixty Years of Photography, 1912-1972*. NY, 1972. Signed. Fine in DJ. $175.
J'aime Paris: Photographs Since the Twenties. NY, 1974 Nicolas Ducrot, ed. VG in dust jacket. $100.

KETHAM, BRYAN E. *Covered Bridges on the Byways of Indiana*. Oxford OH, 1949. $186, signed by author. Very Good-Fine. $60.

KESEY, KEN. *One Flew Over the Cuckoo's Nest*. NY, 1962 1st ed. Very Good. $100. Fine in dust jacket. $200-$400.
Sometime a Great Nation. Viking, 1964 1st ed. Very Good in dust jacket. $125. Fine in dust jacket. $175.
Ken Kesey's Garage Sale. NY, 1973. Paperback. Very Good. $35-$50. Fine in DJ. $95. Signed. $135.

KETON, EDNA. *The Indians of North America*. Harcourt, NY, 1927. Vol. 1. Very Good. $15.

KEYES, DANIEL. *The Minds of Billy Milligan*. NY, 1981 1st ed. Good-Very Good in dust jacket. $20.

KEYES, EVELYN. *Scarlet O'Hara's Younger Sister - My Lively Life in Hollywood*. Lyle Stuart, 1977 1st ed. Fine in dust jacket. $18. Book Club ed. Fine. $8.

KEYES, FRANCES PARKINSON. *The Old Gray Homestead*. Boston, 1919 1st ed. VG. $100-$125.
Dinner at Antoine's. Messner, 1948. Fine in DJ. $8.
Steamboat Gothic. NY, 1952 1st edition. Inscribed. Very Good in dust jacket. $60.
The Frances Parkinson Keyes Cookbook. NY, 1955 1st ed. Very Good in dust jacket. $30.
Roses in December. Doubleday, Book Club ed., 1960. Fine in dust jacket. $12.

KEYHOE, DONALD E. MAJOR. *The Flying Saucer Conspiracy*. Holt, 1955 1st ed. VG. $10.

KEYNES, JOHN MAYNARD. *The Economic Consequences of The Peace*. NY, 1920 1st Amer. ed. VG. $30.

KEYSER, LEANDER. *Birds of the Rockies*. A. C. McClurg, 1902. Good. $12.

KEYSTONE COOK BOOK. The P. D. & Co., 1888. $35.

KIDDER, DANIEL P. *Mormonism and the Mormons*. NY, 1844. Very Good. $65-$100.

KIENE, JULIA. *Betty Furness Westinghouse Cook Book*. Simon & Schuster, 1954 1st ed. VG. $10-$12.

KIERAN, JOHN. *The American Sporting Scene*. New York, 1941 1st edition. J. W. Golinkin illustrator. Very Good-Fine in dust jacket. $15-$30.
The Natural History of New York City. Boston, 1959 2nd edition. Fine in good dust jacket. $25.

KIKI. *Kiki's Memoirs*. Paris, 1930 1st ed. in English, with additonal text. Ernest Hemingway introduction. One of 1,000 copies, paperbound Man Ray illustrations. Banned from entry into U. S. on grounds of obscenity. $275.
The Education of a French Model. NY, 1950. Very poor dust jacket. $45.

KILMER, JOYCE. *Poems, Essays and Letters*. NY, 1918 2 vols. Fine in DJ slipcase. $20.
Main Street and Other Poems. Doran, 1917. $8.

KILVERT, CORY. *The Male Chauvinist's Cookbook*. NY, 1974. Very Good in dust jacket. $18. A fine copy. $35.

KIMBALL, MARIE. *The Martha Washington Cook Book*. NY, 1940. Very Good. $40.

KIMBROUGH, EMILY. *We Followed Our Hearts to Hollywood*. NY, 1943 1st ed. Helen Hokinson illus. Very Good in dust jacket. $30.
Through Charlie's Door. Harper, 1952 1st ed. Signed and inscribed. Fine in DJ. $23. Unsigned. $13.
And a Right Good Crew. NY, 1958. Signed. F in DJ. $12.
The Floating Island. NY, 1968. Signed. VG in DJ. $50.

KIMMEL, STANLEY. *The Mad Booths of Maryland*. Bobbs-Merrill, 1940 1st ed. Illus. VG. $40.
Mr. Davis' Richmond. Coward, McCann, 1958 1st ed. Illus. Very Good in dust jacket. $25.

KINERT, REED. *Early American Steam Locomotives, 1830-1900*. Bonanza Books, 1962. Very Good. $28.
America's Fighting Planes in Action. Macmillan, 1943. Good-Very Good. $15-$20.

KING ARTHUR AND HIS NOBLE KNIGHTS OF THE ROUND TABLE. (Also see Malory, Sir Thomas.) NY, Limited Editions Club, 1936. 3 vols. in slipcase, signed by illus. Near Fine. $100-$150.

KING, CAPTAIN CHARLES. *Starlight Ranch and Other Stories of Army Life*. Lippincott, 1890 1st edition. Spine, corner wear. $45.

Tame Surrender: Story of the Chicago Strike. Lippincott, 1896 1st ed. Good-Very Good. $40.
A Daughter of the Sioux. NY, 1903 1st ed. F. Remington illus. Minor wear, spotting. $50.

KING, CLARENCE. *United States Geological Exploration of the 40th Parallel*. 7 vols. Washington, Govt. Printing Office, 1878-80 1st ed. Chromolithos. Worn, splitting. Internally Very Good. $1,300 auction.
Mountaineering in the Sierra Nevada. London, 1903. Good plus. $30.

KING, CONSTANCE EILEEN. *The Collector's History of Dolls*. NY, 1978 1st ed. Fine in fine DJ. $60.

KING, FRANK M. *Wranglin' The Past, Reminiscences of*. Pasadena, 1946 revised ed. VG in worn DJ. $32.

KING, GRACE. *Monsieur Motte*. NY, 1888 1st ed. Author's 1st book. Yellow cloth. Very good copy. $125.

KING, LARRY L. *The One-eyed Man*. NY, 1966 1st ed. Author's 1st book. Near Fine in VG DJ. $60-$100.
Of Outlaws, Conmen, Whores. NY, 1980 1st ed. Very Good-Fine. $25-$35.

KING, MARTIN LUTHER. *Why We Can't Wait*. NY, 1964 1st ed. Fine in dust jacket. $65.
Strength to Love. NY, no date, 1st ed. VG in DJ. $35.
Where Do We Go From Here. Harper, 1967 1st ed. Very Good-Fine. $40-$50. Same in dust jacket. $75-$125.

KING, MOSES. *King's Handbook of the U. S.* Buffalo, 1891. Over 2,600 illustrators. $25-$50.
Views of the N. Y. Stock Exchange 1897-1898. NY, 1897. 1,061 portraits, illus. Very Good. $80.
King's Views of New York, 1908-1909. King, 1909 1st edition. Fair. $24.

KING, STEPHEN. *Carrie*. NY, 1974 1st ed. VG in slightly worn DJ. $495. Another, Fine in Fine DJ. $375.
The Shining. NY, 1977 1st edition. Very Good in slightly torn dust jacket. $100-$295.
The Stand. Garden City, 1978 1st ed. VG in vg DJ. $125.

KINGSLEY, CHARLES. *The Water Babies*. NY, Dodd-Mead, 1916 1st ed. 12 color plates by Jessie Wilcox Smith. Gilt lettered green cloth, round pictorial label. Near Fine. $250 auction. Same pub. Same year, plain endpapers. 8 plates. $75-$125. London, circa 1916. Fine. $200-$350. Dent, Dutton, no date. With Margaret Tarrant illus. VG. $45. Garden City, 1937 edition with J. W. Smith illus. Worn. $15-$30. Same, VG. $35-$50. Ethel Everett illus. No date. 8 full-color plates. Mild margin foxing. VG. $42.
Westward Ho! New York, Scribners, 1920 1st edition. VG. $50-$100. Same in Library binding. Very Good. $18. Same, 1936 edition. Wyeth illustrator. $40.

KINGSTON, W. H. *A Voyage Around the World*. London, 1870 1st ed. Very Good. $25.

KINNELL, GALWAY. *What a Kingdom It Was*. Boston, 1960 1st ed. Signed. Very Good. $60-$75.
Black Light. London, 1967 1st English edition. Signed. Fine in dust jacket. $60.
The Book of Nightmares. Boston, 1971 1st edition. Fine in dust jacket. $65.

KINSLEY, A. T. *Swine Practice Illustrated*. American Vet. Pub. Co. Chicago, 1921 1st ed. Fine. $20.

KIPLING, RUDYARD. *Barrack Room Ballads*. NY, 1898 1st American edition. Near Fine. $100. 1899. $20-$30. Another, A. L. Burt, 1900 ed. Red leather. $50.
The Jungle Book. London, 1894 1st edition. 2 volumes in blue cloth in DJs. $700-$1,500. Same, NY, 1925. $45. Doubleday, 1948. $15.
Departmental Ditties and Other Verses. 4th ed. Calcutta, 1890. Very Good. $80. Near Fine presentation copy. $150.
Captains Courageous. New York, 1897 1st American edition. Very Good. $125.
The Day's Work. NY, 1898 1st ed. Illus. VG. $-$35-$65.
The City of Dreadful Night. NY, 1899 1st American ed. Charles D. Farrand Illus. Near Fine. $150.
Just So Stories. London, Macmillan, 1902 1st edition. Illus. by author. Good. $143. Another, no place, no date. Gleeson and Bransom illus. Moderate wear. VG. $35.
Just So Stories For Little Children. NY, 1902 1st American ed. Illus. by author. VG. $750. Reprints. $15.
Puck of Pook's Hill. NY, 1906. Arthur Rackham illus. Very Good. $50. Fine. $95. Same, 1916. $20-$45.
Complete Works of Rudyard Kipling. NY, 1907-1908 23 vols. Good-VG. $145. Doubleday, 1898. 14 vols. $165.
Kim. NY, Garden City, 1901 1st American ed. VG. $75.
With the Night Mail: A Story of 2000 A. D. NY, 1909 1st American ed. Illus. Near Very Good. $25.
Soldiers Three. Modern Library 1st ed. 1917. Very Good-Fine in dust jacket. $120.
His Apologies. Doubleday, 1932 "1st ed". Probably a later printing. $20.
The Butterfly That Stamped. NY, 1947, Feodor Rojankovsky illus. VG in DJ. $30.
The Cat That Walked By Himself. Garden City, 1947. Feodor Rojankovsky illus. VG in DJ. $35.

KIRKLAND, ALEXANDER. *Rector's Naughty '90s Cook Book*. Doubleday, 1949 1st edition. VG in fair DJ. $25.

KIRKLAND, FRAZER. *Reminiscences of the Blue and Gray*. Preston Pub., Chicago, 1895. Good. $22.

KIRKLAND, WALLACE. *Recollections of a Life Photographer*. Riverside Press, 1954 1st edition. Fine in dust jacket. $30.
Adventures of a Cameraman. London, 1955. Good. $35.

KIRKMAN, MARSHALL. *Locomotive Appliances*. World Railway, 1902 1st ed. Good, spine missing. $18.

KIRCHTEN, ERNEST. *Catfish and Crystal*. Garden City, 1960 1st ed. Very Good in dust jacket. $12.

KISSELL, MARY LOIS. *Basketry of the Papago and Pima Indians*. Rio Grande Press, 1972 reprint. Fine. $25.

KITTO, JOHN. *Illustrated History of the Holy Bible*. H. Bill, pub. 1871 revised ed. Leather covers. G-VG. $20-$30.

KITTON, E. G. *Dickens and His Illustrators*. London, 1899 1st ed. Rebacked. $300.

KITTREDGE, GEORGE. *Witchcraft in Old New England*. Harvard, 1929 2nd ed. VG in fair dust jacket. $75.

KLAMKIN, Charles. *Weather Vanes, the History, Manufacture and Design of an American Folk Art*. NY, 1973 1st printing. VG in poor dust jacket. $30.

KLAUS, SAMUEL. *New York State vs. Molineux*. NY, 1929. American trials Series. Good in DJ. $75.

KLEE, PAUL. *Pedagogical Sketchbook*. NY, 1953 1st ed. Illus. by author. Fine in fair dust jacket. $50.

KLEIN, BENJAMIN (Editor). *Ohio River Handbook and Picture Album*. Young-Klein, 1958 4th edition. Photo illus. Very Good. $15.

KLEIN, WILLIAM (Photographer). *Home: The City and Its People*. NY, 1959 1st ed. VG-Fine. $150-$300.
Moscow. New York, 1964 1st American edition. Near Fine in dust jacket. $350.
Tokyo. NY, 1964. Ex-library. Rebound. $75.

KLINE, OTIS. *Adelbert, the Planet of Peril*. Chicago, 1929 1st edition. Author's 1st book. Inscribed. Edges worn otherwise Very Good. $200.
Call of the Savage. Clode, 1937 1st edition. Very Good-Fine. $300-$350.

KLONDIKE ALASKA GOLD FIELDS. *The Chicago Record's Book for Gold Seekers*. Chicago, 1897. Photos, maps, etc. $75.

KLOOMOK, ISAAC. *Marc Chagall, His Life & Work*. NY, 1951. Very Good in worn dust jacket. $25.

KLUTE, JEANNETE. *Woodland Portraits*. Boston, 1954 1st ed. With 2 extra plates as issued. Fine. $50.

KNAP, A. H. *Wild Harvest: An Outdoorsman's Guide to Edible Wild Plants in North America*. Toronto, 1975. Illus. by E. B. Sanders. Fine in DJ. $18.

KNEELAND, CLARISSA. *Smuggler's Island*. Boston, 1915. Good. $15.

KNIBBS, HENRY HERBERT. *Sundown Slim*. Boston, 1915 1st ed. Very Good. $50.
Wild Horses. Boston, 1924 1st ed. Fine. $20.
Temescal. Boston, 1925 1st edition. Very Good in DJ. $18.
The Sunglazers. Houghton Mifflin, 1926 1st ed. Fine. $25.

KNICKERBOCKER, DEIDRICH (Washington Irving). *A History of New York from the Beginning of the World to the End of the Dutch Dynasty*. All after 1809 are reprints. Various editions illustrated by Maxfield Parrish, 1900-1915. $150-$250 in Very Good to Fine cond. 1860 revised edition. Geo. P. Putnam. Ex-library. Fair-Good. $10-$24.

KNICKERBOCKER, H. *Danger Forward: The Story of the 1st Divison in WWII*. Wash., 1947. Fine in fine DJ. $95.

KNIGHT, DAMON. *Beyond Tomorrow*. NY, 1965 1st ed. Very Good in dust jacket. $20.
Orbit 4. NY, 1968 1st ed. Fine in dust jacket. $20.
The World and Thorin. NY, 1981 1st ed. Review copy. Fine in dust jacket. $20.

KNIGHT, EDWARD. *Knight's New Mechanical Dictionary 1876-1880*. Boston, 1884 ed. A nice ex-library copy. $75.

KNIGHT, ERIC. *Lassie Come Home*. No place, 1940. Fine in dust jacket. $50-$75.

KNIGHTLEY & SIMPSON. *Secret Lives of Lawrence of Arabia*. McGraw Hill, 1970 1st American edition. Fine in dust jacket. $18.

KNEVELS, G. *The Wonderful Bed*. Juvenile. Indianapolis, 1912 1st ed. Emily Chamberlin Illus. Good. $30.

KNIGHT, JOHN ALDEN. *The Modern Angler*. NY, 1936. Very Good. $25.
Ol' Bill and Other Stories. NY, 1942 1st ed. One of 1,929 copies, signed by author and artist. Near Very Good in dust jacket. $85. Unsigned copy. $45.
Woodcock. NY, 1944 Good-VG. $30.
Ruffed Grouse. New York, 1947 1st edition. Fine in dust jacket. $100.

KNIGHTS OF PYTHIAS MANUAL & TEXT BOOK 1886. Memento Pub, 1886 revised ed. VG. $25.

KNOWER, DANIEL. *The Adventurs of a Forty-Niner*. Albany, 1894. Chipped, cracked leather. $80-$120.

KNOWLES, JOHN. *A Separate Peace*. London, 1959 1st edition. Author's 1st book. Very Good in dust jacket. $50. Same, 1960 1st American edition. Very Good in dust jacket. $125.

KNOWLTON, CHARLES. *The Fruits of Philosophy*. edited by N. E. Himes. Maryland, 1937. 1 of 450 copies of reprint of 1st American book on birth control (1832). $40.

KNOX, DUDLEY W. *The Naval Genius of George Washington*. Boston, 1932 1st edition. One of 550 copies. Very Good. $85.

KNOX, ROLAND. *Essays in Satire*. London, 1928 1st ed. Very Good. $23.
The Three Taps. NY, 1927 1st ed. VG. $40.

KNOX, THOMAS W. *Blacksheesh!* Worthington, 1875 1st edition. Rough copy. $10.
Underground, Life Below the Surface. Burr & Hyde, 1873 1st ed. Fair. $15. 1882 ed. Very Good. $65.
Young Nimrods. Harper, 1881, 1882. 2 volumes. Good. $15-$20. Very Good. $30.

KOBER, ARTHUR. *Having Wonderful Time*. NY, 1937 1st edition. Very Good. $20.

KOCH, ROBERT. *Louis C. Tiffany, Rebel in Glass*. NY, 1965. Illus. VG in dust jacket. $35-$65.

KOCHER & DEARSTYNE. *Colonial Williamsburg-Buildings, Gardens*. Williamsburg, 1949 1st ed. Photo illus. Fine in dust jacket. $14.

KOESTLER, ARTHUR. *The Age of Longing*. NY, 1951 1st edition. Very Good in dust jacket. $15.
Sleepwalkers. New York, 1959 1st printing. Good in dust jacket. $28.
The Call Girls. New York, 1973. Very Good-Fine in dust jacket. $15-$40.

KOLB, ELLSWORTH. *Through the Grand Canyon From Wyoming*. Macmillan, 1970 18th ed. Fine in DJ. $9.

KOLLWITZ, KATHE. *Diaries and Letters*. Chicago, 1955 1st edition. Very Good. $40.

KONIGSBURG, E. L. *The Second Mrs. Gioconda*. New York, 1975 3rd ed. Illus. by author. Fine. $14.
Father's Arcane Daughter. NY, 1977 1st edition. Illus. by author. Fine in dust jacket. $24.
Journey to an 800 Number. NY, 1982 1st ed. Illus. by author. Fine in dust jacket. $40.

KORTRIGHT, FRANCIS. *Ducks, Geese and Swans of North America*. Stackpole, 1953 7th edition. Very Good in poor dust jacket. $12.

KNOBLOCK, BRYON. *Banner-Stones of the North American Indians*. Pub. by author at La Grange, IL, in 1939. Trade ed., signed, worn DJ. $100. Deluxe edition. of 50 copies, signed. $195-$280.

KOONTZ, DEAN R. *Warlock*. New York, Lancer, 1972 1st edition. Paperback original. Fine. $15-$25.
Blood Risk. Bobbs-Merrill, 1973 1st ed. Near Fine in very good dust jacket. $175.
Nightmare Journey. New York, 1975 1st edition. Very Good in dust jacket. $75.
Night Chills. NY, 1976 1st edition. Remainder mark. Fine in dust jacket. $100.

KORZYBSKI, ALFRED. *Science and Sanity*. Lakeville CT, 1959 4th ed. Good-Very Good. $18-$35.

KOUFAX, SANDY. *Koufax*. New York, 1966 1st edition. Very Good in dust jacket. $20.

KOUWENHOVEN, JOHN. *Adventures of America*. NY, 1938 1st edition. Harper's Weekly art, 1857-1900. Very Good in dust jacket. $15-$30.

KOVACS, ERNIE. *Zoomar*. NY, 1957 1st ed. Author's 1st book. Very Good in dust jacket. $75.

KRAEUCHI, RUTH M. *Cocker Spaniel*. Judy Publications, 1956 1st edition. 80 pages. Fine in dust jacket. Signed by author. $16.

KRAFT-EBBING, R. *An Experimental Study in the Domain of Hypnotism*. Putnam's, 1889 1st English ed. VG. $150.
Psychopathia Sexualis. NY, circa 1912. Translation from 12th, final, German ed. VG. $50. Same, 1965 edition. $50.

KRAFT, BARBARA S. *The Peace Ship: Henry Ford's Pacifist Adventure etc*. NY, London, 1978. Ins., Fine. $20.

KRAUS, E. H. *Gems and Gem Materials*. New York, 1947 5th edition. Ex-library. $20.

KRAUS, GEORGE. *High Road to Promontory*. American West, 1969. VG in edgeworn dust jacket. $30.

KRAUSS, RUTH. *A Hole Is To Dig: A First Book of Definitions*. NY, 1952. Maurice Sendak illus. Very Good in dust jacket. $15-$25.
I'll Be You and You Be Me. NY, 1954. Maurice Sendak illus. Ex-library. VG. $8.
Somebody Spilled the Sky. NY, 1979 1st ed. Eleanor Hazard illus. As new in as new DJ. $40.

KREYMBORG, ALFRED. *Troubadour: An Autobiography*. NY, 1925 1st ed. Very Good. $30.
Funnybone Alley. NY, 1927 1st trade edition. Boris Artzybasheff illus. Good. $45.
Selected Poems, 1912-1944. NY, 1945 1st edition. Very Good in slipcase. $10.

KROC, RAY. *Grinding It Out - Making of McDonald's*. Regnery, 1977 1st edition. Good-VG in DJ. $12.

KROEBER, A. L. *Cultural and Natural Areas of Native North America*. Berkeley, 1963. 18 maps. VG plus. $25.

KROEBER, THEODORE AND R. F. HEIZER. *Almost Ancestors - The First Californians*. San Francisco, 1968. Very Good in dust jacket. $30.

KROLASKI, HARRY. *The Fool and His Money*. Gambling. 1911. 328 pgs. Signed by author. Very Fine. $110 auction.

KROMER, TOM. *Waiting for Nothing* New York, 1935 1st edition. Author's 1st book. Good plus. $50.

KRUG, J. A. *The Colorado River*. Dept. of Interior. 1946 1st ed. Including 12 folding maps. Good. $16. VG. $35.

KRUTCH, JOSEPH WOOD (Editor). *A Treasury of Birdlore*. Doubleday, 1926. Illus. Very Good. $35.

KUHNE, FREDERICK. *The Finger Print Instructor*. Munn & Co., 1916 1st ed. VG. $16. Another: 1921 ed., Scientific American pub. Includes 11 loose folding plates in pocket. Very Good. $50-$75.

KUMIN, MAXINE. *Halfway*. NY, 1961 1st. Fine in DJ. $35.
Faraway Farm. NY, 1967 1st ed. Kurt Werth illus. Near Fine in dust jacket. $35.
Up Country. NY, 1972 1st ed. Illus. VG in DJ. $35. Another, signed. $40.

KUNHARDT, DOROTHY. *Little Ones*. NY, 1935 1st ed. Kurt Wiese illus. Near Fine in dust jacket. $35.
Once There Was a Little Boy. Viking, 1946 1st ed. Very Good in dust jacket. $25.
The Tiny Golden Library. Set of 12 miniature story books. NY, 1949 1st edition. Very Good. $110.

KUNITZ, STANLEY (Editor). *Twentieth Century Authors, Biographical Dictionary*. New York, Wilson, 1942 2nd edition. Good plus. $20.

KUNS, RAY. *Automobile Essentials*. 1931 5th edition, textbook. Fine. $14.

KUNZ, GEORGE FREDERICK. *The Curious Lore of Precious Stones*. Lippincott, 1913. Presentation copy, Very Good. $200.
The Magic of Jewels and Charms. Philadelphia, 1915 1st edition. Illus. Fine in dust jacket. $80.
Shakespeare and Precious Stones. Philadelphia, London, 1916. Illus. Inscribed VG in dust jacket. $125.
Rings for the Finger. Lippincott, 1917 1st ed. Fine in slipcase. $350. Another, scuffed, faded, loose. $50.

KUTTNER, HENRY. *Fury*. G&D, 1950. VG in DJ. $60.
Man Drowning. NY, 1952 1st edition. VG in torn DJ. $25.
Ahead of Time. NY, 1953 1st ed. VG in dust jacket. $50.

L

LA CUISINE CREOLE (Will H. Coleman). NY, 1885 1st edition. $250-$400. 2nd edition of same year. $35-$40. Other reprints of these famous recipes. $25-$35.

LABRANCHE, GEORGE M. L. *The Dry Fly & Fast Water*. NY, 1921, 1st ed. Very Good. $20.

LA BELLE. *The Ranger Boys Find the Hermit*. A. L. Burt, 1922. Very Good. $10.

LADD-FRANKLIN, CHRISTINE. *Colour and Colour Theories*. NY, Harcourt, 1929 1st American ed. VG. $40.

LADIES' HOME JOURNAL COOKBOOK. 1963 edition. Doubleday. 728 pages. Good-VG. $12-$15.

LADY'S WORK-BOX COMPANION. NY, 1844. Canvas-work instructions, 29 engravings. Good. $50.

LA FARGE, OLIVER. *Laughing Boy*. Boston, 1929 1st ed. Author's 1st book. Very Good in dust jacket. $180. Franklin Mint, 1977. $15-$25.
Sparks Fly Upward. Boston, 1931 1st edition. Very Good in dust jacket. $25-$35.
The Copper Pot. Boston, 1942. Good. $18.
Pictorial History of the American Indian. Crown, 1956 1st ed. Fine in DJ. $18. 1957 Book Club ed. $15.
American Jesuits. NY, 1956 1st ed. Margaret Bourke-White photos. Fine in dust jacket. $75.
Santa Fe: the Autobiography of a Southwestern Town. Norman OK, 1959 1st ed. VG in dust jacket. $30.
Introduction to American Indian Art. NM, 1973 reprint of 1931 edition. $35.

LAGERLOF, SELMA. *The Miracles of Antichrist*. Boston, 1899 1st edition. Very Good. $20.
The Wonderful Adventures of Nils. Grosset & Dunlap, 1907. G-VG. $16. 1947 Translation. H. Baumhauer illus. Very Good in dust jacket. $35.

LAGRANGE, HELEN. *Clipper Ships of America and Great Britain, 1833-1869*. NY, 1936. 37 wood engravings in color. One of 300 copies. Unopened. $250. Same year, trade edition. G-VG. $40-$95.

LAKE, STUART N. *Wyatt Earp, Frontier Marshal*. NY, 1931 1st ed. ("belly" is spelled "elby" on pg. 54). $40-$50.

The Life and Times of Wyatt Earp. No place, 1956 reprint. Good-VG. $20.

LAKESIDE CLASSICS OF LAKESIDE PRESS. 28 titles. Fine. $15-$20 each.

LAMB and SCHULTZ. *Indian Lore*. 1965 4th ed. Fine in DJ. Signed by Shultz. $25. 1973 8th ed. Fine in DJ. $22. 1977 9th ed. Very Good. $8.
More Indian Lore. Winona IN, 1968 1st ed. Fine in dust jacket. Signed by authors. $35. Unsigned. Fine in DJ. $28.

LAMBERT, HELEN C. *A General Survey of Psychical Phenomena*. NY, 1928. VG plus. $25.

L'AMOUR, LOUIS. *Smoke From This Altar*. Lusk Publications, 1939 1st ed. Author's 1st book. Presentation copy, signed. Fine. $1,250.
Over on the Dry Side. NY, 1975 1st ed. in DJ. $50-$75.
The Sacketts. Doubleday, 1980. 3-in-one vol. *Sacketts Land, To Far Blue Mountains, Warrior's Path*. Book Club edition. Very Good in dust jacket. $8.
Crossfire Trail. Boston, 1980. Fine in DJ. $20.
The Tall Stranger. Boston, 1981 1st hardbound ed. Fine-Very Fine in dust jacket. $30-$40.
Showdown at Yellow Butte. Boston, 1980 reprint of 1953 edition. Fine-Very Fine in dust jacket. $20-$30.

LAMPARSKI, RICHARD. *Whatever Became Of?* Second series. NY, 1967 4th printing. VG in DJ. $25.

LAMPORT, FELICIA. *Scrap Irony*. Boston, no date 1st printing. Edward Gorey illus. Good in DJ. $30.
Cultural Slag. Houghton Mifflin, 1966 1st ed. Very Good in dust jacket. $20-$30.

LANCASTER, CLAY. *Architectural Follies in America*. Tuttle, 1960 1st ed. VG in dust jacket. $20.
Antebellum Houses of the Bluegrass. Kentucky Univ. 1961 1st ed. VG-Fine in dust jacket. $140-$175.

LAND, MARY. *Louisiana Cookery*. 1954 reprint by Cookbook Collector's Library. 376 pages. Very Good. $20.

THE LANDMARKS CLUB COOK BOOK, A CALIFORNIA COLLECTION, ETC. Los Angeles, 1903. Out West Co. A very scarce charity-club cookbook. $150-$300.

LANDON, FRED. *Lake Huron*. Bobbs-Merrill, 1945 reprint. Very Good, no dust jacket. $15.

LANE, C. H. *Rabbits, Cats and Cavies*. NY, 1903. Rosa Bebb illus. Very Good. $60.

LANE, FRANK W. *The Elements Rage*. Philadelphia, 1965. Good-VG in dust jacket. $10-$15.
Kingdom of the Octopus. NY, 1974. Revised ed. Near Fine in dust jacket. $13.

LANE, MARGARET. *The Magic Years of Beatrix Potter*. London, 1979. Illus. Fine in dust jacket. $30.

LANE, ROSE WILDER. *Hill-Billy*. Harpers, 1926 1st ed. Green cloth. Good. $12.
Woman's Day Book of American Needlework. Simon & Schuster, 1963 2nd ed. Fine, No dust jacket. $15.

LANES, S. *The Art of Maurice Sendak*. NY, Abrams, 1980. With original pop-up. Fine in dust jacket. $75.

LANG, ANDREW F. *The Brown Fairy Book*. London, 1904 1st ed. H. J. Ford illus. $95-$200. 1908 reprint. $65-$150.
The Red Book of Romance. London, 1905 1st edition. H. J. Ford illus. $95-$200.
The Lilac Fairy Book. New York, 1910 1st Amer. edition. Ford illus. $50-$75. London, 1914. $35-$60.
The Red Fairy Book. Brundage cover. Saalfield, 1928. $18. London, 1890. $60-$175. 1917 reprint. $25-$50.

LANG, W. *History of Seneca County*. Springfield, 1880. 691 pages, 6 x 9. Worn, stained. $75.

LANGDON, AMELIE. *Just for Two*. Recipes for two persons. MN, 1903. Good. $20.

LANGDON, W. C. *Everyday Things in American Life 1607-1776*. NY, 1937 1st edition. Photos. Damped cover and endpapers. Good. $20.

LANGE, DOROTHEA. *1920s-1960s Photos*. Introductory essay by George P. Elliott. NY, 1966. $20.

LANGE, DOROTHEA and PAUL TAYLOR. *An American Exodus: A Record of Human Erosion*. NY, 1939 1st ed. Photographs by Lange. Fine in dust jacket. $300.

LANGER, SUZANNE. *Philosophy in a New Key*. Harvard, 1942. Fine. $20.

LANGNER, LAWRENCE. *The Importance of Wearing Clothes*. NY, 1959. Illus. Very Good. $25.

LANGSTAFF, JOHN. *Over in the Meadow*. New York, 1957 1st edition. Feodor Rojankovsky illustrator. Very Good in good dust jacket. $25.

LANGSETH-CHRISTENSEN, L. *The Mystic Seaport Cookbook*. NY, 1970. Very Good in dust jacket. $13-$24.

LANGSTON, JANE. *The Majesty of Grace*. NY, 1961 1st ed. 1st book. Illus. by author. Fine in dust jacket. $50.
The Astonishing Stereoscope. New York, 1971 1st ed. Erik Blegvard illustrator. Children's novel. Ex-library. Very Good in dust jacket. $25.
The Boyhood of Grace Jones. NY, 1972 1st ed. Emily A. McCully illus. Fine in dust jacket. $25.

LANGSTROTH, L. L. *Practical Treatise on the Hive and the Honey-Bee*. New York, Saxton-Barker, 1860 3rd edition. 77 engravings. $35-$45.

LANIER, SIDNEY. *The Boy's King Arthur*. NY, 1880. Alfred Kappes illus. Good-VG. $22.
The Boy's Froissart. New York, 1881. Alfred Kappes illus. Good-VG. $18.
The Boy's Mabinogion. NY, 1881. Alfred Fredericks illus. Good-VG. $18.
Poems of Sidney Lanier. NY, 1884 1st. Near VG. $125.
Hymns of the Marshes. New York, 1907 1st edition. Illus. Fine. $35-$50.
The Boy's King Arthur. NY, 1924. N. C. Wyeth illus. Very Good. $30-$50. 1917 ed. $75-$125.

LANMAN, CHARLES. *The Japanese in America*. NY, 1872 1st ed. Very Good. $45.

LANTZ, LOUISE. *Old American Kitchenware 1725-1925*. Thomas Nelson, NJ, 1970. VG in dust jacket. $35.

LANTZ, WALTER. *Oswald Rabbit Plays G-Man*. Racine, Whitman, 1937 1st ed. Illus. from Universal Pictures animated scenes. $75-$125.

LAPP, RALPH E. *Must We Hide?* Cambridge MA, 1949. (atomic bomb) Fine in dust jacket. $18.

LARDNER, RING. *Bib Ballads*. Chicago, 1915 1st ed. Author's 1st book. Very Good. $50.
Treat'em Rough. Bobbs-Merrill, 1918 1st ed. VG. $10.
Symptoms of Being 35. Indianapolis, 1921 1st ed. Helen E. Jacobs silhouettes. Covers slightly discolored. $25.
Say It With Oil. NY, 1923. Very Good. $30.
The Big Town. NY, 1925 1st ed. $25-$40.
The Love Nest & Other Stories. NY, 1926 1st. VG. $75.
Shut Up, He Explained. NY, 1962 1st ed. Edited by B. Rosmond, H. Morgan. Fine in clipped DJ. $35.

LARDNER, RING (In Magazines). *Saturday Evening Post*. May 15, 1915. Illus. fiction. $28.
Saturday Evening Post. Oct 23, 1915. Baseball. $30.
Cosmopolitan. Jan, 1927. Illus. short story (Harrison Fisher cover) $29.
Collier's. Jan 12, 1929. Satire on NY. $18.

LARKIN HOUSEWIFE COOK BOOK. Larkin Co., 1923 4th edition. Very Good. $12.

LARKIN, JAMES. *The Practical Brass & Iron Founder's Guide*. Philadelphia, 1887 5th ed. $40.

LARKIN, PHILIP. *High Windows*. London, 1974 1st ed. Fine. $125.

LARNED, LINDA H. *The Hostess of Today*. Scribners, 1901. 303 pages. Dec. green. cloth. Very Good. $60.

LARNED, WILLIAM T. *Fairy Tales From France*. Volland, 1920. John Rae illus. Wear, soiling. $37.

LARNER, JEREMY. *Drive, He Said*. NY, 1964 1st ed. Very Good in dust jacket. $25.

LAROUSSE TREASURY OF COUNTRY COOKING. Crown, 1975. Fine in dust jacket. $15.

LASSWELL, MARY. *Mrs. Rasmusson's 1-Arm Cookery*. Boston, 1946. Very Good in dust jacket. $35.
Suds in Your Eye. Boston, 1949. Illustrated. $30.
Tooner Schooner. NY, 1953 1st ed. VG in fine DJ. $10.
I'l Take Texas. Boston, 1958 1st ed. VG. $13.
Tio Pepe. Boston, 1963 1st edition. 1st printing, Very Good in dust jacket. $13.

LATHEN, EMMA. *Banking on Death*. NY, 1961 1st ed. Near Fine in dust jacket. $400.
Murder Makes the Wheels Go Round. NY, 1966 1st ed. Fine in dust jacket. $125.
Death Shall Overcome. NY, 1966 1st ed. Fine in DJ. $85.
Murder Against the Grain. NY, 1967 1st ed. F in DJ. $55.

LATHROP, DOROTHY. *Bouncing Betsy*. NY, 1936 1st ed. Illus. by author. VG in poor dust jacket. $50.
Hide and Go Seek. No place, 1938 1st edition. Illus. by author. Very Good. $30.
The Colt From Moon Mountain. NY, 1941 1st ed. Illus. by author. Very Good in dust jacket. $18.
The Skittle Skattle Monkey. NY, 1945 1st ed. Illus. by author. Very Good in dust jacket. $18.

LATHROP, DOROTHY (Illustrator). *The Three Mulla-Mulgars*. By Walter de la Mare. NY, 1919 1st ed. Signed, with note, by Lathrop. Good plus. $135.
Down-Adown-Derry. By Walter de la Mare. London, 1922. Very Good plus. $70.
The Princess and Curdie. By George MacDonald. NY, 1927 1st ed. Very Good in dust jacket. $85.

LATHROP, ELISE. *Early American Inns & Taverns*. NY, 1935. Fine. $25. 1947 ed. Very Good. $16.
Historic Houses of Early America. NY, 1927 1st Tudor ed. Fine in DJ and slipcase. $95. 1937 edition. VG. $36.

LATHROP, GILBERT A. *Little Engines and Big Men*. Caxton, 1955, (Narrow gauge railroads). Good. $25.

LATIMER, JONATHAN. *The Lady in the Morgue*. Doubleday, Crime Club, 1936 1st edition. Near Fine in worn dust jacket. $250.
Dark Memory. Doubleday, Crime Club, 1937 1st edition. Very Good. $35.
Sinners and Shrouds. NY, 1955 1st edition. Very Good-Fine in dust jacket. $25-$50.
Headed For a Hearse. Boston, 1980. Fine in fine DJ. $20.

LAUGHLIN, CLARA E. *The Complete Dressmaker, With Simple Directions for Home Millinery*. 1912. VG. $17.

LAUGHLIN, CLARENCE JOHN. *Ghosts Along the Mississippi*. NY, 1948 1st ed. VG-Fine in DJ. $25-$45.

LAUGHLIN, JAMES. *Some Natural Things*. NY, 1945 1st ed. Poems. VG in good DJ. $75. Another, printed at Prairie Press, CT, 1945 1st ed. VG in dust jacket. $50.

LAUGHTER, VICTOR. *Operator's Wireless Telegraph and Telephone Handbook*. Chicago, Drake, 1918 rev ed. $24.

LAURENCE, WILLIAM L . *Dawn Over Zero: The Story of the Atomic Bomb*. NY, 1946 1st edition. Good-VG. $35. 1947 2nd edition. $12.

LAUT, AGNES. *The Story of a Trapper*. Toronto, 1902. Very Good plus. $49. Another, 1st ed. $35.
The Conquest of the Great Northwest. NY, 1908 2 vols. 1st edition. Very Good. $50.
The Fur Trade of America. NY, 1921 1st ed. VG. $50.
The Blazed Trail of the Old Frontier. NY, 1926 1st ed. Charles Russell illus. Fold maps. $120-$170.
Romance of the Rails. NY, 1929. VG. $20.
The Overland Trail. NY, 1929 1st ed. Illus. Good. $18.

LAUTREC, HENRI DE TOULOUSE. *The Art of Cuisine*. Holt, Rinehart &Winston, 1966 1st ed. VG in DJ. $45-$70.

LAVATER, J. C. *Essays on Physiognomy*. London 1789. Translation 3 vols. 360 engravings. VG plus. $400.
Physiogonmy. London, 1827 1st. Original boards. $85.

LAVENDER, DAVID. *The Fist in the Wilderness*. NY, 1964 1st ed. Fine in DJ. $35.
The Rockies. New York, 1968 1st ed. VG in DJ. $25-$35.
The Great Persuader. New York, 1970 1st edition. Very Good in dust jacket. $15.
Colorado. Doubleday, 1976 1st ed. VG in DJ. $15.

LAVER, JAMES. *Children's Fashions of the Nineteenth Century*. London, 1951 1st. 16 color plates. VG in DJ. $45.
Age of Optimism, Manners & Morals 1848-1914. London, 1966. VG in dust jacket. $25.

LAWES, LEWIS E. *Man's Judgment of Death: An Analysis of the Operation and Effect of Capital Punishment*. NY, 1924 1st ed. Very Good. $30.

LAWRENCE, D. H. *The Widowing of Mrs. Holroyd*. Lon., 1914 1st ed. Very Good. $100.
Touch and Go. NY, 1920 1st American edition. Joint splitting, o/w Very Good. $60.
Kangaroo. London, 1923 1st English ed. VG. $75. Same, New York, 1923. Good. $50.
England, My England. London, 1924 1st English ed. Good in fair dust jacket. $65.
The Plumed Serpent. NY, 1926 1st American edition. Covers stained, soiled. $20.
Pansies. Knopf, 1929 1st edition. Very Good. $100.
The Virgin and the Gypsy. London, 1930 1st edition. Fine in chip dust jacket. $150.
Lady Chatterley's Lover. Tipografia Giuntina, Florence, 1928 1st ed. Limited to 1,000 copies, signed by Lawrence. VG to F. $1,800-$3,000. Worn, hinges cracked. $300-$600. Another, chipped corners. $800. Pirated, unauthorized ed., NY, 1928. Black cloth. $100-$150. London, 1932 1st authorized English ed. Cracked hinges, o/w VG. $50. Grove, 1959 ed. Fine in DJ. $16-$29. Faro, 1930 revised ed. G-VG. $30. 1932 1st American edition. $75-$125.
Apocalypse. London, 1932 1st ed. VG. $125.
Sons and Lovers. University of California, 1977. Facsimile of manuscript. Fine in fine dust jacket. $75.

LAWRENCE. D. H. (In Magazines). *Forum*. Jan-June, 1907. Articles. Ex-library. The lot, $35.
Poetry. July, 1918. Two poems. Good. $35.

LAWRENCE, JOSEPHINE. *The Gingerbread Man*. Whitman, 1930. Very Good. $20-$30.
Man in the Moon Stories. Whitman, 1930. Johnny Gruelle illus. Very Good. $25-$40.
Berry Patch. Cupples Leon, 1925. Very Good. $20.

LAWSON, ROBERT. *Ben and Me*. Boston, 1939 1st ed. Author's 1st book. Illus. by author. VG in DJ. $70-$100.
They Were Strong and Good. Viking, 1940 2nd ed. Illus. by author. Very Good in dust jacket. $14.
The Great Wheel. NY, 1957 4th ed. Fine in DJ. $20.

LAWSON, TED. *Thirty Seconds Over Tokyo*. Blue Ribbon, 1944. Good in dust jacket. $5.

LAY, COL. BEIRNE. *I've Had It*. (WWII) New York, 1945 1st ed. Good plus. $20.

LAYARD, AUSTEN H. *Nineveh and Its Remains*. NY, 1849 1st American edition. 2 volumes. Illus. VG plus. $250. Another, much restored. $95.

LAZARUS, EMMA. *Songs of a Semite: The Dance to Death and Other Poems*. NY, 1882 1st ed. VG. $90.

LEA, TOM. *The King Ranch*. Boston, Little Brown, 1957 1st ed. 1st issue. 2 vol. Trade edition. Signed, in slipcase. $100-$150. Other Limited or Private editions, in fine slipcase. $700-$1,800.
The Brave Bulls. 1949. Good. $12.
The Primal Yoke. Little Brown, 1960 1st edition. Signed. Fine in DJ. $75. Unsigned. $30.
The Wonderful Country. 1952 1st ed. Very Good-Fine in dust jacket. $18-$35.
The Hands of Cantu. Boston, 1964 1st ed. Illus. by author. Very Good in dust jacket. $45.

LEAVITT, JOHN M. *Kings of Capital, Knights of Labor*. Culkey, 1896 edition. Very Good. $15.

LEBLANC, MAURICE. *Arsene Lupin. Super Sleuth*. NY, 1927 1st ed. VG plus. $18.

LE CARRE, JOHN. *Call for the Dead*. Walker, 1960 1st ed. VG in vg dust jacket. $16. 1962 1st American edition. Fine in dust jacket. $50-$65.
A Murder of Quality. NY, 1963 1st American ed. Fine in near fine dust jacket. $750-$950.
The Spy Who Came in From the Cold. NY, 1964 1st American ed. VG in dust jacket. $30.
The Looking Glass War. NY, 1965. G-VG. $8-$15. London, 1965 1st ed. Fine in DJ. $65-$100.
A Small Town in Germany. London, 1968 1st ed. Fine in near fine DJ. $90. Another, signed. $150. Coward McCann, 1st American ed. 1968. VG in DJ. $30-$50.

LE CORBUSIER (Charles E. Jeanneret). *The City of Tomorrow and Its Planning*. London, 1929 1st English edition. VG in vg DJ. $400.
Toward a New Architecture. Lon., 1963. Reprint. G. $15.
The Radiant City. NY, 1967 1st ed. Fine. $40.

LE FANU, SHERIDAN. *Wylder's Hand*. London, 1876 3rd edition. Good. $60.
Green Tea and Other Ghost Stories. Arkham House, 1945. VG in dust jacket. $150.
Uncle Silas. London, 1947. Fine in DJ. $40.

LE GALLIENNE, RICHARD. *The Religion of a Literary Man*. London, 1893 1st ed. Near Fine. $85.
An Old Country House. No place, 1895. Elizabeth Shippen Green illus. VG. $25.
The Romance of Perfume. NY, Paris, 1928. George Barbier illus. Fine. $35.

LEA, HOMER. *The Valor of Ignorance*. No place, 1909 1st edition. Very Good. $45.

LEACOCK, STEPHEN. *Further Foolishness*. NY, Toronto, 1916 1st ed. Very Good in dust jacket. $35.
Nonsense Novels. No place, 1921. VG in DJ. $13.
The Boy I Left Behind Me. NY, 1946 1st ed. VG. $40.

LEADBEATER, C. W. *Some Glimpses of Occultism, Ancient and Modern*. Chicago, 1909. Very Good. $60. 1927 edition, 2 volumes in one. $30.
The Inner Life. Wheaton IL, 1949 3rd edition. 2 volumes. Very Good. $30.
The Hidden Side of Things. 1924 3rd edition. Good-Very Good. $15-$20.

LEAF, MUNRO. *Ferdinand the Bull*. London, 1937 2nd edition. Mostly Very Good. $60.
Noodle. Stokes, 1937. Ludwig Bemelmans illus. G. $22.
Wee Gillis. New York, 1938 1st edition. Robert Lawson illustrator. Fine in dust jacket. $125. Another, Very Good no dust jacket. $40-$60.
The Story of Ferdinand. NY, 1938 6th printing. Robert Lawson illus. Very Good. $16.
John Henry Davis. NY, 1940 1st ed. Illus. by author. Very Good in dust jacket. $40.
Aesop's Fables: A New Version. Heritage Press, 1941. Robert Lawson illus. Reprint. Near Fine. $15.

LEAR, EDWARD. *A Book of Nonsense*. London, 1855 2nd edition. $1,600-$2,200.
Nonsense Books with All The Original Illustrations. Boston, 1888. $150-$250.
Limericks by Lear. World, 1965. Lois Ehlert illus. Fine in frayed dust jacket. $35.
The Nutcracker and the Sugar Tongs. Boston, 1978. Marcia Sewall illus. Good. $10.
Various other reprints, misc. titles 1960-1980. $20-$35.

LEE, GYPSY ROSE. *Mother Finds a Body*. NY, 1942 1st ed. Fine in dust jacket. $65-$100.
Gypsy. NY, 1957 1st edition. $15-$20.

LEE, HARPER. *To Kill a Mockingbird*. London, 1960 1st English edition. Very Good-Fine in dust jacket. $95-$250. Philadelphia, Lippincott, 1960 1st edition. Very Good-Fine in dust jacket. $900-$1,250.

LEE, CAPT. ROBERT E. (Editor). *Recollections and Letters of Gen. Robert E. Lee*. NY, 1904. VG. $225.

LEE, RUTH WEBB. *Victorian Glass. Specialties of the 19th Century*. R. W. Lee, 1944 6th edition. Illustrated. Fine in dust jacket. $18.
Price Guide to Pattern Glass. M. Barrows, 1949 3rd ed. Fine in dust jacket. $10.
Early American Pressed Glass. Lee Pubs., 1960 36th ed. Illus. Fine in dust jacket. $15.

LEECH, MARGARET. *Reveille in Washington, 1860-1865*. New York, 1941. Very Good. $15.

LEEN, NINA (Photographer). *The World of Bats*. Holt, Rinehart & Winston, 1969 1st ed. Printed in Switzerland. Very Good-Fine. $135.

LEHMANN, ROSAMUND. *Dusty Answer*. NY, 1927 1st American edition. VG-Fine in dust jacket. $30-$45.
The Ballad and the Source. NY, 1945. VG. $13.
Gypsy's Baby and Other Stories. NY, 1946 1st American edition. VG in dust jacket. $15.

LEHMANN-HAUPT, HELLMUT. *The Book in America: History of Making & Selling Books*. NY, 1951 2nd ed. Very Good in dust jacket. $65.
The Life of the Book. London and New York, 1957 1st edition. Very Good in dust jacket. $30-$40.

LEHNER, ERNEST and JOHANNA. *Lore and Lure of Outer Space*. NY, 1964. Illus. Very Good in dust jacket. $30.

LEHRER, TOM. *The Tom Lehrer Song Book*. NY, 1954. Illus. Very Good in dust jacket. $18.

LEIBER, FRITZ. *Night's Black Agents*. Arkham House, 1947 1st edition. Inscribed. Very Good. $75-$150.
The Big Time, The Mind Spider and Other Stories. NY, Ace double paperback, 1961 1st ed. Good. $25.

LEICA MANUAL, Morgan & Lester, 1944 10th edition. 551 pages. Very Good in poor dust jacket. $25-$30.

LEIGH, HOWARD. *Planes of the Great War, 1914-1918*. London, circa 1920. Collotype drawings. VG. $25-$45.

LEIGHTON, CLARE. *Four Hedges: A Gardener's Chronicle*. NY, 1935. Illus. by author. VG. $50.
Country Matters. NY, 1937 1st ed. Illus. by author. Very Good in good dust jacket. $30.
Sometime-Never. NY, 1939 1st. Illus. by author. NF. $30.
Southern Harvest. NY, 1942 1st edition. Illus. by author. Fine in dust jacket. $25.
Where Land Meets the Sea: the Tide Line of Cape Cod. NY, 1954 1st ed. Illus. by author. VG in DJ. $45.

LEIGHTON, CLARE (Illustrator). *The Sea and the Jungle*. By H. M. Tomlinson. London, 1930. One of 515 copies, signed by author. 16 woodcuts by Leighton. VG. $200.
Wuthering Heights. By Emily Bronte. 12 wood engravings. NY, 1931 1st Trade ed. Very Good. $35-$75.
Folks Do Get Born. By Marie Campbell. NY, 1946 1st edition. Very Good in good dust jacket. $45.

LEINSTER, MURRARY. *The Last Spaceship*. Fell, 1949. Fine in dust jacket. $60-$70.
Sidewise in Time. Chicago, 1950. Signed. Fine in DJ. $80.
Space Tug. 1953 1st ed. VG in dust jacket. $70.
4 From Planet 5. White Lion, 1974 1st edition. Very Good in dust jacket. $25.

LEINWAND, RITA. *How To Beat Those Cordon Bleus*. Ward Ritchie, 1974 1st edition. cook book. Signed by author. Very Good. $16.

LELAND, E. H. *Farm Homes Indoors & Outdoors*. NY, Judd, 1881 1st ed. 204 pgs. of plans, furnishings, etc. Green dec. gilt cloth cover. $75.

LEMCKE, GESINE. *Chafing Dish Recipes*. NY, 1902. Good-Very Good. $15.

LEMKE, CARL. (Editor). *Official History of the Improved Order of Red Men*. Davis Bros., 1964 1st ed. Fine. $25.

LEMON, MARK. *The Enchanted Doll*. De la More Press, 1903. Richard Doyle illus. Very Good. $25.

LENNON, JOHN. *A Spaniard in the Works*. London, 1965. Lamination wrinkle, o/w Fine. $125.
In His Own Write. NY, 1964 1st edition. Near Fine. $25.
Lennon Remembers. San Francisco, 1971 1st ed. Fine in near fine dust jacket. $25.

LENSKI, LOIS. *Jack Horner's Pie*. NY, 1927 2nd ed. Illus. by author. Very Good. $50.
A Little Girl of Nineteen Hundred. No place, 1928 1st ed. Illus. by author. Very Good. $16.
Johnny Goes to the Fair. Minton Balch, 1932 1st edition. Illus. by author. Very Good. $50.
Phebe Fairchild Her Book. Stokes, 1936. Illustrated by author. Good. $10.
Bound Girl of Cobble Hill. NY, 1938 1st edition. Illustrated by author. VG in DJ. $65.
Strawberry Girl. Philadelphia, 1945 1st ed. Illus. by author. Very Good. $25-$35.
Blue Ridge Billy. Lippincott, 1946 1st ed. VG in DJ. $60.
Berries in the Scoop. Philadelphia, 1956. 1st ed. Illus. by author. VG in good dust jacket. $18.
Shoo-Fly Girl. Philadelphia, 1963 1st edition. Illus. by author. Signed on title page. Near Fine. $93. Auction.

LENT, HENRY B. *Full Steam Ahead*. NY, 1933 1st ed. Earle Winslow illus. Very Good. $20.
Tugboat. NY, 1936 1st ed. Earle Winslow illus. VG. $20.
The Farmer. NY, 1937 1st ed. Illus. by Berta & Elmer Hader. Worn, spine darkened. $35.

LENTZ, HAROLD (Also see Pop-Up). *The Pop-Up Pinocchio*. NY, Blue Ribbon, 1932 1st ed. 4 color pop-ups. Rebacked cover. VG. $357 auction. Another, offered by dealer. Very Good. $125.

LEONARD, JOHN. *The Naked Martini*. NY, 1904 1st ed. Author's 1st book. Near Fine in dust jacket. $75.

LEONARD, JOHN W. *History of the City of New York, 1609-1909*. NY, 1910. Good. $35.

LEOPOLD, ALDO. *Game Management*. New York, 1933 1st ed. Very Good. $45.
A Sand County Almanac. NY, 1949 1st. VG in DJ. $65.

LEQUEX, WILLIAM. *Zoraida*. Stokes, 1895 1st American ed. Good in dust jacket. $45.
The Eye of Istar-A. Stokes, 1897 1st Amer. ed. Fine. $50.

LEROUX, GASTON. *The Phantom of the Opera*. NY, 1911 1st American ed. Andre Castaigne illus. VG. $400.
Bride of the Sun. NY, 1915 1st ed. VG. $125.
Nomads of the Night. NY, 1925 1st American ed. VG-Fine in dust jacket. $60-$80.
The Kiss That Killed. Macaulay, 1934 1st American edition. Very Good. $35.
The Machine to Kill. Macaulay, 1935 1st American edition. Shelfworn in fair dust jacket. $35.

LESLIE, DESMOND. *Flying Saucers Have Landed*. NY, 1953. Photos. Very Good. $15.

LESLEY, LEWIS (Editor). *Uncle Sam's Camels*. (1857-1858). Harvard Univ. Press, 1929 1st ed. VG plus. $135.

LESLIE, ELIZA. *Directions for Cooking, Being a System of the Art*. Philadelphia, 1837 1st edition. Good-VG. $75. 3rd edition, 1838. $50.
The House Book, or a Manual of Domestic Economy. 1840. $300-$375.
Directions for Cookery in Its Various Branches. Philadelphia, 1846 24th ed. Nicely rebound. $55.
Miss Leslie's Seventy-Five Receipts for Pastry, Cakes & Sweetmeats. Boston, 1846. Good-VG. $50.
Miss Leslie's Lady's Housebook: A Manual of Domestic Economy. Philadelphia, 1856 14th ed., enlarged. Ex-library. Near Very Good. $225.
Miss Leslie's New Cookery Book. Philadelphia, 1857. Illus. Front cover loose. $150. Same, VG. $175-$225.
An American Family Cook Book. By a Boston housekeeper. NY, James Miller, 1864. Gold dec. green cloth. 330 pages. Good-VG. $80-$120.

LESLIE, FRANK (Publisher). *Frank Leslie's Illustrated Historical Register of the Centennial Exposition of 1876*. Frank Leslie, 1876 1st ed. 324 pgs. Good, torn spine. $125.
Frank Leslie's Illustrated Famous Leaders & Battle Scenes of the Civil War. Frank Leslie, 1896. 544 pages. 12x16. Very Good- Fine. $65.
Frank Leslie's The Soldier in Our Civil War. Columbia Memorial edition. 2 vols. 1893. As new. $325.
Leslie's Official History of the Spanish-American War. Washington, 1899. Folio, 614 pages. Rubbed, nicked. $70. (See Newspaper Section for more Leslie's items.)

LESLIE, ROBERT C. *A Sea Painter's Log*. London, 1886. Illus. by author. G-VG. $85.
A Waterbiography. London, 1894. Illus. by author. Good-Very Good. $85.

LESLIE, SHANE. *Shane Leslie's Ghost Book*. London, 1955 1st ed. Very Good in dust jacket. $25.

LESSING, DORIS. *The Grass Is Singing*. NY, 1950 1st American ed. Author's 1st book. Near Fine in vg DJ. $65. *The Habit of Loving*. 1947 1st U. S. ed. in DJ. $30-$40. *The Temptation of Jack Orkney*. NY, 1972 1st ed. Fine in dust jacket. $13. *The Marriages Between Three, Four and Five*. NY, 1980 1st edition. Very Good in dust jacket. $20.

LESTER, KATHERINE MORRIS. *Clay Work*. 1908. Good-Very Good. $20. *Historic Costume*. Manual Arts Press, no date. Copyright 1933. Illus. VG in DJ. $25. *Accessories of Dress*. Manual Arts, 1940. Illustrated. Very Good in dust jacket. $65-$95.

LESUEUR, MERIDEL. *North Star Country*. Duell-Sloan, 1945 1st edition. 327 pages. Signed by Author. VG in DJ. $20-$35. Another, No dust jacket. $14.

LESY, MICHAEL. *Wisconsin Death Trip*. NY, 1973. Small town through old photos. Good in DJ. $50.

LE TOURNEAU, R. G. *Mover of Men and Mountains*. Prentice Hall, 1960 2nd ed. Good-VG. $12.

LETTS, J. M. *California Illustrated*. R. T. Young, 1852 1st ed. 2nd state (1st was anonymous). $250-$400. 1853 edition. Very Good. $75.

LEVERING, JULIA. *Historic Indiana*. NY, Putnam, 1909 1st edition. Very Good. $28.

LEVERTOV, DENISE. *With Eyes at the Back of Our Heads*. New Directions, 1959 1st ed. VG in DJ. $45. *O Taste and See: New Poems*. New Directions, 1964 1st edition. Fine in DJ. $60.

LEVI, ELIPHAS. *The Mysteries of Magic*. London, 1897 2nd edition. Translated by A. E. Waite. Fine. $150. *Transcendental Magic*. Chicago, 1910. VG. $125.

LEVI-STRAUSS, CLAUDE. *Introduction to a Science of Mythology*. NY, 1969 3 vols. 1st American ed. Fine in chip dust jacket. $150.

LEVIN, IRA. *A Kiss Before Dying*. NY, 1953 1st ed. Author's 1st book. VG in DJ. $75. Another, quite worn. $35. *Rosemary's Baby*. NY, 1967. Fine in DJ. $13. *The Stepford Wives*. NY, 1972 1st ed. NF in DJ. $20.

LEWIS, ALFRED HENRY. *Wolfville*. NY, 1897 1st ed. Remington illus. Worn, good. $125. *Wolfville Days*. NY, 1902 1st edition. Remington frontis. Very Good. $70. *The Black Lion Inn*. NY, 1903 1st ed. Near Fine. $35. *Peggy O'Neal*. Philadelphia, 1903 1st ed. H. Hutt illus. Very Good. $50.

LEWIS, ANTHONY. *The Day They Shook the Plum Tree*. NY,1963 1st edition. Story of Hetty Green. Ex-library. Good in dust jacket. $8.

LEWIS, C. S. *The Case for Christianity*. NY, 1944. VG in dust jacket. $25-$40. *Screwtape Letters*. Canada, 1945. VG. $15-$20. *Miracles: A Preliminary Study*. London, 1947 1st ed. VG in dust jacket. $30-$50. *The Lion, the Witch and the Wardrobe*. London, 1950 1st edition. Pauline Baynes illus. 1st Narna series book. Very Good in very good dust jacket. $75. *The Horse and His Boy*. NY, 1954 3rd ed. Pauline Baynes illus. Good in worn dust jacket. $25. *The Last Battle*. NY, 1956 1st American ed. Pauline Baynes illus. Very Good in dust jacket. $90.

LEWIS, EUGENE W. *Motor Vehicles: A Saga of Whirling Gears* (Memories of Detroit). Detroit, 1947 1st edition. $15.

LEWIS, G. GRIFFIN. *The Practical Book of Oriental Rugs*. Lippincott Co., 1920 5th ed. VG in fair DJ. $100.

LEWIS, LLOYD. *Chicago: The History of Its Reputation*. NY, 1929. Worn leather cover, o/w Fine. $45. *Sherman, Fighting Prophet*. NY, 1932. G-VG. $12-$24. *Captain Sam Grant*. Boston, 1950 reprint. Fine in DJ. $10.

LEWIS, MERIWETHER & WILLIAM CLARK. *The Journals of the Expedition Under the Command of Capts. Lewis and Clark*. NY, Limited Editions Club, 1962. 2 vols, limited to 1,500 copies. Fine in slipcase. $225-$300. *Original Journals of Lewis and Clark Expedition, 1804-1806*. 8 vols. NY, Arno Press, 1969. As new. $200-$300.

LEWIS, OSCAR. *Bonanza Inn: America's First Luxury Hotel*. NY, 1939 1st ed. Signed VG in DJ. $50 *The Silver Kings*. NY, 1947 1st ed. VG in DJ. $37. *The Town That Died Laughing*. Boston, 1955 1st ed. Very Good in dust jacket. $30. *Here Lived the Californians*. No place, 1957. NF. $25. *War in the Far West, 1861-1865*. Garden City NY, 1961. 1st ed. Good in worn DJ. $25. *The Children of Sanchez: Autobiography of a Mexican Family*. NY, 1961. Very Good. $25. *Sutter's Fort: Gateway to the Gold Fields*. NY,1966. Near Fine in dust jacket. $20.

LEWIS, SINCLAIR. (As Tom Graham) *Hike and the Airplane*. NY, 1912 1st ed. Stokes. Author's 1st book. Arthur Hitchins illustratpr. Repaired, Good plus. $2,200-$3,000. *Babbitt*. NY, 1922 1st ed. 1st state. VG in DJ. $150-$350. No DJ. $50. 1946 paperback ed. Bantam, in DJ. $40. *Dodsworth*. Harcourt Brace, 1929 1st ed. VG in DJ. $225. *Arrowsmith*. NY, 1925 1st Trade ed. Near Fine. $75. *Elmer Gantry*. Harcourt Brace, 1927 1st edition, 1st state, with a C instead of a G on spine. VG in taped DJ. $200.

The Trail of the Hawk. Harpers, 1915 1st edition, later issue. Worn. $90.

Main Street. 1937 Limited Editions Club. Grant Wood illus. Slipcase signed by Wood. VG. $250-$400.

The Godseeker. Random House, 1949 1st ed. VG in ragged dust jacket. $18.

Cass Timberlane. NY, 1945 1st ed. VG in clipped DJ. $35.

The Man From Main Street. Selected essays. Random House, 1953, 1st printing. Shelfworn, VG in DJ. $15.

LEWIS, WYNDHAM. *Childerman*. London, 1928 1st trade ed. Signed. Near Fine in vg DJ. $100.

The Stuffed Owl. London, 1930. Illus. VG. $35.

Apes of God. McBride, 1932 1st ed. VG. $45.

LEY, WILLY. *Rockets*. NY, 1944 1st. VG in poor DJ. $125.

The Conquest of Space. NY, 1950. Chesley Bonestell illus. VG in torn DJ. $20.

Rockets, Missiles and Space Travel. NY, 1951. Good in fair dust jacket. $25-$35.

Salamanders and Other Wonders. NY, 1955 1st ed. Fine in dust jacket. $30.

Events in Space. NY, 1969. Ex-library. $10. F in DJ. $15.

LEYENDECKER, JOSEPH C. (1874-1951). A graduate of the Chicago Art Institute, Leyendecker continued his studies in Paris and returned here in 1899 to begin producing cover art for the *Saturday Evening Post* (40 years, 300 covers). He was employed as an advertising illustrator for The Arrow Shirt Company for 21 years. His *Post* covers are worth from $20 to $50 each. The Arrow Collar ads are also quite collectible.

Saturday Evening Post. May 22, 1915. $50.

Saturday Evening Post. Covers, 1927-1931. $30 each. (Also See Magazine section.)

LIBERMAN, ALEXANDER. *The Art and Technique of Color Photography*. NY, 1957 1st ed. G-VG. $25-$50.

LICHTEN, FRANCES. *Decorative Art of Victoria's Era*. Scribners, NY & London, 1950. Minor chipping, VG. $25.

LIDA. *Pompom, the Little Red Squirrel*. NY, 1936. 1st American ed. Good-VG. $15-$20.

LIDDELL HART, B. H. *T. E. Lawrence in Arabia and After*. London, 1934 5th impression. VG. $50.

The Red Army. NY, 1956 1st Amer. ed. G-VG. in DJ. $15.

A History of the Second World War. NY, 1970 1st edition. Very Good plus. $25.

LIEBLING, A. J. *The Telephone Booth Indian*. Garden City, 1942 1st ed. Good in worn DJ. $125.

The Sweet Science. (Boxing). NY, 1956 1st ed. Very Good in very good dust jacket. $45.

The Wayward Pressman. Doubleday, 1947 1st ed. VG in worn dust jacket. $40-$50.

LIEF, ALFRED. *The Firestone Story*. Company history. Whittlesey, 1951 1st ed. Very Good. $10-$12.

LIFE AND TRAVELS OF JOSIAH MOOSO. Winfield KS, 1888 1st ed. Original cloth. Very Good. $350.

LIFTON, ROBERT JAY. *Death in Life: Survivors of Hiroshima*. NY, 1967. Very Good in dust jacket. $15.

LIFSHEY, EARL. *The Housewares Story*. Chicago, 1973. Kitchenware and houseware history, Victorian to Deco. $8-$16.

LIGGETT, MAJ. GEN. HUNTER. *AEF: Ten Years Ago in France*. NY, 1928. Photos, maps. Fine. $25.

LILES, ALLEN. *Oh Thank Heaven - The Story of the Southland Corp.* Southland, 1976 1st edition. Fine. $15.

LIMPUS & LEYSON. *This Man La Guardia*. E. P. Dutton, 1938 1st ed. Very Good. $10.

LINCOLN, ABRAHAM (Books about). Hundreds of books have been published on the life of Lincoln. Few are of significant value. Most titles, regardless of date, fall in a general price range of $10 to $20, with a few at $30. On the other hand, books *by* Abraham Lincoln are very scarce. His 1860 *Political Debates* is worth between $150 and $225. *The Gettysburg Solemnities*, a 16 page pamphlet sold at auction in 1967 for $15,000.

The Collected Works of Abraham Lincoln. NY, Rutgers Univ., 1953. 8 volume set. History Club Edition. VF. $110.

LINCOLN, JOSEPH C. *Cape Cod Ballads*. Trenton NJ, 1902 1st ed. Author's 1st book. Near VG. $150. Same, NY, 1915. Very Good. $38.

Portygee. NY, 1920 1st ed. Good in DJ. $25.

Galusha the Magnificent. NY, 1921 1st ed. Near VG. $70.

Rugged Water. Appleton, 1924. Endpapers discolored, otherwise Very Good. $8.

Queer Judson. NY, 1925 1st ed. Good in DJ. $20.

Christmas Days. McCann, 1938. One of 1,000 copies. Signed Near Fine. $70.

LINCOLN, MRS. D. A. *Mrs. Lincoln's Boston Cook Book*. Boston, 1884 1st ed. Fine. $600. Disbound, worn $50. Good-Very Good. $200. Editions of 1886, 1888, 1889. Good-Very Good. $50-$75. Revised edition. of 1907. Good-Very Good. $15-$25.

The Boston School Kitchen Text Book. Boston, 1887. Good-Very Good. $30-$55.

Carving and Serving. Boston, 1887. VG. $75.

What to Have for Luncheon. NY, 1904. $45-$65.

LINCOLN, WALDO. *American Cookery Books, 1742-1860*. Worcester MA, 1954. One of 500 copies. Revised and enlarged by Eleanor Lowenstein. Good-VG. $60.

LINDAHR, ANNA and HENRY. *Nature Cure Cook Book*. Chicago, 1918. 13th ed. Very Good. $15.

LINDBERGH, ANNE M. *North to the Orient*. NY, 1935 1st ed. Author's first book. Signed by Anne & Charles. Fine. $1,100. Same, unsigned. G-VG. $25-$100.
Listen! The Wind. Harcourt, 1938 1st ed. in DJ. $18-$24.
A Gift From the Sea. 1955 1st ed., illus. In slipcase. $25-$35. Pantheon, 1955 4th printing. NF in dust jacket. $8.
Dearly Beloved. New York, 1962 1st ed. Fine in DJ. $12.
War Within and Without. No place, 1980. VG in DJ. $15.

LINDBERGH, CHARLES A. *We*. NY, 1927. Autograph ed. of 1,000 numbered copies signed by Lindbergh and publishers, with photographic and photogravure plates. Very Fine in original DJ and box. $1,250. Same, signed by Lindbergh only. Very Good. $150-$450. Same, unsigned, VG. $225. First trade edition, 1927. VG in DJ. $30-$60. Same, Book Club ed. $5-$9. Other editions, 1928-1956, common at $5-$20 each.
Wartime Journals of Charles Lindbergh. NY, 1970. Good in dust jacket. $8.
Boyhood on the Upper Mississippi. St. Paul MN, 1972 1st ed. Inscribed, signed by author. VG. $1,500.
Autobiography of Values. No place, 1977 1st ed. VG $23.
Of Flight and Life. NY, 1948 1st ed. VG to Fine in dust jacket. $20-$28. Another, without jacket. $8. Unsigned trade edition. $10-$20.
The Spirit of St. Louis. NY, 1953 1st ed. Signed presentation copy. Fine in DJ. $800. Trade edition, unsigned. $15.

LINDERMAN, FRANK B. *Indian Why Stories*. NY, 1915 1st ed. Charles M. Russell illus. VG. $75.
Bunch Grass and Blue Joint. NY, 1921 1st ed. VG. No original DJ issued. $40-$50.
Kootenai Why Stories. Burt, 1926. VG. $25.
Recollections of Charley Russell. Univ. of Oklahoma, 1963 1st ed. Fine in DJ. $40-$60.

LINDMAN, MAJ. *Flicka, Ricka and Dicka and their New Friend*. 1st ed. 1942 • *Flicka, Ricka, Dicka and the Three Kittens*, 4th ed. 1943. • *Fire Eye: The Story of a Boy and a Horse*, 2nd ed. 1950. • *Snow Boot: Son of Fire Eye*. 1st ed. 1950. Together, 4 vols. Illus. in color by Lindman. Various sizes, cloth, 1st & 2nd with pictorial cover labels, last 2 in jackets. Chicago: Albert Whitman, various dates. Second with rubbing to cover label, else all are very good or better. $176 for 4 volumes auction.
Individual titles, 1940-1968. Not 1st editions. $15-$20.

LINDNER, ROBERT. *Rebel Without a Cause*. NY, 1944 1st ed. 1st printing. VG. $35.
The Fifty Minute Hour. NY, 1955 1st ed. VG in DJ. $25.

LINDSAY, JACK (Editor). *Ribaldry of Ancient Greece*. NY, 1965. Fine in dust jacket. $15.
Leisure & Pleasure in Roman Egypt. NY, 1966. VG. $25.

LINDSAY, VACHEL. *The Golden Whales of California*. NY, 1920 1st ed. Near Fine. $30-$45.
The Congo and Other Poems. NY, 1922. Inscribed. Corners bumped, o/w Very Good. $55.
Collected Poems. NY 1923 1st ed. VG. $35.
Every Soul Is a Circus. NY, 1929 1st ed. Good. $20.

LINDSEY, ALMONT. *Socialized Medicine in England and Wales*. Chapel Hill NC, 1962 1st ed. Signed. NF. $20.

LILLARD, J. F. B. *Poker Stories*. 1896. 251 pages. VF. $210.

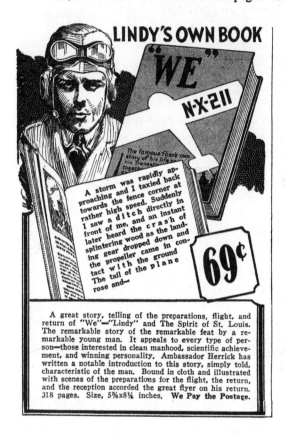

LITTLE PETS LINEN ABC. Children's book, circa 1890s. Very Good. $35.

LITTLE RED RIDING HOOD. Star Soap Company, nursery rhyme series of give-away booklets, 1890s. $20-$30.

LITTLE TOTS DRAWING BOOK. Bengal Baking Powder Company, early 1900s give-away. $20-$30.

LIVELY, PENELOPE. *Astercote*. NY 1970 1st American ed. Ex-library. Very Good in dust jacket. $16.
The Whispering Knights. NY, 1976 1st American ed. Very Good in dust jacket. $12.

LIVERMORE, MARY. *My Story of the War: A Woman's Narrative*. Hartford CT, 1890. VG plus. $45. Another, unbound, Poor. $20.

LIVINGSTON, DAVID. *Adventures and Discoveries of Dr. David Livingston and the Herald-Stanley Expedition*. Hubbard Bros., 1872. Good-VG. $50.
Missionary Travels and Researchers in South Africa. NY, 1858. Illus., maps. $125-$150.

LIVINGSTON, PETER. *How to Cook a Rogue Elephant*. Boston, 1971. Very Good in dust jacket. $45.

LLEWELLYN, RICHARD. *How Green Was My Valley*. New York, 1940 1st American ed. VG in DJ. $80-$100.
None But the Lonely Heart. NY, 1943 1st American ed. Very Good in dust jacket. $18.
A Flame for Doubting Thomas. NY, 1953 1st edition. Fine in dust jacket. $30.
Tell Me Now, and Again. Doubleday, 1978 1st American ed. Fine in dust jacket. $15.

LLOYD, HUGH. *The Copperhead Trail Mystery*. (Hal Keen no. 3). Grosset & Dunlap, 1931 ed. Dampstained in ragged edge dust jacket, o/w Good-Very Good. $80.
The Mysterious Arab. (Hal Keen no. 5) G & D, 1931 ed. VG in Good DJ listing 7 titles on flap. $100.

LLOYD, JOHN URI. *Etidorphia*. No place, 1895. Knapp illus. Loose hinges, frayed, o/w good. $35.
Stringtownon the Pike. Dodd-Mead, 1900 1st edition. 414 pages. Very Good. $10. Near Fine. $25.
Warwick of the Knobs. Dodd-Mead, 1901 1st edition. 304 pages. Very Good. $14.

LOBEL, ARNOLD. *Uncle Elephant*. NY, 1981 1st ed. Illus. by author. Near Fine in dust jacket. $20.
Fables. Harper, 1980 1st ed. Near Fine in DJ. $35.

LOCKE, WILLIAM J. *The Golden Journey of Mr. Paradyne*. London, 1924. Marcia Lane Foster illus. VG. $25.

LOCKHART, JOHN GIBSON. *Curses, Locks and Talismans*. London, 1938. Good. $55.

LOCKRIDGE, FRANCES and RICHARD. *The Client is Cancelled*. Lippincott, 1951 Book Club ed. $5.
Dead as a Dinosaur. Lippincott, 1952. Fine in DJ. $7.
Burnt Offering. Lippincott, 1955 1st ed. Fine in DJ. $25.

LOCKRIDGE, RICHARD. *Death on the Hour*. NY, 1974 1st ed. Fine in DJ. $15. Book Club ed. $5.
The Tenth Life. Lippincott, 1977 1st edition. Fine in dust jacket. $15.

LOCKRIDGE, ROSS. *Raintree County*. Boston, 1948 1st ed. Author's 1st book. VG in DJ. $65-$100.

LOCKRIDGE, ROSS F. *Old Fauntleroy Home. A View of New Harmony Indiana*. New Harmony, 1939 1st ed. Fine. No dust jacket. $22.

LOCKWOOD, FRANK C. *Pioneer Days in Arizona*. NY, 1932 1st ed. Illus. Fine. $45.
Apache Indians. NY, 1938 1st printing. Fine. $85.
Tucson-The Old Pueblo. Phoenix, 1931. Navy blue cloth. Very Good plus. $110.

LOCKWOOD, GEORGE R. *The New Harmony Communities*. Marion IN, 1902 2nd ed. VG. $50.
The New Harmony Movement. NY, 1905 1st ed. Good-Very Good, no dust jacket. $15-$25.

LOCKWOOD, INGERSOLL. *Little Captain Doppelkop*. Rockwell, 1891. VG. $35.
Baron Trump's Marvelous Underground Journey. Boston, 1893. Good. $10.

LOCKWOOD, LUKE VINCENT. *Colonial Furniture in America*. NY, 1901, Scribners, 1st ed. Worn, rubbed, Flaking, but good. $70. Another, Very Good. $100.

LOCKWOOD, SARAH. *Decoration: Past, Present and Future*. NY, 1934. Illus. Good in dust jacket. $15.

LOCKWOOD, T. D. *Electrical Measurement and The Galvanometer*. NY, 1890 2nd edition. Illus. $25.

LOCKWOOD'S DIRECTORY OF THE PAPER AND STATIONERY TRADE. NY, 1920, 45th edition. $50.

LOENING, GROVER C. *Monoplanes and Biplanes*. NY, 1911 1st ed. Good. $95.
Military Aeroplanes. No place, 1918. Good. $65.
Takeoff Into Greatness. NY, 1968. Good. $5.

LOEWY, RAYMOND. *Never Leave Well Enough Alone*. NY, 1951 1st edition. VG in worn DJ. $75. Inscribed presentation copy. $100. Same. 1951 2nd printing. $40.
The New Vision. The Locomotive. London, 1937 1st ed. Very Good in torn dust jacket. $125.

LOFTING, HUGH. *The Story of Dr. Dolittle*. Stokes, 1920 1st American ed. Illus. by author, first book. Good. $100.
Doctor Dolittle's Circus. NY, 1924 2nd ed. Illus. by author. Very Good. $20-$30.
Doctor Dolittle in the Moon. Stokes, 1928 1st ed. Illus. by author. Fine. $50. 1956 edition. $9.
Doctor Dolittle's Return. NY, 1933 1st ed. Illus. by author. Good. $14.
Dr. Dolittle and the Secret Lake. Lippincott, 1948 1st ed. Illus. by author. Good in DJ. $30-$45.
Doctor Dolittle's Puddleby Adventure. Philadelphia, 1952 1st ed. Illus. by author. VG in DJ. $70.
Dr. Dolittle's Post Office. London,1958. 19th impression. Illus. by author. VG plus in chip DJ. $25.

LOMAX, ALAN. *The Folk Songs of North America*. NY, 1960 12th printing. Fine in very good dust jacket. $25.

LOMAX, JOHN A. *Songs of the Cattle Trail and Cow Camp*. No place, 1919 1st ed. Cracked hinges. In fair DJ. $45. Same, NY, 1927. Good. $15-$25.
The Adventures of a Ballad Hunter. New York, 1947 1st edition. Very Good. $35-$50.

LOMAX, JOHN A. and ALAN. *American Ballads and Folk Songs*. NY, 1934 1st ed. One of 500 copies, Signed by Lomaxes. Good-VG. $95-$125.
Cowboy Songs. New York, 1946. Very Good in good dust jacket. $28.

LONDON, JACK. *The Son of Wolf*. Published in 1900 was the author's first book. Original cloth, 1st printing. Fine. $1,000. 2nd state, 1900. Fine. $500. 2nd state, good only, no jacket. $50. A very rare 1st edition, 1st state, in its original dust jacket sold last year at auction for $6,600.
A Son of the Sun. Boston, 1900 1st ed. $200-$450. Doubleday, 19121st ed. VG. $125. Same in VG DJ. $400.
The God of His Fathers. Lon. 1902 1st English. G. $150.
Children of the Frost. NY, 1902 1st ed. VG. $300.
Daughter of the Snows. 1902 2nd ed. $20-$35. Grosset & Dunlap, 1902 reprint. $7.
The Call of the Wild. Macmillan, 1903 1st ed. Near Very Good in repaired DJ. $1,500. Another in original DJ. $3,300 at auction. Another, Near Fine, no DJ. $400. 1912 edition, Paul Branson illus. VG. $40. 1960 LEC. $150.
The People of the Abyss. London, 1903 1st English ed. Good. $125. NY, 1903 1st Amer. ed. $350-$400.
The Faith of Men & Other Stories. NY, 1904 1st ed. Rear endpapers renewed, light spotting, o/w Very Good. $500.
The Game. New York, 1905 1st ed., 2nd state. Henry Hutt illus. Very Good. $65. 1st issue. June 1905. NF. $125.
Love of Life & Other Stories. NY, 1907 1st ed. VG. $125.
Before Adam. Macmillan, 1907 1st ed. VG. $100.
The Iron Heel. Macmillan, 1908 1st ed. Good. $200.
Burning Daylight. NY, 1910 1st ed., 2nd state in DJ. $700. Same, no DJ. $125. Grosset & Dunlap reprint. $8.
Smoke Bellew. Century, 1912 1st ed. VG. No DJ. $100.
The Works of Jack London. 4 volume set. Review of Reviews, 1915. Good. $24.
John Barleycorn. NY, 1913 1st ed. 1st state. $100-$140. 1913 2nd state. F, no DJ. $48. G&D, 1913 reprint. G. $9.
The Abysmal Brute. NY, 1913 1st ed. VG. $225.
White Fang. Macmillan, 1906 1st edition, 8 color plates. Very Good. $100. G&D, 1914 reprint. Good. $8.
The Mutiny of the Elsinore. Macmillan, 1914. Review copy. Good. $400. Sept, 1914 1st edition, rubbed. $175. Fine in rare original dust jacket. $2,300 auction.
The Little Lady of the Big House. Macmillan, 1916 1st edition. Good. $85. Very Good-Fine. $175.
The Acorn Planter. NY, 1916 1st ed. in orig. DJ. $3,000.
The Turtles of Tasman. NY, 1916 1st ed. near VG. $275. Fine in rare original dust jacket. $2,185 auction.
Jerry of the Islands. NY, 1917 1st ed. VG. $100.
The Red One. NY, 1918 1st edition. Good. $750. In rare original Dust Jacket, sold at Auction. $3,025-$4,312.

LONG, FRANK B. *The Hounds of Tindalos*. Arkham House, 1946 1st edition. VG-Fine in dust jacket. $75-$195.
The Horror From the Hills. Arkham House, 1963. Very Good in dust jacket. $60.

LONG, HUEY. *Every Man a King* . New Orleans, 1933 1st ed. Very Good in dust jacket. $35-$50.

LONG, JOHN LUTHER. *Felice*. 1908 2nd prtg. $12-$20.
Billy Boy. Dodd, 1906. J. W. Smith illus. $75-$150.
War. Indianapolis, 1913 1st ed. N C. Wyeth illus. $40-$65.

LONG, MASON. *Life of Mason Long the Converted Gambler*. Chicago, 1878. Good. $25. 4th edition, 1883. Good. $12-$14. A Very Fine copy sold at auction for $60.

LONG, WILLIAM J. *School of the Woods*. Ginn, 1902 1st edition. Illus. by Charles Copeland. Very Good. $35.
Northern Trails. Ginn & Co., 1905 1st. Charles Copeland illustrator. Some shelfwear, seal on endpaper. VG. $30.

LONGFELLOW, HENRY WADSWORTH. *The Song of Hiawatha*. Boston, 1855 1st edition. Endpaper pieces missing, o/w VG. $150. Another, Near Fine. $300-$400. 1909 edition, Reilly & Britton. John R. Neill illustrator. Very Good. $75. 1911 editions: Boston. Parrish, Remington, Wyeth illustrators. $100-$250.
The Courtship of Miles Standish and Other Poems. Ticknor, 1858 1st American edition. $75-$175. London, 1858 1st English edition. $225. Bobbs-Merrill, 1903. Howard Chandler Christy illus. $30-$60. Houghton, 1920. N. C. Wyeth illus. $75-$125.
Tales of a Wayside Inn. Boston, 1863 1st ed. $75-$150.
The New England Tragedies. Boston, Ticknor & Fields, 1868 1st edition. Worn at spine, chipped corners on a few pages. Good-Very Good. $30.
Evangeline. IN, 1905 edition. Christy illus. $50-$75. 1922 ed. Milton Bradley. $25. Houghton, Mifflin, 1897. J. W. Smith illus. $75-$150. Same, Boston, 1916. $35-$60.
Keramos and Other Poems. Boston, 1878. $40.
The Poetical Works of Henry Wadsworth Longfellow. Boston, 1865. Illus. Signed, Fine. $285.
The Complete Poetical Works of --. Boston, circa 1893. 5 volumes. Fine. $40.

LONGSTREET, STEPHEN. *A Century on Wheels: The Story of Studebaker*. NY, 1952 1st ed. Very Good. $30. Another, Ex-library. $12.
The Real Jazz Old and New. Louisiana State University, 1956 1st ed. Very Good in dust jacket. $45.
Sportin' House: A History of New Orleans Sinners & the Birth of Jazz. Sherbourne, 1965 1st edition. Fine in dust jacket. $25.
War Cries on Horseback. Garden City NY, 1970 1st edition. Very Good in worn dust jacket. $25.
Chicago, An Intimate Portrait of Power 1860-1919. McKay, 1973 1st ed. Ex-library. $15.

LONGSTREET, STEPHEN & ETHEL. *A Salute to American Cooking*. Hawthorne, 1968 Book Club ed. Fine in DJ. $14.
The Illustrated Joys of Jewish Cooking. Doubleday, 1974 1st ed. Fine in dust jacket. $20.

LOOMIS, ANDREW. *Figure Drawing for all It's Worth*. OH, 1947 9th ed. Very Good. $20.

LOOMIS, FREDERIC. *Field Book of Common Rocks & Minerals*. New York, Putnam, 13th edition, 1923. Very Good in dust jacket. $15.

LOOS, ANITA. *Gentlemen Prefer Blondes*. NY, 1925 1st ed. Ralph Barton illus. Good-VG. $40-$75.
But Gentlemen Marry Brunettes. NY, 1928 1st ed. Ralph Barton illus. Fine in dust jacket. $95.
A Mouse Is Born. NY, 1951 1st ed. VG in DJ. $18.

LORD, ISABEL (Editor). *Everybody's Cook Book*. Harcourt, 1924 1st ed. Dec. black cloth. 916 pages. Very Good. $55.

LORD, PRISCILLA and DANIEL FOLEY. *The Folk Arts and Crafts of New England*. NY, 1965. VG in DJ. $45.

LORANT, STEFAN. *Lincoln: His Life in Pictures*. Duell, Sloan, 1941 1st ed. VG in dust jacket. $22.
Lincoln: His Life in Photographs. Duell, Sloan, 1941 1st ed. VG, no dust jacket. $18.
Lincoln: A Picture Story of His Life. Harpers, 1952 1st ed. Very Good, no dust jacket. $20.
Pittsburgh, Story of an American City. NY, 1964 2nd printing. Very Good in dust jacket. $20.

LORD, WALTER. *A Night to Remember*. New York, 1955 1st ed. Good in dust jacket. $15.
A Time to Stand. NY, 1961 1st ed. Near Fine in DJ. $30.
The Past That Would Not Die. NY, 1965 1st ed. Very Good in dust jacket. $12.

LORENZ, KONRAD. *Studies in Animal and Human Behavior*. Harvard, 1970 1st American ed. 2 vols. Good-Very Good in dust jacket. $28.

LORSCH, EDWIN. *The Autocrat of the Poker Table*. 1961. 105 pgs. Very Fine. $160 auction.

LOS ANGELES TIMES COOK BOOK NO. 2. *1,000 Toothsome Cooking and Other Recipes by California Women*. Los Angeles, 1905. Very Good. $75.

LOSSING, BENSON J. *Pictorial History of the Civil War*. 3 vols. Hartford, 1866-68. Faded, worn, solid. $85.
History of the Civil War 1861-1865. 16 parts bound together. NY, 1895. G-VG. $65. War Memorial Assoc. edition, 1912. Brady photos. Loose binding, else VG. $60.
Our Country. NY, 1888, 3 vols., 1st ed. Darley illus. Good-Very Good. $75.
History of the United States of America. New York, 1913. 8 volumes. Good. $45.

LOUCHEIM, ALINE B. *5,000 Years of Art in Western Civilization*. NY, 1946. Fine. $20.

LOUDON, JANE WEBB. *The Lady's Country Companion*. London and NY, 1847 3rd ed. Illus. Good. $35.

LOUGHEED, VICTOR. *Vehicles of the Air*. Chicago, 1900. 268 of 270 illus. are present. As is. $40.

LOUYS, PIERRE. *Aphrodite*. NY, Falstaff Press, 1926. Clara Tice illus. Limited ed. $150.
Twilight of the Nymphs. Louys Society, 1927. One of 1,250 copies. Clara Tice illus. Near Fine. $50. London, 1928 Ltd ed. Fine in dust jacket. $75.

LOVECRAFT, H. P. *Beyond the Wall of Sleep*. Arkham House, 1943 1st ed. Near Fine in DJ. $750-$1,500.
Marginalia. Arkham House, 1944 1st ed. VG in DJ. $150.
Something About Cats. Arkham House, 1949 1st ed. Very Good in dust jacket. $130-$150.
The Best Supernatural Stories of H. P. Lovecraft. World, 1950 1st ed. VG in DJ. $65. Tower Books, 1945. $15.
The Dunwich Horror and Others. Arkham House, 1963 1st ed. VG in DJ. $40-$50. Very Fine in DJ. $75.
At the Mountains of Madness. Arkham House, 1964 2nd ed. Very Good in dust jacket. $45. Fine in DJ. $75.
Dagon and Other Macabre Tales. Arkham House, 1965 1st ed. Very Good in dust jacket. $45. Fine in DJ. $75.
Selected Letters of H. P. Lovecraft. Arkham House, 1965. Vol. 1, 2nd ed. VG in DJ. $55.

LOVECRAFT, H. P. (In Magazines). *Weird Tales*. May, July, 1941. 1st appearance of story, "Charles D. Ward". $50. ea.
Weird Tales. for July 1947, Sept 1948, Nov 1949, May 1950, Jan 1951, Jan 1952. $25-$50 each.

LOVELACE, MAUD. *Downtown: a Betsy-Tacey Story*. New York, 1943 1st ed. Lois Lenski illus. VG. $10.
The Tune in the Tree. Crowell, 1950. Eloise Wilkin illus. Good-Very Good. $35.
Trees Kneel at Christmas. Crowell, 1951 1st edition. Fine in dust jacket. $24.

LOVELL, BERNARD. *The Story of Jodrell Bank*. New York, 1968. Very Good in worn dust jacket. $18.

LOWE & JACOBSON. *Fifty Famous Stories*. Neil O'Keefe illus. Whitman, 1920 1st ed. Fine, illus. bds. $17.

LOWELL, AMY. *A Dome of Many-Coloured Glass*. Boston, 1912 1st ed. Author's 1st book. VG. $100.
Pictures of the Floating World. NY, 1919 1st ed. Signed. Very Good. $40.
What's O'Clock. Boston, 1925 1st ed. VG in DJ. $80.

LOWELL, JAMES RUSSELL. *Works*. Boston, 1904. 16 vols. Very Good plus. $95.
Under the Willows. Boston, 1869 1st ed. $40-$50.

LOWELL, ROBERT. *Lord Weary's Castle*. NY, 1946 1st ed. Very Good-Fine. $125-$175.
The Mills of the Kavanaughs. NY, 1951 1st ed. Very Good in very good dust jacket. $75. Fine. $125. Another, signed. Near Fine in dust jacket. $300.
Prometheus Bound. Farrar, 1969 1st ed. Signed. Very Good in clip dust jacket. $175.
The Dolphin. NY, 1973 1st ed. in DJ. $20-$25.
Selected Poems. NY, 1976 1st printing. VG. $15.

LOWNEY'S COOK BOOK. Boston, 1912 revised ed. 421 pages. Poor. $9. Good. $15.

LOWRIE, DONALD. *My Life in Prison*. 1912, and *My Life Out of Prison*. 1915. Mitchell Kennerly. 1st eds. Both VG in chip dust jacket. $45 each.

LOWTHER, GEORGE and JOE SHUSTER. *Superman*. Random House, 1942. No DJ. Good-VG. $80-$180.

LUCAS, E. V. *Playtime and Company*. 1925 1st edition, Methuen. Pictorial cover. Fine. $50. 1925 2nd printing, Doran. Good to Near Fine. $12-$35.
Another Book of Verse for Children. NY, 1907 1st ed., Macmillan. Very Good. $30.
Forgotten Tales of Long Ago. New York, 1906, Stokes. Worn. $25.

LUCAS, JASON. *Lucas on Bass Fishing*. Dodd-Mead, 1962 revised ed. Illus. Fine in dust jacket. $15.

LUCCOCK & HUTCHINSON. *The Story of Methodism*. Methodist Books, 1927 2nd printing. Fine, no DJ. $15.

LUCK, MRS. BRIAN (Editor). *The Belgian Cook-Book*. Dutton, 1915 1st ed. 151 pgs. VG in DJ. $30.

LUDLOW, FITZ-HUGH. *The Hasheesh Eater*. NY, 1857 1st ed. Author's 1st book. Near VG. $125.

LUDLUM, ROBERT. *The Scarlatti Inheritance*. NY, 1971 1st ed. Author's 1st novel. Fine in fragile DJ. $125.
(As Jonathan Ryder:)
The Cry of the Halidon. NY, 1974 1st ed. F in DJ. $45.
The Gemini Contenders. NY, 1976 1st edition. Fine in dust jacket. $28-$40.

LUDWIG, EMIL. *Cleopatra, the Story of a Queen*. NY, 1937 1st ed. Slight cover soil. $15.
Stalin. Putnam, 1942 1st American ed. VG in DJ. $20.

LUDWIG, COY. *Maxfield Parrish*. NY, 1973 1st edition. Fine in dust jacket. $55.

LUHAN, MABEL DODGE. *Lorenzo in Taos*. NY, 1932 3rd printing. Very Good. $20.
Intimate Memories. NY, 1933 1st ed. Good $13.
Movers and Shakers. NY, 1936 1st. VG in DJ. $15-$25.

LUMHOLTZ, CARL. *Unknown Mexico*. NY, 1902 1st ed. 2 volumes. Fine. $185.
New Trails in Mexico. Scribners, NY, 1912 1st ed. Good-Very Good. $50-$110.

LUMMIS, CHARLES. *Some Strange Corners of Our Country*. NY, 1892 1st ed. Good-VG. $30-$75.
The Land of Poco Tiempo. NY, 1893 1st ed. NF. $150.

LUMPKIN, GRACE. *The Wedding*. NY, 1939 1st. VG. $20.

LUNETTES, HENRY. *The American Gentleman's Guide to Politeness and Fashion*. NY, 1857 1st. Overall VG. $85.

LUSK, HILTON. *A General Text on Aeronautics*. New York, 1935 3rd printing. $20.

LUSK, WILLIAM. *The Science and Art of Midwifery*. NY, 1883. VG. $250. 1891 ed. $75. 1896 ed. rev. VG. $50.

LUSTIG, SOUNDHEIM & RENSEL. *Southern Cook Book of Fine Old Recipes*. Culinary Arts, 1939 1st edition. Wood covers. $15.

LUTES, DELLA. *The Country Kitchen*. Little Brown, 1937 12th ed. Gingham cloth covers. Fine. $15. VG. $10.
Home Grown. Little Brown, 1937 1st ed. Very Good. $12.
Cousin William. Boston, 1942 1st edition. VG in DJ. $25.
Country Schoolma'am. Boston, 1941 1st ed. F in DJ. $14.

LYDEKKER, RICHARD. *Library of Natural History in 12 Volumes*. Saalfield, 1901 1st ed. ½ leather on marbled boards. Good. $120.

LYELL, SIR CHARLES. *The Geological Evidences of the Antiquity of Man*. Philadelphia, 1871 2nd American ed. Near Very Good. $60.

LYMAN, GEORGE D. *John Marsh, Pioneer: Life Story of a Trailblazer*. Scribners 1930 1st ed. Slight wear. $55. 1931 edition. Very Good. $12-$25.
Saga of the Comstock Lode. NP, 1937. VG in DJ. $30.
Ralston's Ring: California Plunders the Comstock Lode. NY, Scribners, 1937 1st ed. Very Good. $25-$35.

LYMAN, HENRY, M.D. *The Practical Home Physician*. Albany NY, 1887. Fine. $175. Other Medical titles of the 1880s. Very Good. $75-$150.

LYMAN, WILLIAM DENISON. *The Columbia River: Its History, Its Myths, Its Scenery, Its Commerce*. NY, 1909. 1st American ed. Illus. Near VG. $60.

M

MACARTHUR, GEN. DOUGLAS. *Duty Honor Country*. McGraw Hill, 1965 1st ed., ex-library. VG. $12.

MACDONALD, ALEXANDER. *Design for Angling: The Dry Fly on Western Trout Streams*. Boston, 1947. Good-Very Good. $35-$95.

MACDONALD, BETTY. *Hello, Mrs. Piggle-Wiggle*. Philadelphia, 1957 1st ed. Hilary Knight illus. Very Good in good dust jacket. $25.
Nancy and Plum. Philadelphia, 1952 1st ed. In DJ. $40.

MACDONALD, GEORGE. *At the Back of the North Wind*. Jessie Wilcox Smith illus. David McKay, Philadelphia, 1919 1st ed. Very Good. $50-$95. In DJ. $100-$150.
The Golden Key. Maurice Sendak illus. New York, Straus & Giroux, 1967. Some soil and chipping, else Very Good in dust jacket. $60-$90.
The Light Princess. Putnam, 1893. Maud Humphrey illus. VG. $150-$250.
The Princess and Curdie. NY, 1927. Dorothy Lathrop illus. Very Good in dust jacket. $85. Good, no DJ. $15.
The Princess & the Goblin. Philadelphia, David McKay, 1920 1st ed. Jessie Wilcox Smith illus. VG in fair DJ. $100 auction. Fair to Good, no DJ. $15-$30.1923 ed. $25-$50.

MACDONALD, JOHN D. *The Brass Cupcake*. NY, 1950 1st ed. Paperbound. Author's 1st book. Good plus. $50.
Cancel All Our Vows. Appleton, 1953 1st edition. Very Good. $45.
Death Trap. NY, Dell paperback original, 1957, 1st edition. Very Good. $20.
The Deceivers. NY, 1958 1st edition. Dell paperback original. Fine $75.
No Deadly Drug. NY, 1968 1st ed. VG in vg DJ. $25.

MACDONALD, PHILIP. *The Poleferry Riddle*. NY, Crime Club, 1931 1st ed. Very Good in chip dust jacket. $100. Same without jacket. $25.
The List of Adrian Messenger. New York, Crime Club, 1959 1st edition. Near Fine in dust jacket. $38.

MACDONALD, ROSS (Kenneth Millar). *Blue City*. Dell, 1947. First paperback. Signed. Good plus. $25.
The Drowning Pool. New York, 1950 1st ed. Fine. $85.
Meet Me at the Morgue. NY, 1953 1st edition. Near Fine in very good dust jacket. $400.

The Ferguson Affair. New York, 1960 1st edition. Fine in dust jacket. $110.
The Chill. Knopf, 1963 1st ed. VG in DJ. $60.
The Far Side of the Dollar. NY, 1965 1st edition. Near Fine in dust jacket. $50-$100.

MACFADDEN, BERNARR. *Muscular Power & Beauty*. 1906, Physical Culture Pub. $8.
Vitality Supreme. 1915. Very Good. $7.

MACFADDEN, MARY. *Dumbells & Carrot Strips: The Story of Bernarr MacFadden*. NY, 1953 1st ed. Holt. Very Good, no dust jacket. $35.

MACDOUGAL, ARTHUR R. *Where Flows the Kennebec*. NY, 1947 1st ed. Very Good. $45.
Trout Fisherman's Bedside Book . NY, 1963 1st edition in dust jacket. $35.

MACFALL, HALDANE. *The Book of Lovat*. London, 1923 1st trade edition. C. Lovat Fraser illustrator. Very Good in dust jacket. $100.

MACGREGOR, BRUCE & TED BENSON. *Portrait of a Silver Lady*. 1977, Pruett Pub. Photo illustrations. Very Good in dust jacket and slipcase. $35.

MACGREGOR, ELLEN. *Miss Pickerell Goes to the Arctic*. NY, 1954 1st ed. Very Good in fair dust jacket. $20.

MACHEN, ARTHUR. *Three Imposters*. London, 1895 1st ed. Very Good. $150-$175.
The Anatomy of Tobacco. NY, 1926 1st American ed. VG in worn, chipped dust jacket. $50-$75.
Ornaments in Jade. NY, 1924 1st ed. One of 1,000 copies, signed. Good plus. $30.
Dog and Duck. NY, 1924 1st edition. Very Good. $20.

MACHETANZ, FREDERICK. *On Arctic Ice*. NY, 1940 1st ed. Illus. by author. VG in poor dust jacket. $28.
Alaska Paintings of Fred Machentanz. Peacock, 1977 1st edition. Signed by Machetanz. Very Good. $16-$20.

MACINNES, HELEN. *Pray for a Brave Heart*. NY, 1955 1st edition. Inscribed. VG in clipped dust jacket. $25.
Prelude to Terror. New York, 1978 1st American edition. Fine in dust jacket. $18.

MACK, CHARLES. *Two Black Crows in the A. E. F.* Indianapolis, 1928. (Moran and Mack, comedians.) Inscribed by Mack. Near VG in dust jacket. $50.

MACK, CONNIE. *My 66 Years in the Big Leagues*. NY, 1950 1st ed. Illus. Good plus. $15-$25.
Connie Mack's Baseball Book. NY, 1950 1st ed. Signed. Very Good. $28. Another, unsigned. $24.

MACKAY, DOUGLAS. *The Honourable Company, History of the Hudson Bay Company*. IN, 1938, Tudor. VG. $20.

MACKENZIE, COLIN. *MacKenzie's Five Thousand Receipts in All the Useful and Domestic Arts*. Philadelphia, 1829. Foxing. Good. $95. 1851 ed. Worn. $35.

MACKENZIE, R. SHELTPON. *The Comprehensive History of the Great Civil War*. NY, 1885 1st ed. Exterior fair, interior Good. $25.

MACKENZIE'S 5,000 RECEIPTS IN ALL USEFUL & DOMESTIC ARTS. Philadelphia, 1851, Worn, foxed. $35.

MACKEY, A. G. and W. R. SINGLETON. *History of Freemasonry*. NY, London, 1906 7 vols. Color, black & white illus. Bindings fair, interiors fine. $475.
Encyclopedia of Freemasonry & Its Kindred Sciences. McClure, 1917. G-VG. $20-$30. 1925 rev. ed. Fine. $35.

MACLEAN, ALISTAIR. *Fear is The Key*. NY, 1961 1st ed. Fine in good dust jacket. $23.
Where Eagles Dare. New York, 1967 1st edition. Very Good plus in dust jacket. $15.

MACLEAN, NORMAN. *A River Runs Through It*. University of Chicago Press, 1976 1st edition. Near Fine in dust jacket. $350-$450. Same, subsequent eds. $12-$15.

MACLEOD, W. *Famous Sheriffs and Western Outlaws*. NY, 1944. Torn dust jacket, o/w Very Good. $27.

MACMANUS, SEUMAS. *Donegal Fairy Stories*. McClure, 1901 edition. Verbeck illus. VG. $45. Doubleday, 1927 edition. Verbeck illus. VG. $25.
The Red Poocher. NY, 1903 1st American edition. $30.

MACMARTIN, D. F. *Thirty Years in Hell: The Confession of a Drug Fiend*. Topeka, Capper Printing, 1921 1st ed. Very Good. $60-$90.

MACMILLAN, DONALD B. *Four Years in the White North*. NY, London, 1918 ed. $65-$95. Boston, 1925. $45.
Etah and Beyond. Beston, 1927 1st ed. VG. $35.

MACMULLEN, JERRY. *Paddle Wheel Days in California*. Stanford University, 1944. Illustrated. Very Good in very good dust jacket. $28.

MACPHERSON, JOHN. *Mystery Chef's Own Cook Book*. Longmans, 1936 1st ed. VG, no dust jacket. $10.

MACNEICE, LOUIS. *Holes in the Sky*. NY, 1949 1st American ed. VG in dust jacket. $25.

MADIGAN, THOMAS. *Word Shadows of the Great: The Lure of Autograph Collecting*. NY, 1930 1st ed. VG in tattered dust jacket. $40.

MAETERLINCK, MAURICE. *News of Spring*. NY, 1913 1st ed. Edward Detmold illus. 20 color plates. Soiled, hinge cracked, o/w Good. $125.
The Blue Bird. NY. 1913. Robinson illus. $120-$150.
The Miracle of St. Anthony. Modern Library 1st ed., 1917. Very Good-Fine in dust jacket. $120.
The Children's Life of the Bee. Dodd Mead, 1920. $25.
The Magic of the Stars. NY, 1930. Translation. Ex-library. Fair to Good. $40.

THE MAGICIAN'S OWN BOOK, OR THE WHOLE ART OF CONJURING. NY, 1857. With ads. Good. $200.

MAGNER, D. *The Art of Taming & Educating a Horse*. Battle Creek MI, 1877 and 1884 ed. 1,088 pages. $25-$35.
Magner's Standard Horse & Stock Book. 1906, Saalfield. Fair. $20.

MAGOFFIN, R.V.D. *The Romance of Archeology (formerly Magic Spades)*. NY, 1929. Illus. Very Good. $20.

MAHAN, ALFRED THAYER. *The Influence of Sea Power Upon The French Revolution and Empire, 1793-1812*. Boston, 1894 2 vols, 3rd ed. Near Fine. $150.
The Life of Nelson. Boston, 1897 1st ed, 2 vols. NF. $125.
The South African War. New York, 1900. Remington illus. Very Good. $75.

MAHONEY & WHITNEY. *Contemporary Illustrators of Children's Books*. Circa 1930. 1st ed. VG. $80-$120. Same, 1947. Ex-library. $60.

MAILER, NORMAN. *The Naked and The Dead*. Rinehart, New York, 1948 1st edition. Author's 1st book. Very Good in very good dust jacket. $150-$250. Another, signed by author. $250-$350.
Barbary Shore. NY, 1951. Signed. Chip DJ, o/w VG in very good dust jacket. $150.
Advertisements for Myself. NY, 1959. Signed. Overall VG in very good dust jacket. $95. Same, unsigned. $45.
Tough Guys Don't Dance. Franklin Library, 1984 1st ed. Signed. Fine. $50.
Marilyn, A Biography. NY, 1973 1st ed. Grosset & Dunlap. Very Good in dust jacket. $25-$95.
Of a Fire on the Moon. NY, 1970 1st ed., Little Brown. Signed. Fine in dust jacket. $100.
An American Dream. Dial, 1965 1st ed. in DJ. $30-$35.

MAILS, THOMAS E. *Mystic Warriors of the Plains*. Doubleday, 1972. Color plates. VG in DJ. $42.
The People Called Apache. Prentice hall, 1974 1st ed. Folio, 447 pgs. Illus. Near Fine in DJ. $95.
Pueblo Children of the Earth Mother. Garden City, 1983 2 vols. 1st ed. 44 color plates. Fine in fine DJ. $135.

MAITLAND, LT. LESTER. *Knights of the Air*. Garden City, 1929. Inscribed. Varnished cloth fading. $75.

MAJESTIC MANUFACTURING CO. *Majestic Cook Book*. 1899. 96 pages. $25.
The Great Majestic Range Cook Book. St. Louis (circa 1900). Pictorial wrappers. Includes loose hanging cardboard placard. VG. $50 auction.

MAJOR, CHARLES. *Dorothy Vernon of Haddon Hall*. Macmillan, 1902 1st ed. H.C. Christy illus. VG. $15-$30.

MAJOR, RALPH. *Classic Description of Disease*. Charles Thomas, 1932 1st ed. VG in torn DJ. $75-$95.

MALAMUD, BERNARD. *The Natural*. NY, 1952 1st ed. Author's 1st book. VG in DJ. $750-$850.
Pictures of Fidelman. NY, 1963 1st edition. Fine in very good dust jacket. $35.
The Fixer. NY, 1966 1st edition. Near Fine in DJ. $40. Franklin Mint ed. 1978. Fine Leather. $15-$20.
The Tenants. NY, 1971 1st ed. Very Good. $15.

MALLEABLE CASTING, BRASS FOUNDING, BLACKSMITHING & FORGING. I.C.S. Reference Library Series. Scranton PA, 1901-1905. Good-VG. $10-$20.

MALLET, CAPT. THIERRY. *Plain Tales of the North*. New York, Putnam, 1926 1st American edition. Corners bumped. Good. $35.

MALORY, SIR THOMAS. *Le Morte D'Arthur: The Story of King Arthur & His Noble Knights*. NY, Limited Editions Club, 1936. 3 vols. in slipcase. Signed by illus. Near Fine. $100-$150 auction. London, 1909 2nd ed. Illus. by Beardsley. $350-$600. NY, 1917, Illus. by Rackham. Clothbound. Good-VG. $200-$400.

MALOT, HECTOR. *Nobody's Boy*. Cupples & Leon, 1916. Johnny Gruelle illus. Near Fine. $30-$60.

MALRAUX, ANDRE. *Man's Hope*. NY, 1938 1st American edition. Very Good in dust jacket. $30.
The Voices of Silence: Man and His Art. NY, 1953 1st ed. VG in dust jacket. $25-$75.
The Metamorphosis of the Gods. NY, 1960 Translated. 1st American ed. Fine. $15.

MAN RAY (Photographer). *Self Portrait: Man Ray*. Boston, 1963 1st ed. Fine in slightly worn DJ. $75-$90.

The Photographic Image. Barron's, 1980 1st American edition. Very Good in clipped dust jacket. $65.

MANDERS, OLGA. *Mrs. Manders' Cook Book*. NY, 1968. Good-Very Good. $20-$30.

MANCHESTER, HERBERT. *Four Centuries of Sport in America*. NY, Derrydale Press, 1931. Illus. One of 850 copies. Very Good. $200.
Shadow of the Monsoon. New York, 1956 1st edition. Very Good in dust jacket. $25.
The Diamond Match Company, 1835-1935. NY, 1935. Fine. $35.

MANCHESTER, WILLIAM. *Disturber of the Peace*. New York, 1951 1st ed. Author's 1st book. VG in DJ. $50.
The Death of the President. NY, 1963 1st ed. VG in chip dust jacket. $15.

MANGRUM, LLOYD. *Golf, A New Approach*. New York, 1949 1st ed. Fine in dust jacket. $14.

MANLY, G. B. *Aviation From the Ground Up*. Chicago, 1929. Illus. VG in DJ. $35.

MANLY, WILLIAM LEWIS. *Death Valley in '49*. San Jose CA, 1894 1st edition. Illustrated. Hinges weak, scuffing, darkening. $175. Another, Very Good, lightly rubbed. $250. Same, New York, 1929. Very Good. $40. 1966 Facsimile reprint of 1894 edition. $25.

MANN, HORACE. *Powers and Duties of Woman*. 1853, Hall Mills Co. Very Good. $65.
Lectures on Education. Boston, 1845 1st ed. $125.

MANN, J. J. *Round The World in a Motor Car*. London, G. Bell, 1914 1st ed. illus. Very Good. $125.

MANN, KATHLEEN. *Peasant Costumes in Europe*. Black, 3rd printing, 1937. 2 vols. Fine, no dust jacket. $35.

MANN, THOMAS. *Joseph and His Brothers*. NY, 1934 1st American ed. Good. $20. Same, 6th printing. Signed. $125.
Joseph in Egypt. NY, 1938 2 vols. boxed. VG. $37.
The Beloved Returns. Knopf, 1940 1st U. S. ed. Very Good in dust jacket. $55.
Joseph the Provider. NY, 1944 1st edition. Good to VG. $25-$35. Fine in dust jacket. $45.
Confessions of Felix Krull. NY, 1955 1st American ed. Very Good in dust jacket. $15.

MANO, KEITH. *Bishop's Progress*. Boston, 1968 1st ed. Author's 1st book. Near Fine in dust jacket. $100.

MANSFIELD, HAROLD. *Vision - A Saga of the Sky. Story of Boeing Aviation*. Duell-Sloan, 1956 1st ed. Signed by the Author. VG, no dust jacket. $16-$20.

MANSFIELD, JOHN B. (Editor). *History of the Great Lakes Illustrated*. Chicago, J. H. Beers, 1899. 2 vols. 5 dble maps, 2,141 pgs. Near Fine. $450.

MANSFIELD, KATHERINE. *Poems*. NY, Knopf, 1924 1st American edition. Very Good. $45.

MANSON, G. C. *Frank Lloyd Wright to 1910: The First Golden Age*. Reinhold, 1958. VG in dust jacket. $145.

MANVILLE, BILL. *Saloon Society*. Duell-Sloan, 1960 1st ed. Fine in dust jacket. $16-$20.

MARCH, ELEANOR S. *Little White Barbara*. London, 1902. Illus. by author. Imitation of "Little Black Sambo". Some loose pages. $85.

MARCH, GENERAL PEYTON C. *The Nation at War*. NY, 1932. Illus. Fine. $30.

MARCH, WILLIAM. *Company K*. NY, 1933 1st ed. Author's 1st book. Near Fine in vg dust jacket. $300.
The Bad Seed. NY,1954 1st ed. Very Good. $13.

MARCUS, ADRIANNE. *The Chocolate Bible*. NY, 1979, Putnam's Sons. Very Good. $15.

MARCY, CAPT. RANDOLPH. *The Prairie and Overland Traveller: A Companion for Emigrants, Traders, etc.* London, 1860 1st English ed. Cloth renewed, lettering rubbed, o/w Fine. $425.

MARDIKIAN, GEORGE. *Dinner at Omar Khayyam's*. San Francisco, 1957 8th printing. Signed. Very Good in chip dust jacket. $15.

MARIAS, E. N. *My Friends the Baboons*. NY, 1939. Very Good in dust jacket. $18.

MARIO, T. *Playboy Gourmet*. Playboy Press. 5th printing. Good in dust jacket. $30.

MARITAIN, JACQUES. *The Range of Reason*. NY, 1952 1st edition in English. Very Good in worn DJ. $23.
Bergsonian Philosophy. New York, 1955 1st edition. Very Good in dust jacket. $15.

MARKFIELD, WALLACE. *Teitlebaum's Window*. NY, 1970 Book Club ed. Fine in dust jacket. $5.

MARKHAM, EDWIN. *The Man With the Hoe*. San Francisco, 1899 1st ed. Paperbound. Author's 1st book. VG. $22-$35. Same, 1920 edition. Signed. $50.
California the Wonderful. NY, 1914. Illus. $16. Same, 1923 ed. Signed. Good. $20.
The Real America in Romance. 2 vols. Art edition, NY, 1912. Good. $35.

The Gates of Paradise and Other Poems. New York, 1920. Very Good. $13.
New Poems: 80 Songs at 80. New York, 1932. Inscribed. Very Good. $35.

MARKHAM, HENRY H. *Resources of California*. Sacramento, 1893. 144 pages. 15 plates. VG. $125.

MARKS, JEANNETTE. *Geoffrey's Window*. Milton Bradley, 1921. Juvenile. Clara M. Bird illustrator. Very Good in poor dust jacket. $40.

MARLOW, RALPH. *The Big Five Motorcycle Boys in Tennessee Wilds*. A. L. Burt, 1914. Juvenile. VG. $12.

MARLOWE, DEREK. *A Dandy in Aspic*. NY, 1966 1st ed. Author's 1st book. Near Fine in dust jacket. $50.

MARQUAND, JOHN P. *The Late George Apley*. Boston, 1937 1st edition. Very Good in dust jacket. $100. Franklin Mint edition, 1977. Fine Leather. $15.
Point of No Return. Boston, 1949 1st trade edition. Very Good in dust jacket. $20.
Melville Goodwin, USA. Boston, 1951 1st edition. Fine in fair dust jacket. $20.

MARQUEZ, GABRIEL GARCIA. *One Hundred Years of Solitude*. Cape, London, 1970 1st English edition. Very Good in dust jacket. $175. Same 1970 1st American ed. Near VG in chipped dust jacket. $600.
Innocent Erendia. NY, 1978. Fine in DJ. $50.

MARQUIS, DON. *Danny's Own Story*. Garden City NY, 1912 1st edition. Author's 1st book. E. W. Kemble illus. Very Good plus. $60-$100.
Old Soak's History of the World. NY, 1924 1st edition. Cover fair, o/w Very Good. $13.
A Variety of People. NY, 1929 1st edition. Faded spine, o/w Good. $25.
Her Foot Is On The Brass Rail. Springfield MA, 1935. Privately printed. James Thurber illus. One of 500 copies. Very Good. $50.
Archy and Mehitabel. NY, 1942. George Herrman illus. Very Good in dust jacket. $25.

MARSH, DOROTHY. *Good Housekeeping Cook Book*. 1938-1958 editions. $5-$20.

MARRYAT, FRANK. *Mountains and Molehills or Recollections of a Burnt Journal*. London, 1855 1st ed. 443 pages. 8 chromolithos of Gold Rush, California. Clean, tight copy. $300-$500.

MARSH, GEORGE PERKINS. *Man and Nature: Or, Physical Geography as Modified by Human Action*. NY, 1864. Covers, worn, chipped, internally VG. Early conservation classic. $150.

MARSH, NGAIO. *Death of a Peer*. Boston, 1940 1st ed. Good in dust jacket. $35.
Death and the Dancing Footman. Boston, 1941 1st ed. Near Fine in dust jacket. $60.
Death in Ecstasy. NY, 1941 1st ed. Fine. $25.
Final Curtain. Boston, 1947 1st ed. Fine in poor DJ. $23.
Night at the Vulcan. Boston, 1951 1st American edition. Very Good in dust jacket. $18.
Scales of Justice. Boston, 1955 1st Ameican ed. Near Fine in good dust jacket. $20.
Clutch of Constables. Boston, 1969 1st ed. Very Good in worn dust jacket. $22.
Photo-Finish. London, 1980 1st ed. Fine in vg DJ. $40.

MARSH, REGINALD (Illustrator). *The Big Money. The 42nd Parallel. 1919*. All by John Dos Passos. Boston, 1946 one vol. One of 365 copies, signed by Marsh, Dos Passos. Fine in worn slipcase. $750.
The Fortunes and Misfortunes of the Famous Moll Flanders. By Daniel Defoe. NY, LEC, 1954. One of 1,500 copies. Signed by Marsh. Fine in worn slipcase. $125.

MARSHALL, EVERETT. *Wreck and Sinking of the Titantic*. L. H. Walter, 1912 1st ed. Good. $12.

MARSHALL, H. *Mary Nutting, Pioneer of Modern Nursing*. Johns Hopkins, 1972. Fine in dust jacket. $20.

MARSHALL, JAMES. *Santa Fe-The Railroad that Built an Empire*. Random House, 1945 1st edition. Very Good. $12-$16. Fine. $20.

MARSHALL, JOHN. *American Bastille*. Philadelphia, 1878. Poor binding. $30.

MARSHALL, JOSIAH. *The Farmer's and Immigrant's Complete Guide*. (Cook book). 1840. $124-$145.

MARSHALL, LOGAN. *Our National Calamity of Fire, Flood and Tornado*. 1913. Very Good. $18.
The Sinking of the Titanic and Great Sea Disasters. Myers, 1912. Photo illus. $20-$30.

MARSHALL, NINA L. *The Mushroom Book*. NY, 1901 1st edition. Good. $35.

MARSHALL, S. L. A. *Blitz Krieg*. NY, 1940 1st ed. Signed. Very Good in dust jacket. $25.
Bastogne: The First Eight Days. No place, 1946 1st ed. Fine in vg dust jacket. $25.
Pork Chop Hill. NY, 1956 1st ed. Signed. VG. $24.
Night Drop: The American Airborne Invasion of Normandy. Boston, 1962 1st ed. Very Good. $60.
Battles in Monsoon. NY, 1967 1st ed. Fine. $20.

MARTIN, CHARLES L. *A Sketch of Sam Bass the Bandit*. Univ. of Okla., 1956 reprint of 1880 ed. VF, no DJ. $18.

MARTIN, COLIN. *Full Fathom Five: The Wreck of the Spanish Armada*. NY, 1975. Illus. VG in fair DJ. $19.

MARTIN, GEORGE. *The Family Horse*. Orange Judd, New York, 1889. Good. $45.

MARTIN, H. B. *50 Years of American Golf*. New York, 1936 1st ed. Very Good. $150.

MARTINEZ, PABLO L. *A History of Lower California*. Mexico City, 1960 1st English ed. Very Good. $35.

MARX, GROUCHO. *Groucho and Me*. NY, 1959 1st edition. 1st printing. Very Good. $15-$25.
Memoirs of a Mangy Lover. McFadden, 1964. Paperback. Leo Hershfeld illus. Very Good. $15.
The Groucho Letters. NY, 1967 1st ed. VG in DJ. $10-$12. Near Fine in dust jacket. $20.
The Groucho File. NY, 1976 1st ed. New Fine in DJ. $20.

MARX, HARPO. *Harpo Speaks!* Bernard Geis, 1961 1st ed. Good, no dust jacket. $10. Very Good. $16.

MARX, KARL. *Capital*. Chicago, 1906. Revised & amplified according to the 4th German ed. 3 vols. Fine. $125.

MARZIO, PETER. *The Democratic Art: Chromolithography, 1840-1890*. Boston, 1979. Fine in vg DJ. $50.

MASEFIELD, JOHN. *Philip the King and Other Poems*. London, 1914 1st ed. Fine in slipcase, $65.
Salt-Water Poems and Ballads. NY, 1916. Good. $10.
Reynard the Fox. NY, 1919 1st. VG $40. With DJ. $65.
Poems of. NY, 1935, Macmillan. Very Good. $7.

MASKELYNE, J. N. *Sharps and Flats*. Gambling. 1895. 335 pages. Very Fine. $110.

MASON, BERNARD S. *Roping*. NY, 1940. VG in DJ. $15.
Book of Indian Craft & Costume. NY, 1964. In DJ. $18.

MASON, F. VAN WYCK. *The Singapore Exile Murders*. NY, Crime Club, 1939 1st ed. Good plus. $14.
The Seven Seas Murders. NY, no date. Near VG. $14.

MASORIAK, ROY. *The Curious History of Music Boxes*. Lightner Publishing Co., Chicago, 1943. Includes section on repairs. Good. $45.

MASTERS, EDGAR LEE. *Spoon River Anthology*. NY, 1915 1st ed., 1st issue, in box. Good. $375. 1942 Limited Edition Club. #1,200 of 1,500. Signed. $135.
The Great Valley. NY, 1916 1st ed., no dust jacket. $50.
Lee, A Dramatic Poem. NY, 1926 1st. Inscribed. VG. $65.
The Golden Fleece of California. Countryman's Press, 1930. R. W. Johnson illus. Signed by Masters. One of 550 copies in slipcase. $35.

Lichee Nuts. NY, 1930 1st ed. Spine chip, o/w Fine. $60.
Vachel Lindsay: A Poet in America. NY, 1935 1st ed. Fine in dust jacket. $20.
The Sangamon. Rivers of America Series. NY, 1942 1st edition. No dust jacket. $25.

MASTERS, JOHN. *Nightrunners of Bengal*. Viking, 1951 1st ed. Very Good in dust jacket. $20.
Bhowani Junction. NY, 1954. Good in dust jacket. $4.
Bugles and a Tiger. NY, 1956. Illus. VG. $10.

MATHESON, RICHARD. *Someone Is Bleeding*. NY,1953 1st ed. Author's 1st book. Paperback. Rare. $325.
Third From the Sun. NY, 1955 1st edition. Bantam paperback. Fine. $45.
Beardless Warriors. No place, 1960. Near Very Good in chip dust jacket. $75.
Hell House. NY, 1971 1st ed. Fine in vg DJ. $125.
What Dreams May Come. NY, 1978 1st edition. Signed. Very Good. $95-$125.

MATHEWS, F. SCHUYLER. *The Book of American Trees and Shrubs*. Putnam, 1915 edition. Very Fine in gilt-stamped green. $15.
Field Book of American Wild Flowers. Putnam, 1927 revised ed. Fine in vg dust jacket. $15.

MATHEWSON, CHRISTY. *Pitcher Pollock*. NY, 1914 1st edition. Illus. Near Fine. $40.
Pitching in a Pinch. BSA ed., Grosset & Dunlap, 1912. Ex-library. Good. $18.

MATTHIESSEN, PETER. *The Cloud Forest*. NY, 1961. Illus. Fine in vg dust jacket. $25.
Sand Rivers. NY,1961. Photos. VG in vg DJ. $24.
Under the Mountain Wall . NY, 1962. NF in DJ. $85.
Oomingmak: The Expedition to Musk Ox Island in the Bering. NY, 1967 1st ed. Near Fine in DJ. $55.

MATISSE, HENRI (Illustrator). *Ulysses*. By James Joyce. NY, Limited Editions Club 1935. One of 1,500 copies signed by Matisse. Endpapers browned, o/w VG. $3,500.

MATSUNO, MASAKO. *Taro and the Tofu*. World, 1962 1st ed. Kazue Mizumura illus. Very Good. $15.

MAUGHAM, ROBIN. *The Slaves of Timbuktu*. London, 1961 1st ed. Illus. VG in dust jacket. $15.

MAUGHAM, W. SOMERSET. *The Explorer*. NY, 1909 1st American ed. VG. $70. London, 1915. VG plus. $140.
The Moon and Sixpence. NY, 1919 1st American ed. Author's name misspelled on cover. $125.
Loaves and Fishes. London,1924 1st ed. VG. $125.
Ashenden, or the British Agent. London, 1928 1st ed. Fine. No dust jacket. $150.
Cakes and Ale. Garden City, 1930 edition. In DJ. $35.

Of Human Bondage. Limited Editions Club, 1938 2 vols. John Sloane illus. Signed by Sloane. Fine, lacks slipcase. $350. Another, signed, in case. $275 auction.
The Bread-winner. Doubleday, 1931 1st edition. Very Good in dust jacket. $18-$24.
Summing Up. Doubleday, 1938 1st. VG in DJ. $15-$20.
The Razor's Edge. NY, 1944 1st trade ed. Very Good in good dust jacket. $40.
A Writer's Notebook. NY, 1949. VG. $75.
The Maugham Reader. NY, 1950 1st ed. VG. $100.

MAULDIN, BILL (Author/Illustrator). *This Damn Tree Leaks*. Rome, 1945. Paperback. Near Fine. $30.
Up Front. NY, 1945 1st ed. $10. 6th printing. $5.
Bill Mauldin's Army. New York, 1947 1st edition. Very Good in very good dust jacket. $30.
Back Home. NY, 1947. VG in DJ. $12.
A Sort of a Saga. NY, 1949 1st ed. Fine in DJ. $28.
I Decided I Want My Seat Back. NY, 1965 1st ed. Very Good in dust jacket. $20.
The Brass Ring. NY, 1971 1st ed. Very Good. $27.

MAURIAC, FRANCOIS. *The Desert of Love*. NY, 1951 1st American ed. Very Good. $25.

MAURICE, MAJ. GEN. SIR FREDERICK. *Statesmen and Soldiers of the Civil War*. Boston, 1926 1st ed. Very Good in fair dust jacket. $35. Same, Near Fine. $95.

MAUROIS, ANDRE. *The Thought Reading Machine* . NY, 1938 1st ed. Fine in dust jacket. $20.

MAURY, MATTHEW. *Physical Geography of the Sea*. NY, 1856 edition. 8 folding plates. G-VG. $70.

MAXWELL, MARIUS. *Stalking Big Game with a Camera in Equatorial Africa with Monograph on the Elephant*. Century, New York & London, 1924. Photos by author. Near Fine. $165.

MAXWELL MOTOR COMPANY. *Maxwell Instruction Book*. Detroit, 1918 2nd ed. 64 pages. $25. (Also see Trade Catalog Section.)

MAY, G. *Ballooning: A Concise Sketch of its History and Principles*. London, 1885. Very Good. $45.

MAY, JOHN B. *The Hawks of North America*. New York, Audubon Society, 1935. Very Good. $75. Another, 1936. Good-VG. $35.

MAY, PHIL. *Phil May's Gutter-Snipes*. NY, 1899. Illus. by author. 50 pages. Stained spine. $65.

MAY, SOPHIE. *Dotty Dimples' Flyaway*. Boston, 1897. Illus. Very Good. $10.
Little Purdy's Dotty Dimple. Lothrop, 1865. VG plus. $22.

MAYER, A. M. *Sport With Gun & Rod in American Woods & Waters*. Century, 1883 1st ed. Includes articles by Muir. Beard, Grinnell, etc. Very Good. $130-$150.

MAYER, BRANTZ. *Mexico As It Was And As It Is*. NY, 1844 1st ed. Illus. Five pages out of order. VG. $175.

MAYER, W. *American Telegraphy*. NY, 1897. NF. $65.

MAYHEW, E. *The Illustrated Horse Doctor*. Philadelphia, 1868. Near Very Good. $50.

MAYNE, WILLIAM. *Drift*. NY, 1964 1st American edition. Fine in dust jacket. $25.
Pig in the Middle. NY, 1966 1st edition. Ex-library. Mary Russon illus. VG in dust jacket. $16.
Follow the Footprints. NY, 1968. Shirley Hughes illus. Fine in dust jacket. $35.
A Year and a Day. NY, 1976 1st American edition. Lazlo Kublnyl illus. Fine in dust jacket. $50.

MAYS, WILLIE. *My Secrets of Playing Baseball*. NY, 1967 1st ed. Very Good in torn dust jacket. $10.

McBAIN, ED. *See Them Die*. NY, 1960 1st edition. Near Fine in dust jacket. $175.
The Empty Hours. NY, 1962 1st ed. NF in fair DJ. $125.
Ax. NY, 1964 1st ed. Fine in dust jacket. $150.
Doll. NY, 1965 1st ed. Near Fine in rubbed DJ. $135.
The Sentries. NY, 1965 1st ed. VG in DJ. $20.
Shotgun. Doubleday, 1969 1st. Signed. F in good DJ. $65.

McCAFFREY, ANNE. *The White Dragon*. Del Rey, 1978 1st edition. Fine. $17.
Dragonquest. Del Rey, 1979 1st hardback. Fine DJ. $35.
Dragon Drums. London, 1979 1st English edition. Inscribed. Fine. $20.

McCAHILL, CAPT. WILLIAM P. *First to Fight*. McKay, 1943 1st ed. Good, cover stain. $18.

McCALEB, WALTER FLAVIUS. *The Aaron Burr Conspiracy*. NY, 1936. One of 750 copies. Signed. Good. $50.

McCALL'S GARDEN BOOK. G. Harshbarger. NY, 1968, Simon & Schuster deluxe edition in slipcase. $25.

McCANDLISH, EDWARD. *The Froggies' Diving School*. NY, 1926. Illus. by author. Very Good. $15.

McCANN, E. ARMITAGE. *Ship Model Making. Vol. II. Clipper Ship*. NY, Henley, 1931. Plans in rear pocket. $35.

McCARTHY, CORMAC. *Outer Dark*. NY, 1968 1st ed., 2nd book. Fine in dust jacket. $250-$500.
Child of God. Random House, 1973. Very Good in very good dust jacket. $300.

Blood Meridian: Or, The Evening Redness in the West. Random House, 1985. 1st ed. Fine in DJ. $40.

McCARTHY, DESMOND. *Memories*. London, 1954 1st ed. Good-Very Good. $15.
Portraits. NY, 1954 1st American ed. G-VG in DJ. $30.

McCARTHY, MARY. *Memories of a Catholic Girlhood*. NY, 1957 1st ed. Fine in dust jacket. $18.
The Group. NY, 1963 1st ed. VG in DJ. $15.
Birds of America. NY, 1971 1st ed. Near Fine. $30.

McCLAIN, CHARLEEN. *Holland's Southern Cookbook*. Atlanta, 1952. Good-VG. $15-$20.

McCLELLAN, ELIZABETH. *History of American Costume, 1607-1870*. NY, 1937. Reprint. $40-$65. 1917 edition. 2 vols. Fine. $125.

McCLELLAN, GEORGE B. *Report on Organization and Campaigns, Army of the Potomac*. NY, 1864 1st ed. Maps, etc. $35-$65.
McClelland's Own Story. The War for the Union. C. L. Webster, 1887 1st ed. Bad spine. $22. Another, Very Good. $39-$70.

McCLINTON, KATHERINE M. *Collecting American 19th Century Silver*. NY, 1968. Illus. G-VG in DJ. $40.

McCLOSKEY, ROBERT. *Homer Price*. NY, 1943 1st ed. Illus. by author. Good. $15.
Centerburg Tales. NY, 1951 1st ed. Illus. by author. Very Good in poor dust jacket. $32.
One Morning in Maine. NY, 1952 8th printing. Illus. by author. Very Good in dust jacket. $15.
Make Way for Ducklings. NY, 1955. Illus. by author. Very Good in dust jacket. $15.

McCLURE, ALEXANDER. *The Annals of the Civil War, Written By Leading Participants North & South*. Civil War Times, 1974. Very Good. $33.

McCLURE, J. B. *Edison and His Inventions, Including...* 1879 1st edition. $50-$95.

McCONNELL, H. H. *Five Years a Cavalryman*. Jacksboro TX, Rogers, 1889 1st ed. 319 pages, pink paper stock. Minor spots, else a nice copy. $450.

McCOOK, HENRY. *Tenants of an Old Farm*. NY, 1889. Illus. Fair. $16.

McCORD, DAVID. *Oddly Enough*. Cambridge MA 1926 1st ed. Author's 1st book. Signed presentation copy. VG. $100.

McCORMICK, CYRUS. *The Century of the Reaper*. Boston, 1931 1st ed. Very Good-Fine. $15.

McCORMICK, RICHARD C. *Arizona; Its Resources & Prospects*. NY, Van Nostrand, 1865 1st ed. Very nice in cloth case with gilt-stamped morocco spine label. $225.

McCORMICK, ROBERT. *The War Without Grant*. Bond, Wheelwright, 1950. Fold-out maps. Very Good. $30. Same in dust jacket. $35-$40.

McCORMICK, WILFRED. *The Hot Corner*. NY, 1958. Rocky McCune (baseball juvenile). Inscribed. Fine in very good dust jacket. $20.
Rebel With a Glove. McKay, 1962 1st. G-VG in DJ. $24.

McCOY, HORACE. *No Pockets in a Shroud*. London, 1938 4th English printing. Inscribed. Near Very Good in dust jacket. $100.
I Should Have Stayed Home. NY, 1938 1st . Good. $25.
They Shoot Horses, Don't They? NY, 1948 1st paperback edition. Very Good. $15.

McCRACKEN, HAROLD. *Alaska Bear Trails*. NY, 1931 1st edition. Very Good. $45.
The Great White Buffalo. NY, 1946 1st ed. in DJ. $15.
The Beast That Walks Like a Man. London, 1957. Very Good plus. $25.
The Charles M. Russell Book. Doubleday, 1957 1st ed. Good-VG in dust jacket. $40-$60.
Frederic Remington's Own West. Dial, 1960 1st ed. Fine in dust jacket. $15.

McCRACKEN and VAN CLEVE. *Trapping-Craft and Science of Catching Fur Bearing Animals*. Barnes, 1947 7th ed. Very Good in dust jacket. $10.

McCULLERS, CARSON. *Reflections in a Golden Eye*. Boston, 1941 1st ed. Very Good in dust jacket. $85.
The Member of the Wedding. Boston, 1946. Very Good in fair dust jacket. $90.
Clock Without Hands. Boston, 1961. Very Good in fair dust jacket. $85.

McCUTCHEON, GEORGE BARR. *Graustark*. Chicago, 1901 1st edition. Author's 1st book. Very Good plus. $50. Fine, uncut. $100. Dodd, 1904 & 1906 eds. H. Fisher illus. $10-$25. Grosset & Dunlap reprint. $12.
Castle Craneycrow. Chicago, 1902 1st ed. 2nd printing. Very Good. $35.
Brewster's Millions. Grosset & Dunlap, 1902. 8 Photos from play. Fair. $15.
The Purple Parasol. NY, 1905 1st ed. Fine. $18.
Day of the Dog. Dodd, 1904. H. Fisher illus. $20-$40.
Nedra. Dodd, 1905. H. Fisher illus. $15-$30.
The Alternative. Dodd, 1909. H. Fisher illus. $15-$20.
The Daughter of Anderson Crow. NY, 1906 1st ed. E. Martin Justice illus. Very Good. $28.
The Butterfly Man. NY, A. L. Burt, 1910 reprint. Harrison Fisher illus. Very Good. $10. Dodd, 1910. $15-$30.

A Fool and His Money. NY, 1913 1st edition. Keller illustrator. Red cloth. Fine. $15.

McCUTCHEON, JOHN T. *Drawn From Memory*. Bobbs Merrill, 1950 1st ed. VG, no dust jacket. $14.

McDANIEL. RUEL. *Vinegaroon, the Saga of Judge Roy Bean*. Kingsport TN, 1936 1st edition. Good-Very Good in dust jacket. $15-$35.

McDERMOTT, JOHN FRANCIS. *Travelers on the Western Frontier*. University of Illinois, 1970 1st ed. VG in fine dust jacket. $35.

McDONALD, DANIEL. *History of Marshall County, IN, 1836-1880*. Chicago, Kingman, 1881 1st ed. 154 pages including maps. Good leather. $110.

McDONALD, GENERAL JOHN. *Secrets of the Great Whiskey Ring*. Chicago, 1880 1st ed. VG. $25.

McDOWELL, BART. *The American Cowboy in Life and Legend*. National Geographic Soc., 1972. VG in DJ. $8.

McELHONE, HELEN KIMBERLY. *The Secrets of the Elves*. Devin-Adair. Copyright 1913. Later printing. A. R. Wheelan illus. VG overall. Scarce. $150.

McELROY, JOHN. *This Was Andersonville*. Toledo, 1879. Gilt-dec. blue cloth. G. $50. 1957 reprint. G in DJ. $16.
The Struggle for Missouri. Wash. DC, 1909. $25-$45.

McELROY, JOSEPH. *Hind's Kidnap*. NY, 1969 1st ed. Fine in fine dust jacket. $125.
Lookout Cartridge. New York, 1974 1st edition. Fine in fine dust jacket. $50.

McELROY, ROBERT. *Jefferson Davis: The Unreal and the Real*. NY, London, 1937 2 vols. Near VG. $95.

McELROY, THOMAS P. *The Habitat Guide to Birding*. NY, 1974 1st ed. Illus. Fine. $40.

McFEE, WILLIAM. *Swallowing the Anchor*. NY, 1925 1st edition. Inscribed. Good. $75.
North of Suez. NY, 1930 1st ed. One of 350 copies. Signed. Very Good in worn slipcase. $50.

McGINLEY, PHYLLIS. *On the Contrary*. No place, 1934 1st edition. Poet's 1st book. VG in dust jacket. $65.
The Most Wonderful Doll in the World. Lippincott, 1950. Helen Stone illus. VG in chip dust jacket. $20.
Plain Princess. Lippincott, 1945 1st ed. Very Good. $40.

McGIVERNE, ED. *Ed McGiverne's Book on Fast & Fancy Revolver Shooting*. King-Richardson, 1938 1st edition. Very Good-Fine. $40-$50.

McGLASHAM, CHARLES. *History of the Donner Party. A Tragedy of the Sierras*. Truckee CA, Crowley & McGlasham, 1879. Orig. red cloth, worn and soiled. Paper darkened, pencil notes. $500.

McGRATH, DANIEL. *Bookman's Price Index*. Vols. 1, 8, 9, 10, 11, 12. $40 each.

McGRATH, HAROLD. *The Carpet From Bagdad*. Bobbs-Merrill, 1911 1st edition. Andre Castaigne illustrator. Very Good in dust jacket. $30.

McGUFFEY'S READERS were used in Ameican classrooms for more than 70 years. Wiliam Holmes McGuffey was born in 1800 and schooled at home during his elementary years. By 1826 he had become a university professor.
In 1836 McGuffey sold his series of four readers to Truman and Smith Publishers for $1,000. Since then 122 million copies have been printed.
With so many editions extant, only those bearing 1840-1868 copyrights are worth more than $5 or $10. Some recently advertised examples. *Sixth Reader*, 1857. $20-$25; 1866-1867. $10-$15. *Fifth Reader*, 1849. $25-$35; 1879. $10. *Spelling Book*, 1865. $8-$10. *Primer*, 1867. $22-$28. *Second Reader*, 1865. $10. *Fourth Reader*, 1848. $10; 1866. $9. Revised 1920 ed. $10.

MCGUIRE, MRS. JOHN P. *Diary of a Southern Refugee During the War*. NY, 1867 1st edition. G-VG. $60-$80.

McHUGH, TOM. *The Time of the Buffalo*. Knopf, 1972 1st edition. Illus. Maps. Fine in fine DJ. $15.

McILHENNY, E. A. *The Autobiography of an Egret*. NY, 1939. Very Good in dust jacket. $15-$25.

McILVANE, C. *Toadstools, Mushrooms, Fungi, Edible and Poisonous*. NP, 1912 New ed. Hinges poor, o/w VG. $85.

McINTOSH, J. T. *One of Three Hundred*. NY, 1954 1st ed. Very Good in chipped dust jacket. $25.

McKAY, CLAUDE. *Banjo*. NY, 1929 1st ed. VG. $75-$150.
A Long Way From Home. NY, 1937 1st ed. Near Very Good in dust jacket. $100.

McKEARIN, HELEN. *Bottles, Flasks & Dr. Dyott*. NY, 1970 Crown. Very Good in chipped dust jacket. $25.

McKEARIN, HELEN & GEORGE. *Two Hundred Years of American Blown Glass*. Garden City, NY, 1950 1st Limited ed. #1 of 500 signed by authors. In scuffed case. $75. Crown Pub., 1950-1962 editions. Very Good in dust jacket. $30-$35 each.

McKENNA, DOLORES. *Yellow Bill's Adventures*. Sam'l Gabriel, 1923 1st ed. Juvenile. Very Good. $12.

McKENNON, J. *Horse Dung Trail - Saga of the American Circus*. Carnival Pub., 1975 1st ed. VG in dust jacket. $22.

McKINLAY, WILLIAM L. *Karluk*. NY, 1976. Photos (Ship Crushed by Ice in Arctic). Ex-library. VG. $15.

McKINNEY, F. F. *Education in Violence*. Wayne University Press, 1961. Near VG in chipped DJ. Map intact. $75.

McKUEN, ROD. *Carols of Christmas*. Cheval, 1971 1st ed. 59 pgs. New in dust jacket. $9.
Celebration of the Heart. Cheval, 1975 1st ed. 145 pgs. Fine in dust jacket. $12.
Come to Me in Silence. Simon & Schuster, 1973 1st ed. 120 pages. Signed by author. Fine in dust jacket. $18.

McLAUGHLIN, LOUISE. *China Painting. A Practical Manual*. Cincinnati, 1889. Clippings pasted over ads in back. $40.

McLEAN, ALISTAIR. *The Guns of Navarone*. Doubleday, 1957 1st ed. Near Fine in vg DJ. $35.
Ice Station Zebra. Doubleday, 1963 1st American ed. Near Fine in dust jacket. $25.
Where Eagles Dare. Doubleday, 1967 1st American ed. Fine in very good dust jacket. $15.

McLEAN, GEORGE. *The Rise and Fall of Anarchy in America*. Chicago, 1890. Illustrated. Endpapers missing, o/w Good. $30.

McLUHAN, MARSHALL. *The Mechanical Bride*. New York, 1951 1st ed. Author's 1st book. Good in DJ. $85.
Through the Vanishing Point. NY, 1968 1st edition. Fine in dust jacket. $35.

M'CLUNG, JOHN A. *Sketches of Western Adventure*. L. F. Claflin & Co., 1854. A later edition. Nice copy, lightly frayed. $125.

McMURTRIE, DOUGLAS. *The Golden Book*. NY, 1927. Near Fine. $100.
The Book: The Story of Printing and Bookmaking. Oxford, 1943 Revised 3rd ed. Very Good. $40.

McMURTRY, LARRY. *Horseman, Pass By*. NY, 1961. Author's 1st novel. Near Fine in chipped dust jacket. $575.
The Last Picture Show. NY, 1966 1st ed. NF in good DJ. $300 Book Club edition, Dial Press, 1966. Fine in DJ. $18.
Moving On. NY, 1970 1st ed. Fine in fine DJ. $125. Another, inscribed. $200.
Somebody's Darling. NY, 1970 1st ed. Remainder mark, o/w Very Good in dust jacket. $30.
Terms of Endearment. NY, 1975 1st edition. Fine in fine dust jacket. $75.
Cadillac Jack. NY, Simon & Schuster, 1982 1st ed. 395 pages. Fine in dust jacket. $35.

Anything for Billy. Simon & Schuster, 1988 1st ed. VG-Fine in dust jacket. $30.

McNARY, DONALD. *Ship Models in Miniature*. NY, Praeger, 1975 1st ed. Photos by author. VG. $20.

McNEILL, BLANCHE and EDNA. *First Foods of America*. Los Angeles, 1936 1st ed. Mostly Mexico. VG. $35.

McNULTY, FAITH and ELIZABETH KEIFFER. *Wholly Cats*. NY, 1962 1st ed. Peggy Bacon illus. VG. $22.

McPHEE, JOHN. *A Sense of Where You Are*. NY, 1965 1st ed. Author's 1st book. VG in dust jacket. $225.
Levels of the Game. NY, 1969 1st ed. VG in DJ. $55.
Encounters With the Archdruid. NY, 1971 1st ed. Very Good in dust jacket. $60.
Wimbledon, A Celebration. NY, 1972. Eisenstadt photos. Fine in fine dust jacket. $95.
The Deltoid Pumpkin Seed. NY, 1973 1st ed. Near Fine in dust jacket. $35.

McPHERSON, JAMES. *The Negro's Civil War: How American Negroes Felt & Acted During the War For The Union*. NY, 1965 1st ed. VG in dust jacket. $35.
Battle Cry of Freedom: The Civil War Era. Oxford Univ. Press, 1988. VG in dust jacket. $25.

McREYNOLDS, EDWIN C. *Missouri-History of the Cross-roads State*. Univ. of Okla., 1962 1st ed. Fine, no DJ. $20.

McSHANE, CHARLES. *The Locomotive Up to Date*. Chicago, 1899. Many illus. Fine. $45.

McWATERS, GEORGE. *Knots Untied, Hidden Life of American Detectives*. Hartford, Burr, 1872. Good. $40.

McWILLIAM, CAREY. *California the Great Exception*. NY, 1949 1st ed. Very Good in dust jacket. $25.

MEAD, C. W. *Old Civilizations of Inca Land*. NY, 1924. Very Good. $15.

MEAD, MARGARET. *Male and Female*. 1949 1st ed. Good in dust jacket. $10. VG-Fine in DJ. $40-$60.
Anthropolgist at Work. Boston, 1959 1st. VG in DJ. $20.
Twentieth Century Faith, Hope and Survival. NY, 1972 1st ed. VG-Fine in dust jacket. $25-$45.

MEAD, MARGARET and JAMES BALDWIN. *Rap on Race*. Lippincott, 1971 1st ed. Ex-library. VG in DJ. $12.

MEADE, MARTHA. *Modern Meal Maker*. No place, 1939. Wire bound, Fair. $12.

MEADER, HERMAN LEE. *Motor Goose Rhymes for Motor Ganders*. Illus. NY, Grafton Press, 1905. VG. $100.

MEALS TESTED AND APPROVED. Good Housekeeping Institute, 1930 1st ed. Very Good. $30.

MEANY, TOM. *Babe Ruth*. A.S. Barnes, 1947 1st. VG. $22.
The Boston Red Sox. 1956 1st ed. in dust jacket. $20-$30.

MEATYARD, RALPH (Photographer). *The Family Album of Lucybelle Crater*. No place, 1974 1st edition. Fine in dust jacket. $85.

MECHANICAL DRAWING. International Correspondence Schools, 1904. 550 pgs. Leather bound. VG. $20-$35.

MECH, L. D. *The Wolf: The Ecology and Behavior of an Endangered Species*. NY, 1970. Near Fine in DJ. $18.

MEEKER, EZRA. *A Busy Life of 85 Years*. Seattle, 1916. 1909 ed., expanded. Light Wear. $50.
Ox Team Days on the Oregon Trail. NY 1924. Signed by author. Good. $60.

MEIGS, CORNEILA. *The Covered Bridge*. NY, 1936 1st ed. Marguerite De Angeli illus. Near VG. $35.
Mother Makes Christmas. Grosset & Dunlap, 1940. Lois Lenski illus. Fine in dust jacket. $25.
Railroad West. Little Brown, 1944. Very Good. $18.

MEIKLEJOHN, NANNINE. *Cart of Many Colors*. Dutton, 1938 8th printing. VG in dust jacket. $14.

MELLAND, FRANK. *Elephants in Africa*. London, 1938 1st edition. Fine. $75.

MELLOW, JAMES R. *Charmed Circle - Gertrude Stein & Co*. Praeger, 1974 2nd ed. VG in dust jacket. $15.

MELVILLE, HERMAN. *Typee. A Peep at Polynesian Life*. NY, 1846 1st American ed., 1st book. 2 vols, rebound without paper covers. Moderately rubbed, worn. $750. Another, 1846 ed. 2 vols. in one. 1st printing, 2nd state. Very Good. $300-$500.
Omoo: A Narrative of Adventures in the South Seas NY. 1847 1st American edition. Foxing, dark spine. Two ink stains on front cover. $70.
The Whale. London, 1851 3 volumes. Fine. At least $20,000. Same, New York, 1851. Six blank pages, front and back, and cover blind-stamped make this a first American edition. Worth at least $10,000. Title changed to *Moby-Dick: or, The Whale*.
Moby Dick or, The Whale. NY, 1923 edition. Good-Very Good. $25. Random House, 1930 edition. Rockwell Kent illustrator. Very Good-Fine in dust jacket. $100-$200. Philadelphia, 1931 edition. Pictorial cover. Good. $15.

MELVILLE, HERMAN (In Magazines). *Harper's*. Apr, 1885. Two articles. $45.
Century, May, 1892. Five poems. $38.

MEMORIES OF THE WORLD'S GREATEST EXPOSI-
TION - ST. LOUIS, 1904. James Bayne Co., 1904. Very
Good. $18.

MEN WHO ADVERTISE: AN ACCOUNT OF SUC-
CESSFUL ADVERTISERS. Rowell & Co. 1870
1st edition. $100.

MENCKEN, HENRY L. *A Book of Prefaces*. NY, 1917
1st ed. Inscribed. Very Good. $250.
A Book of Burlesques. NY, 1924 5th printing. Inscribed.
Very Good. $60. Same, London, 1923. $25.
Prejudices. NY, 1919-1927. 6 vols. VG in DJs. $1,200.
The American Language. NY, 1937 4th corrected,
enlarged ed. 6th printing. VG in dust jacket. $15.
Happy Days. NY, 1940 1st edition in dust jacket. $25.
Newspaper Days, 1899-1906. NY, 1941 1st ed. Fine in
dust jacket. $125. Knopf, 1943 ed. Very Good. $12.
A Carnival of Buncombe. Baltimore, 1956 1st ed. Very
Good in dust jacket. $30.
New Dictionary of Quotations. Knopf, 1942. Very Good
in dust jacket. $35.

MENDOZA, GEORGE. *The Crack in the Wall*. NY, 1968 1st
edition. Mercer Mayer illus. VG in DJ. $22.
Beastly Alphabaet. Grosset & Dunlap, 1969. VG-Fine in
dust jacket. $10-$15.

MENEN, AUBREY. *The Backward Bride*. NY, 1950 1st ed.
Very Good. $28.
The Fig Tree. NY, 1959 1st ed. Very Good in DJ. $12.

MENNINGER, KARL. *A Man Against Himself*. NY, 1938.
Signed. $85.
A Psychiatrist's World. Viking, 1959 2 vols. Limited
edition, boxed. $75.
The Crime of Punishment. NY, 1968 1st ed. VG in
slightly worn dust jacket. $23.

MENOTTI, GIAN CARLO. *Help, Help, the Globolinks!*.
NY, 1970 1st ed. Very Good in good dust jacket. $16.

MENZEL, DONALD H. and LYLE G. BOYD. *The World of
Flying Saucers*. Garden City, 1963. Ex-library in dust
jacket. Reading copy. Fair. $10.

MERCK'S INDEX. 1930 4th edition. Good to VG. $9.

MEREDITH, GEORGE. *Diana of the Crossways*. London,
1885 3 vols. Good plus. $150.
Poems. London, 1892 1st edition. Very Good. $35-$50.
The Works of George Meredith. 29 vols set. Gilt-lettered
cloth. Scribner's, 1909-1912. Sunned spines and some
chipping. $70-$100.

MEREDITH, ROY. *Mr. Lincoln's Camera Man: Mathew
Brady*. NY, 1946 1st ed. Many photos. VG. $30.

The Face of Robert E. Lee in Life and Legend. NY, 1947.
Fine in dust jacket. $50. Another, Very Good in DJ. $20.

MERIMEE, PROSPER. *Carmen*. London, circa 1926. 16
color plates. Fine. $95.

MERRIAM, ROBERT. *Dark December: The Full Account
of the Battle of the Bulge*. Chicago, 1947 1st ed. Very
Good in dust jacket. $27.

MERRILL, CATHERINE. *The Soldier of Indiana in the War
For the Union*. Indianapolis, 1896. Rebound $175.

MERRILL, JAMES. *The Seraglio* NY, 1957 1st ed. VG in
DJ. $35. Another, Inscribed in good DJ. $100.
Selected Poems. London, 1961 1st. VG-F in DJ. $75-$100.
Nights and Days. NY, 1966 1st ed. Fine in DJ. $75.
The Rebel Shore. Boston, 1957 1st. VG in chip DJ. $25.

MERRILL, MARION. *The Animated Pinocchio*. Movable
color illus. NY, Cima Pub., 1945 1st ed. $100-$150.

MERRITT, ABRAHAM. *Seven Footprints to Satan*. NY,
1928 1st ed. Near Fine. $85.
The Face in the Abyss. NY, Liveright, 1931 1st edition.
Fine in slightly shelfworn dust jacket with tiny spine piece
missing. $1,500.
Dwellers in the Mirage. NY, Liveright, 1932 1st ed. Cover
spotting, o/w near VG in lightly frayed DJ with small
piece of spine gone. $1,250. 1953 edition, Liveright. VG in
dust jacket. $25. 1944 paperback. Good. $25.

MERRYWEATHER, JAMES. *The Fire Brigade Handbook...For Volunteer Firemen, etc.* London, 1888 1st
edition. Very Good. $75.

MERSHON, WILLIAM B. *The Passenger Pigeon*. NY,
1907. 8 plates. Very Fine in chipped DJ. $150-$175.

MERTON, H. W. *Descriptive Mentality from the Head, Face,
and Hand*. Philadelphia, 1899 1st ed. $45-$65.

MERTON, THOMAS. *Figures for an Apocalypse*. New
Directions, 1947. VG in good DJ. $35. F in good DJ. $80.
The Seven Storey Mountain. NY, 1948 1st ed. Near Fine
in near fine DJ. $300. Same, 1st ed., 2nd state. $200. 3rd
printing, same year. VG in DJ. $20.
The Waters of Siloe. Harcourt, 1949 1st ed. in DJ. $65.
The Ascent to Truth. NY, 1951 1st ed. VG in DJ. $30.
The Silent Life. NY, 1957 1st ed. Fine in DJ. $35.

MERY, FERNAND. *The Life, History and Magic of the Cat*.
Grosset & Dunlap, 1968. Very Good. $18.

MESERVE & SANDBURG. *Photographs of Abraham
Lincoln*. Harcourt Brace, 1944 1st ed. Good. $25. Same,
Fine in chipped dust jacket. $95.

MESSE, GUERDON. *Spaldings' Athletic Library: How to Play Basketball.* Illus. NY, 1910 1st ed. VG. $50 auction.

MESSICK, DALE. *Brenda Starr and the Masked Impostor.* Whitman, 1943 1st ed. VG-Fine. $15-$18.

METHVIN, JOHN J. *Andele, or the Mexican-Kowa Captive.* A story of real life among the Indians. Pentecostal Herald Press, 1899. Orig. red cloth. Spine soiled & rubbed. $150.

METZER, OLIVER. *Nature Rambles.* 4 vols. NY & London, 1931-32 1st ed. 64 color plates. 2 vols. are signed by author and have dust jackets. $75 set of 4.

MEYER, ADOLPHE. *The Post Graduate Cookery Book.* Caterer Pub., NY, 1903. Good-VG. $20.

MEYER, FRANZ. *A Handbook of Ornament, 3,000 Illustrations.* Bridgeman, 1924. VG. $10-$15. Hessling & Spielmeyer, NY, 1894. Worn. $25.

MEYER, J. E. *Protection: The Sealed Book.* Gambling, 1911. 123 pgs. Very Fine. $130 auction.

MEYER, JOSEPH E. *The Herbalist and Herb Doctor.* Ind. Botanic Garden, 1918 revised ed. 400 pgs. Good. $12-$14. 1973 reprint. As new in DJ. $12.
Nature's Remedies. Indiana Botanical Gardens, 1934. Grey cloth. Very Good. $35.

MEYER, ROBERT (Editor). *The Stars and Stripes Story of World War II.* NY, 1960. Good plus. $15.

MEYERS, BARLOW. *The Restless Gun.* Whitman, 1959 1st edition. Very Good. $10.

MICHAEL, ROBERT. *Hudson's Bay: Or Every Day Life in the Wilds of North America.* Boston, 1859 1st American ed. Near Very Good. $125.

MICHAELS, BARBARA. *Greygallows.* NY, 1972 1st ed. Fine in dust jacket. $55.
Patriot's Dream. NY, 1976 1st ed. Fine in DJ. $45.

MICHEAUX, OSCAR. *The Story of Dorothy Stanfield.* NY, 1946 1st ed. Near Fine in dust jacket. $50-$100.
Return to Paradise. NY, 1951 1st ed. VG in DJ. $30.
Alaska. NY, 1963 1st ed. One of 1,000 copies, signed. Fine in slipcase. $90.

MICHELIN GUIDE TO THE BATTLE OF VERDUN. No place, 1919. Very Good. $20.

MICHENER, JAMES A. *The Floating World, the Story of Japanese Prints.* NY, 1954 1st printing. F in vg DJ. $130.
Return to Paradise. Random House, 1951 1st ed. Very Good, no dust jacket. $16.

The Hokusai Sketchbooks. Rutland VT, Tokyo, 1958 1st edition. Illus. Very Good. $95.
The Source. NY, 1965 1st ed. VG in DJ. $25.
Tales of the South Pacific. 1947 1st ed. Good. $10. Macmillan, 1966 13th ed. Fine, no dust jacket. $18.
Sports in America. NY, 1976 1st ed. Fine in clip DJ. $25.
Chesapeake. NY, 1978. VG-Fine. $18-$25.
Space. NY, 1982 1st ed. VG in DJ. $30.
The People and the Land. NY, 1981 1st ed. in DJ. $20.

MICKEY MOUSE STORY BOOK. Walt Disney Studios. Philadelphia, 1931. Color plates. Slight spine wear. $75.

MICKEY MOUSE IN COLOR. Pantheon, 1988 1st ed. $18. (See Disney, Walt for more Mickey Mouse books.)

MILES, CHARLES. *Indian and Eskimo Artifacts of North America.* NY, 1963. Very Good in dust jacket. $40. 1968 Bonanza reprint. Very Good. $25.

MILBANK. JEREMIAH. *The First Century of Flight in America.* Princeton, 1943. VG in dust jacket. $35.

MILES, ALFRED H. *Natural History.* NY, 1895, Dodd Mead. Good-Very Good. $30,

MILITARY MANUALS, UNIT HISTORIES, and other books related to *World War II* are always in demand. We have listed several dozen popular titles alphabetically, by author, but it would take another book to cover this subject in a comprehensive manner.

If you are finding World War II material, it will pay you to order Mark A. George's *Price Guide of World War II Books & Manuals* directly from the author at P.O. Box 36372, Denver CO 80236. (A dealer directory is included.)

MILL, JOHN STUART. *A System of Logic, etc.* NY, 1848 1st American ed. VG-Fine. $125-$225.
Principles of Political Economy. Appleton, 1865 2 vols. Very Good. $60.
Autobiography. London, 1873 1st ed. VG. $250.

MILLAR, KENNETH. (See MacDonald, Ross).

MILLAR, MARGARET. *The Iron Gates.* NY, 1945 1st ed. Fine in dust jacket. $35-$50.
The Listening Walls. NY, 1959 1st ed. VG in DJ. $15.
The Fiend. NY, 1964 1st ed. Signed. Fine in DJ. $40.

MILLAY, EDNA ST. VINCENT. *Renascence and Other Poems.* NY, 1917 1st ed., 1st issue. Author's 1st book. VG. $250. 1927 edition. VG, no dust jacket. $6-$8.
The King's Henchman. NY, 1927 early ed. VG in DJ. $50. 1927 edition. VG, no DJ. $5. Another, 1927, signed one of 500 copies Very Good. $45.

The Buck in the Snow and Other Poems. NY, 1928 1st edition. Very Good in dust jacket. $60.
Fatal Interview. Harper, 1931 1st ed. Good, no DJ. $12.

MILLER, AMY BESS. *Shaker Herbs, A History and Compendium*. New York, 1976 1st ed. Fine in DJ. $27.

MILLER, ARTHUR. *Death of a Salesman*. NY, 1949 1st ed. Fine in dust jacket. $250. G-VG in DJ. $70-$125.
A View From the Bridge. New York, Viking, 1955 1st edition. in dust jacket. $35-$50.
After the Fall. NY, 1964 1st ed. Fine in fine DJ. $50.

MILLER, BENJAMIN. *Ranch Life in Southern Kansas and the Indian Territory*. NY, Fless & Ridge, 1896. 163 pgs. Very Good in new wrapper with original. printed wrap laid down. $1,500.

MILLER, DIANE DISNEY. *The Story of Walt Disney*. NY, 1957 1st ed. VG in dust jacket. $45.

MILLER, EDGAR G. *American Antique Furniture: A Book for Amateurs*. 1937 1st ed., M. Barrows Co. 2 vols. 1,106 pages. Very Good. $100.

MILLER, ELLEN. *Butterfly and Moth Book*. New York, Scribners, 1912. $10-$15.

MILLER, FRANCIS T. (Editor). *The Photographic History Of the Civil War*. NY, 1911 1st eds. 10 vols. Spine fading, overall VG. $125. NY, 1912. 10 vols. ½ leather. $350. 1957, Castle Books. $100-$150. 1987. 5 vols. $100.
The World in the Air. The Story of Flying in Pictures. NY, 1930, Putnams, 2 vols. 1st edition. Gilt decoration. Good-Very Good. $150-$200.
History of World War II. Philadelphia, 1945. $22.

MILLER, HENRY. *Tropic of Cancer*. Paris, 1934 1st ed. Paperbound. Author's 1st book. Fine. $1,200-$5,000. New York, 1940 edition. $25.
The Paris Gun. London, 1930 1st ed. Good. $37.
Black Spring. NY, 1963 1st American ed. Near Fine in dust jacket. $25-$45.
Tropic of Capricorn. Calder Publishing, 1964. 1st English edition. Very Good in dust jacket. $25-$45. Grove, 1961 1st American edition in dust jacket. $50-$75.
Boxed Set of Sexus, Nexus, Plexus. Grove, 1965. Fine in dust jackets, poor box. $125.

MILLER, J. H. *American Polled Durham Herd-Book*. Cattle approved for registry 1894-1912. 6 volumes. Showing shelfwear. $150.

MILLER, JOAQUIN. *Life Amongst the Modocs*. Lond., 1873 1st ed., 3 vols. Tape repairs, leaves reinforced. $150-$250.
First Families of the Sierra. Chicago, 1876 1st edition. Near Very Good. $175.

The Complete Poetical Works of Joaquin Miller. San Francisco, 1897. Hinge weak, o/w Very Good. $50.

MILLER, JOHN A. *Fares, Please*. Appleton, 1941. (Horsecars, trolleys). Illus. Rebound, ex-library. $10.

MILLER, LEWIS B. *A Crooked Trail, Story of a Thousand-Mile Saddle Trip Up & Down Texas*. Pittsburg, Axtell-Rush Pub., 1908. Rubbed & soiled, else VG. $150.

MILLER, MAX. *Where Time Stands Still*. NY, 1943 (Baja California). Fine in fine DJ. $45. Good-VG. $15-$30.
Daybreak for Our Carrier. NY, 1944, VG, chip DJ. $10.

MILLER, OLIVE B. *My Bookhouse*. Chicago, 1925. 6 vols. VG. $140. Pre-1933 7th edition. G-VG. $150. 1937, 12 vols. Fine. $90. 1948, 13 vols. Fine. $130. 1951, 12 vols. VG. $55. 1971, 12 vols. Very Fine. $75.
Tales Told in Holland. 1926. VG. $25-$35.
Nursery Friends From France. No place, 1927. Maude, Miska Petersham illus. Little soiling, o/w VG. $20.
Engines and Brass Bands. Chicago, NY, 1933 1st ed. Illus. Near Fine in chipped dust jacket. $40.
My Book of History. 1930. Very Good. $8.
Treasure Chest of My Book House. 1947. VG. $12.
Flying Sails of My Book House. 1947. VG. $10.
From the Tower Window of My Book House. 1947. Very Good. $12.

MILLER, PERRY. *The New England Mind: the 17th Century*. NY, 1939 1st printing. Damp stains, o/w G. $15.
Orthodoxy in Massachusetts. 1630-1650. Harvard Univ. Press, 1933 1st ed. Very Good. $20.

MILLER, WALTER M. *A Canticle for Liebowitz*. Philadelphia, 1960 1st ed. Inscribed. Fine in vg DJ. $2,500. Same, not inscribed. Ex-library. VG in DJ. $20-$45.

MILLER, WARREN. *The Cool World*. Boston, 1959 1st ed. Very Good in dust jacket. $40.

MILLIGAN, SPIKE. *Puckoon*. London, 1963 1st ed. Very Good in dust jacket. $20.

MILLS, BURT. *Chilton's Auto Restoration Guide*. Chilton, 1975 1st ed. 290 pgs. New in dust jacket. $15.

MILLS, ENOS A. *Wild Life on the Rockies*. Houghton-Mifflin, 1909 1st edition. Photos. Few stained pages, worn covers. $18.

MILLS, G. R. and ZAIDA NELSON. *The Talking Dolls*. NY, Greenberg, 1930 1st edition. Tony Sarg illus. Some tears in jacket, o/w fine. $220 auction.

MILLS, MARJORIE. *Better Home Recipe Book*. Boston Herald-Travaeler, 1933. 500 pgs. Good. $15.

MILNE, A. A. *Winnie the Pooh*. London, 1926 1st ed. Decorations by E. H. Shepard. No DJ. VG. $400. 1st American ed. NY, 1926. G. $75. Dutton rpt, 1961. VG. $8.
When We Were Very Young. London, 1925 10th ed. E. H. Shepard illus. VG. $300. Dutton reprint, 1961. VG. $8.
Now We Are Six . London, 1927 1st edition. $200.
Toad of Toad Hall. London,1929 1st ed. VG in DJ. $90.
Peace With Honor. E. P. Dutton, 1934 1st American ed. Fine, no dust jacket. $35.
Year In, Year Out. NY, E. P. Dutton, 1952 1st American ed. Very Good. $50 auction.
Four Days Wonder. London, 1933 1st ed. in DJ. $40.

MILNE, CHRISTOPHER. *The Path Through the Trees*. NY, 1979 1st American ed. Fine in DJ. $30.

MILTON, JOHN. *Paradise Lost*. NY, Cassell, Petter, Galpin, circa 1880s. Dore illus. Stains, else VG. $100-$150. Another, 1884, Alden. Fair-Good. $25-40. Same, no date, Thomas pub. Good. $15.
Poems in English. London, 1926, Nonesuch Press. 2 volumes. Fine. $195.
The Masque of Comus. Limited Ed. Club, 1954. One of 1,500 copies. Edmund Dulac illus. Fine in slipcase. $225.

MINARIK, ELSE H. *Little Bear*. NY, 1957. Maurice Sendak illustrator. Very Good. $20.
Father Bear Comes Home. Harper, 1959. VG. $20.
Little Bear's Friend. NY, 1960. DJ. $14-$18.

MINGUS, CHARLES. *Beneath the Underdog*. NY, 1971 1st ed. Very Good in dust jacket. $40.

MINNICH, HARVEY C. *William Holmes, McGuffey and McGuffey Readers*. Miami Univ., 1928 1st ed. VG. $14.

MIRSKY, JEANNETTE. *The Westward Crossings*. NY, 1946. Illus. Near Fine in dust jacket. $25.

MISHIMA, YUKIO. *The Sound of Waves*. NY, 1956 1st American ed. Author's 1st book. VG in vg DJ. $40-$70.
Confessions of a Mask. New Directions, 1958 1st English language ed. VG in clipped dust jacket. $65.
After the Banquet. NY, 1963 1st American ed. Near Fine in chip dust jacket. $60.
The Sailor Who Fell From Grace With the Sea. NY, 1965 1st American edition. Very Good in dust jacket. $40. Fine in dust jacket. $100.
Forbidden Colors. NY, 1968 1st American edition. Fine in dust jacket. $30.

MITCHAM, HOWARD. *Creole Gumbo and All That Jazz*. New Orleans cook book. Addison-Wesley, 1978 1st ed. Very Good in dust jacket. $30.

MITCHELL, JOSEPH. *Old Mr. Flood*. NY, 1948. Very Good in chipped dust jacket. $20.

MITCHELL, LEONARD JAN. *Luchow's German Cook Book*. NY, 1952 1st ed. $25-$30. 1956 ed. VG in DJ. $14.

MITCHELL, MARGARET. *Gone With The Wind*. NY, 1936 1st ed., 1st issue. "Published May 1936" on copyright page and no note of further printings. First issue dust jacket lists GWTW in second column of publisher's book list on back panel. Second issue dust jacket has GWTW at top of list in first column. 1st ed., 1st issue as above, and signed by Ms. Mitchell, NF in near fine dust jacket. $5,000 and up. Without signature, $950-$2,500. Less than Near Fine condition reduces price. Second eds. G-VG in dust jacket are worth $400-$500. 13th printing of 1st edition. Sept 1936. Fair, no DJ. $10. Movie ed., 1940. 2nd printing VG in DJ. $25. Another, Good, spine repaired. $15. Facsimile of 1st ed. NY, 1986. As new, $22.

MITCHELL, S. WEIR. *The Collected Poems*. NY, 1896 1st edition. Very Good. $100.
Hugh Wynne, Free Quaker. NY,1899 2 vols. VG. $15.
The Red City. NY, 1908 1st ed. Good-VG. $20-$35.

MITCHISON, NAOMI. *Barbarian Stories*. NY, 1929 1st ed. Very Good. $15.

MITFORD, NANCY. *Love in a Cold Climate*. NY, 1949 1st American ed. Very Good in dust jacket. $35.
Noblesse Oblige. London, 1956 1st ed. VG in DJ. $20.
Madame De Pompadour. NY, 1968 1st. Good in DJ. $7.

MIVART, ST. GEORGE. *The Cat*. London, 1881 1st ed. 200 illustrations. Very Good. $300.

MIZE, JOHNNY. *How to Hit*. NY, 1953 1st ed. Very Good in good dust jacket. $20.

MIZENER, ARTHUR. *The Far Side of Paradise*. Houghton Mifflin, 1951 1st edition. VG in edgeworn dust jacket. $35.

MODERN PRISCILLA COOKBOOK. Boston, Priscilla Pub. Co., 1924. Good. $10.

MOFFIT, ELLA B. *The Cocker Spaniel*. 1935 1st edition, Orange Judd. VG. $15. 1953 ed. $10.

MOHOLY-NAGY, L. (Photographer). *Vision in Motion*. Chicago, 1947 1st ed. Near Fine in vg DJ. $195. Same 2nd printing. Fair-Good. $85.

MOHR, NICOLAUS. *Excursion Through America*. Lakeside Press, 1973. Very Good. $32.

MOLER, A. B. *The Barber's Hairdresser's and Manicurer's Manual*. No place, 1900. Very Good. $35.
The Barber's Manual. No place, 1911. Pocket reference, Very Good. $30.
(Later Moler Manuals, 1930s, 1940s are $15-$25.)

MOLESWORTH, MRS. *A Christmas Child*. London, 1886. Walter Crane illus. Very Good. $40.
Two Little Waifs. NY, 1883. Walter Crane illus. $60-$100.
Us, An Old Fashioned Story. Macmillan, (1886). $50-$75.

MOMADAY, N. SCOTT. *House Made of Dawn*. NY, 1968 1st ed. Fine in dust jacket. $100.
The Way to Rainy Mountain. Albuquerque NM, 1969 1st ed. Fine in dust jacket. $75.
The Names. NY, 1976 1st ed. VG in DJ. $25.

MONAGHAN, JAY. *Diplomat in Carpet Slippers*. Indianapolis, 1945 1st ed. Fine in dust jacket. $10.
Last of the Badmen. Indianapolis, 1946. Fine in DJ. $25.
The Great Rascal. (Ned Buntline). Boston, 1952. $15.
Civil War on the Western Front. NY, 1955. Very Good in very good dust jacket. $20.
Custer. Boston, 1959 1st edition. Near Very Good in worn dust jacket. $55.
The Book of the American West. NY, 1963 1st ed. VG-Fine in dust jacket. $50-$90.

MONCRIEF, A. E. H. *The Romance & Legend of Chivalry*. William Wise, 1934 ed. illus. VG. $13.
London. A. C. Black, 1923. Good, no dust jacket. $15.

MONROE, MARILYN. *My Story*. NY, Stein & Day, 1974 1st ed. Fine to Very Fine in dust jacket. $20-$40. 2nd printing., same year. $15 in dust jacket.

MONROE, MARILYN (In Magazines). All are picture stories or interviews. *Photoplay*. Feb 1963. Near Mint. $25. June 1963. Very Good. $20.
Modern Screen. Sept 1954. Good. $25. Oct 1961. Very Good. $35. Nov 1956, VG. $30.
Playboy. Jan 1964. Near Mint. $25. May 1979. NM. $15. (See Magazine Section for more examples.)

MONSARRAT, NICHOLAS. *The Tribe That Lost Its Head*. NY, 1956. Fine in dust jacket. $8.
White Rajah. NY, 1961. Fine in dust jacket. $7.

MONTESSORI, MARIA. *Pedagogical Anthropology*. NY, 1913. Illus. Binding scuffed and soiled. $100.

MONTEZ, LOLA. *Lectures of Lola Montez, Including Her Autobiography*. NY, 1958 1st ed. Very Good. $50-$80.

MONTGOMERY, FRANCES. *Billy Whisker's Kids*. Saalfield, 1903. W. H. Fry illus. VG in chip DJ. $27. Fair. $17.
Billy Whiskers. Saalfield, NY, 1907. W. H. Fry illus. $15.
Billy Whiskers Jr. Saalfield, 1904. VG. $30.
Billy Whiskers at the Circus. Saalfield, 1908. 1st edition. Good. $14-$25.
Billy Whiskers in Town. Saalfield, 1913. VG. $30.
Billy Whisker's Grandchildren. Saalfield, 1909. Hugo von Hofsten illus. VG in worn, clipped DJ. $50.

Billy Whiskers in An Aeroplane. Saalfield, 1912. Constance White illus. Broken hinge. $9.
Billy Whiskers Tourist. Saalfield, 1929. VG. $35.
Billy Whisker's Pranks. Saalfield, 1925. Frances Brundage illustrator. Very Good plus. $28.
Billy Whiskers, Junior. 1904, • *Billy Whiskers, Jr. and his Chums*. 1907. • *Billy Whiskers Kidnapped*. 1910. • *Billy Whiskers in an Aeroplane*. 1912. • *Billy Whiskers in the South*. 1917 • *Billy Whiskers in Camp*. 1918. • *Billy Whiskers in France*. 1919. • *Billy Whiskers in the Movies*. 1921. Together, 8 vols. Illus. with color plates by various artists. 8¾x7, 3 pictorial cloth, others cloth-backed pictorial boards. First Editions. 8 vols. Normal defects. $85 auction.

MONTGOMERY, JAMES. *The Shaping of a Battle: Gettysburg*. Chilton, 1959 1st ed. Very Good. $40.

MONTGOMERY, L. M. *Anne of Green Gables*. Boston, 1908 1st ed. Covers worn. $85. Reprints. $8-$24.
Anne of Avonlea. Boston, 1909. VG. $20-$35.
Story Girl. Page, 1911 edition. Good. $12.
Rainbow Valley. NY, 1919. Grosset & Dunlap. Light soiling, chip DJ, o/w VG in good dust jacket. $40.
Mistress Pat. Grosset & Dunlap, 1936. VG in DJ. $17.
Jane of Lantern Hill. G&D, 1937. DJ. $25-$35.

MONTROSS, LYNN. *The United States Marines - A Pictorial History*. NY, Bramwell, 1959 reprint. Fine in dust jacket. $15.

MOODY, RALPH. *The Home Ranch*. Norton, 1956 1st ed. Very Good in dust jacket. $25.
Horse of a Different Color. Norton, 1962-1968 eds. VG in chipped DJ. $15-$28.
Mary Emma & Co. No place, 1961 1st ed. Ex-library. Good in dust jacket. $40.
Old Trails West. Promontor, 1963 1st edition. Fine in dust jacket. $18-$24.
Stagecoach West. NY, 1967, Crowell 1st ed. Very Good in dust jacket. $20-$30.

MOON, GRACE. *Singing Sands*. Doubleday Doran, 1936 1st ed. Carl Moon illus. VG-Fine. $20-$30.

MOORE, BRIAN. *The Lonely Passion of Judith Hearne*. London, 1955 1st ed. Author's 1st book. VG in DJ. $100. Paperback, 1957 1st ed. Signed. $75.

MOORE, CARRIE PICKETT. *The Way to the Heart. A Collection of Virginia Recipes*. Richmond, 1905. $50-$75.

MOORE, C. B. *Ways of Mammals in Fact and Fancy*. NY, 1953. Very Good. $10.

MOORE, CHARLES W. *Timing a Century. History of the Waltham Watch Company*. Cambridge MA, 1945 1st edition. $25.

MOORE, CLEMENT C. *The Night Before Christmas*. Houghton, 1912. J. W. Smith illus. $125-$195. Same, (no date) circa 1914. $60-$120. Chicago, 1908 ed. J. R. Neill illus. $30-$50. Lippincott, 1931 ed. Arthur Rackham illus. Very Good. $95-$150. Reprints, 1937-1976. $10-$20.

MOORE, F. C. *Fires: Their Causes, Prevention and Extinction, etc*. NY, 1885 1st edition. $50.
Fire Insurance and How to Build. NY, 1903 1st ed. $35.

MOORE, FRANK. *Women of the War*. Hartford, 1866 1st edition. 9 steel engravings. $25-$38.

MOORE, GEORGE. *The Brook Kerith*. London, 1916. One of 200 copies, signed. Unopened. $75.
Works of George Moore. NY, 1922-1924. 21 vols. Limited ed. Fine. $250.
A Story Teller's Holiday. NY, 1928. 2 vols. Limited ed. Very Good. $35.

MOORE, MERRILL. *Six Sides to a Man*. NY,1935 1st ed. Inscribed. Very Good in dust jacket. $60.
Illegitimate Sonnets. NY, 1950 1st ed. Edward Gorey endpaper illus. Inscribed by Moore. Fine in DJ. $100.
The War Diary of an Army Psychiatrist. No place, 1955 1st ed. Very Good in dust jacket. $20.

MOORE, PATRICK. *A Guide to the Planets*. NY, 1954 1st U. S. ed. Good in worn, chip dust jacket. $20.
The Sun. NY, 1968. Very Good in dust jacket. $15.
The Picture History of Astronomy. Grosset & Dunlap, 1972 4th revised ed. VG in DJ. $22.

MOORE, R. *The Universal Assistant and Complete Mechanic*. Moore, 1881 1st ed. Fair-Good. $15-$20.
Everybody's Guide. NY, 1884. Fair. $24.

MOORE, THOMAS. *Lalla Rookh*. Boston, 1887. Illustrated. Very Good. $45.

MOORE, THURSTON. *Country Music, Who's Who*. 1965-1970. Various editions. $20-$24 each.

MOORHEAD, ALAN. *Gallipoli*. NY, 1956. Good in DJ. $15.
No Room in the Ark. London, 1960. Fine in DJ. $10.
The Fatal Impact. Harper & Row, 1966 edition. 230 pgs. Very Good in dust jacket. $10.

MOSSER, MARJORIE. *Good Maine Food*. NY, 1932 2nd printing. Signed by author. VG. $75. 1947 ed. $25-$40.

MORA, JO. *Trail Dust and Saddle Leather*. Scribners, 1946 1st ed. Review copy. Very Good in dust jacket. $25.

MORATH, INGE (Photographer). *From Persia to Iran: An Historical Journey*. NY,1960 1st ed. Color, black and white photos. Fine in dust jacket. $40.

MORAVIA, ALBERTO. *Two Adolescents*. NY, 1950 1st American ed. Very Good in dust jacket. $28.

MORE, HANNAH. *Memories and Correspondence of*. NY, 1935 1st ed. 2 vols. Very Good. $40.
Old Clock Book. NY, 1936. VG in torn DJ. $30.

MORE, L. T. *The Dogma of Evolution*. Princeton, 1925. Very Good. $15.

MORGAN, ALFRED. *The Boy Electrician*. 1914 1st ed. $30.

MORGAN, BARBARA (Photographer). *Summer's Children: A Photographic Cycle of Life at Camp*. NY, 1951 1st ed. Very Good. $65.

MORGAN, BRYAN (Editor). *The Great Trains*. Bonanza, 1973. Fine in dust jacket. $18.

MORGAN, DALE L. *The Humboldt*. NY, 1943 1st edition. Very Good in dust jacket. $20.
The Great Salt Lake. No place, 1947 1st ed. American Lake series. Illus. Good in dust jacket. $20.
Jedediah Smith and the Opening of the West. Indianapolis, 1953 1st ed. VG in dust jacket. $85.

MORGAN & LESTER. *Graphic Graflex Photography*. Morgan & Lester, 1947 8th ed. 443 pgs. Fine, no DJ. $35.

MORGAN, LEWIS H. *The American Beaver and His Works*. Lippincott, 1868 1st ed. Illus. VG. $150.
House & House-life of the American Aborigines. Wash. DC. 1881. Illus. Very Good. $110.
The Indian Journals 1859-1862. Ann Arbor, 1959 reprint. Very Good in dust jacket. $60.

MORGAN, MURRAY. *The Last Wilderness*. Viking, 1955 1st ed. Fine in dust jacket. $14.

MORISON, SAMUEL ELIOT. *Maritime History of Massachusetts*. Boston, 1922 2nd printing. Good. $22. 1921 1st edition. $50-$75.
Builders of the Bay Colony. Boston, 1930 1st ed. One of 550 copies. Signed, Boxed. VG in DJ. $50.
History of U. S. Naval Operations in WWII. Boston, 1947-1962 15 vols. Good in good DJs. $350.
The Two-Ocean War. Boston, 1963 Good in good DJ. $20.
Spring Tides. Boston, 1965 1st ed., 4th printing. VG in torn dust jacket. $12.
Old Bruin, Commodore Matthew C. Perry. Boston, 1967 1st ed. Very Good in dust jacket. $25.

MORISON & COMMAGER. *The Growth of the American Republic*. Oxford Univ., 1930. Folding map. VG. $25.

MORISON, STANLEY. *First Principles of Typogrpahy*. New York, 1936 1st ed. Fine in DJ. $50.

Four Centuries of Fine Printing. NY, 1960 New ed. Very Good in dust jacket. $23.

MORLEY, CHRISTOPHER. *Where the Blue Begins.* Doubleday, 1922 1st ed. Arthur Rackham illus. Good. $65. Lippincott, 1922 reprint. Inscribed. $100.
Kitty Foyle. G & D, 1939. Photoplay ed. Fine. $35.
The Haunted Bookshop. G & D, 1919 reprint. Good. $8.

MORRELL, DAVID. *First Blood.* NY, 1972 1st ed. Author's 1st book, inscribed. VG in vg DJ. $100-$200. Another, unsigned. Fine in clipped dust jacket. $65.

MORRIS, CHARLES (Editor). *The San Francisco Calamity by Earthquake and Fire.* Philadelphia, 1906 1st ed. World Bible House. Good-VG. $15-$25.

MORRIS, CHARLES. *The Autobiography of Commodore Charles Morris.* Boston, 1880 1st ed. $100-$150.
True Stories of American Blue Jackets. 1902, Winston. Good. $25.

MORRIS, FRANK and EDWARD EAMES. *Our Wild Orchids.* Scribners, 1929. 456 pgs. Good-VG. $30.

MORRIS, JOHN V. *Fires and Firefighters.* Boston, 1953. Good-Very Good. $30.

MORRIS, P. A. *A Boy's Book of Frogs, Toads and Salamanders.* NY, 1957. VG in dust jacket. $10.

MORRIS, WILLIAM. *The Well at the World's End.* Kelmscott Press, 1896. Pictures by Burne-Jones. Goatskin covers, handmade paper. $1,100.
Art and the Beauty of the Earth. London, 1899. Good plus. $70.
Some Hints on Pattern Designing. Kelmscott Press, 1899. Good. $95.

MORRIS, WILLIAM (In Magazines). *The Studio.* (London) Winter 1934. Special issue on Morris. Illus. Essay by G. H. Crow. $125.

MORRIS, WILLIE. *North Toward Home.* Boston, 1967 1st ed. Author's 1st book. VG-Fine. $60. In DJ. $125.

MORRIS, WRIGHT. *The Deep Sleep.* NY, 1953. Very Good in dust jacket. $40.
The Huge Season. NY, 1954 1st ed. VG in DJ. $35.
Love Among the Cannibals. NY, 1957. DJ slightly soiled, edgeworn. Inscribed. $100.
God's Country and My People. NY, 1968 1st ed. B&W photos. Small spine chip, o/w Fine in DJ. $40.
The Inhabitants. NY, 1976. Very Good. $80.

MORRISON, ARTHUR. *Chronicles of Martin Hewitt.* London, 1895 1st ed. D. Murray Smith illus. VG. $300.

The Green Diamond. Boston, 1904 1st American edition. Very Good. $15.
The Hole in the Wall. NY, 1902 1st Amer. ed. VG. $25.

MORRISON, GERTRUDE. *The Girls of Central High...* Grosset & Dunlap, 1914-1915 various titles. Very Good in dust jackets. $15 each.

MORRISON, TONI. *The Bluest Eye.* NY, 1970 1st edition. Good in dust jacket. $25.
Song of Solomon. NY, 1977 1st ed. Inscribed. Fine in dust jacket. $200. Not signed. $50.
Tar Baby. Knopf, 1981 1st edition. Signed. Fine in dust jacket. $100-$150.

MORSE, EDWARD S. *Japanese Homes and Their Surroundings.* Boston, 1886. 307 illus. by author. VG. $175.

MORSE, JOHN T., JR. *Abraham Lincoln.* Boston, Houghton-Mifflin, 1893 1st ed. 2 volumes. with fold out map in pocket. Very Good. $15-$20.

MORSE, SIDNEY & ISABEL CURTIS. *Household Discoveries and Mrs. Curtis' Cook Book.* 1902, Success Co. Very Good. $35. (Later editions omitted "outhouse" plans). 1909-1914. Good-VG. $15-$29.

MORTENSEN, WILLIAM (Photographer). *Pictorial Lighting.* Camera Craft, 1935 1st ed. Photos. VG. $35.
The Model. No place, 1937. Very Good. $15. 2nd ed. San Francisco 1951. Very Good. $15-$20.
Outdoor Portraiture. San Francisco, 1940 1st ed. Near Fine in fair DJ. $40. 1947 edition. $20.
Monsters and Madonnas. San Francisco, 1946 2nd ed., 4th printing. Spiral-bound paperback. Foxing on endpapers, o/w Very Good. $100.
Pictorial Lighting. No place, 1947 2nd ed. VG. $12.

MORTIMER, J. H. *Confessions of a Book Agent, or 20 Years by Stage and Rail.* Chicago, 1906 1st ed. VG. $75.

MOSCOW, ALVIN. *Collision Course: the Andrea Doria and the Stockholm.* Putnam, 1959. G-VG. $20.

MOSELY, EPHRAIM. *Teeth, Their Natural History.* London, 1862 1st ed. Near Fine. $175.

MOSES, GRANDMA. *My Life Story.* O. Kallir, editor. NY, 1952 1st ed. Near Fine in dust jacket. $25.

MOSS, HOWARD. *The Wound and the Weather.* NY, 1946 1st ed. Author's 1st book. Near Fine in DJ. $100.
Toy Fair Poems. NY, 1954 1st ed. VG in DJ. $50.

THE AMERICAN MOTHER GOOSE. By Ray Wood and F. Stokes. 1940 2nd printing. Ed Harris illus. Good-Very Good. $15-$20.

MOTHER GOOSE. *Anonymous.* NY, 1914 1st ed. 12 full page color illus. by Jesse Wilcox Smith. VG. $175-$250.

MOTHER GOOSE. McLoughlin, circa 1882. Kate Greenaway illus. Very Good. $95-$150.

MOTHER GOOSE. Century, 1913. Arthur Rackham illus. Very Good. $150-$250.

MOTHER GOOSE. Dodd, 1912 and 1916 eds. J. W. Smith illus. Very Good. $95-$175.

MOTHER GOOSE. Eulalie Osgood, editor. Volland, 1915. Full pg. color illus. Very Good. $50-$65.

MOTHER GOOSE AND HER WILD BEAST SHOW. By L. J. Bridgman. Boston, 1900. VG. $20.

MOTHER GOOSE, FAMOUS RHYMES OF. Watty Piper, editor. Lois Lenski, illus. Platt & Monk, 1923. VG. $50.

MOTHER GOOSE FOR GROWNUPS. Harper, 1900. Peter Newell illus. Very Good. $75-$100.

THE FANNY COREY MOTHER GOOSE. NY, 1913 1st ed. Anonymous. Fanny Corey illus. G, some pg. Tears. $160.

MOTHER GOOSE IN HAWAII. Tuttle, 1966 3rd printing. Lloyd Sexton illus. Very Good. $25.

MOTHER GOOSE'S MELODIES. Color litho plates throughout with lithographed text, pictorial initials. 9x10¼, orig. gilt-pictorial cloth. Philadelphia, Porter & Coates, circa 1870. Near Fine. $250 auction.

"POP-UP" MOTHER GOOSE. NY, Blue Ribbon Books, 1934 1st ed. Harold B. Lentz illus. VG. $150-$350 auction.

MOTHER GOOSE IN PROSE. Laura R. Smith. 1907 edition. 110 pages. Good-VG. $18.

MOTHER GOOSE TREASURY. By Raymond Briggs. Coward McCann, 1966 1st American ed. VG. $50-$75.

THE NEW MOTHER GOOSE MELODIES. Anon. Chicago, 1895. Paperbound. Worn, Good. $75.

THE REAL MOTHER GOOSE. By Blanche F. Wright. Rand McNally, 1944. Good-VG. $12-$15.

MOTLEY, WILLARD. *Knock on Any Door*. NY, 1947 1st edition. Author's 1st book. Signed presentation copy. Good. $150. Same. Not signed. $45.
We Fished All Night. NY, 1951 1st ed. VG in dust jacket. $20. Another, Fine in dust jacket. $40.
Let No Man Write My Epitah. NY, 1958 1st edition. VG in fair dust jacket. $25.

MOUNTBATTEN, LOUIS. *Combined Operations: The Official Story of the British World War II Commandos*. London, 1943. VG plus. $11.

MOWAT, FARLEY. *The Dog Who Wouldn't Be*. Boston, 1957. Paul Goldone illus. VG in dust jacket. $30.
Women in the Mists. NY, 1957 1st edition. Very Good in dust jacket. $9.
Never Cry Wolf. Boston, 1963 1st ed. Faded spine, o/w VG in dust jacket. $35.

MUDD, NETTIE. *Life of Samuel A. Mudd*. Continental Book, TN, 1975. Reprint of 1906 ed. VG. $25. 1962 reprint, Saginaw. VG. $30. 1955 reprint. $20-$30.

MUENCH, J. and J. *Along Sierra Trails: Kings Canyon National Park*. NY, 1947. VG in good dust jacket. $25.

MUENSCHER, W. C. *Poisonous Plants of the U. S.* NY, 1951. Revised ed. VG plus. $20.

MUIR, JOHN. *Our National Parks*. Boston, 1901 1st edition, 1st issue. Near Fine. $150. Same date but 1920s reprint. $30-$50. 1902 ed. VG. $35-$45.
Stickeen. Boston, NY, 1909 1st ed. Famous dog story. Fine. $200. Another, with name on front paste down. $40. Average copy. $100.
The Yosemite. New York, Century, 1912 1st ed. Original gilt-pictorial cloth. Rubbed but Very Good. $300. Another, ex-library. Good. $50-$60.
The Story of My Boyhood and Youth. Boston, 1913 1st edition, 1st issue. VG. $90 auction. Others, dated 1913. Very Good. $50-$75.
Travels in Alaska. New York, 1915 1st edition. Photo illus. Very Good plus. $75-$95. Boston, 1916. $25-$35.
The Cruise of the Corwin. Boston, NY, 1917 1st ed. One of 500 copies. Large paper copy. Near Fine. $240.
The Mountains of California. Boston, Houghton Mifflin, 1894 1st edition. Original gilt-dec. cloth. Spine rubbed. Very Good. $200-$250. New York, 1922 ed. $20-$40.
My First Summer in the Sierra. Boston, Houghton Mifflin, 1911 1st edition. Original gilt-pictorial cloth. Very Good. $150-$200. Another dealer offers at $100-$125.
A Thousand-Mile Walk to the Gulf. Boston, 1916 1st trade edition. VG. $125-$150.

MUIR, JOHN (Editor). *Picturesque California*. San Francisco, 1888. Over 600 illus, including 120 full-page plates. Bindings fault, o/w VG. $1,200-$1,800.

MUIR, PERCY. *English Children's Books. 1600 to 1900*. NY, 1954 1st American ed. VG in repaired DJ. $60.
Minding My Own Business. London, 1956. VG. $39.

MULDOON, S. and H. CARRINGTON. *The Projection of the Astral Body*. London, 1958. VG in vg DJ. $35.

MULFORD, AMI FRANK. *Fighting Indians in the U. S. Cavalry*. Corning, NY, 1925 2nd ed., paperback. VG. $75.

MULFORD, CLARENCE. *Bar-20*. NY, 1907 1st edition. Author's 1st book. N. C. Wyeth, Frank Schoonover illustrators. Good plus. $50-$75.
Bar-20 Days. Chicago, 1911 1st ed. Maynard Dixon illus. Good. $75-$125.
Buck Peters, Ranchman. Grosset & Dunlap, 1912. G. $8.
The Coming of Cassidy and the Others. Chicago, circa 1913 1st ed. Maynard Dixon illus. VG in DJ. $100.
Hopalong Cassidy Returns. Doubleday, 1924 1st edition. Very Good plus. $30.
Hopalong Cassidy. Dell, 1950 Paperback. Fine. $6.

MULLER, A. and P. FULLER. *The Best of Shaker Cooking*. NY, 1970 1st ed. VG in DJ. $25.

MULOCK, DINAH MARIA. *The Little Lame Prince*. Rand McNally, 1909 1st edition. Hope Dunlap illustrator. Tight, clean. $15. Whitman, 1934 4th printing. Violet Higgins illustrator. Very Good. $18.
Adventures of a Brownie. Saalfield, 1934. J. Dubois illus. VG. $15. Whitman, 1930. Good. $18. 1893 1st Amer. $35.

MUMEY, NOLIE. *A Study of Rare Books*. Denver, 1930. One of 1,000 signed. Illus. Shelf worn, o/w VG. $140.
The Teton Mountains: Their History and Traditions. Denver, 1947. 1 of 700 signed copies. VG in fine DJ. $250.
James Pierson Beckwith, 1856-1866. Denver, 1957 1st edition. One of 500 signed copies. Stained DJ. $125.

MUMFORD, LEWIS. *Sticks and Stones. A Study of American Architecture and Civilization*. NY, Horace Liveright, 1931. Late edition. Signed by author. $20.
The City in History. NY, Harcourt, 1961 1st ed. Signed by author. Very Good in dust jacket. $100.

MUNDY, TALBOT. *King of the Khyber Rifles*. Indianapolis, 1916 2nd ed. Very Good. $30.
Hira Singh. Bobbs-Merrill, 1918 1st ed. VG. $40.
The Ivory Trail. Bobbs Merrill, 1919 1st ed. VG. $25-$35.
Jimgrim. Century, 1931. VG plus. $35.
Gunga Sahib. Appleton, 1934 1st ed. F in fine DJ. $200.
East and West. NY, 1937 1st ed. Good. $30.

MUNSELL, A. H. *A Color Notation. An Illustrated System Defining all Colors*. Baltimore, 1919-1926 eds. $20 each.

MUNSEY, CECIL. *Illustrated Guided to Collecting Bottles*. Hawthorne, 1970. Very Good in dust jacket. $25.
Illustrated Guide to the Collectibles of Coca-Cola. NY, 1967 1st ed. Fine in DJ. $25-$40. 1972. Good. $10.
Disneyana. NY, 1974 1st ed. Fine in dust jacket. $50.

MUNSTERBERG, HUGO. *On the Witness Stand*. New York, 1923. Very Good. $25.

MUNTHE, AXEL. *Memories and Vagaries*. NY, 1930 1st American edition. Very Good. $20.

MUNZ, PHILIP A. *Flora of Southern California*. Univ. of Calif, 1974 2nd ed. 1,086 pgs. VG in DJ. $16-$20.

MURDOCH, IRIS. *Flight From the Enchanter*. NY, 1956 1st American ed. Very Good in dust jacket. $25.
A Severed Head. London, 1961 1st ed. Fine in DJ. $200. NY, 1961 1st American ed. VG in dust jacket. $15.
An Unofficial Rose. NY, 1962 1st American ed. VG in clipped dust jacket. $25.

MURRAY, ALEXANDER. H. *Journal Du Yukon 1847-48*. Ottawa, 1910. 138 pgs., folding map. VG plus. $125.

MURRAY, ARTHUR. *Social Dancing. A Complete Manual*. NY, 1930. Very Good. $25.
Arthur Murray's Dance Secrets. NY, 1946. VG. $20.

MURRAY, CHARLES and CATHERINE COX. *Apollo, The Race to the Moon*. NY, 1989 1st printing. VG in DJ. $26.

MURRAY, H. J. R. *A History of Chess*. Oxford, 1913 1st ed. Illustrated. Fine. $250.

MURRAY, KEITH. *The Modocs & Their War*. Norman OK, 1959 2nd printing. (1st ed. destroyed by fire). VG-Fine in dust jacket. $30-$45.

MURRAY, MARIAN. *Circus: From Rome to Ringling*. Appleton, 1956. Illus. Fine in DJ. $50. Another, Very Good in dust jacket. $25.

MURREY, THOMAS J. *Salads and Sauces*. NY, Stokes, 1889. 297 pgs. Very Good. $45.

MUSSOLINI, BENITO. *My Autobiography*. No place, 1928. Very Good. $25

MUTTER, GLADYS MASON. *Told In Our Neighborhood*. Volland, 1928 2nd ed. Marion Foster illus. VG. $36.

MY BOOKHOUSE, FOR CHILDREN. (See Miller, Olive).

MYERS, GUSTAVUS. *History of Great American Fortunes*. New York, Modern Library, 1936 edition. Very Good in dust jacket. $15.

MYERS, JOHN MYERS. *Doc Holliday*. Boston, 1955 1st ed. Very Good in chip dust jacket. $65.
Death of the Bravos. Boston, 1962 1st ed., 1st printing. VG in fair DJ. $25-$35. Poor or no jacket. $15-$18.

MYRICK, HERBERT. *Cache La Poudre, The Romance of a Tenderfoot in the Days of Custer*. NY, Orange Judd Co., 1905 1st trade ed. Worn, spine splitting. $125.

N

NABOKOV, VLADIMIR. *Laughter in the Dark*. India-napolis, 1938 1st American ed. Author's 1st book. Very Good in near vg dust jacket. $350.
The Real Life of Sebastian Knight. London, 1945 1st English ed. Near Fine in fair DJ. $50.
Lolita. London, 1959 1st English edition. Very Good in dust jacket. $50. 1st American edition. New York, 1955. Near Fine in dust jacket. $100.
Ada. New York, McGraw Hill, 1969 1st edition. Fine in dust jacket. $35-$50.

NADEAU, REMI. *Ghost Towns and Mining Camps of California*. Ward Ritchie Press, 1965. Good in DJ. $15.

NAETHER, CARL A. *The Racing Pigeon*. NY, 1950 1st ed. Fine in dust jacket. $25.

NAGEL, CHARLES. *A Boy's Civil War Story*. St. Louis, 1934. Scarce 1st ed. Fine. $35.

NAILEN, R. L. and J. S. HAISHT. *Beertown Blazes, A Century of Fire Fighting*. No date, no place. Very Good in dust jacket. $30.

NANCY DREW COOK BOOK. Grosset & Dunlap, 1974 ed. Good-Very Good. $12-$20.

NANSEN, FRIDTJOF. *Farthest North*. New York, 1897 1st edition. 2 volumes. Very Good. $125.
The First Crossing of Greenland. London, 1897. Ex-library. Good. $45.
Eskimo Life. London, 1894 2nd ed. Fine. $100.

NAPOLEON: HIS ARMY AND HIS GENERALS. "By an American". NY, 1857, Leavitt & Allen. 20 engravings. Gilt decorated cover. Fair. $50.

NASBY, PETROLEUM V. (David Ross Locke). *Ekkoes From Kentucky*. Boston, 1867 1st edition. Thomas Nast illustrator. 8 full page woodcuts. Ex-library. Loose. $25. Better copy. $35.
Swingin' Round the Cirkle. Boston, 1867 1st ed. Lee & Shepard. Very Good. $50. 1888 edition. Nast illustrator. Yellowed, o/w Very Good. $25.

NASH, E. *Farmer's Practical Horse Farriery*. New York (and Auburn) 1858. Good-Very Good. $35-$45.

NASH, OGDEN. *Hard Lines*. NY, 1931 1st ed. Otto Soglow illus. Author's 1st book. Fine in dust jacket. $100.
Happy Days. No place, 1933 1st ed. Fine in vg DJ. $20.
The Bad Parent's Garden of Verse. NY, 1936 1st ed. Reginald Birch illus. Near VG in chip DJ. $50.
I'm a Stranger Here Myself. Bos., 1938 8th ed. VG. $15.
The Face Is Familar. Boston, 1940 1st ed. Near Very Good in worn dust jacket. $20.
Family Reunion. Little Brown, 1950 1st ed. VG in ragged, soiled dust jacket. $20.
The Animal Garden. Evans and Co., 1961 1st ed. Hillary Knight illus. Fine in fine DJ. $35.

NASH, ROBERT JAY. *Bloodletters and Badmen: A Narrative Encyclopedia of American Criminals*. No place, 1973. Very Good. $30.
Hustlers and Con Men. NY, 1976, 1st ed. VG in DJ. $25.
Look For the Woman - Encyclopedia of Female Miscreants. Evans, 1981 1st ed. 408 pgs. Fine in DJ. $15-$20.

NASH, WALLIS. *Oregon, There and Back in 1877*. London, 1878 1st edition. $40-$50. New York, Appleton, 1882 2nd edition. Fine. $60-$70.
Two Years in Oregon. NY, Appleton, 1882 1st $35-$65.

NAST, THOMAS (Illustrator). Many of Nast's woodcuts appear in Harper's Weekly from 1863 to 1886. Average price: $16 per page. Santa Claus with toys, etc. $25-$100 per pg. Nov 7, 1884 Republican elephant shown for first time. $150. Double-page prints are especially desirable.

NATHAN, GEORGE JEAN. *Mr. George Jean Nathan Presents*. NY, 1917 1st ed. Good. $10.
The Bachelor Life. NY, 1941. Signed VG in DJ. $13.
Beware of Parents. NY, 1943 1st ed. Whitney Darrow, Jr. illus. Fine in fine DJ. $35.

NATHAN, ROBERT. *Peter Kindred*. NY, 1913 1st ed. Author's 1st book. VG plus. $75.
Journey of Tapiola. NY, 1938 1st ed. Near Fine in dust jacket. $55. Good only. $8.
Winter Tale. Knopf, 1940. Advance copy. $35.
Married Look. NY, Knopf, 1950 1st ed. VG in DJ. $16.

NATION, CARRY A. *The Use & Need of the Life of Carry A. Nation*. Topeka, 1905. Illus. Wraps. Very Fine. $125. Good-Very Good. $50-$85.

NATIONAL ALMANAC & ANNUAL RECORD FOR 1863. George Childs, 1963. 698 pgs. Good. $15.

NATIONAL GEOGRAPHIC BOOKS. *Non-Technical* flora and fauna titles published from 1907 to 1957 average. $30-$60 in very good condition. *Technical Titles* from 1896-1954 range from $325 for *Material Culture of Pueblo Bonito*, to $425 for *The Ziegler Polar Expedition.* 1960s and 1970s books on Parks, Peoples of Other Lands, etc. are often seen in dealer catalogs for $8-$12. (See chapter on National Geographics for more information.)

NATIONAL GEOGRAPHIC MAGAZINE CUMULATIVE INDEX, 1899-1946. Pub. in 1948 by N.G.S. 770 pgs. $15.

NAUD, YVES. *UFOs and Extraterrestrials in History.* Ferni, 1978 4 vols. Fine. $125.

NAVAL CRUISE BOOKS. *USS John W. Thompson.* DD-760 Westpac Cruise. Tokoyo, 1961. Illus. $30. *USS Rowan.* DD-782. No place. 1971-1972. J. P. Smith editor. Illus. $30.

NAVAL ORDNANCE. By Officers of U. S. Navy. U.S.N.I., 1939 revised ed. Spine faded. Good. $22. 1946 ed. $15.

NAVAL REVIEW 1962-1963. U. S. N. Academy, 1963. Very Good. $14.

NAVIGATION LAWS OF THE UNITED STATES. Washington, U.S. Bureau of Navigation, 1886. $50.

U.S. NAVY DEPT. *Flags of Maritime Nations.* Washington, 1882 5th ed. Very Good. $45.

NAYLOR, F. *World Famous Chef's Cook Book.* Otto Naylor Corp., 1941. 620 pgs. Very Good. $20.

NAYLOR, IRENE HUME (Editor). *The World Famous Chefs' Book.* Chicago, 1939. Good plus. $25.

NEAL and CLARK. *Hypnotism & Hypnotic Suggestion.* Rochester, NY, 1906 1st ed. Very Good. $40.

NEAL, HARRY. *Telescope.* Messiner, various printings after 1958 1st edition. $12-$15.

NEAL, JOHN. *The Moose Hunter, or Life in the Maine Woods.* NY, 1864 1st ed., 1st issue, paperbound. $350.

NEARING SCOTT. *Reducing the Cost of Living.* Philadelphia, 1914 1st ed. Very Good. $35. *The Organized Destruction and Mass Murder of Civilized Nations.* NY, 1931. Very Good. $35.

NEAVE, AIREY. *The Escape Room.* NY, Doubleday, 1970. Good to Fine in dust jacket. $10-$20.

NEBENZAHL, KENNETH. *Atlas of the American Revolution.* Chicago, Rand McNally, 1974. 54 colored maps, folio. Very Good. $85.

NEELY, FLORA. *Handbook for the Kitchen & Housekeeper's Guide.* New Rochelle, NY (1878). Revised 1910 3rd ed. Good-VG. $20.

NEFF, JACOB K. *The Army and Navy of America from the French and Indian Wars.* Philadelphia, 1845. 624 pages. Folding plates. Very Good. $65.

NEGLEY and PATRICK. *Quest for Utopia: Anthology of Imaginary Societies.* NY, Schuman, 1952 1st ed. Very Good in dust jacket. $40.

NEIHARDT, JOHN G. *Bundle of Myrrh.* New York, 1907 revised edition. $35. *The River and I.* NY, 1910. Good. $20. Macmillan, 1927 Illus. ed. Very Good. $30. *The Song of Hugh Glass.* NY, 1915 1st ed. Very Good-Fine. $30-$60. *Collected Poems of John Neihardt.* NY, 1926 2 vols. One of 250 signed copies. Fine. $175. *Black Elk Speaks.* New York, 1932 1st edition. Standing Bear illus. $50. *The Song of the Messiah.* NY, 1935 1st ed. VG. $18.

NEIL, MARION H. *A Calendar of Dinners.* Proctor and Gamble, 1917 13th ed. Very Good. $25.

NEIL, MARION HARRIS. *Candies and Bonbons and How to Make Them.* Philadelphia, 1913. $15-$20. *Favorite Recipes.* New York, 1917. G-VG. $16.

NEILL, EDWARD. *History of Minnesota, etc.* Philadelphia, 1858 1st ed., half leather, folding map. Good. $60. 1873 2nd ed. Very Good. $75. 1882 reprint. $45. *Glimpses of Nation's Struggle.* St. Paul MN, 1890 2nd series. Very Good. $55.

NEILL, JOHN R. *The Adventures of a Brownie.* Chicago, Reilly, 1908 1st ed. Color illus. by Neill. G-VG. $40. *The Three Little Pigs.* Philadelphia, David McKay, no date. Illustrated. Very Good. $66. *Scalawagons of Oz.* Reilly & Lee, 1941. 1st printing. VG in dust jacket. $150-$250. Reprint, same year. $25-$60. *Lucky Bucky in Oz.* Reilly & Lee, 1942 1st printing. VG in DJ. $150-$250. Reprint, same year, same pub. $25-$60.

NEILL, MISS E. *The Every-Day Cook Book and Encyclopedia.* Lord & Taylor, 1888. Paperbound. Good. $24. Chicago, 1892 edition. Fair. $38.

NELLES, ANNIE. *The Life of a Book Agent.* Cincinnati, 1868 1st ed. $125. 5th. 1892. G. $16. 4th., 1869. VG. $75.

NELSON, BYRON. *Winning Golf.* A. S. Barnes, 1946 1st ed. Very Good, no dust jacket. $12-$14.

NELSON, HENRY. *Uniforms of the United States Army.* NY, 1959. Facsimile color. Good. $40.

NELSON, JOHN L. *Rhythm for Rain.* Boston, Houghton, 1937 1st ed. Very Good. $30.

NELSON, S. A. *Nelson's Wall Street Library.* Garden City, Doubleday-Page, 1904-1916. 6 vols., green cloth. $35.

NELSON, TOTTMAN. *History of the Union Pacific.* New York, 1923. Very Good. $25.

NELSON, W. H. *Small Wonder.* The Amazing Story of the Volkswagen. Boston, 1965 1st ed. Photos. $28.

NEMEROV, HOWARD. *Salt Garden Poems.* Boston, 1955 1st ed. Very Good in vg dust jacket. $45.
Mirrors and Windows: Poems. Chicago, 1958 1st ed. Inscribed. Very Good in worn dust jacket. $69.

THE NERO WOLFE COOKBOOK. NY, 1973. By Rex Stout and editors of the Viking Press. 1st ed. Fine in DJ. $90. Another, Very Good, no dust jacket. $25.

NESBIT, EDITH. *The Story of the Treasure Seekers.* Lon., 1903. G. Browne & L. Baumer illus. Good. $17.
The Bastable Children. NY, 1929. Illus. VG. $20.
The Five Children. NY, 1930. H. R. Millar illus. Contains three Nesbit books. Good. $15.
The Wouldbegoods. London, 1934. Very Good. $20.

NESBIT, WILBUR D. *In Tumbledown Town.* Volland, 1926 17th ed. John Gee illus. Very Good. $22.
A Friend for Two. Volland, 1915 1st edition. Tiny 16mo. Fine in box. $50.
Oh Skin-Nay! Volland, 1913. Good-VG. $20-$35.
The Paths of Long Ago. Reilly & Lee, 1926 1st edition Very Good. $15.

NESBITT, ED. *North American Big Game.* Boone & Crocket, 1977 7th ed. Fine in dust jacket. $15.

NESBITT, FLORENCE. *Household Management.* NY, circa 1918. How poor folks eat. G-VG. $20-$30.

NESS, EVALINE. *Sam, Bangs and Moonshine.* NY, 1966 1st ed. Illus. by author. Ex-library. Very Good. $9.
Yeck Eck. NY, 1974 1st ed. Illus by auth. VG in DJ. $15.

NESS and FRALEY. *Untouchables.* New York, 1957 1st edition. Very Good in dust jacket. $20-$35.

NETBOY, ANTHONY. *The Atlantic Salmon.* Boston, 1968 1st ed. Very Good. $35.

NEUMANN, DOROTHY. *Come Meet the Clowns!* New York, Macmillan, 1941 1st edition. Good-Very Good in dust jacket. $20-$30.

NEUTRA, RICHARD. *Building With Nature.* New York, 1971 1st edition. Illustrated. Very Good in dust jacket. $65.

NEVILL, RALPH. *Old English Sporting Books.* London, 1924 Limited ed. Very Good. $150.

NEVILLE, AMELIA RANSOME. *The Fantastic City; Memoirs of the Social and Romantic Life of Old San Francisco.* Boston, 1932 1st ed. Very Good. $35.

NEVINS, ALLAN. *Fremont: The West's Greatest Adventurer.* New York, 1928 1st edition. 2 volumes. Good-Very Good. $45-$95.
The War For the Union. NY, 4 vols., 1959-1971. Very Good. $45-$95.

NEVINS, WINFIELD. *The Intervale. 1887.* Thin, 58 pgs. $25.
Witchcraft in Salem Village. Boston, 1892. VG. $75.

THE NEW ABC BOOK. Children's cloth book, circa 1917. 12 double pages. Very Good. $35.

THE NEW BUCKEYE COOK BOOK. Home Publishing Company, 1888. More than 1,000 pages. Good-Very Good. $45-$65.

NEW DELINEATOR RECIPES. 1929 1st ed. Butterick pub. 222 pages. Good, no dust jacket. $8-$10.

THE NEW ENGLAND PRIMER. No example of the 1690 1st edition has survived. But this popular children's school book of Biblical rhymes and woodcut illustrations was in print for 150 years and millions were sold. The dozen, or so, editions printed from 1800 to 1826 are in the $150-$175 range. Later editions retail for $35-$55. A 1776 example recently sold at auction for $2,000.

NEW HOUSEHOLD DISCOVERIES - ENCYCLOPEDIA OF RECIPES & PROCESSED. Success Co., NY, 1917. Good-Very Good. $15.

NEWBERRY, CLARE C. *Mittens.* NY, 1936 1st ed. Illus. by author. VG in dust jacket. $50-$60.
Herbert the Lion. NY, 1939 Revised ed. Illus. by author. Good in dust jacket. $100.
Lambert's Bargain. NY, 1941 1st ed. Illus. by author. Very Good in dust jacket. $80.
Drawing a Cat. New York, 1943. Illustrated by author. Very Good. $20.

NEWCOMB, COVELL. *Silver Saddles.* New York, Longman Green, 1943 1st edition. Good-Very Good in dust jacket. $20-$30.

The Secret Door. Story of Kate Greenaway. Dodd-Mead, 1946 1st edition. Very Good in fair DJ. $40.

NEWCOMB, REXFORD. *Franciscan Mission Architecture of California*. NY, 1916 1st ed. VG. $80.
Spanish House for America. Philadelphia, 1927. Good-Very Good. $25-$35.
Old Kentucky Architecture. NY, 1940 1st ed. $35-$45.

NEWDIGATE, BERNARD. *The Art of the Book*. London, The Studio, 1938. Folio. $60. Another, 4to, no place, 1938. Very Good. $50.

NEWELL, G. & A. SMITH. *Mighty Mo: the USS Missouri: A Biography of the Last Battleship*. New York, 1969. Very Good in dust jacket. $25.

NEWELL, GORDON. *Ships of the Inland Sea-Puget Sound Steamboats*. Binsford Mort, 1951 1st ed. Fine. $14.
Ocean Liners of the 20th Century. NY, Bonanza, 1970 1st ed. As new. $15.

NEWELL, PETER. *Pictures and Rhymes*. New York, 1899. Illus. by author. Scratches and wear, o/w VG. $85. Same, 1st edition. VG. $175-$200.
Topsys & Turveys No. 2. New York, 1894 1st edition. Illustrated by author. Soiled covers. $100. VG. $200.
The Hole Book. NY, Harper, 1908 1st ed. Illus. by author. Good. $45. Very Good. $75-$100. Fine. $150-$225.
The Slant Book. Harper, 1910. VG in DJ. $175. Same, early reprint. $50-$95.
The Rocket Book. Harper, 1912. VG. $150-$200. Same, early reprint in DJ. $50-$95.

NEWELL, PETER. (Illustrator). *Fables for the Frivolous*. By Guy Wetmore Carryl Harper, 1898 1st ed. Fine. $86.
The Great Stone of Sardis. By Frank Stockton. New York, 1898. Very Good. $55.
The Enchanted Typewriter. By John Kendrick Bangs. New York, 1899 1st ed. Near Fine. $55.
Whilomville Stories. By Stephen Crane. NY, 1900 1st edition. Good. $85. Very Good. $150-$200.
Mr. Munchausen. By John Kendrick Bangs. Platt, 1901 1st ed. 14 color plates. Very Good-Fine. $50.
Through the Looking Glass. By Lewis Carroll. New York, 1902. Very Good. $75.
The Hunting of the Snark. by Lewis Carroll. New York, 1903. Very Good. $100 up.
Favorite Fairy Tales. NY, 1907. Very Good. $150.

NEWHALL, BEAUMONT. *The History of Photography From 1839 to the Present*. No place, 1949 1st ed. Very Good in dust jacket. $145.
The Daguerrotype in America. NY, 1961 1st ed. Illus. Very Good-Fine. $50-$150.
The Latent Image. Garden City, 1967. 29 plates. Fine in very good dust jacket. $30.

Airborne Camera: The World From the Air and Outer Space. New York, 1969. (Historical study) Good in worn dust jacket. $40.

NEWHALL, NANCY. *Time in New England*. NY, 1950 1st ed. Paul Strand photographs. NF to Fine in DJ. $95-$124.

NEWHOUSE, S. *The Trapper's Guide*. New York, 1869. $35-$50. New York, 1874, Oneida Community. $45. Same, 1893. Good. $20.
(Also see Trade Catalog section.)

NEWMAN, JAMES R. *The World of Mathematics*. NY, 1956 1st ed. 4 vols. Fine in rubbed slipcase. $55.

NEWMARK, HARRIS. *Sixty Years in Southern California*. NY, 1916 1st ed. Very Good. $150. Boston, 1930 3rd printing. $100. Los Angeles, 1970. One of 1,250 copies. Very Good in dust jacket. $60.

NEWSOM, T. M. *Thrilling Scenes Among the Indians*. Chicago, 1884 1st ed. Many drawings. $60. Belford, 1888 and 1889 editions. $20-$30.

NEWTON, A. EDWARD. *The Amenities of Book Collecting*. Boston, 1918 1st ed. Author's 1st book. VG. $75. Rarely found in DJ. $125-$150. Modern Lib. ed. 1935. VG. $10.
This Book Collecting Game. London, 1930 1st English ed. Very Good in dust jacket. $13. Boston, 1928 1st ed. 1 of 990 signed. $100. Another, unsigned. $10.

NEWTON, STAN. *Paul Bunyan of the Great Lakes*. Chicago, 1946 1st ed. Good-VG. $10-$15.

THE NEW YORKER ALBUM. 40 years of New Yorker cartoons. Harper & Row, 1950, 1955, 1965. 3 vols. $45.

THE NEW YORKER ALBUM OF DRAWINGS. 1925-1975. NY, 1975. VG in dust jacket. $28.

NEW YORK FISHERIES, GAME & FOREST COMMISSION REPORT. Albany, 1898. Numerous color lithos and b/w photos. $100-$150.

NIBLEY, PRESTON. *Brigham Young, The Man and His Work*. Deseret, 1937 2nd ed. Very Good. $15. Fine. $20. 1936 1st ed. in dust jacket. $15-$20.

NICHOL, FRANCIS D. *The Midnight Cry*, Review and Herald Pub. Co., 1944. (Defense of the Millerites) VG. $20. Good, no dust jacket. $12.

NICHOLL, EDITH M. *Observations of a Ranchwoman in New Mexico*. Cincinnati, 1901. $50-$75.

NICHOLS, ALICE. *Bleeding Kansas*. Oxford University Press, 1954. Good. $20. Very Good in dust jacket. $30.

NICHOLS, BEVERLY. *Star-Spangled Manner*. Doubleday, 1929 1st ed. Fine in clipped jacket. $45.
Laughter on the Stairs. Dutton, 1953 1st ed. Very Good in edgeworn dust jacket. $50.
Cats XYZ. Dutton, 1961 1st American edition. Fine in dust jacket. $30.

NICHOLS, BOBBY. *Never Say Never*. Fleet Pub., 1965 1st edition. Fine in dust jacket. $9.

NICHOLS, C. and H. SHAW. *Okinawa: Victory in the Pacific*. Washington, 1955. Very Good to Fine in dust jacket. $35-$75. 1989 reprint. $25-$35.

NICHOLS, J. L. *Business Guide: or Safe Methods of Business*. Naperville IL, 1891. Good-VG. $8-$10.

NICHOLS, JOHN. *The Sterile Cuckoo*. New York, 1965 1st edition. Author's 1st book. Near Fine in dust jacket. $200. Advance review copy. Very Good in wraps. $75. Book Club edition. $24.
A Ghost in the Music. New York, 1979 1st edition. Fine in dust jacket. $25.

NICHOLS, JOSEPH (Compiler). *Condensed History of the Construction of the Union Pacific Railway*. Omaha, 1892. Gilt-stamped blue cloth. Very Good. $650.

NICHOLS, LAURA D. *Up Hill and Down Dale*. Lathrop, 1886. Decorative blue cloth. $25-$35.

NICHOLSON, MEREDITH. *The Main Chance*. 1903 1st ed. Harrison Fisher illus. VG. $12-$20.
The Hoosiers. 1915-1916 Centennial edition. Very Good-Fine. $8-$15. Macmillan, 1900 1st edition. Untrimmed, 1st state. Fine. $30.
Little Brown Jug at Kildare Bobbs Merrill, 1908 1st ed. J. M. Flagg illus. Fine, no dust jacket. $15. A. L. Burt reprint, same year. $8.
House of a Thousand Candles. NY, 1905 1st ed. Howard Chandler Christy illus. Good. $12.

NICHOLSON, PETER. *The Practical Cabinet Maker, Upholsterer, and Complete Decorator*. London, 1826. Marbled bds. Worn, chipped, bumped. $485.
The Carpenter's New Guide. London, circa 1857 New edition, revised by Arthur Ashpitel. 74 plates, 3 parts in one. Fraying. $150.

NICKLAUS, JACK. *On & Off the Fairway*. Simon Schuster, 1978 revised ed. VG-Fine in dust jacket. $10.

NICOLAY, JOHN G. *Abraham Lincoln, a History*. NY, Century, 1890. 10 vols. ¾ morocco bound. $150-$250.
Abraham Lincoln, a Short Life. NY, 1919. $12-$15.
The Complete Works of Abraham Lincoln. New York, 1894. 12 vols. $95-$120.

NIEBUHR, REINHOLD. *Self and Dramas of History*. NY, 1955. Very Good in dust jacket. $25.

NIELSEN, KAY (Illustrator). *East of the Sun & West of the Moon*. NY, Doran, circa 1914. Near Fine in dust jacket. $300-$400. Doran, 1920s reprint. VG. $95-$150.
Hans Andersen's Fairy Tales. NY, Doran, 1924. $150-$300. Same, London, no date. $100-$125. Another. $500. NY, Doubleday, no date. VG. $59-$100.
Hansel & Gretel. NY, Doran, 1925. VG. $125-$250.

NIETZSCHE, FRIEDRICH. *Thus Spake Zarathustra*. Modern Library 1917 1st ed. VG-Fine in DJ. $120. Same. NY, Limited Editions Club 1964. Arnold Bank decorations. One of 1,500 copies. Fine. $75.

NIGHTINGALE, FLORENCE. *Notes on Nursing: What it is, and What it is not*. Appleton, 1860 1st American edition. $75-$150.

NIJINSKY, ROMOLA. *Nijinsky*. Simon & Schuster, 1939 9th printing. Shelfworn in poor DJ. Signed by author. $35.

NILES, JOHN J. *The Ballad Book of...* Bramhall House, 1961. VG in dust jacket. $20.

NILES and MOORE. *Songs My Mother Never Taught Me*. NY, 1929. Wallgren illus. VG in DJ. $16.

NIMMO, JOSEPH. *Report on Range and Ranch Cattle Traffic in Western United States*. Washington, 1885. 5 folding maps in this 562 page version. Good-Very Good. $700. Another edition, same year, published without maps. No covers. $200.

NIN, ANAIS. *Winter of Artifice*. NY, 1942. Ian Hugo illus. 1st American edition. $200.
House of Incest. Gemor Press, 1947 1st ed. Very Good, no dust jacket. $200-$250.
The Four Chambered Heart. 1950 1st. VG in DJ. $100.
The Diaries of Anais Nin, 1931-34 and 1934-1943. NY, 1966. 2 vols. 1st ed. Fine in vg dust jackets. $24.

NININGER, ROBERT. *Minerals for Atomic Energy*. NY, 1954 5th printing. Very Good. $30.

NIVEN, LARRY. *A World Out of Time*. NY,1976 1st ed. Fine in dust jacket. $20-$35.
Ringworld. NY, 1977 1st American ed. VG in DJ. $35. Fine in dust jacket. $75.

NIX, EVETT DUMAS. *Oklahombres, Particularly the Wilder Ones*. By a former U. S. Marshall. St. Louis, 1929. VG in darkened jacket. $85.

NIXON, RICHARD. *The Challenges We Face*. NY, 1960 1st ed. Author's 1st book. $50.

Six Crises. New York,1962. Signed (not autopen.) Fine in very good dust jacket. $100.
Memoirs of. NY, 1978 1st ed. Signed. Fine in slipcase. $150. Same, inscribed. No case. VG. $75.
The Real War. NY, 1980. Signed on title page. DJ lightly spoiled. $125.

NOBILE, UMBERTO. *My Polar Flights*. (Dirigibles). NY, 1961 1st ed. VG in dust jacket. $35.

NOBLE, SAM. *Sam Noble, Able Seaman 'Tween Decks in the '70s*. New York, Stokes, 1926. Very Good in worn dust jacket. $30-$45.

NOEL, JOHN. *Through Tibet to Everest*. 1927. VG. $30.
The Story of Everest. Boston, 1927 1st ed. VG. $30.

NOLAN, JEANNETTE C. *Hoosier City - The Story of Indianapolis*. NY, Messner, 1943 1st ed. Fine. $17.

NOLAN, WILLIAM. *Barney Oldfield*. NY, Putnams, 1961. Very Good in dust jacket. $25.

NOLEN, JOHN. *New Ideals In the Planning of Cities, Towns and Villages*. New York, 1919 1st ed. $25.

NORDHOFF, CHARLES. *California for Health, Pleasure and Residence*. NY, 1875. Fine. $50-$100.
Sailor Life on a Man of War. Dodd-Mead, 1881. G. $25.
The Merchant Vessel: A Sailor Boy's Voyages to See the World. NY, no date, Dodd-Mead reprint of 1855 ed. 283 pages gilt dec. cover. Very Good. $45.

NORDHOFF, CHARLES and JAMES NORMAN HALL. *Mutiny on the Bounty*. Boston, 1932 1st ed. 1st issue. Spine faded, covers lightly soiled. Very Good in chip, darkened dust jacket. $250. No date, Chicago, Ferguson reprint. Very Good. $10.
Pitcairn's Island. No place, 1934 2nd ed. Spine faded, o/w Very Good. $18.
Hurricane. Little Brown, 1936 1st ed. Near Fine. $75.
The High Barbaree. Boston, 1945 1st edition. Inscribed by Hall. Fine. $100.
Bounty Trilogy. Boston, 1940. Wyeth illus. $50-$150.

NORRIS, CHARLES G. *Seed: A Novel of Birth Control*. Doubleday, 1930. Faded backstrip. $100.

NORRIS, FRANK. *Moran of the Lady Letty*. NY, 1898 1st ed. Near Very Good. $75.
McTeague: A Story of San Francisco. NY, 1899 1st ed., 2nd issue. Good only. $100. Near Fine. $200.
A Man's Woman. New York, 1900 1st edition. 1st printing. Good. $45.
The Octopus. NY, 1901 1st edition, 1st state, with J. J. Little logo on copyright page. Very Good. $150. Regular edition, same year. $10 up.

The Pit. NY, 1903 1st ed. VG-F. $35-$50. Trade ed. $10.
Complete Works of Frank Norris. New York, 1903. 7 vols. Very Good. $200.

NORRIS, J. W. *Business Advertiser and General Directory of the City of Chicago, 1845-1846*. 1845 1st edition, paperbound with folding plate. $1,750. 1943 Reprint, Anchor Storage. $20.

NORRIS, JUNE. *Katherine the Komical Kow*. Volland, 1926 6th ed. Illus. by author. VG plus. $35.

NORTH, STERLING. *Plowing on Sunday: A Novel of Wisconsin*. NY, 1934, Macmillan, 1st ed. Grant Wood dust jacket illus. Very Good. $45.

NORTHEND, MARY H. *Historic Homes of New England*. Boston, 1914 1st ed. Gilt-dec. grn. cloth. Fine. $55.

NORTHROP, HENRY. *Indian Horrors, or Massacres by the Red Men*. No place, circa 1890s. $30-$40.
Life & Deeds of General Sherman. Phil., 1891. $20-$30.

NORTHRUP, ERIC. *Science Looks at Smoking*. NY, 1957. Good-VG. $20-$25.

NORTON, ANDRE. *The Stars Are Ours*. Cleveland, 1954 1st edition. Near VG in chip DJ. $65.
At Sword's Point. NY, 1954 1st ed. VG in chip DJ. $135.
The Time Traders. Cleveland, 1958 1st ed. F in DJ. $65.
Judgment on Janus. NY, 1963 1st ed. Fine in DJ. $65.
Ordeal in Otherwhere. Cleveland, 1964 1st. NF in DJ. $85.
Victory on Janus. Atheneum, 1966 1st ed. Very Good-Fine in dust jacket. $60-$100.

NORTON, CAROL. *Phantom Town Mystery*. A. L. Burt, 1938 reprint. VG in dust jacket. $10.

NORTON, CAROLINE. *The Rocky Mountain Cook Book*. Denver, 1903. Good-VG. $20-$35.

NORTON, HARRY. *Wonder-Land Illustrated, or, Horse-back Rides Through The Yellowstone National Park*. Virginia City, Montana, 1873. $250.

NORTON, JOHN P. *Elements of Scientific Agriculture*. Albany, 1850. Printed wraps, 135 pgs. $65.

NORTON, MARY. *The Borrowers*. NY, 1953. F in DJ. $16.
The Borrowers Afloat. London, 1959 1st English ed. Diana Stanley illus. F in DJ. $75. Another, VG in later DJ. $45. Harcourt Brace, 1959 1st Amer. ed. VG in DJ. $35.

NORTON, ROY. *The Toll of the Sea*. Appleton, 1909 1st edition. $50-$65.
Plunder. Wattne, 1912. $12-$25.
Canyon of Gold. McCauley, 1935 1st ed. $25-$50.

NOTT, CHARLES C. *Sketches of the War*. New York, 1863 1st ed. $60-$75. Same, 1865 edition. Good. $45.

NOTT, STANLEY CHARLES. *Chinese Jade Throughout The Ages*. NY, 1937. 39 plates in color, 109 in black and white. Very Good. $150. Same, London, 1936. $200. 1962 reprint. Very Good. $25.

NOVTNY, ANN (Editor). *Images of Healing. A Portfolio of American Medical & Pharmaceutical Practice, 18th, 19th, 20th Centuries*. NY, 1980, Macmillan. Illus. $25.

NOWARRA, HEINZ. *The Messerschmitt 109: A Famous German Fighter*. LA, Aero, 1963 1st ed. VG in DJ. $40.

NOWLAN and CALKINS. *The Adventures of Buck Rogers*. Whitman Big Book, 1934 1st ed. Good-VG. $40-$85.

NOWLAND, PHILIP F. *Armageddon 2419 AD*. NY, 1922 1st ed. Very Good in dust jacket. $20.

NOWLIN, WILLIAM. *The Bark Covered House*. Detroit, 1876 1st ed. 6 illus. $1,400-$1,800. Chicago, 1937. Lakeside ed. Very Good. $30.

NOYES, ALEXANDER. *Thirty Years of American Finance, 1865-1896*. New York, 1898. Very Good. $18.

NOYES, ALFRED. *Tales of the Mermaid Tavern*. 1913 1st edition. Fine in dust jacket. $45.
Forty Singing Seamen and Other Poems. NY, 1930. Illus. Very Good. $25.
Walking Shadows. Stokes, 1918 1st. Good-VG. $16-$35.

NOYES, JOHN HUMPHREY. *History of American Socialism*. Lippincott, 1870 1st ed. VG. $95. NY, 1961 reprint of 1870 ed. One of 500 copies. VG in dust jacket. $16-$30.

NOYES, PIERREPONT. *Gentlemen: You are Mad!* Barter Freres, 1946 ed. VG in dust jacket. $25.
My Father's House. No place, 1937. Good-VG. $30.

NOYES and TURNER. *At The Edge of Megalopolis: Salem, New Hampshire*. Town of Salem, 1974 1st ed. Fine in worn dust jacket. $15.

NUCKEL (NUKEL), OTTO. *Destiny, Novel in Pictures*. NY, 1930 1st ed. VG-Fine. $70-$90.

NUNIS, DOYCE B. (Editor). *Letters of a Young Miner, Jasper Hill, during the California Gold Rush, 1849-1852*. San Francisco, 1964 1st ed. Illus. VG plus. $65.

NUTT, FREDERICK. *The Complete Confectioner, or Whole Art of Confectionary Made Easy*. New York, 1807. Good-Very Good. $300. London, 1809 edition. bound in calf. $150-$200. Same, 1819 8th edition. $100.

NUTTING, WALLACE. *Ireland Beautiful*. NY, 1925 1st ed. Very Good in very good dust jacket. $25.
NY Beautiful. Dodd & Mead, 1927 1st edition. Fine. $18.
Furniture Treasury. NY, 1928 2 vols. VG. $100. 12th printing, 1974. Ex-library, VG. $35.
Virginia Beautiful. Garden City, 1935. Illus. $15.
The Clock Book. Garden City, 1935 reprint. $30. 1924 1st edition. Very Good. $60.
Pennsylvania Beautiful. 1924 1st edition. $18-$25. Garden City, 1935 2nd edition. VG. $15. Bonanza, 1970 reprint. Fine in DJ. $10.
Vermont Beautiful. New York, 1936 Deluxe ed. VG. $15.
New Hampshire Beautiful. New York, 1937. Ex-library. Good. $7. Same, 1923 1st edition. Framingham. VG. $20.
Windsor Chairs. Framingham, 1917 1st ed. NF. $75.
Maine Beautiful. Bonanza reprint, 1970s. Fine in DJ. $15.
Furniture of the Pilgrim Century. Boston, 1921 1st ed. $55. Bonanza reprint, 1977. Fine in dust jacket. $28.
Massachusetts Beautiful. Framingham, Old Amer., 1923 1st edition. Very Good. $25.

NYE, BILL (Edgar Wilson Nye). *Bill Nye's History of the United States*. Philadelphia, 1894 1st ed. Some wear. $20.
Billy Nye's Remarks. Neely, 1891. 510 pages. G-VG. $15.
40 Liars & Other Lies. NY, Butler Bros., 1888. Good.$16.
A Guest at the Ludlow & Other Stories. 1897. Fine. $25.

NYE, BILL and F. OPPER. *Bill Nye's History of the United States*. Lippincott, 1894 1st edition. Good in very good dust jacket. $35.

NYE, ELWOOD L. *Marching With Custer: A Day by Day Evaluation of the Abuses and Conditions of the Animals, on the Ill-Fated Expedition of 1876*. Glendale CA, 1964. One of 300 copies. Very Good. $300.

NYE, RUSSELL B. *George Bancroft, Brahmin Rebel*. NY, 1944 1st ed. Good. $10.
Fettered Freedom: Civil Liberties and Slavery. 1949 1st edition. Very Good. $15.
A Guest at the Ludlow and Other Stories. 1897. Gilt-dec. pictorial cover. VG-Fine. $25.

NYE, WILBUR S. *Carbine and Lance: The Story of Old Fort Sill*. 1937 1st ed. Very Good in dust jacket. $110. University of Oklahoma, 1942 edition. Very Good in dust jacket. $30. 6th printing, 1951. $25.

NYE-STARR, KATE. *A Self-Sustaining Woman*. Chicago, 1888 1st ed. Red cloth, portrait. $2,000-$3,000.

NYSTROM, JOHN. *Pocket Book of Mechanics & Engineering. Facts, Practice, Theory*. Philadelphia, 1865 9th edition. $35.

NYSTROM, PAUL H. *Economics of Fashion*. NY, 1928. Illustrated. Very Good. $45.

O

OAKESHOTT, R. E. *The Archeology of Weapons*. NY, 1960. Illus. by author. VG plus. $35.

OAKEY, A. F. *Building A Home*. New York, Appleton, 1881 1st edition. House plans, etc. Decorative pictorial cloth cover . $75.

OAKLEY, VIOLET. *Samuel F. B. Morse*. Philadelphia, 1939. 1 of 500 copies, signed by author-illus. VG. $35.

OATES, JOYCE CAROL. *By the North Gate*. New York, Vanguard, 1963 1st edition. Author's 1st book. Very Good-Fine in dust jacket. $150-$250.
A Garden of Earthly Delights. NY, Vanguard, 1967 1st edition in dust jacket. $125-$150.
Do With Me What You Will. NY, Vanguard, 1973 1st ed. Very Good in dust jacket. $40-$60.

OBER, FREDERICK A. *Camps in the Caribbees*. Boston, 1880 1st edition. Illus. $100.
Travels in Mexico and Life Among the Mexicans. San Francisco, 1884. 190 illus. Leather bound. Fine. $365.

OBERHOLTZER, E. P. *Jay Cooke, Financier of the Civil War*. Philadelphia, 1907 1st ed., 2 vols. VG. $38.

O'BRIEN, EDNA. *The Girls in Their Married Bliss*. NY, 1964 1st American ed. Very Good in dust jacket. $16.
August Is a Wicked Month. NY, 1965 1st American ed. Very Good in dust jacket. $14.

O'BRIEN, P. J. *Will Rogers, Ambassador of Good Will*. 1935, Winston Pub. No dust jacket o/w VG. $10.

O'BRIEN, RICHARD. *The Golden Age of Comic Books*. Ballantine, 1977 1st ed. Card cover. VG. $10.

O'BRIEN, ROBERT. *This Is San Francisco*. Whittlesey, 1948 1st ed. Very Good in dust jacket. $20.
California Called Them: Golden Days & Roaring Camps. NY, McGraw-Hill, 1951. VG in dust jacket. $16.

O'BRIEN, TIM. *If I Die in a Combat Zone*. NY, 1973 1st ed. Fine in fine dust jacket. $100.
Northern Lights. NY, 1975 1st ed. Fine in DJ. $30.
Speaking of Courage. Santa Barbara CA, 1980 1st ed. One of 300 copies, signed. Fine in DJ. $50-$75.

O'CASEY, SEAN. *The Plough and the Stars* NY, 1926 1st American ed. Fine in vg DJ. $75.
Two Plays: Juno and the Paycock: The Shadow of a Gunman. New York, 1945 1st American edition. Near Fine in fair dust jacket. $60.
Oak Leaves & Lavender. Lon. 1946 1st ed. F in DJ. $35.
Cock-A-doodle Dandy. 1949 1st edition. Very Good-Fine in dust jacket. $20-$30.
Under a Colored Cap. St. Martins, 1963. Fine in DJ. $30.

O'CONNELL, FRANK. *Farewell to the Farm*. Caxton Printers, 1962 1st edition. Signed by author. Very Good in dust jacket. $14.

O'CONNOR, EDWIN. *The Oracle*. NY, 1951 1st ed. Author's 1st book. VG in dust jacket. $100.
The Edge of Sadness. Boston, 1961 1st ed. NF in DJ. $30.
Benji: A Ferocious Fairy Tale. Atlantic Monthly Press, 1957 1st ed. Ati Forberg illus. Fine in good DJ. $30.

O'CONNOR, FRANK. *Domestic Relations*. NY, 1957 1st ed. Very Good in dust jacket. $20.
Shakespeare's Progress. Cleveland, NY, 1960. One of 975 copies. Boxed. Very Good. $30-$50.

O'CONNOR, JACK. *Hunting in the Southwest*. NY, 1945 1st ed. Very Good-Fine. $100-$150.
Hunting in the Rockies. NY, 1947 1st ed. VG. $185.
The Rifle Book. NY, 1949 1st ed. 4th printing. VG in poor dust jacket. $30. 1964 2nd revised edition. VG in DJ. $15.
The Big Game Rifle. NY, 1952. Fine in dust jacket. $150.
The Shotgun Book. New York, 1965 1st edition. Fine in very good dust jacket. $60.
The Complete Book of Shooting. NY, 1965. Fine in chip dust jacket. $20.
The Art of Hunting Big Game in North America. NY, 1967 1st ed. Fine in dust jacket. $28.
Horse and Buggy West. NY, 1969 1st ed. 1st printing. Fine in dust jacket. $225.
The Best of Jack O'Connor. Amwell Press, 1977 1st ed. One of 1,000 copies. Fine in DJ slipcase. $250.

O'CONNOR, RICHARD. *High Jinks on the Klondike*. Bobbs Merrill, 1954. Very Good. $25-$35.
Pat Garrett: A Biography. NY, 1960 1st ed. F. $25-$30.
Iron Wheels & Broken Men. Putnam, 1973 1st edition. Fine in dust jacket. $16.

ODD FELLOWS TEXT BOOK AND MANUAL. by Donald Paschal. Moss, revised edition, 1873. Illustrated. Very Good. $20.

O'DELL, SCOTT. *The Dark Canoe*. Boston, 1968 1st edition. Milton Johnson illustrator. Very Good in slightly worn dust jacket. $15.
Journey to Jericho. Boston, 1969 1st ed. Leonard Weisgard illus. Very Good in dust jacket. $15.

ODGERS, GEORGE. *The Air War Against Japan, 1943-1945*. Canberra, 1957. VG-Fine in dust jacket. $35-$50.

ODETS, CLIFFORD. *Three Plays*. NY, 1935 1st ed. Near Fine in chip dust jacket. $125.
Golden Boy. NY, 1937 1st ed. Signed. Near Fine in tanned dust jacket. $150. Very Good in worn DJ. $50.
Night Music. New York, 1940 1st edition. Fine in very good dust jacket. $125.
The Country Girl. New York, 1951 1st edition. Very Good in good dust jacket. $100.

ODUM, HOWARD. *The Negro and His Songs*. Univ. of North Carolina, 1925. Ex-library, o/w VG. $45.
Negro Workaday Songs. University of North Carolina, 1926 1st edition. $50-$65.

O'FAOLAIN, SEAN. *Come Back To Erin*. NY, 1940 1st American ed. VG in dust jacket. $50.
The Man Who Invented Sin. Devin Adair, 1948 1st American ed. Very Good in dust jacket. $40.
I Remember! I Remember!. Little Brown, 1961. Very Good in dust jacket. $8.

OFFICIAL AUTOMOBILE BLUE BOOK. 1920, Vol. 5, (IL, IA, MO) Good, map torn. $24.

OFFICIAL AUTOMOBILE TOURING GUIDE FOR 1924 Vol. I. Auto Blue Books, 1924 1st ed. VG. $24.

OFFICIAL BASEBALL GUIDE. J.G.T. Spink. No place, 1950. Paperback. Near Fine. $40.

OFFICIAL BASEBALL REGISTER. Sporting News, 1940 edition. Blue cloth covers. VG. $39.
Sporting News, 1976 edition. Paper covers. Fine. $12.

OFFICIAL GUIDE BOOK OF THE FAIR. CENTURY OF PROGRESS, CHICAGO, 1933. Exposition Pub., 1933. Very Good. $12-$15.

OFFICIAL GUIDE TO ST. LOUIS WORLD'S FAIR. 1904 1st edition. Fine. $15.

OFFICIAL GUIDE BOOK TO THE NEW YORK WORLD'S FAIR, 1939. Exposition Pub., 1939. Fine, no DJ. $24. Another, Very Good. $12.

OFFICIAL HISTORY OF THE FIFTH DIVISION U.S.A. RED DIAMOND DIV. (WWI). 1919 1st ed., 424 pages, 11 large tissue maps. ½ leather bound. Fine. $115.

OFFICIAL HISTORY OF THE IMPROVED ORDER OF RED MEN. Davis Bros. 1964 1st ed. 810 pgs. Fine. $25.

OFFICIAL HISTORY OF THE NATIONAL LEAGUE. (75th Anniv., 1951). Very Good. $24.

OFFICIAL HISTORY OF THE ST. LOUIS 1904 FAIR. 500 pages. 1904 1st ed. Worn spine. $35.

OFFICIAL RECORDS OF THE UNION & CONFEDERATE NAVIES. Washington, 1895. 16 volumes of 30 volume set. Very Good. $200. Various single volumes. 1895-1914. $20-$25 each.

OFFICIAL SOUVENIR BOOK, NEW YORK WORLD'S FAIR, 1939. Ringbound, loose cover. $28.

O'FLAHERTY, LIAM. *The Informer*. New York, 1925 1st American edition. Rebound in morocco. Inscribed, signed. Very Good. $370. Same. New York, Penguin paperback, 1st edition. Very Good. $15.
Two Lovely Beasts. New York, 1950 1st edition. Very Good in dust jacket. $40.

OGDEN, PETER SKENE. *Traits of American Indian Life & Character*. Grabhorn Press, 1933. VG - Fine. $85-$120.

OGG, FREDERIC A. *The Opening of the Mississippi*. NY, Macmillan, 1904 1st ed. Very Good. $40-$65.
The Old Northwest-Ohio Valley and Beyond. Yale Univ., 1921 subsequent ed. Fine. $15.

OGLESBY and HALE. *History of Grant County, Indiana*. Chicago, 1886. Fair, spine replaced, taped hinges. $45.
History of Michigan City, Indiana. E. J. Widdell, 1908 1st edition. Very Good. $60.

O'HARA, JOHN. *Appointment in Samarra*. New York, 1934 1st edition. Author's 1st book. Very Good in dust jacket. $200-$300. No dust jacket. $50-$100.
Pal Joey. NY, 1940 1st ed. Very Good in dust jacket. $85.
Sweet and Sour. NY, 1954 1st ed. Random House, Near Fine in dust jacket. $15.
From the Terrace. NY, 1958 1st ed. Random House. Fine in dust jacket. $30. VG in dust jacket. $15.

O'HARA, MARY. *Thunderhead, Son of Flicka*. Lippincott, 1943. Good-Very Good. $8-$10.
Green Grass of Wyoming. Philadelphia, 1946 1st ed. Very Good in dust jacket. $15.

OKA, HIDEYUKI. *How to Wrap Five Eggs*. No place, 1967 1st American ed. VG in dust jacket. $125.

OKAKURA, KAKUZO. *The Book of Tea*. New York, 1906. Very Good. $35.
The Ideals of the East. London, 1920. $60.

O'KEEFE & MERRITT COOK BOOK. Circa 1930s, 1st edition. 70 pgs. $8-$10.

O'KEEFFE, GEORGIA. *Georgia O'Keeffe*. NY, 1976 1st ed. VG-Fine in dust jacket. $125-$250.

OLCOTT, FRANCES J. *The Adventures of Haroun El Raschid and Other Tales From the Arabian Nights*. Henry Holt, 1926. Gilt-dec. red cloth. Willy Pogany illus. Good-Very Good. $75. Another, 1925 reprint of 1913 original. Very Good-Near Fine. $55.

OLCOTT, HENRY S. *Old Diary Leaves*. (Theosophical Society). No place, 1895-1904, 3 vols. VG. $65.

OLCOTT, WILLIAM T. *Star Lore of All Ages*. NY, 1911 1st edition. Good. $60.
Sun Lore of All Ages. NY, 1914 1st ed. Fine. $65.
The Book of the Stars for Young People. NY, 1923. Spine spotted, extremities worn. Good. $40. VG. $50.
A Field Book of the Stars. NY, 1935 3rd revised ed. Good in dust jacket. $15. Same, 1936. Very Good in DJ. $40.

OLD MOTHER HUBBARD. Star Soap Company give-away. Children's picture story booklet. 1890's. $20-$30.

OLDER, MRS. FREMONT. *California Missions and Their Romances*. New York, Tudor reprint, 1945. Fine in dust jacket. $15.
Love Stories of Old California. NY, 1940. Very Good, no dust jacket. $20.

OLDS, ROBERT. *Helldiver Squadron*. Dodd & Mead, 1944. Good-VG in dust jacket. $20-$45. 1980 reprint. $15-$20.

OLIPHANT, MRS. *Victorian Age of English Literature*. NY, Lovell Coryell. 1892. 2 volumes. Good-VG. $75-$150.
Cousin Mary. Partridge, London, later edition. Good-Very Good. $20-$35.

OLIVER, A. *Auguste Edouarts' Silhouettes of Eminent Americans 1839-1844*. 1977, Chrittsville, 1st ed. Very Good in dust jacket. $35.

OLIVER, GEORGE A. *Early Motor Cars, 1904-1915*. Stephen Daye Press, 1960. One of 740 copies, 1st American ed. Illus. Very Good in slipcase. $45.
Early Motor Cars, 1919-1930. Stephen Daye Press, 1961. One of 250 copies. Signed. Very Good in dust jacket and slipcase. $45.

OLIVER, RAYMOND. *La Cuisine*. Tudor, 1965 1st American ed. Very Good in dust jacket. $30.

OLLIVANT, ALFRED. *Bob, Son of Battle*. NY, 1898 1st ed. Author's 1st book. Fine. $125. Another, stained. Good. $15. NY, 1901 edition. Worn covers. Good. $20. 1904 edition. Very Good-Fine. $35. Grosset & Dunlap, 1940s. Very Good in dust jacket. $8.

OLMSTEAD, FREDERICK LAW. *A Journey in the Seaboard Slave States*. NY, 1856. Rebound. NF. $85.
The Cotton Kingdom. NY,1861 1st ed. in 2 vols. Green cloth, ex-lib. $60. Knopf, 1953 reprint. Good, no DJ. $12.

OLSEN, JACK. *The Bridge at Chappaquiddick* . Boston, 1970 1st ed. Very Good in dust jacket. $47.

OLSEN, OLUF. *Two Eggs On My Plate*. Chicago, 1952. Good-VG in dust jacket. $15-$25.

OLYMPIC GAMES, 1968 OFFICIAL REPORT. 4 vols., in Spanish & German. $250 each.

OLYMPIC GAMES, 1980 OFFICIAL REPORT. Lake Placid New York, 2 volumes. $175 pair.

OMAN, CHARLES. *Doctors Aweigh: The Story of the U.S. Navy Medical Corps in Action*. NY, 1943 1st ed. G. $16.

OMWAKE, JOHN. *The Conestoga Six-Horse Bell Teams of Eastern Pennsylvania*. Cincinnati OH, 1930. Very Good. $125-$175.

O'NEAL, BILL. *Encyclopedia of Western Gun-Fighters*. Norman OK, 1979 1st ed. VG-F in dust jacket. $40-$65.

O'NEILL, EUGENE. *Thirst and Other One-Act Plays*. Boston, 1914 1st ed. Author's 1st book. Fine. $425.
All God's Chillun Got Wings and Welded. NY, 1924 1st edition. Good. $25.
Desire Under the Elms. Boni, 1925 1st ed. VG. $100.
Lazarus Laughed. NY, 1927 1st American edition. Very Good in dust jacket. $125.
Strange Interlude. NY, 1928 1st ed. Fine in fine DJ. $125.
Emperor Jones . NY, 1928. Alexander King illus. Very Good in slipcase. $200.
Dynamo. Liveright, 1929 1st ed. Good in DJ. $100.
The Hairy Ape. Liveright, 1929 1st ed. One of 775 copies. Dust jacket, boxed. $250.
Anna Christie. Liveright, 1930 1st ed. One of 775 copies. Very Good in dust jacket. Boxed. $250.
Ah Wilderness NY, 1933 1st ed. Good in DJ. $40.
Days Without End. R-H, 1934 1st ed. G in DJ. $75.
A Moon for The Misbegotten. NY, 1952 1st ed. Fine in clipped dust jacket. $75.
Long Day's Journey Into Night. New Haven, 1956 1st edition. Near Fine. $75.

O'NEILL, EUGENE. (In Magazines). *Smart Set*. Oct, 1917. "The Long Voyage Home", 1st published play. $35-$50.

O'NEILL, ROSE (All are illustrated by the author.)
The Loves of Edwy. Lothrop, 1904. VG. $35-$75.
Lady in the White Vail. Harper, 1909. VG. $50-$95.
The Kewpie Kutouts. Stokes, 1914. VG. $500 and up.
Kewpie Primer. Stokes, 1916. VG. $95-$160.
The Kewpies & Dotty Darling. 1912. VG. $150-$250.
Master-Mistress. Knopf, 1922. VG. $35-$65.
The Jell-O Girl Entertains. no date (1920). $65-$100.

O'NEILL, ROSE (In Magazines). *Good Housekeeping* featuring Rose O'Neill's famous Kewpie Dolls, 1914-1919 issues. $15-30 each.

ONO, YOKO. *Grapefruit*. John Lennon introduction. Near Fine in dust jacket. $25.

OPERATION CROSSROADS. NY, 1946. Pictorial record of A-bomb tests. $45-$80.

OPIE, IONA. *The Oxford Nursery Rhyme Book*. Oxford, Clarendon Press, 1955. VG in DJ. $30-$45.

OPIE and OPIE. *Oxford Dictionary of Nursery Rhymes*. Oxford, Clarendon Press, 1952 edition. VG in DJ. $50.

OPPENHEIM, E. PHILLIPS. *The Great Secret*. Boston, 1908 1st American ed. Very Good. $18.
The Governors. Boston,1909 1st ed. Illus. VG. $15.
Havoc. NY, 1911. Howard Chandler Christy illus. Good in dust jacket. $12.
The Double Life of Mr. Alfred Burton. Boston, 1913 1st American ed. Very Good. $18.
The Treasure House of Martin Hew. Boston, 1929 1st American ed. Signed. Rubbed hinges, o/w VG. $50.
Crooks in the Sunshine. Boston, 1933 1st American ed. Near Fine in good dust jacket. $35.
The Battle of Basinghall Street. Boston, 1935 1st American ed. Fine in chipped dust jacket. $35.
General Besserley's Puzzle Box. Boston, 1935 1st edition. Fine in dust jacket. $45.

OPPENHEIMER, J. R. *Science and the Common Understanding*. New York 1954 1st ed. Good-VG. $20-$30.

OPTIC, OLIVER (William T. Adams). *The Do-Somethings*. Boston, 1879. No. 12, Riverdale series. VG. $20.
Our Standard Bearer, Life of Ulysses S. Grant. Boston, 1868. Good-VG. $30-$40.
The Yacht Club. Lee & Shepherd. 1873. VG. $21.
American Boys Afloat. Boston, 1893 VG plus. $35.
Isles of the Sea. 1877. Fine. $75.
Blue & Gray on Land. 1894 1st ed. VG. $35.
Little by Little, or Cruise of the Flyaway. Lee and Shepherd, no date, Good-VG. $10-$15.

ORCUTT, WILLIAM D. *The Flower of Destiny*. Chicago, 1905 1st ed. Charlotte Weber illus. Very Good. $125.

In Quest of the Perfect Book. Boston, 1926. Illus. $25. Another, signed. Fine. $125.
The Magic of the Book. Boston, 1930 1st trade ed. Fine. $65. VG in dust jacket. $30. Signed, 1 of 375. $100.

ORCZY, BARONESS. *The Gates of Kami*. Dodd Mead, 1907 1st ed. Very Good. $35.
The Elusive Pimpernel. London, 1908. Slight cover wear, some yellowing. Good. $15.
Eldorado. London, 1913 1st ed. Very Good. $20-$40.

ORDWAY, SAMUEL H. *Conservation Handbook*. New York, 1949. Good-Very Good. $15-$30.

THE OREGON TRAIL. NY, 1939, Federal Writers Project. American Guide series. VG in dust jacket. $35.

O'REILLY, MAURICE. *The GoodYear Story*. New York, Benjamin, 1983 1st ed. New in dust jacket. $15.

ORGEL, DORIS. *Sarah's Room*. New York, Harper's, 1963 1st edition. Maurice Sendak illustrator. Near Fine in clip dust jacket. $110 auction.

ORMES, ROBERT. *Tracking Ghost Railroads in Colorado*. Colorado Springs, 1975. Fine in pictorial wraps. $18.

ORMOND, CLYDE. *Complete Book of Hunting*. 1969 13th printing, Harper. Very Good. $10.
Bear! Stackpole, 1961. VG in worn dust jacket. $18.

ORMSBEE, THOMAS. *Early American Furniture makers*. Tudor, 1936 2nd ed. Good-VG. $10-$15.
Collecting Antiques in America. 1940 1st ed. VG. $20.
Field Guide to Victorian Furniture. Bonanza reprint, 1950s. Very Good. $8.

ORNDUFF, DONALD. *The Hereford in America*. Kansas City, 1957 1st edition. Very Good in dust jacket. $35-$75. 1960 2nd edition. $25.

ORR, BOBBY. *Orr on Ice*. Prentice Hall, 1970 1st ed. Very Good-Fine in dust jacket. $12-$15.

ORR, JOHN W. *Pictorial Guide to the Falls of Niagara*. Buffalo NY, 1852 1st ed. Engravings, maps. Loose pages. Some damp stains. $40.

ORTON, JAMES. *Underground Treasures: How and Where to Find Them*. Hartford, 1872 1st edition. Light foxing, otherwise Very Good. $200.

ORWELL, GEORGE. *Down and Out in Paris and London*. London, 1933 1st ed. Author's 1st book. VG. $185-$250.
Animal Farm: A Fairy Story. New York, 1946 1st American edition. Worn cover. $65. 1950s Book Club edition. Very Good in dust jacket. $8.

Nineteen Eighty-Four. New York, Harcourt, 1949 1st American edition. Very Good-Fine in dust jacket. $150-$250. London, 1949 1st English edition. Very Good in repaired. dust jacket. $500.

Shooting an Elephant and Other Essays. NY, 1950 1st American ed. Near Fine in dust jacket. $55.

The Road to Wigan Pier. NY, 1958 1st American edition. Fine in dust jacket. $75.

OSBORNE, JOHN. *The Entertainer*. London, 1947 1st ed. Fine in dust jacket. $30.

OSBORNE, WALTER. *The Quarter Horse*. Grosset and Dunlap, no date. VG in dust jacket. $16.

Thoroughbred World. New York, 1971 1st ed. Fine. $35.

OSGOOD, E. S. *Day of the Cattleman*. Minneapolis, 1929 1st ed. 14 plates, maps. Very Good. $125.

OSKISON, JOHN M. *Tecumseh and His Times*. NY,1938 1st ed. G-VG in dust jacket. $30-$50.

OSLER, WILLIAM. *Principles and Practice of Medicine*. New York, 1892. Later issue of 1st edition. Good plus. $550. 1894 edition. Very Good. $250. Same. New York, 1897 2nd edition. Fair exterior, interior Very Good. $55. Same, New York, 1906 6th edition. Very Good. $100.

Science and Immortality: Ingersoll. Boston, 1904 1st edition. Very Good. $40-$60.

An Alabama Student and Other Biographical Essays. Oxford, 1908 1st edition. Covers rubbed, stained. $50. London, 1929 2nd impression. $40.

The Old Humanities and the New Science. Boston, 1920. Almost new in dust jacket. $125.

Evolution of Modern Medicine. New Haven, 1921 1st edition. Very Good. $175.

A Way of Life. Baltimore MD, 1932 1st ed. Browning. fair in dust jacket. $40.

OTERO, MIGUEL A. *The Real Billy The Kid*. NY, Rufus Rockwell, 1936 1st edition. Very Good-Fine. $100-$150.

OTIS, F. N. *Illustrated History of the Panama Railroad*. NY, 1862. Very Good. $85.

OTIS, JAMES. *The Aeroplane at Silver Fox Farm*. Crowell, 1911 1st ed. Green pictorial cloth. G-VG. $15.

Toby Tyler, or 10 Weeks with a Circus. New York, Harper, 1920. Richard Rodgers illustrator. Very Good in dust jacket. $15. Winston,1937. Everett Shin cover illustrator. Very Good. $25. Saalfield, no date. $8.

With the Swamp Fox. A. L. Burt, 1899. Good. $9.

Cruise of the Sally D. Grosset & Dunlap, no date. Very Good in dust cover. $12.

Mr. Stubb's Brother. Harper, 1910. No dust cover. $6.

OUGHTERSON, A. W. (Editor). *Medical Effects of the Atomic Bomb in Japan*. NY, 1956 1st ed. Ex-library. Near Very Good. $75.

OUIDA (LOUISE DE LA RAMEE). *Under Two Flags*. Philadelphia, 1896. 2 vols. 1st Amer. ed. illus. Mint. $250.

Two Little Wooden Shoes. Lippincott, 1897. Pict. cloth cover. $10-$15.

The Nurnberg Stove. Macmillan, 1928 1st ed. Frank Boyd illus. Little Library. Overall Very Good. $12.

Dog of Flanders. Grosset and Dunlap, no date. Very Good in dust jacket. $12.

OUIMET, F. *The Game of Golf*. Boston, 1932 1st edition. Good-Very Good. $25-$45.

"OUR FAVORITES." Charity Cookbooks issued by various ladies' clubs, churches, civic organizations. 1900s-1960s. $10-$15 each. Deluxe eds., up to $25. Pre-1900, up to $50.

OUSPENSKY, P. D. *Tertium Organum*. NY, 1964 3rd ed. Very Good in dust jacket. $15.

OUT OF VERMONT KITCHENS. Rutland Vermont. Local cookbook, 1945 10th printing. Good. $15.

OUTERBRIDGE, PAUL (Photographer). *Photographing in Color*. New York, 1940 1st edition. Color plates. Very Good. $200.

Paul Outerbridge, Jr: Photographs. NY, 1980 1st ed. Fine in dust jacket. $100.

OUTLAND, CHARLES. *Stagecoaching on El Camino Real*. Arthur H. Clark, 1973 1st ed. Fine in DJ. $24.

OVERBECK, ALICIA. *Sven the Wise and Svea the Kind*. NY, 1932 1st ed. Gustaf Tenggren illus. VG. $55.

OVERTON, RICHARD C. *Burlington West*. Cambridge MA, 1941 1st ed. Signed. Very Good. $50.

Burlington Route, A History. NY, 1965. Very Good in dust jacket. $20-$35.

OWEN, ROBERT DALE. *Hints on Public Architecture*. NY, 1849. 15 tinted plates, 99 woodcuts. Poor. $520.

OWENS, BILL (Photographer). *Our Kind of People: American Groups and Rituals*. San Francisco, 1975 1st edition. Signed. Fine in dust jacket. $60.

Working (I Do It For the Money). NY, 1977 1st ed. Signed. Fine in dust jacket. $60.

OWENS, LEE. *American Square Dances of the West and Southwest*. No place, 1949 1st edition. Very Good in dust jacket. $15.

P

PACK, CHARLES L. *War Garden Victorious*. Philadelphia, Lippincott, 1919. Very Good-Fine. $20.

PACKER, ELEANOR LEWIS. *A Story of "Our Gang"*. Whitman Pub., 1929. Very Good. $35.
A Day with "Our Gang". Whitman Pub, 1929 1st ed. $18. Another, color-tinted photos still intact. NF. $55 auction.

PACKARD, ALPHEUS M. *A Guide to the Study of Insects*. 1889 edition, Henry Holt & Co. VG. $55.

PACKARD, FRANK L. *Two Stolen Idols*. Doran, 1927 1st ed. Very Good in dust jacket. $60.

PADDLEFORD, CLEMENTINE. *How America Eats*. Scribners, 1960 1st ed. Very Good in dust jacket. $15-$30.

PAGE, ARTHUR W. *The Bell Telephone System*. Harper, 1941 1st ed. Very Good. $8-$10.

PAGE, THOMAS N. *In Ole Virginia*. Scribners, 1887 1st ed. VG-Near Fine. $75-$150. NY, 1896 1st illus. ed. Frost, Pyle and others. $25-$50. Fair, water stained. $12.
Social Life in Virginia Before the War. Cowles, 1898. Very Good. $10-$15.
2 Little Confederates. Scribner, 1888 2nd printing, illustrated. $40-$50. Same, 1926 and 1927 reprint in pictorial covers. $12-$25.
The Old Gentleman of the Black Stock. Scribners, 1900. H. C. Christy illus. G-VG. $15-$30.
Captured Santa Claus. New York, 1902 1st edition. W. L. Jacobs illustrator. Near Fine. $50.
Bred in the Bone. NY, 1904 1st ed. Near Fine. $40.
Tommy Trot's Visit to Santa Claus. New York, 1908. Very Good. $38.
The Coast of Bohemia. New York, Scribners, 1906 1st American edition. $30.
John Marvel Assistant. Scribners, NY, 1909 1st ed. Orig. green cloth. Fine in uncommon dust jacket. $100. Same without dust jacket. $30-$40.
Among the Camps, or Young People's Stories of the (Civil) War. NY, 1912. Illus. $20.
Novels, Stories, Sketches & Poems. Scribner, 1912. 18 volumes. $36.
History and Preservation of Mount Vernon, 1858-1910, NY, 1910 1st ed. Gilt on red covers. Fine. $25.

PAGE, VICTOR W. *The Model T Ford Car: Its Construction, Operation and Repair*. NY, 1917. Illus. Foldout section view. VG. $65. Another, worn. $40.
Motorcycles, Sidecars & Cyclecars. NY, 1918 1st ed. Good. $35-$70. 1921 revised and enlarged. 691 pgs. $100.
Automobile Starting, Lighting and Ignition. Henley, 1919 5th ed. Very Good. $15.
Everybody's Aviation Guide. Henley, 1928 1st ed. Very Good in dust jacket. $15.
Modern Aircraft - Principles, Operation. Henley, 1928 revised edition. Fine, no dust jacket. $20-$40.
Model T Ford Car, Including Fordson Farm Tractor. NY, Henley, 1926 revised ed. $25.
Modern Gasoline Automobile. NY, Henley, 1912 1st edition, 1st state. $25-$35.

PAIGE, CHARLES. *Experiences of Lieut. Charles C. Paige in the Civil War of 1861*. Journal-Transcript Press, 1911. Inscribed by author. Good-Very Good. $375.

PAINE, ALBERT BIGELOW. *The Great White Way*. NY, 1901 1st edition. Very Good. $40.
The Arkansas Bear. Altemus, 1902. Frank Ver Beck illustrator. Good. $10.
Thomas Nast: His Period and His Pictures. NY, 1904 1st edition. Very Good. $60-$125.
Mark Twain, A Biography. New York, 1912 1st edition. 3 volumes. $45-$95.
The Hollow Tree Snowed-In Books. Harpers, 1912. Ex-library, rebound. Stain, inside VG. $24.
Mr. Rabbit's Wedding. Harpers, 1923. J. M. Conde illustrator. Very Good. $30.
Boys Life of Mark Twain. Harpers, 1944 24th edition. Fine in dust jacket. $8.

THE PAINTER, GILDER AND VARNISHER'S COMPANION. Philadelphia, 1858. 7th ed. $75.

PALAZZO, TONY FEDERICO. *The Flying Squirrel*. NY, 1951 1st ed. Illus. by author. Fine in vg DJ. $30.
The Great Othello: The Story of a Seal. NY, 1952 1st ed. Illus. by author. VG in tattered dust jacket. $25.

PALEY, GRACE. *The Little Disturbances of Man*. NY, 1959 1st ed. 1st book. Very Good in DJ. $60.
Enormous Changes at the Last Minute. NY, 1974 1st edition. Inscribed. Fine in fine dust jacket. $125.

Later the Same Day. NY, 1985 1st ed. Signed. Fine in fine dust jacket. $45. Unsigned in Fine dust jacket. $25.

PALLI, MARCO. *Peaks and Llamas*. NY, 1949. Revised, reset. Fine in vg dust jacket. $35.

PALLISER, MRS. BURY. *A History of Lace*. London, 1875 3rd ed. $80. NY, 1902 4th rev. ed. Very Good. $150.

PALMER, ARNOLD. *Arnold Palmer's Best 54 Golf Holes*. Doubleday, 1977 1st ed. 206 pgs. VG. $16-$20.

PALMER, BROOKS. *The Book of American Clocks*. Macmillan Co., NY, 1950. Lightly soiled dust jacket, chipped. $20. 1969 3rd ed. Fine in dust jacket. $14.

PALMER, ARTHUR J. *Riding High: The Story of the Bicycle*. E. P. Dutton, NY, 1956 1st ed. Good in DJ. $30.

PALMER, RICHARD F. *The "Old Line Mail" Stagecoach Days in Upstate New York*. North Country Books, 1977 1st ed. Very Good in dust jacket. $30.

PAPASHVILY, GEORGE and HELEN. *Yes and No Stories: A Book of Georgian Folk Tales*. NY, 1946 1st ed. Illus. and inscribed by authors. VG in worn DJ. $30.

PARET, J. P. *Lawn Tennis Lessons for Beginners*. New York, 1926. Very Good. $45.

PARKER, DOROTHY. *Men I'm Not Married To*. Garden City, 1922 1st ed. Author's 1st book. VG in dust jacket. $100-$200. Fine. $300.
Sunset Gun. NY, 1928 signed 1st ed. $100-$150. Trade edition in dust jacket. $50. Dial reprint, same year. $7.
Death and Taxes. NY, 1931. $15-$25.
Here Lies... NY, 1939. Very Good in dust jacket. $18-$24.
After Such Pleasures. NY, 1933 1st ed. One of 250 copies, signed. VG in slipcase. $125-$190.
Not So Deep as a Well. NY, 1936. VG in dust jacket. $25.

PARKER, GEORGE F. *Iowa Pioneer Foundations*. Iowa State Hist. Soc., 1940. 2 vols. Fine in glassine wraps. $35.

PARKER, J. W. *The History, Philosophy, and Uses of Human Magnetism, or Mesmerism*. Canfield OH, 1846. Paperbound. Very Good. $250.

PARKER, ROBERT ALLERTON. *A Yankee Saint: John Humphrey Noyes & the Oneida Community*. Putnam, 1935 1st ed. VG to Near Fine in DJ. $60-$75.

PARKER, ROBERT B. *The Godwulf Manuscript*. Boston, 1974 1st ed. The first Spenser novel. Slight foxing, o/w VG in clip DJ. $165. Another signed. Near Fine in DJ. $250.
God Save the Child. Boston, 1974 1st edition. Signed. Near Fine in dust jacket. $350.

Mortal Stakes. Boston, 1975 1st edition. Inscribed. Near Fine in dust jacket. $250.
The Judas Goat. Boston, 1978 1st ed. Fine in DJ. $85. Another, signed. Fine in dust jacket. Same price.
Looking for Rachel Wallace. NY, 1980 1st ed. Signed. Fine in fine dust jacket. $85.

PARKINSON, C. NORTHCOTE. *Parkinson's Law and Other Studies in Administration*. Boston, 1957 1st ed. Robert Osborn illus. VG in DJ. $58.
Devil to Pay. Houghton Mifflin, 1973 1st ed. Very Good-Fine in dust jacket. $15-$20.

PARKMAN, FRANCIS. *The California and OregonTrails*. 1849 1st edition. in 2 vols. $5,000-$12,000. 2nd issue. same year. $1,800.
The Oregon Trail. Boston, 1892 1st edition. Frederic Remington illus. VG. $250. Another, mint, unopened. $375. Same, rebound. $75. Boston, 1901 edition. $25-$50. Boston, 1925. N. C. Wyeth illus. VG. $50-$95. Farrar, 1931 edition. $15-$25. Limited Edition Club, 1943. $75-$95. Doubleday, 1945. Signed by artist, Benton. $150. Literary Guild, 1946 edition. $8-$10.
The Works of Francis Parkman. 1899 edition, 16 vol. set. $200. Scribners, 1915 edition. 16 vols. $150.

PARKS, GORDON (Photographer). *In Love*. Lippincott, 1971 1st ed. Very Good in dust jacket. $45.
Voices in the Mirror. NY, 1990 1st edition. Signed. Fine in dust jacket. $45.

PARLOA, MARIA (Food editor at Good Housekeeping Magazine). *The Appledore Cook Book*. 1878. $70-$85.
Miss Parloa's New Cook Book. Bos, 1881 1st. $45-$60.
Camp Cookery. 1878. $65-$80.
Kitchen Companion. 1887. $45-$60.
Miss Parloa's Young Housekeeper. Bos., 1900. $45-$75.

PARRIS, JOHN. *Mountain Bred*. Parris, 1967 2nd printing. Fine in dust jacket. $18.
These Storied Mountains. Citizen-Times, 1972 1st ed. Signed by author. VG in dust jacket. $18.
Mountain Cooking. Ashville, 3rd printing, 1982. F. $15.

PARRISH, MAXFIELD (Illustrator). *Poems of Childhood*. By Eugene Field. NY, 1904. VG in DJ. $100-$175.
The Arabian Nights. New York, 1909. Near Fine. $225. 1919 edition, worn. $100. 1935 ed. Very Good. $40-$80.
Dream Days. 1902 and *Golden Age*. 1904. 2 volumes at auction $82. Dealers asking $75 each and up.
Troubador Tales. Bobbs-Merrill, 1903. $75. 1929. $25.
A Golden Treasury of Songs and Lyrics. Francis Palgrave, ed. Duffield, 1911. Near Fine. $100-$200.
Annual of Advertising Art. Pub. Print. Co., 1920s editions. Very Good. $35-$70 each.
The Knave of Hearts. By Louise Saunders. New York, 1925 1st edition. Very Good-Fine. $800-$950. Same,

cover erasures, otherwise Very Good condition. $500. Covers by Parrish. 7 magazines, 1897-1935. $10-$80.

PARRY, ALBERT. *Garrets and Pretenders*. Covici-Friede, 1933 1st edition. Cover stains. Good. $20.

PARRY, EDWIN S. *Betsy Ross, Quaker Rebel*. PA Anniv. edition, Winston, 1932. Fine, no DJ. $15.

PARRY, JUDGE. *Don Quixote*. Lane, 1900. W. Crane illus. VG. $75-$100. Same, Dodd, 1926. VG. $50-$75.

PARSON, ALBERT and others. *The Accused The Accusers. The Eight Chicago Anarchists in Court*. Chicago, Socialistic Pub. Soc., 1886. No covers, disbound. $250.

PARSON, HORATIO A. *Steele's Book of Niagara Falls*. Buffalo, Oliver Steele, 1840 8th edition. Worn, foxed, map wrinkled. $45.

PARSONS, JOHN. *A Tour Through Indiana in 1840*. Kale Milner Rabb, editor. NY, 1920 1st ed. in DJ. $40.

PARSONS, JOHN E. *Henry Deringer's Pocket Pistol*. NY, 1952 1st ed. Very Good. $45.
The First Winchester. NY, 1955. VG in DJ. $35.
The Peace-Maker and Its Rivals. NY, 1955 4th edition, William Morrow. Very Good. $45.

PARTON, JAMES. *Daughters of Genius*. Philadelphia, 1885 1st ed. 22 portrait plates. Very Good. $100.

PASTERNAK, BORIS. *Doctor Zhivago*. Pantheon, (1958) 1st American ed. Mint in box. $65. Same, Fine in dust jacket. $50. 1959 1st ed. Very Good in dust jacket. $45.

PATCHEN, KENNETH. *Before the Brave*. NY, 1936 1st ed. Author's 1st book. Damp stain, fading, o/w VG. $25-$75.
Cloth of the Tempest. New York, 1943. Includes "Easy Rider". VG plus. $85. Another in DJ. $125.
Red Wine & Yellow Hair. New Directions, 1949 1st edition. Very Good in dust jacket. $75.
Poemscapes. No place, 1958 1st ed., paperback. Inscribed. Fine. $150.

PATCHIN, FRANK. *Battleship Boys*, various titles in series. Saalfield, 1910-1916. $8-$15.

PATENTS, COMMISSIONER OF. *Annual Report for 1862. Vol II*. Good. $18.
1868 Vol. III. Very Good. $25.
Official Gazette of U. S. Patent Office. 1919 weekly, 150 pages. Illustrated. $34.

PATENT OFFICE REPORT. 1861 Vol. 2. G.P.O., Wash. D.C. 1863. 440 pgs. War related illus. $35.

PATER, WALTER. *Marius The Epicurean*. London, 1924. Very Good. $60-$100.
Studies in Art and Poetry. Mosher Press, 1924. Small spine slit, o/w Very Good in slipcase. $25.
The Marriage of Cupid and Psyche. Limited Editions Club, NY, 1951. Near Fine in slipcase. $175.

PATERSON, KATHERINE. *The Sign of the Chrysanthemum*. NY, 1973 4th printing. Author's 1st book. Peter Landa illus. Very Good in dust jacket. $12.
The Great Gilly Hopkins. NY, 1978 1st ed. Illus. by author. Fine in dust jacket. $50.
Jacob I Have Loved. New York, 1980 1st edition. Very Good-Fine in dust jacket. $25-$50.

PATON, ALAN. *Too Late the Phalarope*. NY, 1953 1st American ed. Fine in DJ. $15. Same, Capetown. $75.
Tales From a Troubled Land. NY, 1961 1st American ed. Very Good in dust jacket. $25.
Cry, the Beloved Country. Franklin Library, 1978. Reissue. New introduction by Paton. Signed. Fine. $75.

PATRICK. Q. *The Grindle Nightmare*. NY, 1935 1st ed. VG in slightly worn DJ. $200. Same, ex-lib. in poor DJ. $19.
Death and the Maiden. NY, 1939 1st ed. Near Fine in slightly frayed dust jacket. $125.

PATTEN, WILLIAM. *Fairy & Wonder Tales*. Collier, 1918. J. W. Smith illus. Red cloth. $35-$60.
Poems Old & New. Collier, 1918. Jr. Classic. VG. $50.

PATTERNMAKING EQUIPMENT AND OPERATIONS. International Textbook Co., Scranton PA, 1923. Good-Very Good. $10-$20.

PATTERSON, ROBERT. *A Narrative of the Campaign in the Valley of the Shenandoah in 1861*. Philadelphia, 1865 1st ed. Signed by author. G-VG. $100-$125.

PATTON, JACOB HARRIS. *Natural Resources of the United States*. New York, Appleton, 1888. Unopened. $60.

PATTON, GENERAL GEORGE. *War As I Knew It*. Boston, 1947 1st ed. Very Good in dust jacket. $28.

PAUL, ELLIOT. *Indelible*. Boston, 1922 1st edition. Author's 1st book. Very Good. $100.
The Last Time I Saw Paris. NY, 1942 1st ed. Very Good in good dust jacket. $35.

PAULDING, JAMES K. *Westward Ho*. NY, 1832 1st ed. 2 vols. Very Good. $300.
Life of Washington. NY, 1836, Harpers Family Library. 2 vol. Good. $37.
Koningsmarke, or Old Times in the New World. New York, Harper, 1836 new revised edition. Leather, worn, scuffed, foxed, $15.

PAULLIN, CHARLES. *Commodore John Rodgers of the American Navy, 1773-1838, A Biography*. Cleveland, 1910. Very Good. $40.

PAULSEN, MARTHA. *Toyland: An Animated Book*. Akron, Saalfield Pub., 1944 1st ed. 4 moveable color plates by Julian Wehr. Good in DJ. $154 auction.

THE P.C. AND CO. KEYSTONE COOK BOOK. Paine, Diehl and Co. No place, 1888. Good-VG. $35.

PEAKE, MERVYN. *Captain Slaughterhouse Drops Anchor*. London, 1939 1st ed. Author's 1st book. Illus. by author. Fine in chip dust jacket. $2,500. Another, VG in DJ. $450.
Rhymes Without Reason. London, 1944 1st ed. Very Good in worn dust jacket. $220-$250.
Titus Groan. London, 1946 1st ed. VG in poor DJ. $600-$650. Same. NY, 1946 1st American ed. Very Good in very good dust jacket. $55-$100.
Gormenghast. London, 1950 1st. VG in DJ. $100-$300.
Titus Alone. London, 1959 1st ed. Fine in DJ. $200.
A Book of Nonsense. London,1972. Previously unpublished poems and drawings. Fine in fine DJ. $35.

PEALE, LOUIS T. *The History of the American Locomotive*. Philadelphia, 1887. Illustrated. Slightly stained covers, o/w Good. $75.

PEALE, NORMAN VINCENT. *The Power of Positive Thinking*. Prentice Hall, 1954. VG. $5.
Stay Alive All Your Life. Prentice Hill, 1957. Good. $5.

PEARL, MINNIE. *Minnie Pearl's Diary: An Inside Look*. 1953 1st ed. Near Fine. $35.

PEARSON, EDMUND. *Dime Novels*. Boston, 1929 1st ed. Very Good in chipped dust jacket. $40.

PEARSON, F. B. *Ohio History Sketches*. Columbus, 1903 1st edition. Good plus. $25.

PEARSON, JOHN. *The Life of Ian Fleming*. McGraw-Hill, 1966 1st ed. Very Good in dust jacket. $10.

PEARSON, T. G. (Editor). *Birds of America*. No date. Nature Lovers' Library. 4 vols. (vol. 4 is Mammals). $50. Another, Garden City, NY, 1942. 832 pgs. VG in fair DJ.$20. Same, 1936 edition. Worn. $12.

PEARY, JOSEPHINE. *The Snow Baby: A True Story*. NY, 1901 4th ed., Fred Stokes. Good-Very Good. $60-$75.

PEARY, ROBERT E. *Northward Over the Great Ice*. NY, 1898 1st ed. 2 vols. VG. $90-$150.
Snowland Folk. NY, 1904. Fair. $75.
Nearest the Pole. NY, 1907 1st ed. VG. $55-$125.
The North Pole. NY, 1910 1st ed. VG in tattered DJ. $85.

PEASE, HOWARD. *Jungle River*. Doubleday Doran, 1938 (1939). Pictorial black cloth. VG in DJ. $15.

PEAT, FERN BISEL (Illustrator). *Sugar Plum Tree & Other Verses*. By Eugene Field. Saalfield, 1930. VG.$45. Edge, spine wear, o/w Very Good. $45.
Friends of the Forest. By Frank Shankland. Saalfield, 1932. Light soiling. $25.
Round the Mulberry Bush. By Marion McNeil. Akron OH, 1933 1st ed. Very Good. $40.
The Cock, the Mouse and the Little Red Hen. Saalfield, 1932. Illus. by author. VG. $25.
Hansel and Gretel. Cleveland, 1932. VG. $25.
Mother Goose. Akron, 1939. Very Good. $40.
Birds. Saalfield Pub., 1943. Soft cover. 16 pgs. $15.

PEATTIE, DONALD CULROSS. *A Book of Hours*. NY, 1937. Lynd Ward illus. VG in DJ. $20.
The Story of the First Men. NY, 1937 1st ed. Naomi Averill illus. Very Good. $25.
The Road of a Naturalist. Boston, 1941 1st ed. Fine in fine dust jacket. $35.
Audubon's America. Boston, 1940 1st ed. 16 double pg. color plates. VG-NF. $30-$50. Revised 1940 ed. G. $20.
Immortal Village. Chicago, 1945. One of 500 copies. Paul Landacre illus. Signed by author and illustrator. Very Good in clip DJ. $175.

PECK. *Art of Fine Baking*. NY, 1961 BCE. G-VG. $8-$10.

PECK, GEORGE. *Peck's Bad Boy and His Pa*. Chicago, 1900. Very Good. $20.
Peck's Bad Boy With the Cowboys. No place, 1907. Very Good. $35. Worn condition. $15.
Peck's Uncle Ike and the Red Headed Boy. Thompson, 1899 1st edition. Good. $15.

PECK, JOHN M. *A New Guide for Emigrants to the West*. Boston, 1836 enlarged ed. Very Good. $175.
Peck's Tourist's Companion to Niagara Falls, Saratoga Springs, etc. NY, 1845. Fair-Good. $60.

PECK, H. *The Book of Rookwood Pottery*. NY, 1968 1st edition. Very Good in dust jacket. $45.

PECK, TAYLOR. *Round-Shot to Rockets*. Naval Institute, 1949 1st edition. Good-Very Good. $15-$35.

PECK, WALTER. *Shelley, His Life and Work*. Houghton Mifflin, 1927 1st ed. 2 vols. Good-Very Good. $40.

PECKHAM, HOWARD (Editor). *Narratives of Colonial America 1704-1765*. Lakeside Press, 1971. VG. $25.

PECKHAM, HOWARD. *Captured by Indians, True Tales of Pioneer Survivors*. New Brunswick, 1954 1st edition. Fine in torn dust jacket. $33.

PECKHAM, JOHN M. *Fighting Fire with Fire*. Walter R. Haessner Inc. NJ, 1972. Good-VG. $20.

PEDDER, JAMES. *The Farmers' Land-Measurer, or Pocket Companion*. Philadelphia, Thomas, Cowperthwait & Co., 1842. Leather, well-scuffed, split. $20.

PEDERSEN, A. *Polar Animals*. NY, 1966. Fine in DJ. $13.

PEEKE, HEWSON L. *Americana Ebriatis: The Favorite Tipple of Our Forefathers and the Laws and Customs Relating Thereto*. NY, Privately printed, 1917 1st ed. Very Good in vg dust jacket. $125.

PEER, FRANK SHERMAN. *The Hunting Field With Horse and Hound*. NY, 1910 1st ed. Illus. and photos. Spine bumped, frontpiece loose, o/w VG. $40.

PEET, BILL. *Dandy Lions*. Boston, 1964 1st edition. Fine in clip dust jacket. $60.
Kermit the Hermit. Boston, 1965 1st edition. Inscribed. Fine in clip dust jacket. $60.

PEGGY: A TALE OF HAIR. No author. Harry Linnell illus. NY, 1907 1st ed. Cover soiled o/w VG. $35.

PEIRCE, JOSEPHINE H. *Fire on the Hearth; The Evolution and Romance of the Heating Stove*. Springfield MA, 1951. Good to Fine in dust jacket. $25-$50.

PIERCE, PARKER. *The Adventures of "Antelope Bill" in the Indian War of 1862*. Marshall MN, 1898 1st ed. 243 pgs. A small crudely printed personal narrative in great demand. Pictorial front wrapper pasted on. Good-Very Good. $935 auction.
Antelope Bill. Apparently a later printing of "The Adventures." Drawings by Mary Mitchell. Minneapolis, 1962. 1 of 550. Fine. $25.

PEIXOTTO, ERNEST. *Romantic California*. NY, 1910 1st edition. Illus. by author. VG. $35-$45.
Our Hispanic Southwest. NY, 1916. Near Fine. $25.

PEMBERTON, MAX. *The Amateur Motorist*. Chicago, 1908. Illustrated. Good-Very Good. $75.

PENDERGAST, A. W. and W. P. WARE. *Cigar Store Figures in American Folk Art*. Chicago, 1953 1st ed. Illus. Very Good. $35-$60.

PENFIELD, EDWARD. *Spanish Sketches*. NY, 1911 1st edition. Illus. by author. Tipped-in color plates. Covers badly soiled. $65.

PENN, IRVING (Photographer). *Moments Preserved*. NY, 1960 1st ed. VG in slipcase. $250-$300.
Worlds in a Small Room. NY, 1974. VG in DJ. $75.

PENNELL, JOSEPH. *Joseph Pennell's Pictures of the Panama Canal*. Philadelphia and London, 1913 4th edition. Very Good. $40.
The Graphic Arts. University of Chicago, 1920 1st ed. Illus. Near Fine. $60.
Pen Drawing/Draughtsman. Macmillan, 1889. $75-$125.
Modern Illustration. Bell, 1895. Pyle illus. $40-$75.
The Glory of New York. Rudge, NY, 1926 1st ed. One of 355 copies, signed by Elizabeth Pennell. 24 watercolor plates. Very Good. $175.

PENNELL, JOSEPH (Illustrator). *The Alhambra*. By Washington Irving. NY, 1895. VG in DJ. $140.
French Cathedrals. By Elizabeth Pennell. NY, 1909 1st American edition. Very Good. $50.
Cycling. By Viscount Bury. Boston, Little Brown, 1887 1st Amer. edition. Very Good. $75.

PENROSE ANNUAL - REVIEW OF THE GRAPHIC ARTS. Hastings House 1958. Fine. $24.

PENNSYLVANIA STATE COMMISSION OF FISHERIES, 1897; 18 color fish plates; 16 color bird plates; numerous b/w photos, intact content, covers worn but tight. $65.

PERCY, WALKER. *The Moviegoer*. NY, 1961 1st ed. Near Fine in dust jacket. $1,600. Same, London, 1963 1st English edition. Very Good in dust jacket. $95.
Love in the Ruins. NY, 1971 1st ed. VG-F in DJ. $50-$75.
The Message in the Bottle. NY, 1975 1st edition, 2nd issue. Very Good in dust jacket. $60.
Lancelot. NY, 1977 1st edition. Signed. Fine in DJ. $75.

PERCY, WILLIAM A. *Lanterns on the Levee*. 1948 edition. Good in DJ. $15. Knopf, 1953 16th ed. Fine in DJ. $10.

PERELMAN, S. J. *Dawn Ginsberg's Revenge*. NY, 1929 1st ed. 2nd printing. VG-Fine in DJ. $300-$500.
Keep It Crisp. NY, 1946 1st ed. Fine in good DJ. $15.
Listen to the Mockingbird. NY, 1949 1st. F in vg DJ. $20.
The Ill-Tempered Clavicord. NY, 1952 1st edition. Fine in good dust jacket. $20.

PERKINS, D. A. W. *History of O'Brien County, Iowa From its Organization to the Present*. Sioux Falls, SD, 1897. First settlement, Indians, emigrants, grasshoppers, etc. Photos of people and businesses. $65-$150.

PERKINS, ELEANOR ELLIS. *News From Notown*. Boston, 1919 1st ed. Lucy Fitch Perkins illus. VG. $60.

PERKINS, FRANCES. *People at Work*. John Day, 1934 1st ed. VG in fair dust jacket. $25.
Roosevelt I Knew. New York, 1946. VG in DJ. $15-$20.

PERKINS, LAUREL. *Laurel Health Cookery*. 1911 edition. Soiled, worn, poor. $35.

PERKINS, LUCY. *The Spartan Twins*. Boston, 1918. Illus. by author. Very Good. $22.
The French Twins. Boston, 1918 1st ed. VG. $20.
The Indian Twins. Houghton Mifflin, 1930. $18-$24.

PERKINS and PECK. *Annals of the West - Discovery of Mississippi to 1850*. Albach, 1851 2nd ed. 818 pgs. Fair, reading copy. $68.

PERRAULT, CHARLES. *The Sleeping Beauty*. London, 1919 1st ed. Arthur Rackham illus. One of 850 copies. Signed by Rackham. Hand-made paper, etc. Fine in fine slipcase. $1,750.
Cinderella and Hansel and Gretel. American Crayon Co. 1943. Fern Bisel Peat illus. Pictorial wraps. Includes two puzzles. As new. $150. Scribner's, 1954. Signed by Marcia Brown illus. Very Good. $80.

PERRY, F. F. *Their Hearts Desire*. Dodd, 1909. H. Fisher color plates. Very Good. $50-$75.

PERRY, GEORGE SESSIONS. *Hackberry Cavalier*. New York, 1945. Very Good. $25.

PERRY, LILLA. *Chinese Snuff Bottles: The Adventures and Studies of a Collector*. Tuttle, 1971, 9th printing. $25.

PERRY, M and B. PARKE. *Patton and His Pistols*. Stackpole, 1957 1st edition. Fine. $45.

PERRY, RALPH BARTON. *Realms of Value*. Cambridge MA, 1954 1st edition. Very Good. $25.

PERSHING, HENRY. *Johnny Appleseed*. VA, Shenandoah, 1930 1st ed. G-VG. $20-$35. Another, ex-lib. Fair. $10.

PERSHING, JOHN J. *My Experiences in the World War*. New York, 1931. Author's autograph edition. 2 vols. VG in dust jacket. $100-$195. Same, cloth, trade ed. $30-$50.
Report of the 1st Army Exped. Forces. Fort Leavenworth, 1923. VG-Fine. $30-$40.

PETER, JOHN. *Masters of Modern Architecture*. NY, Braziller, 1958. Very Good. $25.

PETERKIN, JULIA. *Green Thursday*. NY, 1924 1st ed. One of 2,000 copies. Author's 1st book. Good. $75.
Black April. Indianapolis, 1927 1st ed. Fine in vg DJ. $60.
Bright Skin. Indianapolis, 1932 1st ed. 1 of 250 signed. Fine. $175. Another, unsigned edition, in DJ. $40.
Plantation Christmas. Boston, 1934 1st edition. W. B. Hendrickson illus. Near Fine in dust jacket. $20.

PETERS, ELLIS. *The Funeral of Figaro*. NY, 1964 1st ed. Fine in dust jacket. $125.
The Knocker at Death's Door. NY, 1970 1st edition. Fine in dust jacket. $50.

A Morbid Taste for Bones. London, 1977 1st ed. The first Brother Cadfael novel. Very Fine in dust jacket. $700.
One Corpse Too Many. NY, 1979 1st ed. Fine in DJ. $50.

PETERS, FRED J. *Sporting Prints by Nathaniel Currier and Currier and Ives*. NY, 1930. One of 750 copies, 225 plates. Very Good. $100.
Clipper Ship Prints. NY, 1930. #300 of 500. VG. $80.
Railroad, Indian and Pioneer Prints. New York, 1930. Very Good in dust jacket. $50.

PETERS, HARRY T. *California on Stone*. Doubleday, 1935 1st ed. 501 copy limited edition. VG with dust jacket in slipcase. $450. Fine. $550. 1976 facsimile edition. Shelf worn, soiled. $95.
Just Hunting. NY, 1935, Scribners. $42.
Currier & Ives. Printmakers to the American People. Doubleday, 1942. G-VG. $16-$30. Book Club ed. Wolf. $15. Garden City, 1929 1st ed. 331 pgs. 1 of 501 copies, slipcased. (Volume one only of two. The second appeared in 1931.) Very Good. $200.

PETERS, HERMANN. *Pictorial History of Ancient Pharmacy: With Sketches of Early Medical Practice*. Chicago, 1899, 2nd ed. Illus. $35.

PETERS, JEAN. *Book Collecting, A Modern Guide*. 1978 2nd edition. Good-Very Good. $22.

PETERSHAM, MAUD and MISKA. *The Christ Child*. NY, 1931. Illus. by authors. VG. $22.
Get-A-Way and Hary Janos. NY, 1933 1st edition. Illus. by author. Worn extremities, o/w Very Good. $27.
Milki and Mary: Their Search for Treasures. Viking, 1934 1st ed. Illus. by authors. Edgewear, cover rubbing, o/w Very Good plus. $35.
The Story of Wheels, Ships, Trains and Aircraft. Winston, 1935 1st ed. Illus. by authors. Fine. $20.
Joseph and His Brothers. Winston, 1938. Illus. by authors. Poor dust jacket, interior Good. $15.
American ABC. Macmilan, 1941 1st ed. Illus. by authors. Good plus in DJ. $45. Near Fine. $200.
The Boy Who Had No Heart. NY, 1955 1st printing. Illus. by authors. Very Good. $18.
Silver Mace. NY, 1956. Illus. & signed by authors. Very Good in dust jacket. $70.

PETERSON, H. *Huxley, Prophet of Science*. London, 1932. Very Good plus. $22.

PETERSON, HAROLD L. *Pageant of the Gun*. NY, 1966. Illus. Good in dust jacket. $6.
Daggers and Fighting Knives of the Western World. NY, 1968 1st ed. Fine in dust jacket. $30.
The Last of the Mountain Men. NY, 1969. G in DJ. $4.
Arms & Armor in Colonial America. New York, 1956. Illustrated. $35.

PETERSON, ROGER TORY. *The Junior Book of Birds.* Boston, 1939. Very Good. $8.
A Field Guide to Western Birds. Boston, 1941 1st ed. Very Good in dust jacket. $18.
The Bird Watcher's Anthology. NY, 1957. Very Good-Fine in dust jacket. $20-$30.
Birds Over America. NY, 1948. Signed. VG. $35.
A Field Guide to Birds of All Species. Boston, 1947 2nd edition. Signed. $30-$40.
World Atlas of Birds. NY, 1974 1st ed. Fine in DJ. $25.
Field Guide to Birds of the American West. Easton IL, 1984. Fine. $25.

PETERSON, ROGER W. *Only the Ball Was White.* NY, 1970 1st edition. Very Good in dust jacket. $95-$125.

PETO, FLORENCE. *Historic Quilts.* New York, 1939 1st edition. Good-Very Good. $45-$95.

PETRIE, FLINDERS. *Seventy Years in Archeology.* London, 1931 1st ed. Photo illus. $125.
The Making of Egypt. London, 1939 1st ed. VG. $85.

PETTIGREW, J. BELL. *Animal Locomotion, or Walking, Swimming & Flying, With a Dissertation on Aeronautics.* Illus. engravings. NY, Appleton, 1874 1st Amer. ed. $40.

PHARMACOPOEIA OF THE UNITED STATES OF AMERICA. 1851 ed. VG. $85. 1869 4th ed. $75.

PHELAN, MICHAEL & C. BERGER. *Illustrated Hand Book of Billiards.* NY, Collender, 1874 10th edition. 95 pages. plus 9 pages of ads. $65.

PHELPS, ROBERT DEAN. *The Literary Life: Almanac of the Anglo-American Literary Scene, 1900-1950.* No place, 1968 1st ed. Fine in dust jacket. $20.

PHILLIPS, CABELL. *From the Crash to the Blitz 1929-1939.* Macmillan, 1969 1st ed. Very Good in DJ. $15.

PHILLIPS, COLES. *A Young Man's Fancy.* Indianapolis, 1912 1st ed. Illus. by author. Hinge weak. $250.

PHILLIPS, DAVID. *The Epic of the 101st Airborne.* France, 1945. Good plus. $135.

PHILLIPS, DAVID G. *The Cost.* Bobbs-Merrill, 1904. H. Fisher illus. VG. $25-$40. Same, G & D. VG. $12-$20.

PHILLIPS, D. L. *Letters From California.* Springfield, Illinois State Journal Co., 1877. Ex-library. G-VG. $125.

PHILLIPS, JAYNE ANNE. *How Mickey Made It.* St. Paul MN, 1981 1st. One of 150 cloth copies, signed. Fine. $100.
The Secret Country. Palaemon, 1982 1st ed. One of 50 copies, signed. Fine. $40.

PHILLIPS, JOHN C. *A Sportsman's Scrapbook.* Boston, 1933. Fine in fine dust jacket. $75.
A Sportsman's Second Scrapbook. Boston, 1933. VG. $45. Another, in dust jacket. $70.

PHILLIPS, LANCE. *Yonder Comes the Train.* Barnes, 1965. Very Good in torn dust jacket. $30.

PHILLIPS, W. S. *Totem Tale,* Chicago, 1896, Star Pub. Illus. by author. Very Good. $40.
Indian Tales for Little Folks. NY, 1928, Platt & Munk. Illus. by author. Good. $30. Fine. $50.

PHILLIPS, ULRICH B. *American Negro Slavery.* NY, Appleton, 1918. Very Good. $65. Same, 1928. $18-$40.
Life and Labor in the Old South. Boston, 1929 2nd printing. $15-$30. Same, 1930 & 1931, folding map. $20.

PHILLPOTTS, EDEN. *Farm of the Dagger.* NY, 1904 1st edition. Good. $10.
The Girl and the Faun. Philadelphia, 1919. Illus. Very Good in dust jacket. $20.
Black, White and Brindled. NY, 1923 1st ed. VG. $30.

PHIN, JOHN. *Hints and Practical Information for Cabinet Makers, Upholsterers, etc.* NY, 1884. $75.

PHIPPS, FRANCES. *Colonial Kitchens, Their Furnishing & Their Gardens.* New York, 1972. Illustrated. Very Good in dust jacket. $40-$50. Another, ex-library. Good-Very Good. $20.

PHOTOPLAY ANNUAL. 1947 Hardbound vol. Fine. $95.

PICKARD and BULEY. *Midwest Pioneer, His Ills, Cures, and Doctors.* NY, Henry Schuman, 1st trade ed., 1946 (c. 1945). Original paperboard binding. VG. $15.

PICASSO, PABLO. *Desire: A Play.* Philos Library, 1948 1st edition. Fine in dust jacket. $45.

PICASSO, PABLO (Illustrator). *Lysistrata.* By Aristophanes. Limited Editions Club, 1934. Signed by Picasso. Very Good in torn slipcase. $2,200.

THE PICAYUNE'S CREOLE COOK BOOK. *The Picayune,* New Orleans LA, 1910 4th ed. Worn. $25.

PICTORIAL HISTORY OF THE U.S.S. MASSACHUSETTS (BATTLESHIP) 1942-1945. Mass, 1945 1st edition. Embossed boards. Fine. $28-$35.

PICKERING, H. C. *Neighbors Have My Ducks.* Derrydale Press, 1937. One of 227 copies. Mint. $650.

PICTURESQUE AMERICA. NY, 1872. 2 vols. Lavish steel and wood engravings. G-VG. $195-$350.

PICTURESQUE CALIFORNIA. San Francisco, 1888. 600 illustrations, 120 full-page plates. Bindings fault, o/w Very Good. $1,200-$1,800.

PICTURESQUE EUROPE. NY, Appleton, 1875 1st ed. 3 vols. steel engravings, 9½x12½. Scuffed covers, foxed margins, o/w Very Good. $210 auction.

PIER, A. S. *Boys of St. Timothy's*. NY, Scribner, 1904. Wyeth illus. Very Good. $25-$50.

PIERCE, J. R. *Electrons, Waves and Messages*. NY, 1956 1st edition. Very Good. $40.
Symbols, Signals and Noise. NY, 1961 1st edition. Fine in dust jacket. $40.

PIERCE, R. V. *People's Common Sense Medical Adviser in Plain English*. Buffalo, NY, 1875 1st. 885 pgs. Good. $25.
The People's Medical Advisor. 1888 19th edition. 1,008 pages. Very Good. $12.

PILAT, OLIVER and JO RANSON. *Sodom by the Sea* (Coney Island). Doubleday, 1941. Ex-library. Very Good in good dust jacket. $20. Another, Near Fine. $35.

PILLSBURY'S 4TH GRAND NATIONAL CONTEST COOKBOOK. No place, 1953. 96 pgs. $15. (1950 & 1951 contest cookbooks are worth at least twice as much.)

PILLSBURY'S DIAMOND ANNIVERSARY RECIPES. 1944 paperback. Good plus. $12.

PILLSBURY'S 100 PRIZE WINNING RECIPES BOOK-LETS. Second. VG. $20. Third. Poor-Good. $8-$14. Fourth. G-VG. $12. Fifth. Fair-Good.$10. Sixth. Fair-Good. $7-$10. Seventh-Eighth. Good-VG. $8-$12. Ninth-Eighteenth. Good-VG. $6-$8.

THE PILLSBURY FAMILY COOKBOOK. 1963 1st edition. 528 pages. Ring binder. VG. $24.

PILOT'S HANDBOOK, 1931. 424 pgs. Embossed boards, pocket has 21 Flight Maps. $50.

PINCKNEY, JOSEPHINE. *My Son and Foe*. NY, 1952 1st edition. Very Good in dust jacket. $10.

PINCKNEY, PAULINE. *American Figureheads and Their Carvers*. Kennikat Press, no date. Reprint of 1940 edition. Very Good. $50.

PINCHOT, GIFFORD. *Just Fishing Talk*. Harrisburg, PA, 1936 1st ed. Illus. Good. $75.

PINKERTON, ALLAN. *The Spiritualists and the Detectives*. NY, 1877 1st ed. Good-Very Good. $45.
Spy of the Rebellion . Chicago, 1883. Illus. $40.

Bank Robbers and the Detectives. New York, 1883 1st edition. Very Good. $45.
Bucholz and the Detectives. Carleton, 1880 1st ed. Shelfworn, marred front end plate, o/w VG. $30.
The Gypsies & The Detectives. 1907 reprint of 1879 edition. Very Good. $17.
The Expressman and The Detective. Carleton, 1882 revised ed. G-VG. $10-$15. 1874 1st ed. Wright. $20-$40.

PINKHAM, LYDIA. *Private Textbook Upon Ailments Peculiar to Women*. Lynn MA. Circa 1875. Paperbound. Very Good. $15-$25.

PINKWATER, DANIEL M. *Wizard Crystal*. NY, 1973. Very Good in dust jacket. $30.

PINTO, ORESTE. *Spy Catcher*. NY, 1952 1st edition. Very Good in dust jacket. $18.

PIPER, WATTY (Mabel Bragg). Editor. *Famous Rhymes of Mother Goose*. Platt & Munk, 1923. Lois Lenske illus. Very Good in poor dust jacket. $55.
The Little Engine That Could. Platt & Munk, 1930. Lois Lenski illus. Very Good in slightly soiled DJ. $48. Platt & Munk,1954 edition. George, Doris Hauman illus. $16.
Eight Nursery Tales. 1938 ed. 96 pgs. $18.
Nursery Tales Children Love. Platt-Munk, 1933. Black Sambo cover. Worn, Good. $45.
Tales From Storyland. Platt-Munk, 1941. Illus. G. $40.
The Road in Storyland. Platt-Munk, 1952. L. and H.C. Holling illus. VG in DJ. $40.
My Picture Story Book. NY, 1941. Good-Very Good in dust jacket. $15-$20.

PIPER, WILLIAM. *What Your Town Needs for the Coming Air Age*. Piper Corp. 1946 8th ed. $15-$30.

PIPPERGER, HELMUT. *Coffee Cookery*. George Stewart, 1940 1st edition. Very Good. $20.

PIRANDELLO, LUIGI. *Short Stories*. NY, 1959 1st American ed. Very Good in dust jacket. $35.

PIRSIG, ROBERT M. *Zen and the Art of Motorcycle Maintenance*. NY, 1974 1st ed. Author's 1st book. Signed. Fine in Near Fine dust jacket. $75.

PITTINGER, WILLIAM. *Capturing a Locomotive: History of Secret Service in the Late War*. Washingotn, 1884. Good-Very Good. $15-$30.

PITZA, HENRY and EDWARD WARWICK. *Early American Costumes*. NY, 1929. Illus. Very Good. $45.

PLAIDY, JEAN. *Beyond the Blue Mountains*. NY, 1947 1st American ed. Author's 1st book. Fine in DJ. $20-$40.

PLANCK, CHARLES. *Women With Wings*. NY, 1942 1st ed. Very Good in worn dust jacket. $25.

PLANCK, MAX. *The Philosophy of Physics*. NY, 1936 1st ed. Near Fine. $45.

PLATH, SYLVIA. *Ariel*. NY, 1966 1st ed. Fine in DJ. $70.
The Bell Jar. NY, 1971 1st American ed. Illus. by author. Near Fine in dust jacket. $95.
The Bed Book. NY, 1976 1st American ed. Emily A. McCully illus. Corner wear, mended DJ. $40.
Johnny Panic and the Bible of Dreams. NY, 1979 1st edition. Near Fine in dust jacket. $35.

PLATT, JUNE. *June Platt's Plain & Fancy Cookbook*. Boston, 1941. String Bean Pie to Caramel Parfait. Very Good. $20. 1942 edition. $12.

PLAYBOY CARTOON ALBUM. 20th Anniversary, 1973. Good-Very Good. $12-$15.

PLAYBOY, THE BEST FROM. (Also see Hefner, Hugh, and also Magazine section.) Waldorf Pub., 1954 1st ed. Good in dust jacket. $35. No dust jacket. $25.

PLOWDEN, GENE. *Those Amazing Ringlings and Their Circus*. Caxton, 1968 2nd printing. Fine in DJ. $15.

PLUMBING & GAS FITTING, HEATING, PAINTING, ETC. Intl Textbook Co. Scranton PA, 1903. $10-$20.

PLUMMER, PETER W. *The Carpenters' and Builders' Guide*. Portland ME, 1869 1st ed. $75. 7th ed, 1891. $45.

PODMORE, FRANK. *Apparitions and Thought Transference*. NY, 1895. Very Good. $95.
Modern Spiritualism. Lond., 1902. 2 vols. 1st. NF. $125.
The Newer Spiritualism. London, 1911 2nd printing. $40.
Mediums of the 19th Century. NY, 1963, 2 vols. $50.

POE, EDGAR ALLAN. *Poems*. Boston, 1846. VG. $150.
Poems. with original memoirs. NY, 1864. Fine. $150.
The Works of Edgar Allan Poe. London, NY, Chesterfield Society. 1909. 10 vols. Very Good. $200. NY, 1902 Library edition. 10 vols. $125.
Complete Works of Edgar Allan Poe. Akron OH, 1908. 10 volumes. Very Good. $45. 1943 Heritage Press edition. Fine in slipcase. $22.
The Gold Bug, and Other Tales. Lovell's Library, Vol 8. New York, Sept. 1884. Good. $12.
The Poetical Works of Edgar Allan Poe. NY, circa 1912. Edmund Dulac illus. NF. $175. Doran, 1921. $175-$250. Hodder & Stoughton. circa 1922. VG. $60-$90.
Tales of Mystery and Imagination. NY, 1925. Harry Clarke illus. G-VG. $85-$120. 1933 ed. Fine, no DJ. $145. Same, Tudor Pub., 1935. $45-$80. Lippincott, 1935. Arthur Rackham illus. Very Good. $135-$200.

The Fall of the House of Usher. No place, 1931. One of 1,200 copies. Abner Epstein illus. Good. $38.

POE, EDGAR ALLAN. (In Magazines). *The Gift*. 1840 (Annual). 1st appearance of "William Wilson". Repaired. Very Good. $250.
Ladies' Companion. Nov, 1842, Dec 1842, Feb 1843. "The Mystery of Marie Roget". $40-$60 each.
Graham's Magazine. Apr 1841-June 1842. In every issue. $30-$50 each.
The Gift. 1843 (Annual). 1st appearance of "The Pit and the Pendulum". Foxed, damp stain, o/w Good plus. $150.
Graham's Magazine. Vols. 20, 21, 25. 1842-1844. Poem, stories. Good. $50 each volume.
Godey's Lady's Book. Apr 1844. "Tale of the Rugged Mountains". $30-$50.

POGANY, WILLY ((Illustrator). *Rubaiyat of Omar Khayyam*. No place, 1909 1st ed. 16 tipped-in color plates. Ornate boards. VG plus. $50.
Gulliver's Travels. By Jonathan Swift. NY, 1917 Advance Review Copy. Very Good. $75.
Magyar Fairy Tales. Dutton, 1930. VG. $75-$125.
The Song Celestial. By Sir Edwin Arnold. Philadelphia, 1934. 18 plates in worn box. Contents VG. $75.
Sonnets From the Portuguese. By Elizabeth Browning. NY, 1936. Illus. include 8 tipped-in color plates. Fine in very good dust jacket. $125.
Peterkin. McKay, 1940. 14 color plates. $75-$95.

POGUE. FORREST. *George C. Marshall*. NY, 1963, 1966, 1973, 1987. 4 vols. 1st eds. Fine in fine DJs. $85.

POGUE, JOSEPH E. *Turquoise*. Rio Grande, 1975 10th edition. Very Good. $18.

POHL, FREDERIK. *Undersea City*. With Jack Williamson. Gnome Press, 1958 1st ed. Fine in vg DJ. $50.
Gateway. NY, 1977 1st ed. Fine in dust jacket. $35.

POHL, FREDERIK and C. M. KORNBLUTH. *The Space Merchants*. NY, 1953 1st ed. VG in DJ. $45.

POINT, NICOLAS. *Wilderness Kingdom: Indian Life in the Rocky Mountains, 1840-1847*. NY, Holt, Rinehart & Winston, 1967 1st ed. Full color, folio. VG in Fine DJ. $75.

POLANYI, MICHAEL. *The Logic of Liberty*. Chicago, 1958 1st ed., 2nd printing. VG in chip DJ. $28.
Personal Knowledge. Chicago, 1960 1st ed, 2nd printing. Very Good in dust jacket. $38.

POLITI, LEO. *The Mission Bell*. NY, 1953. Illus. by author. Near Fine in clip dust jacket. $135.
Lito and the Clown. NY, 1964 1st ed. VG plus in DJ. $45.
Poinsettia. Palm Desert CA, 1967. Illus. by author. Fine in fine dust jacket. $75.

POLLARD, ALFRED. *The Romance of King Arthur*. Macmillan, 1917. Rackham color plates. VG in DJ. $120-$160. 1926 ed. B&W illus. $25-$50.

POLLARD, EDWARD A. *The Lost Cause: A History of the War of the Confederates*. NY, 1866 1st edition. Covers detached, contents VG. $40. Another, NP, 1890. G. $28. *Life of Jefferson Davis: History of the Confederacy*. National Publishing. 1869. VG. $33.
Black Diamonds: Gathered in the Darkey Homes of the South. NY, Pudney Russell, 1860 2nd ed. $150-$175.
The First Year of the War. Richmond, 1862 1st ed. Paperbound. $175-$250.

POLLARD, H. B. C. *A History of Firearms*. London, 1926 1st edition. Spine waterstains, o/w VG. $125.

POLLARD, S. *In Unknown China*. Lippincott, 1921. Many photo illus. Very Good. $45.

POOLE, ERNEST. *Avalanche*. Macmillan, 1924 1st edition in dust jacket. $15-$35.

POOLE, HESTER M. *Fruits and How to Use Them. 700 Recipes*. NY, Fowler & Wells, 1890. G-VG. $35.

POOLE'S INDEX TO PERIODICAL LITERATURE. 3 vols, 1882-1891. Very Good. $60.

POOR, CHARLES L. *Men Against the Rule: A Century of Progress in Yacht Design*. Derrydale, 1937 1st ed. One of 950 copies. VG-Fine. $75-$100.

POORE, BEN PERLEY. *Reminiscences of 60 Years in the National Metropolis*. Phil., 1886 2 vols. Soiled. $100.

POPE, ANTOINETTE. *Antoinette Pope Cook Book*. NY, 1973 1st ed. 940 pgs. Fine in DJ. $15-$20.

POPE, ANTOINETTE & FRANCOIS. *Antoinette Pope School Cookbook*. Macmillan, 1951 7th ed. 366 pgs. VG, no DJ. Signed by both authors. $15.

POPE, EDWIN. *Ted Williams, The Golden Year 1957*. Prentice-Hall, 1970 1st ed. VG in dust jacket. $30-$40.

POPHAM, A. E. *The Drawings of Leonardo da Vinci*. New York, 1945. Very Good in DJ. $30. Another, no DJ, $8.

POP-UP BOOKS.   (See large listing at end of "P" section.)

PORTER, C. and M. *Ruxton of the Rockies*. Norman OK, 1950 1st ed. Fine in dust jacket. $20.

PORTER, ADMIRAL DAVID. *The Naval History of the Civil War*. New York, 1886, Sherman Pub. Newly rebound. Very Good. $150.

PORTER, EBENEZER. *The Rhetorical Reader*. Andover, 1839. Pencilling, foxing. Good. $27.

PORTER, ELEANOR H. *Pollyanna*. Boston, 1919. 46th impression. Hinge weak, o/w Very Good. $14.

PORTER, GENE STRATTON. *What I Have Done with Birds*. Bobbs-Merrill, 1907 1st ed. VG-Fine. $175-$225.
Song of the Cardinal, A Love Story. Bobbs-Merrill, 1903 1st ed., photos by author. Orig. red buckram, gilt title. VG-Fine. $95-$175. Good plus. $50-$90
Birds of the Bible. Cincinnati, 1909 1st ed. VG-Fine. $175-$200. Rebacked copy. $65.
A Girl of the Limberlost. NY, 1909 1st ed. Very Good plus in dust jacket. $60. Grosset & Dunlap, 1909 reprint. W. T. Benda illus. VG. $27.
Music of the Wild. Cincinnati, 1910 1st ed. G-VG. $125-$170. Same with broken hinge. 1911 ed. VG. $95.
Moths of the Limberlost. NY, 1912 1st ed. Dark cover and spine. $90-$125. Fine. $140.
Laddie, a True Blue Story. NY, 1913 1st ed. Herman Pfeifer illus. VG-Fine in DJ. $125-$300. Another, VG, no DJ. $35. Same, worn, bumped, no dust jacket. $15-$20.
Freckles. Doubleday, Page & Co., 1904 1st ed. E. Stetson Crawford decorations. 433 pgs., orig. cloth, gilt top. Light wear. Presentation copy. VG. $400. Grosset & Dunlap reprint, 1904. Fine. $15. Another, 1916. VG in DJ. $25. Same, no jacket. $14.
A Daughter of the Land. Doubleday Page, 1918. Good-Very Good. $16-$10.
At the Foot of the Rainbow. Grosset and Dunlap, 1907. Good-Very Good. $14-$20.
Homing With the Birds. Doubleday, 1920 1st ed. Illustrated. Good. $100.
Her Father's Daughter. NY, 1921 1st ed. Good plus. $30. No dust jacket. $20.
Michael O'Halloran. Doubleday Page, 1915 1st ed. Decorative cloth. Good-VG. $15-$45. Grosset & Dunlap reprint, no date. $12.
The Firebird. Garden City, 1922 1st ed. Gordon Grant illustrator. Very Good. $25-$35.
The Magic Garden. New York, 1927 1st ed. VG. $35-$45.
The Keeper of the Bees. Doubleday, 1925 1st ed. Cracked hinges, o/w Good. $150. Another, VG illus. boards. $25. Fair, no dust jacket. $12.
Tales You Won't Believe. Grosset & Dunlap, 1925. Photos. Fine. $75.
Jesus of the Emerald. Doubleday, 1923 1st ed. Inscribed, signed by author. Her scarcest signed book. Good plus. $2,550. Another, not signed. Near Fine. $1,675.

PORTER, KATHERINE ANNE. *Flowering Judas and Other Stories*. New York, 1935 1st trade edition. Near Fine in very good dust jacket. $125.
The Leaning Tower and Other Stories. NY, 1944 1st ed. Good-Very Good in dust jacket. $25-$50.
Ship of Fools. Boston, 1962 1st ed. Fine in DJ. $35-$50.

Collected Stores of Katherine Ann Porter. NY, 1965 1st ed. Fine in dust jacket. $50-$100.

A Christmas Story. Delacorte, 1967 1st ed. Ben Shahn illus. Very Good in dust jacket. $18.

The Never Ending Wrong. Boston, 1977 1st ed. Very Good in dust jacket. $15.

PORTER, ELIOT (Photographer). *In Wilderness Is the Preservation of the World*. Sierra Club, 1962. Loose hinges, o/w Very Good in good dust jacket. $40.

Appalachian Wilderness. NY, 1970 1st. Fine in DJ. $150.

Moments of Discovery: Adventures With American Birds. NY, 1977 1st ed. Fine in DJ. $33.

All Under Heaven: The Chinese. No place, 1983 1st ed. Very Good. $35.

PORTFOLIO OF THE WORLD WAR. No author. NY, 1917. Folio, illus. Good plus. $45.

PORTIS, CHARLES. *True Grit*. NY, 1968 1st ed. Fine in Fine dust jacket. $50. Good in dust jacket. $10.

PORTLAND, MAINE AND WHAT I SAW THERE. Portland, 1920 14th edition. 32 pages of views. $12-$15.

POST, CHARLES C. *Driven From Sea to Sea*. Chicago, 1884, Downey & Co. G-VG. $20-$30.

Ten Years a Cowboy. 1901 ed. Rhodes. Good. $15-$20.

POST, EMILY. *Etiquette*. NY, 1922 1st ed. Near VG. $45.

By Motor To The Golden Gate. NY, 1916 1st edition. Illus. Fine. $45.

Emily Post's Motor Manners. Wash., 1949. 46 pgs. $15.

POST, MAY AUDOBON. *Bunnie Cottontail, A Rabbit's Own Story*. McLoughlin, 1908. Illus. by author. VG. $45.

POST, MELVILLE DAVISON. *Dwellers in the Hills*. NY, 1901 1st ed. Very Good in dust jacket. $30.

The Mountain School Teacher. NY, 1922 1st. VG. $30.

POTOK, CHAIM. *The Chosen*. NY,1967 1st ed. Author's 1st book. Very Good in dust jacket. $100-$150.

Promise. NY, 1969 1st ed. VG-Fine in DJ. $25-$35.

POTTER, BEATRIX. *The Tale of Peter Rabbit*. London, 1902 1st trade issue, color illus. $350-$600. Winston, 1904. Altemus, 1904. 30 color plates. $200-$400. Good. $50. Warne, 1906. $75. Puzzle edition, 1907. $100. G&D reprint. $20 Whitman, 1928. $18.

The Tailor of Gloucester. London, 1903 1st ed., 1st issue. Illus. by author. VG. $425. Warne, NY 1903. $200-$400.

The Tale of Benjamin Bunny. London, 1904. Illus. by author. Near Fine. $450.

The Pie and the Patty-Pan. Frederick Warne, 1905 early ed. Cloth with round pictorial label. 52 pgs. Color plates. Part of spine missing, bumped. $100. Another, VG. $200.

The Story of Miss Moppet. Warne, 1933. VG. $75-$100.

Cecily Parsley's Nursery Rhymes. NY, 1922. $100-$200.

The Fairy Caravan. McKay, 1929. VG. $75-$150.

Peter Rabbit's Almanac. Warne, 1929. VG. $95-$165.

The Tale of Jemima Puddle-Duck. London, 1908 1st ed. Illus. by author. Very Good. $225. Same, 1936 edition in Good dust jacket. $20. 1920 ed. 27 plates. $50.

The Tale of the Flopsy Bunnies. London, 1909 1st ed. Illus. by author. Very Good plus. $285. 1915. $40-$65.

The Tale of Timmy Tiptoes. London, 1911 1st ed. Illus. by author. Very Good. $225.

Roly-Poly Pudding. London, Warne, 1908 1st edition. $250-$400, NY. $250. 1920 reprint. $70.

14 Assorted Titles. Published in USA circa 1903-1910: Mr. Jeremy, Flopsy Bunnies, Timmy Tiptoes, Mr. Tittlemouse, Jemima Puddle-Duck, Ginger and Pickles, Tailor of Gloucester, Peter Rabbit, and 6 others. All in very fine original condition. The lot, $1,500.

Peter Rabbit & Jimmy Chipmunk. 1918 reprint, Saalfield. Good-Very Good. $8-$10.

The Tale of Mr. Toad. 1939. Very Good in DJ. $35.

Wag-By-Wall. Horn Book, 1944 1st ed. J. Lankes illus. Good-Very Good in DJ. $25-$60. Fine in fine DJ. $75.

The Tale of Johnny Town Mouse. NY, 1946. $25-$50.

POTTER, MIRIAM. *The Gigglequicks*. Chicago, 1918 8th edition. Very Good. $18.

POUND, EZRA. *Personae: The Collected Poems*. NY, 1926 1st edition. Very Good. $100.

ABC of Reading. London, 1934 1st ed. Fine overall in chip, soiled DJ. $200. Another, Good, no DJ. $60.

Guide to Kulchur. London, 1938 1st ed. VG in clipped dust jacket. $375. NY, 1952 American ed. $25.

Seventy Cantos. London, 1950. One of 1,633 copies. Fine in worn dust jacket. $110.

POUND, EZRA (In Magazines). *Poetry*. June, 1917. Three cantos. 1st appearance. Cover damp stained. $65.

Poetry. Aug 1917. Three Cantos. Good plus. $60.

POURADE, RICHARD F. *The Colorful Butterfield Overland Stage*. Best West, 1966 1st ed. Good-VG. $12.

The Call to California. Copley, 1968 1st ed. $15-$18.

The History of San Diego. 1961. Very Good. $12-$18.

POWELL, ADDISON W. *Trailing and Camping in Alaska*. NY, 1909 1st ed. Photographs. Good-VG. $50-$75.

POWELL, AGNES BADEN. *Handbook for Girl Scouts*. 1st handbook, 1917. $45.

POWELL, ANTHONY. *A Question of Upbringing*. NY, 1951 1st ed. Fine in dust jacket. $65-$75.

Buyer's Market. London, 1952 1st edition. In DJ. $20.

Hearing Secret Harmonies. Boston, 1975 1st American edition. Fine in dust jacket. $15.

POWELL, DAWN. *The Wicked Pavilion*. Boston, 1954 1st ed. Reginald Marsh illus. VG in fair DJ. $50.

POWELL, FREDERICK. *Bacchus Dethroned*. NY, 1878, National Temperance Society. $50-$75.

POWELL, HICKMAN. *Bali: The Last Paradise*. NY, 1930. Andre Roosevelt photos. VG in DJ. $35.

POWELL, J. C. *The American Siberia, or 14 Years in a Southern Convict Camp*. Chicago, 1893. Good-VG. $60.

POWELL, JOHN WESLEY. *Exploration of the Colorado River of the West and Its Tributaries Explored in 1869, 1871 and 1872*. Washington, 1875. Complete with maps. Moderate wear. VG plus. $395.
Bureau of American Ethnology. First Annual Report, 1879-80. 603 pgs. $30-$50.
Second Annual Report of the Bureau of Ethnololgy, etc. 1880-1881. GPO, 1883. Many plates, some in color. Very Good. $75-$150.
Third Annual Report of the United States Geological Survey. Washington, 1882 Vol. III. VG. $60.
Fourth Annual Report. Vol. III, 1883. Indian Pottery, etc. Very Good. $25-$40.
Sixth Annual Report, 1888. Scuffed ¾ leather. Very Good. $30-$90.
Seventh, Eighth, Ninth Reports. Worn. $30-$90.
Fourteenth & Fifteenth Reports. $30 each.
(All have some color plates. Dealers vary widely on asking prices of all editions listed above.)

POWELL, LYMAN P. *Mary Baker Eddy, A Life Size Portrait*. Macmillan, 1930 1st ed. Fine, Soft leather. $15.

POWELL, PADGETT. *Edisto*. NY, 1984 1st ed. Author's 1st book. Near Fine in dust jacket. $50.
Woman Named Drown. NY, 1987. Fine in DJ. $10.

POWNALL, THOMAS. *Topographical Description of the Dominions of the United States of America*. Pittsburgh, 1949 reprint of 1776 original. 1 of 2,000. VG. $65.

POWYS, JOHN COWPER. *The Inmates*. NY, 1952 1st edition. Fine in dusty DJ. $65.

POWYS, LLEWELLYN. *Ebony and Ivory*. NY, 1923 1st ed. Theodore Dreiser preface. Near Fine in chipped DJ. $50.
Skin for Skin. Jonathan Cape, 1926 1st ed. One of 900 copies. Dust jacket. $35.

POWYS, MARIAN. *Lace and Lace Making*. Detroit, 1981 2nd ed. Very Good. $35-$45.

POWYS, T. F. *The House With the Echo: Twenty-Six Stories*. London, 1928 1st ed. Fine in vg DJ. $75.
Fables. NY, 1929 1st ed. Fine in vg DJ. $85.

THE PRACTICAL AMERICAN COOK BOOK. 1855. Good-Very Good. $110-$135.

PRACTICAL BLACKSMITHING. NY, 1890-1900, M. T. Richardson & Co. Decorative cover. $35.

THE PRACTICAL BREWER. Master Brewers' Association. St. Louis, 1946 1st ed. Very Good. $16.

PRACTICAL HOUSEKEEPING. A COMPILATION OF TRIED & TRUE RECIPES. Anon. 1881, 1887. $45-$65.

PRATT & BAILEY. *A Man and His Meals*. New York, 1947 1st ed. Very Good. $10.

PRATT, CHARLES E. *The American Bicycler: A Manual for the Observer, the Learner and the Expert*. Boston, 1879 1st ed. Chip spine, o/w VG. $200-$250.

PRATT, FLETCHER. *Secret and Urgent*. NY, 1942. Good-Very Good in dust jacket. $15-$35.
Civil War in Pictures. (Harper's and Leslie's repros.) 1955. Book Club edition. Very Good. $18-$22.
Ordeal by Fire. William Sloane, revised edition, 1948. Good plus. $30.

PREBLE, GEORGE. *A Chronological History of the Origin and Development of Steam Navigation, 1543-1882*. Philadelphia, 1883 1st ed. Very Good. $100.

PRESCOTT, KENNETH. *The Complete Graphic Works of Ben Shahn*. NY, 1973. Illus. $25.

PRESCOTT, WILLIAM. *History & Conquest of Peru*. NY, 1847 1st ed, 1st issue. 2 vols. VG plus. $250. 10 vols, 1857 edition. Leather. Fair set. $60.
Conquest of Mexico. NY, no date. Modern Library Giant. Very Good in vg dust jacket. $16.
Conquest of Peru. Heritage, 1957 1st. Fine, No Box. $12.

PRESTON, LYON & BATCHELOR. *Navies of the American Revolution*. Bison Books, 1975 1st ed. Fine in DJ. $16.

PREUSS, ARTHUR. *Study of American Freemasonry*. B. Herder, 1908 2nd ed. 433 pgs. Very Good. $12.

PRICE, GEORGE (Illustrator). *George Price's Characters*. New York, 1955. Good. $28.

PRICE, REYNOLDS. *A Long and Happy Life*. NY, 1962 1st ed. Author's 1st book. Very Good in dust jacket. $90. Another, signed. VG-Near Fine in DJ. $120-$150.
A Generous Man. NY, 1966 1st Fine in clip DJ. $45-$65.
Love and Work. NY, 1968 1st American ed. Signed. Fine in dust jacket $65.
Permanent Errors. NY, 1970 1st edition. Signed. Near Fine in dust jacket. $60.

PRICE, RICHARD. *The Wanderers*. Boston, 1974 1st ed. Author's 1st book. Near Fine in very good DJ. $50.

PRICE, VINCENT & MARY. *A Treasury of Great Recipes*. 1965 1st ed. 546 pgs. Leatherette cover. VG. $40-$60.

PRICE, WILLARD. *Roving South-Rio Grande to Patagonia*. John Day, 1948 1st ed. Illus. by author. VG. $14.
The Amazing Mississippi. John Day, 1963 1st edition. Fine in dust jacket. $12-$15.

PRICHARD, JAMES C. *A Treatise on Insanity and Other Disorders Affecting the Mind*. Philadelphia, 1837 1st American ed. Famous treatise. Overall VG. $250-$400.

PRIESTLEY, J. B. *The Good Companions*. NY, 1927 1st American ed. Good-Very Good. $12-$20.
3 Men in New Suits. NY, 1945 1st Amer. VG in DJ. $40.

PRIESTMAN, MABEL. *Handicrafts in the Home*. Arts & Crafts-style projects. Chicago, 1910 1st ed. $38 auction.

PRINCE, MORTON. *The Dissociation of a Personality*. NY, 1906 1st ed, 2nd printing. Taped hinge. VG. $45.
The Unconscious. NY, 1914 1st ed. Very Good. $75.

PRITCHARD, JAMES A. *Overland Diary. Kentucky to California in 1849*. Old West Pub. Co., 1959 limited edition. 1 of 1,250 copies. Fine. $125.

PRITTIE, TERENCE. *Germans Against Hitler*. Little Brown, 1964 1st American ed. VG in dust jacket. $14.

PROEHL, CARL. *The 4th Marine Division in WWII*. Washington, 1946 1st ed. VG. $125.

PROKOSCH, FREDERICK. *The Conspirators*. NY, 1943 1st ed. Very Good in dust jacket. $35.
A Ballad of Love. Farrar, 1960 1st ed. VG in DJ. $30.
The Wreck of the Cassandra. NY, 1966 1st ed. Very Good in fine dust jacket. $15.
America, My Wilderness. NY, 1972 1st ed. VG in DJ. $25.

PROUST, MARCEL. *Remembrance of Things Past*. NY, 1934. 4 volumes. Very Good. $20.
A Vision of Paris. NY, 1963. Eugene Atget photos. Fine in clipped dust jacket. $175.
Jean Santeuil. Simon & Schuster, 1956 1st U. S. ed. Very Good in worn dust jacket. $15.

PUMPELLY, RAFAEL. *Across America and Asia and Residence in Arizona and China*. NY, 1871 5th ed., revised. Folding maps. Illus. Good. $30. Fine. $40-$50.

PURRINGTON, WILLIAM A. *Christian Science. An Exposition of Mrs. Eddy's Wonderful Discovery*. Treat NY, 1900 1st ed. $35.

PUTER, STEPHEN A. *Looters of the Public Domain*. Portland OR, 1908. Orig. red cloth. Ex-library. $150.

PUTNAM, GEORGE H. *A Prisoner of War in Virginia, 1864-65*. New York, 1912 1st edition. $30-$50. 1914 Preferred 3rd edition. VG-Fine. $30-$50.
Some Memories of the Civil War. NY, 1924 1st edition. Very Good-Fine. $20-$35.
Books & Their Makers During the Middle Ages. NY, 1896. 2 volumes. Good. $100.

PUTNAM, NINA WILCOX and N. JACOBSEN. *Winkle, Twinkle and Lollypop*. P. F. Volland, 1918 28th edition. K. S. Dodge illus. Spine restored. Near VG. $75.

PUZO, MARIO. *The Dark Arena*. NY, 1955 1st ed. Author's 1st book, signed. VG plus in dust jacket. $60-$100.
The Godfather. NY, 1969 1st ed. VG in DJ. $65.

PYE, MRS. JULIA A. *Invalid Cookery*. 1880. $45-$60.

PYLE, ERNIE. *Here Is Your War*. NY, 1943. VG. $4.
Brave Men. NY, 1944. Very Good. $5.
Last Chapter. NY, 1946. 1st printing. G-VG. $15-$25.
Home Country. 1947, W. Sloane. Good. $5.

PYLE, HOWARD. *Pepper and Salt, or Seasoning for Young Folk*. NY, 1886 1st ed. illus. by author. NF in drop-lid case. $500. Later 1922 reprint by Harper. $40-$50.
Otto of the Silver Hand. NY, 1888 1st ed. Rebound in leather. In slipcase, with original cover. $200. Scribner's, 1916 reprint. Illustrated by author. Very Good. $50.
Men of Iron. NY, 1892 1st ed., Harper. Illus. by author. Good-VG. $55-$100.
The Garden Behind the Moon. NY, 1895. VG. $125.
The Price of Blood. Boston, 1899 1st edition. Illus. by author. Very Good. $100.
The Wonder Clock. NY, 1899. VG. $95. 1915 rpt. $25.
The Story of the Champions of the Round Table. NY, 1905 1st ed. Illus. by author. VG. $125-$175
The Ruby of Kishmoor. Harper, 1908. VG. $100.
Howard Pyle's Book of Pirates. Harpers, 1921. Ex-library. Illus. by author. $75. Same, 11 color plates. $150.
Howard Pyle's Book of the American Spirit. NY, London 1923 1st edition. Illus. by author. VG. $100. Same with dust jacket. $250-$300. Harper, 1923 reprint. $95.
The Merry Adventures of Robin Hood. Scribners, 1884. VG. $150. Same, 1917. $85. 1911. 176 pgs. $20. NY, 1924. $50. NY, 1929. Illus. by author. VG. $32. Whitman, 1940 ed. VG in DJ. $15. Scribner's, 1960 reprint. Ex-library. $10.
The Howard Pyle Brandywine Edition, 1853-1933. NY, 1933 5 vols. Illus. by W. J. Aylward, Frank E. Schoonover, Harvey Dunn, Stanley M. Arthurs and Pyle. NF. $350.
Men of Iron. Harper, 1892. Orig. Red cloth. $100-$170. Same, 1919 reprint. Very Good. $40-$60.

POP-UP BOOKS

Books are listed alphabetically by title, omitting prefaces such as "The Pop-up Book of."

ALICE IN WONDERLAND. NY, no date. Paul Taylor. 11 pop-ups. Very Good. $35. Auction lot of 5 different. vols. Illus. with pop-ups. Various publishers, Various Dates. Rubbed, but Very Good. 5 for $357.

ANIMATED ANIMALS. Saalfield, 1943. Julian Wehr. Very Good in fair dust jacket. $55.

ASTRONAUTS ON THE MOON. Hallmark, 1973 1st ed. pop-up. Very Good. $12-$15.

THE BIG JUMP-UP FARM ANIMAL BOOK. By Jean Horton Berg. 4 pop-ups by William Bartlett. NY, Grosset & Dunlap, 1952 1st ed. VG. $38 auction.

BILLY BOY, JACK IN THE BOOK. A Bonnie Book No. 4265. Good-Very Good. $25.

THE BLACK HOLE. Disney Productions, 1979. 4 double pop-ups. $35.

BLINKY BILL. Whitman, 1938. Dorothy Wall. Paper poor, pop-ups good. $56.

BOBBY BEAR. Whitman, 1935. 3 full-color pop-ups. Boards reinforced, o/w Fine. $55.

THE BOLD LITTLE COWBOY. Lon., 1960. 3 pop-ups. $45.

BUCK ROGERS IN THE TWENTIETH CENTURY. NewYork, 1980. Fine. $25.

BUCK ROGERS: STRANGE ADVENTURES IN THE SPIDER SHIP. Chicago, 1935. Three pop-ups. NF. $350.

BUNTY. Racine WI, 1936. 3 pop-ups. Very Good. $85.

CHRISTOPHER COLUMBUS. Los Angeles, 1965. Chuck Coppock. 5 pop-ups. Near VG. $35.

CHRISTMAS TIME IN ACTION. William Kemp Tilley, illustrator. 1949. $30.

COLLECTION. 11 different pop-up books, mostly 1940s. Mostly Very Good. Median price, each. $48.

DICK TRACY: CAPTURE OF BORIS ARSON. Chicago, 1935. Small chip, o/w Near Fine. Three pop-ups. $350.

THE DWINDLING PARTY. New York, 1982. Edward Gorey. Very Good. $42.

THE FACTS OF LIFE. London, 1984. Jonathan Miller & David Pelham. Very Good. $40.

FATHER CHRISTMAS. London, Bancroft, 1961 1st ed. Double-page pop-up by Kubaska. Tab on front cover gone. Taped, o/w Very Good. $165 auction.

FINNIE THE FIDDLER. Cupples & Leon, 1942. Julian Wehr, signed. Worn cover, page stain. $38.

FREDDY AND THE FIRE ENGINE. Crown, 1945. George Zaffo. 4 pop-ups. Spiral bound. VG. $60.

GHOSTLY TOWERS. NY, 1986. Angela Barrett. Fine. $35.

GNOMES, POP-UP BOOK OF. London, 1979. Very Good. $40. Same, New York, 1979. $20.

GOLDILOCKS AND THE THREE BEARS. Blue Ribbon, 1934. 3 pop-ups. Spine chip, o/w Very Good. $50. Another dealer asking $200 same book, same condition.

THE GREAT DINOSAUR POP-UP BOOK. London, 1986. Karen Johnson. Very Good. $18.

GREAT MENAGERIE. 1979 adaptation of 1884 Pop-up. Met. Museum. Fine. $10-$18.

HAUNTED HOUSE. Los Angeles, 1977. Tor Lovig and Jan Plenkowski. Fine. $50.

HERE COMES SANTA CLAUS. London, circa 1960. 4 pop-ups. Spiral bound. Good plus. $38.

THE HUMAN BODY. London, 1983. Jonathan Miller and David Pelham. Very Good. $45.

JACK THE GIANT KILLER. NY, circa 1932. Walter Lenz. 4 pop-ups. Near Fine. $400.

JEMIMA PUDDLE-DUCK. F. Warne, 1985. Beatrix Potter. 9 pop-ups. $25.

JOLLY JUMPUPS. McLoughlin, 1948. 7 pop-ups. Good-Very Good. $30-$70.

LEON JASON'S JINGLE DINGLE CHRISTMAS STOCKING BOOK. No place, 1953. 18 pop-ups. Very Good in broken box. $35.

LET'S GO TO THE CIRCUS. London, circa 1963. Rudolf Lukes. Very Good. $85.

LITTLE BIMBO AND THE LION. Black boy mechanical pop-up. J. C. Winston Co., 1942. Good plus. $70.

LITTLE ORPHAN ANNIE AND JUMBO THE CIRCUS ELEPHANT. Harold Gray. Pleasure Books, Blue Ribbon Pub. 1935. 3 pop-ups, all with minor flaws. Good-Very Good. $150-$300.

LITTLE RED RIDING HOOD. Blue Ribbon, 1934. H. B. Lentz and C. Carey Cloud. Near VG. $45. Chicago, Pleasure Books, 1934 1st ed. Lentz and Cloud illus. Very Good. $121 auction.

LITTLE RED RIDING HOOD. Philadelphia, no date. 9 crepe pop-ups. Foxing, light soiling, o/w Very Good. $125.

THE LITTLEST ANGEL. No place, 1964. $35.

MARCO POLO. London, circa 1960. Kubasta illus. One 2-page intricate pop-up. As new. $450. (Many other pop-ups illustrated by Kubasta run from $150 up.)

MICKEY MOUSE IN KING ARTHUR'S COURT. By Disney staff. Blue Ribbon, 1933 1st ed. Near Fine. Very scarce in this condition. $1,000.

THE POP-UP MINNIE MOUSE. NY, Blue Ribbon, 1933 1st ed. Chipped and stained. $135 auction. Another, unusually fine copy. $325 dealer.

MICKEY MOUSE. by Disney staff. NY, Blue Ribbon Books, 1933. 3 pop-ups, plus illus. Near Fine. $650.

THE MIGHTY GIANTS. Lon., 1988. 4 double pop-ups. $10.

MINNIE MOUSE. NY, Blue Ribbon, 1933. By Disney staff. 3 double page pop-ups. "Unusually fine." $325-$500.

MINNIE MOUSE. 1933, 3-color pop-ups. No dust jacket. Minor wear. $440 auction.

MOTHER GOOSE. NY, 1934. Three double-page pop-ups. H. B. Lentz illus. Scuffed covers, o/w VG. $140. Another, extremely good cond. $350 auction.

THE MOTION PICTURE POP-UP BOOK. No place, 1980. T. Lokvig and C. Murphy. Very Good. $25.

A NUMBER OF BEARS. 1st Counting Book, no date. Hallmark, No. 400. $25.

MY POP-UP BOOK OF BABY ANIMALS. London, 1982. Ann G. Johnstone. Good. $25.

PETER RABBIT. Ottenheimer, 1986. Beatrix Potter. 3 pop-ups. As new in slipcase. $24.

PINOCCHIO. NY, Blue Ribbon, 1932 1st ed. Harold Lentz. 4 color pop-ups. Rebacked cover. VG. $357 auction. Another, offered by dealer. Very Good. $125.

PLAY TRAIN. Saalfield, 1954. Florian. Very Good. $18.

POPEYE AND THE SPINACH BURGERS. No place, 1981. 6 pop-ups. $20.

PUSS IN BOOTS. Prague, 1973. 6 pop-ups. Fine. $38-$45.

PUSS IN BOOTS. NY, 1934. Harold Lentz and C. Cloud. 3 pop-ups. Fine. $75-$100.

THE RED BARN FARM. Hallmark No. 100JE pop-up. $25.

THE ROARING TWENTIES. London, 1984. G-VG. $20.

ROBOT. NY, 1981. 10 pop-ups. Very Good. $30.

RUDOLPH THE RED-NOSED REINDEER. Racine WI, circa 1933. 6 pop-ups. Fine. $35.

SNOW WHITE. Dunewald, 1949. Julian Wehr. 4 pop-ups. Spiral bound. Very Good. $48.

STAR TREK GIANT IN THE UNIVERSE. NY, 1977, Random House. VG. $35-$55.

STAR WARS. NY, 1978. W. D. Barlow. VG. $40. 1983 edition. $15.

STAR WARS: THE EMPIRE STRIKES BACK. NY, 1981. Jim Daly. Very Good. $25.

STARS WARS: RETURN OF THE JEDI. NY, 1983 1st ed. J. Gampert. Fine. $30.

TERRY AND THE PIRATES. Blue Ribbon, 1935. 3 pop-ups. Fine. $425.

THE THREE LITTLE PIGS. Animated Book, 1944. 5 pop-ups. $65.

TOODLES. Racine WI, 1936. 3 pop-ups. Very Good. $65.

TOY BUS. Munich, circa 1984. 4 moveable wheels. As new. $20.

THE TRAIN. John Bradley and Ray Marshall. Fine. $30.

(End of Pop-Up Book Section.)

Q

QUACKENBOS, JOHN D. *Geological Ancestors of the Brook Trout*. NY, 1916. One of 300 copies. Spine poor. Original calf gilt. $70 auction.

QUAD, M. *Field, Fort and Fleet*. Detroit, 1885. Near Very Good. $55.

QUAIFE, MILO M. *Chicago's Highways Old and New*. Chicago, 1923. 3 folding maps, 26 plates. 278 pgs. $65.
Absalom Grimes, Confederate Mail Runner. Yale University, 1926. Very Good. $30-$35.
Checagou: From Indian Wigwam to Modern City. Chicago, 1933 1st ed. Near Fine in good DJ. $30.
Army Life in Dakota. Chicago, 1941. Fine. $24.
Lake Michigan. American Lake Series. 1944 1st ed. Signed by author. Very Good. $25.

QUAIN, RICHARD (Editor). *A Dictionary of Medicine, etc*. Various authors. Appleton, NY, 1884 7th edition. 1,816 pages. Worn morocco. $100-$130.

A QUAKER COOK BOOK. Whittier CA, 1980. First Friends Church. Signed recipes. Very Good. $35.

QUARLES, BENJAMIN. *The Negro in the Civil War*. Boston, 1953. Good-Very Good. $25.
The Negro in the American Revolution. Univ. of North Carolina, 1976 ed. VG in dust jacket. $15-$20.

QUAYLE, ERIC. *Collector's Book of Children's Books*. Potter, 1971 1st American ed. Fine in DJ. $30-$40.
Old Cook Books: An Illustrated History. NY, 1978 1st edition. Near Fine in dust jacket. $35.
Early Children's Books. No place, 1983. Fine in DJ. $25.
The Book of Detective Fiction. London, 1972. Very Good in dust jacket. $60.

QUAYLE, WILLIAM A. *A Book of Clouds*. New York, 1925 2nd printing. Good. $15.
In God's Out of Doors. Cincinnati, NY, 1902. VG. $15.

QUEBBERMAN, FRANCES E. *Medicine in Territorial Arizona*. Phoenix, 1966 Ariz Hist. Foundation. $45-$60.

QUEEN, ELLERY. *The French Powder Mystery*. Stokes, 1930 1st ed. Very Good. $125.

The Adventures of Ellery Queen. Boston, 1934 1st ed. Very Good in good dust jacket. $450.
Devil to Pay. NY, 1938 1st edition. Very Good-Fine in dust jacket. $30-$60.
Ellery Queen, Master Detective. NY, 1941 1st ed. Novelization of film. Near Fine in DJ. $110.
The New Adventures of Ellery Queen. Triangle, 1941 1st edition. Very Good in dust jacket. $15.
The Murderer Is a Fox. Boston, 1945 1st ed. Near Fine in worn dust jacket. $20.
Ten Days Wonder. Boston, 1948 1st ed. Near Fine in nicked dust jacket. $50.
Double, Double. Boston, 1950 1st ed. Very Good in worn dust jacket. $25. Another, in Fine jacket. $45.
The King is Dead. Boston, 1952 1st ed. Near Fine in good dust jacket. $25. Same in fine jacket. $60.
Inspector Queen's Own Case. NY, 1956 1st edition. Fine in dust jacket. $65.

QUEEN OF HEARTS COOK BOOK. NY, Peter Pauper, 1955 1st ed. Very Good in dust jacket. $10.

QUEEN VICTORIA. *Leaves From the Journal of Our Life in the Highlands*. London, 1868. Illus. $700-$800.

THE QUEEN'S BOOK OF THE RED CROSS. London, 1939 1st ed. Deluxe. Contributors include T. S. Eliot, A. A. Milne, H. C. Bailey, Rex Whistler, Edmund Dulac & Frank Brangwyn. G-VG in good DJ and box. $300-$350.

QUEENY, EDGAR M. *Cheechako*. Scribners, 1941. One of 1,200 copies. Illus. Good plus. $90.
Prairie Wings. Duck flight study. Philadelphia, 1946 1st ed. Good. $200. VG in DJ. $400. Ducks Unlimited edition, NY, 1946. VG in dust jacket. $100-$150.

QUENNELL, MAJORIE. *Everyday Life in Roman Britain*. London, 1952. $10-$15.
Everyday Life in Homeric Greece. Putnam, 1930. $10-$20.

QUENNELL, PETER. *Masques and Poems*. London, 1922. Author's 1st book. Very Good. $100-$150.
The Years of Fame. NY, Viking, 1935. Good. $7.
Samuel Johnson: His Friends and Enemies. American Heritage Press, 1973. $10.

QUENTIN, PATRICK. *Puzzle for Puppets*. Simon Schuster, 1944 1st ed. Very Good in dust jacket. $25-$35.

QUICK, HERBERT. *Virginia of the Air Lane*. Bobbs-Merrill, 1909 1st ed. Very Good in DJ. $30-$40.
Vandermark's Foly. Bobbs-Merrill, 1922. VG. $35.
The Invisible Woman. Bobbs-Merrill, 1924. VG. $15.
One Man's Life. Indianapolis, 1925. Good. $10.

QUICK, HERBERT and EDWARD. *Mississippi Steamboatin'*. NY, 1926 2nd printing. Illus. Near Fine. $25. Same, 1st ed., 1st printing. $35-$40.

QUIETT, GLENN. *Pay Dirt, a Panorama of American Gold Rushes*. NY, 1936. $20-$30.
They Built the West. An Epic of Roads and Cities. Appleton-Century, 1934. $20-$30.

QUIGLEY, MARTIN, JR. *Decency in Motion Pictures*. NY, 1937 1st ed. Ex-library. Signed. $12.
Magic Shadows: The Story of The Origin of Motion Pictures. Georgetown University Press, 1948 1st ed. Illus. Very Good in dust jacket. $40.
Films in America. Golden Press, 1970. Very Good-Fine in dust jacket. $30.

QUILLER-COUCH, SIR ARTHUR. *The Sleeping Beauty and Other Fairy Tales*. Dulac illus. Hodder & Stoughton, 1910. Ex-library. Very Good. $75. Near Fine in DJ. $350.
In Powder and Crinoline. London, 1913. Kay Nielsen illus. VG. $300-$450. Fine. $500-$700.
A Treasure Book of Children's Verse. London, no date. M. E. Gray illus. Very Good. $65-$75.
Roll Call of Honor. New York, no date. $20.
The Twelve Dancing Princesses and Other Fairy Tales. NY, no date, 1st Amer. ed. Kay Nielsen illus. VG-Fine in DJ. $85-$275. Doubleday, 1930. $50-$100.
On the Art of Reading. NY, 1920 1st edition. $15.

QUILLER-COUCH, MABEL. *The Treasure Book of Children's Verse*. London, Hodder Stoughton, Circa 1911. Good-VG. $40-$70.

QUIN, MIKE. *More Dangerous Thoughts*. San Francisco, 1941. Illus. Very Good. $30. Another, autographed $40.
The Big Strike. Olema CA, 1949 1st ed. Paperbound. Very Good-Fine. $35.

QUINBY, HENRY COLE. *Richard Harding Davis, A Bibliography*. New York, Dutton, 1924. VG in DJ. $40.

QUINBY, MOSES. *Quinby's New Bee-Keeping*. New York, Orange Judd, 1897 edition. Very Good. $35.

QUINCY, JOSIAH. *The History of Harvard University*. 2 vols. Cambridge MA, 1840 1st ed. Fine. $450.

Figures of the Past. Boston, 1896. Good-Very Good. $20.
History of Boston Athenaeum. 1951 reprint. VG. $15.

QUINCY WOMEN'S CLUB COOK BOOK. Quincy MA, 1915-1916. Nice ads. $25.

QUINE, W.V.O. *Methods of Logic*. Holt, New York, 1959. Revised edition. 1st printing. Inscribed by author. Near Fine in very good dust jacket. $150.

QUINLAN, JAMES E. *The Original Life of Tom Quick, Indian Slayer*. Deposit, New York, 1894 reprint of 1851 edition. $35-$60.

QUINLAN, M. *The Universal Cookbook*. Chicago, 1937. A Good copy. $28.

QUINN, ARTHUR. *History of American Drama*. NY, 1936. A Fine copy. $25.
Edgar Allan Poe: a Critical Bibliography. Appleton, 1941 1st ed. Very Good in dust jacket. $65.

QUINN, JOHN P. *Fools of Fortune: or, Gamblers and Gambling*. Chicago, Howe, 1890 1st ed. VG. $100-$120.
Gambling and Gambling Devices. Canton OH, 1912 1st ed. Illus. VG-Fine. $75-$150.

QUINN, P. T. *Pear Culture for Profit*. NY, 1869. Good. $25.

QUINN, SEABURY, *Roads*. Wisconsin, 1948, Arkham House. Very Good-Fine in dust jacket. $75-$150.

QUINN, T. C. (Editor). *Massachusetts of Today*. 1892. $20.

QUINN, VERNON. *Seeds, Their Place in Life & Legend*. NY, 1936. Illus. Good-VG. $20.
Stories & Legends of Garden Flowers. NY, 1939. Illus. Good-VG in dust jacket. $25-$35.
Shrubs in a Garden and Their Legends. NY, 1940. M. Lawson illus. $15-$25.

QUINT, ALONZO. *The Potomac and the Rapidan*. NY, 1864 1st edition. Good. $40.

QUINTANA, RICARDO. *Eighteenth Century Plays*. Modern Library, NY, 1952 1st edition. Good. $7.

QUINTON, ROBERT. *The Strange Adventures of Capt. Quinton*. New York, 1912. Very Good. $15.

QUISENBERRY, ANDERSON C. *Lopez' Expeditions to Cuba, 1850 and 1851*. Louisville KY, 1906. Original wrappers bound in. Fine. $125.

QUONG, ROSE. *Chinese Wit and Wisdom and Written Characters*. New York, 1944. Good. $12.

R

RACKHAM, ARTHUR (Illustrator). *Tales of a Traveler*. By Washington Irving. NY, 1895 2 vols. Good-VG. $60-$120.
Feats on the Fjord. By Harriet Martineau. London, 1899. Ex-library. $50. NY, Dutton, 1910. VG in DJ. $50-$75.
Mysteries of Police and Crime. By Maj. Arthur Griffiths. London, 1901 3 vols. 14 black and white illus. VG. $150.
Puck of Pook's Hill. By Rudyard Kipling. NY, 1906 1st American ed. VG-Fine. $50-$200. NY, 1916. $25-$50.
The Ingoldsby Legends. NY, 1907 1st American trade edition. Very Good in dust jacket. $200.
Peter Pan in Kensington Gardens. By J. M. Barrie. NY, 1910 and 1929 eds. 16 plates. $60-$80. 1907. $150-$200.
Midsummer Night's Dream. Heinemann, Doubleday, 1908. Good-Very Good. $75-$200.
Little Brother & Little Sister. Dodd & Mead, 1917 1st edition. Red cloth. Good. $60. Very Good. $200.
Grimm's Fairy Tales. London, 1912. Faded spine, endpapers foxed. $200. 1925 reprint, 40 color plates. $150.
The Allies' Fairy Book. London, 1916. 12 plates. Very Good. $125-$250. Philadelphia, 1916. $100-$175.
The Romance of King Arthur and His Knights of the Round Table. New York, 1917 1st American trade edition. 23 plates. Very Good. $160. NY, 1926. VG in DJ. $50.
Cinderella. By Charles Perrault. London, 1919 1st ed. One of 800 copies. Signed by Rackham. Handmade paper. Fine in case. $1,750. Philadelphia, 1919. VG inDJ. $175.
Irish Fairy Tales. By James Stephens. London, 1920 1st edition. Very Good. $200. NY, 1920. VG in DJ. $175.
Where the Blue Begins. By Christopher Morley. New York, 1922 1st edition. Very Good-Fine. $65-$100.
English Fairy Tales. Retold by F. A. Steel. Macmillan, 1924 3rd printing. Very Good. $20. NY, 1919. $125.
The Vicar of Wakefield. By Oliver Goldsmith. Philadelphia, 1929 1st American ed. VG in DJ. $75-$95.
Compleat Angler. By Izaac Walton. London, 1931 Trade ed. VG in DJ. $175-$225. McKay, 1931. $75-$150.
The Night Before Christmas. By Clement C. Moore. Lippincott, 1931 1st ed. VG. $85-$150. NY, 1929. $50.
The Legend of Sleepy Hollow. By Washington Irving. Philadelphia, no date 1st edition. One of 75 copies. Signed by Rackham. NF. $1,850. 1928 trade ed. VG. $150.
The Chimes. By Charles Dickens. London, Limited Editions Club, 1931. No. 303 of 1,500 copies, signed. Very Good in slipcase. $330 auction. Dealer. $500.
The Arthur Rackham Fairy Book. London, 1933 1st American edition. Very Good-Fine. $85-$150.

RADFORD ARCHITECTURAL BOOKS. Average price range. $25-$50. (See Trade Catalog section).

RAE, JOHN. *Grasshopper Green and the Meadow Mice*. Volland, 1922 13th printing. Illustrated. by author. Smudges, o/w Very Good. $48. Same, NY, 1922. $30.
Fairy Tales From France. Illus. by John Rae. Retold by William T. Larned. Volland, 1923 12th edition. Very Good in presentation box. $135. 1920 trade ed. $50-$75.
New Adventures of Alice. Volland, 1917. VG. $75-$125.
The Big Family. NY, Dodd, 1916. VG. $45-$65.
Granny Goose. Volland, 1926. 21 color plates. $75-$125.
Lucky Locket. Volland, 1928. VG. $45-$65.

RAFFALD, ELIZABETH. *The Experienced English House-keeper*. Philadelphia, 1818 New edition. Browned, two plates missing. $35. 1776 edition. Good. $150.

RAINE, WILLIAM MCLEOD. *Big-Town Roundup*. Houghton-Mifflin, 1920 1st ed. VG in good DJ. $28.
Guns of the Frontier: The Story of How Law Came to the West. Boston, 1940. Near Very Good. $45.
45-Caliber Law, 1941 1st edition. Very Good. $16.

RAINEY, GEORGE. *The Cherokee Strip*. Guthrie OK, 1933. Ex-library. Signed. Very Good. $125.

RAINEY, LURETTA. *History of Oklahoma*. Guthrie OK, 1939. Good-VG. $30.

RALLI, PAUL. *Viva Vegas*. House-Warven, 1953 1st edition. Fine, no dust jacket. $24.

RALPH, JULIAN. *Alone in China and Other Stories*. NY, 1900. Inscribed. Illustrated. Near Fine. $35.

RALPHSON, G. H. *Various "Boy Scouts" Titles*. Chicago, M. A. Donahue Co., 1910-1913. Good. $4-$6. Very Good. $10-$12. (Double these prices in dust jacket.)

RAMSAYE, TERRY. *A Million & 1 Nights: History of Motion Pictures*. NY, Simon Schuster, 1926 1st edition. 2 vols., original blue cloth. $150-$300.

RAND, AYN. *The Fountainhead*. Bobbs-Merrill, 1943 1st edition. Very Good in dust jacket. $160. Same, 1943 2nd edition. Rubbed dust jacket. $75. Another, no dust

jacket. $15. Book Club edition, 1943. Worn dust jacket. $14. NY, 1968. 25th anniversary edition. $20.
Atlas Shrugged. NY, 1957 1st edition. Very Good. $75. Another, Fine in dust jacket. $200.
For the New Intellectual. NY, 1961 1st edition. Near Fine in good dust jacket. $75.
The Romantic Manifesto. NY, 1969. Fine in fine DJ. $70.
Night of January 16th. New York, 1968 1st edition. Fine in dust jacket. $30-$40. Another, New York, no date. Paperback. Very Good. $35.
We the Living. New York, 1936 1st edition. Very Good in dust jacket. $60-$80.

RAND MCNALLY & COMPANY. *Atlas of the World*. Various editions, Chicago, 1895-1910. $50-$100. (See Atlas Section under "A", for comparable volumes.)

RANDALL, J. G. and DAVID DONALD. *The Civil War and Reconstruction*. Boston, 1961 2nd ed. VG. $25.

RANDOLPH, SARAH. *The Domestic Life of Thomas Jefferson*. 1871 1st ed. 432 pgs., illus. Tight, clean. $65.

RANDOLPH, VANCE. *Ozark Mountain Folks*. Vanguard, 1932. One of 250 copies, signed. VG in DJ. $25.
We Always Lie to Strangers. Columbia University, 1951 1st edition. Fine in good dust jacket. $30.
Down in the Holler. A Gallery of Oz-Ark Folk Speech. Univ. of Oklahoma, 1953 1st ed. Very Good. $25.

RANHOFER, CHARLES. *The Epicurean*. 1862-1894 menus, recipes. Hotel Monthly Press, 1920. 1,183 pgs. 800 plates. Author was Delmonico chef. Good-Very Good. $85-$150. Dover reprint of recent vintage. 1,183 pgs. Very Good in dust jacket. $35.

RANKIN, MELINDA. *Twenty Years Among the Mexicans: A Narrative of Missionary Labor*. Cincinnati, 1875 1st edition. Very Good. $35.

RANKIN, ROBERT. *Small Arms of the Sea Services: History of Firearms and Edged Weapons*. NY, Flayderman, 1972. Very Good-Fine in DJ. $40-$70.

RANSHAW, G. S. *Manufacturers' Practical Recipes*. Chemical Pubs. 1950 1st ed. Very Good. $12-$15.

RANSOM, JOHN L. *Andersonville Diary*. Auburn NY, 1881 1st edition. $95-$150. Middlebury VT, 1986 reprint. Very Good in dust jacket. $24.

RANSOME, ARTHUR. *Swallows and Amazons*. Philadelphia, 1931 1st ed. Helene Carter illus. Good. $20.
Missee Lee. NY, 1942 1st American ed. Very Good. $45.

RAPAPORT, STELLA F. *A Whittle Too Much*. Putnam's, 1955. Illustrated by author. Very Good in dust jacket. $18.

RAPPORT and NORTHWOOD. *Rendezvous with Destiny: History of the 101st Airborne Division*. Washington DC, 1948 1st ed. Very Good. $150-$175. Enlarged edition of the same year. Very Good in dust jacket. $40.

RASCOE, BURTON. *Belle Starr "The Bandit Queen"*. Random House, 1941 1st ed. Very Good, no DJ. $20.

RASMUSSEN, INGER MARGRETE. *East O'The Sun and West O'The Moon*. Whitman, 1924 3rd edition. Violet Moore Higgins illustrator. Very Good. $25.

RASMUSSEN, KNUD. *Across Arctic America*. NY, 1927 1st edition. Very Good. $75.

RASPE, RUDOLPH. *Singular Adventures of Baron Munchausen*. London, 1869. Engraved illus. and hand-colored frontis. G-VG. $50-$100. NY, 1952 Heritage reprint. Fine in slipcase. $14. Another, 1952 ed. Signed by illus., Fritz Kredel. $75. Altemus, 1903. Good. $8.

RATHBORNE. *The House Boat Boys*. Donohue, 1912. Near Fine. $25.

RAVEN, A. and J. *British Battleships of World War II*. Annapolis, 1976 1st ed. Very Good in dust jacket. $35.

RAVEN, SIMON. *Boys Will Be Boys*. London, 1963 1st edition. Very Good in dust jacket. $20.

RAWLING, CAPT. C. G. *The Land of the New Guinea Pygmies*. Philadelphia, 1913. 48 photos, folding map. Foxing, o/w Very Good. $50.

RAWLINGS, MARJORIE KINNAN. *The Yearling*. NY, 1938 1st edition. Edward Shenton illus. NF in vg DJ. $225. Others with various minor tape repairs. $75-$150. Same, NY, 1938. Wyeth illus. VG in DJ. $95-$150. Same, 1940, in DJ. $60-$95. NY, 1942, 5 plates. $50.
Cross Creek Cookery. NY, 1942 1st ed. Good with owner's name. $20. Another, VG. $40. Another, Fine. $95. Scribner's, 1980, 15th ed. Fine in dust jacket. $14.
Sojourner. New York, 1953. One of 480 copies. Signed presentation copy. Very Good in chip dust jacket. $250. Trade edition, 1953. $25-$45.
The Secret River. Scribner's, 1955. Leonard Weisgard illus. Ex-library. $20. Same, VG. $40. Fine in DJ. $150 up.

RAY, MAN. *Self Portrait*. Boston, 1963 1st edition. Fine in clipped dust jacket. $100.

RAYMOND, ALEX. *Flash Gordon and the Monsters of Mongo*. Whitman, 1935 1st edition. Very Good. $28.

RAYMOND, HENRY J. *Life and Public Services of Abraham Lincoln*. NY, Derby & Miller, 1865. 808 pgs. Full calf. Weak hinge o/w Very Good. $125.

READ, JEAN. *McCall's Book of Entertaining*. New York, 1979. Helpful hints and recipes from the editors of McCall's. Very Good. $15-$20.

READ, MISS. *Miss Clare Remembers*. Riverside MA, 1963. J. S. Goodall illus. Very Good in vg dust jacket. $14.

READ, OLIVER and WALTER WELCH. *From Tin Foil to Stereo*. Indianapolis, 1976 2nd edition. Photos. Near Fine in dust jacket. $30.

READ, OPIE. *A Tennessee Judge*. Chicago, 1893 1st edition. Good-Very Good. $15.
The Starbucks. Chicago, Laird & Lee, 1902 1st edition. Beautiful purple cloth. $75.
An Arkansas Planter. Chicago, 1896 1st ed. Fine. $45.
Bolanyo: a Novel. Way & Williams, Chicago, 1897 1st edition. Very Good. $100.
A Yankee From the West. Chicago, 1898 1st edition. Good-Very Good. $30.

READ, OPIE and FRANK PIXLEY. *The Carpet Bagger*. Chicago, 1893 1st edition. Very Good. $35.

READE, CHARLES. *Cloister and the Hearth*. Heritage, 1932. Lynd Ward illus. 2 vols. Fine in slipcase. $50.

READERS GUIDE TO PERIODICAL LITERATURE. Vols. 10-48, 1935-1988. $495 set.

REAGAN, NANCY. *Nancy*. NY, 1980 1st edition. Signed. Near Fine in dust jacket. $45.
To Love a Child. Bobbs Merrill, 1982 1st edition. Signed. Near Fine in dust jacket. $25.

REAGAN, RONALD. *Where's the Rest of Me?* NY, 1965 1st edition. Fine in dust jacket. $100.

REBOUX, PAUL. *Food for the Rich*. NY, 1958. Near Fine in dust jacket. $65.

RECHY, JOHN. *City of Night*. NY, 1963 1st edition. Fine in dust jacket. $25-$35.
The Sexual Outlaw. NY, 1977 1st edition. Very Good in dust jacket. $15. Another, signed. Fine in DJ. $95.

RECIPES, TRIED AND TRUE. Ladies Aid Society of the First Presbyterian Church, Marion OH, 1909 3rd edition. Very Good. $15.

RECK, FRANKLIN M. *The 4-H Story*. Iowa State Univ. 1962 2nd edition. Very Good. $10.

RECTOR, GEORGE. *The Rector Cook Book*. Milwaukee Railroad, 1923 3rd edition. Fair to Good. $10.
A La Rector. Atlantic & Pacific, 1933. Spine repaired. Inscribed, sgnd. by Rector. Published for World's Fair. $45.

Dine at Home With Rector. NY, 1934, 37. 1st edition. Very Good in good dust jacket. $20.

REDPATH, JAMES. *The Public Life of John Brown*. Boston, 1860 1st edition. Good-Very Good. $20-$40.

REED, ALMA. *The Ancient Past of Mexico*. NY, 1966. Very Good in dust jacket. $40.

REED, EARL. *The Silver Arrow & Other Indian Romances*. Chicago, 1926 1st ed. Signed by author. Good-VG. $18.
Sketches in Duneland. NY, John Lane, 1918 1st ed. Green gilt-dec. cloth. Reed illus. VG. $23. Signed by auth. $30.

REED, G. WALTER (Editor). *History of Sacramento County Calif*. Los Angeles, 1923 1st ed. NF. $75-$100.

REED, HELEN. *Brenda's Summer at Rockley*. Little Brown, 1901. J. W. Smith illus. orig. cloth. $125-$175. Reprint, 1904. VG. $25. Same in dust jacket. $75.

REED, JOHN A. *History of the 101st Regiment of Pennsylvania Volunteers*. Chicago, 1910. $40-$60.

REED, MYRTLE. *The Book of Clever Beasts*. NY, 1904. Peter Newell illus. $20-$25. Putnam, 1902. $30-$45.
White Shield. 1912, signed 1st ed. Very Good. $30.
Weaver of Dreams. Putnam, 1911 1st ed. G-VG. $10-$20.

REES, J. R. (Editor). *The Case of Rudolf Hess*. London, 1947 1st edition. Very Good. $45.

REESE, DAVID M. *Humbugs of New York*. NY, 1838 1st edition. Good. $65.

REEVES, JAMES. *History of the 24th Regiment, New Jersey Volunteers*. Camden NJ, 1889. 45 pages, printed wraps. Very nice copy. $150.

REGARDIE, ISRAEL. *Middle Pillar*. Chicago, 1938. One of 350 copies. Faded spine, soiled slipcase, o/w VG. $125.

REICHENBACH, WILLIAM. *Sixguns and Bullseyes*. 1936 1st edition. Very Good. $35.

REID, HARTELAW. *Rational Cookery Made Practical and Economical*. Edinburg, 1870 5th edition. $65-$80.

REID, MAYNE. *The Quadroon: Or, A Lover's Adventures in Louisiana*. London, 1856 1st edition. 3 vols. Vol. 1 unopened. Some browning, chipping. $400. Dillingham, 1897 edition. Very Good. $15.
Osceola the Seminole. New York, 1858. Rebacked, some foxing edgewear. Good. $215.
The Plant Hunters: or, Adventures Among the Himalaya Mountains. Boston, 1858 1st edition. Good plus. $100. International, 1889 edition. Very Good. $10.

Wild Life, or Adventures On the Frontier. NY, 1859 1st edition. (Early Texas) Very Good. $400.

The Cliff Climbes: Or the Lone Home in theHimalayas. Boston, 1864 1st American edition. Very Good-Fine. $200.

The Headless Horseman: A Strange Tale of Texas. London, 1866 1st edition. 2 vols. Spines frayed, hinges cracked. Good. $300.

The Child Wife: A Tale of Two Worlds. London, 1868 1st edition. 3 vols. Very Good. $325.

The Castaways. NY, 1870 1st American edition. 4 engraved plates. $35.

Bruin: The Grand Bear Hunt. Boston, 1871 Later printing. Very Good. $16.

Scalp Hunters. New York, no date. Many illustrations. Good-Very Good. $50.

REIGER, GEORGE. *Zane Grey: Outdoorsman*. Englewood Cliffs NJ, 1972 3rd printing. Fine in dust jacket. $30.

The Zane Grey Cook Book. Prentice Hall, 1976 1st edition. Near Fine in dust jacket. $25-$75.

REIK, THEODORE. *The Unknown Murderer*. London, 1936 1st edition in English. One of 1,100 copies. VG. $75.

The Compulsion to Confess. New York, 1959 1st edition. Fine in dust jacket. $25.

REILLY, HELEN. *The Man With the Painted Head*. NY, 1931 1st edition. VG in frayed dust jacket. $65.

Murder in Shinbone Alley. NY, Crime Club, 1940 1st edition. Near Fine in chip dust jacket. $30.

Name Your Poison. New York, 1942 1st edition. Fine in good dust jacket. $35.

Ding Dong Bell. NY, 1958 1st ed. Very Good in DJ. $20.

REIT, SEYMOUR. *Masquerade: the Amazing World of Camouflage*. No place, 1978 1st ed. Very Good. $25.

REMARQUE, ERICH MARIA. *All Quiet on the Western Front*. Boston, 1929 1st American edition, 1st printing. Author's 1st book. Very Good. $75. Same. London, 1929 1st edition in English. Very Good in dust jacket. $100. Another, Fine in dust jacket. $250.

REMINGTON, FREDERIC. *Crooked Trails*. NY and London, 1898 1st edition. Illus. by author. Near Fine, $210-$275. 1923 edition, poor dust jacket. $20-$30.

Remington's Frontier Sketches. Chicago, 1898 1st edition. Very Good in slipcase. $600.

Stories of Peace and War. NY, 1899. Illustrated by author. Good. $75.

Done in the Open. NY, 1903. Verses by Owen Wiser. Illustrated by author. Very Good. $350. Same, 1904 edition. Cover rubbed. Good. $68.

Pony Tracks. NY, 1903 ed. 70 illustrations by author. Good. $25. 1923 edition. Very Good, no dust jacket. $24.

The Way of an Indian Fox. Duffield, 1906 1st edition. Illus. by author. Rebound. Good plus. $50.

Frederic Remington's Own West. New York, 1960. Illustrated. Very Good. $18.

REMINGTON, FREDERIC (Illustrator). *The West From a Car Window*. By Richard Harding Davis. London, 1892. Good-Very Good. $65-$85.

The Oregon Trail: Sketches of Prairie & Rocky Mountain Life. By Francis Parkman. Boston, 1892. Near Very Good, largely unopened. $375.

The Old Santa Fe Trail. By Col. Henry Inman. NY, 1897 1st edition. Good plus. $125.

Wolfville. By Alfred H. Lewis. New York, 1897. Scuffed, rubbed. $15.

The Way to The West. By Emerson Hough. No place, 1903 1st edition. Near Fine. $100.

A Journey in Search of Christmas. By Owen Wister. NY, 1904 1st edition. Near Fine. $100.

Prentice Mulford's Story. By Prentice Mulford. Bio, 1953. One of 500 copies. Near Fine. $125.

Many Remington illustrations appear in *Harper's Weekly* from 1875 to 1890. $10-$25 each. A dealer lot of 65 prints from *Colliers* and *Harper's* pre-1903 issues. $600.

REMISE, JAC & JEAN FONDIN. *The Golden Age of Toys*. Edita Lausanne, 1967. Tipped-in color plates. Good. $60. Fine. $100.

REMLAP, L. T. *The Life of General U. S. Grant*. NY, 1888 1st edition. 772 pages. Good-Very Good. $35.

RENAULT, MARY. *The King Must Die*. London, 1958 1st English edition. Fine in clip dust jacket. $45.

The Mask of Apollo. New York, 1966 1st American edition. Fine in dust jacket. $25.

Funeral Games. New York, 1981 1st edition. Fine in dust jacket. $15.

RENDELL, RUTH. *To Fear a Painted Veil*. NY, Crime Club, 1965 1st edition. Fine in dust jacket. $250.

Murder Being Once Done. London, 1972 1st British edition. Fine in dust jacket. $175.

A Judgment in Stone. London, 1977 1st British edition. Fine in dust jacket. $65.

Make Death Love Me. New York, 1979 1st American edition. Near Fine in dust jacket. $35.

REPPLIER, AGNES. *In The Dozy Hours*. Boston, 1894 1st edition. Very Good-Fine. $24.

To Think of Tea! Boston, 1932 Very Good in DJ. $14.

Junipero Serra. 1933, Doubleday Good. $8-$12.

REPORT OF THE COMMISSIONER OF AGRICULTURE FOR 1884. Good. $12.

REPORT TO THE PEOPLE. Stone & Webster Engineering Corp. No place, 1946. Illus. history of atomic energy work in the early years. Good-VG. $75.

RERICK, ROWLAND. *History of Ohio*. Madison WI, 1905 1st edition. ¾ leather. Bumped corners. Good. $50.

RETAIL ADVERTISING, AD ILLUS. International Textbook Co., 1905. Good-VG. $15-$20.

REVERE, JOSEPH WARREN. *A Tour of Duty in California*. NY, Boston, 1849. Rebound. Some foxing. $140-$175. *Naval Duty in California*. No place, 1947. One of 1,000 copies. Very Good. $30. Mint. $50.

REVIEW OF THE INTERNATIONAL LIVESTOCK EXPOSITION. Chicago, 1941 & 1949. 2 vols., maroon cloth. Very Good. $45.

REVOLUTIONARY PAPERS. New York Historical Society, 1879-1881. Vols. 11-13. 3 vols., stains, wear. $35.

REXROTH, KENNETH. *In What Hour*. NY, 1940 1st edition. Fine in dust jacket. $85. *The Signature of All Things*. New Directions, 1949. One of 1,500 copies. Very Good in chip dust jacket. $100. *The Dragon and the Unicorn*. New Directions, 1952 1st edition. Very Good in dust jacket. $50. *Communalism: From Its Origin to the 20th Century*. Seabury, 1974 1st edition. Very Good in dust jacket. $8. *100 Poems From the Chinese*. New Directions, no date 1st edition. Fine. $25.

REY, H. A. *Look for the Letters*. NY, 1945 1st edition. Illustrated by author. Very Good. $50-$100.

REY, MARGARET. *Curious George Flies a Kite*. Boston, 1958 1st edition. H. A. Rey illus. Very Good in DJ. $45.

REYNOLDS, B. S. *Souvenir Books* of Washington DC. Various titles pub. from 1910-1920. $10-$12 each.

REYNOLDS, JOHN. *Pioneer History of Illinois*. Belleville, N. A. Randall, 1852 1st ed. Foxing, spotting. Good. $550.

REYNOLDS, QUENTIN. *The Wounded Don't Cry*. NY, 1941 1st edition, presentation copy. Very Good. $60. Another, trade edition. $14. *Only the Stars are Neutral*. NY, 1942 1st edition. Very Good in dust jacket. $8. *Officially Dead*. Random House, 1945 1st edition. Good-Very Good. $20-$25. *The Fiction Factory, From Pulp Row to Quality Street*. NY, 1955 1st edition. Fine in fine dust jacket. $30-$45.

RHEAD, LOUIS. *The Speckled Brook Trout*. NY, 1902 trade ed. Illus. by author. Very Fine in dust jacket. $195. *The Book of Fish and Fishing*. NY, 1908. Illus. by author. Very Good. $15. *American Trout Stream Insects*. NY, 1916 1st edition. Illus. by author. Good. $25.

Fishermen's Lures and Game-Fish Food. NY, 1920 1st edition. Illustrated by author. Good-Very Good. $40.

RHINE, J. B. *Extra-Sensory Perception After Sixty Years*. NY, 1940 1st edition. Fine in torn dust jacket. $40. *New Frontiers of the Mind*. Farrar, 1937 1st edition. Very Good-Fine in dust jacket. $25-$35.

RHODE, E. S. *A Garden of Herbs*. Boston & NY, 4th printing, 1936. Very Good in dust jacket. $25.

RHODE, IRMA. *The Viennese Cook Book*. NY, 1951 1st edition. Very Good in dust jacket. $12.

RICE, ALICE HEGAN. *Mrs. Wiggs of the Cabbage Patch*. New York, 1901 1st edition, 1st printing. Near Very Good. $45. Grosset & Dunlap reprint. $8. *Lovely Mary*. Century, 1903 1st edition. Illus. $10-$25. *Mr. Opp*. Century Co., 1909 1st edition. Leon Guipon illustrator. Very Good. $45.

RICE, CRAIG. *The Thursday Turkey Murders*. New York, 1943. Fine in fine dust jacket. $125.

RICE, ELMER. *Voyage to Purilia*. Cosmopolitan, 1930 1st edition. Near Fine in dust jacket. $50. *Counsellor at Law*. NY, 1931 1st edition. VG in DJ. $35. *Flight to the West*. Coward, 1941 1st edition. Fine in fine dust jacket. $35.

RICE, LOUISE. *Practical Graphology*. Chicago, 1910. A Good copy. $25.

RICH, PROF. GEO. E. *Artistic Horse-Shoeing. A Practical & Scientific Treatise*. NY, 1890, Richardson. $50.

RICH, LOUISE DICKINSON. *We Took to the Woods*. NY, 1942. Good in dust jacket. $5. *The Coast of Maine - An Informal History and Guide*. Crowell, 1970 3rd edition. Fine in dust jacket. $14.

RICHARDS, EVA. *Arctic Mood*. Caxton, 1949 1st edition. Very Good. $14-$20.

RICHARDS, LAURA E. *Captain January*. Boston, 1891 1st edition, 1st state. Covers badly worn, loose. $35. *Three Margarets*. Boston, 1897. Very Good. $20. *Fernley House*. Estes, 1901. Very Good. $20. *Golden Willows*. Little Brown, 1903 1st edition. $25-$40. *The Silver Crown*. Little Brown, 1906 1st ed. VG. $55.

RICHARD'S PASTRY BOOK. Hotel Monthly, Chicago, 1907 2nd edition. Brown cloth, gilt letters. Good-Very Good. $40.

RICHARDSON, ALBERT D. *The Secret Service, The Field, etc.* Hartford CT, 1865 1st ed. $50-$65. 1866 prntg. $25.

Beyond the Mississippi. Hartford CT, circa 1869. New edition. Stained cover. $95. 1867 1st edition. 572 pgs, 200 illustrations. Discolored. $85.
Personal History of U. S. Grant. Hartford CT, 1868. Leather, shaken. $35.

RICHARDSON, JAMES D (Editor). *A Compilation of the Messages and Papers of the Presidents, 1789-1897.* Complete set of 10 vols. Washington DC, 1896-1899. Very Good plus. $225.

RICHARDSON, LYON. *History of Early American Magazines. 1741-1789*. NY, 1931. VG in worn DJ. $18.

RICHLER, MORDECAI. *Stick Your Neck Out*. NY, 1963 1st American edition. Fine in very good dust jacket. $13.
Jacob Two-Two Meets the Headed Fang. NY, 1975 1st edition. Very Good-Fine in clip dust jacket. $30-$45.
Home Sweet Home: My Canadian Album. NY, 1984 1st edition. Very Good in dust jacket. $18.
Jacob Two-Two and the Dinosaur. NY, 1987 1st edition. Norman Eyolfson illus. Fine in dust jacket. $22.

RICHMOND, C. W. *A History of the County of Du Page, Illinois*. Chicago, Scripps, Bross & Spears, 1857. Worn, frayed, foxed. $350.

RICHMOND, MARY. *Shaker Literature, A Bibliography*. Hancock, Mass., 1977. 2 vols. Very Fine. $50.

RICHMOND, REV. J. F. *New York and Its Institutions, 1609-1873*. 200 illus. Revised, 7th ed. New York, 1873. Dark covers, soiled. $15.

RICHTER, CONRAD. *The Sea of Grass*. New York, 1937 1st edition. Very Good. $40.
The Fields. NY, 1946 1st ed. Fine in fair dust jacket. $35.
Always Young and Fair. NY, 1947 1st ed. VG in DJ. $40.
A Simple Honorable Man. NY, 1962 1st ed. F in DJ. $25.

RICHTOFEN, MANFRED VON. *Der Rose Dampffleger*. Berlin, 1917 1st ed. German WWI ace's own story, illus. Richtofen was killed in action at age 25. Rare. $150.

RICKARD, T. A. *Thru The Yukon & Alaska*. San Francisco, 1909. One of 1,392 copies. Illus. Very Good. $150.
A History of American Mining. McGraw Hill, 1932 1st ed. 418 pgs. Illus. Fine, no DJ. $20.

RICKENBACKER, EDWARD. *Rickenbacker, An Auto-biography*. Prentice Hall, 1967 1st ed. Signed by author. Fine in DJ. $65-$80. Another, unsigned. $15.

RICKETT, H. W. *Wild Flowers of America*. NY, Crown, 1964. Color illus. Fine in dust jacket. $15-$20.
Wild Flowers of the Southern States. 1966. 2 volumes. Fine in slipcase. $75-$125.

RICKETTS, EDWARD and JACK CALVIN. *Between Pacific Tides*. Stanford University Press, 1968 4th edition. Revised by J. W. Hedgpeth. Very Good in dust jacket. $14.

RIDGEWAY, MATTHEW. Soldier: *The Memoirs of Matthew Ridgeway*. NY, 1956 1st edition. Fine. $20.

RIDGEWAY & CLARK REPORT. *Pictorial History of the Korean War, 1950-53*. VFW Memorial Ed, 1954. F. $15.

RIDGEWAY, ROBERT. *A Manual of North American Birds*. Philadelphia, 1887 1st ed. $75-$85. Same, 1896 2nd edition. (enlarged?) $100-$150.

RIDGWAY, J. L. *Scientific Illustration*. Stanford, 1938. Illustrated. Good. $25.

RIDINGS, SAM P. *The Chisholm Trail: A History of the World's Greatest Cattle Trail*. Guthrie OK, 1936 1st edition. Near Fine. $150-$250.

RIDLEY. *Ritz-Carlton Cook Book*. Philadelphia, 1968 2nd edition. Good-VG in dust jacket. $20.

RIDPATH, JOHN CLARK. *A Popular History of the United States of America*. No place, 1880. Full leather. VG. $35.
History of U. S. Civil War and Reconstruction. Vol XI, Jones Bros., 1916 reprint. Good, rebound copy. $12.

RIEGEL, ROBERT. *Merchant Vessels*. NY, Appleton, 1921 1st edition. Illus. textbook. Very Good. $15.

RIESENBERG, FELIX. *The Golden Road: California's Spanish Mission Trail*. NY, McGraw-Hill, 1962. Very Good in dust jacket. $35.
Sea War, the Story of U. S. Merchant Marine in WWII. New York, Rinehart, 1956. $15-$30.

RIIS, JACOB. *How the Other Half Lives*. New York, 1890 1st edition. Very Good. $125.
The Children of the Poor. NY, 1892 1st ed. NF. $125.
Battle With the Slum. NY, 1902. Very Good. $13.
Old Town. NY, 1909 1st edition. Near Fine. $60.

RIKER, JAMES. *Revised History of Harlem*. New York, 1904. 908 pgs., folding map. Good-VG. $75.

RILEY, JAMES WHITCOMB. *Green Fields and Running Brooks*. Bowen-Merrill, 1893 1st edition. Very Good. $14.
Armanzindy. Bobbs Merrill, 1894 1st edition. Special Bound edition of 100, signed and numbered. G-VG. $100-$150. Regular 1894 edition. in green boards. Good. $14.
After Whiles. Bowen Merrill, 1897 revised ed. Good. $9.
A Child-World. Bowen-Merrill, 1897 1st edition. Red cloth. Later printing with London on title page. Few page smudges. Good-Very Good. $60.

Riley Child-Rymes. Will Yowter illustrator. IN, 1898. Good-Very Good. $25.

Boys of the Old Glee Club. Bowen Merrill, 1907 1st edition. Very Good. $18.

Rubaiyat of Doc Sifers. NY, 1897 1st ed. Near Fine. $35.

An Old Sweetheart of Mine. Bobbs-Merrill, 1902 1st edition. Howard Chandler Christy illus. VG-Fine. $20-$50.

The Works of James Whitcomb Riley. NY, 1903 12 vols. Homestead ed. Uncut, unopened. Fine. $200. 1920s, 11 vols. $95. 1916, 10 vols. Memorial ed. VG. $180. 1916, Harper. Christy & Betts illus. Very Good. $75.

Out to Old Aunt Mary's. Bobbs-Merrill, 1904 1st edition. Howard Chandler Christy illus. Very Good-Fine. $20-$50.

While the Heart Beats Young. Bobbs-Merrill, 1906. Ethel Betts illus. Edgewear, o/w Very Good. $60.

The Runaway Boy. Indianapolis, 1906. Ethel Franklin Betts illustrator. Good-Very Good. $20-$50.

Morning. Bobbs-Merrill, 1907 1st edition. October on copyright page. Good-Very Good. $40.

The Raggedy Man. NY, 1907. Ethel Betts illustrator. Edge chip, o/w Very Good. $85.

The Boy Lives on Our Farm. Bobbs-Merrill, 1908. Ethel Betts illustrator. Near Very Good. $55.

Orphant Annie Book. Indianapolis, 1908. Ethel Franklin Betts illustrator. Near Fine. $225.

Songs of Summer. Indianapolis, 1909. Fine. $20.

Riley Roses. Bobbs-Merrill, 1909. Howard Chandler Christy illus. Franklin Booth decorations. VG. $45-$75.

The Rose. IN, 1916. Christy illus. VG. $25-$40.

Riley Farm Rhymes. Bowen Merrill, 1901. Good. $12.

The Out Trail. Doran, 1923. Good plus. $27.

The Red Lamp. Doran, 1925 1st ed. VG, no DJ. $32.

The Great Mistake. NY, 1940 1st ed. VG in DJ. $35.

The Yellow Room. NY, 1945 1st edition. Fine in DJ. $25.

A Hoosier Romance. Canada, 1910 1st edition. Color illustrations. Water stained. $35.

RIMINGTON, CRITCHELL. *Fighting Fleets, 1942*. New York, 1942. Good-Fine. $15-$50.

RIN TIN TIN, ONE OF THE FAMILY. Whitman, 1953 1st edition. Very Good. $12.

RINEHART, MARY ROBERTS. *The Circular Staircase*. Indianapolis, 1908 1st ed. Pict. olive-green cloth. VG. $45. Another, 1st state, with September copyright. $100.

The Man in Lower Ten. Indianapolis, 1909 1st edition. Howard Chandler Christy illus. First crime fiction by author. Very Good. $45-$65. Fine. $100 up.

The Amazing Adventurs of Letitia Carberry. Bobbs Merrill, 1911 1st edition. Howard Chandler Christy illustrator. Very Good plus $15.

The Street of Seven Stars. Houghton Mifflin, 1914 1st edition. Cover spotted. Good-VG. $25.

The Door. Farrar & Rinehart, 1930 1st edition. $30.

Lost Ectasy. Doran, 1927 1st ed. Very Good. $10.

Testing Tonight. Boston & NY, 1918. Illus. $50.

RINZLER, CAROL ANN. *The Book of Chocolate*. NY, 1977. Near Fine in dust jacket. $25.

RIPLEY, OZARK. *Modern Bait and Fly Casting*. NY, 1928 1st edition. Very Good in dust jacket. $28.

RIPLEY, ROBERT. *Believe It or Not!* Simon & Schuster, 1929, 9 part 1st ed. 172 pgs. Good, no DJ. $10. 1930 ed., bright covers. $20. 1946 reprint, Garden City. VG. $5.

RIPPEY, SARAH CORY. *The Goody-Naughty Book*. Rand McNally, 1913 1st ed. Some soiling, else VG. $30-$45.

RITCHEN, RALPH. *Motor's Auto Repair Manual*. 1962 25th edition. Very Good. $16.

RITCHIE, JAMES S. *Wisconsin and Its Resources*. Philadelphia, Desilver, 1858 3rd revised edition. Folding colored map intact. Shaken, else Very Good. $350.

RITTENHOUSE, JACK. *American Horse-Drawn Vehicles*. Los Angeles, 1948 1st edition. One of 1,000 copies. Very Good in very good dust jacket. $35.

RITTER, F. R. *Advantage Card Playing and Draw Poker*. 1905. 117 pages. "Perhaps the rarest and most desired book on cheating and poker." Very Fine. $4,100 auction.

RITUAL OF THE ORDER OF THE EASTERN STAR. Eastern Star, 1916 7th edition. Very Good. $8.

RIVES, AMELIE. *Athel-Wold*. NY, Harper, 1893 1st edition. Orig. dec. cloth, some light soil, o/w clean & bright. $95.

ROBBINS, HAROLD. *The Dream Merchants*. New York, 1949 1st edition. Very Good. $20.

A Stone for Danny Fisher. New York, 1952 1st edition. Fine in very good dust jacket. $35.

The Carpet Baggers. NY, 1961 1st ed. VG in DJ. $40.

ROBBINS, MARY CAROLINE. *The Rescue of an Old Place*. Boston & New York, 1892 1st edition. Author's 1st book. Very Good. $65.

ROBBINS, ROBERT A. *The 91st Infantry Division in WWII*. Washington, 1947 1st ed. VG-Fine. $50-$75.

ROBERTS, CHARLES. *Kindred of the Wild*. Boston, L.C. Page, 1902 1st edition. Illustrated. Very Good. $25.

The Haunters of the Silence. Grosset & Dunlap, 1907. Illustrated. Good-VG. $10-$14.

The Watchers of the Trails. Boston, 1904 1st edition. Illustrated. Very Good. $15.

Secret Trails. Macmillan, 1917 2nd printing. $15-$25.

ROBERTS, DAVID. *Cattle Breeds and Origin*. Wisconsin, 1916. Illustrated. 177 pages. Good-Very Good. $36.

ROBERTS, ELIZABETH MADOX. *Great Meadow*. NY, 1930 limited ed. Signed, in slipcase. Fine. $35.
Song in the Meadow. NY, 1940 1st ed. VG in vg DJ. $40.

ROBERTS, JOHN. *Modern Medicine and Homeopathy*. Philadelphia, 1895 1st ed. Ex-library. $125.

ROBERTS, KENNETH. *The Lively Lady*. NY, 1933. Signed, Very Good. $25.
Rabble in Arms. NY, 1935. Signed. Good. $25.
Northwest Passage. Garden City, 1937 1st edition. Dark green cloth. Inscribed. Very Good. $75. Same in DJ. $125. Doubleday, 1937 2nd edition. Very Good. $8.
Trending Into Maine. Little Brown, 1938. N. C. Wyeth illus. Very Good. $15-22. Another dealer offers at $45.
Lydia Bailey. NY, 1947 Book Club edition. Very Good in dust jacket. $6. Doubleday 1st edition. $20
I Wanted to Write. Doubleday, 1949 1st edition. 470 pages. Very Good, no dust jacket. $14.
Henry Gross and His Dowsing Rod. Garden City, NY, 1951 1st edition. Good in dust jacket. $25.

ROBERTS, STOUDT & KRICK. *History of Lehigh County Pennsylvania*. Includes genealogical records. Lehigh Valley, 1914 1st edition. Very Good. $125.

ROBERTSON, CONSTANCE NOYES. *Oneida Community; The Breakup*. Syracuse, 1972. Fine in dust jacket. $10.

ROBERTSON, H. P. *The History of Thoroughbred Racing in America*. Bonanza reprint of 1963 orig. VG in DJ. $35.

ROBERTSON, JOHN W. *Francis Drake & Other Early Explorers Along the Pacific Coast*. San Francisco, Grabhorn Press, 1927 limited edition. 1 of 1,000 copies. Very Good plus. $250.

ROBESON, KENNETH. *The Man of Bronze*. (Doc Savage). Street & Smith, 1933 1st edition. Paper browned, hinges cracked o/w Very Good. $125.

ROBESON, SUSAN. *The Whole World in His Hands: A Pictorial Biography of Paul Robeson*. Secaucus NJ, 1981. Very Good in dust jacket. $75.

ROBINSON, ALFRED. *Life in California*. NY, Wiley & Putnam, 1846 1st edition. 341 pages, 9 plates, numerous engravings. Rebound, foxing throughout. $400.

ROBINSON, CHARLES. *Modern Civic Art, or the City Made Beautiful*. NY, Putnams, 1903 1st edition. VG. $75.

ROBINSON, EDWIN ARLINGTON. *The Torrent of the Night Before*. Gardiner ME, 1896 1st edition. Author's 1st book. Inscribed. Very Good. $900-$1,400.
The Children of the Night. Boston, 1897 1st edition. Near Very Good. $200.

Tristam. NY, 1927 11th printing. Signed. Very Good. $45.
Amaranth. Macmillan, 1934 1st edition. Very Good in dust jacket which has extra wrapper advertising three more books. $25.

ROBINSON, JERRY. *The Comics, an Illustrated History of Comic Strip Art*. Putnam, 1974. Fine in DJ. $18.

ROBINSON, ROWLAND E. *Uncle Lisha's Shop*. New York, 1887 1st ed. $50. 1888. Very Good. $14.
In New England's Fields and Woods. Boston, 1896 1st edition. Near Fine. $35.
Out of Bondage and Other Stories. Rutland VT, 1936. Very Good. $20.

ROBINSON, WILL H. *Under Turquoise Skies*. New York, Macmillan, 1928. Good. $30.
The Story of Arizona. Phoenix, 1919 1st ed. Berryhill. Signed. Very Good-Fine. $30-$50.

ROBINSON, WILLIAM HEATH (Illustrator). *The Queen's Story Book*. NY, 1898. Fine. $45.
Peacock Pie. By Walter de la Mare. Holt, 1925. Very Good in fair dust jacket. $75.

ROCKFELLOW, JOHN ALEXANDER. *Log of an Arizona Trail Blazer*. Tucson, 1933 1st ed. Fine, tan cloth. $125. Republished, 1955. $20.

ROCKWELL, CAREY. Grosset & Dunlap. Various dates. Corbett Space Cadet Series. All VG dust jackets:
Stand By For Mars. 1953. $25.
Danger in Deep Space. 1954. $20.
The Space Pioneers. 1953. $18.
Revolt on Venus. 1956. $14.
The Robot Rocket. 1956. $14.

ROCKWELL, NORMAN. *My Adventures as an Illustrator*. Garden City NY, 1960, Doubleday 1st ed. Inscribed by author. G-VG. $100-$150. Unsigned 1st ed. $40-$50. 1979 edition. As new. $16.
Willie Was Different. NY, 1969 1st edition. Illus. by author. Good-Very Good. $28.
102 Favorite Paintings of Norman Rockwell. 1978. Very Good in dust jacket. $15.
Norman Rockwell's Counting House. NY, 1977. Illus. by author. Very Good. $15.
Christmas Book. Bookthrift, 1977 edition. Fine in dust jacket. Illustrated. $14.
Tom Sawyer and Huckleberry Finn. Heritage Press, 1936, 1940 2 vols. Color illus. by Rockwell. VG. $65 pair.

ROCKWOOD, ROY. *Through the Air to the North Pole*. NY, 1906 1st ed. Illustrated. As new. $45.
Bomba the Jungle Boy on the Underground River. Cupples Leon, 1930. Very Good in dust jacket. $15. (Other titles. Good, no dust jackets. $5-$8.)

RODDENBERRY, GENE. *Star Trek*. NY, 1979 1st edition. Fine in nicked dust jacket. $30.

ROEDER, RALPH. *Catherine de'Medici and the Lost Revolution*. NY, 1937 1st American ed. Very Good. $20.
Juarez and His Mexico. Viking, 1947 1st ed. 2 vols. in slipcase. Ex-library. $35.

ROERICH, NICHOLAS. *Shambhala*. NY, 1930. Very Good in chip dust jacket. $65.

ROETHKE, THEODORE. *The Lost Son and Other Poems*. NY, 1948. DJ edgeworn. Signed leaf tipped in. $350.
The Collected Poems of Theodore Roethke. Doubleday, 1953 1st ed. Edge wear on dust jacket, o/w fine. $45.
The Waking: Poems 1933-1953. Doubleday, 1953 1st edition. Fair dust jacket, o/w near fine. $165.
The Far Field. Doubleday, 1964 1st. NF in clip DJ. $50.

ROGERS, ALICE. *Poodles in Particular, History, Care and Management*. Orange Judd, 1957 subsequent edition. A Fine copy. $14.

ROGERS, WILL. *Will Rogers Illiterate Digest*. NY, 1924, Boni 1st edition. Good-Very Good. $10-$15.
Letters of a Self-Made Diplomat. 1926. Good. $17.
Ether and Me, or "Just Relax". Putnam, 1931 12th edition. Good. $7.
The Autobiography of Will Rogers. Donald Day, Editor. Houghton Mifflin, 1949 1st ed. Good-VG. $10-$20.

ROHAN, JACK. *Yankee Arms Maker, Samuel Colt*. Harpers, 1935 1st edition. Very Good. $40.

ROHMER, SAX (ARTHUR WADE). *The Green Eyes of Bast*. McBride, 1920 1st ed. Good. $35. VG. $45-$65.
She Who Sleeps. New York, 1928 1st edition. Fine in very good dust jacket. $150-$350.
The Book of Fu Manchu. New York, 1929. $25-$35.
The Mask of Fu Manchu. NY, Crime Club, 1932 1st ed. Near Fine in frayed, chip dust jacket. $400.
President Fu Manchu. Garden City, 1936 1st. $250-$350.
The Island of Fu Manchu. London, 1941 1st edition. Fine in near fine dust jacket. $500. NY, Crime Club 1941 1st edition. Near Fine in written on dust jacket. $250.
Seven Sins. No place, 1943 1st edition. Very Good in chipped dust jacket. $35.
Shadow of Fu Manchu. Crime Club, 1948. Very Good in dust jacket. $65.
The Daughter of Fu Manchu. London, 1955. Fine in dust jacket. $25.
Emperor Fu Manchu. London, 1959 1st ed. Cover stain, dust jacket stain, wear. $30.

ROLL, CHARLES. *Indiana-150 Years of American Development*. Lewis, 1931 1st edition. 5 volume set. Leather bound. Fine. $90.

ROLLINS, PHILIP ASHTON. *Jinglebob*. NY, 1927. VG. $18. Scribners, 1930. Wyeth illus. $75-$150.
The Cowboy An Unconventional History. NY, 1936. Scribners. Good in dust jacket. $35.

ROLLINSON, JOHN K. *Pony Trails in Wyoming*. Caxton, 1940 1st ed. VG in DJ. $30. 1941 ed., no DJ. $15.
Wyoming Cattle Trails. Caxton, 1948 1st ed. Fine in DJ. $35. Same, ex-library. Good. $14.

ROLT-WHEELER, FRANCIS. *Boy With the U. S. Foresters*. Lee & Shepherd, 1910 1st ed. Illus. Very Good. $20.
The Book of Cowboys. Boston, 1921 1st printing. Illus. Very Good. $50.

ROLVAAG, O. E. *Giants in the Earth*. NY, 1927 1st edition. Very Good. $18. Fine. $35.
Their Father's God. NY, 1931 1st ed. F in chip DJ. $50.
The Boat of Longing. New York, 1933 1st edition. Fine in frayed dust jacket. $60.

ROMAIN, J. H. *Gambling*. 1891. 230 pgs. $95 at auction.

ROMAINE, LAWRENCE. *Guide to American Trade Catalogues 1744-1900*. NY, 1960. $40. Another dealer offers at $150. Recent Dover publications, reprint. $10.

ROMBAUER, IRMA. *The Joy of Cooking*. St. Louis, 1931 1st edition. 395 pgs. $800-$1,100. 1931-1975 reprints. Very Good-Fine. $10-$18 each.

ROOSEVELT, FRANKLIN DELANO. *Whither Bound?* Boston, 1926 1st edition. Lecture at Milton Academy. 1st book by FDR. Very Good-Fine. $250-$500.
On Our Way. NY, 1934 1st edition. John Day. Very Good in dust jacket. $60-$75.

ROOSEVELT, ROBERT B. *Five Acres Too Much*. NY, 1869. Spine poor, contents Very Good. $18.

ROOSEVELT, THEODORE. *Hunting Trips of a Ranchman*. NY, 1885 1st trade edition. Very Good. $100-$150. London, 1886 1st British edition. Near Fine. $175-$250.
The Wilderness Hunter. New York, 1893 1st edition. Very Good. $95-$140.
The Rough Riders. NY, 1899 1st edition. Scribners. Gilt dec. cloth. Very Good. $195-$225.
Ranch Life & Hunting Trails. NY, 1902. Frederic Remington illus. Overall Very Good. $90.
Outdoor Pastimes of an American Hunter. NY, 1905 1st edition. Fine. $50-$100.
The Winning of the West. 1906. 6 vol. set. Very Good-Fine. $75. 1904. 4 vol. set. $75-$150.
African Game Trails. NY, 1910 1st edition. Scribners. Good-Very Good. $35-$75. 1919 2 volume set, $55-$65.
Through the Brazilian Wilderness. NY, 1914 1st edition. Illustrated. Good-Very Good. $65-$85. 1920 ed. G. $10.

A Book-Lover's Holiday in the Open. NY, 1916 1st edition. Ex-library. Fine. $65. 1920 edition. $35.
Letters to His Children. New York, 1919 1st edition. $30.
Hunting Adventures in the West. New York, 1927, Putnam. Good-VG. $30-$40.
Rank and File. New York, 1928 1st edition. $30-$50.

ROOSEVELT, THEODORE and KERMIT. *East of the Sun.* NY & London, 1926 1st edition. Very Good. $35.
Trailing the Giant Panda. NY, 1929. Good-VG. $40-$50.

ROOT, A. I. *The ABC of Bee Culture.* Medina OH, 1895 62nd thousand. 428 pgs. plus ads. Very Good. $50-$65. 1920 edition. Good. $24.

ROOT, BENJAMIN. *Halliburton - The Magnificent Myth.* Coward-McCann, 1965 2nd ed. Fine, no DJ. $10.

ROOT, WAVERLY. *The Secret History of the War.* NY, 1945 2 vols. Very Good in dust jacket. $40.

ROPER, STEPHEN. *Hand-book of the Locomotive, Construction, Running, Management.* Philadelphia, 1875. Thin, worn leather. $35.
Hand-book of Modern Steam Fire Engines, etc. Philadelphia, 1889. Thin, worn leather. $100.

RORER, MRS. SARAH T. *Home Candy Making.* 1886, 1889. Good-VG. $90-$110.
Hot Weather Dishes. 1886. $55-$65. 1888 edition. $25.
Mrs. Rorer's Philadelphia Cook Book. 1886 1st ed. Good-VG. $90-$110.
Canning and Preserving. Philadelphia, 1887 VG. $30.
Bread and Bread Making. 1887, $55-$65.
Good Ways in Cooking. 1889. $55-$65.
How to Use a Chafing Dish. No place, 1895 Revised. $15.
Made Over Dishes. No place, 1898 1st ed. VG in DJ. $35.
Mrs. Rorer's New Cook Book. Philadelphia, 1902 1st ed. Good. $40. Fine. $75. Same, 1902 2nd ed. $24.
Rorer's Vegetable Cookery. No place, 1909. $60.

ROSCOE, THEODORE. *U. S. Submarine Operations in WWII.* Naval Institute Press, 1950. Signed by author. $50. Later unsigned editions. $30.
U. S. Destroyer Operations in WWII. Naval Institute, 1953 1st edition. Very Good-Fine. $25-$35. In DJ. $45.

ROSE, BILLY. *Wine, Women and Words.* NY, 1948 1st edition. Illus. by Salvador Dali. Good. $50.

ROSE, FLORA. *The New Butterick Cook Book.* Butterick Pub., NY, 1924 revised and enlarged edition. 740 pgs. Worn, browned pages. Good. $20.

ROSE, JOSHUA. *Modern Machine Shop Practice.* 2 vols. 3,000 engravings. NY, Scribners, 1888. Stains. G. $150.

ROSENBACH, A.S.W. *The Unpublishable Memoirs.* NY, 1917 1st edition. Very Good. $30.
Books and Bidders. Boston, 1927 1st edition. Signed. $55.

ROSENFELD, MORRIS. *The Story of American Yachting Told in Pictures.* Appleton, 1958 1st ed. Near VG. $30.

ROSKILL, S. W. *Churchill and the Admirals.* NY, 1978 1st edition. Very Good in dust jacket. $25.

ROSS, ALEXANDER. *The Fur Hunters of the Far West.* London, Smith, Elder & Co., 1855 1st edition. 2 vols. Rebound in ¾ leather. $850. In original cloth. 333 pgs. VG. $1,000. Many reprints since this edition, e.g., Lakeside, 1924. Good-VG. $30-$40.

ROSS, CLYDE P. *The Lower Gila Region, Arizona.* Washington, USGS. 1923. Three folding pocket maps. Original cloth. $85.

ROSS, MALCOLM. *The Cape Fear.* Holt, 1965 1st edition. Rivers of America series. Fine in dust jacket. $18.

ROSS, MARVIN C. *The Art of Karl Faberge and His Contemporaries.* Norman OK, 1965. 75 color, 100 black and white illus. Very Good. $150-$250.

ROSS, THEODORE. *Illustrated History of Odd Fellowship.* NY, Ross History, 1913 ed. 650 pgs., 4 chomolithos, many line illus. Spine gone, o/w Good. $15.

ROSSETTI, CHRISTINA. *Goblin Markets.* No Place, 1933 1st Amer. trade edition. Arthur Rackham illustrator. VG. $40. Same, Lippincott, no date. $100-$150.

ROSSETTI, DANTE GABRIEL. *House of Life.* Sonnet Sequence, Caldwell ID, 1903 1st ed. VG. $35.
Ballads and Sonnets. Portland ME, 1903. One of 450 copies. Very Good. $35.
Hand and Soul. Mosher Press, 1906. Paperbound, attached dust jacket. Unopened. Fine. $110.

ROSTAND, EDMOND. *Cyrano de Bergerac.* Three Sirens, NY, 1931. VG. $25-$35. Another, Limited Editions Club, NY, 1954. Signed by illus. Very Good. $38-$45.

ROSTENBERG and STERN. *Old & Rare, 30 Years in the Book Business.* NY & London, 1974. Signed presentation copy, in dust jacket. $20.

ROTH, PHILIP. *When She Was Good.* NY, 1967 1st edition. Very Good in dust jacket. $40.
Portnoy's Complaint. NY, 1969 1st trade edition. Very Good in dust jacket. $30. Fine. $60-$75.
The Great American Novel. NY, 1973 1st edition. Fine in very good dust jacket. $30.

ROTHERY, AGNES. *Houses Virginians Have Loved*. No place, 1954. Very Good in dust jacket. $35.
New Roads in Old Virignia. Houghton Mifflin, 1929 1st edition. Very Good , no dust jacket. $18.
Virginia, The New Dominion. Appleton, 1940 1st edition. Library Binding. Fine. $14.

ROUNDS, GLEN. *The Blind Colt*. No place, 1941. Very Good in dust jacket. $40.
Once We Had a Horse. NY, 1971. Good-VG. $10-$15.

ROUSE, PARKE. *The Great Wagon Road From Philadelphia to the South*. New York, McGraw-Hill, 1973. Very Good in dust jacket. $35.

ROUSSEAU, P. J. *Theory of House, Sign and Carriage Painting*. Rousseau, 1878 6th printing, Very Good. $18.

ROVERE, RICHARD. *Waist Deep in the Big Muddy*. Boston, 1968 1st edition. Very Good in dust jacket. $13.

ROWE, EDGAR ROWE. *A Pilgrim Returns to Cape Cod*. New York, 1946. Fine in very good dust jacket. $18.

ROWELL, GEORGE P. *Forty Years an Advertising Agent. 1865-1905*. NY, 1926 2nd edition. 517 pgs. VG. $25.
The Men Who Advertise: An Account of Successful Advertisers, Hints, etc. NY, 1870. 1st ed, 872 pgs. $100.

ROWSE, A. L. *The Annotated Shakespeare*. NY, 1978 1st edition. 3 vols. Over 1,400 illus. Fine in fine DJ. $75.

ROWSOME, FRANK. *Trolley Car Treasury*. 1956. Over 300 photos. Fine in dust jacket. $30.
Verse by the Side of the Road - The Story of Burma-Shave. Rowsome, 17th ed. 1980. Fine in dust jacket.. $5.

ROYCE, JOSIAH. *California from the Conquest in 1846 to the Second Vigilance Committee*. Boston, Houghton Mifflin, 1886 1st edition. Original green cloth. Folding map. Very Good. $80-$120.

ROYCROFT PRESS. (See Hubbard, Elbert.)

ROY ROGERS' BULLET AND TRIGGER IN "WILD HORSE ROUNDUP". Whitman, 1953 1st ed. Fine. $14.

ROY ROGERS AT THE LANE RANCH. Whitman, 1950 1st edition. Very Good. $9.

RUARK, ROBERT. *I Didn't Know It Was Loaded*. NY, 1948, Doubleday. VG in DJ. $30. Another, no DJ. $10.
Horn of the Hunter. New York, 1953 1st ed. Good. Ex-library reading copy. $28.
The Old Man and the Boy. NY, 1957 1st edition. Very Fine in chip dust jacket. $50-$75. Inscribed. $95.
Use Enough Gun. NY, 1966 1st. VG in fine DJ. $25-$35.

The Honey Badger. NY, 1965 1st ed. Very Good in dust jacket. $25. Fine in dust jacket. $45.
The Old Man's Boy Grows Older. Holt-Winston, 1961 1st ed. Very Good in dust jacket. $24. Fine in DJ. $60.

RUBAIYAT OF OMAR KHAYYAM. Translated by Edward Fitzgerald. Many editions have been published since the first 250 copies were printed in London in 1859 ($10,000-$20,000). Examples in extremely limited editions, with sumptuous illustrations and fine bindings, often sell in the $300-$1,000 price range. Some lesser priced volumes: Boston, 1894, gilt decorated cover. VG. $50. Undated, NY & London, $30. Doran, E. Dulac illus. $25. Paul Elder, pub. 1902. G. James illus. VG. $40. NY, Hodder & Stoughton, circa 1915 1st American ed. 11 x 8½ cream buckram, gilt-dec. Worn, soiled, loose. $50 auction.

RUBIN, JERRY. *We Are Everywhere*. NY, 1971 1st edition. Very Good in dust jacket. $20.
Growing Up at Thirty-Seven. NY, 1976. Signed. Fine in dust jacket. $35.

RUDKIN, M. *The Pepperidge Farm Cookbook*. NY, 1965. Eric Blevgad, illus. VG in chipped dust jacket. $15-$25.

RUDOFSKY, BERNARD. *The Unfashionable Human Body*. NY, 1941. Illus. Very Good in soiled DJ. $30.
Are Clothes Modern? Chicago, 1947 1st ed. Very Good in soiled dust jacket. $35-$45.

RUE, L. LEE. *Cottontail*. NY, 1965. Fine in dust jacket. $13.
Sportsman's Guide to Game Animals. NY, 1968. Fine in dust jacket. $12.

RUFFNER, WILLIAM HENRY. *Report on the Washington Territory*. New York, Seattle Lake Shore Railway, 1889 1st edition. Good-VG. $75-$125.

RUKEYSER, MURIEL. *Body of Waking*. NY, 1958 1st ed. One of 950 copies. Very Good in dust jacket. $25-$45.
Waterlily Fire. NY, 1972 1st ed. VG-Fine in DJ. $25-$35.
Orgy. NY, 1965 1st edition. Very Good in dust jacket. $20.

RULES FOR THE MANAGEMENT AND CLEANING OF THE RIFLE MUSKET, MODEL 1863 FOR THE USE OF SOLDIERS. Government Printing Office, 1863. Paperbound. Illus. Fine. $150.

RUMFORD COOKBOOKS. *Various Titles*: 1895-1915. $15-$20 each. 1919-1920. $10-$14 each. 1930s-40s editions. $10-$12 each.

RUNYON, DAMON. *Money From Home*. New York, 1935 1st edition. Near Fine in chipped dust jacket. $125.
Take It Easy. NY, 1938 1st edition. VG in clip DJ. $125.
In Our Town. NY, 1946 1st ed. Garth Williams illus. Fine in fine DJ. $125. Fine in vg DJ. $40. VG in DJ. $28.

RUPORT, ARCH. *The Art of Cockfighting*. Devin-Adair, 1949 1st ed. illus. 211 pgs. VG in edgeworn DJ. $75.

RUSKIN, JOHN. *Modern Painters*. London, 1851 and 1873. 5 vols. Covers worn, spoiled. $150.
Lectures on Architecture and Painting. NY, 1853 1st American ed. Illus. Very Good. $65.
The Seven Lamps of Architecture. George Allen, 1883 4th ed. Fine. $125. 1889 ed, Allen. VG. $60. 1932 ed. $10.
The Stones of Venice. London, 1886 4th edition. 3 vols. Very Good. $135. Same in slipcase. $250.
The Writings of John Ruskin. Boston, 26 vols. Good. $65.
Dame Wiggins of Lee. NY, nd. Greenaway illus. $85.
King of the Golden River. Lippincott, 1932. Rackham illus. Orig. red cloth. Very Good in dust jacket. $75-$150.

RUSLING, JAMES. *The Great West and the Pacific Coast: or Fifteen Thousand Miles by Stage, etc.* New York, Sheldon, 1877 1st ed. Orig. gilt dec. cloth. NF. $100.

RUSS, CAROLYN HALE. *Log of a Forty-Niner, Adventures at Sea and in California Gold Field*. B. J. Brimmer, 1923 1st ed. Illustrated by the author. Fine, no dust jacket. $35.

RUSSELL, BERTRAND. *The ABC of Atoms*. London, 1923 1st edition. Near Very Good. $45.
The ABC of Relativity. London,1925 1st ed. VG. $30-$40.
Our Knowledge of the External World. NY, 1929 2nd edition. Very Good. $35.
Education and the Good Life. NY, 1945. VG. $23. Same in good dust jacket. $35-$40,
Philosophy and Politics. London, 1947 1st edition. Endpapers foxed, o/w Very Good. $23.
Human Knowledge. London,1948. Very Good in DJ. $95.

RUSSELL, CARL P. *100 Years in Yosemite*. Berkeley, 1947. Photos by Ansel Adams. Very Good in DJ. $38.
Guns on the Early Frontiers. Berkeley, 1957 1st edition. Very Good-Fine in dust jacket. $45-$70.
Traps and Tools of the Mountain Men. NY, 1967 1st edition. Very Good in dust jacket. $40.

RUSSELL, CHARLES M. *Back Trailing on the Old Frontier*. Great Falls MT, 1922 1st ed. Paperbound. Illustrated by author. Very Good-Fine. $500-$600.
More Rawhides. Great Falls MT, 1925 1st edition. Illustrated by author. Paperbound. Very Good. $475.
Trails Plowed Under. NY, Doubleday, 1927 1st ed. Illus. by author. VG in DJ to Fine in DJ. $175-$300. 1966 reprint. Very Good, no dust jacket. $18. Book Club ed. No date. Fine in dust jacket. $25-$35.
Good Medicine. Doubleday, 1929 1st ed. Green Buckram cover. Water stained. Good. $50. 1929 Limited ed. on large paper. $800-$1,200. NY, 1930 1st trade ed. Will Rogers intro. Very Good in DJ. $75. Garden City, 1930. VG, ex-library. $25. Another, orig. buckram. Near Fine. $35.

RUSSELL, CHARLES (Illustrator). *My Sixty Years on the Plains*. By W. T. Hamilton. NY, 1905. Very Good. $125.

RUSSELL, DON. *The Lives and Legends of Buffalo Bill*. University of Oklahoma, 1960 1st ed. VG in DJ. $45.
The Wild West, A History of Wild West Shows. Fort Worth, Amon Carter Museum, 1970 1st edition. Torn dust jacket, else Very Good. $60-$90.

RUSSELL, OSBORNE. *Journal of a Trapper*. Oregon Historical Society, 1955 3rd ed. 1 of 750. NF. $100-$150.

RUSSELL, THOMAS H. *Automobile Motors and Mechanism*. Chicago, 1913 1st ed. Fine. $38.
Story of the Great Flood and Cyclone Disasters. Memorial edition, 1913. Very Good. $10.

RUSTRUM, CALVIN. *North American Canoe Country*. Macmillan, 1972. Les Kouba illus. Near VG in DJ. $12.
Chips From a Wilderness Log. NY, 1978 1st edition. Dust jacket. Illus. Very Good. $8.

RUTH, BABE, DIZZY DEAN and TY COBB. *My Greatest Day in Baseball*. As told to John Carmichael. NY, 1945. 1st book ed. Illus. Worn, chip dust jacket, o/w Good. $65.

RUTH, GEORGE HERMAN. *Babe Ruth's Own Book of Baseball*. Putnam, 1928 1st ed. G-VG in DJ. $175-$200. A. L. Burt, 1928 reprint. $60. 1931 edition. $15.

RUTLEDGE, ARCHIBALD. *Old Plantation Days*. NY, 1921 1st edition. Very Good. $85.
Wild Life of the South. New York, 1935. C. E. Pont illustrator. Very Good. $33.
Peace in the Heart. Doubleday, 1945. Signed. Worn dust jacket. $30.
Hunter's Choice. West Hartford VT, 1946. Paul Bransom illus. One of 475 copies signed by Bransom and Rutledge. Overall VG. $110. First Trade Edition, same year. $50.
God's Children: My Negro Friends at Hampton. NY, 1947 1st ed. Very Good in chipped dust jacket. $30.
A Wildwood Tale. NY, 1950 1st edition. Signed. Very Good in mended dust jacket. $15.
Home by the River. Bobbs Merrill, 1941 ed. VG. $10. Signed, in dust jacket. $35. Indianapolis, 1955. Large paper edition. Signed. $30.
Santee Paradise. Indianapolis, 1956. VG in DJ. $35.
From the Hills to the Sea. Indianapolis, 1958 1st. F. $55.

RUXTON, GEORGE F. *Adventures in Mexico and the Rocky Mountains*. London, 1847 1st ed. Ex-lib., o/w near VG. $275. 1855 ed. Fly leaf piece missing. o/w VG. $85.
Life in the Far West. NY, 1849 1st ed. Faded spine, slight foxing, o/w Good. $185. 1951 edition. $40-$50.

RYAN, IRENE & CATHY PINKNEY. *Granny's Hillbilly Cookbook*. Prentice-Hall, 1966. Good in dust jacket. $26.

S

SABIN, EDWIN L. *Kit Carson Days 1809-1868. Adventures in the Path of Empire*. McClurg, 1914 1st edition. $125-$155. 2 vols. illus. by Howard Simon. NY, Press of Pioneers, 1935 revised ed. Stain, tape. Good. $80.
Building the Pacific Railway. Lippincott, 1919 1st edition. Good-Very Good. $24-$35.

SABINE, LORENZO. *Notes on Duels and Duelling*. Boston, First edition. 1855. Good. $135. 1856 edition. VG. $200.

SACHER-MASOCH, LEOPOLD. *Venus in Furs*. Sylvan Press, NY, 1947. One of 1,499 copies. Good. $30.

SACKVILLE-WEST, VITA. *Heritage*. NY, 1919 1st American edition. Author's 1st book. Very Good. $100.
Saint Joan of Arc. London, Cobden, 1936 1st edition. Very Good, no dust jacket. $35.
The Garden. NY, 1946 1st American ed. Fine in DJ. $20.
Nursery Rhymes. London, 1947 1st ed. One of 550 copies. Fine in fine dust jacket. $165.
Faces. NY, 1962 1st American ed. Fine in torn DJ. $20.

SADLEIR, MICHAEL. *Authors and Publishers*. London, 1933 1st ed. Very Good in dust jacket. $60.
Things Past. London, 1944 1st ed. VG in DJ. $30.

SAILING DIRECTIONS FOR ANTARCTICA. Washington, 1943 1st edition. Illus. Map in pocket. $85.

SAINT EXUPERY, ANTOINE. *Night Flight*. Century, 1932 1st edition. Preface by Andre Gide. Fine, no DJ. $25. Another, Fine in chipped dust jacket. $45.
Wind, Sand and Stars. NY, 1939 1st ed. Very Good in very good dust jacket. $18-$30.
Flight to Arras. No place, 1942 1st ed. NF in DJ. $55.

SALA, GEORGE AUGUSTUS. *The Thorough Good Cook*. London, 1895 1st edition. Fine. $75.

SALE, CHIC. *The Specialist*. (Privy builder) St. Louis, 1929 1st printing. Fine. $30. Good-Very Good. $10-$15. Same, 3rd printing. $8. Average copy, $12-$15 with dust jacket. Over 2,000,000 copies sold in 1st three years, still in print. (Specialist Pub. Co., 109 Mesa Drive, Burlingame CA 94010).
I'll Tell You Why. Sequel to "The Specialist". No place, 1930. $12-$15.

SALINGER, J. D. *The Catcher in the Rye*. Difficult to tell if 1st printing, 1st state, 1st dust jacket. Three printings were made in July of 1951. Prices range from $30 (for faded spine in DJ) to $1,700 for a near perfect copy in first DJ. Later 1951 printings. $10-$25. Modern Library, 1958. Very Good in dust jacket. $75. London, Hamish, 1951 1st English edition. $250-$800 in dust jacket.
Nine Stories. Boston, 1953 1st ed. Good in DJ. $450.
For Esme, With Love and Squalor. London, 1953 1st English ed. Very Good in dust jacket. $400.
Franny & Zooey. Boston, 1961 1st edition. Very Good-Near Fine in dust jacket. $50-$75.
Raise High the Roof Beam. Boston, 1962 1st edition, 2nd state. Good in dust jacket. $40.
The Complete Uncollected Short Stories. 1st edition. 2 vols., no place, no date. Fine in orig wraps. $300-$600.

SALISBURY, AL & JANE. *Here Rolled the Covered Wagons*. Superior Pub. Co., 1948 3rd edition. Bumped and rubbed. $22.

SALOMON, ERICH. *Portrait of an Age*. NY, London, 1967 1st American edition. Photographs by the author. Very Good in dust jacket. $75.

SALOMON, JULIAN HARRIS. *The Book of Indian Crafts and Indian Lore*. New York, 1928 1st edition. Cover stained o/w Good. $35.

SALTA, ROMEO. *Pleasures of Italian Cooking*. Macmillan, 1968 5th edition. Signed & inscribed by author. Very Good in dust jacket. $15.

SALTEN, FELIX. *Bambi*. New York, Simon and Schuster, 1928 1st American ed. $50-$100. Subsequent ed. $5-$10.
Bambi's Children. Bobbs-Merrill, 1939 1st edition. Good in dust jacket. $40.
A Forest World. Bobbs-Merrill, 1942 1st edition. Good in dust jacket. $45.

SAMPSON, EMMA SPEED. *Miss Minerva on the Old Plantation*. Reilly & Lee, 1923. Illus. Near Fine. $25.
Billy and the Major. 1920 6th printing, Reilly & Lee. Donahey illus. Very Good. $15. 1924 8th printing. $8.

SAMSTAG, NICHOLAS. *Kay-Kay Comes Home*. 1962 1st printing. Ben Shahn illus. Fine in dust jacket. $30.

SAND, GEORGE. *Tales of a Grandmother*. Philadelphia, 1930. Translated. Harold Hess illustrator. 12 color lithographs. Near Fine. $75.

SANBORN, HERBERT. *Dachshund or Teckel. History, Breeding*. Orange Judd, 1949 revised ed. VG, no DJ. $16.

SANDBURG, CARL. *Chicago Poems*. NY, 1916 1st edition. Very Good in dust jacket. $80.
Smoke and Steel. Harcourt, 1920 1st edition. Signed. Very Good in dust jacket. $200.
Rootabaga Stories. NY, 1922 1st ed. Very Good. $65.
Lincoln: The Prairie Years. NY, 1926 1st ed. 2 vols. Fine. $60. 1954 condensed edition, Harcourt. VG. $12. 1945 edition. 2 vols. Very Fine. $33.
Abe Lincoln Grows Up. NY, 1928. Good. $25.
Lincoln: The War Years. NY, 1939 4 vols. Fine. $40. 1940 3rd edition. Very Good. $35. 1944 4 vols. Fine. $48. 1947 Scribners. Fine, no dust jacket. $10.
Storm Over the Land. NY, 1942 1st ed. Very Good. $30.
Poems of the Midwest. World, 1946 1st edition. 2 vols. Very Good, no dust jacket. $14.
Remembrance Rock. NY, 1948. Minor cover wear, o/w Very Good in dust jacket. $30. Very Good, no DJ. $12.
Always the Young Strangers. NY, 1953. Limited edition, signed. Very Good in box. $125. Unsigned. $35-$45. 2nd edition, 1953, Harcourt Brace. VG in DJ. $15.
Prairie Town Boy. Harcourt, 1953 1st edition. Fine in dust jacket. $15-$20.

SANDBY, GEORGE. *Mesmerism and Its Opponents*. NY, 1844 1st American edition. Good. $85-$150.

SANDERS, ALVIN H. *At the Sign of the Stock Yard Inn*. Chicago, Breeders' Gazette, 1915. 322 pgs., ¾ leather, 32 plates. Some pages creased, o/w nice. $65.

SANDERS, C. *Sanders Young Ladies Reader*. NY, 1860. Half leather, bumped corners, o/w Very Good. $15.

SANDERS, MARTHA. *Alexander and the Magic Mouse*. NY, 1969. Very Good in dust jacket. $20.

SANDERSON, IVAN. *Animal Treasures*. NY, 1937 1st ed. Very Good in worn dust jacket. $10.
The Dynasty of Abu. NY, 1962. Ex-lib. VG in DJ. $10.

SANDOZ, MARI. *Old Jules*. Little Brown, 1936 1st edition. Very Good. $30.
Fantastic Memories. Garden City, 1944 Salvador Dali illus. Slightly stained cover, worn dust jacket. $60.
The Maze. Doubleday, 1945 1st ed. Salvador Dali illus. Fine in very good dust jacket. $85. Same, Very Good. $40.
Cheyenne Autumn. NY, 1953 1st printing. Illustrated. by author. Very Good. $50.
The Buffalo Hunters. Hastings House, 1954 1st edition. Fine in dust jacket. $50.

Crazy Horse, The Strange Man of the Ogalalas. Knopf, 1945 3rd print. VG. $14. Hastings, 1955. Autographed reprint. Very Good in dust jacket. $25.
On the Verge. NY, 1959 1st edition. Salvador Dali illustrator. Very Good. $75.
These Were the Sioux. New York, 1961. Near Very Good in chip dust jacket. $20.
The Story Catcher. Philadelphia, 1962 1st edition. Very Good in dust jacket. $45.

SANDYS, E. *Sporting Sketches*. NY, 1905 1st ed. VG. $25.

SANFORD, P. GERALD. *Nitro-Explosives: A Practical Treatise*. NY, 1906 2nd ed. Revised. Good. $25.

SAN FRANCISCO CITY DIRECTORY. 1854, Strong. 264 pgs. $550 auction. 1867, Langley, 698 pgs. $110 auction. 1869, Langley. 852 pgs. $200 auction.

SANGER, MARGARET. *Woman and the New Race*. NY, 1920 1st ed. No dust jacket. $70-$90.
Motherhood in Bondage. New York, 1928 1st edition. Signed. $85-$100.
An Autobiography. NY, 1938 1st ed. VG in DJ. $30.

SANTAYANA, GEORGE. *Scepticism and Animal Faith*. NY, 1923 1st edition. Very Good. $30.
The Realm of Essence. NY,1927 1st edition. VG. $28.
The Last Puritan. NY, 1936 1st edition. Leather bound . Fine. $125. Same, Very Good in dust jacket. $45.
The Work of George Santayana. NY, 1936 15 vols. One of 940 sets. Signed. Triton ed. Near Fine. $425.
The Realm of Truth. NY, 1938 1st edition. Very Good in soiled dust jacket. $28.
The Poet's Testament, Poems, Plays. Scribner's 1953 1st edition. Fine in dust jacket. $14.

SANTEE, ROSS. *Men and Horses*. NY, 1926. Illustrated by author. Very Good in slipcase. $150.
The Cowboy. NY, 1928 1st ed. Illus. by author. VG. $55.
The Pooch. NY, 1931 1st ed. Illus. by author. VG. $25.
Sleepy Black: The Story of a Horse. No place, 1933 1st edition. Illustrated by author. Very Good in chip dust jacket. $35.
Apache Land. New York, 1947 1st edition. Illustrated by author. Good. $35. Very Good in dust jacket. $60.

SAROYAN, WILLIAM. *The Daring Young Man On The Flying Trapeze*. New York, 1934 1st edition. Author's 1st book. Very Good. $100.
The Trouble With Tigers. NY, 1938. Tattered dust jacket. Inscribed on endpapers. $150.
My Heart's in the Highlands. New York, 1939 1st edition. Fine in dust jacket. $125.
Get Away, Old Man. NY, 1944 1st ed. VG in DJ. $35.
My Kind of Crazy Wonderful People. NY, 1964 1st edition. Review copy. Fine. $20.

The Tooth and My Father. Doubleday, 1974 1st edition. Susan Verrier illustrator. Very Good in dust jacket. $24.

SARTON, MAY. *Miss Pickthorn & Mr. Hare*. Norton, 1966 1st ed. Very Good in dust jacket. $35.
Plant Dreaming Deep. Dutton, 1968 1st edition. Near Fine in very good dust jacket. $35.
Kinds of Love. NY, 1970 1st edition. Very Good in dust jacket. $15.
The House by the Sea. New York, 1977 1st edition. Illus. Very Good in dust jacket. $13.

SARTE, JEAN-PAUL. *Nausea*. New Directions, 1949 1st American edition. Fine in dust jacket. $60.
Being and Nothingness. NY, 1956 1st American edition. Very Good in dust jacket. $50.
The Words. NY, 1964. Very Good. $12.

SASSOON, SIGFRIED. *Memoirs of a Fox Hunting Man*. London, 1929 1st ed. Illus. Signed. VG. $38. Another, undated. Coward McCann, In original slipcase. $70.
Memoirs of an Infantry Officer. London, 1930 1st edition. Fine in worn dust jacket. $30-$45.
Siegfried's Journey 1916-1920. NY, 1946. Good. $20.

SAUER, ELFRIEDA. *The Wingold Cook Book*. Winona MN, 1929 3rd edition. Very Good. $30.

SAUNDERS, JOHN MONK. *Wings*. NY, 1927. Photoplay edition. Good in dust jacket. $25.

SAUNDERS, LOUISE. *The Knave of Hearts*. Scribner's, 1925 1st edition. Maxfield Parrish color illus. Very Good-Fine. Folio. $800-$1,500. Same in quatro. $500-$800. Racine, Wisconsin. Later edition. VG-Fine. $350-$400.

SAVAGE-LANDOR, A. HENRY. *Everywhere: the Memoirs of an Explorer*. NY, 1924 2 vols. Illustrated. Good. $45. Very Good-Fine. $75.

SAVITT, SAM. *The Dingle Ridge Fox*. NY, 1978 1st edition. Inscribed. Very Good in dust jacket. $20.

SAWYER, JOSEPH D. *Washington*. Macmillan, 1927 1st ed. 2 vols. Illus. Gilt-dec. green cloth. $65 set.

SAWYER, RUTH. *Seven Miles to Arden*. 1916 ed. G. $12.
Roller Skates. New York, 1936 1st edition. Valenti Angelo illus. Very Good. $40.
The Long Christmas. New York, 1941 1st edition. Very Good in dust jacket. $30-$45.
This Way to Christmas. NY, 1944. M. W. Barney illustrator. Very Good. $25.
The Enchanted Schoolhouse. New York, 1956 1st edition. Hugh Troy illus. Inscribed. by Troy. Corner and spine wear. $50.
Joy to the World. Little Brown, 1966 1st edition. NF. $20.

SAXON, LYLE. *Father Missippii*. 1927 1st ed. F. $50-$75.
Gumbo Ya-Ya: a Collection of Louisiana Folk Tales. Houghton Mifflin, 1945. Fine in good dust jacket. $30.
Fabulous New Orleans. New Orleans, 1939. Illus. Very Good in DJ. $25. Same, NY, 1950 & 1958 eds. $10-$15.

SAY, THOMAS. *Complete Writings of Thomas Say on the Entomology of North America*. 2 vols. NY, Bailliere, 1859 1st edition. ½ morocco, green cloth. 54 hand-colored plates. Very Good. $1,750.

SAYERS, DOROTHY. *The Omnibus of Crime*. New York, 1929 1st edition, 1st printing. Very Good. $35. Same year, 2nd printing. $15.
Strong Poison. NY, 1930 1st American edition. Good. $35. Very Good-Fine. $60-$95.
The Nine Tailors. London, 1934 1st ed. Very Good. $75.
Busman's Honeymoon. London, 1937 1st ed. paperbound. Near Very Good. $120. 1st American ed. Harcourt Brace, 1937. Very Good in dust jacket. $175.
Gaudy Night. London, 1935 1st edition. Near Very Good in good dust jacket. $160.
In the Teeth of the Evidence and 16 Other Stories. London, 1939 1st edition. Fine in torn dust jacket. $125.

SCARFOGLIO, ANTONIO. *Round the World in a Motor-Car*. London, Grant-Richards, 1909 1st edition. Illustrated 368 pgs. $150.

SCARNE, JOHN. *Scarne on Dice*. Harrisburg, 1945 2nd revised printing. Very Good in good dust jacket. $15.
Complete Guide to Gambling. NY, 1961 Ex-lib. G. $11.

SCHAEFER, JACK. *Shane*. Boston, 1954. VG in DJ. $8. Same, 1st edition. Very Good in dust jacket. $45.
The Pioneers. Boston, 1954 1st edition. Very Good-Fine in dust jacket. $40-$50.
Company of Cowards. Boston, 1957 1st edition. Very Good in dust jacket. $25.

SCHALDACH, WILLIAM. *Coverts and Casts*. NY, 1943. Very Good. $40.
Currents and Eddies. NY, 1944. Very Good. $40.
The Wind on Your Cheek. Rockville Center, 1972. Very Good. $25.

SCHAUFFER, R. H. *Romantic America*. Century, 1913. Maxfield Parrish color plate. Very Good. $65-$100.

SCHECHTER, WILLIAM. *The History of Negro Humor in America*. Fleet Press, 1970 1st ed. Fine in DJ. $14.

SCHENK, GUSTAV. *The Book of Poisons*. NY, 1955. Very Good in dust jacket. $10.

SCHLEBECKER, JOHN T. *Cattle Raising on the Plains 1900-1961*. Lincoln, UNE Press, 1963. Fine. $18.

SCHOTTER, H. W. *The Growth and Development of the Pennsylvania Railroad Co. 1846-1926*. Official Company issued 1st ed. Fine. $60. 1927 2nd printing. $55.

SCHRIBER, FRITZ. *The Complete Carriage and Wagon Painter*. Includes lettering, coloring, etc. NY, 1887. 180 pgs. Good-Very Good. $100.

SCHMITT, MARTIN F. and DEE BROWN. *Fighting Indians of the West*. NY, 1948 1st edition. Very Good in chipped dust jacket. $60-$75.

SCHNESSEL, S. M. *Jessie Wilcox Smith*. NY, 1977, Crowell. Very Good in torn dust jacket. $65.

SCHOLES, SAMUEL. *Modern Glass Practice*. Chicago, Industrial Pub., 1935 1st ed. Very Good. $35.

SCHOOLCRAFT, HENRY R. *The American Indians, Their History*. Rochester, 1851. Original cloth. Some wear. Very Good. $145.
Information, Respecting the History, Condition and Prospects of the Indian Tribes of the United States. Philadelphia, 1853 Part One. Very Good. $500.

SCHOPENAUER, ARTHUR. *Studies in Pessimism*. Modern Library, 1917 1st edition. Very Good-Fine in DJ. $120.
The Essays of Arthur Schopenauer. Wiley Book Co., NY. No date, ex-library. Very Good. $5.

SCHREINER, OLIVE. *Trooper Peter Halket of Mashonaland*. Boston, 1897 1st ed. Very Good. $18.
Dreams. Roberts, 1894 1st edition. Very Good. $50.
Undine. NY, 1928 1st American ed. Fine in vg DJ. $25.
The Story of an African Farm. Limited Edition Club, 1961. One of 1,500 copies. Illus. signed by Paul Hogarth. Ex-library. $35.

SCHREUDERS, PIET. *Paperbacks, USA, A Graphic History, 1939-1959*. San Diego, 1981 1st American ed. Paperbound. Illus. Inscribed. $60. Another, unsigned. $30.

SCHULBERG, BUDD. *The Harder They Fall*. NY, 1947 1st edition. Very Good-Fine in dust jacket. $50-$100.
The Disenchanted. NY, 1950 1st ed. VG in DJ. $20.
Waterfront. NY, 1955 1st ed. Very Good in DJ. $30.

SCHULZ, CHARLES M. *Charlie Brown's All-Stars*. World, 1966 1st edition. Illus. by author. Very Good. $15.
It's The Great Pumpkin, Charlie Brown. World, 1967 1st edition. Illus. by author. Good-Very Good. $10.
You're in Love, Charlie Brown. NY, 1968 1st ed. Illus. by author. Very Good. $15.
Snoopy and His Sopwith Camel. NY, 1969 1st edition. Illus. by author. Fine in very good dust jacket. $20.
Charlie Brown's Yearbook. World Pub., 1969 1st printing. Includes four stories. Very Good. $53.

SCHULTZ, JAMES W. *With the Indians in the Rockies*. Boston, 1912 1st ed. George Varian illus. Good. $85.
On the Warpath. Boston, 1914 1st edition. George Varian illustrator. Very Good. $75.
Blackfoot Tales of Glacier National Park. Boston, 1916 1st edition. Very Good. $50.
Signposts of Adventure. Boston, 1926 1st edition. Signed by author. Near Fine. $250 auction.
Stained Gold. Boston, 1937 1st edition. VG. $85. auction.

SCHWARTZ, DELMORE. *Shenandoah*. New Directions, 1941 1st ed. Paperbound. Fine in dust jacket. $75.
The World is a Wedding. New Directions, 1948 1st ed. Very Good in DJ. $50. Another, Fine in Fine DJ. $125.
I Am Cherry Alive, the Little Girl Sang. NY, 1979 1st edition. Barbara Cooney illus. Fine in fine DJ. $30.

SCHWARTZ, JACOB. *1100 Obscure Points: The Bibliographies of 25 English & 21 American Authors*. 1961 reprint of 1931 1st edition. Fine. $75.

SCHWATKA, FREDERICK. *Along Alaska's Great River*. NY, circa 1855. Good-Very Good. $60-$85.
A Summer in Alaska. St. Louis, 1892 2nd ed. Good. $38.
Nimrod in the North. Boston, circa 1892. Good plus. $25.
In the Land of the Cave and Cliff Dwellers. NY, 1893. Good-Very Good. $10-$15.

SCHWEITZER, ALBERT. *J. S. Bach*. London, 1938. Reprint 2 vols. Spine wear, o/w Very Good. $40.

SCHWIMMER, R. *Tisza Tales*. NY, Doubleday, 1928. W. Pogany color plates. VG in DJ. $65-$95.

SCOTT, FRANK J. *The Art of Beautifying Suburban Home Grounds*. 200 plates, trees, plans, etc. NY, 1886 reprint of 1872 edition. Ex-library. $50.

SCOTT, GENIO C. *Fishing in American Waters*. NY, 1875 New ed. Very Good. $75. Same, 1869 1st ed. Good. $50.

SCOTT, H. HAROLD. *Some Notable Epidemics*. London, 1934 1st edition. Very Good. $50.

SCOTT, JACK DENTON. *The Complete Book of Pasta*. NY, 1968 1st ed. Samuel Chamberlain photos. VG in DJ. $25.

SCOTT, ROBERT P. *Cycling Art, Energy and Locomotion*. Philadelphia 1885. Illus. Some darkening, o/w VG. $150.

SCOTT, SIR WALTER. *The Monastery*. Edinburgh, 1820. 3 vols. 1st ed. Gilt, leather. Very Good. $150.
The Works of Sir Walter Scott. Boston, 1871, James Osgood. 25 vols. Very Good. $750.
Poetical Works of Sir Walter Scott. No date. American News Co. Good-Very Good. $8-$10. Same, 1894 ed. Gilt-leather, VG. $30. Another, Philadelphia, 1871. VG. $36.

Ivanhoe. Boston, 1893 2 vols. One of 1,550 copies, The Parchment Edition. Top edge gilt, deckled edges. $150. Rand McNally, 1922. Milo Winter illus. VG. $25. Heritage Press, 1950. Edward Wilson illus. VG in case. $39.
Letters on Demonology and Witchcraft. London, 1931 2nd edition. Good. $125.
Lady of the Lake. NY, Riverside, 1869. VG. $35. Boston, 1910 ed. Very Good. $5-$8. Bobbs-Merrill, 1910. Christy color plates. Very Good. $35-$65.

SCOVILLE, WARREN. *Revolution in Glassmaking Industry, etc., 1880-1920*. Harvard Univ. 1948 1st ed. VG. $35.

SEABROOK, WILLIAM. *Magic Island*. Literary Guild, 1929. Alexander King illus. VG in good dust jacket. $20.

THE SEAFARERS. 20 vol., Time-Life, 1979. Fine $100-$160.

SEAMAN, AUGUST H. *Sally Sims Adventures It*. Appleton Century, 1942 reprint of 1924 ed. Very Good in DJ. $30.

SEARS, CLARA ENDICOTT. *Gleanings From Old Shaker Journals*. Boston, 1916 1st ed. Illus. Near VG. $65.

SEARS, R. W. *Survey of the Cycle of the Sod & the Livestock Industries*. Wetzel, 1941. VG in DJ. $35.

SEAVER, JAMES E. *The Life of Mary Jemison*. This true story of an Indian captive of 1755 has been published in 23 different editions since its 1824 first printing, which is valued at $1,000-$1,400. 1859 4th ed. Good. $60. 1929 reprint of 1st ed. $20. 1929 Random House Limited ed. of 950. $35. 1949 edition. Good-Very Good. $15.

SECOND DIVISION AMERICAN EXPEDITIONARY FORCE IN FRANCE, 1917-1919. New York, 1937. Illustrated. Near Fine. $35.

SECRETS OF MEAT CURING & SAUSAGE MAKING. B. Heller & Co., 1911 2nd ed. 302 pgs. Fair. $15.

SEEGER, ALAN. *Poems*. NY, 1916 1st edition. Author's 1st book. Very Good plus. $75.

SEELEY, MABEL. *The Crying Sisters*. NY, Crime Club, 1939 1st edition. Very Good plus. $15.
The Whispering Cup. New York, Crime Club, 1940 1st edition. Good plus. $13.
Beckoning Door. Doubleday, 1950 BCE. VG in DJ. $5.

SEGAL, ERICH. *Fairy Tales*. Harper, 1973 1st edition. Very Good in good dust jacket. $14. Fine in fine DJ. $24.

SEITZ, DON C. *The Buccaneers*. Harper, 1912. H. Pyle illus. Very Good. $35-$65.
Famous American Duels. NY, 1929 1st edition. 16 portraits. Very Good. $35.

SELBY, HUBERT, JR. *Last Exit to Brooklyn*. NY, 1964 1st edition. Very Good in dust jacket. $30. Fine in DJ. $50.
The Demon. Playboy Press, 1976 1st ed. VG in DJ. $15.

SELDEN, GEORGE. *Chester Cricket's Pigeon Ride*. NY, 1981 1st ed. Garth Williams illus. Very Good in DJ. $20.

SELIGMANN, KURT. *The History of Magic*. NY, 1948 1st edition. Very Good in dust jacket. $25-$35.

SELWYN-BROWN, ARTHUR. *The Physician Through the Ages*. NY, 1928. 2 vols. Very Good. $75. Fine. $185.

SEMMES, HARRY. *Portrait of Patton*. New York, 1955 1st edition. Fine. $35.

SEMMES, RAPHAEL. *Memoirs of Service Afloat, During the War Between the States*. Baltimore, 1869. Fair. $45.

SENDAK, MAURICE. *Where the Wild Things Are*. NY, 1963 1st edition, 1st issue. Fine in dust jacket. $1,500-$2,400. (Same. Signed, much higher.) New York, 1988. 25th Anniversary issue. One of 220 copies, signed. Fine with original signed illustrations. $1,200.
Higgledy Piggledy Pop!. Harper. 1967 1st ed. Signed. Very Good in clip dust jacket. $80-$100.
In the Night Kitchen. NY, 1970 1st edition. Very Good-Fine in dust jacket. $100-$200.
Seven Little Monsters. NY, 1975 1st American edition. Very Good in dust jacket. $35-$50.
Outside Over There. NY, 1981. Illus. by author. Near Fine in dust jacket. $30. Another, fine, signed by Sendak. $50 auction. Another with signed bookplate by Sendak. $70.
Love for 3 Oranges. No place, 1984 1st ed. One of 200 copies, signed. Fine in slipcase. $200.
Posters. NY, Harmony, 1986 1st edition. VG in DJ. $35.

SENDAK, MAURICE (Illustrator). *A Hole Is to Dig*. By Ruth Krauss. NY, 1952 1st ed. Very Good in dust jacket. $50. Another, Near Fine in dust jacket. $247 auction.
A Very Special House. By Ruth Krauss. NY, 1953 1st ed. Near Fine in dust jacket. $95.
Tell Me a Mitzi. By Lore Segal and Harriet Pincus. NY, 1970 1st edition. Very Good in dust jacket. $60.
Sarah's Room. By Doris Orgel. NY, Harpers, 1963 1st edition. Near Fine in clipped DJ. $110 auction.
Let's Be Enemies. By Janice May Udry. NY, Harper, 1961 1st ed. Good-Very Good in erased DJ. $100 acution.
King Grisly-Beard, a Tale from the Grimm Brothers. NY, 1973. Inscribed by Sendak. Fine. $100.
Fly By Night. By Randall Jarrell. NY, 1976 1st edition. Very Good in very good dust jacket. $30.
Zlateh the Goat and Other Stories. By Isaac Bashevis Singer. NY, 1966 1st ed. Fine in dust jacket. $75.

SENEFELDER, ALOIS. *The Invention of Lithography*. New York, 1911. Very Good in rubbed cloth. $85.

SEREDY, KATE. *The Good Master*. NY, 1935. Illus. by author. Very Good. $45. 7th printing, 1940. $15.
The White Stag. Viking, 1937 1st edition. Illus. by author. Very Good in dust jacket. $125.
The Singing Tree. London, 1940 1st ed. Illus. by author. Very Good in dust jacket. $35.
The Chestry Oak. Viking, 1948 1st ed. Illus. by author. Good-VG in chipped dust jacket. $35.

SERLING, ROD. *Patterns*. NY, 1957 1st ed., Author's 1st book. Near Fine in very good dust jacket. $65.

SERVICE, ROBERT W. *The Spell of the Yukon*. NY, 1907 1st ed. Bound in full calf. Fine overall. $225.
Ballads of a Cheechako. Barse & Hopkins, 1909. 1st ed. Very Good, no dust jacket. $15.
Rhymes of a Rolling Stone. Toronto, 1912 1st edition. Very Good. $65. Rebound in calf. $95.
Rhymes of a Red Cross Man. Barse & Hopkins, 1916 1st edition, Pictorial red cloth. Very Good. $40-$45.
The Trail of the Ninety Eight. Grosset & Dunlap reprint, 1913. Good. $9.
Barroom Ballads. Toronto, 1940 1st edition. Cover stain, o/w Very Good. $40.
Ploughman of the Moon. NY, 1945 1st edition Very Good in good dust jacket. $50.
Lyrics of a Low Brow. NY, 1951. VG in fair DJ. $25.
The Song of the Campfire. NY, 1978. Illustrated. Very Good-Fine in dust jacket. $20.
The Open Gate. Viking, 1943 1st ed. Illus. by author. Very Good in dust jacket. $75.
Philomena. NY, 1955 1st edition. Illus. by author. Spine wear, o/w Very Good. $25.
The Tenement Tree. London, 1960 1st edition. Illus. by author. Near Fine. $35.
Collected Poems of Robert Service. Book Club ed. Dodd & Mead, 1966. Vey Good in dust jacket. $8.

SERVISS, GARRETT P. *Pleasures of the Telescope*. NY, 1910. Fair to Good. $40.
Curiosities of the Sky. Harper, 1921. Good. $25.
Edison's Conquest of Mars. 1947 Limited edition. one of 1,500. Very Good. $55.

SETON, ERNEST THOMPSON. *Lives of the Hunted*. NY, 1901 1st ed. Good. $30. Very Good. $40.
Biography of a Grizzly. Century, 1903 6th impression. Very Good. $18.
Two Little Savages. NY, Doubleday Page, 1903 1st ed. Very Good. $60-$90.
Monarch, the Big Bear of Tallac. NY, 1904 1st edition. Illustrated by author. Very Good. $65.
The Biography of a Silver Fox. NY, 1909 1st edition. Illustrated by author. Near Good. $60.
Animal Heroes. NY, Scribners, 1905 1st ed. VG. $50-$80.
The Natural History of the Ten Commandments. NY, 1907 1st edition. Good. $10.

The Forester's Manual (Boy Scouts series). NY, 1912, Doubleday. $35.
Wild Animals at Home. G & D. 1913. Illustrated by author. Very Good. $6. Doubleday-Page 1913. Good. $12.
Bannertail. Scribners, 1922 1st ed. with 100 illustrations by author. 265 pages. Very Good. $60.

SETTLE, MARY LEE. *O Beulah Land*. No place, 1956 1st American ed. Very Good in dust jacket. $25.
Fight Night on a Sweet Saturday. NY, 1964 1st ed. Signed. Fine in dust jacket. $35.

THE SETTLEMENT COOK BOOK. Settlement Cook Book Co., 1921. 11th ed. Mrs. S. Kander, compiler. Fair-G. $10.

SEUSS, DR. (Theodore Geisel). *The 500 Hats of Bartholomew Cubbins*. NY, 1938 1st edition. Cloth on boards. Seuss's second book. VG in good DJ. $125. Same, inscribed by author. $300-$500.
More Boners. New York, 1931. $20-$40.
The King's Stilts. NY, 1939 3rd ed. VG in vg DJ. $100.
Horton Hatches the Egg. NY, 1940. Very Good. $40.
Thidwick, the Big-Hearted Moose. NY, 1948. Good-Very Good. $20-$40.
If I Ran the Zoo. New York, 1950 1st edition. Very Good in dust jacket. $350.
Scrambled Eggs Supper. NY, 1953 1st edition. Name in crayon, o/w Very Good-Fine. $75.
How the Grinch Stole Christmas. NY, 1957 1st ed. Very Good in good dust jacket. $75.
Dr. Seuss' Sleep Book. NY, 1962. Cover stained, otherwise Good. $7.
You're Only Old Once: A Book for Obsolete Children. Lon., 1986 1st English ed. Paperback. Inscribed. F. $95.
Dr. Seuss From Then to Now. Random House, 1986 1st edition. Fine in dust jacket. $30.
The Tough Coughs as He Plows the Dough. Morrow, 1987 1st edition. Very Good in dust jacket. $20.

SEVAREID, ERIC. *Not So Wild a Dream*. NY, 1946 1st edition. Signed. Fine. $75. Unsigned, $35.

SEWALL, THOMAS. *Examination of Phrenology*. Washington DC, 1837 1st edition. Inscribed to Edward Everett. Scarce. $250.

SEWELL, ANNA. *Black Beauty*. Boston, 1890 1st American edition. Paperbound. Illus. by author. VG. $150-$300. Reilly & Britton, 1908. J. R. Neill illus. VG. $40-$75. London, 1915 edition. Lucy Welch illus. Near Fine. $290. Grosset & Dunlap, 1925 reprint. $6. 1945 edition. Eichenberger illus. $8. McLoughlin, no date. $15. Various other reprints. $6-$25.

SEWELL, HELEN and ELESKA. *Three Tall Tales*. Macmillan, 1947 1st edition. Helen Sewell illus. Near Fine in very good dust jacket. $42.

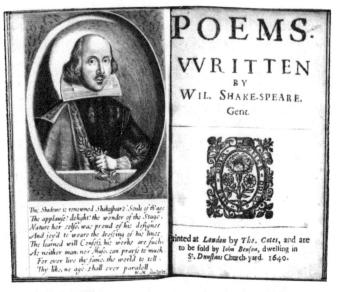

SHAKESPEARE, WILLIAM. *Poems: Written by William Shakespeare, Gent*. Engraved frontis by William Marshall. 5¼ x 3¼ rebound in 19th century gilt-ruled calf. First collected ed. London, Tho. Cotes, 1640. $17,600.
The Plays and Poems of William Shakespeare. First American edition. Corrected from later London editions. 8 vols. Philadelphia, Bioren & Madan, 1795-1796. Contemporary calf, rebacked. $12,500.
The Works of William Shakespeare. Various sets of 3 to 12 vols. published in the 1700s. $600-$6,000 depending upon bindings, illustrations, size and condition. Late 1800s 12 vol. sets pub. in NY & London, for the trade, range from $75-$95 in box. Limited edition sets of the early 1900s have sold for $250-$350. An American actors in engravings, 3 vol set. NY, 1856. Near Fine. $250. London, 1860 2 vols. J. Tallis. Very Good. $70-$95.
Hamlet. NY, 1902. Roycroft Press. Half suede. VG plus. $50. LEC, 1933. Signed by Eric Gill, illus. $200-$300.
The Plays of William Shakespeare. H. C. Selous engravings. London, Cassell, circa 1880. Scuffing else VG. $100-$150. NY, Limited Editions club, 1934-41. 37 volumes. Illus. by 37 artists. Fine. $500 auction.
The Tempest. Doubleday, 1926. Arthur Rackham illus. Very Good. $145-$195.
Titus Andronicus First Quarto 1594. Scribners Facsimile Edition, 1936. Fine. $12.
Merchant of Venice. London, H&S, No date. $25-$40.
Mercury Shakespeare-Merchant of Venice. Harpers, 1939. Fine. $10.
Midsummer Night's Dream. Doubleday, 1908. Rackham illus. VG. $150-$225. Same, LEC., 1939. $200-$300.
Passionate Pilgrim. Clarendon, 1905 Facsimile on vellum. $125. Scribners Facsimile Edition, 1940. Fine. $10.
Romeo & Juliet. NY, Heritage Book Club, 1937. In slipcase. $75-$95. Another, Charles Scribner's Sons, 1936. Signed by artist. $100. Unsigned. $50-$75.
Sonnets of William Shakespeare. Various limited eds. pub. in America, 1901-1971. Octavo, F. $150-$450 each.
Shakespeare's Comedy As You Like It. London and NY, no date. Hugh Thomson color plates. VG. $150-$195.

SHAMBAUGH, BERTHA. *Amana, the Community of True Inspiration*. Iowa City, 1908. Gilt stamped green cloth. Very Good. $40.

SHAND, P. MORTON. *Book of Other Wines Than French*. NY, 1929, Cloister Press. $20.
A Book of Wine. NY, circa 1926. Cloth & rice paper. Ornate. $35.

SHAPIRO, IRWIN. *Casey Jones and Locomotive No. 638*. NY, 1944 1st ed. Donald McKay illus. Good plus. $20.

SHAPIRO, KARL. *Essay on Rime*. Reynal & Hitchcock, 1945 1st ed. Very Good in dust jacket. $38-$45.
Trial of a Poet. NY, 1957 1st ed. Inscribed. Very Good in chip dust jacket. $55.
Poems of a Jew. NY, 1958 1st ed. Presentation copy. Fine in chip dust jacket. $125.
Various later editions of collected poems. $10-$40 each.

SHAPIRO, SAMUEL. *Richard Henry Dana, Jr., 1815-1882*. Michigan State, 1961 1st ed. Fine in dust jacket. $15.

SHAPLEY, HARLOW. *Through Rugged Ways to the Stars, The Reminiscences of an Astronomer*. NY, 1969 1st printing. Very Good in chipped dust jacket. $18.

SHARP, D. L. *The Seer of Slabsides* (John Burroughs). Houghton-Mifflin, 1921. Very Good. $13.

SHARP, MARGERY. *The Rescuers*. Boston, 1959 1st ed. Garth Williams illus. Very Good. $8.
Miss Bianca: A Fantasy. Boston, 1962 1st ed. Garth Williams illus. Very Good in fair dust jacket. $20.
Miss Bianca in the Salt Mines. Little Brown, 1966 1st ed. Garth Williams illus. Good-VG in dust jacket. $45.
The Turret. Little Brown, 1963 1st ed. Garth Williams illus. Very Good in dust jacket. $35-$70.
Miss Bianca in the Antarctic. Boston, 1971. Erik Blegvad illustrator. Very Good. $25.

SHAVER, RICHARD. *I Remember Lemuria and The Return of Sathanas*. Evanston IL, 1948 1st ed. Fine. $45.

SHAER, RUTH M. *Kabuki Costume*. Tuttle, 1966. Illustrated. Very Good in dust jacket, boxed. $85.

SHAW, FRED. *The Complete Science of Fly Fishing and Spinning*. NY, 1915 1st edition. Very Good. $110.

SHAW, GEORGE BERNARD. *This is The Preachment: On Going to Church*. Roycroft Press, 1896. Foxing. $65.
The Intelligent Woman's Guide to Socialism and Capitalism. NY, 1928 1st American edition. Very Good in fair dust jacket. $35.
The Apple Cart (Play). NY, 1931 1st American edition. Very Good in worn dust jacket. $60.

The Adventures of the Black Girl in Her Search for God. Dodd Mead, 1933 1st ed. Good in dust jacket. $40-$80.
Back to Methuselah. John Farleigh illustrator. NY, 1939. Very Good in slipcase. $45.

SHAW, HELEN. *Fly Tying.* New York, 1963 1st edition. Very Good. $45.

SHAW, IRWIN. *Bury the Dead.* NY, 1936 1st ed. Author's 1st book. Near Very Good in dust jacket. $75.
Mixed Company. Random House, 1950 1st edition. Very Good in dust jacket. $40-$50.
Lucy Crown. New York, 1956 1st edition. Very Good in dust jacket. $20.

SHAW, LUELLA. *True History, Pioneers of Colorado* Hotchkiss, Co., 1909. $85.

SHAW, REUBEN COLE. *Across the Plains in Forty-Nine.* Indiana, W. C. West, 1896 1st edition. 200 pgs. Green cloth. Very Good. $250.

SHAW, WILBUR. *Gentlemen, Start Your Engines.* NY, 1955. Very Good. $13.

SHAW, TED. *Gods Who Dance.* NY, 1929. Inscribed. Shelfworn. Good. $25.

SHAY, FRANK (Editor). *Iron Men & Wooden Ships: Deep Sea Chanties.* Garden City, New York, 1924 1st edition. E. A. Wilson illustrator. One of 200 copies, signed by Wilson. Very Good. $200. Another, no date, pictorial wraps. $40.

SHAY, FELIX. *Elbert Hubbard of East Aurora.* NY, 1926 1st edition. Decorated in Roycroft manner. Light stain, o/w Near Fine. $45.

SHEA, JAMES J. *It's All in the Game.* Biography of Milton Bradley. Putnams, 1960. Very Good in dust jacket. $30.

SHEA, JOHN G. *Discovery and Exploration of the Mississippi Valley.* NY, Redfield, 1853 2nd printing. 267 pages plus ads. Some wear, foxing throughout. $150.

SHEARER, EDWIN. *Manual of Human Dissection.* PA, Blakiston, 1937 1st ed. Illus. by author. Fine. $18.

SHEARING, JOSEPH. *The Lady and the Arsenic.* NY, 1944 1st ed. Very Good in fair dust jacket. $28.

SHEFFIELD, LYBA & NITA. *Swimming Simplified.* San Francisco, 1921 2nd edition. $20.

SHELDON, GEORGE W. *The Story of the Volunteer Fire Department of the City of New York.* NY, 1882. Fine. Rebacked. $250. Another copy, average condition. $175.

SHELDON, COLONEL HAROLD P. *Tranquillity, Tales of Sport With the Gun.* Derrydale Press, 1936 1st ed. Nash Buckingham introduction. One of 950 copies. VG. $125.
Tranquillity, Tranquillity Revisited and Tranquillity Regained. NY, 1945. One of 475 sets. Fine. $500.

SHELLEY, C. P. *Workshop Appliances, Lathes, Machine Tools, etc.* NY, Appleton, 1884. Good. $25.

SHELLEY, MARY WOOLSTONECRAFT. *Frankenstein.* Grosset & Dunlap, 1933. Photoplay edition. Stills with Boris Karloff. Good. $20.

SHELLEY, PERCY B. *The Poetical Works of.* London, 1839 4 volumes. Fine. $150. 1853 edition, Moxon. Rubbed, otherwise Very Good. $75.
Complete Poetical Works of. London, 1948. Fine. $30. Another, Ernest Benn. 10 volumes. 1927 Limited. edition. of 780 copies. $800-$1,200.

SHEPHERD, JEAN (Editor). *The America of George Ade.* NY, Putnam, 1960 1st ed. Fine in dust jacket. $20.

SHEPPS WORLD'S FAIR PHOTOGRAPHED. Columbian Exposition, 1893. Autographed by expo president, Harlow Higginbotham. Very Good. $45.

SHERATON, THOMAS. *The Cabinet-Maker and Upholsterer's Drawing Book in Four Parts.* T. Bensley, London, 1802. Boards scuffed, tips bumped. $600.

SHERIDAN, MAC C. *The Stag Cookbook: A Man's Cookbook.* NY, 1922. Good-Very Good. $20-$40.

SHERIDAN, PHILIP. *Personal Memoirs of P. H. Sheridan.* 2 vol set. C. L. Webster, 1888 1st ed. Gilt on green cloth covers. Very Good-Fine. $55-$75. Good. $40-$50.
Outline Descriptions of the Posts in the Military Division of the Missouri. Chicago, 1872 1st ed. with folding map. Good-Very Good. $125-$250.

SHERMAN, HAROLD. *Double Play!* (Home Run Series). Grosset & Dunlap, 1932. Green cloth in dust jacket. Little worn, else Very Good. $40.
Mayfield's Fighting Five. Grosset & Dunlap, 1935 edition. Hinge loose, ragged edge dust jacket. Good-Very Good. $15.
Safe! (Home Run Series). Grosset & Dunlap, 1928. Green cloth, Very Good in dust jacket. $40.

SHERMAN, WILLIAM TECUMSEH. *Personal Memoirs of W. T. Sherman.* NY, 1875 edition. 2 volumes. G-VG. $50-$85. Webster, 1891 4th ed. Good. $20. VG. $35-$70.

SHERRILL, CHARLES H. *French Memories of 18th-Century America.* Scribner's, 1915 1st edition. Very Good in torn dust jacket. $20.

SHERROD, ROBERT. *History of Marine Corps Aviation in World War II*. Washington, 1952 1st ed. Very Good in dust jacket. $45. No dust jacket. $24-$30.

SHERWOOD, MARY MARTHA. *The Happy Choice*. Philadelphia, circa 1825. Very Good. $45.
The Wishing Cup. NY, 1833. Very Good. $35.

SHERWOOD, ROBERT. *The Petrified Forest*. NY, 1935 1st edition. Very Good in pasted dust jacket. $40.
Abe Lincoln in Ilinois. NY, 1939 1st edition. Carl Sandburg foreword. Cover portrait by N. Rockwell. Very Good in dust jacket. $75.

SHETRONE, HENRY CLYDE. *The Mound-Builders*. New York, 1936 2nd edition. End wear, o/w Very Good in fair dust jacket. $175. 3rd edition. $150. 1964 reprint of 1930 edition. Very Good. $60.

SHIEL, M. P. *The Yellow Danger*. NY, 1899 1st ed. VG. $20.
Lord of the Sea. NY, 1901 1st ed. 1st issue. Good. $20.

SHIELDS, G. O. *Hustling in the Rockies*. (Hunting and Fishing). Chicago, 1883. Good. $35.
Big Game of North America. Chicago, 1890 1st edition. Very Good. $110

SHIELS, ARCHIE W. *The Purchase of Alaska*. Univ. of Alaska, 1967 1st ed. Very Good in dust jacket. $9.

SHIPPEN, KATHERINE B. *New Found World*. NY, 1945 1st ed. C. B. Fall illus. Near Fine in chip DJ. $25.

SHIRAS, GEORGE. *Hunting Wildlife With Camera and Flashlight*. National Geographic Society, 1936 2nd ed. 2 vols. Scuffed spines, o/w Very Good. $30-$40.

SHIRCLIFFE, ARNOLD. *The Edgewater Beach Hotel Salad Book*. Chicago, 1929. Illus. Good-Very Good. $40.

SHIRER, WILLIAM. *Berlin Diary*. NY, Knopf, 1941 1st ed. in dust jacket. $10-$20.
The Rise and Fall of The Third Reich. 1960. Very Good in dust jacket. $20. Same, no dust jacket. $8-$15.

SHIRLEY, GLENN. *Toughest of Them All*. University of New Mexico, 1953 1st ed. Fine in fine dust jacket. $25.
Six-Gun and Silver Star. University of New Mexico, 1955 1st ed. Very Good in dust jacket. $30.
Buckskin and Spurs. NY, 1958 1st ed. F in fine DJ. $35.

SHIRLEY TEMPLE EDITION OF "THE LITTLE COLONEL". Burt, 1922. Photos. Slight cover damage, o/w Good. $12.

SHIRLEY TEMPLE EDITION OF "HEIDI". Random House, 1959. Photos from movie. VG. $15. Same, 1937 ed. $20.

SHIRLEY TEMPLE EDITION OF "POOR LITTLE RICH GIRL". Saalfield, 1936 1st ed. Good-VG. $25-$35.

SHOOK, CHARLES A. *Cumorah Revisited or Book of Mormon and Claims of Mormons Re-examined*. Cincinnati, 1910 1st ed. Very Good. $75.

SHOWALTER, MARY EMMA. *Mennonite Community Cookbook*. Mennonite Assn., 1961. G-VG in DJ. $12-$24.

SHOWELL, J. P. M. *The German Navy inWorld War II*. Naval Institute, 1979 1st ed. Fine in fine dust jacket. $25.

SHUCK, OSCAR T. *The California Scrapbook; A Repository of Useful Information*. San Francisco, Bancroft, 1869 1st ed. Very Good. $200-$300.

SHULMAN, CARRIE V. *Favorite Dishes: A Columbian Autograph Souvenir Cookery Book*. Chicago, 1893. Good-Very Good. $50.

SHURCLIFF, W. A. *Bombs at Bikini: The Official Report of Operation Crossroads*. NY, 1947 1st ed. Good. $25.

SHURTLEF, HAROLD. *The Log Cabin Myth*. Harvard Univ. Press, 1939 1st ed. Samuel Eliot Morison editor. VG. $25.

SHUTE, MISS T. S. *The American Housewife Cook Book*. Phil., 1878. $30-$40. Same, 1880 ed. Fair condition. $25.

SIDIS, BORIS. *Multiple Personality*. New York, 1909. Good to Very Good. $50.

SIDNEY, MARGARET. *Five Little Peppers and How They Grew*. Lothrop, 1881. 51st thousand. Soiled back cover, o/w Very Good. $16. Same, Fine. $40. Boston, 1909 edition. Good. $13.
Phonsie Pepper. Boston, 1897 1st edition. Gilt Cloth. McDermott illus. $25-$40.
Various Five Little Peppers titles, 1893-1900 1st eds. Green cloth. 5 vols. $66 all. Auction lot.
The Stories Polly Pepper Told. Boston, 1899. Etheldred Barry illus. Very Good. $10-$12.
Five Little Peppers Abroad. Boston, 1902. Good-Very Good. $20-$30.
The Adventures of Joel Pepper. Boston, 1909. Sears Gallagher illus. Very Good. $10-$12.
Five Little Peppers Midway. NY, Grosset & Dunlap, 1918 reprint. $4.

SIEBERT, W. H. *The Underground Railroad in Mass*. Worcester MA, 1936. Photos. Good. $20.

SILONE, IGNAZIO. *Bread and Wine*. NY, 1937 1st American ed. Very Good in dust jacket. $20-$30.
A Handful of Blackberries. NY, 1953 1st American ed. Very Good in dust jacket. $15.

SILVERBERG, ROBERT. *Mound Builders of Ancient America*. Greenwich CT, 1968 1st ed. VG in chip DJ. $50.

SILVERSTEIN, SHEL. *Different Dances*. NY, 1979 1st ed. Fine in fine dust jacket. $40.
A Light in the Attic. NY, 1981. Fine in dust jacket. $15.

SIMAK, CLIFFORD D. *Ring Around the Sun*. NY, 1953 1st ed. Near Fine in dust jacket. $65.
Strangers in the Universe. NY, 1956 1st ed. Fine in dust jacket. $25. Same, inscribed. $75.
All Flesh is Grass. NY, 1965 1st ed. VG in fine DJ. $75.
Destiny Doll. NY, 1971 1st ed. VG in dust jacket. $55.
Shakespeare's Planet. NY, 1976 1st ed. Fine in DJ. $15.

SIMENON, GEORGES. *Maigret Sits It Out*. NY, 1941 1st edition. Near Fine in slightly worn dust jacket. $165.
Maigret Sets a Trap. London, 1965 1st English ed. Very Good in good dust jacket. $23.
Maigret on the Defensive. London, 1966 1st British ed. Very Good in frayed dust jacket. $35.
Maigret and the Nabour Case. London, 1967 1st ed. Fine in good dust jacket. $40.
Maigret and the Minister. London, 1969 1st edition. Very Good in dust jacket. $10.
Maigret mysteries, all 1st eds., 1963-1978. $35 each.
12 different novels from 1965-1982. 1st American edition. Very Good in very good dust jacket. $15 each.
Inspector Maigret first editions. Published by Hamish Hamilton. Very Good in very good dust jacket, are generally priced at $25-$35. First American editions in similar condition go for $15-$20.

SIMMONS, AMELIA. *American Cookery*. 1815 ed. of first cook book (1796) published in the U. S. by an American author. Asking $3,000. NY, 1958. Facsimile of 1st edition, 1796, with essay by Mary T. Wilson. Fine in slipcase. $40.

SIMMS, WILLIAM GILMORE. *Pelayo: A Story of the Goth*. NY, 1838 1st ed. 2 vols. Very Good. $350.
The Life of Captain John Smith. New York, 1846 1st edition. Good. $60.
The Lily and the Totem. NY, 1850 1st ed. VG plus. $500.

SIMON, ANDRE. *The Art of Good Living*. NY, 1930 1st edition. Very Good. $40.
Andre Simon's French Cook Book. Boston, 1948 New ed. Very Good in dust jacket. $12.
Encyclopedia of Gastronomy. NY, 1952 1st edition. Very Good in dust jacket. $15.
Wines of the World. NY, 1968. Illus. Very Good. $18.

SIMON, ELLEN. *Critter Book*. NY, 1940 1st ed. Illus. by author. Very Good in good dust jacket. $25.

SIMON, HOWARD. *500 Years of Illustration*. Garden City, 1949. Good-Very Good. $50.

SIMON, NEIL. *The Prisoner of Second Avenue*. NY, 1972 1st ed. Frontispiece photo of Peter Falk, Lee Grant. Fine in sunned dust jacket. $40.

SIMONDS, WILLIAM A. *Henry Ford, His Life, His Works, His Genius*. Bobbs-Merrill, 1943. Good. $25.

SIMPSON, CHARLES. *Life in the Mines, or Crime Avenged: Thrilling Adventures Among Miners and Outlaws*. Chicago, 1898. Very Good. $35.

SIMPSON, LOUIS. *Riverside Drive*. NY, 1962 1st ed. Very Good in DJ. $30. Inscribed. Near Fine in good DJ. $60.

SIMS, GEORGE. *The Last Best Friend*. NY, 1968. Very Good in dust jacket. $10.

SIMS, ORLAND L. *Cowpokes, Nesters and So Forth*. Austin, Encino Press, 1970 1st ed. 1 of 250 numbered copies, signed by author. Fine ¾ leather. $120.

SINCLAIR, UPTON. *The Jungle*. NY, 1906 1st ed. Near Fine. $100. London, 1906 1st English ed. Very Good. $75.
The Moneychangers. NY, 1908 1st ed. Very Good. $45.
Profits of Religion. Pasadena CA, 1918 1st ed. Self-published. Very Good. $15.
The Brass Check. Pasadena, pub. by the author, 1920. Presentation to a collector on front flyleaf. Bookplates, otherwise, Very Good. $75.
They Call Me Carpenter. Pasadena by Sinclair, 1922 1st edition. Very Good. $15.
The Goose Step. Sinclair, 1923 2nd edition. Very Good in red cloth. $9.
The Book of Life, Mind and Body. Pasadena, CA, Pub. by author, 1921 1st edition. Worn, torn, paperback. $25.
Oil! A Novel. NY, Boni, 1927 1st ed. Black cloth. VG $35.
Boston: A Novel. Long Beach CA, 1928. Self published. Very Good in good dust jacket. $10. Another, Boston, 1928 in 2 vols. Good-VG. $30.
The Gnomobile. NY, 1936 1st ed. Fine in dust jacket. $75.
The Flivver King. Sinclair, UAW, 1937 paperbound. Very Good. $20. Same. Hardbound in DJ. $45.
Dragon's Teeth. New York, 1942 1st edition. Very Good in good dust jacket. $40.
One Clear Call. NY, Viking, 1948 1st ed. Fine in DJ. $15.
The Return of Lanny Budd. NY, 1953 1st ed. Very Good in dust jacket. $15.

SINDALL, R. W. *The Manufacture of Paper. with Bibliography of Related Works*. New York, 1908, 1st American edition. $25.

SINGER, CHARLES (Editor). *A History of Technology*. London, 1954-58. 5 vols. 1st ed. Profusely illus. Very Good in dust jackets. $200.
A Short History of Medicine. NY, 1928 1st edition. Good-Very Good. $35-$50.

SINGER, ISAAC BASHEVIS. *The Family Moskat*. NY, 1950 1st ed. Author's 1st book. Very Good in DJ. $100.
The Spinoza of Market Street. NY, 1961 1st ed. Very Good in good dust jacket. $35. Fine in Fine DJ. $75.
Short Friday. NY, 1964 1st edition. No DJ. $35.
Zlateh the Goat and Other Stories. NY, 1966 1st ed. Maurice Sendak illus. Fine in dust jacket. $75.
The Estate. NY, 1969 1st ed. Fine in dust jacket. $35.
A Young Man in Search of Love. NY, 1978 1st ed. Raphael Soyer illus. Inscribed by Singer, Soyer. Near Fine in dust jacket. $175.
Old Love. NY, 1979 1st ed. Fine in clip dust jacket. $30.
The Collected Stories of. NY, 1982 1st edition. Inscribed. Fine in dust jacket. $125.
Yentl the Yeshiva Boy. NY, 1983 1st ed. Frasconi illus. Fine in clip dust jacket. $25.

SINGLETON, ESTHER. *The Furniture of Our Forefathers*. NY, 1901, 8 parts in 2 vols. 92 illus. Near VG. $150.
Social New York Under the Georges. NY, 1902 1st edition. Very Good. $25-$35.

SINGMASTER, ELSIE. *Pennsylvania's Susquehanna*. Harrisburg PA, 1950. Illus. Fine in dust jacket. $15.
Little and Unknown. Franklin, 1951. Edward Smith illus. Limited edition in glassine dust jacket. $18-$25.

SINKANKAS, JOHN. *Gem Cutting*. No place, 1955 1st ed. Signed. Fine in worn dust jacket. $50.

SINSABAUGH, CHRIS. *Who Me? Forty Years of Automobile History*. Detroit, 1940 1st edition. Very Good. $35.

SIRINGO, CHARLES A. *A Cowboy Detective*. Chicago, 1912. Good. $100. Very Good. $200-$250.
A Lone Star Cowboy. Santa Fe, 1919 1st ed. Very Good. $100. Another copy, stained, rubbed. $50.
Riata and Spurs: Story of a Lifetime Spent in the Saddle as a Cowboy and Detective. Boston, NY, 1927. Very Good-Fine. $100-$200.

SISCA, MARZIALE. *Caricatures by Enrico Caruso*. NY, 1939 4th edition. Interior good, o/w Poor. $25.

SITWELL, EDITH. *Children's Tales From the Russian Ballet*. London, 1920 1st ed. Illus. Very Good. $35.
Bucolic Comedies. London, 1923 1st ed. Near Fine. $100.
The Queens and the Hive. Boston, 1962 1st American edition. illus. Very Good in dust jacket. $45.
The Last Years of a Rebel. Boston, 1967 1st American edition. Very Good in dust jacket. $15.

SITWELL, H. D. W. *The Crown Jewels*. London, 1953. 40 plates. Very Good in dust jacket. $125.

SIZER, NELSON. *Forty Years in Phrenology*. New York, 1884. Shelfworn, $45.

SLAUSON, H. W. *Everyman's Guide to Motor Efficiency*. New York, 1920 1st edition. Photos, diagrams. Large, limp leatherette. $30.

SLOANE, ERIC. *Our Vanishing Landscape*. NY, 1955 Paperbound. Illus. by author. Fine in dust jacket. $15.
The Book of Storms. NY, 1956. Illus by author. Very Good in chip dust jacket. $18.
American Yesterday. NY, 1956 14th printing. Illus. by author. Very Good in dust jacket. $25.
An Age of Barns. NY, 1961. Illus. by author. Good in dust jacket. $16. 1966 ed. Fine. $12.
Diary of an Early American Boy. Funk, 1962. Fine in dust jacket. $17-$24.
Folklore of American Weather. NY, 1963 2nd printing. Illus. by author. Very Good in torn dust jacket. $20.
The Cracker Barrel. 1967, Funk & Wagnals. Signed by author. Very Good in fair dust jacket. $25.
A Reverence for Wood. Funk, 1965 1st ed. in DJ. $25.

SLOBODKIN, LOUIS. *Clear the Track for Michael's Magic Train*. Macmillan, 1945. Illustrated by author. Very Good in dust jacket. $20.

SLOTE, ALFRED. *Air in Act and Fancy*. Cleveland, 1968. Very Good in dust jacket. $22.
Stranger on the Ball Club. Lippincott, 1970 1st ed. $15.

SMALLEY, EUGENE. *History of the Northern Pacific Railroad*. NY, 1883. 437 pgs., illus. Orig. gilt-stamped cloth. Very Good. $200.

SMITH, ADAM. *An Inquiry into the Nature and Causes of the Wealth of Nations*. Dublin, Whitestone, 1776. Volume 1 of 3. Leather. 391 pgs. Scuffed but clean. $150. Same, with life of the author. 3 volumes complete. London, Maynard, 1811. Worn and foxed, but clean and tight. $125 all. Same, Edinburgh, 1817. 3 vols. Good. $135. Same, London, 1799. 3 vols. Very Good. $220.

SMITH, ARTHUR C. *Turquoise Cup*. NY, Scribners, 1903. Parrish illus. VG. $40-$80. Reprint, 1910. $20-$35.

SMITH, ASA. *Illustrated Astronomy*. NY, 1856. Disbound, foxing, worn covers. $25. 1868 edition. Good. $27.

SMITH, BETTY. *A Tree Grows in Brooklyn*. NY, 1943 1st edition. Very Good. $35.
Maggie-Now. NY, 1958 1st ed. Fine in dust jacket. $45.
Joy in the Morning. NY, 1963 1st ed. Signed Very Good in dust jacket. $25-$40.

SMITH, CHARD. *The Housatonic*. Rivers of America series. NY, 1946 1st ed. Very Good in dust jacket. $15-$30.

SMITH, CLARK ASHTON. *Lost Worlds*. Arkham House, 1944 1st ed. VG in very good dust jacket. $110-$150.

Genius Loci and Other Tales. Arkham House, 1948 1st ed. Very Good in clipped dust jacket. $80-$120. Fine in dust jacket. $125-$175.

The Dark Chateau. Arkham House, 1951 1st ed. Fine in fine dust jacket. $500-$600.

Abominations of Yondo. Arkham House, 1960 1st edition. Fine in fine dust jacket. $150.

Tales of Science and Sorcery. Arkham House, 1964 1st edition. Fine in fine dust jacket. $65-$120.

Other Dimensions. Arkham House, 1970 1st edition. Fine in dust jacket. $50-$75.

SMITH, E. BOYD. *The Story of Noah's Ark*. Boston, 1905 1st edition. Illus. by author. Fine. $35.

Fun in the Radio World. NY, 1923 1st edition. Illustrated by author. Very Good. $43.

SMITH, E. E. *The Skylark of Space*. Providence, 1947 2nd edition. Signed, inscribed. Very Good. $35.

SMITH, EDMUND WARE. *Further Adventures of a One-Eyed Poacher*. NY, 1947 1st ed. E. B. Ripley illustrator. Very Good. $30.

SMITH, ESTHER. *The Official Cook Book of the Hay System*. Pocono Haven PA, 1936 6th printing. VG. $18.

SMITH, FRANCIS HOPKINSON. *A Day at Laguerre's and Other Days*. Boston, 1892 1st trade edition. Good. $13.

American Illustrators. NY, 1892. H. Pyle illus. $65-$95.

Colonel Carter's Christmas. NY, 1903 1st ed. F. C. Yohn illustrator. Very Good-Fine. $15-$30.

The Wood Fire in No. 3. NY, 1905. Kimall illus. VG. $53.

The Works of Francis Hopkinson Smith. NY, 1902-1908. 17 vol. Beacon ed. Uncut, unopened. NF. $175.

SMITH, FRANK. *A Cosy Home. How it Was Built*. Boston, 1887. Ads, floor plans, paint chip samples. (16,000 copies in print.) $125.

SMITH, G. ELLIOTT and WARREN DAWSON. *Egyptian Mummies*. NY, 1924. Fine. $85.

SMITH, GEORGE WASHINGTON. *A History of Southern Illinois*. Chicago, 1912 Vols. 1 & 2. Soiled. $65 each.

SMITH, GRANT H. *The History of the Comstock Lode, 1850-1920*. 297 pgs. Reno NV, 1943. Very Good. $65.

SMITH, H. ALLEN. *Low Man on a Totem Pole*. NY, 1941 1st edition. Very Good. $25.

Lost in the Horse Latitudes. NY, 1944 1st edition. Fine in dust jacket. $10.

Rhubarb. Doubleday, 1946 1st edition. Very Good in dust jacket. $12-$14.

We Went That Way. Doubleday, 1949 1st edition. Fine in good dust jacket. $10.

SMITH, HELENA H. *The War on Powder River, the History of an Insurrection*. McGraw-Hill, 1966. Fine. $20.

SMITH, JESSE WILCOX (Illustrator). *In the Closed Room*. By Frances Hodgson Burnett. Grosset & Dunlap, 1904. Very Good. $95.

A Child's Garden of Verses. By Robert Louis Stevenson. NY, 1905. Good. $25. VG. $125. Another, 1925. $45-$90.

When Christmas Comes Around. By Priscilla Underwood. NY, Duffield, 1915 edition. Ex-library, else VG. $60-$90.

Mother Goose. Dodd, 1912. VG. $150-$250. Same, 1916 ed. VG. $100-$150. NY, 1914 1st ed. Anonymous. 12 full page color plus black/white illustrations. Some foxing, else Very Good. $175-$250. Same, ex-library. $70-$100.

The Little Mother Goose. NY, Dodd, 1918. Very Good. $100-$150.

At the Back of the North Wind. By George MacDonald. McKay, 1919 1st ed. Very Good. $100.

The Water Babies. By Charles Kingsley. New York, Dodd, Mead, 1916 1st edition. Round cover label. Near Fine. $247 auction. Same year. 8 color plates. $75-$150. Garden City, 1937. 4 color plates. $35. Circa 1936. Dodd, Mead, no date, no color. $15-$30.

Dickens' Children. 1912 1st ed. Illus. by author. Slightly soiled, o/w VG. $95. Scribner, 1912. VG. $100-$175.

Heidi. By Johanna Spyri. Philadelphia, David McKay, 1922 1st ed. 10 color plates by J. W. Smith. Pictorial cover label, gilt on blue cloth spine. Near Fine in clean bright dust jacket. $247 auction. Avg. retail. $75-$175.

The Princess and the Goblin. By Geo. McDonald. Philadelphia, David McKay, 1920 1st ed. Very Good in poor dust jacket. $100 auction.

SMITH, LAURA R. *Mother Goose Stories in Prose*. 1907. 110 pgs. Good-Very Good. $18.

SMITH, MARY STUART. *Virginia Cookery Book*. NY, 1885. Near Fine. $75.

SMITH, NORA ARCHIBALD. *Boys and Girls of Book-land*. Cosmopolitan Book, 1923 1st ed. Jesse Wilcox Smith illus. Very Good. $85.

SMITH, MISS PRUDENCE. *Modern American Cookery*. NY, 1835 2nd edition. Very Good. $125.

SMITH, R. (Publisher). *Smiths New Geography*. 1861. 90 pgs. 30 hand-colored maps. $100.

SMITH, THEO L. *The Montessori School*. NY, 1912 1st edition. Very Good in dust jacket. $40.

SMITH, THORNE. *Biltmore Oswald*. NY, 1918 1st edition. Author's 1st book. Very Good plus. $100.

Topper: An Improbably Adventure. NY, 1926 1st ed. Moderate wear. $75.

Lazy Bear Lane. NY, 1931 1st edition. $35-$50.

Night Life of the Gods. Garden City NY, 1931. Near Fine in very good dust jacket. $20-$35.
The Passionate Witch. (completed by N. Matson) NY, 1941 1st ed., Doubleday. Fine. $150. 1942 ed. VG. $16.

SMITH, W. EUGENE. *W. Eugene Smith, His Photographs and Notes*. NY, 1969 1st edition. 120 photographs. Very Good in dust jacket. $40.

SMITH, W. H. B. *Pistols and Revolvers*. 1965, Stackpole Books. Good. $20.

SMITH, WILLIAM. *Dictionary of the Bible*. National Pubs. 1869 revised ed. Fair, leather. $16.

SMITH, WILLIAM M. *Gloves, Past and Present*. NY, 1918. Very Good. $20.

THE SMITHSONIAN COLLECTION OF NEWSPAPER COMICS. Abrams, 1977. Oversize. Very Fine in DJ. $40.

SMITHSONIAN INSTITUTION ANNUAL REPORTS. Washington DC. 12 assorted volumes, 1860-1930. 270 pages to 950 pages. Good. $25 each.

ANNUAL REPORT, SMITHSONIAN INSTUTION, 1901. G.P.O. 1903. Indians of Arizona, Pan-American expo, etc. 452 pgs. 33 in color. Excellent. $80.

SMITHSONIAN SCIENTIFIC SERIES. No place, 1934 12 vols. Good. $75.

SMITHWICK, NOAH. *Evidence of a State, or Recollections of Old Texas Days*. Austin, 1900. Ex-library. Minor foxing. $325.

SMYTHE, WILLIAM E. *The Conquest of Arid America*. NY, 1900. Very Good. $65.

SNEAD, SAM. *How to Play Golf - Professional Tips*. NY, 1946. Good. $25. 2nd ed., 1952. Fine. $9.
The Education of a Golfer. Simon & Schuster, 1962 1st edition. Very Good in dust jacket. $14.
Sam Snead Teaches "Key" Approach. Atheneum, 1975 1st edition. Fine, no dust jacket. $10.

SNEDEKER, CAROLINE DALE. *The Black Arrowhead*. NY, 1929 1st edition. Manning de V. Lee illustrator. Very Good in dust jacket. $30.

SNELL, ROY J. *Sally Scott of the Waves*. Whitman, 1943. Hedwig Meixner illus. Good. $15.

SNELLING, H. H. *The History and Practice of the Art of Photography*. Morgan & Morgan, 1970. Reprint of 1949 edition. As new, $15.

SNOW, C. P. *Death Under Sail*. London, 1931 1st ed. Very Good in dust jacket. $45.
A Time of Hope. NY, 1950 1st Amer. ed. VG in DJ. $20.
Two Cultures and the Scientific Revolution. NY, 1961 1st American ed. 7th printing. Inscribed. Fine in fine DJ. $20.
The Two Cultures and a Second Look. No place, 1964 2nd edition. Very Good in dust jacket. $38.

SNOW, EDWARD ROWE. *Pirates & Buccaneers of the Atlantic Coast*. Boston, Yankee Pub., 1944 1st ed. in DJ. Good-Very Good, $35. Same, signed. $70.
The Romance of Boston Bay. Boston, 1944 1st edition. Overall Very Good. $15.
Famous New England Lighthouses. Boston, Yankee Pub., 1945 1st ed. Fine with an orig. photo laid in. $60.
Legends of the New England Coast. NY, 1957. Illus. Ex-library. Good in dust jacket. $9.
New England Sea Tragedies. New York, 1960. Very Good in good dust jacket. $24.

SNOW, JACK. *The Shaggy Man of Oz*. Reilly & Lee, 1949 1st edition. Very Good, illus. bds. $80.

SNOWDON, LORD. *A Photographic Autobiography*. NY, 1979. Fine in dust jacket. $15.

SNYDER, HARRY. *Bread, a Collection of Popular Papers*. NY, 1930 1st edition. Worn, $35.

SNYDER, W. E. *The Leathercraftsman. A Textbook on Leather*. NY, Bridgman, 1936 1st ed. Very Good. $15.

SOLDIER'S HANDBOOK, FM 21-100. 1941 1st ed. G.P.O. 254 pages. Very Good in wraps. $8-$10.

SOLZHENITSYN, ALEXANDER. *A Day in the Life of Ivan Denisovich*. London, 1963 1st translated ed. Author's 1st book. Near Fine in very good dust jacket. $100. New York, Praeger, 1963 1st American ed. Very Good in dust jacket. $45. Another, Very Good in torn dust jacket. $28.
The First Circle. NY, Harper, 1968 1st ed. Very Good in clipped dust jacket. $45. Fine in fine dust jacket. $60.
Cancer Ward. Dial, 1968 1st ed. VG plus in DJ. $25. Bodley Head, 1968 1st English ed., in dust jacket. $35.
Gulag Archipelago. NY, Harper, 1973 1st edition. Very Good in dust jacket. $30.

SONN, ALBERT H. *Early American Wrought Iron*. NY, 1928 1st edition, 3 vols. Very Good. $200-$400.

SONNICHSEN, C. L. *The Story of Roy Bean*. Old Greenwich CT, 1943 1st edition. Very Good. $35.
Cowboys and Cattle Kings. Norman OK, 1951 2nd printing. Fine in chip dust jacket. $25.
Billy King's Tombstone. Caldwell ID, 1946 2nd printing. Fine in Fair dust jacket. $24. 1951 3rd printing. Fine. $30.

The Mescalero Apaches. Norman, 1958. Univ. of Oklahoma. Near Fine. $75.
Ten Texas Feuds. University of New Mexico, 1957 1st ed. Fine in near fine dust jacket. $45.
Tularosa: Last of the Frontier West. NY, 1960 1st ed. Fine in dust jacket. $60.
Outlaw Billy Mitchell. Denver CO, 1965 1st edition. Fine in fine dust jacket. $35.
Tucson: The Life and Times of an American City. Norman OK, 1982 1st ed. Fine in fine dust jacket. $45.

SONTAG, SUSAN. *The Benefactor*. NY, 1963 1st edition. Very Good in very good dust jacket. $40.
Death Kit. NY, 1976 1st ed. Very Good in DJ. $15.
On Photography. NY, 1977 1st ed. Very Good in DJ. $15.

SOULE, FRANK and JOHN GIHON. *The Annals of San Francisco*. NY, 1855. Binding repaired. $250.

SOUSA, JOHN PHILLIP. *Marching Along*. Boston, 1928 1st edition. Signed presentation copy. VG in shabby DJ. $210.
The Fifth String. IN, Bobbs-Merrill, 1902 1st ed. Christy illus. Fine. $44 auction. (est. $80-$120). 1902 reprint. $15.

SOUTHERN LIVING COOKBOOKS. *Assorted Bread and Dessert Cookbooks (1970-1983)*. $12-$15 each.

SOUTHWORTH, E.D.E.N. *How He Won Her*. NY, no date. Hinges cracked, o/w Good. $10.
Ishmael, or In the Depths. Grosset & Dunlap, no date. Worn spine, loose hinge, o/w Good. $5.

SOWERBY, MILLICENT (Illustrator). *The Gay Book*. By Githa Sowerby. Artists & Writers Guild, 1935. 12 full-page color illus. Overall Very Good. $48.

SOYER, ALEXIS. *Soyer's Cookery Book*. McKay, 1959 reprint. Fine illus. bds. $12.

SPALDING, ALBERT G. *America's National Game*. American Sports Pub. Co., 1911. Folding plates defective, some parts missing. $75. Another, 1st ed. Very Good. $450. Fine. $500-$600.

SPALDING, FREDERICK. *Masonry Structures*. New York, Wiley, 1921 1st ed. $25. 1926 2nd edition, revised. $15.

SPALDING'S OFFICIAL BASEBALL GUIDE. Annual publication, 1878-1939. Early issues worth several hundred dollars. 1900s bring less. (Also see Trade Catalog section).

SPARGO, JOHN. *Early American Pottery and China*. NY, 1938. Fine in very good dust jacket. $40.

SPARKS, MURIEL. *The Prime of Miss Jean Brodie*. London, 1961 1st ed. VG in DJ. $45. Same, NY. $30-$35.

Girls of Slender Means. NY, 1963 1st ed. VG in DJ. $20. Fine in dust jacket. $40
The Mandelbaum Gate. NY, 1965 1st. F in fine DJ. $10.

SPARROW, W. S. *A Book of Sporting Painters*. London, 1931 1st ed. One of 125 copies with two extra hand-colored plates. Very Good. $250.

SPEAKMAN, HAROLD. *Mostly Mississippi*. Dodd & Mead, 1927 1st ed. Good, no dust jacket. $20.

SPEARE, ELIZABETH GEORGE. *The Witch of Blackbird Pond*. Boston, 1958. Very Good in dust jacket. $8.

SPEARMAN, FRANK. *Whispering Smith*. NY, Scribners, 1906. Wyeth illus. VG. $35-$70. 1908 ed. $15-$25.
Nan of Music Mountain. Scribner, 1916. Wyeth illus. Very Good. $20-$40.

SPENCE, LEWIS. *The Problem of Atlantis*. London, 1925 Revised 2nd ed. Very Good-Fine. $15-$35.
The History of Atlantis. London, 1920s. Good plus. $28.

SPENDER, STEPHEN. *Forward From Liberalism*. NY, 1927 1st edition. Fine. $25.
Poems of Dedication. NY, 1927 1st ed. VG in DJ. $35.
Ruins and Visions. NY, 1942 1st Am. ed. VG in DJ. $35.

THE SPICE ISLANDS COOK BOOK. Menlo Park CA, 1961 1st ed. Very Good in fair dust jacket. $15.

SPIEGELBERG, FLORA. *Princess Goldenhair and the Wonderful Flowers*. World Syndicate, 1932. Milo Winter illus. Shelfworn, spotted cover, o/w Very Good. $40.

SPIER, PETER. *London Bridge is Falling Down*. NY, 1967 1st ed. Fine in dust jacket. $16.
The Erie Canal. NY, 1970 3rd printing. VG in DJ. $24.

SPIERING, FRANK. *Lizzie* (Borden). Random House,1984 2nd edition. Fine in dust jacket. $9.

SPILLANE, MICKEY. *I, the Jury*. NY, 1947 1st ed. Author's 1st book. Very Good in dust jacket. $300.
Kiss Me Deadly. NY, 1952 1st edition. Very Good in frayed, chipped dust jacket. $60.
Day of the Guns. NY, 1961 1st ed. Fine in vg DJ. $30.
The Girl Hunters. NY, 1962 1st edition. Very Good in shelfworn dust jacket. $45.
Bloody Sunrise. NY, 1965 1st ed. Very Good in DJ. $25.
The Delta Factor. NY, 1967 1st ed. Fine in DJ. $60

SPILLER, BURTON L. *Grouse Feathers*. NY, Derrydale Press, 1935 1st ed. One of 950 copies. Lynn Bogue Hunt illus. Fine. $250. Same, 1st trade edition. Very Good. $32.
Firelight. Derrydale Press, 1937. Lynn Bogue Hunt illus. One of 950 copies. Very Good-Fine. $175-$350.

More Grouse Feathers. Derrydale Press, 1938. One of 950 copies. Very Fine. $300.

SPINK, J.G.T. *Official Baseball Guide*. No place, 1950. Paperback. Near Fine. $40.

SPOCK, DR. BENJAMIN. *Dr. Spock on Vietnam*. Dell, 1968 Paperback. Slight edge stain, o/w Very Good. $30.

THEW SPORTSMAN'S DIRECTORY & YEARBOOK. Milwaukee, 1892 2nd Annual. Fine illus. $125. Third Annual "Columbian Edition". Shaken. $75.

THE SPORTSMAN'S PORTFOLIO OF AMERICAN FIELD SPORTS. NY, Derrydale Press, 1929. One of 400 copies. $145.

SPRAGUE, ISSAC (Illustrator). *Beautiful Wild Flowers of America*. Boston, 1882. Large 4to. Very Good. $125.

SPRAGUE, MARSHALL. *Money Mountain, the Story of Cripple Creek Gold*. Little Brown, 1953. G-VG. $25. *Newport in the Rockies*. Sage Books, 1961 1st ed. Very Good in dust jacket. $10.

SPRING, AGNES WRIGHT. *Casper Collins: The Life and Exploits of an Indian Fighter of the Sixties*. NY, Columbia Univ., 1927 1st ed. Fine in worn DJ. $80-$100.

SPRY, CONSTANCE and ROSEMARY HUME. *The Constance Spry Cook Book*. New York, 1957 1st edition. Very Good. $45-$60.

SPYRI, JOHANNA. *Heidi*. Boston, 1885 1st American ed. Translated by L. Brooks. Very Good-Fine. $200-$350. Lippincott, 1919 edition. Maria Kirk illus. Very Good-Fine. $75-$125. Philadelphia, David McKay, 1922. Jessie Wilcox Smith illustrator. Original blue cloth, gilt lettered. Pictorial cover label. Near Fine in clean bright dust jacket. $250 auction. Same, by dealer. Good-VG. $45. In DJ. $75-$150. Dial Press, 1935 ed. J. W. Smith illus. VG. $50-$95. *Moni the Goat Boy*. Saalfield, 1926. Translated. Frances Brundage illustrator. Very Good. $22. *Gritli's Children*. A Story of Switzerland. Lippincott, 1924. Maria Kirk illustrator. Very Good. $45. *Children's Christmas Card*. New York, 1957 1st edition. Very Good in good dust jacket. $22. Shirley Temple ed. Random House, 1959. Illustrations from film. VG. $15.

SQUIER, GEORGE. *Incidents of Travel & Exploration in the Land of the Incas*. NY, 1877. Illustrations Overall Very Good. $135.

ST. EXUPERY, ANTOINE. *Night Flight*. NY, 1935 1st ed. Author's 1st book. Very Good in very good DJ. $100. *The Little Prince*. NY, 1943 1st trade edition. Fine in clipped dust jacket. $350.

STACKPOLE, E. J. *Smugglers Luck*. NY, 1931 1st edition. Illustrated. Good. $8. *Privateer Ahoy*. Morrow, 1937. Very Good. $15. *The Sea Hunters, Great Age of Whaling*. No place, 1953. Illustrated. Good in dust jacket. $15. *The Wreck of the Steamer San Francisco*. Mystic CT, 1954 1st ed. Near Very Good, paperbound. $35. *They Met at Gettysburg*. Harrisburg PA, 1956 1st edition. Fine in chip dust jacket. $35. *From Cedar Mountain to Antietam*. Harrisburg PA, 1959 1st edition. Marginal notes, o/w Very Good. $35. *Scrimshaw at Mystic Seaport*. Mystic CT, 1966 2nd ed. Signed. Very Good. $45.

STAFFORD, E. P. *The Big E: The Story of the USS Enterprise*. NY, 1962 1st ed. Very Good in vg DJ. $45.

STAFFORD, JEAN. *Boston Adventure*. NY, 1944 1st ed. Auth's 1st book. G plus, $100. Same. NF in VG DJ. $75. *Children Are Bored on Sunday*. NY, 1953 1st ed. Very Good chip dust jacket. $35.

STAGG, AMOS ALONZO. *Touchdown!* As told to W. W. Stout. NY, 1927 1st ed. Near Fine. $40.

STANDARD, STELLA. *Stella Standard's Cook Book*. World, 1952 1st edition. Near Very Good. $18. *More Than Cooking*. Vanguard, 1946. Very Good. $14.

STANDING BEAR, CHIEF LUTHER. *My Indian Boyhood*. Illus. by Rodney Thompson. Boston, Houghton Mifflin, 1931 1st edition. Near Fine in dust jacket. $150-$200.

STANLEY, HENRY M. *How I Found Livingstone*. NY, 1872 1st ed. 2 maps. Good. $95. Another, poor. $10. *In Darkest Africa*. Scribner's 1890 1st ed. 2 vols. Good-Very Good. $35-$95. Same, 1891. $24-$38. *Through the Dark Continent*. Sampson Low, 1885 5th edition. Very Good. $18.

STANTON, FRANK L. *Songs of Soil*. NY, 1900. VG. $35.

STANTON, G. SMITH. *When the Wildwood was in Flower*. A narrative covering fifteen years' experiences of a New Yorker on the western plains. NY, Ogilvie, 1910, 1909 1st edition. Very Good. $40.

STANTON, SAMUEL W. *American Steam Vessels*. NY, 1895. 500 pgs. Illus. Dull, sunned, shaken. $175.

STARKEY, MARION L. *The Cherokee Nation*. Knopf, 1946 1st edition. Very Good in dust jacket. $20. *The Devil in Massachusetts*. NY, 1950 (Salem witch trials) Very Good in chipped dust jacket. $25.

STARKIE, WALTER. *Raggle-Taggle Adventures With a Fiddle*. Dutton, 1933. Rackham illus. Very Good. $30-$50.

STARR, CHESTER. *From Salerno to the Alps: A History of the 5th Army, 1943-1945*. Wash., 1948. Good plus. $60.

STARR, STEPHEN Z. *The Union Cavalry in the Civil War*. Baton Rouge, 1981-1985 3 vols. Very Good in DJs. $75.

STARRETT, VINCENT. *Murder on "B" Deck*. NY, Double Crime Club, 1929 1st ed. VG in fair dust jacket. $100.
The Private Life of Sherlock Holmes. NY, 1933 1st ed. Good to Very Good. $50. Chicago, 1960 Revised, enlarged. Fine in very good dust jacket. $75.
Penny Wise and Book Foolish. No place, 1929. Ex-library, o/w Very Good. $20.
Dead Man Inside. NY, 1931 1st ed. VG in DJ. $28.

STARS OF THE PHOTOPLAY. No place, 1916. Photos and biographies. Good. $50.

STAWELL, MRS. RODOLPH. *Fabre's Book of Insects*. Dodd Mead, 1921 1st ed. Ex-library, VG. $50.

STEAD, CHRISTINA. *The People With the Dogs*. Boston, 1952 1st American ed. Very Good in chipped DJ. $30.
The Puzzle Headed Girl. NY, 1967 1st edition. Very Good in good dust jacket. $13.

STEARNS, SAMUEL. *The American Herbal or Materia Medica*. Walpole, NH, 1801 1st ed. Leather. $200 and up.

STEELE, FLORA A. *English Fairy Tales*. NY, Macmillan, 1918. 16 Rackham color plates. VG. $150-$250.

STEELE, MATTHEW FORNEY. *American Campaigns*. Adams WA, 1909 2 volumes, map. The set. $60.

STEFFENS, LINCOLN. *Moses in Red*. Philadelphia, 1926, Dorrance. Very Good in scarce dust jacket. $95.

STEICHEN, EDWARD (Photographer). *The Blue Ghost*. Harcourt-Brace, 1947 1st ed. VG in torn DJ. $35.
A Life in Photography. Doubleday, 1963 1st ed., 1st issue. Fine in dust jacket. $35-$70.
U.S. Navy War Photographs. Plates throughout. NY, U.S. Camera, no date, paperbound. VG in orig. wraps. $50-$75.

STEIG, WILLIAM (Cartoonist). *The Lonely Ones*. NY, 1942 24th printing. Author's 1st book. VG in DJ. $15.
Dominic. NY, 1962 1st ed. Illus. by auth. Fine in DJ. $25.
Rotten Island. Boston, 1964. Illus. by auth. F in DJ. $25.
Gorky Rises. NY, 1980 1st ed. Fine in dust jacket. $40.

STEIN, EVALEEN. *Troubadour Tales*. Bobbs-Merrill, 1903. Parrish color plate. VG. $75. Same, 1929. $30.

STEIN, GERTRUDE. *The Autobiography of Alice B. Toklas*. NY, 1933. Faded cloth, no dust jacket, o/w VG. $35.
Portraits and Prayers. NY, 1934. Insc. NF. $200-$450.

Lectures in America. NY, 1935 1st editions, 1st issue. Very Good in good dust jacket. $125. Fine in DJ. $200.
Everybody's Autobiography. NY, 1937 1st edition. Foxed endpapers, o/w Fine in very good dust jacket. $150.
What Are Masterpieces? Los Angeles, 1940 1st edition. Fine in chip dust jacket. $45.
Wars I Have Seen. Batsford, 1945 1st ed. VG in DJ. $75.
Brewsie and Willie. NY, 1946 1st ed. VG in DJ. $40-$75.

STEIN, RALPH. *Sports Cars of the World*. NY, 1952 1st edition. Near Very Good. $15.

STEINBECK, JOHN. *Cup of Gold*. NY, 1936 2nd ed. Author's 1st book. Near Fine in chip DJ. $125.
Of Mice and Men. NY, 1937 1st ed. 2nd issue. VG in worn DJ. $45. Fine in vg DJ. $90. 1979 Ltd Ed. in slipcase. Fine. $100. NY, Triangle, 1940 18th ed. Fine in DJ. $8.
The Moon Is Down. NY, 1942 1st edition, 1st state, Very Good. $75. Good in Fair dust jacket. $8.
The Grapes of Wrath. NY, Viking, 1939 1st ed. VG in DJ. $400. Near Fine to Fine in dust jacket. $600-$900. NY, 5th printing, 1939. $15-$25.
Bombs Away. NY, 1942 1st ed., 1st state. Illus. VG. $95. Good in Fair dust jacket. $25.
Cannery Row. NY, 1945 1st ed. Near Very Good in poor dust jacket. $90. Same, Fine in dust jacket. $125.
The Red Pony. NY, 1945. Illustrated. Fine in slipcase. $45. Very Good, no slipcase, $10.
In Dubious Battle. OH, World, 1946 1st ed. F in DJ. $10.
Pasture of Heaven. OH, World, 1946 1st ed. Fine in Good dust jacket. $8.
Tortilla Flat. NY, 1947 1st ed. Peggy Worthington illus. Near Fine in good dust jacket. $100.
The Pearl. NY, 1947 1st ed. Very Good in vg DJ. $75.
The Wayward Bus. NY, 1947. Fine in dust jacket. $125. Average in dust jacket. $40-$80.
A Russian Journal. New York, 1948 1st edition. Near Fine in dust jacket. $35.
The Steinbeck Omnibus. London, 1950 1st English edition. Fine. $25.
East of Eden. NY, 1952 1st edition. Very Good in dust jacket. $165. Revised 1952 2nd printing. Very Good. $80.
Sweet Thursday. NY, 1954 1st edition. Very Good in chipped dust jacket. $50-$75.
The Short Reign of Pippin IV. NY, 1957 1st edition. Fine in chipped dust jacket. $35.
Once There Was a War. NY, 1958. Very Good. $60.
The Winter of Our Discontent. NY, 1961 1st edition. Near Fine in dust jacket. $100. Same, average in DJ. $35-$60.
America and Americans. NY, Viking, 1966 1st edition. Very Fine, no dust jacket. $17.

STEINER, CHARLOTTE. *Kiki and Muffy*. NY, 1943 1st ed. Illus. by author. Near Very Good. $20.
Kiki Dances. NY, 1949. Very Good, no dust jacket. $8.
Kiki Is an Actress. NY, 1958 1st ed. Illus. by author. Very Good in good dust jacket. $20.

STEINMETZ, ANDREW. *The Gaming Table: Its Votaries and Victims*. London, 1870 1st edition. 2 vols. Light foxing, o/w Very Good. $150.

STEINMETZ, CHARLES. *Four Lectures on Relativity and Space*. NY, 1923 5th printing. Stereoviews in pocket. Spine frayed, o/w Very Good. $30.

STEKEL, WILHELM. *The Homosexual Neurosis*. Boston, 1922 1st ed. J. S. Van Teslaar translator. VG in vg DJ. $38.
Sadism and Masochism. NY, 1939 2 volumes. Louise Brink translator. Good. $40.

STELLE, J. P. *American Watchmaker and Jeweler: Secrets of the Trade*. NY, circa 1870 Paperbound. Good. $25.

STEPHENS, ALEXANDER H. *A Constitutional View of the War Between the States*. National Pub. Co., 1868. Vol. 1. Weak hinge, o/w Very Good. $40.

STEPHENS, MRS. ANN S. *Pictorial History of the War for the Union*. Vol. 1. 1863. Chipped, worn, foxed. $50.

STEPHENS, JAMES. *The Hill of Vision*. Dublin, 1912 1st edition. Very Good. $50.
The Demi-Gods. London, 1914 1st edition. 1st issue. Very Good. $50.
Irish Fairy Tales. London, 1920. Arthur Rackham illus. Very Good. $200. NY, 1920 1st American ed. VG. $75. 1978 reprint. Fine. $30.
The Crock of Gold. NY, 1922 1st American ed. VG. $25. 1928 reprint with Thomas MacKenzie color plates. Very Good. $50. 1926 limited ed. One of 525 copies, signed. Very Good. $300.

STEPHENSON, RALPH W. *Chiropractic Textbook*. Davenport IA, 1927 1st ed. Very Good. $125.

STERLING, GEORGE. *The Testimony of the Suns*. San Francisco, 1904 2nd edition. Very Good plus. $45.
The House of Orchids. San Francisco, 1911 1st edition. Signed. Very Good. $45.
The Caged Eagle. San Francisco, 1916 1st edition. Inscribed. Shelfworn. $38.
Robinson Jeffers. NY, 1926 1st edition. Fine in clip dust jacket. $125.

STERLING, SARA H. *Robin Hood and His Merry Men*. George W. Jacobs, 1921. Rowland Wheelwright illus. Good-Very Good. $25.

STERN, BERT. *The Last Sitting* (Marilyn Monroe). NY, 1982. Fine in dust jacket. $45.

STERN, MADELEINE. *Heads and Headlines: the Phrenological Fowlers*. Norman OK, 1971 1st edition. Very Good in dust jacket. $25.

STERN, PHILIP VAN DOREN. *They Were There: Civil War Action by Combat Artists*. Crown, 1959. Very Good in near very good dust jacket. $30.
The Civil War Christmas Album. NY, Hawthorn Bks, 1961 1st edition. 128 pgs. Illus. Near Fine in DJ. $35.
Prologue to Sumter. Indiana Univ. Press, 1961. Very Good in dust jacket. $20.

STEVENS, SHANE. *Go Down Dead*. NY, 1966 1st ed. Author's 1st book. Fine in fine dust jacket. $85-$100.
Way Uptown in Another World. NY, 1971. Fine in fine dust jacket. $60.

STEVENS, THOMAS. *Around the World on a Bicycle*. Vol. 1 From San Francisco to Teheran. Vol. II From Teheran to Yokohama. NY, 1894. Illus. $100 for 2 vols.

STEVENS, WALLACE. *Harmonium*. NY, 1923 1st edition. 3rd state. 1st book. Very Good. $400.
Opus Posthumous. NY, 1957 1st ed. Good in DJ. $100.
The Collected Poems of Wallace Stevens. NY, 1954 1st edition. Limited edition. Good-Very Good. $50-$200.

STEVENS, WALTER B. *The World's Fair. Official Photographic Views: Saint Louis, 1904*. Thompson Pub. 302 pages. 11 x 13. Weak hinges, chipped spine. $75.

STEVENSON, CHARLES. *Facts and Values*. Yale, 1963. Inscribed. Very Good in dust jacket. $15.

STEVENSON, ROBERT LOUIS. *Treasure Island*. The first edition of this enduring classic was printed in London in 1883. An American edition was published in Boston in 1884. Some of these earliest printings are worth upwards of $1,000. Many limited editions have been published through the years and their comparative values lies in the quality of the illustration and binding. Trade editions are common from 1895 onward. G&D, no date, circa 1900. Good-VG. $5-$15. NY, 1900 edition with Paget illus. Very Good. $20. Scribners, 1911. N. C. Wyeth illus. $65-$175. Same, 1939. $50. Modern Library, 1917. VG-Fine. $120. Rand-McNally, 1919. VG. $50. NY, 1920, Jesse Wilcox Smith illus. $25-$50. Harpers, 1915. VG. $27. Philadelphia, 1930. L. Justis illus. VG, in case. $120. Doran, no date. Edmund Dulac illus. $125. Same, Doubleday. 12 plates. $75-$150. Another, Garden City, circa 1939. $35.
Kidnapped. NY, Scribners, 1913. N. C. Wyeth illustrator. Good. $45. VG. $75-$150. London, 1930. Rowland Hilder illustrator. Very Good. $30. Philadelphia, no date. E. P. Abbott illustrator. Good. $20. Scribner's, 1946. $35.
The Black Arrow. NY, 1916. N. C. Wyeth illustrator. VG. $75-$160. 1927 ed. $35-$65. 1937. $15.
David Balfour. NY, Scribner's, 1924. N. C. Wyeth illustrator. Very Good. $65-$120. Same, 1927. $45.
The Letters of Robert Louis Stevenson. New York, Scribners, 1911. 4 vols. ¾ calf and marbled boards, gilt spines. Near Fine in slipcases. $200.

The Novels of Robert Louis Stevenson. NY, Scribners, 1895. 16 vols. Cloth, Leather spine labels. VG. $100-$150.
A Child's Garden of Verses. London, 1885 1st ed., black cloth, clamshell case. Asking $1,500. Dodge, 1905 & 1908 eds. Gutmann illus. $60-$120. Scribner's. J. W. Smith illus. 1905. VG. $95-$200. 1925. $50-$100. 1944. $25-$50. Rand McNalley, 1919 ed. VG. $50. London, 1931 ed. Willebeek le Mair illus. $100 auction. Platt & Munk, 1932. Eulalie illus. VG in DJ. $45. NY, Limited Editions Club, 1944. One of 1,100 signed by Roger Duvoisin. Near Fine in case. $80-$100. Undated reprints, circa 1900. $10.

STEVENSON, WILLIAM. *Thirteen Months in the Rebel Army*. NY, 1862 1st ed. Ex-library. Loose pages. $30.

STEVENSON, WILLIAM YORKE. *At the Front in a Flivver*. Boston & NY, 1917 1st ed. Illus. Very Good. $25.

STEWART, ANNA BIRD. *Bibi, the Baker's Horse*. Lippincott, 1942 1st ed. Catherine M. Richter illustrator. Stewart inscription. Very Good. $25.

STEWART, D. J. *New Historical Atlas of Seneca County, Ohio*. Philadelphia, 1874. Worn covers, spine gone. $200.

STEWART, DONALD OGDEN. *Mr. and Mrs. Haddock in Paris*. NY, 1926 1st ed. Herb Roth illus. Very Good. $13.

STEWART, GEORGE R. *Ordeal by Hunger: The Story of the Donner Party* . Holt, 1936 1st ed. Centennial edition. Signed. $65. Revised edition, 1960. Good. $8.
Names on the Land. NY, 1945 1st edition. Good. $16.
Man: An Autobiography. NY, 1946 1st edition. Very Good in dust jacket. $13.
Fire. NY, 1948 1st edition. Very Good. $15.
Earth Abides. NY, 1949 1st ed. Signed. Very Good. $30.
The California Trail. An Epic With Many Heroes. New York, McGraw-Hill, 1962 VG in darkened DJ. $25.

STEWART, HENRY. *The Shepherd's Manual, A Practical Treatise on Sheep*. Orange Judd, 1876 1st ed. VG. $24. 1898 edition. 276 pgs. Very Good. $35.

STEWART, JANE L. *Campfire Girls in Summer Camp*. Saalfield, 1914. Very Good in dust jacket. $10.

STICKLEY, GUSTAV. *Craftsman Homes*. NY, 1909 1st ed. Very Good. $250. Paperbound edition of 1913. Near Fine. $65. Undated. 3rd edition. Damaged spine, o/w VG. $175.

STILL, ANDREW T. *Autobiography*. Kirksvile MO, 1897 1st ed. Inscribed by Still. Hinges cracked, o/w VG. $200. Same. Not inscribed. No date. Good. $50. Same, 1908 2nd ed. Revised. Very Good. $145.

STILWELL, HART. *Hunting and Fishing in Texas*. Knopf, 1946 1st ed. Illus. Very Good. $33.

STILES, HENRY REED. *Bundling: Its Origin, Progress and Decline in America*. Albany, 1871 1st ed. Very Good. $30-$60. Private press reprint, no date. Marbled black and gold boards. Very Good-Fine. $35.

ST. LOUIS LOUISIANA PURCHASE EXPOSITION, 1904. *The Greatest of Expositions, Completely Illustrated*. St. Louis, 1904. Good. $65.

STOCKHAM, ALICE B. *Tokology, a Book for Every Woman*. Chicago, 1883 1st ed. Overall Very Good. $125. 1895 reprint. VG. $20-$30. 1901 revised edition. $50.

STOCKMAN, CAPT. J. *The Battle for Tarawa*. Wash DC, 1947 1st edition. Very Good. $20.

STOCKTON, FRANK R. *The Great Stone of Sardis*. NY, 1898. Peter Newell illustrator. Light margin stain, o/w Very Good. $35-$55.
The Late Mrs. Null. NY, 1886 1st ed. 1st state. Worn. $15.
The Girl at Cobhurst. NY, 1898 1st ed. Very Good. $30.
The Vizier of the Two-Horned Alexander. NY, 1899 1st ed., 1st printing. Reginald B. Birch illus. Very Good. $35.

STODDARD, JOHN L. *Stoddard's Lectures*. 1909 (1897 copyright) Balch Bros. 10 volumes plus 5 supplements. Very Good. $3 each or $45 set.
Napoleon, From Corsica to St. Helena. 1902. Many frameable prints. $20.

STOKER, BRAM. *Dracula*. Westminster, 1897 1st ed. Soiled binding, hinges weak. o/w VG in clamshell case. $4,000. Same edition, 1st issue. Near Fine. $2,000. Another, NY, 1975. Saty illus. $50-$75. Limited Editions Club. 1965. Signed by illus. Fine in slipcase. $35-$50.
The Mystery of the Sea. NY, 1902 1st ed. VG. $100.
The Jewel of the Seven Stars. NY, 1904 1st American edition. Very Good. $15.
The Gates of Life. New York, 1908 1st American edition. Cover stained. $35.
The Lair of the White Worm. London, 1911 1st edition. Near Good in very good dust jacket. $95.

STOKES, THOMAS. *The Savannah*. Rivers of America series. NY, 1951 1st ed. Rinehart. VG in DJ. $25.

STONE, I. F. *The Hidden History of the Korean War*. NY, 1952 1st ed. Blue denim cloth cover. Backstrip faded. $28.

STONE, IRVING. *Lust for Life*. Longmans, 1934 1st edition. G-VG in DJ. $20-$50. Heritage Club, 1940s reprint. $15.
Adversary in the House. Doubleday, 1947 1st ed. Very Good in dust jacket. $30.
Most other Stone 1st editions in VG to Fine cond. $30-$40.

STONE, WITMER and W. E. CRAM. *American Animals*. NY, 1902 1st ed. Worn spine. Good. $15.

STONG, PHIL. *Horses and Americans.* NY, 1939 1st ed. One of 500 copies, signed. Illus. by author. Very Good. $65. Same, unsigned 1939 edition. $25.

STOPES, MARIE. *Contraception: Its Theory, History and Practice.* Boston, 1926 1st ed. Good. $75. London, 1928 enlarged edition. Very Good. $25.

STORER, T. I. and L. P. TEVIS. *California Grizzly.* Berkeley, 1955. Very Good. $35.

THE STORY OF CRISCO. Proctor & Gamble, 1914 3rd ed. Includes recipes. Good. $20. 17th edition. $10-$12.

THE STORY OF PLYMOUTH ROCK. Plymouth Rock Gelatine Company give-away, 1908. Children's picture story booklet. $20-$30.

STOUDT, JOHN J. *Sunbonnets and Shoofly Pies: A Pennsylvania Dutch Cultural History.* NY, no date. Circa 1960s. Illus. Very Good in dust jacket. $30.

STOUFFER, SAMUEL. *The American Soldier.* Princeton, 1949 2 vols. 1st ed. VG. One dust jacket torn. $50.

STOUT, REX. *Some Buried Caesar.* NY, 1939 1st ed. Near Very Good, no dust jacket. $50. Same, ex-library. $15.
Black Orchids. NY, 1942 1st edition. Near Fine in very good dust jacket. $1,000.
Not Quite Dead Enough. NY, 1944 1st ed. Fine in very good dust jacket. $575.
Murder By The Book. NY, 1951 1st edition. Near Fine in chipped, worn dust jacket. $40.
The Black Mountain. NY, 1954 1st ed. Good in DJ. $50.
Death of a Doxy. NY, 1966 1st ed. Inscription by Stout. Minor staining on cover edge, o/w Fine in very good dust jacket. $400. Same, unsigned in dust jacket. $30-$60.
Nero Wolfe Cookbook. Viking, NY, 1973 1st ed. Very Good in dust jacket. $15-$50. Fine in dust jacket. $75.

STORYTIME. Children's book, black & white illus. Boston, 1888, Lothrop. 208 pgs. Fair-Good. $28.

STOWE, HARRIET BEECHER. *Uncle Tom's Cabin.* Boston, 1852. 2 vols. 1st ed. Hobart & Robbins. $400-$600. London, 1852 1st English ed. George Cruikshank illus. Riviere and Son binding. $400. 1897 ed. Philadelphia, International Pub. Very Good. $38. Donohoe, circa 1900. Young Folks edition. Fine. $45. Altemus, 1900 reprint. 634 pages. Good. $8. Limited Editions Club, 1938. One of 1,500 copies signed by illustrator. Fine in case. $300. Another, auction. $143.
Pink and White Tyranny. Roberts Bros., 1871 1st edition. Good plus. $60.
The Minister's Wooing. NY, 1859. Good. $10.
A Key to Uncle Tom's Cabin. Boston, 1853 1st edition. Moderate wear. $100.

Dred, a Tale of the Great Dismal Swamp. Boston, 1856 2 vols. Very Good. $50.

STOWE, HARRIET B. and CATHERINE BEECHER. *The American Woman's Home.* (Cookbook). 1869 1st ed. $250-$350.

STRAND, PAUL (Photographer). *Time in New England.* By Nancy Newhall. NY, 1950 1st edition. Near Fine in dust jacket. $85-$125.
Paul Strand: Photographs. NY, 1945. Paperback. Text by Nancy Newhall. Near Very Good. $15.
Paul Strand: A Retrospective Monograph: Photographs, 1915-1945. NY, Museum of Modern Art, 1945. Good in dust jacket. $90-$125.
60 Years of Photographs. NY, Aperture, 1976 1st ed. Fine in dust jacket. $45.
Tir a'Mhurain: Outer Hebrides. London, 1962 1st edition. 145 black/white photos. Some spine fading, o/w VG. $160.
A Retrospective Monograph: The Years 1915-1968. Aperture, 1971 2 vols, bound as one. Near Fine. $160. Average, in dust jacket. $90-$125.
Paul Strand: A Retrospective. NY, 1972 2 vols. Good in dust jackets. $225.

STRATEMEYER, EDWARD (See Dixon, Franklin and Appleton, Victor). *With Washington in the West.* Lee & Shepard, 1901 1st ed. Very Good. $40.
Lost on the Orinoco. Lee & Shepard, 1902 1st. VG. $40.
The Rover Boys on the River. Grosset & Dunlap, 1905. Very Good in fair dust jacket. $25.
Dave Porter at Oak Hall. Boston, Lee Lathrop, 1905 ed. Ballplayer illus. DJ. Good. $17.
Fighting in Cuban Waters. Lee Lothrop, 1930. Very Good in very good dust jacket. $20.
The Fall of Montreal. Lee Lothrop, Shepard, no date. Very Good. $22.
Ruben Stone's Discovery. (Algers No. 99) Street & Smith, 1906 reprint of 1895 edition. Very Good. $12.

STRATTON, EZRA. *The World on Wheels; or, Carriages, Their Historical Associations From Earliest to Present Time.* NY, published by author, 1878 1st edition. 489 pages. Loose hinges. $175.

STRATTON, FLORENCE. *Favaorite Recipes of Famous Women.* No place, 1925. Good-Very Good. $25-$35.

STRATTON, ROYAL B. *Life Among the Indians: Being an Interesting Narrative of the Captivity of the Oatman Girls among the Apache and Mohave Indians.* San Francisco, 1857 1st ed. $1,000-$1,500. (A 2nd edition of same year has shortened title.) 1858 edition was published in New York. $100-$200. Grabhorn Press reprint. San Francisco, 1935. 1 of 550 copies. Good-Very Good. $80-$120.

STRATTON-PORTER, GENE (See Porter, Gene Stratton).

STRAUB, HANS. *History of Civil Engineering, Ancient to Modern Times*. 1960 translation. Brandford Pub. $50.

STRAUS, MONROE B. *Pie Marches On*. Ahrens, 1951 2nd ed. cookbook. Good, no dust jacket. $10.

STRAUS, RALPH. *Carriages & Coaches, Their History and Evolution*. London, 1912 1st edition. Ex-library. Many illustrations. $75. Same, Philadelphia, 1912. Good-Very Good. $75.

STRAUSS, OSCAR. *Roger Williams - Pioneer of Religious Liberty*. NY, 1884, Century. Fine. $15.

STREATFIELD, NOEL. *The Circus Is Coming*. London, 1938 1st ed. Steven Spurrier illus. Good. $30.
Party Shoes. NY, 1947 1st ed. Anne Zinkeisen, R. Floethe illus. Very Good. $30.
The Children on the Top Floor. NY, 1965 1st ed. Jillian Willett illus. Very Good in dust jacket. $9.
Growing Summer. NY, 1966 1st ed. Edward Ardizzone illus. Very Good in dust jacket. $60.

STREETER, EDWARD. *Dere Mable*. NY, 1918 1st edition. Author's 1st book. Very Good in dust jacket. $75.

STREETER, FLOYD B. *Prairie Trails & Cow Towns, The Opening of the Old West*. Boston, 1936 1st ed. Fine. $150.

STRIKER, FRAN. *The Lone Ranger and the Mystery Ranch*. NY, 1938. Paul Laune illustrator. Bob Livingstone photo inserted. Very Fine in dust jacket. $35.
Lone Ranger and Tonto. Grosset & Dunlap, 1940. Very Good in dust jacket. $15.
Various Lone Ranger titles. Grosset & Dunlap, no dates. 13 different titles. $5-$12 each.
Various Lone Ranger titles. dated 1941-1952. $12-$25 ea.

STRIBLING, T. S. *Clues of the Caribbees*. NY, 1929 1st edition. Very Good. $40.
The Store. NY, 1932 1st ed. VG. $25. Franklin Mint edition. Fine leather. $15.
Unfinished Cathedral. NY, 1934 1st ed. Inscribed. Near Fine in dust jacket. $60.

STRINDBERG, AUGUST. *Married*. Modern Library, 1st edition. 1917. Very Good-Fine in dust jacket. $120.

STRONG, A. B. *The American Flora*. NY, 1858 1st edition. Green & Spencer. Very Good. $150-$250.
Illustrated Natural History. New York, 1848, 1849 & 1850. 3 vols. Shaken. $125.

STRONG, JAMES CLARK. *Biographical Sketch of James Clark Strong, Colonel and Brigadier General*. Los Gatos CA, 1910. Maroon cloth, gilt title. Very Good. $350.

STRONG, MOSES. *History of the Territory of* Wisconsin, 1836-1848. Madison WI, 1885. Torn spine, else G. $35.

STROPE, NANCY. *Cattle Country Cook Book*. Portland, 1971, Binfords. Fine. $15.

STUART, GRANVILLE. *Forty Years on the Frontier. Reminiscences of Granvile Stuart, Gold-Miner, Trader, Merchant, etc.* Cleveland, 1925 1st edition. 2 volumes. Near Fine. $200-$300.

STUART, JESSE. *Trees of Heaven*. NY, 1940 1st ed. VG. $45. Same year, Dutton, 4th ed. Good in DJ. $22.
Taps for Private Tussie. NY, 1943 1st ed. VG. $11-$16. Book of the Month Club ed. VG. $5. Same, signed by author. Good in dust jacket. $35.
Album of Destiny. NY, 1944 2nd printing. Signed by author. Good in dust jacket. $50.
The Thread that Runs So True. NY, 1949 1st ed. Good. $23. 1949 revised ed. Very Good. $12. Same, 1958. Inscribed by author. $48.
Kentucky Is My Land. NY, 1952 1st ed. Presentation copy. Fine in fine dust jacket. $65. Fine in browning dust jacket. $50. Another, ex-library. Good. $8.
Year of My Rebirth. NY, 1956. Signed. G in DJ. $45. Book Club edition, 1956. Unsigned. Fine in DJ. $15.
My Land Has a Voice. NY, 1966 1st ed. Ex-library. Very Good in dust jacket. $15-$25.

STYRON, WILLIAM. *Lie Down in Darkness*. Bobbs-Merrill, 1951 1st ed. Author's 1st novel. Near Very Good in very good dust jacket. $125. Fine in dust jacket. $250.
Set This House on Fire. NY, 1960 1st ed. Signed. VG in very good dust jacket. $95.
The Confessions of Nat Turner. NY, 1967 1st ed. Signed. Near Fine in dust jacket. $55.
Sophie's Choice. NY, Random House, 1979 1st ed. Fine in dust jacket. Signed. $60-$95.

STUTZENBERGER, A. *American Historical Spoons: The American Story in Spoons*. Rutland VT, 1971. Illus. Very Good in very good dust jacket. slipcase. $35.

SUGUAD, LOUISA. *Belle Boyd: Confederate Spy*. Richmond VA, 1945 1st ed. Very Good in chip DJ. $30.

SULLIVAN, GEORGE. *By Chance a Winner: The History of Lotteries*. NY, Dodd Mead, 1972 1st ed. 135 pgs. Near Fine in dust jacket. $30.

SULLIVAN, MARK. *Our Times, 1900-1925*. NY, 1926. 2 vols. Good. $15.

SUMMERHAYES, MARTHA. *Vanished Arizona*. Philadelphia, 1908 1st ed. Signed. VG. $135. 2nd edition, Salem MA, 1911. Very Good. $20.

SUMMERS, MONTAGU. *A History of Witchcraft and Demonology* . London, NY, 1926 1st ed. VG. $100. Same, rebound. Very Good. $45.
The Geography of Witchcraft. NY, 1927 1st ed. Illus. Very Good in dust jacket. $125.
Maleus Maleficarum. London, 1928. One of 1,275 copies. Very Good. $225.
Demonolatry. London, 1930. One of 1,275 copies. Very Good. $150.
The Vampire in Europe. London, 1929 1st ed. Good to Very Good. $74.
The Werewolf. London, 1933. Very Good. $50.
The Vampire, His Kith and Kin. No place, 1960 1st American ed. Very Good in dust jacket. $35.

SUN CHIEF, AUTOBIOGRAPHY OF A HOPI INDIAN. Yale Univ. Press, 1963 5th ed. Very Fine in DJ. $28.

SUNNY HOURS. Children's cloth book, circa 1890. 12 dble. pages. Good. $25.

SUSIE SUN BONNET & HOW HER YEAR WAS SPENT. Uncle Milton. NY, 1907 1st ed., Wall illus. $32.

SUTTER, JOHN A. *New Helvetia Diary: A Record of Events Kept by John A. Sutter, 1845-1848*. San Francisco, Grabhorn Press, 1939 1st edition. 1 of 950 copies. Near Fine. $100-$150.

SUTTON, FELIX. *The Big Show: A History of The Circus*. NY, 1971 1st edition. Very Good. $27.

SUTTON, MARGARET. *The Invisible Chimes* (Judy Bolton No. 3). Grosset & Dunlap, 1932. Thick edit. Dust jacket lists 9 other titles. Very Good. $50.
The Living Portrait (Judy Bolton no. 18). Grosset & Dunlap, 1947 1st ed. Wartime paper, o/w Very Good in worn dust jacket. $18.
The Name on the Bracelet (Judy Bolton no. 13). Grosset & Dunlap, 1940 1st ed. Green cloth. VG in torn DJ. $35.
The Clue of the Stone Lantern (Judy Bolton no. 21). G& D, 1950. Rust tweed cloth. VG in dust jacket. $25.
The Phantom Friend (Judy Bolton no. 30). Grosset & Dunlap, 1959 1st ed. VG in fair dust jacket. $95.

SUTTON, RICHARD L. *The Long Trek. Around the World with Camera & Rifle*. St. Louis, Mosby, 1930 1st edition. Near Fine. $65.

SWAN, OLIVER G. *Frontier Days*. NY, Grosset & Dunlap, 1928. Good-Very Good. $20-$30.
Deep Water Days. Grosset & Dunlap reprint, 1929. Very Good, no dust jacket. $22.

SWAN, SUSAN BURROWS. *Plain & Fancy: American Women and Their Needlework, 1700-1850*. NY, 1977. Illus. Very Good in dust jacket. $75-$100.

SWANK, JAMES. *History of the Manufacture of Iron in All Ages, and Particularly in the United States*. Philadelphia, 1884. Very Good. $85.

SWEDENBORG, EMANUEL. *The Apocalypse Revealed*. Philadelphia, 1876. Very Good. $20. 1884 edition. $25.
Treatise Concerning Heaven and Hell. London, 1778 1st English edition. Very Good. $110.
The Delights of Wisdom Concerning Conjugal Love. Philadelphia, 1796 1st American edition. Working copy only. $30. New York, 1870. Good. $45.
Heaven and Its Wonders and Hell. NY, 1885 and 1919 editions. Very Good. $30 each.
Concerning the Earths in Our Solar System, etc. Boston, 1939 1st American ed. Good plus. $45.

SWEET, WILLIAM W. *Circuit Rider Days in Indiana*. Stewart, 1916 1st ed. Orig. cloth, frayed. G-VG. $15-$45.

SWIFT, JONATHAN. *Gulliver's Travels*. Dent, 1904. Rackham illus. $60-$120. Dutton, 1909. $150-$175. NY, circa 1875, Routledge. Color plates. VG. $100. Harpers, 1913 ed. Rhead illus. G-VG. $20. NY, Heritage, 1940. $15. Temple, 1939. $25. Crown, 1947. VG in DJ. $15. Various undated reprints of 1900s. Good. $10.

SYLVESTER, HERBERT. *Indian Wars of New England*. Boston, W. B. Clarke, 1910. 3 vols. Interiors clean, bindings soiled & rubbed. Unopened, untrimmed. $250.

SYMONS, ARTHUR. *The Fool of the World and Other Poems*. London, 1906 1st edition. Fine. $35.

SYMONS, JULIAN. *The End of Solomon Grundy*. London, 1964 1st ed. Very Good in dust jacket. $22.
The Man Whose Dreams Came True. London, 1968 1st edition. Fine in fine dust jacket. $25.

SYNGE, JOHN MILLINGTON. *Riders to the Sea*. Boston, 1911 1st edition. Very Good-Fine. $30-$60.
The Playboy of the Western World. London, 1927. John Keating illus. One of 1,000 copies. Good. $30.

SZASZ, THOMAS. *Law, Liberty and Psychiatry*. NY, 1963 1st edition. Very Good in dust jacket. $25.
The Manufacture of Madness . NY, 1970. Book club ed. Very Good in dust jacket. $18.

SZATHMARY, L. *American Gastronomy*. Chicago, 1974 1st edition. Illus. Near Very Good in dust jacket. $25.

SZEKELY, EDMOND. *The Golden Door Book of Beauty and Health*. NY, 1962. Illus. Very Good in DJ. $12.

SZYK, ARTHUR. *The New Order*. NY, 1941 1st ed. Illus. by author. Very Good-Fine in dust jacket. $100-$250.
The Book of Job. NY, Heritage, 1946. F in slipcase. $25.

T

TABER, GLADYS. *Lyonesse*. Atlanta GA, 1929. Author's 1st book. Very Good plus. $120.
Nurse in Blue. Philadelphia, 1944. Fading spine, o/w Very Good. $30.
The Book of Stillmeadow. No place, 1948. Ex-library. $12. 1948 3rd edition. As new in dust jacket. $13.
Especially Father. McRae-Smith, 1940 and 1950 editions. Very Good. $10-$20.
The First Book of Cats. NY, 1950 1st edition. Bob Kuhn illustrator. Fine in DJ. $50. Same, no dust jacket. $15-$25.
Stillmeadow & Sugarbridge. Lippincott, 1953 1st edition. Very Good in dust jacket. $30.
What Cooks at Stillmeadow. Phila.,1958 1st ed. $25-$35.
Stillmeadow Daybook. Lippincott, 1955 1st edition. Fine in dust jacket. $14.
Stillmeadow Sampler. Lippincott, 1959 1st edition. Fine in dust jacket. $15. Book Club edition. Very Good. $9.
Spring Harvest. 1959, Putnams. Good in dust jacket. $18. No dust jacket. $8.
Stillmeadow Album. Lippincott, 1969 2nd edition. Very Good in dust jacket. $15.
Conversations with Amber. Lippincott, 1978 1st edition. Very Good in dust jacket. $15-$25. Fine, no DJ. $10.
My Own Cook Book. Philadelphia, 1972 1st ed. VG. $35.
Stillmeadow Road. Lippincott, 1962. VG no DJ. $12.
Stillmeadow Cook Book. 1965 1st ed. Good-VG. $25-$35.
Another Path. Lippincott, 1963 1st edition. Fine in clipped dust jacket. $20.
Stillmeadow Calendar. A Country Woman's Journal. Lippincott, 1967 2nd edition. Fine in dust jacket. $15.

TABOR, TROY E. *Mother Goose in Hawaii*. Tuttle, 1966 3rd printing. Lloyd Secton illustrator. Very Good. $25.

TAFT, ROBERT. *Artists and Illustrators of the Old West, 1850-1890*. No place, 1st ed. 90 plates. F in fair DJ. $25.

TAGGARD, DONALD. *History of the 3rd Infantry Division in World War II*. No place, 1947. Good plus. $115. 1989 edition. $50.

TALBOT, FREDERICK A. *Submarines, Their Mechanism and Operation*. Philadelphia, circa 1910. 1st American edition. Good-Very Good. $25.

TALLANT, EDITH. *The Girl Who Was Marge*. Lippincott, 1939. Signed by auth. VG in Fair DJ. $25. Unsigned. $12.
David and Patience. Lippincott, 1940. Dorothy Bayley illus. Signed by author. Very Good in fair dust jacket. $25.

TALLENT, ANNIE. *The Black Hills, or The Last Hunting Grounds of the Dakotahs*. St. Louis, 1899 1st edition. Original gilt-lettered cloth. Fine. $200-$300.

TANSELLE, G. THOMAS. *A Guide to the Study of United States Imprints*. Harvard University Press, 1971. 2 volumes. Fine. $150.

TARBELL, IDA M. *History of the Standard Oil Company*. New York, 1904. 2 volumes. 1st edition. Signed. Ex-library. Soiled. $150.
Life of Abraham Lincoln. Lincoln Historical Society, 1907. 4 vols. Good. $55. 2 volume set of 1917. $25-$33. Sangamon edition, 1924. 4 volumes. $65.
In the Footsteps of the Lincolns. New York, 1924 illustrated edition. $35.

TARKINGTON, BOOTH. *The Gentlemen From Indiana*. NY, 1899 1st ed. Doubleday McClure. Author's 1st book. Good-Very Good. $25-$75. Another, 1899. Ear of corn upside down on spine. VG. $45. 1900 reprint. VG. $10.
The Two Vanrevels. McClure Phillips & Co., 1902 1st edition. Gilt-lettered green cloth cover. $40-$60. Same year, 2nd impression. Good-Very Good. $10-$25.
Monsieur Beaucaire. McClure, 1900 5th impression. C. D. Williams illustrator. Very Good. $24. 1910 Grosset & Dunlap reprint with tipped in letter from author. Very Good. $125.
The Beautiful Lady. New York, 1905 1st edition. Illustrated. Near Very Good. $14.
The Conquest of Canaan. NY, 1905. Lucius Hitchcock illustrator. Very Good. $18.
Cherry. Harper, 1903 1st edition. VG-Fine. $15-$25.
Penrod. Doubleday, Page, 1915 early edition. VG. $20. 1914 1st ed. G. $40-$50. Grosset & Dunlap reprint. $8.
Gentle Julia. NY, 1922 1st ed. Illus. Near VG. $18. Grosset & Dunlap reprint, 1922. $8.
Works of Booth Tarkington. NY, 1918-1929. 21 vols. One of 575 sets signed by Tarkington. Very Good. $300.
Claire Ambler. 1928 Grosset & Dunlap reprint. Good. $5.
Penrod Jashber. Doubleday Doran, 1929 1st edition. Gordon Grant illus. Very Good. $14.
Ramsey Mulholland. Doubleday Page, 1919 1st edition. Gordon Grant illus. Very Good. $15. Reprint, no date. $5.

Seventeen. Harper & Bros., 1916 1st edition. Gilt-lettered cloth. Spine a little pulled at top, o/w Very Good. $100. Grosset & Dunlap reprint, no date. $5.
Mary's Neck. NY, 1932 1st edition. Wallace Morgan frontispiece. Good plus. $16.
Some Old Portraits. NY, 1939, Doubleday Doran 1st edition after the 250 Limited edition. Signed by author. Good in poor dust jacket. $75.

TARRANT, MARGARET W. *Fairy Tales*. NY, 1916. 48 color plates by author. Good plus. $65.

TAVERNER, ERIC. *Birds of Eastern Canada*. No place, 1922 2nd edition. Very Good. $28.
Trout Fishing From All Angles. Lond., no date. VG. $15.

TAYLOR, BAYARD. *Eldorado, or Adventures in the Path of Empire...California, etc.* NY, Putnam, 1850 1st edition, 2 volumes. G-VG. $275 auction. Same, by dealer. $500.
Colorado, A Summer Trip. NY, 1867 1st ed. G-VG. $50.
Picturesque Europe. NY, D. Appleton, 1875 1st edition. 3 vols. Steel engravings, 9½x12½. Scuffed covers, foxed margins, o/w Very Good. $210 auction.
At Home and Abroad. NY, 1889. Original red cloth. $20.

TAYLOR, BENJ. F. *Songs of Yesterday*. Griggs, 1875 1st edition. Fine, gilt edges. $18.

TAYLOR, BERT LESTON. *A Line O'Gowf or Two*. NY, 1923 1st edition. Good. $54.

TAYLOR, DEEMS. *Walt Disney's Fantasia*. NY, 1940 1st edition . Foreword by L. Stokowski. VG in chip DJ. $125.

TAYLOR, E. S. *History of Playing Cards: With Anecdotes of Their Use in Conjuring Fortune Telling and Card Sharping*. 1865. 529 pages. Very Good. $180.

TAYLOR, FRANK HAMILTON. *Philadelphia in the Civil War*. 1861-1865. Published by the City in 1913. Folding map. Average copy, worn. $35.

TAYLOR, FRANCIS HENRY. *50 Centuries of Art*. NY, 1954. 342 color reproductions. Very Good in DJ. $26.

TAYLOR, FREDERICK Winslow. *The Principles of Scientific Management*. NY, London, 1911 1st trade edition. Handsome leather binding. VG. $100-$150. Later printing, 1942. Fine copy. $25.

TAYLOR, HENRY H. *Knowing, Collecting, Restoring Early American Furniture*. Lippincott, 1930 9th impression. Very Good, no dust jacket. $15.

TAYLOR, JANE and ANN. *Little Ann and Other Poems*. London, 1880s 1st edition. Kate Greenaway illustrator. VG. $150-$200. Another, Warne, circa 1900. VG. $100.

TAYLOR, JOSEPH H. *Sketches of Frontier and Indian Life on the Upper Missouri and Great Plains*. Pottstown PA, published by the author, 1889 1st ed. VG. $440 auction.

TAYLOR, MARGARET and FRANCES MCNAUGHT. *The New Galt Cook Book*. Toronto, 1898 revised ed. VG. $40.

TAYLOR, MARY. *Little Mistress Goodhope*. McClurg, 1902. J. W. Smith illus. 1st. VG. $150. Same yr. 2nd prtg. $95.

TAYLOR, NORMAN. *A Guide to Wild Flowers*. 1928, Garden City Pub. Good-Very Good. $30.

TAYLOR, PHOEBE ATWOOD. *Death Blow Hill*. NY, 1935 1st edition. Very Good in dust jacket. $85.
The Crimson Patch. NY, 1936 1st edition. Fine. $20.
Figure Away. NY, 1937. Fine in very good DJ. $100.
The Deadly Sunshade: an Asey Mayo Mystery. NY, 1940 1st edition. Near Fine in dust jacket. $85.
3 Plots for Asey Mayo. NY, 1942 1st edition. Near Very Good in chip dust jacket. $100.
Going, Going, Gone. NY, 1943 1st edition. Near Fine in chipped dust jacket. $60.

TAYLOR, ROBERT LEWIS. *W. C. Fields: His Follies & Fortunes*. 1949 1st ed. Good. $15. VG in DJ. $25.

TEALE, EDWIN WAY. *The Boys' Book of Photography*. NY, 1939 1st edition. Very Good. $65.
The Golden Throng: A Book About Bees. NY, 1940 1st edition. $25. NY, 1945 edition. $10.
The Insect World of J. H. Fabre. NY, 1949. Very Good in good dust jacket. $15.

TEASDALE, SARA. *Sonnets to Duse*. Boston, Poet Lore, 1907. Author's 1st book. Spine label rubbed. $150.
Rainbow Gold. Macmillan, 1927 edition. Dugald Walker illustrator. Cover worn. $35.
Stranger Victory. New York, 1933 1st edition. Fine in very good dust jacket. $45.
Star Tonight. NY, 1930 1st edition. Dorothy Lathrop illustrator. Very Good in dust jacket. $35.

TEBBEL, JOHN. *From Rags to Riches: Horatio Alger, Jr. and the American Dream*. NY, 1963 1st edition. Very Good to Fine in dust jacket. $20.

TELEPHONE DIRECTORY. *New England Telephone and Telegraph Co., District 2*. Published in Boston, 1887. 48 pages, with rules for operating, prices for service and subscribers' names. Printed within 10 years of the invention of the telephone. $225.
Another telephone directory, *Plymouth, Wisconsin*. 1919. 64 pages. $20.

TEMIN, PETER. *Iron and Steel in 19th Century America*. MIT, 1964. Very Good in soiled dust jacket. $10.

TEMPLAR. *The Poker Manual*. 1901. 119 pages. Faded spine, else Very Good. $70.

TEMPLE, SHIRLEY. *My Life and Times*. As told to Max Trell. Saalfield, 1936. Little Big Book No. 116. Fine. $65.
Favorite Tales of Long Ago. NY, 1958 1st edition. 1st printing. Spine bottom missing. $38.
The Shirley Temple Treasury. NY, 1959 1st edition. Illus. with drawings, photos from her movies. VG. $35.

TENNANT, PAMELA. *The Children & Pictures*. Macmillan, 1907. Rackham illus. Very Good. $75-$125.

TERHUNE, ALBERT PAYSON. *Caleb Conover, Railroader*. London, New York, 1907 1st edition. Paul Bransom illustrator. Author's 1st book. Very Good. $75. Special edition, New York, 1907. Very Good. $12.
Lad: A Dog. Dutton, 1919 1st ed. Fine in DJ. $175-$200.
My Friend the Dog. Harper, 1926 1st edition. Illus. by M. Krimse. 11 plates tipped in. Good. $75.
Gray Dawn. NY, 1927 14th edition. Good. $11.
Bumps. Harper, NY, 1927 1st edition. Very Good. $12.
The Book of Sunnybank. NY, 1934 1st ed., 1st issue. Illustrated. Very Good. $125.
Letters of Marque. NY, 1934 1st edition. Very Good. $45.
The Heart of a Dog. Garden City, 1924. Very Good. $45. Cover mildew, else nice. $35. Doubleday, no date. $8.
Real Tales of Real Dogs. Saalfield, 1935 1st edition. Diana Thorne illustrator. Very Good. $25.
A Dog Named Chips. 1931, G&D reprint. Good-VG. $6.
Runaway Bag. A. L. Burt, no date. $6.

TERKEL, STUDS. *Division Street*. NY, Pantheon, 1967 1st edition. Very Good in dust jacket. $30.
Hard Times: An Oral History of the Great Depression. NY, 1970 1st edition. Very Good in dust jacket. $30.
Working: People Talk About What They Do All Day and How They Feel About What They Do. New York, 1974 1st edition. Very Good in dust jacket. $30. Subsequent editions. $7-$10.

TERRY, SAMUEL H. *The Retailer's Manual, Embodying the Conclusions of Thirty Years Experience in Merchandising*. NY, 1869. $75.
How to Keep a Store. New York, 1883 2nd edition of above. Good-Very Good. $25.

TERRY, T. PHILIP. *Terry's Guide to Mexico*. Boston, 1938 revised edition, 34 maps, many ads. $25.
Terry's Mexico, Handbook for Travellers. London, 1911 2nd edition. 26 maps. $65.

TESLA, NICOLA. *Experiments With Alternating Currents*. NY, 1904. New edition. Fine. $100.

TEY, JOSEPHINE. *Miss Pym Disposes*. NY, 1948 1st American edition. Near Fine in dust jacket. $50.

THACKERAY, WILLIAM MAKEPEACE. *Vanity Fair*. Lond., 1848 Leather, gilt edges. $750-$1,500. Lond., 1910. Leather bd. $25-$50. NY, 1931 LEC. 2 vols., in box. $125.
Henry Esmond. Macmillan, 1905. VG. $50.
The Chronicle of the Drum. Scribner, 1882. $30.
The Rose and the Ring. Morgan Library facsimile of original illustrated manuscript. NY, 1947. $25.

THANE, ELSWYTH. *Dawn's Early Light*. NY, 1943 1st ed. VG in DJ. $20. Hawthorne, 1943 reprint. Fine in DJ. $10.
Ever After. Hawthorne, 1947 8th edition. Fine in DJ. $10.

THANET, OCTAVE. *A Book of True Lovers*. Way & Williams, Chicago, 1897 1st edition. Very Good. $100.

THAXTER, CELIA. *An Island Garden*. Boston, 1898. Childe Hassam pictures, illuminations. Fine in slipcase. $24.
Idyls and Pastorals. Lothrop, 1886. Folio. VG. $100.

THAYER, WILLIAM M. *A Youth's History of the Rebellion*. NY, 1865 1st edition. Illustrated. Fine. $75.
From Farm House to White House. 1890. Good. $10.

32ND DIVISION IN THE WORLD WAR, 1917-1919. Int. War Comm., 1920 1st ed. Illustrated. Very Good. $55.

THOLLANDER, EARL. *Back Roads of California*. Lane, 1971 1st edition. Illustrated by author. VG in slipcase. $12.

THOMAS, BENJAMIN. *Abraham Lincoln*. Knopf, 1952 1st edition. Fine in dust jacket. $18.

THOMAS, BOB. *Walt Disney, The Art of Animation*. NY, 1958. Very Good in dust jacket. $35-$45.
Walt Disney, American Original. NY, 1976 1st ed. Very Good in dust jacket. $23.

THOMAS & JOHNSTON. *Disney Animation, The Illusion of Life*. Abbeville, 1981 1st ed. Very Good, no DJ. $18.

THOMAS, DYLAN. *Adventures in the Skin Trade*. New Directions, 1933 1st trade edition. Good in dust jacket. $45. 1955, issue. Very Good in dust jacket. $60.
The World I Breathe. Norfolk CT, 1939 1st edition, 1st issue. One of 700 copies. Fine. $200.
New Poems. Norfolk CT, 1943 1st edition. VG in DJ. $40.
The Doctor and the Devils. New Directions, 1953 1st edition. Dust jacket. Good. $50.
Under Milk Wood. NY, 1954 1st American edition. Near Fine in worn dust jacket. $75.
A Child's Christmas in Wales. New Directions, 1954 1st edition. Very Good in dust jacket. $75.
Quite Early One Morning. New Directions, 1954 1st edition. Some soil, o/w Very Good in ragged DJ. $40.

THOMAS, JERRY. *The Bar Tender's Guide*. NY, Dick & Fitzgerald, 1876. G. $35. New, enlarged 1887 ed. VG. $40.

THOMAS, ISAIAH. *Dictionary of the Bible*. Worcester MA, 1798. Fair-Good. $75.

The History of Printing in America. Albany NY, 1874 2nd ed. 2 vols. $300. 1970 reprint, limited ed., boxed. $65. 1972 Imprint Society Edition. Fine. $250.

THOMAS, JOHN. *The American Fruit Culturist*. NY, Wm. Wood, 1867. Greencloth, 511 pages. Very Good. $30

THOMAS, JOOSEPH. *Hounds and Hunting Through the Ages*. Windward house, 1933 edition. Illus. VG. $35.

THOMAS, LOWELL. *With Lawrence in Arabia*. NY, 1924 1st edition. Near Fine. $30.

The Wreck of the Dumaru. NY, 1930. (Cannibalism in open boat) Very Good. $16.

Tall Stories, Great American Whopper. Blue Ribbon, 1931 10th edition. Very Good. $10.

Lowell Thomas' Book of the High Mountains. NY, 1964 1st edition. Photos in Very Good tattered dust jacket. $15.

The Stranger Everyone Knows. No place, 1968. Signed. Very Good. $25.

THOMAS & MC COWIN. *That Day in June. Teton Dam Disaster*. Ricks College Press, 1977 2nd edition. Fine, no dust jacket. $12.

THOMAS, PIRI. *Down These Mean Streets*. NY, 1967. Advanced review copy of 1st book. Fine in fine DJ. $40.

THOMAS, NORTHCOTE. *Crystal Gazing, Its History and Practice*. NY, 1905 1st edition. Very Good. $30.

THOMAS, CAPT. R. *Born in Battle. Round the World Adventures of 513th Bomber Squadron*. 1944 1st edition. Good. $30.

THOMAS, THOMAS J. *Memoirs of a Southerner, 1840-1923*. Savannah GA, 1923 1st ed. Near Very Good. $95.

THOMAS, WILLIAM S. *Trails and Tramps in Alaska and Newfoundland*. New York, 1913 1st edition. 147 photos. Very Good. $75.

THOMSON, HELEN. *Monarch Cook Book*. Beaver Dam WI, 1910. Good-Very Good. $15.

THOMPSON, KAY. *Vertigo*. New York, 1937 1st edition. Very Good in dust jacket. $195.

Eloise. NY, 1955 18th printing. Hilary Knight illustrator. Very Good in dust jacket. $25.

Eloise at Christmastime. NY, 1958 1st ed. Hilary Knight illustrator. Very Good-Fine in dust jacket. $85-$195.

Eloise in Moscow. New York, 1959 1st printing. Hilary Knight illustrator. Fine in dust jacket. $150. Very Good in dust jacket. $95-$110.

Eloise in Paris. 1957 1st printing. Very Good in DJ. $125.

THOMPSON, MAURICE. *Stories of the Cherokee Hills*. Boston, NY, 1898 1st edition. Very Good. $35.

Alice of Old Vincennes. Indianapolis, 1900 1st edition, 1st printing. VG, green cloth. $20-$40. Another, Good. $10.

THOMPSON, RUTH PLUMLY. *The Perhapsy Chaps*. Volland, 1918. Illustrated by author. Her first book. Very Good plus. $425.

Captain Salt in Oz. Chicago, 1936 1st edition. John R. Neill illustrator. Minor damage $220 (auction). Same, 1st edition. VG in dust jacket. $275. 1936 reprint in DJ. $50.

The Cowardly Lion of Oz. Chicago, 1923 1st edition. John R. Neill illus. Worn. $99. Very Good in DJ. $300-$400. Color reprint, 1923. $75-$150. B&W reprint. $40.

The Enchanted Island of Oz. Kinderhook IL, 1976 1st edition. Pictorial wrappers. Signed by Dick Martin illustrator. $825. (auction).

The Giant Horse of Oz. Chicago, 1928 1st edition. 1st state. John R. Neill illustrator. Cover rubbed. $247. 1928 color reprint. Very Good in DJ. $125.

The Wishing Horse of Oz. 1935 color 1st ed. In DJ. $300.

The Gnome King of Oz. Chicago, 1927 1st ed., 1st state. John R. Neill illust. Worn. $247. (auction). VG. $500.

Handy Mandy in Oz. Chicago, late 1950s reprint. John R. Neill illustrator. Inscribed by Thompson. Minor wear. $605 (auction). Chicago, 1937 probably 1st edition. John R. Neill illus. Near VG. $195. 1937 reprint in DJ. $50.

Kabumpo in Oz. Chicago: Reilly & Lee, 1922 1st edition, 1st printing. John R. Neill illustrator. Chipped cover, $935 (auction). Same, rear hinge repaired. $200. 1922 color reprint. VG in DJ. $150.

Speedy in Oz. Reilley & Lee, 1934 1st ed. Fair, no DJ. $20.

The Lost King of Oz. Chicago, 1925 1st ed., 1st state. John R. Neill illustrator. Minor wear, $330. (auction). Chicago, 1925 1st ed. 2nd printing. John R. Neill illustrator. Hinge reglued, o/w VG. $95-$150. Copp Clarke, 1926. Fair. $10.

Ojo in Oz. Chicago, 1933 1st edition, 1st state. Light rubbing. $330. (auction) Chicago, 1939 printing. John R. Neill illustrator. $250. 1933 reprint, no color. $40.

Ozoplaning With the Wizard of Oz. Chicago, 1939 probably 1st edition. John R. Neill illus. Very Good. $195.

The Pirates in Oz. Chicago: Reilly & Lee, 1931 1st edition, 1st state. John R. Neill illus. Very Good in DJ. $250-$500.

Rinkitink in Oz. Chicago: Reilly & Britton, 1916 1st ed. 1st issue, in dust jacket. Minor wear. $605. (auction).

THOMPSON, WADDY. *Recollections of Mexico*. NY, 1846 1st edition. Lacks end pages. $125.

THOMPSON, WILLIAM T. *Major Jone's Courtship and Travels*. Philadelphia, T. B. Peterson, 1848 1st edition. 2 volumes in one. Signed by the author. Good-VG. $300.

THOREAU, HENRY DAVID. *Walden or, Life in the Woods*. The Boston, 1854 1st edition is quoted in many states of its first printing. The tipped in ads are important points, with April being the earliest and worth $2,000. Later advs.

reduce value as much as two thirds. Boston, Ticknor and Fields, 1864 4th printing. One of 280. Fine. $300-$350. 1909 limited edition, 2 vols. $200-$400. New York, Heritage reprint, 1939. Very Fine. $15.

Cape Cod. Boston, 1865 1st ed. Good-VG. $300-$750.

A Yankee in Canada. 1866 1st edition. includes "Civil Disobedience" and "Life without Principle". VG. $995.

Excursions. 1863 1st edition includes essays "Walking", "Wild Apples", etc. 319 pages. Very Good. $1,100.

Letters to Various Persons. Boston, Ticknor Fields, 1865 1st edition. Gilt on cloth. Very Good. $350.

Men of Concord. Bos., 1936 Wyeth illus. VG in DJ. $200.

THORNBOROUGH, LAURA. *The Great Smoky Mountains.* 1937, Crowell. Signed, no dust jacket. Good. $12.

THORNTON, E. Q., M. D. *Dose Book & Manual of Prescription Writing. Drugs & Preparations.* Philadelphia, 1897. Good plus. $25.

THORNTON, WILLIS. *The Country Doctor.* G&D, 1936. Photoplay edition of Dionne Quintuplet film. $35.

Dionne Quintuplets--We're Two Years Old. Whitman, 1936. Illustrated. Fine. $25.

THORPE, ROSE H. *As Others See Us. Rules of Polite Society, etc.* Detroit, 1895. Good-Very Good. $45-$65.

THORWALD, JURGEN. *The Century of the Detective.* Wolff, 1965 1st edition. Very Good, no dust jacket. $12.

Crime and Science, New Frontiers in Criminology. Wolff, 1967 1st American edition. Fine in dust jacket. $12.

THE THREE LITTLE PIGS. Philadelphia, McKay, no date. Neill illustrator. Cloth-backed pictorial cover with color label. Very Good. $66 auction.

329TH "BUCKSHOT" INFANTRY REGIMENT--A HISTORY. Published by 329th, 1945 1st ed. Fine. $49.

THURBER, FRANCIS. *Coffee From Plantation to Cup.* New York, 1884. Illustrated. Ex-library. $25. Same, 1883 3rd edition. Good. Inscribed. $95.

THURBER, JAMES. *The Seal in the Bedroom.* New York, 1932 3rd printing. Good. $13.

The Last Flower. NY, 1939 1st edition. G-VG. $16-$28.

My World and Welcome To It. NY, 1942 1st edition. Good-Very Good. $20-$35.

Men, Women and Dogs. 1943 1st ed. VG. $24. Worn. $17.

The Thurber Carnival. Harpers, 1943 reprint. Good. $9.

The Great Quillow. New York, 1944 1st edition. Doris Lee illustrator. Very Good in dust jacket. $100.

The White Deer. New York, 1945 1st edition. Don Freeman illustrator. Very Good in dust jacket. $50.

The Thirteen Clocks. New York, 1950 1st edition. Marc Simont illustrator. Very Good-Fine. $125.

Thurber's Dogs. New York, 1955 1st edition. Near Fine in dust jacket. $45.

Further Fables For Our Times. New York, 1956. Very Good in dust jacket. $25. Special, fine paper. $45.

The Wonderful O. New York, 1957 1st edition. Marc Simont illustrator. Very Good in good dust jacket. $25-$30.

THURMAN, ARNOLD. *The Folklore of Capitalism.* New Haven CT, 1937 1st edition. Very Good. $95.

THWAITES, REUBEN GOLD. *Down Historic Waterways: Six Hundred Miles of Canoeing, etc.* Chicago, 1902 2nd revised edition. Ex-library. $25.

On the Storied Ohio. McClurg, 1903 1st edition. VG. $30.

Personal Narrative of James O. Pattie. Cleveland, 1905 1st edition. Very Good. $78.

The Revolution on the Upper Ohio 1775-1777. Madison WI, 1908. One of 1,200 copies. Very Good. $40.

TIBBLES, THOMAS H. *Buckskin and Blanket Days.* Doubleday, 1957 1st edition. Very Good. $20.

TIDYMAN, ERNEST. *Shaft.* NY, 1970 1st ed. Advance review copy. Fine in clipped dust jacket. $25.

Shaft Among the Jews. New York, 1972. Very Good in worn dust jacket. $6.

Good-bye Mr. Shaft. New York, 1973 1st edition. Fine in dust jacket. $25.

Dummy. No place, 1974. Very Good in dust jacket. $15.

TILDEN, JOE. *Joe Tilden's Recipes for Epicures.* San Francisco, 1907. Very Good. $30.

TILDEN, WILLIAM T. *The Art of Lawn Tennis.* NY, 1921 2nd edition. Photos. Very Good. $37.

Singles & Doubles. New York, 1923 1st edition. Photos. Very Good. $45.

It's All in the Game. Doubleday, 1922 1st edition. Good-Very Good in dust jacket. $25.

TILGHMAN, ZOE. *Outlaw Days, A True History of Early Day Oklahoma Characters.* Harlow Pub., 1926. VG. $70.

Marshal of the Last Frontier: Life of William Tilghman. A. H. Clark, 1949. Good plus. $150.

Quanah: Eagle of the Comanches. Oklahoma, 1938 1st edition. Good-Very Good. $35-$45.

TIME-LIFE SERIES. *The Old West.* 12 different titles. All Fine. $8-$12 each.

The Civil War. 28 volumes. Fine. $275.

The Seafarers. 14 assorted titles. Fine cond. $8-$12 ea.

TIME-LIFE BOOKS OF WORLD WAR II. Most, as new. $8-12 each.

TIME-LIFE LIBRARY OF ART. 28 volumes. Fine in slipcases. $150.

TIMLIN, WILLIAM M. *The Ship That Sailed to Mars*. London circa 1923 1st ed. Calligraphic text, 48 color plates, mounted, by auth. Plates fine, book poor-fair. $650. Same, Very Good. $1,200.

THE TINY GOLDEN LIBRARY. 12 story books by Dorothy Kunhardt. Garth Williams illus. NY, 1949 1st ed. Approx. 3 by 4 inches. Overall Very Good. $110 set.

TIXIER, VICTOR. *Tixier's Travels on the Osage Prairies*. University of Oklahoma Press, 1940. $30.

TOBACCO, SMOKING AND HEALTH. Report of the Advisory Committee to the Surgeon General. Wraps. Washington GPO, 1964. Near Fine. $25.

TOBIAS, D. AND M. MERRIS. *The Golden Lemon Cookbook*. NY, 1978 1st edition. VG in dust jacket. $18.

TODD, JOHN. *Early Settlement & Growth of Western Iowa*. Des Moines, 1906. Faded, frayed. $60.

TODD, RUTHVEN. *Over the Mountain*. London, 1939 1st edition. Author's 1st book. Very Good in vg DJ. $75.

TOKLAS, ALICE B. *The Alice B. Toklas Cookbook*. NY, 1954. Sir Francis Rose illustrator. VG in chip DJ. $20-$45. Same, in Very Good dust jacket. $55.
Aromas and Flavors. NY, 1958 1st ed. VG in DJ. $35.
What Is Remembered. NY, 1963 1st ed. F in DJ. 10-$20.

TOLAND, JOHN. *Ships in the Sky: Story of the Great Dirigibles*. NY, 1957 1st. VG in DJ. $35. Fine in DJ. $40.
Dillinger Days. NY, 1963 1st edition. VG in vg DJ. $25.
The Last 100 Days. NY, 1966. 629 pages. WWII events. Very Good in dust jacket. $20.

TOLKIEN, J. R. R. *Farmer Giles of Ham*. Houghton-Mifflin, 1950 1st American ed. Near Fine in very good DJ. $135.
The Lord of the Rings. Boston, 1965. 3 volumes. Revised 2nd edition. Fine in dust jacket and box. $275.
The Hobbitt. Boston, 1938 1st American ed. $200-$500. 1966 reprints. $10-$40.
The Silmarillion. Boston, 1977 1st American edition, 1st issue. Fine in DJ. $20-$35. London, 1977 1st English edition. Fine in dust jacket. $45-$95.
Fellowship of Rings, Two Towers and Return of the King. 3 vols. Ace unauthorized paperback eds. VG. $60.

TOLSTOY, LEO. *Anna Karenina*. NY, 1886 1st American edition. Very Good. $125. Same, Near Fine. $350. Limited Editions Club, 1951. 2 vols. One of 1,500 copies. Signed by illus., Barnett Fredman. Fine in worn slipcase. $150.
Resurrection. Limited Editions Club, 1963. Fair-Good, dented. $18-$20.
War and Peace. Limited Editions Club, 1938. 6 vols. Signed by illus. $95. Simon & Schuster, 1942 ed. $15.

"TOM SWIFT" SERIES. (See Appleton, Victor).

TOMLINSON, H. M. *Gifts of Fortune*. New York, 1926 1st edition. Good. $35.
Gallions Reach. London, 1927 1st edition. Good. $40. Same, NY, 1927 Limited edition. Signed. $20.
The Sea and the Jungle. London, 1930. One of 515 copies, signed. Author's 1st book (1912). 16 woodcuts by Clare Leighton. Very Good. $200. Dutton, 1925. $15.
All Our Yesterdays. London, 1930 1st ed. One of 1,025 copies, signed. Very Good. $80. Same, unsigned. $40.

TORREY, BRADFORD. *Birds in the Bush*. Boston, 1885. Author's first book. Good-Very Good. $30-$35.
A Rambler's Lease. Boston, 1889 1st edition. Green cloth. Good-Very Good. $25.
The Clerk of the Woods. Boston & NY, 1904. G-VG. $12.
The Foot-Path Way. Boston & New York, 1892 1st edition. Good-Very Good. $20.

TOULOUSE-LAUTREC. *The Art of Cuisine*. Holt, Rinehart & Winston, 1966 1st edition. Very Good in DJ. $45-$70.

TOURGEE, ALVIN. *An Appeal to Caesar*. No place, 1884 1st edition. Very Good. $40.
The Story of a Thousand. Buffalo, 1896. Story of Civil War unit. Ex-library. Fair-Good. $95-$150.

TOURTELLOT, ARTHUR. *The Charles*. Rivers of America Series. New York, Farrar & Rinehart, 1941 reprint. Very Good in dust jacket. $20.

TOYNBEE, ARNOLD J. *Lectures on the Industrial Revolution*. Longmans Green, 1912. Very Good. $22.
War and Civilization. NY, 1950. Good in worn DJ. $13.
World and the War. Oxford, 1954. Very Good in DJ. $18.
Acquaintances. NY, 1967 1st American edition. Near Fine in clip dust jacket. $65.
Cities of Destiny. NY, 1967. Fine in dust jacket. $75.

TRADER VIC'S BOOK OF FOOD & DRINK. Doubleday, 1946 1st edition. Signed by "Trader Vic". Fair. $20.

TRAGER, JAMES. *The Big Fertile Rumbling Cast-Iron Growling Aching Unbuttoned Bellybook*. New York, 1972. Very Good in dust jacket. $40.

TRAHEY, JUNE. *A Taste of Texas*. NY, 1949 1st printing. Very Good in fair dust jacket. $20.

TRAIN, ARTHUR. *Page Mr. Tutt*. NY, 1926 1st ed. VG. $20.
Mr. Tutt's Casebook. New York, 1938. Very Good. $25.
Yankee Lawyer. NY, 1943 1st ed. Very Good in DJ. $40.
Mr. Tutt Finds a Way. NY, 1945 1st ed. VG in DJ. $35.

TRAIN, GEORGE. *An American Merchant in Europe, Asia and Australia*. New York, 1857 1st ed. Very Good. $65.

TRAPROCK, WALTER (GEORGE CHAPPELL). *The Cruise of the Kawa*. NY, 1921. Photos. Very Good. $20. *My Northern Exposure*. NY, 1922. Photos, VG. $25.

TRAVEN, BEN. *The Death Ship: The Story of an American Sailor*. New York, 1934 1st American edition. Author's 1st book. Very Good in good dust jacket. $250.
The Night Visitor and Other Stories. New York, 1966 1st American edition. Near Fine in dust jacket. $40.
General From the Jungle. New York, 1972 1st American edition. Fine in dust jacket. $15. 1954 English edition. Very Good. $35.

TRAVER, ROBERT (JOHN P. VOELKER). *Trouble-Shooter: The Story of A Northwoods Prosecutor*. NY, 1943 1st edition. Author's 1st book. Good-Very Good in fair dust jacket. $100-$125.
Small Town DA. New York, 1954 1st edition. Inscribed. Near Fine in chip dust jacket. $75.
Trout Madness. NY, 1960 1st edition. Fine. $25-$30.
Hornstein's Boy. New York, 1962 1st edition. Fine in frayed dust jacket. $23.
Anatomy of a Fisherman. NY, 1964 1st edition. Very Fine in chip dust jacket. $90.
The Jealous Mistress. Boston, 1967 2nd printing. Fine in dust jacket. $35.

TRAVERS, P. L. *Mary Poppins Comes Back*. NY, 1935 1st American edition. Near Fine in chip dust jacket. $45.
Mary Poppins and Mary Poppins Comes Back. NY, 1937 1st deluxe edition. Mary Shepard illustrator. Fine. $70.
Happily Ever After. New York, 1940. One of 1,000 copies. Very Good. $45.
Mary Poppins From A to Z. New York, 1962 1st edition. Mary Shepard illustrator. Very Good. $15.

TREADWELL, M. E. *The Women's Army Corps (WWII)*. GPO, 1971. Very Good. $40.

TRIMMER, GEORGE. *At The Zoo*. Linen children's book. Merrill, 1946. $10-$15.

TRIPLETT, COL. FRANK. *The Life, Times and Treacherous Death of Jesse James*. Chicago, 1882. 3 versions appeared in 1882. $300-$500.

TRIPLETT, JUNE. *Salt Water Taffy*. G. D. Putnam, 1929 8th edition. Very Good, no dust jacket. $8.

TRISTRAM, W. OUTRAM. *Coaching Days and Coaching Ways*. London & New York, 1893 edition. Good-Very Good. $35-$50. London, 1924. Hugh Thomson & Herbert Railton Illustrators. Fine binding. $50.

TROWBRIDGE, JOHN. *What Is Electricity?* NY, 1896, Appleton, 1st edition. $50. Circa 1900 reprint. $25.
Electrical Boy. Boston, 1891. Very Good. $35.

TRUMAN, HARRY S. *Memoirs*. Doubleday, 1955 & 1956 2 vols. Inscribed. Slight discolor, o/w Very Good in dust jacket. $150. Another signed set. Fine in dust jacket. $350.
Mr. Citizen. New York, 1960. Inscribed to Carl Laemmle Jr. Near Fine in worn dust jacket. $200. Another, one of 1,000 signed. 1960. Fine in box. $350-$500.

TRUMBO, DALTON. *Washington Jitters*. New York, 1936 1st edition. Very Good in worn dust jacket. $125.
Johnny Got His Gun. Lippincott, 1939 1st edition. Very Good-Fine in dust jacket. $75-$150.
The Remarkable Andrew. Lippincott, 1941 1st edition. Very Good in dust jacket. $40.

TRUMBLE, ALFRED. *The Mott Street Poker Club*. 1888 hard cover, 50 pages. Very Fine. $200. Same in scarce paper edition. $300.

TRUMBULL, HENRY. *Indian Wars*. History of engagements with Indians in New England 1620-1679. Boston, 1830, George Clark. Color lithos. Good. $320.

TRUMPS. *The American Hoyle*. 1864 rule book. 518 pages. Very Good-Excellent. $75.

TRYCKARE & CAGNER. *The Lore of Sportfishing*. Crown Publishers, 1975 1st edition. Fine in dust jacket. $25.

TSCHIRKY, OSCAR. *The Cook Book by Oscar of the Waldorf*. Chicago, 1896. Near VG. $75. Fine. $120.

TSELEMENTES. *Greek Cookery*. NY, 1954. VG. $20.

TUCHMAN, BARBARA. *Stilwell and the American Experience in China, 1911-1945*. NY, 1970 1st edition. Very Good in very good dust jacket. $18.

TUCKER, ELIZABETH S. *Baby Folk*. New York, Frederick Stokes, 1898. 1st edition. Illustrated by Maud Humphrey. Rubbed, else Very Good. $70.
Book of Fairy Tales. NY, 1892. Maud Humphrey illus. Very Good. $500.
Little Ones. Stokes, 1898. 12 Maud Humphrey plates. Very Good. $250-$400.

TUCKER, SOPHIE. *Some of These Days*. The Autobiography of Sophie Tucker. Garden City, 1946 reprint. Signed dedication by author. Very Good in DJ. $35.

TUCKERMAN, BAYARD. *The Life of General Philip Schuyler, 1733-1804*. New York, 1904 1st edition. Dodd, Mead. Very Good. $25.
The Life of General Lafayette. New York, 1889 1st edition, 2 volumes. Very Good. $40.

TUCKERMAN, FREDERICK GODDARD. *The Cricket*. Cummington Pres MA, 1950. F in original envelope. $200.

TUCKERMAN, HENRY T. *America and Her Commentators, With a Critical Sketch of Travel in the United States*. New York, 1864 1st edition. Some foxing, shelf wear, otherwise Good. $85.

TUDOR, TASHA. *The White Goose*. NY, 1943 1st edition. Illustrated by author. Good. $100.
The Dolls' Christmas. Oxford University Press, 1950 1st edition. Illustrated by author. Fine in dust jacket. $150. Very Good in dust jacket. $100.
Edgar Allen Crow. Oxford Univ. Press, 1953. Illustrated by author. Darkening jacket, else Very Good. $100-$150.
First Graces. Oxford Univ. Press, 1955 1st ed. Illus. by author. Soiled and clipped dust jacket, else VG. $100.
Becky's Birthday. NY, 1960. Illus. by author. VG. $18.
The Tasha Tudor Book of Fairy Tales. NY, 1961 1st ed. Illustrated by author. Fine. $15.
First Delights. Platt & Munk, 1966 1st ed. Illus. by author. Near Fine in dust jacket. $60.
First Poems of Childhood. Platt & Munk, 1967. Illustrated by author. Fine. $15.
Tasha Tudor's Bedtime Book. New York, 1977. Illustrated by author. Very Good. $20.
Rosemary for Remembrance: A Keepsake Book. NY, 1981 1st ed. Illustrated by author. VG in slipcase. $30.

TUDOR, TASHA (Illustrator). *Fairy Tales From Hans Christian Andersen*. NY, 1945. Very Good in DJ. $23.
Mother Goose. Oxford, 1944 3rd printing. $25.
A Child's Garden of Verses. By Robert L. Stevenson. Oxford, 1947 1st ed. Very Good in slightly worn DJ. $75.
A Little Princess. By F. H. Burnett. Philadelphia, 1963 Reprint. Fine in dust jacket. $30.
The Real Diary of a Real Boy. By A. Shute. Richard Smith, 1967. Fine in fine dust jacket. $43.
The Christmas Cat. By Efner Tudor Holmes. New York, 1976. Fine. $35.

TUER, ANDREW W. *History of the Horn Book*. New York, 1979 Arno Press reprint of 1897 London edition. Very Good in dust jacket. $45.

TULLIDGE, EDWARD. *The Life of Brigham Young*. NY, 1876 1st edition. Very Good. $120. Another, repaired. $85.

TUNIS, EDWIN. *Chipmunks on the Doorstep*. NY, 1971 1st edition. Illustrated by author. Fine in dust jacket. $25.

TUNNEY, GENE. *A Man Must Fight*. Boston, 1932 1st edition. One of 500. Signed. Hinge loose. $300.

TURGEON, CHARLOTTE. *Cooking for Christmas*. NY, 1950 1st edition. Inscribed. Good plus. $15.
The Creative Cooking Course. New York, 1982. Very Good in dust jacket. $16.
Encyclopedia of Creative Cooking. Weathervane, 1985 reprint. Fine in dust jacket. $35.

TURNER, GEORGE. *Narrow Gauge Nostalgia*. Corona del Mar, 1971 3rd revised ed. Very Good in dust jacket. $25.

TURNER, GRACE. *The Celebrities' Cookbook*. NY, 1948. Very Good in dust jacket. $32.

TURNER, J. B. *Mormonism in All Ages: Rise, Progress, Causes*. An anti-Mormon book published two years before Joseph Smith was killed. Illinois College, Jacksonville, NY. Platt & Peters, 1842 1st edition. Very Good. $350.

TURNER, TIMOTHY G. *Bullets, Bottles and Gardenias*. Dallas, 1935 1st edition. Fine in dust jacket. $150.

THE TURNER'S COMPANION. Ornamental woodworking instructions. Philadelphia, 1866. Good. $75.

TURRILL, GARDNER S. *A Tale of the Yellowstone*. Jefferson IA, Turrill Pub., 1901. Stained, mildewed. $132 auct.

TUTHILL, MRS. L. C. *History of Architecture From Earliest Times, Its Present Condition in the United States*. Philadelphia, Lindsay & Blackiston, 1848. 34 plates, 103 engravings. $100.

TUTTLE, CHARLES R. *New Centennial History of the State of Kansas*. Inter-State., 1876. Rubbed. $85.

TWAIN, MARK (SAMUEL CLEMENS). *The Innocents Abroad*. Hartford, 1869 1st ed., 3rd state. Spine cloth torn, o/w Very Good. $75. Same, 2nd issue. Very Good. $125.
The Adventures of Tom Sawyer. Hartford, 1876 1st American edition. 2nd printing. Overall Very Good. $700-$2,000. 1917 edition, Harper. Good. $10. 1936 Rockwell edition. Heritage Press. $24-$37. Cambridge, Limited Editions Club, 1939. Signed by Thomas Hart Benton. Fine, no slipcase. $300. 1946 G&D reprint. $6-$12. Winston, 1931. Wyeth illus. Very Good. $25-$40.
A Tramp Abroad. Hartford, 1880 1st. 2nd state. G. $125. Same, Harper, 1907 ed. Very Good. $15-$25.
The Prince and the Pauper. Boston, 1882 1st American edition. Very Good. $95-$180.
The Adventures of Huckleberry Finn. NY, 1885 1st Amer. ed. E. W. Kemble illus. VG overall in slipcase. $2,500. Same in grn. cloth. $800. LEC, 1942. Signed by Benton. In slipcase. VG. $250. Whitman, 1939 ed. F. $20.
A Connecticut Yankee in King Arthur's Court. NY, 1889 1st edition, 1st state. 'S' ornament between The & King on page 59. Cracked hinge, rubbed. $150. Another, Very Good . $350. Harpers, 1926 reprint. $14. G&D. $8.
The American Claimant. NY, Charles Webster, 1892 1st edition. Dan Beard illus. Good. $25. VG-Fine. $75-$150.
The Curious Republic of Gondor and Other Whimsical Sketches. NY, Boni & Liveright, 1919 1st ed. Orig. white cloth & yellow print boards. Very Good. $120-$150.
The Mysterious Stranger. Harper's 1916 1st ed. N. C. Wyeth illus. VG. $125. Same date, reprint. VG. $65-$95.

The Gilded Age, A Tale of Today. Hartford, 1874 1st ed., later printing. In orig. 1/2 leather. VG. $200.

The 1,000,000 Pound Bank Note. New York, Charles L. Webster & Co., 1893 1st ed. Good-Very Good. $100-$150.

Tom Sawyer Aboard. London, 1894 1st British edition. Dan Beard illustrator. Good. $125. G&D reprint. $5-$10.

Life on the Mississippi. Boston, Osgood, 1883, 1st state, 1st ed. Gilt-dec. cloth. VG. $300. 1883 later printing. VG. $125. 1944 Heritage Press edition. VG, no DJ. $22. Harpers, 1900, Gilt-dec. red cloth. Good. $12.

Following the Equator: A Journey Around the World. Hartford, American Pub., 1897 1st ed., 1st issue. Orig. blue cloth with color pictorial label, gilt decor. VG. $80-$150.

Pudd'nhead Wilson. Hartford, 1894 1st American edition. $100-$175. Rebound in fine dec. bds. $300.

English As She Is Taught. Mutual Book Co., 1900 1st edition. Very Good. $100.

A Double Barrelled Detective Story. New York, 1902 1st edition. Lucius Hitchcock illustrator. $75-$150.

An Unexpected Acquaintance. NY, 1904. G-VG. $50-$100.

A Dog's Tale. New York, 1904 1st American edition. W. T. Smedley illustrator. VG. $250. Another, 1905. $20.

A Horse's Tale. Harper & Bros., 1907 1st edition. Corners bumped, spine pulled, o/w Very Good. $100.

The Works of Mark Twain. Author's National Edition New York, London, 1911 25 volumes. Very Good. $150.

The Favorite Works of Mark Twain. NY, 1939, Garden City. 1,178 pages in dust jacket. $15.

The Adventures of Huckleberry Finn. New York, London, 1923. Worth Brehm illustrator. Near Fine. $40.

Mark Twain's Notebook. Harper & Bros., NY & London, 1935 2nd edition. $30.

Tom Sawyer, Detective. G&D, no date. VG in DJ. $15.

Tom Sawyer and Huckleberry Finn. Heritage Press, 1930 and 1940, 2 volumes. Norman Rockwell color illustrations. Very Good. $65.

The Washoe Giant in San Francisco. San Francisco, 1938. Very Good. $100.

Roughing It. Hartford, American Pub., 1872 1st Amer. ed. 2nd state, word missing pg 242, line 21. VG. $200-$300.

Report From Paradise. Charles Locke illus. NY, 1952 1st edition. Very Good. $35.

Mark Twain's Autobiography. 2 vols. NY, Harpers, 1924 1st ed. Fine, no dust jacket. $75. Same, Good-VG. $30.

St. Joan of Arc. Harpers, 1919. Howard Pyle color plates tipped in. Very Good. $50-$100.

U

UDRY, JANICE MAY. *Let's Be Enemies*. NY, Harper, 1961 1st edition. Maurice Sendak illus. G-VG in erased dust jacket. $100 auction.

UELSMANN, JERRY N. (Photographer). *Silver Meditations*. NY, 1975. Photographs from 1968 to 1975. Very Good in dust jacket. $45.

ULANOFF, STANLEY M. *Fighter Pilot*. Garden City, 1962 1st edition. Good. $15.

ULLMAN, JAMES R. *Other Side of the Mountain*. NY, 1938 1st edition. Fine. $15.
Americans on Everest. Lippincott, 1964. Good in DJ. $25.
The Age of Mountaineering. New York, 1954 1st U.S. edition. Very Good in dust jacket. $15.

ULLOM, JUDITH. *Folklore of the North American Indians*. Washington, G.P.O., 1969 1st edition. $15-$20.

ULMANN, DORIS (Photographer). *Roll, Jordan, Roll*. Indiapolis, New York. 1933. Dust jacket worn, otherwise very good. $225.

UNCLE WIGGILY AND THE RED MONKEY. American Crayon Co. give-away premium booklet, 1943. $25-$40.

UNDERHILL, EVELYN. *The Mystic Way*. London, 1913. 2nd printing. Good to Very Good. $30.

UNDERHILL, FRANCIS. *Driving for Pleasure: or Harness, Stable and its Appointments*. Appleton, 1897. Good-Very Good. $250-$400.

UNDERWOOD, LORING. *The Garden and Its Accessories*. Boston, Little Brown, 1907. Pictorial green and white cloth. Very Good. $50-$80.

UNDERWOOD, PRISCILLA. *When Christmas Comes Around*. Illus. including color plates by Jessie Wilcox Smith. NY, Duffield, 1915 1st edition. Ex-library, rubbed, else Very Good. $60-$90. Same, VG-Fine. $150-$175.

UNDSET, INGRID. *Christmas and the 12th Night*. NY, 1932 1st ed. Fine in dust jacket. $15.
Ida Elisabeth. NY, 1933 Translated. Good plus. $7.
Mistress of Husaby. Grosset & Dunlap, 1928. Good. $7.

UNGER, F. W. *Roosevelt's African Trip*. NY, 1908. Illus. Very Good. $20.

UNGERER, TOMI. *The Mellops Go Diving for Treasure*. NY, 1957 1st ed. Illustrated by author. Good. $24.
The Mellops Strike Oil. NY, 1958 1st ed. Illus. by author. Very Good in dust jacket. $60.
Compromises. NY, 1970 1st ed. Illustrated by author. Very Good in dust jacket. $15-$25.

UNITED STATES BREWERS' ASSOC. *American Beer, Glimpses of its History and Manufacture*. New York, 1909 1st edition. $50.

UNITED STATES GEOLOGICAL EXPLORATION OF THE 40TH PARALLEL. Clarence King. 7 volumes with beautiful chromolithos. Washington, U. S. Government Printing Office, 1878-1880 1st edition. Worn, splitting. Internally Very Good. $1,300 auction.

UNITED STATES STRATEGIC BOMBING SURVEY. U. S. Government Printing Office, 1946 First edition. (Effects of Atom Bomb on Hiroshima and Nagasaki). Paperbound. Very Good. $150.

UNTERMEYER, LOUIS. *The Donkey of God*. NY, 1932. J. MacDonald illustrator. Signed. Good. $20.

UNTRACHT, OPPI. *Metal Techniques for Craftsmen*. Doubleday, 1975 15th edition. 509 pgs. 769 illus. Fine in dust jacket. $17.

UP DE GRAFF, F. W. *Head-Hunters of the Amazon*. London, 1923. Illustrated. Very Good plus. $35.

UPDIKE, JOHN. *The Carpentered Hen*. NY, 1958 1st ed. Author's 1st book. Near Fine in dust jacket. $450. Another, 1st edition, 1st state. Fine in dust jacket. $850.
The Same Door. NY, 1959 1st edition. 1st collection of stories. Near Fine in dust jacket. $175.
The Poorhouse Fair. New York, 1959 1st edition. Cover spots, bumping, otherwise Near Fine in dust jacket. $250. Another, signed. $375.
Rabbit Run. NY, 1960 1st ed. Signed. Fine in DJ. $600. NY, 1960 1st ed. Unsigned. Near Fine in DJ. $280-$400.
Couples. London, 1968 1st British ed. VG in chip DJ. $35.
Bech: A Book. NY, 1970 1st ed. VG in dust jacket. $40.

Rabbit Redux. NY, 1971 1st ed. Fine in DJ. $30-$50.
Marry Me. NY, 1976 1st ed. As new in dust jacket. $40.
Note: "BOOK PRICES, USED." 1993 edition, published by The Spoon River Press of Peoria IL, lists 150 different prices and titles for Updike.

UPFIELD, ARTHUR W. *Murder Down Under*. Garden City, 1943. Advance review copy. Corner creases, o/w VG. $30.
The Mystery of Swordfish Reef. NY, Crime Club, 1943. Very Good in fair dust jacket. $30.
Wings Above the Claypan. NY, Crime Club, 1943 1st edition. Near Fine in good dust jacket. $75.
The Devil's Steps. NY, Crime Club, 1946 1st American ed. Fine in chip DJ. $50. A. Robertson, 1965 ed. VG. $30.
Murder Must Wait. NY, Crime Club, 1953 1st edition. Very Good in dust jacket. $25-$40.

UPHAM, CHARLES W. *Life, Explorations of John Charles Fremont*. Boston, Ticknor & Fields, 1856. Green cloth. Foxed, browned pages, o/w Very Good. $50. Same in worn cloth. $17-$35.

UPHAM, ELIZABETH. *Little Brown Bear*. 1942, Platt & Munk. Marjorie Hartwell illustrator. Good-VG. $18-$20.
Little Brown Monkey. 1949. Platt & Munk. VG. $23.
The Merry Adventures of Little Brown Bear. Platt & Munk, 1965. Majorie Hartwell illustrator. Very Good in dust jacket. $25.

UPSON, WILLIAM HAZLITT. *Earthworms in Europe*. New York, 1931 1st edition. Signed. Good. $15.
Keep'Em Crawling: Earthworms at War. New York, 1943 1st edition. Fine in fine dust jacket. $40.
No Rest for Botts. New York, 1952 1st edition. Fine in very good dust jacket. $40.

UPTON, BERTHA. *The Golliwog's Bicycle Club*. London, 1896 1st edition. Florence K. Upton illus. 31 full page color plates. Boards soiled, worn. Lacks endpaper. Text, illus. Very Good. $250.
The Golliwog at the Sea-Side. London, 1898. Florence K. Upton illustrator. 31 full page color plates. Boards soiled, worn, hinge taped, o/w Very Good. $250.

UPTON, EMORY. *Infantry Tactics*. New York, 1874. 390 pages. Illustrated. Binding loose. $85.

UPTON, FLORENCE. *The Adventures of Two Dutch Dolls and a Golliwog*. London, NY, no date 1st edition, 1st book in series. Illustrated by author. Overall Very Good. $125.
The Golliwog's Air Ship. NY, London, 1902. Illustrated by author. Good. $175.

URBAN, J. W. *Battle Field and Prison Pen*. Edgewood, 1882. $30-$40. A signed copy. Good. $50.
In Defense of the Union. Washington, 1887 1st ed. $35.

URBINO, L. B. & HENRY DAY. *Art Recreations*. (Victorian Crafts). Tilton, Boston, 1864. Near Fine. $45.

URBUART, F. A. *The Monarch Butterfly*. Toronto, 1960. Color plate illus. Good in dust jacket. $60.

UREY, HAROLD. *The Planets: Their Origin and Development*. Yale, 1952 1st edition. Very Good. $20.

URIS, LEON. *The Angry Hills*. New York, 1955 1st edition. Very Good in dust jacket. $25.
Armageddon. New York, 1964 1st edition. Fine in very good dust jacket. $35.

URQUHART, D. H. *Cocoa*. New York, 1956. Very Good in dust jacket. $10.

U. S. CAMERA ANNUAL. 1936 1st issue. Very Good. $30. 1937-1949 annuals. Average. $15 each.

U. S. DEPARTMENT OF AGRICULTURE YEARBOOK. In 1871 the U. S. Government Printing Office (GPO) published 250,000 hardbound copies of the *Agriculture Yearbook*. Most volumes, before and after that date, sell in the $8 to $18 range.

USHER, ABBOTT P. *A History of Mechanical Inventions*. Harvard University, 1954 revised ed. Very Good. $35.

U. S. INFANTRY AND RIFLE TACTICS. Philadelphia, Lippincott, 1863. 450 pages. Illustrated. Very Good. $100.

U. S. NAVY. *Blue Jackets Manual*. Appleton, 1918 6th edition. Fair, stained. $10. Annapolis, 1940 10th ed. $6. Annapolis, 1943 11th ed. Fine. $8.
Hand to Hand Combat. Annapolis, 1943. Fine in DJ. $15.

U. S. ONE, MAINE TO FLORIDA (WPA GUIDE). New York, Modern Age, 1938 1st edition. Good in DJ. $39-$45.

U. S. S. CLEVELAND (LPD-7) WESTPAC. Ship's cruise book, 1982. 154 pages. Good-Very Good. $15.

U. S. S. SHANGRI-LA AND AIR GROUP THREE - CRUISE 1956. Shangri-La, 1956. 250 pages. Fine in dust jacket. $25.

USTINOV, PETER. *We Were Only Human*. Boston, 1961 1st edition. Very Good. $10.

UTLEY, ROBERT M. *Frontier Regulars, the U. S. Army and the Indians, 1866-1890*. NY, 1973 1st ed. Inscribed by author. Near Fine in dust jacket. $75.

UZANNE, OCTAVE. *The Book Hunter in Parris*. London, 1893. Very Good. $45.

V

VAIL, ROBERT W. G. *Voice of the Old Frontier*. Philadelphia, 1949 1st ed. 1,800 annotations. VG. $55. 1970 Reprint. Fine. $35.

VAILLANT, GEORGE C. *Aztecs of Mexico: Rise & Fall of the Aztec Nation*. Doubleday, 1941 1st ed. VG. $25-$35.

VAILLE & CLARK. *The Harvard Book*. Historical sketches by various authors. Cambridge, 1875. 2 volumes. Heavy tooled covers. Good-Very Good. $150.

VALE, ROBERT. *How to Hunt American Game*. Harrisburg, 1946 subsequent ed. VG-Fine in dust jacket. $15-$20.

VALENTINE, DAVID T. *History of the City of New York*. New York, 1853 1st ed. Maps, lithographs. Good. $110.

VALERY, PAUL. *Variety, Second Series*. New York, 1938 1st American edition. Translated. Good-Very Good. $40.
Monsieur Teste. NY, 1947 1st American ed. Translated. Good in dust jacket. $35.

VAN ALLSBURG, CHRIS. *Jumanji*. New York, 1981 10th printing. Very Good in dust jacket. $20.
Ben's Dream. Boston, 1982 1st edition. Binding design by Jarmila Sobota. Handsewn. Signed. In slipcase. As new condition. $450.
The Z Was Zapped. Boston, 1987 1st edition. Signed. Fine in dust jacket. $35-$50.

VAN ALSTYNE, LAWRENCE. *Diary of An Enlisted Man, 1862-1864*. (Civil War). New Haven, 1910 1st. $40-$50.

VAN BUREN, SARA. *Good Living: A Practical Cookery-Book for Town and Country*. New York, 1908 3rd edition. Good plus. $45.

VANCE, JACK. *The Dragon Masters*. Easton Press, no date. Steven V. Johnson illus. Charles N. Brown introduction. Leather binding, gilt edges. Fine. $25.
To Live Forever. New York, 1956 1st edition. Fine in dust jacket. $500.
Emphyrio. Doubleday, 1969 1st ed. VG in DJ. $150.

VANCE, LOUIS JOSEPH. *The Lone Wolf*. Boston, 1914 1st American edition. Near Very Good. $75.
Encore the Lone Wolf. Lippincott, 1933. NF in DJ. $60.

VANDERBILT, AMY. *Amy Vanderbilt's Complete Cook Book*. 1961. Very Good. $15-$25.
Amy Vanderbilt's Complete Book of Etiquette. Revised edition. 1978. Very Good. $7.

VANDERCOOK, JOHN W. *Black Majesty*. Literary Guild, 1928 1st edition. Mahlon Blaine illus. Very Good. $30. 1930, 13th printing. $7.

VANDERCOOK, MARGARET. *The Ranch Girls at Boarding School*. Winston, 1913. Fine. $5-$10.
The Campfire Girls Behind the Lines. Winston, 1918. Fine in Very Good dust jacket. $10.

VANDERPOEL, EMILY. *Color Problems. A Practical Manual*. 117 color plates. New York, 1902 1st edition. Chart in rear pocket. Very Good. $75.

VANDERVEER, HELEN. *Little Slam Bang*. Volland, 1928 1st edition. Very Good. $50.

VAN DEVENTER, H. R. *Telephonology. A Description of Modern Telephone Appliances*. NY, McGraw Hill, 1910 1st edition. Very Good. $50.

VAN DE WATER, FREDERIC. *The Family Flivvers to Frisco*. NY, Appleton, 1927 1st edition. Very Good. $35.
Glory Hunter, A Life of General Custer. Bobbs Merrill, 1934 1st edition. Very Good. $45. Fine in dust jacket. $95. New York, Argosy, 1963 reprint. 1 of 750. Fine. $27.

VAN DE WETERING, JAN WILLEM. 9 mysteries by, 1976-1985 All Fine in dust jackets. $25 each.

VAN DINE, S. S. *The Dragon Murder Case*. NY, 1933 1st edition. Very Good. $28. Same in dust jacket. $90-$150.
The Garden Murder Case. NY, 1935 1st ed. VG. $35. Same, Ex-library. $8.
The Kidnap Murder Case. Grosset & Dunlap, 1936. Very Good in dust jacket. $35.
The Gracie Allen Murder Case. NY, 1938 1st edition. Very Good plus in very good dust jacket. $50-$150.
The Winter Murder Case. NY, 1939 1st edition. Very Good in chipped dust jacket. $95.

VANDIVER, FRANK. *Rebel Brass*. Baton Rouge, 1956. Signed. Very Good in dust jacket. $25-$35.

VAN DOREN, CARL. *Benjamin Franklin*. NY, Viking 1938 1st trade ed. 3 volumes in DJ. Very Good. $18-$24.

VAN DOREN, HAROLD. *Industrial Design. A Practical Guide*. NY, 1940 1st edition. $25.

VAN DYKE, HENRY. *The Lost Word, A Christmas Legend*. Scribner's, 1898. Dec. green cloth. Faded. $20.
The Ruling Passion. NY, 1901 1st edition. Illus. VG. $12.
The First Christmas Tree. Scribners, 1897. H. Pyle illus. Very Good. $25-$45.
The Blue Flower. Scribners, 1902. H. Pyle color plates. Very Good. $25-$50.
Even Unto Bethlehem. Scribners, 1928. N. C. Wyeth illus. Very Good. $20-$40.
The Story of the Other Wise Men. NY, 1920 Limited autograph edition. Illustrated. Near Fine. $45.
Ships and Havens. NY, Crowell, 1898 edition. 42 pgs. illustrated boards. Fine. $12.
The Toiling of Felix and Other Poems. NY, Scribners, 1904 edition. 88 pages. Fine. $12.
Music and Other Poems. NY, Scribners, 1905 1st edition. Spine faded. Very Good. $12-$14.
Days Off and Other Digressions. NY, Scribners, 1907 1st edition. 322 pages. Frank Schoonover illus. Fine. $20-$24.
The Lost Boy. Harper, 1914 1st edition. N. C. Wyeth illustrator. Very Good. $15-$25.

VAN LOON, WILLEM H. *The Story of Wilbur the Hat*. Liveright, 1925 1st ed. Illus. by author. Near VG. $40.
An Elephant Up a Tree. NY, Simon & Schuster, 1933 1st edition. Green cloth pictorial cover. Very Good. $50-$80.
The Golden Book of the Dutch Navigators. Appleton, 1938 Revised edition. Illus. Very Good in dust jacket. $18.
Van Loon's Lives. Simon & Schuster, 1942 ed. VG. $8.

VAN METRE, T. W. *Tramps and Lines*. NY, 1931 1st ed. Good-Very Good. $20-$35.
Trains, Tracks & Travel. NY, 1939. Very Good. $30.

VAN ORMAN, R. *A Room for the Night, Hotels of the Old West*. IN, 1966. Good-Very Good. $20-$35.

VAN RIPER, GUERNSEY. *Lou Gehrig: Boy of the Sand Lots*. Bobbs-Merrill, 1949 1st ed. in dust jacket. $15-$20.

VAN SLYCK, J. D. *Representatives of New England Manufacturers*. 2 volumes of factory engravings. 588 pages. Boston, 1879. Fine, rare. $300.

VAN TASSEL, C. *The Book of Ohio*. No place, 1903 3 volumes. Very Good. $50. Centennial Edition, no date. Ohio. 2 volumes. 11½x15 leather. 996 pages. Worn extremies o/w Very Good. $225.

VAN RENSSELAER, MARTHA. *Manual of Home-Making*. NY, 1920. Rural Manual Series. Good-VG. $20-$30.

VAN STRUMPELL, DR. ADOLF. *A Text-book of Medicine for Students and Practitioners*. Appleton, 1911 subsequent edition. 2 vols. Fine. $18-$24.

VAN VALKENBURG, JOHN. *Knights of Pythias Manual & Text-Book 1886*. Memento Pub., 1886 rev. ed. VG. $25.

VAN VECHTEN, CARL. *Spider Boy*. NY, 1928 1st trade ed. Near Fine in dust jacket. $100.
Nigger Heaven. G & D, no date. VG in DJ. $30.

VAN VOGT, A. E. *Slan*. Arkham House, 1946 1st edition. Very Good in dust jacket. $150.
The World of A. New York, 1948 1st edition. Good-Very Good in dust jacket. $100-$175.
The Book of Ptath. Fantasy Press, 1947 1st edition. Fine in dust jacket. $75.

VARGAS, LLOSA M. *The Time of the Hero*. Grove, 1966 1st American edition. Near VG in dust jacket. $40.
The Cobs and Other Stories. New York, 1979 1st edition. Fine in dust jacket. $30.

VARNEY, ALMON. *Our Homes and Their Adornments, or How to Build, Finish and Furnish a Home, etc.* Chicago & Philadelphia, 1885 edition. $50.

VAUGHN, ROBERT. *Then and Now, or 36 Years in the Rockies*. Minneapolis, 1900 1st edition. Good-Very Good. $50-$150.

VAUGHN, SNOW and SNOW. *This Was Frank James*. Dorrance, 1969 1st edition. Fine in DJ. $15-$20.

VAVRA, ROBERT. *Lion and Blue*. NY, 1974 2nd edition. Fleur Cowles paintings. Very Good in worn DJ. $25.
Romany Free. NY, 1977 1st edition. F. Cowles illus. Good-Very Good. $20-$45.
All Those Girls in Love With Horses. NY, 1981. Fine in fine dust jacket. $45.

VEBLEN, THORSTEIN. *The Higher Learning in America*. NY, 1918 1st edition. Minor cover wear. $75.

VEECK, BILL. *Veek as in Wreck*. Putnam, 1962 1st edition in dust jacket. $30-$40.

VELIKOVSKY, IMMANUEL. *Worlds in Colision*. Macmillan, 1950 1st edition. Very Good. $25.

VERNE, JULES. *The Tour of the World in Eighty Days*. Boston, 1873 1st American edition. Near Fine. $275. London, no date, 20th edition. $20.
Adventures in the Land of the Behemoths. Boston, 1874 1st American ed. VG. $150. Water damaged, worn. $50.
A Floating City and the Blockade Runners. NY, 1875 2nd American edition. Very Good. $125.

A Journey to the Center of the Earth. London, 1876. Illustrated. Very Good. $50. Boston, no date. $20-$25.
Michael Strogoff. NY, 1927. N. C. Wyeth illus. VG. $100.
Twenty Thousand Leagues Under the Sea. NY, Scribner, 1935 ed., W. J. Aylward illus. Good-VG in dust jacket. $20-$30. Limited Editions Club, 1956. E. A. Wilson illustrator. Signed by Wilson, boxed. $60. Undated Grosset & Dunlap reprints. $8-$10.

VERNON, ARTHUR. *History and Romance of the Horse*. Boston, 1939 1st ed. $40-$55. NY, 1941 ed. Good. $28.
California Tin Types. Los Angeles, no date. Photo illustrations. $20-$30.

VERPLANCK, W. *Sloops of the Hudson*. NY, 1908 1st ed. 13 illustrations. VG in dust jacket. $40-$50.

VERRIER, E. *Practical Manual of Obstetrics*. New York, 1884 1st edition. Very Good. $95.

VERRILL, A. HYATT. *Lost Treasure: True Tales of Hidden Hoards*. Appleton, 1930 1st ed. Fine in DJ. $40.

VESTAL, STANLEY. *Fandango: Ballads of the Old West*. Boston, 1927 1st edition. Author's 1st book. Very Good-Fine in dust jacket. $100-$150.
The Old Santa Fe Trail. Boston, 1939 1st edition. Very Good in dust jacket. $28.
Short Grass Country. NY, 1941 1st edition. Fine. $30.
King of the Fur Traders. Houghton-Mifflin, 1940 1st edition. Ex-library. Fair. $10.
Bigfoot Wallace. Boston, 1942 1st ed. Very Good. $50.
Jim Bridger, Mountain Men. NY, 1946 1st edition. Very Good in dust jacket. $25-$40.
Joe Meek, the Merry Mountain Men. Caldwell ID, 1952 1st edition. Very Good. $75.
The Missouri. NY, 1945 1st edition. Farrar. Rivers of America Series. VG in dust jacket. $24. No DJ. $19.

VFW PICTORIAL HISTORY OF WWII. Vols. 1, 2 & 3. 1950s. $15 each.

VICK, EDWARD. *Audels Gardeners and Growers Guide*. NY, 1928. 4 vols., thin cloth. $24.

THE VICTROLA BOOK OF THE OPERA. Victor Co., 1925 to 1929 editions. $8-$15 each. (Also see Catalog Section, Victor Talking Machine Co.)

VIDAL, GORE. *Williwaw*. New York, 1946 1st edition. Author's 1st book. Very Good. $185.
In a Yellow Wood. E. P. Dutton, 1947 1st edition. Very Good in dust jacket. $25.
The City and the Pillar. NY, 1948 1st edition. Signed. Fine in very good dust jacket. $150.
Death in the Fifth Position. NY, 1952 1st edition. Very Good in chipped dust jacket. $200.

Myra Breckenridge. New York, 1968 1st edition. Very Good in dust jacket. $25-$35.

VIELE, MRS. *Following the Drum. A Glimpse of Frontier Life*. New York, 1858 1st edition. Original cloth, some soil. Good-Very Good. $100-$150.

VIEMEISTER, PETER E. *The Lightning Book*. Garden City, 1961. Very Good in worn dust jacket. $25.

VIEWS OF BRATTLEBORO, VT. Brattleboro, C. L. Howe & Son, , 1886. 32 photo-prints. $50.

VIGNON, PAUL. *The Shroud of Christ*. Westminster, England, 1902. Good-Very Good. $65.

VILLIERS, ALAN J. *Whaling in the Frozen South*. Bobbs-Merrill, 1925 1st edition. Illustrated. Very Good in chip dust jacket. $75.
Falmouth for Orders. NY, 1929. Very Good. $40.
The Last of the Wind Ships. Morrow, 1934. $18-$40.
Whalers of the Midnight Sun. NY, 1934 1st American edition. Very Good. $17-$35.
Sons of Sinbad. Scribner's, 1940 1st edition. Very Good, no dust jacket. $16.

VINCENT, GILLIAN. *Writers' Favorite Recipes*. New York, 1979. Very Good. $24.

VIRGINIA, GUIDE TO THE OLD DOMINION. Pub. by W.P.A. in 1941. Rebound, Ex-library. $15.

VISSCHER, WILLIAM L. *Black Mammy: A Song of the Sunny South*. Cheyenne, 1885 1st edition. Author's 1st book. $80-$100.
A Thrilling and Truthful History of the Pony Express. Rand McNally, 1946 2nd edition in DJ. $30-$40.

VIZETELY, HENRY. *A History of Champagne*. London, 1882 1st ed. Illus. Good-VG. $150-$300.

VOGEL, JOSEPH. *At Madame Bonnard's*. NY, Knopf, 1935 1st ed. Very Good in poor dust jacket. $40.

VOISIN, GASTON. *French Cooking For All*. New York, Stokes, 1930. $15.

VONNEGUT, KURT. *Player Piano*. Scribner, 1952 1st ed. Author's 1st book, 1st state. Inscribed. NF in DJ. $300.
The Sirens of Titan. Orig. Dell Paperback, 1959. $30-$50.
God Bless You, Mr. Rosewater. Holt, Rinehart, 1965 1st edition. in dust jacket. $90-$130.
Slaughterhouse-Five. Delacorte, 1969 1st edition. Near Fine in dust jacket. $300.

VOYNICH, E. L. *The Gadfly*. NY, 1897 1st edition. Author's 1st book. Near Fine. $75.

W

WADE, BLANCHE ELIZABETH. *Garden in Pink*. Chicago, 1905, McClure. Good-VG. $35-$45.
Anne, Princess of Everything. 1916, Goldsmith. Good-Very Good. $12-$20.
Ant Ventures. Chicago, 1924 1st edition. Harrison Cady illustrator. Near Fine. $95.

WADSWORTH, WALLACE. *The Stubborn Dirigible and Other Stories*. Chicago, 1935. Ruth Eger illus. Spine restored, otherwise Very Good. $75.

WAGGONER, J. FRED. *The Home Cook Book*. No place, 1874. $75-$90.

WAGNER, CHARLES. *The Story of Signs. An Outline History*. Boston, 1954. Very Good. $35.

WAGNER, HENRY R. *Califiornia Voyages, 1539-1541*. No place, 1925 1st editions. Inscribed. Very Good. $100.
Sir Francis Drake's Voyage Around the World. No place, 1926. One of 100 copies. Signed. Very Good. $175.
Spanish Explorations in the Strait of Juan de Fuca. Fine Arts Press, 1933 1st edition. Very Good. $600.
Plains & Rockies: Bibliography of Narratives. San Francisco, 1937. Fine. $150. 1953 3rd ed. Fine. $195.

WAGNER, RICHARD. *Ring of the Niblung*. Garden City, 1939. Rackham illus. VG inDJ. $50-$110.
Tannhauser. Brentario's, no date. Pogany illus. VG. $65.
Lohengrin. Crowell, 1913. Pogany illus. VG. $75-$125.
Story of Bayreuth. Boston, 1912. Very Good. $40.

WAGNER, WILLIAM. *Ryan the Aviator*. McGraw Hill, 1971 1st edition. Signed by Ryan & the author. Fine in DJ. $35.

WAIN, JOHN. *A Travelling Woman*. NY, 1959 1st American edition. Very Good in dust jacket. $27.

WAITE, A. E. *Doctrine and Literature of the Kabala*. London, 1902 1st edition. Very Good. $175.
Pictorial Key to the Tarot. London, 1911. Inscribed. Front hinge loose, o/w Very Good. $350.
The Book of Black Magic. Chicago, 1940. Light soiling, o/w Very Good. $30.
The Book of the Holy Grail. London, 1921 1st ed. Near Fine in vg dust jacket. $95.
The Secret Tradition in Alchemy. NY, 1926 1st. NF. $95.

WAKEFIELD, DAN. *Island in the City*. Boston, 1959 1st ed. Author's 1st book. NF in very good dust jacket. $35-$50.

WAKEFIELD, H. R. *Clock Strikes 12*. Arkham House, 1946 1st edition. VG-Fine in dust jacket. $40-$80.

WAKEFIELD, JOHN. *The Strange World of Birds*. Macrae Smith, 1964. Fine. $40.

WAKEFIELD, RUTH. *Toll House Tried and True Recipes*. 1937 edition, signed by author. Very Good. $25. New York, 1945 20th printing. Revised and enlarged. Very Good in dust jacket. $15.

WALDEN, HOWARD II. *Angler's Choice*. No place, 1947 1st edition. Very Good in dust jacket. $15.
Upstream and Down. Derrydale Press, 1938. M. C. Weiler illustrator. One of 950 copies. Very Good. $75.
Familiar Freshwater Fishes of America. New York, 1964 1st edition. New York, 1964 1st edition. Illustrated. Fine in dust jacket. $12-$15.

WALDO, MYRA. *The Diners' Club Cook Book*. NY, 1959 1st edition. Very Good in dust jacket. $8-$14.
The Complete Round the World Cookbook. No place. 1967. $15-$20.

WALKER, ERIC. *The Great Trek*. London, 1965 5th edition. Very Good in dust jacket. $35.

WALKER, FRANKLIN. *San Francisco's Literary Frontier*. NY, 1943 2nd edition. Good-Very Good. $25.

WALKER, JOSEPH. *How They Carried the Mail*. Sears Pub., 1930 1st edition. Very Good. $16.

WALKER, STANLEY. *Home to Texas*. NY, 1956 1st edition. Good in dust jacket. $20.

WALL, BERNHARDT. *Following General Sam Houston*. Austin TX, 1935 1st edition. Illus. by author. Signed. Slight stain, o/w Very Good. $40.

WALL, E. J. *Photographic Facts & Formulas*. Boston, 1924 1st edition. Very Good. $40.

WALL, O. W. *Sex & Sex Worship*. St. Louis, 1922. VG. $50.

WALLACE, ALFRED RUSSELL. *Island Life*. London, 1880 1st edition. Very Good-Fine. $275.

WALLACE, EDGAR. *Terror Keep*. Garden City, 1927 1st American edition. Near Fine in good dust jacket. $100.
People. Garden City, 1929 1st American edition. Autobiography. Minor wear. $20.
Mr. Commissioner Sanders. Doubleday, 1930. Very Good in good dust jacket. $40.
The Green Ribbon. The Crime Club, 1930. Fine in very good dust jacket. $30.
Various Titles. Subsequent editions, 1927-32. $10-$20.

WALLACE, LEW. *Ben Hur, A Tale of Christ*. NY, 1880 1st edition, first issue has 1880 date on title page and six-word dedication. $225-$350. Other versions in same year are common at $15 in good condition. Harper's Play edition, with photos, 1901. Illus. bds. Good. $25. 1904 printing, Harpers. 560 pages. Fine, no dust jacket. $8. 1908 revised edition. Good. $5.
Fair God. Houghton Mifflin, 1890. Good-VG. $12-$18.
Prince of India. NY, Harper, 1893 1st ed. 2 vols. Good-Very Good. $20-$45. Ex-library set. Very Good. $15.
Autobiography. New York, 1906 1st edition. 2 volumes. Very Good-Fine. $90-$125.

WALLACE, PHILIP. *Colonial Ironwork in Old Philadelphia*. Measured drawings. NY, 1930 1st ed. VG. $75.

WALLACE, WILLIAM N. *MacMillan Book of Boating-History of American Sail*. Ridge Press, 1964 1st edition. Fine in dust jacket. $16.

WALLING, DR. W. H. (Editor). *Sexology: Family Medical Edition*. Philadelphia, 1904. Illustrated. Fine. $40.

WALLIS, CHARLES. *Stories on Stone*. American epitaphs. Oxford Univ. Press, 1954 1st edition. VG in poor DJ. $20.

WALLOP, DOUGLAS. *The Year The Yankees Lost the Pennant*. NY, 1954 1st ed. Very Good plus in DJ. $50.

WALPOLE, HUGH. *The Wooden Horse*. London, 1909 1st edition. Author's 1st book. Very Good. $50.
Portrait of a Man with Red Hair. NY, Doran, 1925 1st edition in dust jacket. $18-$40.
Rogue Herries. London, 1930 1st ed. Inscribed. VG. $30.
Vanessa. London, 1933 1st edition. Very Good in DJ. $45.
The Killer and the Slain. NY, 1942 1st ed. VG in DJ. $10.

WALSH, WILLIAM. *Handbook of Literary Curiosities*. Philadelphia, 1893. Very Good. $45.

WALTON, IZAAK. *The Compleat Angler: or the Contemplative Man's Recreation*. Charles Cotton is sometimes listed as co-author. He wrote a special section on fly-fishing and making flies. Walton enlarged his classic considerably after the first publication in 1653. The first edition has 13 chapters, the 5th 21. Many very limited, illustrated editions, circa 1800-1900, have sold for $500-$3,000. For example, a copy of the Samuel Bagster edition of 1808, lavishly rebound, was offered for nearly $500. Some common editions: Boston, 1867. $45. Great Britain, 1925, J. Thorpe illus. Good. $30. David McKay, 1931, Rackham illus. $125. Penguin paperback, 1929. VG. $20. Dutton, 1927, illus. ed. $50. Heritage Press, 1948. G. $12. Same, Fine in case. $18. Harrap of London, 1979. F. $25.

WALTON, PERRY. *The Story of Textiles*. NY, Tudor, 1937 edition. Fine in chipped dust jacket. $18.

WARD, ARCH. *Frank Leahy and the Fighting Irish*. Putnam, 1947. Very Good in dust jacket. $15.

WARD, ARTEMUS, (Charles F. Browne). *Artemus Ward, His Book*. Carleton, 1865 1st ed. Good. $14.
The Grocers' Handbook & Directory for 1886. Philadelphia, 1886. $50-$75.
The Grocers' Encyclopedia. NY, 1911. $65.
The Encyclopedia of Food. 1923 reprint. VG. $35-$50.

WARD, AUSTIN. *Male Life Among the Mormons*. Philadelphia, 1863. $55.

WARD, CHRISTOPHER. *The War of the Revolution*. Macmillan, 1952. 2 vols. in slipcase. Fine. $16.

WARD, MARIA E. *The Commonsense of Bicycling*. NY, 1896 1st edition. Photo illus. Very Good. $225.

WARD, WILLIAM. *Harry Trace, The Death Dealing Oregon Outlaw*. Cleveland, circa 1908. 191 pages, illustrated. Stained cover. $35.

WARE, E. H. *Wing to Wing: Bird Watching Adventures in Five Countries*. Harper, 1946. Illus. Good in torn DJ. $25.

WARNER, GERTRUDE CHANDLER. *The Boxcar Children*. Scott, Foresman, 1942. Kate Deal illustrator. VG. $30.

WARNER, MATT & MURRAY KING. *The Last of the Bandit Riders*. 1940, Bonanza Books. Photo illustrations. Good reading copy. $35.

WARNER, JUAN and others. *An Historical Sketch of Los Angeles County, 1771-1876*. 88 pages, 2nd issue. Los Angeles, Louis Lewin, 1876 1st ed. Good-VG. $300-$500.

WARNER, OLIVER. *Great Sea Battles*. Macmillan, 1963 1st edition. Illustrated, 4to, 304 pages. Very Good in DJ. $24.

WARNER, SYLVIA TOWNSEND. *Loly Willows*. NY, 1926 6th printing. Very Good in dust jacket. $25.
The Salutation. NY, 1932 1st ed. Fine in dust jacket. $25.

WARREN, W. C. *The House and Sign Painters' Book. Valuable Recipes, etc.* Indiana, 1907. 96 pgs. 5th ed. $35.

WARWICK, EDWARD & HENRY C. PITZ. *Early American Costume.* New York, 1929. Illustrated. Covers spotted, o/w Very Good. $65.

WASHBURN, CEPHAS. *Reminiscences of the Indians.* Presbyterian Committee Pub., 1869. Worn and frayed. Good plus. $300.

WASHBURN, ROBERT C. *The Life and Times of Lydia E. Pinkham.* NY, 1931 1st edition. Good-Very Good. $20.

WASHINGTON, BOOKER T. *The Future of the American Negro.* Boston, 1899 1st edition. Author's 1st book. Fine. $200. Very Good. $25.
The Story of My Life & Work. J. L. Nichols, 1901. Good-Very Good. $18-$25.
Up From Slavery. 1901 1st edition, original red cloth. $75-$100. NY, 1902. Rubbed o/w Very Good. $30.
Working With the Hands. Doubleday, 1904 1st edition. Good. $50. Very Good. $75.
Putting The Most Into Life. NY, 1906 1st ed. NF. $125.

WASON, BETTY. *Bride in The Kitchen.* New York, 1964. Peach cake to cucumber soup. $15-$20.

WATERHOUSE, KEITH. *Billy Liar.* W. W. Norton, 1960 1st American edition. Very Good in dust jacket. $40.

WATERS, L. L. *Steel Trails to Santa Fe.* University of Kansas, 1950. Hinge repaired, o/w Good. $37. Another, Very Good in torn dust jacket. $60.

WATKINS, LURA. *American Glass and Glassmaking.* NY, 1950 1st edition. Illustrated. Very Good. $25.

WATROUS, GEORGE. *The History of Winchester Firearms.* New York, Winchester Press, 1975 4th edition. Near Fine in slipcase. $35.

WATSON, WILBUR J. *Bridge Architecture.* New York, 1927. 200 historical illus. Fine. $100.

WAUGH, ALEC. *Hot Countries.* Literary Guild, 1930. Lynd Ward illustrator. Very Good. $12.
My Brother Evelyn. New York, 1967 1st American ed. Inscribed. Very Good in dust jacket. $40.

WAUGH, AUBERON. *The Foxglove Saga.* London, 1960 1st ed. Author's 1st book. Near Fine in dust jacket. $50.

WAUGH, EVELYN. *Brideshead Revisited.* Boston, 1945 1st American edition. Very Good in dust jacket. $30-$55.
The Loved One. Boston, 1948 1st American edition. Very Good in dust jacket. $40-$75.

Wine in Peace and War. London, 1949. Stained endpapers, o/w Very Good. $100.
The Holy Places. Queen Ann Press. 1953 1st American edition. #139 of 1,000 copies. Fine. $95.
Tactical Exercise. Boston, 1954 1st American edition. Fine in dust jacket. $70.
Officers and Gentlemen. Boston, 1955 1st American edition. Good. $20.
The Ordeal of Gilbert Pinfold. Boston, 1957 1st American edition. Very Good in dust jacket. $40.
Tourist in Africa. Boston, 1960 1st edition. Illustrated. Very Good in dust jacket. $35.
End of the Battle. Boston, 1961 1st ed. VG in DJ. $25.

WAUGH, SIDNEY. *The Art of Glass Making.* New York, Dodd-Mead, 1939. Very Good. $20.

WAY, FREDERICK, JR. *The Log of the Betsy Ann.* NY, 1933. Good-Very Good. $30. Same, inscribed. $55.
The Allegheny. NY, 1942 1st ed. Rivers of America series. Good-Very Good. $20-$35.
Pilotin' Comes Natural. NY & Toronto, 1943 2nd ed. $25.

WEAVER, LOUISE. *Bettina's Best Desserts.* 1923, Burt, Very Good. $14.

WEAVER, WARREN A. *Lithographs of N. Currier and Currier & Ives.* NY, Holport Pub., 1925. G-VG. $25-$50.

WEAVES, FABRICS, TEXTILE DESIGN. International Textbook Co., 1921. Very Good. $20.

WEBB, WILLIAM SEWARD. *California and Alaska and Over the Canadian Pacific Railway.* NY, Putnam, 1890 1st ed. No. 161 of 500 copies. Good-VG. $110 auction.

WEBB, WALTER PRESCOTT. *The Great Plains.* Ginn, 1931 1st ed., 1st printing. Some spotting, o/w VG. $85. Another, VG no DJ. $16-$30. 1936 edition. VG in DJ. $40.
The Texas Ranger. Boston, 1935 1st. One of 200 copies. Illus. Signed. In worn slipcase. $500. Unsigned, no DJ. Very Good. $50-$60. 1965 reprint. Very Good in DJ. $30.

WEBSTER, DANIEL. *Works of Daniel Webster.* Boston, 1851 1st ed., 6 vols. Subscriber's copy, signed. Fine. $150.

WEBSTER, HELEN N. *Herbs, How to Grow Them and How to Use Them.* 1942 revised ed. VG in DJ. $10-$12.

WEBSTER, H. T. *Webster's Poker Book.* 1925. 126 pages. Very Good. $45. Same with chip compartment, and cardboard chips. Ex. $190.

WEBSTER, H. T. and PHILO CALHOUN. *Life With Rover.* Appleton, 1949. Illus. by Webster. VG in chip DJ. $25.

WEBSTER, JEAN *Daddy Long Legs.* NY, 1914. G plus. $14.

WEBSTER, KIMBALL. *The Gold Seekers of '49*. Manchester NH, 1917. Ex-library, orig. cloth. Faded spine. $85.

WEBSTER, NOAH. Served in the American Revolutionary War, became a lawyer in 1781 and published a three-part speller, grammar and reader in 1783-85. By 1850 Webster's *Elementary Spelling Book* was selling a million copies per year. An 1804-1829 edition of the so-called "Blue-backed Speller" is worth $50-$60. Webster's *Dictionaries* for *Primary* and *Common Schools* published in the early 1800s have been listed between $400 and $500 in some catalogs. His *American Dictionary of the English Language*, first published in 1828, eventually achieved annual sales of 300,000 copies. An 1828 1st edition with two pages of ads inserted might fetch more than $3,000. Various versions from 1832-1858 have been offered by dealers for $25 to $200. The huge 2,600 to 3,000 page editions of *Webster's New International Dictionary* of the 20th century are common at $25-$50.

WEEGEE (Arthur Fellig). *Naked City*. NY, 1945 1st edition. Near Fine. $100. Good-Very Good. $25-$35.
Weegee's People. New York, 1946 1st edition. Gilt stamped brown cloth. $30-$40.

WEEGEE and MEL HARRIS. *Naked Hollywood*. NY, 1953 1st edition. Very Good in chip dust jacket. $200.

WEEKS, LYMAN H. *History of Paper Manufacturing in the United States, 1690-1916*. Lockwood Trade Journal Co., 1916 1st edition. Illustrated. Very Good. $45.

WEEMS, MASON L. *The Life of George Washington*. Philadelphia, 1812. 12th edition worn. Original leather binding. $45. Jospeh Allen, 1838, 27th edition. Poor. $18. Philadelphia, 1840 edition. Very Good. $95.
The Life of Benjamin Franklin. Uriah Hunt, 1845 1st edition. Poor. $15.

WEGMANN, EDWARD. *The Design and Construction of Dams*. NY, Wiley, 1907 5th edition. Fine. $50.

WEHR, JULIAN. *Raggedy Ann & Andy*. Akron, Saalfield Publishing, 1944 1st edition. Animated with moveable color illustrations by Wehr. Near Fine. $247 auction.
Puss in Boots. Duenewald, 1944. Very Good. $50-$70.

WEINBERGER, BERNHARD WOLF. *An Introduction to the History of Dentistry*. C. C. Mosby, 1948. 2 volumes. Many illustrations. Fine in dust jackets. $150.

WEINER, NORBERT. *The Human Use of Human Beings*. Houghton-Mifflin, 1950. Near Fine in dust jacket. $70.

WELLING, WILLIAM. *Photography in America: The Formative Years, 1839-1900*. New York, 1978 1st edition. Fine in dust jacket. $60.

WELLS, CAROLYN. *A Parody Anthology*. NY, 1904. $20.
Mother Goose's Menagerie. Noyes, 1901. $100-$175.
Beauties. Dodd, 1908. Fisher illus. VG. $175.
Seven Ages of Childhood. 1909 1st ed., Moffat. Jessie W. Smith illustrator. Very Good in dust jacket. $100.
Marjories Vacation. NY, 1907, Grosset & Dunlap. G. $8.
Patty's Success. New York, Dodd, 1910. Good. $7.
Such Nonsense. 1918. Good. $15.
The Doomed Five. Phil., 1930 1st ed. VG in DJ. $20.

WELLS, CARVETH. *Six Years in the Malay Jungles*. NY, circa 1923. Very Good. $12.
In Coldest Africa. NY, 1931. Very Good in DJ. $25.

WELLS, HELEN. *Cherry Ames, Army Nurse*. Grosset & Dunlap, 1944. Fine. $10.

WELLS, H. G. *Select Conversations With an Uncle, etc.* London, 1895 1st edition. Very Good. $150. Same, NY, 1895. Near Fine. $350.
The Time Machine. London, 1895 1st ed. VG overall. $750. NY, 1931 edition. Dwiggins illus. Very Good. $30.
War of the Worlds. London, 1898 1st edition. Very Good-Fine. $300-$400. Same, NY, 1898 1st American edition. Additional illus. Very Good-Fine. $150-$350.
When the Sleeper Awakes. NY, 1899 1st American ed. Illustrated. Near Fine. $125.
The Invisible Man. Harper, 1898. Good. $50. NY, 1907. Dell paperback. Very Good. $25.
Tales of Space & Time. NY, 1899 1st Am. ed. $50.
Tono-Bungay. NY, 1909 1st American edition. Near Very Good in dust jacket. $95.
War in the Air. Modern Library, 1917 1st ed. Very Good-Fine in dust jacket. $120. 4th printing, no date. VG. $30.
Men Like Gods. London, 1923 1st ed. Very Good. $40.
Works of H. G. Wells. NY, 1924. Atlantic edition. 28 vols. with prospectus. One of 1,000 signed copies. Fine. $1,000.
The Adventures of Tommy. NY, 1929. 1st American ed. Illus. by Wells. Fine in fine glassine dust jacket. $50.
Autocracy of Mr. Parnham. Doubleday, 1930. In dust jacket. $30-$50.
The Work, Wealth and Happiness of Mankind. London, 1932 1st edition. Very Good in fair dust jacket. $20.
Star-Begotten. Viking, 1937 1st ed. Good in DJ. $15.

WELLS, S. R. *New Illustrated Self-Instructor*. Phrenology-Physiology. 1890s edition. 176 pages. Good-VG. $17-$20.

WELTY, EUDORA. *Delta Wedding*. NY, 1946 1st ed. Signed. Fine in mended DJ. $200. Another, unsigned in Very Good dust jacket. $100.
The Bride of the Innisfallen. NY, 1955 1st ed. Inscribed. Fine in near fine dust jacket. $190.
The Shoe Bird. NY, 1964 1st edition. Beth Krush illus. Signed by Welty. Fine in fine dust jacket. $175-$250.
Losing Battles. Random House, 1970 1st edition. Very Good in dust jacket. $40. 2nd edition. Fine in DJ. $10.

WENDT, HERBERT. *Out of Noah's Ark*. Boston, 1939 1st American edition. Spine tear, o/w Good. $7.
In Search of Adam. 1956 1st American edition. Good-Very Good. $8-$15.
The Sex Life of the Animals. Simon & Schuster, 1965. Fine, no dust jacket. $10.

WENDT & KOGAN. *Lords of the Levee*. Bobbs Merrill, 1943 1st edition. Very Good, no dust jacket. $18.

WENTWORTH, EDWARD N. *America's Sheep Trails: History, Personalities*. Iowa State Univ. Press. 1948 1st edition. Very Good. $80. Same, presentation copy. $100.

WENTWORTH and FLEXNER. *Dictionary of American Slang*. New York, 1960. Very Good. $25.

WENTWORTH, PATRICIA. *The Case is Closed*. Philadelphia, 1937 1st edition. Ex-library. $18.
Miss Silver Deals With Death. Philadelphia, 1943 1st edition. Very Good in worn dust jacket. $50.
Poison in the Pin. Philadelphia, 1954 1st edition. Very Good in good dust jacket. $19.

WENTZ (Chef). *Gastronomy*. New York, 1960 1st edition. Very Good. $16.

WERTHAM, FREDRIC. *Dark Legend*. New York, 1941 1st edition. Very Good in chip dust jacket. $25. Same, no dust jacket. $15.
The Show of Violence. NY, 1949 1st edition. Inscribed. Very Good in dust jacket. $15-$25.
Seduction of the Innocent. NY, 1954 1st edition. Good-Very Good in dust jacket. $35-$75.

WEST, C. *Second to None: The Story of the 305th Infantry in WWII*. Washington, 1949 1st edition. Fine. $110.

WEST, JERRY. *Happy Hollisters and the ....* Doubleday, Juvenile series 1953-1964 Book Club edition. Very Good in dust jacket. $7 ea.

WEST, MAE. *Goodness Had Nothing to Do With It*. NY, 1959 1st edition. Very Good. $20.
Mae West on Sex, Health and ESP. W. H. Allen, 1975. Illustrated. Very Good in dust jacket. $30.

WEST, NATHANAEL. *Miss Lonelyhearts*. NY, 1933. Very Good in dust jacket. $40. Undated reprint. Very Good. $20.
A Cool Million. NY, 1934 1st edition. Very Good-Fine in dust jacket. $700-$900. Same, London, 1954 1st English edition. Near Fine in dust jacket. $235.
The Day of the Locust. New York, 1939 1st edition. Very Good-Fine in dust jacket. $500. Same, Good-Very Good, no dust jacket. $35-$75.
The Complete Works of Nathanael West. NY, 1957 1st edition. Near Fine in dust jacket. $50.

WEST, REBECCA. *Black Lamb and Grey Falcon*. New York, 1941 2 volumes. in slipcase. Very Good. $50. 1943 edition in one volume. Fair dust jacket. $20.
The Meaning of Treason. New York, 1947 1st American edition. Very Good in dust jacket. $25.
Birds Fall Down. NY, 1966 1st American edition. Very Good in good dust jacket. $15.

WEST, RICHARD S. *Lincoln's Scapegoat General: A Life of Ben Butler*. Houghton Mifflin, 1965. Very Good in worn dust jacket. $18.

THE WEST COAST OF MEXICO AND CENTRAL AMERICA. U. S. Hydrographic Office. Washington, 1887. Map included. Very Good. $65.

WEST, WOOD & WENDER. *Second to None. The Story of the 305th Infantry in World War II*. Infantry Press, 1949 1st edition. Fine, no dust jacket. $45-$55.

WESTCOTT, GLENWAY. *Twelve Fables of Aesop*. NY, 1954. One of 975 copies, boxed. Near Fine. $125.

WESTERMARCK, EDWARD. *The History of Human Marriage*. Allerton, 1922 5th edition. 3 vols. Very Good. $50.

WESTERMEIER, CLIFFORD. *Trailing the Cowboys*. Caxton, 1955 1st edition. Very Good in dust jacket. $28.

WESTERNERS BRAND BOOKS. 1944-1986 editions in fine condition. $45-$125 each. 1940s editions bring top price.

WESTLAKE, DONALD. *Killy*. NY, 1963 1st edition. Near Fine in nicked dust jacket. $150.
The Spy in the Ointment. NY, 1966 1st edition. Fine in fair dust jacket. Signed. $33.
The Busy Body. New York, 1966 1st edition. Near Fine in clipped dust jacket. $40.
Cops and Robbers. NY, 1972 1st ed. Near Fine in DJ. $20.

WESTON, EDWARD (Photographer). *Leaves of Grass*. by Walt Whitman. New York, 1942. Limited Editions Club. 2 vols. Copy 1,333 signed by Weston. Slipcase. Slight spine wear. $700.
My Camera on Point Lobos. Boston, 1950 1st edition. Spiral bound. Fine. $350.
The Daybooks of Edward Weston. Vol. 1, Mexico, NY, 1961 1st edition. Vol. II, NY, 1966 1st edition. Both, in near fine dust jacket. $75-$100 each.
California and the West. NY, Duell, Sloan, 1940 1st edition. $70-$100.

WESTOVER, W. *Suicide Battalions*. (WWI). New York, 1929. Illustrated. Fine. $30.

WETMORE, MRS. HELEN C. *Last of the Great Scouts: The Life Story of Buffalo Bill*. Duluth, 1899 1st ed. Clippings tipped in, 1st printing. Fine. $175. Fair. $40. Good-Very Good. $75-$100. 1918 ed. with Zane Grey forward. NY, Grosset & Dunlap. VG in DJ. $75. Without DJ. $20-$25.

WEYGANDT, CORNELIUS. *Philadelphia Folks*. Appleton, 1938 1st edition. Very Good, no dust jacket. $14.
Heart of New Hampshire. Putnam, 1944 2nd ed. VG. $10.

WHARTON, DON (Editor). *The Roosevelt Omnibus*. Knopf, 1934 1st ed. Illustrated. Very Good, no DJ. $15.

WHARTON, EDITH. *The Touchstone*. Merrymount Press, 1900 1st edition. Very Good. $120.
The House of Mirth. NY, 1905 1st ed. Fine. $65. Limited Editions Club, 1975. One of 2,000 copies, signed by illustrator. Very Good. $35.
The Fruit of the Tree. Scribners, 1907 1st ed. Faded. $50.
A Motor Flight Through France. New York, 1908 1st edition. Very Good. $100.
Hermit and the Wild Woman. NY, Scribner, 1908 1st edition. Original red cloth. Fine. $125.
Ethan Frome. NY, 1911 1st edition, 1st issue. VG. $150-$165. Limited Editions Club, 1939. Henry Varnum Poor illustrator. One of 1,500 copies, signed by Poor. Very Good in slipcase, $85. Fine, no case. $50.
The Custom of the Country. NY, 1913 1st ed. Fine. $125.
The Glimpses of the Moon. Appleton, 1922 1st edition, 1st printing. Very Good. $25. Fine in DJ. $125.
A Son at the Front. New York, 1923 1st edition. Fine in fair dust jacket. $125.
The Children. New York, 1928 1st edition. Very Good in dust jacket. $95.
The Age of Innocence. Appleton, circa 1920. $7-$15. LEC, 1978. One of 2,000 copies. Signed by illustrator. Boxed. $35. Modern Library ed. 1940s. VG, no DJ. $8.

WHARTON, EDITH (Editor). *The Book of the Homeless (Le Livre des Sans-Foxer)*. New York, Scribners, 1916 1st ed. Rubbed corners, else Very Good. $70-$100.

WHARTON, EDITH & OGDEN CODMAN. *The Decoration of Houses*. New York, Scribner's, 1897 1st edition. Marbled boards. Scuffed, faded. Good. $225. VG. $285.

WHARTON, JAMES GEORGE. *Indian Basketry and How to Make Indian and Other Baskets*. Pasadena CA, 1903 3rd edition. 21 vols. Near Fine. $75.
California, Romantic and Beautiful. Page, 1914 2nd edition. Very Good. $65.
The Grand Canyon of Arizona. Boston, 1910. 2 vols. illus. from photos. Both bright and tight. $45-$90 pair.
Indian Blankets and Their Makers. Chicago, 1914 1st edition. Illustrated. Very Good. $300.
Arizona the Wonderland. Boston, 1917 1st edition. Near Very Good. $45.
New Mexico, Land of the Delight Makers. Boston, 1920 1st edition. Pictorial and gilt cloth. Very Good. $75.

WHARTON, M. *Doctor Woman of the Cumberlands*. Pleasant Hill TN, 1953 1st ed. 208 pgs. VG in DJ. $20.

WHAT SHALL WE EAT? *A Manual for Housekeepers, etc.* Anonymous. Putnam, NY, 1868. Very Good. $50.

WHEAT, CARL. *Maps of the California Gold Region, 1848-1857*. Grabhorn Press, 1942. $800 up.
Books of the California Gold Rush. Grabhorn Press, 1949 1st edition. Very Good-Fine. $225.
The First 100 Years of Yankee California. Washington, 1949 1st edition. 1 of 500. Good-Very Good. $20-$30.
Mapping the Transmississippi West...1540-1861. San Francisco, 1957-1967. 5 volumes of 6. Many folding maps. 14 x 10 half cloth & buckram. 1 of 1,000 sets, ex-library. $2,475 auction.

WHEATLEY, DENNIS. *File on Bolitho Blaine*. NY, 1936 1st American edition. Crimefile No. 1. One of four such in which clues were inserted in book. U. S. title: *Murder Off Miami*. Very Good. $45.

WHEELER, F. G. *Billy Whiskers at the Fair*. Saalfield, 1909 1st edition. Very Good. $30-$35.
Billy Whiskers' Travels. Saalfield, 1907. Very Good. $32. (The better-known "Billy Whiskers" author is Frances Montgomery.)

WHEELER, ELIZA ANN. *The Frugal Housekeeper's Kitchen Companion, or Guide to Economical Cookery*. NY, 1848. Good-Very Good. $100.

WHEELER, JANET. *Billie Bradley on Lighthouse Island (No. 3)*. Sully, 1920 1st edition. Blue cloth. Very Good in fair dust jacket. $20.

WHEELER, OPAL. *Sing Mother Goose*. Dutton, 1945. Illustrated. Very Good in dust jacket. $30-$35.

WHIPPLE, FRED L. *Earth, Moon and Planets*. Harvard University Press, 1968 3rd edition. Good. $15.

WHIPPLE, MAUREEN. *This is the Place: Utah*. Knopf, 1945 1st edition. Very Good. $10.

WHISTLER, JAMES A. M. *The Gentle Art of Making Enemies*. NY, 1890. Near Very Good. $45.

WHITE, ANDREW D. *A History of the Warfare of Science With Theology in Christendom*. NY, 1917 2 volumes. Very Good. $85. 1955 reprint in one volume. $25.

WHITE, E. B. *The Lady is Cold*. NY, 1929 1st ed. Author's 1st book (poems). Very Good. $150. NY, 1944, New enlarged edition. Very Good in dust jacket. $15.
One Man's Meat. NY, 1942 1st edition. Very Good-Fine in dust jacket. $40-$100.

Stuart Little. NY, 1945 1st edition. Garth Williams illustrator. Fine in dust jacket. $110-$175. Very Good in dust jacket. $50-$95. Same without dust jacket. $35.
Charlotte's Web. NY, 1952 1st ed. Garth Williams illus. Near VG. $185. Near Fine in dust jacket. Dealer. $150. Auction. $275. Same year, 2nd printing. $20-$60.
The Second Year From the Corner. NY, 1954 1st trade edition. Very Good in dust jacket. $50.
The Points of My Compass. NY, 1962 1st edition. Fine in dust jacket. $40. Very Good in dust jacket. $30.

WHITE, EDWARD L. *Song of the Sirens*. Dutton, 1934 revised edition in dust jacket. $20-$50.

WHITE, HENRY ALEXANDER. *Robert E. Lee and the Southern Confederacy, 1807-1870*. NY, 1897 1st edition. Illustrated. Very Good. $100.

WHITE, LEONARD. *The Jeffersonians*. NY, 1951 1st edition. Good. $20.

WHITE, MINOR (Photographer). *Mirrors, Messages, Manifestations*. NY, 1969 1st ed. VG dust jacket. $165.

WHITE, OWEN. *Them Was the Days*. NY, Minton Balch, 1925 1st edition. $30-$60.
Frontier Mother. NY, 1929. Good-Very Good. $50-$75.

WHITE PINE SERIES OF ARCHITECTURAL MONOGRAPHS. NY, 1915-1928. Vol I, No. 1-Vol XIV, No. 6. A total of 64 issues; not a complete run. Some wear, but Very Good. $100.

WHITE, RAY B. *The Trail of the Desert Sun*. NJ, Pillar of Fire, 1931. Rubbed, spotted cover. $25.

WHITE, STEWART EDWARD. *The Claim Jumpers*. NY, 1901 1st edition. Author's 1st book. Very Good. $40-$60.
The Westerners. G&D, 1901 reprint. Very Good. $8-$10.
The Forest. NY, 1903 1st ed. Very Good-Fine. $15-$20.
The Mountains. NY, 1904 1st edition. Very Fine. $35. Reprint, 1910. Very Good. $25.
The Pass. NY, 1906 1st edition. Fine. $25.
Arizona Nights. McClure, 1907 1st edition. N. C. Wyeth illus. VG in dust jacket. $250. No DJ. $50-$75.
The Mystery. With Samuel Hopkins Adams. NY, 1907 1st edition. Will Crawford illustrator. Very Good. $35.
The Riverman. McClure, 1908 N. C. Wyeth illus. Very Good. $40-$60. Reprint, 1908. VG. $20.
The Sign at Six. Indianapolis, 1912 1st edition. M. Leone Bracker illustrator. Very Good. $35.
The Land of Footprints. New York, 1912. Photos. Hinge poor, o/w poor. $45.
African Camp Fires. Garden City, 1913 1st edition, 1st printing. Very Good. $50.
The Rediscovered Country. Garden City, 1915 1st edition, 1st printing. Very Good. $40.

Lions in the Path. Garden City, 1926 1st edition, 1st printing. Very Good. $50.

WHITE, T. H. *England Have My Bones*. New York, 1936 1st American edition. Fine in very good dust jacket. $65.
Mistress Masham's Repose. NY, 1946. Fritz Eichenberg illustrator. Very Good in dust jacket. $35.

WHITE, TRUMBULL. *Our War With Spain for Cuba's Freedom*, Monarch Books, 1898. Illustrated. G-VG. $16.

WHITE, WILLIAM ALLEN. *The Martial Adventures of Henry and Me*. New York, 1918 1st edition. Tony Sarg illustrator. Very Good. $12-$18.
A Puritan in Babylon. NY, 1938 1st edition. VG. $15.

WHITEHEAD, ALFRED NORTH. *Science and the Modern World*. NY, 1925 1st edition. Very Good. $65.
Adventures of Ideas. NY, 1933 1st American edition. Very Good in torn dust jacket. $50.
Philosophy of Alfred North Whitehead. Northwestern, 1941. Very Good. $28.

WHITEHEAD, DON. *The FBI Story*. New York, 1956. Signed by Hoover. $40.
Border Guard. McGraw Hill, 1963 1st ed. VG in DJ. $14.
The Dow Story-History of Dow Chemical. McGraw Hill, 1968 1st edition. Fine in dust jacket. $16.

WHITEHEAD, JESSUP. *The Steward's Handbook and Dictionary and Guide to Party Catering*. Chicago, 1903 6th edition. Good. $60.

THE WHITE HOUSE COOK BOOK. Hugo Ziemann and Mrs. F. L. Gillette. 1887-1894 edition. $50-$65, 1897 printing. $30-$35. 1905 edition. $25-$30. 1911-1924 printing. $20-$24. 1964 edition. $10-$12. All prices for volumes in very good condition. Deduct for torn, worn or shaken examples. Add to value for fine copies.

WHITER, LEONARD. *Spode, a History of the Family, Factory and Wares From 1733 to 1833*. NY, 1970. Illus. Good-Very Good in dust jacket. $100-$150.

WHITING, GERTRUDE. *Tools and Toys of Stitchery*. NY, 1928. Illustrated. Soiled dust jacket, o/w VG. $100-$150.

WHITLOCK, H. P. and M. L. EHRMANN. *The Story of Jade*. NY, 1949. Illustrated. Good-Very Good. $40-$55.

WHITLOCK, R. *Rare and Extinct Birds of Britain*. London, 1953. Near Fine in dust jacket. $24.

WHITMAN, WALT. *Leaves of Grass*. Boston, 1860-1861 3rd edition. Worn. $125-$200. Philadelphia, 1884. Yellow cloth. $100. Same, with Autobiography. McKay, 1900. Green gilt dec. covers. Good. $28. 1919, Mosher Press,

facsimile of 1855 text. One of 100 copies, unopened. 1st edition, 1st facsimile. Dust jacket slightly browned, o/w Fine. $250. New York, 1919, Doubleday Page. Good. $7. Another, no date. NY, Heritage Press, and London. One of 1,000 copies, signed by Rockwell Kent, illus. In slipcase. VG plus. $175. NY, 1966 Facsimile of 1st ed. Fine in vg slipcase. $25. Halcyon House, 1942. Fine in slipcase. $14.
November Boughs. Philadelphia, 1888. Minor soiling, Good-Very Good. $225-$325. Fair. $90.
Song of Myself. Roycrofters, 1904. Deluxe binding, gilt and red morocco roses. Near Fine. $175 auction.

WHITMAN, WALT (In Magazines). *North American Review.* Jan, 1856. Edward Everett Hale review. "Leaves of Grass." $20-$30.
The Critic. Jan 15, 1881 (1st issue) 1st of Series: "How I Get Around Sixty." $30-$50.
U. S. Review. Apr 1885-Nov 1885 bound vol. "Leaves of Grass" reviewed. Spine cracked. $20.

WHITNEY, MRS. A. D. T. *Just How, a Key to the Cookbooks.* Boston, 1879 1st edition. Bibliographical. VG. $50.

WHITNEY, DR. DANIEL H. *The Family Physician and Guide to Health.* Penn-Yan, NY, 1833. Leather, crude illustrations. Foxing. $125.

WHITNEY, HARRY. *Hunting With the Eskimos.* NY, 1910 1st edition. Very Good. $50-$75.

WHITTEMORE, REED. *Heroes and Heroines.* NY, 1946 1st edition, 1st book. Inscribed. Covers faded. $50.

WHITTIER, JOHN GREENLEAF. *Ballads of New England.* Boston, 1870 1st edition. Near Fine. $45.
The King's Missive. Boston, 1881 1st edition. Good. $20.
The Tent on the Beach and Other Poems. Boston, 1899 1st American edition. Very Good. $25.
Snowbound. Reilly, 1909. John R. Neill illustrator. Very Good-Fine. $40-$65.

WHITTIER, JOHN GREENLEAF (In Magazines). *The Democratic Review.* Aug, 1843. Poem, Hampton Beach. Very Good. $30.
Literary World. Dec, 1877. John Greenleaf Whittier issue. $30-$40.

WHO'S WHO IN BASEBALL. 1939 annual. Good. $25.

WHO'S WHO IN CALIFORNIA, 1958. Moore, revised edition, 1958. Good. $15.

WHO'S WHO IN CHICAGO & ILLINOIS. A. N. Marquis pub., 1945. 8th edition. Fine. $20.

WHO'S WHO IN COLORED AMERICA. Burckel, editor/publisher. 1950 7th edition. $16.

WHO'S WHO IN THE NATION'S CAPITAL, 1923-24. W.W. Publishing Co., 1924 2nd edition. 488 pages. Good-Very Good. $30.

WHY CREMATION IS PREFERABLE TO EARTH BURIAL. All the facts. Boston, 1917. Illustrated. $35.

WHYMPER, ROBERT. *The Manufacture of Confectionery.* New York, 1923. Everything you need to know to run a candy factory. $40.

WICKERSHAM, JAMES. *A Bibliography of Alaskan Literature.* Cordova AK, 1927. $100-$250.
Old Yukon Trails, Washington DC, 1938 1st edition. Good-Very Good. $35-$50.

WICKS, WILLIAM. *Log Cabins: How to Build & Furnish Them.* New York, 1889 1st edition. Very Good. $200. 1904 5th edition. Good. $45.

WIDDIFIELD, HANNAH. *Widdifield's New Cook Book.* 1851. $225-$300.

WIDE-AWAKE. *The Wide-Awake Gift; A Know-Knothing Token for 1855.* J. C. Derby, NY, 1854. $65.

WIENER, NORBERT. *Cybernetics.* NY, 1948 1st edition. Fine, no dust jacket. $200. VG in fair, but rare, DJ. $350.
The Human Use of Human Beings. Boston, 1950 1st ed. Signed, dated 1950. VG in clipped dust jacket. $300.

WIESE, KURT (Illustrator). *Freddy the Pied Piper.* By Walter Brooks. NY, 1946 1st edition. Good. $40.
Freddy the Magician. By Walter Brooks. NY, 1947 1st edition. Good. $40.

WIGGIN, KATE DOUGLAS. *A Summer in a Canon, A California Story.* Boston & NY, 1889. Some soil. $35.
The Village Tower. Boston, 1895. Very Good. $40. Another listed at $10.
The Birds Christmas Carol. Houghton Mifflin, 1886 edition. $10. Cambridge, 1897 edition. $15. 1901 printing (now over 261,000). Fine $25. 1914 printing. VG. $8.
Penelope's Progress. Boston, 1898 1st edition. Good. $10. Very Good. $25. Fine. $35.
Penelope's Irish Experiences. Boston, 1902. C. E. Brock illustrator. Very Good-Fine. $25-$40.
Rebecca of Sunnybrook Farm. Boston, 1903 1st edition, inscribed by author. $125. Unsigned. VG. $40. Another, no inscription. Fair. $14. 1911 Popular Edition. Good. $20. 1910 Grosset & Dunlap reprint. $5. 1959 Random House "Shirley Temple Edition". Fine. $15.
New Chronicles of Rebecca. Boston, 1907 1st ed. F. $40.
Old Peabody Pew. NY, 1907 1st edition. Inscribed. Very Good. $59. Another, not inscribed. $16.
Susanna and Sue. Houghton Mifflin, 1909 1st edition. N. Wyeth illustrator. $25-$45.

Mother Carey's Chickens. NY, 1911. Good. $30.

Bluebeard: a Musical Fantasy. NY, London, 1914 1st edition. Signed with note by author. Very Good. $125.

The Works of Kate Douglas Wiggin. Boston, 1917 10 vols. One of 500 signed, numbered, sets. NF. $400-$500.

Homespun Tales. Boston, 1920. Good. $30.

My Garden of Memory. Boston, New York, 1929. Good-Very Good. $15-$30.

WIGGIN, KATE DOUGLAS & NORA A. SMITH. *The Arabian Nights*. NY, 1909 and 1919 eds. VG. $95-$195. 1921. 12 Maxfield Parrish color plates. Worn cover. $95. 1935 and 1937 editions. VG. $45-$75.

WILBUR, RICHARD. *Ceremony and Other Poems*. NY, 1950 1st edition. Very Good. $25.

Poems, 1943-1956. London, 1957 1st edition. Very Good in dust jacket. $25. Another, signed. $120.

WILCE, J. W. *Football: How to Play It and How to Understand It*. NY, 1923 1st edition. Photographs, diagrams. Near Fine in chipped dust jacket. $75.

WILCOX, ELLA WHEELER. *The Beautiful Land of Nod*. Conkey, 1892. Louise M. Mears illus. Very Good. $15.

WILCOX, R. TURNER. *The Mode in Footwear, from Antiquity to the Present Day*. NY, 1948. Illustrated. Very Good in worn dust jacket. $50.

The Mode in Furs: The History of Furred Costume of the World from the Earliest Times to the Present. NY, 1951. Illustrated. Very Good in worn dust jacket. $50.

Five Centuries of American Costume. Scribners, 1963. Very Good in dust jacket. $25.

The Mode in Costume. Scribners, 1965. DJ. $15-$20.

WILDE, OSCAR. *The Happy Prince and Other Tales*. Boston, 1888 1st American edition. Walter Crane, Jacob Hood illustrators. Rubbed, o/w Good. $75.

The Picture of Dorian Gray. London, 1890 1st edition, 1st issue. Spine head repaired, paper browning. $850. Same, NY, 1890 1st American ed. Paperbound. VG in box. $1,850. Another, Modern Library, 1917 1st ed. Very Good in dust jacket. $250.

The Harlot's House. John Luce, circa 1900 1st edition. Althea Gyles illustrator. Very Good. $75. John Luce Pub., 1910. $35-$70. NY, 1929. John Vassos illustrator. One of 200 copies. Very Good. $200.

A House of Pomegranates. London, 1891 1st edition. Hinges failing, o/w Very Good. $550. Same, Mosher Press, 1913. Very Good. $15.

De Profundis. NY, 1905 1st American edition. $50-$75. NY, 1926 Modern Library. Near Fine. $30.

Salome: A Tragedy in One Act. Heritage Press, 1945. Valenti Angelo illustrator. Cover fade, o/w Very Good. $20. New York, Limited Editions Club, 1938. 2 volumes. Fine in case. $175-$250.

The Satyricon. Hogarth Press, no date. Translated by Wilde. Alexander King illus. 1 of 2,500 copies. VG. $45.

Poems of Oscar Wilde. New York, 1927. Jean de Bosschere illustrator. $30-$65. Same, NY, 1935, Boni. Good. $8. Same, NY, 1937, Boni. Fine. $60.

The Ballad of Reading Gaol. Heritage reprint, 1937. Zhenya Gay illustrator. Fine in slipcase. $23.

WILDER, LAURA INGLALLS. *Little House in the Big Woods*. New York, 1932 1st edition. Helen Sewell illustrator. Very Good. $40.

Farmer Boy. New York, 1933 1st edition. Helen Sewell illustrator. Very Good. $50.

On the Banks of Plum Creek. NY, 1937 1st ed. Helen Sewell, Mildred Boyle illustrators. Cover soiled, o/w VG. $50. Another, no DJ. $10.

By the Shores of Silver Lake. NY, 1939 2nd edition. Helen Sewell, Mildred Boyle illustrators. VG in worn dust jacket. $110. 1946 edition, no dust jacket. $45.

The Long Winter. Harper, 1953. Garth Williams illus. Very Good in chip DJ. $15. 1940 ed., lacks fly leaf. $20. Most Laura Ingalls Wilder 1st editions sell for $35-$45 in very good condition with original dust jackets, and about $25 without jackets.

WILDER, THORNTON. *Cabala*. NY, 1926 1st edition, 1st issue. Author's 1st book. Fine, inscribed, in dust jacket. $600. Same, VG, no dust jacket. $200.

The Woman of Andros. NY, 1930 1st ed. VG in DJ. $45. Fine in chipped dust jacket. $58.

Angel That Troubled the Waters. Coward McCann, 1933. Signed. Very Good in dust jacket. $55.

The Skin of Our Teeth. NY, 1942 1st edition. Reading copy in dust jacket. $60.

The Ides of March. NY, 1948 1st trade edition. Very Good in dust jacket. $17.

Theophilus North. NY, 1973 1st edition. Stain, o/w Very Good in dust jacket. $12.

Our Town. Cordovan Press, 1974. One of 2,000 copies Signed. Fine in slipcase. $125.

WILEY, BELL IRVIN. *The Life of Johnny Reb*. Indianapolis and New York, 1943. $25-$45.

The Plain People of the Confederacy. Baton Rouge, 1944 1st edition. Very Good in dust jacket. $50.

WILKINS, HAROLD T. *Flying Saucers on the Attack*. Citadel, 1954 1st edition. Very Good. $15.

Mysteries of Time and Space. London, 1955. Good. $10.

WILKINS, SIR HUBERT and HAROLD SHERMAN. *Thoughts Through Space*. House-Warven Pub., 1951 1st edition. Very Good in dust jacket. $25.

WILKINS, MARY E. *The Wind in the Rose-Bush and Other Stories*. NY, 1903 1st edition. Peter Newell illustrator. Dec. green cloth. Very Good. $50-$75.

WILKINSON, GERTRUDE. *The Attic Cookbook*. Penguin, 1972 1st edition. Fine in dust jacket. $9.

WILLARD, FRANCES E. *A Wheel Within A Wheel. How I Learned to Ride the Bicycle*. New York, 1895, Revell 1st edition. Fine. $75-$100.

WILLIAMS, A. *A Boy's Books of Pirates and Great Sea Rovers*. NY, 1913. Very Good. $55.

WILLIAMS, BEN AMES. *The Happy End*. Derrydale Press, 1939. One of 1,250 copies. Fine. $125-$175.
Fraternity Village. Boston, 1949 1st edition. DJ illustrated by Andrew Wyeth. Good-Very Good in dust jacket. $45.
Various Titles. BCE, etc., 1940s. Not illustrated. $5 each.

WILLIAMS, CHARLES. *All Hallow's Eve*. NY, 1948 1st edition. Fine in near fine dust jacket. $50.
The Place of the Lion. NY, 1951 1st American edition. Fine in near fine dust jacket. $40.

WILLIAMS & FISHER. *Elements of the Theory & Practice of Cookery*. Toronto, 1902 2nd printing. Good. $20.

WILLIAMS, GARTH (Illustrator). *Stuart Little*. By E. B. White. NY, 1945 1st edition. VG in dust jacket. $125.
In Our Town. By Damon Runyon. NY, 1946 1st edition. Fine in very good dust jacket. $40.
The Tiny Golden Library. By Dorothy Kunhard. NY, 1949 1st edition. 12 books. Very Good. $110.
Charlotte's Web. By E. B. White. NY, 1952 1st edition. Very Good in fair dust jacket. $200.
The Long Winter. By Laura Ingalls Wilder. NY, 1953 1st edition. Very Good in chip dust jacket. $15.

WILLIAMS, HENRY S. *Modern Warfare*. New York, 1915. Very Good. $23.

WILLIAMS, JOEL S. *A Missourian in the Far West*. Carrollton MO, 1906. 72 pages. Red cloth cover. VG. $85.

WILLIAMS, LEONARD. *Illustrative Photography in Advertising*. San Francisco, 1929 1st edition. $25.

WILLIAMS, MARY FLOYD. *History of the San Francisco Committee of Vigilance of 1851*. Berkeley CA 1921. Good-Very Good. $50-$125. Fine. $150.

WILLIAMS, LT. COL. REGINALD. *Fifteenth Army Group History*. Vienna, 1945. 215 pgs. 18 fold-out maps. F. $85.

WILLIAMS, R. R. *The American Hardware Store. A Manual of Approved Methods of Arranging and Displaying Hardware*. NY, 1901 enlarged edition. $75.

WILLIAMS, T. H. *Lincoln and His Generals*. NY, Knopf, 1952 1st edition. Very Good in good dust jacket. $25.

WILLIAMS, TED. *My Turn at Bat*. NY, 1969 1st edition. Very Good in dust jacket. $20-$35.
The Science of Hitting. New York, 1971. Ex-library. Good in dust jacket. $6.

WILLIAMS, TENNESSEE. *The Glass Menagerie*. NY, 1945 1st edition in dust jacket. $75-$150.
A Streetcar Named Desire. NY, 1947 1st edition. Near Fine in Very Good dust jacket. $350-$475.
The Rose Tattoo. New Directions, 1951 1st edition. Good in dust jacket. $60. London, 1954 1st British edition. Fine in clip dust jacket. $100.
Hard Candy. Norfolk VA, 1954 Limited Edition. Near Fine in very good dust jacket. $75-$125.
The Night of the Iguana. NY, 1962 1st edition. Very Good in dust jacket. $75.
Cat on a Hot Tin Roof. NY, 1955 1st ed. in DJ. $50-$100.

WILLIAMS, VALENTINE. *The Fox Prowls*. Boston, 1939 1st edition. Very Fine in dust jacket. $40.

WILLIAMS, WALTER. *State of Missouri, An Autobiography*. State, 1904 1st ed. 592 pgs. Very Good. $35.

THE WILLIAMSBURG COOK BOOK. Colonial Williamsburg Foundation, 1971. Near Fine, no dust jacket. $9.

WILLIAMSON, HAROLD. *Winchester: The Gun That Won the West*. Combat Forces Press, 1952 1st ed. VG. $30.

WILLIAMSON, SCOTT GRAHAM. *The American Craftsman*. NY, 1940. Fine in very good dust jacket. $30.

WILLIS, N. P. *Outdoors at Idlewild*. NY, 1855. Fine. $60.
Forrest Rock and Stream. 1886. 20 engravings by Barlett.. Very Good. $150.
Picturesque American Scenery. Boston, 1887. VG. $75.

WILLS, MAURY. *It Pays to Steal*. NY, 1963 2nd edition. Fine in very good dust jacket. $10.

WILLS, ROYAL B. *Houses for Good Living*. Illustrated. NY, Architectural Book Co., 1940 1st ed. Very Good. $25.

WILMERDING, JOHN. *A History of American Marine Painting*. Boston, 1968 1st edition. Illustrated. Very Good in dust jacket. $100.

WILSON. *San Francisco's Horror of Earthquake, Fire and Famine*. 1906. 500 pgs. Photo illus. Very Good. $35.

WILSON, CAROL GREEN. *Gump's Treasure Trade: A Story of San Francisco*. New York, 1949 3rd printing. Signed by author and Richard Gump. Near Fine. $40.

WILSON, COLIN. *The Outsider*. Boston, 1956 1st American edition. Author's 1st book. Very Good in DJ. $30-$40.

Religion and the Devil. London,1957 1st edition. Very Good in chipped dust jacket. $23.
Ritual in the Dark. Boston, 1960 1st edition. Fine in fine dust jacket. $30.

WILSON, F. E. *Advancing the Ohio Frontier*. Long, 1937. Good-Very Good in dust jacket. $45.

WILSON, HARRY LEON. *Lions of the Lord*. Lothrop, 1903. Rose O'Neill illus. VG. $50.
The Seeker. Doubleday, 1904. VG. $20-$35.
Somewhere in Red Gap. NY, 1916 1st ed. in DJ. $40-$65.
Merton of the Movies. Doubleday, 1922 1st ed. Good. $18.
So This is Golf! NY, 1923. Good. $40.
Cousin Jane. Cosmopolitan, 1925 1st ed. VG in DJ. $25.

WILSON, JOHN LAIRD. *Pictorial History of the Great Civil War*. Danks & Co., 1881 1st edition. Good. $40.

WILSON, JOSEPH T. *The Black Phalanx: A History of the Negro Soldiers of the United States in the Wars of 1775-1812, 1861-1865*, Hartford, 1888 1st edition. Good-Very Good. $175-$350.

WILSON, MITCHELL. *American Science and Invention, A Pictorial History*. New York, 1954. Very Good in dust jacket. $25. Bonanza reprint, same year. Very Good in dust jacket. $15.

WILSON, NEILL & FRANK TAYLOR. *Southern Pacific, The Roaring Story of a Fighting Railroad*. NY, 1952, McGraw-Hill. Good-Very Good. $15-$20.

WILSON, RUFUS ROCKWELL. *Lincoln in Caricature*. New York, 1953. Very Good. $20.

WILSON, WOODROW. *A History of the American People*. NY, 1902, 5 volumes. Good. $40. VG. $75-$100.
George Washington. NY & London, 1896. Howard Pyle illustrator. Backstrip faded. Uncut. $25. 1897. VG. $50.

WILSTACH, FRANK J. *Wild Bill Hickok, The Prince of Pistoleers*. Doubleday, 1926. $12-$24.

WILSTACH, PAUL. *Potomac Landings*. Garden City NY, 1921 1st edition. Good. $35.
Patriots Off Their Pedestals. Bobbs-Merrill, circa 1927. Paper labels. Signed. Very Good. $17.
Mount Vernon. Doubleday, 1916. Very Good. $17. Bobbs-Merrill, 1930. Very Good. $15.

WINANT, LEWIS. *Firearms Curiosa*. NY, 1955 1st edition. One of 1,050 copies. Very Good in dust jacket. $40.

WINCHESTER, CLARENCE (Editor). *Railroad Wonders of the World*. London, 1935. 2 volumes. Illustrated. 1 volume has torn spine, o/w Very Good. $115.

WINCHESTER, JAMES DALY. *Capt. J. D. Winchester's Experience on a Voyage to San Francisco and the Alaskan Gold Fields*. Salem MA, Newcomb & Gauss, 1900. 251 pages, 27 plates. Good-Very Good. $200.

WINCKLER, ELSNER, et. al. *The Techno-Chemical Receipt Book*. (Fireworks, matches, tobacco, etc.) Philadelphia, 1896. Fine and bright. $70-$100.

WIND, HERBERT WARREN. *The Story of American Golf, Its Champions*. Simon & Schuster, 1956 1st edition. Fine in dust jacket. $20.

WINDSOR, EDWARD, DUKE OF. *A King's Story*. NY, 1951 1st American edition. One of 385 copies signed. Fine in slipcase. $450.

WINKLER, J. *Tobacco Tycoon-Story of James Buchanan Duke*. 1942 1st edition. 337 pages. Very Good. $25.

WINN, MARY DAY. *The Macadam Trail. Ten Thousand Miles by Motor Coach*. Knopf, 1931 1st ed. Good. $24.

WINSLOW, JOHN. *Famous Planes and Famous Flights*. Platt & Munk, 1940 1st edition. Fine in dust jacket. $24.

WINSLOW, OLA ELIZABETH. *Harper's Literary Museum*. Harper, NY & London, 1927 1st ed. Good-VG. $20-$25.

WINSOR, KATHLEEN. *Forever Amber*. NY, 1944 1st ed. Author's 1st book. Signed. VG in dust jacket. $100. Macmillan, 1945 12th printing. $5-$10.

WINTER, WILLIAM. *The Life and Art of Edwin Booth*. NY, 1893. Illustrated. Good-Very Good. $55.

WINTERICH, JOHN T. *Books and the Man*. Greenberg, 1929 1st edition. Fine. $165.
Squads Write! A Selection From The Stars and Stripes (WWI). NY, 1931. Illustrated. Fine. $55.
Early American Books and Printing. Boston, 1935 1st edition. Very Good. $35.

WIRT, MILDRED. *The Wishing Well* (Penny Parker no. 8). Cupples & Leon, 1942 1st edition. Last title on list. Very Good in fair dust jacket. $25.
Pirate Brig. Scribners, 1950 1st ed. VG in fair DJ. $20.

WISE ENCYCLOPEDIA OF COOKERY. 1949, Wise & Co. Very Good. $15.

WISSLER, CLARK. *Indian Cavalcade*. NY, 1938 1st edition. Illustrated. Very Good in chip dust jacket. $20.
Indians of the Plains. NY, 1941 3rd ed. Illus. G-VG. $18.

WISTER, OWEN. *The Dragon of Wantley*. Lippincott, 1892. Very Good. $35.

The Virginian. NY, 1902 1st ed. $75-$200. Macmillan reprint, 1902. Good, no DJ. $8. Tan cloth, 11th printing. VG. $40. Grosset & Dunlap reprint, 1904. VG. $10.
Red Men and White. 1895 1st. Remington illus. VG. $25.
Journey in Search of Christmas. NY, 1904 1st edition. Remington illustrator. NF. $100. 1905 printing. VG. $30.

WITKIN, LEE & BARBARA LONDON. *The Photograph Collector's Guide*. Boston, 1979 1st ed. F in DJ. $75-$95.

WITNEY, DUDLEY. *The Lighthouse*. New York Graphic Society, 1975 1st American edition. Fine in DJ. $35-$40.

THE WIT AND HUMOR OF AMERICA. No place, 1911. 10 volumes. Very Good. $45.

WODEHOUSE, P. G. *The Intrusion of Jimmy*. NY, 1910 1st American edition. Edge wear, spine fade, o/w VG. $275. Later reprint, Grosset & Dunlap. Very Good. $10.
Leave It to Psmith. NY, 1924 1st American edition. Very Good plus. $100.
Bill the Conqueror. NY, 1924 1st American ed. NF. $75.
Fish Preferred. NY, 1929 1st American ed. Good. $15.
Very Good, Jeeves. 1st British edition. Good. $75. Same, NY, 1930 1st American ed. Very Good. $20-$30.
Nothng But Wodehouse. Edited by Ogden Nash. NY, 1932 1st edition. Good-Very Good. $25-$30.
Heavy Weather. Boston, 1933 1st American ed. Fine. $45.
Thank You, Jeeves. Boston, 1934 1st American edition. Near Fine in fair dust jacket. $85.
Uncle Fred in the Springtime. NY, 1939 1st. in DJ. $50.
Angel Cake. NY, 1952 1st American edition. Some cover fade, o/w Very Good. $19.
Return of Jeeves. NY, 1954 1st Amer. ed. VG. $25-$50.
Young Men in Spats. NY, 1936. Very Good. $25.
Summer Moonshine. NY, 1937 1st ed. Ex-lib. Fair. $10.
Bertie Wooster Sees It Through. NY, 1955 1st edition. Near Fine in very good dust jacket. $75-$125.

WOLF, DICK. *Fishing Tackle & Techniques*. E. P. Dutton, 1961 1st edition. Fine in dust jacket. $12.

WOLFE, THOMAS. *Look Homeward, Angel*. NY, 1929 1st ed. Author's 1st book. VG-NF in DJ. $800-$1,300. Same. Fine in DJ. Inscribed. $6,000. Another, London, 1930 1st English ed. One of 3,000 copies. Fine in fine DJ. $1,750.
The Web and the Rock. NY, London, 1939 1st edition. Near Fine in dust jacket & slipcase. $200. Same, NY, 1939 in dust jacket. $75-$125.
You Can't Go Home Again. NY, 1940 1st edition. Fine in fine dust jacket. $250. Good-Very Good in DJ. $40-$150.
Of Time and the River. NY, 1935 1st edition. VG, no DJ. $40-$60. Same in Very Good dust jacket. $100-$250. Same year, 7th printing. Very Good, no dust jacket. $12.

WOLFE, TOM. *The Painted World*. NY, Farrar-Strauss, 1975 1st edition. Fine in dust jacket. $37.

WOLFF, MARTITA. *Whistle Stop*. NY, 1941 1st edition. Author's 1st book. Signed. Very Good in DJ. $50.

WOLFF, PAUL (Photographer). *Dr. Paul Wolff's Leica*. NY, 1937. 150 Photos of Berlin Olympics. VG. $30.

WOLFF, WERNER. *Island of Death*. (Easter Island) NY, 1948 1st edition. Photo illustrations by author. Very Good in chip dust jacket. $55.

WOODWORKING, PATTERNMAKING, ETC. I.C.S. Ref. Library Series. Scranton PA, 1901-1905. $10-$20.

WOMEN'S CITY CLUB OF DETROIT RECIPE BOOK. 1946. Spiral bound. Very Good. $12.

WOMAN'S HOME COMPANION COOKBOOK. New York, 1942 1st edition. Very Good in dust jacket. $40. 1950 Revised edition. Very Good. $10-$12.

WOMAN'S INSTITUTE LIBRARY OF COOKING. Scranton PA, 1923. Good. $15.

WONDRISKA, WILLIAM. *The Stop*. NY, 1972 1st edition. Illustrated by author. Very Good in dust jacket. $30.

WOOD, C. J. *Reminiscences of the War*. Union Army sketches. No place, 1880. Very Good. $150.

WOOD, EDWARD. *The Wedding Day in all Ages and Countries*. New York, Harper, 1869 1st American edition. Very Good. $35.

WOOD, H. C. *Nervous Diseases & Their Diagnosis*. Lippincott, 1887 1st edition. Very Good. $110.

WOOD, REV. J. G. *Animal Traits and Characteristics*. London, 1855-1856. Harrison Weir illustrator. Rebound 2nd edition. $95.
The Common Objects of the Country. London, 1858. W. S. Coleman illustrator. Light spotting, foxing. $125.
The Common Objects of the Seashore. London, 1858 2nd edition. G. B. Sowerby woodcuts. Very Good. $105.
Homes Without Hands. NY, 1866. Animal habitations. Heavily illustrated. Covers poor, contents good. $40.
Illustrated Natural History. London, no date, circa 1870. 2 volumes, rebound. Very Good. $155.
Animate Creation. New York, 1885. 3 volume set, chromolithos. Good. $75. Same, 6 volumes. $90.
Our Living World's Edition of Wood's Natural History. 1885. Vol. II. Prang bird plates. $95.

WOOD, MARY C. *Flower Arrangement Art of Japan*. Tuttle, 1962 popular edition. As new, in case. $16.

WOOD, RAY and F. STOKES. *The American Mother Goose*. 1940 2nd printing. Ed Harris illus. G-VG. $15-$20.

WOOD, SYLVESTER. *The Uncivilized Races of Men in All Countries of the World*. Hartford, 1877 1st American ed. 2 vols. Over 1,500 illustrations. Very Good. $100.

WOOD, STANLEY. *Over the Range to the Golden Gate*. Chicago, 1891. Torn map, o/w Very Good. $55. 1901 & 1906 editions. Good. $20-$35. VG-Fine. $50-$75.

WOOD, WALES W. *A History of the 95th Regiment Illinois Infantry*. Chicago,1865 1st edition. $150-$175.

WOOD, WILLIAM. *Captains of the Civil War*. NY, 1921. Gilt pictorial covers. Maps. Very Good. $25-$35.

WOODBURY, C. *The Fire Protection of Mills, etc.* NY, Wiley, 1895 3rd edition. Fine. $100.

WOODBURY, DAVID O. *The Giant Glass of Palomar*. NY, 1939 1st ed. Good. $50. 1940 edition. VG in fair DJ. $20.

WOODBURY, GEORGE. *The Story of a Stanley Steamer*. NY, 1950 1st edition Inscribed. VG in dust jacket. $20.

WOODHOUSE, BARBARA. *Show Dogs*. London, 1959. Very Good in chipped dust jacket. $25.

WOODROW, MRS. WILSON (Nancy). *The Silver Butterfly*. Bobbs-Merrill, 1908 1st edition. H. C. Christy illustrator. Minor foxing, o/w Very Good. $8-$15.

WOODWARD, GEORGE E. *Woodward's Architecture and Rural Art. No. II*. New York, 1868. Good. $60.

WOODWARD, NANCY HYDEN. *The Mariners Cookbook*. Castle Books, 1969. Very Good. $10.

WOODWARD, W. E. *Meet General Grant*. Literary Guild edition, 1928. Good. $15.

WOOLF, VIRGINIA. *The Common Reader*. Hogarth Press, 1925 1st edition. Good. $100.
A Room of One's Own. NY, 1929 1st American edition. Covers sunned, dust jacket darkened. $275.
The Waves. London, 1931 1st edition. Chip dust jacket, spine darkened. Scarce in DJ. $200-$400. Same. 1st Amer. edition. NY, 1931. VG in DJ. $100. Same, no DJ. $25.
Between the Acts. Harcourt, 1941 1st ed. VG in DJ. $65.

WOLLE, MURIEL S. *Bonanza Trail*. Indiana Univ., 1958 3rd edition. 510 pages. Fine in dust jacket. $24.

WOOLLEN, WILLIAM WESLEY. *Biographical & Historical Sketches of Early Indians*. Indianapolis, 1883 1st edition. Cracked hinge, else fine. $48.

WOOLNER, FRANK. *Grouse & Grouse Hunting*. NY, 1973 4th printing. Fine in dust jacket. $16-$24.

WOOLRICH, CORNELL. *The Dancing Detective*. Lippincott, 1946 1st edition. Near Fine in very good DJ. $250.
Dead Man Blues. Lippincott, 1948 1st edition. Fine in very good dust jacket. $250.
Hotel Room. NY, 1958 1st ed. Fine in dust jacket. $65.
Nightwebs. NY, 1971 1st edition. Fine in dust jacket. $65.

WOOLWORTH, F. W. *50 Years of F. W. Woolworth*. NY, 1929. Good-Very Good. $15-$20.
Woolworth's First 75 Years. NY, 1954. Good-VG. $30.

WORLD TREASURY OF CHILDREN'S LITERATURE. World Pub., 1946. Good. $30.

WORLD'S FAIR. *Official Souvenir Book, New York World's Fair, 1939*. Ringbound, loose cover. $28.

THE WORLD'S CONGRESS OF REPRESENTATIVE WOMEN. No place, 1894. 2 volumes. Very Good. $50.

WORSHAM, J. *One of Jackson's Foot Cavalry: 1861-1865*. 1912, 1st edition. Very Good. $45.

WORTHAM, LOUIS J. *A History of Texas-From Wilderness to Commonwealth*. Wortham, 1924 1st edition. Volume V from set. ½ leather, Very Good. $16.

WOUK, HERMAN. *The Caine Mutiny*. NY, 1951 1st edition. Very Good in very good dust jacket. $100. Near Fine in chip dust jacket. $150. Book Club Edition, 1951. Very Good in worn dust jacket. $16.
Marjorie Morningstar. New York, 1955 1st edition. Fine in dust jacket. $150.
Youngblood Hawke. Doubleday, 1962 1st edition. Fine in dust jacket. $40.
The Winds of War. Boston, 1971 1st edition. Very Good in dust jacket. $25.

WPA GUIDES. (Also see Federal Writers Project.) First editions of *State Guides* in good to very good condition with maps & dust jackets intact. Average $20-$35. Least populated states bring highest prices: *Alabama*. $60. *Delaware*. $80. *Iowa*. $75. *Nebraska*. $80. *North Dakota*. $150. *Oklahoma*. $65. *United States One, Maine to Florida*. $35. All are circa late 1930s.
Oklahoma. 1941 2nd edition. Ex-library. $8.
Oregon. 1940 1st edition. Map in pocket. $15.
Rochester and Monroe County, NY. 1937 1st edition. 3 large maps. Fine. $28.
San Francisco. Hastings House, 1947 2nd edition. Maps. Fine. $10.
Washington, City and Capital. American Guide Series. 1937 1st edition. 3 maps. Very Good. $38.

WREN, PERCIVAL C. *Beau Geste*. Grosset & Dunlap, 1926. Photoplay edition. Good. $8.
Beau Ideal. Stokes, 1928 1st edition. VG in good DJ. $20.

Rough Shooting. London, 1938 1st edition. Near Very Good in dust jacket. $50.
Port of Missing Men. Macrae Smith, 1943 1st American edition. Fine in dust jacket. $20.

WRIGHT AND DITSON'S LAWN TENNIS GUIDE FOR 1895. Boston, 1895. Paperbound, Illus. Fair to good. $35.

WRIGHT, BLANCHE F. *The Real Mother Goose*. Rand McNally, 1944. Illus. by author. Good. $12.

WRIGHT, CALEB E. *Frances Slocum the Lost Sister*. PA, R. Baur, 1889 1st edition. Fine. $35.

WRIGHT, DARE. *The Lonely Doll*. NY, 1957. Photo illus. of dolls, bears, toys, etc. $35.
The Doll & the Kitten. New York, 1960 4th edition. Very Good in dust jacket. $30-$40.
The Lonely Doll Learns a Lesson. NY, 1961. Issued without dust jacket. Very Good. $30.

WRIGHT, E. W. *Lewis & Dryden's Marine History of the Pacific Northwest*. Portland, 1895. Good-Very Good. $110 auction. (est. $200-$300).

WRIGHT, FRANK LLOYD. *An Autobiography*. NY, 1932 1st edition. Very Good. $250. 1943 Revised edition. Very Good in chipped dust jacket. $125-$150.
The Disappearing City. NY, 1932 1st edition. VG. $175.
When Democracy Builds. University of Chicago Press, 1945 1st edition. Ex-library. Good. $6.
Genius and the Mobocracy. NY, 1949 1st edition. Soiled cover, o/w Good plus. $65. Revised edition. 1971. Fine in repaired dust jacket. $50.
The Future of Architecture. NY, 1953 1st edition. Very Good in chip dust jacket. $45-$75.
The Natural House. NY, 1954 1st edition. Many illus. Very Good in chip dust jacket. $75. Fine, no dust jacket. $95. 1970 7th edition. Fine. $8.
An American Architecture. NY, 1955 1st edition. Edited by Edgar Kaufmann. 250 illustrations. VG in chip DJ. $75.
A Testament. Horizon Press, 1957. Fair, tattered dust jacket. Good-Very Good. $50.
Architecture: Man in Possession of His Earth. NY, 1962 1st edition. Fine in dust jacket. $95.

WRIGHT, FRANK LLOYD (In Magazines). *House Beautiful*. Nov, 1955. Frank Lloyd Wright issue. Good. $65.
Arizona Highways. Feb, 1956. Article by. Fine. $20.
Esquire. Feb, 1958. Photo essay about, plus son's memoirs. Very Good. $17.

WRIGHT, HAROLD BELL. *That Printer of Udell's*. Chicago, 1903 1st edition. Author's 1st book. John C. Gilbert illustrator. Very Good. $40-$60. Fine. $100-$125.
Shepherd of the Hills. No place, 1907 1st edition. Weak hinge. Good. $75.

Their Yesterdays. Book Supply, 1912 1st ed. Fine in good DJ. $32. A. L. Burt, 1912 rpt. Fine, no DJ. $12. Fair. $5.
The Winning of Barbara Worth. Chicago, 1911 1st edition. F. G. Cootes illustrator. Very Good in dust jacket. $75. No dust jacket. $25. Reprint, same year A. L. Burt. 512 pages. Cootes illustrator. Fine, no DJ. $12. Grosset & Dunlap, 1966 reprint. Very Good in DJ. $8.
The Uncrowned King. Book Supply, 1910 1st. VG. $40.
The Eyes of the World. Chicago, 1914 1st ed. Fine. $14. Another, Book Supply, 1914. VG. $7. Fine, no DJ. $15.
Re-creation of Brian Kent. Book Supply, 1919 1st ed. Fine, no dust jacket. $15.
When A Man's a Man. Book Supply, 1915 1st edition. Fine, no dust jacket. $15.
Helen of the Old House. Appleton, 1921 1st ed. Very Good. $45. 3rd edition. Very Good, burgundy cloth. $15.
The Mine With the Iron Door. No place, 1923 1st edition in DJ. $25-$50. Same, no dust jacket. $12-$15.
Exit. NY, 1930 1st ed. VG in dust jacket. $28-$75. Same with no dust jacket. $17-$25.
God and the Groceryman. Triangle, 1942 reprint. Fine in dust jacket. $13.
Ma Cinderella. Burt, 1932 reprint. Very Good. $18.

WRIGHT, JULIA M. *The Complete Home. Encyclopedia of Domestic Affairs*. Philadelphia, 1879. Good-Very Good. $50-$75. Fine. $100.

WRIGHT, MABEL OSGOOD and ELLIOTT COUES. *Citizen Bird*. Macmillan, 1898 2nd printing. Good. $45.

WRIGHT, RICHARD. *Native Son*. New York, 1940 1st edition. Good plus. $50-$75.
Black Boy. NY, 1945 1st edition. Good-Very Good. $20-$35. Fine in very good dust jacket. $50.
Black Power. NY, 1954 1st edition. Very Good in DJ. $45.
White Man, Listen! NY, 1957 1st edition. VG in DJ. $60.

WRIGHT, RICHARDSON. *Hawkers and Walkers in Early America*. Philadelphia, 1927 1st ed. Illus. Very Good. $10.
The Gardener's Bed Book. Philadelphia, 1929. VG. $15.
Flower Prints & Their Makers. New York, 1948. Illustrated. Very Good. $75.

WRIGHT, ROBERT. *Dodge City. The Cowboy Capital and the Great Southwest*. Undated reprint of 1913 1st edition. $50-$95.

WRIGHT, SOLOMON A. *My Rambles as East Texas Cowboy, Hunter, Fisherman, Tie-Cutter*. Austin, Texas Folklore Society, 1942. Very Good. $60.

WRIGHT, THOMAS. *The Life of Charles Dickens*. NY, Scribners, 1936. Good. $35.

WRIGHT, WILLIAM. *The Oil Regions of Pennsylvania*. NY, 1865 1st edition. Spine ends worn, o/w Very Good. $100.

WRIGHT, WILLIAM. *The Grizzly Bear*. NY, 1913 and 1922 eds. Photo illus. Good-VG. $35-$75.

WRIGHTMAN, W.P.D. *The Growth of Scientific Ideas*. Yale, 1953. Illustrated. Very Good. $18.

WURLITZER, CENTENNIAL COOK BOOK. 1856-1956. No place, 1956. Near Fine. $45.

WYCHERLEY, GEORGE. *Buccaneers of the Pacific*. Indianapolis, 1928. Spine, cover wear, o/w Very Good. $35.

WYETH, ANDREW. *Brandywine*. No place, 1941 1st ed. Fine in dust jacket. $40.
Four Seasons. NY, 1962. Very Good-Fine. $50-$95.
Wyeth at Kuerner's. No place, 1976 1st edition. Fine in dust jacket, boxed. $60.

WYETH, ANDREW (Illustrator). *The Sea Bird Island*. By Agnes C. Foote. Boston, 1935. Jacket, illustrated by Wyeth. Signed by Wyeth. Fine. $300.

WYETH, JOHN A. *The Life of General Nathan Bedford Forrest*. New York, 1899 1st edition. Good-Very Good. $95-$150.

WYETH, NEWELL C. (Illustrator). *Arizona Nights*. By Stewart Edward White. McClure, 1907 1st edition. Very Good in chipped dust jacket. $250. No DJ. $50-$75.
Hiawatha. By Henry Wadsworth Longfellow. Boston, 1911. Very Good. $195.
Little Shepherd of Kingdom Come. By John Fox. NY, 1931. 14 color plates. Very Good. $105-$125.

Anthology of Children's Literature. Boston, 1940. 15 color plates. Very Good in dust jacket. $125.
The Black Arrow. By Robert Louis Stevenson. NY, Scribners, 1916. 14 color plates. $150.

WYLER, SEYMOUR. *The Book of Old Silver*. NY, various subsequent editions. 1940-1973. Good-VG. $15-$25.

WYLIE, ELINOR. *Nets to Catch the Wind*. NY, 1921 1st edition. Author's 1st book. Very Good. $60-$100.
The Orphan Angel. NY, 1926. Limited edition, signed. Fine in box. $175.
The Venetian Glass Nephew. New York, 1928 trade edition. Very Good. $25-$35.

WYMAN, ARTHUR L. *Los Angeles Times Cook Book No. 3*. California, Spanish and Mexican Dishes. Los Angeles, 1911. Very Good. $75.

WYMAN, WALKER D. *Wild Horse of the West*. Caldwell ID, 1946. Very Good in good dust jacket. $18.

WYNDHAM, JOHN. *The Day of the Triffids*. Garden City NY, 1951 1st edition. Fine in dust jacket. $30. Doubleday, Book Club edition, 1951. Very Good, no dust jacket. $13. Same. London, 1951 1st English edition. Fine in DJ. $125.
The Kraken Wakes. London, 1953 1st ed. VG in DJ. $15.
The Midwich Cuckoos. NY, 1957 1st edition. Very Good-Near Fine in dust jacket. $50-$120.

WYSS, JOHANN. *Swiss Family Robinson*. Grosset & Dunlap, 1949. Junior Library. Lynd Ward illustrator. Very Good. $25.

Y

THE YACHTSMAN'S ANNUAL GUIDE. Boston, 1891. 180 pages of sea charts and ads. $150.

YAGGY and HAINES. *Museum of Antiquity*. 1881 to 1884 editions. Very Good. $35-$45 each.

YANNER, F. M. *Yanner Baking*. 1894. $35-$50.

THE YANKEE COOK BOOK: A NEW SYSTEM OF COOKERY. Anonymous. Dick & Fitzgerald, circa 1860s. Worn. $40.

YARDLEY, HERBERT. *American Black Chamber*. Indianapolis, 1931 1st ed. Good-VG in dust jacket. $25-$35.
The Education of a Poker Player. NY, 1957. Very Good in dust jacket. $15.

YATES, GEORGE W. *Body That Wasn't Uncle*. Morrow, 1939 1st edition. in dust jacket. $35-$65. Triangle, 1941 2nd edition. $8-$12.

YATES, RAYMOND F. *ABC of Television or Seeing by Radio*. NY, 1929. Illustrated. Very Good. $65.
Antique Fakes and Their Detection. New York, 1950. Illustrated. VG in worn dust jacket. $25. Gramercy ed. $10.
Under Three Flags. Henry Stewart, 1958 1st edition. Fine in dust jacket. $15.
Boys' Book of Rockets. Harpers, 1947. G-VG. $25-$35.

YATES, RICHARD. *Revolutionary Road*. Little Brown, 1961 1st edition. Author's 1st book. In DJ. $125-$200.

YBARRA, T. R. *Young Man of Caracas*. NY, 1941 1st edition in dust jacket. $15-$25.

YEAGER, BUNNY. *How I Photograph Nudes*. NY, 1965. Very Good in dust jacket. $20.

YEARBOOKS. *College Yearbooks of the 1900s* are often found in the $15-$25 range unless they bear a celebrity autograph.

YEARNS, WILFRED B. *The Confederate Congress*. Univ. of Georgia Press, 1960 1st ed. Very Good in DJ. $23.

YEARY, MAMIE. *Reminiscences of the Boys in Gray*. Dallas, 1912 1st ed. Very Good-Fine. $150-$275.

YEATS, WILLIAM BUTLER. *Poems*. London, 1895 1st trade edition. Very Good. $295. Same, Boston, Copland, 1895. $200. London, 1904 4th edition. $75-$100.
The Shadowy Waters. London, 1900 1st edition. Signed. Good. $45.
The Green Helmet and Other Poems. New York, 1912. Very Good. $50.
The Land of Heart's Desire. Mosher Press, 1906 5th edition. One of 950 copies. Spine rubbed, otherwise Very Good. $23.
Reveries Over Childhood. NY, 1916 1st ed. $50-$100.
Plays for Dancers. NY, 1921 1st American edition. Edmund Dulac illustrator. VG in chip dust jacket. $150.
The Winding Stair and Other Poems. London, 1933 1st edition. Very Good-Fine in dust jacket. $250-$375.
Last Poems and Plays. New York, 1940 1st edition. Very Good in dust jacket. $125.
Later Poems. Macmillan, 1924 1st American edition Very Good in dust jacket. $300. London, 1922 1st edition. One of 1,500. Green cloth in dust jacket. Good-VG. $350-$375.

YEE, CHIANG. *The Silent Traveller in San Francisco*. Norton, 1964 1st edition. Near Fine in dust jacket. $25.

YERKES, ROBERT. *Psychological Examining in the U. S. Army*. Wash. D.C., 1921 1st ed. Ex-library. $100-$125.

YERKES, ROBERT M. and ADA W. YERKES. *The Great Apes*. Yale University Press, 1929 1st edition. Photo illustrations. Fine. $200.

YLLA. *Two Little Bears*. NY, 1954 1st edition. Photos by author. Fine in dust jacket. $30.
Dogs. London, 1949. Photos by author. VG in DJ. $20.

YOAKUM, HENDERSON. *History of Texas 1685-1846*. NY, Redfield, 1856 1st ed., 2nd printing. VG. $300-$500.

YODER, ROBERT M. *Saturday Evening Post Carnival of Humor*. Prentice Hall, 1958 edition. VG in DJ. $16-$20.

YOGANANDA, PARAMAHANSA. *Whispers From Eternity*. No place, 1929 2nd edition. Ex-library. Signed, inscribed. $65.
Autobiography of a Yogi. NY, 1946 1st edition. Good plus. $85. Same, 4th edition. Very Good. $25.
Science of Religion. Los Angeles, 1957. Near VG. $15.

YONGE, CHARLOTTE M. *The Little Duke*. NY, 1927. Marguerite de Angeli illustrator. Very Good. $35.
Book of Golden Deeds. Thomas Nelson, no date, Good-Very Good. $15-$25.
Unknown to History. Harper, circa 1927. VG. $30.

YOST, KARL. *Charles M. Russell, The Cowboy Artist*. Pasadena, 1948 1st edition. One of 500 copies. $90-$100.
A Bibliography of the Published Works of Charles M. Russell. University of Nebraska Press, 1971 1st edition in dust jacket. $60-$80.

YOST, NELLIE *Buffalo Bill - His Family, Friends, Fame, Failures*. Swallow, 1979 1st ed. Photos. Fine, no DJ. $15.

YOUATT, WILLIAM. *On The Structure and the Diseases of Horses*. New York, Orange Judd, 1883. Foxing, o/w Very Good. $45.
Youatt's Treatment & Diseases of the Horse. No place, 1880. Good. $45.

YOUNG AMERICA'S COOK BOOK. NY, 1949 edition. Good plus. $18.

YOUNG, ANDREW. *Wayne County, Indiana. From Its First Settlement to the Present*. Young, 1872. VG. $90.

YOUNG, ANN ELIZA. *Wife No. 19, or the Story of a Life in Bondage*. Dustin Gilman, 1876 1st edition. Poor, spine chipped. $28.

YOUNG, ART. *Hell Up to Date*. Chicago, 1893. Illustrated by author. Very Good. $100.
Art Young's Inferno. NY, 1934 1st edition. Good. $60.
Art Young, His Life and Times. NY, 1939 1st edition. Near Fine in very good dust jacket. $45.

YOUNG, CHIC. *Blondie & Dagwood in Footlight Folly*. Dell, 1947 1st edition. Paperback. $20-$30.

YOUNG, CLARENCE (Edward Stratemeyer). *The Motor Boys Across the Plains*. NY, 1907 1st edition. Illustrated. Very Good. $15.
Motor Boys After a Fortune. NY, Cupples & Leon, 1912. Scarce in dust jacket. $25.
The Motor Boys Series was launched in 1906 by the Stratemeyer syndicate. The series was an immediate success and didn't slow down for 20 years. It went through 22 titles, 35 editions and sold 5 million copies.

YOUNG, DESMOND. *Rommel, the Desert Fox*. NY, Harper, 1950 1st. VG in DJ. $15-$25. Same, no DJ. $10.

YOUNG, E. R. *Stories from Indian Wigwams and Northern Campfires*. NY, 1893 1st ed. Good-Very Good. $40-$60.
By Canoe and Dog Train Among Cree and Salteaux Indians. London, 1895. Very Good. $35.

Three Boys in the Wild Northland. NY, 1896 1st ed. Illus. Pictorial cover. $100 up. Same, Charles Kelly, 1898. J. E. Laughlin illus. Gilt-dec. cover. $75-$95.

YOUNG, GORDON R. *Savages*. NY, Doubleday, 1921 1st ed. Good-VG. $20-$35.

YOUNG, HARRY. *Hard Knocks: A Life Story of the Vanishing West*. Portland and Chicago, 1915. $40-$60.

YOUNG, HAZEL. *The Working Girl Must Eat*. Boston, 1938 1st edition. Spiral bound Very Good in DJ. $18.
The Working Girl's Own Cook Book. Boston, 1948 1st edition. Very Good in dust jacket. $13.

YOUNG, JAMES HARVEY. *The Medical Messiahs*. Princeton Univ. Press, 1969 2nd printing. VG in DJ. $10.
The Toadstool Millionaires: A Social History of Patent Medicine in America. Princeton Univ. Press, 1974 2nd edition. (Original 1961) Near Fine. $25.

YOUNG, JOHN P. *San Francisco: A History of the Pacific Coast Metropolis*. 2 volumes. Limited ed. San Francisco, S. J. Clarke, 1912. Very Good. $165 auction.
Journalism in California. San Francisco, 1915 1st ed. Very Good. $50-$80.

YOUNG, JOHN RUSSELL. *Around the World with General Grant*. No place, 1879. 2 vols. ½ leather. $50-$75.

YOUNG, MARGUERITE. *Prismatic Ground*. NY, Macmillan, 1937 1st ed. Signed by author. Fine, no DJ. $55.
Angel in the Forest - A Fairy Tale. NY, Reynal-Hitch, 1945 1st American ed. Fine in Very Good dust jacket. $55. Scribners, 1966. Fine in DJ. $25.
Miss Makintosh My Darling. NY, 1965 1st edition. Very Good in dust jacket. $20-$30.

YOUNG, PAUL H. *Making and Using the Dry Fly*. Birmingham, 1934. Very Fine. $300.

YOUNG, S. H. *Alaska Days with John Muir*. NY, 1915. Very Good to Fine. $30-$45.

YOUNG, S. P. *The Wolf in North American History*. Caxton, 1946. Near Fine. $47.
Other titles in Animal Series. Washington DC, 1940s, 1950s. Very Good 1st editions. $30-$45 each.

THE YOUNG WIFE'S COOK BOOK. No place, 1857. Good. $95-$135.

YOUNGBLOOD, CHARLES. *Adventures of Chas. L. Youngblood During Ten Years on the Plains*. Indianaa, 1882 1st ed. Very Good. $250-$275.
Mighty Hunter. The Adventures of Chas. L. Youngblood. Chicago, 1890 rpt. of 1882 ed., on cheap pulp stock. $195.

Z

ZACHARIAS, E. M. *Secret Missions (WWII)*. No place, 1946 1st edition. Signed. As new in fair dust jacket. $35.

ZAEHMSDORF, JOSEPH. *The Art of Bookbinding*. London, 1880. Woodcut illus. Good. $95-$125. Third edition, 1897. Color plate illus. $100.

ZAFFO, GEORGE. *Big Book of Real Airplanes*. Grosset and Dunlap, 1951. Illustrated by author. G-VG. $16-$30.

ZAHARIAS, BABE DIDRIKSON. *This Life I've Led*. NY, 1955 1st edition in dust jacket. $25.

ZANGWILL, ISRAEL. *The Master*. NY, 1895 1st edition. Gilt dec. covers. Very Good. $30.
Children of the Ghetto. NY, 1896. Good. $28.

ZAVALLA, JUSTO. *The Canning of Fruits & Vegetables: Based on Methods Used in California*. NY, 1920. Photo illustrations. Good-Very Good. $20.

ZELAZNY, ROGER. *Lord of Light*. Doubleday, 1967 1st edition. Marred endpapers and library stamps. Good-Very Good in dust jacket. $50.

ZERANSKA, ALINA. *The Art of Polish Cooking*. Doubleday, 1968 reprint. Very Good in dust jacket. $9.

ZERBE, JEROME (Photographer). *Happy Times*. No place, 1973 1st edition. Text by Brendan Gill. Fine in fine dust jacket. $45.

ZERN, ED. *To Hell With Fishing*. NY, 1945 1st edition, 1st printing. Fine in fine dust jacket. $30.
To Hell With Hunting. NY, 1946. Fine in fine DJ. $25.
How to Catch Fishermen. NY, 1951. Fine in good DJ. $35.

ZIEBER, EUGENE. *Heraldry in America*. Philadelphia, 1909. Very Good. $95.

ZIEL, RON. *The Twilight of Steam Locomotives*. Grosset & Dunlap, 1963. Illus. Very Good. $18.

ZIEMANN, HUGO and MRS. F. GILLETTE. *The Whitehouse Cook Book*. 1887-1894 ed. $50-$65. 1897 printing. $30-$35. 1905 edition. $25-$30. 1909 enlarged edition. $35. 1911-1924 printing. $20-$24. 1964 edition. $10-$12.

ZILBOORG, GREGORY. *The Medical Man and the Witch*. Baltimore, 1935 1st edition. $45.
A History of Medical Psycholology. NY, 1941 1st edition. Fine. $40-$65. Fair. $20.
The Psychology of the Criminal Act and Punishment. NY, 1954 1st edition. Very Good. $30.

ZIM, HERBERT. *Air Navigation*. NY, 1943. F in DJ. $30.
Rockets & Jets. Harcourt, 1945. Illustrated. VG. $16.

ZIMMERMAN, A. A. *Points for Cyclists with Training*. England, 1893. First English edition. Very Good. $125.

ZIMMERMAN, A. A. and C. H. POPE. *The Development and Growth of the Rattle of Rattlesnakes*. Chicago, 1948. Signed by both authors. $28.

ZIMMERMAN, ARTHUR. *Francisco de Toledo*. Caldwell, 1938 1st edition. VG-Fine in dust jacket. $16-$25.

ZIMMERMAN, O. B. *Internal Combustion Engines & Tractors*. Intl Harvester, 1919 4th ed. VG. $15-$20.

ZIMMERMAN, PAUL. *The Los Angeles Dodgers*. Coward McCann, 1960 1st ed. Very Good-Fine in DJ. $15-$25.

ZISTEL, ERA. *The Golden Book of Cat Stories*. Ziff Davis, 1946. Very Good in dust jacket. $15.

ZITTLE, CAPTAIN JOHN H. *Correct History of the John Brown Invasion*. Hagerstown, 1905 1st ed. G-VG. $95.

ZOGBAUM, RUFUS F. *Horse, Foot and Dragoons: Sketches of Army Life*. New York, 1888 1st edition. Illustrated. Very Good. $250.

ZORNOW, WILLIAM. *Kansas. A History of the Jayhawk State*. Norman OK, 1957 1st edition. VG in DJ. $30.

ZURIER. *The Firehouse; An Architectural and Social History*. New York, 1982. Very Good. $35.

ZWEIG, ARNOLD. *The Case of Sergeant Grischa*. NY, 1928 1st American ed. Very Good in good dust jacket. $28.

ZWEIG, STEFAN. *Mental Healers*. (Mesmer, Eddy, Freud). NY, 1932 1st ed in English. Good to VG. $40.

NO AUTHOR?

A hundred years ago, a newly published book in London stretched for 829 pages to list over 41,450 books and pamphlets whose authors had sought anonymity over the centuries. Most of these publicity-shy scribes feared political or social repercussions.

Many of the same reasons have made American writers apprehensive since Colonial times, and today knowledgeable bookhunters know better than to toss aside any unattributed book from the early 1800s. It could be worth hundreds of dollars.

Here are 25 titles to watch for:

1. *AB-SA-RA-KA*. Philadelphia, 1868.
   Mrs. Henry B. Carrington. $100-$250.

2. *The Adventures of Robin Day*. Philadelphia. 1839. 2 volumes.
   Robert Montgomery Bird. $200-$350.

3. *The Adventures of Timothy Peacock, Esquire*. Middlebury VT. 1835.
   Daniel Pierce Thompson. $400-$500.

4. *The Adventures of a Yankee*. Boston, 1831.
   John Ledyard. $325-$425.

5. *Altowan: or Incidents of Life and Adventure in the Rocky Mountains*. New York, 1846.
   Sir William D. Stewart. $500-$850.

6. *The American Cruiser*. Boston, 1846.
   Capt. George Little. $120-$140.

7. *The American Shooter's Manual*. Phil.,1827.
   Jesse Kester. $2,000-$3,000.

8. *Atalantis*. New York, 1832.
   William Gilmore Simms. $350-$750.

9. *The Autocrat of the Breakfast Table*. Boston, 1858. Oliver Wendell Holmes. $500-$600.

10. *A Biographical Note of Commodore Jesse D. Elliott*. Philadelphia. 1835.
    Russell Jarvis. $125-$150.

11. *A Book of Commandments for the Govt. of the Church of Christ*. Independence MO, 1833.
    Joseph Smith, Jr. $25,000-$30,000.

12. *Border Beagles: A Tale of Mississippi*. Philadelphia, 1840.
    William Gilmore Simms. $300-$400.

13. *A Brief Description of Western Texas*. San Antonio.
    W. G. Kingsubry. $900-$1,500.

14. *The Brothers: A Tale of the Fronde*. NY, 1835. 2 volumes.
    Henry William Herbert. $250-$300.

15. *Calavar: or the Knight of the Conquest*. Philadelphia, 1834. 2 volumes.
    Robert Montgomery Bird. $350-$450.

16. *California Illustrated by a Returned Californian*. New York, 1852.
    J. M. Letts. $550-$850.

17. *California Sketches, With Recollections of the Gold Mines*. Albany NY, 1850.
    Leonard Kip. $850-$1,000.

18. *Captain Smith and Princess Pocahontas: An Indian Tale*. Philadelphia, 1805.
    John Davis. $2,000-$2,500.

19. *Carl Werner, An Imaginative Story*. New York, 1839. 2 volumes.
    William Gilmore Simms. $350-$450.

20. *Castle Dismal: or, the Bachelor's Christmas*. New York, 1844.
    William Gilmore Simms. $250-$350.

21. *The Child's Botany*. Boston, 1828.
    Samuel G. Goodrich. $100-$175.

22. *A Christmas Gift From Fairy Land*. New York, 1838.
    James Kirk Paulding. $200-$250.

23. *College Musings: or, Twigs from Parnassus*. Tuscaloosa AL, 1833.
    William Russell Smith. $750-$800.

24. *Count Julian: or, the Last Days of the Goth*. Baltimore, 1845.
    Walter Savage Landor. $350-$450.

25. *Cromwell: An Historical Novel*. New York, 1838. 2 volumes.
    William Henry Herbert. $200-$350.

For your convenience we have cross indexed these titles alphabetically within this guide.

OLD MAGAZINES

Harvard University realized the importance of magazines in relation to popular culture when they commissioned Frank Luther Mott's *History of American Magazines* in the late 1920s. The huge five-volume work was completed in 1968.

Three other important references covering the universe of older periodicals are: *Magazines in the United States* by James P. Wood, 1971; *American Magazines 1890-1940* by Dorey Schmidt, 1979; and the five-volume *Union List of Serials* published by H. W. Wilson, in 1965, which catalogs the magazine collections of every major library in the country.

Between 1820 and 1860 more than 1,000 new magazines were launched—many by entrepreneurs who had more money than editorial talent. Not surprisingly, most of these titles died quickly and quietly. Others, like *Godeys* and *American Ladies* merged and prospered by combining fashion, music, cooking and literature departments in a single publication; at a subscription rate of only $3 per year.

Other survivors of the period—which are quite collectible today—were *Graham's Magazine of Literature and Art* (1840), *Peterson's Magazine* (1842), *Harper's Monthly* (1850), *Gleason's Pictorial Drawing-Room Companion* (1851), *Frank Leslie's Illustrated Weekly* (1855), *Harpers Weekly* (1857) and *Harpers Bazaar* (1867).

These journals endured because they appealed to wide markets and hired the best writers, editors and illustrators available.

As subscriptions mushroomed advertisers gobbled up all available space to hawk everything from newly-invented pedal sewing machines to shower-baths and bust-developers. Those wildly imaginative ads, combined with flowery Victorian prose, hand-colored fashion prints and fine wood engravings, are what make early magazines so desirable today.

As magazines progressed into the 20th century in-depth news reporting evolved, and photography added documentation to cold print. During this period, magazines such as *The Saturday Evening Post*, *Country Gentleman*, *McCalls* and *Woman's Home Companion* grew by leaps and bounds. By the 1920s *Pictorial Review* and *Literary Digest* had also joined the top producers in advertising income, with gross ad sales of nearly $7,000,000 a year.

Children and college students were employed as delivery people and subscription salesmen. *The Youth's Companion*—with a record-breaking circulation of 500,000 at the turn of the century—published an annual "Premiums Issue", which was a huge folio filled with illustrations of toys, sporting goods and housewares offered to readers for signing up new subscribers.

Cover artists and story illustrators such as Winslow Homer, Frederic Remington, Jessie Wilcox Smith, Arthur Rackham, Charles Dana Gibson, Maxfield Parrish, Howard Chandler Christy, Harrison Fisher, James Montgomery Flagg, N. C. Wyeth, Norman Rockwell and J. C. Leyendecker became famous through the medium of magazines and have become household names in the field of collecting.

Today the fact that the first published writings of many famous authors (including such luminaries as Noah Webster, Ben Franklin, Edgar Allan Poe, Horace Greeley, Harriet Beecher Stowe and John Greenleaf Whittier) initially appeared in periodicals has become widely recognized. A new breed of "first edition" collectors is actively seeking these issues.

"To break, or not to break." That is the question. The art of clipping old magazines has developed to a degree which never could have happened to traditional books. Many magazine values can easily be tripled or quadrupled by clipping.

By contrast, a book loses much of its worth if the dust jacket is missing, a page torn, or a plate removed. But a magazine often brings much more when taken apart than if left intact. The cover can be sold to a decorator, the advertising to a collector, the illustrations to a third party, and various articles to a fourth, fifth or sixth customer.

Who else buys old magazines or pieces of them? Antique dealers, picture framers, editors, writers, publishers, film-makers, historians, teachers...and people with birthdays that match cover dates.

If you have attended any good-sized flea market or antique show recently you have probably seen entire booths filled with matted or shrink-wrapped magazine covers and full page ads devoted to trains, planes, automobiles, babies, children, toys, Coca Cola, Cream of Wheat, Campbells Soup, Hires Root Beer, Jello, Planters Peanuts, paper dolls, RCA Victor, Winchester Arms, fashions, food, fountain pens, furniture, fishing lures, houseware, hardware, carpenter tools, tobacco products and hundreds of other graphics related to whatever antiques or collectibles happen to be in vogue. Prices for attractively packaged pages range from five dollars for a 1930s Lucky Strike ad to fifty dollars for a full color Maxfield Parrish center spread.

Not everyone has the inventory (or stamina) necessary to do a major antique show or flea market, so where else can a person find potential customers for his or her wares? Three publications which we have used are: *Paper Collectibles Marketplace*, PO Box 128, Scandinavia, Wisconsin 54977; *The Illustrator Collector News*, PO Box 1958, Sequim, Washington 98382; and the *Paper and Advertising Collector,* PO Box 500, Mount Joy, Pennsylvania 17522. General antiques publications such as the *Antique Trader Weekly*, PO Box 1050, Dubuque, Iowa 52004, or *Antique Week*, PO Box 90, Knightstown, Indiana 46148 are also inexpensive advertising mediums that reach thousands of collectors of everything from cigar labels to Marilyn Monroe and Elvis memorabilia.

A valuable inventory of active buyers can be obtained by clipping classified ads from these periodicals and building an alphabetical card file. Most of the "wanted to buy" ads are good for many months after first appearing.

It is very important that you properly grade any magazines you offer for sale to mail order customers. An accurate description in your catalog or advertisement, including all defects, will virtually eliminate returns and build long term customer loyalty.

Condition and grading terms.

MINT: Straight from the publisher, probably unopened. No mailing label.

FINE or VERY FINE: Very slight traces of wear, the lightest fading of cover or spine. No writing or mailing label. No browning. Very Fine has a minimum of wear traces and fading.

VERY GOOD: If lamination is present, peeling may be obvious. Cover luster is gone, there is slight browning, and spine may be a bit loose. No tape repairs.

GOOD: Color cover badly faded, spine rolling, cover folded too often. Some pages may be brittle. Creases and flaking present. but nothing is missing.

FAIR: Major defects. Badly worn, torn and soiled. Part of cover may be missing. Stains common. However, the item is still complete. Equals the reading copy of a hardcover book.

Established dealers have many opportunities to buy magazines in bulk at auctions, from libraries, and off the street as a result of their Yellow Page advertising. So bear in mind that although book shops are always interested in nicely bound old volumes, magazine dealers often buy cheaper from established sources.

Bob Mainard, proprietor of The Magazine Shop in San Francisco, warns that "While most first issues are worth a premium, generally only first issues of famous, long-running titles (Time, Life, Sports Illustrated, Saturday Evening Post, Fortune, Vogue, etc.) have substantial value." Bob would like to see price guides stress the importance of condition and the fact that dealers (as opposed to collectors) can pay only a fraction of retail value.

If you are looking to buy a particular issue, or run, of magazines, here are a few dealers who are specialists in the field. (Be sure to enclose a self-addressed stamped envelope when making inquiries.)

John Alk	The Magazine Shop
414 Lazarre Avenue	731 Larkin Street
Green Bay, WI 54301	San Francisco, CA 94109
Back Number Wilkins	Periodicals Paradise
Box 247M.	3430 S.E. Belmont
Danvers, MA 01923	Portland, OR 97214
The Magazine Baron	Periodyssey
1236 S. Magnolia	1650 Argonne Place
Anaheim, CA 92804	NW Washington, DC 20009

Check the Yellow Pages in any large metropolitan area phone book for additional used magazine dealers. Many more may be found in the collector publications listed at the top of this page.

Prices vary widely from dealer to dealer and state to state. We have listed "asking prices" from mail-order dealers. You may do better, or worse, according to where you offer your wares for sale.

The most valuable part of most any magazine is its cover. If you have the ability to mat and frame attractive covers by Rockwell, Parrish, Wyeth and other popular illustrators, you should find a ready market.

Stick to magazines at least 35 years old for best results, and try to purchase complete runs or large accumulations rather than individual issues.

Run an "Old Magazines Wanted" ad in your local newspaper and see what treasures come out of the woodwork.

A

ABEL NEW ENGLAND FARMER'S ALMANAC.
1839-1854. $15-$30.

ACCENT MAGAZINE.
13 issues, 1940-1950s. The lot. $35.

ACE HIGH. 1930s. $5.

ACE SPORTS. 1930s. $10.

ACTUAL DETECTIVE STORIES. 1930s-1940s. $5-$10.

ACTION-PACKED WESTERN. May 1950. $5.

ACTUAL DETECTIVE. 1930s-1940s. $5-$10.

ADVENTURE. 1900-1920. $10-$30.
1930-1940. $5-$10.

THE AERO. Vol. 1, No. 1, May 1909, to Vol. III, No. 62,
July 1910. London. 2 bound vols. $500.

AERO DIGEST. 1930s. $7-$10. 1940s. $4-$6. 1950s. $5.

AERONAUTICAL ENGINEERING REVIEW.

Complete run, 1942-1958. 32 vols. Full calf. $110.

AERONAUTICS.
9 issues, 1940-1941. The lot. $15.
Average issue. $3.

AFTER DARK. 1973-1977. $5-$10.

AIR FORCE. 16 issues, 1943-1945. $5 each.

AIR LIFE.
Vol. 1, No. 1, March 1942. Tabloid-size. $25-$50.

AIR PROGRESS.
Nov 1941. $15.
Annual, 1941. $24.
June 1943. $25 up.
Mixed 1930s, 1940s avg. $5-$10.
Great articles may triple value.

AIR SERVICE JOURNAL. 1918-1919. $10.

AIR TRAILS MAGAZINE.
1941-1942. $8-$15.
1951-1956. Annuals. $24 each.

AIR TRAVEL NEWS.
1920s. $3-$6.
Dec 1928. Zeppelin. $10.

AIRCRAFT MAGAZINE.
Vol. 1 Mar 1910-Feb 1911.
Leather bound. VG. $300-$500.
64 issues, June 1910-June 1916. $240.

THE ALDINE, A TYPOGRAPHIC JOURNAL.
Vol VI, 1873. $100.
Vol VII, 1874-1875. Folio. 22 issues. $295.
Jan 1871 to Dec 1873. Bound as one. $150.
1880s-1950s individual issues. $8-$10.

ALFRED HITCHCOCK'S MYSTERY MAGAZINE.
1950s-1970s. $5-$10.

AMAZING DETECTIVE. Dec 1960. $5.

AMAZING STORIES.
March 1929. $30.
June 1929. $20.
May 1930. $30.
Oct 1930. $20.
Nov 1930. $20.
Oct 1932. $20.
Most others, 1929-1932. $10.
April 1967 issue. Signed by Philip Dick
and Richard Matheson. VG. $100.
Vol 1, 1976, Nos. 6, 9, 10. $70-$75 each.
Vol 2, No. 7. $65.
Vol 3, Nos. 4, 7. $60 each.

THE AMERICAN.
Boston, July 1744. 1st successful
American magazine. Poor condition. $23.
1890s-1950s. $5-$20.
Sept 1934. $12.

AMERICAN AGRICULTURALIST.
5 issues, 1854. The lot. $15.
Vol. 28, 1869. $25.

Other bound vols. 1 yr. $35-$75.
Single issues. 1850-1950. $3-$10.

THE AMERICAN AMATEUR PHOTOGRAPHER.
54 issues, 1891-1907. The lot. $375.

THE AMERICAN ANGLER. 1888-1891.
Nine bound, Nine unbound vols. Approximately 460 issues. Ex-library. Scarce journal. $3,950 all.

AMERICAN APHRODITE.
9 vols. of quarterly erotic magazine. No date. Good. $150.

AMERICAN AQUATIC MAGAZINE.
Yachting, rowing, canoeing. Vol. 1, No. 1, Jan 1884. $35.

AMERICAN ARCHITECT.
1870s. $12-$15.
1882 issue. $8.
12 issues, 1909-1912. $95 all.

AMERICAN ARTISAN & TINNER. 35 issues, 1895-1905.
The lot. $250.

AMERICAN ARTIST.
1930s-1970s. Avg. $3-$5.
Special illustrators. $6-$12.

AMERICAN AVIATION. 1950s. $3-$5.

AMERICAN BEAUTIES.
Vol. 1, No. 1. Oct 1925. Pinups. $20.

AMERICAN BEE JOURNAL.
Vol. 1, issues 1-4, 1861. Some illus. removed. $150.
Vols. VII and VIII, 1872-1873. Both. $75.
1860-1890 issues $4-$10.
1900-1940s. $3.

AMERICAN BOOK COLLECTOR.
Special issues, $40-$65 each: Jack London, James Joyce, James T. Farrell, Jean-Jacques Rousseau, Jesse Stuart, Frank Baum, Rockwell Kent, Sherlock Holmes, Soren Kierkegaard, Vardis Fisher, W. W. Denslow. 233 issues, 1950-1976. Very Good. $650.
63 issues, 1968-1980. The lot. $65.

AMERICAN BOY.
Bound vol., Nov 1913-Oct 1914. 11 issues. Waterstains, some spotting. Good. $75.
March 1904. $20. Avg. issue, 1899-1940. $5-$10. Exceptional graphics might bring four times the price.

AMERICAN BUILDER.
20 issues, 1922-1926. $12 each.
1917-1925. Avg. $6-$12.
Mixed, 1930s. $3-$5.

AMERICAN CHAP-BOOK.
Vol. 1, Nos. 1 and 2, Sept and Oct 1904. $50 each.

THE AMERICAN CHAUFFEUR.
Avg. 1915-1930s issue. $3-$5.
August 1916. New autos. VG. $20.

AMERICAN CITY.
(Fire truck, municipal supplies, etc.)
Bound vol., 1927. $50.
Sept 1915. $25.
76 bound vols., ex-lib., 1919-1941 and 1949-1956. The lot. $500.
Avg. issue, 1916-1960. $8-$10.

AMERICAN COLLECTOR.
5 issues, 1934, 1935. The lot. $10. 1940s. $5-$8 ea.

AMERICAN COOKERY.
(Formerly The Boston Cooking School Magazine)
Avg. $4-$6 ea. Special articles. $20.

THE AMERICAN COTTON PLANTER AND SOIL OF THE SOUTH. Vol. 1, No. 11, Nov 1857. $50.

AMERICAN DETECTIVE. 1930s. $4-$6.

AMERICAN DRUGGIST.
1920s-1950s. Avg. $4.
Special covers, ads, etc. $10-$35.

AMERICAN ENGINEER. 1880s. $5 each.

AMERICAN FABRICS.
8 issues, 1960s. The lot. $120.
15 issues, 1950s (all with swatches). The lot. $225.

AMERICAN FAMILY.
Mixed issues from July 1952 to Aug 1953. $5 each.

AMERICAN FIELD.
1890s-1920s. $4.
1930s-1940s. $3.

THE AMERICAN FLORIST. Bound vol. 1891-1892. $110.

AMERICAN FORESTRY.
Bound vols. 1910-1918. $10-$12 ea.
Individual issues. 1890s-1930s. $3.

AMERICAN FORESTS & FOREST LIFE.
77 issues, 1924-1933. The lot. $100.

THE AMERICAN FREEDMAN.
16 monthly issues, 1866-1868. $160.

THE AMERICAN FURNITURE GAZETTE.
Single issue, 1891. Nice engravings. $100.

AMERICAN FURRIER.
  1910s. Avg. $9-$11.
  1920s-1930s. $4-$8.

AMERICAN GIRL.
  1917-1919. $5-$8.
  1920s. $4-$7.
  1930s, 1940s. $3.

AMERICAN GLASS REVIEW.
  1880s. Avg. $10-$15.
  1900-1950. $4-$10.

AMERICAN GOLFER.
  Nov 1931 & Dec 1932. Bobby Jones. $10-$15.
  Avg. issue. $6-$8.

THE AMERICAN GUN.
  Vols. 1, 2, 3. 1961. The lot. $48.

AMERICAN HERITAGE.
  Average 1950s-1970s issue. $3-$5.
  Dealers ask more for Mickey Mouse (1968)
  and Maxfield Parrish issues (1970).
  Library discards usually are $1-$2 each.

AMERICAN HISTORICAL REVIEW.
  1890s. Avg. $6.
  1900s-1940s. $3-$4.

AMERICAN HOME.
  1920s-1930s. $5-$10.
  50 issues, 1937-1958. The lot. $37.
  1930s-1960s. Good. $3-$6.

AMERICAN HOROLOGICAL JOURNAL.
  Bound vols., 1870, 1871, 1872, 1873. $75 each.

AMERICAN HORSE BREEDER.
  1890s. $5-$15.
  174 issues, 1905-1918. $450 all.

AMERICAN HOUSEKEEPER'S ALMANAC.
  1851-1854. $25-$50.

AMERICAN JOURNAL OF INSANITY.
  19th Century issues. $25-$45.
  Vol. 58, No. 3, 1912. $25.

AMERICAN JOURNAL OF NUMISMATICS.
  Complete run. 1866-1924. Auction. $5,775.

AMERICAN JOURNAL OF PHILATELY.
  12 issues, 1895, 1896. Covers soiled. The lot. $35.
  Vol. XIII 1909. $20.

AMERICAN LADY. Late 1930s. $5-$8.
  Vol. 1, No. 1. Sept 1938. $15-$20.

AMERICAN LEGION.
  50 issues, 1924-1946. The lot. $45.
  4 issues, 1927. All have H. C. Christy covers. The lot. $30.
  120 issues, 1938-1951. Many war issues. The lot. $35.

AMERICAN MAGAZINE.
  Various issues from May 1931 to May 1933. $10 ea.
  Others with Rockwell covers, 1918, 1920s. $15-$35.

AMERICAN MACHINIST.
  18 issues, 1912-1915. VG-Fine. $14 each.
  Average issues, 1878-1920s. $3-$5.

AMERICAN MAGAZINE OF ART.
  Jan, March, April 1934. $20 each.
  Various issues from teens and twenties. $8-$15.

AMERICAN MAGAZINE OF FASHION.
  Vol. 1, Nos. 1 and 2, Nov-Dec 1871. The pair. $35.

AMERICAN MECHANICS.
  1825-1826. Vols. 1, 2. Very Good. $150 pair.

AMERICAN MERCURY.
  Vol. 1, No. 1. Jan 1924-Dec 1925. 24 issues in one vol.
  with all covers and ads bound in. Fine. $300.
  17 bound vols, 68 issues. Ex-library. $750.
  1920s. $5-$10 each.
  1950s. Avg. $3.
  April 1932. $8.

AMERICAN MONTHLY. 1830. $12-$15.

AMERICAN MOTORCYCLIST AND BICYCLIST.
  1925-1926 issues. $25-$50 each.

AMERICAN MUSEUM. 1790-1792. $38-$72.

AMERICAN NATURALIST.
  Vol. 1, March 1867-Feb 1868.
  12 issues, with 16 plates. $150.
  Average issue, 1860-1950. $5-$10.

THE AMERICAN NEPTUNE.
  Vol. 1, 1941, through Vol. 15, 1955.
  Uniformly bound. $275.
  Average issue, 1940-1960. $5-$10.

AMERICAN NEEDLEWOMAN.
  1920s-1940s. $3.
  Exceptional issues. $6-$12.

THE AMERICAN PENMAN. 1912 issue. $10.

AMERICAN PHOTOGRAPHY.
  121 issues, Straight run, 1936-1941 and 1924-1935.
  The lot. $120. 4 issues, 1913-1915. $15 all.
  1928-1941 issues avg. $8 each.

AMERICAN PHILATELIST.
Stamp collecting. 1880 to present. $1-$5.

AMERICAN PHRENOLOGICAL JOURNAL.
1847. New York monthly. $26.
Vol. XII, 1850. $75.
1865. Andrew Johnson cover. $12.

AMERICAN POULTRY.
1870s-1920s. $3 each.
1870s-1900s. $6-$10.
1920s-1950s. $3-$4.

THE AMERICAN PRINTER. 1930s. $4-$8.

AMERICAN QUARTERLY OBSERVER.
Vol. 1, July-Oct 1833. Light foxing. $275.

AMERICAN REVIEW.
1890s-1930s. $6-$10.
Automobile & bicycle issues. $15.

AMERICAN RIFLEMAN.
1925-1926. $5-$10 ea.
1927-1942. $3-$4 ea.
1946-1949 (48) bound issues. $48.
1950-1977 (286) issues. $169 all.

AMERICAN ROD & GUN.
Vol. 1, No. 1. June 1954. $15-$25.

AMERICAN SPECTATOR. 1930s. $5 each.

THE AMERICAN SPORTSMAN.
1968-1970. 12 vols. Fine. $150.

AMERICAN STOCK JOURNAL.
Bound vols. I & II. 1859-1860. 380 pgs.
Many illus. 3/4 morocco, gilt lettering. $175.

AMERICAN WEST. 1960s. $3 each.

AMERICAN VEHICLE.
1907 issue. 37 pgs. of carriages. Fair. $20.

THE AMERICAN WOMAN.
Bound vol., Apr 1901-Feb 1903. $70.
9 issues, 1917 to 1920. The lot. $35.
33 issues, 1901 to 1907. $60 all.
11 issues, 1904 to 1915. Scuffed spines. $15 all.
Average issue. $4-$6.
With paper doll insert. $18-$25.

AMERICAN WOODSMAN. 1930s. $4. 1950s. $2.

AMERICANA. 83 issues, 1909-1943. Most bound.
The lot. $75.

THE ANTIQUARIAN.
15 issues, 1926, 1929-1931. The lot. $60.
Nov 1931. $9.
Most issues 1918-1960. $4-$8.

ANTIQUES MAGAZINE.
18 bound volumes, ex-library. 1947-1960. $150.
1920s-1930s. $6-$15.
1940s to present. $4-$5.

ANYTHING GOES.
Vol. 1, No. 1. Jan 1956. Scandal magazine. Fine. $25.

APERTURE.
Run of 23 vols., 1982-1987. Fine. $190-$250 the lot.
10 issues, 1958-1962. Many well-known photographers:
Weston, Coburn, White, Lange, Hine. $30-$45 each.
Vol 15, No. 1, 1969. French Primitive Photography. $20.
Monograph on W. Eugene Smith. 1969. $20.

APPLE PIE.
Vol. 1, No. 1. March 1975. Bathroom humor. $10-$20.

APPLETON'S JOURNAL.
Bound vol. July-Dec 1870. $35.
Single issues. 1870s-1880s. $8-$15.

APPLETON'S MAGAZINE. 1900-1907. $5-$10.

APPLETONS' MECHANICS MAGAZINE.
Bound vol. 1851-1852. 768 pgs. $40.

ARCHITECTURAL DIGEST.
Vol. XIV, No. 1. Los Angeles, 1934-35. $15.
Other 1930s-1940s issues. $4-$8.

THE ARCHITECTURAL FORUM.
1929. $10-$15.
October 1936. $15
Jan 1938. Frank Lloyd Wright. $15.
1956 issue. Frank Lloyd Wright. $12.

ARCHITECTURAL RECORD.
14 issues, 1904-1907. The lot. $120.

ARGOSY.
1880s. $20-$30 each.
39 issues, 1929-1938. $253 all.
1929-1939. $3-$6.
Issues with E. R. Burroughs stories. $10-$20.
8 issues, 1932. The lot. $45.
November 1927 to December 1927. Six issues. Incl.
 Hulbert Footner novel before book publication. $50.
Nov 1, 1930. John R. Neill illus. $5.
Oct 5, 1940. $5.
Exceptional art brings up to $20 per issue.

ARIZONA HIGHWAYS.
   Mixed issues 1944-1955. $5 each.
   59 issues. 1945-1959. The lot. $49.
   12 issues, 1948-1956. mint. $3 each.
   July 1975. Indian Basket issue. $8-$15.
   Feb 1955. Frank Lloyd Wright. $20.
   1947 Annual, hardbound. $45.
   1949 Bound vol., 12 months. $25.

ARMOURS FARMERS ALMANAC.
   1929. Worn, bent. $9.

THE ART AMATEUR. 1892-1893 issues. $25 each.

ART & ARCHEOLOGY.
   23 issues, 1923-1929. The lot. $25.

ARTS & DECORATIONS.
   1920s-1930s. $8-$25.
   10 issues 1926-1928. $30 all.

ART DIGEST. 30 issues, 1932-1940. The lot. $25.

ART IN AMERICA. 1960s. $3-$4 each.

THE ART JOURNAL.
   21 bound vols. $1,155 auction.
   1852 vol. Good. $75.
   Sept 1856. $50.
   1865 vol. Fine. $125.
   1877 vol.3. $75.
   These are great "breakers" for framing.

ART LOVERS.
   Vol. 1, No. 1. Jan 1925. Nudes, fiction, pinups. $25.
   Feb 1925. Risque movie, theatre. Fine. $14.

ART PHOTOGRAPHY.
   Avg. 1950s issue. $8-$10.
   Marilyn Monroe, Sophia Loren, etc. $25-$40.

ARTHUR'S HOME MAGAZINE.
   1870s. $8-$10.
   1890s. $4-$8.

ARTHUR'S LADY MAGAZINE. 1860s-1870s. $8-$12.

THE ARTS. 23 issues. 1923-1927. The lot. $38.

ASIA. 1900-1930. $5-$8. Exceptional covers bring more.

ASSOCIATION BELGE DE PHOTOGRAPHIC.
   Brussels, 1875-1906 bound. 10 annual vols., various years.
   Text in French. The lot. $1,600.

ASTOUNDING SCIENCE FICTION.
   22 issues, 1955-1958. $4 each.

ASTOUNDING STORIES. 1930s. $8-$10.

ASTRONOMICAL JOURNAL.
   1850-1900. $4-$10.
   1930s-1940s. $2-$4.

ATHLETIC JOURNAL. 1920s. $2-$3 each.

ATLANTIC MONTHLY.
   1st two vols., 1858. $75 the pair.
   Dec 1867. Railroad ads. $15.
   1880s avg. issue. $5-$12.
   50 issues, 1906-1944. The lot. $35.
   32 issues, 1919-1926. Some ads clipped. $28.
   Maxfield Parrish and Norman Rockwell. $25-$50.

ATLANTIC SPORTSMAN.
   Nov, Dec 1932. $10 each.

AUDUBON MAGAZINE.
   1890s-1940s. $3-$8.
   405 issues, 1940s-1970s. The lot. $200.

AUTO AGE.
   November 1955. $9.
   Other 1950s. $4-$8.

AUTO CAR. 1950s. $5-$7.

AUTOMOBILE DIGEST.
   Various issues, 1925. $8-$20.
   Assorted, 1939-1941. $5 each.

THE AUTOMOBILE.
   Vol. 1, No. 4. Jan, 1900. $50.

AUTOMOBILE TRADE JOURNAL.
   1918-1930. $20-$40.
   May-June 1929. $18-$24.
   1931-1940. $10-$15.

AUTOMOTIVE INDUSTRIES.
   July-Oct 1924. 5 issues. $40.
   1930s-1950s. $5-$15.

AUTO RACING JOURNAL. 1940s. $8-$10.

AVANT GARDE.
   11 issues, 1969-1971. Fine. The lot. $44.
   Issues 1-13. The lot. $35. Avg. issue. $3-$4.
   Issues 1-14. Near Fine. The lot. $100.
   Issue No. 8. Picasso erotic gravures. $15-$30.
   Issue No. 11. Lennon's erotic lithographs. $13.
   March 1968. Marilyn Monroe. $15-$45.

AVIATION.
   13 issues, 1924-1927. The lot. $75.
   54 issues. 1925-1927. $6 each.

AVIATION AERONAUTICAL ENGINEERING.
   (Later AVIATION WEEK).
   96 bound vols., ex-library, 1919-1960,
   lacks 1st half of 1942. The lot. $2,000.
   $20-$25 avg. price per volume.

AVIATION WEEKLY.
   20 issues, 1947-1948. Dealer lot. $20.
   1950s. $3-$15 each.

AVON FANTASY READER.
   1947-1952. Most $7-$10.
   Feb 1947. $15.

AVON SCIENCE FICTION READER.
   1951 issues. $7-$8 each.

AYERS AMERICAN ALMANAC.
   3 issues, all 1881. $9 lot.

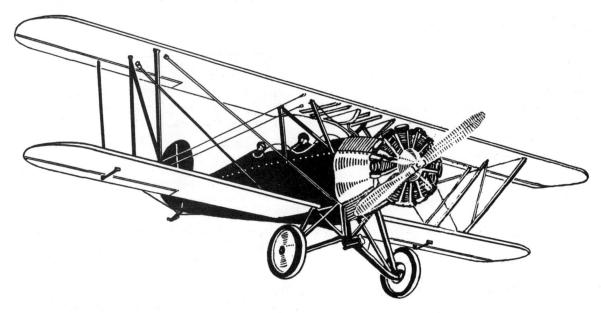

Hess-Warrior powered Argo

B

BABYHOOD. 12 issues, 1885-1886. In ring binder. $75.

BACHELOR.
Vol. 1., No. 1. April 1937. Gypsy Rose Lee, etc. Fine. $45.

BAGOLOGY MAGAZINE. Chase Bag Co. June 1937. $14.

BADMAN.
Vol. 1, No. 1. 1971. Old West outlaws, etc. Mint. $20.

THE BAKER STREET JOURNAL.
NY, 1946 Vol. 1, Nos. 1-4. The lot. $150.
NY, 1947 Vol. 2, Nos. 1-4. The lot. $150.

BALLOU'S PICTORIAL DRAWING ROOM COMPANION.
Bound vol. July-Dec 1885. $75.
1850s issues. $12-$25.
April 1858. Winslow Homer illustrations. $50.
1870s. $7-$10.
July 28, 1885. Sandwich Islands. $15.

BALLYHOO.
4 issues, 1934-1936. $10 each.
2 issues, 1932. Both, $18.
Cartoon issues. $20-$25.

BARBER'S GAZETTE.
NY, Sept 1939. Gambling issue. Girlie cover. $35-$50.

BARBER'S JOURNAL. 35 issues, 1937-1942. $5 each.

BARKER'S ALMANAC.
1878. $25-$50.
1886-1930. $5-$10.

BARNES & PARK FAMILY MEDICAL ALMANAC.
1851-1854. $25-$50.

BASEBALL DIGEST.
1940s........$9-$15.
1950s........$7-$15.
1960s........$6-$9.
1970s........$3-$8.
1980s........$3-$5.
NOTE: Prices are for non-special issues in very good to fine condition. Star-slanted and event-slanted issues can go as high as $30.

World Series issues. $7-$10. issues featuring such stars as Joe DiMaggio, Ted Williams, Lou Gehrig, etc. $15-$30.

BASEBALL MAGAZINE.
1910s....:.........$100 up, in fine condition.
1920s..............$40-$50.
1930s..............$25-$40.
1940s..............$15-$25.
1950s..............$10-$20.
NOTE: Prices are for non-special issues in very good to fine condition. Star-slanted and event-slanted issues can go much higher.
World Series issues:
1908-1919......$100-$500.
1920-1929......$75-$90.
1930-1939......$40-$50.
Cy Young number, Sept 1908-1919. $450-$550.
Ty Cobb number, Mar 12, 1912. $400-$500.
Honus Wagner number, Jan 15, 1915. $150-$250.

BEAUTIFUL WOMANHOOD.
10 issues, 1922-1923, including Vol. 1, No. 1. Large photos of film stars. The lot. $50.

BEAUTY PARADE.
Jan 1955. Peter Driben cover. Bettie Page pin-up. Chipped. $20.
Lot of 31 issues. 1920s-1930s. $150.

BEDTIME STORY.
Vol. 1, No. 1. 1932. A spicy pulp magazine. $35.

BEECHAM'S ALMANAC. Most years. $15-$30 each.

BEGGS PRACTICAL ALMANAC. $20-$40.

BEST TRUE FACT DETECTIVE. June 1951. Good. $12.

BETTER HOMES AND GARDENS.
90 issues, 1940s. VG. The lot. $125.
21 issues, 1938 and 1939. $39 all.
9 issues, 1928-1936. The lot. $34.
10 issues, 1944. The lot. $40.
12 issues, 1943. The lot. $60.
13 issues, 1926-1929. Fair. The lot. $15.
Individual issues. 1922-1940. $4-$10;
1941-1950. $2-$5 each.

BEYOND FANTASY FICTION. July 1953. $5.

BEYOND REALITY.
Vol. 1, No. 1. Oct-Nov 1972. Occult magazine. Mint. $15.

THE BIBELOT.
21 vols., VG to Fine. $125-$300.
Individual issues. $3-$4.

THE BIG STORY.
Vol. 1, No. 1. Oct 1951. Digest-size, press stories. $22.

BIG-TIME RECORD STARS.
Vol. 1, No. 1. Nov 1959. Elvis, etc. Mint. $35.

BILLBOARD.
4 issues, 1937-1941. All $35.
12 issues, 1937-1940. G-VG. The lot. $120.
3 issues, 1941, 1944 and 1948. $10 each.
Aug 6, 1921. $20.
Individual issues. 1880s-1948. $5-$20.

BIOREN'S TOWN & COUNTRY ALMANAC. 1821. $25.

BIRD LORE.
1929-1943. $3-$6.
Late teens, early 20s. $5-$12.

BIRDS.
April 1897. 10 full-page bird photos in color. $25.
Other 1890s-1900s issues. $10-$35.

THE BLACK CAT. 1890s. $9-$12 each.

BLACK BOOK DETECTIVE.
1940s. Avg. $25 each in very good condition.

BLACK MASK. Probably the most important American crime literature magazine ever published. Founded in 1920 by H. L. Mencken and George Jean Nathan, it utilized the talents of writers such as C. J. Daly, G. H. Coxe, Erle Stanley Gardner, John D. MacDonald and the hardboiled school of Hammett and Chandler. Fine examples of pulp magazines are very scarce. 1920-1937 issues of Black Mask are worth $100-$300 in fine to very fine condition. 1938 to 1951 issues are often quoted in the $25-$40 range.

THE BLACKSMITH & WHEELWRIGHT. 1897 issue. $28.

BLISS NATIVE HERBS ALMANAC.
1900-1929. $5-$10 ea.

BLUE BOOK MAGAZINE.
March 1939. VG. $25.
Aug 1945. Good. $5.
Early 1900s avg. $5-$15 each.

BLUNT'S NAUTICAL & ASTRONOMICAL ALMANAC. 1856. 150 pgs. $18.

BOILERMAKERS & BLACKSMITHS JOURNAL.
1880s-1890s. $15.
Early 1900s. $8-$10.

BOOK DIGEST OF BEST SELLERS.
Vol. 1, No. 1. Feb 1937. Digest size magazine. $15.

BOOK LEAGUE MONTHLY.
Dec 1928, bound Thomas Hardy issue. VG. $35.

BOOKBUYER.
1890s. $5-$7 each. (Maxfield Parrish illus. much higher.)

BOOKLOVERS. 1900-1906. $7-$15.

THE BOOKMAN.
1920s. $4-$8 each. (Maxfield Parrish illus. much higher.)

BOSTON COOKING SCHOOL MAGAZINE.
Nov 1901 to July 1903. $5 each.
1890s issues. $5-$8.

THE BOSTON MAGAZINE.
March 1874. $37.

BOSTON MEDICAL AND SURGICAL JOURNAL.
223 issues, 1888-1902. The lot. $340.

THE BOTANICAL MAGAZINE.
London, 1796-1800. Vols. I-XIV bound in 7 volumes. 503 engraved plates, hand-colored. $8,500.
London, 1796 Vol V. 35 hand-colored plates. VG. $1,250.

BOXING.
1950s. $5-$15 each.
7 issues, 1989. The lot. $10.
47 issues, 1977-1986. $65 all.
Annuals. $15.

BOX OFFICE.
312 issues, most from 1970s and 1980s. Most fine. The lot. $150.
10 issues 1940s & 1950s. $2 each.
Assorted 1920s, 1930s. $5-$15.

BOX OFFICE BAROMETER.
1946-1956. $8 each.

BOY'S LIFE.
Norman Rockwell drew 40 covers for this magazine from 1913 to 1945. In VG-Fine condition such issues range in value from $10 to $80. Older issues are the most valuable. 19 issues, 1933-1939, G-VG. $6 each.
Avg. issue. 1912-1935. $6-$12.

BRANDRETH'S ALMANAC.
1859-1868. $20-$40 each.
1872-1882. $10-$20 ea.

THE BREEDER'S GAZETTE. 1890s. $5-$7 each.

BREWER'S DIGEST. 1920s. $3-$5 each.

BRIDES MAGAZINE. 1930s. $4-$6 each.

BRISTOL'S FREE ALMANAC.
1843. $100-$200.
1844. $50-$100.
1847-1848. $25-$50.

BRISTOL'S ILLUSTRATED ALMANAC.
1860-1915. $15-$25 each.

THE BRITISH JOURNAL OF PHOTOGRAPHY.
London, 1862. Nos. 157-179. Important early periodical.
Some foxing. $225.

BROADCASTING. 1930s. $3-$5 each.

BROADCAST NEWS.
1946, issues no. 43 to 50, bound as one. $22.
1957, issues no. 93 to 98, bound as one. $14.

BROOM & BROOM CORN NEWS. Aug 1943. $18.

THE BROOM MAKER. May 1920. $24.

BROTHERHOOD OF LOCOMOTIVE FIREMEN AND
ENGINEERS.
8 issues, mostly 1922. The lot. $39.
Dec 1942 issue. $10.

BROWN'S IRON BITTERS ALMANAC.
1893-1895. $20-$40 ea.

BROWN HERB CO. ALMANAC. 1908-1911. $10-$20 each.

BROWN SHAKESPEARIAN ALMANAC.
1881-1896. $10-$20 each.

BROMO-SELTZER ALMANAC. 1908-1915. $10-$20 each.

BRUSH AND PENCIL MAGAZINE.
1890s. $10-$15 each. (Special illustrators bring more.)

BUBIER'S POPULAR ELECTRICIAN. April, 1893. $18.

BUDDIES. 1928 number. Sold by unemployed ex-
Servicemen. Fine. $25.

BUICK MAGAZINE.
1948-1952. 10 issues. $20 all.
1953 issue. 20 pgs. $17.

BUILDER. 1860s. $7-$9 each.

BUILDING AGE.
Aug 1911. VG. $15.
March 1927. VG. $7.
Average issue. $5-$8.

BULL'S SARSAPARILLA ALMANAC.
Most issues. $25-$50 ea.

BULL'S UNITED STATES ALMANAC.
1856-1860. $20-$40 each.

BUNGALOW. Seattle, 1912. Vol. I, No. 5. $20.

BURDOCK BLOOD BITTERS ALMANAC.
1895-1935. $8-$15 each.

BUSINESS WEEK.
50 issues, 1940. The lot. $50.
1930s. $2-$4 each.
1950s. $1-$3.

BURR-MCINTOSH MONTHLY.
December 1907. Mucha cover art. $100-$150.
June 1904. $25-$35.
Average issue 1890s-1900s. $10-$20.

THE BUTTERFLY. London. 2 vols. VG. $85 the pair.

C

CABARET MAGAZINE.
Feb 1957. Fine. $12-$15.

THE CALIFORNIAN.
1880s. $15-$25.
1890s. $12-$20.

THE CAMERA.
Avg. issue, 1922-1940. $2-$4.
105 issues, 1910-1949. VG. $5 each.
38 issues, 1926-1940. The lot. $30.
24 issues, 1940s. Good. The lot. $12.

CAMERA ARTS. 22 issues, Nov 1980-June 1983. Complete run. The lot. $95.

CAMERA CRAFT.
Five issues: Dec 1910, June 1910, Jan 1911, May 1911, Sept 1911. Near Fine. The lot. $45.
35 issues from 1940s. The lot. $60.

CAMERA WORK.
Nos. 1, 2, 7, 11, 19, 31, 34, 36 and 40 of this famous periodical, 1902-1912. Hand-pulled gravures in each issue. Price range for individual issues: $850-$2,750.
No. 11, July 1905, 11 plates. Cover edges chipped. $275.
Special number, June 1913. Illustrations of paintings by Cezanne, Picasso, Van Gogh. Good. $250.

CAMPER AND HIKER. 3 issues, 1928. $15 all.

CAMPING MAGAZINE. 1920s-1930s. $2-$4 each.

THE CANADIAN MONTHLY AND NATIONAL REVIEW.
Vols. 1 & 2, 1872. $24 for both.

THE CANADIAN MOTORIST. Aug 1921. $15.

THE CANNING TRADE.
Jan 27, 1913. 42 pg. trade magazine. $25.

CAR AND DRIVER.
27 issues, 1973-1979. Good. The lot. $35.
Avg. 1960-1980 issue. $3.
Special issues. $4-$8.

THE CARPENTER. 25 issues, early 1920s. $49 all.

CARPENTRY AND BUILDING.
10 issues, 1886-1889. Fine. The lot. $100.
Other 1880s. $5-$10 each.

CARRIAGE MONTHLY.
60 issues 1879-1890. The lot. $850.
Philadelphia, 1900, No. 12. $60.

CARTOON HUMOR.
Vol. 1, No. 1. Jan 1939. Top artists of the 30s. $20-$35.

CARTOONS MAGAZINE.
Jan 1912. Vol. 1. No. 1. $25-$50.
Nov 1914. 50 war-related cartoons. $30.
Dec 1915 and Oct 1917. VG. $18 each.
1920-1921. $18 each issue.
Misc. 1915-1920. $10-$25 each.

CASANOVA. Vol. 1, No. 1 May 1957. Playboy magazine copycat. Fine. $20.

CASHBOX. 1950s. $6-$8 each.

THE CASKET. 1830s-1850s. $35-$40 each.

CASSIER'S MAGAZINE.
Marine number, 1897. 184 pgs. illus. $50.

CATERER & HOUSEHOLD MAGAZINE.
Volumes I-IV. Philadelphia, 1882-1886. Black sheepskin and marbled boards. Worn, cracked. Contents VG. $175.

CATTLEMEN. 1920s. $2-$4 each.

CELEBRITY. Vol. 1, No.1. April 1954. Pocket-size. $10-$20.

CENTAUR ALMANAC. 1876-1881. $20-$40 each.

CENTAUR ATLAS-ALMANAC. 1882-1886. $15-$30 each.

CENTURY MAGAZINE.
Bound vols. for 1882-1883, 1884-1885, 1895-1896, 1885-1886, 1883-1884. $16-$19 each.
6 mos. in 3/4 leather, 1894 & 1895. $18 each.
6 mos. 1884-1885. Very tight. $25 each.
39 issues, 1903-1919. The lot. $100.
Bound vol. May-Oct 1888. $24.

Dec 1907. 14-page article on Kate Greenaway. $35.
Feb 1920. $17.
Mar 1885. $15.
Jan 1901. Parrish illus. Fair. $24.
Aug 1912. Parrish illus. VG. $30.
Misc. issues, loose covers, 1890s. $5 each.

THE CHAP-BOOK.
Stone & Kimball, Chicago, 1894-1895. Vols. 1-4. Unbound. Flaked edges, o/w VG. $150.
Vol. 2, 1894-1895. 12 issues and index. Loose covers. $60.
Individual issues, 1894-1906. $6-$10.

CHASE'S CALENDAR ALMANAC. 1910-1938. $10-$20 ea.

THE CHATAQUAN. 1880s-1900s. $3-$9.

CHATTERBOX ANNUALS.
Bound vols. 1878-1926. Good-VG. $19-$30.
Fine. $40-$50.

CHESS WORLD. Vols. 1-3. $30.

CHIC. Vol. 1, No. 1. Oct 1976. Published by Larry Flynt. Mint. $20.

CHICAGO. Aviation number, Sept 1911. $24.

THE CHICAGOAN MAGAZINE.
July, 1934. Very Good. $5.

THE CHILDRENS HOUR.
1866-1880s. $6-$12 each.
1900s. Some with paperdolls. $3-$15.

CHRISTIAN EXAMINER.
53 vols., 1824-1869 (plus 106 loose issues). G-VG. $475.

CHRISTIAN HERALD.
1890s. $2-$3 each.
Later issues, some Rockwell illus. $1-$8.

CIBA REVIEW. (Textile Trades).
Bound Vol. VII, 1949-1952. $125.
Bound Vol. VIII, April 1951-Feb 1953. $125.

CIGAR & TOBACCO JOURNAL.
Minneapolis MN. June, 1947. $15-$20.

CINEMA.
Winter 1972-1973. "A Clockwork Orange". $20.

CIRCUS. 1940s. $8-$10 each.

CIRCUS REVIEW. 1950-1953. $3-$7.

CITY GOVERNMENT.
7 issues, 1898-1899. The lot. $85.

CIVIL WAR HISTORY.
March 1962 to Dec 1965. 16 issues. Good. $30 all.

CIVIL WAR TIMES & CIVIL WAR TIMES ILLUSTRATED.
Complete run. 1959-1966. VG. $197.
37 issues, 1963-1967 and (9) from 1978. The lot. $50.

CLARKS ALMANAC. 1870s. $25-$50 each.

THE CLASS STRUGGLE.
Vol. 1, No. 4, Nov-Dec 1917. New York. Essays by Lenin, Trotsky. VG. $20.

CLICK.
1930s Girlie mag. $8-$10.
Feb & Mar 1938. $20-$25.
July 1941. $7.
April 1944. $7.

CLYDE BEATTY'S CIRCUS. 1940s-1950s. $5-$15.

THE CLOAK JOURNAL. A Monthly Review of the Women's & Children's Wear Trades. NY, 1892. 98 pgs. Folio. $45.

COLLECTIBLES ILLUSTRATED.
13 issues, 1982-1985. Fine. $3 each.
Nov-Dec 1982. Monroe cover. $10.
Sept-Oct 1984. Political buttons cover. $10.

THE COLLECTOR. 1975-1977. $3 each.

COLLEGE HUMOR.
1920s-1930s. $8-$10. More with Armstrong covers.

COLLEGE SISTER MAGAZINE.
1910s issue with Betty Bonnet paperdoll outfits. $15-$20.

COLLIERS.
50 issues, 1940s and 1950s. VG. The lot. $95.
42 issues, 1914, 1915. No covers. The lot. $50.
34 issues, 1938. Few covers, missing. The lot. $169.
Avg. 1880s issue. $8-$15.
1930s. $5-$10.
May 1905. Jessie Wilcox Smith cover, C. D. Gibson & W. A. Clark foldout. $40.
Sept 15, 1905. Feb 24, 1906. May 26, 1906. Jessie Wilcox Smith covers. $25-$40 each.
May 5, 1906. Earthquake. $50.
Sep 1905. Frederic Remington article. $21.
July 1911. Remington cover. $18.
Oct 1910. Harrison Fisher print. $20.
Sep 2, 1911. Bowser color cover. $8.
Feb 17, 1912. N. C. Wyeth cover. $24.
June 1915. Leyendecker baseball cover. $10.
Mar 6, 1912. C. D. Gibson cover. $20.
April 1923. Maxfield Parrish cover. $25-$50.
July 1908. Maxfield Parrish cover. $30.
Feb 20, 1915. Leyendecker cover. $15.

COLLIERS (continued).
    May 14, 1904. Remington illus. $10.
    Dec 3, 1904. Parrish cover. $25-$50.
    July 24, 1909. Parrish cover. $25-$50.
    Sept 12, 1903. Gibson illus. $15-$18.
    Oct 1940, Jan 1942. Lawson Wood covers. Fine. $10 ea.
    Apr 8, 1933. $8.
    Apr 1, 1944. $8.
    Oct 9, 1948. KKK. $8.
    Oct 13, 20 and 27, 1962. Eugene Burdick novel, "Fail-Safe" (True 1st ed.) Near Fine. $45.
    Feb 6, 1943. Hitler and Nazi caricature. Fine. $15.
    July 10, 1943. Gen. Wainwright cover. VG. $6.
    Jan 27, 1945. F. D. Roosevelt cover. VG. $8.
    July 9, 1954. Marilyn Monroe. $30.

THE COLOPHON.
    Complete run, 44 vols. plus indices. Total 48 vols. Very Good to Fine. $485.
    10 issues, 1931-1934. Ex-library. The lot. $65.
    Avg. 1930s issue. $6-$10.

COLUMBIAN ALMANAC FOR 1855. $12.

THE COLUMBIAN MAGAZINE.
    Philadelphia, Sept 1787. Probably 1st magazine printing of the U. S. Constitution. $2,450.
    Philadelphia, Dec 1787. Pennsylvania ratifies the Constitution. $45.
    Avg. 1787-1792 issue. $8-$20.

COLUMBIAN LADY'S & GENTLEMAN'S MAGAZINE.
    Vols. 3 & 4, 1845. 10 color fashion plates. Foxing. $160.
    Vols. 5 & 6, 1846. 3 color plates. Many engravings. Foxing, o/w Very Good. $60.

COMFORT.
    1880s-1900s. $5-$10.
    1931-1938. $2-$6.

THE COMMENTATOR.
    Vol. 1, No. 1. Feb 1937. Digest-size magazine by leading radio commentators. $10-$20.

THE COMMERCIAL PHOTOGRPAHER.
    14 issues. 1932-1935. $90 the lot.
    12 issues. 1948-1953. $14 the lot.

COMPLETE DETECTIVE CASES. Oct 1951. $9.

THE COMPLETE PHOTOGRAPHER.
    105 issues. 1941-1943. Some dupes, Good. $79.
    58 issues. 1941-1943. The lot. $80.
    1941-1943 most issues. $2 each.
    Disney animation issues. $25 each.

COMPLETE BASEBALL.
    1940s-1950s. $15-$50. Top players bring top dollar.

THE COMRADE: AN ILLUSTRATED SOCIALIST MONTHLY. Oct 1903. Predecessor of THE MASSES. Very Good. $10-$20.

COMSTOCK'S ALMANAC. 1844-1847. $50-$75 ea.

THE CONFEDERATE VETERAN.
    1971 facsimile copy of all 1895 issues. The lot. $18.
    6 issues, 1897-1899. Near Good. The lot. $35.

CONFIDENTIAL.
    Vol. 1, No. 1., Dec 1952. $20.
    May 1956. Jane Russell cover. $9.
    Other 1950s-1970s. $5-$15.

CONNOISSEUR. 1900s-1950s. $5-$8.

CONTEMPORARY PHOTOGRAPHER.
    1962-1968. $20-$35.

THE CONTRIBUTOR.
    Salt Lake City, 1880 issue, Mormon youths' monthly. $19.

CONTROVERSY.
    Vol. 1, No. 1. May 1959. Earl Wilson, Salvador Dali cover. $15-$25.

COOL & HEP CATS. Oct 1958. Elvis Presley. $24.

COPPER ROMANCES.
    Vol. 1, No. 1. Nov 1953. Maybe the only Black Romance magazine ever published. $20-$50.
    Avg. 1950s-1960s issue. $5-$10.

CORONET.
    Dec 1913. Jack London. $10.
    July 1914. Christy illus. $6.
    1932-1933 issues, Harrison Fisher illus. $25-$45 each.
    1940s-1950s. 40 good issues. $30 all.
    1948-1961. 33 issues. $50 the lot.
    Feb 1956. Masters of Mystery issue. $25.
    Jan 1966. Marilyn Monroe. $10.
    Avg. 1930s-1960s issue. $2-$5.

COSMOPOLITAN.
    June 1894. Buffalo Bill. $25.
    Assorted 1896-1897. $12-$15 each.
    March 1899 issue. Indians. $20.
    Early 1900s bound vols. in poor cond. $15.
    Aug 1903. Rose O'Neill. $20.
    Aug 1912. H. Fisher cover. $15.
    Avg. 1900-1929 issue. $5-$8.
    1933-1934. H. Fisher covers. $12.
    1932-1936 lot of 28 issues. $250.
    Avg. 1930-1945 issue. $4-$6.
    July 1936 Crandall cover. $12.
    May 1953 Marilyn Monroe. $25-$40.
    Assorted 1950s issues. $5 each.

COUNTDOWN.
First 3 issues of underground magazine. The lot. $18.

COUNTRY GENTLEMEN.
1883-1940 avg. issue. $5-$8.
20 issues, 1926-1930. $10 each.
26 issues, July 1931-Dec 1935. $5 each.
76 issues, 1937-1945. The lot. $220.
135 issues, 1940s. The lot. $125.
Misc. 1940s issues. $4-$6 each.
Nov 1944, Wyeth color cover. $18.
Dec 1946 issue. $15.
44 issues, 1940-1953. The lot. $89.
50 issues, 1929-1953. $50 for all.
N. Rockwell & N. C. Wyeth covers. $25-$30.

COUNTRY LIFE IN AMERICA.
Early 1900s-1920s. Avg. issue. $5-$10.
Famous illustrators. $25-$75.
15 issues. 1912-1923. $109 all.
May-Oct 1903. 6 issues bound in one vol. $95.
Feb 1914. Pool table adv. $17.
May 1921. Cole Phillips adv. $16.
1924-1927. 6 issues bound in buckram. $180.

THE NEW COUNTRY LIFE. Early 1900s. $6-$12.

THE COVENT GARDEN MAGAZINE.
12 issues, 1774. $605 auction.

COVER GIRLS. 1950-1954. $5-$10.

THE CRAFTSMAN.
Gustave Stickley, editor, Mission-style furniture maker.
Avg. issue. $15-$25.
5 issues, 1907, leather-bound. Fine. $60.
Issues of July, Aug and Nov 1907. Good. The lot. $67.
Issues of Nov 1912, Aug 1914 & Dec 1914. The lot. $125.
Oct 1909. Walter Crane, automobiles. $40.
Jan 1908-Dec 1908. 12 issues bound in 1 vol. No covers or ads. $300.
Jan 1911-Dec 1911. Ditto. $300.

CRAM'S MAGAZINE. Jan 1901. $20.

CRIME DETECTIVE. 1940s-1960s. Avg. $5.

THE CRITIC.
Bound vols. Jan-June 1902, July-Dec 1903. $30 each.
Bound vol. July-Dec 1905. Ex-library. $15.

CROCKETT'S ALMANAC, 1850. $24.

THE CROSS AND THE FLAG. Vols. for 1962, 1965, 1966.
36 issues. Gerald L. K. Smith's anti-Semitic rag. The lot.
$200-$300.

CUE MAGAZINE. 1950s. $4-$5 each.

D

THE DAILY TATTLER. All 13 numbers. Chicago, 1896.
Attempt at daily literary periodical by Stone & Kimball.
Scarce, fragile. $1,025.

DANCE MAGAZINE.
1920s-1950s. $5-$7.
15 bound vols. Nos. $25-$40. $300 for all.
1931 issues with Varga covers. $50-$100 each.

DARING CONFESSIONS.
Vol. 1, No. 1. October 1937. $10.

DAREDEVIL ACES. 1930s-1940s. $15-$40.

DARING DETECTIVE. 1930s-1950s. $3-$10.

DAVIS PAINKILLER ALMANAC. 1870s. $15-$30 each.

THE DECORATOR AND FURNISHER.
Oct 1883 to Sept 1884. 12 issues, original.
orange wraps. $200.
Later individual issues. $25 each.

THE DELINEATOR. Founded in 1873 by Mr. Ebenezer
Butterick, the pattern publisher, to promote his clothing
patterns. A pure fashion magazine until early 1900s when
fiction and general interest were added. Became an
impressive folio-size in 1909. Full color ads, fashion plates
and paper dolls from 1909 onward are very desirable.
Feb 1884. $25.
Mixed issues. 1891-1895. $12 each.
Oct 1896. $40.
1900-1903. $25 each.
June 1921. Golf. $35.
May-July 1927. Art Deco covers, up to $50 ea.
1930s. $8-$10 each.
12 issues 1936. $45 all.
Dec 1905. Leyendecker. $75.
Bound volume, Jan 1914-Dec 1914 including all
paper dolls and ads. $225.
Bound volume, 1915. Paper dolls plus
Rackham and Wyeth illus. $225.
July 1917. Paper dolls. $50.
May 1928. Rose O'Neill, Kewpies. $20.
Values range from $7 to $75 depending
upon ads, covers and illustrators.

DEMOCRATIC REVIEW.
1850s. $10-$30 each.

DEMOREST'S MONTHLY.
1860-1900. $5-$20.
March 1891. $18.
8 issues, 1865-1884. Good. $15 ea.

THE DENTAL DIGEST.
165 issues, 1915-1929. Some repeats, The lot. $85.
Single issues rarely bring over $2.

DESIGN. 1890s. $5-$15.
1950s. $4-$6.

THE DESIGNER.
1910s. $6-$10 each.
Jan 1902. $15.
June 1903. Fashions. $14.
Exceptional covers or plates can raise values by 100%.

DETECTIVE MAGAZINE. 1940s. $6-$9.

THE DETECTIVE. Jan 1892. $17.

DETECTIVE WORLD. April 1948. $10.

DIAL MAGAZINE.
17 bound vols. Ex-library. 1910-1917. The lot. $100.
Avg. issue 1880-1929. $5-$8.

DIAMOND DYE ALMANAC.
1888-1892. $5-$10 each.
1887. $15.

THE DIGEST.
Vol. 1, No. 1, July 17, 1937. Joining of Review of Review and Literary Digest. $10-$20.
Avg. 1930s issue. $2.

DIMENSIONS. No. 14, May-July 1954. Harlan Ellison's fanzine. Front cover tear, o/w Very Good. $95.

DISCOVERY.
Nos. 1-6, 1952-55. Complete run. Good-VG. $35.

DISNEY MAGAZINE.
Jan, Feb 1966. $4 each.
Other 1960s, $7-$10.

DISNEYLAND. 7 Fawcett Publications magazines, 1972, 1973. Disney characters in color. $50. All.

DISPLAY WORLD.
1920s. $3-$5 each.
Feb 1958. $10.

DISQUES. Vol. 1 March 1930-Feb 1931. Spine cover partially off o/w VG. $40.

DODD'S ALMANAC.
1890s-1940s. $8-$15 ea.

DOG WORLD.
Teens. $5-$10.
1920s. $3-$6.
1930s-1940s. $1-$4.

DOLLAR MAGAZINE: A MONTHLY GAZETTE. NY, Vols 1, 2 1841-1842. many plates. VG. $125 the lot.

THE DOLPHIN.
No. 1, 1933 by Limited Editions Club. One of 1,200 copies. Very Good. $175.
The same, No. 2. Near Fine. $175.
Fall 1940. Foxing, VG. $15.
Facsimile reprint. 4 vols. 1933-1941. VG. $159.

THE DOME.
London, 1897-1898 5 vols. in one. Articles by Yeats, Housman, etc. Art Nouveau illus. Good plus. $200.

DOMESTIC MONTHLY. 1870s. $4-$6 each.

DOWNBEAT.
5 issues, 1942, 1943. The lot. $10.
Avg. 1950s issue. $3-$4.

DR. MILES NEW WEATHER ALMANAC.
1927. Foxed, bumped. $8.

DRAMA MAGAZINE. 1920s-1930s. $3-$5 each.

DRAMATIC.
152 issues. 1944-1960. Some repeats. The lot. $55.

DRUG AND COSMETIC INDUSTRY.
55 issues. 1946-1959. The lot. $40.

DRUG STORE RETAILING. May 1935. $25.

DUKE. Vol. 1, No. 1. June 1957. The Black version of Playboy Magazine. Mint. $45-$75.

DWIGHT'S JOURNAL OF MUSIC.
1850s-1880s. $4-$8 each.

DYN MAGAZINE.
A Review of Modern Surrealist Art. Nos. 1-6 in five issues, 1942-1944. Work by Henry Miller, Anais Nin, Calder, Covarrubias. Asking $695 the lot.

DYNAMIC SCIENCE FICTION.
Dec 1952. $5.

Berret for Little Boys.

E

EBONY.
46 copies, 1946-1957.
Most VG to Fine. $8-$15 each.
Mixed 1963-1982. $5-$7.
Another mixed lot, 1952-1972. $4 each.

ECHO.
Vol. 1, No. 1. 1959. Includes 5 LP records,
Astaire, Thurber, Nichols & May. $22.

ELECTRICAL EXPERIMENTER.
1912-1920s. $4-$8 each.

ELECTRICAL MERCHANDISING.
4 issues, 1930. Covers stained. $6 each.

ELLERY QUEEN'S MYSTERY MAGAZINE.
36 issues, 1943-1951. $35 the lot.
Nov 1943. $8.
Jan 1949. $20.
1956-1990. $2-$4 each.
1968-1988. Lot of five. $8.

ELSA MAXWELL'S CAFE SOCIETY.
Vol. 1, No. 1953. Zsa Zsa Gabor cover. Many celebrities.
Mint. $45. Another, fine. $35.

EMPIRE ALMANAC.
1898-1903. $10-$20 each.

ENCOUNTER.
Vol. 1 through Vol 3. 132 issues. Good. The lot. $200.

ENGINEERING AND MINING JOURNAL.
Vols. 23, 24, 25, 26, 27, 28, 1877-1879. $95 per vol.

ENGINEERING DIGEST.
3 issues, 1909. The lot. $15.

THE ENTERPRISE.
Vol. II, issue 8, 1881. Grocery business
news. Illustrated ads. $35.

THE EPICURE.
Magazine catalog of S. S. Pierce, Boston. 1892. $35.
1917-1928. $15.
1935. $20.

EROS.
Vol. 1, Nos. 1, 2, 3 and 4, 1962. Incl. Marilyn Monroe
issue. VG-Fine. The set. $95.
Marilyn Monroe issue alone. As new. $40.
Vol. 1, Issues 1, 2, 4. 1965. Fine. $33 each.
Vol. 1, No. 1, 1962. Cover soil. $30.
Vol. 1, No. 2. 1962. Worn cover. $45.

ESCAPE. Vol. 1, No. 1. Oct 1955. Good-VG. $15-$25.

ESCORT.
Vol. 1, No. 1. Jan-Feb 1959. Girlie mag. Fine. $15.

ESQUIRE.
Vol. 1, No. 1. Oct 1933. $40-$85.
July 1934. Rockwell Kent. $50.
Sept 1934. Rockwell Kent. $10.
1936-1939. 3 issues, Petty Girls. $45 all.
Dec 1939. Petty Girl fold-out. $40.
1937 Advance Christmas Preview. $25.
Oct 1940. Varga illus. $40.
Dec 1940. Varga fold-out. $50-$85.
Early 1940s issues. $15-$45.
1941 Bound volume, 12 issues with all Petty and
Varga fold-outs. Fine. $600.
June 1948. Al Moore. $15.
Sept 1951. Marilyn Monroe. $35-$50.
Jan 1952. Calendar issue. $20.
Sept 1952. Esther Williams. $25-$40.
Feb 1954. $20.
Nov 1955 with fold-out. $15-$25.
Nov 1960. Lenny Bruce. $6.
Assorted 1950s, 1960s. $3-$10 ea.
1970s avg. $3-$5 each.

ETUDE.
1880s-1900s. $5-$15.
Dealer lots: 50 issues, 1913-1944. $40.
50 issues, 1920-1940. $75.
35 issues, 1924-1926. $100.
Mixed 1940s-1950s. $2-$5 each.

EVE. Vol. 1, No. 1, May 1949. Tabloid-size magazine,
sports, pinups. etc. $15-$22.

EVERGREEN REVIEW.
Vol. 1, No. 1, 1957. Original wraps. $45.

EVERY SATURDAY.
    1870s. Avg. $5-$7. Some to $15.
    Oct 15, 1870. $12.
    Christmas issue, 1870. $27.
    Oct, Nov 1871. 3 Chicago fire issues. $18-$21 each.
    Aug 12, 1871. $12.

EVERYBODY'S ALMANAC.
    Jackson/Hoofland. 1850s and 60s. $20-$40 ea.

EVERYBODY'S MAGAZINE.
    Early 1900s. avg. $5-$10. Parrish illus. $25-$35.
    August 1908 & April 1909. Rose O'Neill illus. $20-$30.
    1910s. $5-$7 each. July 1912. $10.
    Two 1953 Coronation issues. $10 each.

EVERYWOMAN'S MAGAZINE.
    1940s-1950s. $3-$6.
    1960s. $1-$2.

EVERYLAND.
    Circa 1915. Avg. issue. $4-$8.
    Watch for Norman Rockwell art.

EXCELLENT STORIES OF REAL LIFE.
    Similar to Cosmopolitan. June 1925. $9.

EXCELSIOR (BRANDRETH) ALMANAC.
    1870-1871. $15-$30 each.

EXCITING WESTERN. 1950s. $10-$20.

EXCLUSIVE. 1950s. $5-$10.

EXHIBITOR MAGAZINE.
    Lot of 10 early 1940s. $35.
    Avg. 1950s issue. $2.

EXHIBITORS HERALD WORLD.
    Jan & Sept 1930. $ each.

EXHIBITORS TRADE REVIEW.
    3 issues. 1916-1920. $35 all.

EXOTIC ADVENTURES.
    Issues 2, 3, 4. Fine. The lot. $35.

EXPOSED. 1950s. $10-$15.

EYE MAGAZINE.
    Vol. 1, No. 1. May 1949. $15-$22.
    Avg. 1940s-1950s. $4-$10.
    Some pin-ups may raise value.
    1960s issues. $3-$5.

F

FAHNESTOCK FREE ALMANAC.
    1848-1851. $20-$40 ea.
    1860-1870. $15-$30 ea.

FAMILY CIRCLE.
    Early 1930s. $3-$10.
    Nov 1934. Good. $7.
    1940s-1950s. $4-$8.
    1952-1969. $4-$6 ea.
    1960s-1970s. $1-$12.
    11 assorted, 1930s-1940s. $10 all.

THE FAMILY MAGAZINE.
    67 issues, beginning with No. 1, April 20, 1833.
    Foxing, worn. $40 all.
    5 Bound vols. 1836-1840. Worn. $125 all.
    1838 volume in VG cond. $50.

FAMOUS FANTASTIC MYSTERIES.
    1939-1953, avg. issue. $4-$10.

FANTASTIC. Science fiction magazine.
    1930s-1950s. $5-15.
    1960s-1970s. $1-$5.

FANTASTIC ADVENTURES.
    May 1939. $20.
    Sept 1939. $20.
    Others, 1939-1949. $5-$15 each.
    27 issues, 1942-1950. $200 all.

FANTASTIC NOVELS.
    1958-1951. 17 issues. $60 all.
    Individual issues. $6-$10 each.

FANTASY BOOK. Vol. 1, No. 1. 1947. Sci-fi.
    Autographed by two authors. Fine. $65-$120.

FANTASY & SCIENCE FICTION.
    Vol. 1, No. 1, 1949. $25-$50.
    Avg. 1950s issue. $10-$20.
    1960s-1970s. $4-$8.
    1980s. $1-$2.

FARM AND FIRESIDE.
    Late 1800s-1930s. $3-$6.
    Much more if Rockwell cover.

FARM JOURNAL.
    5 issues, 1884-1905. The lot. $15.
    Early 1900s. $2-$4.
    Assorted 1940s issues. $5 ea.

FARM LIFE. 1890s. $3-$8 each.

FARMER'S ALMANAC FOR THE YEAR OF OUR
    LORD 1841. By Thomas Spofford. Worn, darkened. $15.
    Same, 1843. $20.

FARMER'S ALMANAC. Pinchot, Bruen & Hobart.
    1870-1881. $5-$10 ea.

FARMER'S ALMANAC.
    Fred Clarke. 1880s. $8-$15 ea.

FARMER'S ALMANAC.
    C. B. Smith & Co. $8-$15 ea.

FARMER'S & DAIRYMAN'S ALMANAC.
    A. C. Grant. 1850s-1861. $12-$25 ea.

THE (OLD) FARMER'S ALMANAC.
    1850. Robert B. Thomas, Boston. $8.
    76 issues, 1800-1891. The lot. $185.
    31 issues, 1838-1849 and 1854-1866. $75.

FARMER AND MECHANIC.
    Bound vols., 1846-1856. $75 each.

FARMER'S CABINET.
    Aug 1836-July 1838. 2 vols., library buckram. $100.
    Single issues, 1839, 1840. $12 each.

THE FARMER'S REGISTER.
    1835-1836 issues. Petersburg VA periodical. $12 ea.

THE FARMER'S WIFE.
    1910. $3-$4 each.
    July 1932. $6.
    Nov 1935. $10.
    June 1935. $15.
    Rockwell, Leyendecker and Parrish covers, or artwork,
    can quadruple values.

FASHION DIGEST. 1930s-1940s. $2-$ each.

FASHIONABLE DRESS.
   The Magazine for M'Lady. Sept 1922. $30.

FATE.
   Avg. issue, 1940s-1960s. $2-$6.
   11 issues, 1951-1958. The lot. $20.
   Spring 1948. $5.

FBI DETECTIVE STORIES.
   Vol. 1. February 1949. $20-$40.

FEAR!
   May 1960. $9.
   July 1960. $15.

FIELD & STREAM.
   1897-1920. $5-$20.
   Sept 1916. $10.
   June 1925. $12.
   Nov. 1947. $5.
   Mixed. 1930s. $4 ea.
   74 issues. 1945-1953. The lot. $200.

FILM CURB.
   Trade publication, theater owners. Dec 1934. $35.

FILM COMMENT.
   155 issues, 1960s-1980s. The lot. $65. Avg. $4 ea.

FILM FACTS. 5 bound vols. of 12 magazines per year,
   1958-1962. The lot. $70-$100.

FILM FUN.
   1930s-1940s. $10-$25.
   Pin-up covers are the most valuable.

FILM QUARTERLY & FILM HERITAGE.
   1960s and 1970s. $2 each.

FILMLAND.
   June 1952. Susan Hayward. $8.
   Sept 1956. James Dean. $25.
   Other stars, 1950s. $10-$20.

FILMS IN REVIEW.
   5 hardbound vols., 1961-1971. $25 all.
   1960s. $10. 1970s. $7. 1980s. $5.
   50 issues. 1956-1961. $10 each.

FINAL.
   Vol. 1, No. 1. Sept 1950. Tabloid-
   size, sensational-type. $15-$22.

FIRE AND WATER. NY, May 4, 1895. 24 pgs., folio.
   Weekly news, fire protection & water supplies. $35.

FIRE CHIEF. May-June 1930. $8.

FIRE ENGINEERING.
   Pre-1940. $8-$10.
   1940-1950. $5-$7.
   1950-1960. $3-$4.

FIRE PROTECTION. June 1931. $8.

FIREHOUSE.
   Vol. 1-No. 1. Sept-Oct 1976. $75.
   All others. $2 each.

FIREMAN. 1940-1940. $2-$4.

FIREMAN'S HERALD. $15.

FIREMAN'S STANDARD. $15.

THE FISHERMAN. 1940s. $5-$6 each.

FITCH FAMILY HEALTH ALMANAC.
   1842-1850. $50-$100 ea.
   1856-1867. $15-$30 ea.

FLAIR.
   First 12 issues, Vol. 1, No. 1. Feb. 1950. $20-$45.
   Good-VG. $120.
   11 issues, 1950-1951. Spine wear. The lot. $75.
   6 issues. 1950. VG. $10 each.
   1953 Annual. Fine. $20.

FLEMING'S FARM & LIVESTOCK ALMANAC. $5-$10.

FLIGHT MAGAZINE.
   Bound vol. 12 issues. Jan-Dec 1909. $500.

FLORIDA AGRICULTURIST. Sept 1880. $20.

FLYING.
   1943-1946 issues. $8-$15 each.
   Dealer lot, 50 issues 1945-1953. $150.
   Avg. 1940-1950. $5-$10.

FLYING ACES.
   May, July, Oct, 1941. $15 each.
   Other 1930s-1940s. $10-$22.

FLYING SAUCERS.
   Dec 1959. $9.
   Aug 1960. $9.

FOCUS. 1950s. $4-$5 each

FOLEY ALMANAC. 1906-1921. $5-$8.

FOLLIES MAGAZINE. 1957-1960. $5-$10 each.

FOOD MAGAZINE. Boston, 1907. $25.

FOR PEOPLE EVERYWHERE.
Vol. 1, No. 1. March 1939. Myrna Loy,
Black Voodoo, etc. $18-$35.

FOOD DEALER AND OWNER.
Spet 1924 issue. 144 pgs. $15.

FORD NEWS. March, May 1937. $6 each.

FORD TIMES.
Early 1920s-1930s. $5-$15 ea.
68 issues, 1952-1958. Good. The lot. $65.
17 issues. 1945-1951. G-VG. The lot. $35.

FOREST & STREAM.
1883-1885. Good. $25 ea.
Jan-Dec 1912. $10 each.
1923 and 1924 issues with cover art by
Schaldach, Hunt and Rhead. Up to $25 each.
Other 1920s. $8.

FORTUNE.
Vol. 1, No. 1. Feb 1930. $50.
Single issues: 1930-1935. $15-$25.
1936-1940. $12-$20.
1941-1950. $8-$15.
1951-1960. $4-$10.
All above in VG to Fine cond.
Advertising and famous illustrators
determine value within price range.
March 1932 $40.
June 1932. $12.
Aug 1932. $10.
Feb 1933. Coke, Cigar bands. $50-$75.
March 1933. Cigar art. $50.
Nov 1933. $18.
March 1937. Cassandre posters. $40.
Dec 1939. Train photos, Packard adv. $22.
Feb 1940. 10th Anniv. issue. Mint. $20.
Bound volumes:
5 years, 1930-1935. $250.
Feb 1930 (1st year) to Nov 1948, missing
July 1938. Good. $1,800 for 18 year run.
155 issues. Feb 1930-Dec 1942. Fine. $1,800.
92 issues. 1930-1950. The lot. $385.
72 issues. 1930-1955. The lot, $189.
46 issues. 1962-1969. The lot. $125.

FORUM.
1890s. $2-$4 each. 1920s issues. $5.

FOTO PARADE. 1930s. $8-$10 each.

FOUR TRACK NEWS. 1890s. $3-$4 each.

FOWLER & WELLS AMERICAN WATER CURE
ALMANAC. 1840s, 50s & 60s. $15-$30 ea.

THE FRA. A Roycroft publication.
Early 1900s single issues. $1 to $5 ea.
Bound volumes. $35.
April 1908. Vol. 1, No. 1, Denslow art
on back cover. $10-$25.

FRANK LESLIE'S PUBLICATIONS.
(See "L", also see Newspaper section).

THE FREEMAN. 1870s. $5-$7 each.

FRESH. Vol. 1, No.1. Nov 1940. Tabloid-size magazine,
pinups and cartoons. $20-$28.

FRIARS FABLES.
1960s issues. $5-$10.

FRIDAY.
Sports, show biz, horse racing.
Vol. 1, No. 1. March 1940. $15-$22.
March 1941. Hitler. $15.
Avg. 1940s issue. $4-$8.

FROLIC. 1952-1959. $5-$10 each.

FROM UNKNOWN WORLDS.
Anthology, 1948. $15.

FRONT PAGE DETECTIVE.
Avg. issue, 1940s-1960s. $3-$5.

FRONTIER STORIES. 1940s-1950s. $5-$12.

FRONTIER TIMES.
Jan-Dec 1930. 12 mos. The lot. $40.

FRUIT GROWER. 1940s. $3-$8.

FUR, FISH & GAME.
Apr, June, Aug 1935. $12 each.
Sept 1945. $8.
Assorted. 1928-1933. $12 each.
Avg. price range. $3-$8.

THE FURNITURE MANUFACTURER & ARTISAN.
Various dates. 1921-1926. $5 each.

FURNITURE TRADE REVIEW.
Various, 1900. $20 each.

FURNITURE WORKER.
Trade magazine, Dec 1893. $15.

FURNITURE WORLD.
Various. 1907 issues. $10 each.

FUTURE. May, June 1950. $10 the pair.

G

THE GAGE MAGAZINE. 1901. $6-$8.

GAGS. A cartoon magazine of tabloid size.
Vol. 1, No. 1. 1941. $18-$20.
Most issues. $4-$8.

GALA. 1958-1960. $5-$10 each.

GALAXY.
May 1866-Jan 1878. Vols. 1-25, bound. $1,250.
Jan 1870-June 1871. 18 issues bound in 3 vols.
Contents fine. $125.

GALAXY SCIENCE FICTION.
26 issues from 1955-1958. $4-$5. each.
Vol. 1, No. 1. Oct 1950. Fine. $15.
Jan-Mar 1952. Bester's "Demolished Man".
True 1st ed. of sci-fi novel. $20.
1960s-1970s. Avg. $3 each.

G-MEN. 1930s-1940s. $10-$15.

THE GAME BREEDER. 1930s. $4-$5.

GAMES DIGEST. Vol. 1, Sept 1937. $12.

GARDEN AND HOME BUILDER.
1920s. $5-$6 each.
Mar 1925. $12.

THE GARDENER'S MONTHLY: HORTICULTURE,
ABORICULTURE, BOTANY, & RURAL AFFAIRS.
8 issues. 1860-1862, Philadelphia. Very Good. $25 all.

GAY BROADWAY. Undated striptease magazine,
circa 1940s. Vol. 1, No. 1. $20.

GEN. TAYLOR'S ROUGH & READY ALMANAC.
1848. Facsimile reprint. Dallas, no date. $16.

GENESIS WEST. Vol. 1 through 7. $23.

GENII - THE CONJURER'S MAGAZINE.
1930s. $3-$5. each.

GENT. Vol. 1, No. 1. Sept 1956. $25-$40.

THE GENTLEMAN FARMER. 1890s. $4-$8 each.

GENTLEMAN'S MAGAZINE.
18th Century English magazine with
many articles relating to America.
Bound vol. for 1736. $148.
Bound vol. for 1745. $141.
Bound vol. for 1778. $325.
Bound vol. for 1796. (six issues only) $42.
Important single issues:
Apr 1874. Treaty ending Revolutionary War. $48.
July 1780. Charleston surrender. $64.
Feb 1772. Folding map of Southern states. $245.
March 1784. Washington resigns. $85.
Aug 1776. Declaration of Independence. $1,850.
Oct 1763. Early map of America. $285.
Jan 1793. Louis XVI beheaded. $97.
May 1752. Ben Franklin and Electricity. $45.
Dec 1783. Montgolfier's 1st flight. $55.
Nov 1805. Trafalgar, Nelson's death. $85.
Nov 1756. $65.
May 1757. $65.
Apr 1792. Death of Mozart, Bounty mutiny. $150

GENTLEMAN'S QUARTERLY.
Christmas 1928. $18.

GENTLEWOMAN.
1870s-1920s. $4-$7.
1930-1973. $3-$5.
Better covers bring $10-$15.

GENTRY.
Summer, 1952 issue, contains real trout fly. $12.

"GIRLIE MAGAZINES".
Various titillating titles, from ADAM to WILDCAT,
1955 to 1993. $5 to $10 each in very good condition.
16 mixed Vol. 1, No. 1's. 1960-1970. $10 ea.
Early Men's Magazines, 1940s-1950s. 1st eds.,
Vol. 1, No. 1. VG-Fine. Avg. $15-$25 each.

GLAMOR PARADE.
1957-1958. $5-$10 each.

GLAMOROUS MODELS.
1950-1952. $5-$10 each

THE GLASS PACKER.
Jar and bottle trade publication.
Ogden-Watney. NY, Nov 1934. $25.

GLEASON'S PICTORIAL DRAWING
ROOM COMPANION.
May 1851. Calif. Gold Rush. $50.
Jan, 1852. New York Police. $8.
July 1854. Harper's Ferry. $20.
Avg. issues sell for $8-$10.
Prices are subjective and individual 1850s
to 1880s copies range from $8 to as high as $60.
Bound volumes of the 1850s-1860s are offered
at $150 to $250 each.

GODEY'S LADY BOOK.

Two failing magazines merged in the mid-1830s to produce America's first really successful women's magazine. Godey's subscription base of 150,000 households was a record breaker for its day.

In 1830 Louis Godey began publishing *The Lady's Book*, which originated the idea of special departments for cooking and household hints. The venture limped along because Godey, while imaginative, could not edit. His production was thrown together in scrapbook style.

In 1828, Sara Josepha Hale had become editor of *The Ladies Magazine* in Boston. Widowed at 40, Mrs. Hale was more interested in crusading for women's education than in the standard fashion magazine fare. By the mid-1830s her magazine was also in deep financial trouble.

Godey persuaded Mrs. Hale to edit a combined periodical called *Godey's Lady's Book and American Ladies Magazine* (later, simply *Godey's Lady's Book*). It became, in one writer's words, "the alpha and omega of the world of women's rights, fashion, etiquette and cookery." *Godey's Lady's Book* also predated the first mail-order catalog by offering a "shopping service" to subscribers. In the 1860s Godey's spurred the Americanization of foreign fashion with the help of the new mass-produced Singer sewing machine. Mrs. Hale edited the magazine from 1837 to 1877.

Although *Godey's Lady's Book* continued publication until 1898, the early issues, with hand-colored plates, are the most popular with collectors. Ironically, that part of her magazine in which Mrs. Hale was perhaps the least interested (fashions), is what makes *Godey's Lady's Book* so much in demand today.

Early single issues of *Godey's Lady's Book* range in value from $12 to $35, depending upon the quality of the hand-colored plates. Bound volumes sell for $55 to $75 each.

GOOD HOUSEKEEPING MAGAZINE.
1880s-1890s. $5-$10.
1900s-1920s. $5-$10.
1930s-1950s. $3-$8.
Jan 1915. Kewpie cover. $25.
July 1918. J. W. Smith cover. $25.
1912-1917. Cole Philips covers. $20-$30.
June 1911. Gibson illus. $12.
1914-1919. Kewpie dolls. $15-$25.
Feb 1931. J. W. Smith cover. $35.
July 1938. Cafron cover. $12.
1917-1939 (25) bound vols. No covers. Ex-library. $385.
Jan-June 1918 bound vol. $48.
Dealer lot. 50 issues 1933-1960. $48.
11 issues, 1932-1933. Jesse Wilcox Smith covers. $100.
74 issues, 1926-1938. $525.

GOLDEN BOOK.
32 issues, 1925-1928. $250 all.
Nov 1925. Very Good. $12.

GOLDEN DAYS. 1880s. $3-$5 each.

GOLF ILLUSTRATED.
Aug 1926. Bobby Jones wins. Some staining. $135.

GOLFING. 1940s. $2-$4 each.

GOOD FURNITURE MAGAZINE.
Aug 1915 issue. $12.

GOOD STORIES.
Bound vol., 1917 and 1918. $30.
1880s issues. $5-$9.

GOOD WORDS.
Bound vol., Nov 1870-Oct 1871. Includes George MacDonald's "The Princess and the Goblin" in 8 installments. Covers fair to good. $110.

GOURMET.
1940s-1960s avg. $3 each.
12 issues, 1944, bound. The lot. $20.

GRAEFENBURG ALMANAC.
1850-1886. $15-$30 each.

GRAHAM'S MAGAZINE.
Avg. 1840s-1850s issue. $8-$10.
1841 bound volume. Contains "The Murders in the Rue Morgue" and other Edgar Allan Poe tales. Good-VG. $1,500.
Vol. 24, Jan-June 1844. Three color plates. Worn, but tight. $85.
12 issues bound in one. 1847. VG. $80.
Bound vol. 1855-1856. Binding fair. $65.

BATHING SUITS.

THE GRAPHIC.
    1880s. $7-$10 each. Feb 17, 1894. $12.

GRAY'S SPORTING JOURNAL.
    9 issues, 1976-1979. The lot. $15.

THE GREAT DIVIDE. 1880s. $5-$8 each.

GREATER AMUSEMENTS.
    20 issues, 1945-1946. $10 each.

GREATEST DETECTIVE.
    Misc. 1940s issues. $3-$6 each.

G. G. GREEN ALMANAC. 1884-1916. $8-$15 ea.

THE GREENBAG MAGAZINE.
    Bound vols. 1 and 2, 1889 and 1890. $55 pair.

GREEN BOOK.
    Assorted early 1900s stage mag. $3-$10.

GREEN MAGAZINE. 1940s. $7-$8 each.

GREENLEAF'S NEW YORK, CONNECTICUT AND
    NEW JERSEY ALMANAC FOR 1792. $75.

GREEN'S ATLAS AND DIARY ALMANAC.
    Woodbury NJ, 1880. $15.

GRIN. 1940s. $6-$10 each.

GRIT & STEEL.
    1890s-1940s. $2-$10.

GROCERS' MERCANTILE REVIEW.
    Sept 1881. 4 weekly issues. $20.

H

HADLOCK'S PULMONIC ALMANAC. $35-$75.

HALLER ALMANAC. 1900s-1920. $7-$15.

HALL'S FAMILY ALMANAC. $20-$40.

HARDWARE AGE. March 3, 1927. $8.

HARDWARE DEALERS' MAGAZINE.
   June 1897. $20-$30.
   1922 Directory with ads. $20.
   Dec 1911. Holiday Issue. $25-$50.
   Oct 1912. Guns, Bicycles. $25-$35.

THE HARLEY-DAVIDSON ENTHUSIAST.
   1920-1923 issues of Company magazine. $25 each.

HARNESS GAZETTE. Aug 1900. $30.

HARPER'S MONTHLY.
   The four Harper brothers, James, John, Joseph and
   Fletcher, grew up on a farm on Long Island, New York.
   James, born in 1795, was apprenticed to a New York
   printer at the age of 16. John went with him to the city,
   working for another master. In 1817 they went into the
   business for themselves. Caution was the byword with the
   Harper brothers. Before publishing a new book or
   reprinting an old one they would scout all the wholesale
   houses for tentative orders.
   Their first big job was 2,000 copies of "Seneca's Morals"
   for another New York publisher. In 1818 they printed 500
   copies of Locke's "Essay upon Human Understanding" for
   their own customers. In 1823 and 1826 Joseph and
   Fletcher Harper joined the firm. By 1825 their publishing
   business was the City's largest, employing 50 men and
   boasting 10 hand-presses. Steam power arrived later on
   the scene.
   The launching of *Harper's Magazine* in 1850 created
   quite a stir in the periodical trade. "Godey's Lady's Book",
   and "Graham's" and "Sartain" magazines were soon
   outstripped by Harper's, who spent lavish amounts on the
   best talent here and in England. Beautifully printed and
   illustrated, the magazine became a national institution.
   Every library in the country was a subscriber and they all
   bound the monthly into 6 or 12 issues per volume. Many
   more of these smaller format magazines survived the
   ravages of time than have the fragile *Harper's Weekly*

(which has larger, more exciting illustrations and often
brings ten times as much on today's market).
Tired and worn bound volumes of *Harper's Monthly* are
common at $5 to $15 each. Pristine copies in better leather
bindings run from $25 to $35 each. 45 bound vols. dating
from 1850 to 1879 recently were offered as a lot for $450.
51 vols. with index brought. $650. Later years bring less.
67 issues 1905-1920. $130 the lot. 6 mos. 1880s. $25.
6 mos. 1860s. $35. Single issues 1850-1880. $3-$10 each.
32 issues 1906-1916. $30 the lot.

HARPER'S BAZAAR.
   1860s tabloids. $7-$20 ea.
   1872. 2 bound vols. Good, with plates. $225.
   1872 Bound vol., stained, worn. $80.
   1875 bound vol. Fine. $125.
   December 1886 (Christmas issue). $20.
   1890 6 mos. vol. Fine. $80.
   1902-1904 13 issues. Good. The lot. $200.
   1929-1934 5 issues. The lot. $30.
   Aug 1930. $10.
   Feb and Apr 1929, July 1931, Jan 1943. $6 each.
   Maxfield Parrish art, or covers, greatly increases value.
   Also watch for Rose O'Neill Kewpie illustrations.

HARPER'S ROUND TABLE.
   3 issues, 1890s, with Maxfield Parrish covers. $75 all.
   Average issues are $6-$8 each.
   Nov 1897-Oct 1899. 24 issues bound in 2 vols. Fine. $125.

HARPER'S WEEKLY (Also see Newspaper Section).
   These periodical-sized magazines are larger format and
   printed on different paper, than Harper's Monthly. They
   are also much more valuable to collectors. Copying Frank
   Leslie's successful *Illustrated News*, Harper's went on to
   exceed their rival's circulation during the Civil War.
   Featured regularly were the works of Winslow Homer,
   Thomas Nast and other prominent illustrators. Harper's
   editor, G. W. Curtis, was perhaps the most influential
   editor of his day.
   Some examples of recently offered bound volumes:
   Vol. 1, No. 1 to Vol. 4, No. 209. Jan, 1857-Dec, 1860.
   4 vols. $2,200.
   Jan 1860-Dec 1860. 52 issues. $450.
   Vol. 5. 1861. $800. (Civil War news.)
   Jan 1863-Dec 1863. 52 issues. Bound in half-leather. $800.
   Jan 1866-Dec 1866. 52 issues. $450.

Jan 1867-Dec 1867. 52 issues. Half-leather. $525.
Jan 1870-Dec 1870, 53 issues. $525.
Jan 1871-Dec 1871. $450.
Jan-Dec 1876. $425.
July-Dec 1901. includes 5 color plates. $110.

HARPER'S WEEKLY (Single issues).
Nov 20, 1858. Steam Fire Engine. $12.
June 25, 1859. Queen Victoria. $12.
Aug 30, 1862. Stonewall Jackson. $30.
Oct 11, 1862. The Battle of Antietam. $20.
Nov 22, 1862. McClellan Surrenders. $15.
Lincoln Death and Funeral, May 6, 1865. $50-$100.
Oct 28, 1865. Sioux Indians. $20.
Baseball Match, Nov 18, 1865. $75.
Aug 18, 1866. Mormons and Salt Lake. $42.
May 29, 1869. Pacific Railroad Completed. $23.
Sept 3, 1869. Brigham Young. $24.
June 18, 1870. U. S. Grant & Indians. $10.
Dec 24, 1870. Franco-Prussian War. $11.
July 1, 1871. Communist Revolution. $10.
Oct 6, 1877. Twelve Apostles, Mormon. $14.
Sept 14, 1878. Lawn Tennis. $33.
Nov 17, 1883. Modern David, Puget Sound. $15.
Mar 8, 1884. Thomas Nast cover. $15.
Aug 3, 1884. Black Bass Fishing. $23.
June 18, 1870. U. S. Grant & Indians. $10.
July 9, 1887. Howard Pyle illus. $20.
Dec 14, 1889. Death of Jefferson Davis. $14.
1892 World's Fair issues. $20.
Dec 1894. E. Penfield cover. $25.
Nov 27, 1897. Peter Newell cover. $20.
June 25, 1904. Charge of San Juan Hill. $17.
June 18, 1910. Teddy Roosevelt. $15.

HARPER'S YOUNG PEOPLE.
Bound vol., 1893, with supplements. $50.
Bound vol., 1894, with supplements. $55.
10 issues, 1895. The lot. $37.
Avg. issue, 1880s-1890s. $8.

HARTER'S ALMANAC.
1870s-1897. $5-$10 ea.

THE HARVARD LAMPOON.
Vol. 1, No. 1, Feb 10, 1876.
Plus 14 issues same year. Rare. $150.
Vol. 1, No. 1 to Vol. IV, No. 10 (June 1878).
50 issues in 5 volumes. $400.
Avg. issue, 1876-1989. $3-$15.

HAZELTINE/PISO ALMANAC.
1870-1878. $20-$40.
1879-1919. $8-$15.

HEADQUARTERS DETECTIVE.
May 1940. $10. Avg. issue. $5-$6.

HEALTHWAY ALMANAC.
Illinois Herb Co. 1930-1970. $4 ea.

HEARST'S MAGAZINE.
Avg. issue. $6-$10.
5 issues, 1918 and 1919. Christy, Flagg illus. $65 all.
Apr 1916. Christy illus. $30.
Oct 1916. Christy , Flagg, Wyeth illus. $40.
July 1921. Cover damage. $25.
(Watch for Rose O'Neill and Maxfield Parrish issues.)

HEARTH AND HOME.
1868-1930s. $2-$10.
8 issues, 1920s. The lot. $12.
35 issues, 1920-1930. $35 all.

HERBALIST ALMANAC. 1920s-1970s. $5 ea.

HERRICKS ALMANAC. 1860-1895. $5-$9.

ALFRED HITCHCOCK MYSTERY MAGAZINE.
1971-1984. $3-$4 each.

HITES POPULAR ALMANAC. $20-$40.

HOBBIES MAGAZINE.
1930s-1960s. Avg. $2-$6.
Lot of 8 different, 1942-1944. $10.
Lot of 14 different, 1950s. $28.
Lot of 6 different, 1960s. $9.

HOLDEN'S DOLLAR MAGAZINE. Vols. 3, 4, 1849.
12 monthly issues. Binding wear. Good. $50.

HOLDEN'S FREE CALIFORNIA ALMANAC. $25-$50.

HOLIDAY MAGAZINE.
Vol. 1, No. 1. March 1946. $20-$40.
45 issues, 1946-1954. $5 each.
49 issues, 1950-1966. $1 each.

HOLLYWOOD FAMILY ALBUM. Apr 1952. $10.

HOLLYWOOD GLAMOR GALS.
Vol. 1, No. 1, 1955. Anita Ekberg. Near Mint. $25.

HOLLYWOOD MAGAZINE.
1911-1940s. $10-$25.
June 1934. $25.
July 1936. $20.
March 1937. $25.
May 1940. Grant. $30.
Dec 1940. Lamour. $12.
Jan 1941. Cooper. $25.
Feb 1941. DeHavilland. $12.
Aug 1941. Lane. $12.
Sept 1942. Tierney. $15.

HOLLYWOOD LIFE STORIES. 1950s-1960s. $10-$20.

HOLLYWOOD LIFE STORIES. 1950s-1960s. $10-$20.

HOLLYWOOD REPORTER. 1930s-1950s. $6-$15.

HOLLYWOOD STUDIO.
    1969-1989 issues. $6-$8 each.

HOME. 1890s. $4-$5 each.

HOME ARTS.
    May, 1935. Maud Toussey Fangel cover. $10.
    Assorted issues 1937-1940. $3 each.

HOME CIRCLE. 1920s. $2-$3 each.

HOME & FARMER'S ALMANAC.
    Shakman & Loewy. $15-$30.

HOME & FIELD.
    7 issues, 1933. The lot. $30.
    Avg. 1930s-1940s. $2-$4.

HOME JOURNAL. 1840s-1900. $5-$10 ea.

HOME PROGRESS.
    10 issues, 1915-1916. The lot. $6.

HOMEOPATHIC NEWS. 1890s. $3-$5 each.

HOOD'S FARM ALMANAC. 1900-1916. $10-$20.

HOOEY. 1930s. $10-$12.

HOP BITTERS ALMANAC. 1877. $20-$40.

HORIZON (AMERICAN).
    Vols. 2-6. The lot, $23.
    Hardbound, 1960s. $2-$4 each.
    Wyeth, Erte, etc. $5-$10.

HORIZON (LONDON).
    119 issues. Incomplete run. $275.

HORN BOOK. 1940s-1970s. $2-$4.

HORSE LOVER. 1951-1965. $2-$5.

THE HORSEMAN.
    1880s $6-$12.
    1900-1939. $3-$10.
    1940-1960. $1-$4.

HORTICULTURE. 117 issues. 1933-1945. $69.

THE HORTICULTURIST AND JOURNAL OF
    RURAL ART AND RURAL TASTE.
    Vols. 1-7, 1846-1862. Foxing, stains. $925.

Vol. 3, 1848-1849. 12 issues, bound. No covers. $50.
Vol. 4. Contains 16 engravings. $100.
Vol. 1-Vol. 6. 1846-1851, 66 issues bound in 6 vols.
Fine plates. $1,500.

HOSTETTER'S CALIFORNIA ALMANAC. $10-$20.

HOSTETTER'S U. S. ALMANAC.
    1862. $25-$50.

HOT ROD MAGAZINE.
    Sept 1954. $7.
    Various 1960s. $5 each.
    Annuals. $5-$8.

HOT POTATO.
    Vol. 1, No. 1. June 1932. The Evils of Prohibition
    in a humorous vein. $20.

HOUSE AND GARDEN.
    Early 1900s. $8-$10.
    1937-1949. $5-$7.
    1950s. 49 issues. VG. The lot. $60.
    Sept 1934. $12.
    Sept 1927. $12.
    (Watch for Norman Rockwell & Maxfield Parrish illus.)

HOUSE AND HOME. 1890s. $3-$4.

HOUSE BEAUTIFUL.
    1890s-1900s. $5-$15.
    10 issues. 1927-1928. The lot. $85.
    31 issues. 1940s. The lot. $55.
    Various, 1937-1955. $3-$7 each.
    Dec 1946. Golden Jubilee. $8.
    Oct 1959. Frank Lloyd Wright. $10.
    (Watch for Norman Rockwell & Maxfield Parrish illus.)

HOUSEHOLD. 1880-1930s. $3-$6.

THE HOUSEWIFE.
    1880s. $3-$5 each. 1890/91 bound vol. $25.
    1896 issue, 100 pgs. $12. 5 issues, 1906-1907. All. $14.

HUNTER, TRADER, TRAPPER.
    1860s-1880s. $10-$20.
    1900-1940s. $4-$15.

HUNTING AND FISHING.
    15 issues from 1943-1948. The lot. $45.
    1930s issues. $5-$8.

HUNT'S MERCHANT MAGAZINE & COMMERCIAL
    REVIEW.
    NY, Vols. 1-44, 1839-1861 (Vols. 3, 4, missing).
    Mostly bound. VG. $750.
    1841-1843 monthly issues. $18-$20 each.
    11 Gold Rush issues. 1849-1851. VG. $195 all.

I

ICE SKATING.
100 issues. 1975-1992. The lot. $75.

IDEAL WOMAN.
Vol. 1, No. 1, Nov 1941. Mary Pickford. $20.

IF, WORLDS OF SCIENCE FICTION.
1952-1969. $4-$6 each.

THE ILLUSTRATED AMERICAN.
1893 weekly magazine. $15 each.

ILLUSTRATED FAMILY ALMANAC.
Reed & Austin, 1856-1858. $15-$30.

ILLUSTRATED LONDON NEWS.
Bound volumes:
July-Dec 1849. Worn. $75.
Jan - June 1894. VG. $120.
1916-1919. 8 vols. $525 all.
Single issues:
1843 misc. issues. $5-$7 ea.
Oct 18,1856. Czar Alexander. $10
1861-65. Civil War issues $11-$20 ea.
Sept 16, 1871. Princess Louise. $7.
April 29, 1865. Lincoln Assassination. $75.
May 15, 1937. Coronation number. $17-$25.
1953. Double Coronation number. $33.
1960s. Misc. issues. $5-$15 each.
82 issues, 1966-1968. $22 all.
7 issues, 1949-1964. $14 the lot.
5 issues, 1916-1918. $45 the lot.
15 issues, 1934-1955. $45 all.
Covers, ads, artists and articles determine value
of individual issues. Generally speaking 1842-
1900s issues sell in the $5-$20 range.
World War II issues are $3-$15 each.
1950s rarely exceed $2-$3 each.

ILLUSTRATED SPORTING & DRAMATIC NEWS.
1870s-1890s. $10-$20.
1900-1949. $3-$9.

ILLUSTRATED WAR NEWS.
1898. $40-$55 each.
Other sources list these at from $10 to $12 ea. &
$50-$100 each. (We will take the middle ground).

ILLUSTRATED WORLD.
1920s. $5-$8 each.

IMAGINATION.
Vol. 1, No. 1. Oct 1950. $10-$20.
Avg. issue. $3-$5.

THE INDEPENDENT MAGAZINE.
10 issues, 1882, 1891, 1892.
Spine wear, o/w Very Good. $75 the lot.
Avg. issue 1850-1920s. $4-$8.
1912. Titantic sinks. $15-$20.

INFINITY SCIENCE FICTION.
Nov 1955. $6.
Other 1950s issues. $3.

INLAND PRINTER.
Avg. issue 1895-1919. $10-$12.
Feb 1916, July 1923, June 1921, May 1922,
July 1924. Spine chips, o/w Fine. $9 each.
1896 and 1897 issues with perfect covers by
illustrator, Joseph Leyendecker. Up to $100 ea.
6 issues, 1898. Art Nouveau covers. $150 all.

INSIDE DETECTIVE.
1930s-1940s. $3-$5. Nov 1960. $5. Sept 1965. $6.

INSIDE BASEBALL.
1950s. Avg. issue. $15-$30.

INSIDE TV.
Vol. 1, No. 7. Jan 1954. Guy Madison cover. $12.
Dec 1959. Fabian cover. $8.

INTERNATIONAL STUDIO.
Bound vols. for 1913 & 1914. $50 each.
8 bound vols. 1911-1913. $175 all.
12 issues, 1912-1916. Loose covers, spine chips.
The lot. $15.
12 issues, 1930, 3 duplicates. The lot. $45.
June 1931. $6.
Dec 1922. Art of the Poster. $35.
Avg. issue 1850-1950. $5-$8.

INTIMATE DETECTIVE STORIES.
Mar 1943. Good. $8.

J

JACK AND JILL.
  1940s-1950s avg. $2-$3 each.
  Sept 1950-Jan 1953 with paper dolls. $6-$8 ea.

JADE.
  Typical late 1950s girlie magazine. Undated. $8.
  Vol. 1., No. 1. In fine condition. $15.

JAYNE MEDICAL ALAMANAC.
  1844-1845. $50-$100.
  1846-1847. $20-$40.
  1857-1896. $8.
  1900-1933. $4-$6.

JAZZ RECORD. Avg. 1940s issue. $8-$16.

THE JEWELERS' CIRCULAR.
  55th Anniversary number 1924. Torn pgs. Fair. $20.
  59th Anniversary number 1928. VG. $40.

JET SET.
  Vol. 1., No. 1. Sept 1973. Jackie O. cover. Mint. $16.

JOKES MAGAZINE. Various issues from Mar 1959 to
  Aug 1967. Bob Hope, Red Skelton, etc. $6 ea.

JONES FAMILY MAGAZINE. 1893-1894. $15-$30.

JOURNAL OF AMERICAN HISTORY.
  Vol. 1, No. 1. Assoc. Pub., 1907. $15.
  Vol. 1, No. 11. Very Good. $12.
  Bound vol., 16 issues, 1907-1910. Ex-library. $90.

JOURNAL OF THE AMERICAN INSTITUTE OF
  ARCHITECTS. (10) 1917 issues. The lot. $100.

THE JOURNAL OF HEALTH.
  Philadelphia, 1830-1833. 4 vols. Foxing, endpapers missing. The lot. $200.
  24 issues, 1829-1830. $125 all.
  Single copies. $5-$8.

JOURNAL OF THE NATIONAL DENTAL ASSOC.
  8 issues, 1917-1938. The lot. $39.

JOURNAL OF UFO STUDIES.
  3 issues, 1979-1983. The lot. $10.

JUBILEE.
  Vol. 1, No. 1. Sept 1950. Tabloid girlie magazine.
  Fine. $20.

JUDGE.
  Often sold for cover art. Hard to pinpoint value.
  General price range 1880s-1900s. $5-$20.
  Jan 4, 1919. James M. Flagg cover. $18.
  Aug 16, 1924. Ku Klux Klan satire. $40.
  Jan 26, 1895. Blacks, color cartoon. $50.
  Dec 1, 1917. Leyendecker cover. $50.
  Oct 14, 1922. Baseball news. $15.
  Oct 26, 1953. Modern revival of the old magazine.
  Mint. $15-$20.
  Bound vol., 1905. 10 issues. Fine. $100-$125.
  62 issues, 1925-1932. Binder holes. The lot. $239.
  9 issues, 1912-1918. The lot. $39.
  49 issues. 1924. The lot. $150.

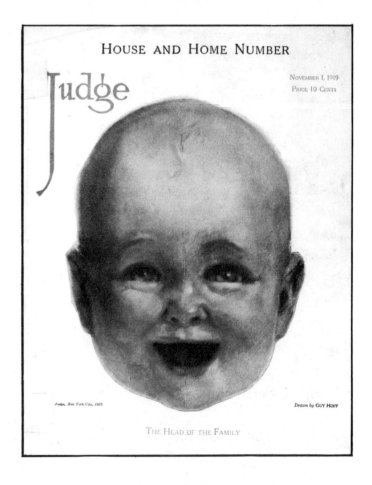

HOUSE AND HOME NUMBER

Judge

NOVEMBER 1, 1919
PRICE 10 CENTS

Judge, New York City, 1919

Drawn by GUY HOFF

THE HEAD OF THE FAMILY

K

KANSAS MAGAZINE.
Vol. 2, July-December 1872. 12 issues. $60.

KEN. Late 1930s high class tabloid-size magazine.
Some pinups.
95 copies, 1938. Vols. 1-7. Some duplicates.
Fine. The lot. $300.
Vol. 1, No. 1. April 7, 1938. Very Good. $20.
Fine. $25-$40. Mint. $75.
Avg. 1939 issues are $7-$15 each.

KENDAL'S EXPOSITOR.
Washington, Mar 17, 1841. Harrison inaug. $24.

KENTUCKY FARMERS' ALMANAC FOR 1852.
Worn and darkened. $25.

KENYON REVIEW. 1944-1945. $9-$15 each.

KERAMIC STUDIO.
Magazine of pottery and china decorating.
Sept-Dec 1914. $5 each.
1900s-1920s. $5-$12.

KEYHOLE DETECTIVE CASES.
Vol. 1, No. 1. Mar 1942. True crime. Fine. $20.

THE KEYSTONE. Jewelry trade magazine.
Holiday Number. Philadelphia, 1904. $45.
Easter Number & 7 other issues, 1899 to 1908,
bound as one. 1,000 pgs. $80.
Avg. 1890s-1900s issue. $15-$20.

KICKAPOO ALMANAC.
1892-1904. $35-$75 ea. Torn or worn. $15 each.

KIPLINGER MAGAZINE.
November 1948 issue. Special ed. announces Dewey
wins presidency. With letter admitting error. $25.

KITE'S TOWN & COUNTRY ALMANAC FOR
1831. Darkened, else VG. $25.

KIWANIS MAGAZINE.
1937-1938 issues. $4 each.

THE KLUXER. 1924. $15-$20 each.

KNAVE MAGAZINE.
Vol. 1, No. 1. Jan 1959. Typical late 50s girlie magazine.
$15-$25. Subsequent issues are worth less.

KNICKERBOCKER.
1837 issue. $15.
1840s-1850s. $10-$20.
1860s-1880s. $5-$10.

KNIGHT. June 1964. Good. $9.

KODAKERY.
63 issues,1920-1930. The lot. $225.
25 issues, 1919-1921. The lot. $19.
12 issues, 1930-1931. The lot. $28.

KODOL ALAMANAC.
1900-1909. $7-$15 ea.

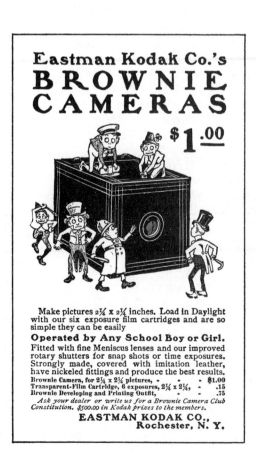

L

LADIES BIRTHDAY ALMANAC.
Pre-1894. $10-$15.
1898-1949. $5 ea.

LADIES CABINET MAGAZINE.
Jan-June 1848. 15 handpainted fashion plates. $65.

LADIES CIRCLE.
Avg. 1960s issue. $2-$3.

THE LADIES COMPANION.
1839 New York monthly. $15.

LADIES HOME COMPANION.
Vol. 14, Nov 1840-Apr 1841.
Worn, foxing. No color plates. $45.

LADIES HOME JOURNAL.
No average price range here. Each issue is subject
to cover art, collectible ads and interesting articles.
Paperdolls, Palmer Cox Brownies or Rose O'Neill
Kewpies run $12-$16 per issue.
Harrison Fisher, Norman Rockwell, James M. Flagg,
M. Fangel, M. Parrish and Coles Phillips covers,
or full page art work, are in the $20-$50 range.
21 issues, 1894-1909. Good plus. $8-$25 each.
25 issues, 1894-1908. The lot. $85.
3 issues, 1901, 1908, 1909. $7 each.
63 issues, 1932-1940. VG. $8 each.
23 issues, 1921-1929. $20 each.
25 issues, 1940s. VG. The lot. $150.
Aug 1912 and Aug 1913. Harrison Fisher covers.
The pair. $40.
Misc. 1950s-1960s issues. $5 each.

LADIES HOME MAGAZINE.
1860. Bound vol. 7 colored fashion plates. $38.

THE LADIES MAGAZINE. 1829. $25 each.

LADIES REPOSITORY.
Bound vol., 1867. Stains. $30.
Full year, 1870. $25.
1855 issue, 60 pgs. $12.

LADIES STANDARD MAGAZINE.
April 1894. Special Bicycle edition. VG. $40.

LADIES WORLD MAGAZINE.
Avg. 1890s issue. $5-$9.
July 1896. Bicycle Number. $45.
1897-1913. 34 issues for $120.
June 1913. Gibson cover. $18.
1915 issue w/Cream of Wheat ad. $20.

THE LADY'S REALM.
London. Nov 1908-April 1909. Coburn photos. Fair. $25.

LAFF MAGAZINE. 1940s. $6-$12.

L'ALBUM. 10 issues, 1901. Illus. by Job, Guillaume, Robida
and others. The lot. $175.

L'ILLUSTRATION, (PARIS).
117 issues, 1915-1932. VG-Fine. $14-$20 each.
34 issues, 1933 and 1938. The lot. $195.
13 issues, 1930-1932 and 2 from 1924. The lot. $99.
2 vols., 1932 L'Album de la Guerre, 1914-1919. Color
plates, photos. Very Good. $300.
June 27, 1931. $18.
Christmas issue, 1938. Color plates. $16.
July 1939. New York World's Fair. $22.

THE LAND OF SUNSHINE.
Vol. II, Nos. 3 & 4. $30 each.

THE LARK.
Vol. 1, No. 1, May 1895-April 1897. 24 issues, complete
run in 2 vols. Fine, $240-$300.

LARKIN CLUB.
1929. Premium offers. $8.

LARKIN IDEA. 1900s. $10.

L'ART DE LA MODE.
February 1906. 6 full color plates. Cover Fair. $48.

LA VIE PARISIENNE.
Bound vol. July 1871-April 1872. Illus. Rubbing,
o/w Very Good. $75.
Bound vol. 1872, July 1871-Apr 1872. Engravings.
Very Good. $75.
Bound vol. 1872-1873, May-Sept 1872, Aug 1873-Dec
1873. Engravings. Very Good. $75.

LAWSON'S CURATIVE ALMANAC.
Most issues. $25-$50 ea.

LE COSTUME ROYAL.
Misc. 1914-1919 issues. $20-$30 each.
Sept 1913............$8.
Dec 1914.............$20.
Feb 1919.............$20.

LE RIRE.
1897. Bound vol. Plates by Toulouse-Lautrec
and others. Very Good. $450.
6 issues, July-Dec 1900. $75 all.

LE SOURIRE (French erotic magazine).
57 issues from 1923 to 1927. Lavishly illus. $375.

LEATHERNECK. 21 issues, 1945-1947. The lot. $89.

FRANK LESLIE'S BOYS AND GIRLS WEEKLY.
1860s.................$8-$10 each.
1870s.................$3-$8.

FRANK LESLIE'S BUDGET OF FUN.
July 1875. $15.
Two year run, 1880s. Great woodcuts. (Very few have
survived). $1,000.

FRANK LESLIE'S COMIC ALMANACK. 1874. $25.

FRANK LESLIE'S CHATTERBOX.
1880s. $5-$7 each.

FRANK LESLIE'S ILLUSTRATED WEEKLY.
Frank Leslie apprenticed with the *Illustrated London
News* and *Gleason's Pictorial* before launching his own
weekly in December of 1855. Leslie was successful
because he was able to print woodblock-illustrated stories
as fast as conventional newspapers could publish dull, un-
illustrated pieces. Not highbrow, but definitely melo-
dramatic, Leslie's issues are highly collectible.
1861-1869. 14 bound volumes. $3,600 auction.
Sept 1868-1869. 52 issues bound in 2 vols. Fine. $750.
Jan 1913-Dec 1913. 52 issues bound in 2 vols. with all
covers and ads. $300.
Aug 3, 1861. Battle of Bull Run. $25.
Aug 13, 1864. Civil War Generals. $30.
May 20, 1865. Booth body, Lincoln funeral. $23.
June 9, 1866. California trees. $7.
July 22, 1876. Custer massacre. $85.
Aug 26, 1882. Jessie James killed. $545.
May 9, 1912. Airplanes. $30-$40.
Mar 15, 1919. Leyendecker cover. $40.
Average issue, news of the day. $9-$15.
Special interest issues: Cowboys, Indians, Outlaws, Civil
War, etc. $25-$65.
Norman Rockwell covers. $25-$35.

FRANK LESLIE'S LADY'S MAGAZINE.
May 1863. Fashion plates. $15.

FRANK LESLIE'S POPULAR MONTHLY.
4 issues, 1878-1881. The lot. $18.
Assorted 1870s. $6-$8 each.

THE LEISURE HOUR. London, 1853. Illus. $50.

THE LIBERATOR.
November 1918. John Reed articles. $12-$25.
Avg. issue. 1830s-1920s. $6-$12.

LIBERTY.
60 issues, 1920s-1940s. The lot. $140.
16 issues, 1937-1945. The lot. $45.
25 issues, 1937-1947. The lot. $50.
1920s. Coles Phillips covers. $25 each.
Average 1920s-1940s issue. $3-$5.
Oct 25, 1941. Hitler cover. $20.
May 1942. Donald Duck cover. $12-$15.
Winter 1973. Peanuts cover. $7.

LIBRARY MAGAZINE. 1890s. $3-$4 each.

LIFE (Early humor magazine).
218 issues, 1916-1920. VG-Fine. $1,250.
Bound vol., July-Dec 1891. Near VG. $45.
Bound vol., Jan-Mar 1909. VG. $38.
Various, 1880s. $5-$8 each.
Christmas number, 1904. $15.
Apr 14, 1904. J. M. Flagg illus. $20.
Apr 28, 1904. Pope bicycle on back cover. $25.
Oct 1909. Coles Phillips cover. $25.
May 10, 1917. N. Rockwell cover. $40.
July 21, 1921. Leyendecker cover. $40-$50.
Dec 1922. Maxfield Parrish cover. $50-$60.

LIFE MAGAZINE.
Miniature issue of Nov 1936. $25-$40.
Most single issues of *Life* sell in the $5-$10 range.
Here are a few popular issues, in Very Good to
Fine condition, which exceed the norm:
Nov 30, 1936. West Point. $30.
Dec 7, 1936. Ski issues. $25.
Jan 4, 1937. Franklin Roosevelt. $20.
May 17, 1937. Dionne Quints. $25-$45.
Nov 8, 1937. Greta Garbo. $35.
May 3, 1937. Jean Harlow. $30.
June 20, 1938. Rudolph Valentino. $35.
May 1, 1939. Joe DiMaggio. $45.
May 22, 1939. World's Fair. $45.
Sept 11, 1939. Mussolini. $15.
July 15, 1940. Rita Hayworth. $15.
April 4, 1940. Rookie Rucker. $12.
Sept 2, 1940. Dionne Quints. $20.
Oct 7, 1940. Gary Cooper. $20.

LIFE MAGAZINE (continued)
Oct 11, 1940. Tom Harmon. $14.
Dec 9, 1940. Ginger Rogers. $15.
Oct 13, 1941. Turner/Gable. $12.
Jan 6, 1941. Katherine Hepburn. $15.
Aug 11, 1941. Rita Hayworth. $15.
Dec 8, 1941. Far East Commander. $22.
Mar 29, 1942. Shirley Temple. $15-$25.
June 1, 1942. Hedy Lamarr. $12-$20.
Nov 16, 1942. N. C. Wyeth adv. illus. $15.
July 12, 1943. Roy Rogers. $35.
July 19, 1943. Wasp Pilot. $20.
Oct 16, 1944. Lauren Bacall. $25.
Dec 11, 1944. Judy Garland. $15.
Nov 12, 1945. Ingrid Bergman. $14.
Dec 3, 1945. Spencer Tracy. $20.
Dec 24, 1945. Overseas A.F. edition. $20.
Feb 4, 1946. Hope & Crosby. $20.
April 1, 1946. Cardinal Pitcher. $12.
July 19, 1946. Vivien Leigh. $15.
Nov 25, 1946. 10th Anniv. issue. $25.
July 14, 1947. Elizabeth Taylor. $15.
Nov 10, 1947. Rita Hayworth. $15.
May 3, 1948. Israeli War. $20.
Dec 6, 1948. Montgomery Clift. $14.
Aug 1, 1949. Joe DiMaggio. $25-$40.
May 8, 1950. Jackie Robinson. $25-$40.
June 12, 1950. Hopalong Cassidy. $20-$35.
April 16, 1951. Esther Williams. $15.
April 7, 1952. Marilyn Monroe. $15-$25.
July 21, 1952. Ike Nominated Pres. $12.
Sept 1, 1952. Hemingway story. $23.
Nov 17, 1952. Ike Elected Pres. $12.
Feb 2, 1953. Ike Inaugurated. $12.
April 6, 1953. Luci, Desi Arnaz. $11.
May 25, 1953. Monroe & Russell. $30.
Feb 22, 1954. Disney Undersea Movie. $11.
April 26, 1954. Grace Kelly. $15.
Sept 13, 1954. Judy Garland. $20.
Jan 31, 1955. Spencer Tracy. $15.
April 23, 1956. Jayne Mansfield. $12.
June 25, 1956. Mickey Mantle. $20-$30.
April 28, 1958. Willie Mays. $15-$20.
April 20, 1959. Marilyn Monroe. $15-$20.
Sept 5, 1960. Hemingway story. $25.
Dec 16, 1960. Hemingway story. $25.
Aug 18, 1961. Mantle & Maris. $15-$30.
April 13, 1962. Mantle & Maris with baseball card insert
(volatile price, check with sports-card dealers).
Aug 17, 1962. Memories of Marilyn. $22.
Aug 28, 1964. Beatles cover. $15-$30.
May 7, 1965. John Wayne. $25.
Jan 7, 1966. Sean Connery. $20.
Sept 1, 1968. Beatles cover. $15-$20.
April 16, 1971. Paul Mc Cartney. $12.
Dealer lots and bound volumes:
1,747 issues, 1936-1972, including 1st issue.
Mostly Good-Fine. $3,899.

800 issues, 1937-1960. Fine. $1,100.
600 issues, 1937-1967. Fine. $1,000.
12 bound vols., 1936-1940, 3 issues missing.
VG-Fine. $1,600.
50 issues, 1950s and 1960s. VG. $65.
75 diff. 1979-1988. $95.
50 issues, 1937-1970. The lot. $60.
25 issues, 1950. Fair tc Fine. $20.
1939, 13 issues. Professionally bound. VG. $55.

LIMELIGHT.
Vol. 1, No. 1. 1955. Marlon Brando. Fine. $20-$25.

LINKING RING. Feb 1959. $5.

LION'S ROAR.
A "Fortune"-style MGM movie magazine which was
sent to the trade only.
Sept 1941. Vol. 1, No. 1. Folio. $100.
Dec 1941. $75.
Oct 1942. $75.
Average issue, 1940s. $20-$40.

LIPPINCOTT'S MONTHLY.
1870s-1900s. $5-$10 each.

LISTEN. Vol. 1, No. 1. Oct 1959. Leonard Bernstein.
Fine. $15-$20.

LISTENERS DIGEST.
Vol. 1, No. 1. Feb 1939. Toscanni cover. $15-$20.

LITERARY DIGEST.
72 bound vols. Ex-library. 1914-1937. The lot. $500.
50 loose issues 1930s. Good. $75.
35 assorted, 1933-1935. $75.
1890s-1900s avg. issue. $5-$10.
1920s-1930s. $3-$4.
May 9, 1907. Leyendecker cover. $15-$25.
March 6, 1909. Mucha cover. $40-$50.
April 27, 1918. Wyeth cover. $15-$20.
March 1921. Rockwell cover. $20-$25.
April & May 1921. Rockwell. $20-$25.
June 25, 1927. Lindberg cover. $20.
Nov 15, 1930. $8.
Dec 27, 1930. $8.
Aug 13, 1932. $8.

THE LITERARY PASTIME.
Sept 12, 1868. $8.

LITERATURE.
Weekly magazine. Oct 27, 1888. Article on racist
language of J. C. Harris. $30.
Most other 1880s issues are only $2 each.

LITHOGRAPHERS JOURNAL.
1920s-1940s. $2-$4 each.

LITHOPINION.
   26 issues, 1966-1975. VG-Fine. $5 each.

LITTELL'S LIVING AGE.
   4 hardbound vols., 1854-1856. $20.

LITTLE FOLKS.
   1870s. $3 each.
   9 issues, 1914-1926. The lot. $14.

LIVING ROMANCES. 1930s-1940s. $6-$12.

THE LOCOMOTIVE. 1906 issue. Fine. $25.

THE LONDON MAGAZINE.
   Bound vols. for 1734, 1736, 1749, 1750 & 1770.
   $115-$290 each. Others, w/plates missing. $60.

THE ILLUSTRATED LONDON NEWS.
   (See Newspaper Section).

LONDON MERCURY. Nov 1902. $10.

LOOK MAGAZINE.
   1937-1939. $9-$15.
   1940-1947. $8-$10.
   July 20, 1937. Tarzan. $15.
   March 15th & 29th, 1938. Flash Gordon. $20 ea.
   May 1937. Jean Harlow. $25.
   July 18, 1939. Gone With the Wind. $20.
   Dec 5, 1939. $12.
   Nov 21, 1939. $12.
   May 11, 1937. Mae West. $25-$35.
   Feb 13, 1940. Terry and Pirates. $40.
   Feb 27, 1940. Superman. $40-$75.
   May 7, 1940. Garland & Rooney. $20.
   Dec 3, 1940. Don Winslow. $25.
   Oct 20, 1942. Flash Gordon. $15-$20.
   Nov 18, 1941. Admiral Kimmel. $15.
   Nov 2, 1943. Flying Tigers. $15.
   Oct 29, 1946. Basil Rathbone. $20.
   Oct 15, 1946. Ted Williams. $35-$50.
   June 30, 1953. Monroe, Bacall, Grable. $20.
   Various 1950s-1960s. Monroe covers. $10-$15.
   April 6, 1971. Disney World opens. $15.
   Oct 19, 1971. Last issue. Mint cond. $10.

LOS ANGELES TIMES (magazine section).
   Midwinter Number, Jan 1, 1912. Six parts: Panama
   Canal, California, sports, etc. $35.

LOUDEN'S PEOPLES ALMANAC.
   1850-1861. $20-$40 ea.

LUMBER TRADE MAGAZINES.
   9 issues of two titles, 1907-1911. The lot. $35.

M

MAD MAGAZINE.
Early issues were comic books and range from $1,800 for
no. 1, to $100 for no. 30.   (Consult a comic book dealer).
1970s-1980s magazine format average $2-$5 each.

MADEMOISELLE.
1940s. $4-$8 each.
1950s. $3-$5.

MAGAZINE OF ART.
4 issues, 1881 and 1887. Covers
poor. The lot. $15.
1895 bound vol. 683 pages. $75.
1930s-1950s issues. $3-$6 each.

MAGAZINE OF FANTASY.
Fall 1949 issue. $9.

MAGAZINE OF FANTASY & SCIENCE FICTION.
1950-1989. $2-$4 each.

MAGAZINE OF WESTERN HISTORY ILLUSTRATED.
No. 1, Nov 1884. Good. $45.

THE MAGNET.
NY, 1842-1843. 14 issues bound together. Animal
magnetism, mesmerism. The lot. $150.

THE MAGAZINE ANTIQUES.
28 bound vols. 1947-1960. Ex-library. The lot. $150.
1920s-1930s. $6-$15.
1940s to 1980s. $3-$5.

MAJOR LEAGUE BASEBALL.
1941. Phil Rizzuto cover. Fine. $15.
1948. Ted Williams cover. VG. $12.

MAN, MYTH & MAGIC.
Cavendish Corp, 1970.
24 vol. set. Fine. $100.

MANHUNT MAGAZINE.
Vol. 1., No. 1. January 1953. Fine. $65.
1953-1966. Avg. issue. $5-$7.

MANSFIELD'S FAMILY ALMANAC.
Most issues. $15-$30.

MANUFACTURER & BUILDER.
April-June 1894. $50 all.
May 1869. $10.

MARSHALLS ILLUSTRATED ALMANAC.
1880-1916. $5-$10 ea.

MASTER DETECTIVE.
April 1934. Dillinger. $18-$24.
Avg. 1940s issue. $3-$5.
Nov 1960. $4.
May 1970. John Dunning. Fine. $20.

MC CALLS.
Mc Call's circulation grew from 12,000 per month
in 1893 to over a million subscribers in 1908.
50 issues, 1927-1960. The lot. $49.
10 issues, 1930s. The lot. $85.
80 issues, 1950s. The lot. $150.
1873-1960s issues run from $2 to $20 each.
Rockwell, Parrish & J. W. Smith art can raise price to $45.
Paper dolls of the 1920s boost value to $20 an issue.
Aug 1932. $29.
1936, assorted. $6 each.
July 1931. $20.
May 1907. $10.
Oct 1916. $20.
Nov 1908. $15.

MC CALL'S FASHION QUARTERLY.
1920s issues. $15-$25 each.
Mc Call's Needlework issues, 1936-1943. $3-$5.

MC CLURE'S.
Bound vol., Nov 1896-May 1897. 30 portraits of
George Washington. $40.
Bound vol. 1899. $15.
Nov 1896. Daguerrotype in America. $75.
Oct 1906. Maxfield Parrish cover. $20.
Jan 1910. Leyendecker cover. $35.
1893-1898. Various issues. $5-$10 each.
1900-1929 issues. $3-$8.
McClure's magazine of 1893 boasted of 100 pages
and 100 illustrations at a price of 15 cents per copy.

MC CONNON'S ALMANAC.
1900-1939. $5-$10 each.

MC DONALD'S ALMANAC.
  1900-1960. $3-$5 each.

MC LEAN'S ALMANAC.
  Pre-1875. $15-$20.
  1877-1883. $8-$15.
  1885-1918. $6-$10.
  1920-1960. $5 each.

MECHANICS MAGAZINE.
  1880s. $8-$15 each.

MECHANICS & HANDICRAFTS.
  7 issues, 1936-1937. The lot. $32.

MECHANIC'S MAGAZINE & JOURNAL OF
  ENGINEERING, AGRICULTURE, ETC.
  London, 1865. Vol. 12. 26 weekly numbers.
  Worn, no backstrip. $75.

MECHANICS TODAY.
  Vol. 1, No. 1. Nov 1953. $12-$20.

MECHANIX ILLUSTRATED.
  1920s-1930s. $5-$12.
  1940s-1950s. $3-$6.
  1960s-1980s. $1-$2.

THE MENTOR.
  Vol. 1, Nos. 1-24. Bound vol. $50.
  Apr 1, 1914. Wright brothers balloon race. $45.
  Average 1920s issue. $3-$6.
  July 1921. Motion Pictures, D. W. Griffith. $6.
  Mar 1922. Maxfield Parrish illus. $10-$20.
  June 1922. Indian Blankets. $10.
  June 1927. Pyle, Parrish illus. $10.,
  Bound volume 1924. $25.
  March 1924. $13.
  Dealer lot. 28 issues. 1921-28. All $15.
  22 issues 1926-1928. All $25.

MERCHANTS GARGLING OIL ALMANAC.
  1860-1887. $8-$15 ea.

MERCHANT'S TRADE JOURNAL.
  Des Moines, 1912. $35.

MERCURY MYSTERY BOOK.
  March 1956. $45.

MERRITT'S FARMER'S ALMANAC.
  Most issues. $8-$15.

MERRITT'S FANTASY MAGAZINE.
  Vol. 1, No. 1. Dec 1949. $15.
  Vol. 1, No. 4. July 1950. $11.

METALWORKER.
  37 issues, 1891-1903. The lot. $250.
  Avg. 1850s-1880s issue. $12-$20.
  1880s. Bound vols. $75 each.
  Misc. 1870s issues. $8-$10 ea.
  Great full-page cast iron stove ads in
  most issues of this trade journal.

METEORITICS.
  Vol. 12, No. 4, 1977. $12.

THE METHODIST MAGAZINE FOR THE YEAR
  OF OUR LORD 1818.
  12 issues. Browning, foxing. $35 all.

THE METROPOLITAN.
  June 1897. $12.
  Jan 1899. $9.
  Most 1900s issues $8-$15 each.
  6 issues, color covers. 1897-1899. $40 all.
  Famous illustrators can boost prices to $25-$50 range.

MICKEY MOUSE MAGAZINE.
  Vol. 1, No. 1. 1935. $75-$150.
  Vol. 1, No. 12. 1936. $25-$50.

MIDLAND MAGAZINE.
  1920s. $3-$4 each.

MIDDLE EAST JOURNAL.
  First four issues, 1947. Bound. $14.

MIDNIGHT FROLICS.
  Vol. 1, No. 1. Circa 1943. $15-$25.

MIDWEEK PICTORIAL (NY TIMES).
  July 27, 1918. $13.
  June 20, 1931. $20.
  Aug 15, 1931. $7.

MIKE SHAYNE MYSTERY MAGAZINE.
  1970-1985. $2-$3 each.

DR. MILES NEW WEATHER ALMANAC.
  1922. $7.
  1939-1942 editions. $5 ea.

MILLENIAL DAWN.
  Allegheny PA. Vols. 1-3. 1886-1891.
  Jehovah's Witnesses publication.
  Original printed wrappers. Rare. $375.

MILLINERY TRADE REVIEW.
  Jan 1924. $20.

MINING JOURNAL.
  12 issues. 1966-1968. The lot. $10.

MINUTEMAN MAGAZINE.
   55 issues. 1943-1946. The lot. $25.

MISS LESLIE'S MAGAZINE.
   Vols. 1 and 2, 1843. 9 color plates. First mezzotint
   in America. Foxing, worn backstrip, o/w VG. $150.
   Avg. 1840s issue. $15-$30.

MISSILES & ROCKETS.
   12 bound vols. Ex-library. 1958-1963. The lot. $150.

MODEL AIRCRAFT ENGINEEER.
   1930s. $5-$10 each.

MODEL AIRPLANE NEWS.
   Sept, Oct, Nov 1954. $5 each.
   6 issues, 1931-1932. $6 each.

MODEL RAILROADER.
   1930s-1950s. $2-$10.

MODERN BREWERY AGE.
   1930s. $3-$5 each.

MODERN BRIDE.
   1960s. $2 each.

MODERN GAME BREEDER.
   1930s. $2 each.

MODERN MAN.
   Avg. 1950-1960 issue. $5-$10.
   Vol. 1, No. 1. July 1951. Jane Russell $30-$45.
   March 1955. Marilyn Monroe. $45.
   March 1961. Jayne Mansfield. $25.
   Annual, Vol. 2. Spring 1955. Mint. $35.

MODERN MECHANIX.
   8 issues, 1935-1937. The lot. $40.

MODERN PACKAGING.
   1929-1930. $15-$30 each.

MODERN PHOTOGRAPHY.
   30 issues, 1950-1953. The lot. $25.
   Wide price range, depending upon subjects
   featured. $5-$35 each issue.
   Marilyn Monroe brings top dollar.

MODERN PRISCILLA.
   5 issues, mid-1920s. Fair condition. The lot. $33.
   Aug 1924 and March 1925. $7 each.
   1880s - early 1900s. $8-$15.
   Famous illustrator covers bring. $15-$35.

MODERN RAILROAD. 1940-1950. $3-$10.

MODERN ROMANCE. 1940s-1950s. $5-$10.

MODERN SCREEN.
   65 issues. 1930s. $20 each.
   95 issues. 1940s. $15 each.
   67 issues. 1950s. $10 each.
   95 issues. 1960s. $5 each.
   75 issues. 1970s. $3 each.
   Sept 1931. Nancy Carroll. $15-$30.
   Sept 1933. Clark Gable. $15-$25.
   March 1934. Meriam Hopkins. $20-$30.
   Dec & Jan 1935. Christy illus. $20-$30.
   Jan 1939. Shirley Temple. $25-$35.
   Feb 1940. Judy Garland. $25-$35.
   Oct 1943. Betty Grable. $15-$25.
   Nov 1946. C. Wilde. $10-$15.
   Dec 1949. W. Powell. $10-$15.
   Jan 1954. J. Leigh. $8-$12.
   1955. Marilyn Monroe pinups. $35-$50.

MONTHLY ILLUSTRATOR.
   3rd Quarter, 1895. $15.

MONTHLY REVIEW OR LITERARY JOURNAL.
   36 vols. 1757-1809. Good. $375.

MORNING NOON AND NIGHT.
   Plantation Bitters Almanac for 1869,
   1870, 1871-72. $10 each.

MORRILL'S MEDICAL ALMANAC.
   Most issues. $25-$50 each.

MORSE'S ALMANAC.
   1889-1939. $8-$15 each.

MOTHER'S MAGAZINE.
   Early 1900s issues. $6-$12.

MOTOR LIFE.
   1900s-1920s. $15-$30.

MOTION PICTURE.
   1910-1929. $20-$50 each.
   1930s-1940s. $15-$25.
   1950s-1960s. $7-$10.
   A small sampling of star-studded covers:
   June 1916. Ruth Ruland. $20.
   March 1917. Violet Mersereau. $25.
   June 1921. $20.
   July 1920. $35.
   Oct 1926. $30.
   March 1928. $25.
   April 1931. Dietrich cover. $40.
   July 1935. Harlow cover. $50.
   April 1938. $45.
   July 1939. $20.
   Nov 1939. $15.
   Sept 1941. $18.

MOTION PICTURE CLASSIC.
  14 issues, 1910s. Very Good. $30-$45 each.
  Mixed lot, 1916-1927 issues. Good. $15 each.
  Super stars of the 20s and 30s, Clara Bow to
  Claire Windsor. $25-$40 each.

MOTION PICTURE HERALD.
  1920s. $18-$35 each.
  1930s. $15-$30.
  1940s. $10-$20.
  1950s. $5-$8.

MOTION PICTURE & TV MAGAZINE.
  4 issues. 1950s. $10-$17 each.

MOTOR.
  42 issues. 1929-1950. $5 each.
  Avg. price range. $4-$12.
  Sept 1922. Christy cover. $35.
  Annual Show Numbers. 1923, 1937,
  1938, 1940, 1941. $30-$50 each.

MOTOR AGE.
  Early 1900s. $15.
  1947-1952. $4 each.
  May 1925. Indy 500 cars. $13.

MOTOR LIFE.
  1910s. $20-$25 each.
  Nov 1955. $9.

MOTOR SERVICE.
  Early 1950s. $3 each.

MOTOR TREND.
  1940s avg. $5 each.
  1951-1967. $3-$4.
  May 1954. $8.

MOTORCYCLING & BICYCLING.
  Nov 1922 issue. $20.

MOVIE ALBUM.
  Aug 1948 issue. $10.

MOVIE CLASSIC.
  7 issues. 1930s. $20-$30 each.

MOVIE FAMILY ALBUM.
  1965 issue. Fine. $10.

MOVIE FAN.
  March 1955. $12.

MOVIE LIFE.
  1940s-1950s. $10-$15.
  1960s issues. $8.
  July 1941. Gene Autry. $35.

Nov 1942. Lana Turner. $25.
Jan 1945. Roy Rogers. $20.
1958-1968. Elvis covers. $25-$45.
Mar 1956. Liz Taylor. $25.
Year Books, 1949-1965. $12-$20.

MOVIE MAKERS MAGAZINE.
  12 bound issues, 1929. As new. $60.

MOVIE MIRROR.
  40 issues. 1930s. $20-$35 each.
  67 issues. 1960s. $6-$10 each.
  July 1937. Jean Harlow. $35.
  April 1937. J. Crawford. $25.
  March 1940. P. Lane. $15.
  May 1935. G. Rogers. $18.
  Nov 1937. C. Colbert. $18.

MOVIE PLAY.
  May 1950. VG. $10.

MOVIE SCREEN YEARBOOK.
  1960s. $10-$20.

MOVIE SHOW.
  Nov 1946. Very Good. $10.
  Major Stars of the 1940s. $15-$20.

MOVIE STARS PARADE.
  1949-1958. $10-$20.
  Feb 1942. Judy Garland. $18.
  April 1961. Elvis. $30-$40.

MOVIE STARS TV CLOSEUPS.
  June 1959. $10.

MOVIE STORY.
  1937-1942 issues. $15-$35 each.
  Mixed, 1943-1951. Closeout. $10 each.

MOVIE WORLD.
  1958-1969. $8-$10.
  May 1959. Elvis. $30.

MOVIELAND.
  Jan 1945. Shirley Temple. $20.
  March 1949. $10.

MOVIES.
  Jan 1942. Rita Hayworth. $15.
  Nov 1944. Lucille Ball. $15.

MUNSEY.
  Bound vols., 1903, 1906, 1910, 1919. $30-$40 each.
  1904 vol. $25.
  1907 vol. $22.
  4 vols., 1898 and 1899. VG. The lot. $75.
  3 issues. July 1895. March 1896, July 1905. $32 all.

May 1896. Bicycle number. VG. $30.
Feb 1899. Klondike. $10.
Oct 1907. Great ads. $10.

MUNYON'S ALMANAC.
1905-1920. $10-$20 each.

MUSCLE POWER.
8 issues, 1950s plus 3 other strength & health mags.
Total 11 issues. $20.

MUSIC MAGAZINES.
60 issues of various titles, 1872-1902. The lot. $59.
Most musical digests and quarterlies of the early
1900s sell for $2-$4 each.

MUSICIAN MAGAZINE.
1890s. $5 to $10 each depending on advertising.
Mostly band instruments.

MUNYON'S ILLUSTRATED WORLD.
1880s. $5-$10 each.

MYSTERY BOOK MAGAZINE.
July 1945. 1st issue. VG. $65.
Aug 1946. $11.

MYSTIC MAGAZINE.
Nov 1953. $7.

MYSTIQUE. Occult magazine.
Vol. 1, No. 1. April 1973. $15-$20.

N

THE NATION MAGAZINE.
  1860s-1960s. $3-$16 each.
  29 issues, 1931-1938.
  Fair to Good. The lot. $75.
  30 issues, 1933-1946. $4 each.
  Feb 22, 1912. Parrish article. $16.
  1965 100th anniversary issue. Frost,
  Pound, Mencken etc. Fine. $25.

NATIONAL FARM JOURNAL.
  1920s. $4-$5 each.

NATIONAL GEOGRAPHIC.
  (See chapter on National Geographic publications.)

NATIONAL HERD CO. ALMANAC. $5-$10 ea.

NATIONAL HORSEMAN.
  1910-1920. $3-$10.

NATIONAL JEWELRY & OPTICIAN.
  1911-1915. $10-$20.

NATIONAL MAGAZINE.
  Vol. 1. July-Dec 1852. Foxing. $20.
  Vol. 2. Jan-June 1853. Foxing. $20.
  1850s single issues. $4-$8 each.
  Sept 1915. Five and Dime Store. $15.

NATIONAL SPORTSMAN.
  Sept 1923-Nov 1923. $13 each.
  12 issues 1939. $50 all.
  Avg. 1890s-1940 issue. $5-$8.

NATIONAL STOCKMAN AND FARMER.
  1870s issues. $3-6 each.

NATION'S BUSINESS.
  1900s issues. $1-$3 each.

NATURAL HISTORY.
  1860s-1950s. $2-$10.

NATURE MAGAZINE.
  Early 1900s issues. $3-$8 each.
  4 issues, 1924-1925. $9 all.
  1940s. $1-$2 each.

NAUTILUS MAGAZINE OF NEW THOUGHT.
  1900s-1920s. $6-$16.

NAVY LOG.
  40 issues, 1920s, 1930s. $3 each.

NEEDLECRAFT.
  88 issues, 1926-1940. $2 each.
  8 issues, 1925-1933. The lot. $10.
  Early 1900s issues. $2-$12.
  Misc. Jello, Cream of Wheat ads. $10-$20.

NEW AGE.
  1860s-1890s. $3-$5.

THE NEW DAGUERREIAN JOURNAL.
  July 1975. Vol. 3, No. 4. $25.

NEW ENGLAND.
  1830s issues. $8-$40 each.
  Bound vol. Mar 1905-Aug 1905. Ex-library. VG. $22.
  Bound vol. Sept 1903-Feb 1904. Near Fine. $75.

NEW ENGLAND ANTI-MASONIC ALMANAC.
  1832-1835 edition. $60-$100 ea.

NEW ENGLAND FARMER.
  Boston, 1849. 408 pgs. Cover detached. $15.
  1854, Nos. 1-12. $15.
  Bound vol. 1858-1859. $25.
  Bound vol. 1850-1851. $35.

NEW ENGLAND MEDICAL ALMANAC.
  Most issues. $20-$40 ea.

NEW ENGLANDER.
  1840s. $4-$6 each.
  Mixed issues to 1890. $8-$15 ea.

THE NEW LADY'S MAGAZINE.
  London, 1788. $16.

NEW LETTERS.
  J. D. Salinger story. 1978 issue. Fine. $15.

NEW MASSES.
  33 copies, 1931-1946. $8 each.

THE NEW MOVIE.
 34 issues, 1930-1932. VG. $25-$35 each.
 Feb 1934. Hepburn cover. VG-Fine. $40.
 July 1934. VG-Fine. $30.

NEW REPUBLIC.
 44 issues. 1936. Edges browned. The lot. $35.
 75 issues. 1950s. $2 each.
 1929-1935. $2-$5.
 1949-1953. $1-$2.

NEW STARS.
 1940s. Avg. $8-$10.

NEW WEST.
 1976. $4-$6 each.

NEW YORK ARCHITECT.
 June 1909. Water stains. $13.

NEW YORK (CENTAUR) ALMANAC.
 1887-1910. $10-$20 ea.

NEW YORK CLIPPER.
 March 29, 1884. Baseball. $15.
 Other baseball related issues. $12-$20.

NEW YORK ILLUSTRATED NEWS.
 1880s. $8-$18 each.
 June 29, 1861. Nast engravings. $50.

NEW YORK LUMBER TRADE JOURNAL.
 1880s. $8-$12 each.
 1900s-1930s. $4-$8.

NEW YORK MIRROR.
 1830s. $10-$15.

NEW YORK TIMES MIDWEEK PICTORIAL.
 Bound vol., 1918-1919. $75.

NEW YORK TIMES MAGAZINE SECTION.
 Dealer lot. 100 issues, 1930s-1940s. VG. $3 each.

THE NEW YORKER.
 24 bound vols., 1947-1952. Some browning,
 o/w VG-Excellent. The lot. $1,750.
 59 issues. 1933-1937. Good-VG. $5 each.
 10 issues. 1930s. VG-Fine. The lot. $45.
 1960s. Good. $2-$4 each.
 1961-1968. $1-$4 each.
 Exceptional ads or famous illustrators
 can raise value to $10 or more.

NEW FLASH DETECTIVE.
 Oct 1946. VG. $10.

NEWSWEEK MAGAZINE.
 1930s. $2-$5 each.
 1940s-1960s. $1-$4 each.
 Bound vols., 3 mos. each, 1948-1963. $25 ea.
 First issue, Feb 17, 1933. VG-Fine. $25-$50.
 Oct 4, 1937. Hitler & Mussolini. $15-$25.
 Dec 1942. F. D. Roosevelt. $5.
 Oct 3, 1943. Carl Hubbell cover. $5.
 April 23, 1945. FDR death cover. $5.
 May 17, 1954. Grace Kelly cover. $50.
 June 25, 1956. Mickey Mantle. $5-$10.
 Feb 24, 1964. The Beatles. $10-$20.
 93 WWII issues, 1940-1943. VG. The lot. $250.

NICKEL PLATE ROAD.
 15 issues. Jan 1955-Sept 1964. $25 all.

NIGHT AND DAY.
 Vol. 1, No. 1. Nov 1948. Lili St. Cyr cover. $20-$35.

NORTH AMERICAN ALMANAC.
 1920-1927. $5-$10 ea.

NORTH AMERICAN REVIEW.
 48 bound vols., ex-library, 1901-1904, 1913,
 1916-1924, 1936-1939. The lot. $250.

NORTH DAKOTA HISTORICAL QUARTERLY.
 Oct 1926-July 1932. Bound vol. 24 issues.
 Custer, gold rush, etc. $175.

NORTH PACIFIC COAST.
 Dec 1879 to Sept 1881. Bound vol. Published in
 New Tacoma, Washington Territory. VG. $1,500.

NORTHWEST.
 1880s-1890s. $8-$12.
 1900s-1920s. $5-$10.
 1930s-1940s. $2-$4.

NORTHWESTERN MILLER.
 Jan-June 1880. Engravings of machines. $55.

NOVAE TERRAE.
 British sci-fi magazine. Dec 1937, Jan 1938,
 December 1938. Arthur C. Clarke. 3 issues. $100.

NUDIST MAGAZINES.
 Approximately 250 issues, 1950s and 1960s.
 Including Sunshine and Health. VG. $5 each.

NUGGET.
 Vol. 1, No. 1. Nov 1955. Betty Brosmer cover. $15-$35.

THE NURSERY.
 Boston 1873. Vols. 13 & 14, bound in leather. Pair, $45.

NATIONAL GEOGRAPHICS

Don Smith has been dealing in National Geographic Society publications for nearly 25 years. The latest edition of his value guide is the Bible for anyone collecting or dealing in Geographic material. Most of the data below has been extracted from Don's guide, with his permission. Condition for any item cited is assumed to be very good to fine.

The National Geographic has sported six different cover designs since 1888, the first year of issue.

The value of individual issues is determined by age and subject matter. From 1888 to May, 1905, prices remain above $100. Collectors covet issues published between 1888 and the beginning of World War I.

Special issues featuring Monkeys, Head Hunters, Birds, Cattle, Dogs, Butterflies, Sea Shells, Military Medals, etc., command a premium over other numbers.

1905 to 1909 issues, **in very good to fine condition**, are worth from $35 to $80 each. 1910 to 1919, $10-$25. 1920s, $9-$13. 1930s, $8-$10. 1940s, $7-$13. 1950s, $6-$7. 1960 to 1980, $3-$6.

Bound volumes from 1888 to 1914 are the heart of any serious collection, according to Don Smith. Values are as follows:

1888-1889	$7,500	1902	$650
1890	$3,500	1903	$650
1891-1892	$1,500	1904	$800
1892-1893	$3,500	1905	$650
1893-1894	$2,250	1906	$300
1884-1895	$1,500	1907	$225
1896	$650	1908	$225
1897	$650	1909	$225
1898	$700	1910	$225
1899	$1,000	1911	$200
1900	$625	1912	$200
1901	$650	1913-1914	$175

Collectors demanding fill-in issues persuaded the National Geographic Society to run off *reprint issues* and *volumes* in 1964. The period from 1888 through 1907 was chosen. All issues were marked REPRINT at the bottom of the front cover. The bound volumes are scarce today and worth from $75 to $125 each.

Among the rarities, scarcities, and novelties published by the National Geographic Society are:

1. A technical book, *The Material Culture of Pueblo Bonito*. 1954. $325.

2. Set of 10 monographs published in 1895. Sample title: *Present and Extinct Lakes of Nevada*. $375 each.

3. Sixteen technical books were issued between 1896 and 1954. Sets are rare. Individual titles run from $275 to $425.

4. Most non-technical books published from 1907 to 1957 average $30 to $60 each. The most sought-after are: *Australia and New Zealand*, a 1943 issue is worth $400, and *The Valley of 10,000 Smokes* published in 1922, which is valued at $235.

5. Curiosa include bookmarks made from fabric of the Explorer II, which set a world altitude record in 1935, $100 or more. MAD Magazine's 1958 parody issue, *The National Osographic Magazine*, sells for $300 or more. Among the articles: *Why Pygmies Smell Bad, New Zealand's Jails are Nicer,* and *I Got Lost in Patterson, New Jersey*.

6. Pictorial supplements totaling 33 were featured in the National Geographic between 1903 and 1958. They range in value from $10 in 1958 to $60 in 1903. Most of these supplements were glued between the initial ads and the first page, but some were inserted loose. A pictorial on the Alaskan Wrangell Mountains in the November 1903 issue which is rated at $60. Another, of ships, in 1938 is worth $50.

Map sections are also collectible. The most valuable National Geographic map supplements are those issued from 1889 to 1918:

Oct 1889	$100	March 1896	$65
March 1892	$75	Oct 1896	$40
April 1893	$65	April 1898	$100
Jan & Feb 1896	$40 ea	May 1898	$65

1906 to 1918 average $10-$20 each. Most 1920 to 1960 maps are only worth a dollar or two. A total of more than 300 maps have been issued.

For more information on National Geographics and their values, send a stamped and self-addressed envelope to:

Don Smith
3930 Rankin Street
Louisville, Kentucky 40214.

O

OBJECTIVIST MAGAZINE. (Ayn Rand).
   7 copies, all VG. $7 each.

THE OCEAN.
   1st number, March 1907. Fair-Good. $15.

THE OFFICE MENTOR.
   Vol. 1, No. 1, Oct 1926. $15-$30.

THE OFFICE MAGAZINE.
   Vol. 1, No. 1, Feb 1932. $17-$35.

OFFICE LIFE, THE MAGAZINE OF OFFICE PEOPLE.
   Vol. 1, No. 1, July 1926. $15-$30.

OFFICIAL DETECTIVE STORIES.
   1940s issues. $6-$12 each.
   1960s. $5 each.

OFFICIAL GAZETTE OF THE U. S. PATENT OFFICE.
   Various monthly issues from the 1870s. $15-$25 each.

OLD FARMERS ALMANAC.
   31 issues, 1870-1906. $125 all.
   (Also see "Farmers Almanac".)

OLIVER OPTIC'S MAGAZINE.
   1860s. $6-$10 each.
   Aug 1874. Baseball cover. $25.

OLYMPIA.
   Vol. 1, No. 1. No place or date. Fine. $35.

OMNI.
   Oct 1978 to Sept 1990. $250.
   March, Sept 1981. $5 each.

OMNIBOOK.
   Vol. 1, No. 1. Dec 1938. Tabloid size, book
   reviews. $20-$35.

ONCE A WEEKLY.
   Oct 13, 1894. $11.

1,000 JOKES.
   1959-1967 issues. $5 each.

ON THE QT. "Stories newspapers won't print."
   Vol. 1, No. 1. Jan 1950. $15-$25.
   Avg. 1950s-1960s issue. $10-$15.

THE OPAL.
   Utica NY, 1853. Edited by insane asylum inmates.
   One issue. $54.

ORANGE JUDD FARMER.
   1880s-1890s issues. $5-$10 each.

ORBIT SCIENCE FICTION.
   1953 issues. $5 each.

ORIENTAL RUG MAGAZINE.
   1930s. $3-$6 each.

OTHER WORLDS SCIENCE FICTION.
   1949-1953. Most $4-$6 each.
   1950, 1951. $3-$6.
   Nov 1949. Lemuria. $8-$9.

OUR CONTINENT.
   Philadelphia, 1882. Albion Tourgee, ed. Vol. 1, No. 1,
   Feb 1882, to Vol. 1, No. 21, 1882. Complete. $95.

OUR DUMB ANIMALS.
   1860s-1890s. $5-$6 each.

OUR LITTLE MEN AND WO MEN.
   1890 children's magazine with premium section of toys
   and games offered for selling subscriptions. $35.

OUR YOUNG FOLKS.
   An Illustrated Magazine for Boys and Girls. Bound Vol.
   1866. 772 pgs. $45.
   Bound vols. 1866-1869. 42 issues in 7 vols. Red leather
   and green cloth. $250 all.
   Avg. single issue, 1860s. $3-$5.
   With full page Winslow Homer engravings. $20-$40 ea.
   1867 Baseball article. $15.

OUTDOOR AMERICA.
   April 1931 issue. $7.
   Other 1920s-1960s. $2-$12.

OUTDOOR LIFE.
  1890s-1900. $6-$15.
  1910-1920. $2-$5.
  Nov 1924. $9.
  Dec 1936. $10.
  Mar 1944. $6.
  1950s-1980s. $1-$5.

OUTDOORS.
  19 issues from 1941-1944. The lot. $75.
  Single issues. $2-$4 each.

OUTING.
  Single issues from 1882-1923 sell in a wide
  price range of from $3 to $65 each.
  Sept 1891. $10.
  Jan 1896. $25.
  1909 Maxfield Parrish covers and July 1910
  Baseball heroes bring top dollar.
  Bound vols: Oct 1885-Mar 1886. $40.
  7 vols. 1898-1902. Fine. $300 all.
  Assorted single issues 1906-1908. $20 ea.

OUTING AND THE WHEELMAN.
  Bound Vol. 1884-1885. $50-$75.

THE OUTLOOK.
  Bound vol. Dec 1895-Nov 1896. VG. $65.
  April 3, 1909. Woman suffrage. Fine. $10.
  5 issues, 1918-1929. The lot. $15.
  Mar 2, 1912. $6.
  Dec 1, 1915. $6.
  Avg. 1870-1935 issue. $3-$8.

THE OUTSIDER.
  Nos. 1 and 2, 1961-1962.
  Work by Bukowski, Kerouac, Corso. $35.

OVERLAND MONTHLY.
  Vol. 1, No. 1, July 1868-Dec 1870. 30 issues,
  bound. Near Fine. Asking $800.
  1907-1912. Fine. $25 each.
  1920s issues. $3-$5 each.

OZOMULSION ALMANAC.
  Any issue. $25-$50.

P

PACIFIC MONTHLY.
1907-1910. Fine. $25 each.
Avg. 1900s-1920s. $5-$10.

PACIFIC RURAL PRESS.
4 vols. 1900-1901. The lot. $300.

THE PAINTER'S MAGAZINE.
Trade publication for coach painters.
Vol. XII. Nos. 1-12. Bound volume 1886.
Includes 3 large folding stencils. $125.
Jan 1886, Dec 1888. 2 vols. 684 pgs. Good. $150.

PANSY.
Child's magazine of the 1880s. $1-$3.

PARABOLA.
Winter 1981. 8 Paul Caponigro photos. Good. $20.

PARENTS.
1930s. $1-$3 each.
20 issues 1941-1951. $5 ea.
Norman Rockwell illus. bring up to $25.

PARIS REVIEW.
43 issues, 1930s-1960s. The lot. $160.
Summer 1966 issue. James Salter article. Signed. $30.

PARKER'S MEDICAL ALMANAC.
Any edition. $50-$100.

PARLEY'S MAGAZINE FOR CHILDREN & YOUTH.
1833. 14 issues, incl. Vol. 1, No. 1. Woodcuts. Good.
The lot. $40.

PARTISAN REVIEW.
25 issues, 1930-1960s. The lot. $70.

PATHFINDER.
21 World War I issues. The lot. $50.
1919-1930. $3-$5 each.
1940s-1950s. $2.
90 issues. 1940s and 1950. The lot. $75.

PAXTON'S MAGAZINE OF BOTANY.
London, 1834. Vol. 1. 41 hand-colored
plates. Very Good. $1,500.

PEARSON'S MAGAZINE.
1900-1910. $4-$8 each.
Oct 1901. Fine. $18.
June 1906. Good. $6.

PENCIL POINTS.
1920s. $3-$5 each.
Maxfield Parrish illus. bring more.

PENNSYLVANIA MAGAZINE.
Philadelphia, May 1775. Edited by Thomas
Paine at beginning of Revolutionary War. $355.
April 1776. Revolutionary War news. $285.

PENNY MAGAZINE.
London, 1832-1836. Vols. 1-5.
Heavily used. As is, $150.
Nov 30, 1833 issue. $5.
Other single copies. $5-$10.

PENTHOUSE.
70 issues, including Vol. 1, No. 1, 2, 3, 4.
Mint. $2,450. Dupes. $35 each.
1969 issues. $10-$30.
Most issues since 1970. $5 each.
1970-1983. $3-$7 each.
1980s. Madonna, Vanessa Williams, etc. $20-$30.

PEOPLE MAGAZINE.
42 issues. 1974-1977. All complete. Fine. $3 each.
Jan 1975. Elvis issue. $10.
Other stars. $4-$8.

PEOPLE'S FREE ALMANAC.
Most issues. $20-$40 ea.

PEOPLE'S HOME JOURNAL.
1885-1899. $8-$15.
1910-1920. $5-$12.
Leyendecker, Parrish and Rockwell. $20-$35.

PEOPLE'S POPULAR MONTHLY.
1910-1920. $3-$8 each.
1917-1923 issues with Rockwell covers. $30-$50.

PERUNE ALMANAC.
1890-1919. $5-$10 ea.

PETERSON'S LADIES MAGAZINE.
Bound vol. 1864. $120.
Bound vol. 1860. $60.
Bound vol. 1879. $120.
Bound vol. 1862. 2 plates, several pp missing. $32.
Bound vol. 1864. Cover, spine poor, o/w Good. $48.
6 issues. 1872. Interior VG. $37.
1842-1898. Avg. $12-$22 ea.
With hand-colored plates. $25 each.
1865-66 issues, 70 pgs. $22 each.
3 issues. 1884-1886. The lot. $20.
Missing handcolored fashion plates and color
needlepoint patterns account for lowest quotes.

PHANTOM DETECTIVE.
1930s. $10-$12.

PHILADELPHIA PUBLIC LEDGER ALMANAC.
1881-1900. $8-$10.

THE PHILISTINE.
Roycroft Press. March 1899. (A Message to Garcia). $5.
Most issues 1895-1915. $1-$2.
Bound vols. up to $15 in VG condition.

PHILOBIBLION.
25 issues. 1861-1863. Loose in binder. The lot. $22.

THE PHOTO AMERICAN.
115 issues. 1891-1903. VG. $800.
12 issues. 1882-1893. The lot. $25.

PHOTO-GAZETTE.
8 vols. French photo magazine. 1897-1910.
Covers fair, contents VG. The lot. $350.

PHOTO-GRAPHIC ART.
Vol. 3, No. 2. 1917. $20.

THE PHOTO MINIATURE.
63 issues, turn of century. The lot. $600.
Vol. 1, No. 1. Apr 1889. VG. $45.
Five issues. 1899-1901. $80.

THE PHOTOGRAPHIC JOURNAL.
8 issues. 1931. The lot. $10.
Avg. issue. $3-$5.

PHOTOGRAPHIC MAGAZINES. (Mixed).
Several titles, 49 issues, 1940s and 1950s. The lot. $39.
60 issues, various titles, 1940s and 1950s. The lot. $60.

PHOTOGRAPHIC TIMES.
1890s. $3-$6 each.

PHOTOGRAPHY YEAR BOOK
1970. Very Good. $20 each.

PHOTOPLAY MAGAZINE.
VG to Fine, all with cover mailing label.
1910-1929. Most VG. $25-$30. Good. $18-$24.
1930-1939. $18-$30.
1940-1949. $10-$20.
1950-1959. $9-$17.
1960-1969. $7-$10.
1970-1979. $5-$10.
Special star covers, such as Gish, Pickford, Coogan,
Talmadge, etc. $25-$35.
Misc. dealer lots:
25 issues. 1910s. VG. $35-$60 each.
70 issues. 1920s. $20-$35 each.
90 issues. 1930s. $20-$35 each.
6 issues. 1952. VG-Fine. The lot. $41.
9 issues. 1954. Fine. The lot (much Marilyn Monroe). $60.
12 issues. 1955. The lot. $55.
9 issues. 1948. VG-Fine. The lot. $41.
Individual Issues:
Stars of the Photoplay issue, 1930. $75.
Barbara Stanwick. Sept 1931. $22.
Mary Astor. Feb 1932. $20.
Sidney Fox. May 1932. $14.
Ann Harding. Nov 1935. $17.
Norma Shearer. Oct 1936. $12.
Ginger Rogers. Nov 1942. G-VG. $14.
Olivia DeHavilland. Sept 1942. $15.
Paulette Goddard. Dec 1943. $15.
Greer Garson. Jan 1944. $14.
Joan Fontaine. March 1944. $10.
Olivia DeHavilland. June 1944. $14.
Ingrid Bergman, June 1945. $25.
Lauren Bacall. June 1945. G. $30.
Diana Lynn. August 1945. $15.
Claudette Colbert. Dec 1945. $14.
Jennifer Jones. April 1946. $15.
Jeanne Crain. May 1946. $14.
Ingrid Bergman. June 1946. $18.
Esther Williams. July 1946. $13.
Ingrid Bergman. Feb 1947. G. $9.
Olivia DeHavilland. Oct 1947. $16.
June Haver. Jan 1948. $13.
Betty Grable. April 1948. $15.
Esther Williams. July 1948. $14.
Ava Gardner. Dec 1948. $16.
Lana Turner. Feb 1949. $16.
Bing/Kids. March 1949. $18.
Betty Grable. April 1949. $20.
Jane Wyman. May 1949. $12.
Liz Taylor. Jan 1950. $15.
James Stewart. March 1950. $18.
Alan Ladd. Sept 1950. $14.
Liz Taylor. Oct 1950. $14.
June Allyson. Dec 1950. $14.
Lana Turner. Jan 1951. $15.
Esther Williams. April 1951. $12.

PHOTOPLAY (Continued).
Ava Gardner. Feb 1952. $15.
Liz Taylor. May 1952. $12.
June Allison. June 1952. $10.
Doris Day. Dec 1952. $12.
Debbie Reynolds. Jan 1953. $12.
Janet Leigh. Oct 1953. $13.
Piper Laurie. Nov 1953. $15.
Kim Novak. Nov 1955. $16.
Annual. 1955. $22.
Natalie Wood. Dec 1956. $15.
Photoplay Year of 1947. Hdbk. $95.
Elizabeth Taylor. 1963 Annual. $12.

PHRENOLOGICAL ALMANAC.
1847 edition. $20.

PHRENOLOGICAL JOURNAL.
1820s-1860s. $8-$12.

PHYSICAL CULTURE.
27 issues. 1920s and 1930s. Mint. $8 each.
27 issues. 1921, 1924, 1926 and 1928. The lot. $40.
50 issues. 1930s. The lot. $250.
31 issues. 1921-1931. $6 each.
1903-1920. $5-$8.
1920s-1940s. $2-$6.

PIC MAGAZINE.
1938-1957. $6-$15.

PICTORIAL REVIEW.
10 issues form 1906. $40 all.
Dolly Dingle Paper Doll Issues:
Dec 1917. $25. Feb 1923. $20.
Jan 1923. $22. Mar 1923. $22.
July 1923. $25. June 1927,
July 1927, Aug 1927, May 1928,
June 1928. $15 each.
1930s. $10-$15 per issue.

PICTURE PLAY.
25 issues, 1920s. VG. $20-$25 each.
Nov 1932. Dietrich cover. VG-Fine. $50.
Nov 1933. Garbo cover. VG-Fine. $50.
Aug 1930s issue. $10-$20.

PIPE LORE.
Wally Frank Co. 3 issues, 1942-45. $29.

PLANET STORIES.
7 issues, 1949-1954. $45 all.
Winter, 1939. $25.
Spring, 1940. $15.

PLANTER AND STOCKMAN.
1880s. $5-$7 each.

PLANTER'S & FARMER'S ALMANAC.
Most issues. $15-$30.

PLAYBOY.
No. 1, Dec 1953 Marilyn Monroe. Fine. $1,500-$2,000.
Most issues since 1970, $4-$5 each.
Annual No. 1, 1956. VG in DJ. $23.
Holiday Anniverary issue. Jan 1966. $11.
Holiday Anniverary issue. Jan 1929. $13.
Oct 1958. $25.
Mar 1959. $15.
Aug 1959. $15.
Oct 1960. $25.
May 1960. $15.
Feb 1962. $12-$15.
July 1962. $10.
Oct 1961. $10.
Feb 1960. Jayne Mansfield. $35.
Playboy Special Editions:
Best of Playboy No. 5. $15.
Wet N Wild. $8.
Sensuous Society, 1973. $15.
Sporting Women, 1966. $12.
Cover Girls. 1966. $12.
Playmate Review Premier Issue. $44.
Playmate Review 3rd Edition. $22.50.
Girls of Winter. 1963. $32.
Holiday Girls. 1967. $30.

PLAYMATE.
1950s. $5-$12 each.
Lot of 10 from 1947-1951. $30.

PLEASURE.
Brief Esquire rival. 1st issue, 1937. $25-$50.
Avg. 1930s edition. $5.

PLUCK AND LUCK.
With color-litho firefighting scenes on covers. $15-$20.

PM: An Intimate Journal for Production Managers, Art Directors and Their Associates. 33 issues, 1936-1941. Articles, by Gropius, Bruce Rogers, etc. Includes paper samples. VG. $250 all.

POETRY MAGAZINE.
1910-1920. $2-$5 each.
7 issues. 1925-1926. $10 each.
Sept 1955. $5.
Dec 1955. $8.
Dec 1968. $3.
Other 1960s issues. $1.

POLICE GAZETTE (NATIONAL POLICE GAZETTE).
1880s. $8-$10 each.
8 issues, 1917-1921. $40 all.
28 issues, 1950-1975. $60 all.

POLICE GAZETTE (Continued).
    April 1940. Carole Landis. $7.
    1961 Marilyn Monroe cover. $25.
    Feb 1963. Kim Novak. $6.
    Apr 1963. Hitler. $6.
    Aug 1964. Liz Taylor. $6.

POLICE RECORD DETECTIVE.
    Oct 1949. $9.

POPULAR ASTRONOMY.
    Complete years (10 issues per year) 1931,
    1933, 1934, 1935, 1947, 1948, 1949, 1950.
    First four years unbound, the rest bound with-
    out original covers. Each annual volume. $70.
    4-year run, 1936-1939 Bound with covers. $280.
    10-year run, 1942-1951. Bound without covers. $600.
    23-year run, 1918-1940. Bound without covers. $1,200.
    All are ex-library copies in good condition.

POPULAR AVIATION.
    1938, 1939, 1940 issues. $8 each.
    Setp 1941. Special US Army Air Force issue. $12.
    Avg. 1930s-1940s. $8-$15 each.

POPULAR HORSEMEN.
    11 issues from early 1950s. The lot. $10.

POPULAR HOT RODDER.
    Vol. 1, No. 1. 1962. Fine. $25.

THE POPULAR MAGAZINE.
    1900s-1920s. $5-$8.
    Rockwell and Leyendecker covers. $40-$60.

POPULAR MECHANICS.
    1902-1910. $5-$10.
    1920s-1940s. $6-$8.
    Most 1950s. $3 each.
    July 1908. Airship collapses. $25.
    Aug 1909. Night Baseball. $10.
    Misc. 1907-1909. $15 ea.
    5 issues 1931-1936. $30 all.
    Jan 1952 Anniversary issue. $15.
    Early Aviation covers. Up to $25.

POPULAR PHOTOGRAPHY.
    9 issues. 1913-1916. The lot. $100.
    67 issues. 1937-1952. VG. $5-$10 each.
    50 issues. 1937-1965. The lot. $65.
    Vol. 1, No. 1. May 1937. $20-$30.
    1930s Glamour girls. $10-$20.
    Various issues, 1941. $5-$7 each.
    1942-1948. $3-$6 each.

POPULAR RADIO.
    1920s-1930s. $8-$10 each.

POPULAR SCIENCE.
    1872, 1st edition, 1st issue. 6 mos. bound vol. $65.
    50 issues. 1941-1958. The lot. $47.
    20 issues. 1934-1938. The lot. $50.
    13 issues. 1930-1935. $7 each.
    17 issues. 1932-1937. The lot. $90.
    Oct 1920. Norman Rockwell cover. $50-$150.
    Various issues. 1940s. Mint. $6 each. G-VG. $4 each.
    4 issues. 1918-1920. $25 all.

POPULAR SONGS MAGAZINE.
    1930s. $7-$9 each.
    (Some hits are twice the price.)

THE POSTER.
    1890s. $12-$25 each.
    Maxfield Parrish. $75-$125.

POULTRY MAGAZINES.
    11 issues, 1897-1900. Various titles. The lot. $20.

PRAIRIE FARMER.
    1840s. $7-$10 each.
    1940s. $4 each.

PRATT'S ALMANAC.
    1900s-1920. $5-$10.

PRIMARY EDUCATION.
    6 issues. 1893-1902. The lot. $15.

PRINCETON TIGER.
    Sept 26, 1938. $6.

PRINTERS INK.
    1920s. $5-$7 each.
    Famous illustrators. $10-$40.

PROFESSIONAL ART QUARTERLY.
    June 1936. Rockwell Kent articles. $12.

PSYCHEDELIC REVIEW.
    Vol. 1, No. 1. Summer 1963. Fine. $100.
    Vol. 1, No. 4. 1964. VG. $23.

THE PSYCHOANALYTIC REVIEW.
    NY, 1913-1916. Vols. 1, 2, 3. $600 all.

PSYCHIC DIMENSIONS.
    Vol. 1. No. 1. May 1973. Mint. $16.

PSYCHOLOGY TODAY.
    May 1967-December 1984. 212 issues.
    Few reprints. Good. $300.

PUBLISHERS WEEKLY.
    1870s onward. $3-$4 each.

PUCK.

Avg. 1877-1918. $12-$30.

Vols. 11-12, 1882-1883. 2 years of political
cartoons in color. Ex-library. VG-Fine. $600.

Oct 25, 1882. Fine. $25.

Oct 10, 1883. Cowboys. $25.

9 issues, 1885-1888. $12-$18 each.

1890s. Rose O'Neill and Harrison Fisher
covers. $50-$95.

June 16, 1886. $15.

Christmas issue Dec 5, 1888. $27.

Nov 15, 1893. Framable covers. $25.

Vol. 40, Aug 19, 1896-Aug 11, 1897.

52 issues in 2 vols. Fine. $500.

PUNCH.

London. 1st 45 years, 1841-1885. In bound vols.
Shelf wear. Ex-library. $1,250 all.

15 half-year vols. 1870s-1890s. VG. $10 each.

Vols. 111, 112, 1896, 1897. Bound. Fine. The lot. $85.

Avg. 1840-1940 issue. $5-$15.

8 issues, most 1935, 1936, others 1914, 1916
Hitler, Mussolini cartoons. The lot. $25.

Assorted issues, 1953-1955. $4 each.

PURE-BRED DOGS.

1890s issues. $8-$20 each.

1900-1940. $5-$12.

PUTNAM'S MONTHLY MAGAZINE OF AMERICAN LITERATURE, SCIENCE AND ART.

Vols. I-III, 1853, 1854. VG. The lot. $150.

Avg. 1850s-1900s issue. $10-$12.

A RATIONAL LAW, OR—TAMMANY.

Q

THE QUEEN.

1880s. $5-$12 each.

QUICK MAGAZINE.

50 issues, 1949-1953. VG. The lot. $65.

Vol. 1, No. 1. Oct 1964. $15.

Avg. 1949-1959. Good. $2-$5. Fine. $5-$10.

Cowboys, military heros and movie stars
can raise value to $25.

R

THE RADICAL.
2 bound volumes, 1865, 1867. Worn. $150 pair.

RADIO ALBUM.
Summer, 1949. $12.

RADIO AND TELEVISION MIRROR.
70 issues. 1940-1945. $10-$15 each.
118 issues. 1950s. $8-$10 each.
105 issues. 1960s. $5-$10 each.
9 issues. 1951-1954. The lot. $60.
1939-1941. $10 each.

RADIO & TELEVISION RETAILING.
5 issues. 1939-1940. The lot. $15.
October 1940. $8 each.
June 1945. $5.

RADIO AND TV NEWS.
1950s. $5-$10 each.

RADIO ART. 1930s. $3-$12 each.

RADIO BROADCAST.
1920s. $9-$12 each.

RADIO-CRAFT.
1930s. $4-$8 each.

RADIO DIAL.
1930s. $3-$9 each.

RADIO DIGEST.
1930s. $8-$10 each.

RADIO GUIDE.
1930s-1940s. $10-$20.

RADIO MIRROR.
42 issues. 1930s. $10-$18 each.
20 issues. 1940s. $5-$10.
Selected issues. $15-$30.

RADIO NEWS.
8 issues. 1940-1948. The lot. $16.
1929-1933. $8-$10 each.
1930-1932. $6 each.

RADIO RETAILING.
7 issues. 1935-1939. The lot. $20.

RADIO STARS.
1930s. $10-$20 each.
(The bigger the star, the higher the price.)

RADWAY'S ALMANAC. 1861-1906. $10-$20.

RAILROAD MAGAZINE.
April 1942. Women's Pictorial. $6.
April 1946. Penn. Central. $5.
Jan-Dec, 1950. Kokomo IN.
12 unbound issues. VG. $30.
1947-1962. 50 issues. Mostly VG. The lot. $120.

RAILWAY AGE. 1920s. $7-$10 each.

RAILWAY MASTER MECHANIC.
98 issues. 1907, 1098, 1909, 1914, 1915. Stains,
some spines poor, covers loose. Good. $100 all.

RAMPARTS. 1960s. $8-$10 each.

RAWLEIGH ALMANAC.
1900-1904. $8-$10.
1928-1970. $3 each.

READER'S DIGEST is the largest circulation magazine
in the entire world. Old issues are tough to sell.
Bound vols. can be hollowed out for craft projects.
4 issues. 1928-1933. $3 each.
7 issues. 1930-1940. $5 all.
50 issues. 1923-1944. $55 the lot.
1950s-1970s. $1 each.

REAL DETECTIVE. 1920s-1930s. $4-$5.

REAL LIFE STORY.
Vol. 1, No. 1. Nov 1939. Fine. $35.
Avg. 1930s-1940s issue. $15-$20.

REAL SECRETS.
Vol. 1, No. 1. Oct 1957. James Dean article. Fine. $25.
Avg. 1960s issue. $2.

REAL WESTERN. Dec 1952. Good. $5.

THE REALIST.
 The magazine of mob violence.
 "Free thought" ideas on newsprint.
 Feb 1961. $20.

RECREATION.
 12 issues. 1896-1903. The lot. $95.
 6 issues. 1890s. Worn. $24 all.
 1897-1906. Some Rockwell covers.
 Fine. $25 each.

REDBOOK.
 1903-1920s. $5-$10.
 1930s-1940s. $3-$6.
 1950s-1960s. $2-$4.
 Movie stars may increase value.

RED CROSS MAGAZINE.
 1920s. $3-$4 each.
 June 1917. $7.
 Aug 1917. $15.
 June 1918. Rockwell cover. $25-$35.
 1918 Cole Phillips cover. $15.

THE REVIEW OF REVIEWS.
 1910-1920. $1-$3 each.
 1920s. $1-$2 each.
 Collectible ads increase value.

REX STOUT'S MYSTERY MAGAZINE.
 1945-1946. Avg. $5-$6 each.

REXALL ALMANAC.
 1918, 1920-1927. $5-$10 ea.
 1929-1976. $3 ea.

RHEUMATIC SYRUP ALMANAC.
 Any issue. $20-$40.

RING MAGAZINE.
 1920s. $6-$9 each.
 Many issues. 1928-1949. G-VG. $5-$25 each.
 100 issues. 1930s-1950s. Good plus. The lot. $400.
 Complete run, 1934-1950. $1,100.
 8 issues. 1948-1952. The lot. $35.
 6 issues. 1989. The lot. $10.
 9 issues. 1988. The lot. $13.
 Various 1960s. $6 each.

RINGLING BROTHERS.
 1930s-1940s. $8-$20.
 1950s. $7-$10.
 Quality of illus. determines price.

RINGMASTER.
 Vol. 1, No. 1. May 1936.
 Tabloid size, caricature art. $30-$40.

ROAD & TRACK.
 23 issues. 1971-1982. Good. The lot. $40.
 Avg. 1950s-1980s issue. $2-$8.
 Jan 1956. $8.
 Annuals. $6-$12.

ROD & CUSTOM.
 Oct 1955. $8.
 Other issues. $4-$6.

ROD & GUN.
 Vol. 1, No. 1. May 1957.
 L. B. Cole cover. $15-$25.
 Avg. 1950s-1960 issue. $3-$5.

ROLLING STONE.
 Vol. 1., No. 1. 1967. John Lennon. $75-$200.
 Ten issues 1976-1977 in bound vol. $95.
 1960s prices range from $20-$200.
 1970s-1980s. $3-$15.
 Top stars of the 60s and 70s such as Dylan, Elvis, Hendrix, Lennon and Morrison command highest prices.

ROMANTIC MOVIE STORIES.
 1920s-1930s. $15-$45 each.

ROSICRUCIAN DIGEST.
 98 copies. 1930-1931.
 $3 each. The lot. $120.

ROUND TABLE. 1860s. $5-$10 each.

ROYCROFT QUARTERLY.
 3 issues published, May 1896:
 Reprint of Stephen Crane story. $105.
 2nd issue. G. B. Shaw "On Going to Church". $65.
 3rd issue. $25-$35.
 Note: Most monthly issues of Roycroft Magazine are one dollar or less.

THE RUDDER.
 Jan-June 1910. 11 color plates. VG. $28.

THE RUMELY MAGAZINE.
 Farming photos. 1930. $5 each.

RURAL MESSENGER.
 1870s-1880s. $5-$10 each.

RURAL NEW YORKER JOURNAL.
 1871. Bound vol. Jan-July. $50-$75.
 1900-1901. 48 issues. $25 all.
 1936-1937. 23 issues. $60 all.

RUSSELL'S MAGAZINE.
 1850s. $8-$10 each.

S

THE SAILORS' MAGAZINE.
1882-1885. 3 issues. $12.

SALUTE MAGAZINE.
Tabloid-size magazine devoted to ex-
servicemen returning home from WWII.
Vol. 1, No. 1. Apr 1946. $15-$35.

THE SARTORIAL ART JOURNAL (Tailoring).
January to December 1892. $100.
January-June 1910. Ex-library. Fair. $65.

SATAN MAGAZINE.
Feb 1957. Feature, Tina Louise. $8.

THE SATURDAY EVENING POST went through
a series of ups and downs after its founding in
1821. During 1877 the magazine's assets were
sold at a sheriff's sale to A. E. Smythe who soon
after unloaded it on Cyrus Curtis for a thousand
dollars. Curtis threw out the old four-page format
and hired George H. Lorimer to edit his new
magazine. Circulation rose from 1,800 subscribers
in 1900 to 3,000,000 a week in 1937.
A great portion of Post's success was due to the
choice of cover artists. Joseph Leyendecker, a
Chicago Art Institute graduate, went to work
for Mr. Curtis in 1899 at the age of 25 and produced more than 300 Post covers during a 40 year
period.
Norman Rockwell painted his first Post cover at the
age of 22 and over a fifty year span Curtis published
more than 315 Rockwell renderings. The most
popular covers were produced in the 1930s and
1940s. The last one was printed in 1963. Rockwell's
first cover of May 20, 1916 is worth from $125 to $250
in very good to fine condition.

BOUND VOLUMES AND DEALER LOTS:
4 bound vols., 1918 & 1919. Mostly Fine. $640.
9 issues. 1907-1911. $10-$20 each.
22 Civil War issues. $5-$15 each.
50 issues. 1924-1961. The lot. $62.
28 issues. 1938. 4 Rockwell, 5 Leyendecker covers.
The lot. $279.
19 issues. 1955. Fine. The lot. $32.
Assorted non-Rockwell issues. 1904-1938. $8 each.

SATURDAY EVENING POST (Single Issues).
Feb 9, 1901. Harrison Fisher. $15-$25.
June 12, 1907. Harrison Fisher. $18-$35.
Aug 6, 1912. Coles Phillips. $15-$20.
May 22, 1915. J. C. Leyendecker. $35-$50.
May 20, 1916. Norman Rockwell. $50-$250.
Mar 20, 1919. Norman Rockwell. $25-$40.
Jan 3, 1920. Leyendecker & Parrish. $20-$30.
Dec 8, 1923. J. C. Leyendecker. $10-$15.
July 17, 1926. J. C. Leyendecker. $25-$40.
Dec 24, 1927. J. C. Leyendecker. $30-$40.
June 30, 1932. Norman Rockwell. $25-$40.
Nov 30, 1940. Norman Rockwell. $15-$25.
June 27, 1942. Norman Rockwell. $15-$25.
Jan 1, 1944. Norman Rockwell. $15-$25.
May 26, 1945. Norman Rockwell. $18-$35.
Dec 29, 1956. Norman Rockwell. $20-$30.
Other Rockwell issues from the 1950s range
from $12 to $20 each.

THE SATURDAY MAGAZINE.
4 half-year vols. of illus. weekly, 1835-1842.
Botany, art travel, etc. Fine. The lot. $100.

SATURDAY REVIEW (LONDON).
35 vols., starting in 1921. Library bound.
Fine. $10 per volume.
Single issues. 1920s-1950s. $1-$2 each.

SATURDAY REVIEW OF LITERATURE.
125 issues. 1940s, 1950s. $2 each.

SAWENS ALMANAC.
1870-1888. $10-$20 each.

SCHOOL ARTS MAGAZINE.
18 issues. 1925-1931. The lot. $165.
58 issues. 1915-1937. Ex-library.
VG to Fine. $5-$10 each.
Other 1920s-1950s. $2-$8 each.

SCIENCE.
Complete run. Nov 1979-Aug 1986. $60.
1920s-1950s. $5-$10 each.

SCIENCE & TECHNOLOGY INTERNATIONAL.
1962-1969. $6-$8 each.

SCIENCE DIGEST.
 1940s-1950s. $2-$5 each.

SCIENCE FICTION PLUS.
 1953. $7-$9 each.

SCIENCE FICTION QUARTERLY.
 Vol. 1, No. 1. May 1951. $12.
 Vol. 1. Nos. 2, 4. $10.
 Vol. 5, No. 1. May 1957. $10.

SCIENCE ILLUSTRATED.
 Vol. 1, No. 1 April 1946. $15-$25.

SCIENCE MECHANICS.
 1920s-1930s. $6-$10 each.
 1940s-1970s. $1-$5.

SCIENCE & INVENTION.
 1920s issues. $10-$20 each.

SCIENCE WONDER STORIES.
 1929-1930 quarterlies. $25-$60.

SCIENTIFIC AMERICAN.
 Newspaper size weekly from 1845 to 1921.
 Monthly magazine from 1921 to present.
 Bound vol. 1846-1848. (104 issues). $100.
 Bound volumes of 6 mos. to one year:
 1860s-1880s. $75-$150 each.
 1890s-1921. $40-$50.
 Single issues: 1860-1920s avg. $5-$15 each.
 Jan 14, 1911. Automobile issue. $25-$50.
 Single issues 1921 to 1960s avg. $1-$5 each.
 (Also see Newspaper Section.)

SCIENTIFIC MONTHLY.
 1920s. $4-$6 each.

SCOUTING.
 1930s. $2-$4 each.
 (4) issues 1932-1941. $32.
 May 1, 1918. No. 9. $10.
 Modern issues. $1-$2.

SCREEN ALBUM.
 1935-1939. $15-$25 each.
 1940-1950. $5-$10.

SCREEN BOOK.
 Avg. 1930s issue. $15-$20.
 Jan 1934. K. Hepburn. $30-$50.
 Mar 1934. R. Keeler. $30-$50.
 April 1932. C. Bennett. $20-$3.
 April 1937. C. Colbert. $20-$30.

SCREEN GUIDE.
 Avg. 1930s issue. $15-$30.
 12 issues, 1940s. VG or better. $15-$25 ea.
 6 issues, 1943-1945. $8 each
 May 1944. Sheridan. $15.
 Feb 1947. Goddard. $15.
 Sept 1946. Johnson. $10.
 Feb 1950. Crain. $7.

SCREEN PLAY.
 Oct 1931. Jean Harlow. $25.
 July 1933. Mae West. $15.
 Feb 1934. Garbo. $30-$40.
 Feb 1937. Ida Lupino. $15.

SCREEN PLAY SECRETS.
 Aug 1930. VG-Fine. $25.

SCREEN ROMANCES.
 1930-1939 avg. $15-$20 each.
 1940s-1950s. $5-$15.
 June 1936. Coleman-Colbert. $20.
 Dec 1936. Dionne Quints. $45.
 Nov 1933. Jean Harlow. $30.
 July 1940. Greer Garson. $24.
 Jan 1942. Judy Garland. $25.

SCREEN STORIES.
 June 1951-April 1966. $10 each.

SCREEN STARS.
 1940s-1960s. $8-$20.

SCREEN LAND.
 1920s-1930s. $20-$35.
 1940s-1950s. $8-$18.
 1960s. $5-$10 each.

SCRIBNER'S MAGAZINE.
 33 bound vols., 1887-1912. Good.
 $24-$35 per vol.
 Bound volumes:
 6 mos. 1872. $35.
 6 mos. 1879. VG. $25.
 Jan-June 1890. $45.
 6 mos. 1880. $45.
 July-Dec 1896. $25.
 6 mos. 1901. Parrish illus. $60.
 38 issues. 1891-1898. The lot. $85.
 Single issues:
 Dec 1898. M. Parrish. $50-$65.
 June 1895. Bicycle ads. $8.
 June 1899. T Roosevelt. $8.
 May 1903. Jesse Wilcox Smith illus. $18.
 Mar 1904. Christy, Fisher, Wilcox illus. $10.
 Dec 1903. M. Parrish illus. $25.
 Mar 1905. Edward Curtis photos. $18.

SCRIBNER'S (Continued).
  Mar 1906. N. C. Wyeth illus. $18.
  Oct 1906. N. C. Wyeth illus. 25.
  Feb 1907. Many famous illustrators. $35.
  Feb 1909. Indian Houses. $30.
  Jan 1910. Teddy Roosevelt. $15.
  Dec 1911. J. Wilcox Smith. $24.
  Aug 1912. M. Parrish illus. $28.
  Dec 1911. Dicken's children. $20.
  1912 & 1913. Automobile covers. $25.
  Aug 1918. N. C. Wyeth illus. $18.

SEE MAGAZINE.
  1940s-1950s. $5-$8.
  July 1942-Jane Russell. $25.
  July 1953. Terry Moore. $7.

SENSATIONAL DETECTIVE CASES.
  April 1941. $10.

THE SENSUOUS STREAKER.
  Vol. 1, No. 1. 1974 magazine about
  running naked in public. $20.

SEPIA. Sept 1960-Dec 1962. $6 ea.

SEVENTEEN. 1950s. Avg. $2-$4 each.

SHADOWLAND.
  Avg. 1920s issue. $20-$30.
  Vols. 1, 2. Mint. $1,000.
  39 issues. 1920-1922. The lot. $400.
  7 issues, 1921-1923. Good. $25 each.

SHAKER ALMANAC.
  1889-1897. $50-$100 ea.

THE SHERLOCK HOLMES JOURNAL.
  Vol. 1, No. 1. 1952. VG. $45.

SHIELDS MAGAZINE.
  April 1905. Fine. $25.

SHOE & LEATHER REVIEW.
  Bound vol., 1884, 27 issues. $135.

SHORT WAVE & TELEVISION.
  Jan 1937 issue. $15.

SHORTHORN WORLD.
  Apr 1946, Centennial number. $15.
  1939 issue. $12.

SHOW MAGAZINE.
  Vol. 1, No. 1. June 1940. $15-$20.
  1940s-1960s. Avg. $5-$8 each.
  14 issues, 1971-1973. VG-Fine. $4-$5 each.

SHOW BUSINESS ILLUSTRATED.
  Vol. 1, No. 1. Sept 5, 1961. $18-$35.
  Avg. 1960s issue. $10-$14 each.
  8 mixed, 1961. The lot. $20.

SIERRA CLUB BULLETIN.
  6 issues, 1929-1940. many Ansel Adams plates.
  Very Good. The lot. $65.

SIGNAL.
  Hitler's propagana organ. Berlin, 1940-1944. 4 bound
  vols. Total of 90 issues. G-VG. In German. $600.

SIGNS OF THE TIMES.
  22 issues. Outdoor advertising. 1923-1929. The lot. $195.

SILVER SCREEN.
  Bound vol. 1930-1931. $300.
  Early 1930s issues. $20-$30 ea.
  1936-1956. $8-$18.
  1960s-1970s. $3-$7.
  Aug 1936.   Colbert. $18.
  June 1937. Rogers. $18.
  Feb 1937.   Young. $18.
  July 1937. Faye. $18.
  Oct 1937.   MacDonald. $18.
  Nov 1937.   Carroll. $18.
  Dec 1938.   Oberon. $18.
  Mar 1939.   Davis. $15.
  June 1939. Rogers. $15.
  July 1939. Lombard. $15.
  Aug 1939.   Arthur. $15.
  Oct 1939.   Garbo. $30.
  Jan 1940.   Lane. $15.
  Mar 1940.   Bennett. $15.
  Feb 1941.   Rogers. $15.
  Nov 1942.   O'Hara. $15.
  Dec 1949.   Sheridan. $10.
  Mar 1950.   Colbert. $7.
  Nov 1951.   Leigh. $7.
  Feb 1953.   Williams. $6,
  Apr 1960.   Elvis. $25.

SIMMONS LIVER REGULATOR ALMANAC.
  1877-1907. $15-$25 ea.

SKATING.
  20 issues. 1968, 1969. 1971, 1972.
  Good. The lot. $125, or $8 each.

THE SKELLY ALMANAC.
  Skelly Oil Co. 1949. $5.

SKIN DIVER MAGAZINE.
  400 issues. 1966-1988.
  Some repeats. The lot. $100.
  June and Aug. 1960. $8 pair.

SKY AND TELESCOPE.
  1950s. $1-$2 each.
  July 1961. VG. $4.

SKY FIGHTERS.
  1933-1943. $15-$30 each.

SKYWAYS.
  10 issues. 1949-1950.
  Good. The lot. $15.
  Avg. 1940s issue. $3 ea.

SLOAN'S ALMANAC.
  Any issue. $25-$50.

THE SMART SET.
  1910-1920. $8-$10 each.
  Sept 1901. Light soiling. $7.

SMITH'S BILE BEANS ALMANAC.
  Any issue. $20-$40.

SNAP.
  1940s. $5-$10 each.

SNAPPY STORIES.
  Dec 1915. Good. $15.

SOCIAL JUSTICE.
  Father Coughlin's tabloid.
  150 issues. 1930s. $3 each.

SONG FAN.
  Vol. 1, No. 1. March 1954.
  Lyrics and photos. $12-$25.
  Avg. 1950s issue. $5-$10 ea.

SONG HITS.
  1940s. $4-$5 each.

SONGS & WORDS.
  Vol. 1, No. 1. Sept 1954.
  Music and lyrics. $12-$25.

SOUTHERN BOTTLER.
  Coke & Root Beer ads. May 1947. $24.

SOUTHERN LITERARY MESSENGER.
  18 vols., 1834-1854. $800 at auction.

SPACE AGE.
  First six issues. 1958-1960. VG. The lot. $90.
  Nov 1948 issue. $10.

SPACE HORIZONS.
  Vol. 1, No. 1. 1965. $25.

SPACE JOURNAL.
  Vol., 1, No. 1. Summer 1957. $15-$25.
  Spring, Summer, Fall 1958. $9 each.

SPACE SCIENCE FICTION.
  May, Sept 1952. $5 each.

SPARROW MAGAZINE.
  Nos. 1 to 72. 6 year run, 1972-1978.
  7 issues are signed. $350 all.

THE SPHINX.
  A Magazine for Magicians.
  Jan 1973. $8-$10.
  8 issues. 1946-1947. $35 all.
  1951 issue. $16.

SPINNING WHEEL.
  Antique collecting.
  1950s-1970s. $5-$10 each.

SPICY MYSTERY.
  1935-1938. $75-$150.
  1940s issues. $35-$50.

SPIRIT OF THE TIMES.
  A chronicle of the turf, agriculture, field
  sports, literature and the stage.
  Bound vols., 1847-1848. Folio. $175.
  Individual issues, late 1800s. $15-$25.

SPIDER.
  1933-1938. $45-$95 each.
  1939-1943. $30-$40.

SPORT MAGAZINE.
  1940s..........$10-$25 each.
  1950s..........$8-$25.
  1960s..........$5-$12.
  1970s..........$2-$4.
  Prices are for non-special issues in very good
  to fine condition. Star-slanted and event-slanted
  issues can go higher.

SPORTING NEWS.
  1930s..........$24-$30 each.
  1940s..........$18-$24.
  1950s..........$14-$24.
  1960s..........$8-$12.
  1970s..........$5-$8.
  10 issues. 1944-1946.
  VG to Fine. $25-$40 each.
  Jan 31, 1946 (DiMaggio, Williams).
  Fine. $85.
  Star-related and event-related issues
  can go higher.

SPORTS AFIELD.
 Hunting & Fishing.
 1880s-1920s. $10-$20 ea.
 1930s-1940s. $4-$8.
 1950s-1960s. $2-$6.

SPORTS ILLUSTRATED.
 First issue, Aug 16, 1954 has a 3-pg.foldout
 insert of Topps baseball cards. $150-$300.
 Second issue is the most valuable, Aug 23, 1954,
 with NY Yankees and Mickey Mantle cards. Has
 golf bag on cover. $250-$300.
 April 11, 1955 and April 18, 1955 issues also contain reproductions of baseball cards and sell for
 $50-$15 each.
 Swimsuit issues begain in 1964 and commonly
 sell for $10 to $50 ea.
 1964-1965 issues in mint cond. $40-$50.
 1966-1969 mint or near mint. $25-$40.
 1970-1979 issues. $10-$25 each.
 Non-special issues:
  1954-1960. $7-$15.
 1961-1970. $5-$10.
 1971-1980s. $3-$7 each.
 Dealer and auction lots:
 1964-1979. $2-$3 per magazine in lots of
 24 or more.
 According to specialist dealers, at present the most
 requested issues are: 1955 Ted Williams at $75;
 1956 Mickey Mantle at $75; 1961 Roger Maris at
 $40 and 1964 Bill Bradley at $15. (Next year others
 will head the list.)
 Some broad guidelines are:
 Vol. 1, No. 1. 1949...$75-$110.
 1950s issues..............$8-$20.
 1960s.........................$5-$15.
 1970s.........................$3-$10.
 Swimsuit and baseball stars often go higher, e.g.
 Jan 3, 1955. R. Bannister. $25-$35.
 April 11, 1955. Al Rosen. $50-$75.
 July 2, 1962. M. Mantle. $35-$45.
 1964-1968 Swimsuit issues. $25-$60.
 If you have a large accumulation of 1950s & 60s
 issues it might pay to consult a Sports Collectibles
 price guide or a specialist dealer for up-to-date values.

THE SPORTSMAN.
 1920 issues. $5-$15 each.

SPORTSMAN'S NEWS.
 1950s-1960s. $2-$8 each.

SPORTSMEN'S REVIEW.
 1908-1915. VG to Excellent. $25 each.

SPORTING GOODS JOURNAL.
 1930s. $6-$8 each.

THE SPUR MAGAZINE.
 5 issues. 1924 and 1939. The lot. $30.

THE SQUARE DEAL. June 1914. Good. $7.

ST. JOSEPH'S ALMANAC.
 1916-1924. $10-$20 ea.
 1925-1943. $4-$8 ea.

ST. NICHOLAS.
 Complete run. 1873-1939. All bound, ex-
 library. Few covers missing. 800 issues. $925.
 6 bound vols., 1873-1883. Mostly VG. $60-$75 each.
 Bound vols:
 Nov 1886-Oct 1887. $18.
 1888-1889, 6 months. $35.
 1890. $35.
 1891, 6 months. $27.
 Nov 1893-Apr 1894. $30.
 1915-1916. 6 months. $24.
 Dealer lots:
 18 issues, 1895-1896. The lot. $45.
 15 issues. 1907-1912. The lot. $45.
 6 issues. 1908. Ex-library. Fine. The lot. $12.
 9 issues. 1922-1924. The lot. $35.
 12 issues. 1923. The lot. $15.
 10 issues. 1920s and 1930s. The lot. $22.
 120 issues. 1879-1889. Bindings poor. The lot. $150.
 Individual issues:
 1890-1895 avg. issue. $3-$6.
 June 1902. Jack London story. $20.
 Nov 1908. Denslow illus. $18.
 Feb 1909. Leslie Brooke illus. $13.
 May 1909. Denslow illus. $10.
 N. Rockwell and M. Parrish covers greatly increase value.

STAGE.
 1930s. VG. $12-$20 each.
 Ex-library issues. $4-$5.
 11 issues. 1934-1939. VG. The lot. $90.
 1933-1939. $7-$10 each.
 7 issues. 1930s. The lot. $50.
 3 issues. 1933-1937. The lot. $25.
 2 issues. 1939. Both, $15.
 May 1933. $32.
 Aug 1935. $9.
 Aug 1936. Commemorative issue. $20.
 Aug 1937. $10.
 April 1939. $7
 Aug 1938. $25.

THE STAGE PHOTOPLAY NEWS.
 May 1922 with press book in center. $20.
 Jan 1922. $20.

STANDBY RADIO MAGAZINE.
 Various issues from 1937. $5 each.

STANDARD OIL CO. FARMERS ALMANAC.
Most issues. $10-$20 each.

STARTLING DETECTIVE.
Nov 1959. $5.

STARTLING DETECTIVE ADVENTURES.
Feb 1937. Good. $8.

STARTLING NOVELS.
19 issues. 1940-1954. The lot. $123.

STARTLING STORIES.
Jan 1939. $5.
May 1939. $10.

STORY MAGAZINE.
Early 1940s issues. $20-$35 each.

STRAND (British).
1902-1906. $25 each.
Dec 1918, Oct 1916, Nov 1930. $25-$35 each.
Coronation Souvenir. 1937. Cover loose, o/w
Fine. $35.

STREET & SMITH'S BASEBALL.
Avg. 1950s-1970s. $6-$15.
Star players bring much more.

STREET AND SMITH'S LOVE STORIES.
Many issues. 1930s and 1940s. $2-$14 each.

STRENGTH AND HEALTH.
3 issues. 1930s-1940s. The lot. $14.

SUCCESSFUL FARMING.
1900s-1930s. $3-$12 each.
1940s-1950s. $2-$6.

SUNSET.
1900s-1930s. $4-$20.
1940s-1960s. $2-$3.

SUNSHINE & HEALTH.
Nudist magazine. 1940s-1960s. $5 each.

SUPER SCIENCE STORIES.
1940s-1950s. $9-$15.

SURVEYING AND BUILDING NEWS.
Bound vol. 6 issues, 1883. $30.

SUSPENSE.
Spring, Summer, Fall 1951. $4-$6 each.

SWANK MAGAZINE.
1940s-1950s $5-$12 each.

T

TATTLER MAGAZINE.
  1930s issues. $5-$6 each.

TECHNICAL WORLD.
  Oct 1908. Article on mechanical dolls. $15.
  Avg. 1900s issues. $5-$10.
  Lot of 5 from 1907-1910. $30.

TELEPHONE REVIEW.
  Bell Telephone Co.
  Bound vol., 1919. 12 issues. $30.

TELEPHONY.
  1915 issue. $15.

TEMPO MAGAZINE.
  1953-1960. $4-$8 each.

TEN-STORY FANTASY.
  Spring 1951. $10.

TERROR TALES.
  1934-1941. $30-$70.

THACHER'S ALMANAC.
  1900-1925. $7-$15 ea.

THEATRE MAGAZINF.
  24 issues, 1924-1931. VG. The lot. $200.
  Jan 1923. VG. $20.
  Nov 1930. Fine. $20.
  Avg. 1920s-1930s. $12-$15.

THEATRE ARTS MONTHLY.
  16 bound vols., ex-library. 1936-1940,
  1940, 1950, 1952 & 1960. The lot. $200.
  7 vols., 42 issues. 1944-1947. Two numbers
  missing. Ex-library o/w Fine. The lot. $200.
  224 issues. 1950-1963. Some repeats. The
  lot. $80.
  Individual issues sell in wide range. $5-up.
  Oct 1938. $12.
  Aug 1939. $10.

THERAPEUTIC DIGEST.
  Cincinnati, Dec 1905. Covers missing. $20.

THIS QUARTER.
  Vol. 1, No. 1. Paris 1928.
  Hemingway, Stein, Joyce,
  Boyle, etc. Good. $250.

THIS WEEK.
  Avg. 1940s-1960s issue. $1-$3.

THRILLING RANCH STORIES.
  May 1935 issue. $6.

THRILLING WESTERN STORIES.
  Jan 1935 issue. $6.

THRILLING WONDER STORIES.
  13 issues. 1941-1952.
  G-VG. The lot. $84.
  Winter 1954. Good. $4.

THE TICKER.
  Wall Street news.
  Nov 1907 to April 1908.
  Bound vol. 6 issues. $125.

TIGER.
  Vol. 1, No. 1. Aug 1956.
  Another Playboy imitator. $12-$20.

TIME MAGAZINE.
  March 3, 1923. Vol. 1, No. 1. $50-$85.
  Dec 27, 1937. Disney. $25-$40.
  Aug 3, 1942. Artzybasheff. $10-$20.
  April 1945. Gen. Patton. $12.
  May 1945. Adolf Hitler. $15.
  Oct 4, 1948. Joe DiMaggio. $15-$20.
  Feb 22, 1963. Cassius Clay. $20-$30.
  Average issue 1930s-1960s. $2-$10.
  Famous illustrators increase value.

TIP-OFF.
  Vol. 1, No. 1. April 1958. Scandal
  magazine. $15-$25.
  Avg. 1950s issue. $10-$14.

TIP TOP WEEKLY.
  June 1904. 2 issues on baseball. $50 pair.

TITTER.
   April 1955. Peter Driben cover.
   Lilli Christine pin-up. Fine. $20.

TNT MAGAZINE.
   Vol. 1, No. 1. March 1941.
   Tabloid size humor, cartoons.
   G-VG. $22.

TOBACCO JOBBER.
   April 1948 issue. $38.

TOBACCO WORLD.
   Early 1900s. $15-$25.

TODAYS WOMAN.
   Assorted, 1946-1947. $4 each.

THE TOPS.
   An Independent Magazine of Magic.
   60 issues. 1938-1943.
   VG. The lot. $350.

THE TOUCHSTONE.
   1920s. $5-$10 each.

TOWN & COUNTRY.
   Avg. 1920s-1940s. $5-$8 each.
   Watch for Maxfield Parrish illus.

JACOB TOWNSEND'S ALMANAC.
   Any edition. $35-$75.

TOWNSEND'S MONTHLY.
   4 hand-colored fashion plates. 1857. $23.

TRACTOR & GAS ENGINE REVIEW.
   1920s issues. $7 each.

THE TRADESMAN.
   Scarce Southern trade journal.
   Many ads. Chatanooga, 1903. $50.

TRAIL AND TIMBERLINE.
   1920s. $2-$4 each.

TRAINS MAGAZINE.
   26 issues. 1949-1953. The lot. $50.
   1940s issues. $4-$10 each.

TRANSITION.
   1920s. $3-$9 each.

TRAVEL.
   Dec 1915. Santa Claus. $15-$25.
   1926 folo-sized monthly. $12.
   1937-1938 issues. $3-$8.

TREAT'EM SQUARE.
   July 1930. WWI Vets. $22.

TRU-CRIME DETECTIVE STORIES.
   March 1941. Good. $12.

TRU-LIFE DETECTIVE CASES.
   July 1944. $9.

TRUE DETECTIVE.
   1930s-1960s. $3-$15.
   Dec 1933. Pretty Boy Floyd. $25.

TRUE CONFESSIONS.
   12 issues from 1946-1957. The lot. $15.
   1935-1950s. $4-$6.

TRUE EXPERIENCES.
   May 1938. $10.
   March-Dec 1939. $10 each.
   Other 1930s-1940s. $8-$20.

TRUE. "The Man's Magazine."
   Avg. 1940s-1960s without pinups. $3-$6.
   Alberto Varga and George Petty pinups and
   gatefolds are $10-$30 each.
   Feb 1961 Anniversary Number. $7.

TRUE OR FALSE.
   Vol. 1, No. 1. April 1958. $15-$20.

TRUE PICTORIAL STORIES.
   1940. $6-$7 each.

TRUE POLICE.
   Jan 1960 issue. $4.

TRUE ROMANCE.
   May, June, Dec 1938. $10 each.
   Mixed issues. 1948-1955. $6 each.

TRUE STRANGE STORIES.
   Vol. 1, No. 1. Oct 1956. $15-$25.

TRUE STORY.
   62 issues from 1941-1957.
   The lot. $50.
   11 issues. 1946-1947. The lot. $35.
   Assorted 1939-1942. $2-$10 each.
   May 1933. Good. $17.
   1931. Jean Harlow cover. $8.
   Sept 1938. D. Durbin. $15.
   Nov 1951. M. Monroe. $20.

TRUE WEIRD MAGAZINE.
   ⁃Vol. 1, No. 1, June 1966.
   Ripley's Believe It or Not. $15-$25.

TRUMPET & UNIVERSALIST MAGAZINE.
    Boston, April 15, 1837. $7.

THE TRUTH.
    Vol. 1, No. 1. Feb-March 1958.
    Scandal magazine. $15-$25.
    1980s issues. $3-$4 each.

TURF. 10 issues. 1930s. Mint. $7 each.

TURKISH REMEDY CO. ALMANAC.
    1870-1877. $16-$30 each.

TV GUIDE.
The first issue of TV Guide was published on June 14, 1948 as Television Guide. It is not as valuable as the issue of April 3rd 1953. Walter Annenberg bought the magazine in late 1952 and on his first cover featured Ricky, the baby of Lucy Ricardo (Lucille Ball). Thousands of copies were bought at 15 cents each. Today a very nice copy is worth $600. (A specialist says he can get twice as much for a flawless mint example.) A few other exceptional issues are:
    Nov 6, 1948. Howdy Doody. $75.
    May 6, 1950. Hopalong Cassidy. $150.
    Sept 18, 1953. Fall Preview. $150.
    Sept 25, 1953. Superman (George Reeves). $315.
    Sept 15, 1956. Elvis Presley. $175.
Most issues for the first four decades of publication range in value as follows, in VG or better condition:
1st national issue: April 3, 1953. $250-$1,000.
Next two issues: $100 each and up.
    1953. $20-$40 (with average being about $24).
    1954. $10-$24 (average $20 each).
    1955-1956. $7-$20 (average $15 each).
    1957-1959. $7-$15 (average $10 each).
    1960s. $5-$12 (average $8 each).
    1970s and 1980s. $2-$5 each.
    1980 to 1994. $1 each.
Fall preview issues and issues dealing heavily in top-rated programs and personalities can be trouble or triple the value.
Bound volumes:
    17 issues. 1956. G-VG. $145.
    13 issues. 1957. G-VG. $125.
    13 issues. 1958. G-VG. $95.
    42 issues. 1976-1980. Fine. $1 ea.
    25 issues. 1956-1968. The lot. $50.
Some recently advertised single issues:

1952: Oct 31. $45.

1953:

April 23. $35	May 1. $35.	May 8. $35.
May 15. $45.	May 22. $40.	June 12. $35.
June 19. $35.	June 26. $35.	July 3. $35.
July 10. $35.	July 24. $50.	July 31. $40.
Aug 7. $40.	Aug 14. $35.	Aug 21. $35.
Aug 28. $35.	Sept 4. $25.	Sept 11. $20.
Sept 18. $50.	Sept 25. $45.	Oct 23. $30.
Nov 6. $25.	Nov 13. $35.	Nov 20. $25.
Nov 27. $25.	Dec 4. $30.	Dec 18. $30.

1954:

April 23. $50.	July 17. $50.	Aug 14. $50.
Oct 9. $75.	Oct 23. $75.	Dec 25. $55.

1955:

July 3. $35.	Aug 6. $20.	Sept 24. $50.
Dec 10. $50.		

1956: July 14. $15.

1957:

Jan 26. $10.	Feb 2. $15.	Mar 2. $15.
Mar 9. $15.	April 20. $15.	April 17. $20.
May 4. $10.	May 11. $25.	June 1. $10.
June 15. $20.	July 27. $15.	Aug 3. $15.
Aug 16. $15.	Aug 17. $20.	Aug 24. $15.
Aug 31. $25.	Sept 14. $75.	Oct 12. $15.
Oct 5. $15.		

1958:

April 26. $75.	June 14. $20.	June 21. $15.
June 28. $25-$50.	July 5. $15.	July 12. $25.
July 19. $25.	July 25. $15.	Aug 2. $20.
Aug 9. $15.	Aug 16. $25.	Aug 23. $15.
Sept 6. $15.	Sept 27. $15.	Oct 4. $20.
Oct 11. $15.	Dec 27. $25-$50.	

1959: July 4. $55.   Sept 19. $60.
1962: Sept 8. $55.   Sept 15. $50.
1963: April 30. $50.   Sept 14. $50.
1964: Feb 22. $50.
1965: Jan 2. $75.
1966: Mar 26. $50.   Sept 10. $50.
1967: Jan 28. $50.   Mar 4. $65.   Nov 18. $50.
1968: Aug 24. $65.
Prices drop if any cover wear or address labels. Filled-in crossword puzzles also lower value considerably.

TV PICTURE LIFE.
    1950s issues. $10-$20.
    March 1967. VG. $8.
    Other 1960s avg. $5-$9 each.

TV-RADIO TALK.
    Nov 1975. Rick Nelson cover. Fine. $12.

TV-RADIO MIRROR.
    36 issues. 1956-1973. Fine. $175 all.
    Aug 1975. Michael Landon cover. Fine. $15.

TV RADIO SHOW.
    Aug 1967. Elvis & Priscilla. $15.

TWENTIETH CENTURY HOME.
    Aug 1904 and Feb 1906.
    Rose O'Neill illus. VG. Both. $23.

THE TWILIGHT ZONE.
    1982-1987. $6-$10 each.

TYPE FOUNDER.
    Bound vol. (contains first issue).
    Chicago, 1876-1882. $850.

TYPOGRAPHIC MESSENGER.
    12 issues. 1866-1872. The lot. $250.

U - V

UNCLE SAM'S FAMILY ALMANAC.
    1870s-1890s. $15-$30 each.

THE UNION MAGAZINE.
    NY, 1848. January-May. Engravings.
    Disbound. Edges rubbed, o/w VG. $75.
    1850s single issues. $6-$10 each.

U. S. CAMERA.
    Vol. 1, No. 1. Fall 1938. $30-$40.
    13 assorted 1938-1940. The lot. $300.
    Avg. 1930s-1950s issue. $3-$12.
    Feb 1939. $20. Jan 1940. $10.
    Annuals: 1942-1962. $15 each.

U. S. NEWS & WORLD REPORT.
    1940-1966. $1-$4 each.

UNITED STATES REVIEW.
    1854 issues. $15 each.

U. S. SERVICE MAGAZINE.
    Most Civil War issues. $15-$25 ea.

VANITY FAIR.
    Vol. 1, No. 1. Dec 1859. $30-$40.
    1859-1960 issues sell in a very
    wide price range with famous illustrator
    covers bringing $30-$75 each.
    At a recent auction 15 bound volumes,
    1869-1883, brought $5,200.
    Feb 1914. F. X. Leyendecker. $50-$75.
    Misc. 1920s Rockwell Kent illus. issues.
    $30-$50 each.
    April 1923. Fashions, autos, golf. $30.
    May 1922. Thomas Hart Benton. $25.
    May 1924. Benito cover. $35.
    Misc. 1926-1927 issues. $12 ea.
    Nov 1929. Art Deco cover. $40.

VERMONT LIFE.
    1930s. $1-$3 each.

VERVE.
    Vol. 1, No. 2. Dec 1937. Printed in France.
    Lithos by Leger, Miro, Bores and Ratner.
    Very Good. $150.

Vol. 1, Nos. 1-4. Paris, 1937-38. English text.,
    Bound in decorated silk. VG. $750.
    Spring, 1938 edition. Lithos. Fine. $375.
    No. 4, 1939. $200.

VETERAN'S SERVICE MAGAZINE.
    1930 number. Miss Liberty cover plus leading
    cartoonists of the day. Very Good. $25.

FREDERICK VICTOR REMEDIES ALMANAC.
    1890-1915. $5-$10 ea.

VICKS ILLUSTRATED.
    1870s-1890s issues. $3-$15 each.
    Bound vol. 1880. 12 color plates. $95.
    Most single copies under $8 each.

VIEW. 1940s issues. $2-$3 each.

VIRGINIA MAGAZINE OF HISTORY & BIOGRAPHY.
    13 vols., 1894-1906. Leather bound. The lot. $250.

VIRGINIA QUARTERLY.
    1920s issues. $4-$5 each.

VISITING FIREMAN.
    1954-1960. $12-$16.
    1961 onward. $5 each.

VIVA.
    Oct 1973 Collector's Edition. $20-$40.

VOGUE.
    Avg. issue 1890s-1950s. $4-$10.
    1909 issue missing back cover. $14.
    Same in VG condition. $16-$20.
    March 1917. Leyendecker cover. Mint. $75.
    Misc. 1920s-1930s issues. $20 each.
    Art Deco covers, Lepape illus., 1927-1931.
    Mint. $50-$70 each.
    Oct 1923. Lepape cover, chipped. $20.
    Aug 1920. Platt cover, back cover gone. $14.
    April 1925. George Plank cover. $40.
    April 1922. P. Brussard cover. $40.

VON NOSTRAND'S ECLECTIC ENGINEERING.
    NY, 1869. Vol. 1. 12 monthly nos. Well worn. $50.

W

WAKEFIELD ALMANAC.
Pre-1875. $15-$30.
1876-1906. $5-$10 each.

WALT DISNEY'S MAGAZINE.
Avg. 1950s-1960s. $7-$20 each.
Vol. 1. Nos. 1 & 2. 1956. $25-$50 ea.

WARD'S ALMANAC.
Most editions. $7-$15 ea.

WASHINGTON HISTORICAL QUARTERLY.
Vol. 1, No. 1. Oct 1906. $25.

WATER-CURE JOURNAL.
1851 bound vol. 24 issues.
Illus. Some wear. $125-$150.

WAR CRY.
1884-1890s. $2-$5 each.

WATER GAS & STEAM.
June 1880. $9.

WATKINS ALMANAC.
1900s-1949. $5-$10 each.

WEIRD TALES.
1920s-1930s. $25-$75.
1940s-1950s. $10-$50.
July 1947. Good. $30.
Sept 1948. Very Good. $50.
Jan 1951. Very Good. $25.

THE WELLSPRING.
Children's magazine.
Bound vol. 39 issues. 1897. $14.

WEST SHORE.
An illustrated Western magazine.
Jan-Dec 1888. 12 issues.
94 duotone lithos. Some tears.
Orig. covers. $800-$1,200 all.

WESTERN FAMILY.
Assorted 1940s-1950s. $5 each.

WESTERN FIELD MAGAZINE.
1905-1908. Fine. $25 each.

WESTERN HORSEMEN.
1950-1966. $4 each.

WHAT'S WHAT IN FOOTBALL.
33 issues. 1938-1941. VG. $10 each.

THE WHEEL.
A Journal of Cycling.
NY, Oct 4, 1882. $75-$100.

THE WHEEL AND CYCLING TRADE REVIEW.
NY, April 5, 1889. $75-$100.

WHEELWOMAN.
Costumes, wheels and bicycling news.
Feb 1896. $125.

WHIG ALMANAC.
1885 edition. $18.

WHIRL.
1956-1959. $5-$10 each.

WHISPER.
1940s-1960s. $8-$9 each.
Some pinups are more.

WIDE AWAKE.
1880s. $10-$12 each.
1890s. $6-$10 each.
With color-litho firefighting
scenes on covers. $12-$15 ea.

WILD FLOWERS OF AMERICA.
Bound Vol. 1, Nos. 2-19, 1894.
Each issue bears a rear wrapper. $150.

WILD WEST WEEKLY.
25 issues. 1915-1916. Leather bound.
Very Good. $75.

WILDER'S ALMANAC.
Most issues. $25-$50 ea.

WOMAN'S HOME COMPANION.
Country boys were offered a real live pony
as a reward for signing up new subscribers
in the 1880s. The magazine had achieved a
circulation of 4 million by 1950.
Average issue from 1896-1952. $5-$6 ea.
3 mint issues, 1930s. $15 ea.
20 from 1930-1938. Rockwell and Wyeth
illus. $149 all.
April 1926. $20.
Dealer lot. 50 issues 1930-1955. $50.
Famous illus. covers, early 1900s. $25-$75 each.
Rose O'Neill Kewpies. $20-$30.
Paperdolls of the 1920s. $20-$30.

WILFORD'S MICROCOSM.
A Religio-Scientific Monthly Magazine.
NY, 1881, 1883 issues bound. $95.

WILL CARLETON'S MAGAZINE.
1890s issues. $4-$10 ea.

WILSON'S MONARCH ALMANAC.
1890s-1920. $10-$20 ea.

THE WINDSOR MAGAZINE (BRITISH).
Vol. 15, Dec 1901-May 1902. $23.
Vol. 18, June-Nov 1903. $25.

WIRELESS WORLD.
Oct 1945. Arthur Clarke's proposal for an
orbital satellite for global TV. $20-$30.

WNYF MAGAZINE.
NY Firemen.
6 issues, 1943-1953. $44 all.

WOMEN'S DAY.
49 issues. 1948. VG. The lot. $85.
17 issues. 1945-1951. The lot. $45.
1940s, 1950s, 1960s. $4-$6 each.

THE WOOD WORKER.
13 issues. 1929-1933. The lot. $59.
1928 issues. $8 each.

WOODHULL'S MAGAZINE.
1870s. $9-$11 each.

WOODS ALMANAC.
Most issues. $35-$75.

THE WORKSHOP.
NY, 1868-1871. 4 vols. bound in 2 books.
Furniture craftsmanship, decorative arts.
Lacks 6 numbers. Covers worn, stains. $450.

WORLD'S FAIR MAGAZINE.
San Francisco, Jan 1893. VG. $30.

THE WORLD'S MONTHLY.
Vols 1 and 2, 1926.
Covers worn, spines chipped.
Work by Ezra Pound, Arthur
Machen, etc. $30.

WORLDS OF FANTASY.
Vol. 1, No. 1. 1968.
Only issue published.
Near Fine. $45.

WORLD'S WORK.
1890s-1920s avg. $3-$10 ea.
6 issues. 1903-1908. The lot. $29.
September 1914. War outbreak. $15.
April 1920. $5.
November 1921. $15.

WRESTLING WORLD.
July 1954. Vol. 1, No. 4. VG. $15.
Various other Wrestling magazines,
mixed titles, 1960s, 1970s. $6 each.

WRIGHT'S ALMANAC.
Pre-1853. $30-$40.
1860-1899. $8-$15 ea.

Y

YACHTING MAGAZINE.
  1950s. $3-$4 each.

YALE LITERARY MAGAZINE.
  1936 Centennial Number.
  "Literature is a Business" by
  Sinclair Lewis. $30.

YALE REVIEW.
  17 bound vols. ex-library. 1924-1971.
  The lot. $100.

YANK.
  Average 1940s issue. $3-$5.
  Jan 1944. Ranger in Scotland. $5.
  VE Day Edition, no date. $20.
  Death of Roosevelt. 1945. $20.
  July 1945. GI Sketch Book. $5.
  British Edition. 35 issues 1943. $50.

YANKEE MAGAZINE.
  127 issues. 1947-1962. The lot. $50.
  Maxfield Parrish covers. $10-$30 ea.

YOUNG LADIES JOURNAL.
  1889 American edition with
  32" x 48" fashion fold-out. $24.
  Most 1877-1911 issues. $9-$18 each.

YOUTH'S COMPANION.
  2,000 issues. 1870-1908. $425 the lot.
  Avg. non-premium issue. $5-$8 each.
  Bound vol., 1886. 52 issues. $150.
  Bound vol., 1889. $90.
  65 issues. 1911-1926. VG. $10-$14 each.
  50 issues. 1895-1923. The lot. $40.
  12 issues. 1898-1914. The lot. $25.,
  9 issues. 1912-1914. Includes "Premiums"
  issue of 1913. The lot. $18.
  4 issues. 1925. The lot. $15.
  8 issues. 1928-1929. Worn. $17 all.
  Oct 1896. Premium issue. $15-$20.
  Oct 1918. Premium issue. $30.
  Nov 1925. 100th Birthday issue. $30.

  Maxfield Parrish and Norman Rockwell
  illus. $15-$30.

Only Chicago Evening Newspaper With All Leading News Services—Associated Press, International News and Universal Service

Hold Woman in Slaying Quiz

CHICAGO AMERICAN

7TH RACE SPORTS COMPLETE

WILL ROGERS KILLED
DIES WITH POST IN CRASH

WING TO DEATH. ENGINE FAILS, PLANE FALLS IN REMOTE

READ EVERY ARTICLE
THE BEST AUTHORS

Kaiser and Party Prisoners in Holland
CHICAGO AMERICAN SECOND EDITION

WAR OVER

The Youngstown Telegram
EXTRA

FIND LINDY BABY DEAD

DOLLAR BANK RE-OPENING IS SET FOR MAY 18

DERBY WINNER WILL RUN IN PREAKNESS

FIND BODY OF KIDNAPED CHILD

OHIO PRIMARY DOOMS POWER

BRUNO DIES IN CHAIR AT 8:20 P.M.
Klein Hits 2 Homers. Cubs Beat Dodgers, 9-5

CHICAGO AMERICAN

8 STAR SPORTS COMPLETE

ONE LIFE FOR ANOTHER---
Two Full Pages of Lindbergh Case Pictures on Pages 6 and 7

HAUPTMANN BREAKS IN CELL

HERALD CHICAGO AMERICAN

FIRST SATURDAY EDITION

HITLER, DUCE WAR ON U.S.

Surviv...
How...
Wales...

Cecil...
Saved...

NEW YORK JOURNAL

HE'S HERE!
MILLIONS CHEER CROWD BATTLES

FINAL COMPLETE · MONDAY, JUNE 13, 1927 · THREE CENTS · FINAL COMPLETE!

No. 14,922—DAILY

SPIRIT OF ST. LOUIS CRIPPLED

WELCOME

VICTORY

V-E EDITION

CLEVELAND NEWS

EXTRA
HOME EDITION

NAZIS QUIT!

Germany's Surrender is Unconditional; Enemy Signs Terms at Eisenhower's Headquarters; Time, 8:41 P.M. Sunday

BY EDWARD KENNEDY, Associated Press Staff Correspondent

LONDON—The greatest war in history ended today with the unconditional surrender of Germany at 2:41 a. m. French Time (8:41 p. m. Sunday, Cleveland time).

The surrender of the Reich to the western Allies and Russia was made at General Eisenhower's headquarters at Reims, France, by Colonel General Gustaf Jodl, chief of staff for the German Army.

The news came in an Associated Press dispatch from Reims. Earlier German broadcasts told the German people that Grand Admiral Karl Doenitz had ordered the capitulation of all fighting forces, and called off the U-boat war.

Joy at the news was tempered only by the realization that the war against Japan remains to be resolved.

The end of the European warfare, greatest, bloodiest and costliest war in human history—it has claimed at least 40,000,000 casualties on both sides in killed, wounded, and captured—came after five years, eight months, and six days of strife that over-
spread the globe. Hitler's arrogant onslaught began with the beginning the agony that convulsed the world for 2,076 days.

Unconditional surrender of the beaten remnants of his legions first was an-nounced by the Germans.

The historic news began breaking with a Danish broadcast that Norway had been surrendered unconditionally.

Then the new German foreign minister, Ludwig Schwerin von Krosigk, an-nounced to the German people, shortly after 2 p. m. (8 a. m. Eastern War Time), that "after almost six years struggle we have succumbed."

Von Krosigk announced Grand Admiral Karl Doenitz had "ordered the un-conditional surrender of all fighting German troops."

The world waited tensely. Then at 9:35 a. m. E.W.T. came the Associated Press Flash from Reims, France, telling of the signing at General Eisenhower's head-quarters of the unconditional surrender at 2:41 a. m. French time (8:41 p. m., E.W.T.) Germany had given up to the Western Allies and to Russia.

London went wild at the news. Crowds jammed Piccadilly Circus. Smiling throngs poured out of subways and lined the streets.

A war note came from the German-controlled radio at Prague. A broadcast monitored

Here's Text of Nazi Surrender Broadcast

Save This V-E Day Edition

Microphones Set Up in White House

Last Minute News

Los Angeles Examiner

NAZIS SURRENDER
EUROPE WAR COMES TO END

REIMS, France, May 7—(AP)—Germany surrendered uncondition-ally to the Western Allies and Russia at 2:41 a. m. French time today.

The surrender took place at a little red school house which is the headquarters of General Eisenhower.

The surrender which brought the war in Europe to a formal end after five years, eight months and six days of bloodshed and destruction was signed for Ger-many by Colonel General Gustav Jodl.

Jodl is the new chief of staff of the German Army.

It was signed for the Supreme Allied Command by Lieutenant General Wal-ter Bedell Smith, chief of staff for General Eisenhower.

It was also signed by General Ivan Sousloparoff for Russia and by General Francois Sevez for France.

Only the First Half Is Over—LET'S KEEP ON THE JOB!

YESTERDAY'S NEWS

Newspapers are the diaries of history. In 1880 more than 7,000 newspapers were being published in America. If you multiply this by an average of say, 2,000 subscribers, the answer is 14 million papers hitting street corners and doorsteps every day. Folks were frugal—by nature and necessity—and most of those newspapers were recycled. They were used in business as packing material, book backing and fish wrapping. Household copies found their way to the bottoms of barrels, drawers, trunks and outhouses. They also made useful scrapbook pages, shelf liners, and shoe innersoles. Local libraries and historical societies kept every issue and dutifully bound them into handsome six-month volumes. So, you see, it is no wonder that the average old newspaper is worthless, too many survived. Only the most exciting examples are valuable today.

Certain old newspapers are collectible in at least 25 ways, according to Jim Lyons' book, *Collecting American Newspapers*. (Available from the author at 24745 Summerhill Ave. Los Altos, CA 94024.)

History, reported as it happened, is the number one motivator. But some collectors just love to soak up the "atmosphere" of a particular place in time. Also coveted are first and last issues, "Centennial" and "Anniversary" issues, unusual titles and extremely bold graphics.

Many newspaper buffs belong to the Newspaper Collectors Society of America, which has an official journal, *Collectible Newspapers*. Rick Brown, the journal editor, has been dealing in newspapers for over 30 years. For newcomers, he has written, *A Primer on Collecting Old and Historic Newspapers*. The booklet costs $1.50 plus a self-addressed, stamped envelope. (Order from NCSA, Box 19134, Lansing MI 48901.)

Here are some key points made by Mr. Brown's publication: The front page layout and contents weighs heavily in determining value. If a newspaper from the 1790s offers only minor events, its age is not an asset. Hard core collectors will not be interested. By contrast, very bold 20th century headlines featuring disasters, heroes, villans and war news are highly sought after.

Newspapers lacking significant historical news are called "atmosphere" newspapers. Some are bought just for reading enjoyment. Local history buffs and collectors of information about particular subjects—slavery, sports or the Western movement, for example—can sometimes find jewels in "atmosphere" papers. An issue that carries the first report of an important national event is very collectible. For example, the *New York Herald's* 2 a.m. edition of April 15, 1865, has a higher price tag than other papers which carried the news of Lincoln's assassination several hours later, on April 15th.

Longer articles, larger headlines or bigger graphics add to desirability. If the front page is very displayable, the issue will be much more valuable than a competitor's edition with less "eye appeal."

The wise collector never folds a newspaper in half. Keeping the paper flat helps prevent brownness and deterioration. Newspaper issues that are brittle, stained, badly browned, dirty, wrinkled or have pieces missing are generally to be avoided. Plastic lamination may prevent such issues from complete disintegration, but destroys collector value. Better to store them in individual 16 x 24 inch clear poly bags with backing boards.

When buying "blind" by mail, collectors need an honest description which includes all defects. Be sure to accurately grade your offerings and you will be rewarded by regular repeat sales and no returns.

NEWSPAPER GRADING

The grading system of the Newspaper Collectors Society of America is as follows:

VERY FINE: Newspaper can have a minor tear but it cannot extend into the body affecting any articles. Small amounts of staining or mottling may be present. The texture of the paper can show some usage and have some fold lines.

FINE: Newspaper can have some staining, mottling or browning and can have some spine separation. The texture of the paper will show signs of handling (limp, wrinkles, etc.). Margins can show some wear or even a portion may have a small area torn away, but it must not affect any part of the text.

GOOD: The spine is separated completely. The texture of the paper will show obvious wear and tear. Considerable staining, mottling and browning are present. Small areas of the page missing, including portions of text. Only truly rare paper is collectible in this condition.

POOR: Anything less than the definition of "good." Paper entirely separated at the half-fold, etc. Has no collector value unless it is the only known example of the paper.

Many newspaper collectors use a simpler grading system. If a 20th Century newspaper is solid, intact, relatively clean with no stains and only mild browning, it is in collectible condition.

A newspaper printed before 1870, on rag stock, that has become limp from use, with pieces missing and lots of wrinkles, might only be worth 25 percent of one that is in collectible condition.

Be on the lookout for reprints. Reprinting began as early as 1825. If you find a newspaper of the following title and date, the odds are a hundred to one that it is not an original. Many copies of these issues have been run off as advertising giveaways or for outright deception:

BOSTON NEWS-LETTER, April 24, 1704. (The first regularly published newspaper in America.)

NEW ENGLAND COURANT, February 11, 1723. (Ben Franklin was the publisher.)

BOSTON GAZETTE AND COUNTRY-JOURNAL, March 12, 1770. (Boston Massacre.)

NEW YORK MORNING POST, November 17, 1783. (Washington's farewell address.)

GAZETTE OF THE UNITED STATES, May 2, 1789. (Washington's inauguration.)

NEW YORK SUN. September 3, 1883. (First issue.)

PHILADELPHIA PUBLIC LEDGER, March 25, 1836. (First issue.)

VICKSBURG DAILY CITIZEN, July 2, 1863. (Printed on the back of a sheet of wallpaper.)

NEW YORK HERALD, April 15, 1865. (Lincoln assassination.)

The most frequently reprinted antique newspaper is the *Ulster County Gazette* of January 4, 1800. It contained a report of George Washington's death and funeral. Although this news was not unique or exclusive, somehow the Ulster County version became the most copied. Thousands of reproductions have been issued, some as early as 1825. Many were distributed at the Centennial Exposition of 1876. In reality only two originals are known to exist today and both were found in the 1930s.

In 1958 the Library of Congress issued a circular exposing all the reprints and listing the points present in the originals. The first clue to a copy is that none were printed on hand-made rag paper, which has remained soft and pliable for 195 years. Also present should be the fleur-de-lis watermark which can be observed when held to a light. Reproductions might be worth $10 or $20 each, but only as curiosity items.

Before the late 1880s all newspapers and magazine artwork was hand engraved on wooden blocks or metal plates. Only a few tabloids were copiously illustrated, most of these used stock cuts for printing and advertising.

Frank Leslie started the nation's then-most-popular newsweekly in December of 1855. Using experience garnered as an apprentice in the *London Illustrated News* and at *Gleason's Pictorial Drawing Room Companion*, Mr. Leslie developed a faster artist-to-engraver reporting and printing procedure than any rival publication.

The Harper Brothers took note of his success and launched *Harper's Weekly* in January of 1857. Their highly paid professional illustrators covered every historic event from the Civil War onward to Reconstruction and the Westward movement. Once *Harper's* passed *Leslie's* circulation they never looked back and are perhaps the most collected newspaper of today. Bound volumes from the Civil War years sell for as much as $500 each.

The following descriptions and prices are from specialist newspaper dealer catalogs. They may be lower than the asking prices for old newspapers offered in antique shops and bookstores.

AFRICA'S LUMINARY. Monrovia, Liberia, 1839. Missionary Society paper, $29.

THE AGE. Augusta, ME. Dec 11, 1846. Polk state of union address. $17.

THE ALASKAN. Sitka, June 12, 1886. Vol. 1 issue. $23.

ALASKA FORUM. Rampart, AK, 1901. Vol. 1 issue of northernmost paper. $74.

ALBANY WEEKLY JOURNAL. NY, Aug 14, 1847, and Dec 29, 1849. Indian news, Mexican war, Gold Rush. VG. Both, $25.

THE ALBION. Weekly of foreign news. NY, Mar 13, 1847. General items of interest. $7.

AMERICAN FARMER. Baltimore, MD. 1822-1824 issues of 8 pages each. $25.

AMERICAN MERCURY. Hartford, CT. Jan 16, 1800. Famous funeral oration for George Washington, $255.

THE AMERICAN SOCIALIST. Oneida, NY. 1876. Newspaper of famed Utopian commune. $25.

AMERICAN TRAVELER. Boston, May 8, 1832. $6.

ARIZONA SILVER BELT. Globe, AZ, 1885. Rare. $57.

ARMY AND NAVY JOURNAL. NY, Nov 28, 1863. Text of Gettysburg Address. $235.
NY, Oct 15, 1864. Sherman's official report on capture of Atlanta. $23.

ASHEVILLE NEWS AND HOTEL REPORTER. NC. Vol. 1, No. 1, Feb 2, 1895 to July 20, 1895. 25 issues, disbound. Names underlined. $100.

BALLOU'S PICTORIAL. Oct 11, 1856. $4.

BERKSHIRE EVENING NEWS. Pittsfield, MA. June 5, 1931. Aviation news. $20.

BERLINER ILLUSTRIERTE ZEITUNG. Bound vol., Nov 1918-Dec 1919. Best known German illustrated weekly newspaper. Browning, some tears. Good. $90.

BISMARCK TRIBUNE. North Dakota, Nov 3, 1932. $5.

THE BLACK DWARF. London, 1919. Famous satirical paper. $17.

BODIE MORNING NEWS. Bodie, CA, 1880. Bodie once a famous mining town. $35.

BOSTON DAILY ADVERTISER. Boston, MA, Apr 13, 1861. Civil War begins. $135.
May 17, 1868. Results of Johnson Impeachment. $50.

BOSTON GAZETTE. Boston, MA, Mar 12, 1770. Paul Revere woodcut of Boston Massacre. (This is a facsimile paper done in 1876). VG. $75.
Sept 10, 1759. Siege of Quebec and Niagara. $54.
Jan 18, 1790. Washington's 1st State of Union address. $185.
May 3, 1790. Ben Franklin dies. $57.
Mar 13, 1809. Madison inaugurated. $27.
July 3, 1810. General news of the day. $12.

BOSTON HERALD. Boston, MA, Aug 13, 1892. Lizzie Borden plea in court. $24.
Sept 4, 1939. British steamer torpedoed. $22.

BOSTON MORNING POST. Boston, Nov 8, 1834. $45.

BOSTON NEWS-LETTER. Boston, MA, Nov 13, 1760. 1st successful American newspaper. $285.

BOSTON PATRIOT. Boston, MA. A semi-weekly. Bound vol., May 9, 1812-Feb 10, 1813. Approx. 78 issues. Fair-Good. The lot, as is. $350.

BOSTON TRANSCRIPT. Boston, MA, July 6, 1844. $9.
July 1, 1879. Article on Sarah Bernhardt. $35.
Aug 29, 1879. Plans to build Panama Canal. $35.

BOSTON WEEKLY MESSENGER. Boston, Aug 4, 1815. Wellington Rerport on Waterloo battle. $175.
Jan 27, 1831. General news of the day. $12.

BRADFORD OPINION. Bradford, VT, Mar 24, 1877. How Bell's telephone works. $34.

BUFFALO COURIER EXPRESS. 10 assorted issues 1939-1945. The Lot. $12.

BUFFALO EVENING NEWS. Buffalo, NY, Jun 6 & May 7, 1945. War Victory issues. $4 each.

CALIFORNIA DAILY COURIER. Dec 24, 1850. 4 pages. Gold Rush news. $150.

THE CALIFORNIA STAR. San Francisco, CA, Mar 27, 1847. State's second newspaper. $1,150.

CALL-CHRONICLE EXAMINER. San Francisco, Apr 19, 1906. 3 papers combine for quake news. $655.

CAMP DIX TIMES. Oct 3, 1918. New Jersey Army camp. $8.

CBI ROUNDUP. VE Day. 1945. Yank paper in China, Burma, India. Headline: ONLY JAPS LEFT. $9.

THE CHEROKEE ADVOCATE. Tahlequa, Cherokee Nation. Apr 1, 1871. Repaired, browning. As is. $85.

CHEROKEE PHOENIX AND INDIANS ADVOCATE. New Echota, Indian Nation, Aug 3, 1833. Rare Indian newspaper. $385.

CHICAGO AMERICAN. Chicago, IL, June 22, 1938. Max Schmeling vs. Joe Lewis. $20.

CHICAGO DAILY TRIBUNE. Chicago, IL, Nov 3, 1948. Famous blooper headline, "Dewey Defeats Truman." $300-$1,000.

CHICAGO EXAMINER. July 3, 1939. "Chamberlain Warns Britain Ready For War!" $7.

CHRISTIAN WATCHMAN. Boston, MA, June 20, 1834. $5.

CINCINNATI DAILY GAZETTE. 1861-1865. General news. $8-$14 per issue.

CLEVELAND DAILY PLAIN DEALER. Cleveland,
OH, Nov 28, 1854. Charge of the Light Brigade. $38.
Feb 14, 1859. Oregon Joins the Union. $58.
Oct 19, 1859. John Brown's raid. $45.

CLEVELAND HERALD. Cleveland, OH, July 10, 1865.
Lincoln shooting conspirator hanged. $46.
July 8, 1876. Custer Massacre. $155.
Mar 11, 1881. Garfield inaugurated. $23.
July 16, 1881. James Gang robs Rock Isle train. $46.
July 21, 1881. Sitting Bull surrenders. $85.

COLUMBIAN CENTINEL. Boston, MA, May 25, 1793.
Trial of Louis XVI, $26.
Sept 16, 1797. Frigate Constellation launched. $115.
Dec 10, 1803. General news of the day. $11.
June 26, 1816. Maine to separate from Mass.? $11.
Mar 29, 1817. General news of the day. $8.

COMMERCIAL APPEAL. Memphis, TN, August 17,
1977. Elvis Presley dies. $28.

CONNECTICUT COURANT. Hartford, CT, Mar 14,
1780. British name Cornwallis commander. $235.
Sept 9, 1783. Washington's farewell address. $865.
July 16, 1792. General news of the day. $25.

CONNECTICUT HERALD. New Haven, CT, 1811.
General news of the day. 10 issues. The lot. $28.

CULTIVATOR & COUNTRY GENTLEMEN. 1875
Weekly folio newspaper of farm and garden. State by
state news and ads. $15.

DAILY ARGUS LEADER. South Dakota, Aug 25,
1928. Saloons. $7.

DAILY AMERICAN STAR. Mexico City, Dec 20, 1897.
Mexican War. $145.

THE DAILY DELTA. New Orleans, LA, May 24, 1846.
Map, battle of Palo Alto, Mexico. $27.

DAILY FREE PRESS. Bodie, CA, Sept 17, 1880. Boom
town now a ghost. $75.

DAILY DISPATCH. Richmond, VA, Aug 14, 1861.
Battle of Manassas. $130.

DAILY EVENING BULLETIN. San Francisco, Dec 22,
1855. Murder, taxes. $100.

DAILY EVENING JOURNAL. San Francisco, July 3,
1852. Gold in San Joaquin River. $100.

DAILY GRAPHIC. NY, Mar 22, 187. Mormon murder
case involving 18th wife. $15.
Sept 26, 1879. Famous foot race in Madison Square
Garden. $7.

DAILY JOURNAL-GAZETTE. Mattoon, IL. Aug 12,
1940. Nazis Open Aerial Battle. $5.

DAILY MISSOURI DEMOCRAT. St. Louis, July 6,
1863. Battle of Gettysburg. $78.

DAILY MONTANA POST. Butte (?) 1868. First newspaper in state. $59.

DAILY TOMBSTONE. Tombstone, AZ, 1886. Very
rare title. $145.

DAYTON NEWS. Dayton, OH, May 21, 1927.
Lindbergh Over Ireland. $23.

DENISON DAILY NEWS. Denison, Tx, Sept 10, 1876.
"Boss" Tweed jailed in Spain. $8.

DES MOINES REGISTER. Jan 18, 1936. Rudyard
Kipling dies. $11.

DESERET NEWS. Salt Lake City, UT, 1854. Very early
issue of famous Mormon newspaper. $37.
Dec 10, 1856. Mormon Church president dies. $43.
Sept 3, 1877. Brigham Young dies. $135.
1886-1889, 5 issues. General news of the day. $33.
Sept 6, 1886. Geronimo, $67.
Mar 18, 1892. Jack the Ripper. $17.

DOLLAR NEWSPAPER. Philadelphia, PA, May 10,
1848. Interview with original Siamese twins. $12.
Oct 31, 1849. Long California Gold Rush letter. $45.

DUNLAP'S AMERICAN DAILY ADVERTISER. Philadelphia, PA, July 29, 1793. Ship and slave ads. $24.

EASTERN ARGUS. Portland, ME, June 30, 1929.
General news of the day. $6.
Nov 11, 1865. Lincoln assassination conspirator
Capt. Wirtz executed. $35.

THE EMANCIPATOR. Boston, MA, Nov 23, 1837.
Elijah Lovejoy, abolitionist, killed. $46.

EUGENE CITY GUARD. Eugene City, OR, Dec 15, 1877. General news of the day. $11.

EVANSVILLE DAILY JOURNAL. Evansville, in Mar 9, 1853. President Pierce Inaugural. $16.
Mar 7, 1857. Dred Scott decision Supreme Court. $145.
Mar 11, 1857. Buchanan inaugurated. $16.
Mar 5, 1861. Lincoln inaugurated. $147.
Mar 5, 1869. Grant inaugurated. $25.
July 6, 1876. Early reprint on Custer massacre. $155.
Nov 3, 1880. 8 x 17 inch woodcut of an American eagle. $18.
Oct 6, 1892. End of Dalton Gang. $225.

EVENING ADVERTISER. Portland, ME, Feb, 1832. Notice of Henry Clay running for president. $5.

EVERY SATURDAY. New York, Oct 28, 1871. Chicago Fire. $21.

FRANK LESLIE'S ILLUSTRATED WEEKLY. See *Leslie's Illustrated*. (Also see magazine section.)

THE FRIEND. Honolulu, HI, Jan 1, 1855. Kamahameha III dies. $46.

THE FRIEND. Phil., Nov 27, 1852. Slave traffic. $24.

GACETA DE MEXICO. May, 1772. 1st hemispheric newspaper published outside of Boston and Philadelphia. $485.

GAZETTE OF THE UNITED STATES. NY, Sept 13, 1789. Preface to the Bill of Rights. $2,550.
Mar 10, 1790. First national census ordered. $445.
Apr 14, 1790. Patent Act created. $315.
Philadelphia, Jan 23, 1794. U. S. flag altered for first time. $245.

GOLD HILL DAILY NEWS. Gold Hill, NV, July 12, 1875. General news of the day. $7.

GOLDEN AGE. NY, Apr 1, 1871. General news. of the day. $7.

GUINEA GOLD. New Guinea, Aug 8, 1945. GI newspaper. Atom bomb dropped on Japan. $26.

HAMPSHIRE GAZETTE. Northampton, MA, May 1, 1790. Much on newly-dead Ben Franklin. $56.

HAPPY DAYS. Civilian Conservation Corps camp paper. No place given. 1935. $27.

HARPER'S WEEKLY. (Bound volumes). *Also see Magazine Section.* Vols. 1-19, 1857-1875. Very Good. $7,600 (auction).
Bound Civil War issues:
Vol. 4, 1860. $200-$250. Water-stained margins.
Vol. 5, 1861. $250-$350. Water-stained margins.
Vol. 6, 1862. $300-$350. Water-stained margins.
Vol. 7, 1863. $250-$350. Water-stained margins.
Vol. 8, 1864. Recently rebound. $300-$350.
Vol. 9, 1865. Recently rebound. $300-$350.
Jan 1863-Dec 1863. 52 issues bound in half leather. Very Good condition. 800.
Complete years, bound, for 1862, 1870, 1871, 1875, 1876. $275 each, auction (Dealer asking $450 each).
June-Dec 1894, bound vol. $110.
July-Dec 1901, bound vol. sports, airships, 5 color plates. $110.

HARPER'S WEEKLY (Single issues). *Also see Magazine Section.*
1857 (First year of pub.) 16 page typical issue. $35.
Sept 3, 1859 Brigham Young, Horace Greeley. $24.
Nov 2, 1861. Rebel Steamer Merrimac. $15.
Jan 3, 1863. Nast's 1st Santa Claus. $25.
May 6, 1865. Lincoln death, funeral. $340.
Nov 16, 1867. Black man votes after 14 Amendment passes. $125.
May 29, 1869. Pacific RR done. $23.
Dec 8, 1877. Sitting Bull. $35.
July 27, 1879. Black baseball. $18.
Oct 1, 1881. Garfield killed. $15.
Mar 2, 1895. Frederick Douglass dies. $69.
Spanish American War: , 1898. $14-$28 each.
Christmas issue, 1903. $13.
Apr 30, 1910, Mark Twain dies. $35.

HARPER'S WEEKLY (Supplements).
July 8, 1872. Centerfold bird's eye view of Boston area. $10.
Aug 30, 1873. Foldout view of Newport, RI. $13.
Dec 14, 1872. Foldout of Boston after fire. $8.
Sept 30, 1876. Balloon view of Centennial Exposition, near Philadelphia. Foldout. $16.

HARPER'S WEEKLY (Prints). Various subjects illustrated with full or part-page prints in specific issues of this famous illustrated periodical.
Santa Claus: by Thomas Nast. $25-$100 each.
Blacks: 17 issues, 1860-1869. $14-$39 each.
Indians: issues of 1/27/66-10/27 and 12/8/77, 7/24/80 and 4/10/86. $13-$59 each.
Gambling: issues of 10/3/57, 7/15/65, 2/17/66, 2/23 and 3/30/67, 5/2/74 and 3/31/83. $18-$31 each.

Firefighting engravings: 1860-1900. $25 each.
Winslow Homer: April 25, 1863. Pirate ship. $20.
March 28, 1864. Army of the Potomac. $50. Nov 5,
1863. Great Russian Ball. $60. Feb 28, 1863. Army
Payday. $50.

HARTFORD DAILY STAR. Hartford, CT, 1865. Extra,
Lee surrenders. Light wear. $50.

HELENA DAILY HERALD. Helena, MT, May 31,
1882. General news of the day. $9.

THE HERALD: A GAZETTE FOR THE COUNTRY.
NY, Aug 11, 1794. Whiskey Rebellion. $44.

HERALD OF FREEDOM. Bethel, CT, Feb 19, 1834.
Editor is P. T. Barnum, before circus career. $17.

HONOLULU ADVERTISER. May 30, 1944. Yanks
Lunge on Rome; 14,000 Planes Slash Europe. $5.

HONOLULU STAR-BULLETIN. Honolulu, HI. Dec 7,
1941. First of four editions issued this day. Pearl
Harbor, eyewitnesses of attack. $1,875.

I. F. STONE'S WEEKLY. Jan 17, 1953-Dec 19, 1955.
Complete run of 1st 3 vols. Bound in buckram, signed
by Stone. VG. $100.

IDAHO DEMOCRAT. Boise City, ID, 1870. Rare. $64.

IDAHO ENTERPRISE. Malad City, ID, 1889. Rare. $58.

IDAHO HERALD. Boise City, 1872. Rare. $68.

ILLUSTRATED AMERICAN. NY & Chicago, Jan 27,
1894. Vanderbilt mansion. $10.
Oct 20, 1894. Article on Charles Dana Gibson. $23.

THE ILLUSTRATED LONDON NEWS.
(Bound volumes.)
   July-Dec 1849. Worn, torn. $75.
   31 vols. 1887-1897. $1,250 (auction).
   Jan-June, 1894. Spine wear, o/w VG. $120.
   8 bound vols. 1916-1919. The lot, $525.
(Multiple issues.)
   82 issues, 1966-1968. Fine. The lot, $22.
   7 issues, 1949-1964. The lot. $14.
   5 issues., 1916-1918. Fine. The lot. $45.
(Single issues.)
   Oct 18, 1856. Czar Alexander crowned. $10.
   Feb 21, 1857. $8.

1861 issues. $20 each.
May 15, 1927. King George VI crowned. $17.
May 1937. Coronation number. $17-$25.
Apr 21, 1945. FDR death. $17.
1953. Coronation issue. $33.
1960s. Misc. issues. $5-$15 each.

INDEPENDENT CHRONICLE. Boston, Sept 19, 1782.
British talk of granting independence to U. S. $220.
Boston, April 11, 179. Chronicle editor on trial for
sedition. $45.
Mar, 1802. Hint Louisiana to be bought. $15.
Nov 15, 1817. General news of the day. $6.

INDEPENDENT GAZETEER OR CHRONICLE OF
FREEDOM. Philadelphia, PA, May 26, 1787.
Washington elected president. $345.

KENDALL'S EXPOSITOR. Washington, DC, Mar 17,
1841. Harrison inauguration. $24.
Apr 17, 1841. President Harrison dies. $67.

KINGSPORT TIMES. April 8, 1934. Clyde Barrow is
sought in killing. $19.

LANCASTER DAILY EAGLE. Lancaster, OH, Jan 5,
1933. President Coolidge dies. $14.

LANCASTER DAILY GAZETTE. Lancaster, OH, May
23, 1934. Bonnie and Clyde killed. $68.

LANCASTER INTELLIGENCER. Lancaster, PA. Jan
18, 1825. General news of the day. $6.

THE LAND MARK. Salem, MA, Nov 29, 1834. $5.

THE LATTER-DAY SAINTS MILLENIAL STAR.
Liverpool, Eng. 1851. Bound vol., 24 issues. $125.

LESLIE'S ILLUSTRATED WEEKLY. 1850s. $9-11
Each issue. 72 issues, 1870s and 1880s. $8-$65 each
(Average $15).
May 13, 1865. Booth killed, Lincoln funeral. $29.
June 3, 1865. Jefferson Davis caught. $62.
Aug 26, 1876. Indian scenes. $32.
Mar 31, 1877. Bell telephone exhibit. $58.
Apr 15, 182. Jesse James' house. $23.
Apr 22, 1887. Jesse James killed. $545. (Newspaper
specialist Timothy Hughes says "This could well be
the most sought-after issue of any illustrated
newspaper.")

Jan 7, 1860. Wm. Seward, Central Park, etc. $15.
Oct 6, 1860. Garibaldi, Pittsburgh Expo. $9.
Oct 13, 1860. Prince of Wales. $9.
Jan 3, 1874. United States Navy. $12.
Sept 11, 1875. New York City Police. $11.
Oct 7, 1882. Political Circus Leap. $15.
Jan 26, 1884. Steamship Columbus Wreck. $14.
June 8, 1889. Harlem Aquatic Regatta. $15.
Aug 1, 1885. U. S. Grant Dies. $23.
Nov 6, 1865. Statue of Liberty. $37.
1861-1865 Average Civil War issues. $18-$20 each.
1870-1910 Misc. issues. $6-$12 each.
1914-1917 Assorted issues. $5-$15 each.

THE LIBERATOR. Boston, MA, Apr 16, 1831. William
Lloyd Garrison's anti-slavery paper. $68.
Dec 24, 1847. Slave auction woodcut. $28.

LITTLE FORT PORCUPINE. Little Fort, IL, Apr 30,
1845. $27.

LONDON CHRONICLE. Aug 5, 1775. Washington
named Commander in Chief. $215.
Feb 28, 1789. Early boxing. $12.
Nov 10, 1796. Washington's farewell address. $135.

LONDON DAILY MAIL. London, June 30, 1919.
Printed in gold ink to mark war's end. $46.

LONDON GAZETTE. London, Feb 16, 1684. King
Charles II, funeral. $97.
July 21, 1690. William Penn sought on treason
charge. $78.

LOS ANGELES TIMES. Los Angeles, CA, May 7,
1945. European war ends. Extra. $31.

LOS ANGELES WEEKLY HERALD. July 10, 1875.
General news of the day. $25.

LOUISVILLE DAILY COURIER. Louisville, KY, 1862.
5 issues. $28.

LOUISVILLE DAILY JOURNAL. 1840-1860. General
news. $8-$10 per issue.

LYNCHBURG VIRGINIAN. Mar 10, 1845. Small ad,
"Negro woman to be sold at auction." $24.

THE MADISONIAN. Washington, DC. Dec 18, 1841.
General news of the day. $15.

THE MANIFESTO. Canterbury, NH, 1885. Shaker
commune paper. $8.

MASSACHUSETTS MERCURY. Boston, MA, Dec 31,
1799. George Washington dies. $390.

THE MILITARY MONITOR. NY, 1813. 1812 War
news. $20.

MILWAUKEE SENTINEL. Milwaukee, WI, Apr 19,
1865. Lincoln shot. $34.
Apr 5, 1968. Martin Luther King Shot. $27.

MINNEAPOLIS STAR. Minnesota, Jan 29, 1936.
General news of the day. $7.

MINNEAPOLIS TIMES TRIBUNE. Minnesota, Apr 9,
1940. Hitler seizes Norway. $6.

MISSOURI REPUBLICAN. St. Louis, MO, Apr 9,
1882. Article on Jesse James. $43.

MODOC INDEPENDENT. Alturas, CA, May 9, 1889.
General news. $14.

MOORE'S RURAL NEW YORKER. 1868 bound
volume. $75. Single issues. $10.

MONTROSE VOLUNTEER. Montrose, PA, Feb 7,
1839. General news. $5.

MORNING CHRONICLE. Washington (DC) Apr 14,
1866. Anniversary of Lincoln assassination. Black
columm rules. $25.

THE MORNING GUIDE. San Jose, CA, Oct 19, 1871.
Chicago fire. $26.

NATIONAL ERA. Washington, DC, Nov 29, 1849.
California statehood. $8.

NATIONAL GAZETTE. Philadelphia, PA, Aug 28,
1824. Lafayette tours America. $20.

NATIONAL INTELLIGENCER. Washington, Aug 10,
1801. Benedict Arnold dies. $18.
Aug 21, 1801. Front page has long list of govern-
ment officials. $36.
Apr 10, 1819. $8.
June, 1939. $10.
Mar 6, 1845. Polk inaugurated. $27.

NATIONAL POLICE GAZETTE. New York City crime newspaper. July 29, 1876. Great engravings. $30.
Feb, 1882. John L. Sullivan wins fight. $13.
June 15, 1889. Johnstown Flood. $16.

NEVADA STATE JOURNAL. Reno, NV, Mar, 1878. General news of the day. $14.
May 15, 1880. General news of the day. $7.

NEW BRUNSWICK FREDONIAN. New Brunswick, NJ, Apr 10, 1865. Lee surrenders. $39.

NEW ENGLAND CHRONICLE. Cambridge, MA, July 6, 1775. Bunker Hill casualty list. $650.

NEW-ENGLAND COURANT. Feb 4-11, 1723. Ben Franklin's 1st newspaper. (Facsimile done Sept 17, 1856). VG. $35.

NEW ENGLAND PALLADIUM. Boston, MA, 1801. 5 issues, news of the day. The lot. $17.

NEW HAMPSHIRE PATRIOT. Sept 23, 1817. Mississippi joins the Union. $22.

NEW JERSEY STATE GAZETTE. Trenton, NJ, July 2, 1852. Henry Clay dies. $26.

NEW YORK AMERICAN. Aug 13, 1831. Eyewitness on bear-alligator fight. $12.
Aug 26, 1831. Discussion of Mormon success. $75.
Aug 29, 1831. Nat Turner Rebellion. $65.

NEW YORK DAILY GRAPHIC. 1870. 10 issues. News of the day. The lot. $24.

NEW YORK DAILY NEWS. July 21, 1969. Moon landing. $40.

NEW YORK HERALD. Apr 15, 1861. Civil War begins. $170.
Dec 9, 1941. Congress Votes War; 1,500 Dead in Hawaii Raid. $5.
April 13, 1945. President Roosevelt is Dead; Truman Sworn In. $5.

NEW YORK WEEKLY HERALD. June 28, 1845. Andrew Jackson funeral. $17.
June 12, 1876. $10.

NEW YORK HERALD-TRIBUNE. Aug 7, 1945. First atom bomb dropped on Japan. $25.

NEW YORK ILLUSTRATED NEWS. (1859-1864). Not to be confused with similar titles of 1850s.
Jan 26, 1861. Negro sale at Atlanta. $35.
Feb 9, 1861. Negro Ball in Charleston. $35.
Mar 9, 1861. Lincoln's journey by T. Nast. $50.
June 29, 1861. U.S. Army on shores of Potomac. $50.

NEW YORK JOURNAL AND WEEKLY REGISTER. July 30, 1789. State Dept. of U. S. created. $125.

NEW YORK MIRROR. Apr, 1834. News of the day. $8.

NEW YORK MORNING EXPRESS. Apr 1, 1847. Mexican War. $14.

NEW YORK SEMI-WEEKLY TRIBUNE. June 26, 1860. Pony Express. $23.

NEW YORK SEMI-WEEKLY TIMES. 10 Civil War issues. $63.
Mar 6, 1877. Hayes inaugurated. $22.

NEW YORK SPECTATOR. Feb 15, 1800. Text of Washington's will. $290.
Feb 17, 1815. Andrew Jackson reports on New Orleans battle. $37.
July 14, 1826. John Adams and Thomas Jefferson deaths. Both died on July 4.
April 10, 1841. President Harrison funeral. $48.

THE NEW YORK SUN. Vol. 1 issue, 1834, of first penny newspaper in U. S. $7.
May 14, 1835. News of the day. $5.

NEW YORK DAILY TIMES. (Now the NEW YORK TIMES). Aug 20, 1852. Issue from Vol. I. $9.
Nov 16, 1852. Daniel Webster dies. $13.
Sept 19, 1862. Battle of Antietam. $135.
Jan 28, 1861. Louisiana secedes. $29.
Sept 23, 1862. Emancipation Proclamation. $265.
Nov 9, 1864. Lincoln elected. $140.
Apr 6, 1865. Taking of Richmond. $47.
Apr 17, 1865. Lincoln shot. $97.
May 5, 1865. Lincoln buried. $27.
May 14, 1865. Jerfferson Davis captured. $135.
July 20, 1865. Miss Harris, Lincoln plot "conspirator," acquitted. $17.
Sept 9, 1924. Morro Castle burns. $26.
Apr 13, 1945. FDR dies. $34.
Aug 15, 1945. War with Japan ends. $31.
Nov 23 & 25, 1963. JFK Assassination. The Pair. $50.
Jan 21, 1965. Johnson takes oath of office. $14.

Jan 25, 1965. Churchill dies. $18.
Dec 27, 1972. Truman dies. $18.
Aug 9, 1974. Nixon resigns. $24.
Mar 31, 1981. Reagan shot. $63.

NEW YORK TIMES. 1940. 14 issues, Several on London Bombing. $25 all.

NEW YORK (DAILY) TRIBUNE. May 27, 1844. First news dispatch made by telegram. $158.
Oct 29, 1859. John Brown insurrection. $115.
Feb 28, 1860. Lincoln's Cooper Union speech. $87.
Apr 5, 1860. Pony Express begins $89.
May 19, 1860. Lincoln nominated. $78.
1961-1865. General news issues. $10-$15 each.
8 Civil War issues. The lot. $52.
Mar 5, 1861. First Lincoln inauguration. $195.
July 22, 1861. Battle of Bull Run. $56.
July 26, 1861. Full account, Bull Run. $53.
Sept 23, 1862. Emancipation Proclamation. $245.
Apr 4, 1865. Colored Troops 1st to enter captured Richmond. $365.
Apr 15, 1865. Lincoln dying. Many details. $1,250.
Apr 26, 1865. Lincoln funeral. $118.
May 15, 1865. Jefferson Davis captured. $135.
June 21, 1865. Sherman reports on march. $17.
May 12, 1869. Celebration of Transcontinental Railroad Completion. $185.
June 11, 1870. Charles Dickens dies. $33.
Nov 30, 1872. Horace Greeley dies. $36.

NEWPORT NEWS. Newport News, RI, July 23, 1934. Dillinger killed. $190.

THE NEWS. Garden Grove, CA, Feb 21, 1962. John Glenn in space flight. $10.

NEWS-EXTRA. St. Anthony and Minneapolis, MN, Mar 5, 1861. Lincoln inaugural broadside. $435.

NIAGARA FALLS GAZETTE. NY, June 6, 1944. Normandy invasion. $24.

NILES WEEKLY REGISTER. Feb 4, 1815. Battle of New Orleans. $22.
Misc. 1820s-$10-$20 each.
Dec 6, 1823. Monroe Doctrine announced. $115.
Apr 24, 1830. President Jackson says, "Our Federal Union. It Must Be Preserved." $168.
June 21, 1845. Andrew Jackson dies. $38.

NORFOLK CHRONICLE. England. Dec 1, 1781. Cornwallis surrenders at Yorktown. $1,250.

NORFOLK VIRGINIAN. Jan 31, 1872. Frederick Douglass insulted by hotel clerk. $26.

NORTHERN STAR. Snohomish, WA, 1878. General news of the day. $34.

OAKLAND INQUIRER. Oakland, CA, July 14, 1894. General news of the days. $7.

OAKLAND TRIBUNE. April 25, 1945. Hitler's Hideout Bombed. $5.

ONEIDA CIRCULAR. Oneida Community, NY, 1872. Utopian colony newspaper. $11.

THE OPAL. Utica, NY, 1853. Edited by lunatic asylum inmates. $54.

OREGON CITY ENTERPRISE. Oct 17, 1873. $5.

OREGON HERALD. Portland, Apr 22, 1871. General news of the day. $5.

OREGON SENTINEL. Jacksonville, Feb 20, 1875. General news of the day. $15.

OREGON STATE SENTINEL. Eugene. Mar 16, 1878. Edison interview on phonograph invention. $235.
Aug 1, 1885. Ulysses S. Grant dies. $53.

OROVILLE MERCURY. Oroville, CA, Jan 16, 1874. Part of Mark Twain novel, "The Gilded Age". $26.

THE PACIFIC NEWS. San Francisco, CA, Nov 10, 1849. 4th newspaper in California. $1,850.

PANAMA AMERICAN. No place. Nov 11, 1948. Prince Charles born. $16.

PASADENA INDEPENDENT. Pasadena, CA, Nov 9, 1960. Kennedy elected. $20.

THE PATRIOT. Harrisburg, PA, Oct 15, 1916. Theodore Roosevelt shot. $13.

PENINSULA TIMES TRIBUNE. Palo Alto, CA, Aug 30, 1982. Ingrid Bergman dies. $15.

PENNSYLVANIA CHRONICLE. Philadelphia. Feb 1, 1768. One of Farmer Dickinson's famous letters attacking England. $255.

PENNSYLVANIA JOURNAL AND WEEKLY ADVERTISER. Philadelphia, Mar 27, 1776. British evacuate Boston. $785.

PENNSYLVANIA PACKET. Philadelphia, Oct 26, 1786. Gov. Patrick Henry of Virginia issues proclamation. $36.
Oct 9, 1789. First national Thanksgiving proc. $265.
Sept 24, 1789. Fall of the Bastille. $155.

PEOPLE'S CAUSE. Red Bluff, CA, 1878. General news of the day. $8.

PHILADELPHIA INQUIRER. 1861-1865. General news. $10-$15 per issue.
Apr 20, 1865. Front page illustration of Lincoln funeral. $315.
July 8, 1865. Lincoln conspirators hanged. $88.

PITTSBURG SUN-TELEGRAPH. Apr 4, 1933. Dirigible crash. "Akron Breaks to Pieces: 73 Dead." $15.

PITTSBURGH RECORDER. Sept 5, 1826. July 24, 1827. Sept 11, 1827. The lot. $60.

PM WEEKLY. New York City, July 21, 1940. 5th issue of this experimental tabloid. $5.

PORTLAND DAILY TELEGRAM. Oregon, May 2, 1879. General news of the day. $6.

PORTLAND OREGONIAN. Oct 24, 1871. 2 columns on Peshtigo fire. $13.

PORTLAND STANDARD. OR, May 12, 1882. General news of the day. $5.

THE PRESS. Philadelphia, PA, Aug 26, 1858. First Lincoln-Douglas debate. $89.

PRETORIA FRIEND. South Africa, June 26, 1900. Boer War. $16.

PROVIDENCE GAZETTE. RI, Mar 14, 1821. Monroe inauguration. $25.

PUBLIC LEDGER. Philadelphia, PA, July 13, 1853. General news. $11.

THE REPUBLIC. Washington (DC), Aug 20, 1849. California Gold Rush. $13.

RICHMOND INQUIRER. VA, 1840-1860. General news. $8-$12 per issue.

RICHMOND EXAMINER. VA, Sept 20, 1864. Confederate newspaper. $125.

RIVERSIDE DAILY PRESS. CA, June 20, 1927. General news of the day. $5.

RIVINGTON'S NEW YORK GAZETEER, or WEEKLY ADVERTISER. Nov 2, 1775. Famous Tory newspaper. $235.

ROANOKE WORLD NEWS. VA, Dec 8, 1941. Pearl Harbor Attacked. $25.

SACRAMENTO BEE. CA, Nov 22, 1963. Kennedy shot. $25.

SACRAMENTO DAILY UNION. CA, Sept 10, 1867. General news of the day. $5.

SACRAMENTO DAILY RECORD-UNION. CA, Mar 22, 1882. Doc Holiday, the Earps. $90.

SACRAMENTO UNION. CA, Jan 1859. Pre-Gold Rush issue. $17.
Aug 8, 1860. Stephen Douglas talks at Harvard. $20.
Bound volume. Jan-June 1867. Near Fine. $475.

SALEM RECORD. OR, Mar 6, 1875. General news of the day. $5.

SALEM WEEKLY MERCURY. OR, Apr 16, 1875. General news of the day. $6.

SALT LAKE DAILY JOURNAL. UT, Aug 6, 1873. (Early Utah are all collectible). $5.

SALT LAKE SEMI-WEEKLY HERALD. UT, 1875-1876. 10 issues. The lot. $65.

SALT LAKE WEEKLY HERALD. UT, July 7, 1881. Garfield assasinated. $79.

SAN ANTONIO DAILY EXPRESS. TX, July 31, 1872. U. S. Grant for president. $15.

SAN FRANCISCO CALL. Aug 6, 1926. Gertrude Ederle swims English Channel. $15.

SAN FRANCISCO CHRONICLE. May 9, 1878.
General news of the day. $5.
Nov 8, 1962. Mrs. Rosevelt dies. $12.
Mar 7, 1982. John Belushi dies. $13.

SAN FRANCISCO DAILY HERALD. Aug 2, 1851.
Indian treaty, Wholesale prices current. $125.

SAN FRANCISCO EVENING BULLETIN. Bound vol.
Jan-June, 1880. 157 issues. The lot. $48.
Dec 1, 1880. Mauna Loa erupts. $13.

SAN FRANCISCO EXAMINER. Sept 11, 1889. Jack
the Ripper. $245.
June 10, 1899. Jeffries knocks out Fitzsimmons. $125.
Apr 20, 1906. First issue after the quake. $85.
Feb 10, 1917. Tom Mooney convicted. $10.
July 27, 1956. Andrea Doria sinks. $20.
Nov 25, 1963. Oswald killed. $15.
Oct 16, 1964. Kruschev out. $17.
Feb 21, 1972. Nixon meets Mao, Winchell dies. $25.
Oct 15, 1977. Bing Crosby dies. $12.
June 12, 1979. John Wayne dies. $17.

SAN FRANCISCO MORNING CALL. Oct 29, 1868.
General news of the day. $7.

SAN JOSE MERCURY. CA, Apr 6, 1976. Howard
Hughes dies. $14.
Aug 13, 1982. Henry Fonda dies. $17.
Aug 6, 1984. Richard Burton dies. $15.

SAN JOSE NEWS. CA, Dec 19, 1980. John Lennon
killed. $15.

SANTA CRUZ SENTINEL. CA, June 8, 1872. Buffalo
Bill. $38.

SANTA FE DAILY NEW MEXICAN. May, 1881.
Reward for Billy the Kid. $95.

SATURDAY EVENING POST (Newspaper format).
Philadelphia, 1859 early issue. $5. 6 issues, 1859. The
lot. $15.
Mar 15, 1862. Monitor and Merrimac. $49.

SCIENTIFIC AMERICAN (Newspaper format).
Bound vols. 1846-1848. 104 issues. $400.
Bound vols. 6 months, 1860s-1880s. $75-$100 each.
Bound vols. 12 months. 1862-1880s. $95-$150 each.
Individual issues featuring famous events, or inven-
tions of historic importance. $25-$40 each.

Bound vol., July-Dec 1908. Much on Wright
Brothers. Library binding. $100.
Other 1900-1910s vols. $40 each.
As a general rule value drops from 1890s onward
when photographs replaced line engravings. Bound
vols. from 1890s to 1920s average. $35-$50 each.
(Scientific American, single issues.)
NY, May 20, 1854. New $3 gold coin. $19.
Misc. issues. 1861-1884. $8-$25 each.
Mar 31, 1877. Bell's new telephone. $40-$50.
Mar 30, 1878. Edison's phonograph. $40-$50.
Aug 7, 1880. Wine making in NY. $17.
Sept 15, 1888. Kodak camera. $48.
Jan 28, 1905. Much on autos. $32.
June 30, 1906. (Supplement). The Lusitania. $17.
June 12, 1909. Wright brothers. $65.
Apr 15, 1916. Houdini escapes from strait jacket. $33.
Scientific American was a weekly from 1845 to 1921
and issued in a smaller magazine format thereafter.

SEATTLE POST-INTELLIGENCER. Apr 28, 1912.
Interview with Titantic survivor, etc. $40.

SEMI-WEEKLY CONSTITUTION. Washington City,
WA, May 7, 1859. Treaty with Nez Perce. $15.

THE SHAKER SHAKERESS. Mt. Lebanon, NY, 1873.
Scarce title. $28.

THE SHAMROCK HIBERNIAN CHRONICLE. NY,
Apr 20, 1811. Irish in U. S. $8.

THE SHEEPSCOT ECHO. Wiscasset, ME, 18992.
General news of the day. $11.

SILVER STATE. Winnemucca, NV, July 8, 1876. Custer
Massacre. $47.

SPIRIT OF THE TIMES. NY, 1847-1849. 8 issues.
Sporting news. The lot. $22.

SPORTS EVENTS: NEWSPAPERS NOT NAMED.
(Some issues are folded, with ring marks).
March 10, 1888. Sullivan-Mitchell Fight. $10.
July 9, 1889. Sullivan-Kilrain. Worn. $15.
Mar 18, 1897. Corbett-Fitzsimmons match. $60.
Oct, 1906. World Series. $25.
Oct, 1907. World Series. $30.
Aug 25, 1908. Burns fights Squires. $10.
Feb 10, 1912. Jack Johnson's bigamy charge. $10.
Oct 24, 1912. More on Johnson. $8.
July 29, 1913. America Wins Davis Cup. $8.

Feb 26, 1918. Dempsey beats Brennan. $8.
July 5, 1919. Dempsey beats Willard. $10.
July 13, 1923. Firpo beats Willard. $10.
July 16, 1923. Bobby Jones golf chap. $8.
Dec 11, 1923. Tunney beats Greb. $10.
July 25, 1924. Tunney beats Frenchman. $10.
Oct 1924. World Series. $30.
Oct 1925. World Series. $35.
Dec 26, 1925. Tunney KOs Madden. $10.
Oct 13, 1931. Sharkey beats Carnera. $10.
June 20, 1946. Louis KOs Conn. $15.

ST. LOUIS GLOBE-DEMOCRAT. MO, Dec 29, 1880.
Billy the Kid captured. $245.
Aug 20, 1883. Frank James on trial. $14.

THE ST. LOUIS TIMES. May 21, 1927. Extra, Extra.
"Lindbergh Arrives in Paris." $25.

ST. PAUL (MN) DISPATCH. Jan 15, 1925. Nazis win
election, Jimmy Doolittle speed flight. Lindbergh
kidnaping. $8.
May 29, 1927. Lindbergh starts Paris flight. $25.
Mar 4, 1929. Hoover takes oath. $10.
Jan 5, 1933. Coolidge dead of heart disease. $15.
Jan 19, 1933. Kidnaped millionaire Hamm freed. $8.
Jan 14, 1935. Lindbergh kidnaping testimony. $8.
Jan 29, 1937. Mississippi flood. $5.
Feb 14, 1914. Mass air flight over Eng. Channel. $7.
Jan 11, 1935. Amelia Earhart lost in fog. $7.
Feb 10, 1942. Singapore Lost. Japanese advance. $11.
Mar 28, 1945. U. S. Army advances in Europe. $10.
May 2, 1945. Nazi Army quits in Italy. $10.
May 5, 1945. Last Nazi army units surrender. $12.
May 8, 1945. City to mark V-E Day. $10.

ST. PAUL (MN) PIONEER PRESS. Feb 4, 1924.
Woodrow Wilson dies in sleep. $15.
May 22, 1927. Lindbergh lands in Paris. $20.
Nov 7, 1928. Hoover wins White House. $12.
May 18, 1931. Stunt aviator killed in crash. $7.
Mar 6, 1932. Roosevelt orders bank holiday. $10.
Jan 6, 1933. Coolidge funeral details. $12.
Apr 4, 1933. Dirigible Akron crashes. $6.
Jan 13, 1945. Amelia Earhart lands at Oakland. $14.
Mar 21, 1936. New England floods leave 270,000
victims. $5.
Jan 27, 1943. Roosevelt in Casabanca. $10.

THE STANDARD. London. 24 issues from 1838-1843.
In bound vol. Very Good. $195.

THE STAR. Colorado Springs, CO, Aug 1, 1889. Tiny
newspaper (4½ by 6 inches). $13.

THE STARS AND STRIPES. France, Oct 18, 1918. War
news in Yank newspaper. $8.

STOCKTON INDEPENDENT. CA, June 29, 1926.
General news of the day. $10.

STOCKTON WEEKLY. CA, Dec, 1870. General news
of the day. $10.

THE SUMMARY. Elmira. NY, 1912. Prison inmates
publication. $7.

SUNDAY FUNNIES. Complete color sections from a
variety of U. S. newspapers. $8-$16 each. Dealer lots,
10 sections for $40.

TOLEDO NEWS-BEE. OH, Apr 16, 1912. Titanic sinks.
$115.

TRANS-CONTINENTAL. Niagara Falls, NY, Vol. 1,
No. 1. Probably 1st newspaper published aboard a
train. Only 4 issues printed. Very Good. $100.

THE UNION. Washington (DC) May 16, 1846. Polk
declares war on Mexico, $89.

UNIVERSAL YANKEE NATION. Boston, MA, Feb 13,
1841. 26 by 32 inches. Claims to be "the largest"
paper in the nation. $18.

UTICA MORNING HERALD. New York, July 4, 1863.
Battle of Gettysburg. $120.

WAPAKONETA DAILY NEWS. OH, July 21, 1969.
Hometown boy, Neill Armstrong steps on moon. $42.

THE WAR. New York. Sept 28, 1813. Perry victory on
Lake Erie. $78.

WASHINGTON OBSERVER. Washington, PA, Apr 16,
1912. Titanic sinks. $650.
Sept 29, 1920. World Series thrown. $21.
Feb 15, 1929. St. Valentine's Day Massacre. $140.
June 6, 1931. Al Capone indicted. $17.
Apr 4, 1933. Dirigible Akron lost. $15.

Courtesy Newspaper Collectors Society of America.

WEEKLY ALTA CALIFORNIA. San Francisco, July 11, 1863. Full 3-day account of Gettysburg battle. $175.

THE WEEKLY REGISTER. Baltimore, MD, Dec 21, 1812. Historic letter by Stephen Decatur. $25.

WESTCHESTER HERALD. Sing Sing, NY, May 15, 1849. New gold dollar. $9.

WEST YELLOWSTONE JOURNAL. Miles City, Montana Terr. Nov 20, 1886. Yellow paper. $75.

WILLIAMSPORT GAZETTE. PA, June 6, 1968. Robert Kennedy killed. $17.

WILLIAMSPORT SUN. NY, Jan 6, 1919. Theodore Roosevelt found dead in bed. $15.

THE WOMAN'S JOURNAL. Boston, MA, Feb 15, 1908. Famous suffrage paper. Photo of Susan B. Anthony. $38.

WOODHULL & CLAFLIN'S WEEKLY. NY, Jan 16, 1875. Women's rights on child-bearing. $30.

THE WORLD. NY, 1876. Baseball Season Review. $65.

ZION'S HERALD. Boston, MA, Jan 28, 1824. John Quincy Adams nominated for president. $11.

TRADE CATALOGS

In 1744 Ben Franklin issued the first American trade catalog "to make publications available to readers living in remote areas." Although commercial printers were established in the United States as early as 1639, very few tradesmen issued any advertising other than an occasional folded broadside or a posted handbill. A typical American trade catalog of the early 1800s rarely exceeded twelve pages, while European "pattern books"—published since 1542—were evolving into thick, full-color sales catalogs.

Before the Civil War there was no reason for merchants or factories to expand their markets beyond state or county lines. Most craftsmen, tradesmen and foundries had all the local business they could comfortably handle. But by the end of the conflict excess industrial capacity evolved which prompted many American manufacturers to seek wider distribution.

Trade catalogs were first the tools of "drummers" (traveling salesmen and factory reps). As transportation routes and postal service improved, catalogs were mailed directly to farmers, merchants and housekeepers across the land. The term "trade catalog" encompasses a broad spectrum. These are the main varieties:

Retail Catalogs such as Sears Roebuck and Company's giant wish books, are the type most often found. These general merchandise catalogs appeal to a wide spectrum of collectors, publishers, historians, librarians, and even your neighborhood instant printer, who uses them for "clip art." Hollywood movie studios and documentary film makers are also active buyers of old retail catalogs. Set designers and prop men often refer to them during production.

Wholesale Catalogs were issued by jobbers and distributors to retail establishments such as hardware, grocery, auto supply, and variety stores. Wholesale catalogs often have larger illustrations and less written copy than retail catalogs. Volumes produced prior to 1910 are most coveted because their engraved "line art" illustrations are much clearer than the murky halftone photo reproductions which appear in early 20th Century trade catalogs.

Manufacturer's Catalogs were issued directly to wholesale houses and industrial customers such as railroads, municipalities, military installations, mining companies and large factory complexes. These trade catalogs usually were 9 x 12 inches or larger and are sought after by publishers, museums and libraries.

Picture framers, interior decorators and antique dealers often break up these wonderfully illustrated old volumes for resale to institutions and collectors.

Ninety-five percent of current demand is for pre-1935 catalogs. Most fashions and products designed after 1935 still closely resemble those of today, and are not yet "antique" in the eyes of senior collectors (like the authors). However, many younger dealers are beginning to stockpile recent catalogs; some dating as late as the 1980s. By the year 2000 they will have a ready market among a new generation of collectors.

Tools of the Trade. Booksellers cite "Romaine" when advertising their trade catalogs for sale. About 35 years ago a Middleboro, Massachusetts, rare book dealer, Lawrence Romaine, took it upon himself to compile the first comprehensive bibliography of American trade catalogs. In his book Romaine lists thousands of catalogs located in 200 of the nation's largest libraries, historical societies and museum archives—and goes on to describe their individual merits.

Before Romaine wrote his *Guide to American Trade Catalogs, 1744-1900*, most bookmen relied upon Charles Evans' *American Bibliography* and the catalogs of other notable booksellers, such as Brigham, McKay, Sabin and Silver. You will still encounter references to these book catalogs in the sales lists of modern dealers, who cite them for prestige more than any other reason. Anyway, Romaine's is the one you ought to own. (It has been reissued in paperback by Dover Publications, 21 East 2nd Street, Mineola, NY 11501.)

Two other reference volumes which librarians and trade catalog dealers often cite or consult are: Charles Evans' *Chronological Dictionary of Books, Pamphlets and Periodical Publications Published in the United States of America from 1639 to 1820* (published in 1903), and Richard McKinstry's *Trade Catalogs at Winterthur, A Guide to the Literature of Merchandising, 1750-1950* (published in 1984).

PRISTINE CONDITION is not an important factor to most buyers of old trade catalogs. As a group they are generally users rather than collectors. They are interested in the contents of old catalogs as a direct source of information. Detached covers and missing spine backs are commonly overlooked if all pages are intact and undefaced by any medium that might hamper reproduction.

Specialist dealers often place disclaimers at the front of their catalog listings which state "Normal signs of wear, such as chips, creases, pencil notations and company or library stamps are to be expected." Serious defects, such as missing pages, broad tears, clipped or defaced illustrations should be noted in any promotional literature you mail out.

How to sell. Let's suppose you have just acquired a hoard of older trade catalogs and wish to move them rapidly without incurring a huge selling expense. You could start by placing an inexpensive classified advertisement in widely-read collector publications such as: *The Antique Trader Weekly,* PO Box 1050, Dubuque, IA 52004-1050; *Antique Week*, Box 90, Knightstown, IN 46148; *The Paper and Advertising Collector*, Box 500, Mount Joy, PA 17552; or *Paper Collectors' Marketplace,* PO Box 12899, Scandinavia, WI 54977.

One can often reach collectors directly, through their club affiliation. You will find related names and addresses listed in a huge book called *The Information Collectors Clearing House, An Antiques and Collectibles Resource Directory*, by David J. Maloney, published by Wallace-Homestead Book Co. of Radnor, Pennsylvania. It is available at most bookstores and libraries and contains data on 7,000 buyers, dealers, experts, auction houses, restorers, clubs, collectors, museums and periodicals.

If your stock of old trade catalogs contains important 19th century material, you might try sending a list to university libraries and historical libraries in the cities where the catalogs were published. Also contact a few of the institutions listed in Romaine's Guide.

Probably the quickest way to unload your goods would be to wholesale them to a dealer who specializes in buying and selling old trade catalogs. You can ask for specific offers or quote a price for the whole collection (at 25 to 50 percent of estimated retail.) Exceptionally scarce catalogs could bring offers of up to 80 cents on the dollar.

As you read further in this section you will find that the big money ($150-$900 per volume) is in pre-1900 trade catalogs featuring Baseball Equipment, Bar Supplies, Gambling Paraphernalia, Horse Tack, Stable fittings, Dental Supplies, Drafting Instruments, Firefighting Gear, Art Glass, Pottery, Popcorn Machines, Type Specimen Books, Soda Water Dispensers, Bicycles, Barbershop Fixtures, Billiard Tables, Knives, Razors, Locks and Keys, Fishing Tackle, Fireworks, Guns, Toys, Dolls, Lamps, Cigar Labels, Tobacco, Perfume, Commercial Wagons and Carriages, Ornamental Ironwork, Amusement Machines, Telephone Switchboards, Windmills, Airplanes and Weather Vanes.

We have devoted very little space to low-end, low-demand, quite common catalogs such as those featuring:

Heavy Machinery, Wire Rope, Roofing Materials, Well Drilling Supplies, Rubber Goods, Building Materials, Construction Equipment, Electrical Goods, Pumps, Heaters and Pet Supplies. We could only scratch the surface of many broad areas of consumer goods such as Shoes, Clothing, Underwear, Jewelry, Automotive Accessories, Agricultural Supplies, Stoves, Furniture, Housewares, Hardware, Drugs and Groceries. Again, we stress the fact that rarely will you find a gem among mass-market volumes published after 1935.

There are only a dozen or so dealers in the nation who specialize in old trade catalogs. We have listed some major players below. Be sure to enclose a large stamped, self-addressed envelope when making inquiries.

Broken Kettle Books
702 E. Madison
Fairfield, IA 52556

Steve Finer Books
Box 758
Greenfield, MA 01302

Hesson Collectables
1261 S. Lloyd Ave
Lombard, IL 60148

High Ridge Books
PO Box 286
Rye, NY 10580

Hillcrest Books
Rte 3, Box 479
Crossville, TN 38555

Kenneth E. Schneringer
271 Sabrina Ct
Woodstock, GA 30188

THE POPE MFG. CO.
MAKERS OF BICYCLES AND TRICYCLES

Columbia Direct-Spoke Light Roadster.

383

TRADE CATALOGS

ABERCROMBE, DAVID T. *Articles for Sportsmen and Travelers*. New York, 1900. 12mo, 64 pages. $45.

ABERCROMBIE & FITCH. *Camp Outfits*. NY, 1905. $50.
Fishing & Hunting Catalog. New York, circa 1917. 8vo, 166 pgs. $25. 1918 edition. 4to, 166 pgs. $25.
Complete Outfits for Explorers. 1907. 320 pgs. $75-$100.
Tents & Camping Outfits. 1922. $25.
Fishing & Camping Catalog. 1952. 132 pgs. $30.

ACME CHAIR CO. *Wooden Folding Chairs*. Reading MI, 1928. 4to, 40 pgs. $30.

ACME CYCLE CO. *Acme Bicycles - 1898*. Elkhart IN, 1898. 12mo, 30 pgs. $40-$80.

ACME MFG. CO. *Stormer Bicycles*. Reading PA, 1895. 32 pgs. $35-$70.

ACME FOLDING BOAT CO. *Acme and Eureka Folding Canvas Boats and Canoes*. OH, 1897. 36 pgs. $50-$65.

ACME ROAD MACHINERY CO. *Catalog No. 11*. Steamrollers, graders, excavators. Frankfort NY, circa 1920. 63 pgs. $30-$50.
Traction Garders, Wagons, Street Sweepers. NY, 1927, 4to, 48 pgs. $40.

ADAMS CARRIAGE CO. *Baby Carriages*. Victorian wicker with parasols. Dover OH, 1906. 4to. 76 pgs. $80.

ADAMS & KELLY. *Millwork, Cabinets, Leaded Glass*. 1902. 360 pgs. $75-$100.

MARTHA LANE ADAMS CO. *Spring & Summer, 1921*. 192 pgs. of fashions. $70.

ADAMS & WESTLAKE MFG. *Every Day Cookery*. Recipes with a 40-page store catalog section. Chicago, 1884. $85.

ADAMS & WESTLAKE CO. *Adlake Camera Catalog*. Plus bicycles & accessories. Chicago IL, 1898. 32 pgs. $50.

ADDER MACHINE CO. *Business Machines*. 1912. 12 mo, 48 pgs. $20-$30.

ADJUSTABLE FIXTURE CO. *Lamps of All Kinds*. Milwaukee, 1924. 8vo, 64 pgs. $40-$50.

ADMIRAL CORPORATION. *Admiral Radio & Television*. 1949 full-color catalog. 54 pgs. $50-$95. 1950 foldout brochure. 12x24. $35.

ADVANCE THRESHER COMPANY. *1903 Catalog of Money Making Machinery*. Die-cut catalog in shape of a hand holding a wallet. 72 pgs. $95-$135.

AEOLIAN COMPANY. *Pianola and Pianola Piano*. Player piano catalog. New York, 1911. 4to, 32 pgs. $35-$50.

C. W. AEPPLER & CO. *Honey Packaging Equipment & Supplies, Maple Syrup Supplies*. Oconomowoc WI, 1936. 8vo. 40 pgs. $30.

AERMOTOR COMPANY. *12th Annual Windmill Catalog*. Chicago IL. 1900. 40 pgs. $40.

AERO SUPPLY MFG. CO. *Airplane Parts Catalog*. Corry PA, 1940. 200 pages of precise drawings, pre-war aircraft parts. $150.

AHRENS FIRE ENGINE COMPANY. *Fire Engine Catalog*. Cincinnati, 1906. 64 pgs. $175.

WM. AINSWORTH & SONS. *Catalog of Precision Engineering & Surveying Instruments*. Denver CO, 1909. 63 pgs. $100. Catalog B-1, 1926. 96 pgs. $85.

AJAX FIRE ENGINE WORKS. *Ajax Chemical Fire Engine*. 4 models, illus. Brooklyn, circa 1910. 4to, 8 pgs. $45.

AKRON TOOL CO. *Kraus & Akron Sulky Cultivators*. Akron OH, 1890. 31 pgs. $40.

ALADDIN COMPANY. *Aladdin Homes. Catalog No. 29*. Bay City MI, 1917. $25-$50.
Readi-cut Houses. 1929. 4 pgs. $15.
Aladdin Interiors. 12 pgs. $40.
Aladdin Readi-cut Homes. 1936. $20-$40.
The New Look in Homes, 1950. $15.

ALDENS *Christmas Catalogs*.
    1939 to 1949........................$75-$100.
    1950 to 1965........................$75-$100.
    1966 to 1970........................$65-$75.
    1971 to 1975........................$40-$50.
    1976 to 1982........................$30-$40.

ALDENS *Fall & Winter Catalogs*.
    1927 to 1930........................$60-$80.
    1931 to 1935........................$50-$70.
    1936 to 1941........................$45-$65.
    1942 to 1946........................$35-$55.
    1947 to 1950........................$45-$55.
    1951 to 1955........................$30-$45.
    1956 to 1960........................$30-$40.
    1961 to 1965........................$25-$35.
    1966 to 1970........................$20-$30.
    1971 to 1982........................$17-$20.

ALDENS *Spring & Summer Catalogs*.
    1927 to 1930........................$60-$80.
    1931 to 1935........................$50-$70.
    1936 to 1941........................$45-$65.
    1942 to 1946........................$35-$55.
    1947 to 1950........................$45-$55.
    1951 to 1955........................$30-$45.
    1956 to 1960........................$30-$40.
    1961 to 1965........................$25-$35.
    1966 to 1970........................$20-$30.
    1971 to 1982........................$17-$20.

ALDINE MFG. CO. *Artistic Mantles & Grates*. Grand Rapids MI, 1895. 32 pgs. $40.

A. B. ALLEN. *New York Agricultural Warehouse*. Rare 1846 catalog of Horticultural and Agricultural Tools. 80 pgs. $300-$500.

BENJ. ALLEN & CO. *Illustrated Catalog of Watches, Jewelry, Clocks and Silverware*. Chicago, 1891. 760 pgs. $75. 1933 edition. 668 pages. $35-$60.
Tools & Jeweler's Supplies. No. A28. circa 1912, Tools, signs, fixtures. 606 pages. $100-$150.

ALLEN & MC ELWAIN. *Vegetable and Flower Seeds*. Springfield MA, 1860. 70 pgs. $75.

S. L. ALLEN & CO. *Planet Jr. Garden Implements*. Philadelphia, 1893. $25-$35.
1895 Farm Machinery. 34 pgs. $30.
1912 edition. 64 pgs. $30-$40.
1927 photo illus. cat. 72 pgs. $25.
Flexible Flyer Sleds. 4 page brochure, 1908. $20.

W. D. ALLEN MFG. CO. *Catalog No. 28, 1906*. Factory and Mill Tools and Supplies. Village fire engine, hoses, belts, pullies. Chicago. 638 pgs., 7 x 10, hard cover. $100-$150.

ALLIED RADIO CORP. 1934 to 1936 catalogs of 86-136 pages each. $12-$16.
1938 issue. 160 pgs. $20-$30.

ALLIS-CHALMERS CO. *Corliss Engines*. Milwaukee, 1901. 8vo. 179 pgs. $65.
Thresher Parts. 1936. $15.

A. S. ALOE CO. *Catalog No. 159, Surgical Supplies*. St. Louis MO, 1935. 498 pgs. $35.

THEO. ALTENEDER & SONS. *Drawing Instruments*. 1892 Edition. 80 pgs. $45. Philadelphia, 1947. 36 pgs. $20.

B. ALTMAN & CO. *Catalog No. 50*. Fashions, home furnishings. New York, 1885. 4to, 112 pgs. $135.
Spring & Summer, 1915. 92 pgs. $25-$35.
Fall & Winter, 1921-22. 136 pgs. $35-$70.
Book of Styles. 1921. 160 pgs. $50-$75.

AMERICAN BICYCLE CO. *Bicycle Sundries Catalog*. Hartford CT, 1901. 52 pgs. $35.
Stormer and Pennant Bicycles. 1900. $35.
Juvenile Bicycles. 1900. 8 pgs. $35.

AMERICAN BRASS CO. *Anaconda Architectural Bronze*. Waterbury CT, 1930. 4to, 190 pgs. $50. 1937 edition. $25.

AMERICAN CARRIAGE CO. *Seventh Annual Catalog - 1893*. 12mo, 68 pgs. $100.
Price List No. 14. 1899. 24 pgs. $40.
Catalog No. 17. 1902. 96 pgs. $195.
Wagon and Pony Vehicles. 1903. $75.
Catalog No. 36, Pony Line. Cincinnati, 1905. 36 pgs. $100.

AMERICAN CRAYON CO. *Catalog of Prang Crayons & Watercolors*. Cambridge MA, circa 1920. 28 pgs. $25.

AMERICAN ELECTRICAL NOVELTY CO. *Flashlights, Searchlights, Clocks, Electric Candles, etc*. New York, circa 1902. 12mo, 64 pgs. $35.

AMERICAN FEATHER PILLOW COMPANY. *Book of Truth*. Feather pillows and how they are made, plus a price list. Photo illus. Nashville TN, 1915. 40 pgs. $45.

AMERICAN FIRE ENGINE CO. *American Fire Engines Catalog*. Seneca Falls NY, 1902. 96 pgs. $200.
World's Fair Souvenir Edition. NY, 1893. 24 pgs. $225.

AMERICAN FLAG MFG. CO. *How to Decorate Artistically for Celebrations*. Catalog of flags, bunting, pole holders, etc. Easton PA, 1912. 16 pgs. Color. $50.
Catalog No. 20. Circa 1913. 191 pgs. Color. $125.
Catalog No. 22. New York, 1927. $40.

AMERICAN FLYER. *Miniature Railroads Catalog*. Circa 1920s. 20 pgs. $35.
American Flyer Trains. Chicago, 1937. 24 pgs. Full color. $50-$75.

AMERICAN FORK & HOE CO. *True Temper Tools*. Cleveland, 1927. 136 pgs. 8vo. $30.

AMERICAN GONG CO. *Illustrated Price List of Bicycle Bells*. East Hampton CT, circa 1900. 16mo. 4 pgs. $25.

AMERICAN HORSE EXCHANGE. *"Woodburn Farm" Trotting Horses*. Auction sale catalog. New York, 1892. 12mo, 58 pgs. $40.

AMERICAN LA FRANCE. *Metropolitan Stream Fire Engines*. 1906 Catalog. 48 pgs. $175.
Fire Fighting Apparatus, No. 20. Chicago, 1923. $125.
Fire! Dingville F. D. Cartoons. 1922. $60.
Modern Fire Fighting Equip. No. 38. 1938. 144 pgs. $45.

AMERICAN LAMP & BRASS CO. *Illustrated Catalog of Lamps*. Trenton NJ, circa 1900. 40 pgs. $100.

AMERICAN LEGION. *Emblem Catalog*. Indianapolis IN, 1930. 64 pgs. $50.

AMERICAN LITHOGRAPH CO. *Cigar Label Sample Book*. No date. 100 pgs. Auction. $1,200.

AMERICAN LOCOMOTIVE CO. *Various Locomotive Catalogs*. NY, circa 1905. 48 to 60 pages. $60-$75 each.

AMERICAN MACHINE CO. *Hardware Specialties & Recipes for Ice Cream*. (Ice cream machines). Philadelphia PA, 1887. 48 pgs. $50.

AMERICAN MECHANICAL TOY CO. *The American Model Builder*. Erector set-type instruction book. Dayton OH, 1915. $20-$40.

AMERICAN NEWS COMPANY. *Illustrated Catalog of Holiday Goods*. NY, 1905. 4to, 168 pgs. plus 20 pg. insert catalog for McLoughlin Bros. toys, books, games. $100.

AMERICAN NOVELTY CO. *Catalog of Guns, Knives, Razors, etc.* Circa 1923. 106 pgs. $40-$70.

AMERICAN ROAD MACHINE CO. *Champion Road Machinery*. Kennett Square PA, 1896. 40 pgs. $50.
Road Graders. 1890. 22 pgs. $50.

AMERICAN MOTOR CAR SALES CO. *The American Roadster & Tourist*. 1908 5th edition. 24 pgs. $100.

AMERICAN MOTORS. *Rambler Family Album*. 1961. 114 pgs. Photo illus. $15. (Also see Nash Motors Co.)

AMERICAN SEATING COMPANY. *Furnishings of Modern Churches*. Chicago, 1920s. 21 plates. $25.

AMERICAN SKATE CO. *1916 Roller Skate Catalog*. 34 pgs. $29.

AMERICAN SNUFF CO. Almanac/Catalog, 1945. $20.

AMERICAN SODA FOUNTAIN CO. *First in the Industry*. Boston MA, 1922. 24 pgs. $65.
Instructions & Sundry Catalog. Philadelphia. circa 1900. 299 pgs. $325.

AMERICAN STEEL & WIRE CO. *American Fences*. Chicago, 1903. 16mo, 34 pgs. $20.
Fence Posts. 1913. 12mo, 22 pgs. $30.
Catalog No. 26. Binghampton NY, 1921. 8vo, 60 pgs. Including tools. $30.

AMERICAN THEATRE EQUIPMENT CO. *Advertising & Announcement Slides*. Ohio, circa 1920. 32 pgs. $40.

AMERICAN TYPE FOUNDERS CO. *Various Type Specimen & Border Catalogs:*
Dallas, 1895. 727 pgs. $300.
Cleveland, 1897. 934 pgs. $200.
Baltimore, 1897. 236 pgs. $95.
Boston, 1902. 132 pgs. $50.
Chicago, 1900. 1,188 pgs. $100.
New York, 1900. 1,168 pgs. $100.
No Place, 1912. 1,301 pgs. $125.
No Place, 1912. 102 pgs. $80.
No Place, 1923. 4 inches thick. $65.
Specialty Catalogs of 8 to 16 pgs. $15 each.

AMERICAN WHOLESALE CORPORATION. *General Merchandise, Holiday Goods*. Nov 1927. 602 pgs. $50-$100. Baltimore MD, 1928. 438 pgs. $45-$60.

AMERICAN WRINGER CO. Horseshoe Brand Clothes Wringers. New York, 1910. 104 pgs. $75-$100.

AMERICAN WRITING MACHINE CO. *The Calligraph*. Hartford, 1888. Typewriter catalog. 12mo, 25 pgs. $35-$50.

AMES SWORD CO. *Regulation Army Uniforms and Equipment for Officers*. Chicago, circa 1885. 36 pgs., 8vo. Illus. clothing and decorations. $150-$190.

AMESBURY CARRIAGE CENTRE. Co-op catalog listing many carriage companies and their products. Amesbury MA, 1893. 42 pgs. $75.

ANDERSON-BARNGROVER MFG. CO. *Catalog No. Y-100. Canning Machinery*. San Francisco CA, 1930. $45.

ANDERSON SHOE CO. *Made in 110 Styles, Direct to Wearer*. Baltimore, 1918. 64 pgs. $20.

A. M. ANDREWS. *Office Furniture*. 1903. 88 pgs. $40-$80.

ANNIN & CO. *Fine Flags - Wholesale Catalog No. 225*. New York, 1920. 8vo, 310 pgs. $100. Same, 1931. $100.

ANSCO CAMERAS. *1916 Catalog*. 64 pgs. $25-$50. *1914 Edition*. 56 pgs. $25-$50.

ANSONIA BRASS & COPPER CO. *Brass Housewares, etc.* Ansonia CT, 1883. Folio, 454 pgs. $250-$300.

APPERSON BROS. AUTOMOBILE COMPANY. *The Apperson Anniversary Eight*. Kokomo IN, 1919. 20 pgs. $50. 1920 Standard Eight. 16 pgs. Fine renderings. $95.

ARBUTHNOT - STEPHENSON CO. *Korrect-Way Store Fixtures*. Pittsburgh PA, 1931. 8x10. 32 pgs. $32.

ARCADE TOY COMPANY. *Catalog No. 35*. Full line of 1917 toys. 237 pgs. $825 auction. (Wild bidders?)

ARCHITECTURAL DECORATING CO. *Plaster, Cement and Composition Carvings*. 1909. 229 pgs. $75-$100.

ARCHITECTURAL LEAGUE OF NEW YORK. *Catalog/ Year Book*. 1907 to 1931 editions. $35 to $50 each.

ARMSTRONG CORK COMPANY. *Helpful Hints*. Lancaster PA, 1918. 4to, 52 pgs. $40.
Portfolio of Interiors. 1929. 32 pgs. $45.
A Story of Floors. 1929. 28 pgs. $15.
Cork, The Story of. 1930. 32 pgs. $18.
Linoleum Pattern Book. 1937. 375 pgs. $50.
Floors, Furniture and Color. 1924. 52 pgs. $35.

ART BRASS CO. *Catalog B - Fine Bath Room Ware*. NY, 1909. 96 pgs. $75.

ART METAL COMPANY. *Catalog R947. Residential Lighting*. Cleveland OH, 1947. 20 pgs. $20.

HENRY ARTHUR & CO. *Boots & Shoe Uppers, Leather and Findings*. New York, 1880. 56 pgs. $50. 1874 Edition. Includes machinery, 100 woodcuts. $200.

THEO. ASCHER CO. *Correct Millinery at Correct Prices*. Chicago IL, Fall 1900. Hats and Trimming. 24 pgs. $20.

ASSOC. OF AUTOMOBILE MANUFACTURERS. *Hand Book of Gasoline Automobiles*. NY, 1910. A great catalog of all the car makers combined in one volume featuring 1910 models. 199 pgs., 8vo. $300-$450.

E. C. ATKINS & CO. *Atkins Silver Steel Saws*. Pocket catalog, circa 1930. 48 pgs. $20. Catalog No. 31. Indianapolis, 1935. 4to, 151 pgs. $25. Catalog No. 18, 1919. 264 pgs. $20-$30.

ATLANTIC AMMUNITION CO. *Chamberlin Cartridge Catalog*. Includes color plates of game birds, etc. New York, 1886. 32 pgs. $100.

ATLAS PORTLAND CEMENT. *Catalog of 1924*. 42 pgs., color. $39. (If anyone is interested.)

ATLAS TRICK AND NOVELTY CO. *Catalog No. 11, Magical Specialties*. Chicago IL, circa 1910. 78 pgs. $75.

ATWATER KENT MFG. CO. *Atwater Kent Radio Instruction Book*. Philadelphia, 1928 4th edition. 9x6 47 pgs. $25.

AULTMAN, MILLER & CO. *Buckeye Harvesters, Annual Catalog*. Akron OH, circa 1894. 34 pgs. $75. *Chieftain Hay Rakes & Tedders*. OH, 1895. 8 pgs. $40.

AULTMAN-TAYLOR CO. *The Aultman-Taylor Thresher*. Mansfield OH, 1878. 24 pgs. $45.

AUTOMOBILE CATALOGS

Between the years 1900 and 1908 more than 500 American car companies were formed. Henry Ford started his first venture, The Detroit Automobile Company, on August 5th, 1899. In 1910 there were 300 car makers in the U. S. By the end of World War I only 23 automobile factories remained in Detroit, with another handful scattered around the country.

We have listed a few showroom brochures and maintenance manuals alphabetically by maker. The average 1950-1970 advertising folder will fall in a $15 to $50 range. The rarer the car, the higher the price in literature. A Ford Model A Taxi catalog might fetch $250 or more, while a 1928 instruction manual would bring only $25. Packard, Cadillac and Lincoln accessory catalogs before 1941 are worth $100 and up.

Other desirable catalogs worth big money are: Auburn, American Austin, Cord, Duesenberg, Franklin, LaSalle, Locomobile, Pierce-Arrow, Scarab, Moon and Simplex. Older foreign car literature is also scarce and anything featuring children's toy pedal cars is hot!

The markets for all of the above are automobile clubs, restoration firms, auto museums, and old car swap meets like the big annual event in Hershey, Pennsylvania.

Hemmings Motor News is the monthly trade publication most often consulted by old car buffs. It's available at news stands or bookstores. The antique automotive hobby has more devotees than coin, stamp and Barbee doll collectors combined. Keep your eyes peeled for everything from old road maps to registration certificates. It's all collectible.

B. F. AVERY & SONS. *Plows, 1878-79*. Louisville, KY. 64 pgs., 12 mo. $50-$85. 1872 edition in larger 8vo. size. 38 pgs. $75-$100.

AVON GIFTS. *Dealer Catalog. Christmas Gifts*. 1957 ed. 46 pgs. $45-$60.

B

BABCOCK MFG. CO. *Improved Self Acting Chemical Fire Apparatus.* Chicago IL, circa 1870. 24 pgs. $135.

H. H. BABCOCK COMPANY. *Builders of Fine Carriages.* Miniature catalog. Watertown NY, 1892. 2½ x 3½ in. 96 pgs. Illus. $125. 1902 catalog, 4to, 90 pgs. Fine color print of blacksmith. Detailed illus. of late models. $150-$250.

BABCOCK & WILCOX. *Steam Engines.* New York, 1891. 154 pgs. $75.
Steam. 27th edition. New York, 1893. 174 pgs., 4to. Hardcover ed. $90.

BAGBY FURNITURE CO. *Catalog No. 38, Spring 1906.* Baltimore MD, 1906. 76 pgs. $50-$70.

BAGG & BATCHELDER. *Catalog of Flower & Vegetable Seeds.* Springfield MA, 1875. 96 pgs. 8vo. $75.

C. C. BAILEY & CO. *Rubber Goods, Soap, Brushes.* Boston, circa 1890. 16mo, 58 pgs. $35.

JAMES BAILEY COMPANY. *Sporting Goods and Specialties.* Portland ME, 1925. 8vo, 94 pgs. $50. Another, 1930. 4to, 120 pgs. $50.
Saddlery & Horse Furnishings. Portland, 1913. 8vo, 32 pgs. $55.

J. W. BAILEY & SONS. *Catalog of Wood Mantels, Brackets, Mouldings.* Boston MA, 1879. 40 pgs. $100.

BAILEY'S INC. *Riding Clothes and Horse Goods.* Chicago, 1937. 18 pgs. $18.

BAIRD-NORTH CO. *Jewelry, Silver, Notions.* Various retail catalogs issued by this firm from 1895 to 1921. 160 to 232 pages. Fine. $40-$75. Fair to good. $25 each.

BAKER & BENNETT TOYS. *Catalog of 1922.* New York, 1922. 16mo, 36 pgs. $35.

BAKER, HAMILTON & PACIFIC CO. *General Hardware, Catalog No. 11.* SF, circa 1938. 3,116 pgs. $150-$200.

BAKER-LOCKWOOD MFG. CO. *Catalog of Awnings, Tents, Etc.* Includes flags, lamps, gypsy tents. Kansas City MO, 1907, 128 pgs. $75.

Catalog of Circus Tents & Show Equipment. Kansas City MO, 1920. 16 pgs. $100.

WALTER BAKER & CO. *Cocoa and Chocolate. A Short History.* Dorchester MA, 1899. 72 pgs. $50.

BALDWIN LOCOMOTIVE WORKS. Philadelphia, circa 1872. 132 pgs. 16 original photos tipped in. $500-$750.
Mallet Articulated Locomotives. 1910. 36 pages of drawings. $85.
Catalog of Locomotives. 1910. Hardbound. 128 pgs. $150.
Gasoline Locomotives. 1914. 32 pgs. $50.
Assorted Baldwin Catalogs. Average 30 pages each. Oblong 8vo. Circa 1898-1917. All for $775.

BALL & BALL. *Furniture Brasses.* West Chester PA, 1936. 28 pgs. $30.

BANCROFT CO. BOOKS. *Christmas Catalog for 1888.* San Francisco, 1888. 8vo. 40 pgs. $25.

BANNER BUGGY CO. *Banner Buggies.* One of the last really great carriage catalogs, 1911. Color covers, hundreds of 2-color illus. Big folio size, in orig. mailing tube. 112 pgs. Fine. $350-$550.

FRANCIS BANNERMAN. *Catalog of Guns, Swords & Military Goods.* Brooklyn, 1889. 28 pgs. $100-$175. 1907 edition. 9 x 12. 258 pgs. $150. 1911 edition. 19 pgs. Folio. $90. 1940 75th Anniversary. 286 pgs. $35. 1933 Catalog No. 22. 354 pgs. $100-$200. 1934 circular. 18 pgs. $25.

BARAWIK COMPANY. *Radio Catalog, Spring-Summer, 1929.* 260 pgs. including household and sporting goods. $25. 1925 edition, 50 pgs. Radio kits and parts. $50.

W. T. BARBEE IRON & WIRE WORKS. *Supplement No. 22.* Crestings, stable fixtures, brackets, hitching posts, weathervanes. Very decorative. 4to, 32 pgs. $75-$150.

BARLOW HARDWARE CO. *This is Our Salesman 1902.* Corry PA. 6 x 8, 208 pgs. $35.

BARNES CYCLE CO. *Barnes Bicycles - The White Flyer.* Syracuse NY, 1896. 8vo, 32 pgs. $100.

JOHN & W. F. BARNES & CO. *Barnes' Patent Foot-Powered Machinery*. Rockford, IL, 1885. Pedal-style jigsaws, lathes, etc. 8vo, 88 pgs. $75-$125. 1897 edition. 40 pgs. $48. 1921 edition. 36 pgs. $40.

BARNHART TYPE FOUNDRY. *Stock Cut Catalog*. Chicago, 1910-15. 199 pgs. $75.
Pony Specimen Book. Chicago, 1891. 444 pgs. $125.

E. T. BARNUM CO. *Catalog of Reservoir Vases*. Detroit MI, 1889. 20 pgs. $200.
Catalog No. 274. Wrought iron fences, weather vanes, hitching posts. Circa 1900. 40 pgs. $250.
Catalog No. 710. Park, garden and mausoleum gates, weather vanes, etc. 1927. 66 pgs. $35-$50.
General Catalog No. 690. Ornamental iron for builders. Jails to mausoleums. Detroit, 1925. 66 pgs. $70.
No. 734 Builders' Catalog. 1928. 66 pgs. $50.

GEORGE F. BASSETT AND CO. *Gibson (Girl) Picture Plates*. Circa 1910 catalog, 12mo. $35-$50.

BATEMAN MFG. CO. *Iron Age Farm Implements*. Grenloch NJ, circa 1910. 40 pgs. 8vo. $20. Same, 1900. $40.

BATES MACHINE & TRACTOR CO. *Bates Steel Mule*. Joliet IL, 1920. 8 x 11, 10 pgs. $25.

FRED BAUER, CATALOG. *Cake Art. Flower & Ornamenting Tools*. Chicago, circa 1924. 16mo, 16 pgs. $20.
The Bakers Library, Cake Art Craft. Chicago, 1924. 140 pgs. $100.

BAUER GAS FIXTURE WORKS. *Catalog No. 5, Electric Fixtures*. Lanterns, newels, ceiling lights, globes. Philadelphia, circa 1905. 156 pgs. 10 x 13. $125-$175.

BAUSCH & LOMB OPTICAL CO. *Photographic Lenses, Shutters*. 1894. 32 pgs. $75.
Apparatus for Chemical Laboratories. 1904. 438 pgs. $75.
Photographic Lenses. 1907. $50.
Handbook for Engineers. 1912. $20.
Polarizing Microscopes. 1918. 18 pgs. $35.
Microscopes & Scientific Instruments. 1929. 318 pgs. $65-$75.

J. BAUSCHER, JR. *Sunflower Poultry & Seed Farm*. 2nd ed. Freeport IL, 1904. 64 pgs. $35.

GEO. M. BEARCE. *The Mexican Curio Company*. San Antonio TX, circa 1905. 38 pgs. $50-$100.

BEARDSLEE CHANDELIER MFG. CO. *Catalog No. 17 Electric/Gas Light Fixtures*. Chicago, circa 1906. Folio, plates 1024-1228. $150-$250. Another, 1915. $200.

BEATTY'S ORGANS & PIANOS. 1881. 48 pgs. Color. $195.

A. C. BECKEN. *1901 Jewelry Catalog*. Chicago. Hardbound. 4to, 608 pgs. $75-$120. Another, 1908. Folio, 692 pgs. $95. 1905 edition. Silverware, glassware, watches, etc. Folio, 768 pgs. $100-$200. (1915 to 1920 editions were smaller, 64 pgs. $15-$20 ea.)
1931 Optical Goods. 96 pgs. $40.

BECKLEY-RALSTON COMPANY. *Automotive Parts Catalog No. 98*. 1926. 448 pgs. $35. 1923 edition. $70.

L. BECKMANN CO. *Catalog No. 9. Surveying Instruments*. Toledo OH, 1925. 82 pgs. $75-$100.

BEDELL CO. *Spring & Summer, Ladies Fashions*. 1916. 102 pgs. $80. 1913. 96 pgs. $75. 1921. 194 pgs. $80.

BEE AUTOMOBILE COMPANY. *Catalog No. 26*. Supplies, parts for all makes. Allentown PA, 1925. 288 pgs. $75.

BEE KEEPERS' SUPPLIES. Hundreds of regional firms kept the nation's honey producers well supplied. Average catalogs from 1890s to 1920s sell for $15-$35. Exceptional graphics would double value.

BELCHER & LOOMIS HARDWARE. *Automobile Supplies & Sporting Goods*. New York, 1928. 320 pgs. $45.

BELCHER & TAYLOR. *Catalog No. 24. Agricultural Implements*. Chicopee Falls, circa 1908. 80 pgs. 8vo. $50. Another, 1895. 72 pgs. $35.

BELDING BROS. & CO. *Hints on Art Needlework*. Chicago IL, 1888. 52 pgs. $35. Another, 60 pgs. $25.
Fifty Years. (Co. History). No place, 1913. 48 pgs. $35.

BELDT'S AQUARIUM CATALOG. *Everything for the Fishbowl*. St. Louis MO, 1936. 4to, 48 pgs. $35.

BELKNAPP HARDWARE CO. *1925 Trade Catalog*. Largest wholesale hardware company in the U. S. (Took over E. C. Simmons Co.) 3,436 pgs. $100-$175.
1950 Edition. Hardware, tools, sporting goods, auto supplies, etc. 3,548 pgs. $100.

C. S. BELL CO. *Catalog No. 908. Steel Alloy Church & School Bells*. No date. Hillsboro OH. 38 pgs. $75.

BELLAS HESS. FALL & WINTER.
1915 to 1920. $40-$60	1941 to 1951. $25-$30.
1921 to 1930. $35-$45.	1952 to 1970. $25-$30.
1931 to 1940. $30-$40.	

BELLAS HESS. SPRING & SUMMER.
1925 to 1935. $25-$45	1941 to 1950. $20-$30.
1936 to 1940. $25-$35.	1951 to 1970. $20-$30.

BENJ. ALLEN CO. (See Allen.)

BENNET BROS. CATALOGS.
 1947 to 1955. $40-$45   1961 to 1970. $30-$35.
 1956 to 1960. $35-$40.   1971 to 1983. $20-$25.

BERGER BROS. *Catalog No. 7 Tinplate, Roofers Supplies.* Philadelphia, 1910. 174 pgs. $50-$75.

C. L. BERGER & SONS. *Engineering and Surveying Instruments.* Boston, 1900. Engraved illustrations. $180. Another, 1904. 212 pgs. $75. 1915 edition. 213 pgs. $50.

OSCAR BERGER. *Cuckoo, Quail & Trumpeter Clocks.* New York, circa 1905. Very ornate. 32 pgs. $75.

BERLIN PHOTOGRAPHIC CO. *Fine Art Publishers - 1905.* New York. Reproductions of famous artists' work. 8vo, 246 pgs. $20.

EUGENE BERNINGHAUS CO. *Barber Supply Catalog.* Cincinnati OH, circa 1910. Everything from poles to chairs; razors mugs, etc. 4to, 120 pgs. $250.
Barber Chair Furniture & Supplies. 1920. 4to, 56 pgs. $125.

FRANK S. BETZ CO. *Physicians & Surgeons Supplies.* Betzco line for 1925. 7 x 10, 256 pgs. $125-$150.

BICKFORD & HUFFMAN. *The Farmers Favorite Grain Drill.* 20 page catalog, NY, 1890. $25.

```
BICYCLE CATALOGS are listed throughout this
section at $85 to $200 each. Circa 1878 to 1905
examples featuring high-wheelers bring top dollar.
```

JAMES G. BIDDLE. *Catalog No. 525. "Roentgen" Coils & X-Ray Apparatus.* Philadelphia, 1904. 52 pgs. $100.
Roentgen Radiographic Table, etc. 1906. 16 pgs. (stained). $50.

BIDDLE HARDWARE CO. *Wholesale Hardware and Cutlery.* Philadelphia, Fall, 190. 48 pgs. 8 x 11. $50.
Farm and Household Items. 1889. 36 pgs. $40.

BIDWELL BEAN THRESHER. 1897. 16mo, 14 pgs. $10-$15.

JULIUS BIEN CO. *Quality Cigar Labels.* 16 fine sample pages. New York, 1911. $150.

BIGELOW-HARTFORD CARPET CO. *Century of Carpet and Rug Making in America.* New York, 1925. 98 pgs. $60.

BINGHAM TRUNK CO. *Catalog of 1912.* Buffalo, 1912. 8vo, 80 pgs. $50-$75.

W. BINGHAM CO. *Wholesale Hardware, Housewares.* 1918. 1,148 pgs. $95. 1931 ed. 11x12. 3 in. thick. $125.
1927 General Catalog. 1,171 pgs. Electrical, automotive, fishing equipment, kitchen items, bicycles, etc. $150-$250.

BINGHAMTON WAGON CO. *1890 Catalog of Fine Wagons, Buggies, etc.* Binghamton NY, 1890. 16mo. 64 pgs. $95.

JAMES H. BIRCH. *The Celebrated Birch Carriages, Harnesses & Horse Goods.* Burlington NJ, 1892. 8 x 11. (7) pieces laid in, plus 9 x 15 flyer. In orig. envelope. $350. 1907 edition. 144 pgs. $250.

BIRELY & CO. *Steam Yachts and Small Boats.* Oshkosh WI, 1890. 16 pgs. $95.

BIRMINGHAM STOVE & RANGE CO. *Red Mountain Stoves & Ranges.* Circa 1920s. 140 pgs. $30.

FRED F. BISCHOFF & CO. *Bischoff Patent Steel Ceiling.* Catalog of architectural components. Chicago, circa 1890. 32 pgs. Folio. $100-$200.

BISHOP & BABCOCK CO. *Cleveland Beer Pumps, 19th Annual Catalog.* Cleveland OH, 1898. 44 pgs. $195.
Eureka No. 9 Beer Pump. Cleveland, 1895. 44 pgs. $90.
1901 Edition. Pumps bar supplies. 3½ x 5½, 100 pgs. $60.

BISSELL CARPET SWEEPER CO. *Promotional Pamphlet,* Xmas 1921. 4to, 18 pgs. $15.

BLACK & CLAWSON CO. *Illus. Catalog of Paper Mill Machinery & Supplies.* Hamilton OH, 1886. 77 pgs. $50.

BLAIR CAMERA COMPANY. *The Hawk Eye Camera.* Boston, 1889. 12mo, 12 pgs. $75.
Instruction Book. 1890. 6 pgs. $50.

J. C. BLAIR, MANUFACTURING STATIONERS. *Keystone Stationery.* Tablets, note-books, etc. Huntington PA, 1902. 4to, 104 pgs. $75-$100.

BLAIR MANUFACTURING CO. *Lawn Mower Catalog.* Springfield MA, circa 1900. 13 pgs. $25.

O. M. BLANCHARD & CO. *Oswego Planing Mill. Mouldings, Doors, Brackets, etc.* Chicago IL & Oswego NY, 1872. 84 pgs. $200.

BLICKENDERFER MFG. CO. *Blickensderfer Typewriters.* Stamford CT, circa 1905. 8vo, 32 pgs. $35-$65.

E. W. BLISS. *Catalog of Industrial Machinery.* Presses, drop hammers, etc. Brooklyn, 1897. 8vo, 509 pgs. $100-$200.
Another, 1892. 389 pgs. $50-$100.

BLOCH BILLIARD TABLE CO. *Pool, Billiard and Saloon Supplies.* Cleveland OH, 1895. 80 pgs. $175.

J. G. BLOUNT CO. *Catalog of Speed Lathes.* Everett MA, circa 1924. 32 pgs. $20.

BMC PEDAL CARS. *Circa 1950 Catalog* of 38 pgs. $85.

BOBBINK & ATKINS. *Hardy Herbaceous Plants.* 1932. 84 pgs. $25.

BOGGS & BUHL. *Fashion Catalog & Fashion Review.* Holiday goods. Fall & Winter, 1888-89. 80 pages. $95.

BOEING AIRCRAFT CO. *First in Design, First in Production.* Boeing Corp. circa 1945. 24 pgs. Illus. $20.

JOHN L. BOLAND BOOK & STATIONERY CO. *Book cases, Stationery, etc.* St. Louis, 1902-03. $75.

BOOMER & BOSCHERT PRESS CO. *Cider and Wine Presses.* First catalog, 1876. 12 pgs. $100. 1888 edition, Syracuse NY. 62 pgs. $100. 29th Annual Circular, 1902. 8 pgs. $30.

GEO. BORGFELDT & CO. *Department Store Catalog.* New York, 1916. 16 pgs. $50.
China & Pottery. 1905. 8vo, 96 pgs. $100.

HENRY BOSCH CO. *Wall Paper Samples.* NY & Chicago. 1909. 160 leaves. $100.

UNITED AMERICAN BOSCH CORP. *The Automatic Maestro Radio.* 12 page catalog of 1936. $20.

BOSTON REGALIA CO. *Masonic Ritual Items.* Boston, 1909. 16mo, 48 pgs. $45.

BOSTON STORE. *Spring/Summer 1898 Ladies' Clothing.* 24 pgs. $25.
Holiday Gifts, 1898. 48 pgs. $50.
Fall/Winter, 1911 Women's Fashions. 96 pgs. $70.
Fashions. Chicago, 1920. 160 pgs. $70.

BOSTON WOVEN HOSE & RUBBER CO. *Catalog of Rubber Goods, Mechanical.* Cambridge MA, 1924. 72 pgs. $25.

BOSTWICK-BRAUN CO. *Catalog No. 38.* 1932, cloth cover. 1,337 pgs. Misc. goods, including 200 pgs. of toys. $75-$95.

JOHN W. BOUGHTON, MFG. *Interior Decorations & Artistic Floors.* Boston, 1893. 64 pgs. $150.

BOYLSTON STEAM SPECIALTIES. *1919 Catalog.* Boston, 94 pgs. $25.

BOY SCOUTS OF AMERICA. *Scouting Equipment, Uniforms.* 1927. 32 pgs. $50-$75.
Executive Equipment Number. 1929. 50 pgs. Contains everything a Boy Scout could want. $25-$50.
Various "Camp" catalogs. 1930-1950. 8-24 pgs. $15-$30.

BRADLEY & CURRIER CO. *Illustrated Catalog of Balusters, Railings, Stairs.* New York, 1896. 64 pgs. $50.

MILTON BRADLEY & CO. *Bradley's Patent Croquet, Magic Hoops & Other Games.* Springfield MA, circa 1870. 12 pgs. $100.
School Supplies. 1889. 130 pgs. $100.
Bradley's Kindergarten Material. 1899. 80 pgs. $95. *1913 Edition.* $20. *58th Year.* 1918. 48 pgs. $15.

F. E. BRANDIS, SONS & CO. *Precision Instruments For Civil Engineers, etc.* Brooklyn NY, 1902. 236 pgs. $75-$125.

BRANFORD LOCK WORKS. *Supplementary Lock Catalog.* Branford CT, 1879. Pgs. 840-1024. $125.

J. G. BRAUN CO. *Catalog No. 29, Drapery Hardware.* Chicago, 1929. 32 pgs. $25.

W. C. BRAUN. *Braun's Radio Catalog.* 1929. Radios, lamps, auto, sports. 200 pgs. $25-$35.

BRAZEL NOVELTY MFG. CO. *4th of July Special Catalog. 1920.* Fireworks, etc. 8vo, 54 pgs. $65.
Catalog No. 40. Circa 1920s. 8vo. 40 pgs. of novelties and fireworks. $100-$175.

BRECHT CO. *Machinery & Accessories for Retail Sausage Makers.* St. Louis, circa 1900. 49 pgs. $35.
General Catalog. circa 1910. Everything for butchers and meat packers. 144 pgs. $95-$135.

JOSEPH BRECK & SONS. *Agricultural Hardware, Implements, Machines.* Also includes weather vanes. Boston, 1900. 350 pgs. $200-$275.

BREYMANN BROS. *Awnings, Tents, Flags, Covers, etc.* Toledo OH, 1891. 24 pgs. $75-$150.

BRIDGEPORT ATHLETIC MANUFACTURING CO. *Tennis & Gold Rules.* Retail catalog, golf & tennis equip. New York, 1904. 12mo, 120 pgs. $150.

BRIDGEPORT GUN IMPLEMENT CO. *Price List.* Loaders, recappers, molds, shell extractors, compasses, knives. Bridgeport CT, 1882. Large illus. 8vo, 40 pgs. $75-$100.
Golf Goods of Every Description. New York City & Bridgeport CT, 1901. 12mo, 95 pgs. (Early golf catalogs are scarce). $250.

BRIDGE & BEACH MFG. CO. *Stove Catalog, 69th Year*. St. Louis, July 1, 1905. 142 pgs. $40.

BRIGGS CARRIAGE COMPANY. *Electric Railway Car Catalog*. Amesbury MA, circa 1890. 36 pgs. $200.

NEAL BRINKER CO. *Catalog No. 14*. Stanley and Starret brand, hardware, tools. Plus mill supplies, etc. $65.

WM. BRINCKERHOFF & CO. *Wholesale Hats, Furs, Robes*. New York, 1871. 32 pgs. $100.

BROADWAY POSTCARD CO. *Illus. Catalog & Price List*. Circa 1900. 280 postcards pictured on 16 pgs. (Chipped, folded, etc.) $35.

GEO. T. BRODNAX. *Catalog No. 39*. Memphis TN, 1938. Jewelry, notions, silver, luggage, etc. 8 x 11, 100 pages. $35-$50.

BRONSON AND TOWNSEND CO. *Wholesale Distributor's Catalog*. Tools, farm & house furnishings, etc. New Haven CT, 1920. 538 pgs. $125.

BROOKLYN CHAIR CO. *Catalog No. 12*. Brooklyn NY, 1925. 80 pgs. $35.

BROOKS MANUFACTURING CO. *Brooks Boats No. 32*. Saginaw MI, 1917. 8vo. 64 pgs. $40.

ARTHUR BROWN & BROS. *Artists' Materials Catalog*. NY, 1942. 224 pgs. $15. 1958. 208 pgs. $20.

BROWN BROTHERS. *Fruit & Flower Catalog*. Rochester, 1903. 4to, 100 pgs. Full color. $50. Another, 1902. 82 pgs. $75.

BROWN CARRIAGE CO. *Pony Vehicles and Harness*. Cincinnati OH, 1910. 64 pgs., 8vo. $125-$175.

BROWN FENCE & WIRE CO. Cleveland, 1916. All types of fences, including barbed wire. 4to, 80 pgs. $40. 1932-1936 editions. $40 each.

BROWN & HIRTH. *Enterprise Gun & Machine Works*. Catalog of guns, sporting goods, handcuffs, clay pigeons, etc. Pittsburg, circa 1880. 8vo, 48 pgs. $150.

BROWN & WILLIAMSON TOBACCO CORP. *Premium Catalog No. 17*. Louisville KY, circa 1940. 44 pages. $15-$20.

BROWN & SHARPE MFG. CO. *Catalog of Machinists' Tools*. Providence RI, circa 1900. 20 pgs. $15.
Catalog No. 31, Small Tools. 1929. $20.
Catalog No. 139, Machinery & Tools. 1929. 655 pgs. $30.
Same, 1935-1941 catalogs. $25-$35 each.

JIM BROWN'S 1935 BARGAIN BOOK. *Farm Supplies*. 64 pgs. $10-$15.

BROWNELL CAR COMPANY. *How A Good Car Differs From A Poor One*. Railway car catalog of 1895. $125.

CHARLES BRUNING. *No. 13 Drafting & Surveying Equipment*. 1938. 388 pgs. $35-$50.

BRUNSWICK-BALKE-COLLENDER CO. *Billiard and Pool Table Supplies, No. 644*. NY, 1911. 134 pgs., 8vo. $125-$175.
Brunswick Phonographs. Chicago, circa. 1925. 28 pgs. $50-$70.
Billiard and Bowling 1937-1938. 1937. 39 pgs., 4to. Some color plates. $50-$60.

BRUNSWICK RADIO CORP. *Catalog, Models 15 and 32*. New York, 1930. 12 pgs. $25.

A. M. BUCH & CO. *Hair Goods, Theatrical & Street, Wigs & Toupees*. Philadelphia, circa 1910. 8vo, 24 pgs. $40.

BUCKEYE CHURN CO. *16 page pamphlet promoting churns*. Carey OH, circa 1889. $50-$85.

BUCKEYE INCUBATOR CO. *Brooder, Incubator Catalog*. Springfield OH, 1893. 48 pgs. $35-$50.

BUDDE & WESTERMANN. *Hotel Supplies*. 1930s china, coolers, butcher blocks, kitchen utensils. 128 pgs. $36.

BUEGELEISEN & JACOBSON. *Musical Merchandise-Catalog No. 160*. Guitars to harmonicas, wholesale. New York, 1930. 4to, 176 pgs. $50-$75.

BUERGER BROS. SUPPLY CO. *Shoeshine Parlor Furniture*. 16 page catalog of 1924. $75.
Barber Supplies. Denver, circa 1900. 94 pgs. $300-$400.

BUESCHER BAND INSTRUMENT CO. *Buescher True Tone Instruments*. Elkhart IN, ca 1923. 4 folio pgs. $30.
True-Tone Drums & Trays. 1913 catalog. 32 pgs. $40.

BUFF & BERGER. *Handbook & Catalog of Surveyors Instruments, etc.* Boston MA, 1895. 150 pgs. $150.
Engineers & Surveyors' Instruments. Catalog of 1887. 148 pgs. $220.
Astronomical Instruments, etc. Catalog of 1879. 27 pgs. $100.

BUFF & BUFF MFG CO. *Makers of Fine Instruments, Transits, etc.* 1918 catalog. 124 pgs. $100.
Adjustments and Instructions. MA, 1925. 36 pgs. $20.

BUFFALO DENTAL MANUFACTURING CO. *Dentists Appliances*. Catalog "A", 1914. 48 pgs. $75.

BUFFALO FORGE CO. *Illustrated General Catalog*. Buffalo NY, 1896. 398 pgs. $35-$75.

BUFFALO MFG. CO. *Water Coolers, etc.* Buffalo NY, 1903. Everything from spittoons to bathroom fixtures. 8vo, 128 pgs. $95.

BUFFALO STAMPING WORKS. (Sidney Shepard & Co.) *Hardware & Housewares*. Buffalo NY, 1889. 183 pgs. $200-$300.
Tinware. 1892. 125 pgs. $90.
Bird Cages. 1889. 48 pgs. $200-$250.
Tinware. 1885. 23 pgs. $35.

WILLIS N. BUGBEE CO. *Minstrel and Accessories Catalog*. Equipment, wigs, makeup, costumes. New York, circa 1933. 8vo, 24 pgs. $40-$50.

BUICK MOTOR CO. *1916 Buick Sixes*. 24 pgs. $50.
Buick Valve-in-Head Motor Cars. 1921. $75.
1922 Buick. 47 pgs. $65.
Suggestions on Buying. 1925. $75.
1940 Buick. 4-fold. $12.
Buick Puts Best Foot Forward. 1948. $75.
Front and Center for 1952. $35.
Buick Smart Buy for 1949. $17.
1963 Buick. 10 x 14 brochure. $14.
Buick Magazine. 1948-1953. $5-$15.

ROBERT BUIST CO. *Buist Garden Guide, 1925*. Philadelphia, 1925. $30.

BULOVA WATCH CO. *It's Time You Knew. Strange and Interesting Facts*. 1944. 254 pgs. $20.

J. H. BUNELL & CO. *Telegraphy Catalogs & Manuals*. New York, 1891. 72 pgs. $50. 1895 edition. 96 pgs. $40. 1915 36th edition. 80 pgs. $40.

BURLEY & TYRELL. *Lamps*. Chicago, 1889. Victorian-style. 12mo, 144 pgs. $95-$150.
Catalog No. 104. Fall, 1902. China, lamps, dinnerware, glass. 9 x 10. 160 pgs. $150-$275.

CHARLES L. BURLINGAME & CO. *Gambling & Magic Catalog*. Chicago, 1898. 74 pgs. $100.

W. ATLEE BURPEE & COMPANY. *Burpee's Annual for 1918*. Philadelphia. 216 pgs., color. $40-$50.
Annual Garden Book, 1929. 8vo, 172 pgs. $15.
The Plain Truth About Seeds. Phila., 1898. 144 pgs. $35.

C. R. BURR & CO. *Flowers, Trees*. Color plate catalog. Manchester CT, circa 1910. 78 pgs. $100.

E. T. BURROWES. *Catalog No. 81. Home Billiard & Pool Tables*. Portland ME, 1908. 8vo, 24 pgs. $85. 1916 edition.

32 pgs. $100-$195.

G. H. BUSHNELL CO. *Cider & Wine Press*. Circa 1888-90. 40 pgs. $50.

BUSSEY & MC LEOD STOVE CO. *Gold Coin Stoves & Ranges*. Troy NY, 1896. 151 pgs. $50.

BUTLER BROS. (Nation's largest wholesaler). *Our Drummer, Wholesale Dry Goods. Toys and Holiday Goods*. 1918. 490 pgs. $135. 1903 to 1933 issues of approx. 250-600 pages ea. $40-$95 depending upon the size and scope of Toy Sections.
1880s Housewares, etc. 24 pgs. $45.
1882 Christmas Catalog. 58 pgs. $50.
1885 Our Drummer. 24 pgs. $45.
1890 Edition . 48 pgs. $75.

BUTLER BROS. *Pennant Baseball Uniforms*. Wholesalers. Chicago, 1916. (19) mounted swatches. 8 pgs. $225.

E. H. BUTLER & COMPANY. *Catalog of Approved School Books*. Philadelphia, 1872. Numerous woodcut illus. of pages from various text books. 96 pgs., 12mo. $75.

BUTTERICK PUBLISHING CO. *Patterns, Summer, 1871*. 32 pgs. $50. *Fall, 1872*. 32 pgs. $45. *Spring, 1873*. $35. *Winter 1876-77*. 270 pgs. $25-$50. *Patterns, 1878*. 32 pgs. $25.
Metropolitan Fashions, 1892. 90 pgs. $75.

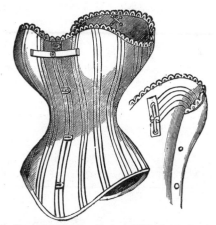

5. EHRICHS' NO-PAD CORSET. This Corset has a bust distended by bones, so that a pad becomes unnecessary. A tape extends across front, preventing the dress from falling in. Well made of heavy Satteen, and well boned............$0.95

Cork Bosom Pads, Improved.

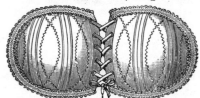

22. The lightest and most desirable bosom pad to be found. Price.......................$0.40

C

CADILLAC MOTOR CAR COMPANY. *1911 Brochure*. Fine airbrush plates. 32 pgs. $100.
Cadillac Motor Cars. Detroit, circa 1920. 16 pgs. $35.
Cadillac Accessories. Pre-1941 catalogs. $100 and up.

CALIFORNIA PERFUME CO. *Avon and Perfection Products*. NY, Kansas City, Montreal, 1934. Leatherette binder, 7 x 10½. 120 pgs. $120.

CALIFORNIA REDWOOD ASSOCIATION. *Redwood Home Plans*. San Francisco CA, 1928. Numerous color plates. 48 pgs. $50.

CALIFORNIA REDWOOD ASSOCIATION. *Redwood Home Plans*. San Francisco CA, 1928. Numerous color plates. 48 pgs. $50.

ALFRED J. CAMMEYER. *Illustrated Catalog of Boots, Shoes, Slippers*. New York, 1890. 48 pgs. $50.

CAMPANA ART CO. *Catalog No. 7. Artist's Materials*. Chicago IL, circa 1910. China painting patterns, brushes, etc. 64 pgs. $15-$20.

JOSEPH CAMPBELL & CO. *Campbell Soups From A to Z*. Camden NJ, circa 1915. 16 page photo tour of factory. $50.

CANTON STEEL CEILINGS. *Ornamental Sheet Metal*. Canton OH, circa 1920. 144 pgs. $50.

CAREY BROS. & GREVEMEYER. *3rd Annual Catalog of Holiday Goods*. Stationery, toys, mechanical banks, etc. Philadelphia, 1888. 4to, 128 pgs. Fine. $350-$500.

CARLISLE & FINCH. *Electrical Novelties and Scientific Toys*. Cincinnati, 1898. 24 pgs., 8 vo. Electric trains, etc. $95-$175.
Catalog B, No. 8. Ohio, 1903. 56 pgs., 8vo. Electric trains, dynamos, generators. $100-$225.

GEO. B. CARPENTER. *Boat & Marine Supplies*. Chicago, 1912. 4to, 432 pgs. $85.
Tents, Flags, Awnings, Wagon Covers. Chicago, 1910, 92 pgs. $75-$95.

CARVED COTTON GIN CO. *Boot & Shoe Machinery*. East Bridgewater MA, 1893. 45 pgs. $25.

CARRIAGE, BUGGY & WAGON catalogs were printed by the tens of thousands between 1865 and 1910. Small, thin, booklets with common vehicles are worth from $30 to $75 each. Large, well-illustrated volumes featuring deluxe and commercial vehicles, run from $95 to $350 or more. (See individual listings.).

CARY SAFE CO. *Catalog of Safes on Wheels*. Buffalo NY, 1898. 32 pgs. $50.

J. I. CASE THRESHING MACHINE CO. *Steam Road Roller Catalog*. Racine WI, 1909. 24 pgs. 9 x 12. $60.
Case Machinery Catalog. 1917, 4to, 102 pgs. $75.

CASH BUYERS UNION. *Catalog No. 354*. Carriages, Buggies, etc. Chicago, 1899. 128 pgs. $75-$125.
Oakwood, Arlington, Maywood Bicycles. Chicago, 1896. 42 pgs. $85.
Special Catalog 1896. Carriages, buggies, saddles, harnesses. 128 pgs. $150.

CASSELL'S BOOK CATALOG. New York, 1874. 4to, 64 pgs. $75.

CATERPILLAR TRACTOR CO. *Farm Survey, Demo. Plan*. Peoria IL, 1932. 36 pgs. $30.
Caterpillar Diesel D4 Tractor. Parts catalog, line dwgs. August 1943. 147 pgs. $22.

CATTLE AUCTION. *Various auction catalogs*. Offering registered animals. 48-72 pages, 8vo, 1880s. $35-$75.

CENTRAL ELECTRTIC CO. *Catalog of Light Fixtures*. Plus electrical appliances, radio supplies, etc. Chicago, 1924. 12mo, 804 pgs. $80.

CENTRAL IRON & WIRE WORKS. *Catalog No. 530*. Milwaukee, 1928. Fences, gates, mausoleums, jail cells. 8vo, 64 pgs. $65.

CENTRAL NEW YORK NURSERIES. *Flowers & Trees*. Geneva NY, circa 1905. Full-color catalog. 100 pgs. $125. Another, 1900. 200 pgs., 8vo. Hardcover, 100 full color illus. $250-$300.

CENTRAL SCIENTIFIC. *School Laboratory Apparatus, Glass, etc.* 1904 Cat. No. M. 308 pgs. $75. 1914-1932 editions, (72 to 336 pgs. ea.) $25-$35 each. 1936 Catalog No. J-136. 1,636 pgs. $40.

CENTURY FURNITURE CO. *Reproductions of Early Styles.* Grand Rapids, 1928. 12mo. 156 pgs. $40.

CENTURY LIGHTING FIXTURES. *Catalog No. 49.* 1933. 44 pgs. $45.

CERAMIC ART COMPANY. *Artistic China & Porcelain.* 1903. 86 pgs. $95.

CHALLENGE WINDMILL & FEEDMILL CO. *Challenge Windmills.* Batavia IL, 1885. 8vo, 44 pgs. $55. Folding circular in color. Circa 1890. 8 pgs. $50-$75.

CHALMERS DETROIT MOTOR CO. *1909 Models.* 36 pg. catalog. Fine illus. $100.

H. B. CHAMPION CO. *Forge & Blower Catalog.* Lancaster PA, 1912. Hardbound, 300 pgs. $50.
Catalog No. 60. 1936. 126 pgs. $40.

CHAMPION IRON FENCE CO. *Fence & Railing.* Miniature catalog. Kenton OH, 1890s. 32 pgs. $40.
Cresting Catalog No. 11. 1886. Finials, windmills, park benches, etc. 4to, 24 pgs. $75-$150.

CHANDLER & FARQUHAR. *Tools & Supplies For Mechanics, etc.* Boston, 1883. 56 pgs. $100.

CHANNON COMPANY. *Machinery, Tools, Supplies.* Chicago, 1916. 1,152 pgs. $45. 1930 edition. Everything from diving gear to barb wire. 1,271 pgs. $50.

H. CHANNON CO. *Camp Guide Catalog No. 58.* Chicago IL, 1914. 8vo, 120 pgs. $75.

CHAPMAN MFG. CO. *Dog Collars & General Dog Furnishings.* Meriden CT, 1890. 46 pgs. 1st ed. $100.

CHARIG BROS. *Catalog of Diamonds, Watches, Jewelry.* New York, circa 1890. 4to, 142 pgs. $75.

CHARLES & CO. *Wholesale Food, Tobacco, Beverages.* NY, 1928-1933 catalogs of approx. 350-390 pgs. $50-$75 each.

CHARLES WILLIAMS STORES. (See Williams.)

CHEVROLET.
New Chevrolet Six. Detroit, 1933. 12 pgs. $50.
1925 Touring Car. Brochure. $15-$25.
1939 Chevrolet Trucks. 20 pgs. $35.
1953 Accessories. 32 pgs. $22.

1958 Accessories. Color catalog. $39.
1937-1965 assorted catalogs, etc. 7 pieces. $150.

CHICAGO APPARATUS CO. *Catalog No. 41. Scientific Instruments, Lab. Supplies.* 1929. 497 pgs. $35. 1936. 832 pgs. $35.

CHICAGO ARTIFICIAL FLOWER CO. *Parade Floats and Decorations Catalog No. 38.* Chicago, 1935. 32 pgs. $25.

CHICAGO FLAG & DECORATING CO. *Catalog No. 30. Flags, Tents, etc.* Chicago, circa 1915. 32 pgs. $25.

CHICAGO FLEXIBLE SHAFT CO. *Stewart's Horse Clipping Machines, Cat. No. 18.* Chicago, 1902. 43 pgs. $75.

CHICAGO FUR CO. *Fine Furs and Seal Garments - 12th Annual Catalog, 1900-1901.* 48 pgs, 12mo. $35.

CHICAGO GALVANIZED WIRE FENCE CO. *Barbed Wire Advertising* in a memorandum book of 16 pages. Chicago, 1882. $75.

CHICAGO HOUSE WRECKING CO. *Catalog No. 138. Machinery, Supplies, etc.* Chicago, 1905. 348 pgs. $35.
Catalog No. 52. Architectural Goods. 1898. 16 pgs. $35.
Catalog No. 162. General merchandise. From sheriffs' sales. 1910. 442 pgs. $50-$75.
Catalog No. 64. 1914. 64 pgs. $30.

CHICAGO MAGIC CO. *Catalog of Superior Magical Apparatus, No. 6.* Chicago, 1914. 159 pgs. $50.

CHICAGO MAIL ORDER COMPANY.
1914 Catalog No. 37....................................$30.
Fashions, 1912...$80.
Fall & Winter, 1920....................................$80.
Fall & Winter, 1923-24..............................$45.
Fall & Winter, 1932-33..............................$60.
Spring & Summer, 1928............................$50.

CHICAGO SIGN BOARD CO. *Manufacturers of Sign Boards, etc.* Chicago, circa 1920-30. 30 pgs. $25.

CHICKERING PIANO CO. *Illus. Catalog of Piano-Fortes.* Boston, ca 1876. 36 pgs. $125. 1863 ed. 11 plates. $100.

CHARLES A. CHILDS & CO. *Catalog H. Farm Tools.* Utica NY, circa 1918. 72 pgs. $75.

GEORGE F. CHILD CHAIR CO. *Wheel Chairs, Invalid Furniture.* New York, 1886. Detailed and elaborate. 8vo, 24 pgs. $150.

CHILDREN'S VEHICLE CORP. *Peerless Collapsible Go-carts, Pullman Sleepers, Baby Carriages, etc.* East Templeton, MA, 1914. 16mo, 28 pgs. $75.

O. J. CHILDS CO. *Childs Ford Fire Apparatus & Equip.* Utica NY, circa 1915-20. 12 pgs. $75.

CHILTON'S AUTOMOBILE MUTLI-GUIDE. *Spring 1930.* Statistics, ads. Hardbound, 536 pages. Soiled covers, else Fine. $30-$45.

CHRIS-CRAFT. *1950 Motor Boats.* 71 pgs. $15.

CHRYSLER CORPORATION. *Thrilling Movie Shots of Dodge in Action.* 1933 Exposition. 24 pgs. $35. Dealer lot 8 pieces. Show-room catalogs; Chrysler, Dodge, Imperial. 1949-1977. $150 for all.
All About Your New Plymouth. Detroit, 1956. 32 pgs. $15.

THOMAS CHUBB. *Chubb Rods are Built on Honor.* Vermont, 1926. 78 pgs., 8vo. Detailed illus. of fishing rods. $150-$295.

> CIGAR BOX LABEL SAMPLE BOOKS. Salesman's sample books with full-sized labels on each page are valuable! We have seen (12) sheet volumes sell for $75 to $350 each. Recently an American Lithograph Company 100-page sample book sold at auction for $1,210. A smaller Louis Wagner Company volume went for $715. A Johns & Co. 16 page catalog with 10 color labels sold for $275. (See individual listings.)

CINCINNATI COFFIN CO. *Catalog of Wood Coffins & Caskets.* Cincinnati OH, 1875. 16 pgs. $100.

CINCINNATI IRON FENCE CO. *Catalog of Iron Fences & Gates.* 1928. 96 pgs. $60.
Catalog No. 10. Victorian-style iron fences. Cincinnati, circa 1910. 8vo, 88 pgs. $75.

CINCINNATI REGALIA CO. *Catalog No. 803. Uniforms For Parades, etc.* Cincinnati, 1934. 24 pgs. $25.

J. R. CLANCY INC. *Catalog No. 33, Theatrical Stage Hardware.* Syracuse NY, 1925. 64 pgs. $60.

CLAPP & JONES MFG. CO. *Builders of Steam Fire Engines, Hose Carriages, Tenders, Etc.* Hudson NY, 1872. 60 pgs. $275.

W. B. CLAPP & CO. *Watches & Jewelry.* Chicago IL, 1876. Cloth bound. 176 pgs. $50.

GEORGE M. CLARK & CO. *Cat. No. 62. Jewel Gas Stoves.* Lots of cast iron kitchen tools. Chicago, 1905. 64 pgs. $45

CLARK HUTCHINSON. *Shoe Findings, Shoe Store Equip.* 1901. 46 pgs. $25-$30.
Manufacturers' Shoe Catalog. Spring, 1901. 64 pgs. $18.

B. CLARKE & CO. *Catalog of Watches, Diamonds & Jewelry.* New York, 1895. 42 pgs. $95.

CLARK'S O.N.T. DESIGNS. *Gift Catalog.* Items made of lace. Newark, 1921. 4to, 22 pgs. $20.

CLAUSS SHEAR CO. *Scissors, Razors, etc.* Fremont OH, circa 1915. 30 pgs. $40.

CLAYCRAFT POTTERIES. *Mantels and Fountains.* Los Angeles, circa 1920-30. 32 pgs. 4to. $150.

CLEVELAND FOUNDRY CO. *Oil & Gas Stoves, Sad Irons.* 1896. 49 pgs. $25.

CLEVELAND RUBBER COMPANY. *Specimen Book of Rubber Stamps.* Cleveland, ca 1882. 12mo, 122 pgs. $75.

CLEVELAND MODEL AIRPLANES. *1938 Catalog.* Photos of model planes, trains and boats. Cleveland OH, 1938. 47 pgs. $40. Same, 1944 edition. $20. 1955 issue. $10.

CLEVELAND TRACTOR CO. *Model "W" Crawler Tractor.* Late 1920s sales brochure. 3-fold. $25.

CLEVELAND TYPE FOUNDRY. *Catalog of Type Specimens.* Cleveland OH, 1880. 176 pgs. $275. 1893 edition. 408 pgs. $150-$200.

CLIFFORD PERFUME MFG. CO. *Wholesale Barber's Supply Catalog.* Boston, 1884. 62 pgs. $175. 1888 Barber and Dentist furnishings. 160 pgs., 12mo. $250-$350.

CHARLES A. COLE. *Power Models, Steam Train Engines, etc.* 1960 Catalog No. 18. 100 pgs. $50-$95.

COFFEE MACHINERY CATALOG. ca 1930, 14 pgs. $25

COLEMAN LAMP CO. *Coleman Quicklite Catalog No. 36.* Wichita KS, circa 1920. 64 pgs. $50.
Household Appliances, etc. 1938. 30 pgs. $25.

COLGATE & CO. *Colgate's Barber's Premiums.* Jersey City NJ, 1918. 48 pgs. $35.
Bee Soap. Premium Catalog. NY, 1906. 8vo. 32 pgs. $20.

COLLIER-KEYWORTH CO. *Rockaway Baby Carriage Catalog.* Gardner MA, circa 1908. 6 pgs. $45.

COLT'S PATENT ARMS MFG. CO. *Catalog of Colt Revolvers and Automatic Pistols.* 1911-12 Edition, 40 pgs. $100. 1920 to 1933 Editions. $50-$75 each.

COLUMBIA BICYCLES. (See Pope Mfg. Company.)

COLUMBUS CART CO. *Road, Speeding, Phaeton & Sulky Carts.* Springfield MA, 1888. 12 pgs. $35.

COLUMBIA DENTAL CHAIRS. *1913 Catalog*. 101 pp. $35.

COLUMBIA MOTOR CAR CO. *Advance Particulars of 1912 Columbia Cars*. New York, 1912. Fine illustrations. 16 pgs. $50.

COLUMBIA PHONOGRAPH CO. *Graphophone Catalog*. Bridgeport CT, 1899. 52 pgs. $150. Same, 1900 edition, 36 pgs. $125.
1946 Columbia Records. 499 pgs. $40. 1921 edition. $25.

COLUMBUS CARRIAGE & HARNESS CO. *33rd Annual Catalog. Buggies*. Columbus OH, 1909. 102 pgs. $100.
35th Annual Catalog. 1910. 80 pgs. $85.

COMBINATION LADDER CO. *Catalog No. 53. Brass Goods & Fire Dept. Supplies*. Providence RI, circa 1900. 12mo, 64 pgs. $50.

COMSTOCK-CASTLE STOVE CO. *Catalog No. 73*. Quincy IL, circa 1910. 236 pgs. $25-$35.

CONANT-BALL CO. *Colonial Furniture Catalog No. 46*. Boston, 1928. 56 pgs. $35.

CONFECTIONERS & BAKERS SUPPLY CO. *Catalog No. B2. Tools for Confectioners*. Chicago, circa 1910. $75.

CONGDON & CARPENTER CO. *Automobile Supplies*. Emphasis on Ford accessories. Providence RI, circa 1916. 4to, 124 pgs. $50.

CONN CO. *Band & Orchestra Instruments*. 1940. 56 pgs., illustrated. $35.

CONNECTICUT MFG. COMPANY. *General Merchandise, Novelties, etc.* A monthly illustrated catalog. Hartford CT, circa 1885. 48 pgs. $35.

CONSOLIDATED BICYCLE, HARDWARE & TOY CO. *Catalog No. 38*. New York, 1939. 4to, 24 pgs. $25-$35.

CONSOLIDATED DENTAL MFG. CO. *Dental Equipment Catalog*. New York, 1908. 8vo. 500 pgs. $75-$95.

CONSOLIDATED LAMP & GLASS CO. *Catalog No. 2. Oil, Glass & Electric*. Coraopolis PA, 1909. 82 pgs. Folio. $225.

CONSOLIDATED MANUFACTURING CO. *Yale Motor Cycles Catalog*. Ohio, 1912. 16 pgs. $95-$125.

CONSOLIDATED MERCHANDISE SYND. *1944 Catalog. Sundries, Notions, Toys*. General 5 & 10 cent items. $20.

ALBERT CONSTANTINE & SON INC. *Woodworking Supplies*. New York, 1930. 8vo, 48 pgs. $15.

CONTINENTAL MUSIC COMPANY. *Musical Merchandise Catalog*. New York, 1930. Violins, banjos, etc. 221 pgs. 4to. $75.

CONTINENTAL TOBACCO CO. *Save Your Tags*. Premium catalog. St. Louis MO, 1980. 28 pgs. $20-$30.

DAVID C. COOK PUBLISHING CO. *Annual Catalog, 1915*. Elgin IL. 4to, 80 pgs. $40.
Sunday School & Holiday Supplies, 1937. 152 pgs. $35.
Illus. For Church Printing. Chicago, 1937. 64 pgs. $20.

G & D COOK CO. *Illustrated Catalog of Carriages and Special Business Advertiser*. New Haven CT, 1860. $500-$1,200. 1866 Edition. 226 pgs. $1,000-$1,200. This very exceptional catalog has been reprinted by Dover Publications, Mineola NY.

COOKE & BEGGS. *Catalog of Railway & Steamship Supplies*. New York, 1879. 176 pgs. $100.

COOKE & CO. *Engines & Boilers*. NYC, 1891. Steam engines, pumps, etc. 52 pgs. $45.

A. COOLEY, CO. *Illustrated Jewelry Catalog*. New York, circa 1890. 96 pgs. $75.

CORBIN LOCK CO. *Corbin Locks*. New Britain CT, 1904. 4to, 788 pgs. $175. *No. 30*. 1920. $120.
Catalog No. 38. Locks, Keys, Hardware. 1928. 4to, 662 pgs. $75-$125.
Catalog No. 22. Desks, Safes, Door Knobs. 1907. 8vo, 237 pgs. $75-$95.
Railroad Padlocks. Circa 1940. 16 pgs. $30.

P. & F. CORBIN HARDWARE. *Illus. Catalog of Hardware*. New Britain CT, 1895. 678 pgs. $175-$250.

CORGI TOYS. *1960 Catalog*. 20 pgs. $25.

R. P. CORMULLY CO. *High Wheel Bicycles & Accessories*. Chicago, 1883-84. 16mo, 16 pgs. $60-$75.

CORTLAND WAGON COMPANY. *Carriage Builders*. Cortland NY, 1905. 88 pgs. $75-$100.

COUCH AND SEELEY CO. *Catalog E - Switchboards, Telephones*. Boston, circa 1905. A rare early telephone catalog of 48 pgs. $225.

JOHN S. COX. *Aviation Catalog*. Terre Haute IN, 1920-30. Uniforms, parachutes, tools, etc. $65-$125.

CRANDALL & GODLEY CO. *Bakers', Confectioners, Ice Cream Makers' and Soda Water Dispensers*. NY, 1902. Everything from machines to tiny candy molds. Hard cover catalog of 180 pgs. $175-$235.

CRANDALL PETTEE CO. *Catalog No. XIV*. For bakers, confectioners, ice cream makers. New York, 1922. 328 pgs. $65.

CRANE CO. *Homes of Comfort, Crane Fixtures*. Sinks, showers, toilets, etc. St. Louis MO, 1926. 87 pgs. $25.

CRAY BROS. *Carriage and Auto Supplies*. Cleveland, 1915. 512 pgs. $45. Another, 1916. $65.

CHARLES CRITTENTON. *Proprietary Articles for the Drug Trade*. NY, 1886. 352 pgs., 12 mo. $75-$125.
Proprietary Medicine. Pharmacy supply list with many ads for patent medicines. NY, 1888. 12mo, 310 pgs. $65.

CROWN HAIR GOODS. *Beauty Hints for the Beauty Salon*. Catalog of everything necessary to open a beauty shop. New York, 1928. 4to, 48 pgs. $45.

CUDAHY PACKING CO. *Year Book, 1931*. 72 pgs. $15.

CULLEN & NEWMAN CO. *Southern Bargain House*. Knoxville TN, 1900. Importers & jobbers of everything from corsets to chewing gum. 9 x 15. 30 pgs. $30.

CURTIS COMPANIES, INC. *1914 Millwork, Leaded Glass*. 383 pgs. $100.
Curtis Cabinet & Stairwork. Clinton IA, circa 1927. 47 pgs. $20.
Architectural Interior & Exterior Woodwork. 1920. 238 pgs. $40.

CURTISS AEROPLANE CO. Hammondsport NY, 1913. Planes and their prices, from the early days of aviation. 4to, 28 pgs. Scarce. $250-$350.

CURTISS MANUFACTURING CO. *The Curtiss Motors and Motorcycles*. Hammondsport NY, 1907. 16 pgs. $125.
Curtiss Motorcycle Achievements. Single folio, folded sheet. 1907. $50.

CURTISS WRIGHT. *Aero Supplies, 1933-34*. 36 pgs. 9 x 11. $60-$100.

CUSHMAN MOTOR WORKS. *The Farm Cushman Engine*. Lincoln NE, 1914. 40 pgs. $20.

CUSSINS & FEARN CO. *Catalog No. 36*. General Merchandise, Farm Tools, etc. Columbus OH, 1920-21. 176 pgs. $55-$65.

CYCLONE PROPERTY PROTECTION. *Fence Catalog No. 16*. Everything from barbed wire to iron railing. Circa 1930. 20 pgs. $20.

CYPHERS INCUBATOR CO. *9th Annual Catalog*. Buffalo, 1905. 8vo, 228 pgs. $50-$75.

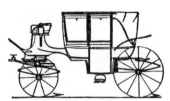

Five-Glass Landau.

Tally-Ho Mail Coach.

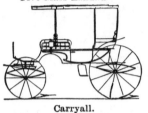

Carryall.

Six-Pass. Rockaway.

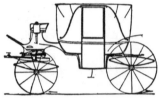

Leather Top Landau.

Double Suspension Brougham.

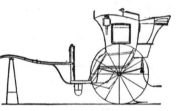

Hansom Cab.

Physicians' Phaeton.

Victoria Cab.

Omnibus or Gurney.

Democrat Wagon.

Body-Break Wagon.

Berlin Coach.

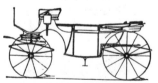

Landaulette.

Dog Cart.

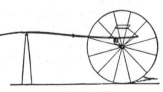

Two-Wheel Sulky.

D

DADANT & SONS. *1916 Catalog of Beekeepers' Supplies.* Hamilton IL. 8vo, 42 pgs. $20.

DALTON & INGERSOLL CO. *Plumbing Fixtures.* Boston, 1896. Folio, 148 pgs. of bathroom fixtures, etc. $150. 1889 edition. 4to, 200 pgs. $250.

DALY & GALES SCHOVERLING. *Miniature Catalog No. 21.* Guns, sporting equip., etc. NY, 1903. 25 pgs. $50.

W. S. DARLEY & CO. *Police & Municipal Equipment.* 1937. 52 pages. $100. Another 1937 edition. including firefighting equipment. 92 pgs. $100.
Firefighting Champions. Fire trucks & equipment. 1944. 99 pgs. $75.

DAVIS-BIRELY TABLE CO. *Tables. Spring 1909 Styles.* Shelbyville IN, 1909. 206 pgs. $85.

DAVIS SEWING MACHINE CO. *The Davis Vertical Feed Sewing Machine.* Dayton OH, 1893. 24 pgs. $35.
Best on Earth. Catalog & Manual. ca. 1895. 48 pgs. $25.
Directions for Davis Vertical Feed. ca. 1915. 48 pgs. $25.

DAVIS & STEVENS MFG. CO. *Cyclone Bicycle Pumps, Accessories.* Seneca Falls NY, 1897. 32 pgs. $35.

C. S. DAVISSON & CO. *1899 Embroidery and Lace Catalog.* Philadelphia PA. 8vo, 104 pgs. $40.

DAYTON MOTOR CAR CO. *The Stoddard Dayton for 1909.* 32 pgs. Good-VG. $40-$100.

W. DAZIAN. *Theatrical Goods, Church and Military Trimmings, etc.* New York, 1892. 12mo, 159 pgs. Everything from ostrich plumes to underwear; swords, sequins & armor. $150.

DECKER & CO. *Grand, Square, Piano-Fortes.* New York, 1866. 26 pgs. $150.

DECORATORS SUPPLY COMPANY. *Catalog of Period Ornaments, Compo and Wood Fibre.* Chicago, 1909. 108 pgs. $50-$75.
1925 Edition. 4to, 343 pgs. $40.
Mantels, Catalog No. 120. 80 pgs. $25.

DECORATORS WALL PAPER CO. *Book No. 4, Samples.* Chicago & NY, circa 1895-1900. Folio of 80 leaves. $150.

DEERE & CO. *John Deere Implements.* Moline IL, circa 1912. Plows, harrows, planters, cultivators, etc. 9 x 11 in., 156 pgs. $125.

JOHN DEERE PLOW CO. *Vehicles Catalog.* Carriages. Syracuse NY, 1915. 4to, 60 pgs. $125.

DEERE AND WEBBER CO. *Sleigh Catalog No. 27.* Minneapolis MN, 1907. 43 pgs. $100.

WILLIAM DEERING & CO. *Catalog of Grass Cutting Machinery.* Chicago, 1890. 8vo, 24 pgs. $50.
One of the Triumphs of the 19th Century. Engravings & descriptions of the firms many machines. Circa 1890. 16mo, 32 pgs. $30.
Harvesting Machinery. Chicago, 1887. 20 pgs. 8vo. $45-$75.

DEERING HARVESTER COMPANY. *Official Retrospective, Harvesting Machinery For the Paris Exposition of 1900.* Paris, 1900. 125 pgs. $25-$35.

DEFIANCE MACHINE WORKS. *Catalog No. 14 Woodworking Machinery.* Defiance OH, 1904., 473 pgs. $75.
Catalog No. 200. 1910. 533 pgs. $50-$100.

DEFIANCE MFG. CO. *Drawing Materials, Architects' Supplies, etc.* New York, 1916. 399 pgs. $95. 1930 Edition. 318 pgs. $45.

DE LAVAL SEPARATOR CO. *Keeping Cows for Profit.* New York, 1899. 32 pgs. $30.
Farm and Diary Improved 20th Century Cream Separators. New York, 1901. 12mo, 44 pgs. $25.

DELTA POWER TOOLS. *1939 Catalog.* 63 pgs. $25.

DE MOULIN BROS. & CO. *Costumes for Order of Red Men.* Greenville IL, 1903. 10 pgs., 8vo. $75-$120.
Burlesque and Side Degree Specialties. Catalog No. 306. 1910. 164 pgs. $100-$200. Catalog No. 331. 1924. 182 pgs. $75-$85.
1902 Catalog of Wigs & Robes. 192 pgs. $80.

WM. DEMUTH & CO. *Illustrated Catalog of Smokers' Articles and Show Figures*. New York, 1875. 9 x 12 in. 56 pgs. Everything from carved pipes to cigar store Indians, for the trade only. $600-$1,500.

DENNISON MFG. CO. CATALOGS are among the most commonly found today.
The Uses of Tissue Paper. 1895. 32 pgs. $50.
Art & Decoration in Crepe & Tissue Paper. Framingham MA, 1900. 88 pgs. $50.
Crepe & Tissue Paper. Including samples. 96 pgs. Very elaborate. 1914. $60.
How to Make Paper Costumes. 1922. $15.
Moulding, Decorating and Painting with Wax. 1925. 36 pgs. $25.

DENT HARDWARE CO. *Illustrated Catalog of Iron Toys*. Fullerton PA, ca 1905. 39 pgs. 7x10. $75-$100.
Dent Toys, Catalog No. 10. Cast iron & cast aluminum cars, planes, stoves, cap pistols, etc. Circa 1930. 47 pgs. VG-Mint. $95-$120.
Refrigerator Hardware, Catalog B. 1911. 358 pgs. $75.

DENTON BROTHERS. *Butterfly Hunter's Guide*. Catalog of supplies, instructions for catching and mounting. Wellesley MA, 1900. 20 pgs. $50.

DENVER DRY GOODS. *Western-Style Clothing Catalog*. Denver, 1940. 4to, 54 pgs. $25-$40. 1945-46 edition. 12mo, 40 pgs. $25-$40.

DERBY SILVER CO. *Silverplated Wares*. Derby CT, circa 1920. Folio. 75 pgs. $75.

DE SOTO. *Sketch Book of the 1941 De Soto*. Showroom booklet. $24.

DETRA FLAG CO. INC. *Detra Flags*. Oaks PA, 1927. 216 pgs. $125.

DETROIT STOVE WORKS. *Stove Catalog*. Detroit, 1901. 8vo, hardbound, 300 pgs. $75.
Jewel Stoves, Ranges & Furnaces. 1913 hardbound catalog, 228 pgs. Good. $45.

F. W. DEVOE & CO. *Artists' Materials Catalog*. NY, circa 1885. 8vo, 407 pgs. $75-$125. 1890 ed. 248 pgs. $35-$50.

DEVOE & RAYNOLDS CO. *Harmony in the Home*. New York, 1917. 23 pgs. $20.

DIAMOND MATCH CO. *Catalog of Beekeeper's Supplies*. 1916. 56 pgs. $35.

DIEBOLD SAFE & LOCK CO. *Burglar Proof Safes, Jail Doors*. Canton OH, 1887. 112 pgs. $250.

DIETZ, FRED. *A Leaf From the Past, Dietz Then and Now*. Lanterns and history. New York, 1914. 194 pgs. $35.

EUGENE DIETZGEN CO. *Drafting & Surveying Supplies*. Chicago, 1925. 495 pgs. $25-$40. 1928 13th edition. 495 pgs. $25-$40. 1931 edition. 520 pgs. $30-$50. Editions No. 1, 2, 3 and 5 are worth $100-$250.

DINGEE CONARD CO. *Our New Guide to Rose Culture*. West Grove PA, 1896. 110 pgs. $50.
Sixty Years Among the Roses, 1850-1909. West Grove PA, 1909. 114 pgs. $35.

HENRY DISSTON (& SONS). *Keystone Saw & Tool Works*. Philadelphia, 1860. 20 pgs. $185. 1884 to 1895 Editions. $75-$85 each. 1914 Edition. 113 pgs. $65. 1914. $30.

OLIVER DITSON CO. *Guide Book for Buyers of Musical Instruments*. Boston MA, circa 1905. 184 pgs. $80-$95.

DIXON PENCILS. Color catalog, 1910. $35.

WILLIAM DIXON. *Jewelers Tools*. Newark, 1926. 8vo, 75 pgs. $50-$95.

DODGE-HALEY COMPANY. *Hardware, Steel & Iron, Machinists Supplies*. Cambridge MA, 1928. 316 pgs. $65.

DOMESTIC SEWING MACHINE CO. *Catalog of Fashions & Spring Styles*. New York, 1877. 24 pgs. $35-$65.
Patterns for Fall Fashions. 1883. $50.

DOVER STAMPING & MFG. CO. *Catalog of Automobile Specialties, Funnels, etc.* Cambridge MA, 1916. $40.

DRAPER & MAYNARD. *Boxing Gloves, Striking Bars, Footballs*. Ashland NH, 1895. 20 pgs. $60.

DUNHAM BROTHERS COMPANY. *Spring and Summer, Shoe Catalog*. Brattleboro VT, 1934. 40 pgs. $15.

JAMES H. DUNHAM & CO. *1918 Catalog*. Many fabric swatches and inserts. New York, 1918. 4to, 280 pgs. $125. 1923 edition. Includes swatches. $95.

JOHN A. DUNN. *Reed and Rattan Furniture*. Gardner MA, circa 1920. 64 pgs. Includes baby carriages. $50-$95.

DUNNING & BOSCHERT CO. *Catalog of Cider and Wine Presses*. Syracuse NY, circa 1920. 70 pgs. $70-$125.

DURANT-DORT CARRIAGE COMPANY. *Blue Ribbon Buggies, Surreys, Spring and Road Wagons*. Flint MI, circa 1895-1900. Large 8vo, 48 pgs. $50-$100.

DURANT MOTORS. *Durant, Just a Real Good Car*. 1929. 12 pages. Illus. $45.

E

EAGLE CARRIAGE CO. *Pony Vehicles and Harness, Catalog No. 24*. Cincinnati OH, circa 1923. $100.

EAGLE LOCK CO. *Trunk, Chest, Cupboard & Drawer Locks*. Terryville CT, 1867. 10 x 12, 56 plates. $550-$750.

EAGLE PENCIL CO. *Pens, Pencils & Displays*. Color Illus. New York, 1915. $150-$250.

EASTERN ESTATE TEA CO. *Catalog of Food Products and Premium List*. New York, circa 1905. 44 pgs. $40.

EASTMAN KODAK CO. *Cameras and Accessories*. NY, 1911. 64 pgs. $25-$50.
Kodak Cameras. 1914. VG. $15-$20. 1919 edition, 64 pgs. $40. 1925 edition. $30.
Pocket Kodak Portraiture. 1900. 39 pgs. $35-$45.
Hawk-eye Cameras. 1900. 30 pgs. Color cover. $50-$95.
Century Camera. 1909. 44 pgs. Color cover. $95-$150.

H. S. ECKELS & CO. *Catalog of Embalming Fluids, Supplies*. Philadelphia, 1903. 464 pgs. $75.

W. EDDY PLOW CO. *Catalog No. 31*. Greenwich NY, 1912. 50 pgs. $15.

THOMAS A. EDISON, INC. *Edison's Life & Favorite Invention*. Combination biography and phonograph catalog. Orange NJ, 1911. 36 pgs. $25.
A Phonograph in Every American Home. Chicago, circa 1910. Full-color ads. 64 pgs. $150-$200.
Edison Blue Amberol Records. 1913. $50.
Edison Diamond Disk Phonographs. Orange NJ, 1915, 8vo, 24 pgs. $50.

EDISON ELECTRIC APPLIANCE CO. *Simplex Electric Appliance Catalog*. Chicago, 1928-29. 24 pgs. $15.

H. D. EDWARDS. *Catalog No. 50*. Marine hardware, machines, flags, accessories. Detroit, 1892. Hardbound folio. 568 pgs. $150.

EHRICH BROS. *Fall, 1875*. 28 pgs. Furs, dresses, toys. $35.
Fashion Quarterly, Summer 1881. Including toys & dolls, bathing suits, etc. 65 pgs. $65.
Spring, 1883. 12mo, 24 pgs. $35.
Spring, 1886. 168 pgs. $85.

EIMER & AMEND. *Catalog of Chemical Apparatus, etc.* New York, 1907. 445 pgs. $60.
1892 Edition. 329 pgs. $150.
Laboratory Supplies & Assayers Materials. New York, 1920. 608 pgs. $125.
Discontinued Stock. 1929. 62 pgs. $15.

THE ELECTRIC CORP. *Catalog No. 31*. LA, circa 1931. Appliances, lamps, fans. 260 pgs. $50-$75.

ELECTRIC VEHICLE COMPANY. *Columbia Electric Commercial Vehicles*. Hartford, 1904. 24 pgs. Trucks, delivery wagons, etc. $200.

ELGIN WATCH CO. *Thru Ages with Father Time*. Evanston, 1922. 8vo, 196 pgs. $65.

ELKHART CARRIAGE & HARNESS MFG. CO. *Catalog No. 58*. 20 illus. buggies & wagons. IN, 1907. $60.
Catalog No. 31. Tiny 64 pg. ed. 1893. $75.
Catalog No. 32. 1894. 24 pgs. $45.
1904 Catalog. 230 pgs. $50-$100.
1911 Pratt-Elkhart Cars. 16 pgs. $95.

B. K. ELLIOTT & CO. *Drawing & Surveying Instruments*. Pittsburgh, circa 1910. 440 pgs. 8vo. $50. 1920 edition. $45.

ELMIRA ARMS CO. *Catalog of Fire Arms & Ammunition*. Elmira NY, 1916. 4to, 80 pgs. $65.
Spring, Summer, Fall, Winter. Sporting Goods, 1931. 180 pgs. $65.
Spring & Summer, 1923. 108 pgs. $60.

EMBALMERS SUPPLY CO. *Embalming Fluids and Instruments, etc.*. A very comprehensive catalog with history. Westport CT, circa 1925. 200 pgs. $60.
Good Equipment for Good Undertakers. 1925 catalog of 64 pages. $30.
Catalog of Fluids, etc. Circa 1915. 200 pgs. $40.

EMERSON PIANO CO. *Catalog of Grand & Upright Piano-Fortes*. Boston, 1878. 12 pgs. $50.

C. V. ENGSTROM CO. *Catalog of Leather Shoe Store Supplies, Shoe Machinery*. Stands, displays, tools. Peoria IL, 1912. 8vo, 200 pgs. $50.

ENTERPRISE CARRIAGE CO. Miamisburg OH, 1893. Color illus. catalog. 12mo, 64 pgs. $195.

ENTERPRISE MFG. CO. *Pflueger Fishing Tackle Pocket Catalog No. 155*. Akron OH, 1935. 128 pgs. $25-$50. *Catalog No. 156 for Every Species of Game Fish, etc.* 128 pgs. $50.

ENTERPRISE MFG CO. *Grinders and Special Food Recipes*. 1887. 64 pgs., 8vo. $100-$150. *Illustrated Catalog of Patented Hardware*. Coffee grinders, spice mills, meat choppers, etc. Philadelphia, 1889. 64 pgs. $75-$100. *Patented Hardware Specialties*. 1899. 112 pgs. $95. *1927 Edition*. 24 pgs. $50. *The Enterprising Housekeeper*. Catalog & Cookbook Comb. 1898. 80 pgs. $20-$40.

ENTERPRISE TEA CO. *Catalog No. 4*. A premium catalog for a food company which advertises on front cover "Not in the Trust". Cedar Rapids IA, circa 1905. $35.

M. C. EPPENSTEIN. *Watches & Jewelry, etc.* 1894. 208 pgs. 8½ x 12. $80.

ERIE ENGINE WORKS. *Stationary Detached Portable Engines*. Erie PA, 1895. 40 pgs. $100.

ERKER BROS. OPTICAL COMPANY. *Catalog of Motion Picture Apparatus*. St. Louis MO, circa 1918. 144 pgs. $45. 1914 edition, 120 pgs. $50.

ERKINS STUDIOS. *Garden Ornaments, Catalog No. 54*. NY, circa 1920. 30 pgs. $25.

ESSEX MOTORS. *The Five Passenger Touring Car*. Detroit MI, 1920. 12 pgs. $35.

ESTERBROOK STEEL PEN MFG. CO. *Steel and Metallic Pens*. 1916 Catalog. 39 pgs. $60.

ESTEY ORGAN CO. *Illustrated Catalog of Organs*. Brattleboro VT, 1882. 36 pgs. $75. 1883 Edition. 36 pgs. $50-$80. 1884 Edition. 16 pgs. $45-$65.

EUREKA CARRIAGE CO. *Catalog of Vehicles*. Rock Falls IL, circa 1890. 16mo, 40 pgs. $75-$95.

EUREKA FLOWER CO. *1882 Catalog*. 8vo, 16 pgs. $25. 1887 Edition. Utica NY. 24 pgs. $40.

EUREKA TRICK & NOVELTY CO. *Conjuring Tricks & Magicians Articles*. New York, 1877. 80 pgs. $250. *Agents Catalog for 1883*. 32 pgs. $85.

GEORGE EVANS & CO. *See What You Will Save*. Philadelphia, 1889. 96 pgs., 8vo. China to cosmetics. $75.

Owl-Wool Uniforms. For Bands, Fire, Military. Philadelphia, circa 1916. Black & white illus. 30 pgs. $20.

H. C. EVANS & CO., CATALOG. *Manufacturers of High Class Amusement Concessions: Sporting Goods, Casino Supplies, Trade Stimulators*. Chicago, 1923-24. 64 pgs. Illus. $100. *The Blue Book. Private & Confidential*. Chicago, 1930s. 32 pgs. $50. *1936 Edition*. 72 pgs. $65.

EVANS MANUFACTURING CO. *Catalog "A". Bob Sleighs*. Hammond NY, circa 1900. 12 pgs. $50.

EVANS, MC EVOY & CO. *Cabinet Hardware, Tools, etc.* Boston, circa 1890-95. 8vo, 96 pgs. $100.

VAL EVANS CO. *Catalog of Magic*. Lynn MA, circa 1920. 32 pgs. $35.

EVERSON-ROSS CO. *Fire Department Badges-Caps, Helmets, etc.* NY, circa 1915. 36 pgs., 8vo. $150. *Police and Fire Department Badges*. NY, circa 1910. 44 pgs., 8vo. $100.

EVINRUDE OUTBOARD MOTORS CORP. *1929 Outboard Motor Catalog* . $27. 1936 Edition. 16 pgs. $35.

EXHIBIT SUPPLY CO. *Exhibit Amusement Machines*. Chicago, 1929. 72 page catalog of penny arcade games. Very scarce. Fine condition. $300-$400.

F

S. W. FABER CO. *Faberware Holloware, Electrical & Fancy Goods, No. 35*. 72 pgs. $75.

FAIRBANKS CO. *Auto & Service Station Equipment*. 1920. 4to, 94 pgs. $50.

FAIRBANKS COMPANY. *Some Speed Boats*. New York, 1917. 8vo, 16 pgs.$35.

FAIRBANKS & CO. *Patent Platform and Counter Scales*. St. Johnsbury VT, circa 1852. 16mo, 54 pgs. $150.
Railroad, Hay and Counter Scales. Circa 1875. 16mo, 12 pgs. $35.
Illus. Price List of 1891. 118 pgs. $75.
Fairbanks Scales, Catalog No. 880. Johnsbury VT, 1918. 197 pgs., 16mo. $50.

FAIRBANKS, MORSE & CO. *Small Vertical Engines Catalog No. 80-C*. Chicago IL 1907. 36 pgs. $35.
General Catalog No. 60. Mining, drilling, railroad equipment & scales. 1908. 8vo, 658 pgs. $150.

FALCONER MFG. CO. *Bee Hives and Bee Keepers' Supplies*. Jamestown NY, 1894. 28 pgs. $35.
Falcon Bee Supplies. 1923. 5 x 9 in. 22 pgs. $8.

FALKER & STERN CO. *Holiday Lines, 1907*. European & Oriental Imports. Chicago, 1907. 52 pgs. $50.

FARMER, LITTLE & CO. *New York Type Foundry Specimens*. NY, 1887. 135 pgs. $200.

FARMER SEED & NURSERY CO. *1932 Catalog*. 84 pgs. $25-$45.

A. B. FARQUHAR, LTD. *Engine, Boilers, Saw Mills*. York PA, 1895. 64 pgs. $85.

FAVOR, RUHL & CO. *Artists Materials*. New York, circa 1905. 4to, 144 pgs. 10 color plates. $75-$100.

FECHEIMER BROS. CO. *Catalog for Letter Carriers*. Uniforms, hats, accessories. Cincinnati, 1914. 16mo, 16 pgs. $35.

FEICK BROTHERS CO. *Surgical Supplies*. Circa 1910. 576 pgs. $125. Another, Pittsburgh, 1929. 8vo, 458 pgs. $95.

FASHIONS, CLOTHING. Novice dealers tend to overprice their Victorian fashion magazines and catalogs. Hand-colored illustrations are not rare among these volumes. Most were mass-produced on assembly lines, using paint-by-number stencils. Unless the illustrations are very large or unusual (such as children with toys, sporting scenes, etc.) you will be fortunate to average five dollars each for frameable plates. Look for additional priced examples in the magazine section of this book.

FENTON METALLIC MFG. CO. *Fenton High Grade Bicycles*. Jamestown NY, 1896. 12mo, 31 pgs. $100.

THE FERGUSON COMPANY. *Manufacturers of Harness*. Horse collars, strap work, riding saddles. Paducah KY, 1930. 104 pgs., 4to. $50-$75.

MARSHALL FIELD & CO. *Notions and Fancy Goods 1890-91*. With large toy section. $450.
Jewelry Department. Chicago, 1893. 300 pgs. $95.
Counter Sales Book 1914-15. Jewelry, silverplate, china. Hardbound. $75.
"Fashion of the Hour". Catalogs of 1925, 1926, 1928 & 1930. $20 each.

FIRESTONE TIRE & RUBBER CO. *Farm Tire Catalog*. Includes auto supplies. Akron OH, 1936. 40 pgs. $30.
Auto Supplies. Spring & Summer 1944. 52 pgs. $25.
Home & Auto Supply. 1940. $15.

FIREWORKS CATALOGS are very scarce. A typical 4-page illustrated folder from the 1880s might bring up to $200. Larger 32-page catalogs of the 1930s are worth $100 and up. An 1890s "Fourth of July Goods" catalog was recently advertised at $450.

FIRST NATIONAL NURSERIES. *Full Color Catalog*. Trees, fruit, flowers. Circa 1900. Bright. 100 plates. $250.

CARL FISCHER CO. *Competition Catalog of Stringed Instruments*. New York, 1902. 120 pgs. of violins, guitars, mandolins, etc. $195.
18th Edition, Band Instruments & Specialties. NY, circa 1910. 44 pgs. $50.
Reed & Wood Wind Instruments. ca 1922. 63 pgs. $50.

FISCHER & JIROUCH CO. *Decorative Plaster Wall Ornaments*. Cleveland, 1925. 254 pgs. $75. Another, 1931. 206 pgs. 4to. $35.

HOMER FISHER. *Rifles, Shot Guns, Revolvers & Ammunition*. NY, 1880. 80 pgs., 8vo. Fine woodcuts. $275.

FISCHER SCIENTIFIC CO. *Laboratory & Chemical Supplies*. Pittsburgh PA, 1926. 630 pgs. $95-$150.

FISKE HOMES & CO. *The Open Hearth, A Catalog of Designs*. Makers of Boston Fire Brick. Boston, 1897. 4th edition. $35-$50.

J. W. FISKE IRON WORKS. *Copper Weather Vanes*. New York, 1925. 36 pgs. $150.
Ornamental Iron Work for Buildings. New York, circa 1885. 122 pgs. $500.
Stable Fixtures. Including lamps, weather vanes. New York, circa 1912. 4to, 184 pgs. $200-$300.
Ornamental Iron Settees, Chairs. NY, 1924. Park benches, plant stands, etc. 40 pgs., 4to. $100-$150.
Ornamental Iron and Zinc Fountains. NY, 1927. Many ornate designs. 64 pgs., 4to. $125-$175.

EDWIN A. FITCH CO. *Embroideries and Laces Catalog*. New York, 1906. 94 pgs. Worn. $20.

FITZWATER WHEEL CO. *Fitz Over Steel Overshoot Water Wheel*. Hanover PA, 1928. 84 pgs. 8vo. $40.

A. FLANAGAN CO. *School Furniture and Playground Equip*. Chicago, 1932-1933. 8 x 10. 94 pgs. $50-$75.

FLEMISH ART CO. *Woodburning Tools, etc.* New York, circa 1905. 64 pgs. $40.

FLEXIBLE FLYER SLEDS. 1910. 16 pgs. $50-$100.

FLINT & WALLING MFG. CO. *Star Wind Engine*. 1891. 24 pgs. $75.
Star Windmills. Catalog No. 46. Ft. Wayne IN, 1905. 64 pgs. $75.
Catalog No. 57. Kendallville IN, 1909. 48 pgs. $35.

FLORENCE STOVE CO. *Oil Stoves*. 1882. 8 pgs. $25.
Price List & Receipts. Florence MA, 1883. 26 pgs. $35.
Oil Ranges. 1937. 72 pgs. $20.

H. & D. FOLSOM ARMS CO. *Reach Goods*. Football & boxing items. 1914. 8vo. 34 pgs. $40.
Ammunition & Sporting Goods Catalog No. 45. 1935. 240 pgs. $50.
Catalog No. 53. New York, 1940. 4to, 115 pgs. $40.

FORBES SILVER CO. *Catalog No. 14 - Wares in Silver Plate*. Meriden CT, 1909-10. 181 pgs. $165.

FORD MOTOR COMPANY. *Illustrated Catalog of 1906*. 24 pgs. $100.
Ford Motor Cars. Nov, 1911. 24 pgs. $40.
Ford, The Universal Car. 1918. 24 pgs. $35.
Ford Instruction Book and Wholesale Price List. (Model T). 2 items for $25.
Model A Taxi Catalog. 1929. $250-$400.
Model A Town Car. 1928-29. $350-$500.
Private Preview of New 1961 Thunderbird. 10 pgs. $25.
Thunderbird Soft-Top Convertible. 1958. 4 pgs. $25.
Price List Parts and Accessories Ford Model T, 1909-1917. 64 pgs. $25.
Ford Motor Cars. Detroit, 1911. 24 pgs. $50.

FORDSON TRACTOR. 1930s Instr. Manual. 52 pgs. $15.

FOREST CITY FURNITURE CO. *Desks, Library Cases, etc.* Rockford IL, 1887. 4to, 68 pgs. $125.

FORT DEARBORN WATCH & CLOCK CO. *1928 Gift Book & General Catalog*. From silver to furniture. Color plates. 612 pgs. $85. 1936 ed., includes toys. $75-$120.

FOSTORIA GLASS COMPANY. *Manufacturers of Decorated Lamps, Globes, Shades and Table Glassware*. Moundsville WV, circa 1895. 24 pgs. $250.
Table Glassware and Novelties. Moundsville, 1901. 72 pgs. Folio. $150. 1898 edition, 28 pgs. $100-$200. 1912 Catalog No. 1. $250-$500. (2 versions. 99 pgs. & 131 pgs.)

H. C. FOX & SONS, INC. *Glass Manufacturers Catalog*. Philadelphia, circa 1905. 53 pgs. $75-$100.

WALLY FRANK, LTD. *Pipe Smokers Catalog*. Christmas, 1942. 44 pgs. $25-$40.
Pipe Lore. "Magalog" 6 issues. 1942-1945. $30 all.

H. FRANKE - STEEL RANGE CO. *Stoves & Broilers*. Cleveland, circa 1895. 4to, 52 pgs. $50.

FRANKELITE CO. *Catalog No. 31. Refinement in Lighting*. Fixtures, lanterns, shades. Cleveland, ca 1931. 56 pgs. $50.

FRANKLIN AUTOMOBILE CO. *Runabouts, Touring-Cars, Town Carriages*. 1907 Price List. $45.
The Franklin Car. Types, Principles. Syracuse NY, 1918. 80 pgs. $75.
1921 Sales Brochure. 16 pgs. $15.
Series 15 Deluxe, Transcontinental. 1931. 22 pgs. $75.

FRANKLIN JEWELRY CO. *Illustrated Catalog, Wholesale*. Philadelphia, circa 1890. 80 pgs. $100.

FRANKLIN MANUFACTURING COMPANY. *Franklin Automobiles for 1909*. 16 pages, illus. A fine copy. $125.
Franklin Runabouts, Touring Cars, Town Carriages. NY, 1908. 36 pgs. Lovely illus. $150.

FRANKLIN SIMON. *Spring & Summer, 1921*. Correct Dress for Women, etc. 126 pgs. $80.

WILLIAM FRANKFURTH CO. *Hardware & Housewares, Revolvers*. Milwaukee WI, 1886. Wholesale catalog with large, clear engravings. 9 x 12. 976 pgs. $300-$450.

FRANZ & POPE KNITTING MACHINE CO. *Hand and Power Knitting Machines*. Bucyrus OH, circa 1880. 16 pgs. $75.

WM. H. FREAR & CO. *Fall & Winter, 1901-02*. Troy NY, Department store catalog. 4to, 148 pgs. $35.

E. FREDERICS INC. *For the Hair of Women Who Care*. NY, 1927. Beauty parlor equip. 8vo, 24 pgs. $45.

C. A. FREES. *Artificial Limbs Catalog*. New York, 1886. 50 pgs. $135.

THE FREIDLANDER CO. *Lamps & Home Decorations*. Sports figures, statuettes, book-ends, etc. Chicago, circa 1910. 33 pgs. 10 x 13 in. $225.

W. A. FRENCH & CO. *Builder's Supplies*. Camden NJ, 1882. Decorative glass panels, ornamental cornices, ads for carriage suppliers, etc. 8vo, 208 pgs. $195.

FRICK CO. *Refrigerating and Ice Making Machinery*. Waynesboro PA, circa 1885. 176 pgs. $50.

FRIEDLEY-VOSHARDT CO. *Weather Vane Catalog*. Very unusual designs. Chicago, 1919. 4to, 16 pgs. $195.

FRIEDMAN-SHELBY SHOES. *"Red Goose Shoes". Mens, Ladies, Childrens*. 1928. 96 pgs. $50-$75.

E. H. FRIEDRICHS. *Artist's Canvas and Supplies*. New York, circa 1885. 84 pgs. $35.

FRIGIDAIRE AUTOMATIC REFRIGERATION. *Color Catalog of Refrigerators*. Dayton OH, 1929. 34 pgs. $35.

FROST & ADAMS. *Pyrography Supplies*. Circa 1900 woodburning equip. Full color edition. 44 pgs. $125. *Artist Materials, Mathematical Inst.* Boston, circa 1910. 654 pgs. $65.

FUNK WIG COMPANY. *Wigs & Beards, Makeup. Catalog No. 15*. Chicago IL, 1929. 32 pgs. $25.

FUNSTEN BROS. & CO. *Trappers Supply Catalog*. St. Louis, 1911. 8vo, 36 pgs. $55.

FURNITURE DIRECTORY. *1905 Directory of Furniture Mfgs. in the US*. Wholesale manufacturers & suppliers to the trade. Many illus. ads. 8vo, 694 pgs. $85-$125.

FURNITURE CATALOGS.
The average furniture catalog published between 1895 and 1935 is only worth from $50 to $75 because similar furniture illustrations can be found in many department store catalogs. The exceptions are earlier 1860-1880 volumes and broadsides. Bentwood, Mission Oak, and fancy wicker style catalogs also bring premium prices even though many have been reproduced. A *Thonet Brothers* 12 page Bentwood furniture album of 1883 recently sold for $350. See individual listings for additional prices.

Our $13.95 Combination Bookcase.
No.1T1326 Combination Bookcase. 6 feet high, 3 feet 4 inches wide, with a French pattern bevel mirror, 16x18 inches; the carving is hand made, the glass in the door is of extra double thickness; the inside of desk is pigeonholed and has a drawer in center; there are three large drawers below the desk and each drawer has lock and key. This bookcase is made of solid oak and is finished in golden oak. The shelves are adjustable, the drawer pulls are solid cast brass. The back of case is solid oak and paneled inside; the inside is well finished, the casters are ball bearing. Shipping weight, 200 pounds.
Price, each.................................$13.95

Great Bargain at $15.75.

No. 1T1480 High Curtain Office Desk, 4 feet long, 2 feet 6 inches wide, 4 feet 1 inch high; dust and knife proof curtain. Solid oak, finished golden; extension slides, finished back, quarter sawed sycamore pigeonhole case, six pasteboard pigeonhole filing boxes. Combination lock on drawers, spring lock with duplicate keys on curtain. Four drawers on left side; book closet on right hand side. Weight, 220 pounds. Price, without closed back..... $15.75
No. 1T1481 Same desk as No. 1T1480, but with closed panel full finished back. Price........ $16.45

G

GATEWAY SPORTING GOODS. *Catalog No. 21*. 1939. 134 pgs. $35.

GEISER MANUFACTURING COMPANY. *Self Regulating Grain Separator, Cleaner and Bagger.* Plus traction and steam engines. Waynesboro PA, 1880. 8vo, 60 pgs. $40.

W. B. GEISER & CO. *Fancy Dry Goods, Notions, etc.* San Francisco, 1913. 64 pgs. $45.

GEM CRIB & CRADLE CO. *Catalog of Bassinets, Cribs, Wardrobes, Infant Furniture.* Gardner MA, 1929. $25.
The Gem Line of Babies' Carriages and Strollers. Ontario Canada, 1928. 20 pgs. $45.

GEMCO MFG. CO. *Catalog of Popular Automobile Accessories.* Milwaukee WI, 1917. 52 pgs. $35.

GENERAL ELECTRIC CO. *Edison Incandescent Lamps.* Schenectady NY, 1900. 110 pgs. $125.
Brochure. 1893. 3 x 7 in. unfolds to 15 x 24 in. $50.
Electrical Appliances. 1939. 56 pgs. $40.
Monitor Top Refrigerators. Binghamton NY, circa 1940. 22 pgs. $25-$45.

GENERAL FIRE EXTINGUISHER CO. Providence, 1903. Hardbound catalog of misc. fire fighting apparatus. 12mo, 384 pgs. $75.

GENERAL RADIO. *Catalog No. G. Radio Supplies.* 1932. 174 pgs. $30.

GENERAL MOTORS. *A Car For Every Purpose.* 1927 illus. brochure. $30. (See individual makers, Chevrolet, Pontiac, Oldsmobile, etc.) .

F. W. GESSWEIN CO. *Fine Tools, Machinery & Supplies.* For nearly all trades. New York, 1899. 504 pgs. $135.

GIBSON AUTOMOTIVE EQUIPMENT. *Catalog No. 29.* 1927. 376 pgs. $35.

GIBSON CO. *Guitar Catalog* . circa 1920. 112 pgs. $50.

GIBSON & PERIN OFFICE SUPPLY. *Catalog No. 34.* Furniture, ink, pens, pencil sharpeners, etc. Cincinnati, 1930s. 156 pgs. $25.

GIFFORD, JOHN & SON. *Automobile Hardware and Trimmings.* NY, 1911. Leather bound. 292 pgs. $150.

GIFFORD-WOOD CO. *Ice Tools and Ice Handling Machinery.* Chicago, 1905. 64 pgs. $75-$100.
1907 edition. 32 pgs. $40. 1911 edition. 132 pgs. $95.

A. C. GILBERT CO. *Hello Boys! Look at These Gilbert Toys.* New Haven, circa 1910-15. 18 pgs. $25.
Instruction Manual. Electrical set. 1916. 8vo. 48 pgs. $39.
How to Make'm Book. 1936. 8vo, 56 pgs. $20-$40.
Fun & Thrills American Flyer Erector. New York, 1939. 4to. 40 pgs. $45.

GILBERT CLOCK COMPANY. *Fall Supplement of New Designs.* Winsted, CT, 1898. 16 pgs. $75.

GILLETTE SAFETY RAZOR CO. *Silver Jubilee, Gillette Blade Catalog.* 1928. 144 pgs. $50-$100.
"The Gillette Blade". 7 bound vols., 1918-1928. $900.
Gillette Razor Catalogs. Pre-1910. $100-$150 each.

GILLIAM MFG. CO., CATALOG. *Horse Boots & Racing Specialties.* Canton OH, 1902. 40 pgs., color plates. $100.

GIMBEL BROS. *Fall & Winter, 1907-08.* Fashions, housewares. Philadelphia, 1907. 248 pgs. $75.
Paris, London & American Styles. Circa 1915. 176 pgs. $25-$35.

GIRL SCOUTS, INC. *Fall Equipment Catalog.* New York, 1936. 4to. 47 pgs. $25-$40.
Silver Anniversary Catalog. NY, 1937. 48 pgs. $30-$40.

W. W. GLECKNER & SONS. *Harness Collars & Saddlery Catalog.* Canton PA, circa 1907. Profusely illus. with everything a horseman could need. 128 pgs. $125-$175.

GLOBE LIGHTING. *Cast Iron & Bronze, Exterior Equip.* 1928. 84 pgs. $60.

GLOBE-WERNICKE. *File Cabinets, Supplies.* Cincinnati, 1899. $65-$85. Same, 1907 edition. $40. 1925. $15.

GODFREY, CHARLES. *Warren Bicycle Catalog*. NY, 1894. 24 pgs., 16mo. $100.

GOERZ CAMERA. *Cameras, Lenses, Binoculars*. 1913 ed. 68 pgs. $30-40.

GOES LITHOGRAPHING CO. *Printer's Helps. Certificates, Borders, etc*. NY, early 1900s. 20 sample plates. $40.

GOETZE NIEMER. *Standard Surgical Instruments*. 1922. 416 pgs. $100.

C. H. GOLDTHWAITE. *Goldthwaite's 1904 New Drug Prices*. Many patent medicine ads, etc. Brockton MA, 1904. 80 pgs. $50.

GONDER CERAMIC ARTS INC. *Catalog of Art Pottery*. Zanesville OH, circa 1925. 16 pgs. $35.

GOODELL PRATT CO. *Toolsmiths. Pocket Catalog No. 11*. Greenfield MA, 1913. 344 pgs. $20. 1922 Pocket Catalog. 448 pgs. $50.

L. W. GOODELL'S CATALOG. *Rare Fruit Trees, Flower & Garden Seeds*. Dwight MA, 1888. 31 pgs. $35. *Bulbs, Roses, Water Lilies, etc*. 40 pgs. with inventory marks. 1895. $25.

GOODNOW & WIGHTMAN. *Price List of Tools*. Boston. Various editions from 1875 to 1886, fine illustrations. $100-$125 each.

B. F. GOODRICH COMPANY. *Mechanical Rubber Goods*. 1910. 171 pgs. Mining to medical. $30.

GEORGE C. GOODWIN & CO. *Patent Medicines, Drugs, Chemicals, etc*. 1000's listed, many ads. Boston, 1892. 8vo, 670 pgs. $100-$150.

GOODYEAR'S INDIA RUBBER GLOVE MFG. CO. *Catalog of Sporting Goods*. NY, circa 1880s. 16 pgs. $45.

GOODYEAR'S RUBBER CURLER CO. *Illustrated Price List*. Everything from toys to life preservers. New York, circa 1883. 24mo. (small). 96 pgs. $75.

GOODYEAR'S RUBBER MANUFACTURING CO. *Boots and Shoes, Season of 1905*. 16mo, 62 pgs. $20.

GOODYEAR RUBBER SPECIALTIES. *Illustrated Catalog of 1901*. Door mats, fire buckets, spittoons. 12 pgs. $30.

GOTHAM SPORTING GOODS. *Motorcycles Supplies*. NY, 1921. 8vo. 72 pgs. $60. Another, circa 1910. 72 pgs. $65. Same, 1917. 66 pgs. $60-$100.

GRAF, MORSBACH CO. *Catalog No. 38. Harness and Saddlery*. Cincinnati OH, 1908. 348 pgs. $200. *Gemco Harness*. 1910. 24 pgs. $75.

GRAHAM PAPER CO. *Salesman's Pocket Sample Book of Printer's Papers*. St. Louis MO, circa 1905. $40.

GRAHAM-SELTZER CO. *Automotive Equipment & Parts*. Service station supplier. Peoria IL, 1929. 224 pgs. $30.

GRAND RAPIDS REFRIGERATOR CO. *Cold Facts About the Leonard Cleanable Refrigerator*. Grand Rapids MI, 1901. 32 pgs. $35.

GRAND RAPIDS SHOWCASE CO. *The New Way*. 1916. 68 pages. Folio catalog of men's clothing fixtures. $95-$150. *Catalog A - Department and General Stores*. 1916. 88 pgs. Racks, counters, marble, showcases, etc. $125-$175.

GRAND RAPIDS STORE EQUIP. CORP. *The Road to Success Runs Through Every Town*. 32 page catalog of 1930. $25.

A. W. GRAY'S SONS. *Horse-powered Threshing & Sawing Machines*. 1890s-1900s. 50 page catalogs. $35-$60.

GREAT NORTHERN MFG. CO. *Aluminumware, Cooking Utensils, etc*. Chicago, circa 1920. 4to, 56 pgs. $25-$50.

GREAT WESTERN GUN WORKS. *Gun & Revolver Catalog No. 33*. Pittsburgh PA, 1883. 16 pgs. $100. *10th Annual List, 1873*. 63 pgs. $200.

W. GREEN & CO. *Catalog of Jeweler's Supplies*. Massive folio of tools & supplies. NY, 1911. 563 pgs. $100-$150.

GREENFIELD. *Small Tools Catalog*. 1937. 85 pgs. $20.

GREENHUT-SIEGEL COOPER CO. *Latest New York Styles–Spring 1911*. 236 pgs. $50.

GREVEMEYER & CAREY BROS. *Third Annual Illustrated Catalog of Holiday Goods*. A stationery company with a large section of mechanical and other toys. Philadelphia PA, 1888. 128 pgs. $350-$500.

PALMER GRISWOLD & CO. *Fashion Catalogs, 1887-1896*. Avg. 40 pgs. ea. $60-$95.

GUARANTEE BARBERS SUPPLY CO. *Catalog of 1911*. Everything from shaving mugs to barber bottles. Many color plates. 174 pgs. 4to. $400-$500.

GUNN FURNITURE CO. *Sectional Book Case Catalog*. Grand Rapids MI, 1906 to 1915 editions. $15-35 each.

W. & L. E. GURLEY. *Manual of American Engineering & Surveying Instruments*. Troy NY, 1858. 125 pgs. $175. 1873 edition. 182 pgs. $75-$150. 1895 ed. 438 pgs. $100. *1903 Catalog/Manual*. 446 pages. $90. 1918 ed. $60-$75.

H

HAGERSTOWN SHOE CO. *Fall & Winter, 1931.* 40 pgs. $15-$20.

JOSEPH HAGN CO. *Catalog No. 405. Housewares, Gifts.* 1941. 80 pgs. $32.
Jewelry, Clocks, Furniture. 1951. 678 pgs. $50-$65.
Jewelry, Silver, General Merchandise. 1957. 840 pgs. $60-$70.

HALL & CARPENTER. *Catalog of Tinsmiths' Tools & Machines.* Philadelphia, 1878. 120 pgs. $150.

HALL CHINA CO. *Fireproof China Cookware.* East Liverpool OH, circa 1925. 8vo, 72 pgs. Color. $50.

H. W. HALL CO. *Hog Ringing Instruments.* Decatur IL, 1875. 8 pgs. $75.

HALL & SON. *Jewelry, Watches, Clocks, Silver. Catalog No. 20.* San Francisco, 1913-1914. 292 pgs. Folio. $50-$95.

HALLAHAN CO. *Catalog for Fall & Winter, 1891-92.* Shoes, boots, slippers. 64 pgs. $65-$85.

HAMILTON BROWN SHOE CO. *Catalog No. 40, Shoes.* Buster Brown brand. 1929-30. 69 pgs. $50-$70.

HAMILTON MFG. CO. *Printers Furniture.* Type cabinets, office equipment, etc. 1907. 192 pgs. $85. Another, circa 1910-1915. 192 pgs. $25-$35.

HAMLEY'S COWBOY CATALOG. *Saddles, tack, bits, blankets, holsters.* OR, 1939. Three-color cover. $80.

C. T. HAMM MFG. CO. *Lanterns & Lamps.* Rochester, circa 1920s. 16 pgs. $45.

HAMMACHER, SCHLEMMER & CO. *Catalog No. 600.* "A Landmark catalog of tools and hardware." Hardbound. New York, 1924. 762 pgs. $95-$125.

HAMMER BLOW TOOL CO. *Stream Line Supplement to 1936 Century of Progress Trailer Builders Guide.* Wausau WI, 40 pgs. $27.

J. L. HAMMETT & CO. *School Furniture, etc. Including Bradley's Kindergarten Gifts.* Bos. 1887-88. 80 pgs. $125.

Catalog of School Supplies. Boston, 1900-01. 116 pgs. $40. 1928 Edition. 158 pgs. $25.

HARDIN-LAVIN CO. *Plumbing & Heating Supplies.* Chicago, 1916. 5 x 8. 222 pgs. $35.

H. J. HARDIN & CO. *One Price Cash Hat House.* New York, 1897. 7 x 10. 20 pgs. $30.

HARDWARE CATALOGS.

Thousands of retail and wholesale hardware firms issued beautifully illustrated catalogs between 1880 and 1930. Many were 9 x 12 inches, containing a thousand or more pages. The most desirable have large wood engravings, rather than photo illustrations. Catalogs featuring guns, sporting goods, and toy sections are premium items.

The 1880-1905 hardcover editions of Sargent, Simmons, Winchester, Russell & Erwin, William Frankfurth, P. F. Corbin and Eagle Lock Company catalogs are worth from $200 to $500. Later hardware catalogs, printed on thin paper, with small illustrations or photos are not worth more than $75 or $100 unless they contain color sections which can be framed. (See individual listings for specific values.)

HARGRAFT & SONS. *Everything for Smokers.* Chicago, 1925. 92 pgs. $35-$50.

HARLEY-DAVIDSON. *Motorcycles.* 1940. Fold-out. $75.

F. S. HARMON & CO. *Chairs, Baby Carriages & Brass Goods.* Tacoma WA, 1897. 86 pgs. 4to. $150.

HARPER & BROS. *Book Catalog.* "More Than 3,000 Books described." New York, 1922. 306 pgs. $25.
1886 Holiday Catalog. 32 pgs. $15.
1888 General Trade List. 56 pgs. $30.

HART SCHAFFNER & MARX. *Style Book for Young Men.* Chicago, Winter, 1920-21. 24 pgs. 8vo. Color illus. by famous artists. $50-$75.

HARTFORD SILVER PLATE COMPANY. *Electro Gold & Silver Plated Ware*. Hartford CT, 1885. 8vo, 54 pgs. $95.

HARTMAN FURNITURE CO. *Furniture, Stoves, Rugs*. Chicago, 1914. 416 pgs. $100. Another, 1918. 460 pgs., 4to. Everything but the kitchen sink, and all low-end quality. $85. 1915. 64 large pages. Victrolas, glassware, hardware, furniture, rocking horses, go karts. $65.

G. F. HARVEY CO. *Manufacturing Chemists*. Saratoga Springs, 1900. 232 pgs. $50. 1896 Catalog, 144 pgs. $40. 1897 Catalog, 200 pgs. $75.

HARRINGTON AND RICHARDSON ARMS CO. *Catalog No. 7 Guns & Revolvers*. Worcester, 1903. 32 pages. $40. *Cat. No. 6 Pocket Revolvers*. 1900-1901. 28 pgs. $50-$95. *Cat. No. 21. Revolvers & Shotguns*. ca 1930s. 28 pgs. $35.

GEO. S. HARRINGTON. *Cabinet Hardware, Furn. Mfg. Supplies*. Boston, 1884. 120 pgs. $250. 1889 edition. 108 pgs. $175.

HARRIS BROS. *Building Materials. Catalog No. 187*. 1923. 200 pgs. $50.

HARRIS, FLIPPEN & CO. *Catalog No. 17. Fall, 1900*. Sporting goods, guns, etc. Richmond, Virginia. 1900. 28 pgs. $75.

GEORGE HARRIS & SONS. *Catalog of New Labels*. (Cigar box). New York & Chicago, 1890s. $250.

HART SCHAFFNER & MARX CO. *Autumn & Winter Styles for Men & Boys, 1922 & 1923*. Chicago, 1921. 24 pgs. $25. *Style Book, Autumn & Winter*. New York, 1910-11. 32 pgs. $25.

HARTFORD CYCLE CO. *Hartford Safety Bicycle Catalog*. Hartford CT, 1892. 24 pgs. $70.

HARTMAN FURNITURE and CARPET CO. *Shopping Guide for the Millions*. Chicago, 1918. Furniture, rugs, household items. 4to, 460 pgs. $70. 1914 edition, 416 pgs. $75-$100. 1915, 64 pgs. $20-$30.

HARTMANN-SANDERS CO. *The Pergola, Catalog No. 39*. Lattice work, pergolas, balustrades, gazebo trim and lawn ornaments. Chicago IL, 1928. $50.

C. H. HARTSHORN. *Reed Carriages, Collapsibles, Strollers, Sulkies*. Gardner MA, 1919. 59 pgs. $85.

THEODORE HAVILAND & CO. *The Book of Theodore Haviland China*. New York, 1924. 10 pgs. $20.

T. G. HAWKES & CO. *Catalog of Cut Glass*. Corning NY, circa 1900. 32 pgs. $75.

HAYES & WILLIS MFG. CO. *Outing Bicycles-1896*. Indianapolis IN, 1896. 12mo, 18 pgs. $45.

HAYDEN, GERE & CO. BRASS FOUNDERS. *Manufacturers of Plumbing Materials*. Haydenville MA, 1877. 297 pg. catalog, 10 color lithos. $275.

H. F. HEACOCK. *Grocers', Butchers' & Confectioners' Fixtures*. Philadelphia PA, circa 1892. 56 pgs. 8vo. $65.

HEANEY MAGIC CO. *Professional Catalog of Wonders, No. 24*. 6 x 9, 96 pgs. $25. Catalog No. 25. Berlin WI, 1924. 224 pgs. $50.

D. H. HECKMAN, MFR. *Yachts, Boats & Canoes*. Kennebunk ME, 1899. 64 pgs. $100.

HEDSTROM-UNION BABY CARRIAGES. *1936 Catalog*. 32 pgs. $15.

HENRY HEIL CHEMICAL CO. *Catalog of Chemical Apparatus, etc*. St. Louis, 1903. 521 pgs. $50-$75. *Catalog of Physical Apparatus, Drawing Instruments, etc*. 1909. 170 pgs. $75-$95.

H. J. HEINZ CO. *The Home of the "57"*. Pittsburgh PA, circa 1908. 32 pgs. of photos and business history. $25.

HELLER ALLER CO. *Catalog No. 34-Windmills & Towers*. Circa 1926. Clothbound. $75.

HENDEE MANUFACTURING CO. *Indian Motorcycles*. Springfield MA, 1914. 28 pgs. $100. (Also see Indian Motorcycles.)

HENDERSON AMES CO. *Catalog No. 1. Paraphernalia, Regalia and Costumes for I.O.O.F. Lodges*. Kalamazoo MI, 1897. 4to, 120 pgs. $100. 1897 edition. 80 pgs. $75. Circa 1900 edition. 148 pgs. $150. 1919 edition. 16 pgs. $50. (Most have fine color plate sections.)

PETER HENDERSON & CO. *Everything For The Garden*. New York, 1904. 180 pgs. $35-$45. Another, 1907. 64 pgs. $20. Another, 1917. 208 pgs. Worn. $35.

HENDRYX BIRD CAGES. New Haven, circa 1925. 4to, 24 pgs. Bird cages and accessories. $25.

WILLIAM G. HENIS. *Illustrated Catalog of Copper Weather Vanes*. Phila., ca 1885. 4to, 58 pgs. $275-$375.

HENLEY SKATE COMPANY. *Henley Roller Skates*. Richmond IN, circa 1905. 32 pgs. 8vo. $65.

C. HENNECKE & CO. *Catalog No. 2. Art Studies*. Plaster anatomical casts for classroom. Milwaukee, 1885. 4to, 72 pgs. $100.

A. C. HENSCHEL & CO. *Cigar Bands, Private Brands.* Chicago IL, circa 1900. 26 plates in color. $150-$250.

HERBRAND QUALITY TOOLS. *1939 Catalog.* $30.

ALLAN, HERCHELL CO. *Carousels for Parks and Carnivals.* N. Tonawanda NY, circa 1915. 12 pgs. 4to. Among the rarest of catalogs. $400.

B. HERDER. *Illus. Catalog of Church Vestments.* St. Louis MO, circa 1900. 72 pgs. $65.

HERRESHOFF MFG. CO. *Yacht Catalog.* Bristol RI, circa 1930. 4to, 58 pgs. $85.

FREDERICK HERRSCHNER. *Catalog No. 11. Embroideries & Fancy Goods.* 1912. 176 pgs. $35.
Catalog No. 25. Drygoods. 1925. 66 pgs. $20.
Catalog No. 32 Art Needlework. 1928-29. 87 pgs. $15.

HERTER'S INC. *Fly Tyers-Rod Builders-Materials & Tools.* Waseca MN, 1950. 224 pgs. of everything needed to tie flys and make rods. $50-$75.

HETTRICK BROS. *Awnings, Tents, Banners and Flags.* Toledo OH, 1896. 48 pgs. 12mo. $75.

HEX MFG. CO. *Catalog 48.* Prizes for bazaars, carnivals, fairs. Lots of flashy goods. Buffalo NY, 1934. 94 pgs. $65. 1935 edition, 88 pgs. $40.

HEYWOOD-WAKEFIELD CO. *Upholstered Reed Furniture.* Chicago, 1903. 48 pg. catalog. $150.
Catalog No. 8. Cane & Reed Rockers, Doll carts, etc. 1911, 223 pgs. $175.
Wakefield Carriages. Gardner MA, 1912. 245 pgs. $100.
A Completed Century 1826-1926. Boston, 1926. 112 pgs. $35-$50.
Cane & Wood Furniture. ca 1920. Folio, 80 pgs. $40-$50.
Baby Carriages. 1925. 4to, 48 pgs. $75.
Streamline Furniture. 1938. 32 pgs. $20.

HIGGINS and SEITER. *Catalog No. 8. Fine China, Cut Glass.* New York, 1897. 196 pgs. $175. Another, circa 1900. 257 pgs. $200-$250.

HILL BROS., CATALOG NO. 27. *Dealers in Cards, Dice, Inks & Tools.* Salida CO, no date. 32 pgs. $50.
Parlor Tricks and Exposure of Crooked Gambling Methods, etc. Circa 1915. 32 pgs. $75.

HILL, CLARKE & CO. *Machinery Blue Book.* Machine tools, lathes, planers. Boston MA, 1897. 402 pgs. $85.

N. N. HILL BRASS COMPANY. *Illus. Catalog No. 40, Bells.* East Hampton CT, 1921. 31 pgs. $75.

HILLES & JONES CO. *Catalog No. 6 Machine Tools.* Wilmington DE, 1900. 176 pgs. $35.

CAL HIRSCH & SONS. *Fall & Winter Fashions, 1914-15.* St. Louis MO, 1914. 32 pgs. $30.

HODGE & HOMER. *Catalog, Builders' Hardware & Tools.* Chicago, 1887. 219 pgs. $100.

E. F. HODGSON CO. *Hodgson Portable Homes.* Boston, 1917. 12mo, 16 pgs. $35.
Hodgson Houses & Outdoor Equip. 1933. 48 pgs. $20.
Hodgson Houses & Camps. 1937. 80 pgs. $35.

R. HOE & CO. *Catalog of Printing Presses & Materials.* New York, 1881. 171 pgs. $200.
Misc. pamphlets & flyers. from above, 1861-1880. $50-$80 each.

WM. HOEGEE CO. *Catalog No. 14. Tents, Awnings, Camping Goods.* Scarce West Coast catalog. Los Angeles, circa 1910. 8vo, 112 pgs. $75.

M. HOHNER, INC. *How to Play the Chromonica.* New York, circa 1927. 12 pgs. $15.
Hohner Harmonicas. 4 page catalog, circa 1920. $25. 1936 Edition. 22 pgs. $20.

J. R. HOLCOM & CO. *Violins, Bass Viols, etc.* Cleveland OH, 1887. 32 pgs. $75.

HOLMES & BLANCHARD CO. *Illustrated Catalog of Machinery, etc.* Everything from chocolate to fertilizer-making machines. Boston, 1895. 8vo. 200 pgs. $45.

HOLSMAN CO. *Fall & Winter 1929.* Jewelry, etc. Chicago, 1929. 240 pgs. $25.

C. I. HOOD & CO. *Hood's Pansy.* Flower-shaped 16 page Hood's Sarsaparilla brochure. Lowell MA, ca 1890s. $20.

HOOSIER MANUFACTURING CO. *Planning the Modern Kitchen.* Newcastle IN, circa 1920. 32 pgs. $40.

HOOSIER STOVE CO. *Stove Catalog.* 1908. 64 pgs. $45.

OLIVER HOOVER & CO. *Illus. Catalog of Queens, Bees & Bee Keepers' Supplies.* Snydertown PA, 1890. 36 pgs. 12mo. $35.

HOOVER WAGON CO. *Blue Print Catalog.* Ice Wagons. York PA, 1912. 13 pgs. $80. Hardbound catalog of mail, butcher, ice, furniture and plumbers wagons. 1909. 4to. 150 pgs. $250.

HENRY HOPE & SONS. *Leadwork for the Garden*. Catalog of garden ornaments. New York, 1931. 4to, 38 pgs. $50.

HIBBARD, SPENCER, BARTLETT & CO. *General Hardware Catalog No. 70*. 2,756 pages of everything from guns, to buggy whips, to baby cribs. Chicago, 1923. $150-$250. 1927 ed. Ripped spine. $65. 1932. Catalog No. 77. Tools, Hardware, Office Supplies. 1,800 pgs. $85-$125.

HOPKINS & ALLEN ARMS CO. *Catalog No. 15*. Norwich CT, 1913. 16mo, 24 pgs. $30.

HOPKINS & DICKINSON MFG. CO. *Catalog of Locks, Builders' Hardware*. Darlington NJ, 1879. 12mo, 408 pgs. $350-$400.

HOPKINS MARINE HARDWARE. *Yacht Supplies, Marine Hardware, Sporting Goods*. New York, circa 1905. 8vo. 164 pgs. $95. 1910 Catalog. 114 pgs. $40.

HOPP CARRIAGE COMPANY. *1909 Catalog*. Mifflinsburg PA. 32 pgs. $95.

HORDER CO. *Christmas & New Year Greeting Cards*. 1928. 32 pgs. $40.

WM. H. HORSTMANN. *Art Embroidery, Linens, Fancy Goods*. Philadelphia, circa 1905. Crafts catalog. 8vo, 100 pgs. $30-$40.

HORTON MANUFACTURING CO. *"Lucky Strike" Bristol Steel Fishing Rods*. Bristol CT, 1907. 48 pgs. 8vo. $65.

HOTCKIN & WILDER. *Fine Open & Top, Buggies & Carriages*. 1884. 5 x 7, 28 pgs. $50-$70.

HOVEY & CO. *Catalog of Trees, Shrubs, Plants*. Cambridge Nurseries, 1846. 16 pgs. $175.

HOWARD CLOCK COMPANY. *Regulators, Office and Bank Clocks*. Boston, 1900. 44 pgs. $100.

HOWE MACHINE COMPANY. *History of the Sewing Machine*, with catalog section. New Haven, circa 1867. 44 pgs. $35-$50.
Sewing Machine Instructor. New York, circa 1875. 32 pgs. $45-$60.

W. M. HOYT. *Groceries*. Canned goods, tobacco, small hardware, fixtures. Chicago, 1915. 80 pgs. $35.

HUBBARD, ELDREDGE & MILLER. *Furniture*. Rochester NY, 1923. Folio, 120 pgs. $45-$65.

HENRY HUBER & CO. *Illustrated Catalog of Plumbing Specialties*. Numerous woodcuts and color plates. New York, 1888. 222 pgs. $475.

HUDSON BARN EQUIPMENT. *1933 Catalog*. 166 pgs. $18-$24.

HUDSON BAY FUR CO., INC. *Indian Curios*. Furs, Rugs, etc. Circa 1920. 8vo, 16 pgs. $50.

HUDSON MOTOR CAR CO. *The Hudson "20" 1910 First Announcement*. 12 pgs. $40-$80.
Greater Hudson "8" for 1929. Color fold-out brochure. $15-$30.
New Hudson "8" for 1932. Showroom brochure. 16 pgs. color. $15-$30.
Various owner manuals. 1949-1951. $15-$20 each.

HUEG & COMPANY. *Ornamental Confectionary and the Art of Baking*. New York, 1893. 16 pgs. $35.
1901 Edition. 223 pgs. incl. trade catalog. $75.
Catalog and Price List for Bakers, Confectioners, etc. Circa 1900. 48 pgs. $45.

MAX HUNCKE CHEMICAL CO. *Embalming Fluids, 5th Edition*. All kinds of morticians' supplies. Brooklyn, 1922. 8vo, 112 pgs. $55.

HOWARD C. HUNT PEN COMPANY. *Steel Pens, Boston Pencil Sharpeners*. Folio size catalog. NJ, 1928. 28 pgs. $50-$75.

HUNTINGTON, HOPKINS & CO. *Illustrated Catalog of Hardware, etc*. A rare West Coast trade catalog with numerous extra flyers bound in. San Francisco & Sacramento, 1884. 4to, gilt-stamped cloth, 296 pgs. $350.

G. W. HUNTLEY & CO. *Jewelry, Clocks, Furniture*. Summer, 1918. 320 pgs. $80.
1920 General Merchandise. Silverware, furniture, baby carriages, dolls. 684 pgs. Folio. $125.

HUPP MOTOR CAR CORP. *The 1930 Hupmobile*. 16 pg. brochure. $35.

HURD SHOES. *Fall, 1916*. 54 pgs. $35.

HURST & CO. *Brook Catalog*. New York, circa 1880. Games, magic, dime novels, etc. 8vo, 64 pgs. $25.
New Catalog, Books, Games, Stationery. Circa 1885. 48 pgs. $35.

W. H. HUTCHINSON & SON. *Catalog of Bottler's Supplies*. 1928. 64 pgs. $50.

HYDE WINDLASS CO. *Steam & Hand Windlasses*. And cuts of many other shipfittings. Bath ME, 1915. $60.

HYMAN & OPPENHEIM. *Coiffures of Style & Quality*. New York, 1918. 78 pgs. $50.

I

IDEAL MANUFACTURING COMPANY. *Handbook of Useful Information for Shooters No. 8*. Ammunition and accessories. New Haven CT, 1888. 8vo, 96 pgs. $50.

ILLINOIS BOARD OF PRISONS. *Furniture Catalog*. 1908. 76 pgs. $75-$100.

ILLINOIS GLASS COMPANY. *Illustrated Catalog and Price List*. Alton IL, 1911. Glass containers, wooden boxes, etc. 275 pgs. 16mo. $90.

ILLINOIS SURGICAL SUPPLY CO. *Physicians & Hospital Supplies*. Chicago, circa 1920. 64 pgs. $40. Another, no date. 145 pgs. $50.

ILLINOIS WATCHES. Springfield IL, circa 1925. 9 x 12. 24 pgs. $24.

IMPERIAL AUTOMOBILE SUPPLY CO. *Automobile Supplies Catalog*. NY, 1912. 96 pgs. 8vo. $75.

INDIAN MOTORCYCLE. *Operators Manual*. Springfield, 1914. 48 pgs. $125. (Also see Hendee Mfg. Co.)

INLAND TYPE FOUNDRY. *Specimen Book and Catalog*. St. Louis, 1897. 431 pgs. $125. 1907 edition. 243 pgs. (Soiled). $50. 1883 ed. 12 leaves gone. $125.

INTERNATIONAL BUSINESS MACHINES CO. *Scales, Keypunch Machines, Card Sorters, etc.* New York, 1925. 42 pgs. $40-$75.

INTERNATIONAL HARNESS MACHINERY CO. *Catalog of Harness Machinery*. Cincinnati OH, 1917. 26 pgs. $35.

INTERNATIONAL HARVESTER CO. *International Motor Trucks*. 400 photos. Chicago, circa 1907. 140 pgs. $150. *Champion Horse-Drawn Harvest Equip*. ca 1910. $30. *Deering Corn Machines*. 1910. 24 pgs. $25. *Bluebell Cream Separator*. 1910. $40. *Motor Vehicles*. Chicago, 1915. 24 pgs. $50. *Gasoline Engines*. circa 1915. 55 pgs. $25-$50. *Farmall Tractors*. circa 1936. 48 pgs. $35. *I. H. McCormick-Deering*. WWII. Cream separators, milkers, parts. 72 pgs. $30. *Catalog No. 40*. Tractors, plows. 1940s. 612 pgs. $50.

INTERNATIONAL MOTOR CAR CO. *The International Motor Car. Vol. I, No. 3*. Electric vehicles, not gas buggies. Toledo OH, 1902. 32 pgs. $25.

INTERNATIONAL SHIRT & COLLAR CO. *Catalog of 1899-Men's Fashions*. Troy NY, 1899. 32 pgs. $35.

INTERNATIONAL SILVER CO. *Catalog No. 147 - 1847 Rogers Bros*. Meriden CT, circa 1925. 4to, 48 pages. $50. *Holloware Catalog*. 1931. 96 pgs. $35. Another, 1915. 54 pgs. $40.

INTER-STATE AUTOMOBILE CO. *Inter-State Motor Cars*. Muncie IN, 1911. 32 pgs. $75.

ISLAND CYCLE SUPPLY CO. *Wheel Goods, Bicycles, Pedal Cars, etc.* Minneapolis, 1938. 108 pgs. $50-$75.

ITHACA GUN COMPANY. *The New Ithaca Gun*. NY, 1930. 22 pgs., folio. Color lithos throughout. $125-$175.

IVER JOHNSON ARMS & CYCLE WORKS. *Bicycles, Motorcycles, Firearms*. Fitchburg MA, 1913. 12mo, 64 pgs. Color plates. $90. Another, 1914. 80 pgs. $125. *Fishing Tackle*. Boston, circa 1925. 108 pgs. $40.

IVER JOHNSON SPORTING GOODS CO. *Bicycles*. Boston MA, circa 1908. 8vo, 52 pgs. $60. *Lovell Diamond Bicycles*. Circa 1910. 12mo, 77 pgs. $55. *Firearms, Ammunition, Novelties*. Circa 1910. $100. *Reliable Firearms*. 1931. 20 pgs. $35.

IVES, JULIS & CO. *Universal Clothes Wringer*. NY, circa 1864. 2 pages, 2 woodcuts. $40.

IVES MANUFACTURING CO. *Ives Toy Catalog*. Electric trains, miniature bldgs. Bridgeport CT, 1915. 32 pgs. $160. Another, no date. 7 x 10 in. 24 pgs. $175. *Ives Miniature Railway System*. Bridgeport CT, Circa 1900. 22 pgs., 4to. Color wraps and illus. $175-$350.

J. W. IVORY. *Catalog of Dental Specialties*. Philadelphia PA, circa 1910. 48 pgs. $70.

J

JACKSON HARDWARE CO. *General Catalog*. Aberdeen SD, 1923. 457 pgs. 9 x 11. $64.

JACOBS BIRDHOUSE COMPANY. Waynesburg PA, 1917. 32 pgs. of birdhouse photos. 12mo. $35.

JACOBSON & CO. *Architectural and Decorative Ornaments. Catalog No. 2*. NY, 1929. 255 pgs. $125. Another, 1925. 192 pgs. $85. Another, 1914. 187 pgs. $35.

JACOBY ART GLASS CO. *Illustrated Catalog*. Circa 1920s. 32 pgs. $35.

JAMES MFG. CO. *Catalog No. 60. Barn Fixtures*. Ft. Atkinson WI, 1928. 160 pgs. $35.
Dairy Barns, Catalog No. 21. 1916. 313 pgs. $35.

JANUSCH MFG CO. *Fireplace Fixtures*. NY, 1925. Fancy implements, andirons, etc. 248 pgs., 4to. $75-$100.

JARBURG BROTHERS. *The Best of Everything for Bakers*. New York, 1916. 336 pgs. $85.

THOMAS B. JEFFERY & CO. *The Rambler Automobile*. Kenosha WI, 1902. 21 pgs. $150.

JENNINGS & GRAHAM. *Books, Art Calendars, Christmas Cards*. Cincinnati, 1906-07. 144 pgs. $25.

GEORGE W. JERRARD CO. *Jerrard's Seed Potatoes and Early Seeds*. Caribou ME, 1892. 40 pgs. $35.

> JEWELRY CATALOGS are beautiful, but they are very common. Many deluxe hardbound examples of up to 400 pages were published from 1875 to 1935 and are worth only $50 to $100 each. Cheaper quality paperback versions sell for $25 to $35. Catalogs featuring designer creations, art deco or art nouveau-style jewelry are worth more than general-line volumes. Victorian jewelry catalogs are not scarce. Most will have extra sections devoted to clocks, watches, silverware, cut glass, optical goods, sewing notions, handbags, combs, brushes, etc.

JOHNS & CO. *Cigar Labels-Sample Catalog*. Cleveland, circa 1880. 16 pgs. 10 labels in color. $275.

JOHNS-MANVILLE CO. *Electrical Catalog No. 14*. 1905. 349 pgs. $30. (9) catalogs and booklets, 1930s. $32 for all.

JOHNSON AIRPLANE SUPPLY CO. *1932 Aeronautical Supplies*. Dayton OH. 80 pgs. Drawings of pilots, parts, instruments. $150.

H. A. JOHNSON CO. *Supplies, Machinery, Fixtures, Ovens,* for the Baker, Confectioner and Ice Cream Mfr. Boston, 1915. 200 pgs. $125.

J. H. JOHNSTON, GREAT WESTERN GUN WORKS. *Wholesale Illustrated Price List No. 2*. Pittsburgh PA, 1879. 48 pgs. $175.
List No. 38. Rifles, Shot Guns, etc. 1887. 32 pgs. $100.

JOHNSON & LUND. *Dental Catalog*. Philadelphia, 1881. 8vo, 322 pgs. $150-$250.

NATHANIEL JOHNSON. *Illustrated Catalog of Church & School Furniture*. New York, circa 1880. 17 pgs. $75.

S. C. JOHNSON CO. *Various circulars* advertising wax & hardwood floors. ca 1890-1900. 12 to 16 pgs. $20-$30 ea.
A Fold-out panel with actual mounted wood samples. 8vo. A scarce item. $75.

JOHNSON SMITH & CO. *Novelties, Puzzles, Tricks, Joke Goods*. Racine WI, 1929. 768 pg. catalog. $95. Another, same year. 579 pgs. $55. 1937 edition. $50. 1942 edition. $28. 1950 "We're in Business for Fun." $20.
Millions of these novelty catalogs have been issued since Alfred Johnson Smith brought his mail order business to Chicago, from Australia, in 1914.

JOHNSTON HARVESTER CO. *Farm Machinery Catalog*. Batavia NY, circa 1910. 64 pgs. $30.

J. & C. JOHNSTON. *Historical Calendar and Fashion Catalog*. New York, 1880. 64 pgs. $75.

J. H. JOHNSTON & CO. *The Christmas Spoon*. New York, circa 1890. Jewelry and gift catalog of 112 pages. $75.
Diamonds, Watches, Silver. NY, 1894. 4to, 8 pgs. $60.

W. & A. K. JOHNSTON. *Maps & Globes*. Chicago, 1912. 4to, 39 pages. $85.

E. D. JONES & SONS. *Paper Mill Machinery*. Pittsfield MA, 1899. 8vo, 118 pgs. $75.

THOMAS W. JONES. *Catalog of Copper Weather Vanes, Finials, etc.* New York, circa 1884. 72 pgs. $250-$400.

W. H. JOSEPH & SON. *Catalog No. 30. Badges for Fire & Police Departments*. New York, circa 1925. 44 pgs. $50.

JORDAN MARSH & CO. *Dept. Store Catalog*.
  1881. 8vo. 32 pgs.....................................$40.
  Fall & Winter, 1882-83. 208 pgs............$125.
  Spring & Summer, 1884........................$50.
  Fall & Winter, 1886. 4to, 128 pgs.........$100.
  1889..$50.
  1892..$65.
  1893..$40.
  1896..$35.
  1900..$60.
  The Jordan Marsh Story. 1911.............$40.

STERLING SILVER BELT CLASPS AND BROOCHES.
BAIRD-NORTH COMPANY, GOLD AND SILVER SMITHS, SALEM, MASS.

K

KAISER-FRAZER AUTOMOBILE CO. *Various showroom flyers* from 1951-52. 4-8 pgs. ea. $40-$50.

KANKAKEE MFG. CO. *Kankakee Art Bicycles.* IL, 1896. 20 pgs., 12mo. 8 illus. of safety-style bicycles. $100-$150.

S. KARPEN & BROS. *Furniture Catalog.* Chicago, 1906. 216 pgs. $20.

KASBACK HARDWARE. *No. 34 Wholesale Hardware.* 1934. 806 pgs. $100.

J. M. KASE & CO. *National Glass Manufacturers.* Reading PA, 1918. 64 pgs. 32 color plates. $240.

KAYSER & ALLMAN. *Wallpaper Sample Book.* NY, circa 1909. $50-$75.

H. H. KAYTON. *Imported Watch Materials and Jeweler's Findings.* Plus optical goods, etc. NY, 1896. 456 pages, 4to. $60-$80.

KEARNS GORSUCH BOTTLE CO. *Catalog of Packers' Glassware.* Zanesville OH, 1920. 99 pgs. $40.

KEEN KUTTER. (See Simmons Hardware Co., and also Shapleigh. Hardware Co.)

KEIL & SON. *Key Blanks Catalog.* NY, 1916. 339 pgs. $75.

WALTER T. KELLEY CO. *Bee Supply Catalog.* Paducah KY, 1936. 8vo, 32 pgs. $30.

O. S. KELLY MFG. CO. *Engines, Threshers, Feedmills.* Iowa City IA, 1902. 32 pgs. $50-$75.

THE KELSEY COMPANY. *Bicycle & Automobile Supplies.* 1904. 118 pgs. $35.

KELSEY PRESS CO. *Do Your Own Printing, Money Made and Saved.* Catalog of type & cuts, plus presses. Meriden CT, circa 1919. 32 pgs. $35. 1925 Catalog with loose brochures. 4to, 36 pgs. $25.

KENNEDY & CURTIS. *4th Annual Catalog. Guns, Rifles, Pistols.* Includes repair manual. Phila., 1891. 88 pgs. $150.

KEN-WEL SPORTING GOODS CO. *Baseball Mitts, Golf and Tennis Equipment.* Utica, NY, 1931, 56 pgs. $50.

KEUFFEL & ESSER CO. *Catalog of Drawing Materials & Surveying Instruments.* 21st edition, 1890. $75-$150. 34th edition, 1913. 566 pgs. $35-$75. *Various other editions* up to 1936. $35-$75 each.

KEYSTONE MFG. CO. *Toy Boats.* Toy power and sail boats. Boston, 1940. 12 pgs. $45.

KEYSTONE TYPE FOUNDRY. *Type Specimen Book.* Philadelphia, 1899. 405 pgs. $75. 1906 edition, 632 pgs. soiled. $60. *Newspaper Headlines.* 1899. 9 pgs. $50.

KILBOURNE-JONES CO. *Hardware and Metal Catalog.* Philadelphia, 1901. 1,220 pgs., 4to. $175-$295.

S. D. KIMBARK. *Carriage and Wagon Hardware.* Chicago, 1888. 8vo, 402 pgs. Copious illustrations. $250-$300.

KINFOLKS, WORLD'S MOST FAMOUS RAZOR. Little Valley NY, circa 1910. 20 pg. catalog. $40.

KING FOLDING CANVAS BOAT CO. *Catalog No. 23.* MI, 1920. $45-$70.

KINGERY MANUFACTURING CO. *Kingery Popcorn Poppers and Peanut Roasters.* Cincinnati OH, 1928. 12mo, 72 pages. $140. Another, also includes candy vending carts. Ohio, 1913. 64 pgs. Color illus. covers. Mint. $250-$450.

SAMUEL KIRK & SON. *Sterling Silverware By Kirk.* Baltimore MD, 1935. 64 pgs. $20.

W. STOKES KIRK. *Guns, Ammunition, Cutlery, Sport & Army Clothing.* Philadelphia PA, 1916. 44 pgs. $35. *Catalog No. 20.* Circa 1920s. 50 pgs. $45-$65.

KIRSCH MFG. CO. *The 1929 Kirsch Book, Window & Door Draping.* Sturgis MI, 1928. 32 pgs. $20.

KITSELMAN BROS. *Ornamental Fences & Gates.* 1929. 64 pgs. $24.

KNICKERBOCKER WALL PAPER CO. *Catalog of Samples*, Folio, 18 x 16 in. NY, 1909. 126 leaves. $95.

L. E. KNOTT APPARATUS CO. *Scientific Instruments Catalog No. 26*. Boston, 1921. 8vo. 326 pgs. $35-$50.

KNY SCHEERER CO. *Surgical Instruments*. New York, circa 1895. 8vo, 336 pgs. $135.
Vacuum Apparatus. 1905. 32 pgs. $50.
X-Ray Coil. Circa 1903. 16 pgs. $75.
Surgical Instruments. 1928 edition. $95.

THEO A. KOCHS & SON. *Illustrated Catalog of Barbers' Supplies*. 1894 edition, color plates. $375. 1902 edition, 198 pgs. $200-$350. 1926 edition. $95-$125.
Beauty Shop Chairs. 1932, 16 pages. $50.
Chrometal Barber Shop Equipment. Catalog No. 58. 1936. 32 pgs. $65.
1937 Barber Supplies. 98 pgs. $65.

KODAK (See Eastman Kodak).

F & F KOENIGRAMER. *Reliance Beauticians & Barbers Chairs*. 1941. 16 pgs. $30.

HERMAN KOHLBUSH. *Balance Scales, Precision*. New York, 1888. 26 pgs. $125.

KOKEN-CHISHOLM CORP. *Beauty Shop Chairs and Equipment*. New York, circa 1925. 4to, 96 pgs. $75.

ERNEST E. KOKEN. *Illustrated Catalog of Barbers' Supplies*. St. Louis MO, 1905. Color plates. $375. 1980 reprint of above. $35-$50.

KOKOMO FENCE MACHINE CO. *20th Illus. Catalog of Ornamental Fence*. Kokomo IN, circa 1910. 48 pgs. $40.

KOLYNOS COMPANY. *Kolynos Disease Preventer.* "A Scientific Dental Cream." New Haven CT, circa 1920-25. 16 pgs. $25.

FR KRAUS, SON. *Ice Cream Molds for Every Occasion*. Cincinnati OH, 1928. 24 pgs. $40.

KRETCHMER MFG. CO. *Bee Keeper's Supplies. 92nd Edition*. Council Bluffs IA, 1907. 80 pgs. $15.

JOHN KRODER, INC. *Illustrated Catalog of Brass Goods & Curtain Poles, etc.* New York, 1894. 64 pgs. $100.

E. KRONMAN. *Complete Catalog of Kitchen Equipment.* For restaurants & hotels. New York, 1921. 88 pgs. $65.

KOKEN BARBER'S SUPPLY

L

LANA LABELL. *Spring & Summer, 1960. Juniors, Misses.* 64 pgs. $15.
Holiday Catalog, 1961. 64 pgs. $15.

LAFAYETTE RADIO. *Radios, Sound Systems, Supplies.* 1938. 174 pgs. $30.

LAMSON BROTHERS CO. *Your Baby Needs.* Clothes to furniture. 1925. 44 pgs. $24.
Dry Goods Catalog. Infant wear, carriages. Toledo OH, circa 1915. $30.

LANE BRYANT. *Slenderizing Fashions For Stout Women.* 1924 to 1954 editions of 82 to 144 pgs. ea. $25-$50 each.

LANDERS, FRARY & CLARK. *Fine Table Cutlery, Butchers' & Household Tools.* New Britain CT, 1905. 437 pgs. $150-$200.
Table Cutlery and Hardware. 1869. Folio, 222 pgs. $350-$400.

LANSING WHEELBARROW CO. *Catalog No. 7. Trucks and Barrows.* Lansing, 1900. 8vo. 128 pgs. $75.

LARKIN SOAP MANUFACTURING CO. *Can We Break the Crust?* Premium catalog, circa 1882. 12mo, 18 pgs. $50. Another, circa 1895. $50.
Club Premium List. Buffalo NY, 1897. 4to, 22 pgs. $40. Another (soiled). $15.
Soap & Premium Catalog. 1899. 12mo, 24 pgs. $40.
Larkins Products & Premiums. Circa 1900. 12mo, 24 pgs. $15.
Premium Catalogs. 1900 to 1915. 16mo. $15.
1908 Products & Premiums. 4to, 88 pgs. $35.
Furniture & Housewares. 1905. $35.
The Larkin Plan, Factory to Family. 1915. 32 pgs. $15. 1923 edition, 196 pgs. $50.
Fall & Winter. 1919-1920. 196 pgs. $65. 1923-1935 General merchandise 184-196 pgs. $35-$70 each.

W. H. LASSELLE. *Annual Illustrated Catalog.* Jewelry, silverware, talking machines, cameras. Berlin MA, circa 1902. 704 pgs. $95.

F. B. LATHAM. *Electrical Appliances.* Heaters, fans, lighting, etc. New York, 1912. 527 pgs. $60.

HOMER LAUGHLIN CHINA CO. *Catalog of Decorated Table & Toilet Wares.* Virginia and Ohio, 1912. 40 pgs. $150.

THOMAS LAUGHLIN CO. *Catalog No. 75, Marine Hardware.* Portland ME, 1912. 448 pgs., 8vo. Worn and waterstained. Fair. $80. Catalog No. 80. 1920. 490 pgs. Good-VG. $100.

LAWRENCE, BRADLEY & PARADEE. *Carriages and Sleighs.* Also includes harness, saddles, tack. "200 of the finest engravings ever produced." New Haven CT, 1862. 148 pgs., 8vo. $1,000-$1,250.

LAZERUS BROS. *Clothing Bargains for Men and Boys.* New York, 1927. 32 pgs. $16.

JOS. LAZARUS & CO. IMPORTERS. *Ladies Hats, Bonnets, Trimmings.* Cincinnati, Spring 1900. 9x12. 28 pgs. $28.

WILLIAM LEAVENS & COMPANY. *Catalog of Cottage Furniture.* Popular furn. of the period. Mission oak and Windsor reproductions, rattan chairs, cottage-style pine. Boston, circa 1910. 260 pgs. $100.

LEEDY MFG. CO. *World's Finest Drummer's Instruments.* Elkhart IN, circa 1926. 70 pgs. $70.

FRANCIS H. LEGGETT & CO. *The Premier Enquirer.* NY, 1909. 128 pg. catalog of food brands. $45.

LEHIGH PORTLAND CEMENT CO. *Build The Castle of Your Dreams.* Allentown PA, 1925. 31 pgs. $25.
Plans for Concrete Houses. Chicago, 1925. 79 pgs. $35.
28 Better Homes. 1925. 32 pgs. $15.

E. LEITZ, INC. *Leica Camera Catalog.* New York, 1936. 54 pgs. $20.

LENOX INCORPORATED. *Catalog of Lenox Belleek.* Trenton NJ, 1909. 31 pgs. $50.
Lenox China. NJ, 1922. Color catalog, 34 loose-leaf pgs. $60-$125.

CHARLES LENTZ & SONS. *Catalog of Surgical Instruments, etc.* Philadelphia, 1898. 598 pgs. $150.

RICHARD LEVICK'S SON & CO. *India Rubber Goods, Druggists' Sundries, Stationers' and Fancy Goods.* Philadelphia, 1889. 76 pgs. $100.

G. B. LEWIS COMPANY. *York Honey and Bee Supply Co.* Watertown WI, 1907. Newspaper format. Folio, 18 pgs. $35. 1920 edition. 4to, 40 pgs. $25.

WM. LEWIS & SON. *Stringed Musical Instruments.* 1930. 96 pgs. $50-$75.

C. A. LIBBEY CO. *Catalog No. 26. Modern Barn Equipment.* Oshkosh WI, 1924. 191 pgs. $35.

LIBRARY BUREAU. *Handbook of Library Fittings and Supplies.* Boston, 1899. 172 pgs. $65.

LIBERTY STORE CATALOGS. *Fashions, Gifts, etc.* Circa 1925. $25.
Fabrics, Rugs, Vases. Circa 1930. $25.
Dresses, Blouses, Hats. Circa 1937. $25.

LICHTENSTEIN'S FASHION CATALOG. *Spring and Summer, 1889.* New York. 4to, 160 pgs. $85-$125.

A. LIETZ COMPANY CATALOG. *Surveying Instruments, etc.* Revised edition. San Francisco, 1896. 200 pgs. $150.

LIGHTOLIER. Lighting Fixture Catalog. New York, 1922. 4to, 112 pgs. $50-$65.

M. C. LILLEY & CO. *Military Clothing and Equipment.* Circa 1880. 25 pgs. in full color. No prices. $350-$550.
Masonic Lodge Supplies. Columbus OH, 1886. 52 pgs. $60-$95.
Knights Templar. Shrine dress. Circa 1888. 20 pgs. $25.
Police Uniforms and Supplies. 1907. $100.
Modern Woodsmen. 1905. 88 pgs. $45.
Masonic Lodge Supplies. 1903 to 1930 Catalogs. $40-$75 each.

ELI LILLY CO. *Handbook of Pharmacy & Therapeutics.* Indianapolis, 1919. 279 pgs. $35-$50. 1920 edition. 8vo. 286 pgs. $65. 1925 edition. 295 pgs. $35-$50.

E. H. LINLEY SUPPLY CO. *Railroad Supply Catalog.* St. Louis, 1898. 12mo, 470 pgs. $100.

C. M. LINNINGTON. *Agents Supply House.* Wholesale Jewelry, Notions, etc. Chicago, 1890. 48 pgs. $35.

LIONEL CORPORATION. *Lionel Electric Trains. Accessories.* NY, 1928. 44 pgs., 4to. $150-$295.
Lionel Trains. NY, 1938. 36 pgs., 8vo. $25-$40.
Lionel Trains in Action. 1945. 6x9. 17 pgs. $20.
Dealer Lot of Lionel Train Catalogs: (16) catalogs dated 1957-1978. Mint condition. $175 all.

1942 Lionel Trains Catalog. $35.
Lionel Hudson 5344. NY, 1937. 16 pgs. $25.
Assorted Lionel Trains Catalogs. 1954-1957. 44 pgs. Color. $8-$10 each. 1952 ed. 34 pgs., 4to. Color. $25-$40.

CHARLES LIPPINCOTT & CO. *Catalog of Apparatus for Making and Dispensing Soda Water.* Philadelphia, circa 1885-90. 218 pgs. $250. 1892 edition. 289 pgs., 4to. $250. Another, circa 1895. 92 pgs., 8vo. $175.

LITHGOW MFG. CO. *Catalog No. 65-A.* Very ornate stoves & ranges, plus kitchenware. Louisville KY, circa 1900. 104 pgs. $75.

LIVESTOCK CATALOGS. Local productions put together for auction sales, etc. May contain 16 to 200 pages and sell for $25 to $125 each. Horse engravings, suitable for framing, are tops in this value range. Colorful poultry catalogs with stone lithographed plates are also desirable.

LIVINGSTON'S SEED ANNUAL. *1920 Catalog.* 96 p. $35.

LOCKWOOD OUTBOARD MOTORS. *Catalog for 1929.* 17 pgs. 8½ x 11 in. $22.

LOCKWOOD'S DIRECTORY OF THE PAPER, STATIONERY TRADE. NY, 1920, 45th ed. 848 pgs. $50.

LOCOMOBILE COMPANY OF AMERICA. *14th Annual Catalog of Motorcars.* Bridgeport CT, 1912. 194 pgs. $50.
The Locomobile Book. The Car of 1912. History, products, etc. 210 pgs. $95.
Instructions for Owners. 1915. $25.
Gasoline Touring Cars. 1905. 32 pgs. $150-$250.

LOFTIS BROS. CO. *Jewelry, Watches, Sterling, etc.* Chicago, 1912. 6x9, 97 pgs. $30.

THEODORE LOHR. *Catalog of Zithers, Strings, etc.* New York, circa 1900-05. 19 pgs. $35.

LONDON, BERRY & ORTON. *Machinery For Working Wood.* Philadelphia, 1888. 198 pgs. $150.

LORD & TAYLOR. *Catalog No. 28, Spring & Summer, 1882.* Women's and children's clothing. New York, 1882. 149 pgs. $85.

P. LORILLARD CO. *Catalog of Presents.* A tobacco co. premium catalog with ads. New York, circa 1916. 8vo, 128 pgs. $15-$30. Another, 1913. 88 pgs. $45.

LORILLARD REFRIGERATOR CO. Oak iceboxes in halftone & color. New York, 1898. 24 pgs. $50.

LOS ANGELES SADDLERY AND FINDING CO. Los Angeles, 1912. A huge horse goods catalog of 479 pages. Oblong 8vo. Saddles, straps, harness, etc. Some color plates. $500-$1,000.

LOUDEN MACHINERY CO. *Barn Equipment*. Farm items. Fairfield IA, circa 1910. 50 pgs. $15-$25.
Building Plans for Barns. 112 pgs. $50.
Catalog No. 52. 1923. 240 pgs. $50.
Catalog No. 54. 1929. 211 pgs. $40.

JOHN P. LOVELL ARMS CO. *Guns, Rifles, Revolvers*. Boston, 1890. Leading brands are superbly illustrated. 96 pgs., 4to. $150.

DANIEL LOW & CO. *Jewelry Year Books*. 1905 ed. $65. 1911 to 1925 editions of 172-218 pgs. $20-$50 each.

LOZIER MOTOR COMPANY. *Lozier Motor Cars. Four Cylinders and Six*. NY, 1910. 32 pgs. $125.

LUDENS EASTER CANDIES. *1934 Catalog*. 65 pgs. $30.

LUFKIN RULE CO. *Precision Tool Division, Catalog No. 7*. Saginaw MI, circa 1930. 128 pgs. $32.
Measuring Tapes, Rules, etc. 1924. $35.
Catalog No. 8. circa 1930s. 160 pgs. $20.

DAVID LUPTON'S SONS COMPANY. *Fire Proof Windows, Architectural and Ornamental Sheet Metal Work*. Philadelphia, 1906. 164 pgs. $100.

LYDIA E. PINKHAM MEDICINE CO. *Lydia E. Pinkham's Private Text-Book*. "Upon Ailments Peculiar to Women". Lynn MA, circa 1900. $15-$20.

LYMAN WOOD MFG. *Buggy, Wagon, Saddlery Specialties*. Circa 1900. 178 pgs. $100.

J. LYNN & CO. *Wholesale Catalog*. New York, circa 1880. Novelties, etc. 8vo. 80 pgs. $50. 1897 edition. 96 pgs. $30.
Latest Catalog & Guide to Rapid Wealth. New York, circa 1890. Knives, toys, musical instruments, watches, etc. 46 pgs. $35.
Jewelry, etc. 1904. 80 pgs. $40.

LYON BROTHERS. *Bargain Bulletin No. 17*. Misc. popular priced merchandise. Chicago IL, 1903. 32 pgs. $25.
Fall Specialties for 1899. Stoves, housewares, clocks. 32 pgs. $45.
Guns, Jewelry, Furniture. 1899. 4to, 72 pgs. $50.

LYON & HEALY. *Illustrated Catalog of Band Uniforms*. Chicago, 1880. 44 pgs. $225. 1883 edition. Color lithos. 72 pgs. $200-$400. 1890 edition. 8 pgs. only. $55.
Musical Handbook. circa 1905. Includes instruments and talking machines. 288 pgs. $195.

SURCINGLE BLANKETS.

Surcingle Blankets fit close to the horse, have two surcingles with patent clasps, and can not be pulled off. Particularly adapted for stable or shipping horses. Note our specially close prices.

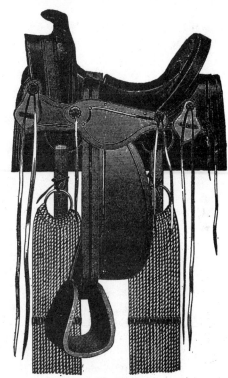

No. 7503.

No. 7503 Colorado Saddle (buh), fine quality russet leather, double tie girth or cinches, large fenders, full underskirts, leather covered rings, 2 inch lined and laced stirrup leathers, high Cheyenne cantle, strictly high class workmanship and material, and one of the best sellers in this style saddle we have; best quality Louisville tanned leather, each $13 75
No. 7504 Same as 7503, with llama pockets, each $17 00

M

MACK TRUCK. *1939 Brochure* , 3 pg. fold-out, color. $35. Ditto, 2 pgs. $22.
1930s Maintenance Manual. 136 pgs. $20.
Mack Truck Catalogs. Dating from 1931 to 1981. Auction, $3,800 for a lot of 12.

MACKELLAR, SMITHS & JORDAN CO. *Specimens of Printing Type.* Philadelphia, 1890. 510 pgs. $175.

WALTER MACKINTOSH. *Scientific Kite Catalog.* Springfield MA, 1899. 16 mo, 10 pgs. $35.

MACY FURNITURE CO. *Office Furnishings Catalog.* Grand Rapids MI, 1921. 36 pgs. $25.

R. H. MACY & CO. *Fall & Winter Catalog, 1909-1910.* 8vo. 448 pgs. $100.
Spring & Summer, 1911. New York. 454 pgs. $75.
High Quality Groceries. New York, 1919. 92 pgs. $20.

THOMAS MADDOCKS SONS CO. *Catalog G., Bathroom Fixtures.* NJ, 1916. 162 pgs. Morocco binding. $50.

AUGUST MAGG. *Bakehouse Utensils & Tools.* Baltimore, 1890. 42 pgs. $75.

MAGNAVOX COMPANY. *Magnavox Anti-Noise Telephones.* Oakland CA, 1922. 36 pgs. $65.

E. F. MAHADY CO. *Catalog of Surgical Instruments, etc.* Boston, circa 1915. 416 pgs. $75. Another, 458 pgs. stained. $35.

MAHER & GROSH CUTLERY. *A Good Razor. How to Choose It.* Toledo OH, circa 1895-1900. 32 pgs. $35-$45.
Hand Forged, Razor Steel Pocket Cutlery. Catalog No. 32. Circa 1900. Knives, razors, revolvers, fishing gear, etc. 80 pgs. $125.
1916 Pocket Cutlery. $65. 1886 ed. 56 pgs. $150.
Catalog No. 48. 1927. 8vo, 96 pgs. $65-$100.

MAIL POUCH TOBACCO CO. *Catalog of Premiums.* Wheeling WV, 1917. 8vo, 32 pgs. $20-$30.

MAINE MFG. CO. *White Mountain Refrigerators.* Maine, 1901. 16mo, 32 pgs. $50-$75.

MAJESTIC MFG. CO. *Range Comparison.* Woodstoves. St. Louis, circa 1915. 16 pgs. $20.

MALLEABLE STEEL RANGES. *Wood Stoves.* 1902. 40 pgs. $25.

MANCHESTER LOCOMOTIVE WORKS. *Amoskeag Steam Fire Engines and Hose Carriages Catalog.* Manchester NH, 1899. 54 pgs. $250. 1903 edition. $225.

MANDEL BROS. *Shopping Guide No. 58.* Chicago, 1884. 4to. 136 pgs. $125.
Great January Sale. 1897. 33 pgs. $20.
Spring & Summer 1911. 128 pgs. $35.
Fall & Winter 1903. 206 pgs. $45.
Christmas Catalog 1914. 40 pgs. $25.

MANHATTAN ELECTRICAL SUPPLY CO. *Descriptive Pamphlet of Electric Telephones.* New York, circa 1895 2nd ed. 48 pgs. $85. 1898 edition includes toy trains, lamps, household items. 872 pgs., 8vo. $125-$175.

MANHEIM CO. *Jewelry Catalog.* NY, 1942. Folio. 334 pgs. $25-$45.

MANNING, MAXWELL & MOORE. Huge Catalog of railway, steamship, machinist, factory and mill supplies. Thousands of line drawings. New York, 1902. 1,000 pgs. $150-$200.
1885 Catalog of Portable Forges. from same distributor. 24 pgs. $50-$75.

MARBLE ARMS & MFG. CO. *Outing Equipment.* Knives, gun sights. Gladstone MI, 1931. 12mo, 48 pgs. $25.

MARCH BROTHERS. *Catalog No. 132. Books for Teachers.* Includes holiday decorations, etc. Lebanon OH, 1913. 80 pgs., 12mo. $30.

MARLIN FIREARMS CO. *Manufacturers of Marlin Repeating Rifles, etc.* New Haven CT, 1897. 190 pgs. Illustrated. $150.
Firearms. Handbook for Shooters. 1910. 160 pgs. $35.
1911 Catalog. 12mo, 122 pgs. $35.

MARMON. *Automobile Catalog.* Circa 1923. 24 pgs. $45.

JOHN MARSELLUS CASKET COMPANY. *Casket Catalog.* Circa 1915. 112 pgs. $50.

MARSHALL FIELD. *Notions & Fancy Goods 1890-91.* 359 pgs. Large Toy Section. $450.
Jewelry Department. Chicago, 1893. 9x11, 300 pgs. $150.
Jewelry, Watches, Silverware, Cut Glass. Counter Sales Book. 1914-15. 264 pgs. $100.
Fashions of the Hour. Christmas 1957. $25.

W. E. MARSHALL CO. *Marshall's Matchless Seeds.* 1933 catalog. 120 pgs. $12.

MARSHALL-WELLS HARDWARE CO. *Catalog No. 40. Mining, Railway, etc.* MN, OR & Canada. 1903. 1,136 pgs. $75.

MARSHFIELD MFG. CO. *Bee Keepers Supplies.* Marshfield WI, 1927. 34 pgs. $15.

MARVIN SAFE CO. *Folder, 10 panels.* New York, circa 1880. $65.

MASON FENCE CO. *Wirefencing & Fence Supplies.* Leesburg OH, 1906. 32 pgs. $12.

MASON & HAMLIN ORGAN CO. *Illus. Catalog of Cabinet Organs.* Boston MA, circa 1871. 20 pgs. $125-$175.

MASSBACK HARDWARE. *Wholesale Catalog.* 1931. 796 pgs. $75.

MAST, FOOS & CO. *Catalog No. 10 Pumps and Windmills.* Springfield OH, circa 1890. 144 pgs. $100.

P. P. MAST & CO. *Descriptive Circular of Buckeye Agricultural Tools.* Springfield OH, 1882. 12 pgs. $25.

MASTEN & WELLS. *Assorted Fireworks.* Boston, 1887. 72 pgs., 16mo. $125.
Fireworks, Flags, Lanterns. 1882. 4to. 8 pgs. $80.
New England Laboratory Fireworks. 72 pgs. Fine and clean complete. $300.
Price List for 1908. 88 pgs., illus. Near Mint. $300-$400.

MATCH BOX TOYS. *1971 Catalog, USA Edition.* $25.

JOHN MATTHEWS. *Matthews Catalog of Soda Fountain Apparatus.* New York, 1886. 104 pgs. $500.

MAULE SEED BOOK FOR 1906. Philadelphia, 1906. 152 pgs. $60.

L. & C. MAYER. *Jewelry.* New York, 1925. Silverware, clocks, watches. 4to, 106 pgs. $50.
Wholesale Catalog. 1932. 220 pgs. $50.
Jewelry and Giftware. 1949. $30.

MAXWELL MOTOR COMPANY. *Catalog for 1913* (all models). 4to, 31 pgs. $65.
The "25". 1912-13. 24 pgs. $35.
The "25". 1915. 45 pgs. $75.
Catalog for 1915. (all models). $65.
The Maxwell. NY, 1907. 32 pgs. $65.

F. MAYER & CO. *Illus. Catalog of Furniture for 1886.* Chicago, 186. 64 pgs. 4to. $120.

MC ALLISTER & BROTHERS. *Spectacles, Telescopes, Photo Equipment.* 3rd edition. Philadelphia, 1855. 84 pgs. $450.

T. H. MC ALLISTER. *Stereopticons and Magic Lanterns.* NY, 1890. 194 pgs., 8vo. $195-$350. Dec, 1891. $95. 1901, 88 pgs. $125. 1906, 84 pgs. $75.

ARTHUR MC ARTHUR & CO. *Manufacturers & Dealers.* Furniture, carpets, house furnishing goods. Boston, circa 1880. 264 pgs. $200.

MC ARTHUR, WIRTH & CO. *Butchers & Packers Tools & Machinery.* Syracuse NY, 190. 84 pgs. of everything from showcase, to scales, to fly fans. $40-$50.

MC CALL QUARTERLY. *Winter 1923 Fashion Pattern Catalog.* VG. $30. May 1938. 12x14. 718 pages. $65.

MC CINTOSH COMPANY. *Stereopticon Catalog.* Chicago, circa 1895. $60.

C. M. MC CLUNG & CO. *Wholesale Hardware Catalog.* Knoxville TN, 1891. 762 pgs. 4to. $250-$400.

A. C. MC CLURG & CO. *Catalog of Stationery & Sundries.* Chicago, 1918-1919. 11x14 in. 338 pgs. $85.

MC CORMICK HARVESTING MACHINE CO. *The Pride of the New Century.* Catalog of reapers, binders, mowers. Chicago, 1901. 40 pgs. $75.
58th Annual Catalog. 1889. 40 pgs. $100.
(Also see International Harvester.)

MC CURDY POULTRY EQUIPMENT. *Catalog of founts, feeders, egg sizers, brooders, etc.* OH, 1934. $16.

MC KEE GLASS CO. *Catalog No. 2, Baking Ware.* Jeannette PA, 1917. 22 pgs. $20.

MC LAUGHLIN BROS. *Catalog of Valentines, Comics and New Novelties.* New York, 1891. 12 pgs. $100-$180.

MC LISTER BROS. KENNELS. *Coon Hounds.* Tennessee, circa 1925. 4x7. 100 pgs. $25.

MC WHORTER WEAVER & CO. *The Buyers Guide No. 118*. Wholesale general merchandise. Nashville, 1924. 112 pgs. $50-$75.

E. C. MEACHAM ARMS CO. *Sporting & Military Ammunition, Guns, Rifles & Pistols*. St. Louis, 1881. 96 pgs., 8vo. Full pg. plates of guns & accessories. $250-$325. *Catalog for April, 1887*. Baseball, guns, tackle, bicycles, etc. 130 pgs. $125.

MEAD CYCLE COMPANY. *The Oldest Bicycle House in America*. Chicago, 1910. 28 pgs. $35.
"Ranger" Bicycles & Supplies. 1918. 64 pgs. $80. 1920. 12 pgs. $50.
1000 Reasons to Ride a Ranger Bicycle. Chicago, 1914. 12mo. 48 pgs. $30.

JAMES MEANS & CO. *James Means $3 Shoe*. Boston, 1887. 21 pgs., 12mo. Color and line illus. of various occupations wearing Means shoes. $60-$75.

MECO. *Guaranteed Motorcycle Supplies*. Hammondsport NY, 1928. 10x7. 40 pgs. $40.

MEGOW'S CATALOG NO. 10. *Model Airplanes, Boats, Trains*. 1941. 128 pgs. $50-$75.
Catalog No. 9. 1941. 32 pgs. $25.

GEO. H. MELLEN CO. *Seed Catalog*. Springfield OH, 1907. 96 pgs. $15.

MENEELY BELL COMPANY. *Manufacturers of Church, Tower, Factory, Fire and Other Bells*. Troy NY, 1880. 48 pgs. $125. 1906 ed. 44 pgs. $60. 1926 ed. 20 pgs. $25.

MERIDEN BRITANNIA CO. *Electro Plated Nickel Silver Goods*. Meriden CT, circa 1867. 4to, 190 pgs. $300. Another, 1867. Folio, 152 pgs. $350-$450. Another, 1873. Folio, 78 pgs. $150.
The Silver Standard. Vols. 4 and 5. 1908. $25.
"1847 Rogers Bros." Silverplated Spoons. 1881 price list. 68 pgs. $60.

J. S. MERRELL DRUG CO. *Catalog of Drugs & Medical Supplies*. St. Louis MO, 1914. 80 pgs. $80-$125.

MERSMAN TABLES. *Furniture Catalog*. Celina OH, 1936. 88 pgs. $25.

C. S. MERSICK & CO. *Catalog No. 19H. Factory Supplies*. New Haven CT, 1919. 969 pgs. Hard cover. $40.

GEORGE L. MESKER & CO. *Metal Store Fronts*. Circa 1895. 32 pgs. $175.
Catalolg of Standard Store Fronts. Evansville IN, 1904. 32 pgs. $95.

THE METALLIC CAP MFG. CO. 8 pgs. of Blasting Caps. NYC, 1870s-80s. $40.

METROPOLITAN SEWING MACHINE CO. *Instruction Book and Illustrated Price List*. NY, 1910. 100 pgs. $20.

METROPOLITAN WASHING MACHINE CO. *Doty's Clothes Washer*. New York, 1867. 16 pgs. $45.

MEXICAN ART & CURIOSITY STORE. *Catalog of Mexican Art & Curios*. Jewelry, Pottery, Blankets, etc. El Paso, 1888. 12mo, 88 pgs. $85.

FRED C. MEYER & CO. *Musical Instruments Catalog*. Philadelphia, 1924. 48 pgs. $75.

S. F. MEYERS & CO. *Catalog No. 98*. Jewelry, watches, silverware, etc. New York, 1898. 740 pgs. $200.

WILLIAM MEYERS CO. *Bargain House Catalog No. 26*. Philadelphia, 1900. 160 pgs. $75.

E. B. MEYROWITZ. *Sun Dials, Catalog*. New York, 1914. 56 pgs. $40.

MIAMI CYCLE & MFG. CO. *The Racycle*. Early safety bike. Middletown OH, 1903. 24 pgs. $60.

MICHELL'S SEEDS. *Bulbs, Plants*. 1928. 184 pgs. $35.
Wholesale Seeds. 1928. 10 pgs. $20.

MIFFLINBURG BUGGY CO. *Catalog No. 8. High-Grade Work*. Circa 1900. 37 pgs. $75.

MILBURN WAGON CO. *Booklet No. 105. The Milburn Way*. Toledo OH, circa 1910. 48 pgs. $70.

MILES KIMBALL CO. *Christmas Toy Catalog*. 1957. 63 pgs. $15.

CHARLES A. MILLEN & CO. *Mouldings, Trim, Stair Rails, Balusters, Wash Stands, Mantels, etc.* Boston, 1891. 12mo, 96 pgs. Fine illustrations. $125.

MILLER HARNESS COMPANY. *Catalog No. 33*. New York, 1934. Sadles, bridles, etc. 40 pgs. 8vo. $40.

MILLER LOCK CO. *Champion Locks, Catalog No. 9*. Philadelphia, circa 1890. 16 pgs. $75.

MILLER, SAMUEL C. *Neon Signs. Manufacture, Installation, Maintenance*. NY, 1935. Illustrated. Fine. $50.

MILLER STOCKMAN SUPPLY CO. *Western Wear, Saddles, Tack, etc.* Catalog No. 71, Denver CO, 1946. 34 pgs. $35. 1951 edition. 64 pgs. $25.

MILLERS FALLS TOOLS. *Catalog No. J*. Millers Falls MA, 1912. 16mo. 173 pgs. $30.
Catalog No. L. Circa 1916. 16mo, 219 pgs. $20.

THOMAS MILLS & BRO. INC. *Ice Cream Manufacturers' Equipment*. Philadelphia PA, circa 1915. 60 pgs. $30.
Confectioners' Machinery and Equip. 1924 catalog. 219 pgs. $125.

MINE & SMELTER SUPPLY. *Catalog No. 24 Assayers' & Chemists' Supplies*. Denver, El Paso, Salt Lake, NY, 1912. 595 pgs. $50.

MISSOURI TENT & AWNING CO. Catalog of tents, awnings, canvas feed bags, wagon covers, circus tents, etc. St. Louis, 1883. 24 pgs. $95-$125.

MITCHELL MOTORS CO. *1915 Specifications*. 24 pgs. $30.

ROBERT MITCHELL FURNITURE CO. *Catalog No. 38. Mantels & Fireplaces*. Cincinnati OH, 1903. 72 pgs. $75.

M. MITSHKUN CO. *Catalog G*. Detroit MI, 1915. Everything from toys to farm equip. and railway supplies. Very unusual. 408 pgs. 8x11 in. $200.

MODEL PORTRAIT & FRAME CO. *Catalog No. 21*. Chicago, 1913. Picture frames, stereo views. 36 pgs. $40.

MODERN WOODMEN OF AMERICA. *Supply Department Catalog*. Rock Island IL, 1928. 72 pgs. $25.
1905 edition. Uniforms, banners, flags, ribbons. 12mo, 236 pgs. $100.

A. B. MOLER. *The Barbers' Hairdressers' & Manicurers Manual*. NY, 1900. Instructions, materials and prices. 117 pgs., 16mo. $50. (Also see Book Section.)

MONEY IN MUSHROOMS. National Spawn & Mushroom Co. Boston, 1907. 32 pgs. $20.

MONTGOMERY WARD. (See Ward, Montgomery)

MOORE BROS. *Our Silent Salesman - 14th Edition*. Catalog of Veterinary Supplies. Albany NY, 1915. 64 pgs. $100.

MOORE & EVANS. *Watches, Diamonds, Silverware, Clocks*. Chicago, 1898. 4to, 392 pgs. $85.
Our Monthly Salesman. 1913. 4to, 32 pgs. Jewelry and sporting goods. $35.
General Merchandise Catalog. 1913. 424 pgs. $50-$75.
Our Salesman No. 66. 1936. 320 pgs. $45.

MORGAN WOODWORK CO. *Building With Assurance*. Millwork catalog. Stained glass, etc. Oshkosh WI, 1921. 408 pgs. $50-$100. Another, 1923. 439 pgs. 79 color plates of interiors. $80-$100.

MORRIS & CO. *Meat products packed by Morris*. Chicago, circa 1905. 199 pgs., 12mo. Color illus. $75-$100.

ANDREW J. MORSE & SON, INC. *Diving Apparatus and Submarine Appliances*. Boston MA, 1937. 51 pgs. 4to. $200-$300.

MORTON & BRET. *The Blue Book of Speed*. Wholesale racing accessories. Indianapolis, 1931. 32 pgs. $75.

C. M. MOSEMAN & BROS. *Moseman's Illus. Guide For Purchasers of Horse Furnishing Goods*. New York, circa 1879. Folio, 305 pages. Mint in orig. box. "The most outstanding record ever issued." (6) brilliant color plates. $1,000-1,500. Modern reprints. $25-$50.

MOTORLA INC. *Motor Golden View Television*. Chicago, 1949. 42 pgs. 4to. $50.
Motorola Radios. 1946. 32 pgs. $20.

J. L. MOTT IRON WORKS. *Plumbing and Sanitary Dept.* New York, 1881. 248 pgs. From toilets to sinks. Very elaborate. $250-$350. Reprint by Dover. $15.
Ornate iron settees, chairs, tables, tree guards. NYC, 1906. 64 pgs. $200.
Metal Stable, Barn & Pig Pen Fittings. New York, 1892. 232 pgs. $250.
Modern Plumbing. 1911. 79 pgs. $35.

W. H. MULLINS. *Sheet Metal, Architectural Ornaments*. Salem OH, 1894. 168 pgs. $150.
Sheet Metal Finials, Weather Vanes, etc. Circa 1894. 22 pgs. Folio. $300.
Mullins Pressed Steel Boats. Circa 1908. 48 pgs. 8vo. $100-$200. Another, 1903. 36 pgs. $85.

WILBER H. MURRAY MFG. CO. *World-Renowned Buggies and Harness*. Cincinnati OH, 1889. 8vo. $100.
Everything You Need for a Horse. Cincinnati, 1890. 146 pgs. $150-$200.
Carriage Catalog for Season of 1905. Cincinnati, 1905. 146 pgs. $125.

FRED W. MUTH CO. *1923 Bee Supply Catalog*. Cincinnati OH, 1923. 8vo, 40 pgs. $30.

S. D. MYRES SADDLE CO. *Fine Stock Saddles, Ranch Supplies and Art Leather Goods*. El Paso, circa 1930. 8vo, 80 pgs. $65.
Officers' Equipment. 1939. 31 pgs. $60.

S. F. MYERS & CO. *Catalog of Watchmakers' Supplies*. New York, circa 1890. 155 pgs. $150.

MYSTO MFG. CO. *Supplement Catalog of Magic, Illusions*. New Haven CT, circa 1920. 42 pgs. 8vo. $35.

N

NARRAGANSETT MACHINE CO. *Catalog of Gymnastic Apparatus*. Providence RI, 1925. Hardcover. 250 pgs. $75-$95.

NASH MOTORS COMPANY. *The New 400 Series Enclosed Cars*. Kenosha WI circa 1926. 24 pgs. $40.
Get Ready to Drive a New Kind of Car. Nash, 1941. 28 pgs. $28.
The Nash Special Six. 1927. 16 pgs. $30.
Nash Family Album. 1954. 80 pgs. $15.

E. NASON & CO. *Wholesale Catalog*. Novelties, notions. New York. 1881-1891 editions. $25-$35 each.

NATIONAL CASH REGISTER CO. *Catalog, Testimonials, etc*. Circa 1890. 12mo, 344 pgs. $75.
Illustrated Cash Registers. Circa 1905, 22 pg. fold-out. $80-$95.
Storekeeper's Dream. Dayton OH, 1909. 8vo, 32 pgs. $35.

NATIONAL CASKET COMPANY. *Catalog No. 19. Mechanics of Embalming*. USA, 1907. 332 pgs. $50.

NATIONAL CLOAK & SUIT CO. *1909-1926 Catalogs*. Fall & Winter and Spring & Summer editions of 140 to 500 pages. Some have H. C. Christy covers. $75-$100 each. Smaller catalogs of 20 to 90 pages sell for $25-$35.

NATIONAL COLORTYPE CO. INC. *Safety on the Highways with Fireball Signs*. Bellevue KY, 1939. 32 pgs. $25.

NATIONAL DAIRY MACHINE CO. *Cream Separator Catalog*. Newark, 1900. 8vo, 16 pgs. $20.

NATIONAL HARNESS CO. *Catalog of Oak Tanned Harnesses*. Buffalo NY, 1886. 20 pgs. $45.

NATIONAL LEAD COMPANY. *Paint and Decorating Catalogs*. New York, 1906. 40 pgs. $25. 1909, 26 pgs. $30. 1910. 6 pg. folder with color chips. $50.

NATIONAL MAGIC CO. *No. 7. Magic Supplies and Novelties*. 1947. 350 pgs. $50.

NATIONAL MOTOR VEHICLE CO. *National "40"*. Indianapolis, 1910. Many racing victories. 20 pgs. $100.

NATIONAL PHONOGRAPH CO. *Edison Phonographs*. Orange NJ, 1899. 24 pgs. $150-$200.
1903-1905 Editions. $50-$100 ea.
British, European Records. 1907. $40.
American Selections, Edison Records. Orange NJ, 1909. 68 pgs. $40.

NATIONAL SCHOOL FURNITURE CO. *Catalog of New School and Church Furniture*. NY, 1873. 46 pgs., 8vo. Chairs, bells, maps, clocks, globes, etc. $75-$100.

NATIONAL SPORTSMAN. *Encyclopedia of Sports Goods*. Boston MA, 1908. 384 pgs. $65.

NATIONAL SUPPLY CO. *Oil and Gas Well Supplies. Cat. No. 25*. Pipes and Tools for oil drilling rigs. Toledo OH, 1917. 761 pgs. $125.

NATIONAL WASHBOARD CO. *Catalog of Washboards*. Chicago, circa 1925. 8vo, 36 pgs., full color. $75.

NEIL NIELSON. *Barber's Supplies*. Buffalo NY, circa 1905. 96 pgs. 4to. $125-$150.

NEIMAN MARCUS. *Christmas Catalogs*.
1961 to 1975...................................$20-$30.
1976 to 1983..................................$10-$15.

M. L. NELSON CO. *Wholesale Furniture Catalog*. Chicago, circa 1910. 224 pgs. $75.

LOUIS E. NEUMAN & CO. *Cigar Box Labels*. Sample Book. (7) plates, circa 1890. $150.

NEW HAVEN FOLDING CHAIR CO. *18th Annual Illustrated Catalog*. New Haven CT, 1880. 72 pgs. $135.

NEW HOME SEWING MACHINE CO. *The World's Best Sewing Machine*. Orange MA, 1919. 16mo, 16 pgs. $20.
Directions for Using. Circa 1880. 8vo, 24 pgs. $35-$50.

NEWHOUSE STEEL TRAPS. *Catalog for Hunter, Trapper*. Oneida Community Limited. Kenwood NY, circa 1890. 16 pgs., 16mo. $50.

NEW JERSEY BRUSH CO. *Brush Catalog*. Bloomfield NJ, circa 1905. 72 pgs. $45.

A. G. NEWMAN. *Illus. Catalog of Fine Hardware*. NY, circa 1895. Folio, 416 pgs. Fine engravings. $250-$300.

NEW YORK BATH MFG. CO. *Infant Bath & Toilet Tables*. Nursery clothes drier, swings, doll tubs, etc. Circa 1910. 30 illus. $40.

NEW YORK BIRD STORE. *Illustrated Catalog of Live Birds, Talking Parrots*. Pittsburgh PA, circa 1910. 64 pgs. 12mo. $75.

NEW YORK LIGHTING FIXTURE CO. *Catalog of Exclusive Designs*. New York, circa 1920. 55 pgs. $35.

NEW YORK SPORTING GOODS CO. *Catalog No. 53*. New York, 1912. 12mo. 434 pgs. $40.
No. 66D, Sporting Goods Blue Book. 1916-17. $95.
Sportsmen's Hand Book. Hunting, fishing, camping, bicycles, skates, baseball. 1914. 12mo, 472 pgs. $60.
Bicycles & Bicycle Supplies, 1913-1914. 12mo. $35.

NICHOLAS-BEAZLEY AIRPLANE CO. *Aeronautical Parts & Supplies*. Early barnstorming days catalog. Marshall MO, 1931. 4to, 96 pgs. $125-$175.

NICHOLS AND STONE CO. *Catalog No. 5. Chairs and Settees*. Gardner MA, 1921. 88 pgs. $75.

NICHOLSON FILE CO. *File & Tool Catalog of 1894*. $75.
File Filosophy - 12th Edition 1922. Providence RI, 1922. 12mo, 48 pgs. $25.

NOKES & NICOLAI. *Musical, Equip*. 1910. 96 pgs. $60.

T. NOONAN & SONS. *Barber's & Hairdresser's Furniture*. Boston MA, circa 1914. 32 pgs. $45-$65.

NORDYKE & MARMON CO. *International Champion. The Marmon Automobile*. Indianapolis, 1911. 32 pgs. $75.

B. F. NORRIS, ALISTER & CO. *13th Annual Catalog. Jewelry, Clocks, Optical Goods*. Chicago, 1893. 544 pgs. $95-$150.

NORTH BROS. MFG. CO. *"Yankee" Tool Book*. Spiral-drive drills, screwdrivers. Philadelphia. 1900 to 1925 editions. $25-$35 each.

NORTHERN FURNITURE CO. *Catalog No. 33*. Bedroom & dining room. Sheboygan WI, 1921. Folio, 79 pgs. $50.

NORTHWESTERN SCHOOL OF TAXIDERMY. *Catalog No. 67. Taxidermist's Supplies*. Omaha, 1925. 26 pgs. $12.

NORWALK LOCK CO. *Locks and Builders Hardware*. Folio size, highly illus., hard cover. Norwalk CT, 1890. 380 pgs. $250-$375.

Number 490 BREAST PIN

This magnificent Pin is gold-plated. The American flag at top is hand-painted in red, white, and blue enamel colors. Beneath swings the Star of Cuba, hand-painted in red, white, and blue.
SAMPLE, by mail, **6 CENTS**
One Dozen, by mail, **60 Cents**
One Dozen, by express, **55 Cents**

PERFUME REVOLVER.
SAMPLE, by mail, 3 CENTS.

This Perfume Revolver, size of our en graving, has a rubber handle. By putting the end of the barrel into perfume, and squeezing the rubber handle, you fill the revolver with perfume; then by pressing the handle again you can send a spray of perfume twenty feet. The Perfume Revolver

Number 456 BREAST PIN.

This is a beautiful gold-plated pin, shape of a key. From the key swings a blue turquoise heart.
Sample, by mail...............................12 cents

NOVELTY CATALOGS. Between 1885 and 1910 dozens of small mail-order firms issued cheaply printed paperback catalogs of 32 to 64 pages. These were aimed at young people and unsophisticated rural folk. The exaggerated line drawings featured pocket knives, watches, sewing notions, novelties, gadgets, jewelry, and small toys. Average price range for these pulp-paper productions is $25 to $35.

HENRY NURRE. *"The First Moulding Factory in the West."* Cincinnati, circa 1905. 272 pgs. of pictures and frames. $200.

WALLACE NUTTING. *Supreme Edition*. Catalog of Early American furniture reproductions. 1930. $85-$125.
7th Edition. 1928. 80 pgs. $75.

O

OAKLAND MOTOR CAR CO. *Oakland Sensible Six*. Circa 1925. 16 pg. sales brochure. $50. Same, ca 1915. $50-$60.

OAKLAND POULTRY YARDS. Bantams to Game cocks, etc. Wonderful color litho catalog. Oakland CA, 1891. 84 pgs. $350.

THOS. OAKS & CO. *Police Uniforms*. 1913. 16 pgs. Color illustrations. $95.

ODIN STOVE MFG. CO. *Gas Cooking Appliance Catalog*. Erie PA, 1932. 24 pgs. $20.

OHIO CARRIAGE MFG. CO. *Split Hickory Vehicles*. Columbus OH, 1914. 140 pgs. $125. 1917. 188 pgs. $135. *Annual Bargain Catalog*. Circa 1923. 98 pgs. $50.

OHIO RAKE CO. *Agricultural Implements*. 1906. 8vo, 56 pgs. $30.

OHIO CULTIVATOR CO. *Catalog of Sulky & Walking Cultivators*. Bellevue OH, 1894. 16 pgs. $35.

OIL WELL SUPPLY CO. *Catalog of Oil Well Supplies*. 1907. 368 pgs. 6x9. $49. 1916. 690 pgs. 16mo. $45.

OLD HICKORY CHAIR CO. *1910 Chair Catalog*. Rustic-style. Martinsville IN. 40 pgs. $45-$75.

OLDSMOBILE. *Hydra-matic Drive*. Lansing, 1947. 16 pgs. "No clutch pedal in the car." $15.
Oldsmobile for 1952. Rockets to New Highs. Showroom brochure. $20.
1958 Brochure with specs. $9.
1961 Oldsmobile Classic 98. Folder. $25.

OLDS MOTOR WORKS. *Refined Oldsmobile Six is Here*. Lansing MI, circa 1926. 4 pgs. $25.
Oldsmobile. 1910-11. 20 pgs. $125.

OLIVER CHILLED PLOW WORKS. *8 pg. fold out advertising sheet*. South Bend IN, 1885. $25.

OLIVER TYPEWRITER CO. *The Oliver Typewriter*. 1902. 24 pgs. 8vo. $25-$45. 1904. $40. 1907. $25.

ONANDAGA INDIAN WIGWAM CO. *The Lively Line for Lively Youngsters*. Syracuse NY, 1914. 36 pgs., 8vo. Playsuits, from policeman to Indian Chief. $50.

ONEIDA CARRIAGE WORKS. *Vehicles for the Trade*. Oneida NY, circa 1895. 32 pgs. $95.

ONEIDA COMMUNITY LTD. *Hardware Specialties Catalog*. Kenwood NY, circa 1898-1900. 102 pgs. $75. *Newhouse Steel Traps*. NY, circa 1890. 16 pgs. $50.

ORINOKA MILLS. *Draperies & Color Harmony Catalog*. Circa 1920. 24 pgs. $20.

ORNAMENTAL PRODUCTS CO. *Catalog No. 9 Lignine Wood Carvings*. Detroit MI circa 1925. 38 pgs. $50.

ORNAMENTAL WOOD CO. *Natural Wood Ornaments*. Drawer pulls, rosettes, cherubs, etc. Bridgeport, 1877. 67 pgs. $175.

ORR, PAINTER & CO. *Sunshine Stoves & Ranges*. Reading PA, circa 1880s. 8 pgs. $20.

J. J. OSBORN & CO. *Manufacturers of Fine Carriages*. New Haven CT, circa 1885. 14 pgs. Fine line illus. $100.

C. S. OSBORNE & CO. *Trimmer's Tools, Catalog No. 10*. Leather working supplies. Newark NJ, circa 1925. 28 pgs. $25-$35.

D. M. OSBORNE & CO. *Harvesting Machinery - 28th Annual Catalog*. Auburn NY, 1884. 8vo, 16 pgs. $50.
Osborne 20th Century Book No. 8. 56 pgs. of woodcut illustrations. Circa 1893. $50.
Care of Stock and Other Valuable Information. Circa 1900. 56 pgs. Farm equip. $75.

OSHKAMP NOLTING & CO. *Optional Goods*. OH, 1905. Oculist supplies, lenses, etc. 4to, 110 pgs. $75.

OVERMAN WHEEL COMPANY. *Victor Tricycles*. Springfield MA, 1883. 24 pgs. $125.
Victor Sunlights. 1885. 14 pgs. color. $150. Boston, 1894. 12 pgs. 5 color plates of bicycle scenes. $75-$100.
Victor Bicycles. Pocket catalog. 1899. 16 pgs. $75.

P

PACKARD MOTOR CARS. *1928-1941 Accessory Catalogs.* $75-$150 each.
1936 Senior Cars Accessories. $75-$150.
1936 Junior Cars. $50-$100.
1956 The New Clipper. 8 pgs. $15-$25.
1929-1930 Deluxe Boxed Color Portfolios. 9-11 color plates. Mint. $150-$300.
1940 Super 8. Hardbound. $175.
Pre-1941 Accessory Catalogs. $100 and up.

EMIL J. PAIDAR CO. *Catalog No. 32 Barber Shop and Beauty Parlor Equip.* 1928. 123 pgs. (damp stained). $100. 1921 Edition. (soiled, worn). $125.

PAINE FURNITURE MANUFACTORY. *Eastlake Black Walnut Furniture.* Boston MA, circa 1880. 28 pgs. $100. *Catalog of Folding Beds, etc.* Circa 1880. 24 pgs. $100. *Showcase Catalog.* circa 1880s. $100.

PALM LETTER CO. *Sample Book of Transfer Letters.* Cincinnati OH, 1899. 11x16. 24 pgs. Some in color. $125.

PARAMOUNT ELECTRICAL SUPPLY. *Artistic Lighting Fixtures.* 1920s catalog. 88 pgs. $35.

PARIS MANUFACTURING CO. *Catalog of Children's Sleds.* Paris, Maine, circa 1910. 20 pgs. $75-$125.

PARKE DAVIS & CO. *1887 Catalog.* 116 pgs. $65.
Catalog of the Laboratories. 1898. 224 pgs. $25-$50.
Manufacturing Chemists. 1904. 399 pgs. $50-$75.
Standardized Products. 1911, 16mo, 50 pgs. $25.

EDWIN PARKER CO. *Illustrated Catalog of Natural Wood Ornaments.* New York, 1891. 28 pgs. $60.

PARKER & WOOD. *Illustrated Catalog of Agricultural Tools, Machines.* Boston MA, 1891. 216 pgs. $125.

PARLIN & ORENDORFF MACHINERY CO. *Catalog No. 69. Agricultural Implements.* Later merged with International Harvester. 1911 edition, 444 pgs. $125.

HORACE PARTRIDGE CO. *Catalog No. 112. Athletic Goods.* Cleveland OH. Fall & Winter 1925. 80 pgs. $35.

PASSAIC AGRICULTURAL CHEMICAL WORKS. *Catalog of Standard Fertilizers.* 1878. Bird's eye view of plant. 64 pgs. $50.

PATRICK & CARTER CO. *House Goods and General Electrical Supplies.* Philadelphia, 1896. 152 pgs., folio. Bells, burglar alarms, electric clocks, etc. $160-$225.

PATRICK, CARTER & WILKINS. *Catalog of Electrical House Goods.* 1906. 72 pgs. $63.

COMFORT, PAXSON & CO. *Undertakers' Hardware.* Philadelphia, 1886. 4to, 36 pgs. $75.

PEARCE, INNIS & CO. *Furniture Catalog for 1893.* Rushville IN, 1893. 48 pgs. $95.

BEN PEARSON, INC. *Catalog No. 16. Bows & Arrows.* Pine Bluff AR, 1941. 31 pgs. $40.

A. G. PECK & CO. *Axes and Edged Tools.* Cohoes NY, 1891. 32 pgs., 8vo. $35.

PECK & SNYDER. *Illustrated Price List A Guide for Sportsmen.* NY, 1878. 192 pgs. 12mo. Baseball, firemen's equip., magic, toys, sporting goods. $600-$1,200.
Sporting Goods. Similar catalog to above. 1879 ed. Falling to pieces. $150. Larger 1887 edition. 400 pgs. Colored wraps of sports activities. Mint. $1,000.

PECK, STOW & WILCOX CO. *Tinsmiths Tools, etc.* NY & CT, 1890. 504 pgs. $200.
Catalog No. 10A. Circa 1900. 168 pgs. $50.
Catalog No. 25A. 1927. 4to. 136 pgs. $35.

PEEK & SON. *"Opera" Pianos.* 1892. 24 pgs. $36.

PEERLESS MOTOR CAR COMPANY. *Peerless Motor Cars, 1913.* 32 pgs. $100.
Peerless Motor Cars, 1909. 32 pgs. $125.

PEIFFER BROTHERS. *Seals, Stencils, Stamps.* Office supply firm. Philadelphia, circa 1890. 8vo, 32 pgs. $45.

PENINSULAR STOVE CO. *Catalog of Heating & Cooking Stoves.* Chicago, 1900. 128 pgs. $50-$100.
Catalog No. 625 Peninsular Stoves. 1925. 51 pgs. $45.

PENN METAL CEILING AND ROOFING CO. *Catalog of Roofing, Siding, Cornices, etc.* 34th edition, Boston, 1906. 62 pgs. $75.

PENN WALL PAPER MILLS. *Penn Wall Papers for 1942.* Approx. 80 diff. wallpaper samples in full color, 9x16 in. Bridgeton NJ, 1942. $35.

J. C. PENNEY. *Christmas Catalogs.*
1963 to 1965...........................$65-$100.
1966 to 1970...........................$40-$75.
1971 to 1975...........................$25-$50.
1976 to 1980...........................$20-$40.

J. C. PENNEY. *Fall & Winter Catalogs.*
1963 to 1965...........................$25-$40.
1966 to 1970...........................$20-$35.
1971 to 1975...........................$17-$30.
1976 to 1980...........................$15-$25.

J. C. PENNEY. *Spring & Summer Catalogs.*
1963 to 1965...........................$25-$40.
1966 to 1970...........................$20-$35.
1971 to 1975...........................$17-$30.
1976 to 1980...........................$15-$25.

J. C. PENNEY. *Summer Catalogs.*
1963 to 1975...........................$10-$15.

PEP BOYS. *Automobile Accessories.* 1932. 96 pgs. $50.

J. W. PEPPER'S COMPLETE CATALOG. *Musical Instruments & Trimmings.* Philadelphia, 1899. 128 pgs. $125.

PERFECTION STOVE CO. *New Line of Oil Cook Stoves.* Cleveland OH, 1914. 26 pgs. $20. 1920-1929 eds. $10 ea.

PERRY DAME CO. *Fall & Winter 1920. Ladies, Mens, Fashions.* 178 pgs. $80.

PERRY PICTURES. *1926 Catalog.* Includes several frameable prints. 64 pgs. $26. Another, 1925. VG. $10.

PETERS & JONES. *Wholesale Dealers in Children's Carriages.* Boston MA, 1886. 12 pgs. $100.

PETERSBURG TRUNK & BAG CO. *Manufacturers of Trunks, Bags, Cases.* Petersburg VA 1916. 52 pgs. $50.

M. PETERSON, HUMAN HAIR PRODUCTS. *Hair Jewelry, Ornaments, Goods.* Including items for Black people. 1904. 36 pgs. $75-$100.

PETTIBONE BROS. MFG. CO. *Odd Fellows Lodge Regalia.* Cincinnati, 1901, 16 pgs. $35.
Band Uniforms, Catalog No. 353. 1903. 4to, 48 pgs. $45. 1909 edition. 56 pgs. $75-$95.

Police Uniforms & Equipment. Catalog No. 302. Circa 1910. 64 pgs. $125.

PFLUEGER FISHING TACKLE. *1926 Catalog.* 120 pgs. $75. Another, circa 1931. 5x8. 130 pgs. $25.

PHILADELPHIA IRON WORKS. *Boiler Tank Catalog.* 1897. 40 pgs. $18.

PHILIPSBORN. *Fall & Winter Fashions, 1917-18.* $30.

PHOENIX GLASS CO. *The Illuminator.* Pittsburgh PA, 1918. 18 pgs. $25.

ALBERT PICK CO. *General Catalog No. E47.* Houseware, china, kitchen items. Chicago, 1947. 32 pgs. $30.

PICKARD STUDIOS. *Secrets of Correct Table Service.* Catalog/etiquette/cookbook. Chicago, 1912. $30-$60.

PICTORIAL PRINTING CO. Catalog of ornate druggist labels, billheads, etc. 4,000 examples including whiskey, cologne. Chicago, 1890's. 9x12. $750.

PIERCE, BUTLER & BUTLER. *Bathroom Fixtures.* 1903. 60 pgs. $50-$75.

PIERCE-ARROW MOTOR CAR CO. *Brilliant New Series of Eights.* Buffalo NY, 1932. 2 brochures 12 pgs. and 16 pgs. $125 both.
Quiet... Buffalo NY, 1930s. 8 pgs., black & gold. $50.

BENJAMIN PIKE'S SON & CO. *Catalog of Instruments. Drawing, Surveying & Engineering.* New York circa 1880. 110 pgs. $125.

PIONEER BUGGY CO. *1893 Catalog.* Columbus OH. 8vo, 32 pgs. $125.

PIONEER GRAIN & BEAN THRESHERS. *1924 Catalog.* 16 pgs. $15.

PIONEER MFG. CO. *Photo Buttons, Medallions.* New York, 1902. Lockets, brooches and frames for photos. 8vo, 40 pgs. $40.

PITTSBURGH ART GLASS CO. *Book of Designs.* Circa 1910. 8vo, 64 pgs., 32 in color. $100.
Catalog A. Pittsburgh Plate Glass Co. Circa 1910. 8vo, 286 pgs., 32 of stained glass. $95.
Glass, Paints and Varnishes. Pittsburgh, 1923. 184 pgs., 4to. Much color. $125.

PITTSBURGH FIREARMS CO. *Guns, Rifles, Fishing Tackle & Sporting Goods.* Pittsburgh, 1885. 60 pgs., 4to. Everything from powder flasks to baseball mitts. $200.

PITTSBURGH LAMP, BRASS, & GLASS CO. *Catalog No. 20. Portable Electric Lamps.* Circa 1920. Art glass and painted glass shades. Approx. 100 collectible lamps in full color on 68 pgs. $250-$500.

PITTSBURGH MIRRORS. *Catalog No. 406.* 1940. $10.

PITTSBURGH STOVE & RANGE CO. *Tremont Stoves, Ranges, Furnaces.* Pittsburgh, 1900. 90 pgs. $55-$95.

ADRIANCE, PLATT CO. *Mowers, Reapers, Binders.* Poughkeepsie NY, 1911. 48 pgs. $24.

FAVETTE R. PLUMB, INC. *Catalog of Hammers, Axes, Sledges, etc.* St. Louis MO, 1925. 34 pgs. $35.

PLUMBING & BATHROOM fixture catalogs of 1875-1890 are collectible if they feature engravings of ornate Victorian tubs, showers and commodes. We've seen 9x12 hardbound volumes of 200 pages sell for $200 to $450. Photo-illustrated examples from 1900 to 1930s are common at $25 to $50. See individual listings.

PLYMOUTH. *Deluxe Plymouth, 1939.* Showroom booklet. 20 pgs. $25.
All About Your New Plymouth. 1956. 32 pgs. $15.

P & O VEHICLES. *1915 Buggies, Wagons.* 92 pgs. $75.

A. POMERANTZ & CO. *Stationery & Office Furniture Catalog.* Philadelphia, circa 1908. 364 pgs. $100.

A. H. POMEROY. *Price List of Fancy Woods & Scroll Saw Material.* Hartford CT, 1895. 32 pgs. Fair cond. $40.

PONTIAC. *Pontiac's Fabulous 1956 Star-Chief 4-door Catalina.* Color flyer. $20.
Pontiac 1967. Color catalog. $15.

POPE MANUFACTURING CO. *Columbia Bicycles 1885 Catalog.* 8th ed. 48 pgs. Fine engravings. $350. Another, Boston, 1894. 16mo, 12 pgs. $40. Another, Hartford, 1896. 8vo, 50 pgs. $125.
Columbia & Hartford Bicycles. 1899. 16 pgs. $95.
Fay Bicycles. 1905. 12 pgs. $35.
Columbia Bicycle Co. 1913. $75.

PONTIAC SPRING AND WAGON WORKS. *Catalog No. 45.* Pontiac MI, 1906. Hundreds of horse drawn vehicles, including tradesman wagons. Includes paint chip samples. 124 pgs., 4to. $200-$300.

N. PORTER CO. *Cowboy Catalog No. 18.* Phoenix AZ, 1935. 232 pgs. $75. Another, 1947, 4to, 64 pgs. $35.

PORTER SADDLE & HARNESS CO. 1924-1940 Catalogs. $75-$150 each.

PORTLAND CEMENT ASSOCIATION. *Concrete in Architecture.* No place, 1927. 59 pgs. $25.

FREDERICK POST CO. *New Post Drafting Materials.* Chicago, 1949. 416 pgs. $20.

POST MFG. CO. *Sports Equipment, Uniforms.* Spring & Summer, 1932. New York, 30 pgs. $35.

POWER, TAINTER & CO. *Builders of Wood Working Machinery.* Philadelphia, 1874. 56 pgs. $40.

PRAIRIE STATE INCUBATOR CO. *Illustrated Catalog of 1895.* Homer City PA, 1895. 114 pgs. $65.

L. PRANG & CO. *Christmas and New Year Cards, Novelties.* New York, 1887. 46 pgs. $65.
The Prang Bulletin. Chicago, 1922. Arts and crafts materials. 64 pgs. $24.

PRATT & CO. CATALOG & PRICE LIST. *Locks, Builders, Housekeepers Hardware.* Buffalo NY, 1861. 420 pgs. $350.

PRATT & WHITNEY CO. *Small machine tools,* dies, etc. Hartford CT, 1899. 12mo. 104 pgs. $35. Another, 1911. 248 pgs. $35.
Lathes. 1907. 9x6, 106 pgs. $30.

PREMIER CYCLE WORKS. *Catalog No. 117.* 1910. 4to, 32 pgs. $45.
Bicycles & Accessories. Chicago, 1913. 4to, 62 pgs. $75.

PREMIER MOTOR MFG. CO. *Automobiles.* Indianapolis, 1912. 4to. 32 pgs. Color illus. cover. $100.

PREMO CAMERA CATALOG. *Cameras and Supplies.* 1915. 48 pgs. $25-$45.

WM. R. PRINCE'S CATALOG. *Fruit & Ornamental Trees & Plants.* Flushing NY, 1841. 52 pgs. $175.

PRISCILLA PUBLISHING CO. *The Priscilla Needlework Book.* Boston, 1905. 26 pgs. $20.
1912 Supplement to Priscilla Catalog. 50 pgs. $25.

JAMES W. QUEEN & CO. *Catalog of Microscopes, Telescopes, etc.* Philadelphia, circa 1880. 32 pgs. $100.
Catalog of Meteorological Equipment. 1882. 126 pgs. 8vo. $145.
How to Fit Glasses. 1888. 114 pgs. Many ads. $85.
Catalog of Physical Apparatus. 1900. 154 pgs. $100.
Self-Regulating Xray Tube. 1902. 36 pgs. $200.

R

RADFORD ARCHITECTURAL CO. *Radford's Artistic Bungalows. 208 Designs.* Chicago IL, 1908. 219 pgs. $75. *Practical Carpentry.* NY, 1907. 264 pgs. $25. *The Radford Ideal Homes, 100 House Plans.* Chicago IL, 1902. 110 pgs. $40. *Radford's Artistic Homes, 250 Designs.* 1908. $50. *Radford American Homes, 100 House Plans.* 1903. $50.

RADIO CORPORATION OF AMERICA. *Radiolas.* Early radio catalog; all are battery operated. New York, circa 1923. 22 pgs. $50. *RCA Victor, Bluebird Records.* 1940. 612 pgs. $40. *RCA Receiving Tube Manual.* 1947. 256 pgs. $15.

RAMBLER AUTOMOBILE. Thomas B. Jeffery Co. imprinted sales catalog. Kenosha WI, 1902. 21 pgs. $150.

RAMOND ROSEN & CO. *High Grade Tools for Barbers.* Philadelphia, circa 1905. 16 pgs. $40-$60.

L. B. RAMSDELL. *Children's Wagons, Chairs.* So. Gardner, circa 1880. 40 pgs. $125.

RAND & AVERY. *Type Specimen Catalog.* Boston, circa 1868. 126 leaves. $300.

RAND & LEOPOLD DESK CO. *The Leopold Desk. Catalog No. 19.* Burlington IA, 1898. 12mo, 48 pgs. Many styles, including huge telescoping banker's model. $150-$250.

RAPIDS FURNITURE CO. Boston MA, 1924. 176 pgs. Folio. $75.

RAWLINGS MFG. CO. *Spring & Summer Sports.* St. Louis, 1940. 72 pgs. $20-$40. Another. 84 pgs. $50.

A. J. REACH CO. *Catalog of Base Ball Goods.* Philadelphia, 1911-12. 32 pgs. $95-$150.

WM. READ & SONS. *The New Mail.* 1889 High Wheel Bicycle Catalog. 48 pgs. $150. *Guns and Sporting Goods.* Boston, circa 1899. 4to, 104 pgs. Guns, golf, etc. $100.

READING HARDWARE CORP. *Catalog No. 21, Builders Hardware.* Reading PA, 1931. 578 pgs. $40.

RED WING UNION STONEWARE CO. *Home Packing the Red Wing Way.* Catalog and Recipe Book. Early 1900s. 32 pgs. $55.

REDDING & CO. *Catalog of Masonic Works and Outfits.* New York, circa 1883. 24 pgs. $90. *Catalog No. 2.* 1885. 16 pgs. $75.

REED & BARTON. *Sterling Silver Tableware.* Newburyport, 1926. 8vo, 44 pgs. $35. *Catalog No. 47D.* Chests & cases of pewter & bronze. Taunton MA, 1912. 4to, 176 pgs. $175.

REGAL MFG. CO. *Iceless Gem. Refrigerator.* Salt Lake City, 1915. 12 pgs. $25.

A. H. REID CREAMERY & DAIRY SUPPLY. *Commercial Diary Supplies.* Philadelphia, circa 1927. 65 pgs. $40.

RELIABLE FURNITURE MFG. CO. *Catalog of Spring Styles.* Baltimore MD, 1899. 28 pgs. $50-$65.

REMINGTON ARMS CO. *Bicycle Catalog.* Ilion NY, 1894. 48 pgs. $75. *Cartridges and Ammunition.* 1913. 212 pgs. $75. *Catalog No. 107. Modern Firearms.* 1923. 192 pgs. $85. *Kleanbore Shells.* 1931. 16mo, 36 pgs. $20.

E. REMINGTON & SONS. *Military, Sporting Rifles, Pistols.* Ilion NY, 1876. 5th edition. $300. *Breech Leading Firearms.* 1879. 111 pgs. $350. *Revised Price List.* 1886. 16 pgs. $175. *1880 Catalog.* $250.

REMINGTON TYPEWRITER CO. *The Remington Typewriter.* NY, 1914. 44 pgs., 12mo. Includes other office machines as well. $25-$45. *Remington Standard Typewriter.* Office furniture and typewriter catalog issued in 1890s by Seamans and Benedict Wyckoff. 32 pgs. $50.

REO MOTOR CAR CO. *Reo The Fifth, 1913.* 20 pgs. $50. *The 1929 Reo Flying Clouds.* A sumptuous catalog. 16 pgs. Color. $75. *A New Reo-Royale.* 1927. 8 pgs. $35. *Presenting The New Reo for 1936.* 11x17 folder. $20.

REVERE MOTOR CAR CORP. *America's Incomparable Car*. Logansport IN, circa 1915. 4to, 20 pgs. $125.

JOHN REYNDERS & CO. *Veterinary Instruments & Turf Goods Catalog*. New York, 1898. 126 pgs. $200-$300.

RICE & HUTCHINS, INC. *The Story of Bicycle Shoes*. Boston, 1896. 16mo, 16 pgs. $25-$50.

RICHARDSON & BOYNTON. *Cooking Ranges*. New York, 1882. Folio, 15 pgs. $65-$95.
The Richardson Line. New York, 1925. 8vo, 410 pgs. $50.

RICHMOND CEDAR WORKS. *Wooden Ware Catalog*. Ice cream freezers, churns, mop buckets. Richmond VA, 1937. 29 pgs. $35.

RICH PUMP & LADDER CO. *Catalog No. 21. Spruce Ladders*. Cincinnati OH, 1926. 38 pgs. $30.

F. RICHTER & CO. *The Toy the Child Likes Best*. Building block sets. NY, circa 1880. 12mo, 56 pgs., color. $115.

RIDABOCK & CO. *Catalog No. 400. Army Uniforms*. New York, 1923. 32 pgs. $40.

ED. N. RIDDLE COMPANY. *Originalities in Toledo Lighting Fixtures*. 1930. 8x11. 12 pgs. $32.

HERBERT N. RIDGWAY AMUSEMENT DEVICES. *The Pit*. Boston MA, 1910. 20 pg. catalog illustrating devices made for commercial amusement parks. $150.

RIGGS & BRO. NAUTICAL WAREHOUSE. *Navigational Supplies*. Philadelphia, 1901. 8vo, 152 pgs. $95.
Nautical Almanac with catalog for sextants, binnacles, etc. 1916. 8vo, 98 pgs. $125.

RILEY, SCHUBERT, CROSSMAN. *Catalog No. 52. Home-Farm Supplies*. 1917. 256 pgs. $75.

J. K. RISHEL FURNITURE CO. *Bedroom & Dining Room Furniture*. Williamsport PA, 1912. Folio, 132 pgs. $75. Another, 1925. 105 pgs. $50.

RISHELL PHONOGRAPH CO. *1918 Catalog*. Williamsport PA. 20 pgs. $35.

RISK CRAWFORD CO. *Niagara Blue Ribbon Wall Paper*. Belfast NY, ca 1920s. 28 sample leaves of wall paper. $25.

ROACH & MUSSER CO. *Universal Design Book No. 25*. Builder's woodwork catalog. IA, 1927. 356 pgs. $125.

E. L. ROBERTS & CO. *Blinds, Doors, Sashes, etc*. Chicago, 1900. 350 pgs. Many color plates. Fold-out missing. $75.

ROCHELLE CLOCK & WATCH CO. *Victorian-Style Clocks*. Rochelle IL, 1908. 8vo, 48 pgs. $50.

ROCHESTER OPTICAL CO. *Premier Camera*. NY, circa 1900, 36 pgs. $50.
Premo Cameras. NY, 1914. 48 pgs. $45.

ROCHESTER SHOW CASE WORKS. *Illustrated Catalog and Price List*. NY, 1882. Indoor and outdoor commercial display fixtures. 48 pgs., 8vo. $150-$200.

ROCK ISLAND SASH AND DOOR WORKS. *Catalog of Sash, Door, Blinds*. Very extensive, staircases to stained glass. Rock Island IL, 1900. 492 pgs. $150.

E. V. RODDIN & CO. *31st Catalog Diamonds, Watches, Jewelry, Silverware*. Chicago, 1887. 8vo, 202 pgs. $75.

LEWIS ROESCH CO. *Catalog of Grape Vines, Fruit, etc*. Fredonia NY, 1891. 20 pgs. $35.

ROGERS & BROTHERS. *Electro Silver Plated Spoons, etc*. 1877. 48 pgs. $25-$35.
Catalog No. 49. Waterbury CT, circa 1890. 136 pgs. $100.

JOHN ROGERS. *Statuary Catalog*. Includes lawn ornaments. New York, 1877. 6 pg. fold-out. $100.

WILLIAM A. ROGERS, LTD. *Silverware*. NY, 1920. 42 pgs., 8vo. Holloware of all kinds. $20.
Rogers Silver Plated Flatware. 1922. 28 pgs. 4to. $30.

ROOKWOOD POTTERY COMPANY. *Founded in 1880. Its History & Aims*. Cincinnati, 1920. 16mo, 16 pgs. $40.

A. I. ROOT CO. *Bees & Honey, Our 79th Edition*. Medina OH, 1894. 50 pgs. $35. 1916 edition. 64 pgs. $14.
Everything for the Beekeeper. 1937. $12.

ROOT BROTHERS BO. *Cobblers' Outfits and Saddlery Hardware*. Plymouth OH, 1905. 154 pgs. 8vo. $65.

ROSENOW COMPANY. *Book of Type Faces, etc*. Chicago, 1930. 219 pgs. $45.

ROSENTHAL CORN HUSKER CO. *Catalog, Feed Cutters & Silo Fillers, etc*. Milwaukee WI, 1916. 20 pgs. $26.

ROSEVILLE POTTERY INC. Circa 1930s rare catalog of art pottery: Cosmos, Ivory, Iris, Pincone, etc. 28 pgs. 10x13 in. (showing 409 pieces). $280-$500.

ROSTLAND MFG. CO. *Brass & Iron Fireplace Fixtures*. Milford CT, 1921. 76 pgs. 4to. $50-$75.

ROUND OAK FURNACE CO. *Catalog No. 32*. Dowagiac MI, 1933. 4to, 60 pgs. $40.

CHARLES BROADWAY ROUSE. *Wholesale Dry Goods Catalog*. New York, 1926. 4to. 150 pgs. $65.
Monthly Auction Trade Journal. New York, 1910. Folio. 338 pgs. of clothes, guns, toys, harness, etc. $100.

ROYAL DOULTON. *Catalog No. 1. Figurines*. 1949. 32 pgs. $20-$40. 1955. 68 pgs. $30.
Royal Doulton Statuary. Circa 1930, 16 pgs, color. $30.

ROYAL TOURIST CAR COMPANY. *Royal Tourist, 1909*. Early motor car catalog from Ohio. 24 pgs. $85.

ROYAL TYPEWRITER CO. *The Master Key to Typewriter Service*. Hartford CT, circa 1920. 12 pgs. $15.
The World of Tomorrow. New York World's Fair, 1939. 16 pgs. $25.

ROYCROFT SHOPS. *Hand Made Furniture, etc.* East Aurora NY, 1906. $100-$150. 1915 edition. 64 pgs. $50.

RUBY LAMP CO. *Sketch Book, Lighting Fixtures*. 1934. 47 pgs. $45.

J. A. RUBRECHT. *Thorough-Bred Poultry*. Fine catalog, woodcuts of breeding stock. Telford PA, circa 1910. 24 pgs. $25.

RUMSEY & CO. *Catalog of Force Pumps for Gardens and Fire*. Seneca Falls NY, 1870. 64 pgs. $225.
Hand & Power Pumps. 52nd ed. 1899. 16mo, 192 pgs. $35.
53rd Edition. 1902. 8vo, 256 pgs. Includes Fire Fighting equip. $150. Another. 1909. 257 pgs. $300.

J. H. RUSHTON MFR. *Sporting Boats & Canoes*. Canton NY, 1879. 24 pgs. $150.

RUSSELL & ERWIN MFG. CO. *Catalog of American Hardware*. New Britain CT, 1865. 436 pgs. (Needs rebinding). $500.
Vol. III Locks, Tools, Hardware. 1875. $300.
Vol. IV. Misc. Hardware. 1877. $300.
Vol. XI. New Britain, 1899. 997 pgs. $200.

J. RUSSELL & CO. *Catalog and Price List of 1919*. Huge wholesale hardware, auto & railway supply catalog. Holyoke MA, 1919. 1,101 pgs. $125.

JOHN RUSSELL CUTLERY COMPANY. *Catalog of Cutlery & Electro-plated ware*. Turners Falls MA, 1883. 144 pgs. $300-$500.

RUSSELL UNIFORM CO. *Catalog No. 35*. Police, Fire, Military Uniforms. New York, 1929. 64 pgs. $70.

RYAN & MC DONALD. *Wide-Awake Thresher & Separator*. Steam engines, etc. 16 pgs. 1888. $50.

RUSSELL & ERWIN MANUFACTURING CO.

Full size cut of No. 330.

Full size cut of No. 318.

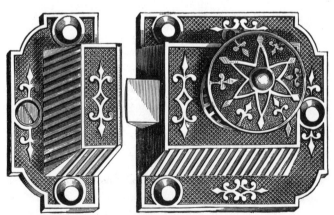

Full size cut of No. 320.

S

JOHN A. SALZER SEED CO. *Salzer's Surprize Collection.* Illus. garden catalog. La Cross WI, 1897. 28 pgs. $25.

SARGENT & CO. *Hardware and Lock Catalog.* New Haven CT, 1884. 900 pgs. $300. 1927 edition (damp stained). $75.

E. H. SARGENT & CO. *Scientific Supplies.* Chicago, 1922. 4to, 554 pgs. $100-$150.

SARGENT MFG. CO. *Reclining Chairs.* Muskegon, 1890. 32 pgs. $100.
Catalog C. NY, 1895. 24 pgs. of reclining chairs. $125.

SAVAGE BROS. *Candy Machinery & Copper Work.* Chicago, circa 1905. 144 pgs. $69.

M. W. SAVAGE. *Fall & Winter 1928.* General Merchandise. Minneapolis MN. 512 pgs. $70.
Catalog No. 62. 1933. 256 pgs. $60.

SAXON MOTOR CAR CO. *Saxon Days.* 30 pg. sales catalog. Detroit, 1915. $95.

SCHACK ARTIFICIAL FLOWER CO. *Schack's Floral Parade Decorations.* Chicago IL, circa 1930. 22 pgs. $25.

SCHALL & CO. ARTISTIC CONFECTIONERS. *Catalog of Ice Cream Molds, Cake Decorations.* New York, circa 1910. 80 pgs. $60.
Individual Ice Cream Molds. New York, 1921. 12mo, 29 pgs. $20.

J. W. SCHERMERHORN & CO. *Descriptive Catalog of Joslin's Terrestial and Celestial Globes.* New York, circa 1875. 12 pgs. $100.

W. H. SCHIEFFELIN & CO. *General Prices Current. Drugs, Medicines, Chemicals, Pharmaceuticals.* New York, 1885. 12mo, 555 pgs. Many illus. ads. $75.
1891 Edition. Includes fancy goods, perfumes, drugs, etc. 671 pgs. $100.

JOS. SCHLITZ BREWING COMPANY. *A Token of Remembrance.* Milwaukee WI, 1895. 22 leaves. $100.

A. SCHOENHUT COMPANY. *Humpty Dumpty Circus.* NY, circa 1915. 32 pgs. $50-$75.
All Wood Perfection Art Doll. 1915 catalog. 28 pages., 4to. $75-$150.
Schoenhut's Marvelous Toys. Philadelphia, 1918. Full color. 47 pgs. $200-$300. 1923 edition. 96 pgs. $300.

SCHUMACHER & ETTLINGER LITHO. CO. *Cigar Box Labels.* 7 leaf sample book with extra sheets inserted loosely, including cigar band samples. Chicago & San Francisco, 1898. $300.

F. SCHUMACHER & CO. *Catalog No. 7 - Taxidermists' Supplies.* Jersey City NJ, circa 1925. 32 pgs. $45.

SCHWAHN-SEYBERTH CO. *Harness, Saddles, Western Wear, etc.* 1920s catalog of 548 pgs. $125.

F. A. O. SCHWARTZ. *Christmas Catalogs.*
1956 to 1965..$50-$75.
1966 to 1970..$40-$65.
1971 to 1977..$30-$50.

J. W. SCOTT & CO. *Catalog of American & Foreign Coins.* New York, 1875. 45 pgs. $100.

SEARS ROEBUCK. *Christmas Catalogs.*
1934 to 1941..$100-$195.
1942 to 1945..$70-$80.
1946 to 1954..$65-$100.
1955 to 1965..$60-$85.
1966 to 1970..$45-$70.
1971 to 1982..$20-$40.

SEARS ROEBUCK. *Fall & Winter Catalogs.*
1920 to 1930..$60-$85.
1931 to 1935..$45-$65.
1936 to 1940..$40-$60.
1941 to 1945..$35-$55.
1946 to 1950..$30-$50.
1951 to 1955..$25-$45.
1956 to 1960..$20-$40.
1961 to 1965..$18-$35.
1966 to 1975..$15-$25.
1976 to 1985..$10-$20.

SEARS, ROEBUCK. *Spring & Summer Catalogs.*
1920 to 1930	$60-$85.
1931 to 1935	$45-$65.
1936 to 1940	$40-$60.
1941 to 1945	$35-$55.
1946 to 1950	$30-$50.
1951 to 1955	$25-$45.
1956 to 1960	$20-$40.
1961 to 1965	$18-$35.
1966 to 1975	$15-$25.
1976 to 1985	$10-$20.

(14 million copies of the last big Sears Catalog were printed in 1993.)

SEARS ROEBUCK. *Toy Catalogs.*
1961 to 1970	$50-$75.
1971 to 1975	$20-$35.
1976 to 1980	$15-$30.
1981 to 1985	$10-$20.

SEARS ROEBUCK. *Wallpaper Catalogs.*
1929 to 1940	$15-$25.
1941 to 1950	$10-$20.
1951 to 1955	$8-15.

SEARS ROEBUCK. *Misc. Early Catalogs.*
1896 Edition. The first "Big Book." $195-$250.
Special Vehicle, Harness & Saddlery. 1898. $75.
Bicycles. 1901. 4to, 36 pgs. $50. Another, 1898. Girl on cover. 36 pgs. $100-$150.
Guns, Fishing Tackle. 1898. 64 pgs. $100.
Patent Medicines. 1902. 52 pgs. $75.
General Catalogs. 1899-1912. (1,000 or more pages.) $125-$250.
Buggies & Carriages. 1903. $65.
Furniture. Circa 1900. 4to, 72 pgs. $50.
Solid Comfort Vehicles. 1906. 96 pgs. $60.
Mantels and Fireplace Furn. 1915. $25.
Beckwith Pianos. 1913. 24 pgs. $25.
Annual White Goods. 1914. 156 pgs. $35.
Honor Bilt Modern Homes. 1928. 120 pgs. $35.

SEBASTIAN-MAY CO. *Catalog No. 6.* Planers, circular saws, lathes, drills and hand tools. Sidney OH, 1892. 8vo, 63 pgs. $50.

ALBERT SECHRIST MFG. CO. *Electric Lighting Fixtures.* Denver CO, 1903-1908 editions. $150-$250 each.
Special Designs. 31 plates, 11x14. Circa 1915. $100.

SEGELKE & KOHLHAUS. *Design Book.* Millwork, leaded and stained glass, etc. 1920. 320 pgs. $75-$100.

SEITZ & KLEINERT. *The Original Fireworks Depot.* Philadelphia, circa 1880. Only four pages, 4to. Prices, listings. $100-$175.

E. G. SELCHOW & CO. *Wholesale Games & Home Amusement.* New York, 1879-80. Fine toy illustrations. 46 pgs. $400-$500.

SELCHOW & RIGHTER. *Wholesale Toy Catalog.* 1892-1893 edition. 8vo, 144 pages. $350-$450. 1896 edition. 128 pgs. $300.
Fourth of July Goods. Firecrackers, Balloons, Flags, Lanterns. NY, 1890. 32 pgs., illus. $320-$450.

SELL HORSE GOODS CO. *Catalog No. 53. Boots, Harness, etc.* Canton OH and Portland ME. 1908. 103 pgs. $100.
Catalog No. 58. Horse Goods. Harness racing supplies, etc. 1915. 184 pgs. $95.

SENECA CAMERA MFG CO. *Camera Catalog.* Indian maid on cover. Rochester NY, 1911. 76 pgs. $35.

SENOUR MANUFACTURING COMPANY. *Monarch Mixed Paint.* Sample book with 16 colored paint chips. Chicago, 1888. 12mo, 16 pgs. $75.

SETH THOMAS CLOCK CO. *Seth Thomas Clock Movements.* NY, circa 1910. (This is a parts catalog. The clocks themselves can be found in most Jewelry Trade catalogs of the period.) 14 pgs. $25-$50.

B. A. SHACKMAN & CO. *Catalog of Shackman Favors.* Ephemeral gifts, toys, novelties. NY, 1906. 190 pgs. $100.
Catalog No. 70. Circa 1910. 112 pgs. $35.
Catalog No. 166. 60th Anniversary. 1958. 35 pgs. $20.

SHADBOLT & BOYD. *Car and Truck Equipment.* 1919. 321 pgs. $75.
Auto, Blacksmith & Machinist's Supplies. 1917. $95.

SHAPLEIGH'S HARDWARE CATALOG. *Diamond Edge and Keen Kutter Brands.* St. Louis, 1942. 2,586 pgs. $175-$250.
Shapleigh's Auto Equip. & Supply. 1920. 452 pgs. $100.
Shapleigh Sporting Goods. Catalog No. 308. 220 pgs. circa 1929. $125.

ARTHUR B. SHEPARD CORP. *Catalog No. 20, Service Station Buildings.* New York, 1922-25. 28 plates. $125.

SIDNEY SHEPARD & CO. *Stamped Metalware, 1889.* Buffalo, NY, 1890. 184 pgs., 4to. $195-$275.

SHERWIN WILLIAMS CO. *Catalog of Stencils & Materials.* Cleveland OH, 1912. 40 pgs. $15.
Paint & Varnishes For the Home. 1922. 12-page fold-out. Point of purchase lit. $20.
The Home Designer. Ohio, 1913. 36 pgs. plus paint chips. Point of purchase lit. $35.
Paint & Color Style Guide. 1940. 120 pages. Full color, limited edition. $75.

SHOE CATALOGS are a drug on the market. If you laid all the old footwear catalogs printed since 1880 end-to-end, they would stretch to the moon and back. Large shoe sections also appear in old Sears and Wards catalogs so don't pay more than $15 to $30 for average old shoe literature. Shoe-making machinery catalogs frequently are offered at $50-$75 each.

SHOEMAKER CO. *Almanac & Fine Illustrated Catalog of Poultry*. Freeport IL, 1894. 64 pgs. $35.
Catalog & Almanac of Incubators, Brooders & Poultry. 1905. 224 pgs. $60-$75.

B. SHONINGER ORGAN CO. *Illustrated Catalog & Price List*. New Haven CT, 1878. 12mo, 24 pgs. $75. 1884 edition. 16mo, 24 pgs. $35.

SHREIBER CARRIAGE MFG. COMPANY. *High Grade Carriages, Buggies and Wagons*. Chariton IA, 1906-1907. 8vo, 20 pgs. $50-$70.

SHRYOCK-TODD NOTION CO. *Novelties for Street Vendors & Auctioneers*. St. Louis, circa 1904. 8vo. 64 pgs. $35.

A. SHUMAN & CO. CLOTHIERS. *1890 Catalog*. Color covers. $40.

N. SHURE CO. *Jewelry, Gifts, Toys, Novelties*. 1940. 1,216 pgs. $60-$100.

HIRAM SIBLEY & CO. *Seed Catalog-1884*. Partially illus. catalog for farmers. New York, 1884. 136 pgs. $35.

SIDNEY SHEPARD & CO. (Buffalo Stamping Works). *Hardware & Housewares*. Buffalo NY, 1889. 183 pgs. $200-$300. *Tinware*. 1892. 125 pgs. $90.

SIDWAY BABY CARRIAGES. *1913 Catalog*. Some color. 71 pgs. Worn. $70.

SIEGEL COOPER. *General Merchandise*. Chicago, 1895-1896. 208 pages. $150-$200.
Artists Materials, Sporting Goods, Cameras. New York, circa 1900. 32 pgs. $20-$35.
World's Greatest Store. New York, 1906. 264 pgs. $50.
Spring & Summer Styles, 1909. Plus guns, toys. $75-$95.

SIMMONS HARDWARE CO. *House Furnishings & Hardware*. St. Louis, 1881. 285 pgs. $250-$350.
1909 Keen Kutter. 4,200 pgs. Auction. $850.
1880 Tools & Hardware. Huge hardbound. 4to . $500.
1887 Hardware, etc. 1,636 pgs. $400.
1927 E. C. Simmons/Winchester. $390.
1935 E. C. Simmons, Keen Kutter. $295.

FRANKLIN SIMON & CO. *Spring & Summer 1918*. $40.
Correct Dress-Fall and Winter, 1905. 30 pgs. $35.

SIMPLEX MOTION PICTURE PROJECTORS. 1940s catalogs and maintenance manuals. $35-$50 each.

SIMPLEX MOTOR CAR CO. *Mechanical Masterpiece, American Simplex*. Mishawaka IN, 1909. 24 pgs. $75.

SIMPSON CRAWFORD. *Spring & Summer, 1910. Ladies, Childs Fashions*. 154 pgs. $90.

SIMPSON, HALL, MILLER & CO. *Catalog for 1891. Electro-Plated Ware*. 4to, 432 pgs. Hardbound, rich illustrations. $200-$275.

SINGER & CO. *Fall & Winter 1924-1925*. Sporting goods, clocks, toys, musical instruments. 64 pgs. $45.

SINGER SEWING MACHINES. *Instruction Manual, 1920*. 28 pgs. $10. Earlier small green booklets. $10-$15 each.

SLACK MFG. CO., NOVELTIES. *Catalog No. 128. Everything for Amusements, etc*. Chicago, 1920s. 96 pgs. $50.
Celebration Goods. Decorations, Novelties, Jewelry, Candy, etc. Chicago, 1923. 80 pgs. $35.

SLOAN MFG. COMPANY. *Sloan's Shirts, Collars and Cuffs*. New York, circa 1888. 25 pgs. $50.

J. T. SLOCOMB CO. *Machinists Measuring Tools*. Providence, 1920. 12mo, 127 pgs. $35-$50.

SMITH BROTHERS, BARBERS SUPPLIES. *Price List of Hair Dresser's Sundries*. Boston MA, 1882. 16 pgs. $75.

SMITH-COURTNEY CO. *General Hardware Catalog*. Richmond VA, 1905. 1,009 pgs. $150-$250.

HERBERT S. SMITH. *Wheel Chair Catalog for 1894*. New York, 1894, 24 pgs. $85.

MARVIN SMITH CO. *Catalog No. 30. Farm Machinery, Agricultural Implements*. Chicago, 1899. 320 pgs. $135.

SMITH & POMEROY. *"Eureka" Self-Regulating Windmills*. Kalamazoo MI, 1891. 12 pgs. $75.

SMITH PREMIER TYPEWRITER CO. *Improvement, The Order of the Age*. Syracuse, NY, circa 1892. 20 pgs. $65.
Typewriters and Office Furniture. NY, 1902. Includes roll-top desks. 32 pgs. 4to. $125-$250.

SMITH & WESSON. *Revolver Catalog*. Springfield MA, circa 1880. 24 pgs. $150. 1908 edition, with history. $75.

S. A. SMITH MFG. CO. *Shoo Flys, Horses, Wagons, Carts, Toys*. Brattleboro VT, 1917. 106 pgs., 8vo, $175.
The *Famous "Kon-Struct-It"*. Vermont, 1920. 90 pgs. Wagons, carts, horses and other toys made of wood. Several in color. $180-$220.

WILLARD P. SMITH CO. *Catalog of Premiums*. New York, 1911. 44 pgs. $35.

ISAAC SMITH'S SON & CO. *Catalog of Umbrellas & Parasols*. New York, 1884. 20 pgs. $75.

JOHN M. SMYTH & CO. *General Merchandise Catalog*. (Similar to Sears). Chicago, 1901. 4to, 1,052 pgs. $120.
1903 Edition. 1,082 pgs. $125.
Catalog No. 60. 1906. 1,164 pgs. $100.
Bicycle and Auto Supplies. 1916. 4to, 64 pgs. $50.
Groceries and Provisions. 1908. 48 pgs. $30-$40.

SNAP-ON TOOLS CORP. *25th Anniversary Catalog*. 1945. 8x11 in. 96 pgs. $15.

SNOW & NEALLEY. *Tools for Lumber Jacks*. 1937. $30.

W. A. SNOW & CO. *Catalog B. Cast Iron Stable Fixtures*. Including weather vanes. Boston, 1894. 148 pgs. $250.
Catalog C. 1898. 4to, 78 pgs. $250.
Catalog of Weather Vanes. 1913. Folio, 10 pgs. $75.

SNYDER ENGINE COMPANY. *Horizontal and Vertical Marine Engines*. New York, 1883. Woodcuts of launches, motors, etc. 20 pgs. $60.

E. G. SOLTMANN. *Drawing Materials, Architects & Engineers' Supplies*. New York, 1886. 8vo, 272 pgs. $50.
Buff Edition of Mammoth Catalog. New York, 1908. Folio, 96 pgs. $100-$150.

G. SOMMERS & CO. *Catalog No. 415. Our Leader*. Wholesale, general merchandise. St. Paul MN, 1928. 350 pgs. $75.

SOSYMAN & LANDIS. *Scenery Catalog, Opera Houses & Halls*. Chicago IL, circa 1883. 8 pgs. $65.

SOUTH BEND BAIT COMPANY. *Fishing. What Tackle and When*. South Bend IN, 1932 to 1939 editions. $35-$55 each. 1947 to 1949 post-war editions. $10-$12 each.

SOUTH BEND TOY MFG. CO. *Illus. Catalog of Croquet and Children's Wagons*. Includes rocking horses, fire engines, etc. South Bend IN, 1919. 80 pgs. $100.
1922 and 1924 editions. 8vo. $90.
1928 Doll Carriages. 72 pgs. $95.

SOUTHERN FURNITURE CO. *Catalog No. 44*. Furniture, Appliances. Circa 1940. 348 pgs. $50.
Catalog No. 50. 1950. $45.

A. J. SOUTHWICK & CO. *Dexter Windmills*. Decatur IL, 1872. 24 pgs. Many ads. $195.

A. G. SPALDING & CO. *Catalog B, Athletic Uniforms*. New York, 1891. 8vo. 68 pgs. $195.
Catalog No. 101. Sporting Goods. Fall &Winter, 1893. 4to, 40 pgs. $75.
Winter Sports. Circa 1880. 36 pgs. $50.
Bicycle Sundries. 1899. 32 pgs. $45.
College Athletics. 1894. 46 pgs. $40.
Spring & Summer, 1903. 98 pgs. $45.
Fall & Winter, 1906-07. 128 pgs. $95.
Fall & Winter, 1912. 40 pgs.$30.
Court Games. 1914. 126 pgs. $35.
Spring & Summer, 1915. 48 pgs. Much baseball, major league. $95.
1927. Mixed sports. 112 pgs. $45.

SPEAR & CO. *Christmas Savings Sale*. Pittsburgh PA, circa 1920. $50.
Spear's Dollar Sale. 1926. $25.
General Catalog No. K100. 1920. 216 pgs. $70.

SPELMAN BROTHERS. *Fancy Goods*. Wholesale notions, clocks, toys, laces, etc. New York, 1880, 76 pgs. $60. 1882. 24 pgs. $35. 1881. 118 pgs. $85.
Fancy Goods Graphic. Magazine-style catalog. 1882. 54 pgs. $65.

EDWARD E. SPENCER & CO. *Shoemakers' Tools & Supplies. Supplement No. 1*. Everything for the cobbler. New York, circa 1901. pages 213-355. $50.

SPENCER FIREWORKS CO. *Fireworks Headquarters*. Spring 1936 catalog. Polk OH. 32 pgs. $100-$150.

L. G. SPENCER BABY CARRIAGES. *Tenth Annual Illustrated Catalog*. Chicago, circa 1880. Includes toys, dolls, baby carriages, etc. 32 pgs. 12mo. $150.

SPERRY & HUTCHINSON. *Green Stamps Premiums*. New York, 1910. 12mo, 56 pgs. $25.

SPIEGEL. *Christmas Catalogs*.
1944 to 1950...........................$50-$100.
1951 to 1955...........................$50-$85.
1956 to 1969...........................$40-$75.
1970 to 1980...........................$30-$50.

SPIEGEL. *Fall & Winter Catalogs*.
1931 to 1939...........................$50-$70.
1940 to 1945...........................$40-$60.
1946 to 1950...........................$35-$55.
1951 to 1955...........................$30-$45.
1956 to 1965...........................$25-$40.
1966 to 1980...........................$15-$30.

SPIEGEL. *Spring & Summer Catalogs.*
 1931 to 1939..........................$50-$70.
 1940 to 1945..........................$40-$60.
 1946 to 1950..........................$35-$55.
 1951 to 1955..........................$30-$45.
 1956 to 1965..........................$25-$40.
 1966 to 1980..........................$15-$30.

SPRAGUE MOWING MACHINE CO. *Catalog of Horse-drawn Mowers.* Providence RI, 1872. 24 pgs. $75.

STANDARD FISHING ROD CO. *Illustrated Catalog & Price List.* West Brookfield MA, 1904. 110 pgs. $100.

STANDARD MAIL ORDER CO. Clothing catalog with a nice toy section. New York, 1916. 4to, 346 pgs. $75.

STANDARD OIL COMPANY. *Polarine Pointers.* NY, circa 1908. Early oil products catalog. 20 pgs. 16mo. $25.

STANDARD SILVERWARE CO. *Tableware, Cutlery.* Plus jewelry, watches, spectacles, etc. Boston, circa 1890. 80 pgs. $75.

STANDARD SANITARY MFG. CO. *Standard Bath Tub Decorations.* 342 pgs. (2 plates missing). $175.
Porcelain and Enameled Baths. Pittsburgh, 1906. 484 pgs. $125.
Modern Bathrooms. 1901. 54 pgs. $50. 1908 edition. 100 pgs. $75.
Brass Goods. 1909. 8vo, 251 pgs. $70.
Standard Plumbing Fixtures. No date. 80 pgs. $25.
Bathroom Furnishings & Decoration. 1929. 55 pgs. $75.
The Bathroom, A New Interior. (Art Deco). 1931. 95 pgs. $50.

STANDARD TEXTILE PRODUCTS CO. *Sanita's Wall Covering Catalog.* New York, circa 1915. 28 pgs. $25.

STANLEY MOTOR CARRIAGE CO. *Stanley Steam Cars, Season of 1913.* Newton MA, 1913. 32 pgs. $50.
The Magic of Steam. 1918. $25.

STANLEY RULE & LEVEL CO. *1879 Price List.* $50-$75.
1883 Bailey's Patent Bench Planes. $50.
1888 Improved Labor Saving Tools. Hardcover. $250 and up.
1907 Tool Catalog, 2nd ed. $70.
1912 Condensed Price List. $50-$75.
1914 Pocket Catalog. $25-$50.
1927 to 1958. No. 34 Catalogs. $25-$50 each.
No. 134 Dealer Catalog. $175.

STAR GLASS & SUPPLY CO. *Soda Fountains, Glassware, Billiard Tables, etc.* Fostoria OH, circa 1910. 144 pgs. Folio. $450. This catalog combines 3 hot collectibles.

STAR STEEL SLEDS. *Coasters and Bobs. Catalog No. 26.* Harvard IL, circa 1900. 16 mo, 16 pgs. $50.

L. S. STARRETT CO. *Catalog No. 18.* Small hand tools for machinists. Athol MA, circa 1898. 8vo. 232 pgs. $35. Another, NY, circa 1905. 176 pgs. $25.
Catalog No. 20. 1900. 320 pgs. $45.
Book for Machinists' Apprentices. 1915. 175 pgs. $30.
50th Anniversary Catalog. 1930 $15-$25.

STATIONERY & OFFICE SUPPLIES. Catalogs from various local and national suppliers, 1880-1920, are now bringing only $10-$40 each. However, office supplies and business machines have become hot collectibles in Germany and well-illustrated old office machine and office supply catalogs could skyrocket in price if the fad reaches our shores.

STAVER CARRIAGE COMPANY. *The Staver Line for 1913.* Chicago IL, 1913. 4to, 112 pgs. $125.

GEO. STEERE. *Sign Letters.* Circa 1910. Slim 8vo. $35.

STEIFF. *Realistic Animal Catalogs.* Stuffed toys. 1956 thru 1961. $50 each.

STEINFELD BROTHERS. *Holiday Specialties and Toys.* New York, circa 1905. 70 pgs. 8vo. $195.

STEINWAY & SONS. *Pianofortes Catalog.* New York, 1923. 32 pgs. $60.

STERN BROTHERS. *Fashion Catalog No. 115.* NY, 1908. 120 pgs., 4to. Illus. include early automobiles. $65.

S. STEERNAU & COMPANY. *Sternauware.* NY, 1909. 307 pg. catalog full of Art Nouveau serving pieces. $100-$175.

STERLING CYCLE WORKS. *Sterling Bicycles, Built Like a Watch.* Kenosha WI, 1896. 8vo, 32 pgs. $100.

STERLING WHEELBARROWS. *1923 Catalog.* Concrete carts, etc. 40 pgs. $20.

A. W. STEVENS & SON. *The Stevens Threshing Machine.* Auburn NY, 1887. 40 pgs. 4to. $50.

B. A. STEVENS. *Catalog B. Billiard and Bar Supplies.* Toledo OH, 1892. 209 pgs. $450-$650.
Butcher's Catalog. Newspaper-type format, 15x22 in., 12 pgs. 1883. $25.

CHARLES A. STEVENS & BROS. *Fall & Winter Catalog. Cloaks & Silks.* Chicago, 1893-94. 52 pgs. $50.

STEVENS-DURYEA COMPANY. *Catalog of Automobiles.* Chicopee Falls MA, 1905. 64 pgs. $125-$200.

J. STEVENS ARMS & TOOL CO. *Rifles, Pistols. Pointers For Those Who Shoot.* 1896. 36 pgs. $100.
Firearms Catalog No. 53. Chicopee Falls MA, 1911. 72 pgs. $50.
Stevens Firearms. 1901. 128 pgs., 8vo. Color covers. $250-$350.
Sports Rifles. 1900. 128 pgs., 12mo. $65.

J. E. STEVENS CO. *Export Catalog of Iron Cap Pistols & Banks No. 51.* 1924. 26 pgs. $250-$400. Another. $125.
Illustrated Catalog of Iron Toys. Cromwell CT, circa 1900. 48 pgs. $250.

STEVENSON, VAN SCHAAK & CO. *Annual Prices Current.* Medicines, dyes, paints, medical instruments. Great illus. Chicago, 1884. 12mo, 593 pgs. $150-$225.

STEWART IRON WORKS CO. *Catalog No. 60A. Fences, Gates, etc.* Cincinnati OH, 1910. 84 pgs. $45.
Standard Wrought Iron Designs. 1928. 32 pgs. $25.

STICKLEY BROTHERS. *Institutional Furniture by Stickley.* Grand Rapids MI, circa 1920. 80 pgs. $60.

GUSTAVE STICKLEY. *Chips From the Workshops of United Crafts.* Eastwood NY, 1901. Stickley's first furniture catalog. Woodcuts and tipped-in photos. 30 pgs., 8vo. A rare find. $500-$850.
Chips. Furniture and accessories. Circa 1901-1905. 16mo, 64 pgs. $200.
Craftsman Homes. NY, circa 1910. 36 designs. $500.

L. & J. G. STICKLEY. *The Work of L. & J. G. Stickley.* Furniture. Fayetteville NY, circa 1925. 56 pgs. $150.

ST. LOUIS LIGHTNING ROD CO. *Lightning Rods & Balls.* Circa 1920, color illus. 108 pgs. $85-$100.

ST. LOUIS STAMPING CO. *How to Cook.* Cookbook plus 7 pages of pots and pans advertising. St. Louis, 1878. 16mo. 64 pgs. $50.

STOCKMAN-FARMER SUPPLY CO. *Catalog No. 60.* Denver, 1941. $50.
Catalog No. 64. 1942-43. Western Goods. $30.

GILBERT STODDARD CO. *Wholesale Grocers, Tobacconists and Importers.* New Haven CT, 1911. 92 pgs., 8vo. $25.

STODDARD MOTOR CAR CO. *Stoddard Dayton.* Dayton OH, 1910. Fold-out with pics of large cars of the 1910 period. 8 pgs. $20.

A. F. STOEGER. *Catalog of Arms & Ammunition.* 1924. 4to, 126 pgs. $75. 1931. 144 pgs. $50. 1934. 304 pgs. $35. *The Shooters' Bible.* 1936, 1947, 1948 & 1951. (4) for $32. 1960s, 1970s. $5 each.

WM. A. STOKES & CO. *Woodenware & Furniture.* NY, 1897-1898. 72 pgs. $75.

STOKES KIRK. *Military Supplies.* Philadelphia, circa 1925. Guns, uniforms, saddles. 30 pgs. $30.
Catalog 20B. Circa 1920. 50 pgs. $25-$35.

G. STOMPS & CO. *Chair Manufacturer's Catalog.* Dayton OH, 1885. 190 pgs. $150.

STOVER MFG. & ENGINE CO. *Samson Windmills and Parts.* Freeport IL circa 1915. 64 pgs. $90.

STOVES & HEATING EQUIPMENT.
Although Victorian stove catalogs are among the most beautifully illustrated price books of the period, they are not scarce.
In 1877 The National Association of Stove Manufacturers issued a directory of stove and heater names and trademarks listing 4,275 in use.
An average old stove catalog of the 1880-1920 period is worth between $25 and $60. Volumes containing 200 to 300 large pages of exceptional material might fetch $100 or more.

HERMAN STRATER & SONS. *Catalog No. 71, Bar Sundries.* Boston, circa 1900. Lemon squeezers to beer steins. 58 pgs. $125-$200.

STRATTON & TERSTEGGE CO. *Catalog No. 75. 1937-1938.* Auto parts, household, farm machinery. Includes 22 pg. toy section. 1,674 pgs. $45-$55.

MATHEW STRAUSS. *Catalog No. 50.* Auto supplies. Buffalo NY, circa 1910. 48 pgs. $45.

SIMON STRAUSS. *Tobacco Machines, Cigar Store Equip. & Figures.* New York, 1885. 32 pgs. 8vo. $185-$250.

DAVID L. STREETER. *Ideal Styles in Shoes.* Catalog of 1885. 30 pgs. $45.

CHARLES STRELINGER & CO. *Catalog of Tools, Supplies, Machinery.* Detroit MI, 1907. 502 pgs. $75.
1897 edition. Approx. 400 pgs. $75.

C. W. STUART & CO., NURSERYMAN. *Descript. Plate Book in Natural Colors.* Newark, New York, circa 1900. 192 pgs. $75.

STUDEBAKER BROS. MFG. CO. *Makers of Farm, Freight, Truck & Spring Wagons.* South Bend IN, 1884-1885. 16 pgs. $75.

STUDEBAKER CORP. OF AMERICA. *Trade Catalog No. 604.* Giant edition combining 4 catalogs of horse drawn buggies. South Bend IN, 1912. 387 pgs. $495. *The Studebaker. 3 Models, The "25", The "35", The "Six".* Detroit, 1910. 1915. 32 pgs. $100.

STUDEBAKER AUTOMOBILE CO. *1932 Studebaker.* 20 pgs. 5 full-page color illus. Mint. $100-$140. *Miracle Ride Studebaker Champions.* 1935. 24 pgs. $75. *Big Six & Special Models.* 1922. 28 pgs. $28. *Studebaker For 1953.* Color flyer. $25.

OTTO STUMPF CO. *Jewelry Catalog.* Chicago, 1910. 7x9 in. $75-$85.

SUNSET SEED & PLANT CO. *California Seeds Direct From Growers.* San Francisco, 1898. 64 pgs. $50.

SUPERIOR TOOL & SUPPLY. *Superior Baker's Machinery.* Cincinnati OH, 1907. 48 pgs. $35.

SURE HATCH INCUBATOR CO. *9th Annual Catalog of Incubators, Brooders.* Clay Center NE, 1906. $20.

J. H. SUTCLIFFE & CO. *Our Salesman, No. 7.* Everything from buggies, to guns, to potato mashers. Louisville KY, 1896. 242 pgs. $75.

ABRAM SWANN HAT COMPANY. *Circa 1910 catalog of men's hats.* Louisville KY. 19 pgs. $20.

SWARTCHILD CO. *Watchmakers & Jewelers Supplies.* 1932. 576 pgs. $50-$75.

SWEETSER, PEMBROOK AND CO. *Treatise on Wash Fabrics.* New York, 1899. 40 pgs. folio with color illustrations of fabrics. Also black and white illus. of fashions of the day. $100-$200.

SWEET'S ARCHITECTURAL CATALOG.
1922. 2,175 pgs. $100.
23rd Annual, 1929. 1,347 pgs. $125.
3 vols. 1928. 4,128 pgs. $125.
1926. 4to, 990 pgs. $75.
1906 First Edition. $80.

SWIFT & CO. *Swift Illustrated.* Chicago, 1900. catalog of 30 pgs. Factory view, etc. $25-$50.

SYRACUSE ORNAMENTAL CO. *"Syroco" Wood Carvings.* Syracuse NY, circa 1923. 10 x 13. 432 pgs. line drawings true to period styles. $50-$100.

Bakes Equally at the Same Time.

6 Sizes without Ovens.

3 Sizes with Ovens.

2 Sizes with High Top.

2 Sizes Parlor Heaters.

Send for Circular

AND

Price List.

1877

T

TABORS MODERN HOMES. *Practical Designs for City Suburban Residences, Stores, Churches, Schools*. 1889. 50 pgs. $75-$125.

GEO. H. TAY CO. *Catalog of Plumbing Fixtures*. San Francisco, 1905. 481 pgs. $50.

ALEX TAYLOR CO. *Catalog No. 30. Fall & Winter Sports*. New York, 1921. 8vo, 108 pgs. $40.

C. A. TAYLOR TRUNK WORKS. *Taylor Trunk Catalog*. Chicago, 1909. 12mo, 32 pgs. $25.

F. C. TAYLOR FUR CO. *Trappers Merchandise*. St. Louis MO, 1927. 4to, 48 pgs. $35. 1948-49 edition. $20.

H. E. TAYLOR CO. *Undertakers' Supplies*. New York, 1878. Well illustrated. 8vo, 32 pgs. $100.

TAYLOR INSTRUMENT CO. *Thermometers, Barometers, Hydrometers*. 1912. 208 pgs. $60.
Tycos Catalog. New York, 1923. 4to, 24 pgs. $25.

THAYER & CHANDLER. *Pyrography Catalog*. Chicago, 1906. H. Christy cover. 92 pgs. $60.
Artists' China Plates. 1925. 78 pgs. $20-$40.
Idea Book. 1930. 32 pgs. $15.

THAYER MANUFACTURING CO. *Quality Magic - Catalog No. 6*. Los Angeles, 1972. 240 pgs., 8vo. Fully illus. $55.

RICHARD E. THIBAUT. *Peerless Wall Paper Sample Book*. NY & elsewhere, 1909. 120 leaves. $50-$75.

F. H. THOMAS CO. *Surgical Supplies*. Boston, circa 1905. 576 pgs. $95. Another, 1917. Hardbound, includes electrical and X-Ray apparatus. 692 pgs. $125. Another, surgical only, 1917. 672 pgs. $75.

THOMAS MANUFACTURING CO. *Shears, Razors and Fine Cutlery*. Dayton OH, 1906. 62 pgs., 4to. $75.

SETH THOMAS SONS & CO. *Mantel Clocks*. NY, 1872. 8vo, 48 pgs. $150-$225.
Clock Movements. Circa 1910, 8vo, 15 pgs. $50.

THOMPSON BROS. *Outboard Motor Boats, Canoes*. 1929. 32 pgs. $25. 1933. Sail, duck, row boats. $50.

THOMPSON BROS. BOAT MFG. COMPANY. *Catalog No. 21. Canoes, Row Boats, etc.* Peshtigo WI, 1916-1918. 48 pgs. $50.

CLEON THROCKMORTON INC. *Theatre Scenery, Lighting, Hardware*. New York, 1932. 72 pgs. $25.

THURSTON MANUAL TRAINING SUPPLY. *Catalog of Hard to Get Materials*. 1926-27. 56 pgs. $12.

W. & J. TIEBOUT. *Catalog No. 17, Marine Hardware*. NYC, circa 1915. 300 pgs. $75-$125.

TIFFANY & CO. *Tiffany Favrile Glass, Windows, Mosaics, Granite*. (Ecclesiastical). New York, 1922. 128 pgs. $95.

TIFFANY GLASS COMPANY. *Tiffany Favrile Glass*. New York, 1896. 18 pgs. $225.

TIFFANY STUDIOS. *Bronze & Wrought Iron Catalog*. New York, 1912. 24 pgs. $125.
Ecclesiastical Department. New York, 1922. 64 pgs., 8vo. Stained glass, bronze, stone, etc. $175.

TIGER VEHICLES. *Catalog No. 1, Buggies, Wagons, Surreys*. Freeport IL, circa 1900. 114 pgs. $100-$175.

B. C. TILLINGHAST. *General Rubber Goods, Clothing, etc.* Philadelphia, 1913. 108 pgs. $50.

TODD-DONIGAN IRON CO. *Tool & Carriage Hardware*. Louisville KY, 1893. 4to, 390 pgs. $250.

TOLEDO SCALES. *Automatic Scales Catalog*. Ohio Match Co. Oct, 1921. $25.
Toledo Weight Control. OH, 1943. 90 pgs. $35.

TOPPING BROTHERS. *Heavy Hardware. Catalog No. 8*. NY, 1913. Tools, hardware, machinery for ship chandlery, contractors, miners, railroads. 8vo, 358 pgs. $60.

TOWLE MFG. CO. *Silverware Catalog*. Newburyport MA, 1905. 35 pgs. $39. Historical series. 1899. $50-$60 each.
Paul Revere, Artist-Patriot. 3rd Colonial Series. MA, 1901. Silverware. 8vo. 44 pgs. $60.

TOY & DOLL CATALOGS are always in demand even though the best examples have been reproduced by publishers such as Dover. We recently paid $450 for a 1890 Marshall Field Holiday Catalog which we will reprint as part of a Victorian Toy Book. At a recent auction event two determined bidders drove a 1917 Arcade Toy Truck Catalog up to $825. Not every old toy or doll catalog is worth this kind of money, but as a group they are among the most collectible. Even modern catalogs featuring Barbie Dolls and Hot Wheels are worth acquiring. Also, the toy sections from old department store catalogs such as Sears or Butler Bros. can be sold for $5 to $20 a page. See individual listings for more examples.

TRANSOGRAM. *Toys, Games, Craft Sets.* 1949. 36 pgs. $50.

TREMONT RUBBER CO. *Rainy Day Clothes.* Raincoats for men, boys, police, firemen. Boston, 1912. 8vo, 32 pgs. $25.

TRENTON IRON CO. *Wire Rope Tramways.* Illus. showing operation of tramway. 1892. 44 pgs. $100.

TRICYCLE MFG. CO. *Bean's Patent Wheelbarrows, Boys' Tricycles, Bicycles, Wagons, Carriages.* Springfield OH, 1883. 40 pgs., 8vo. $200-$250.

HENRY TROEMNER. *Manufacturer of Scales & Weights.* Philadelphia, 1921. 160 pgs. $150-$200.

CHARLES GREEN TRUAX & CO. *Catalog of Veterinary Instruments.* Chicago, 1893. 8vo, 238 pgs. $125.

EDWARD K. TRYON JR. & CO. *Shot Guns, Rifles, Revolvers, Ammunition and Sporting Goods.* Philadelphia, 1899. 112 pgs. 4to. $125. Another, 1891. $150.

JAMES W. TUFTS CO. *Soda Water Apparatus Catalog.* Boston, 1880. 16mo, 110 pgs. $200. 1884 edition. 256 pgs. 4to. Fantastic soda fountain equipment. $450-$650.

TUTTLE & BAILEY. *Warm Air Registers, Ventilators, Screens.* 1899. 46 pgs. $95.

TUTTLE & CLARK. *Catalog No. 56. Bluebook of Horse Goods.* 1920. 109 pgs. $50-$75.

20TH CENTURY RADIO MAIL ORDER CORP. *Catalog No. 1. 1930.* 40 pgs. of radio sets, cabinets, parts. $16.

C. H. TYLER & CO. *Business Desks for Railroads, Banks, Insurance, etc.* St. Louis, 1882. 38 pgs., 4to. Woodcuts of Victorian office furniture. $250-$400.

TYPEWRITER HEADQUARTERS. E. N. Miner's catalog of all makers; from Blickensderfer to Underwood. New York, circa 1896-1900. 16mo, 32 pgs. $75.

U

UNDERTAKERS' SUPPLIES
Yes, some people do collect this stuff, (caskets, embalming chemicals, instruments, etc.). Catalogs of the 1880 to 1925 period are worth from $40 to $100 each. A large collection of (90) undertaking catalogs was recently offered for sale at $1,800.

UNCLE SAM'S SHOEMAKERS. *Wholesale Shoe Catalog*. Boston, circa 1910. 12mo, 32 pgs. $20.

UNDERTAKERS SUPPLY CO. *The Superior Line*. "Everything for the Mortician." Chicago IL, 1924. 160 pgs. $40.

UNDERWOOD TYPEWRITER CO. New York, circa 1910. 32 pgs. $45.

UNION BRASS MANUFACTURING CO. *Railway Coach & Fine House Hardware*. Chicago, 1884. 209 pgs. $175.

UNION CYCLE MANUFACTURING CO. *Union Bicycles*. Boston MA, 1894. 32 pgs. $75. 1897 edition. 32 pgs. $40.

UNION GAS ENGINE CO. *Union Stationary and Marine Gas & Oil Engines*. San Francisco, ca 1905. 52 pgs. $60.

UNION GOSPEL PUBLISHING CO. *Sunday School Supplies*. Cleveland, 1923. 8vo, 124 pgs. $15.

UNION IRON WORKS. *Catalog No. 3 Mining Machinery*. San Francisco, 1896. 8vo, 204 pgs. Including birds-eye view of San Francisco. $250.
Catalog No. 26. $270 pgs. $60.

UNION MANUFACTURING CO. *Catalog of Wooden Ware*. Toledo OH, 1876. 24 pgs. $95.

UNION STOVE WORKS. *Catalog No. 78*. New York, 1912. 8vo, 144 pgs. $40.

UNION TYPE FOUNDRY. *Type Specimen Book*. Chicago, 1884. 336 pgs. $250.

UNION WIRE MATTRESS CO. *Beds of All Kinds*. Chicago, 1901. Simple hospital-style to elaborate Victorian folding beds and children's cribs. 4to, 144 pgs. $75.

UNITED CASKET CO. *Catalog*. Louisville, 1922. 4to, 78 pgs. $40.

UNITED CIGAR STORES. *Premium Catalog*. 1928. 48 pgs. of gifts. $12.

UNITED COMPANY. *Thoroughbred Poultry*. New York, circa 1905. 180 pgs. $75. Poultry Supplies. 1900. $75.

UNITED FACTORIES. *Stoves, Furniture, Sewing Machines*. Cleveland, 1912. Hardware, farm-related items, carriages, etc. 4to, 270 pgs. $75.

UNITED LEAD CO. *Architectural Ornamental Leadwork*. 1928. 60 pgs. $75. Another, pipes, gutters, etc. $45.

UNITED MOTORS SERVICE. *Catalog No. 25 Service Parts*. Detroit MI, 1922. 146 pgs. $48.

UNITED PROFIT SHARING CO. *Premium Catalog*. United Cigar Store certificates. NY, 1930s. 8vo, 68 pgs. $15.

UNITED SHOE MACHINERY CO. *The Shoe in Romance and History*. Boston, early 1900s. 32 pgs. $15.

UNITED STATES CARTRIDGE CO. *Firearms Collection Catalog*. Lowell MA, circa 1905. Crossbows to revolvers. 8vo, 140 pgs. $60-$120.

UNITED STATES QUARRY TILE CO. *Pattern Book, Floor and Garden Tiles*. Parkersburg WV, 1931. 48 pgs. $40.

UNITED STATES RUBBER CO. *Automobile Tire and Accessory Catalog*. Chicago, 1917. 362 pgs. $20.

UNIVERSAL STUDIOS. *Movie Rental Catalog*. 30th Anniversary edition, 1946-1976. 264 pgs. $20.

U. S. BANK FURNITURE CO. *Bank Fixtures and Furniture*. Indianapolis IN, 1911. Signs, grills, gratings, desks. 8vo, 80 pgs. $50.

U. S. WIND ENGINE & PUMP CO. *Halladay's Standard Wind Mills Catalog*. Batavia IL, 1879. 40 pgs. $150. 1886 edition. 92 pgs. $135.

UTTERBACK BROTHERS CO. *Carriages, Harness, Horse & Stable Goods*. Bangor ME, ca 1910. 4to, 144 pgs. $125.

V

VAN CAMP HARDWARE & IRON CO. *Sporting Goods & Auto Accessories*. Indianapolis, 1914. 4to, 134 pgs. $100. 1933 edition, 2,423 pgs. $95-$125.

VANGUARD CYCLE CO. *Vanguard and Climber Bicycles*. Indianapolis, circa 1900. 16mo, 16 pgs. $50.

PETER VAN SCHAACK & SONS. *Annual Illustrated Drug Catalog*. Everything from glassware to paint and perfume. Philadelphia, 1887. 739 pgs., Many color plates. $350-$500. Another, Chicago, 1905. 1,389 pgs. $150.

VARNEY ELECTRICAL SUPPLY CO. *Catalog No. 3, 1913*. Distributors of everything from toasters to telephone booths. 7 x 10 , 906 pgs. $100-$175.

VAUGHAN'S GARDENING. *Illustrated Catalog*. 1929. $25.

VERMONT FARM MACHINE CO. *Davis Swing Churn*. 24 pg. catalog, circa 1896. Mint. $45.
The Improved United States Separator. Bellows Falls VT, 1904. 19 pgs. $30.

VERMONT MARBLE CO. *Tombstone Catalog*. Proctor VT, 1923. 570 pgs. $25.
Vermont Marble Cos. Designs. 1905. 386 pgs. $35.

VICK, JAMES. *Vick's Illustrated Guide for Flower Garden & Catalog of Seeds*. 7th ed., NY, 1868. 96 pgs., 8vo. $50.
Vick's Illustrated Catalog of Hardy Bulbs. New York, 1872. 32 pgs. $20.
Vick's Monthly Magazine-Catalog. 1885, 1886. $15-$25 each.
Vick's Illustrated Monthly . Bound volume for entire year 1880. $95. October, 1885. $15. Aug, 1886. $25. Various issues, 1890s. $10.

VICTOR PICTURE PROJECTORS. *Steropticans, Motion Picture Projectors*. Davenport IA, 1918. 8vo, 24 pgs. $50.

VICTOR TALKING MACHINE CO. *Victor & Monarch Records*. Philadelphia, 1901. 8 pgs. $35.
1908 Edition. (18 pgs.) $15. (126 pgs.) $50.
Victrola Catalog. 1921. 12 pgs. $20.
Victor Book of the Opera. 1925 to 1929 eds. $8-$15 each.
Victor Records. 1922-1930. $25 each.

VICTOR SAFE & LOCK CO. *Office Desks*. Cincinnati OH, 1896. 20 pgs. $50.
Safes, Vaults, Boxes. 1901. 142 pgs. $100. 1904 edition. 200 pgs. $100. 1911 edition. 152 pgs. $75.
Safes & Desks. 1907. 24 pgs. $30.
One Hundred and Fifty Thousand Now in Use. Cincinnati, 1904. 160 pgs., some color. $100.

VICTOR SEWING MACHINE CO. *The New "Victor" Sewing Machine*. Middletown CT & Philadelphia PA, circa 1880. 16mo fold-out to 8 panels. $20.

VICTOR SPORTING GOODS CO. *1906 Catalog*. Baseball, boxing, football, golf, tennis. Springfield MA, 1906. 58 pgs. $75.

VISALIA STOCK SADDLE CO. *Catalog No. 31, Western Gear*. San Francisco CA, 1935. 128 pgs. $35.

F. VOGEL & SONS. *Art Embroideries & Fancy Goods*. Chicago, circa 1900. 4to, 32 pgs. $30.

WILLIAM VOGEL & BROS. *Tinware Catalog*. New York, circa 1880. Packaging products, etc. 40 pgs. $65.

VOGUE PATTERN BOOK. Conde Nast Pub. Co. March, 1939. 96 pgs. $20.

VOIGTLANDER & SHON. *Catalog of Cameras, Lenses*. 1914. 48 pgs. $25-$45.

VOLKSWAGEN. *Volkswagen Sedans*. Brochure. Wolfsburg, Germany, circa 1950. 8 pg. 4to. Full-color cutaway. $25.
What Happens When You Drive a Volkswagen and Why. 1964, 16 pgs. $25.

VOM CLEFF & CO. *Hardware and Cutlery*. New York, 1906. Everything from nippers to razors & scissors. 7 x 10. 128 pgs. $100.

EDWARD VOM HOFF. *Fine Fishing Tackle*. New York, 1929. 6 x 9. 173 pgs. $35.

VON GERICHTEN ART GLASS CO. Columbus OH, 1897. Clear and colored glass, leaded, bent. Windows, storefronts, churches, etc. 7 x 10. 96 pgs. $125.

W

WADDELL COMPANY. *Catalog No. 19*. Decorative architectural elements. Grand Rapids MI, 1903. 200 pgs. $40.

WADSWORTH HOWLAND & CO. *Artists & Draftsmens Supplies*. Boston, 1912. 224 pgs. $35-$50.
1885 Edition. 92 pgs. $40.

LOUIS WAGNER CO. *Cigar Label Sample Book*. No date. (More pages than most examples). Auction. $715.

WAKEFIELD RATTAN CO. *Children's Carriages*. Boston, 1894. 68 pgs., 4to. More than fifty different styles of baby buggies in woven rattan, etc. $130-$165.

WALKER & COMPANY. *Catalog of Fruits For Sale*. Boston, 1847. 20 pgs. $175.

WALKER & GIBSON. *A List of Druggists' Sundries*. Illus. cat. of 1905. 284 pgs. $100.

WALKER-STETSON. *News for Buyers*. Jan, 1902. Fancy dry goods catalog. 4to, 48 pgs. $35-$45. 1920 edition. $20.

W. & H. WALKER. *Clothing Catalog*. Pittsburgh PA, 1912 to 1916. Avg. 100 pgs. $20-$25 each.

WALLACE & SONS MFG. CO. *Catalog of Prize Cups & Trophies*. Wallingford CT, 1909. 24 pgs. $40.
Catalog of Pewter Utensils. 1930. 4to, 16 pgs. $30.
Silverware. 1928. 4to, 96 pgs. $95.

WALTHAM MANUFACTURING CO. *Orient Bicycles*. "Up to 10 riders". Waltham MA, 1898. 8vo, 32 pgs. $150. 1899 edition. smaller, 12mo. 32 pgs. $100.

WALTHAM WATCH COMPANY. *Home of the Waltham Watch*. Waltham MA, 1912. Factory views. 36 pgs. $25.

WALWORTH MFG. CO. *Plumbing Fixtures, Tools, Gas Engines*. Boston, 1924. 615 pgs. 7 x 10. $75.

JOHN WANAMAKER. *China, Cut Glass, Art Wares, Lamps*. 1895. 52 pgs. $95-$150.
Wanamaker Diary. NY, 1907. 12mo, 445 pgs. $65-$75.
Wanamaker's Correct Horse Goods. New York, 1908. 190 pgs. $150.
Fashion Catalogs. 1906 to 1918. $45-$90 each.

C. E. WARD CO. *Catalog No. 41. I.O.O.F. Costumes & Regalia*. Circa 1910. 4to, 73 pgs. 8 color plates. $75.
Catalog No. 109 - Odd Fellows Costumes. New London OH, circa 1922. 128 pgs. $35.

MONTGOMERY WARD. *Christmas Catalogs*.
1933 to 1935.....................................$65-$125.
1936 to 1940.....................................$55-$100.
1941 to 1945.......................................$45-$95.
1946 to 1966.......................................$40-$80.
1967 to 1980.......................................$20-$30.
1981 to 1985.......................................$15-$20.

MONTGOMERY WARD. *Fall & Winter Catalogs*.
1920 to 1925.......................................$75-$90.
1926 to 1930.......................................$65-$80.
1931 to 1935.......................................$60-$70.
1936 to 1940.......................................$50-$65.
1941 to 1945.......................................$45-$60.
1946 to 1955.......................................$35-$50.
1956 to 1960.......................................$30-$45.
1961 to 1970.......................................$25-$35.
1971 to 1985.......................................$15-$20.

Note: Spring and Summer editions are less.

MONTGOMERY WARD. *Misc. Early Catalogs*.
Catalog No. 42. 1887. 364 pgs. $225.
No. 47. 1890. 540 pgs. $175-$195.
Furniture Catalog, 1890. 124 pgs. $75.
General Catalog. 1904. $125-$150.
Spring & Summer. 1898. 812 pgs. $150-$195.
House Furnishings. 1911. 114 pgs. $25.
Jan-Feb Sale. 1915. 112 pgs. $45.
15th Annual Sale. 1917. 96 pgs. $30.
Fashions. 1914. 272 pgs. $70.
No. 89. 1917. $100-$125.

MONTGOMERY WARD. *Specialty Catalogs*.
Camera Catalogs. 1949 to 1963. $15-$20 each.
Farm Catalogs. 1948 to 1980. $12-$20 each.
Fishing & Hunting. 1949 to 1960. $15-$25 each.
Pure Food Groceries. 1897 to 1919. $25-$40 each.
Garden Catalogs. 1951 to 1965. $10-$15 each.
Wallpaper Catalogs. 1920 to 1954. $15-$35 each.

WARDER, BUSHNELL & GLESSNER CO. *Champion Harvesting Machines*. Chicago, ca 1890-95. 16 pgs. $50-$65.

WARNER & SWASEY COMPANY. *Astronomical Instruments*. Cleveland, 1900. 4to, 36 halftone plates. $75.

WARNER'S SAFE YEAST CO. *Rheumatic Cure*. Patent medicine catalog. Rochester NY, 1883. 66 pgs. $20. *Nature's Great Secret*. Log cabin remedies. 1887. $15.

WARREN FEATHERBONE CO. *Book of Gowns*. Three Oaks MI, 1912. Feminine supports revealed. 12mo, 24 pgs. $15.

J. D. WARREN MFG. CO. *Standard Hardware Store Fixtures*. Chicago, 1913. Color plates of display fixtures for axes, guns, saws, brooms, etc. 144 fabulous pages. $250-$325.

WARRIOR MOWER CO. CATALOG. *Mowers, Reapers, Horse Rakes*. Buffalo NY, 1886. 32 pgs. $50.

WASHBURN CO. *Kitchen Utensils, etc*. 1924. 116 pgs. $50.

E. G. WASHBURNE & CO. *Copper Weather Vanes*. New York. 1914 Catalog. 32 pgs. $250. 1920 Catalog. 32 pgs. $250.

```
WASHING MACHINES have been around since the
early 1800s. They were a spontaneous folk invention.
By the year 1900 nearly 2,000 washing machine-
related patents had been filed and 100 factories were in
full production. Motors were added in 1910 and
bottom-mounted agitators followed in 1922. Maytag
was first on the market with a non-rusting aluminum
tub and captured 60% of the business. Washing
machine catalogs circa 1915-1930, of 16 pages or less,
are common at $10-$25 each.
```

WATERBURY CLOCK CO. *Waterbury Clock Co*. Waterbury CT, 1875. 8vo, 84 pgs. $200. *Catalog No. 155*. Folio. 1909. 92 pgs. $150-$250.

WATERBURY WATCH CO. *Treatise on Duplex Escapement*. 1880. $40.

WATERLOO GASOLINE ENGINE CO. *Catalog of Waterloo Boy Gas Engines*. Waterloo IA, circa 1912. 32 pgs. $100.

WATSON PAINTERS SUPPLIES. *Catalog No. 54*. Paints, brushes, etc. Chicago, Circa 1932. 144 pgs. $25.

WAVERLEY CO. *Waverley Electric Car Catalog*. Color plate centerfold. Indianapolis IN, circa 1905. Folio size. 28 pgs. Mint cond. $250.

```
WEATHER VANES are important pieces of
Americana. Almost any circa 1870-1925 catalog with
a good-sized group of figural weather vane illus-
trations is worth between $150 and $400.
```

WEBB MANUFACTURING CO. *Catalog "B". Plumbers Supplies*. Boston, 1900. 321 pgs. $125.

F. WEBER & CO. *Illustrated Price List of Artist's Materials and Draughtsmen's Supplies*. Includes sign painters and coach painters materials. Philadelphia, circa 1885. 16mo, 321 pgs. Worn. $50. 1900 edition. 280 pgs. $75. *Architects & Engineers Supplies. Vol. III*. Dec, 1895. $85.

WEBER LIFELIKE FLY CO. *Catalog No. 17*. 1936. 6 x 9. 78 pgs. $40.

WEBSTER BASKET CO. *Catalog of Fruit Packages and Baskets*. Webster NY, 1922. 40 pgs. $30.

JOSIAH WEDGWOOD & SONS LTD. *Wedgwood*. Etruria, United Kingdom, circa 1925. 95 pgs., folio. Color & b/w plates of china, lustre, etc. $500.

WEED & COMPANY. *"1818 Brand" Hardware Catalog*. Axes to dog muzzles. New York, 1915. 4to. 808 pgs. $75.

A. J. WEED & CO. *Venetian Iron*. New York, 1893. 8vo, 24 pgs. $40.

WEEDEN MFG. CORP. *Weeden Toy Steam Engines*. 19 page catalog, 1939. $75. *Miniature Steam Engines, etc*. New Bedford MA, circa 1905. 28 pgs. $150.

WEEKS & POTTER. *Foreign and Domestic Drugs*. 1890. 600 pgs. $65. *Soda Water Supplies*. Combination soda fountain syrup catalog and "cookbook" for soda jerks. Boston MA, 1893. 106 pgs. $150.

W. M. WELCH, SCIENTIFIC CO. *Catalog G*. Physics-Chemistry items. Chicago, 1919. 318 pgs. $35. *Laboratory Apparatus*. 1922. 445 pgs. $35. 1928 edition. 476 pgs. $35-$65. *Scientific Apparatus For Schools*. 1934. 510 pgs. $60.

WESTERN AUTO. *Automobile Parts, Radios, Sports Equip*. 1932. 132 pgs. $30-$40. *Christmas Catalogs*. 1954 to 1974. $15-$30 each.

WESTERN ELECTRIC CO. *Electro-Medical Surgical Apparatus*. Chicago IL, 1875. 77 pgs. $200.

WESTERN RANCHMAN OUTFITTERS. *Fall & Winter, 1940-41*. Clothes, saddles, tack. 52 pgs. $35.

WESTERN WHEEL WORKS. *Cresent Bicycles*. Chicago, 1897. 8vo, 40 pgs. $75.

A. B. & W. T. WESTERVELT. *Catalog No. 3 Stable Fittings*. New York, 1881. 64 pgs. $200.

WESTINGHOUSE ELECTRIC CO. *Catalog of Household Appliances*. New York, 1934. 24 pgs. $25.
Electrical Supplies, full line. 1921. 1,310 pgs. $80. 1936. 637 pgs. $30.
Cars and Car Equipment. New York, 1920. Trolley car catalog. 4to, 87 pgs. $100.

WESTMORLAND GLASS CO. *Early American Glassware Catalog*. Reproductions. 1953. 35 pgs. $25.

WESTON ENGINE CO. *High Speed Engines*. 1897. $45.

WEYERHAUSER SALES CO. *4 Square Book of Homes*. House plans and renderings. St. Paul MN, 1942. $50.
Good Houses. 1922. 4to, 64 pgs. $45.

WHEELER, EDWIN W. *Type Specimen Catalog*. Boston, 1900. VG. $50.

WHEELER & WILSON MFG. CO. *Sewing Machines*. Albany NY, 1859. 16 pgs. $100. No place, 1860. $50. Chicago, 1873. 8 pgs. $40. Albany, 1878. 16 pgs. $25.

WHEELING CORRUGATING CO. *Catalog No. 290*. Sheet metal coverings, stores & offices. 1911. 192 pgs. $40.
Catalog No. 260. 1907. 110 pgs. $40.
Catalog No. 313. Ceilings. 1914. 270 pgs. $80.

WHITALL, TATUM & CO. *Glassware and Druggists' Sundries*. Philadelphia, 1891. 200 pgs., 8vo. Some color plates, show jars, etc. $250.
Druggists Sundries Price List. 1877. 21 pgs. glassware, drawer pulls, etc. $75.
Druggists', Chemists and Perfumers' Glassware. 1916. 190 pgs. $125.

WHITE COMPANY OF CLEVELAND. *White Bulletin No. 14*. Steam car brochure. Cleveland, 1907. 32 pgs. $150.

WHITE & DAVIS. *Saddlery and Cowboy Goods*. Spring & Summer 1932. $35-$70. 1941 edition. 34 pgs. $25-$45.

E. WHITE, LETTER-FOUNDRY. *Specimen of Printing Types and Ornaments*. New York, 1829. 8vo, marbled boards, 128 leaves. Superb cuts of the period. Columbia University has one copy; if you find another it may fetch up to $2,500.

WHITE FROST REFRIGERATOR CO. *In the Great White Frost There is a Place for Everything*. Jackson MI, 1915. 28 pgs. $25.

JOHN A. WHITE CO. *Some Woodworking Machinery*. Dover NY, 1894. 88 pgs. $75.

WHITE MFG. CO. *Hearse Mountings*. Plumes, rails, handles. Circa 1900. 37 pgs. $40.

R. H. WHITE & CO. *Spring & Summer Fashions*. Boston, 1883. 256 pgs. $7.

WHITE SEWING MACHINE CO. *The White Bicycle*. Color illus. catalog. Cleveland OH, 1897. Superb. $275.
Eldridge Special Sewing Machines. Boston, 1906. 16 pgs. $20.
Incomparable White at Army Maneuvers. Cleveland, 1904. Steam automobiles. 32 pgs. $200.

S. S. WHITE DENTAL MFG. CO. *Instruments, Appliances for Crown and Bridgework*. Philadelphia, 1894. 64 pgs., 8vo. $100-$150.
Catalog of Dental Engines and Equipment. 1895. 104 pgs. $90. 1892. 84 pgs. $125.
World's Premium Procelain Teeth. Philadelphia, 1911. 216 pgs. $75.

WHITEHEAD & HOAG CO. *Catalog No. 143 Badges & Awards*. For winners of dog and stock shows. NJ, circa 1905. 20 pgs. $40.
Fireman's Badges. Catalog No. 26. NJ, 1895. 18 pgs., 4to, color illus. $125.
Catalog of pins and medals, fraternal. 1895. 4to. $75.
Union Made Badges. 1896. 20 pgs. $25.

WHITELY FASSLER & KELLY. *Reaping & Mowing Machine Catalog*. 1878. 64 pgs. $45.

WHITING-ADAMS CO. *Brush Manufacturers*. Almanac & Catalog. Boston, 1915. $15.

JOHN L. WHITING & SON. *Catalog No. 45*. Hundreds of Brushes. Boston, 1910. 257 pgs. 10 color plates. $45.
Whitings Celebrated Brushes. Boston, circa 1910. 12 pg. folio. $20-$30.

B. M. WHITLOCK. *Clothing & Furnishings for Officers and Crews of Yachts*. NY, 1889. 78 pgs., 8vo. $250-$325.

P. A. WHITMORE. *Catalog No. 2 Barber Supplies*. Portland ME, 1926. 12mo, 72 pgs. $75.

HARLEY WICKHAM CO. *Sporting Goods*. Erie PA, 1928. 4to, 32 pgs. $25.

JASON WIELER & SON. *Jewelry Catalog, 1917*. Boston, 1917. 128 pgs. $35.

GEORGE WIEDERHOLD. *Illustrated Catalog of Ladies Undergarments*. Lots of Hoops and Bustles. New York, 1883. 16 pg. $40-$50.

WILCOX AND WHITE. *Organ Catalog*. Meridien CT, 1884. 8vo. $75.

WILLIAM WILER. *Stair Rods, Brass Beds, Cornice Poles*. Philadelphia, 1889. 71 pgs. $150.

WILKINS TOY CO. *Malleable Iron Toys*. Keene NH, 1916. Fire engines, trucks, trains, etc. 8vo, 50 pgs. $250.

A. J. WILKINSON & CO. *Patent Foot, Hand & Steam Engines*. Boston MA, 1893. 8vo, 36 pgs. $100.
Tools & Supplies. Carpenters' blacksmiths, etc. Boston, circa 1910. 4to, 215 pgs. $75.
Machinists' Tools & Supplies, Hardware, For Blacksmiths, Pattern Makers, Model Makers, etc. Boston, 1879. 112 pgs. $150.
Folding & Adjustable Draw Knife. Boston, 1889. 6 pgs. $50-$70.

JOHN WILKINSON CO. *Scientific Roller Skates*. Chicago IL, 1882. 8 pgs. $50.
Scroll Saws, Lathes, Tools. 1885-1886. 9 x 12. 56 pgs. $50-$75.
Gymnasium, Theatrical & General Sporting Goods. 1886. 36 pgs. $100.

A. C. WILLIAMS. *Toy Catalog Supplements*. Pair, dated 1908. Auction. $358.

WILLIAMS BROTHERS MFG. CO. *Price List, Electro Silver Plated Spoons, Forks*. Hartford CT, 1884. 42 pgs. $150.

WILLIAMS CO. *Gold & Rolled Plate Jewelry*. 1883. $40.

CHARLES WILLIAMS STORES. *General Merchandise*, similar to Sear's Catalog. Fall & Winter 1914. 1,186 pgs. $100. 1915 to 1920 editions. $45-$95 each. 1921 to 1935. $35-$70 each.
Automobile Supplies. NYC, 1916. 48 pgs. $48.

FRANK W. WILLIAMS CO. *Picture and Picture Frames*. Various catalogs issued from 1902-1913. $25-$40 each.

WILLIAMSPORT FURNITURE MFG. *Dining & Bedroom Furniture*. 1912. 50 pgs. $25-$50.

E. J. WILLIS CO. *Sail and Motor Yacht Equipment*. Lamps, stores, hardware, accessories. NY, 1929. 96 pgs. $65.
1936 Edition, 6 x 9 in. 264 pgs. $28.

WILLIS MANUFACTURING CO. *Catalog No. 6, Twentieth Anniversary*. Galesburg IL, 1911. Architectural Sheet Metal, Tin ceilings, Weather vanes, etc. 180 pgs. $150.

WILLMARTH FISHING TACKLE. *1937 Catalog*. $30.

WILLYS-OVERLAND CO. *Overland Whippet*. Owners manual, Model 96. Toledo OH, 1926. 36 pgs. $50.
1930 Willys Knight. 4 double pgs. $40.

WILSON MFG. CO. *Plumbers' Supplies of Every Description*. Baths, sinks, closets, traps, etc. Rome NY, circa 1897. 4to, 49 pgs. $100.

WILSON SPORTING GOODS. *Gateway to Golf for 1937*. $40. Spring & Summer 1948. $30.

WILSON'S. *17th Annual Seed Catalog*. Fruits, Vegetables, etc. with poultry section. Mechanicsville PA, 1893. 112 pgs. $35-$55.

WINCH BROTHERS. *The Little Drummer - Boots, Shoes, Rubbers*. Boston, circa 1897. 126 pgs. $50. 1901 edition. 148 pgs. $20. 1889 edition. 80 pgs. $25.

WINCHESTER REPEATING ARMS CO. *Catalog No. 82, Rifles & Shotguns*. New Haven CT, 1920. 208 pgs. $100.
Catalog No. 78. 1913. 212 pgs. $75.
Catalog No. 81. 1918. 216 pgs. $95.
Catalog No. 70. 1903. 160 pgs. $100.

GEORGE WINDHEIM. *Catalog of Saddlery, Horse Goods*. Utica NY, 1906. 190 pgs. $100.

WING & SONS. *Complete Information About Pianos*. New York, 1900. 114 pgs. Folio. $95-$150. Smaller version, 1897. 8vo. $45-$75.

WINTON MOTOR CAR COMPANY. *The Winton Six for 1913*. Cleveland OH, 1913. 62 pgs. $100.

WIRE GOODS CO. *Hardware, Kitchenware Specialties*. 1915. 256 pgs. $75-$125.

R. H. WOLFF & CO. LTD. *Wolff-American High Art Cycles*. NY, 1896. 32 pgs. of hard-working dwarfs making bicycles. 8vo. Near Mint. $175.

WOLF, SAYER & HELLER. *Packer's, Butchers' & Sausage Makers' Tools, Supplies*. New York, 1904. 286 pgs. $50.

WOLLENSAK. *Camera Lenses, Shutters*. 1914. 40 pgs. $35.

J. R. WOOD & SON. *Jewelry, Watches, etc.* 1918. 160 pgs. $80.

WALTER A. WOOD. *Mowing and Reaping Machines*. Hoosic Falls NY, circa 1857. 36 pgs. $150. 1868 edition, 48 pgs. $85. 1879. $50. 1883-1894. $40-$55. 1895. $30.

WOODHOUSE MFG CO. *Fire Department Supplies*. New York, 1929. 250 pgs. $65-$95.

WILLIAM WOOD & CO. *Ice Tools Catalog*. Arlington MA, 1903. Everything for the icehouse owner. 8vo, 56 pgs. $75-$100.

BENJ. WOODS. *Type Specimen Catalog*. Boston, 1874. 287 pgs. $200.

WOODWARD CO. *Catalog "A". Saddlery*. Harness, Saddles, Tack, etc. Syracuse NY, 1908. 409 pgs. $75.

F. W. WOOLWORTH. *1956 Christmas Catalog*. 64 pgs. $30. *Fifty Years of Woolworth*. 1929 booklet. 48 pgs. $30.

WORCESTER CORSET COMPANY. *The Ladies' Companion, WCC Corsets*. Worcester MA, 1891. 30 pgs. $40.

WORLD MFG. CO. *Standard Household Items for Agents*. New York, 1881. Toys, guns, watches, jewelry, books, etc. 8vo, 64 pgs. $45.
Fall and Winter Catalog. Books, novelties. New York, 1883. 8vo. 48 pgs. $65.

GEO. WORTHINGTON CO. *Christmas Gifts & Toys*. 1935. 108 pgs. $50-$95.

WRIGHT AERONAUTICAL ENGINES. *1929 Catalog: Whirlwind, Cyclone and Gipsy Engines*. Paterson NJ. 36 pgs. 9 x 11. $75.

WRIGHT AIRPLANES. *"Wright, Your Plane is Ready Sir."* Sikorsky, Vought, Stinson, etc. 25 planes pictured. Paterson NJ. circa 1920-1930. $75.

WRIGHT & DITSON. *Illustrated Catalog of Out and Indoor Games and Amusements*. Boston, 1886, 1st ed. $250.
Catalog of Games & Apparatus for Physical Exercise Boston, 1886. 64 pgs. $85.
Lawn Tennis Guide for 1895. Boston, 1895. Dark end pgs., chips. $50.
Fall & Winter Trade Price List, 1919. Illus. with sports equipment and some bicycles. 72 pgs. $100-$150.

WRIGHT CO. *Catalog of Kitchen Gadgets*. Cleveland, circa 1920. 8vo, 66 pgs. $30.

WM. E. WRIGHT & SONS CO. *Bias Fold Tape, Sewing Catalog No. 25*. Xmas issue. New Jersey, 1925. $25.

WRIGHT & WILHELMY CO. *Catalog No. 23, Wholesale Hardware*. Omaha NE, 1923. Guns, knives, auto supplies, houseware. 9 x 11. 1,096 pgs., some in color. $100-$150.

WURLITZER MUSICAL INSTRUMENTS. *Catalog No. 50*. 1901-02. 410 pgs. $125.
Catalog No. 110. 1917. 154 pgs. $95.
Catalog No. 125. 1922. 144 pgs. $75.

X-RAY EQUIPMENT.
Medical supply catalogs from the early 1900s featuring X-Ray equipment (Roentgen, Roentgenography, etc.) are often listed in dealer catalogs in the $100 range. The very earliest X-Ray catalogs, from the late 1890s, sell for $200 and up.

Y

YALE & TOWNE MFG. CO. *Trade Catalog of Locks & Hardware, No. 18*. NY, 1905. 207 pgs. 8vo. Hard cover, embossed boards. $100-$150.
Keys and Blanks. NY, 1918. 8vo, 52 pgs. $30.

YAWMAN & ERBE MFG. CO. *Suggestions for Office Filing*. Rochester NY. Various card filing, duplicating and typing machines described in catalogs issued from 1900-1910. 8vo, 24 to 68 pgs. $20-$30.

YOST & CO. *Conjuring Apparatus*. Philadelphia, ca 1910. Over 500 tricks described & priced. 8vo, 125 pgs. $75.

YOUNG AMERICAN PRESS CO. *Printing Press Catalog*. 1888. 62 pgs. 6 x 9. $75.

OTTO YOUNG & CO. *Watches, Diamonds, Jewelry, Silver*. Chicago, 1898. 495 pgs. $100-$150.
Jewelers' Tools & Materials. 1898. 720 pgs. $85.

PAUL YOUNG FINE, FISHING TACKLE. *1935 Catalog, "More Fishing, Less Fussing"*. Detroit MI, 1934. 132 pgs. $35.

BIBLIOGRAPHY

One of the first things we notice when we enter an antique shop or a used book store is the long shelf full of well-worn reference books sitting behind the proprietor's desk. They have probably been accumulated over a period of several years and are the most valuable tools of his or her trade.

No single volume can possibly list every collectible book published during the last two centuries; there are millions of titles extant. Most bookmen own five or six general price guides and take them all (including this one) with a grain of salt. It requires several years of dealing to figure out what the market will bear.

Some of the reference books listed here may still be in print and available from their publishers, but many are not. Watch the classified ads in *AB Bookman's Weekly* for secondhand copies or consult your local librarian. Now is the time to begin accumulating your own tools of the trade.

As an aspiring collector, book scout, or dealer, you should begin your quest for knowledge by subscribing to two or three of the trade periodicals listed immediately below. Some of the publishers will send you a freebie, others will require payment for a sample issue. It is important to be familiar with these publications if you are serious about the book business!

PERIODICALS

AB BOOKMAN'S WEEKLY. Box AB, Clifton NJ 07015.

BOOK QUOTE. 2319-C West Rohman Ave, Peoria IL 61604.

FIRSTS: COLLECTING MODERN FIRST EDITIONS. PO Box 16945, North Hollywood CA 91615.

THE BOOKSELLER. PO Box 8183, Ann Arbor MI 48107.

THE PAPER COLLECTOR'S MARKETPLACE. Box 127, Scandinavia WI 54977.

THE PAPER AND ADVERTISING COLLECTOR. PO Box 50, Mount Joy PA 17552.

THE ILLUSTRATOR COLLECTOR'S NEWS. Box 1958, Sequim WA 96382.

ANTIQUE WEEK. PO Box 90, Knightstown IN 46148.

GENERAL BOOK PRICE GUIDES

AMERICAN BOOK PRICES CURRENT. Washington CT, Bancroft, Parkman. Annual.

BOOKMAN'S PRICE INDEX. Daniel and Virginia McGrath. Detroit MI, Gale Research, Biannual.

BOOK PRICES: USED AND RARE. Edward M. Zempel and Linda Verkler. Peioria IL, Spoon River Press: 1992, 1993, 1994 annual vols.

HUXFORD'S OLD BOOK VALUE GUIDE. Bob Huxford, Paducah KY, Collector Books: 1993 5th ed., 1994 6th ed.

MANDEVILLE'S USED BOOK PRICE GUIDE. Mildred Mandeville. Kenmore WA, Price Guide Publishers: New 5-year edition in 1994.

COLLECTED BOOKS: THE GUIDE TO VALUES. Allen and Patricia Ahearn. New York, Putnam's: 1991.

THE BOOK COLLECTOR'S HANDBOOK OF VALUES. Van Allen Bradley. New York, Putnam's: 1982-1983.

THE OFFICIAL PRICE GUIDE TO OLD BOOKS. Tedford & Goudey. NY, House of Collectibles: 1994.

THE OFFICIAL PRICE GUIDE: PAPERBACKS. Jon Warren. New York, House of Collectibles: 1991.

PAPERBACKS AT AUCTION, 1994. Gorgon Books. 102 JoAnne Drive, Holbrook, NY 11741: 1994.

TOMART'S PRICE GUIDE TO 20TH CENTURY BOOKS. John Wade. Dayton OH, Tomart Pub: 1994.

HANCER'S PRICE GUIDE TO PAPERBACK BOOKS. Kevin Hancer. Radnor PA, Wallace-Homestead: 1990 3rd.

THE COLLECTOR'S BOOKSHELF VALUE GUIDE. Jos. LeFontaine. Buffalo NY, Prometheus Books: 1990.

BOOKS: IDENTIFICATION AND VALUE GUIDE. Nancy Wright, New York: Avon Books, 1993.

SPECIALIZED PRICE GUIDES

AUTHOR PRICE GUIDE SERIES. Allen Ahearn. Rockville MD, Ahearn; 1970s. continuing.

THE BOOK OF AUTOGRAPHS. Charles Hamilton. New York, Simon and Schuster: 1978.

THE PRICE GUIDE TO AUTOGRAPHS. George Sanders. Radnor PA, Wallace-Homestead: 1992.

THE BLUE BOOK ON THE RED COVER: (LIFE MAGAZINE). Robert Lenson. Newton Centre MA, Fondest memories: 2nd ed 1994.

BOOKMAN'S GUIDE TO AMERICANA. Lee Shiflett. Metuchen NJ, Scarecrow Press: 1991 10th ed.

CHILDREN'S MODERN FIRST EDITIONS: THEIR VALUE TO COLLECTORS. Joseph Connolly, Philadelphia, Trans-Atlantic Pubs: 1988

CIVIL WAR BOOKS: A PRICED CHECKLIST. Tom Broadfoot. Wendell NC, Broadfoot Rte 3, Box 318: 1990 3rd edition.

COLLECTIBLE ADVERTISING: AN ILLUSTRATED VALUE GUIDE. Sharon and Box Huxford. Paducah KY, Collector Books: 1993.

COLLECTIBLE MAGAZINES: IDENTIFICATION AND PRICE GUIDE. David K. Henkel, New York, Avon Books: 1993 1st ed.

COLLECTING LITTLE GOLDEN BOOKS: A COLLECTOR'S IDENTIFICATION AND VALUE GUIDE. Steve Santi. Florence AL, Books Americana: 1994.

COLLECTING AMERICAN NEWSPAPERS. Jim Lyons, 24745 Summerhill Ave, Los Altos CA 94024: 1990.

COLLECTING BOOKS AND PAMPHLETS SIGNED BY THE PRESIDENTS OF THE UNITED STATES. Stephen Koschal. Verona NJ, Patriotic Press: 1982.

COLLECTING PAPER, PRICE GUIDE. Gene Utz. Florence AL, Books Americana: 1994.

COLLECTOR'S ENCYCLOPEDIA OF DISNEYANA. David Longest and Michael Stern. Paducah KY, Collector Books: 1992.

THE COLLECTOR'S GUIDE TO BIG LITTLE BOOKS AND SIMILAR BOOKS. Lawrence F. Lowery. Box 1242, Danville CA 94526: 1983.

COOKBOOKS WORTH COLLECTING. Mary Barile. Radnor PA; Wallace-Homestead: 1994

A GUIDE TO COLLECTING COOKBOOKS. Col. Robert Allen. Paducah KY, Collector Books: 1993.

PRICE GUIDE TO COOKBOOKS & RECIPE LEAFLETS. Linda Dickinson. Paducah KY, Collector Books: 1993.

COYKENDALL'S SPORTING COLLECTIBLES. Ralf Coykendal Jr. New York, Lyons & Burford: 1991.

THE ILLUSTRATED PRICE GUIDE TO CULT MAGAZINES. Allan Betrock. Shake Books. 449 12th St., Brooklyn, NY 11215: 1994.

FAMOUS FACES: PRICE GUIDE AND CATALOG FOR MAGAZINE COLLECTORS. Frank Zawacki. Radnor PA, Wallace-Homestaed: 1985.

GOLF ANTIQUES (WITH PRICE GUIDE). J. M. and M. W. Olman, Cincinnati OH, Market Street Press: 1993.

MALLOY'S SPORTS COLLECTIBLES VALUE GUIDE. Roderick Malloy. Radnor PA, Wallace-Homestead: 1993.

THE MASTER'S PRICE AND IDENTIFICATION GUIDE TO OLD MAGAZINES. Denis C. Jackson, Box 1958, Sequim WA 98382: 1993.

MODERN FIRST EDITIONS: THEIR VALUE FOR COLLECTORS. Joseph Connolly, Philadelphia PA, Trans-Atlantic Pubs: 1987 3rd ed.

MODERN LIBRARY PRICE GUIDE. Henry Toledano. Books Etc, 538 Castro St, San Francisco CA 94114: 1993.

MODERN LIBRARY PRICE GUIDE. Joseph D. Hill. 312 Turquoise Drive, Hercules CA 94547: 1993.

NATIONAL GEOGRAPHIC MAGAZINE: 1888-1992. Don Smith. 3930 Rankin St., Louisville KY 40214: 1992.

NEW PRICING GUIDE FOR MATERIAL PRODUCED BY THE ROYCROFT PRINTING SHOP. Paul McKenna. PO Box 306 North Tonawanda, NY 14120: 1991 3rd ed.

1993 PRICE GUIDE FOR WORLD WAR II BOOKS AND MANUALS. Mark A. George, PO Box 36372, Denver CO 80326: 1993.

OFFICIAL PRICE GUIDE TO AMERICAN ILLUSTRATOR ART. Anne Gilbert. New York, House of Collectibles: 1991 1st ed.

OFFICIAL IDENTIFICATION AND PRICE GUIDE TO MOVIE MEMORABILIA. Richard De Thuin, New York, House of Collectibles: 1990 1st ed.

OLD MAGAZINES PRICE GUIDE. Anon. L-W Books. Gas City IN 46933: 1994.

PRICE GUIDE & BIBLIOGRAPHY TO CHILDREN'S & ILLUSTRATED BOOKS. Edward S. Postal. M & P Press. 1475 Glenneyre St. Laguna Beach CA 92651: 1994.

PRICE GUIDE TO CHILDREN'S AND ILLUSTRATED BOOKS FOR THE YEARS 1880-1950. E. Lee Baumgarten. 718½ West John St., Martinsburg W VA 25401: 1993.

VALUE GUIDE TO BASEBALL COLLECTIBLES. M. D. and R. Raycraft. Paducah KY, Collector Books: 1992.

TOMART'S PRICE GUIDE TO GOLDEN BOOK AND RECORD COLLECTIBLES. Rebecca Greason. Dayton OH, Tomart Pubs: 1991.

STERN'S GUIDE TO DISNEY COLLECTIBLES. M. Stern. Paducah KY, Collector Books: Vol 1, 1992. Vol 2, 1993.

WARMAN'S PAPER (Advertising ephemera, etc). Martinus & Rinker. Radnor PA, Wallace Homestead: 1994.

BIBLIOGRAPHIES AND DIRECTORIES

ANNOTATED INDEX OF AMERICAN NEWSPAPERS KNOWN TO HAVE BEEN REPRINTED. Rick Brown. Box 191341, Lansing MI 48901: 1993.

ANTIQUARIAN BOOKMAN'S ANNUAL. PO Box AB, Clifton, NJ 07015.

ANTIQUARIAN, SPECIALTY & USED BOOK SELLERS DIRECTORY. Omnigraphics, Penobscot Bldg. Detroit MI 48226: Annual.

BASEBALL, A COMPREHENSIVE BIBLIOGRAPHY. Myron J. Smith Jefferson, NC: 1986.

GUIDE TO BASEBAL LITERATURE. Anton Grobani. Detroit, MI: 1975.

A BIBLIOGRAPHICAL INTRODUCTION TO SEVENTY-FIVE MODERN AUTHORS. Gary M. Lepper. Serendipity: 1975.

BIBLIOGRAPHY OF AMERICAN COOKERY BOOKS, 1742-1860. Eleanor Lowenstein. Massachusetts, American Antiquarian Society: 1972.

BIBLIOGRAPHY OF AMERICAN LITERATURE. Jacob Blanck. Yale University Press. 6 vols: 1955-1973.

BIBLIOTHECA: A DICTIONARY OF BOOKS RELATING TO AMERICA. Joseph A. Sabin. Metuchen NJ, Scarecrow Press. INDEX to this well-known work: 1974.

BOOKS IN PRINT. New Providence NJ, R. R. Bowker: Annual Directory of all books in print.

BUY BOOKS WHERE: SELL BOOKS WHERE. Ruth E. Robinson. Rte 7, Box 162A, Morgantown W VA 26505: This important biannual guide lists hundreds of current buyers and sellers for all types of books. A valuable tool for mail-order dealers.

CHRONOLOGICAL DICTIONARY OF BOOKS, PAMPHLETS AND PERIODICALS PUBLISHED IN THE U.S. FROM 1639 TO 1820. Charles Evans. 1903.

CULINARY AMERICANA, 100 YEARS OF COOKBOOKS PUBLISHED IN THE UNITED STATES, 1860-1960. Bob and Eleanor Brown. NY, Roving Eye Press: 1961.

DICTIONARY OF AMERICAN CHILDREN'S FICTION, 1859-1959. Alethea K. Helbig and Agnes R. Perkins. Westport CT; Greenwood Press: 1985.

THE DICTIONARY OF LITERARY BIOGRAPHY. Detroit MI, Gale Research: 1984-1993, 42 vols.

GASTRONOMIC BIBLIOGRAPHY. Katherine Bitting. San Francisco CA, A. W. Bitting: 1939.

GUIDE TO AMERICAN TRADE CATALOGS, 1744-1900. Lawrence Romaine. New York, Bowker: 1960 (also a 1990 Dover reprint).

TRADE CATALOGS AT WINTERTHUR, A GUIDE TO THE LITERATURE OF MERCHANDISING, 1750-1950, McKinstry. Winterthur Museum, Rte 52, Winterthur DE 19735: 1984.

GUIDE TO THE STUDY OF U.S. IMPRINTS. G. T. Tanselle. Cambridge MA, Belknap Press: 1971.

INFORMATION COLLECTOR'S CLEARING HOUSE: AN ANTIQUES AND COLLECTIBLES RESOURCE DIRECTORY. David J. Malone. Radnor PA, Wallace-Homestead: 1993. Hundreds of collector addresses.

NINETEENTH CENTURY PHOTOGRAPHY: AN ANNOTATED BIBLIOGRAPHY, 1839-1879. William Johnson. Boston MA, G. K. Hall: 1990.

THE SANTA FE TRAIL. Jack Rittenhouse. Albuquerque NM, Univ. of New Mexico: 1971.

SCIENCE FICTION AND FANTASY LITERATURE, 1975-1991. Robert Reginald. Detroit MI, Gale Research: 1992.

SIX GUNS AND SADDLE LEATHER: A BIBLIOGRAPHY OF WESTERN OUTLAWS AND GUNMEN. Ramon Adams. Norman OK, Univ. of Oklahoma Press: 1969.

US IANA 1700-1950. Wright Howes. New York, R. R. Bowker: 1982. Grades 11,620 important U. S. Books.

THE COMPREHENSIVE GUIDE TO COLLECTABLE AUTHORS, ILLUSTRATORS & PHOTOGRAPHERS. Robert A. Juran, Box 10554, Burke VA 22009: 1993.

HAWK'S PSEUDONYMS FOR BOOK COLLECTORS. Martin P. Hawk. 1740 Sunshine Lane, Southlake TX 76092: 1993.

HISTORY OF AMERICAN MAGAZINES. Frank Luther Mott. Harvard University Press: 1930-1968.

THE COLLECTOR'S BOOKSHELF: A LISTING OF AUTHORS AND PSEUDONYMS. Joseph LeFontaine. Buffalo NY, Prometheus Books: 1990.

GUIDE TO FOOTBALL LITERATURE. GUIDE TO BASEBALL LITERATURE. Anton Grobani. Detroit MI, Gale Research: 1975.

FIRST PRINTINGS OF AMERICAN AUTHORS. M. J. Bruccoli and C. E. Frazer Clark Jr. Detroit MI, Gale Research: 1977-1979, 5 vols.

PETER PARLEY TO PENROD. A BIBLIOGRAPHY OF AMERICAN JUVENILE BOOKS: 1974.

THE WHO'S WHO OF CHILDREN'S LITERATURE, AUTHORS & ILLUSTRATORS. Brian Doyle, ed. NY, Schocken Books: 1968.

WHO'S WHO IN TWENTIETH CENTURY LITERATURE. Martin Seymour-Smith. New York. Holt, Rinehart, Winston: 1976.

OTHER USEFUL BOOKS

ABC FOR BOOK COLLECTORS. John Carter. Revised by N. Barker New York, Bowker 1992: 6th ed.

THE ADVENTURES OF A TREASURE HUNTER. Charles Everitt. Glenwood IL, Meyerbooks: 1987 (Reprint).

AMERICAN CHILDREN THROUGH THEIR BOOKS, 1700-1835. Monica Kiefer. Philadelphia, Univ. of Pennsylvania Press: 1948.

AMERICAN PICTURE BOOKS FROM NOAH'S ARK TO THE BEAST WITHIN. Barbara Bader. New York, Macmillan: 1976.

AMERICAN ILLUSTRATOR ART. Anne Gilbert. New York, House of Collectibles: 1991.

AMERICAN POPULAR ILLUSTRATION: A REFERENCE GUIDE. James Best. Westport Ct, Greenwood Pub: 1984.

ILLUSTRATOR PRICE GUIDES. A Series is available from Denis C. Jackson, Illustrator Collector News. Box 1958, Sequim WA 98282.

AUCTION MADNESS. Charles Hamilton. New York, Everest House: 1981.

AUDUBON AND OTHER CAPERS. John Jenkins. San Angelo TX, Pemberton Press: 1976.

THE BARGAIN HUNTER'S GUIDE TO ART COLLECTING. Steven Naifeh. New York, Quill: 1982.

BIBLIOPHILE IN THE NURSERY. William Targ. New York, World Pub: 1957.

THE BLACK MASK BOYS: MASTERS IN THE HARD-BOILED SCHOOL OF DETECTIVE FICTION. William R. Nolan. New York, Morrow: 1985.

BOOK COLLECTING: A COMPREHENSIVE GUIDE. Allen Ahearn. New York, Outnam's: 1989.

BOOK COLLECTING: A MODERN GUIDE. Jean Peters, New York, Bowker: 1977.

BOOK PUBLISHING IN AMERICA. Charles A. Madison. New York, McGraw-Hill: 1966.

THE BOOK QUOTER'S BOOK. J. C. Vincent and D. Ruth Adams, Laguna Beach CA, Buccaneer Books: 1985.

BOOK SCOUTING: HOW TO TURN YOUR LOVE OF BOOKS INTO PROFIT. Barbara Johnson. New York, Prentice-Hall: 1981.

THE BOOKMAN'S GLOSSARY. Jean Peters. New York, Bowker: 1983.

BOOKS IN MY BAGGAGE. Lawrence Clark Powell. New York, World Pub: 1960.

BOUILLABAISSE FOR BIBLIOPHILES. William Targ, ed. New York, World: 1953.

THE CARE OF FINE BOOKS. Jane Greenfield, New York, Lyons & Burford: 1988.

CAROUSEL FOR BIBLIOPHILES. William Targ. Metuchen NJ. Scarecrow Press: 1967 Reprint.

CHILDREN AND BOOKS. May Hill Arbuthnot. Chicago, Scott-Foresman: 1964.

CHILDREN'S BOOK COLLECTING. Carolyn Michaels. Hamden CT, Shoe String Press: 1993.

CLEANING AND CARING FOR BOOKS. R. L. Shep. London, Sheppart Press: 1982.

COLLECTING OLD PHOTOGRAPHS. Margaret Haller. New York, Arco Pub: 1978.

COLLECTING RARE BOOKS FOR PLEASURE AND PROFIT. Jack Matthews. Athens OH, Ohio Univ. Press: 1981 Revised ed.

THE COLLECTOR'S BOOK OF BOOKS. Eric Quayle. New York, C. N. Potter: 1971.

THE COLLECTOR'S BOOK OF CHILDREN'S BOOKS. Eric Quayle. New York, C. N. Potter: 1971.

THE COLLECTOR'S GUIDE TO 19TH CENTURY PHOTOGRAPHS. William Welling. NY, Collier: 1976.

COOK BOOKS. Patrick L. Coyle. NY, Facts on File: 1985.

DANGER IS MY BUSINESS: AN ILLUSTRATED HISTORY OF THE FABULOUS PULP MAGAZINES. Lee Server. San Francisco, Chronicle Books: 1993.

DUKEDOM LARGE ENOUGH. David A. Randall. New York, Random House: 1969.

EARLY AMERICAN BOOKS AND PRINTING. John T. Winterich. Boston, Houghton-Mifflin: 1935.

84 CHARING CROSS ROAD. Helen Hanff. New York, Grossman Pub: 1970.

EVERYBODY'S GUIDE TO BOOK COLLECTING. Charlie Lovett. Write-Brain Publications, 10714 W. 128th Ct. Overland KS 66213: 1993.

FIRST EDITIONS, A GUIDE TO IDENTIFICATION. Edward N. Zempel and Linda Verkler. Peoria IL, Spoon River Press: 1989.

A HISTORY OF BOOK ILLUSTRATION. David Bland. Berkeley CA, Univ. of California Press: 1969.

HOW TO IDENTIFY PRINTS. Bamber Gascoigne. New York, Thames and Hudson: 1986.

HOW TO IDENTIFY AND COLLECT AMERICAN FIRST EDITIONS. Jack Tannen. New York, Prentice-Hall: 1985.

HISTORY OF AMERICAN MAGAZINES. Frank L. Mott. Harvard University Press: 1930-1968. 5 volumes.

MAGAZINES IN THE UNITED STATES. James P. Wood. New York, Ronald Press: 1971 3rd ed.

MAGAZINE MAGIC. How to Buy and Sell. Marjorie M. Hinds. Laceyville PA: 1972.

MEMOIRS OF A BOOKMAN. Jack Matthews. Athens OH, Ohio University Press: 1989.

MODERN BOOK COLLECTING. Robert Wilson. New York, Lyons & Burford: 1980.

NINETEENTH CENTURY FICTION. Michael Sadleir. Berkeley CA, Univ. of California Press: 1951.

OLD COOK BOOKS: AN ILLUSTRATED HISTORY. Eric Quayle. New York, Dutton: 1978.

THE OXFORD COMPANION TO CHILDREN'S LITERATURE. H. Carpenter and M. Prichards. New York, Oxford Univ. Press: 1984.

PAPERBACKS, U.S.A.: AN ILLUSTRATED HISTORY, 1939-1959. Piet Schreuders. San Diego, Blue Dolphin Enterprises: 1981.

THE PHOTOGRAPH COLLECTOR'S GUIDE. Lee D. Witkin and Barbara London. New York, New York Graphic Society: 1979.

PHOTOGRAPHS: A COLLECTOR'S GUIDE. Richard Blodgett. New York, Ballantine Books: 1979.

POCKET GUIDE TO THE IDENTIFICATION OF FIRST EDITIONS. Bill McBride. 157 Sisson Ave, Hartford CT 06105: 1985.

POINTS OF ISSUE: A COMPENDIUM OF POINTS OF ISSUE BY 19TH AND 20TH CENTURY AUTHORS. Bill McBride. See above.

THE PRACTICAL GUIDE TO BOOK REPAIR AND CONSERVATION. Arthur W. Johnson. New York, Thames and Hudson: 1988.

A PRIMER OF BOOK COLLECTING. John Winterich and David Randall. NY, Crown Pub: 1966 3rd revised ed.

PRINTS AND THE PRINT MARKET. Theodore B. Donson. New York, Crowell: 1977.

RARE BOOKS AND ROYAL COLLECTORS. Maurice Ettinghausen. New York, Simon & Schuster: 1966.

THE SPORTS COLLECTORS BIBLE. Bert R. Sugar. New York, Bobbs-Merrill: 1983 4th ed.

STEIN AND DAY BOOK OF WORLD AUTOGRAPHS. Ray Rawlins. New York, Stein and Day: 1978.

THIS BOOK COLLECTING GAME. A. Edward Newton. New York, Little: 1928.

TURNING PAPER INTO GOLD. Joseph LeFontaine. White Hall VA, Betterway Pub: 1988.

200 YEARS OF AMERICAN GRAPHIC ART. Clarence P. Hornung. New York, George Braziller: 1976.

THE WORLD OF SCIENCE FICTION. Lester Del Rey. New York, Ballantine Books: 1979.

UNION LIST OF SERIALS. Catalogs all magazine collections of major U. S. Libraries. H. W. Wilson Co: 1965.

THE USED BOOKLOVER'S GUIDE:
  To the Midwest.
  To New England.
  To Mid-Atlantic States.
  To South-Atlantic States.
  Locations and descriptions of thousands of shops. Compiled by David and Susan Siegel. Book Hunter Press, Yorktown Heights, New York: 1994.

BROWSING THE BEST WEST COAST USED BOOK STORES: A Series of Guides to the Foremost General Stock Used and Out-Of-Print Establishments in Los Angeles, Berkeley, Seattle, San Francisco, San Diego, Portland, Sacramento, Orange County, Silicon Valley and Vancouver. Browsing the Best Publications, P. O. Box 7263, Berkeley, CA 94707-0263

PRESERVATION SUPPLIES

Items to preserve or enhance collectible books, magazines and newspapers, including mylar jackets, polyethylene bags, backing boards, repair tapes, binding supplies, subject signs, display shelves and stands, bookends, book trucks, book ladders and step stools, are available from the following sources. Write on your business stationery when requesting a catalog.

Archivart
301 Veterans Boulevard
Rutherford NJ 07070

The Hollinger Company
PO Box 8360
Fredericksburg VA 22404

Brodart Company
1609 Memorial Avenue
Williamsport, Pa 17705

Library Binding Company
2900 Franklin Avenue
Waco TX 76710

Conservation Resources
8000-H Forbes Place
Springfield VA 22151

Light Impressions
439 Monroe Avenue
Rochester NY 14603-0940

Demco
PO Box 7488
Madison WI 53707

Richard Novick Products
17 Abbey Lane
Marlboro NJ 07746

Document Preservation Ctr
Postal 821
Yonkers NY 10702

University Products, Inc.
PO Box 101
Holyoke MA 01041-0101

FOLIO.

QUARTO, "4to."

Duodecimo, "12mo."

OCTAVO, "8vo."

BOOK SIZES
4to (quarto) aprox. 12 inches high.
8vo (octavo) approx. 9 in. high.
12mo (duodecimo) approx. 7 to 8 inches high.
16mo approx. 6 to 7 inches high.
24mo approx. 5 to 6 inches high.
32mo approx. 4 to 5 inches high.
48mo approx. 4 inches high.
64mo approx. 3 inches high.
Miniature, below one inch high.
Folio, approx 13 in. or higher.
Elephant folio, 23 in. or larger.
Atlas folio, 25 inches.
Double elephant folio, larger than 25 inches.

Victorian Houseware, Hardware and Kitchenware

At last, a price guide that actually covers the antiques we most often find: the house furnishings, hardware, and farm tools of our greatgrandparents. Ronald S. Barlow (author of *The Antique Tool Collector's Guide to Value*), and Linda Campbell Franklin (author of *300 Years of Kitchen Collectibles*), have combined their talents to produce this giant 376-page catalog of the Victorian period. Seven other experts — in such fields as Oak and Wicker, Locks and Keys, Lanterns and Oil Lamps, Silverplate and Brassware, Doorknobs and Drawer Pulls, Clocks and Corkscrews, Sad Irons and Sewing Machines — have contributed over a hundred and fifty years of collector knowledge to this work. Dozens of priceless old trade catalogs were photographed, and over 2,000 wood engravings are reproduced in their original 9 x 12 inch page size. Exceptionally nice Graniteware ads from the 1880's are also included, along with current prices. You will be amazed at the variety of material goods that surrounded our Victorian ancestors: brass birdcages, wind-up fly fans, catch'em-alive mouse traps, handcranked peach pealers, tin-plated toddy warmers, string holders, nutmeg graters, sugar augers, and coffee roasters. All this information, plus copyright-free use of the wonderful old wood engravings, makes this new book an indispensable tool for any artist, designer, craftsman, historian, antique dealer, or collector. First edition. **376 pages. 9 x 12 Paperback $19.95**

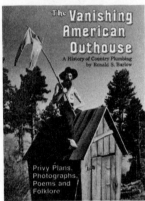

The Vanishing American Outhouse

Rave reviews in *The New York Times, Los Angeles Times, and Washington Post.* ''A funny, fascinating book,'' says the American Library Association. For some unexplained reason, scholars have ignored (or avoided) this important part of our architectural heritage, and only recently have historians begun to appreciate the ''necessary house'' as a true form of folk architecture. Privies which were once routinely burned or demolished are now quickly sold to landscape designers who move these quaint buildings into the backyards of wealthy clients, where they become transformed into playhouses, pool cabanas, and Victorian-style garden sheds. The author's serious research begins with biblical references to elimination etiquette, and ends twenty-two chapters later in a salute to plumbing pioneers Henry Moule and Thomas Crapper. The book contains nearly 200 color photographs and plan drawings of American privies constructed between 1820 and 1940. In addition to a great deal of technical information, it features many humerous anecdotes, old poems, bits of folklore, Victorian bathroom fixture ads, and a collection of rarely seen privy postcards. Also included is a reprint section containing U.S. Government pamphlets on outhouse construction, and a bibliography which features very candid reviews of nearly every outhouse book ever published. The 9 x 12 inch format and extra large typeface make this colorful paperback an excellent gift for the over-fifty crowd, and an enlightening cultural history for baby boomers who have never used an authentic outdoor convenience. **144 pages. Paperback $15.95**

The Antique Tool Collector's Guide to Value

Old woodworking tools are one of today's hottest new areas of collecting. Long neglected by all but a few sophisticated insiders, this field is growing rapidly. Several Stanley/Bailey carpenter planes are already selling in the $500–$900 range, and an early plow plane sold for over $6,000 at a recent tool auction. Ronald Barlow has spent three years working full-time on this guide . . . recording dealer and auction prices from all over the world for every kind of old tool imaginable. Just a few of the over-5,000 items described and priced: adzes, anvils, axes, books, trade catalogs, braces, bitstocks, chisels, cobbler's tools, cooper's items, compasses, dividers, hammers, hatchets, pocket knives, lathes, levels, planes, pliers, plumb bobs, routers, rules, saws, scorps, screwdrivers, shears, spar & spoke shaves, surveying instruments, tinsmith's tools, trammel points, wrenches & wheelwright's tools. Contains historical data on inventors and manufacturers, as well as an extensive bibliography which includes the names and addresses of major antique tool auctioneers, dealers, and collector organizations. Over 2,000 illustrations. Extra-large 9 x 12 inch paperback volume. A best seller, over 75,000 copies now in print. Order your copy today. Just one ''find'' in an attic, barn, or garage could pay for this price guide many times over. (Includes 1991 Auction Update.) **236 pages. Paperback $12.95**

How To Be Successful In The Antique Business

OPENING AN ANTIQUE SHOP? This 185-page Start-up Manual can help you to succeed where others often fail. Some of the dozens of chapters are: Wholesale Antique Outlets, Nationwide List of Wholesale Giftware Centers, How to Purchase Estates, How to Become a Licensed Appraiser, How to Make a Living at Antique Shows, An Introduction to the Jewelry Business, Professional Furniture Refinishing & Restoring, Consignment Sales, Cash Flow & Profit Projections, Shopping Center Leases, Mail-Order Selling, Proven Advertising Techniques, Container Importing from Europe, Dealer Trade Publications, Selling Rare Books & Prints, Finding and Dealing with ''Pickers,'' plus over 45 charts, photos, and sample forms. (Fifth printing.) **185 pages. Paperback $9.95**

Order from your favorite bookstore, or directly from Windmill Publishing Co., 2147 Windmill View Road, El Cajon, California 92020